THE NEW WESTMINSTER DICTIONARY OF LITURGY AND WORSHIP

Also published by The Westminster Press

THE WESTMINSTER DICTIONARY OF CHRISTIAN SPIRITUALITY
edited by Gordon S. Wakefield

THE WESTMINSTER DICTIONARY OF CHRISTIAN THEOLOGY
edited by Alan Richardson and John Bowden

THE WESTMINSTER DICTIONARY OF CHRISTIAN ETHICS
edited by James F. Childress and John Macquarrie

THE NEW WESTMINSTER DICTIONARY OF THE BIBLE
edited by Henry Snyder Gehman

THE NEW WESTMINSTER DICTIONARY OF LITURGY AND WORSHIP

EDITED BY
J. G. DAVIES

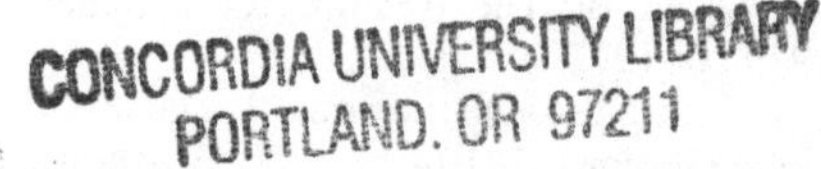

THE WESTMINSTER PRESS
PHILADELPHIA

First published in Great Britain in 1986
under the title *A New Dictionary of Liturgy & Worship*

First American edition

Published by The Westminster Press®
Philadelphia, Pennsylvania

PRINTED IN THE UNITED STATES OF AMERICA
4 6 8 9 7 5 3

Library of Congress Cataloging-in-Publication Data

The New Westminster dictionary of liturgy and worship.

British ed. published under title: A New dictionary of liturgy & worship.
Rev. ed. of: The Westminster dictionary of worship. 1979, © 1972.
1. Liturgics—Dictionaries. I. Davies, J. G. (John Gordon), 1919- . II. Westminster dictionary of worship.
BV173.N49 1986 264'.003'21 86-9219
ISBN 0-664-21270-0

PREFACE

To explain in what ways this *New Westminster Dictionary of Liturgy and Worship* differs from its predecessor is in fact to call attention to the main trends in liturgy and worship that have become evident over the past one and a half decades.

Perhaps the leading feature can be most easily identified if the period is named the harvest time of liturgical revision. Throughout the 1970s the impact of the Liturgical Movement continued to make itself felt. Via the decrees of the Second Vatican Council, this resulted in a whole series of revised orders of worship for the Roman Catholic Church. The churches of the Anglican Communion were not far behind with, for example, the Book of Common Prayer of the American Episcopal church (1979) and the Alternative Service Book (1980) for Britain. Nor have other churches been idle; for instance, the British Methodists have issued their own revision. Consequently this new dictionary not only has a major fresh article on liturgical revision itself, but a number of the previous composite entries have had to be updated, in particular those relating to baptism, burial, liturgical books, marriage, and ordination. This process of reworking, both of content and bibliography, has been undertaken wherever there was fresh material requiring notice.

Other movements of thought, more recent in time than what may be called the yeastlike activity of the Liturgical Movement, that have affected both the form and understanding of worship, are perhaps to be regarded as more radical. Women's Liberation in its non-exaggerated activities demands a fresh approach to the role of women—hence there are additional entries: the Feminist Liturgical Movement, Inclusive Language, the Ordination of Women, and Women and Worship. Indeed, anyone sensitive to this current of thought could no longer begin this preface with the sentence that stood at the outset of its predecessor: namely, 'Ritual would appear to be natural to man.' Ritual is natural to all human beings, whether male or female.

Then, typical of the modern age in the West has been the increasing attention paid to the bodily aspect of human nature. Medicine had shown the way by emphasizing the psychosomatic, and theologians have not been slow to point out parallels with the biblical approach. The relevance of this to worship is recognized in articles on the dance choir, liturgical dance, and movement-prayer, together with expanded ones on Gestures and Posture. While Intercommunion is a perennial issue, Ecumenical Worship and Inter-Faith Worship have acquired increased importance. Pastoral Care and Worship seeks to redress an overindividualistic attitude to the cure of souls. Cremation is becoming more popular—hence another new article.

There are also distinct groups of people for whom the previous dictionary did not cater, so there are now entries relating to children and worship, family services, and school worship, as well as to handicapped people, including the blind and the deaf. Greater space (fifty percent more) has allowed an increase in the number of religious bodies whose worship is described: e.g., the Armenian Church, the United Reformed

Church, the Liberal Catholic Church, the Presbyterian Church, the Church of Jesus Christ of Latter-day Saints, Rastafarians, Shakers, and Unitarians. Specialized studies are devoted to Drama and Worship, House Churches, Indigenization, Laity and Worship, Law and Worship, Liberation and Worship, and Media Worship—indeed, nearly seventy completely new entries have been included, which meant that space could be found for such topics as the Cult of the Saints and Pilgrimages.

There is still no section under the sole heading of Worship, but this is because the entire dictionary is devoted to the subject. Nevertheless, the biblical basis of Christian worship is now covered by additional entries on the Old and New Testaments, while two other major ones consider its sociology and its theology.

The selection of subjects is always a difficult task. What one would include, another would omit. The existence of companion volumes, such as *The Westminster Dictionary of Christian Ethics, The Westminster Dictionary of Christian Spirituality,* and *The Westminster Dictionary of Christian Theology,* has enabled me to have a greater latitude than would otherwise have been the case, for it has seemed unnecessary to repeat what is to be found in these works of reference. While I must bear the responsibility for the final choice, I am grateful to those who have given their advice and to all the contributors, without whose ready cooperation this project could not have been completed.

In particular, I would like to record my appreciation of the invaluable assistance of Monsignor J. D. Crichton, who has not only revised his own original entries and written many new ones but has also checked for factual errors many other contributions which contain references to Roman Catholic liturgical practice. Invaluable, too, have been the painstaking efforts of Margaret Lydamore, Associate Editor of SCM Press, who, while preparing the manuscript for publication, has paid great attention to details and has ensured the removal of not a few disparities—for any that remain, I must accept responsibility.

The liturgical ferment of recent times has inevitably stirred up oppostion: some Roman Catholics hanker after the Tridentine mass; some Anglicans wish to cling to the forms of the seventeenth century. Indeed, if anything, the contemporary scene is witnessing a recrudescence of a conservatism that could well impede further liturgical experimentation and even blur the impact of what has been achieved. There would be nothing to regret in this if worship is intended simply to provide a refuge, but if, on the contrary, it is an occasion of encounter with the living God, should it not be liberating and challenging, and therefore is not the undercurrent of resistance to change to be itself resisted, so that in another decade and a half a further revision could give evidence of continuing liturgical creativity?

J. G. DAVIES

PREFACE TO THE 1972 DICTIONARY OF LITURGY & WORSHIP

Ritual would appear to be natural to man. When even birds and animals engage in it, as for example in sex play, it is not surprising to discover that human beings practise it almost universally. This formalization of natural actions lies at the basis of worship, which is the expression in corporate gatherings of adoration, praise and thanksgiving to God in response to his activity in the world. This response precedes doctrinal formulation, so that one may say that worship is primary and theology secondary. In Christian terms, this means that the early church worshipped Christ long before it had reached an intellectual understanding of his person and work. It is this sequence that explains the Latin tag *lex orandi, lex credendi*, i.e. what is to be believed is derived from the practice of worship. Consequently, worship has always been regarded as the living heart of any religion. Because of this centrality, a knowledge of worship is essential for a sympathetic appreciation of all religious movements.

Worship can be either 'free' or formal. In the latter case it is offered according to fixed rites and it is customary to use the term 'liturgy' in reference to these. Liturgy also bears a narrower sense in that it can refer in particular to the eucharist as the church's corporate and official act of worship. Because of this distinction, it has seemed appropriate to use both worship and liturgy in the title of this Dictionary.

As a reference book, this present volume is intended to provide background knowledge about worship for those who are regularly involved in it or would learn something about it. It seeks to concentrate upon the information that Christians today need in order to participate with understanding in the worship of the traditions to which they belong. At the same time, it aims to assist them to appreciate traditions and contemporary practices other than their own, familiarity with which is required to further the case of ecumenical co-operation.

The separate articles are not confined to simple definitions, but give the historical background to the subject treated and seek to relate this to the contemporary scene. However, while a reliable factual content is essential, emphasis is laid upon its interpretation, with particular reference to the principles upon which the practice, object, etc. is founded or used. In this way the reader will be enabled to understand not only what has been or is done but why it has been or is done. Hence, the Dictionary is concerned not only with the structures but also with the rationale of worship, the tracing of patterns and influences, and the underlying basis.

The entries relate not only to the historic Christian churches, such as the Anglican, the Lutheran, the Presbyterian and the Roman Catholic, but also to those bodies which have intimate links with the biblical and Christian inheritance, such

as the Pentecostals and the Unitarians. In addition, accounts are given of the worship of other major world religions, e.g. Judaism and Islam.

In order to ensure representative accounts, the contributors to the Dictionary have been chosen from recognized liturgical experts within the different churches, so that, for example, Eastern Orthodox scholars have written on subjects pertaining to their own church, similarly Old Catholics, etc. The result of this is that some of the major articles are composite. The accounts of baptism, matrimony, liturgies, etc., are divided into sections, each one detailing the practice of a major denomination. The opening three sections of each composite article are in historical sequence, so that the first is devoted to the patristic period, the second to Eastern Orthodoxy, and the third to Roman Catholicism, mediaeval and modern; the remainder follow in alphabetical order, beginning with Anglicanism.

One consequence of this composite authorship is that different viewpoints are expressed, so that, e.g. in the entry on Ordination, varied and sometimes conflicting understandings of the subject are to be found. This lack of uniformity is inevitable if the positions of the several Christian churches are to be presented faithfully. Not only has each contributor been left free to give his own denominational interpretation, but no attempt has been made to achieve a consensus on matters of minor importance; e.g. the date of the *Apostolic Tradition* of Hippolytus is variously given, according to the predilection of the individual writers, as *c.*215, *c.*217 or even *c.*222.

While the majority of entries are devoted to the principal aspects of liturgy and worship, others treat of its ancillaries, e.g. its architectural setting, vestments, etc.

Worship today is, of course, not simply a matter of history. The Liturgical Movement, to which a major article is devoted, and the many revisions that are currently being produced witness to a desire to formulate patterns of worship relevant to contemporary man. But to say this is to recognize that worship is undergoing a crisis. To some it has lost its meaning. Hence the need, which is emphasized in several entries, for experimental forms, for attention to the problems of indigenization, to secularization, to the relation of liturgy and culture and liturgy and mission.

It is hoped that the *Dictionary* will be found useful by several types of reader. It is intended to appeal to church leaders, clergy and ministers, to laity and to students who wish to increase their understanding of the history and contemporary practice of worship and liturgy.

J. G. DAVIES

CONTRIBUTORS

Ronald J. Allen, *Assistant Professor of Preaching and New Testament, Christian Theological Seminary, Indianapolis.*
Burial 6. Christian Church; Marriage 6. Christian Church

†Henry Ashworth OSB, *late of Quarr Abbey, Ryde.*
Books, Liturgical 3. Mediaeval and Roman Catholic (1)

Frank Baker, *Professor Emeritus of English Church History, Duke University, North Carolina.* **Love Feast**

T. G. A. Baker, *Dean of Worcester.*
Bible, Use of in Worship; Law and Worship

John M. Barkley, *Professor Emeritus, Union Theological Seminary, Belfast.*
Baptism 14. Reformed; Burial 13. Reformed; Ordination 13. Reformed

Paul Bayes, *University Chaplain in the West London Chaplaincy.*
Drama and Worship

B. B. Beach, *Department of Public Affairs and Religious Liberty, General Conference of Seventh-day Adventists, Washington.*
Baptism 15. Seventh-day Adventist; Books, Liturgical 15. Seventh-day Adventist; Burial 14. Seventh-day Adventist; Liturgies 15. Seventh-day Adventist; Marriage 14. Seventh-day Adventist; Ordination 14. Seventh-day Adventist; Seventh-day Adventist Worship

George Bebawi, *Lecturer at St John's College, Nottingham.* **Coptic Worship**

Mary Berry, *Director of the Schola Gregoriana of Cambridge and Member of the Faculty of Music, Cambridge University.*
Antiphon; Byzantine Chant; Chants of the Proper of the Mass; Church Modes; Divine Office, The; Gregorian Chant; Hymns 1. Latin; Motet; Music in the Mass of the Roman Rite; Notation and Rhythm; Polyphony; Psalmody; Psalm-Tones; Responsorial Psalmody, Responsories

Paul F. Bradshaw, *Associate Professor of Liturgy, University of Notre Dame, Indiana.* **Eucharist**

Eugene L. Brand, *Secretary for Ecumenical Relationships, Worship and Ecclesiological Research, Lutheran World Federation, Geneva.*
Books, Liturgical 9. Lutheran (2) USA; Liturgies 9. Lutheran; Lutheran Worship

Marcus Braybrooke, *Executive Director of the Council of Christians and Jews, London.* **Inter-Faith Worship**

F. F. Bruce, *Emeritus Professor, University of Manchester.*
Baptism 13. Plymouth Brethren; Books, Liturgical 13. Plymouth Brethren; Burial 12. Plymouth Brethren; Liturgies 13. Plymouth Brethren; Marriage 12. Plymouth Brethren; Plymouth Brethren Worship

Colin Buchanan, *Bishop of Aston.*
Burial 4. Anglican; Cremation; Liturgies 4. Anglican

R. F. Buxton, *Careers Adviser and Honorary Lecturer in Liturgy, University of Manchester.*
Advent; Ascension Day; Ash Wednesday; Calendar; Christmas; Corpus Christi; Easter; Epiphany; Good Friday; Holy Saturday; Holy Week; Lent; Low Sunday; Maundy Thursday; Octave; Palm Sunday; Pentecost; Quinquagesima; Santification of Time, The; Sunday; Transfiguration; Trinity Sunday

†H. Ellesworth Chandlee, *Late Professor of Liturgics, St Andrews Theological Seminary, Manila.* **Liturgical Movement**

C. E. de C. Chittenden, *Formerly Chaplain for the Deaf, Birmingham Diocese.*
Deaf People and Worship

Neville Clark, *Principal of the South Wales Baptist College, Cardiff.*
Children and Worship

†J. Connelly, *Late parish priest, St Giles Church, Cheadle, Stoke-on-Trent.*
All Saints; All Souls; Fast Days; Ferial; Mariological Feasts; Rogation Days; Saints Days

†Gilbert Cope, *Late Deputy Director, Institute for the Study of Worship and Religious Architecture, University of Birmingham.*
Colours, Liturgical; Gestures; Posture; Vestments

Frederick Coutts, *Formerly of the Salvation Army International Headquarters, London.* **Salvation Army Worship**

M. A. Creasey, *Formerly Director of Studies, Woodbrooke College, Selly Oak, Birmingham.* **Quaker Worship**

J. D. Crichton, *Retired parish priest; formerly Editor of* Life and Worship.
Altar, Stripping of; Altar, Washing of; Ashes; *Asperges;* Baptism 3. Mediaeval and Roman Catholic; Bible Services; Books, Liturgical 3. Roman Catholic (2); Catechism; Catechist; Catechumen, Catechumenate; Lay Ministries; Liturgies 3. Mediaeval and Roman Catholic; Marriage 3. Mediaeval and Roman Catholic; Mass, High; Mass, Low; New Fire; Ordination 3. Mediaeval and Roman Catholic; Paschal Candle; Pascal Vigil; Penance; Roman Catholic Worship; Tabernacle; *Tenebrae;* Unction

C. J. Cuming, *Formerly Lecturer in Liturgy, King's College, London and Ripon College, Cuddesdon.*
Baptismal Vows, Renewal of; Books, Liturgical 4. Anglican; Churching of Women; Commination; Marriage 4. Anglican; Sick, Visitation of the

Horton Davies, *Professor Emeritus of the History of Christianity, Princeton University.*
Baptism 7. Congregationalist; Books, Liturgical 7. Congregationalist; Burial 7. Congregationalist; Congregationalist Worship; Liturgies 7. Congregationalist; Marriage 7. Congregationalist; Ordination 7. Congregationalist

J. G. Davies, *Edward Cadbury Professor of Theology and Director of the Institute for the Study of Worship and Religious Architecture, University of Birmingham.*
Ablutions; Absolution; Absolution Prayer; Absolutions of the Dead; Aisle; Alms; Amen; Apse; Architectural Setting; Atrium; Baptistery; Basilica; Blessing; Books, Liturgical 1. Early Church; Burial 1. Early Church; Canticles; Centralized Building; Ceremonial; Chancel; Chantry; Chapel; Choir (Architectural); Choir (Dance); Christmas Crib; Commixture; Common of Saints; Communion; Consecration of Churches; Cult, Cultus; Dance, Liturgical; Dedication; Directions,

Liturgical; Dismissal; Disposal of Eucharistic Remains; Easter Garden or Sepulchre; Ember Days; Font; Fraction; Gallery; Grace; Handicapped People and Worship; Indigenization (Introduction); Intinction; Invocation; *Lavabo;* Lord's Supper, The; Marriage 1. Early Church; Martyrium; Mission and Worship; Mixed Chalice; Movement-Prayer; Movements in Worship; Narthex; Nave; Noonday Prayer; Office Hymn; Ordination 1. Early Church; Orientation; Requiem Mass; Riddle, Ridle; Rite; Ritual; Rubrics; Sacramentals; Sacristy; Saints, Cult of the; Sanctuary; Secularization and Worship; Sentences; Shaker Worship; Transept; Vestry; Viaticum; Vigil; Votive Mass; Whitsunday; Words of Administration

F. Debuyst OSB, *Benedictine Monk of St André, Ottignies, Belgium.*
Architectural Setting (Modern) and the Liturgical Movement

Peter Dickinson, *Composer and Emeritus Professor of Music, University of Keele.*
Music, Modern; Organ

C. W. Dugmore, *Emeritus Professor of Ecclesiastical History in the University of London.* **Canonical Hours**

J. H. Eaton, *Reader in Old Testament Studies, University of Birmingham.*
Alleluia; Old Testament Worship

John C. England, *Program Co-ordinator, Tao Fong Shan Ecumenical Centre, Hong Kong.* **Indigenization 4. South-East Asia**

J. D. C. Fisher, *Canon Emeritus of Chichester.*
Baptism 1. Patristic; Catechumen, Catechumenate; Insufflation

Paul Fisher, *Team Leader of the Lay Training Team, Diocese of Southwark.*
Culture and Worship

J. H. Foy, *Bishop of the Moravian Church, and a former member of the Governing Board of the Moravian Church in Great Britain and Ireland.*
Advent Star; Candle Service, Moravian; Christingle; Moravian Worship

R. H. Fuller, *Professor Emeritus, Virginia Theological Seminary.*
Lectionary; Sermon

†T. S. Garrett, *Formerly a Member of the CSI Synod Liturgy Group.*
Church of South India Worship

A. Raymond George, *Warden, John Wesley's Chapel, Bristol.*
Anniversary; Baptism 10. Methodist; Books, Liturgical 10. Methodist; Burial 10. Methodist; Extempore Prayer; Methodist Worship 1. Britain; Ordination 10. Methodist; Prayer Meeting

Mark Gibbs, *Executive Director and Editor, The Audenshaw Foundation.*
Laity and Worship

Paulos Mar Gregorios, *Metropolitan of Delhi and the North.*
East Syrian Worship; Ethiopian Worship; Mar Thoma Church Worship; West Syrian Worship

W. Jardine Grisbrooke, *Formerly Lecturer in Liturgical Studies at The Queen's College, Birmingham, and at St Mary's College, Oscott.*
Agnus Dei;* Anaphora; Antidoron; Baptism 2. Orthodox; Books, Liturgical 2. Orthodox; Cathedral Office; Collect; Consecration, Prayer of; Diptychs; Doxology; Enarxis; Entrance, Great; Entrance, Little; Incense; Intercession; *Kyrie;* Litany; Liturgies 2. Orthodox; Lord's Prayer, The; Oblation; Ordinary; Preface; Presanctified Mass; Proper; Prothesis; *Sanctus;* Shinto Worship; Silent Prayer; Suffrages; *Super Oblata;* Synaxis; *Trisagion

John Gunstone, *Secretary of the Greater Manchester Ecumenical Council.* **Blessing of Children**

Sergei Hackel, *Reader in Russian Studies, University of Sussex and Vicar-general, Russian Orthodox Church in the British Isles.* **Orthodox Worship**

D. W. Hardy, *Senior Lecturer, Department of Theology, University of Birmingham.* **Thanksgiving (USA)**

Joseph G. Healey MM, *Parish priest and writer, Tanzania.* **Indigenization 1. Africa**

P. Hinchcliff, *Fellow of Balliol College, Oxford.* **Acolyte; Bishop; Cantor; Catechist; Celebrant; Chairman of District; Class Leader; Crucifer; Deacon; Deaconess; Elder; Lay Preacher; Lector; Local Preacher; Presbyter; Reader; Server; Subdeacon; Superintendent; Thurifer**

W. J. Hollenweger, *Professor of Mission, University of Birmingham.* **Camp Meeting; Community and Worship; Experimental Forms of Worship; Liturgies 12. Pentecostal; Open-Air Meeting; Ordination 12. Pentecostal; Pentecostal Worship; Spirituals**

Antony Howe, *Chancellor of the Archdiocese of Westminster.* **Papal Rites**

†Clifford Howell SJ, *Late author, preacher and lecturer.* **Vernacular**

John M. Hull, *Senior Lecturer in Religious Education, Faculty of Education, University of Birmingham.* **School Worship**

E. D. Hunt, *Lecturer in Classics and Ancient History, University of Durham.* **Pilgrimages**

R. C. D. Jasper, *Dean Emeritus of York.* **Anglican Worship; Canon; Liturgies 1. Patristic; Ordination 4. Anglican; Procession; Remembrance Sunday; Revisions, Liturgical**

Klaus Klostermeier, *Professor in the Department of Religion, University of Manitoba.* **Indigenization 2. India**

S. Kraft, *Member of the Liturgy Commission of the Old Catholic Church in Germany.* **Baptism 11. Old Catholic; Books, Liturgical 11. Old Catholic; Burial 11. Old Catholic; Liturgies 11. Old Catholic; Marriage 11. Old Catholic; Old Catholic Worship; Ordination 11. Old Catholic**

†John A. Lamb, *Late Librarian of New College, Edinburgh.* **Books, Liturgical 14. Reformed; Liturgies 14. Reformed**

Gordon Lathrop, *Professor, Lutheran Theological Seminary, Philadelphia.* **Burial 9. Lutheran; Marriage 9. Lutheran**

Stewart Lawton, *Canon of Chester Cathedral and formerly Warden of St Deiniol's Library, Harwarden.* **Blind People and Worship**

Paul Lazor, *Dean of Students and Lecturer in Liturgics, St Vladimir's Orthodox Theological Seminary.* **Burial 2. Orthodox; Marriage 2. Orthodox; Ordination 2. Orthodox**

Rosemarie A. Loft, *Public Communications Department, Church of Jesus Christ of Latter Day Saints, London.* **Church of Jesus Christ of Latter Day Saints Worship**

A. J. Long, *Principal, Unitarian College, Manchester.* **Unitarian Worship**

Kilian McDonnell OSB, *President of the Institute for Ecumenical and Cultural Research and Professor of Theology at St John's College, Collegeville, Minnesota.* **Baptism 12. Pentecostal; Books, Liturgical 12. Pentecostal**

I. Howard Marshall, *Professor of New Testament Exegesis, University of Aberdeen.* **New Testament Worship**

†William D. Maxwell, *Late Professor of Ecclesiastical History, University of Fort Hare, Cape Province, SA.* **Reformed Worship**

Wilfrid Mellers, *Emeritus Professor of Music, University of York.* **Music as Worship**

Basil S. Moss, *Formerly Provost of Birmingham Cathedral.* **Cathedral**

Brian Newns, *Parish priest, St John Fisher, Widnes.* **Burial 3. Mediaeval and Roman Catholic; Epistle; Exorcism; Gospel; Last Gospel; Lesson**

Denise Newton, *Deputy Director, Institute for the Study of Worship and Religious Architecture, University of Birmingham.* **Sociology of Worship**

†A. Niebergall, *Late Professor of Practical Theology, University of Marburg.* **Burial 9. Lutheran; Marriage 9. Lutheran**

Geoffrey Parrinder, *Emeritus Professor of the Comparative Study of Religions, University of London.* **Buddhist Worship; Hindu Worship**

Stephen Pattison, *Lecturer in Pastoral Studies, Department of Theology, University of Birmingham.* **Pastoral Care and Worship**

Thomas Phelan, *Professor of History and Dean of the School of Humanities and Social Sciences, Rennsselaer Polytechnic Institute, Troy, New York.* **Offertory**

†C. E. Pocknee, *Late parish priest.* **Alms-dish; Altar; Altar Hangings; Ambo; Aumbry; Baldachin; Candles, Lamps and Lights; Cathedra; Chalice and Paten; Chrismatory; Ciborium; Corporal; Cross, Crucifix; Cruet; Fan; Frontal; Iconostasis; Monstrance; Pall; Piscina; Purificator; Pyx; Rostrum; Screen; Stoup; Thurible; Tower; Veil**

Marjorie Procter-Smith, *Assistant Professor of Liturgy, Perkins School of Theology, Southern Methodist University, Dallas.* **Women and Worship**

Bernarr Rainbow, *Director, The Curwen Institute, London.* **Anthem; Carol; Chants; Choir (Musical); Hymns 2. Vernacular; Metrical Psalms**

G. D. W. Randall, *Teacher of Religious Education, Broadland High School, Norfolk.* **Altar Hangings; Altar Rails; Aumbry; Bells; Cathedra; Ciborium; Communion Table; Corporal; Cross, Crucifix; Frontal; Iconostasis; Lectern; Pascal Candle; Pew; Piscina; Pulpit; Reredos; Rostrum; Screen; Tabernacle; Veil**

†Alan Richardson, *Late Dean of York.* **Creed, Creeds**

Rosemary R. Ruether, *Georgia Harkness Professor of Theology, Garrett-Evangelical Seminary and Graduate Faculty of Northwestern University, Evanston, Illinois.* **Feminist Liturgical Movement; Inclusive Language**

Letty M. Russell, *Professor of the Practice of Theology, Yale University Divinity School.* **Ordination of Women**

Peter Selby, *Bishop of Kingston-upon-Thames.* **Prayer**

David Sibrey, *Information Office of Jehovah's Witnesses, London.* **Baptism 8. Jehovah's Witnesses; Books, Liturgical 8. Jehovah's Witnesses; Burial 8. Jehovah's Witnesses; Jehovah's Witnesses Worship; Liturgies 8. Jehovah's Witnesses; Marriage 8. Jehovah's Witnesses; Ordination 8. Jehovah's Witnesses**

E. J. R. H. S. von Sicard, *Lecturer, Selly Oak Colleges, Birmingham.*

Baptism 9. Lutheran; Books, Liturgical 9. Lutheran (1) Europe; Ordination 9. Lutheran

John E. Skoglund, *Cornelius Woelfkin Professor Emeritus of Preaching, Colgate Rochester Divinity School.*
Baptist Worship; Burial 5. Baptist; Liturgies 5. Baptist; Ordination 5. Baptist

Norman Solomon, *Director, Centre for the Study of Judaism and Jewish-Christian Relations, Selly Oak, Birmingham.* **Jewish Worship**

Kenneth Stevenson, *Anglican Chaplain and Lecturer in Liturgy, University of Manchester.* **Blessing of a Marriage; Eucharistic Sacrifice; Family Services**

B. M. Sutcliffe, *Sign Language Interpreter.* **Choir (Sign Language)**

Eric S. Taylor, *Presiding Bishop of the Liberal Catholic Church in England.*
Liberal Catholic Church Worship

John B. Taylor, *Secretary General, World Conference on Religion and Peace.*
Islamic Worship

Anthony C. Thiselton, *Principal, St John's College, Nottingham.* **Sign, Symbol**

Joyce V. Thurman, *Teacher.* **House Churches**

Angela Tilby, *Producer, Religious Programmes, BBC Television.*
Media, Worship on the

C. Tol, *Pastor Emeritus, Old Catholic Church.*
Baptism 11. Old Catholic; Books, Liturgical 11. Old Catholic; Burial 11. Old Catholic; Liturgies 11. Old Catholic; Marriage 11. Old Catholic; Old Catholic Worship; Ordination 11. Old Catholic

Oliver Tomkins, *Formerly Bishop of Bristol and Chairman of the Faith-Order Commission, World Council of Churches.* **Ecumenical Worship; Intercommunion**

H. R. Tonks, *Minister of Carrs Lane Church, Birmingham.*
United Reformed Church Worship

David Tripp, *Lecturer in Liturgy, Lincoln Theological College.*
Covenant Service; Watch-Night

Geoffrey Wainwright, *Professor of Systematic Theology, Duke University, North Carolina.* **Theology of Worship**

C. J. Walsh, *Lecturer in Liturgy, Ushaw College, Durham.*
Benediction; Concelebration; Exposition; Forty Hours Devotion; Reservation; Rosary; Sacred Heart; Stations of the Cross; Veneration of the Cross

Keith Watkins, *Professor of Worship, Christian Theological Seminary, Indianapolis.*
Baptism 6. Christian Church; Books, Liturgical 6. Christian Church; Christian Church Worship; Liturgies 6. Christian Church; Ordination 6. Christian Church

E. C. Whitaker, *Canon Emeritus of Carlisle.*
Ante-communion; Baptism 4. Anglican; Bidding Prayer; Confirmation; Harvest Thanksgiving; Three Hours Devotion

James F. White, *Professor of Liturgy, University of Notre Dame, Indiana.*
Baptism 10. Methodist; Liturgies 10. Methodist; Marriage 10. Methodist; Methodist Worship 2. USA

James A. Whyte, *Professor of Practical Theology and Christian Ethics, University of St Andrews.*
Books, Liturgical 14. Reformed; Liturgies 14. Reformed; Marriage 13. Reformed; Presbyterian Worship

Gabriele Winkler, *Professor of Liturgical Studies, St John's College, Collegeville, Minnesota.* **Armenian Worship**

S. F. Winward, *Minister, Four Oaks Baptist Church, Sutton Coldfield.* **Baptism 5. Baptist; Books, Liturgical 5. Baptist; Marriage 5. Baptist**

Theo Witvliet, *Lecturer in Ecumenism, University of Amsterdam.* **Indigenization 3. Latin America; Liberation and Worship; Rastafarian Worship**

Thomas F. Zimmerman, *General Superintendent, The General Council of the Assemblies of God.* **Assemblies of God Churches' Worship**

† Deceased.

ABBREVIATIONS

ASB	Alternative Service Book 1980
AV	Authorized Version (King James Version) of the Bible
BCP	Book of Common Prayer
DACL	*Dictionnaire d'Archéologie Chrétienne et de Liturgie*, 1903
DTC	*Dictionnaire de Théologie Catholique* ed A. Vacant, E. Mangenot and E. Amann, 1903–50
ET	English Translation
IDB	*Interpreter's Dictionary of the Bible*
IKZ	*Internationale Kirchliche Zeitschrift*
ISWRA	Institute for the Study of Worship and Religious Architecture, University of Birmingham
JEH	*Journal of Ecclesiastical History*
NDCT	*A New Dictionary of Christian Theology* ed Alan Richardson and John Bowden, 1983
NEB	New English Bible
NT	New Testament
OT	Old Testament
RSV	Revised Standard Version of the Bible
RV	Revised Version of the Bible
SJT	*Scottish Journal of Theology*
TDNT	*Theological Dictionary of the New Testament*, ET of *TWNT* tr and ed Geoffrey Bromiley, 1964ff.
TWNT	*Theologisches Wörterbuch zum Neuen Testament* ed Gerhard Kittel, 1933ff.
WCC	World Council of Churches

* An asterisk following a word indicates a separate entry under that or a similar heading.

ACKNOWLEDGMENTS

We are grateful to the following for permission to reproduce copyright illustrations:

A. C. L., Brussels, *Plate 47*; *L'Art Sacré*, Paris, *Fig. 11*; James Austin, *Plate 5*; Bernsen's International Press Service Ltd, *Plate 55*; D. X. Botte, *Plate 15*; James Brooks, *Plate 10*; Courtauld Institute of Art, *Plates 7 & 8*; Margaret Eaton, *Figs 1 & 24*; Graphion, London, *Plate 41*; Louis Grosse Ltd, *Fig. 33*; C. V. Hancock, *Plates 6 & 34*; Photo Krongold, London, *Plate 40*; The Mansell Collection, *Plates 1 & 3*; Fritz Metzger, Zürich, *Plate 13*; National Gallery, London, *Plate 53*; *North American Moravian*, *Plate 22*; Pax House, Ipswich, Suffolk, *Plate 25*; Otto Pfeifer, Lucerne, *Plates 14, 56 & 57*; Poppe, Bad Kissingen, *Plate 11*; Rheinisches Bildarchiv, *Plate 12*; R. C. Swift, University of Birmingham, *Plates 37 & 44*; Andrew Sydenham, *Plate 27*; Uffizi, Florence, *Plate 32*; Victoria and Albert Museum, Crown Copyright, *Plates 46 & 54*; *Watch Tower*, *Plate 18*; Colin Westwood, *Plate 29*; C. D. and A. Willmott, *Plate 2*; World Council of Churches, *Plate 26*.

Ablutions

The ceremonial cleansing of the eucharistic vessels and of the minister's fingers after communion. In the patristic period this took place in the sacristy* when the service was ended (*see* **Disposal of Eucharistic Remains**). But in the tenth and eleventh centuries it became customary to do this immediately after the act of communion itself, i.e. before the end of the service proper. This transference of the ablutions to a position within the mass was realized in two stages. The first stage comprised the washing of the priest's hands, the water being poured down the piscina*. The second stage involved the cleaning of the chalice with the consumption of the liquid used. The ablutions as finally evolved were the product of the fusion of these two, and so the Roman practice, regulated by the missal of Pope Pius V, requires the cleansing of the chalice with wine and then of the fingers and chalice with wine and water.

W. Lockton, *The Treatment of the Remains at the Eucharist after Holy Communion and the Time of the Ablutions,* 1920.

EDITOR

Absolution

A formal act of pronouncing the forgiveness of sins. In the early church this was a public event, in the sense that sinners were reconciled in the presence of the congregation, after they had previously made private confession; the church leaders were thus acting upon the commission of Christ to 'bind' and 'loose' (Matt. 16.19; 18.18). By the side of this public system of discipline, there was also the practice of confessing one's sins privately to a spiritual director without absolution. In the Celtic monasteries of the sixth century these two systems were amalgamated, the absolution, in front of the congregation, being transferred to private confession. The confession (*see* **Prayer** 2) entered the liturgy soon after the year 1000 and the accompanying absolution was either declaratory or precatory, i.e. God's forgiveness was either declared or prayed for. In the thirteenth century the indicative form was adopted, i.e. 'I absolve you.'

Absolution continues to be given privately, e.g. in the Anglican, Lutheran, Orthodox and Roman Churches. Liturgically it is included in most services, such as the daily offices or in the eucharist.

EDITOR

Absolution Prayer

A prayer, which reached its final form in the thirteenth century, used in the Divine Office* after the psalms and before the lessons of each nocturn.

EDITOR

Absolutions of the Dead

The name given to the mediaeval service after a Requiem Mass*. It consisted of prayers for the departed and the censing and asperging of the body while the *Pater noster* was said. These absolutions were changed into a final farewell to the dead (*see* **Burial** 3) in the RC *Ordo Exequiarum* in 1969.

EDITOR

Acolyte

Strictly one of the minor orders of the ministry, the office existed in the church in Rome by the middle of the third century. It was subsequently introduced into the other parts of Western Christendom and is still one of the stages through which aspirants to the priesthood in the Roman Catholic Church pass. In this sense it is part of the ordained ministry. The acolyte's functions were originally similar to those of the modern server* and included the carrying of ceremonial lights. The term is commonly used generally of those who serve at the altar, and more particularly of those who carry candles in a liturgical procession.

P. HINCHLIFF

Adoration

see **Prayer** 1

Advent

The word is derived from a Latin root which means 'coming' or 'arrival', and the season was developed in the Western church as a preparation for the festival of the nativity. Councils held in Gaul in the sixth century refer to a penitential period of six weeks before Christmas. There was fasting on Mondays, Wednesdays and Fridays. But the season was already known to Gregory of Tours in the latter part of the preceding

century. It may be affirmed that fifth-century Gaul was the place of origin of the fully organized period of six Sundays, and that the structure of Advent, with regard to its length, was modelled on Lent. Various lectionaries dating from the seventh and eighth centuries, or representing the use of that time, show the six Sunday pattern in Gaul and north-west Italy. At a greater distance from Gaul, that is, in Spain, north-east Italy and south Italy, we find five Sundays, clearly representing a modification of the original structure. The Würzburg manuscript, *Mp.th.fol.62*, containing in a table of epistles the oldest Roman lectionary, commences with Christmas and places a five-Sunday Advent at the end. So at Rome the logic of the invention of Advent had not been completely accepted. Eventually at Rome Advent was reduced from five to four Sundays. As the Roman rite gradually triumphed over the native uses of the West the four-Sunday Advent became the norm.

Advent has come to mark preparation for the coming of Christ in a double manner, first in his incarnation as the babe of Bethelehem, which is obvious, and in his second coming at the end of time, which is perhaps less so. Also involved is commemoration of the ministry of John the Baptist as Christ's forerunner and, for Anglicans and other followers of the tradition of the Book of Common Prayer, the place of scripture in worship and life, because of the prayer book collect for the second Sunday.

Modern observance of Advent tends to be overshadowed by the all but universal anticipation of Christmas, necessary in scholastic institutions, unfortunate if perhaps inevitable elsewhere. Likewise it can be questioned whether the Joint Liturgical Group Calendar, with its nine-Sunday approach to Christmas, can be combined with the traditional Western four-Sunday Advent, as the Alternative Service Book of the Church of England has done. Perhaps a penitential analogue to Lent for the period before Christmas is otiose anyway, a piece of unnecessary Gallican elaboration, and something like the Joint Liturgical Group approach should be adopted without further complication.

For bibliography *see* under **Calendar**.

R. F. BUXTON

Advent Star

In Moravian homes and churches all over the world what is known as the 'Advent Star' is hung up on the first Sunday in Advent and left in place until Epiphany. The custom originated in Eastern Germany around 1850 where stars were made by a family named Verbeek who later founded a small star-making factory in Herrnhut, which is now the headquarters of the Moravian Church in Eastern Germany. The factory is still operating and makes and exports the stars all over the world.

Originally the triangular shaped paper 'points' of the stars were affixed to a solid metal core; later a smaller and simpler version was evolved in which the 'points' could be joined together using paper fasteners. The stars are illuminated from within by a low wattage electric bulb powered according to the size of the star. (*See* Plate 28.)

The star has a threefold symbolism. It recalls the star which guided the wise men from their homes to Bethlehem where they found and worshipped the infant Christ (Matt. 2). It testifies to the greatness of God the Creator who made the numberless stars (Gen. 1.16). And it points to Christ, 'the bright and morning star' (Rev. 22.16).

J. H. FOY

Adventist Worship

see **Seventh-day Adventist Worship**

Agape

see **Love Feast**

Agnus Dei

The anthem * *Agnus Dei*, for many centuries sung between the fraction * and communion in the Roman mass, has recently been restored to its original purpose as a *confractorium*, i.e. anthem to be sung during the fraction. It appears to have been introduced into the Roman rite in the seventh century, perhaps during the pontificate of Sergius I (687–701), for it is clearly of Eastern origin – the word 'lamb' is commonly used in the Eastern liturgies to designate both Christ and the consecrated bread of the eucharist, and the West Syrian liturgy

contains *confractoria* which speak of 'the Lamb of God who takes away the sins of the world' – and this was a period of considerable Eastern, and especially Syrian, influence at Rome: Syria had recently been overrun by the Muslims, and many Syrian clergy found their way to Rome, among them Pope Theodore I (642–9), while Sergius I was a Syrian by descent.

A prayer addressed specifically to Christ present in the eucharist as a sacrificial offering, the anthem originally comprised simply as many repetitions as necessary of the single sentence 'O Lamb of God, who takes away the sins of the world, have mercy upon us'. When the fraction was shortened through the introduction of unleavened bread, the number of repetitions was fixed at three, probably about the middle of the ninth century, and during the tenth and eleventh centuries, when the fraction had all but disappeared, and the anthem in practice therefore accompanied the kiss of peace (*see* **Gestures**) immediately following, the third clause was given the appropriately variant ending it has had ever-since – '. . . of the world, grant us peace'. As early as the eleventh century, too, a further variant appears, which persisted until 1969: at requiem masses, the first and second petitions ended '. . . grant them rest', and the third '. . . grant them rest everlasting'. The present *Ordo Missae* has suppressed this variant, and provision has also been made for additional repetitions of the opening sentence when, for whatever reason, the fraction is more prolonged than usual.

The *Agnus Dei* was retained in the BCP of 1549 as a communion anthem, but suppressed in that of 1552, as in most of the reformed liturgies of the sixteenth and later centuries. Its use was (unofficially) restored in many Anglican churches in the nineteenth and twentieth centuries, and, in varying translations or paraphrases, it has been incorporated in many twentieth-century revisions of the eucharistic liturgy, either as a *confractorium* or as a communion anthem.

See also **Music in the Mass of the Roman Rite; Ordinary**.

J. A. Jungmann, *The Mass of the Roman Rite*, II, 1955, pp. 332–40.

W. JARDINE GRISBROOKE

Aisle

From the Latin *ala* and the French *aile* meaning 'a wing', aisle refers to an adjunct of a main church building. It is a lateral division, being the part on either side of the nave*. In the patristic period in certain areas it was customary to assign the south aisle to the men and the north to the women. The application of this word to the gangways up the centre of a nave or elsewhere is of course incorrect, and the expression 'centre aisle' is a contradiction in terms.

EDITOR

Alb

see **Vestments** 1(*a*)

All Saints

Many martyrs and non-martyrs were unrecorded and therefore unhonoured on earth. On the other hand, places like Antioch and Rome had more known martyrs than there were days of the year. So a common feast for all martyrs was instituted, and this is the origin of the later All Saints feast. A feast of All Martyrs was observed on Easter Friday in Syria at the beginning of the fifth century, and the octave day of Pentecost was the day for a similar feast in the Byzantine liturgy. In Rome, Boniface IV had the relics of many martyrs moved from the catacombs to the Pantheon, and on 13 May 610, he consecrated the building as *St Maria ad Martyres*. This became known as the feast of All Martyrs and All Saints and of Our Lady. These three feasts, especially the Syrian one, were closely connected with the Easter season and therefore with Christ's victory. This paschal connection was broken and eventually rather lost sight of after the Roman feast of 13 May was transferred in 835 to 1 November, with the title of All Saints.

J. CONNELLY

All Souls

Most Christians who were remembered each year were neither martyrs nor confessors – people not distinguished by their death or by their way of life. At such anniversaries the eucharist was offered, not in thanksgiving as for the martyrs, but in petition to God and in the hope that God

would give the departed to share in the victory of the risen Christ. The funeral service is a glowing testimony to Christian hope in a 'blessed resurrection', and to Christian love for departed relatives and friends.

Besides the funeral or anniversary rites, a general commemoration or *memento* of the dead is found in the eucharistic prayer of liturgies. There has also been for centuries, a day set apart for the general commemoration of the dead. Holy Saturday* was designated in the Syrian rite as a 'memorial day of all priests and monks and of all the faithful departed'. This shows the connection between Easter and the liturgy of the dead, and between All Saints and All Souls.

There is evidence of many local 'memorial days' in the West in earlier centuries, but All Souls, as now observed, is due to Odilo of Cluny. This solemn 'memorial day', first kept in Cluniac houses (from about 1000), eventually became an official part of the Roman rite.

During the 1914–18 war Benedict XV allowed priests to celebrate the eucharist three times on All Souls' Day (2 November). This permission was given partly because of the 'useless slaughter' of the war and also because the confiscation of church property at, and since, the Reformation had made it impossible to carry out the obligations for anniversary masses which had been the conditions of so many gifts and legacies.

J. CONNELLY

Alleluia

One of the richest words in religious vocabulary, it comes to English through the Greek and Latin transliterations of the Hebrew phrase (sometimes written as one word) *hallelu yah*. The Hebrew is a plural imperative with, as object, the short form of the name of God (Yahweh): 'Praise Yah' (AV 'Praise ye the Lord'). It aptly condenses the themes of Israel's worship as the exaltation of the Creator, who, for all his mystery and terrible power, has revealed himself in personal and accessible form. The plural imperative itself is also typical of Israelite worship, where the leading motif of the hymns is the summoning of the worshippers and the world to praise the Lord. Thus praise is seen especially as the response of the community of creatures before their Creator, one encouraging another in the great work which banishes

Fig. 1 Praising God in Ancient Egypt. Trumpeter with singing and clapping priests at the outset of the festal procession of Amun. *See also* Fig. 24.

pre-occupation with self and worship of false gods and rejoices in God's triumph. (*See* Fig. 1.)

In the Hebrew Bible the phrase occurs only in the psalms, where (apart from 135.3) it lies outside the main text, appearing as a preliminary or a concluding summons or as both. Thus it is found at the beginning of 111 and 112; at the end of 104, 105, 115–117; and at the beginning and end of 106, 113, 135, 146–150. Although in 147 it can be understood to connect grammatically with the main text, it can generally be regarded as an independent liturgical cry, common no doubt in oral usage and perhaps very ancient, but only occasionally happening to be written with the text of hymnic psalms, especially from around the fourth century BC. The textual witnesses, including the Dead Sea Scrolls, show considerable variation in the frequency and placing of the expression. The Greek translators, from the third or second century BC, found it generally only at the beginning of psalms. They seem to have known it in worship in its Hebrew form, for they simply transliterated it. It occurs likewise in transliteration in the Greek of 3 Maccabees (7.13, *c*.100 BC), where rescued Jews break into rejoicing, with 'the priests and the whole multitude shouting the Alleluia'. In the Greek book of Tobit (13.18) it is a cry of praise appropriate to the new Jerusalem. The tradition is taken up in the New Testament, where 'Alleluia' leads the praise in heaven (Rev. 19.2, 3, 4, 6). In the Odes of Solomon, which survive in Syriac, Coptic and Greek, and which may be early Christian psalms, each ode ends with an Alleluia.

It was adopted into the Christian liturgy at an early date as an expression of joy and praise particularly suitable for Eastertide. Gregory the Great determined the Roman usage prescribing it for mass and the offices throughout the year except during the penitential season from Septuagesima to Easter. It was later omitted from the funeral offices but the Greek church retained it for all.

In the Western rite, together with a verse from scripture, it follows the Gradual immediately preceding the gospel, but in the Mozarabic rite it is sung after the gospel, as in the East where it precedes the Great Entrance*. In the 1549 BCP it was appointed to be said after the first *Gloria Patri* at morning and evening prayer from Easter to Trinity; it was replaced by a versicle and response in 1552 but was allowed in the Irish PB of 1877 to be sung after the gospel. In the American BCP (1979) it appears as an invocation at the beginning of the communion service for use from Easter to Pentecost. The ASB (1980) follows suit for Rite A and also suggests it as an invitation to communion as well as printing it as an opening sentence for morning and evening prayer. The United Lutheran Church of America prescribes its use when 'the Gradual for the day is omitted'. It is printed in the *English Hymnal* under 'Introits and other Anthems'.

See also **Chants of the Proper of the Mass; Music in the Mass of the Roman Rite**.

F. Delitzsch, *Commentary on the Psalms*, III, 1889, on Ps. 104.35; J. H. Eaton, *The Psalms Come Alive,* 1984, pp.5, 95, 128; H. Gunkel, *Einleitung in die Psalmen,* 1933, pp.37–8.

J. H. EATON

Alms

Ultimately derived from the Greek word *eleemosune* meaning 'mercy', the term alms refers to charitable gifts. The necessity for generous giving was recognized by the first Christians as the right response to Christ's own self-giving (II Cor. 8.9). The presentation of these gifts early became an integral part of worship, especially at the eucharist associated with the offertory*, and they were a portion of the offerings made either in kind or in money.

At the present day the tendency is to speak of the 'collection' and the word 'alms' has a certain archaic character. In liturgical usage, however, the correct phase would be 'the collection of alms'.

EDITOR

Alms-dish

The duty of sharing material things with those less fortunately placed occupies a prominent place in the teaching of the OT and NT (Matt. 6.3–4; Acts 11.27–30), and the subject is often mentioned by early Christian writers, such as Justin Martyr and Cyprian. In earlier times, the method was sometimes to collect alms* for the poor outside the church; in many English

mediaeval churches there was an alms-chest with a slot in the lid, as at Heckfield, Yorkshire. Pope Innocent III ordered such chests to be placed in English churches in the time of King John for collections for the Crusades. In the time of King Edward VI many of the alms-chests disappeared, but there remained the poor men's box.

Some commentators have wrongly concluded that the alms-dish or basin was entirely an innovation of the post-Reformation rites introduced in the English prayer book; but this is incorrect, as there are fifteenth-century examples still extant, and there are references to such dishes in the fourteenth century (*Test Ebor.* i. 114, Surtees Soc.).

It is, however, interesting to notice the changes that have taken place in the method of collecting alms in the various editions of the English prayer book. That of 1549 says, 'While the clerks do sing the Offertory, so many as are disposed shall offer to the poor men's box, everyone according to his ability.' But in the 1552 book the rubric was altered thus, 'Then shall the churchwardens or some other by them appointed gather the devotion of the people, and put the same into the poor men's box.' It was not until 1662 that the present custom appeared, following the Scottish Liturgy of 1637, 'The deacon or (if no such be present) one of the churchwardens shall receive the devotions of the people there present, in a bason provided for that purpose. And when all have offered, he shall reverently bring the said bason, with the oblations therein, and deliver it to the presbyter, who shall humbly present it before the Lord, and set it upon the Holy Table.'

This was a return in principle to the custom of earlier centuries when the elements of bread and wine as well as other offerings in kind were brought up by the people and received on tray-shaped patens (*see* **Chalice and Paten**).

C. E. POCKNEE

Almuce

see **Vestments** 2(*e*)

Altar

Derived from the Latin *altare*, the word means a place or structure where sacrifice is offered. In Christian worship it is associated with the chief act of Christian worship, the Lord's Supper*, the eucharist*, the holy communion* or the mass*.

There can be little doubt that at the institution of the sacrament of the Lord's body and blood in the Upper Room Jesus presided at a wooden table; and that structures of this kind were used in the house-churches when the eucharist was celebrated on the first day of the week during the first three centuries of the Christian era. References to the eucharist in the NT are not frequent since it was the normal function of the Christian assembly on Sundays.

It has been mistakenly supposed that the term 'altar' can only be applied to a structure of stone rather than wood. Paul, referring to the disorders at Corinth in connection with the eucharist, speaks of 'the Lord's table' (I Cor. 10.21); but this is an oblique reference to the sacrament itself rather than to the structure of the table. The writer of the Epistle to the Hebrews says, 'We have an altar from which those who serve the tent have no right to eat' (Heb. 13.10). There can be little doubt that the writer is referring to the eucharist in distinction from the sacrifices of the old covenant. It is important to take note that he refers not simply to an altar in the new dispensation but to a place where eating takes place, a sacrificial act. In the Greek text of this passage the term for altar is the normal term used to describe both Jewish and pagan altars of sacrifice in the Septuagint, e.g. Lev. 6.9 and Judg. 6.25. The fact that this term is applied to the eucharist is of considerable significance. The reference to the eucharist as 'a pure sacrifice' by the writer of the *Didache,* ch. 14, about AD 100, also underlines this fact. Ignatius of Antioch in his epistles, written about 107, also makes numerous references to the altar (the same term) and the eucharist, thus 'Be careful to use one eucharist, for there is one flesh of our Lord Jesus Christ, and one cup for union with his blood, one altar, as there is one bishop' (*Ep. Phil.* 4.1). The Greek fathers during the first four centuries sometimes use the term 'table' and sometimes 'altar' for the structure upon which the eucharist is celebrated. The Latin fathers, such as Tertullian and Cyprian in the third century, also use the terms *mensa* and *altare* for the eucharistic table. Augustine of Hippo (d. 430) uses the term *altare* in connection with a wooden table (*Ep.* 185), thus

disproving the idea that a distinction was drawn between a communion table of wood and a sacrificial altar of stone. Wooden altars seem to have been of various shapes, square, round and semi-circular.

There can be little doubt that the custom of having stone altars is directly connected with the celebration of the eucharist at or near the tomb of a saint in the catacombs, thus linking altar with tomb. With the building of permanent churches in the fourth century at Rome, Jerusalem and elsewhere, the idea was carried a step further and the altar was built over the martyr's or confessor's tomb or shrine. Hence the words martyrium* or confessio. In the more important churches the body of a celebrated saint was buried under the altar, but in the smaller churches which were used simply as a place of assembly for public worship it became the custom to require that some kind of relic associated with a saint should be buried in a cavity in the top of the altar. In some instances a consecrated host was used instead. Thus eventually it became the more usual custom to require that no altar was used without such relics. (*See also* **Saints**, **Cult of the.**)

While in the first three centuries the mere fact of celebrating the eucharist on an altar-table was considered to be sufficient to hallow it, it gradually came to be the custom that no altar should be used without its formal consecration by a bishop. This consisted in the placing of relics in the altar, to which we have alluded; in addition, the

Plate 1 Altar with ciborium c.1000, Castel S. Elia, Italy

altar-top had five crosses engraved on it and these were anointed with chrism by the bishop (*see* **Consecration of Churches**). Nevertheless, it is possible to produce evidence for the use of altars which had received no such consecration. Also, we know that wooden altars were in use in England until quite late in the Middle Ages.

In the earlier centuries the altar was of equal dimensions, i.e. it was cube-shaped. Prominence was given to this type of altar by surmounting it with a canopy mounted directly on four columns, and known as a ciborium* (*see* Plate 1). This kind of canopy and its columns were made of wood, stone, or precious metal. In the West, as the centuries went on, the altar tended to be lengthened, until in the late Middle Ages we find very long altars such as that at Tewkesbury Abbey (13 ft) and that of the Lady Chapel at Ely (over 16 ft). The result was that the ciborium resting on its four columns became dismembered; the posts or columns remained round the ends of the lengthened altar, while the canopy became suspended as a separate tester hanging from the roof. Sometimes the posts were surmounted by carved angels holding candles (*see* **Riddel**). This type of altar was more prevalent in northern Europe, and it has been mistakenly termed an 'English altar', as though it was something peculiar to the Church of England. (*See also* Fig. 26.)

Another development in Western Christendom in the Middle Ages was the multiplication of altars in churches associated with guilds and fraternities, in contrast to the primitive era when there was only one altar and one celebration of the eucharist in any one church on any one day. In this respect the Eastern Orthodox Church, with its one altar and one eucharist on any one day, has remained closer to the primitive church.

For many centuries, too, except possibly in churches of the East Syrian rite, the altar was normally free-standing and accessible on all sides. In the West, however, the altar came to be placed against a wall or screen*. In the greater churches such as abbeys and cathedrals, this screen often separated the altar from the reliquary containing the body of the patron saint, as we can still see at Westminster Abbey and St Albans Cathedral. The separation of the altar from the saint's reliquary in the later Middle Ages was to permit the crowds to pray at the shrine of the saint without interrupting the service in progress at the high altar.

The placing of candlesticks (*see* **Candles, Lamps and Lights**) and a cross* on the altar was also a very late innovation in the West, the candlesticks and cross originally being used in processions and placed on the pavement around the altar. Only at the end of the Middle Ages did these ornaments sometimes come to be set upon the altar. The idea that all altars must have a cross standing on them is an error of the nineteenth-century ecclesiologists. Also, the custom of having precisely six candlesticks on the altar was a development that arose from the Counter-Reformation movement in the Roman Catholic Church in the sixteenth century. Nor did flower vases find a place on the holy table in olden times; instead flowers were thrown on the pavement before the altar.

At the Reformation many stone altars were destroyed and replaced by wooden tables because stone altars had become associated with a particular view of the eucharistic sacrifice*. Through a revived biblical theology and the wider study of comparative religion we realize that both mediaevalists and Reformers were too limited in their conception of sacrifice which they associated exclusively with death or immolation. Today we should prefer to say that the sacrifice of Christ recalled in the eucharist is the whole of his atoning work culminating in the cross, resurrection and ascension.

J. Braun, *Der Christliche Altar,* 2 vols, 1924; D. R. Dendy, *The Use of Lights in Christian Worship,* 1959; C. E. Pocknee, *The Christian Altar,* 1963.

C. E. POCKNEE

Altar Hangings

In the first two centuries of the Christian era it is unlikely that the table at which the eucharist* was celebrated was regarded as a permanent feature and ornament. But in the third century, rooms came to be adapted permanently in the larger houses as the eucharistic room, and the altar-table was looked upon as the focal point of Christian worship (*see* **Architectural Setting**). Over the table was thrown a cloth of silk, damask or brocade which enveloped it on all sides,

the altar* being cube-shaped in structure at that time. As time went on, this cloth was decorated with emblems in embroidery and with jewels; John Chrysostom in the fourth century had to give a warning that too much attention should not be paid to this kind of thing. We can see, in a sixth-century mosaic in the church of San Vitale, Ravenna, a depiction of an altar arrayed in this kind of altar-cloth or pall.

Over the decorated cloth there was spread at the time of the offertory* the fair linen cloth upon which the eucharist was celebrated. The altar arrayed in this vesture was regarded as the symbol of Christ in the midst of his church.

This type of throw-over altar cloth was revived in the Church of England in the seventeenth century and has somewhat misleadingly come to be termed a 'Jacobean' altar frontal; but it is, as we have stated, a revival of the vesture of the early Christian centuries.

In the second part of the Middle Ages in the West, when altars came to be placed close to screen and walls, the throwover cloth was abandoned for a frontal*, a flat silk cloth which was suspended on the side of the altar visible to the congregation.

In the earlier centuries there were also silk or damask curtains suspended on rods between the columns or posts that supported the ciborium* (*see also* **Baldachin; Riddel**). These curtains were also embroidered and decorated with jewels in the larger and more affluent churches. In the later Middle Ages, when the altar came to be lengthened, these curtains were hung between the riddel-posts that enclosed the ends of the altar, while at the back of the

Plate 2 Altar with carved reredos and riddel posts, vested with frontal and frontlet, Tring, England

altar, if there was not a reredos* of wood or stone, a cloth with embroidered figures and emblems was hung. This back-cloth is properly termed a dorsal or super-frontal. (*See* Plate 2; Fig. 26.)

A fair linen cloth is spread on the top of the altar at the time of the celebration of the eucharist. As the shape of the altar has changed over the course of the centuries, this cloth has had to be adapted in form to meet such changes.

P. Dearmer, *The Linen Ornaments of the Church*, [2]1950; J. M. Petersen, *Altar Frontals, their history and construction*, 1962; C. E. Pocknee, *The Christian Altar*, 1963; The Warham Guild, *The Warham Guild Handbook*, rev ed 1963.

C. E. POCKNEE/G. D. W. RANDALL

Altar Rails

Altar rails were unknown in England before the Reformation and they began to come into use in the last part of the reign of Queen Elizabeth I, but a considerable impetus was given to their use by William Laud who, as Dean, Bishop and finally Archbishop (he was appointed to Canterbury in 1634), insisted that the altar should be placed in the traditional position in the sanctuary* and fenced off with rails to protect it from irreverence. To quote the words of Bishop Wren of Norwich, 'the rayle be made before the communion table reaching crosse from the north wall to the south wall, neere one yarde in height, so thick with pillars that doggs may not gett in.'

Although, therefore, they were not designed to provide support for kneeling communicants during the administration, and, indeed, were often rather high for convenience, it was the existence of the rails which suggested to the Laudian clergy the practice of the communicants coming to the altar to receive rather than the clergy going to them in their seats. Sometimes, especially in the eighteenth century, rails were provided on three and even four sides of the communion table rather than crossing the chancel from north to south in the approved Laudian fashion. Rails were also used to define the sanctuary and protect the altar in European Baroque churches which had no screen*.

Once the menace of dogs had diminished in the nineteenth century, lower, more open rails were installed, but liturgical reforms now taking place seem to indicate that both rails and benches alike may become obsolete with the increasing custom of standing to receive holy communion. It should be realized that for over a thousand years throughout Christendom the normal posture for receiving holy communion was that of standing: only in the thirteenth century did the custom of kneeling come into fashion in connection with the introduction of the ceremony of the elevation of the host. Standing at the holy communion has never been abandoned in the Eastern Orthodox rite.

G. W. O. Addleshaw and F. Etchells, *The Architectural Setting of Anglican Worship*, 1948; G. Randall, *Church Furnishing and Decoration in England and Wales*, 1980.

C. E. POCKNEE/G. D. W. RANDALL

Altar, Stripping of

A rite that took place (and in some Anglican churches still does) at the end of the liturgy on Maundy Thursday*. The altar cloth(s) and frontal* were removed during the recitation of Ps. 21 (22).

From a very early time altars, which were simple and unpretentious structures, were covered with a single cloth, for such was the custom of the Roman empire at the time. Of this we have probably the first witness in the Gnostic *Acts of Thomas* (5th act, ch. 49), and by the fourth century Optatus of Milevis certainly refers to the linen cloth. This was removed without ceremony at the end of the eucharist and the altar stood bare throughout the week. This remained the custom for centuries, although by the sixth century, at least in some places (e.g. Ravenna), the altar was richly clothed. This practice, together with the later allegorizing tendencies, led to a symbolic interpretation of the rite.

There were two factors that led to the development of the rite summarily described above. The altar itself came to signify Christ's body and the cloth(s) and frontal or pallium the members of Christ's body, namely Christians. The place in the Passion according to St John (which was and is still sung on Good Friday) where Ps. 21 (22) is quoted (John 19. 23, 24) led to a dramatization of the rite. By the second half

of the eighth century (*Ordo Romanus* XXVII), two deacons standing at either end of the altar took away the cloth 'in the manner of thieves', furtively. Later still (*Ordo Romanus* XXXI–*c.* 850–900), the cloth was taken from the altar at the words 'They divided my vesture among them'. In the tenth century the rite was associated with the rending of the veil in the Temple, and two cloths were prepared which at the appropriate moment were parted and taken away.

The rite then signified the stripping of Christ before his crucifixion and the separation of Christ from his members, the church. All this was summed up in the (allegorical) commentaries of Beleth (d. 1165) and Durandus of Mende (d. 1296), with sundry additions. For the former, the rite signified the kenosis of Christ who in the passion was stripped of his glory, his stripping by the soldiers before crucifixion and the abandonment of him by the apostles. The rite reminds Durandus of Isa. 53 and of the rending of the Temple veil. The ancient action, then, of removing the cloth from the altar after every eucharist and then on Maundy Thursday without ceremony was now transferred to Good Friday with the significance that it symbolized the stripping of Christ before his crucifixion. Combined with the washing of the altar*, it ultimately signified the church's mourning for its dead Lord.

In the Roman Catholic revision of the Holy Week liturgy of 1970, there has been a return to the earliest tradition. Both on Maundy Thursday and Good Friday the cloth is removed without ceremony.

See also **Altar Hangings**.

M. Andrieu, *Les* Ordines Romani *du Haut-Moyen Age*, ORI, OR XXVII, OR XXI; J. Beleth, *Divinorum Officiorum . . . explicatio*, c. 104; G. Durandus, *Rationale Divinorum Officiorum*, Lib. V. c. LXXVI; M. Righetti, *Manuale di Storia Liturgica*, II, [2]1955, p. 168.

J. D. CRICHTON

Altar, Washing of

A rite now observed only at St Peter's, Rome, on Maundy Thursday*, it was, in the Middle Ages, practised very generally (e.g. Spain, France, England) at least in cathedrals and larger churches on the same day.

Originally it was a utilitarian rite whose purpose was to clean the whole church in preparation for the celebration of the Easter festival. Thus Isidore of Seville (*De Ecclesiasticis Officiis*, I, 29) speaks of the altars, walls, floors and vessels being washed on Maundy Thursday. This statement is juxtaposed to one referring to the Lord's washing of his disciples' feet, thus discreetly suggesting a symbolism: the church in the person of the disciples is washed, cleansed from sin.

A Gallic writer, St Eloy or Eligius of Noyon (588–659), repeats this statement, which would seem to indicate that the custom was common at this time to Spain and Gaul. It does not appear in the Roman books until the tenth-century *Romano-Germanic Pontifical* (ed C. Vogel, 1963, II, p.57) where Isidore's words are reproduced almost *verbatim*. It would seem to be a clear inference that the custom came from Spain through France to Rome under German influence. Thence it spread throughout Europe. It is found in J. Beleth (d. 1165) and in Durandus of Mende (d. 1296), the Sarum books and in the English writer John Myrc (*fl.* 1400), who provides a commentary on the Sarum use.

1. *Symbolism.* As can be seen from the origin of the observance, its meaning is partly suggested by its place in the Holy Week* liturgy. It was associated with the commemoration of the Last Supper and of the Passion. But during all the Middle Ages the altar acquired an ever richer symbolism and became more and more the focus of attention. It became the principal symbol of Christ. At its consecration, five crosses were carved in the table (*mensa*) to represent the five wounds of Christ, and the cloths and covering (frontal or *antependium*) were regarded as the members of Christ's (mystical) body. The stripping of the altar* was a sign of death and, as the present rite indicates, the washing with wine and water signifies the mourning over the dead Christ. In other words, it is a funeral rite.

But the mediaeval writers, after their fashion, allegorized the rite. Thus for Beleth, the washing with wine and water signifies the blood of redemption and the water, the water of regeneration. There is naturally a reference to the water and blood that flowed from Christ's side, and there is the comment that the church washes the

altar because his body was sprinkled with blood and water on the cross. The branches or sprigs with which the wine and water were spread over the altar suggest the crown of thorns, and therefore the branches must have rough leaves. But he also refers to the cleaning of the floor with similar branches, and this symbolizes our being cleansed from vice. Durandus repeats much of this, sometimes using the very words of Beleth, and offering very little of his own. In the Sarum use we note that it was the five crosses themselves that were washed, thus emphasizing that it was a funeral rite. John Myrc repeats Beleth and Durandus.

The twigs or branches were scattered upon the altar after the washing, and even in recent times, the palms from the previous Palm Sunday were put on the (now unwashed) altars (*see* Herbert Thurston, *Lent and Holy Week*, 1904, pp.302f.).

2. *The present rite*. It is performed by seven canons of St Peter's after the last office of Maundy Thursday. With the other clergy of the basilica, they go in procession to the Altar of the Confession, Ps. 21 (22) is intoned and the canons then pour wine mixed with water on the altar. The cardinal archpriest approaches and with a branch of yew spreads it over the altar and the canons do likewise. Afterwards, they dry the altar with sponges and towels. All now retire from the altar and kneel while the responsory *Christus factus est* (Phil. 2.8) is sung. The rite concludes with a silent recitation of the Lord's Prayer and the collect used at the day's office (*see* Mario Righetti, *Manuale di Storia Liturgica*, II, [2] 1955, p.168).

J. D. CRICHTON

Ambo

Also spelt ambon, a Greek term in origin. A structure often approached by a flight of steps and surrounded by a parapet, and made of wood, stone or marble. It was used for the reading of the gospel at the eucharist and was usually larger than the mediaeval pulpit * as its platform not only accommodated the readers of the gospel but also the attendant taperers or candle-bearers. The ambo was used also on the eve of Easter by the deacon * who sang the *exultet* at the blessing of the Paschal candle*. In the larger basilicas* the ambo was often decorated with carved or tessellated designs, a frequent one being Jonah and the whale, a type of Christ's resurrection (Matt. 12.40).

There were sometimes lesser ambos, as at St Clement's, Rome, from which the other lessons at the eucharist were read or a pair, as at St Mark's, Venice. All these structures

Plate 3 Ambo, thirteenth century, Ravello cathedral, Italy

usually had a desk upon which the liturgical book was placed.

From the steps of the ambo a portion of psalmody was sung by the chanters in between the reading of the epistle and the gospel. Hence this chant came to be known as the gradual, from the Latin *gradus*, a step. The ambo was not primarily designed as the place from which a sermon was delivered, as this was done by the bishop from his throne or cathedra*.

See Plate 3.

C. E. POCKNEE/G. D. W. RANDALL

Amen

A Hebrew word meaning 'firm' or 'established', and then, as an adverb, 'certainly' or 'assuredly'. It is used often in the OT as an acknowledgment that a saying is valid and binding and constitutes a claim which is accepted. In synagogue worship it served as a community response of assent and confirmation.

In the NT it is frequent on the lips of Jesus, being translated in the AV by 'verily' and in more recent versions by 'truly'. It stands, however, at the beginning and not at the end of Jesus' sayings to show that the words are reliable and true and are so because he acknowledges them as his own and hence makes them valid.

Following the example of Jesus and the practice of the synagogue, it was adopted into Christian liturgical usage, and so Paul speaks of the amen of the assembly at the giving of thanks (I Cor. 14.16). According to Justin Martyr the people say amen after prayer and thanksgiving and 'this word amen answers in the Hebrew language to *genoito*, i.e. so be it'. Cyril of Jerusalem states that the Lord's Prayer is 'sealed' with an amen.

In the eucharist the amen is especially noticeable as the people's response to the prayer of consecration and, in many liturgies, to the words of administration. It is, however, not only an assent but also a proclamation of faith, for Jesus himself is 'the amen' (Rev. 3.14), i.e. he himself is the response to the divine Yes in him. So the worshippers proclaim their belief that in Christ the faithfulness of God has been vindicated.

TDNT, I, pp.335–8.

EDITOR

Amice

see **Vestments** 1(*b*)

Anamnesis

see **Anaphora** 7

Anaphora

A Greek word, meaning 'offering', from the verb *anaphero*, 'I carry up', 'I offer up (in sacrifice)', 'I offer up (to God on high)', which has from a very early date been the normal Greek name for the eucharistic prayer, commonly called in English the prayer of consecration*, and is universally the name most widely used by liturgical scholars. The oldest name for this prayer is probably *eucharistia* (Gk and thence Lat 'thanksgiving'); other ancient names are *actio sacrificii* (Lat 'the act of sacrifice'), *oratio oblationis* (Lat 'the prayer of offering'), and simply *oratio* or *prex* (Lat '*the* prayer'). In the Roman rite for many centuries this prayer has been entitled canon* (Lat 'rule', the exact sense of which in this application is uncertain); in the revised *Ordo Missae* of 1969 it is entitled *prex eucharistica* (Lat 'eucharistic prayer').

The common opinion of earlier generations of liturgists, that there was originally a single basic pattern of the eucharistic prayer, has fallen increasingly out of favour in the present century, partly as a result of the greater number of early documents now available, and partly as a result of the more scientific detailed study both of these and of documents previously known, to such an extent that there are some writers who deny that there was even an approximation to such a pattern. This assertion, however, appears to rest upon an inability to see the wood for the trees, as well as, in some cases, speculations belonging to the realm of fantasy rather than to that of sober scientific scholarship, and sometimes involving positive mishandling of the evidence. A serious study of all the available evidence, and of the work done upon it, suggests that the earlier opinion may be right after all, in principle although not in detail.

For the apparently considerable differences between the anaphorae of the historic rites, and between all of them and such primitive evidence as is available, all reveal themselves, when carefully examined, to be the consequence of secondary elements added

to the primitive structure or elaborated from it – secondary elements which were added or elaborated in different ways and at different points in the common basic structure. (I abstain from discussion of the prayers in the *Didache* which may or may not constitute eucharistic prayers: if they are, as I suspect they are, eucharistic prayers in embryo, then this is very important evidence of a very early stage in Christian worship, at which Jewish prayers were simply and minimally Christianized, but by that very token is still part of the 'pre-history' rather than of the 'history' of the Christian eucharistic prayer proper.) That common basic structure appears to be preserved in the oldest actual text of an anaphora which, so far as is at present known, survives, that in the *Apostolic Tradition* of Hippolytus of Rome, written *c.*215. The integrity of the textual tradition of this document has been disputed, notably by Dix and Ratcliff (in different ways and with different, and mutually incompatible, implications), but it has been established beyond reasonable doubt by the editor of the definitive critical edition, Bernard Botte, who has also vindicated the authorship and date of it.

The eucharistic prayer of the *Apostolic Tradition* may be divided into the following parts (the definition and description of which we leave to a later point): introductory dialogue; thanksgiving; narrative of the institution; anamnesis; epiclesis; concluding doxology. With one exception (apart from certain Hispano-Gallican and Ethiopic documents which are in such a manifest state of textual confusion that no reliance can be placed upon them), there is no known anaphora in any of the historic rites which does not contain, or has not contained at some time, all these parts in this order. The one exception is the mid-fourth-century Egyptian Anaphora of St Serapion, in which the narrative of the institution and the anamnesis are conflated; a second apparent exception, the East Syrian Anaphora of the Holy Apostles Addai and Mari, from the existing texts of which the institution narrative is missing, once contained it. So much is agreed by recent competent scholars who have investigated the problem, although they differ in the details of their reconstruction of the original text: Dom Botte's reconstruction still seems to be the most likely, on both internal and external grounds. (If they are all wrong, then the original text of this prayer is very early indeed, and joins the texts in the *Didache* as another stage in what I have called the 'pre-history' of the eucharistic prayer.) There are one or two other ancient prayers which have an institution narrative of what we would call an unconventional form, without the actual 'words of institution', but this only presents a problem if seen anachronistically through later liturgical spectacles.

Absent from the anaphora of the *Apostolic Tradition* are three elements, two of which are all but universal, and one of which is not uncommon, in the historical anaphorae: the anthem *Sanctus*, which occurs in the course of the thanksgiving or at its close in almost every other complete anaphora at present known, with the single significant exception of that in a fourth-century (?) Syrian document, the *Testament of our Lord Jesus Christ*, closely dependent on the *Apostolic Tradition*; the intercessory prayers technically called the diptychs, which occur in every other anaphora but those of the ancient Hispano-Gallican rites, where they are placed between the offertory* and the anaphora; and a preliminary epiclesis before the institution narrative, which occurs in the Alexandrine and Roman rites. The varying arrangement of these elements, in itself a strong indication of their addition to an original common structure which did not include them, is the principal means by which the anaphorae of the historic rites are classified, and the great liturgical families distinguished one from another. (It should, however, be added that passages corresponding both to the *Sanctus* and to the intercessions occur in some of the Jewish *berakoth* which, it is generally agreed, are the original starting-point from which the Christian eucharistic prayer was developed: it may be, then, that from the very beginning the Christian prayer in some places included these elements, and in others did not.)

In order to clarify the issue, we will first enumerate the possible component parts of a developed anaphora of classical structure, and then examine their disposition in the anaphorae of the great liturgical families. The possible component parts are as follows: 1. introductory dialogue; 2. preface

or first part of the thanksgiving; 3. *Sanctus*; 4. post-*Sanctus* or second part of the thanksgiving; 5. preliminary epiclesis (alternative or additional post-*Sanctus*); 6. narrative of the institution; 7. anamnesis; 8. epiclesis; 9. diptychs or intercessions, which may be divided; 10. concluding doxology.

The expansion of the postulated original common structure in the anaphorae of the Antiochene or West Syrian family of liturgies (which includes the second most widespread of the great historic rites, the Byzantine, commonly called, through the anachronistic application of denominational labels to the ancient liturgies, 'Orthodox') is clear from a comparison of the anaphora in the *Apostolic Tradition*, that in the *Testament of our Lord Jesus Christ*, and those of the developed Antiochene type. The order of the first of these is: 1 2 6 7 8 10. The order of the second is: 1 2 6 7 8 9 10. All the developed anaphorae of this family follow the order: 1 2 3 4 6 7 8 9 10. (Some of them conclude 8 10 9 10, a variant which clearly reveals the way in which (9) was added to an existing complete structure. But again it has to be added that something not unlike this arrangement can be found in some of the Jewish forms.) The distinguishing features of the Antiochene anaphora are the absence of any preliminary epiclesis (5), together with the continuation of the thanksgiving, often indeed the greater part of it, in the post-*Sanctus* (4), and the insertion of the diptychs between the epiclesis and the doxology.

The anaphorae of the East Syrian family follow the order: 1 2 3 4 6 (absent, as already noted, from the existing text of one of them, but undoubtedly originally present) 7 9 8 10.

The anaphorae of the Alexandrine family exhibit a number of internal variants (although many of these are due to the textual confusion of the Ethiopic anaphorae, which constitute the majority of the family). The normal order appears to be that found in the Liturgy of St Mark, the principal liturgy of the family: 1 2a 9 2b 3 5 6 7 8 10. This exhibits the principal distinctive features of this type of anaphora: the insertion of the diptychs (9) in the middle of the thanksgiving, and the presence of a preliminary epiclesis (5) before the institution narrative, together with the absence of any further thanksgiving (4) after the *Sanctus*. Certain variants deserve notice. The conflation of the institution narrative and the anamnesis in the Anaphora of St Serapion has already been noted; the same anaphora has no intercessory insertion in the preface, but a brief one after the epiclesis, in the position characteristic of the Antiochene type. Some liturgists suggest, on fragmentary evidence and technical grounds, that originally the Alexandrine diptychs may have been divided, like those of the Roman rite (*see below*). A feature common to a number of the Ethiopic anaphorae is the substitution of a post-*Sanctus* thanksgiving (4) for a post-*Sanctus* preliminary epiclesis (5), but this probably originated in direct borrowing from Antiochene liturgies; one ancient Alexandrine liturgical fragment, however, has a post-*Sanctus* succinctly combining (4) and (5).

The surviving texts of the ancient Hispano-Gallican liturgies of the West are in a state of evident confusion similar to that of the Ethiopic texts in the East. It is, however, possible to reconstruct from them a normal form of their anaphora (which was almost entirely composed of variable prayers appropriate to the day or season). The diptychs (9) were recited between the offertory and the anaphora, and the structure of the latter appears to have originally been that of the *Apostolic Tradition* with the sole addition of the *Sanctus* with a post-*Sanctus* continuation of the thanksgiving: 1 2 3 4 6 7 8 10; in the extant texts the anamnesis (7) is often reduced to a minimal form and combined with the epiclesis (8).

The most distinctive feature of the historic Roman canon is the division of the diptychs, half being placed before and half after the central prayers. Its order is as follows: 1 2 3 9a 5 6 7 8 9b 10. The new eucharistic prayers of the Roman rite abandon this particular distinctive feature, being structured thus: 1 2 3 4 5 6 7 8 9 10. Like the Roman canon itself, therefore, their structure falls midway between those of the Antiochene and Alexandrine types, although they have moved a stage nearer the former. From this consideration of the structure of the anaphorae in the primitive and historic liturgies, we pass to a more

detailed examination of its component parts.

1. *The introductory dialogue*. Like the Jewish forms of thanksgiving from which it is derived, the Christian thanksgiving begins with a dialogue inviting the participants to remembrance of God and thanksgiving for his mercies. That still in use in the Roman rite and its derivatives is the basic form, closely resembling that preserved in the *Apostolic Tradition* of Hippolytus; most of the Eastern rites elaborate it to a greater or lesser extent, as did the ancient Hispano-Gallican rites in the West. But in all the Christian forms the basic content remains the same: mutual greeting; an invitation to lift up the heart to God, with a response declarative of doing so; an invitation to give thanks, with a response declaring the propriety and duty of doing so. It is the third versicle, 'Let us give thanks', and response, which explain the universality and necessity of the dialogue: before he may proceed with the thanksgiving, the president of the assembly must receive the assembly's authority to do so in the name of all, and its assent to what he is about to say. (This is even more clearly marked in the otherwise very different Jewish forms of the dialogue.)

2. *The preface or* (*first part of the*) *thanksgiving*. The significance of the word 'preface' in the context is explained elsewhere (*see* **Preface**). The thanksgiving is the foundation of all that follows it in the anaphora: the church gives thanks for God's mighty works in the past, in creation and redemption, and thereby proclaims its faith in their continuance in the future, the faith which is the source and spring of the prayers which follow.

During the formative centuries of the liturgy a clear distinction arose between two types of this thanksgiving: the one variable, stressing from day to day one part or aspect after another of the saving work of Christ, and the other fixed, longer, and presenting a general view of the whole history of salvation at each celebration of the eucharist. The first type came to predominate in the West, and the second in the East. Each has its advantages and disadvantages: the variable thanksgiving, or 'proper preface', makes it possible to think more deeply and appositely of the mystery appropriate to the day or season than does the invariable type, while the latter enables thanksgiving to be made at one eucharist for the whole action of God in creation and redemption more fully than does the variable type. The proper preface has the advantage of comparative brevity, the invariable thanksgiving that of maintaining a better balance between thanksgiving and prayer in the anaphora. It is perfectly possible to have both types of thanksgiving in one rite, either by providing a full general thanksgiving into which proper clauses or paragraphs can be inserted when appropriate, or by including one or more such general thanksgivings among a full range of proper prefaces, for use either on certain occasions or at will. It is also possible to have a number of alternative forms of the full internally invariable thanksgiving, as is common in the Eastern rites.

The content of the preface is also affected by the insertion of the anthems *Sanctus* and *Benedictus* in the anaphorae of all the historic liturgies. In certain rites, notably the historic Roman canon, now called eucharistic prayer I of the Roman rite, these anthems conclude the thanksgiving; in others, including most of the great Eastern liturgies (and the new eucharistic prayers III and IV of the Roman rite), they divide the thanksgiving, and in the latter case it is common either for the preface to be essentially no more than a formal ascription of praise, the detailed thanksgiving for the works of creation and redemption being postponed until after the *Sanctus* (*see below*), or alternatively for the greater part of the thanksgiving to be made in the preface, leaving only, e.g., a specific reference to Christ's passion to be made after the *Sanctus*, as an introduction to the institution narrative. Other divisions of the thanksgiving matter are also found, and in some anaphorae there is a considerable amount of repetition. Further reference to this question will be found below, in the consideration of the post-*Sanctus*.

3. *The* Sanctus*. In all the great historic liturgies the preface ends with the singing or saying of the anthem *Sanctus*, to which is added in all but the Alexandrine anaphorae the anthem *Benedictus qui venit*. In

the oldest surviving texts these anthems are either missing or apparently interpolated. This interpolation, while it provides for the the congregation to join vocally in the climax of the thanksgiving, has not been an unmixed blessing: it has done as much as anything to confuse the clarity of structure which ought to be apparent in the anaphora. Whether, as in most rites, the thanksgiving originally led directly to the narrative of the institution as the account of the divinely-given means of making the thanksgiving truly effective, or, as in the Roman and Alexandrine rites, to a prayer for the acceptance or hallowing of the offerings within which the narrative was set, the transition from the thanksgiving by word to the thanksgiving by act was clear: we thank God . . . and therefore we *offer*. Once the *Sanctus* and *Benedictus* are interpolated, this sequence is obscured: it is all too easy for the thanksgiving (especially the first part of it, when it is divided) to be seen as a mere preliminary, concluding with these anthems – we thank God . . . and therefore we *sing* . . .

For these reasons some have suggested the suppression of these anthems in contemporary liturgical revision. This, however, is unnecessary; it is perfectly possible so to integrate them into the thanksgiving that the sequence of thought is clear and uninterrupted. It is also undesirable; they provide a valuable opportunity for the whole assembly to join its voice with that of the celebrant at this climactic point. Moreover, the question of the date and circumstances of their introduction into the anaphora is a far from simple one, and those who argue that in some places they may have formed part of it from the beginning are not without evidence which may reasonably be held to support their thesis, not least the presence of markedly similar passages in certain Jewish thanksgivings of this type. Nor is there sufficient reason for dividing them, or suppressing the *Benedictus*, or transferring *Sanctus* and *Benedictus*, or *Benedictus* alone, to the end of the anaphora: the arguments which have been put forward for these courses all rest on debatable hypotheses based on evidence carefully selected and interpreted for the purpose, and while they may be of great interest to liturgical scholars, they are not an adequate foundation for practical liturgical reform.

4, 5. *The post-*Sanctus *and preliminary epiclesis*. Whether the *Sanctus* was inserted in the middle or at the end of the thanksgiving, its insertion necessitated the provision of a passage linking it with what follows. It has already been noted that the post-*Sanctus* may take one of two forms, so far as its content is concerned: it may be either a continuation of the thanksgiving, or a prayer consequent upon the thanksgiving called for convenience the preliminary epiclesis; it may comprise both, as in the new Roman anaphorae. In most of the historical liturgies in which it is a continuation of the thanksgiving, it is linked to the *Sanctus* by the device of opening it with some such phrase as 'Holy in truth and blessed in truth . . .', thus taking up the themes of the divine holiness and blessedness from the *Sanctus* and *Benedictus* respectively. In the Alexandrine anaphorae, in which the post-*Sanctus* takes the form of a preliminary epiclesis, the theme of fullness is taken up from the preceding anthem, the prayer asking that as the heaven and earth are full of God's glory, so the gifts now offered in sacrifice may be filled with his blessing, or some equivalent petition. Only in the historic Roman canon is any link of this kind all but absent, and the sequence of thought obscured by the insertion of the diptychs of the living at this point.

In liturgical revision, the form and content of the post-*Sanctus* should be determined by two principal considerations: first, the content and structure of the thanksgiving, and in particular by whether the preface is variable (in which case an invariable thanksgiving is desirable in the post-*Sanctus* making mention of the whole economy of creation and thanksgiving, however briefly) or invariable (with or without variable insertions, in which case the post-*Sanctus* needs to be so worded as to make a smooth transition from the verbal thanksgiving to the ritual thanksgiving with the bread and cup); second, the theology of consecration which the rite is intended to embody, a preliminary epiclesis being required in the post-*Sanctus* if the theory of consecration by the recitation of the words of institution is held, although the presence of a preliminary epiclesis does not necessarily imply such a theory of consecration. This issue will be considered further in connection with the epiclesis.

6. *The narrative of the institution.* The recital of the narrative of the institution of the eucharist at the Last Supper (not anciently necessarily always including the actual 'words of institution', although it nearly always does) is universal in the primitive and historic anaphorae (the one apparent exception being, as already remarked, due to demonstrable textual corruption). It appears always to have been held necessary, whether or not the recitation of our Lord's words in it is regarded (as in the West from quite early in the Middle Ages) as itself constituting the whole consecration. In almost every anaphora the narrative is elaborated to a greater or lesser extent; in many, congregational responses are provided in the course of it or at the close of it, an enrichment which has been introduced into the new eucharistic prayers of the Roman rite, the historic Roman canon having none, although one has now been introduced into it as well. Theologically, in those traditions which do not regard the recitation of the words of institution as by themselves operating the consecration, their essentiality is understood in the sense that they are the authority for proceeding to the anamnesis and the epiclesis, an authority which must be invoked in order that the anamnesis and epiclesis may be effectual.

7. *The anamnesis.* A Greek work expressing a Semitic concept, *anamnesis* is all but untranslatable into English. Memorial, commemoration, remembrance – all these suggest that the person or deed commemorated is past and absent, whereas anamnesis signifies exactly the opposite: it is an objective act, in and by which the person or event commemorated is actually made present, is brought into the realm of the here and now. And the eucharist, as the early church understood it, is 'the "re-calling" before God of the one sacrifice of Christ in all its accomplished fullness so that it is here and now operative by its effects in the souls of the redeemed' (Dix, *Shape of the Liturgy*, p.243: so far as the doctrine of the early church is concerned, he ought to have written 'bodies and souls').

As a liturgical term, then, the anamnesis signifies that part of the anaphora in which it is explicitly stated that the church is offering the bread and cup with this meaning and for this purpose, in obedience to Christ's command so to do. The normal form of the anamnesis, which is all but universal in the primitive and historic liturgies, comprises a statement of the memorial and a statement of the offering, inseparably linked by making the former grammatically dependent on and relative to the latter. (This important syntactical link has been broken in some modern vernacular translations, notably in the English one of the historic Roman canon.) The former always mentions at least the passion, resurrection and ascension of our Lord; other aspects of the mystery of redemption, such as the incarnation, the burial, and the mediation of the ascended Christ at the right hand of the Father are added in some anamneses, and most contain also a reference to the second coming which sets the eucharist in its eschatological perspective. The statement of offering in the ancient liturgies always explicitly offers the bread and cup, either using those words or some elaborated equivalent; certain anaphorae, notably those of the Byzantine rite and the historic Roman canon, contain clauses emphasizing that in this offering the whole of the created order is representatively offered, but all make it clear that the offering is dependent upon its identification, in virtue of Christ's institution, with his own offering of himself. The anamneses in the new eucharistic prayers III and IV of the Roman rite carry this to lengths unprecedented in expression although not in content in the ancient anaphorae, a consequence of the formal embodiment in these prayers of the mediaeval and post-mediaeval Western doctrine that the consecration is effected solely by the recitation of the words of institution.

8. *The epiclesis.* Though the Greek word *epiclesis* simply means 'invocation', it has long been commonly used only of the prayer for the consecration of the bread and cup in the anaphora (although there is now a tendency to extend its use), and it is usually restricted to that form of it which asks the Father to send the Holy Spirit upon them to change them into the body and blood of Christ. This restriction appears, when the evidence is examined with care and without *a priori* presuppositions, to have little or no historical or theological justification, and to be partly the result of,

and partly responsible for, the unfortunate controversies which have raged about this prayer, notably that which arose between East and West in the Middle Ages concerning the 'moment of consecration'.

A prayer at this point in the anaphora is universal, and the essential content of it, as distinct from its formulation and elaboration of the content, is also universal: it asks for the divine response to the church's obedience to Christ's command in the preceding anamnesis. The epiclesis in the anaphora of the *Apostolic Tradition* comprises a petition for the descent of the Holy Spirit on the elements and a statement of the ends for which this is sought, the fruits of communion. It does not specify the change of bread and cup into body and blood (although this is clearly implied throughout the prayer), and has therefore been called by some a 'communion epiclesis' as distinct from a 'consecration epiclesis'. This distinction is anachronistic, in that it implies a later and more sophisticated theology of the eucharistic action. It is also inaccurate, in so far as it is the prayer for the descent of the Spirit which is the actual petition for consecration in later and more elaborate Spirit-epicleses, the specification of the effect of this descent as the change of bread and cup into body and blood being essentially no more than a descriptive elaboration of it. The first certain evidence for the fuller form is the Greek Alexandrine Anaphora of St Basil, the basis of the Byzantine Anaphora of St Basil (which has been proved to be the work of Basil), and a document which cannot date from later than the first half of the fourth century and may well be older. From the middle of the fourth century the fuller form, comprising 1. the petition for the operation of the Spirit, 2. the description of the effects of this operation as the change of the bread and cup into the body and blood of Christ, and 3. the statement of the ends for which this is sought, the fruits of communion, has been universal in the Eastern liturgies. The Anaphora of St Serapion has an epiclesis asking for the descent of the Logos or Word instead of that of the Spirit, but this is an isolated theological variant, as there is evidence of an epiclesis of the Spirit in Egypt before it as well as after it. Some Eastern epicleses ask for the descent of the Spirit on the people as well as on the elements, a prayer clearly related to that for the fruits of communion with which they conclude.

In the West the epiclesis asking for the descent of the Spirit to effect the consecration appears to have been common in the ancient Hispano-Gallican rites. It has commonly been asserted that the historic Roman canon contains no epiclesis, but this assertion is based on the *a priori* presupposition that the epiclesis must ask for the descent of the Spirit, and specify the effect of this as the change of the elements, in so many words. In fact, so far from not containing an epiclesis at all the Roman canon contains one of an unusually rich and elaborate kind: it comprises two paragraphs (not one as in most anaphorae), the first (*supra quae* . . .) praying for the acceptance of the gifts, with profound typological scriptual references, and the second (*supplices te* . . .) asking for their translation to the heavenly altar (i.e. Christ himself), followed by the statement of the ends for which this is sought. A more explicit, or theologically more precise, petition for consecration than the latter of these two prayers would be difficult to conceive.

The issue has been confused both by the development in the West of the doctrine of consecration by the recitation of the words of institution and by the presence of the clause describing the change of the elements in a preliminary epiclesis (*quam oblationem*). The Alexandrine anaphorae, as previously noted, also have such a preliminary epiclesis, the division of the epicletic material between this and the epiclesis after the anamnesis varying somewhat from one anaphora to another, and in some involving considerable repetition. The origin of this division or duplication of the epiclesis is by no means clear, for there is no adequate evidence for concluding that either is a later interpolation in those anaphorae in which they occur.

In the new eucharistic prayers of the Roman rite the preliminary epiclesis is definitely 'consecratory', in content, introducing the institution narrative, while the second epiclesis is specifically a prayer for the fruits of the eucharist: the operation of the Spirit is invoked in both. This arrangement is clearly designed to embody a particular doctrine of the moment of conse-

cration; and this is true of the arrangement of the epicletic material in most modern eucharistic prayers. But it would be anachronistic to regard the double epicleses of the ancient Roman and Alexandrine traditions as the result of considerations of this kind. On the other hand, it is not now possible to eliminate them from the mind in the work of contemporary liturgical revision; given that the issue of a 'moment of consecration' has been raised, even the attempt to abandon such a concept by saying that the whole prayer consecrates merely results, in practice, in regarding the conclusion of the prayer as that moment.

In the Antiochene tradition, which has no preliminary epiclesis, as well as in the Alexandrine tradition which has, the conclusion of the epiclesis after the anamnesis has from a very early date been regarded as 'the moment of consecration'. This should not, however, be understood as an exact parallel to the developed Western doctrine of consecration by the recitation of the words of institution, although in controversy some Eastern writers have themselves tended so to regard it; the classical Eastern position is that the epiclesis is necessary to the consecration, and therefore that its conclusion is the moment when the latter is complete, but this insistence on the necessity of the epiclesis is not exclusive – the narrative of the institution and the anamnesis are equally so.

9. *The diptychs**. The origins of the diptychs, or eucharistic intercessions, in the historic anaphorae are considered in the article devoted to them, and it has been pointed out both in that and earlier in the present article that their insertion at different points in the prayer is one of the principal structural distinctions between the anaphorae of different traditions. A word must be added on the theological rationale of intercessory prayers in the anaphora, in view of the current tendency in some quarters to eliminate such prayers from the eucharist proper altogether, which appears to owe more to liturgical archaeologizing (and that on a rather slender basis) than to serious theological and pastoral consideration. To remove all intercessory prayer from the memorial of Christ's one all-sufficient sacrifice cannot but obscure the fact that we can offer this, like any other prayer, only as members of Christ, redeemed through that sacrifice, and in the power of that sacrifice. Nothing can make this clearer, nor more effectively express the co-inherence of all redeemed humanity in Christ, than placing the intercessions in the anaphora, in the context of the offering of the eucharistic sacrifice, and of the prayer for the supreme gift of God which we ask for ourselves and for all men, the fruits of unity with Christ in communion. This is most clearly apparent when the intercessions are placed, as in the Antiochene anaphorae and the new Roman eucharistic prayers, after the central prayers of the anaphora as a continuance of the prayer for the fruits of communion. In the words of Alexander Schmemann:

> . . . before we partake of the heavenly food there remains one last, essential and necessary, act: the *intercession.* To be in Christ means to be like him, to make ours the very movement of his life. And as he 'ever liveth to make intercession' for all 'that come unto God by him' (Heb. 7.25), so we cannot help accepting his intercession as our own. The Church is not a society for escape – corporately or individually – from this world to taste of the mystical bliss of eternity. Communion is not a 'mystical experience': we drink of the chalice of Christ, and he gave himself for the life of the world. The bread on the paten and the wine in the chalice are to remind us of the incarnation of the Son of God, of the cross and death. And thus it is the very joy of the Kingdom that makes us *remember* the world and pray for it. It is the very communion with the Holy Spirit that enables us to love the world with the love of Christ. The Eucharist is the sacrament of unity and the *moment of truth*: here we see the world in Christ, as it really is, and not from our particular and therefore limited and partial points of view. Intercession begins here, in the glory of the messianic banquet, and this is the only true beginning for the Church's mission. It is when, 'having put aside all earthly care', we seem to have left *this world*, that we, in fact, recover it in all its reality. Intercession constitutes, thus, the only real preparation for communion (*The World as Sacrament*, 1966, p.53).

10. *The doxology**. The anaphora ends as it begins with praise and thanksgiving, all but universally in the form of a particularly solemn Trinitarian doxology. The concluding *Amen** by the people is of equal importance with their responses to the introductory dialogue, expressing their assent to, and participation in, all that the president has said in their name.

Further reading: So many works have been devoted to this subject that it is impossible to recommend even an adequate representative selection, and any less adequate selection would tend to reflect the personal preferences of the present writer to an undesirable extent. Four books should, however, be mentioned. A. Hänggi and I. Pahl, 1968, *Prex Eucharistica*, contains the most complete documentation of the subject available; R. C. D. Jasper and G. J. Cuming, *Prayers of the Eucharist, Early and Reformed*, 1975, contains convenient English renderings of a number of ancient anaphorae; E. G. C. F. Atchley, *On the Epiclesis of the Eucharistic Liturgy and in the Consecration of the Font*, 1935, and J. H. McKenna, *Eucharist and Holy Spirit*, 1975, are the most fully documented treatments of the epiclesis.

W. JARDINE GRISBROOKE

Anglican Worship

Anglican worship was a unique product of the Reformation, in that it is a development from the traditional Western Christian cultus and not merely another variant of continental Protestantism. Its base was a liturgy whose use was obligatory and whose contents conformed to what was believed in the sixteenth century to be a truly primitive pattern. Its principles were set out in the 1549 BCP in the preface and in the tract entitled *Of Ceremonies*.

First, instead of a series of local variations of the mediaeval Roman rite, there was now to be a single 'use' for the whole country. Furthermore, the ceremonies connected with it were essential to the rite and conducive to order, reverence and intelligibility. Secondly, all services were to be in English instead of Latin, in the interests of intelligibility and lay participation. Thirdly, there was an emphasis on edification, particularly through scripture, whereby men might profit in the knowledge of God and 'be the more inflamed with the love of his true religion'. To this end there was a daily office of morning and evening prayer – a unique Anglican feature among the worship of the Reformed Churches – involving the systematic recitation of the psalter and the reading of the Bible in accordance with a drastically simplified calendar. Fourthly, the central act of public worship was to be the eucharist, to be celebrated at least on Sundays and holy days, and possibly even daily. Finally, the liturgy was to be loyal to scripture and loyal to tradition – it was to contain nothing repugnant to the word of God and was to be expressive of the mind and purpose of the early fathers.

With the passage of time these basic principles have been modified, either by law or by common consent. Strict uniformity is no longer recognized as tenable: a church as comprehensive as the Church of England must make provision for differing attitudes – the sacramental and the prophetic, the corporate and the individual, simple austerity and rich splendour, the other-worldly and the this-worldly. It now attempts to have 'a tendency to conservatism in respect of the past; a passion for freedom in respect of the present; a reverence for the institution which incorporates its life; and an inveterate individualism in living that life'. Anglican worship has therefore moved away from a rigid and universal adherence to a single 'use' towards a conformity to a general pattern within fairly wide but nevertheless prescribed limits. This was recognized in the report of the Royal Commission on Ecclesiastical Discipline in 1906: 'The *law* of public worship in the Church of England is too narrow for the religious life of the present generation.' The report therefore recommended that this law should be modified in the light of the comprehensiveness of the Church of England and its existing needs. A great part of the twentieth century has been occupied in attempting to implement that recommendation, and the operation still continues.

Secondly, although English is still the language of liturgy, it remained unchanged from 1662 until the present day; in consequence it is now increasingly thought to be irrelevant and unintelligible. Only in recent decades has the task of creating a truly

contemporary liturgical language been undertaken, and this task is far from completion.

Thirdly, the system of public daily worship shared by both clergy and laity has never really worked, because the practising Christian layman has never been more than a Sunday worshipper. Broadly speaking, corporate worship of the entire community of clergy and laity is now a weekly event, while the daily round of worship is largely maintained by clergy and the members of certain institutions – religious communities, theological colleges, college chapels and cathedrals. But this in itself has produced another element in worship which is unique in the Church of England, the choral daily office, and around this has developed a corpus of church music such as no other church possesses (*see* **Divine Office, The**).

Fourthly, it is now recognized that worship cannot be static; it is affected not only by developments in theology but also by the changing pattern of life in the world. The church today cannot be committed to the precise doctrinal positions of Anglican reformers and revisers of the sixteenth and seventeenth centuries. It can only be committed to their general appeal to scripture and the early church, and it must take into account fresh and contemporary understanding of the gospel. It is true that the ideal of the eucharist as the basic act of public worship has become generally accepted, but the way in which that rite is celebrated and the circumstances in which it is celebrated are beginning to change. Anglican worship has begun to combine with the sense of order and tradition a greater degree of freedom and spontaneity, largely under the influence of the Ecumenical and Liturgical Movements*. This is particularly evident in those acts of worship which now take place outside the traditional church building. There is a growing recognition of the connection between worship and the mission of the church (*see* **Mission and Worship**), and of the need to relate worship to a variety of situations.

Nowhere has this been seen more clearly than in the developing worship of the Anglican Church overseas. Until the twentieth century, with relatively few exceptions, the 1662 prayer book was the basis of all public worship throughout the whole Anglican Communion. But the Lambeth Conference of 1920 sounded the note of reform with the assertion that the development of self-conscious and indigenous churches had created a demand for new forms of worship and for local adaptations of the prayer book. The principle of uniformity as expressed in the preface to the prayer book was not applicable to Anglican churches overseas, nor was it necessary as a bond of union between churches which possessed a unity of faith. This note was repeated by the Lambeth Conferences of 1930 and 1948, while the Conference of 1958 urged that each part of the Anglican Communion must be free to order its worship in ways which were real and meaningful in its own area. Anglican worship therefore began to assume different forms in different parts of the world, although the basic appeal to scripture, to the primitive church and to reason was maintained.

In the last quarter of a century liturgies have proliferated throughout the Anglican Communion. Some have been experimental and ephemeral; but there is evidence that the period of liturgical revision is being replaced by a period of consolidation. A number of churches and provinces – e.g. America, Australia, England, Ireland, Wales – have already produced new prayer books, thereby indicating that no major changes in forms of worship are contemplated for some time – perhaps not until the turn of the century; although experiment in some areas will undoubtedly continue. What have been emerging, however, are patterns of worship which are ecumenical rather than distinctively Anglican. The Lambeth Conferences of 1958 and 1968 prepared documents – published in 1965 and 1970 – which set out to establish basic guide-lines, first for the eucharist and then for the daily office, which would commend themselves to all provinces of the Anglican Communion. These were concerned with structure and not with texts, language or doctrine. But neither document exerted much influence and in effect were overtaken by events.

Liturgical dialogue between Anglican and non-Anglican churches has developed enormously since the Second Vatican Council, while the liturgical creativity of the united Church of South India proved to be extremely influential. Although earlier prayer

books have served as valuable quarries from which phrases and prayers have been extensively hewn, there has been a great deal of cross-fertilization. Agreed texts of creeds and canticles have transcended both denominational and national barriers: the borrowing of prayers, hymns and lectionaries has been considerable: and there has been a remarkable convergence in ceremonies (e.g. the westward position, and the peace), in vesture, and in the ordering of churches. This ecumenical activity has also been expedited by the general desire to use forms of worship in contemporary language. It must not be assumed, however, that all this change has produced a dull uniformity. The needs of local cultures and institutions are sufficiently met to produce regional variety and colour. Furthermore, in some parts of the Anglican Communion the earlier distinctive Anglican ethos of worship will remain side by side with the new. In England, for example, the new Service Book of 1980 has not replaced the 1662 BCP, but is simply an alternative to it. The same is true of Australia. It means, therefore, that those congregations who wish to continue worshipping in a traditional Anglican manner will be free to do so.

See also **Books, Liturgical** 4; **Liturgies** 4.

F. E. Brightman, *The English Rite*, 1955; C. O. Buchanan, *Modern Anglican Liturgies 1958–1968*, 1968; *Further Anglican Liturgies 1968–1975*, 1975; Church of England Liturgical Commission, *Prayer Book Revision in the Church of England*, 1957; G. J. Cuming, *A History of Anglican Liturgy*, [2]1982; P. Dearmer, *The Parson's Handbook* (revised by C. E. Pocknee), 1966; C. Dunlop, *Anglican Public Worship*, 1953; E. Underhill, *Worship*, 1936.

R. C. D. JASPER

Anniversary

An annual celebration in the life of a church. A church or chapel anniversary is the Free Church equivalent of what others call a dedication festival (*see* **Dedication**). It usually commemorates so many years of worship in the building, but sometimes the continuous history of a congregation, even though the building is not that which was used originally. Particular departments of church life also have anniversaries, e.g. choir anniversary, sisterhood anniversary. Anniversaries are often divorced from the original starting-date of the department; they are simply annual festivals. The chief of these is the Sunday school anniversary, usually held in the spring. At these services Sunday school scholars sing hymns and anthems during the services. Sunday school anniversaries have been held, especially in Methodist churches, since at least the early part of the nineteenth century. Many local customs attached themselves to them, e.g. the building of a special platform for the scholars, the wearing of white dresses. They were for long the best-attended services of the year. They are still held, but are not as popular as formerly.

A. RAYMOND GEORGE

Annunciation

see **Mariological Feasts**

Ante-communion

The BCP provides that 'if there is no communion' the communion service shall be said to the end of the prayer for the church and concluded with a collect and the blessing. Such a service is known as ante-communion, and for a short time the expression achieved official currency in the Series 2 experimental Order for Holy Communion in the Church of England to describe that part of the service which included the introduction, the ministry of the word, and the intercessions. However in the ASB the two main parts of the service are distinguished by the expressions Ministry of the Word and Ministry of the Sacrament, and the word 'ante-communion' does not appear.

The name was a relatively recent innovation. From the seventeenth century until the nineteenth both the communion service and the ante-communion were commonly called the second service; during this period of infrequent communion the ante-communion was more frequently observed for the second service. It was 'second' in relation to mattins* and the litany* which came before it, since the strict observance of the Act of Uniformity required mattins, litany, and holy communion every Sunday morning.

This service is comparable to the mass of the catechumens of the patristic age, when catechumens* were dismissed after the

lessons and sermon (but before the prayers of the faithful), and also to the dry mass of the Middle Ages, which consisted at the least of the epistle, gospel, Lord's Prayer and blessing and at the most of the whole rite of the mass except the canon and the use and presence of the elements and their vessels. The dry mass came to be associated with superstitious notions and practices, and came to be regarded as quasi-sacramental in character, and so incurred the disapproval of the Reformers. Another name for the dry mass was *memoria*, and it is noteworthy that Archbishop Grindal and others described the ante-communion as 'a commemoration of the holy communion'.

The position from which the priest read the ante-communion was a matter of contention in the seventeenth century. The Puritans read it from the reading desk, and their 'exceptions' included a demand that the rubric should require it. The high churchmen read it from the altar, 'the church thereby keeping her ground, visibly minding us of what she desires and labours towards, our more frequent access to that Holy Table' (Sparrow, *Rationale*). It was one of the charges against Laud at his trial that he 'read the Second Service at the Communion Table or Altar'.

W. E. Scudamore, *Notitia Eucharistica*, 1876, pp.814ff.

E. C. WHITAKER

Anthem

Although various alternative derivations for the term anthem have been suggested, it is almost certainly an anglicization of the word antiphon*. Traditionally a musical setting of words drawn from the psalms or from scripture, the anthem may be regarded as a vernacular equivalent of the Latin motet*, authority for its place in the liturgy being conferred by the rubric in the BCP. *In choirs and places where they sing, here followeth the anthem.* Regarded in that light, to justify its place in a service, an anthem should be chosen not only for its musical excellence but as making a valuable and relevant contribution to an act of worship. When selected on a seasonal or *de tempore* basis, and when the words are made known to the listening congregation, that result becomes possible; but the precarious performance of an anthem beyond the choir's abilities must inevitably cause distraction to the listener, thus contradicting its true function.

Anthems may be accompanied or unaccompanied, for 'single' or 'double' choir, and with or without soloists, a particular type in which the full choir is employed alternately with a soloist or group of soloists being known as a 'verse anthem'. The wide repertoire is perhaps best considered chronologically:

1. *Tudor, Elizabethan and Jacobean.* Tallis and Tye, who were active as composers both before and after the Reformation, provide a direct link between motet and anthem, the Latin or English of their texts, rather than questions of musical style, frequently marking the distinction. Other representative composers of the period are Tomkins, Byrd, Farrant, Morley, Mundy, Weelkes, Orlando Gibbons, Bevin and Batten. Characteristic of the period is a general absence of independent organ* accompaniment – though many sixteenth-century anthems sung unaccompanied today probably received light organ support in contemporary performance.

2. *Restoration.* The type of anthem written for the Chapel Royal under Charles II was influenced by the French idiom made familiar to the monarch during his exile at Versailles. Accompanied by a string band and organ, such anthems were often lightly rhythmic and contained solo passages and sections in recitative. Perhaps most familiar in Purcell's 'Bell Anthem' (Rejoice in the Lord alway), the style was first introduced by Pelham Humphrey, to be continued by Blow, Wise and Turner – all of whom, like Purcell himself, had been Chapel Royal choristers.

3. *Hanoverian.* Representative of the English Baroque manner, and recalling Handelian conventions, the anthems of Boyce, Croft, Green, Battishill, and Handel himself are marked by a dignity which sometimes approaches ponderousness; but which fades into dullness with Nares and Kent.

4. *Late Georgian and Early Victorian.* Sometimes influenced by Mozart and Mendelssohn, the best anthems of Crotch, Attwood, Goss and Walmisley yet preserve an integrity of their own. Those of S. S.

Wesley introduce a new emotional content coloured by the chromaticism of Spohr, but avoiding excess. S. S. Wesley and Walmisley were the first to write the important independent organ accompaniments at this time which became a feature of most later anthems.

5. *Later Victorian and Edwardian.* Few of the multitude of anthems produced during the age of 'fashionable' churchgoing have earned a lasting place in the repertoire, the emotionalism and lack of dignity of much of Stainer, Sullivan, Barnby and their successors proving unacceptable to modern tastes. Recovery began with Stanford, whose anthems include several masterpieces, and Parry, whose coronation anthem, 'I was glad', in particular affords luxurious harmonies and sonorities without offending propriety. Charles Wood continued the new tradition to produce several rich anthems which still satisfy.

6. After the founding of the Motet Society in 1841, the anthem repertoire was further widened and enriched by the inclusion of works by Catholic composers such as Palestrina, Victoria, and their succcessors, often with an English paraphrase of the original texts. In the present century, the advent of radio brought about a general rise in musical awareness which stimulated the revival after 1920 of many sixteenth-century compositions hitherto regarded as merely archaic. The same development encouraged a new astringency in composers as diverse as Vaughan Williams and John Joubert. There is today no shortage of modern anthems written by English composers of international standing who have managed to discipline their writing successfully so as to avoid making impossible demands upon the church choirs anxious to perform their works. It is perhaps in that direction that the biggest challenge to the modern anthem composer is presented.

C. Dearnley, *English Church Music, 1650–1750*, 1970; E. H. Fellowes, *English Cathedral Music*, revd Westrup, 1969; M. B. Foster, *Anthems and Anthem Composers*, 1901; P. le Huray, *Music and the Reformation in England*, 1967; C. H. Phillips, *The Singing Church*, revd Hutchings, 1968; E. Routley, *The Church and Music*, 1970.

BERNARR RAINBOW

Antidoron

Antidoron (Gk lit. 'instead of the gift') is the name given to the blessed bread which is distributed to the congregation after the eucharistic liturgy in the Byzantine rite.

The purpose of this distribution is threefold: 1. to consume what remains of the bread offered by the faithful for the eucharist but not used for it (*see* **Oblation; Prothesis**), 2. to provide immediate sustenance for communicants who have been fasting at least since midnight, and 3. to provide an additional element of participation in the service for non-communicants. It is from the third of these that the name 'antidoron' is derived: for non-communicants it to some extent takes the place of *the* gift, the eucharistic elements themselves. In recent years, with the spread of ecumenical contacts, this third purpose of the antidoron has been extended to provide an additional element of participation, and of fellowship with the congregation, for non-Orthodox visitors.

Similar usages have existed, and in some places still exist, outside the Byzantine rite; the distribution of blessed bread after the liturgy is a feature also of the Armenian and Syrian rites in the East, and it was once common in many parts of the West as well, surviving in France until recent years. The widespread recovery of more frequent communion has no doubt been a contributory factor in the dying out of such survivals of mediaeval usage.

C. Kucharek, *The Byzantine-Slav Liturgy of St John Chrysostom*, 1971 (see index under 'Antidoron').

W. JARDINE GRISBROOKE

Antiphon

This word is derived from a Greek term *antiphonos* (= responsive), adopted without translation at an early date by the Latin Church. In early texts the term may mean either 'antiphony', i.e., a type of psalmody in which the two sides of the choir respond to each other in alternation; or it is the name given to a short chant sung in association with a psalm. This is the meaning that has generally prevailed. Antiphons are normally sung before and after the psalms and canticles of the Divine Office*. The antiphons of the weekly psalter are gen-

erally one of the verses of the psalm about to be sung, often the first verse or part of it. Other antiphons have texts from scriptural or other sources and provide matter relevant to the Sunday or feast day or feria. The antiphon determines which of the psalm-tones should follow and which cadence ('difference') should be used. Some later mediaeval offices have sets of antiphons composed in rhyming verse. The music of these antiphons often follows the order of the Church Modes*, e.g., the first antiphon will be in Mode 1, the second in Mode 2, and so on. Another group of antiphons includes chants that have come to be detached from psalmody altogether: these are the famous Marian Antiphons composed in honour of the Blessed Virgin Mary, of which the best-known are the four large-scale chants *Salve regina, Alma redemptoris mater*, *Ave regina caelorum* and *Regina caeli.* To these must be added the ancient *Sub tuum praesidium*, whose original Greek text survives in a third-century papyrus. A further group of antiphons detached from psalmody is a category containing processional antiphons, which include those sung with the Palm Sunday procession and those of the Major Litanies of 25 April.

Michel Huglo, 'Antiphon', *The New Grove Dictionary of Music and Musicians*, 1980.

MARY BERRY

Apse

An architectural term denoting a semicircular structure roofed with a half dome. It was the standard form of the sanctuary in the early Christian basilica*, and could either project beyond the east end, as in the Latin or Roman type, or be enclosed by a wall, thus providing side chambers, as in the Hellenistic form found in Syria.

EDITOR

Architectural Setting

The nature of Christian worship is such that it does not of itself require any particular architectural setting. It does not centre in a cult object, such as an image, that has to be protected within a shrine. It does not require a large item of liturgical furniture, such as a stone altar*, that has to be housed in a special way. It can be and has been celebrated in a dining room, a hospital ward or an open field. Nevertheless, throughout the centuries, it has had an architectural setting, which has expressed the Christian understanding of worship. Hence the study of worship historically cannot be divorced from a knowledge of the buildings in which it was conducted.

Yet it has to be recognized that the minutiae of liturgical change can have little architectural effect. The addition of a prayer here or a petition there is not reflected in the buildings. New ideas only produce alterations if they are related to 1. new concepts of the nature of worship and of the church; 2. movement; 3. different ways of doing things. The development of Christian architecture in terms of church plans is in part an account of the operation of these three 'laws', but the elevation of these buildings also changed as different 'styles' emerged.

Primitive Christian worship, centring in the eucharist, was essentially domestic and so was celebrated in the private house. The shape and location of these house-churches differed therefore according to the several forms of domestic architecture throughout the empire. In the east, where one-family buildings up to four storeys high were the norm, worship took place in the dining room which was usually on the top floor. In Rome, on the other hand, tenement dwellings were general, with apartments horizontally across them, and not necessarily having a dining room, so that the largest chamber available would have been used.

In time, houses were bought by or given to the church and these were then specially adapted to the needs of the cult. So the one at Dura Europos, built shortly after 200, had two rooms made into one, by removing a wall, and a dais was set up, while, to the right of the entrance, a small chamber was transformed into a baptistery*, complete with font and wall decorations.

After the victory of Constantine, with Christianity replacing the pagan cults as the state religion, worship ceased to be a family gathering and became a public occasion. Its architecture accordingly was made to correspond with civic and imperial forms, and so the basilica became general in both east and west. The basilica* was a large meeting hall, belonging to a recognizable class of public

buildings, with nave* and aisles*, possibly galleries* and clerestories. These pagan forms were given religious overtones by the presence of the emperor's image. The Christian basilica was a similar monumental place of public gathering with religious associations, devotion to God as emperor of heaven being substituted for the imperial cult. Here, then, is an example of the operation of 'law' 1 above, i.e. a new concept of worship, public instead of private, being embodied in fresh architectural forms. Since the genus basilica did not have a uniform plan, the early Christian examples differed, but by the end of the fourth century they had assumed a recognizable identity.

Its general aspect was that of a single room, with the altar standing towards one end on the middle axis. This was the focal point of the building, and around it priesthood and laity gathered for the celebration of the liturgy, each section having its prescribed place. In the centre of the semi-circular apse*, roofed by a half-dome, the bishop had his throne (*see* **Cathedra**), on either side of which were the seats of the presbyters. The superior clergy were separated from the rest of the congregation by the altar around which the deacons were grouped. It could stand on the chord of the apse or even in the body of the church, well down the central nave. The rectangular hall was divided by parallel rows of columns into areas of which there was always an odd number. The centre one, the nave, corresponded to the apse in width and was equivalent to the sum of the aisles. Its walls rose above them and were pierced with windows to form a clerestory and allow the access of light (*see* Fig. 2 and Plate 4). As is appropriate for a pilgrim people, the basilica belongs to that type of structure best designated a 'path': it has all the necessary features to define it clearly. The nave walls present firm edges; there is continuity and directionality in the parallel colonnades whose converging lines lead to an unmistakable terminal, i.e. the altar.

In the eighth and ninth centuries in Western Europe, the operation of 'law' 2 above,

Plate 4 The Christian basilica, Abbey of Pomposa, Italy – a path

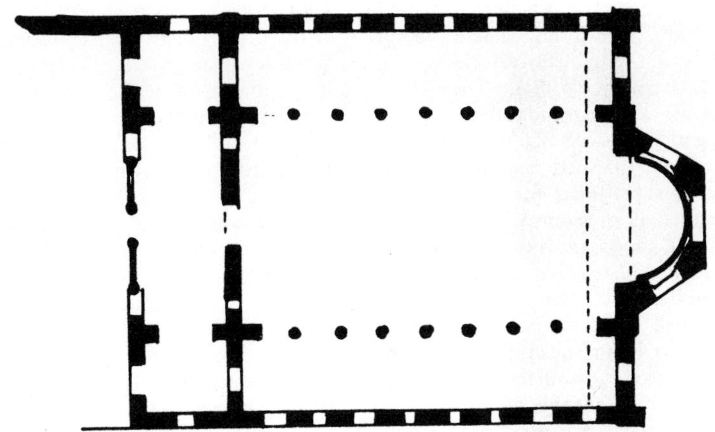

Fig. 2 Basilica of St John of Studion, Constantinople, Turkey

i.e. movement, produced a new type of church, known as the porch-church or *Vollwestwerk*. In effect this was still a basilica but with its west end completely transformed and composed of two elements: a crypt at ground level and, above it, an upper church with aisles and galleries. Externally this was provided with a central tower and two smaller ones on each side gave access to the upper church. This porch-church was in fact to provide for the services of Holy Week and was modelled in part on the Holy Sepulchre complex at Jerusalem; it allowed for the many processions, i.e. movement, as well as for the celebration of the eucharist, the adoration of the cross, etc. The first examples, from *c*.775, include St Riquier near Abbeville. In the tenth century there was a change in liturgical observance – the operation of 1 above – which immediately had an architectual effect. Whereas in the heyday of the porch-church, worship was something in which all actively participated, it gradually became a spectacle at which the people were passive onlookers. This meant that the plan could be simplified, circulation space being no longer required, and so the porch-church steadily atrophied, first losing its crypt, as in St Pantaleon, Cologne, then being transformed into a western apse, e.g. the cathedral of Paderborn, and finally only surviving as a decorative feature of the western facade, as in the triple towers of Maria-Laach in the twelfth century or the twin towers which appear on the front of so many Gothic buildings (*see* Plate 5).

The passivity of the congregation, which played so important a part in the decline of the porch-church, had, as its obverse, the increasing importance of the clergy who now ceased to conduct the liturgy 'on behalf of' and celebrated it 'instead of' the congregation. The architectural result of this was that the place of the clergy, which had usually occupied the east end of the nave together with the apse, was removed out of the body of the church to create a second room (*see* Fig. 3). Hence the two-room plan of the Middle Ages – the sanctuary* being for the ordained ministers, the nave for the laity (*see* Plate 6). In terms of the eucharist, this had involved a shift of emphasis from the communion to the consecration with the elevation as its climax – all that was needed, therefore, since non-communicating attendance was widespread, was a distant view of the raised host, dimly glimpsed through the chancel screen beneath the rood at the far end of the choir. The priest had also moved from facing the people across the altar to standing with his back to them and so looking towards the east – here 'law' 3 is in operation.

The mediaeval church plan was not only the product of a different concept of worship – primarily a sacrifice in the presence of an audience – and of the church – a hieratically structured institution rather than an organism with interdependent functions – nor just of a new concept of the eucharist – centred in the consecration –

Plate 5 The porch-church, Jumièges, France

but also of the developed cult of the saints*. For this we have to go back to the fifth century and to recognize the existence of a building type other than the basilica.

With the cessation of persecution, the period of the martyrs came to be looked upon as a golden age with the martyrs themselves as the heroes of the faith. Christians then began to enclose their remains in martyria*. These copied the form of pagan tombs and were roofed with domes, the symbol of heaven and the bliss of eternal life. The domes were supported by round or octagonal structures and in some cases abutted at all four points of the compass to

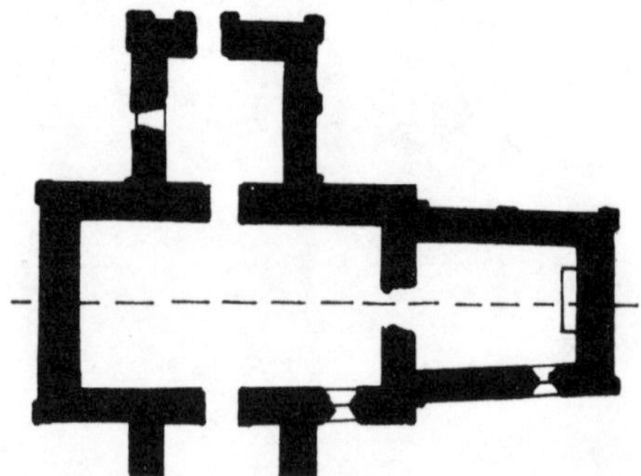

Fig. 3 St Laurence, Bradford-on-Avon, England

produce the shape of a cross (*see* Plate 7). This so-called centralized architecture was in origin a type of funerary monument and it provided for the cult of the saints side by side with the Jesus-cult in the congregational basilicas. The fusion of the two cults in the east brought the two building types into relation and the result was a new form which perpetuated that of the martyrium but modified it, sometimes by the addition of a basilican east end, to create centralized churches. This became the standard plan for Eastern Orthodoxy. One had only to add side chambers to the apse and an iconostasis * with its doors, and a type which has remained traditional to the present day had been created (*see* Fig. 4). In this instance a developed understanding of the eucharist – 'law' 1 – relating it to the intercession of the saints, has had long lasting architectural effects.

In the West, however, this cult did not have the same result; there the relics were placed in direct association with the main altar, either enclosed therein or connected by a shaft. Nevertheless the translation of relics did leave its mark on the internal arrangement of churches in Western Christendom, in so far as each and every relic had its own altar. This, together with the practice of votive masses and the belief that every priest must celebrate every day – further instances of 'law' 1 – led to the multiplication of altars which was such a feature of the mediaeval cathedrals and, to a lesser degree, of the parish churches.

As for style, the Middle Ages produced two very different ones, namely Romanesque and Gothic. Each of these owes its distinctiveness to the vaults. At first the Roman barrel vault was used, making the nave into an uninterrupted continuum of space, but from 1000 onwards the cross-vault became the norm and this divided the nave into a series of bays, slowing the eastward drive and requiring large pillars to carry the weight of the stone. Sculptural decoration abounded on both the exterior and interior. Gothic vaults, created out of pointed arches, replaced the separation of the Romanesque bays with a vigorous continuity and an emphasis not on horizontality but on verticality.

Plate 6 Two-roomed mediaeval plan, Heath chapel, Shropshire, England

Plate 7 Centralized cruciform church, Djivari, Georgia, USSR

The Reformation inevitably marked a watershed in the architectural setting of worship, since the Protestants had their own ideas about the cult, which differed radically from those embodied in the mediaeval buildings. Within the Roman Catholic Church, however, there was no such break with the immediate past, although the Renaissance initiated a new phase in church design. The Renaissance was a rebirth of classical culture, based upon a careful study of the writings and ruins of ancient Rome coupled with an imaginative re-creation of that past era as a golden age in which consolation and refreshment could be sought. For centuries a church had been regarded as a sacred edifice, and the effect of this concept within the Renaissance context was to equate churches and temples, and so the temples of pagan Rome served as models for Christian buildings. The result was twofold: first,

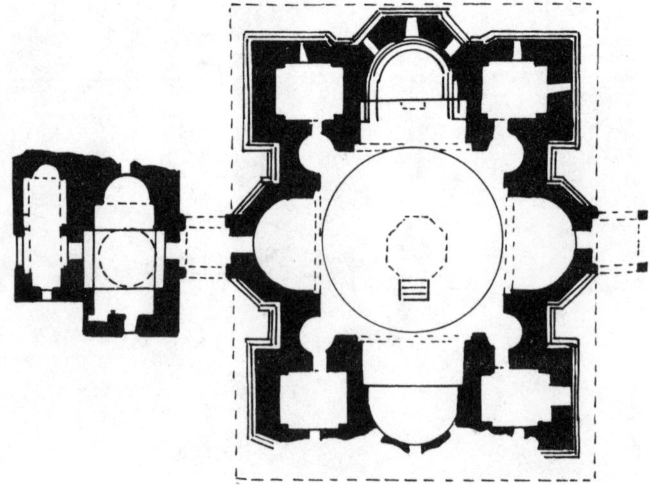

Fig. 4 Typical Eastern Orthodox plan, Djivari, Georgia, USSR – a place

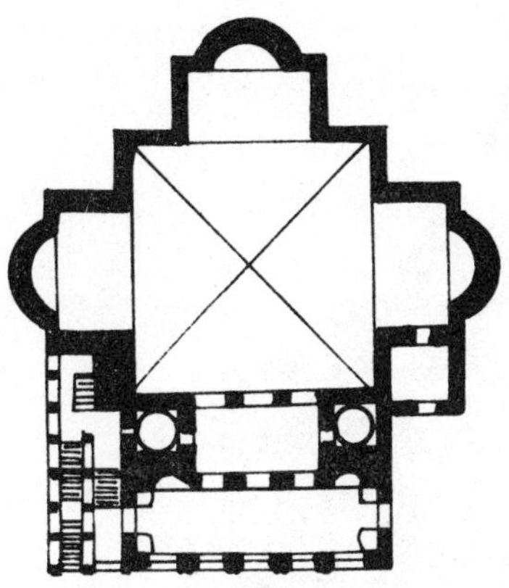

Fig. 5 Centralized Renaissance plan, S. Sebastiano, Mantua, Italy

a centralized* plan was favoured, e.g. S. Sebastiano, Mantua; and, second, aisles were suppressed, since these had no place in pagan temples, and were replaced by side chapels (*see* Fig. 5 and Plate 8).

Out of Renaissance classicism grew the Baroque – an exuberant proclamation of the triumph of the Counter-Reformation. Here the prototype was no longer the temple but the theatre which, through the opera, had become the cultural focus of the period. Churches were now erected to provide distant vistas, with a scenic progression along the horizontal axis. The church was now a place for an occasion, similar to a *soirée* at court complete with a *divertissement* by Lully. The focal point of worship became the exposition* of the reserved sacrament – 'law' 1 above was operative – and in this

Plate 8
The Renaissance temple, Maser, Italy

divine presence a kind of heavenly grand opera was performed, with the high altar, profusely decorated and housing the sacrament, providing the centre piece (*see* Fig. 6 and Plate 9).

The further operation of 'law' 1 is nowhere better to be observed than in the churches of Protestantism. Many of the Reformers rejected the sacrificial interpretation of the mass and emphasized its communion aspect; they laid stress on the ministry of the word and denied a rigid dichotomy of ordained and lay. The circumstances of the time – wars, religious strife – precluded any large-scale new building programme, and consequently Protestants re-used or re-ordered the existing mediaeval churches that they had taken over. Anglicans may serve as an example of the first and Calvinists of the second.

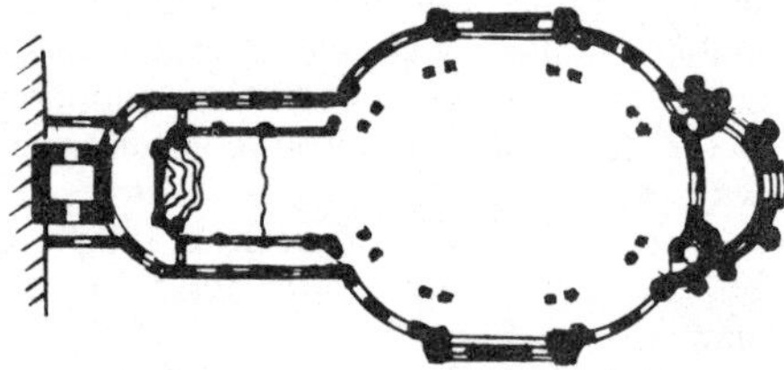

Fig. 6 Baroque theatrical architecture, Die Wies, Germany

The Church of England authorities recognized that the mediaeval plan did indeed consist of two rooms; it was therefore decided to use them as such for different functions. So the nave was the place for the ministry of the word and the sanctuary became the scene for the celebration of the eucharist, the altar being moved forward into the middle of the choir and the worshippers arranging themselves around it. This was a different way of doing things –'law' 3 – under the influence of new concepts of worship and of the church – 'law' 1.

The Calvinists replanned the interior of their churches, as illustrated by St Pierre, Geneva. The mediaeval building, oblong with transepts, had the bishop's throne in the eastern apse, the altar in the choir and

Plate 9 Baroque theatrical architecture, Vierzehnheiligen, Germany

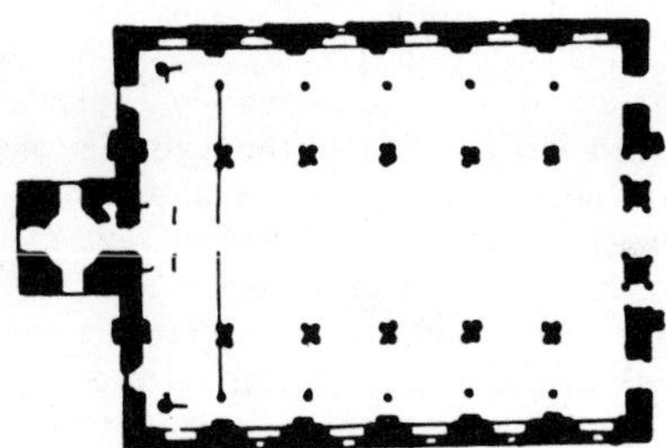

Fig. 7 The Wren auditory church, Christ Church, Newgate Street, London

the pulpit* at the same level as the rood screen separating the priest from the congregation. In 1541 rood screen and choir were demolished; the pulpit was moved to the first pillar on the left and the congregation was arranged in the form of a star at the front of the nave, in the transepts and the ancient choir. A table was brought in only on communion days and baptism was administered from a basin.

Within Anglicanism 'law' 1 continued to operate during the seventeenth century and is particularly noticeable during the Laudian controversy. The mobility of the altar under the Elizabethan settlement – being carried forward into the centre of the choir – led on occasion to its being treated with lack of reverence and even profaned. To prevent this, William Laud initiated a policy of protecting it with rails and fixing it permanently against the east wall. Although the archbishop's ideal was repudiated by the Puritans, it came back into favour at the Restoration and by the end of the century the majority of churchmen were shocked when they found an altar not so placed and fenced in. Laud and his later imitators had to deal with the two-room plan, but with Sir Christopher Wren a new type was introduced, usually referred to as the auditory church, and this was in effect a one room design. Wren was convinced that Anglicanism, unlike Catholicism, required its worship to be both visible and audible. His stress therefore was not only on the sermon but on the services as a whole. This involved, according to his calculations, small churches with galleries to seat not more than 2000 people. He suppressed the projecting chancels, dispensed with the screens, and produced a single volume with three liturgical centres instead of well-defined places. So he sited the font by the door; he installed pulpit and reading-pew, and finally the altar (*see* Fig. 7).

A similar concern to stress the importance of both the auditory and visual aspects of worship resulted within Lutheranism in the *Prinzipalstück*. The declared ideal was that of an oblong building, minus Gothic chancel, with a single space at the east end in which were combined all the principal liturgical acts. Altar, font* and pulpit were thus assembled together – 'law' 3 operating under the influence of 1. This concept was first advocated by Joseph Fürttenbach, writing in 1649, and was taken up by L. C. Sturm in two works of 1712 and 1718. Influenced by the plan of the classical theatre, Sturm supported the adoption of the *Zentralbau*, or centralized auditorium with *Prinzipalstück*.

A somewhat similar concept of the place of assembly as an auditorium, with the emphasis on the sermon – 'law' 1 – was embodied in the chapels built by the English Nonconformists, first licensed after the Declaration of Indulgence of 1671–72. Most of these were of a modest and domestic nature, without spires or obvious ecclesiastical features on the exterior. The design was rectangular, without chancel or transepts. Galleries were introduced into the larger buildings, mainly to provide greater accommodation, and the pulpit was big and prominent.

There was, therefore, a general tendency within the Protestant church to affirm both the visual and auditive elements in worship, to favour a single room design and even, especially with Calvinism, to adopt a centralized plan. This tendency was completely reversed by the Gothic Revival which was to affect all Christian communions.

To the adherents of the Gothic Revival each religion produces its own supreme architectural form that best expresses its ethos and spirit. Renaissance architecture, in so far as it sought inspiration from the heathen temples of ancient Rome, was to be dismissed as pagan. Only Gothic represented the full flowering and ideal embodiment of the Christian faith. The pioneers of this movement within Anglicanism were influenced to no small degree by the Tractarians, whose teaching about the church and the sacraments was meant to be both biblical and patristic but frequently

did not achieve more than an echo of the mediaeval understanding. The same ideas were shared on the Catholic side by another great leader of the movement, A. W. N. Pugin. 'Law' 1 now came into its own. The emphasis upon the nature of the ministry and the sacrificial character of the eucharist required the two-room plan which had originally expressed these same ideas. The ecclesiologists therefore advocated and secured the all but universal adoption of the mediaeval church design with elongated chancel; the tyranny of an architectural orthodoxy was imposed (*see* Plate 10 and Fig. 8).

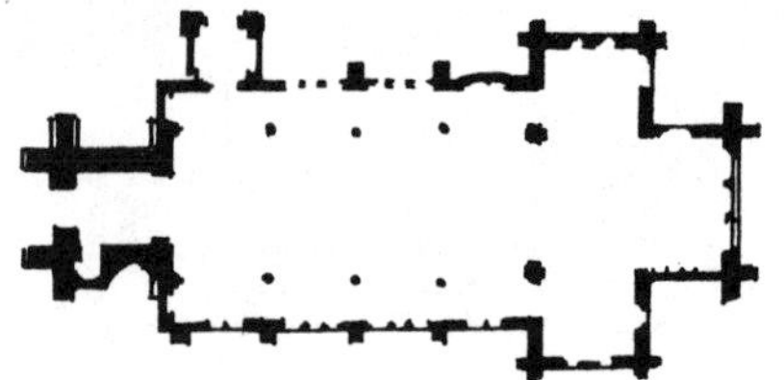

Fig. 8 Gothic revival, two-roomed plan, Privett church, England

Plate 10 Gothic revival, two-roomed plan, St Chad, Nicholas Square, London

Wherever British influence extended, thither the Gothic plan and elevation was exported, so that churches of the period, whether in the USA, in Australia or even in India, followed the same revivalist norm. No church escaped this mixture of antiquarianism and romanticism. Roman Catholic buildings were frequently indistinguishable from Anglican, apart from certain details of the furnishings. Even the Free Churches submitted themselves to the prevailing fashion, but more under the pressure of social considerations than of theological ideas. Anxious to demonstrate that they were as socially respectable as the Established Church, Methodists, Congregationalists, Baptists, all vied with one another in adopting the full mediaeval plan with nave, aisles, transepts and chancels. For a hundred years, from approximately 1850 to 1950, revivalism dominated church design and it was only when the Liturgical Movement* had sufficiently come of age and had wedded itself to the modern movement in architecture that any liberation from the dead hand of the past was achieved and new forms began to emerge. These embodied new concepts of the nature of worship (e.g. that it is corporate), and of the church (e.g. that it is an organic whole with interdependent functions), different movements (e.g. offertory processions) and different ways of doing things (e.g. celebration facing the people) – so 'laws' 1, 2, and 3 were once again stimulating a development of Christian architecture in relation to the liturgy (*see also* **Architectural Setting (Modern) and the Liturgical Movement**).

G. W. O. Addleshaw and F. Etchells, *The Architectural Setting of Anglican Worship*, 1948; A. Biéler, *Architecture in Worship*, 1965; A. Blunt et al, *Baroque and Rococo. Architecture and Decoration*, 1978; B. F. L. Clarke, *Church Builders of the Nineteenth Century*, 1938; K. J. Conant, *Carolingian and Romanesque Architecture 800 to 1200*, 1959; J. G. Davies, *The Secular Use of Church Buildings*, 1968; *Temples, Churches and Mosques*, 1982; P. Frankl, *Gothic Architecture*, 1962; C. Heitz, *Recherches sur les rapports entre architecture et liturgie à l'époque carolingienne*, 1963; R. Krautheimer, *Early Christian and Byzantine Architecture*, 1965; T. F. Mathews, *The Early Churches of Constantinople: Architecture and*

Liturgy, 1971; P. Murray, *The Architecture of the Italian Renaissance*, 1969.

EDITOR

Architectural Setting (Modern) and the Liturgical Movement

To guide us amidst the stupendous and almost chaotic diversity of forms and structures which are characteristic of modern church architecture, we have two main criteria: the human consistency of the architectural setting, and its intrinsic relation to the needs of the Christian community, in other words, hospitality and celebration.

Modern architecture and the Liturgical Movement* are very complex phenomena. Their parallel evolution, and in our case their interaction, depend upon a great variety of factors. To avoid overcomplication, we shall concentrate upon a few particularly significant examples. They alone are able to give us insight into the principles (theological, liturgical, functional, etc.) which inspired the evolution of modern church-building. These architectural facts cover a period of half a century of continual change, stretching from approximately 1925 to the present day.

1. *From 1925 to 1945.* Many authors take as the starting point for modern church architecture the church at Le Raincy near Paris, by A. Perret (1923), both for its thoroughly honest reinforced-concrete structure and for its one-room plan, which foreshadows in a measure the liturgical spaces of the German and Swiss churches of the following decade. But Le Raincy had only a slight influence upon subsequent church building, and one has to remember that the Liturgical Movement was still almost non-existent in France at that time.

Therefore it is preferable to start with something more decisive, a real and living *centre* of liturgical and architectural renewal. The obvious choice is Schloss Rothenfels-am-Main, the castle which served as headquarters to the Catholic Youth movement in Germany between 1927 and the Second World War. (Other centres, like Maria-Laach or Klosterneuburg, had only slight contact with modern architecture.)

Schloss Rothenfels was remodelled in 1928 under the direction of its chaplain, the already famous liturgist Romano Guardini, and of the architect Rudolf Schwarz, who was to become later one of the greatest church builders in Europe. It possessed a regular chapel, but the most interesting feature was the main hall, occasionally used for the eucharist (*see* Fig. 9).

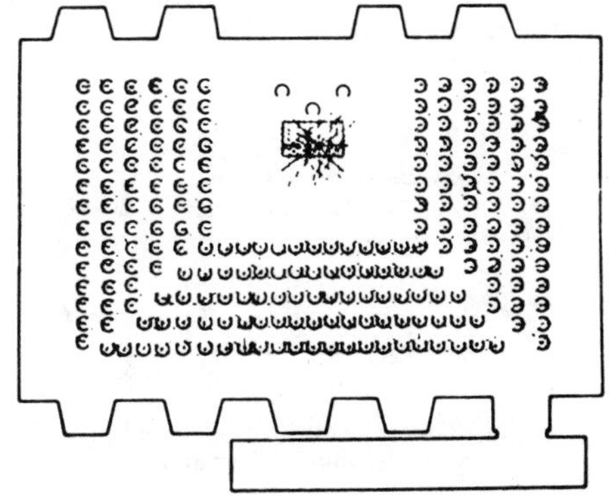

Fig. 9 The main hall, Schloss Rothenfels, Germany

This hall was a large rectangular space, with pure white walls, deep windows and a stone pavement. It was void of decoration. The only furniture was a hundred little black cuboid stools. The disposition of these stools could be easily changed according to the different functions of the room and the nature of the assembly. For example, it was different for a discussion, a recital, a conference, or for a festive occasion. On the days of liturgical celebration, a provisional altar was set up in the hall and the faithful surrounded it on three sides. On the fourth side, facing them from behind the altar, the celebrant closed the circle. In the autobiographical book which Schwarz wrote many years later about his own churches, we find a description of these celebrations and a record of the extraordinary climate of active unity which characterized them (R. Schwarz, *Kirchenbau*, 1960, pp.37–46). Rothenfels was frequented by an *élite*. Its influence on the Liturgical Movement in Germany and in Switzerland has been enormous, even if we had to wait

almost thirty years to find a really consistent application of its principles to parish churches. We can say that the liturgical arrangement at Schloss Rothenfels was probably 'optimal', the best possible solution for an active participation of the faithful in word and sacrament. The liturgy was celebrated and understood as a totally corporate affair, to be expressed with the greatest possible simplicity and flexibility. This included celebration facing the people, a free grouping of the faithful and an overall interpretation of the place of worship where the interior symbol (the living community itself) took precedence over the exterior, the world of persons over that of objects, and hospitality (the pluri-functional room) over monumentality.

Some of these principles were refounded in a measure in the first parish church planned by Schwarz, Böhm and Guardini shortly after Rothenfels: Corpus Christi at Aachen (1928–30) (*see* Plate 11). Aesthetically, its relation to the *Bauhaus* is unmistakable. The plain cubic exterior fits perfectly into its industrial surrounding. The interior, with its white walls and colourless windows, is a rectangular space of absolute geometrical strictness. It unites in a single space the space for the altar and that for the faithful. But this space is still a *Langbau*, i.e. a narrow rectangle at the end of which the altar remains somewhat isolated. The architect has clearly concentrated on *visual* participation, and thus primarily on the visibility of the altar, which dominates the room with almost dictatorial power. It has almost no connection with the pulpit* situated at the centre of the nave*. Schwarz insisted on the fact that his church was not 'christocentric' (as the hall at Rothenfels) but 'theocentric' and even 'trinitarian', having, so to speak, three 'regions': first the area of the faithful with its black pavement and long rows of benches, image of this earth, realm of the Holy Spirit; then the space of transition with the steps leading to the altar, region of Jesus Christ, the Mediator; finally the great white void of the back wall, image of heaven, the region of the Eternal and Invisible Father, and of the glorified Lord.

There is no doubt that, notwithstanding its concentration on essentials and its functional honesty, the lofty, over elevated interior of Corpus Christi still kept a strong symbolic expressivity (which was to be carried even farther in the great post-war 'theological' churches of Rudolf Schwarz). It is interesting to note that this symbolism was explicitly sanctioned by Romano Guardini, who related it to the 'theocentric' movement of liturgical prayer itself.

Plate 11 Corpus Christi, Aachen, Germany

The influence of Corpus Christi was instrumental in the planning of some of the best churches of the early thirties, particularly the church at Norderney by Dominikus Böhm (1930), St Theresa at Zürich by Fritz Metzger (1932) and the delightful little country church of Leversbach by Schwarz himself (1932). The first two look literally like smaller 'sisters' of the great geometrical church of Aachen. At the same time, their more human scale points already (and this is even more true of Leversbach) towards the *domus ecclesiae*, i.e. a church building considered primarily as the 'house' of the local community.

The two leading architects in Switzerland, Metzger and Baur, had been in direct contact with Schwarz, Guardini and the

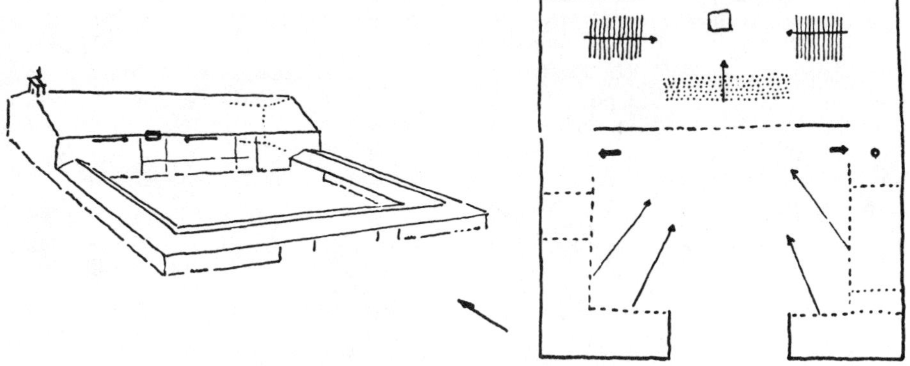

Fig. 10 Project for a church in the diaspora (Steffann)

Rothenfels movement. This was to prove a very happy circumstance. The coming to power of Hitler put an end to almost any further development of church building in Germany. From now on, and at least until 1945, the new spirit was, so to speak, a Swiss responsibility. Northern Switzerland became the only place in Europe where one could find authentically modern churches. Most of them were one-room, rectangular spaces, well lighted, and in some cases, of beautiful human proportions. But they kept, as a rule, the over-elevated altar at the far end of their elongated plan. One hesitates to speak here of 'free-standing' altars, because in all these churches, the altar remains rather away from the people, hardly detached from the back wall and much too broad or too monumental to allow the assistants any kind of enveloping movement. Even the most progressive liturgists of that time still considered the church as a building to house primarily an altar and only secondarily the community. Therefore, the altar *had to be* a big static object, the visual and monumental focus of the whole space.

A memorable exception to this situation was provided by three projects for a diaspora church by the German architect Emil Steffann. They show us: (*a*) exteriors which are much closer to a barn, a farm house or a simple family house than to a religious building in the then accepted meaning of the word; (*b*) an organization of the area of celebration which (at least for projects 1 and 3) is that of the main hall at Rothenfels, i.e. a free-standing altar surrounded on three sides by the faithful; (*c*) an extension of the function of the church to other needs of the community than mere worship. (The drawings were published in *Die Schildgenossen*, 1938, pp.279–81. *See* Fig. 10.)

These plans, however, could not be realized at the moment. The first one foreshadows the famous barn church arranged by Steffann at Bust near Thionville (1942–45). The third is a very close anticipation of one of the most interesting churches of the late fifties: Maria-in-den-Benden at Düsseldorf-Wersten (1958), an almost perfect example of a *domus ecclesiae*.

Before closing this short review of the pre-war period, we must remember that the really authentic modern churches of that time were an extremely small minority. Between 1925 and 1945, the concept of the church remained by and large the old traditional and monumental concept, or at best a compromise between this concept and the new vision of things. All the examples given above are Roman Catholic. This does not mean that the Reformation did not sponsor any good church buildings before 1945. The experiments of Otto Bartning (project for the 'Star church' in 1924; 'Steel church' in 1928; 'Round church' at Essen in 1930), and later, in the Swiss context, the *Johanneskirche* at Basel by Egender and Burckhardt (1936) or the beautiful church of Zürich-Altstetten by Werner Moser (1941), had a real influence on contemporary religious architecture. But their liturgical inspiration remained somewhat ambiguous. One of the reasons for this limitation is that the Reformed

theology of the first part of the century pointed less in the direction of a more active participation of the congregation in the liturgy than towards a re-integration of the symbolic values of the church building itself ('The Evangelical place of worship is not only a meeting-place, it is a "Word in stone" – "*ein gebautes Wort*"', Paul Girkon). One may add that the churches at Basel and Altstetten were too close to the passive *auditorium* to be representative of the Liturgical Movement.

2. *From 1945 to 1963.* After the interruption of the war, a new period opened and stretched from 1945 (or rather 1950) to Vatican II, i.e. at least until 1963.

The main characteristic of this new period was the progressive abandonment of the rectangular plan and of the traditional symmetry. This process was realized by two very different, and almost opposite, groups of churches.

The best examples of the first group present in general a very rational vision of space, an interior which is simple, functional, of human scale and of good proportions. Their plan is most of the time based on the *square* (or on a broad rectangle), where the assembly has a real chance to approach the altar and to surround it on three sides. This is not yet the case in the Illinois Institute of Technology chapel of Chicago, by Mies van der Rohe (1952), nor in the church of Maria Königin at Köln, the last work of Dominikus Böhm (1954), two classical examples of the early fifties. But we find this arrangement fully realized (with even the presidential seat and the possibility of celebrating the eucharist facing the people) in a remarkable series of churches by Emil Steffann: St Laurentius at München (1955), St Elisabeth at Opladen (1957), St Maria-in-den-Benden at Düsseldorf-Wersten (1958) (*see* Fig. 11) and St Laurentius at Köln-Lindenthal (1962). Their architecture is not pointedly modern (some critics call them heavy and slightly 'archaeological') but they have a deep human quality and their liturgical synthesis, with the accent on the living community, is probably the best of the whole period, better even than that proposed as 'ideal' in a famous text of the German Liturgical Commission, the 'Guiding Principles for the design of churches according to the spirit of the Roman liturgy' (1947 and 1955). Together with excellent proposals, this text remains somewhat prone to exalt monumentality. It speaks of objects more than of persons and still insists, in the case of large churches, on a distinct sanctuary (two-room building).

To these churches, we must add some other sober, hospitable, liturgically very sound buildings, for instance, the lovely little Episcopalian church of St James the Fisherman at Cape Cod, Connecticut, by Olav Hammerstrom and the then priest-in-charge, James A. Pike. In this wooden

Architectural Setting (Modern)

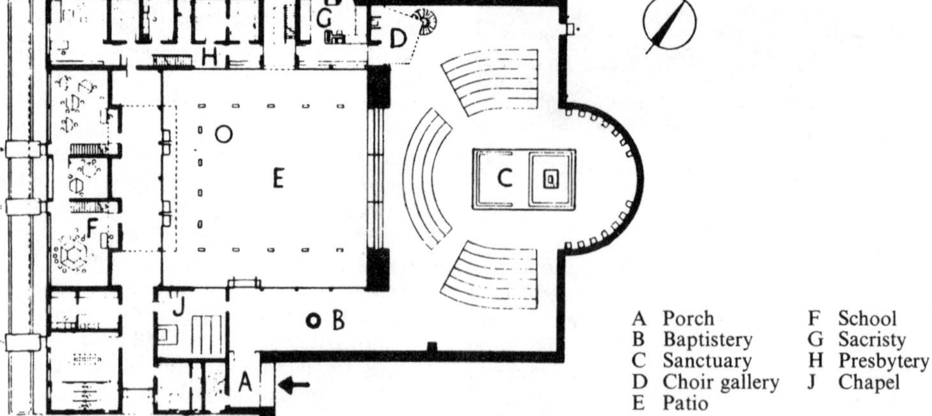

Fig. 11 St Maria-in-den-Benden, Düsseldorf-Wersten, Germany

structure, the central, square altar is entirely surrounded by *four* groups of pews – an arrangement which would probably be dangerous in a big church, but which works perfectly in a fifty-eight feet square space. As other good examples, we may recall here St Paul at Bow Common, by Maguire and Murray (1960), the prefabricated churches of Rainer Senn in Eastern France, the churches of Le Donné at Marienau (1955), Mulhouse (1956), Vitry-sur-Seine (1964), and the last churches by Rudolf Schwarz, particularly St Christophorus at Köln-Niehl (1962). In drastic contrast with the 'theological' schemes developed in his book *Vom Bau der Kirche*, Schwarz allowed this small, unassuming church no other symbolism

Plate 12 St Christophorus, Köln-Niehl, Germany

than the fundamental one of the *domus ecclesiae*. Its climate of simplicity, of tranquil harmony, of plain and radiant humanity, is the very kind of architectural setting which points towards the future of the liturgy. (*See* Plate 12.)

The second, very different direction taken by church-building after 1950 is by way of a much more organic vision of space and symbol. The typical examples, here, are of course strongly individualized. Their forms become more and more lyric. All the elements of architecture: walls, ceilings, floors, etc., become parts of each other. Continuity is everywhere, in the materials and the furnishing as well as in the functions. Applied to the space of worship, this organic character becomes the symbol of the organic, hierarchized body of the faithful.

One of the first experiments in this direction is the church of St Franziskus at Basel-Riehen, by Fritz Metzger (1950) (*see* Plate 13). Its sanctuary and the nave (an ellipse and trapezium) blend in one symbolic form, whose meaning is to express, and at the same time to activate, the participation in the celebration. The floor of the nave follows a slight declivity, where the benches are disposed in a segment of a circle. Everything is organically concentrated on the sanctuary and particularly on the altar. This kind of direct, quasi-physical symbolism is always dangerous in architecture. We must admit that in the case of Riehen, it remained rather discreet.

But directly after 1955, the impact of Le Corbusier's chapel at Ronchamp accelerated the normal pace of the evolution to the point of almost changing its nature. It led to a complete break away from the axial symmetry and other rules which had governed Christian churches since Constantine. Not a bad thing in itself, this liberation unfortunately resulted in the attempt to infuse into every new country church the lyrical creativity of Ronchamp. Many German and practically all Swiss architects were intoxicated by this. It is evident that in this unhealthy, competitive atmosphere, it was difficult to avoid overdoing things, and to escape a touch of megalomania. And what is true of the Swiss churches could be repeated of a large number of 'organic' churches designed between 1955 and 1965 all over the world. From our point of view in the 1980s, we realize that there was little more in this movement than a new metamorphosis of the old temptation to monumentality – a climate in which the liturgical functions were either swallowed up in the *décor* (the form of the space, the dazzling rhythm of the lighting, the heavy fixation of the liturgical poles, etc.) or stressed in a one-sided way.

One has to remember that Ronchamp,

Plate 13 St Franziskus, Basel-Riehen, Switzerland

the most famous of all 'modern' churches, had been the embodiment of a very special programme (a pilgrimage chapel at the top of a hill). It had only little to do with normal, everyday worship. It had almost no connection with the Liturgical Movement in France, which had become at that time the thinking and living *milieu* which laid the basis for the liturgical revolution of Vatican II.

This does not mean that the organic direction in church building is necessarily to be condemned. It is not lyricism as such which is wrong, but lack of coherence, of human scale, of ecclesiastical and functional fitness. However, when trying to point out the churches which really anticipated the 'post-conciliar' church, we see that the examples are generally found in the other group, illustrated by the works of Steffann, Le Donné, etc. They are the best churches liturgically, and also architecturally, in so far as they unite strictness with poetry, and architectural seriousness with a sufficient amount of creative liberty.

3. *From 1963 to 1970*. We have now reached the period of Vatican II. Its importance in the realm of church building does not depend only upon the 'Constitution on the Sacred Liturgy' (1963), but also upon other later texts and statements such as the 'Constitution on the Church and the World' (1965) and the 'Declaration on Religious Liberty' (1965). Even more important was the general climate of freedom, research and the need for authenticity.

Strictly speaking, the 'Constitution on the Liturgy' did not do much more than 'officialize' the major tenets of the Liturgical Movement of the post-war period, particularly the principle of *assembly* worship (considered as the living sign of the universal body of the faithful) and the close link which unites liturgy and mission. But this was enough to suggest a new image of the church building, completely at the 'service' of the assembly. It meant a break with the image still familiar to the great majority of Christians, the 'monumental' image which came from the beginning of the Middle Ages and remained ours even – as we have seen – in the most recent

metamorphoses of organic architecture. This break could not be achieved in a single day.

It seemed easier to start from the *functional* modifications implied by the new liturgy and to comply with the demands of the Constitution by a simple readjustment of the poles of celebration.

Before the Council, many liturgists still arranged everything in church in strict subordination to *one pole*: the altar. The new emphases on the liturgy of the word, celebration facing the people and concelebration*, obliged them now to give prominence also to the chair of the celebrant and to the pulpit, i.e. to the two poles of the liturgy of the word, and to find a distinct location for the tabernacle (for example, against the wall or on a pillar). These three or four poles have to be at the same time clearly differentiated and formed into a living synthesis. The liturgical arrangements of the years immediately following 1963 display an extraordinary variety of solutions. But these arrangements have one thing in common: the *fixity* of all the liturgical furniture. Chair, pulpit, and altar remain firmly bound in stone, concrete and marble. In the organic climate of the Swiss churches, for example, one is confronted with a sanctuary full of huge stones, themselves over-activated by the talent of the sculptor. We are still very far from the place of *interpersonal* communion supposed by the new liturgy of word and eucharist.

The same is true for the liturgy of baptism. In the earlier stages of the Liturgical Movement, the baptismal font* was still located in its traditional chapel, or elsewhere near the entrance area. A special stress was thus given to the initial rite of entry into the church. But the act of incorporation into the community, which is the *living* image of the church, is far more important. Therefore, some liturgists looked for other solutions. They located, for instance, the font in one of the lateral spaces of the church, largely open to the assembly (*see* **Baptistery**). We find examples of this arrangement in some churches by Rudolf Schwarz, like St Anna at Düren (1955) and St Christophorus at Köln-Niehl (1962) (*see* Plate 12).

Other liturgists think that baptism should normally be celebrated facing the assembly; thus the best position for the baptismal font is in a symmetrical relation to the ambo *. Apart from its communal value, this position emphasizes the close tie that binds

Plate 14 St Pankratius, Oberkirch, Lucerne, Switzerland (Fritz Metzger)

baptism to the liturgy of the word and to the eucharist. The danger of this new location is of overcrowding the area of celebration, and this is exactly what happened in the Swiss churches mentioned above (*see* Plate 14). The baptismal font added one huge stone to others.

Real progress in the general arrangement of the church and especially of the sanctuary was to be found by way of more suppleness, simplicity and mobility. Paradoxically, this was first realized in countries like Austria or Belgium, where the movement of modern churches had remained, at least up to 1960, practically sterile. It is these countries, too, which offered the first truly post-conciliar churches – completely and uncompromisingly so.

The idea coming to life in these churches can be summed up in one phrase: the serving of the assembled community in the simplest possible form. Beyond the limited perspective of pure liturgical functionalism, this means humility, limpidity, and above all a great opening to a living dialogue. But dialogue excludes any kind of rigid confrontation between the celebrant and the faithful, and thus also rigidity in the form, material and location of the liturgical objects. The Belgian architect Marc Dessauvage was probably the first to accept this evolution and to draw the consequences. In the parish churches he built after 1963, the altar, the pulpit, the chair and the font are generally mobile (*see* Plate 15).

An even more important change, introduced by the Austrian architect Ottokar Uhl, was the possibility of movement for the assembly itself. In his students' chapel of the Peter Jordanstrasse at Vienna (1965), the single space is divided into two distinct areas. The first is furnished by benches and occupied by the assembly during the liturgy of the word. The second is an open, free space for the eucharist. The faithful enter this space after the sermon and stand in a semi-circle around the altar. Provision for movement is carried even farther in another chapel by Uhl, arranged at the school of

Plate 15 St Rochur, Aarschot, Belgium

Plate 16 Chapel for students, Melk, Austria

the Benedictine abbey of Melk (1967) (*see* Plate 16).

The question of movement in church is related to the question of number and to other fundamental problems. At the New York Congress on Religion, Architecture and the Visual Arts (1967), which is another major milestone in the evolution of modern church building, the main theme in discussion was not any more the liturgical fitness of the church, but the very question of still building churches in a situation of acute mobility, anonymity, urbanization and secularization. The parochial system, i.e. the frame of Christian life and worship which the faithful had known for centuries, and until a very recent time, appeared now clearly to be in the process of crumbling away. The question was: how to replace it? In the conclusions of the Congress, Professor Houtart demonstrated the need to develop the new solutions on three levels: the small group (a homogeneous meeting of no more than twenty people), the congregation (a flexible, not strictly territorial adaptation of the parochial assembly) and the large community (an occasional grouping of many hundreds or even thousands of faithful). These three levels of ecclesial belonging and expression have to be simultaneously ordered for several functions: not only the liturgy, but also communication, social action, etc. (*Revolution, Place and Symbol*. Journal of the New York Congress, 1969, pp.57–9).

The small group is characterized by the openness and simplicity of its contacts, and, in the liturgy, by the reduction of external rites. It does not need any specialized space for worship. Because the centres of life and worship coincide, everything can normally take place in the homes of individuals. For the large community, there is no architectural problem either: it will use great, pre-existing spaces (a cathedral, a theatre, a cultural centre, a stadium, etc.). Only the group called 'congregation' will still need and ask for specialized church buildings.

The problem is to adapt these buildings fully to the new situation. It is evident that the majority of the churches built between 1967 and 1970 do not differ very much from the churches of the early 'sixties. In a few cases, however, we find a real attempt to integrate the new values. Good examples are the Church of St Paul at Waterloo, Belgium (1968) and the church at Neuville near Liège (1970), both by Jean Cosse. In the second of these buildings, especially, which has a demountable podium and movable furniture, the space for worship is occasionally used for conferences, concerts, etc. It can be extended towards the reception room (with open firehearth, adjacent kitchen, cloakroom and other facilities). The dominant character of the main space remains thus that of a place of worship, but it is flexible enough to accommodate other functions. Although at least 150 people take part in worship, the liturgy in this church has a real family climate: it is a domestic liturgy, thanks to the very hospitable setting. (*See* Fig. 12.)

Neuville is thus a kind of multi-purpose church. This new concept, elaborated between 1965 and 1967, supposes a real synthesis, and not only a juxtaposition, of the liturgical and the secular functions. In his important book on *The Secular Use of Church Buildings* (1968), Professor J. G. Davies has demonstrated that the union of liturgical and secular functions is deeply traditional and corresponds to the very nature of Christianity. In the modern context, the experiments of multi-purpose churches point towards a plurality of solutions. The church at Neuville is a prudent but quite acceptable one. Another possibility is to keep a fixed sanctuary, and to screen it off when using the nave for other purposes. This solution is best known, probably because it is the easiest to put into practice, but its future is very uncertain if

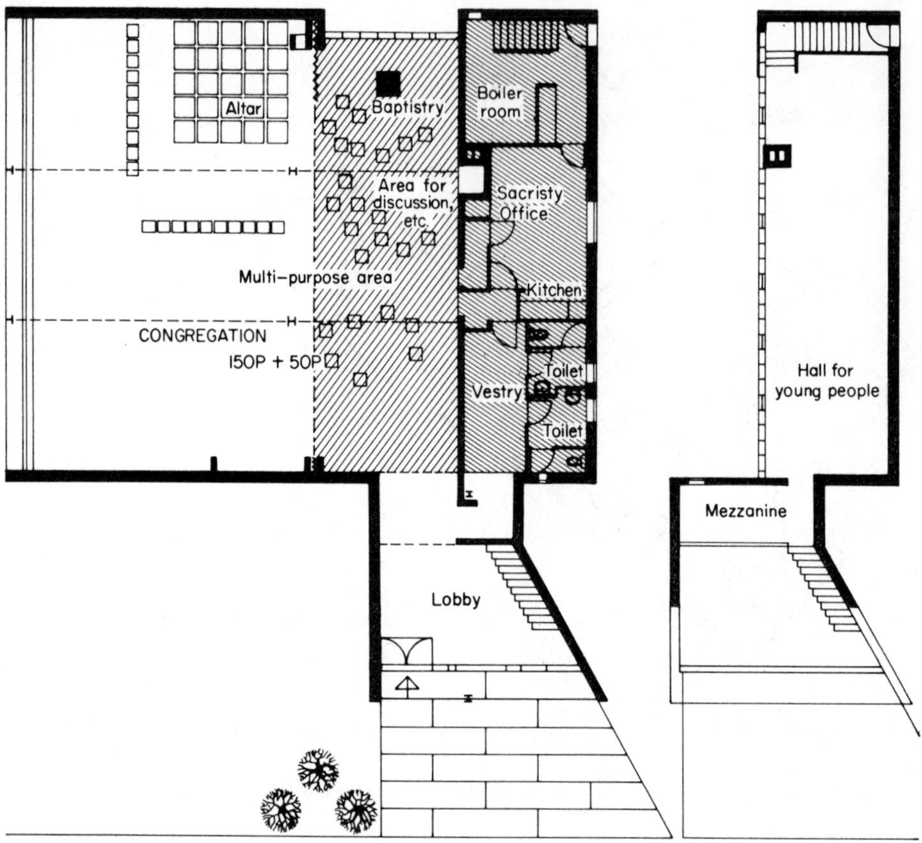

Fig. 12 Church at Neuville, Liège, Belgium

only because it is not really honest, and is better defined as dual-purpose rather than multi-purpose.

The Institute for the Study of Worship and Religious Architecture of the University of Birmingham, and Professor Davies himself, have inspired multi-purpose churches of another type, where the worship area includes a fixed and defined space for the sanctuary, choir and the font, but without any screen to shield them during secular use (*see* Fig. 13). This enables the unity of the functions 'to be demonstrated and to be lived' (*The Secular Use of Church Buildings*, pp. 243–8).

A fourth kind could be illustrated by the new pastoral centre at Kessel-Loo near Louvain, in Belgium, by Dessauvage (1970). The very flexible main space, which offers pluri-dimensional possibilities, serves for worship on Sundays and feast days only, and has no permanent liturgical furniture. Normally, it is used for secular purposes (like the hall at Rothenfels). However, in the quietest part of the centre, a much smaller room, liturgically fully equipped, is reserved for daily worship and personal meditation. This could seem a regressive arrangement. But by 1970, 'secularization' was no longer the only problem. One had to take into account the rediscovery of meditation and intense personal prayer. The same could be said of the need for new and vital forms of festivity and celebration. The Liturgical Movement still had to integrate better these two, almost opposite, forms of worship: and so had the church building, if it was to remain faithful to its never-ending quest for adaptation and authenticity.

4. *From 1970 to 1985.* Compared with the years which immediately preceded or

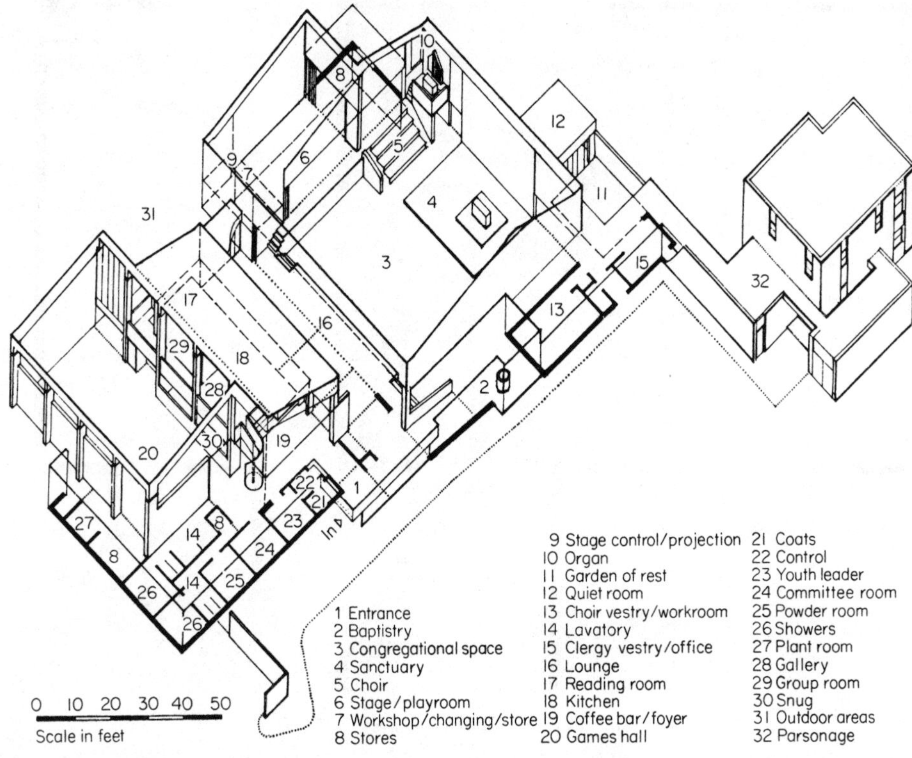

Fig. 13 St Philip and St James, Hodge Hill, Birmingham, England

followed Vatican II, the churchbuilding of the seventies and early eighties will evidently seem rather uneventful. The great liturgical and architectural battles were over; interest ebbed considerably. The obvious prediction is that from the mid 1980s on evolution will concern only minor matters. There is also the impact of the economic crisis, felt everywhere: fewer churches are built, most of them relatively small and modest – not a bad thing in itself.

On the other hand, many Roman Catholic pastors and architects are still struggling with the liturgical data of the Council, not always knowing how to apply them with real coherence and harmony. A typical instance is the location and volume given to the freestanding altar. In many new arrangements, or in the rearrangements of older churches, it remains too far from the faithful, too high placed, too broad, too big, and because of its heavy frontality, a hindrance to a good location of the other poles of the liturgy, and certainly not the radiant, active presence it is supposed to be.

This does not imply a regression of liturgical 'functionalism'. Most of the churches built around 1975 were entirely designed and organized as liturgical settings, even if they were at the same time more or less open to other uses (multi-purpose).

We have already described the reappearance of the old 'house church' (*domus ecclesiae*) of the first centuries, with its plurality of spaces and its domestic climate. This tendency is now gaining power with the more and more frequent passage from the 'one-cell' to the 'multi-cell' church, an organic body where each space is used again for a specific purpose. We find examples of this in Germany (Rosing; *see* Fig. 14), Austria (Rainer), England (Williams and Winkley), Belgium (de Boe), USA (Quinn; *see* Fig. 15). These churches express a *living* plurality which corresponds to the complexity of the Christian life-style of today and its multiple values, practical, social, festive, meditative, liturgic, etc. An interest-

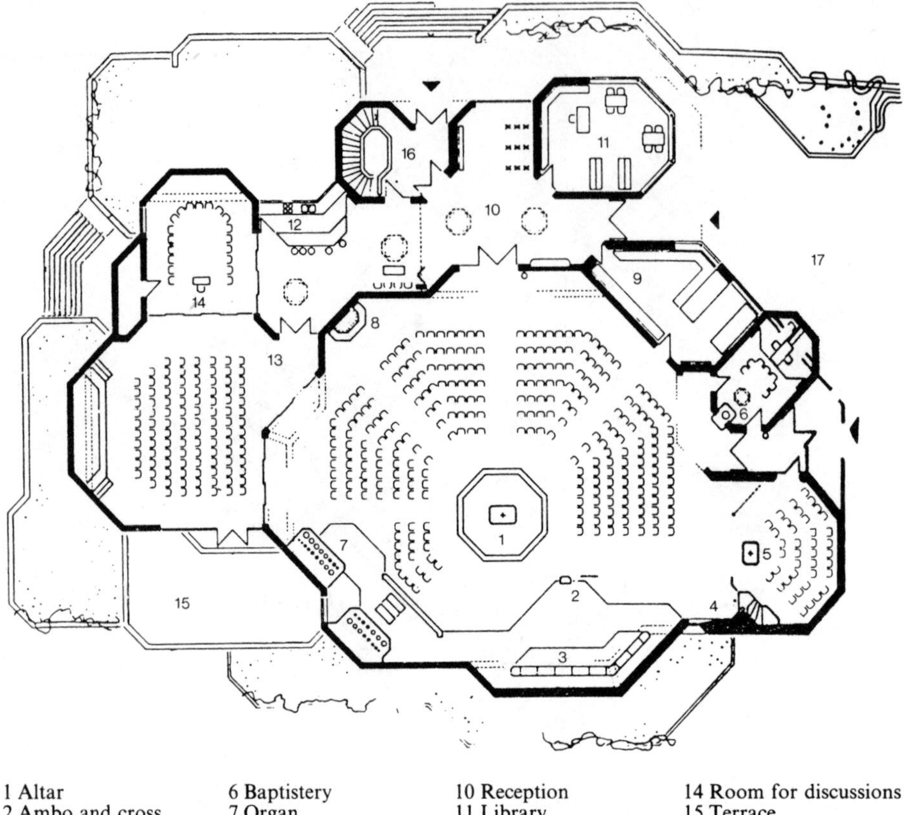

1 Altar
2 Ambo and cross
3 Clergy seating
4 Reserved sacrament
5 Weekday chapel with mobile altar
6 Baptistery
7 Organ
8 Virgin Mary
9 Sacristy
10 Reception
11 Library
12 Kitchen
13 Parish room
14 Room for discussions
15 Terrace
16 Descent to youth area
17 Open space

Fig. 14 St Laurence, Plettenberg, Germany, by Nicolas Rosing, 1975

ing element in this respect is the reception hall, not limited in these churches to the entrance area but penetrating to the heart of the building. This hall is an artery of communication, activation, synthesis, which links the celebration area organically to the other communal spaces and to the more meditative space of the weekday (or adoration) chapel.

At least from 1978 or 1980, the religious spirit seems to become once again all-embracing, and reintegrates values which had been more or less neglected in the previous years. This seems to be particularly true of the 'sacred', an ambiguous religious value which used to be exaggeratedly linked to monumentality and to the objects of the liturgical space. The danger is of course to go simply back to this old sacrality. Between the monumentally sacred, which concentrates on the object, and the desacralized world, the sacred has to be reorientated towards its truly Christian meaning, which is that of the personal mystery of presence and communion given by the risen Christ to his congregation.

To express this in the church building and the liturgical setting is not easy. The experiments we know of (for instance the small church at the monastery of Clerlande in Belgium by Jean Cosse; *see* Plate 17) tend to combine: architecturally, a domestic character, truly accepted, and the rediscovery and reinterpretation of some fundamental elements of the old church

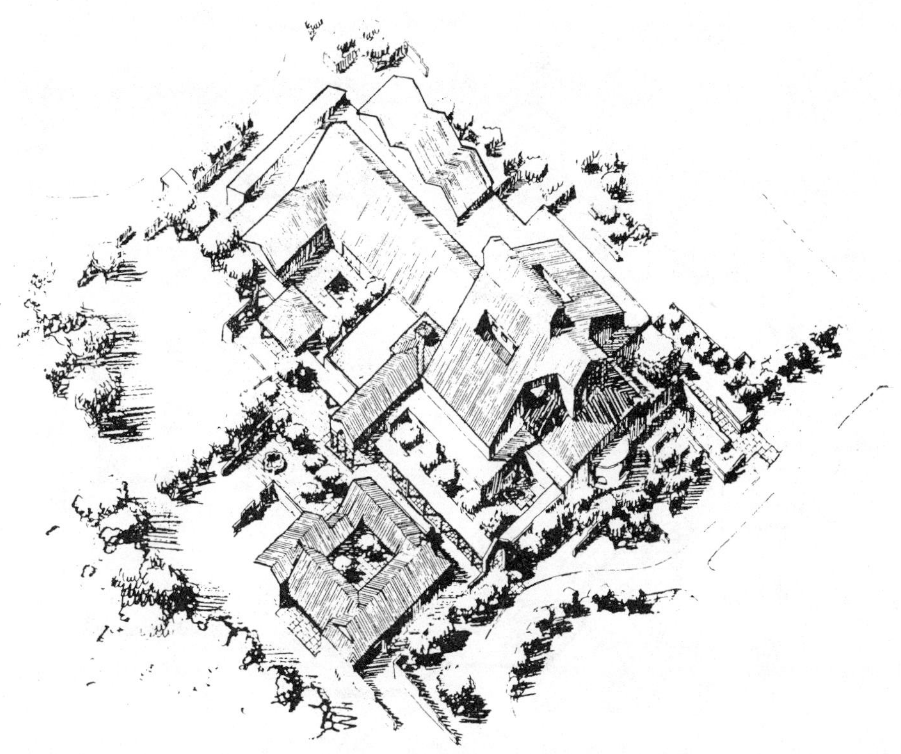

Fig. 15 Project for St Jude, Boca Raton, Florida, by Patrick Quinn, 1980

architecture, like the apse, the columns, the complexity of higher and lower spaces, the gradation of the light, the icon – and liturgically, a synthesis between the enveloping movement of the assembly around the altar, and the axial, symmetrical orientation which expresses reverence, adoration. To make this kind of 'total' image more definite will probably be the specific liturgical task of the next decade.

F. Debuyst, *Modern Architecture and Christian Celebration*, 1968; 'In Praise of the Uncertain', *Art d'Eglise*, 193, 1980, A, B; P. Hammond, *Liturgy and Architecture*, 1960; R. G. Kennedy, *American Churches*, 1982; R. Maguire, K. Murray, *Modern Churches of the World*, 1965; J. Plazaola, *Futuro del arte sacro*, 1973.

F. DEBUYST

Armenian Worship

1. *Introduction.* Armenia was first evangelized from the South-West, probably by Edessa, and later also from the West by missionaries from Cappadocia. Thus Syrian and Greek influences were present at the very onset of Armenia's Christianization.

The conversion of the royal house took place either at the end of the third or the beginning of the fourth century through Gregory the Illuminator, who had been educated in Cappadocia. The tendentious insistence on the religious significance of Gregory and his connections with Cappadocia was meant to obliterate the originally close relationship between Armenia and Edessa which has been known to us through legendary reports. Recent scholarship has shown that Armenia's original theological concepts were moored in the theological tradition of Edessa with its close ties to Antiochene christology.

Another factor contributed to the complexity of Armenia's doctrinal and liturgical evolution. Armenia was divided in 386/7 between Persia and Byzantium with the

Plate 17 Chapel of the monastery, Clerlande, Belgium, by Jean Cosse, 1981

greater portion falling under Persian domination and the smaller part under Byzantine rule. The political and ecclesial difficulties arising from this break-up of the nation were partially overcome by the invention of the Armenian alphabet at the beginning of the fifth century and the creation of a national church in the sixth century which signalled Armenia's attempt to attain greater independence from Byzantine tutelage and Nestorian doctrinal positions in Persia by taking over Alexandrian christology.

With regard to the formation of the liturgical tradition, we can say that Syrian influence prevails in the rites of initiation, whereas parts of the liturgy of the hours were decisively formed through the influence of Jerusalem, and the Armenian anaphoras integrated borrowings from Byzantium. Latin dominance came into play during the twelfth century, which led to the Latinization of the Armenian rite. Given this multifaceted background of Armenian worship, it is wrong to subordinate the Armenian to the Byzantine rite as is often done.

2. *Liturgical Books*. The most important include the *Mashtoc'* (ritual), *Pataragamatoyc'* or *Horhrdatetr* (missal), *Tonac'oyc'* (typikon), *Tshashoc'* (lectionary), *Žamagirk'* (horologion); several different books exist for the hymns: the oldest is the *Sharaknoc'* or *Sharakan* (tropologion); the *Ergaran* (hymnary) and *Tagharan* (songbook) developed later. (*See also* **Books, Liturgical** 2.)

3. *Rites of Initiation*.

(*a*) *Theology*. The Armenians and the Maronites have preserved the most ancient characteristics of the initiation rites, both having kept the earliest stratum of the Syrian baptismal theology. The original Syro-Armenian type of initiation is based on what one could determine as 'Genesis-mysticism' and on John's baptismal theology (John 3) with its characteristic pneumatic emphasis (no exorcisms!), in contrast to the Graeco-Latin type which developed out of Paul's christocentric 'death-mys-

ticism' (Rom. 6) and the increase of exorcisms. Thus the original emphasis lies on 1. the dawn of creation and the creative force of the Spirit, 2. Christ as the Adam who was baptized in the Jordan with the Spirit resting upon this 'Adam', and 3. the outpouring of the Spirit at Pentecost who transformed the disciples into apostles just as Jesus emerged from the Jordan as the 'Sent One'.

This imagery is best preserved throughout the Maronite baptismal liturgy, whereas the Armenians show these archaic features especially in their hymns. The over-riding emphasis of these rites rests on the pneumatic underpinnings of the entire baptismal liturgy, where verbal exorcisms are originally absent. Not the expelling of the evil spirit, not the extinction of the previous life during the immersion, not the assimilation to Christ's death and resurrection formed here the basis from which the rite took its inspiration; what happened through the life-giving force of the Spirit, whose creative power became manifest at the creation, the Jordan, and Pentecost, was the guiding principle for the unfolding of the rites.

(*b*) *Structure*. The Armenian *textus receptus* differs only marginally from the oldest manuscripts of the ninth and tenth centuries. The evidence of the manuscripts needs to be compared with the patristic documents of the third to fifth centuries. The Armenians preserved the original structural transparency of the initiation rites: A. Preparatory rites, traces of which are reflected in the initial rubric; B. Prebaptismal rites on the day of baptism including: I. The rites in front of the church: 1. invitatory; 2. two juxtaposed prayers with respective intercessions (of which the second with its exorcistic flavour is clearly of a later date); 3. archaic form of the baptismal vows with no exorcisms; II. Entry into the church with Ps. 117, then 1. the blessing of the oil with an allusion to the original prebaptismal anointing (which was later dropped); 2. blessing of the water with its imagery of rebirth and its referral to Jesus' baptism (no exorcisms! no reference to Paul's baptismal theology of Rom. 6!); C. Baptism proper: only the rubric (later introduced) refers to Christ's death, which is re-enacted through the immersion, whereas the reading of Matt. 3.13–17 (= Jesus' baptism) maintains the older stratum of Jesus' beginning at the Jordan; D. Postbaptismal anointing, which originally was absent since the anointing took place before the immersion as in the oldest Syrian tradition. (*See also* **Baptism** 1.)

4. *Anaphora.** Today, only the anaphora attributed to Athanasius is celebrated. According to Catergian and Dashian, the anaphora of Cappadocia attributed to Basil was translated into Armenian during the fifth century. This Armenian version has to be considered among the oldest redactions of the liturgy of Basil. Later the Armenians attached the name of Gregory the Illuminator to this anaphora. Towards the end of the fifth century other Cappadocian formularies were also rendered into Armenian, namely the so-called anaphora of Sahak, Gregory of Nazianzus, Cyril, and Athanasius. These anaphoras derive, according to Catergian, from Gregory of Nazianzus. However, the anaphora of Sahak apparently also shows a close affinity to the anaphora of Basil. The anaphora of Cyril has nothing in common with its Syriac or Coptic counterpart, but ought to be compared with the Constantinopolitan anaphora of Basil of the ninth century and the Egyptian, Greek and Coptic liturgy of Gregory. (*See also* **Liturgies** 2.)

After the tenth century the anaphora of Basil once more became rendered into Armenian and, probably between the twelfth and thirteenth centuries, also the liturgy of Chrysostom. During the eleventh to fourteenth century two Syriac anaphoras and the Latin mass were also taken over. The anaphora of Athanasius prevailed over all the other formularies; of importance for the study of its evolution is the tenth-century commentary by Chosrov.

5. *Liturgy of the Hours* (*see also* **Canonical Hours**). The cathedral hours comprise the morning (*aṙawotean*) and evening (*erekoyean*) hours, both of which have kept archaic features. The evening office apparently consists of two juxtaposed cathedral offices (with the universal evening psalm, 140), with no traces of monastic influence. The first one was probably adopted through outside (Constantinopolitan?) influence, whereas the second office seems to reflect the authentic Armenian tradition. The Armenian morning office (like the East-Syrian) does not have Ps. 62 (the universal

morning psalm of Antioch, Palestine, including possibly also Cappadocia). The central part of the office consists (as in East Syria although in a different order) of Pss. 50, 148–150, followed by the *Gloria in excelsis*.

The Sunday cathedral vigil derives in its nucleus from Jerusalem. This vigil now consists of: 1. the monastic office of the night (*gisherayin*), 2. the cathedral vigil proper (*iwghaberic'*), and 3. the morning office (*ar̃awotean*). This vigil or 'office of the spice-bearing women', which commemorates the resurrection of the Lord, is patterned after the Easter vigil with its three canticles of Moses (Ex. 15.1ff.), Azarias (Dan. 3.26ff.), and the Three Youths (Dan. 3.52ff.). The canticles are followed by the gospel of (the burial and) resurrection. Originally the canticles were sung with a responsory (*kc'urd*) which later developed into a troparion (*sharakan*). These troparia then assumed such overriding importance that they threatened to suffocate the original element. The original structural transparency of the tripartite Sunday vigil became obscured with the introduction of NT canticles in the morning office (*Magnificat*, Zachariah, Simeon) and the increase of troparia and other hymnodic elements, which culminated in the subsequent disintegration of the psalmody of the night office.

The main structure of the night office (*gisherayin*) originally consisted of a christological doxology with the invitatory (Ps. 3) and the variable psalmody arranged in numerical order. The invitatory then became expanded (3 + 87, 102, 142) and more doxologies were introduced, followed by intercessions and the variable psalmody. In the Middle Ages hymns were added, two of them artificially inserted between the intercessions (*k'aroz*) and their collect (*aghot'k'*). Under the weight of an increasing adoption of hymnodic material and the insertion of the office of the dead (on days when the liturgy is celebrated), the original main element (the variable psalmody) disintegrated into a few psalm verses.

The following remaining hours await closer investigation in regard to their historical evolution: *arewagali* (sunrise office), *tshashu* (midday office), *chaghaghakan* (peace office), and *hangstean* (rest office). Further study also awaits the development of the feasts in Armenia. Thus far it is determined that the Armenians preserved the oldest structure of the feast of Epiphany,* celebrating both Christ's baptism and birth on 6 January.

6. *Hymnography*. Some of the Armenian baptismal hymns, which are also sung on Epiphany, are very ancient and show close contacts with the baptismal theology of Syria.

Other hymnodic material derives from the responses (*kc'urd*) taken from the canticles and psalms of the Sunday vigil. Quite soon non-biblical refrains were being used to elucidate the meaning of the main dominical feasts such as Easter and Epiphany. The Armenian name for these troparia (*sharakan*) is apparently of Syriac origin and associated with the three canticles of the Easter and Sunday vigil. These troparia are older than those sung with the morning psalms (50, 148–150). Both the Armenian and Byzantine structure of the *kanon* of troparia grew out of the Easter and Sunday vigil of Jerusalem. During the seventh century these troparia, originally restricted to the main feasts of the Lord, then also taken over by the Sunday vigil and later even by the ferial office, must have steadily increased. By the turn of the eighth century the troparia were grouped in the various *kanons* by Step'annos Siwnec'i. By then the Armenian *kanon* (in contrast to the Byzantine) includes not only the troparia of the canticles but also those of the morning psalms. Later the troparia were also spreading to the evening office. The increase of troparia (*sharakan*) reached its peak by the twelfth century with Nerses Shnorhali.

Besides the older *sharakan*, the *erg* (hymn) and the *tagh* (song) also developed later and they became collected in the *ergaran* (hymnarium) and *tagharan* (songbook).

The importance of the Armenian evidence lies in the fact that with the help of Armenian sources we can unravel the oldest layers of Christian worship, often the original structure and meaning of the Syrian rites, and to a considerable extent the early shape of Byzantine worship.

See also **East Syrian Worship**; **Orthodox Worship**; **West Syrian Worship**.

A. Renoux, *Le codex arménien Jérusalem*

121, 2 vols, 1969–71; P. Ferhat, A. Baumstark, A. Rücker, 'Denkmäler altarmenischer Messliturgie', *Oriens Christianus*, new series 1, 1911; 3, 1913; 7–8, 1918; third series 1, 1927; G. Winkler, *Das armenische Initiationsrituale*, 1982; 'The Armenian Night Office', *Revue des Études arméniennes* 17, 1983.

GABRIELE WINKLER

Ascension Day

The commemoration of the Ascension of Christ on the fortieth day after Easter* builds into liturgical tradition the chronology used by Luke in the Acts of the Apostles. Originally the Ascension and the coming of the Spirit at Pentecost were celebrated as a unitive festival at Pentecost* itself, but their evolution into two festivals was probably taking place during the last quarter of the fourth century, originating in the region Constantinople – Asia Minor – Antioch. Apart from appropriate lections and prayers, there are no particular liturgical ceremonies associated with the day. It used to be the custom for the paschal candle* to be lit for the last time at the eucharist on Ascension Day, and then extinguished after the reading of the gospel, but modern custom is to continue lighting it at services until Pentecost.

For bibliography *see* under **Calendar**

R. F. BUXTON

Ash Wednesday

The first day of Lent, the Wednesday of the seventh week before Easter* (for an account of why Lent begins on this day, *see* **Lent**). The day derives its name from the ceremonial imposition of ashes* on the foreheads of worshippers in the liturgy of the day, a rite that goes back to at least the tenth century, and the fact that all participate in it is one of the signs that Lent was no longer the preserve of those doing formal penance prior to readmission to communion at Easter and had become a general period of penitential devotion observed by all.

In the modern Roman rite, and in the 1985 service produced by the Liturgical Commission of the Church of England, the imposition takes place in the eucharist after gospel and sermon, though the eucharistic context is not obligatory. The ceremony itself consists of a blessing or prayer over the ashes, traditionally made by burning the palms from the previous year's Palm Sunday*, followed by imposition on the forehead accompanied by a verbal formula which is either a reminder of human mortality or an exhortation to faithfulness to the gospel or both. This combination of word and acted symbol can and should be a spiritually powerful inauguration of the season of Lent.

See also **Commination**.

For bibliography *see* under **Calendar**

R. F. BUXTON

Ashes

Ashes are a symbol of 1. purification (cf. Num. 19.9, 17f.; Heb. 9.13); 2. penitence (cf. Judith 9.1; Jonah 3.6; Luke 10.13; Matt. 11.21).

The former symbolism could be seen in the consecration of a church* according to the Roman rite. Water, called Gregorian water, was mingled with wine, salt and ashes, and with this mixture the bishop sprinkled the altar and the walls of the church in different places. It was an exorcistic rite intended to purify the building before it was consecrated by the anointing with chrism (*see* **Chrismatory**). The use of 'Gregorian Water' was abolished by the *Rite of the Dedication of a Church*, 1977.

The latter symbolism, common to many religions and part of the common stock of OT and NT religion (cf. texts quoted), is to be found in the rite of the imposition of ashes on Ash Wednesday*. In the earlier centuries of the church, when the discipline of public penitence was in force, penitents sometimes sprinkled ashes on their heads or alternatively received from the bishop a rough garment on which ashes had been sprinkled. In the tenth to eleventh century, when the primitive discipline had become obsolete. Christians generally associated themselves with the modified discipline and came to church on the Wednesday before the first Sunday in Lent (subsequently called Ash Wednesday) to have blessed ashes (made of the palm branches of the previous year) put on their foreheads (*see* **Commination**). The prayer(s) used indicate that the rite is a penitential one and one formula used for the imposition of the ashes

suggests the necessary abasement before God if forgiveness is to be achieved: 'Remember, man, that you are dust and into dust you shall return' (cf. Gen. 3.19).

Formerly the rite took place before the mass. Since 1970 it takes place within it, after the homily.

A. G. Martimort, I. H. Dalmais, P. Jounel (eds), *L'Eglise en Prière*, IV, 1983, pp.81–82; M. Righetti, *Manuale di Storia Liturgica*, I, 1950, pp.54–55, II, [2]1955, pp.120–123.

J. D. CRICHTON

Asperges

The word comes from Ps. 50.9 in the vulgate psalter: 'Thou shalt *sprinkle* me with hyssop and I shall be cleansed: thou shalt wash me and I shall be made whiter than snow', which in the Roman rite is recited when holy water is sprinkled over the people, when holy communion is given in the home and on some other occasions. Formerly other verses of the psalm were sung or said during the sprinkling, which took place usually in a procession of celebrant, ministers and servers around the church before the principal mass on Sunday. The rite (now to be performed after the entrance chant) is no longer of obligation in parish churches.

Originally, it would seem, an exorcistic rite (though there is a reference to sprinkling of the people in the ancient prayer of the blessing of baptismal water of the Paschal vigil*) for the cleansing of a building or place where a liturgical service was to take place, and also more strictly so when fields were sprinkled, it has become in the course of centuries connected with baptism. It is seen both as a reminder of baptism and as a means of renewing its grace. This is indicated both by the sprinkling of the people after the renewal of their baptismal promises at the Paschal vigil and by the change of text for the Sunday sprinkling in Paschal time. The *Asperges* is replaced by a text based on Ezek. 47.1, 8, 9: 'I saw water coming out from the temple on the right side and all whom this water touched were saved.'

The rite of the Sunday *Asperges* probably had its origin in the monastic custom of sprinkling the monastery on that day. In the Middle Ages in some parts of Europe the procession for the sprinkling with holy water went through the whole village.

In modern Roman Catholic churches the rite is replaced for ordinary masses by the custom of taking holy water from stoups placed at the entrance to the church. The people are supposed to recite the *Asperges* while doing so.

R. Berger, *Kleines Liturgisches Wörterbuch*, 1969, pp.44, 471–2; A. G. Martimort (ed), *L'Eglise en Prière*, 1961, pp.165, 639.

J. D. CRICHTON

Assemblies of God Churches' Worship

The Assemblies of God, with international headquarters in Springfield, Missouri, was organized in 1914, and ten years later the Assemblies of God, Great Britain and Ireland was constituted by about seventy independent Assemblies agreeing to form a recognized fellowship. It is one of the denominations brought into existence as a result of the Pentecostal revival of the late nineteenth and early twentieth centuries (*see also* **Pentecostal Worship**). In addition to being a church of the evangelical tradition, the Assemblies of God is known for an emphasis on the manifestation of the gifts of the Holy Spirit as described in I Cor. 12–14.

In many ways the architecture of Assemblies of God churches is similar to that of other non-liturgical churches. Almost invariably the pulpit* is in the centre of the platform, indicating the emphasis placed on the centrality and authority of the scriptures. Ordinarily a communion table is directly in front of the pulpit at the level of the congregation; altar rails or benches are either made a part of the platform or placed between the congregation and the platform, symbolizing the direct access man has to God through Jesus Christ. A baptistery* is usually located behind the platform.

The Assemblies of God considers the mission of the church to be threefold. The ministry of the church towards God involves worship and obedience (Acts 13.2). Its ministry towards it members provides for edification and maturation (Eph. 4.11–16). Its ministry towards unbelievers emphasizes the need of personal regeneration (John 3.3). The Assemblies of God ministry

to unbelievers includes a missionary programme built on indigenous principles which reaches around the world.

Assemblies of God services are informal and non-liturgical. Vestments are not worn by officiating clergy. In expression of the threefold mission of the church, regular services may have one of three major emphases. The Sunday morning service usually emphasizes worship, but it is also designed for the edification of the worshippers. The Sunday evening service usually emphasizes the need of regeneration and is intended to bring unbelievers to a personal commitment to Christ. A midweek service is most often thought of as a time for Bible study and prayer. Special services of the local congregation include evangelistic meetings, Bible conferences, mission conventions, and training courses. Because the Assemblies of God has a basic congregational polity, there are variations of the emphases mentioned, and the degree of informality varies.

The order of the services usually includes congregational singing of hymns and gospel songs, often accompanied by a variety of musical instruments, public prayer, ministry of music by a choir and/or individuals, receiving of tithes and offerings, and the ministry of the word. Quite often opportunities are given for members of the congregation to share personal testimonies concerning scripture portions which have been especially meaningful to them or experiences in which they feel God has helped them in a special way. The testimonies may be interspersed with the singing of choruses by the congregation. Enthusiastic congregational participation is an important aspect of worship in Assemblies of God churches.

Ways in which an Assemblies of God service differs from other non-liturgical evangelical services include times of united audible prayer and worship; manifestations of the gifts of the Holy Spirit, such as speaking in tongues, interpretation of tongues, and prophecy; and prayer for the sick, including anointing with oil. In many instances, especially in smaller congregations, opportunity is given in a service for members of the congregation to mention needs which they feel should be remembered during public prayer. Most services end with an invitation for those present to kneel at the altar rail or at their seats for a time of prayer.

The Assemblies of God recognizes two ordinances and considers both symbolic rather than being inherently efficacious.

Baptism by total submersion is considered essential as an act of obedience and outwards sign of the believer's identification with Christ in his death, burial, and resurrection. Baptism is administered only on profession of faith in Christ, and for this reason infants are dedicated to God rather than baptized. Baptismal services are conducted either in a church baptistery or in an outside natural body of water.

The Lord's Supper*, usually celebrated monthly, is considered a memorial of Christ's substitutionary death and a reminder of Christ's second coming. Faith in Christ, rather than membership in an Assemblies of God church, is the basis upon which worshippers are invited to participate in this ordinance. Communicants partake of both elements, usually at their seats, served by laymen.

The Assemblies of God without exception accept the Bible as the infallible and authoritative rule of faith and conduct.

THOMAS F. ZIMMERMAN

Assumption

see **Mariological Feasts**

Atrium

The entrance or fore-court of a basilica*. It was usually open in the centre and surrounded by covered colonnades.

EDITOR

Aumbry

A cupboard or recess in the wall of a church or the sacristy* in which the sacred vessels and books, and sometimes also reliquaries, were kept. Aumbries were also used to house the three oils used in certain sacramental rites; these were stored in a chrismatory*. They were also used with a locked door for the reservation* of the blessed sacrament usually in a wall near the altar, but sometimes in the sacristy. This method of reserving the consecrated elements has been revived in the Church of England during the last hundred years, and the door and surround of the aumbry sometimes have elaborate decoration, as we can see in the examples at St Mary-le-Bow,

London, and St Philip and St James, Oxford. But an even longer standing tradition for this method of reservation exists in the Scottish Episcopal Church, to which reference is made in the 1929 Scottish prayer book as 'the long standing custom in the Scottish Church'; this custom is to be traced back to the Liturgies of the Non-jurors in the eighteenth century, where we are told 'that some of the consecrated Elements be constantly reserved in the vestry or some other convenient place in the church under a safe lock'.

While the wall-aumbry does not appear to have been used very much in mediaeval English churches as the place of reservation, it was undoubtedly employed in pre-Reformation Scottish churches, where it was termed 'sacrament house'. Those at Fowlis Easter, Angus, and Deskford, Banff (dated 1551), have elaborately carved surrounds. At Auchindoir, Aberdeen, it is carved to resemble a monstrance*. The wall-aumbry was also in use for reservation in Sweden, Germany and Italy. With the post-Tridentine legislation in the sixteenth century the use of such cupboards was abandoned in Italy and some of these were converted to housing the oil for the sick, as at St Egidio, Florence, by having the legend *Oleum Infirmorum* inscribed on the plinth; but the original sculpture displays a chalice and host with adoring angels.

The wall-aumbry was also termed 'sacrament house' in Germany; but there and in the Low Countries this term came to be applied at the end of the Middle Ages to a large spire-like structure standing on a pedestal in which the reserved sacrament was housed.

J. S. Coltart, *Scottish Church Architecture*, 1936; A. A. King and C. E. Pocknee, *Eucharistic Reservation in the Western Church*, 1965; E. Maffei, *La Réservation Eucharistique jusqu'à la Renaissance*, 1942.

C. E. POCKNEE/G. D. W. RANDALL

Baldachin

Also spelt balddachino, baldachinum or baldaquin. This term is often used rather loosely to describe any kind of canopy over an altar* but it should only be applied to a canopy of woven fabric and not to wooden, stone or metal canopies. Baldachin is derived from the Italian *Baldacco*, meaning Baghdad, where woven textiles of silk woof and metal thread were first made. Canopies made from such textiles first appear in the Renaissance period, and particularly where the altar was near or attached to a wall or screen. Fabric canopies known as baldachins were also placed over the thrones of kings and princes. A canopy resting directly on four columns and made of wood, stone or metal is more correctly described as a ciborium*. Sometimes the reserved sacrament was suspended in a pyx* hanging from under the canopy.

In the return to the more cube-shaped altar that is now being made under modern liturgical reforms, such an altar tends to appear insignificant and the provision of a ciborium over the holy table will give an emphasis that is likely to be otherwise lacking in the focal point of Christian worship.

C. E. Pocknee, *The Christian Altar*, 1963.

C. E. POCKNEE

Baptism

The rite whereby a person is made a member of the church. From the Greek *baptizein*, to dip, baptism has especial reference to the water rite, but it can be used of Christian initiation as a whole and may therefore, on occasion, include both the water rite and confirmation*.

1. *Patristic*. The principal authorities for the patristic rite of baptism are: in Africa, Tertullian, Cyprian and Augustine; in Rome, Hippolytus and John the Deacon; in North Italy, Ambrose; in Spain, Isidore and Hildephonsus; in the East, Cyril of Jerusalem, Chrysostom, Theodore of Mopsuestia and Pseudo-Dionysius Areopagiticus.

In the West baptism was normally administered at Easter, Pentecost being an alternative season. The font* was blessed by the bishop with a prayer invoking the Holy Spirit upon the water so that baptism should not be a mere physical washing. Anointed with the oil of exorcism*, the candidates renounced Satan. Asked successively whether they believed in the Father, the Son and the Holy Spirit, they replied in the affirmative to each question and were dipped in the water, this threefold series of question, answer and dipping

constituting baptism in the name of the Trinity. Emerging from the font, they were anointed on the head by a presbyter to signify their incorporation into the royal and priestly body of Christ. During this period it became customary for them to be vested in white robes after their baptism. From the privacy of the baptistery* they were led into the church, where all the faithful were assembled with the bishop, who then prayed over them, invoking the sevenfold Spirit upon them, laid his hand upon them and signed them with chrism on the forehead. Finally, regenerated by water and the Spirit and sealed with the Spirit of adoption, they took part in the corporate prayers and received communion* for the first time, never before having been allowed to see the last part of the eucharist*, or even know what happened at it. There was no strict uniformity throughout the West, the African church, for instance, having only one unction* after baptism and placing more emphasis on the episcopal hand-laying, and the Gallican churches including the ceremony of washing the candidates' feet.

In the East there were some notable differences. The negative renunciation of Satan was followed by a positive declaration of adhesion to Christ. The trinitarian formula of baptism, 'N is baptized in the name . . .', goes back at least to Chrysostom's time, thus anticipating by several centuries the appearance of the formula 'N, I baptize thee in the name . . .' in the West. There was only one anointing after baptism, a sealing with chrism not only of the forehead, as in the West, but also of the breast and organs of sense. At an early date hand-laying disappeared from Eastern usage. In some Syrian rites from the third to the seventh centuries the gift of the Holy Spirit was associated with the unction before baptism, in the opinion of some scholars the original sequence of events.

The rite was essentially corporate, presided over by the bishop*, assisted by his clergy, and with all the faithful involved. Candidates might be of any age from infancy upwards, the rite itself, though not the catechumenate, remaining unchanged long after infant candidates began to outnumber all others. There was as yet no question of infants being prevented by their age from receiving the grace conveyed by one part of the rite as opposed to another. Liturgically and theologically the patristic rite possessed far more unity than modern Western students can easily appreciate. Everything from the renunciation of Satan to the final episcopal unction could be covered by the word *baptisma*, Tertullian describing baptism, anointing and hand-laying under the heading *De Baptismo*. The episcopal unction was the moment when the candidates received the Pentecostal gift of the Spirit, and were anointed with chrism, or christened with the same Spirit with whom Christ, the anointed one, was endowed at his baptism. What is now called confirmation* was that part of baptism which signified and conferred the baptismal gift of the Holy Spirit.

The rite could be administered in its entirety only if a bishop were present. This was impossible in the case of adult catechumens* suddenly taken ill, or newborn infants not expected to survive, as soon as it became generally accepted that they must not be allowed to die unbaptized. While the Eastern Church solved this problem by delegating the whole rite to presbyters* when a bishop was not available, in the West the rule was gradually established that the post-baptismal unction and hand-laying must be reserved to the episcopate, a decision for which scriptural justification was claimed in the apostolic laying on of hands in Acts 8.17. Consequently, where this rule was in force and baptism was required in haste, presbyters, being instantly available, gave baptism and communion, hand-laying and anointing being, in the case of those who recovered, deferred until the next episcopal visitation.

Thus, while the Eastern Church has been able to keep the unity of the patristic rite of initiation intact even to the present day, the Western Church allowed it gradually to be divided into the seemingly independent rites of baptism and confirmation. So arose the need to define the activity of the Holy Spirit in each of these rites. A sermon preached by Faustus of Riez in the late fifth century, in which he said that the Holy Spirit restores to innocence at the font and in confirmation confers an increase in grace, was one of the main sources on which mediaeval theologians based their solution of this theological problem.

J. D. C. FISHER

2. *Orthodox*. More correctly, Byzantine. The baptismal service of the Byzantine rites, like those of the other historic rites, is a conflation of a number of short services designed to be spread over a period of time – originally Lent, leading to baptism at Easter – but now celebrated together, one after another. Its shape and content have changed remarkably little for at least eleven hundred years, and probably very much longer, even to the extent that although it is, and has been throughout that time, used far more often for the baptism of infants than for that of adults, the rubrics for the most part still seem to presuppose the latter.

The service falls into two halves, the order for the making of a catechumen*, and the order of holy baptism, and this division is still clearly retained in the service books, the two halves being printed separately, each with its own title.

The order for the making of a catechumen comprises four separate acts: (*a*) the prayer for the admission of a catechumen; (*b*) the exorcisms; (*c*) the renunciations; (*d*) the profession of faith.

The prayer for the admission of a catechumen asks for the deliverance of the candidate from error, and the bestowal upon him of the gifts of faith, hope and love, that he may come to know God, to follow his commandments, and to be united to God's flock, that in him God's name may be glorified; it is preceded by a triple breathing upon the candidate by the priest (*see* **Insufflation**), and a triple signing of him with the sign of the cross (*see* **Gestures** 3) on brow and breast, and commences with a laying-on of hands in the name of the Trinity.

The exorcisms*, four in number (although the modern Greek books print the third and fourth together), all beseech the expulsion from the catechumen of all evil spirits and their influence, while the fourth beseeches also the gift of the guardian angel. Each was originally accompanied by the laying on of hands, but this is no longer customary now that they are all said together immediately after the admission of the catechumen, with the laying on of hands at the beginning; at an appropriate point in the fourth the priest breathes upon the brow, mouth and breast of the catechumen.

The renunciations follow the exorcisms. The catechumen, turned towards the west, and with arms upraised, three times renounces Satan, all his works, all his angels, all his worship, and all his pomp; confirms the renunciation; and then blows and spits as an expression of his contempt for all that he has renounced.

The profession of faith follows at once; its inclusion in the order for the making of a catechumen rather than in that of holy baptism may occasion surprise, in the light of the intimate connection between the profession and the baptism in the early liturgy, but it is probably due to an historical accident in the arrangement of the books, an issue too involved to go into here, consequent upon the conflation of the several baptismal rites into one service and their celebration at times other than Easter. The essential element of the profession of faith, to which are added various decorative questions and answers, is the recitation of the Nicene-Constantinopolitan Creed, the candidate facing east. The order for the making of a catechumen is then concluded with a prayer for the grace of baptismal renewal and enlightenment.

The order of holy baptism comprises: (*a*) the hallowing of the baptismal water; (*b*) the pre-baptismal anointing; (*c*) the baptism itself.

The hallowing of the font* is introduced by a litany, based on the common greater litany (*see* **Litany**) with several appropriate additional petitions – for the hallowing of the water by the coming of the Holy Spirit, for the descent upon it of the grace of redemption, for illumination by the power of the Holy Spirit, for the averting of every device of evil spirits, and six petitions for the candidate, that he may truly acquire all the benefits of baptism. During this litany, sung by the deacon, the celebrant prays secretly for the divine assistance in the administration of the sacrament. The litany concluded, he proceeds to bless the font, with a very lengthy prayer, following the pattern of the eucharistic prayer or anaphora*, commencing with a thanksgiving for God's manifestations of himself in creation and redemption, continuing with a prayer for the hallowing of the water by the descent of the Holy Spirit, and concluding with a petition for the effects of this hallowing to be operative in him who is to be baptized, with a closing doxology. The cere-

monial accompanying this prayer is of the simplest, the essential act being a triple breathing on the water in the form of the cross at an appropriate point.

The pre-baptismal anointing is preceded by the blessing of the 'oil of gladness' corresponding to the Western 'oil of catechumens', and a triple signing of the water with this oil – a typical early mediaeval addition to the blessing of the water, paralleled in the other historic rites, which adds nothing to the clarity of the liturgical structure of the rite. The candidate is then anointed on brow, breast and back (*see* **Unction**).

The baptism itself then follows immediately. Orthodox theology and canon law require total immersion, except in emergency; the candidate is held upright in the font, with his face towards the east, and is immersed three times, at the naming of each person of the Trinity, with the formula: 'The servant of God N is baptized in the Name of the Father, Amen; and of the Son, Amen; and of the Holy Spirit, Amen.' Psalm 31 (32) is then sung (while the newly-baptized is dried), after which the new white clothing is put on the newly-baptized, with appropriate formulae.

The administration of the sacrament of chrismation (the Byzantine name of what is called confirmation* in the West) follows at once, for infants as well as adults. The administration, like that of baptism and the eucharist, is of course delegated to the priest, although he uses episcopally consecrated (in modern practice patriarchally or primatially consecrated) chrism (*see* **Unction**). The celebrant says a prayer giving thanks for baptism, beseeching the gifts of the seal of the Holy Spirit and participation in the eucharist (which anciently also followed without a break). He then anoints the newly-baptized with the chrism, making the sign of the cross on the brow, the eyes, the nostrils, the mouth, the ears, the breast, the hands and the feet, saying at each anointing 'The seal of the gift of the Holy Spirit, Amen.'

The baptismal rites are concluded by a brief form of the synaxis* with an appropriate epistle and gospel; originally, of course, this was the synaxis of the baptismal eucharist. It is still the custom in many Greek churches, unless the celebration of the eucharist is to follow shortly, to give the newly-baptized and confirmed (especially if he is an infant) communion from the reserved sacrament at the end. With the spread of liturgical reform it is reasonable to hope that before long the restoration of the baptismal eucharist will be achieved at least in some places, in which case the Byzantine baptismal liturgy will again manifest the integrity of the rites of Christian initiation as they were celebrated in the early church; as it is, it has for many centuries done so more fully than has any of its Western counterparts, a situation which has only begun to change in very recent years, with a movement towards the reintegration of the rites of Christian initiation becoming slowly but increasingly evident in revised Western liturgies, a movement of which the outstanding manifestation is the magnificent *Rite for the Christian Initiation of Adults* of the Roman rite.

W. JARDINE GRISBROOKE

3. *Mediaeval and Roman Catholic*. In Rome from the sixth century, since adult baptism had become rare, the custom of baptizing infants became general. The ritual of the catechumenate* was retained and elaborated, but the adult catechumenate became obsolete.

The child was necessarily passive, and, as it were to compensate for this, the scrutinies (examinations) were increased to seven; since instruction could not be given to unconscious children, a rite of the 'tradition' of the gospels was substituted for it. The questions about faith formerly put to the candidate during the action of baptism were now anticipated and addressed to the parents and godparents. The formula, said by the priest, 'I baptize you, in the name of the Father, etc.', is attested in eighth-century Rome. Gradually, too, the traditional liturgical days of scrutiny and the giving back (*redditio*) of the Lord's Prayer* and the creed* were separated from the traditional days of Lent when these acts had taken place. By the eighth century there were only two assemblies in church, the first for the enrolment and giving of salt (indicating that the child was now a catechumen) and the 'tradition' of the gospels which consisted of no more than the reading of the first phrases of each of the four gospels. Neither of these observances required the response of the candidate.

With the compilation of the Romano-German pontifical of the tenth century, the ceremony of the giving of the white garment was accompanied with a prayer giving its sense, a prayer that passed into the Roman rite of baptism of a later age, and the giving of the lighted candle, a symbol of Christ the light of the world, was added. This, too, has survived in the Roman rite. Later still, in the fourteenth century, baptism by 'infusion', the pouring of the water on the head, replaced the ancient custom of immersion, though immersion was still known in the thirteenth century (witness Thomas Aquinas, *Summa Theologiae*, III.66.7) and the practice of baptism by immersion has never been forbidden in the Roman Catholic Church.

All traces of a catechumenate as a separate ceremony were finally wiped out by the ever more prevalent custom of baptizing infants as soon after birth as possible, a custom that became general from the tenth century onwards. By the thirteenth century all the pre-baptismal ceremonies of catechumenate, renunciation of Satan and the anointing with the oil of catechumens had been combined into one service which is first found in the *Ordo ad cathecumium* (sic) *faciendum* of the Pontifical of the Roman Curia of the same century. The books of the local churches, e.g. the *Manuale* of Salisbury, merely endorsed this situation. But local usages remained, and in the post-Tridentine period, it became necessary to introduce order into the administration of baptism. The *Rituale Romanum*, issued by Pope Paul V in 1614, tidied up the situation and this book remained in force until the new order of baptism of 1969. Unfortunately, it was no more than a work of compilation. No effort was made to construct an order of infant baptism that would meet the changed conditions of the church. The compiler merely took two orders found in the tradition, one longer and one shorter: the longer, which comprises all the ancient rites of the catechumenate in one service, was destined for adults and the other, shorter, for infants.

A new order for the baptism of infants was promulgated on 15 May 1969 and came into force on 8 September of the same year.

It was issued with two introductions, one on baptism in general and the second on the baptism of infants. The whole is to be seen as part of a fuller document, *The Order for the Christian Initiation of Adults*, issued in 1972, which contains the rites of the (restored) catechumenate and of adult baptism, confirmation and holy communion which normally take place at the Pascal vigil*. Both introductions are documents of considerable theological importance, a summary of which would, however, take up a good deal of space. It may be noted, however, that the faith of the parents, who play a central role in the service, is the crucial factor in accepting infants for baptism. They, with the gathered community, profess the faith of the church which they represent, a faith they are required to communicate to the child as it grows up.

Baptisms are to be celebrated normally on Sundays in the presence of the local community whether at mass or at some other time of the day.

The celebrant welcomes the baptismal party at the church door and asks the first questions establishing the willingness of the parents to bring their child up in the Christian faith. He then signs the child on the forehead with the cross and the parents and godparents are invited to do likewise. This is a relic of the ancient enrolment ceremony.

There follows 'the celebration of God's word', consisting of one or two passages from scripture, a homily, intercessions for the child, the family and all baptized persons.

There is a single prayer of exorcism* and the anointing of the breast (only) with the oil of catechumens. Local conferences of bishops may allow, for good reasons, the omission of the whole of this rite.

'The celebration of the sacrament' follows with the blessing of the water (three forms provided, to be used at choice), the parents' renunciation of evil (two forms given) and profession of faith with the gathered community, the act of baptism (either by immersion or affusion), the anointing with chrism, the giving of the white garment, and of the candle.

The service concludes before the altar where a blessing is given to the mother (replacing churching*), to the father and the assembled congregation.

The new order is both new and traditional. It is adapted to circumstances of infant baptism, it addresses itself to the

parents and their friends and it requires a genuine commitment. Traditional elements will be found in the ministry of the word, parallel to the ancient vigil, the anointings and the ceremonies after the act of baptism. In one respect it fails to keep the ancient order: the renunciation of evil is separated from the exorcism.

J. D. CRICHTON

4. *Anglican*. After it had separated from the Roman Communion, the teaching and practice of the Church of England in respect to the sacrament of baptism remained largely those which had become commonly accepted in Western Catholicism. The attention of the English Reformers was occupied chiefly with the presentation of a strong apologetic for continuing the practice of infant baptism, the provision of instructional material, and the revision of the baptismal service. The order for baptism in the first English BCP of 1549 was a combination of materials drawn from the pre-Reformation Latin service and early Lutheran sources. It followed closely the structure of the Latin rite, but abridged the catechumenal introduction which had become prefixed to the baptismal rite in the Middle Ages. The traditional ceremonies of signing with the cross (*see* **Gestures** 3), exorcism*, unction*, and bestowal of the white baptismal dress were all retained. Many of the words translated or paraphrased the Latin. There were a number of new compositions, chiefly prayers and exhortations; in these the influence of the Reformation is the most apparent. Reformed influences, however, were much more evident in the second BCP of 1552. The baptismal order in this book reduced the introductory section still more, made a number of changes in the words of the service, and added a thanksgiving section. With the exception of signing with the cross, which was transferred to follow the baptism, all the traditional ceremonies were omitted. Without significant alteration, the 1552 baptismal rite passed eventually into the 1662 BCP. All of the orders for baptism in the various Anglican prayer books derive from the 1662 order, and all follow it closely, while differing from it and each other in details.

The Anglican baptismal rite begins with an introductory section consisting of prayers, addresses, and a reading from the gospel. The baptismal vows or promises follow. These are made personally in the case of adult candidates, by sponsors in the case of infants. The promises are in the form of a series of questions and answers involving a set of renunciations, a promise of adherence to the Christian faith as stated in the Apostles' Creed, and a promise to follow the Christian way of life. The baptismal water is then consecrated according to a form adapted from that prescribed for monthly use in the first BCP. The baptism then takes place. Water is poured upon the candidate or he is dipped into water – the latter rarely in actual practice – while the Trinitarian baptismal formula is recited. The newly-baptized are then signed with the cross and declared received into the church. A thanksgiving and address to the sponsors or a blessing concludes the service. The Anglican prayer books design baptism as a public liturgy, and make provision for the insertion of the baptismal service into the regular services of worship. However, in common practice, baptisms have been more generally held before or after regular services or at specially arranged times, with only those immediately concerned present.

Anglican teaching about baptism has changed but little since the Reformation, and is very much the same in all the churches which make up the Anglican Communion. Most of its baptismal doctrine Anglicans hold in common with other parts of the Christian church, and it is difficult to discern anything distinctively Anglican about it. Anglicans have always regarded baptism as a sacrament instituted by Christ and, except in the presence of most unusual conditions, necessary for salvation. The sacramental sign is water, poured upon an unbaptized person, or into which he is dipped. The form of words which must accompany this action are: 'N, I baptize thee in the Name of the Father, and of the Son, and of the Holy Ghost.' Any baptism carried out by means of this sign and formula Anglicans regard as true baptism, and all persons thus baptized are accounted members of the Christian church. While it is baptism which Anglicans hold to be necessary for admission into the Christian church, the Anglican churches have generally required confirmation* as well as baptism for admission to communion and full participating membership in the church,

thus in effect regarding baptism by itself as incomplete; some Anglicans have taught that this is the case. The spiritual gifts of baptism may be summed up in the words: 'A death unto sin, and a new birth unto righteousness'. Repentance and faith are the necessary requirements for the effective reception of the sacrament. Baptism is to Anglicans a mystical washing away of sin both original and actual. It is a sharing in the death and resurrection of Christ, a rebirth into the saving community of the church. By means of it one is incorporated into Christ's mystical body, made a child of God, and an inheritor of the Kingdom of Heaven. While Anglicanism has always taught that the baptism is of water and of the Spirit, and that the Holy Spirit is active and in some way given in baptism, it has never clearly defined the activity and gift of the Spirit in baptism in relation to those in confirmation. Everywhere in Anglicanism, from the Reformation to the present day, infant baptism has continued to be defended and to be the norm of practice.

During the last three decades there has been a debate about baptism which has gathered force and has spread to all parts of the Anglican Communion. The present pastoral situation, insights gained from the Liturgical Movement*, and increasing ecumenism have all combined to produce a growing dissatisfaction with traditional Anglican teaching and practice. A Baptismal Reform Movement has been started and is doing much to further investigation of baptism in relation to the modern situation of the church and to awaken the church to the needs for change and revision. A major point in the discussion has been the practice of baptizing all infants presented for baptism, and the relevance of infant baptism in the contemporary pastoral scene. It is also believed in some quarters that the rites of baptism in use at present are but one part of Christian initiation, and that a re-integration of baptism, confirmation, and first communion into a single rite of Christian initiation is necessary to a full appreciation of the meaning of the sacrament in the life of the church.

In recent years new orders of baptism and confirmation have been adopted in most provinces of the Anglican Communion. The ASB takes account of the current situation, in which some parents hesitate to commit their infants to the responsibilities of baptism but the number of adults seeking baptism increases. Three orders of service are provided. The first is for the baptism and confirmation of adults and allows also for occasions when infants and children are to be baptized with their parents. This order provides the liturgical basis for the other two, 'the baptism of children' (i.e. not only or necessarily infants) and 'the confirmation of those already baptized'. Provision is made for all of these to take place in the context of public worship, and very commonly they do. While the confirmation rite says nothing clear about the activity of the Holy Spirit in confirmation, the orders of baptism include the petition 'Send your Holy Spirit upon them' in the prayer over the baptismal water. The rubrics allow that oil may be used for the signing with the cross in the baptismal rite and in the imposition of the hand in confirmation: but the meaning of this is nowhere indicated. By contrast the significance of the sign of water in baptism is made abundantly clear. It is seen not only as a symbol of washing as in the BCP, but also of life, of refreshment, and of death, in accordance with the imagery of the OT and NT. The BCP implies that baptismal washing conveys the remission of sins to infants. Today it is widely doubted whether sins can be imputed to infants and the ASB meets this with phraseology which allows a wider interpretation of the remission of sins in baptism. In accordance with the classic rites of the Western church, the renunciations have been detached from the credal interrogations. The latter have been restored to their original place in close association with the baptismal washing, the former appear in a section called The Decision in the preliminary part of the rite, and may be accompanied by the signing with the cross.

In America, the Book of Common Prayer of 1979 provides an order for holy baptism, which it describes as a sacrament, and an order for confirmation, which is grouped with the blessing of a civil marriage and the ministration to the sick and other matters in a section entitled pastoral offices. The latter consists of a renewal of baptismal commitment and a ceremony in which the bishop 'lays hands upon each one' and prays 'Strengthen your servant with your Holy Spirit.' This is not described as a

sacrament. The one order of baptism provides for the baptism both of adults and of infants. The baptismal washing is followed by a ceremony in which 'the bishop or priest places a hand on the person's head', signs him on the forehead with the cross 'using chrism if desired', and says 'N, you are sealed with the Holy Spirit in Baptism and marked as Christ's own for ever.' This ceremony is performed with adults and infants alike. The prayer for the consecration of the chrism prays 'that those who are sealed with it may share in the royal priesthood of Jesus Christ'. This seems to indicate that the function of the chrism is to illuminate what happened in baptism rather than to add anything to it.

E. C. WHITAKER

5. *Baptist*. The use of the title Baptist may account for the belief, now widespread, that the baptism of believers by immersion is the basic principle of that denomination. It is, in fact, secondary and derivative. Believers' baptism rests on three primary convictions about authority, faith, and the church. The source of authority is God manifest in Christ, and the medium of his authority is scripture. The only baptism found in the NT is the baptism of believers. On the authority of scripture, baptism is administered only to those who have professed repentance towards God and faith in Jesus Christ. Conversion must precede baptism. This personal response to the activity of the Holy Spirit is essential for membership in the body of Christ. For the Christian society consists of those who have heard the gospel with faith; it is the fellowship of believers. It follows from these three convictions that it is not the *mode* but the *subject* of baptism which is of primary importance. The mode is immersion; the subject is the believer. The Anabaptists and the early English Baptists baptized by affusion or pouring. When circumstances, such as sickness or extreme age, make it advisable, baptism is occasionally administered in that way today. It was to exhibit the full meaning of the rite that immersion was eventually adopted. The actions of going down into, of being buried beneath, and raised up from the water, proclaim the death, burial, and resurrection of Christ. The mode has importance because of what it signifies, but what really matters is *who* is baptized, not *how* the rite is administered. The emphasis on personal response is characteristic of the teaching and practice of all Baptists. The candidate is said to be following the example and obeying the command of Christ, making a confession of faith in him, pledging allegiance to him. This stress on the human response has been and is accompanied by a widespread tendency to ignore or deny the activity of God, not prior to, but in the sacrament. To many Baptists, baptism is represented as a purely symbolic rite, a dramatic portrayal of what has already taken place in the experience of the candidate. It would be misleading to generalize on this matter, and among Baptists today, as in the past, there are marked differences of teaching. Recent Baptist scholarship has emphasized the relationship between baptism, the Holy Spirit, and the church. On the question of when baptism should be administered to a believer, there are two conflicting points of view. On the one hand, since conversion and baptism belong together, there is a desire to minimize the period between the initial response and the administration. On the other hand, especially on the mission field, the need for an adequate period of preparation is recognized. Candidates are usually, though not always, taught before baptism. Baptists have no prescribed liturgy, but administer the rite in the threefold context of the fellowship, the word, and the prayers. Baptism is not regarded as a private or domestic occasion, but is administered in the setting of the congregation at worship, and of the reading and preaching of the word. There is a marked evangelistic quality about the service. The candidates bear witness, sometimes verbally, and always in the act of baptism, and it is expected that this witness, together with the preaching of the gospel, will be used to make disciples from among those present. Baptism is regarded as a converting ordinance, and the service often concludes with an appeal for others also to respond. After the preaching it is the usual, though not invariable custom, to put questions to the candidates. Typical answers include a confession of faith in the Holy Trinity, the acceptance of Jesus Christ as Lord and Saviour, and a pledge to follow and serve him. The occasion is often preceded by prayer meetings, and in the service itself a prayer for the candidates precedes or follows the questions and answers. In the baptistery, the names of the candidate, and words indicative of

personal response, often precede the traditional Trinitarian formula. 'N, on thy profession of repentance towards God and of faith in our Lord Jesus Christ, I baptize thee in the name of the Father, and of the Son, and of the Holy Spirit.' Immersion takes place in one of three ways. The candidate stands in the water, and is lowered backwards into it until submerged, and is then lifted up again. The candidate may kneel in the baptistery, and then be immersed forwards. When the rite is administered in a river or pool, as often in Africa, Asia, or Latin America, the candidate is led out into the water until it reaches the neck, and then, after the formula, the head is pressed under. In many churches, the Aaronic blessing* is said or sung after each immersion. The baptisms may be followed by an appeal for decisions; the service then concludes with a hymn and the blessing. In some churches, the laying on of hands after baptism, practised by the early General Baptists of Britain, and always adhered to by a small minority of Baptist communities, has been restored. The practice of baptizing at the Lord's Supper is also on the increase. The desire to enrol the candidates as members of the church at the baptismal service itself is one outcome of the new emphasis upon baptism as initiation into the body of Christ.

S. F. WINWARD

6. *Christian Church* (*Disciples of Christ*). Although the major founders of the Christian Church (Disciples of Christ) stood in the Reformed tradition, they early set aside the practice of infant baptism in favour of the baptism of believers by immersion. Alexander Campbell (1788–1866) took the lead in the examination of the NT that led to the conclusion that the 'one baptism' mentioned in scripture required a specific action, upon certain candidates, with a particular meaning. The action was defined as immersion, to the exclusion of other modes, and that mode was single immersion as contrasted with trine immersion practised by people in the various Brethren churches. The proper candidate was a penitent believer. The meaning ascribed to the act was phrased in this way by Campbell: 'Baptism is, then, designed to introduce the subjects of it into the participation of the blessings of the death and resurrection of Christ.'

In his writings Campbell regularly translated the Greek terms into immerse and related words instead of into baptize and its related words. Yet his discourses clearly indicate that he was talking about the Christian sacrament of baptism rather than merely a water rite. Furthermore, his views constituted a high doctrine of baptism. He claimed that regeneration and conversion were both equivalent terms to immersion (by which he meant the sacrament of baptism). Therefore wherever the scripture discusses regeneration or conversion that teaching must be applied to baptism. The scripture, said Campbell, calls for 'an actual coming' to the Lord Jesus. But 'Where shall we find him? Where shall we meet him? Nowhere on earth but in his institutions, the first of which is the institution for remission of sins – the sacrament of baptism.'

It is clear in early writings of the Disciples that salvation was seen as the free gift of God; in this way they stood firmly in orthodox Christianity as interpreted by the churches of the Reformation. The new element in their view was the emphasis upon active participation of the one coming to baptism. Faith was considered to be a requisite of baptism, faith understood as trust in Christ and therefore an act of complete obedience to Christ. Repentance was to follow from faith and was understood to be a complete turning around of life. Then would come immersion, death and resurrection with Christ, the first act signifying complete surrender to Christ's will. The result was that a person was changed to a new relationship with God.

This careful synthesis has suffered from abuse through the years since it was first articulated. Some have stressed the active participation of the baptizand to the degree that the free gift of God has been compromised. Some have stressed the idea of obedience to the degree that divine grace and the imperative to lead a new life have been neglected. Some have emphasized the mode of the act so much that the equivalence of regeneration, conversion, and baptism has not been recognized.

At first Disciples admitted only persons immersed as penitent believers into membership in their churches. If there had been previous baptism in some other mode, baptism by immersion would be administered anew, under the rubric of 'completing

one's obedience to Christ'. The severity of this closed membership policy has been moderated by open admission to communion, so that persons from other denominations may share freely in the liturgical and congregational life of a Disciple church even when not admitted to formal membership because of irregular baptism. An increasing number of congregations have, since about 1900, received by transfer of membership Christians from churches who baptize by other modes. Furthermore, there is a growing resistance in the denomination to what is now widely recognized to be rebaptism.

There has been a widespread custom in Disciple congregations for a simple act of blessing and dedication to be ministered shortly after a baby is born into one of the families of the church. This rite has sometimes included the naming of the child. More characteristic has been the practice of asking parents to pledge that they will rear the child in the Christian faith. The congregation is asked to share in this responsibility and a prayer of dedication concludes the service.

The baptismal rite, as commonly practised, has two parts which may be separated in time and place. The first is called confession of faith and always takes place in a regular service of worship. During an invitation hymn, usually following a sermon, the believer walks to the front of the church and is met by the minister. The minister, usually drawing upon Peter's confession in Matt. 16 asks: 'Do you believe that Jesus is the Christ, the son of the Living God; and do you accept him as your Lord and Saviour?' The person answers affirmatively, after which the minister speaks a brief word of commendation, usually drawing upon some appropriate passage of scripture. At some later date, again at a regular service of worship, the baptism takes place. Although the rite is occasionally performed in running water, it is ordinarily administered in a baptistery constructed so as to be visible to people in the main worship room of the church. The minister may read a passage of scripture dealing with baptism, and then pronounces: 'By the authority of our Lord Jesus Christ, in whom you have confessed your faith, I baptize you (N) in the name of the Father and of the Son and of the Holy Spirit. Amen.' Single immersion, the baptizand leaned backwards into the water, then takes place.

Current discussions among Disciples indicate that the theological position first developed continues to be widely supported. There is somewhat less emphasis now upon the absolute necessity of immersion, although that mode continues to be the only one practised. There is ambivalence about the appropriate age of baptism. As a general rule children from church families are received for instruction and baptism at about the age of twelve; only then are they received at the communion table.

KEITH WATKINS

7. *Congregationalist.* The early Congregationalists (or Independents, as they were then known) held the same views about baptism as the English Presbyterians. Both groups dissented from three characteristics of the Anglican administration of the sacrament according to the BCP. First, they objected to signation with the cross as an additional ceremony for which there was no biblical warrant. Secondly, they disliked the godparents taking the role of the parents in making the promises that the child should be brought up as a Christian, since this was the duty of the parents. Thirdly, they objected to private baptism. In their view baptism was a sacrament of the gospel, giving assurance of forgiveness of sins and of eternal life, which ought to be celebrated in the church.

John Cotton's *The True Constitution of a Particular Visible Church* (1642) describes the classical Independent administration of baptism:

> As for Baptism, it is to be dispensed by a Minister of the Word unto a Believer professing his Repentance, and his Faith, being a member of the same Church Body as also unto his seed, presented by the Parent unto the Lord and his Church at which time the Minister in God's roome calleth upon the Parent to renew his Covenant with God for himselfe and his seed and calleth upon God as the nature of the Ordinance requireth, for the pardon of originall sinne, and for the sin of the Parents and for a blessing upon the Sacrament and Infant and then calling

> the Childe by the name, which the Parent hath given it for his owne edification, and the Childes, he baptizeth it either by dipping or sprinkling into the name of the Father, the Son, and the Holy Ghost.

Plainly, early Congregational baptism was the claiming of the covenant promise of God to be with his children and his children's children, a solemn inclusion of the child of believing parents within the company of the elect, by baptism in the triune name, and accompanied by the parental promise to bring up the child in the nurture and admonition of the Lord, until this promise should be honoured by the child when he reaches physical and spiritual maturity. The only point of difference between Independent and Presbyterian usage was that the latter used to require the parent to recite the Apostles' Creed as a test of orthodoxy in belief, whereas the Independents insisted that a covenant (or affirmation of loyalty) was more appropriate than a creed, which was a historical summary which could be recited with 'the top of the mind'.

In the early and middle part of the twentieth century, when theology had become increasingly more immanental, there was a tendency for baptismal orders of worship to stress the human profession of faith rather than the divine initiative in baptism. This meant that baptism came to look increasingly like infant dedication. *A Manual for Ministers* (1936) in its baptismal order affirms that there are three purposes in baptism: to acknowledge God as the source of all good; to affirm the divine fatherhood of all children; and that 'we solemnly re-dedicate ourselves in the presence of God, and ask for His help worthily to fulfil these new and sacred duties' (p. 73).

A richer theological exposition of the meaning of baptism will be found in the 'Order for the Baptism of Children' in *A Book of Public Worship* (1948). It reads:

> This Sacrament is a sign and seal of the covenant of grace, of union with Christ in his body, of remission of sins in his blood, of resurrection unto eternal life through him, and of our calling and engagement to be his for ever. It declares that the children of Christian parents belong, with us who believe, to the membership of the Church; and that Christ claims them as his own (p.159).

Surveying contemporary Congregational baptismal practice in the USA, and that of the United Reformed Church* in England and Wales (before its further union with the believer-baptism Churches of Christ in 1981, since when both forms have been normative), it could be stated with confidence that a typical administration of baptism would comprise the following elements, though not necessarily in the order given:

1. Warrant for baptism (usually Matt. 28.18–20; occasionally Mark 10.13–16).
2. Exhortation on the meaning of baptism.
3. Questions to the parents to elicit solemn promises from them.
4. Prayers for the sanctification of the child to be baptized.
5. The act of baptism by sprinkling of water on the child's head, mentioning the child's name, and saying, 'N, I baptize thee in the name of the Father, and of the Son, and of the Holy Ghost.' The Aaronic blessing* follows.
6. A declaration by the minister, with the congregation as witnesses, that the child is now received into the congregation of Christ's flock.
7. A concluding prayer for the child, parents and congregation, that they may be protected and guided by God to fulfil their vows and to recall their own baptism, and finally attain to everlasting life.

A similar service, with the necessary adaptation, is used for the baptism of believers.

In recent times Congregationalists, like other Christians, have been disturbed by the relatively small percentage of infants baptized who come to confirmation or full church membership at maturity. They have attempted to meet this problem in two ways. They have made the explanatory section of the rite fuller and clearer, and they have required of parents both a confession of faith and solemn promises to bring up their children in the Christian faith and life. But in both Britain and the USA the problem is still a major one.

HORTON DAVIES

8. *Jehovah's Witnesses.* Baptism has been part of Christianity since its beginning. The word 'baptize' is taken from the Greek word *baptizein*, meaning 'to dip, to plunge'. Accordingly, Jehovah's Witnesses follow this pattern in their public baptisms.

For any individual to come into a relationship with Jehovah God, the following fundamental steps are needed: (*a*) Taking in accurate knowledge of God's Word (Rom. 10.13–15); (*b*) exercising faith (Heb. 11.6); (*c*) repentance (Matt. 4.17); (*d*) conversion (Acts 3.19); (*e*) dedication (Luke 9.23); and (*f*) baptism (Matt. 28.19). It is when this final step of baptism has been taken that the individual enters into a relationship with his heavenly Father, his baptism symbolizing his dedication to Jehovah, hence constituting his ordination as a minister (*see* **Ordination** 8).

Those who are baptized as Jehovah's Witnesses have to be recommended by the elders of the congregation with which they associate. A period of instruction in Christian doctrine is essential. When all the elders are convinced that the candidate has a firm grasp of the scriptures, and can vouch for his or her moral standing as being exemplary, arrangements are made for baptism. Baptism on a false premise would be invalid. There must be evidence of a 'new personality' replacing the 'old personality' possessed before coming to a knowledge of the truth of God's Word (Col. 3.5–10). The dedication of the individual is also a 'request made to God for a good conscience', the good conscience resulting, not from doing works of self-righteousness, but from doing God's will (I Peter 3.21).

In view of the fact that 'hearing the word', 'embracing the word heartily', and 'repenting' precede water baptism (Acts 2.14, 22, 38, 41) and that baptism requires the individual to make a solemn decision, it is apparent that one must at least be of age to hear, to believe, and to make this decision. It follows that babies and young children are not baptized by Jehovah's

Plate 18 'Kingdom Increase' convention held at Twickenham RFU ground on 28 July 1984. Part of a mass baptism of 181 people.

Witnesses. Jesus was 30 years old when baptized and the commission of Matt. 28.19, 20 points to accurate knowledge as a prerequisite for dedication and baptism.

The mass baptisms performed by Jehovah's Witnesses each year are well known (*see* Plate 18). During the course of 1984, 179,421 individuals were baptized world-wide as servants of Jehovah God.

DAVID SIBREY

9. *Lutheran*. Baptism, according to the Lutheran confessional writings, is an ordinance commanded by God and instituted by Jesus Christ, through which a special promise of inward grace, regeneration and incorporation into Christ's body the church, is offered in conjunction with an outward material sign, water. It is therefore one of the true sacraments and normally necessary for salvation (*Large Catechism* IV; *Apol. der Conf. Aug* XIII, 3ff., *Smalcaldic Articles* III, 4; *Augsburg Confession*=*CA* IX). It summons the baptized to lifelong trust and obedience and the expectation of perfect renewal at the last day.

The Lutheran doctrine of baptism developed during the Reformation period both as a reform of the Roman Catholic view and as a defence against more radical teachings, e.g. those of the Anabaptists.

The main points emphasized were:

(*a*) That the effective working of baptism is *by faith*, not by the objective performance of the rite. Faith is not just an outward profession but is the fruit of God's grace growing within man until it is manifested outwardly. Faith is not proved empirically (*CA* IV, 57).

(*b*) That since baptism is God's act, infant baptism is the clearest demonstration of this (Luther, *Werke*, Weimar, 1883ff.=WA 26, 157; American edition, 1958ff., 40,244). Luther held that baptism calls forth faith in infants, though he agreed that we do not understand how (WA 16,157; Amer. ed. 40,243). Child faith is inferred from child baptism, not vice versa.

(*c*) The relationship of baptism to sin. Baptism is seen as a continuing work of God, preparing a Christian for the last day. The entire Christian life with its struggle against sin is a constant return to one's baptism. This eschatologically oriented view of baptism helps to establish a tone of trust and prayerful responsibility and offers a key to the Christian quest for sanctification.

(*d*) The responsibility of all who are baptized to the word of God and to the people of God.

(*e*) The exaltation of the baptismal vow of faithfulness to Christ in all walks of life.

Luther's interpretation generally set the pattern for the Lutheran church. Lutheran orthodoxy, however, as it developed in the sixteenth and seventeenth centuries transformed Luther's flexible, paradoxical view into a more fixed and institutionalized conception. In the background was what eventually became a complex and rigid analysis of the 'order of salvation' with a sharp distinction between justification and sanctification. The rise of rigid state-church systems also helped to externalize baptism.

At the Reformation, Luther conservatively simplified the traditional rite and laid the emphasis on earnest prayer for the child (WA 12,38ff.). In the *Taufbüchlein* of 1523 he retained the mediaeval practices. In his revised order of 1526, which attained great popularity in Germany, he made some editorial revisions and omitted a number of symbolic features, such as the two anointings (*see* sections 1–3 above, and **Unction**). His positive contribution was a collect known as the 'Flood prayer'. For the mode of baptism he preferred immersion as more adequate to signify the drowning of sin, but he did not insist on this mode. Lutherans have agreed that immersion is not essential; pouring and sprinkling have become the most common modes in Lutheran churches.

During the eras of pietism and rationalism exorcism* and renunciation generally dropped out of the Lutheran rite, though the latter has returned in many orders.

In many churches the admonition to the sponsors and the salutation have been added to the liturgy. In many of the churches the custom of signing the child with a cross (*see* **Gestures** 3) was retained or has reappeared. The renunciation of the devil is retained in most liturgies except that of the Church of Sweden.

The German churches experienced a proliferation of baptismal liturgies, basically on the lines of either Luther's rite of 1526 or Bugenhagen's of 1535. Since 1961 most of them have a common one which closely follows Luther's.

In view of Luther's doctrine of the

priesthood of all believers any Christian may in an emergency perform baptism according to the order laid down for such situations. Such a baptism, which is to be reported to the authorities of the church, is considered a proper function of the church (WA 12,181; 31,211).

The place of baptism in the worship of the church is less prominent in Europe, where the practice of private baptism in homes or at the church after public worship has developed, than in the American tradition, where there is a strong tendency to administer baptism at a public service to emphasize the communal significance of the sacrament.

E. J. R. H. S. VON SICARD

10. *Methodist.* John Wesley's *Sunday Service of the Methodists in North America*, 1784, is the foundation for subsequent initiation rites in Methodism. Its baptismal services were adopted from the 1662 BCP of the Church of England, but with some drastic alterations.

The private baptism of infants was omitted. All references to godparents were omitted, though the 'Friends of the Child' were asked to give the name; consequently the vows of renunciation, belief and obedience in the name of the infant were omitted. In 1784 two references to regeneration were removed, but that in the prayer 'Almighty and Immortal God' was retained, as was the phrase 'that he may be born again' in the prayer 'Almighty and Everlasting God, Heavenly Father'. These prayers were both omitted, among other changes, in 1786; the prayer for the sanctification of the water was then still retained, but the central petition was in some subsequent editions modified and in the others wholly omitted. In 1784 Wesley added to the modes of baptism 'or sprinkle', but omitted the possibility of pouring water. A few of the 1784 copies retained the signing with the cross and the reception, but the others omitted them. Other changes were aimed at shortening the service.

In Great Britain there were further changes in the Wesleyan Church in 1846, 1864 and 1882 (in *Public Prayers and Services*), as well as in very different services produced in the non-Wesleyan Churches. After the union, *The Book of Offices*, 1936, produced a further revision, in which a leading feature of the service was the promises made by the parents.

In America the Methodist Episcopal Church (MEC) in 1864 and the Methodist Episcopal Church South (MECS) in 1866 added reference to others than parents, and the term 'sponsors' appeared in MEC in 1916 and is retained in the *Book of Worship* (*BW*), 1964. The prayer for the sanctification of the water lasted till 1858 in MECS and 1916 in MEC. The 1792 *Discipline* allowed sprinkling, pouring or immersing, all of which are provided for in the 1964 rite, though sprinkling is almost always used.

In American Methodism today baptism is almost always performed in the presence of a congregation. Baptized children are regarded as 'preparatory members' in the United Methodist Church.

An office for the 'Baptism of Children and Youth' appeared in 1914 (MECS) and remained till 1964.

Wesley's treatment of the ministration of baptism to such as are of 'riper years' was, in general, similar to his treatment of infant baptism. Several references to baptismal regeneration disappeared, rubrics and exhortations were dropped, and, in this case, the sign of the cross was definitely omitted in all editions of the Sunday service. The renunciation, creed and vow of obedience were retained, though the 1786 editions dropped the phrase in the creed (put interrogatively): 'that he went down into hell', and the same editions dropped the petition for the sanctification of the water. The British books made various changes, in the same years as for infants, though the changes did not always correspond. In America, Wesley's version remained remarkably intact until twentieth century revisions began pushing in the direction of brevity. Alternate gospel lessons were provided, four choices appearing in the *BW*, 1944. The American service of 1964 for baptism of 'youth and adults' remains brief, but represents a move away from the watering down of sacramental doctrine of the recent past with more emphasis on remission of sins and the reception of the Holy Spirit.

Wesley's most significant change was the omission of a confirmation* rite. Not till 1864 did MEC add an office for the reception of members and MECS followed in 1870. In 1886 MECS added a rubric to adult baptism to allow the minister to 'lay

his hands on the subject . . . with suitable invocation'. Beginning in 1964 the term 'Confirmation' replaced 'Reception into the Church'. In Britain the Wesleyan Conference did not adopt a service for the 'Public Recognition of New Members' till 1894. There was a new form in 1936.

In general, the black Methodist churches have done less pruning of the Wesleyan services than the predominantly white churches, though the African Methodist Episcopal and the Christian Methodist Episcopal churches have alternate brief orders for infant baptism.

New theological, liturgical, and ecumenical currents led in the 1970s to reconsideration of the entire process of Christian initiation. This became manifest in America in *A Service of Baptism, Confirmation, and Renewal* published in 1976, revised in 1980, and included in *The Book of Services* (1985) as 'The Baptismal Covenant: Holy Baptism, Confirmation, Reaffirmation of Faith'. Chief concerns have been to recover the unity of Christian initiation and yet to provide for general acts of individual and congregational reaffirmation of God's work in baptism. Recovered have been the renunciation of sin and profession of faith (Apostles' Creed interrogatively), thanksgiving over the water, and laying on of hands of the newly baptized.

In Britain, *The Methodist Service Book*, 1975, following an experimental draft of 1967, has as its first section 'Entry into the Church'. The service for the baptism of infants has a fresh structure: preparation, lessons, including three gospel passages, homily, baptismal prayer, promises by the congregation, the parents, the sponsors (the sponsors are optional), Apostles' Creed or shorter creed, presentation of the child by the parents, baptism, signation, reception. Aaronic blessing, giving of a lighted candle (optional), final prayers, grace. This may be inserted into the main service of public worship or used separately. Then follows 'Public Reception into Full Membership, or Confirmation'; and then finally 'The Baptism of those who are able to answer for themselves, with the Public Reception into Full Membership, or Confirmation'. This proceeds as follows: hymn, prayer, OT lesson, epistle, hymn, gospel, sermon, hymn, homily, the baptismal prayer, promises by the congregation and the candidates, Apostles' Creed, further questions to the candidates, baptism, homily when there are others to be confirmed who have been baptized previously, confirmation and reception, prayer, hymn, Lord's Supper, with alternative ending 'if, in exceptional circumstances and for good reason, Confirmation does not immediately follow the baptism of those who are able to answer for themselves'. An appendix deals with the reception of persons from other Christian Communions.

A. RAYMOND GEORGE/JAMES F. WHITE

11. *Old Catholic*. The teaching of the Old Catholic churches of the Utrecht Union on baptism is that of holy scripture and the catholic church. Baptism is administered with water 'in the name of the Father and of the Son and of the Holy Spirit', usually by affusion. The baptismal water is blessed in the liturgy of Easter night and kept in the font. The baptism of infants is generally practised.

Grace received at baptism is completed and developed by the sacrament of confirmation*, bestowed on children by the bishop, after the children have received instruction in the Christian faith. In the Old Catholic Church of the Netherlands confirmation is brought into closer connection with baptism by the renewal of baptismal vows. In other countries, this takes place on receiving first communion. In the Polish National Catholic Church in America, baptism and confirmation together are regarded as a single sacrament: 'The Word of God, heard and preached', is regarded as the seventh (or second) sacrament.

The former baptismal rite of the Old Catholic churches was based on the *Ordo Baptismi Parvulorum* of the *Rituale Romanum* of Paul V; it is partly an exact translation and partly a free revision. In the German and Swiss rites of baptism there is a clear concern to explain the sacred actions by accompanying words.

In the Netherlands, baptism was administered in Dutch as early as the eighteenth century, according to formulae which were a complete literal translation of the *Ordo Baptismi Parvulorum* from the *Rituale Romanum*. In 1902 the bishops introduced a revised text. Though they kept to the old Roman pattern for the most part, the exsufflation and the exorcisms disappeared.

After the threefold renunciation of Satan the promise 'to love the Lord your God with all your heart and with all your soul, and with all your strength, and with all your mind, and your neighbour as yourself' is required. At the first anointing a prayer for Christ's grace was added, for strength to fight the good fight.

Between World War I and World War II it became the practice more and more to baptize the child in the presence of the mother, and therefore after a few weeks rather than immediately after birth, as the strict Dutch practice had been before. Also, increasingly, baptism took place immediately after the eucharist, in the presence of the congregation. For the past few years there has been a tendency to baptize during the eucharist, after the gospel and the sermon.

As an example of an Old Catholic order of baptism, there follows here a short description of baptism in the Old Catholic Church in Germany. The original rite of baptism of the Old Catholic Church was a translation of the *Ordo Baptismi Parvulorum* of Pope Paul V. In recent years considerable thought has been given to this matter and in Germany two forms of the baptismal rite have been published, the first suitable for infants and the second for older children and adults. The new order of baptism of infants, which was issued in 1983 and excludes any specific promises by the sponsors, addresses the parents and sponsors directly and not, as it were, as proxy for the child. This is also the reason why the congregation also makes the confession of faith for and on behalf of the child. A renunciation of Satan is not included in this rite as the child is not yet capable of making one. The child, together with its parents and sponsors, is met at the portal and the parents present their child to the congregation. The priest makes the sign of the cross (*see* **Gestures** 3), on the child's forehead. The parents, sponsors and other representatives of the congregation may also do likewise. A liturgy of the word follows if the christening does not take place during the celebration of the eucharist. This is followed at the font by a prayer for protection from evil, the anointing with oil and the confession of faith. After baptism (with the sign of the cross), there follows the anointing of the head with the oil of chrism and the bestowal of a white baptismal garment. The father or a sponsor then lights the baptismal candle on the Paschal candle. The blessing is given after the Lord's Prayer has been said. In the order of service for older children and adults the rites of the catechumenate* can be given during the course of preparation for baptism. In this service, which was issued for experimental use in 1985, the candidate makes a renunciation of the devil and a confession of faith. In place of the anointing with oil an adult can be confirmed immediately after baptism.

S. KRAFT/C. TOL

12. *Pentecostal.* In classical Pentecostalism (*see* **Pentecostal Worship**), many churches have no given rite of baptism but improvise a ceremony according, as it is said, to the movement of the Spirit. A rite of baptism which I observed in the Bahama Islands consisted of a procession from the church to the sea, accompanied with singing, hand clapping, ejaculatory prayers. On the beach the pastor addressed the faithful, admonishing them to repent of their sins and to accept Christ as their personal Saviour. Baptism was by immersion. The spontaneity of the people and deep sense of prayer and celebration made it evident that the participants were not going through a prescribed rite, but were deeply involved in prayer. In many classical Pentecostal groups the baptismal rite is accompanied with tongues, prophecies, and in one African church, the rite is accompanied with a prayer for healing. In the Church of the Twelve Apostles (Nackabah), an African church, the baptismal candidates are properly soaped and bathed (W. Hollenweger, *The Pentecostals*, 1971, p.391). Within classical Pentecostalism one can also find baptismal rites written down and printed in a disciplinary book or a minister's manual. These would include prayers, exhortations, and either the trinitarian baptismal formula or a formula mentioning only the name of Jesus. These rites would be used with great freedom by the ministers.

Most classical Pentecostals (e.g. Assemblies of God*) follow a Baptist conception of baptism, that is, for adults who have made a personal commitment to Christ. But there is a sizeable minority of classical Pente-

costals who use sprinkling: the majority of Chilean Pentecostals, the largest of the German churches, a Yugoslav group, and in the beginning, the Finnish and Norwegian movements (Hollenweger, *The Pentecostals*, p.392). Often the pastor dips his hand in a bowl of water and rubs the head of the candidate. One American directory says that 'the candidate shall have the right to choose whatever mode of baptism he prefers' (*Discipline of the Pentecostal Holiness Church*, 1961, p.78). The Quaker Pentecostals think the whole baptismal controversy peripheral. Both a Chilean and a German church allow adult baptism *and* infant baptism and therefore have baptism by immersion or sprinkling. In addition to these groups, all of which are trinitarian, there are the Pentecostal modalists, or 'Jesus only' groups, which take Acts 2.38 to mean that the trinitarian formula is not to be used, but rather candidates should be baptized only in the name of Jesus. Among some of the Churches of God (USA) there are groups which baptize only in the name of the Father (E. Clark, *The Small Sects in America*, 1949, p.105).

Neo-Pentecostals (*see* **Pentecostal Worship**) would tend to follow the rite of their respective churches. Some Lutheran Pentecostals have taken over the patterns of classical Pentecostals and have been rebaptized by immersion, not necessarily because their baptism by pouring was thought invalid. When a Catholic priest who is involved in the charismatic renewal baptizes a child of a Catholic charismatic couple, the rite of the Roman Catholic Church would be followed but there can, in addition, be quiet praying in tongues, interpretation, prophecy, and free prayer.

In Chile men and women admitted that they were deeply moved the first time they attended a Pentecostal service: 'Not because of the beauty of the ceremonial – oh, no, it is not as beautiful as with Catholics – but because people spoke to me, the pastor shook my hand, and I was able to sing and pray with them' (C. Lalive d'Epinay, *Haven of the Masses*, 1969, p.49).

At their worst, Pentecostal baptismal liturgies can be theologically impoverished and too subjectivistic. At their best, Pentecostal baptismal liturgies are successful because each individual is a participant, because their liturgies are essentially oral rather than printed (and usually oral even when printed), because they are simple, direct, and personal, because baptism is more immediately a prayer act than an external ritual, because whether dealing with a pre-literate or post-literate culture they know how to elicit a personal commitment through involvement in an experience which is self-explanatory, because the baptismal rite is itself an instrument of evangelization.

Finally, their rites are not techniques and are not separable from their spirituality, which is fullness of life in the Spirit and the exercise of the gifts of the Spirit.

For bibliography *see* under **Pentecostal Worship**.

KILIAN MCDONNELL

13. *Plymouth Brethren*. The Open Brethren almost without exception practise the baptism of believers only, on personal confession of faith, and the accepted mode is, almost invariably, total immersion. If immersion is impracticable for reasons of health or age, such token baptisms as affusion or sprinkling are not employed: the will is simply accepted for the deed. In these respects they closely resemble the Baptists; they do not, however, treat their baptismal doctrine and practice as so essential a feature of their church life that they could properly be described as Baptists.

Baptism is commonly understood among them as an act of public confession and Christian obedience, not as a vehicle of grace or as necessary to salvation. Probably the majority of those baptized among them are young people who have either grown up in the fellowship with their families or have become attached to it through various departments of its youth work; but one finds people of all age-groups asking for it and receiving it. It is normally administered before a congregation; most of the Open Brethren's meeting-places have suitable baptisteries sunk in the floor and boarded over when not in use.

Open Brethren do not, for the most part, treat any particular mode of baptism as an indispensable condition for admission to the communion table or to church membership; this would unfairly exclude, for example, Christians who have been baptized in infancy and cannot conscientiously recognize any obligation to receive 're-

sponsible' baptism. But the baptismal teaching given at their meetings is uniformly that connected with believers' baptism.

Among the Exclusive Brethren the situation is much less uniform. Those who adhere most closely to the Darbyite tradition follow J. N. Darby in baptizing the infant children of their church members; this practice is commonly called 'household' baptism (on the basis of Acts 16.15, 31–34; I Cor. 1.16, etc.). In the Taylorite connection such baptized children are regularly admitted to church fellowship at the age of twelve, if not earlier. Some of Darby's closest associates who disagreed with infant baptism found it expedient not to press their views: when an argumentative lady once asked him what his principal lieutenant, George Vicesimus Wigram (1805–1879), held about baptism, he is said to have replied, 'Madam, he holds his tongue.' And when the first major division took place within the Exclusive ranks (1881), although the issue had nothing to do with baptism, practically all those who held 'Baptist' views seceded with William Kelly (1820–1906), while the paedobaptists went 'nearly solid' for Darby (W. B. Neatby, *A History of the Plymouth Brethren*, 1901, pp.273f.).

An interesting situation arises when reunions take place (as they happily do from time to time) between groups or congregations which have incidentally differed from each other in baptismal doctrine or practice; there proves in practice to be no obstacle to the peaceful coexistence of the two ways (believers' baptism and infants' baptism). Tension is perhaps prevented by the fact that among the paedobaptist Exclusives infants are in any case baptized at home whereas Open Brethren and others who baptize believers do so in public.

F. F. BRUCE

14. *Reformed.* The baptismal rites in the Western church at the eve of the Reformation show that many ceremonies had been added to the practice of the early church, but these were not essential to the sacrament and their omission in cases of emergency did not affect its validity. This led to revision. In 1523, Luther published his *Das Taufbüchlein verdeutscht* (*Works*, Weimar XII, 42–48), which with minor alterations was a German translation of the mediaeval order in use at Wittenberg. When Diebold Schwarz translated the order in use at Strasbourg in 1524, he drew heavily on this. This was revised in 1525 (Hubert, *Die Stras. lit.*, 37–52), but it was now more than a translation, for the whole rite was re-cast. Under the influence of Bucer, further revisions were carried out during the years 1525–33, and it was on these Farel based his *La Manière et façon.* To Farel and Bucer, Calvin was much indebted for his Strasbourg rite. This later was simplified for use in Geneva (Op., VI, 184–191) and became the determining influence in the *Form of Prayers* (*FP*, 1556) of the English exiles there and the Scottish *Book of Common Order* (*BCO*, 1564).

Calvin's Strasbourg order, as found in the 1545 edition published by Paul Garnier, is:

1. Scripture sentence (Ps. 124.8).
2. Question: Do you present this child to be baptized, earnestly desiring that he may be engrafted in the mystical body of Christ?
3. Long exposition and exhortation.
4. Prayer for grace and reception of the child into the Kingdom of Christ.
5. The Lord's Prayer.
6. Question: Do you wish this child baptized in the name of the Father and of the Son, and of the Holy Spirit?
7. Apostles' Creed, said by parents.
8. Exhortation to parents.
9. Baptism with water in the triune name.
10. Declaration that the child is a member of Christ's church.

In *FP* and *BCO* the order is altered to 2 3 7 4 5 9 and a concluding prayer of thanksgiving and for the blessing of the Holy Spirit.

In the Reformed Church baptism was always placed in the setting of the worship of the people of God, the rite following the reading and preaching of the word. It was to be administered only 'in the face of the congregation'. Baptism, being a sacrament of the gospel, could only be administered by a minister of the word. For this reason also, the font* was removed from the church door and placed near the pulpit*.

The Reformed Church sought to remove all non-scriptural elements from the rite and to make it relevant to the baptism of infants. Whereas some other traditions super-

impose a baptismal order upon the existing mediaeval rite, which was designed in the first place for the baptism of adult believers, in Reformed rites no vicarious profession of faith is required of the parents or godparents, the children being admitted to baptism on the grounds of the covenant of grace. For this reason also, exorcism* and renunciations are laid aside as being inappropriate to the baptism of children of Christian parents. The Creed is repeated by the parents as the faith which they themselves believe as members of the church of Christ and into which they wish their children baptized, they taking a vow to bring them up therein. While there is no objection to godparents, the chief sponsor is, generally speaking, the father of the child.

In the early Reformed rites there is no epiclesis (*see* **Anaphora** 8) in the baptismal prayer. The reason for this could be that in the mediaeval church the consecration of the font had become a separate rite, or perhaps it was held that the declaration of intention of baptism was sufficient. Baptism is normally by affusion, but nothing is prescribed as to whether it should be single or triple. The latter has always been the practice of the Reformed churches in France, Switzerland, Germany and Hungary.

The order in *FP* (1556) and *BCO* (1564) remained the practice in the Reformed churches in Britain until it was replaced by that in the *Westminster Directory for the Public Worship of God* in 1645. Its order is:

Exhortation.
Prayer, including epiclesis.
Inquiry as to name.
Baptism with water in the triune name.
Prayer of thanksgiving and for the blessing of the Holy Spirit.

Here no profession of faith is required of the sponsors, but the adopting Act of the General Assembly of the Church of Scotland shows that the same requirement was continued. This is also true of Irish Presbyterianism. The *Directory*, being really only one extended rubric, resulted in a period of decadence. Renewal did not begin until the Church Service Society published the first edition of its *Euchologion* in 1867.

(*a*) *Rites in English*. The editors of *Euchologion* (1867) said concerning the baptismal order: 'The following Service is based upon the Baptismal Service in John Knox's *Book of Common Order*. It is condensed and considerably curtailed; but may be regarded as presenting the original and genuine doctrine of the Scottish Church regarding the sacrament of Baptism.' Several revisions followed, and the fifth (1884) may be said to have become normative. It is:

Scripture sentence (Ps. 124.8).
Scripture readings: Matt. 28.18–20; Mark 10.13–16; Acts 2.38–39.
Vows: Apostles' Creed, or alternative, answered by parents; upbringing of child.
Prayer: based on Greek, BCP and Catholic Apostolic rites with epiclesis from Westminster *Directory*.
Baptism with water in the triune name.
Apostolic or Aaronic blessing (optional).
Declaration that the child is received into the church: from 'Savoy Liturgy' (1661).
Prayer: from *BCO* (1564) and 'Larger Catechism'.
The Lord's Prayer.
Apostolic benediction.

This rite won its way into most of the English Reformed rites, and became almost universally accepted, remaining substantially unaltered in the Scottish *BCO* (1940) and American *Book of Common Worship* (*BCW*, 1946). In recent years, however, revision has taken place as a result of continental, Scottish and Irish research.

The Irish *Book of Public Worship* (*BPW*, 1965) may be taken as representing a transitional stage between the old and the new, (i) having references in the scripture readings to God's covenant with Abraham and the baptism of Jesus, (ii) requiring the congregation to take a specific vow; and (iii) departing from the traditional wording of the parents' vow to bring up the child in the Christian faith by adopting the form in *BCW* of the Church of South India.

Good examples of the new rites are *BCO* (Presbyterian Church, Canada, 1964), *Public Service Book* (*PSB*, England and Wales, 1968) and the Scottish 'Order for Holy Baptism' (1969). With minor alterations the last has been incorporated in the *BCO* (1979). While there are variations in these orders the last may be outlined. It is:

Liturgy of the word.
Scripture readings: Matt. 28. 18–20 (reference by Jesus to baptism), Acts 2.38–39 (statement on end of baptism), Mark 10.13–16 (Jesus and children).
Vows of parents, added first in Calvin's rite.
Congregation accepts responsibility by reciting Apostles' Creed.
Prayer: *Sursum corda*, adoration, epiclesis.
Baptism with water in the triune name.
Aaronic blessing.
Declaration that the child is received into the church.
Matt. 18.5, 6, 10 may be read.
Prayer: supplication and intercession.
The Lord's Prayer.
Psalm or hymn.
Benediction: 'The peace of God . . .'

The English-Welsh and Canadian rites both open with Ps. 124.8. In the former the reference to the baptism of Jesus is omitted, but in the latter Mark 1.9–11 is read. In both the Apostles' Creed is said by the congregation before the parents take their vows. The Scottish rite, in 1963, re-introduced Calvin's first question to the parents. The other two do not do so. The English-Welsh rite adds a vow for godparents, if there are any. In the baptismal prayer the *Sursum corda* is omitted by both, the Canadian also omitting the epiclesis. Both conclude with the apostolic benediction.

While theologically these rites add nothing new to what was always the doctrine of baptism in the Reformed Church, they do give fuller expression to it.

The United Reformed Church in England is a union of Congregational Churches, the Presbyterian Church, and the Churches of Christ. It produced *A Book of Services* (1980) in which the Order for the Baptism of Infants follows substantially the Reformed tradition. With the incorporation of the Churches of Christ, who practice believers' baptism, into the original Congregational/Presbyterian union it has already been agreed to produce a revision of *A Book of Services*. The effect of this union 'has been to make the service of baptism of believers and the act of thanksgiving for the birth of children more important and widely used in the denomination'.

The Presbyterian Churches in America used the 1788 revision of the Westminster *Directory*, and this practice, apart from the experiments of individuals continued until the formation of a Church Service Society, on the Scottish model, in 1897. Its instigators and leaders were Henry van Dyke and Louis Benson. This led eventually to the *BCW: Prepared for the Committee of the General Assembly of the Presbyterian Church in the USA for Voluntary Use* (1906), in which the baptismal rite was firmly based on a 'covenant theology', but rather defective structurally. This was revised in 1932, when it was also adopted by the Southern Presbyterians 'for the optional and selective use of our ministers'. The impetus for a third edition came from the publication of the *BCO* (1940) by the Church of Scotland, and this appeared in 1946. The new baptismal rite was considerably influenced by the Scottish and it reveals a more careful handling of the theological implications of baptism.

In 1955, the Presbyterian Church in the USA set up a committee to revise the *BCW*, and in this work three things are of note: (i) the United Presbyterian Church of North America and the Presbyterian Church in the United States (Southern) decided to participate together in the project: (ii) in 1961 a revision of the old *Directory* was published setting out basic principles; and (iii) before issuing a revised *BCW*, a *BCW: Provisional Services* (1966) was prepared for use and report. After a decade of experimental use, with a few minor alternations, this Baptismal Order was published in *The but in French-speaking Switzerland and Worshipbook* (n.d., *c*.1977) for use in The Cumberland Presbyterian Church, the Presbyterian Church in the United States, and the United Presbyterian Church in the United States of America. This is the baptismal rite now in use, and is noteworthy for three distinctive features: (i) 'the service is designed to be used both for the baptism of adults and for the baptism of infants'; (ii) opportunity is provided for an elder representing the session to take a part in the service; and (iii) 'the service includes opportunity for the whole congregation to renew baptismal vows in a unison prayer'.

(*b*) *Rites in French*. The liturgical movement in the Reformed Church in France begins with *La Liturgie d'Eugène Bersier* (1874). This work was destined to exercise a wide influence not only in France

but in French-speaking Switzerland and elsewhere. The result of this movement may be illustrated by the Genevan rite (1945):

Scripture sentence: (Ps. 124.8).
Declaration of intention.
Scripture readings: Ezek. 36.25–28; Matt. 28.18–20; Acts 2.38–39.
Baptismal instruction.
Vows.
Exhortation to parents.
Baptism with water in the triune name.
Prayer of supplication and intercession.
The Lord's Prayer.
Benediction (Phil. 4.7; Rom. 15.33).

Here, as in the English-speaking rites, recent research has exercised a great influence. While they differ structurally, good examples of the new rites are those in the Canton de Vaud (1962) and in France (1963). The order for the latter is:

Welcome based on Mark 10.13 and Ezek. 36.24–27.
Invocation and adoration.
Apostles' Creed said by congregation.
Institution: Matt. 28.18–20.
Prayer.
Baptismal instruction.
Exhortation to parents.
Desire of parents.
Involvement of congregation.
Baptism with water in the triune name.
Vows of parents, may be placed before baptism.

The rite for Vaud adds Mark 1.9–11 and Acts 2.38–39 to the readings, which are followed by the creed and a prayer based on Geneva (1542) and *La Liturgie des Églises du Pays de Vaud* (1725). Then come the vows, institution, and a prayer from the Roman rite. Neither rite contains an epiclesis, although the Vaud rite has a petition that the child may be 'baptized with water and the Spirit'. The baptismal instruction (omitted in Vaud) is based on Strasbourg (1536) and Geneva (1542). In the French rite the vows are presented as laid upon the parents by the church, which itself is a 'witness' to the baptism and required to take upon itself 'responsibility' for the baptized. Baptism is always with water 'in the name of the Father, and of the Son, and of the Holy Spirit'. The concluding prayer is based upon Genevan, French or Vaudoise sources. The Vaud rite ends with a declaration, 'We receive you into the family of God, the church of Jesus Christ.'

(*c*) *Rites in German*. The baptismal order in the German rites, broadly speaking is:

Scripture readings: Matt. 28.18–20, Mark 10.13–16.
Baptismal instruction.
Prayer: supplication and intercession.
Apostles' Creed, sometimes said by the congregation.
Vows of parents and godparents.
Baptism with water in the triune name.
Exhortation to parents and congregation.
Prayer of thanksgiving.

This may be taken as representative, even though some service-books in addition include the form in *Der Taufordnung der Pfälzischen Kirchenordnung* (1563).

The scripture readings from Matthew and Mark are always included as the warrant for baptism. The baptismal instruction is drawn from many sources – Strasbourg (1524), a'Lasco (1550), Geneva (1542), Pfalz (1563) and Basle (1572), as are the questions to the parents. The words introducing the Apostles' Creed are drawn from Micronius (1554), Pfalz (1563), or Basle (1572). Baptism is with water 'in the name of the Father, and of the Son, and of the Holy Spirit'. The exhortation is based on Zurich (1529) and Pfalz (1563). The supplications and intercessions have a common content but vary considerably in different rites, according to whether or not they are derived from Zurich (1525), Strasbourg (1536), Geneva (1542), a'Lasco (1550), Scottish *BCO* (1564), Basle (1572), Bern (1598), Cassel (1657), or St Gallen (1699). None includes an epiclesis. Generally speaking several thanksgivings are provided, but they almost always include a'Lasco (1550) and Pfalz (1563).

(*d*) *Confirmation, Baptism of the Sick, Baptism of Believers*. All these rites contain an order for confirmation*. In cases of sickness and emergency, private baptism is permitted. The liturgy of the Reformed Church in France provides a separate rite for this, and others contain special prayers. Here it might be worth making into a universal practice the decision of the Perth Assembly (1618):

> That the minister shall the next Lord's day after such private baptism declare in the

church that the infant was so baptized, and therefore ought to be received as one of the true flock of Christ's fold.

The early Reformed liturgies and the *Westminster Directory* make no provision for the baptism of adult believers. The first such rite was prepared by the Dutch Reformed Church in 1604. The first in English is in the third edition of *Euchologion* (1874). The latter casts the rite as baptism-confirmation, for the baptism is followed by prayer 'with imposition of hands'. This theological position remains basic in all the rites, and the changes taking place are parallel to those in the rites for the children of believers.

(*e*) *Theology*. Baptism is a gift of God to men through his church, in which he 'presents' and 'seals' Christ to them, admitting them to the fellowship of the church and demanding from them the response of faith and a life of godliness through the power of the Holy Spirit. All these rites do set forth clearly the Reformed doctrine of 'the grace of baptism'. At the same time, two questions require to be raised: (i) If in a sacrament God, through the 'visible sign', 'presents and seals Christ', should the prayer before the act of baptism not always include a petition that the 'visible sign' may fulfil God's purpose? (ii) Does the eschatological significance of baptism always receive adequate expression?

JOHN M. BARKLEY

15. *Seventh-day Adventist*. Seventh-day Adventists believe that baptism is the ceremony of initiation into the Christian church, and is therefore a solemn ordinance, the proper form of which is to be administered by immersion. Baptism is the antitype of the Genesis flood, which prefigured the freely accepted 'reduced flood'. It typifies the death, burial, and resurrection of Christ, and openly expresses faith in his saving grace. As such it is a condition of entrance into church membership (*Church Manual*, 1981, p.57). In addition to the etymological argument stemming from the basic meaning of the Greek word *baptizo* ('to dip', 'to plunge', 'to overwhelm'), Seventh-day Adventists hold that the soundest argument for baptism by immersion is the theological one derived from Paul's symbolism (Rom. 6.1–11) of baptism as representing death, burial and resurrection. Baptism signifies death to sin, moral resurrection in this life and corporal resurrection in the life to come. The practice of another mode of baptism by the apostolic church would have rendered meaningless the significance of the symbolic character Paul gave to the baptismal ceremony.

In harmony with other followers of the Baptist tradition, Seventh-day Adventists reject infant baptism, believing that there is no biblical support for this custom. Accordingly they practice believer's baptism, administering it only to those who have reached accountability and meet the prerequisite of active faith.

Baptism is not just a momentary act, but should be a continuous sign witnessing to the believer's acceptance of Jesus Christ as his personal Saviour. Persons joining the SDAC, who have already been baptized by immersion, are not rebaptized, except when they desire rebaptism. Seventh-day Adventists who have apostatized and have publicly violated the faith and principles of the SDAC, thus nullifying the sign and witness of baptism, are in the case of reconversion asked to enter the church as in the beginning, namely by baptism (*Church Manual* 1981, p.74).

Adventists do not view baptism as a ritual washing with some kind of supernatural power or magical cleansing of sin *per se* without true repentance. In common with their Protestant heritage, they therefore reject the sacramentalist view of baptism as imparting grace *ex opere operato*, that is, as an act or sign that, in and of itself, imparts grace and effects salvation. Though baptism does not automatically convey grace, it is intended to be a public sign of grace that comes through incorporation into the family of God.

Baptismal candidates are thoroughly instructed in the Christian faith, and prior to baptism an examination takes place either before the church board or at the baptismal service itself, when they are asked to affirm publicly their assent to the teachings of the SDAC. Baptism is usually administered by an ordained minister, but 'when none is available the local church elder may officiate' (*Manual for Ministers*, 1977, p.95), after making proper arrangements with the conference or mission president.

A typical baptismal service is preceded by a hymn, prayer and short discourse on the meaning of baptism. As each candidate is immersed, the congregation often sings a stanza of some appropriate hymn. Where the local church does not have a baptistery, a stream, lake or other aquatic facility is used.

Before the candidate is immersed, the minister performing the baptism raises his right hand and pronounces the following formula (or a very similar one): 'My brother or sister, upon the profession of your faith in Jesus Christ as your personal Saviour, I now baptize you in the name of the Father, and the Son, and of the Holy Spirit. Amen' (*Manual for Ministers* 1977, p.99).

B. B. BEACH

Baptism and Confirmation. Prayer Book Studies I, 1952; *Baptism and Confirmation,* Report of the Church of England Liturgical Commission, 1959; J. Baillie, *Baptism and Conversion*, 1964; J. M. Barkley, *Worship of the Reformed Church*, 1966; G. W. Bromiley, *Baptism and the Anglican Reformers*, 1953; J. D. Benoit, *Initiation à la liturgie de l'Eglise Reformée de France*, 1956; British Council of Churches, *The Child in the Church*, 1976; *Understanding Christian Nurture*, 1981; Church of Scotland, *Biblical Doctrine of Baptism*, 1958; J. D. Crichton, *Christian Celebration: The Sacraments*, 1973, pp. 40–87; J. G. Davies, *The Spirit, the Church and the Sacraments*, 1954; N. Dixon, *Troubled Waters*, 1979; M. Dujarier, *The Rites of Christian Initiation: Historical and Pastoral Reflections*, 1979; W. Elert, *The Structure of Lutheranism*, 1962; J. D. C. Fisher, *Christian Initiation in the Medieval West*, 1965; J. D. C. Fisher, *Christian Initiation – The Reformation Period*, 1970; B. G. Holland, *Baptism in Early Methodism*, 1970; R. Josefson, *Luthers tära omdepet*, 1944; C. Jones, G. Wainwright, E. Yarnold (eds), *The Study of Liturgy*, 1978, Part II, Ch. II; W. G. Johnsson, *Clean: The Meaning of Christian Baptism*, 1980; A. Kavanagh, *The Shape of Baptism: the Rite of Christian Initiation*, 1978; U. Kury, *Die altkatholische Kirche* (Die Kirchen der Welt II), 1966, pp.185–187 (Old Catholic); G. W. H. Lampe, *The Seal of the Spirit*, 1967; M. Luther, *The Holy and Blessed Sacrament of Baptism* (*Works*, American ed, vol 35), 1960; A. J. Mason, *The Relation of Confirmation to Baptism*, 1893; K. F. Müller and W. Blankenburg (eds), *Liturgia. Handbuch des evangelischen Gottesdienstes*.5. Taufe, Konfirmation, 1952; H. M. Riley, *Christian Initiation*, 1974; A. Schmemann, *Of Water and the Spirit*, 1976; M. Searle, *Christening. The Making of a Christian*, 1977; E.-P. Siman, *L'expérience de l'Espirt par l'Eglise d'après la tradition syrienne d'Antioche*, 1971; L. H. Stookey, *Baptism: Christ's Act in the Church*, 1982: E. C. Whitaker, *Documents of the Baptismal Liturgy*, 1960; E. Yarnold, *The Awe-Inspiring Rites of Initiation*, 1972.

Baptismal Vows, Renewal of

The idea of a solemn renewal of vows seems to appear first in the confirmation service of Hermann's *Consultation* (1545). The BCP of 1549 mentions it in the prefatory rubric as the first purpose of confirmation, but does not provide for it in the service. This is first done in the revision of 1661. The *Durham Book* introduces a form consisting of a new question by the bishop to which the candidates 'audibly answer, I do'; they then repeat the vows, and the bishop adds a prayer from the Ordering of Priests. In the 1662 BCP only the new question remains. An actual repetition of the vows was proposed in the 1928 BCP and forms part of the service in most modern revisions.

Such a renewal may be made also on other occasions such as New Year by the whole congregation, as in the first Methodist covenant service* (1780). The ASB (1980) provides a form for use on its own, consisting of a verbatim repetition of sections 13, 18 (part) and 19 of the baptism service with introductions by the minister and a selection of prayers (sections 35–39). When included in baptism or confirmation, it follows the sermon or the welcome, and consists simply of the repetition of the vows. It is also included in the Easter vigil service issued in 1985.

In the American BCP (1979) a renewal forms part of the baptism service, with the title 'The Baptismal Covenant', and consisting of the Apostles' Creed and five questions about the Christian life. It is made by the whole congregation. For candidates who had been baptized in infancy, this is preceded by two questions about reaffirming renunciation of evil and

renewing commitment to Jesus Christ. With this addition the form is also included in the Easter vigil.

In the Roman Catholic baptism service the congregation renew their profession of faith by repeating the creed, and in confirmation the candidates repeat the vows made at their baptism. In the Easter vigil, after an introduction by the priest, the congregation repeat the vows and are then sprinkled with holy water.

F. E. Brightman, *The English Rite*, 1915, II, pp.776, 793; G. J. Cuming, *The Durham Book*, 1961, pp.222–5; ASB, pp.275–8; BCP, pp.292–4, 303–5; R. C. D. Jasper (ed), *The Alternative Service Book: A Commentary*, 1980, p.119; M. J. Hatchett, *Commentary on the American Prayer Book*, 1979, pp.248, 271–3, 281–3.

G. J. CUMING

Baptist Worship

Baptist worship can only be understood from the Baptist understanding of the church. For Baptists, the chief manifestation of the visible church is the gathered congregation. The gathered or local congregation which is faithful has within it, according to Baptist ecclesiology, the fullness of the church visible. It is made up of persons who have committed themselves to Jesus Christ and his church and upon profession of faith have been baptized and received into church membership. Such a congregation 'gathers' for worship. Worship is celebration of the gospel; i.e. the good news in Jesus Christ. Thus worship for Baptists is primarily a time of praise and thanksgiving, but it is also marked by private and corporate confession, by petition and intercession. The worshipper seeks a living presence of Christ and that spiritual renewal which will enable him to live as a Christian in the world. Congregational worship can take place where two or three are gathered together in the name of the Lord, and he is in the midst of them. Robert Browning's recollection of his Christmas visit to a nonconformist chapel describes well Baptist worship at its heart:

> I remember, he did say
> Doubtless that, to this world's end,
> Two or three should meet and pray,
> He would be in the midst, their friend;
> Certainly he was there with them!
> (*Christmas Eve and Easter Day*)

The modern Baptist movement had its beginnings in the early years of the seventeenth century as a part of English separatism. It manifested itself first in a congregation of separatists which had fled persecution in England and settled in Holland. Under the leadership of John Smyth this group in the first decade of the seventeenth century separated from the parent congregation over the question of believer's baptism. Smyth's group felt that a local congregation (church) should be made up of those who were baptized after they had made their personal professions of faith. Such 'gathered' congregations met regularly for worship, yet little is known of the form and content of their worship. No manuals of worship have come down to us, for they did not exist. For these early Baptists, such books would have been hindrances to what Smyth called 'spiritual worship'. Smyth himself left a few directions which doubtless reflect the way in which the Baptist congregation of Amsterdam worshipped. He wrote:

1. We hold that the worship of the New Testament properly so called is spiritual proceeding originally from the heart: and that reading out of a book (though it is a lawful ecclesiastical action) is no part of spiritual worship, but rather the invention of the man of sin, it being substituted for a part of spiritual worship.
2. We hold that seeing prophesying is a part of spiritual worship: therefore in time of prophesying it is unlawful to have the book (i.e. the Bible) as a help before the eye.
3. We hold that seeing singing a psalm is a part of spiritual worship: therefore it is unlawful to have the book before the eye in time of singing a psalm (John Smyth, *The Differences of the Churches of the Separation: Contayning a Description of the Leitourgie and Ministerie of the Visible Church*, 1609, in W. T. Whitley, *The Works of John Smyth*, 1915, p.273).

According to a contemporary description, the Sunday service in Smyth's church would begin at 8 a.m. with a reading from the Bible. The book would then be set aside.

Sermons up to five in number, as time would permit, would be preached on the text. These would be interspersed with prayers (from the heart). Psalms from memory would be sung. At 12 noon the service would be concluded with prayer. Another service following the same pattern would begin at 2 p.m. and go on until 5 or 6 o'clock.

Smyth's worship pointed to the centrality of the remembered and experienced word and the freedom of the Spirit in worship. In these points he made a permanent contribution to Baptist worship. When the refugee congregations returned in part to England and the Baptist movement began to grow, the main stream of Baptist church life that developed, while remembering Smyth's stress on freedom in worship, took on the worship patterns of its Presbyterian and Congregational counterparts. (*See also* **Congregationalist Worship; Presbyterian Worship.**) The typical worship of these churches consisted of the reading and proclamation of the word preceded and followed by scripture sentences, prayers and the singing of psalms, particularly at communion services. Later, hymns came into general usage.

With the Congregationalists and others, Baptists became a part of the Free Church Movement. While the term 'free', when used in relation to the church, has a variety of meanings, such as freedom from clerical control, freedom from the state, freedom to organize and maintain churches, freedom of worship, etc., in relation to worship it means primarily freedom from prescribed liturgical forms. Thus the Baptists, as other Free Churches, have no required orders of worship such as the divine liturgy of the Orthodox churches, the Roman mass, or the forms of worship of the Anglican BCP.

To say that Baptists have no required orders for public worship does not mean that Baptists believe that worship should be disordered. Worship that is careless and undisciplined is an offence to God and may be the means of destroying rather than of building the faith of a congregation. Baptists frequently quote Paul's well-known words on spiritual gifts. He urged that 'all things should be done decently and in order' (I Cor. 14.40). He further directed the Corinthian congregation: 'When you come together, each one has a hymn, a lesson, a revelation, a tongue, or an interpretation. Let all things be done for edification . . . For you can all prophesy one by one, so that all may learn and all may be encouraged . . . For God is not a God of confusion but of peace' (I Cor. 14.26, 31,33). Baptists believe in ordered worship but not required ordered worship. For them, as for others, word and table are the two basic points for the ordering of Christian worship, for here the primary foci of God's revelation are presented. The believer responds to this revelation by acts of adoration, repentance, thanksgiving, petition, dedication, and intercession. The response comes in the forms of prayers, litanies, doxologies, *Glorias*, sung psalms and hymns, the spoken word, and the breaking of bread and drinking of wine.

In a Baptist church, the responsibility for public worship lies with the congregation. No hierarchy hands down required forms and materials for worship. This means that great variety characterizes Baptist worship. Some Baptist churches, particularly those that have been influenced by the movement for liturgical renewal, have formal services. They use set prayers which are read from printed orders distributed to the congregation beforehand. Choirs and clergy are robed, and church buildings are often neo-Gothic in architecture. In such churches one can find lamps, candles and crosses, often set upon altars backed by a reredos and decked out in seasonal liturgical colours. On the other hand, Baptist worship may be completely informal and spontaneous. Such informality and spontaneity would characterize most black church worship in America. While black church worship does have a structure or pattern, the structure is not allowed to interfere with the free flow of the spirit. The congregation gathers to find joy in the Lord and it feels that such joy can only be hindered by set forms. In between the highly formalized and the completely informal, most Baptists worship according to a pattern generally developed over a period of time by the congregation and yet sufficiently free to allow for considerable spontaneity.

Baptist worship has been largely conditioned by the culture in which it has found itself. Reference was made above to the informality and spontaneity of black church worship. This spirit goes back to the

days when black people were slaves and the church was the only place where they could express their human freedom. Thus in the church they turned themselves loose and lived, at least during the time of worship, as persons free in the sight of God. On the American frontier the characteristic Baptist service was the revival meeting. Here lively singing, testimonies as to the freedom and forgiveness which has come in Christ, and spontaneous prayer characterized the first part of the revival service. These 'preliminaries' prepared the congregation for the reading and the preaching of the word and the call to repentance, followed by the response of the sinner or 'backslider'. When these revival services resulted in churches, the people who formed them had become used to the style of the revival meeting and the services of worship tended to be planned as a repetition of the revival service. In Germany and the Scandinavian countries where Baptists arose out of the pietistic ferment of past centuries, worship still has strong overtones of pietistic devotional life. Bible reading and meditation, spontaneous prayer and introspective hymns tend to characterize such services. In England as well as New England, Baptist worship has been strongly influenced by the plain and decorous character of the chapel service.

In the Baptist mission fields worship has moved in two directions. There has been a strong tendency to copy the forms of the sending church. But increasingly the younger churches are finding their own forms of worship. In South India, particularly in the villages, indigenous music and *Kalakkala*, a form used by the village story teller to relate the myths of Hinduism, are used to proclaim the gospel. As the story teller (the preacher) sings out the good news, the congregation responds antiphonly.

Historically, Baptists have been strong exponents of the Reformation doctrine of *sola scriptura*. Nothing is to be done that is unscriptural and everything that is done is to be done in accordance with the scriptures. Reading and proclamation of the word have occupied a central place in Baptist worship. The Baptist stress upon the importance of preaching has produced a striking number of 'great' preachers. From John Bunyan to Charles Haddon Spurgeon, Harry Emerson Fosdick, Billy Graham and Martin Luther King, Jr, Baptist preachers have gained hearings far beyond their own churches and denomination. So central is preaching to worship for Baptists that most Baptists when asked to evaluate worship will immediately turn to the sermon, and the success or failure of a given worship service will stand upon the fact as to whether or not the sermon is good or bad. In some areas Baptists tend to distinguish or to separate worship and preaching. The morning service is called a service of 'worship *and* preaching'. Or the worship segments are characterized as 'preliminaries'. The *pièce de résistance* is invariably the sermon. In the most Baptist worship it occupies the concluding and climactic point of the service. It is often followed by a hymn of invitation in which an opportunity is offered for non-believers to give themselves to Christ and for believers to rededicate themselves to the Christian life. This self-offering is doubtless related to what has been called the offertory in the traditional liturgy. Preaching in Baptist churches has followed no set pattern. Baptists have used textual, expository and topical methods, the form dependent upon the preacher's preference. But increasingly Baptists are turning to lectionary preaching as they are becoming more and more involved in the observance of the Christian year.

While the Lord's Supper* is regarded highly by Baptists, it is not frequently practised. Relatively few churches observe weekly communion. Most churches will hold communion on a monthly or a quarterly basis. Formerly communion was often separated from the preaching service. At the conclusion of the preaching service the congregation would be dismissed and only those who were members of the local congregation would remain for the Lord's Supper. For those who were included, communion was indeed a high and holy time in which the congregation remembered in deep solemnity the life and passion of their Lord, and renewed their hope in his return in power and glory. Today the services of word and table are generally one service.

Baptists differ on the issue of open and closed communion. Many churches invite all who believe in Jesus Christ to participate. Others seek to restrict communion

to Baptists and in some places reserve communion to those who are members of the local congregation. The pastor of the congregation generally presides at the communion service, but if no pastor is available, a layperson can be designated by the congregation to officiate. Baptism, as well as other elements of worship, can be performed by a layperson if no ordained minister is available or present. Such lay leadership is done by licensing. The congregation votes to designate one or more of its members to serve its needs.

The communion service is primarily a memorial meal. 'Real presence' comes as the individual believers renew their faith and fellowship in Jesus Christ. In most Baptist churches today, the elements of bread and wine are distributed by the deacons to the congregation as they sit in their places. They eat the bread simultaneously as the minister repeats the words of Jesus. 'Take, eat. This is my body which is broken for you. Do this in remembrance of me.' Then, as the minister says, 'Drink of it, all of you; for this is my blood of the covenant, which is poured out for many for the forgiveness of sins,' the congregation drinks the wine (*see* **Communion**).

The structure of the Sunday morning preaching service in a Baptist church is relatively simple. The service generally begins with a scripture sentence followed by a prayer of invocation and a hymn of praise. A responsive reading, usually from the psalms, is read, followed by the singing of the *Gloria*. Then comes the pastoral prayer which covers such elements as adoration, confession, thanksgiving, and intercession. Following the prayer, church announcements are made and the offering is received with the singing of the doxology. A hymn may then be sung followed by the reading of the scripture and the sermon. After the sermon a hymn of dedication and invitation is sung and the benediction is pronounced. If a choir is present, suitable anthems come at various places in the service and responses, introits, etc. provide introductions and conclusions to the spoken parts of the service.

Baptists have no official manuals of worship or books of common prayer. In Britain Ernest A. Payne and Stephen F. Winward compiled *Orders and Prayers for Church Worship* (1960), and in the USA John E. Skoglund published a *Manual of Worship* (1968). While books like these have no official endorsement, they have received denominational encouragement. The orders which are included in the books are not in any way required of the congregations, but are intended to provide guide lines for worship done 'decently and in order'.

Baptists have not been at the centre of the movement for liturgical renewal. Individuals have participated in liturgical conferences and have written on the issues of worship, but for the most part church life has not been greatly influenced. The freedom allowed in worship in Baptist congregations has afforded opportunities for a number of experiments. Baptist worship can be readily adapted to such informal gatherings as house churches, to services with high lay participation, and to other experimental forms (*see also* **Experimental Forms of Worship**). In this Baptists may make in the future a significant contribution to liturgical renewal.

See also **Books, Liturgical** 5; **Liturgies** 5.

James W. Cox, *Ministers Worship Manual* (revision of the Payne/Winward Manual for use in the USA), 1965; Winthrop S. Hudson and Norman H. Maring, *A Baptist Manual of Policy and Practice*, 1963; Ernest A. Payne, *The Fellowship of Believers*, 1952; John E. Skoglund, *Worship in the Free Churches*, 1965; Stephen F. Winward, *The Reformation of our Worship*, 1965.

JOHN E. SKOGLUND

Baptistery

Baptism does not of itself require any particular building type or indeed any building at all, any more than does any other form of Christian worship (*see* **Architectural Setting**). Nevertheless, to study Christian initiation upon a textual basis alone is to indulge in something of an abstraction, for the rites need to be considered in their setting, which was both architectural and iconographical. In such a context the documents assume a deeper and more real meaning, and conversely the conjunction of text and monument illuminates the latter, which tends to be no more than an empty shell if there is ignorance of what took place within it.

The story of the baptistery does not begin

until the opening decades of the third century. Baptisteries may have existed before then, but of these no literary evidence survives and no archaeological traces have been discovered. In the apostolic age and during the second century, baptism was administered in rivers and pools, while the gatherings for eucharistic worship were held in private houses. When at length special architectural provision was made for the latter, we may assume that it would embrace the former, so that as accommodation was created for the liturgical assembly of the church, it was also set aside for the sacrament of initiation into the church.

The earliest baptisteries of the third and fourth centuries were square or rectangular with or without an apse at one end. This type persisted in such areas as Greece, Palestine and North Africa until the seventh century. In other parts of the empire, notably France and Italy, the quadrilateral was superseded from the middle of the fifth century by round or octagonal designs. In many provinces these baptisteries were either detached from or loosely attached to the main building for worship, but in Greece they frequently formed part of the church, being an adjoining room opening off the narthex*.

The adoption of the quadrilateral in the first instance was the outcome of three factors. First, when baptism ceased to be administered out of doors and a baptistery was arranged in the house church, it naturally had the shape of an ordinary room, i.e. it was quadrilateral, and as such is to be found at Dura Europos. Second, since the baptismal rite had affinities with bathing, the *frigidarium* of the Roman baths, often a square or rectangle, had its influence. Third, from NT times baptism was understood in terms of a death and resurrection with Christ; the baptistery was therefore a kind of tomb, and since many pagan funerary monuments were domed quadrilaterals it was natural to reproduce this design. Its persistence in certain areas is explicable because it was in precisely the same provinces that the square tomb was and continued to be the norm.

This last factor provides the clue to the reason for the adoption of other shapes in Italy and in those countries under her direct influence. Here there was a transition from the square to the circle and also to the hexagon and octagon. The circular plan with ambulatory was the plan of many tombs and this funerary association was also expressed through the six- and eight-sided design. The symbolism of the hexagon refers to the sixth day of the week, i.e. Friday, upon which Christ was crucified and buried, so it declared the baptismal co-death with the redeemer. The octagon represented the day of Christ's resurrection, i.e. the first day of the new week, and so it served to emphasize co-resurrection with Christ in baptism and the dawn of the Age to Come.

Other less widespread forms derived from the same association of ideas. Thus trefoil and quatrefoil baptisteries reproduced the designs of tombs and martyria*, and the few cruciform examples relate directly to the manner of Christ's death. The iconographical scheme of baptisteries is further evidence of the close connection in belief between baptism and death, for the mosaics which decorated many of them reproduced the same themes as sepulchral art, e.g. the Good Shepherd who lays down his life for the sheep, the star-studded domes which represent heaven and eternal life.

Baptism itself was gradually elaborated into a complex rite which included the disrobing of candidates, their affirmation of faith, their entry into the water, their anointing, their clothing in white robes and their procession to the main building for the eucharist. In planning their baptisteries, Christians could have produced a series of rooms, each corresponding to one element in the rite as a whole. Indeed this is what took place, and although, probably due to lack of material resources, some were no more than a single room, others had two or more adjoining the one in which the font* was placed. As an example we may take the complex opening out of the north end of the narthex of Basilica A at Philippi (*see* Fig. 16). There are three rooms: the first cannot be anything other than a vestibule; the second is the baptismal area with font, and beyond that is a third with an apse in one of its walls. There is every reason to suppose that the apse was constructed with a specific purpose in view, namely to enshrine the episcopal throne. This permits the identification of the room as a *chrismarion*, i.e. the place where the bishop administered the chrism which completed the rite of initiation. Sometimes, in default of other rooms,

'confirmation'* could take place in the area of the font, and where there is an apse* such as the one at Tropaeum Traiani, this was almost certainly to provide a space for the cathedra*.

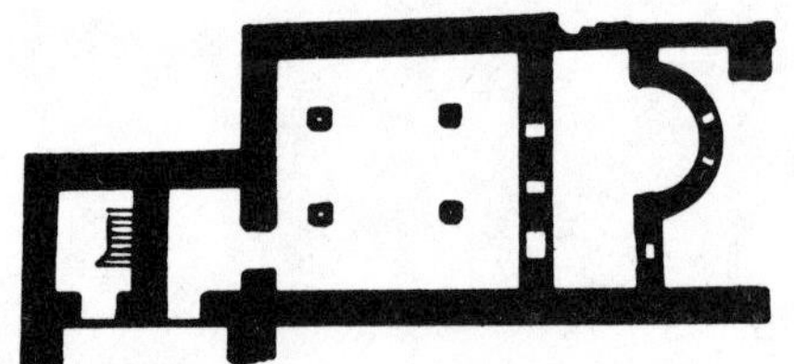

Fig. 16 Basilica A, Philippi, Macedonia

Whether simple or complex, baptisteries were at first erected only in episcopal cities, since it was the bishop's office to confirm and since baptism and confirmation were for centuries united. The occasional baptisteries in non-episcopal centres existed to spare candidates too long a journey. In the East, where priests were eventually allowed to confirm in place of the bishop, using for the purpose oil that had been episcopally blessed, baptisteries became more numerous, and were therefore not confined to episcopal centres. In parts of Syria in the sixth century, each town had its baptistery, not infrequently two and sometimes three. In the West, on the other hand, where the bishop did not delegate this authority, it was not until baptism and confirmation were finally separated that each parish came to possess its own.

From the seventh to the fourteenth centuries, detached baptisteries (*see* Plate 19), after the model of the early Christian ones and with the same plan and ideological content, continued to be erected, of which the ones at Florence (*see* Fig. 17) and Pisa are perhaps the most well known. But the later Middle Ages witnessed a complete transformation of the architectural setting of baptism in so far as the detached type ceased to be built and the font was placed within the church itself. The factors that contributed to this result were all different aspects of the situation that obtained when the whole population of a country had become nominally Christian. The virtual cessation of adult initiation and the corresponding preponderance of infant baptism meant that provision for undressing and privacy for the nude were no longer required. The public nature of baptism, with all present accepting the Christian faith, meant that a separate building was no longer necessary. Hence there was no reason why a simple font should not be introduced into the nave, usually by the main door to indicate that baptism is the means of entrance into the church. The result of this movement was that baptism ceased to have an architectural setting properly so called. However, in a number of churches a baldachin* or ciborium* was erected over the font and occasionally a low wooden railing surrounded it, thus defining a space and dignifying the celebration of the first gospel sacrament.

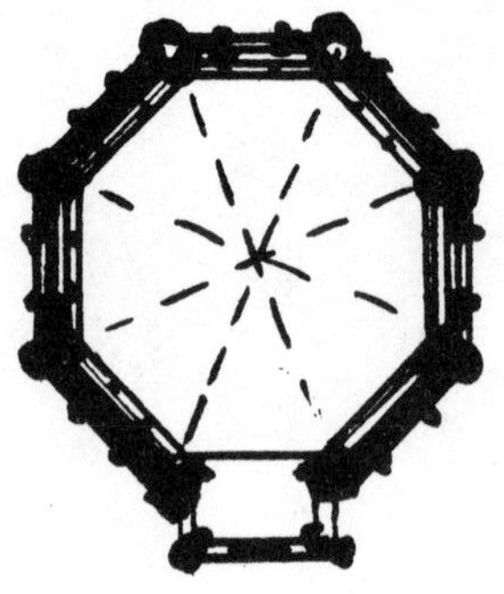

Fig. 17 Baptistery, Florence, Italy

Within the Roman Catholic Church this practice was fostered by Charles Borromeo who issued directions for his diocese of Milan in 1559. In legislating for parish churches, Borromeo ordained that 'an oratory or chapel should be built, inside close to the chief doorway and on the gospel side, and it should be alike to the other lateral chapels erected to contain altars'. So he advocated the creation of a defined space which was to be enclosed by iron or wooden railings, with the font sunk in the centre to the depth of several steps. Being of a practical turn of mind, he had to acknowledge that there were some buildings in which even this would not be feasible, and so he was prepared to allow the font to stand alone at the rear of the church in the mediaeval fashion, but this was clearly not his ideal, and this ideal, formulated in great detail, has continued to have its effect upon the architectural setting of baptism within

Plate 19 Detached baptistery, Parma, Italy

Roman Catholic churches right down to the present.

Within Protestant churches the baptistery proper ceased to exist. Anglicans were content with a font by the church door, following the mediaeval practice. Calvinists used shallow basins placed either on the holy table or in brackets fixed to the pulpit. The Lutherans eventually adopted the *Prinzipalstück* (*see* **Architectural Setting**) and located the font close to the table and pulpit at the east end.

With the Gothic Revival the mediaeval precedent continued to be observed, but about the middle of the nineteenth century influences were at work to produce exceptions to this norm and ultimately to issue in a new approach to the architectural setting of baptism and indeed in the restoration of the baptistery. The first of these influences was a growing awareness of the detached baptisteries still standing in Italy. As more and more architects made the grand tour, ignorance of the baptistery proper was no longer possible. The second influence was the contemporary Roman Catholic practice. Pugin argued forcibly that the font should be given prominence by an enclosing

Plate 20 Macgregor chapel, Afikpo teacher training college, Eastern Nigeria

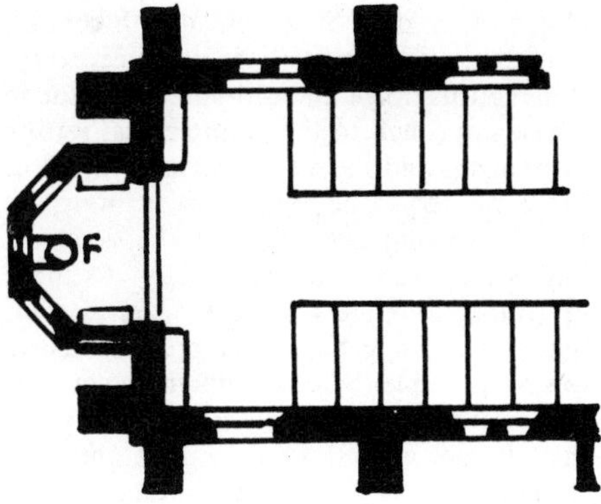

Fig. 18 Dodford Church, England

chancel and in several of the churches he designed he did create a baptistery at the west end. Architects working for Anglican patrons began to adopt the same concept and they were further affected by the gradual re-use of the many chapels and chantries in the English cathedrals for weekday services; this suggested that one of them could house the font, so creating a baptistery. In existing buildings, where the font had been an isolated object, baptisteries were introduced by defining the space with rails. In some new churches western apses were deliberately planned as baptisteries (*see* Fig. 18).

In the twentieth century this movement has continued. Architects and their clients began to think no longer in terms simply of a font but in spatial categories. It was thought that the rite required not only certain necessary items of furniture but a defined space suitable to its importanc and meaning. Consequently the practice increased of creating baptisteries within existing churches and making provision for them within those that were rebuilt after damage or destruction during the Second World War.

In the majority of modern Roman Catholic churches, unlike those of Eastern Orthodoxy, the idea of a separate baptistery apart from the main assembly hall for worship, has predominated. The baptistery may project from the western facade; it may be located to one side of the church, usually the north; it may be contained within the entrance hall or narthex. Other denominations represent a greater variety, with no one concept entirely to the fore.

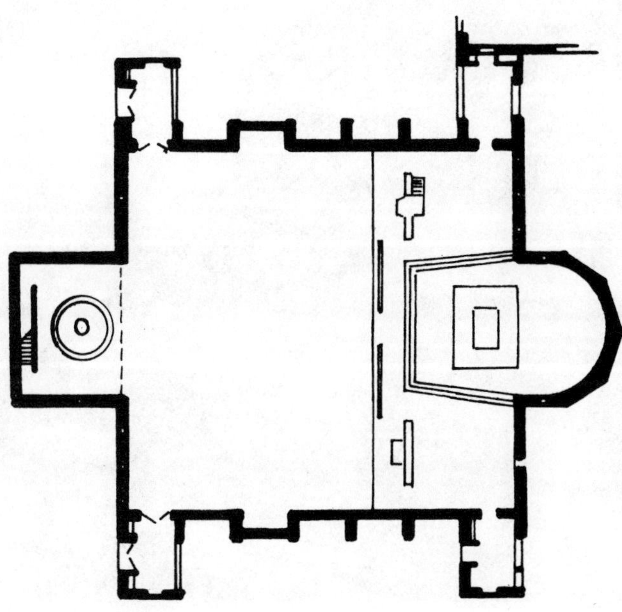

Fig. 19 Siegburg St Joseph, Germany

In some modern Anglican churches the mediaeval disposition continues; in others the baptistery is combined with the porch, while in others again the idea of the *Prinzipalstück* is being reproduced with the font inside or close to the sanctuary (*see* Plate 20). This last arrangement, which was for centuries the Lutheran norm, has now commended itself to many Calvinists and is frequent in Holland, but in some recent Lutheran designs the font is actually at the rear of the congregation in mediaeval style and occasionally within its own baptistery (*see* Plate 21 and Fig. 19). Within the Free Churches the *Prinzipalstück* has been widely accepted, while the Baptists necessarily give prominence to the font, to which they apply the term baptistery, by placing it at the sanctuary end, although since it is for submersion and so below floor level, it is covered and so lost to sight except when actually in use.

Plate 21 St Andrew, Malmö, Sweden

As we look to the future, it may be said that past history and the understanding of the nature of baptism suggests three principles to be observed. These are 1. the need to make provision for congregational participation; 2. the need to give the setting a visual importance that accords with the celebration of the first gospel sacrament; 3. the need to devise a shape and décor that conveys some of the meaning of the rite. Clearly these can be applied in a variety of ways and no one can say that there is any single correct solution.

See also **Baptism**.

J. G. Davies, *The Architectural Setting of Baptism*, 1962; A. Khatchatrian, *Origine et typologie des baptistères paléochrétiens*, 1982.

EDITOR

Basilica

The basilica is an early form of church building derived from pagan prototypes (*see* **Architectural Setting**). Although initially there were many varieties, from the late fourth century four main types may be distinguished.

1. *Roman or Latin*. Its main characteristics were: (*a*) a projecting apse*; (*b*) an architrave or continuous beam supported on the abacus of each column; (*c*) a covered porch; (*d*) an atrium*; (*e*) a transept* – although this is also found in the second type.

2. *Hellenistic*. Its main characteristics were: (*a*) the apse was polygonal on the outside or was flanked by side chambers which, especially in Syria were contained within one wall to preserve the rectangular shape; (*b*) archivolts, i.e. arches linking the columns; (*c*) galleries over the aisles for the women; (*d*) there was often but not invariably an atrium; (*e*) transepts were included in Greece and the adjoining lands, but in North Africa no examples are known and only one in Palestine and one in Syria; (*f*) a narthex* was attached (*see* Fig. 20).

3. *Oriental*, also known as the barn or hall church (*Hallenkirche*), originating in Mesopotamia and found in Anatolia, Armenia, Crete, Cyprus and Greece. In plan, it is indistinguishable from the previous one (*see* Fig. 20), but it differed in elevation, in that the walls of the nave were not carried up above the roofs of the aisles

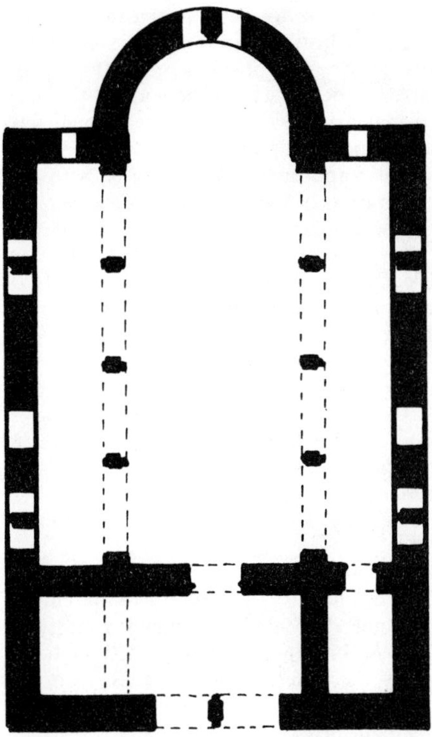

Fig. 20 Church No. 4, Bin Bir Kilisse, Turkey

to form a clerestory. Hence its characteristics are: (*a*) a blind nave; (*b*) windows in the apse and aisles; (*c*) no atrium; (*d*) a narthex; (*e*) it was usually vaulted.

4. *Transverse*. This is a primitive Mesopotamian form found in Armenia, Cappadocia, the Hauran and the Tur Abdin. It consisted of a single nave at right angles to the line connecting the entrance door with the apse.

Under the impact of the modern Liturgical Movement* in its somewhat archaeological phase, a number of churches were built in the twentieth century which reproduce the basilica plan.

EDITOR

Basilican Position

see **Posture** 2

Bells

The earliest church bells used to announce services were made of thin sheets of an alloy of copper and tin, bent into a quadrangular shape and riveted together. They were not fixed to a building but carried by a handle and struck with a mallet. Some, used by missionary saints such as Patrick, were later venerated and housed in metal shrines. Later bells have always been cast.

Traditionally the introduction of bells fixed to church buildings is ascribed to Paulinus of Nola, *c.*400, but the first solid evidence is provided by Gregory of Tours, *c.*585. According to Bede the first such bells in England were introduced from Italy *c.*680, and Abbot Turketul gave a peal of seven to Croyland Abbey in the eighth century. From the ninth century onwards they were increasingly hung in bell-towers. The invention of the clapper enabled them to be rung by means of a rope from below, though the custom of striking the bell by hand survived in parts of Europe until quite recent times. Although bells first became general in monasteries, their use in parish churches is attested by the Capitulary of Charlemagne in 802.

In the Middle Ages bells were chimed by pulling a rope attached to the spindle on which the bell hung, but the gradual introduction of the wheel and the slide, which enabled the bell to rest in the upside-down position until required to sound again, led to the development in the seventeenth century of the peculiarly English art of change-ringing. On the continent, especially in the Low Countries, chimes and carillons were developed instead. These are stationary bells rung by levers operated mechanically or by hand.

In the Middle Ages it was the custom to baptize new bells in the name of the Trinity in a ceremony involving unction* and washing with salt water. The prayers in this service reflected the belief that bells could guard against storm damage to the church and also drive away evil spirits. When the last part of the new *Rituale Romanum* was issued in 1984, a fresh Order for the Blessing of Bells was authorized. This omits unction and washing and all references to demonology. The bells are sprinkled with holy water and then censed; the prayers strongly emphasize that the function of bells is to call to worship, although they may mark other occasions in people's lives. In the Reformed churches a simple dedication ceremony is generally used instead, but bells still often bear names.

Belief in the power of bells to drive away

evil spirits was reflected in the use of the passing bell, tolled when a parishioner was dying. It was followed by the death knell, still sometimes used, in the form either of a single tolling bell or of a muffled peal. Bells are still sometimes rung for baptisms and frequently for weddings, and in Roman Catholic countries the angelus is still rung three times a day. Backward peals, ringing from tenor to treble, were formerly used as alarms.

The sacring or sanctus bell was used in the Middle Ages, as it still is in the Eastern Orthodox rite, to mark the beginning of various parts of the liturgy. The most important of these moments is the Elevation of the Host, and the ringing of a bell at this point has survived also in the West. Though the sacring bell was often small and hand-held, sanctus bell turrets survive on the chancel gables of a number of English mediaeval churches.

F. Cabrol-H. Leclerq, *DACL*; S. M. Coleman, *Bells, their history, legends, making and use*, 1928; *Rituale Romanum: De Benedictionibus*, 1984; H. B. Walters, *The Church Bells of England*, 1913.

G. D. W. RANDALL

Benediction

A Roman Catholic service with the reserved sacrament, benediction seems to have derived from two different liturgical sources, the liturgy of the hours and the Corpus Christi* procession. From at least the tenth century it had been customary to conclude the divine office with a Marian hymn or anthem, known as *laude* in Italy, *salut* in France. In the fourteenth century solemnity was often added to these evening devotions by exposing the blessed sacrament in a monstrance* and blessing the people with it at the end. This closely parallels a custom, first recorded in Germany in the fourteenth century, of interrupting and concluding the Corpus Christi procession with a solemn blessing of the people with the monstrance. Later in that century, similar processions concluding with benediction were found on the occasion of other major feasts, civic celebrations and secular crises.

These origins suggest that benediction was not originally an independent ritual but served as a solemn conclusion to another liturgy. This situation is still reflected in the post-tridentine *Roman Ritual* of 1614, where it is never referred to as an independent liturgy. The Sacred Congregation of Rites (established 1588 to regulate liturgy) was constantly cautious and restrictive in its regulations, and was generally reluctant to provide official rites for it. (It was not until 1958 that the SCR explicitly affirmed that benediction is a 'true liturgical function'.) The model (for Corpus Christi) in the 1614 Ritual consisted of an incensation, the *Tantum ergo* stanzas from the hymn *Pange lingua*, the Corpus Christi collect, and the blessing of the people with the monstrance in the form of a cross. From the seventeenth to the twentieth centuries this basic format was expanded in unofficial publications and practice with further hymns (e.g. *O salutaris hostia*), prayers, litanies and acclamations.

In early nineteenth-century Britain benediction was often celebrated as the conclusion of Sunday vespers, but with the spread of 'continental' devotions in the middle of the century it became more often attached to a devotional evening service of rosary and sermon, and was itself often accompanied by litanies and other Marian devotions and, at the end of the century, by the set of acclamations known as the 'divine praises'. With the introduction and spread of evening mass since the 1950s, the frequency and popularity of benediction, with or without other devotions, has declined sharply in most parishes, though it continues in revised form in most religious houses.

The revised *Roman Ritual* (1973) classifies and regulates benediction as a 'brief exposition', governed by the same theological principles and broad liturgical guidelines as exposition*. The reformed rite consists of four stages: 1. exposition of the sacrament in a monstrance or ciborium* on the table of the altar (no longer on a 'throne' or pedestal) and its incensation; 2. a period of adoration including scripture reading, prayer, song and silent worship; a homily may be given; this period concludes with a eucharistic hymn (*Tantum ergo* is no longer mandatory), incensation and a collect at choice; 3. the minister puts on a humeral veil (*see* **Vestments** 2[*j*]) and blesses the congregation with the monstrance in silence; 4. while the sacrament is taken back to the tabernacle*, the people may sing or say an acclamation. Any Marian prayers or

anthems may follow only after the sacrament has been returned to the tabernacle. Exposition may not be held simply for the purpose of giving benediction.

N. Mitchell, *Cult and Controversy: The Worship of the Eucharist outside Mass*, 1982.

C. J. WALSH

Benedictus

See **Anaphora** 3; **Canticles**; **Music in the Mass of the Roman Rite**; **Ordinary**

Bible Services

In the Roman Catholic Church these services are the fruit of the Liturgical Movement* and the biblical revival of more recent years and they received official recognition in the *Constitution on the Liturgy* (35.[4]) of the Second Vatican Council.

They remain a free form of service, may be conducted by a lay person, though where, for want of an ordained minister they replace the mass, it is recommended that they follow the order of the ministry of the word in the new *Ordo Missae*.

They consist of three main elements, the reading of God's word, homily or homilies on it, the response of the people by word, song or silence and intercessions or other forms of prayer.

The Council saw them as a useful means of giving the people a deeper appreciation of holy scripture and strongly urged that the clergy should organize such services especially during the great seasons of the year, such as Lent and Advent, and as vigils of preparation before the greater feasts.

These services are much used in informal groups of laity, and in those parts of the church where there is a lack of ordained ministers they are used (and must be used) as a preparation before communion from the reserved sacrament.

Instruction for Implementing the Liturgical Constitution (37–39); commentary 'Bible Services' by Edmund Jones OSB in *The Liturgy and the Future* ed J. D. Crichton, 1966.

J. D. CRICHTON

Bible, Use of in Worship

The Bible of the early church was the OT in its Septuagint (i.e. Greek) version. Following the practice of the synagogue, passages from it were read out in the course of Christian worship along with a sermon. This formed part of the first half of the eucharist*, known variously as the ministry of the word, the synaxis* and the mass of the catechumens*. To these lections were added Christian writings from documents believed to be of apostolic authorship, and eventually collected into an authoritative canon of scripture. These readings were eventually brought together in several books, the gospels in the 'evangelarium', the epistles in the 'epistolarium', the psalms in the 'psalterium', the OT lections in the 'lectionarium' (*see* **Books, Liturgical** 3). Even after the production in the sixth century of MSS copies of the entire Bible, separate volumes continued in use for convenience. Meanwhile the daily office was developed (*see* **Canonical Hours**), the scripture readings being controlled by a lectionary*.

The invention of printing, and the production of more manageable complete Bibles did not greatly affect former practice. The Orthodox Churches still have several volumes, while the Roman Catholic Church has grouped the mass lections in the missal, and the office readings in the breviary. The churches of the Anglican communion print the OT readings, epistles and gospels in full, but provide only tables of lessons for morning and evening prayer. Other churches (e.g. the Church of Scotland, of South India, the Methodist and Presbyterian Churches) give tables for all lections so that the complete Bible is in regular use.

In the Church of England the Bible usually remains permanently on the lectern, although in the seventeenth and eighteenth centuries it was common for copies of the Bible and the BCP to stand upright at the back of the altar. In the French Reformed Church it lies open continually on the holy table. In the Church of Scotland it is carried in at the beginning of a service. The Bible is used as a liturgical object in the gospel procession, the little entrance* and in ordinations*.

In this century liturgical revision has affected the use of the Bible at the eucharist. In the revised liturgies of the Roman Catholic, Anglican and other Churches the biblical readings have been increased by the addition of an OT lesson to the epistle and gospel (all read in a modern translation), often with a psalm and canticle provided

together with a generous sprinkling of isolated sentences, the readings following a two or three year cycle, and held together by a common theme. Many have welcomed these changes, but others have objected that the new rites have been produced with too little consultation with contemporary theologians, and still less regard for two hundred years of careful biblical criticism.

It is argued that, at a time when ignorance of the Bible has never been greater, and the problems posed by it never been so serious, the new rites are so heavily biblical that no place is left for enrichment and clarification from non-biblical sources. Little trace can be found in them of the fundamental (and sometimes creative) changes in theological perspective occasioned by the combined effects of criticism and scientific discovery, nor of the principle that biblical texts must be seen in their historical and cultural context, nor of the growing conviction that the world view of the biblical writers was in almost every respect widely different from our own, thus precluding any direct application of the text to our times. Also the new rites are said to emphasize God's alleged acts from the distant past to the virtual exclusion of his presence now. Their Christo-centricity is claimed to be aggressive and obsessional. As for the biblical images, there seems little sign of any serious attempt to consider whether these still carry resonance, intelligibility or relevance. Nor is there any serious attempt to *give* them such resonance or relevance. Instead they are presented in so bald, stark and prosaic a way, and with so little selectivity, that a fundamentalist interpretation is invited, as it is also by the words 'This is the word of the Lord' after each reading. Those who are critical of the new rites are not suggesting that biblical words and images should *not* be used, nor that modern (and possibly ephemeral) imagery should be in a wholesale fashion substituted, but rather that the revisers show an alarming insensitivity to the problems and the opportunities which are presented by biblical criticism and contemporary thought.

In answer to this the supporters of the new rites claim that biblical language is *sui generis* and irreplacable, and that the images used are of an archetypal and universal potency; that the critics do not offer alternatives; that the incorporation of modern theological insights into liturgy is impractical; that the critics betray an inadequate doctrine of the inspiration of scripture; that a freer and more selective use of the images will lead not to a re-interpretation but to a *change* of doctrine; and that in any case the alleged popularity of the new services gives the lie to their detractors.

In conclusion the polarization between critics and supporters need not be complete. The critics do not deny that many of the biblical words and images must still be used in liturgy. The supporters seem prepared to agree that *some* of the images need to be changed to meet changing contexts and cultures, and that they must in any case be handled sensitively and responsibly. Some hope that at the next full-scale revision of the liturgy the Bible will be used more realistically and imaginatively than is the case at present.

C. Byworth (ed), *Using the Bible in Worship*, 1977.

T. G. A. BAKER

Bidding Prayer

The element of intercession* in the eucharistic rites of the Western church has been variable. The Good Friday *orationes solemnes* of the Roman rite survive as the only example of the earliest known form of the prayers of the faithful at the beginning of the mass of the faithful. In the sixth century their place was taken by a litany* of Eastern origin, found among the introductory material in the rite, and the *kyries* survive as a relic of this litany. When the litany fell out of use after about a century, the element of intercession virtually disappeared from the Western liturgy, apart from the brief prayers for the living and the dead in the canon of the mass, until the bidding of the bedes appeared in the unofficial vernacular element in the Latin rite known as the prone. The prone is an example of a measure of pastoral concern in the Middle Ages, and was a vernacular passage in the course of the mass consisting of a sermon, which was preceded or followed by the bidding of the bedes, notices, and instruction in the Decalogue, the Lord's Prayer, and similar formularies. The word 'bid' in Anglo-Saxon means 'pray', and the 'bidding of the bedes' means

the 'praying of the prayers': cf. 'Ye shulle stonde up and bydde your bedys . . .' in a fourteenth-century example of the bidding prayer which was used at Worcester. In its earlier and better examples the prayer covered the full range of matters for intercession, the church, the state, the departed, and all men in their various callings: it was flexible and gave scope to the initiative of the celebrant. With the passage of time it became formalized, and at the time of the Reformation, when such freedom was not acceptable, precise forms were laid down, as appears in Canon 55 of 1604. The canon lays down that the bidding prayer shall be said before sermons, although so far as the sermon at the eucharist is concerned this seems pointless, since the prayer book since 1549 has restored the provision for intercession which the old rite lacked. Canon B19 of 1967 leaves the bidding prayer optional. The association between the sermon and the intercessions which is found in the liturgical forms of some of the Reformed churches is probably derived from their association in the prone. In the Roman Catholic Church today the missal provides for intercessions after the creed and these are commonly known as bidding prayers.

F. E. Brightman, *The English Rite*, 1921; H. O. C(oxe), *Forms of Bidding Prayer*, 1840.

E. C. WHITAKER

Bishop

The highest order in the traditional pattern of the ministry, though there was a mediaeval view that bishops are not to be reckoned as an order entirely separate and distinct from the priesthood but are merely priests with additional powers and functions. This view arose from contemporary eucharistic theology which stressed the importance of the sacrament as a sacrifice and made it difficult to imagine an order of ministry higher than the priesthood. NT evidence is not entirely clear, but there are passages which suggest that originally the terms 'bishop' (*episcopos*, overseer) and presbyter* were interchangeable (Acts 20.17–28). It has been widely assumed that the early Christian communities were governed by colleges of elders, as Jewish synagogues were, and that in the course of time a monarchial episcopate developed. Disagreement about when and how this happened is notorious. It is possible that the need to have a liturgical president (like the ruler of the synagogue) may have contributed to the process. By the time of Ignatius of Antioch it was possible to claim that the presence of the bishop or his authorized representative was essential for the eucharist*, and in Cyprian's writings the same argument is further developed. But by this later date the process of delegation had had to be taken further. In earlier days the presbyters had been associated with the bishop in his liturgical as well as his governmental function. They had a place if not a separate liturgical activity and were gathered round the bishop as he celebrated. But by the middle of the third century it was evidently no longer possible for the Christian community in the larger centres to assemble in a single congregation. Presbyters were given authority to take charge of separate districts and there to preside over celebrations of the eucharist. There is evidence for this in Rome and Carthage and in rural areas. But the bishop remained in theory the chief minister in all sacramental acts. Ordination and confirmation* remained in some sense the bishop's special prerogative, though not in quite the absolute sense that has sometimes been suggested. There is some evidence that persons not in episcopal orders have on rare and extraordinary occasions been authorized by the papacy to ordain. And in the East confirmation is administered by the priest at the same time as baptism*, using chrism that has been blessed by the bishop.

At the Reformation the office of bishop was retained by Anglicans and some Lutherans. In some cases it was the intention to retain the historic succession (e.g. in England and Sweden), in other cases it was deliberately not so (e.g. in Denmark). The *Unitas Fratrum* (Moravians) also preserved the episcopal order and claim an unbroken succession through the Bohemian Brethren, but they have not always regarded the laying on of the bishop's hands as necessary for ordination. In some parts of the Methodist Church the title is used, particularly in America where Thomas Coke introduced it, having been set apart by John Wesley as superintendent of Methodist work there. Methodist bishops have the power of appointing ministers and exercise a pastoral

and disciplinary oversight over them. They also perform all ordinations but not confirmations. In the third decade of the twentieth century German Lutherans adopted the title for the majority of those ministers who had been called superintendents up to that date. In the united churches formed by the reunion of separate denominations in the Indian subcontinent bishops are an order of the ministry and all ordinations are performed by them, though confirmation is not necessarily an episcopal act. Most reunion proposals of the second half of the twentieth century have included provision for an episcopally ordered ministry.

K. M. Carey (ed), *The Historic Episcopate*, 1954; R. P. Johnson, *The Bishop in the Church*, 1966; K. E. Kirk, *The Apostolic Ministry*, 1946; G. Simon, *Bishops*, 1961; W. Telfer, *The Office of a Bishop*, 1962.

P. HINCHLIFF

Blessing

1. A blessing is an authoritative declaration of divine favour addressed to persons. It is used liturgically: (*a*) Immediately before the act of communion*. Although not primitive, this was customary in all eucharistic rites by the end of the fourth century, being an encouragement and preparation for those about to communicate. It assumed elaborate forms in the Gallican rite and survives in the ritual of the Church of Lyons. It was omitted from the Roman rite *c.*500, and no post-Reformation order has retained it. (*b*) At the end of the eucharist. Although not prescribed in the missals, this became customary in the late Middle Ages, and probably derived from the blessing by the bishop of his flock as he went out. This mediaeval feature has been perpetuated in most reformed rites (except the Zwinglian), with the Aaronic form (Num. 6.24–26) appearing in the Lutheran, Calvinist and derived orders, and Phil. 4.7, with the mediaeval episcopal blessing as the second half, in the Anglican and most British churches. (*c*) During the eucharist and other services, e.g. the blessing of the deacon who is to sing the gospel and of the penitent about to make confession. (*d*) Frequently at the end of other services, e.g. the Sunday service of the Free Churches, confirmation in the BCP, etc.

2. A blessing can also be a verbal formula for the sanctification of objects, which include the water at baptism, oil for exorcism or for the anointing of the sick (*see* **Unction**), the Paschal candle*, etc.

EDITOR

Blessing of Children

Baptists and other Protestant congregations who baptize only believers have long recognized that there is a deep need in parents to acknowledge the gift God has made them in the birth of their child. The earliest Baptists, taking as their example Christ's blessing of children in the gospel story, brought their newly-born infants to the assembly of believers to be blessed. With the blessing the parents dedicated themselves to the Christian upbringing of their offspring – hence the title, 'service of dedication'.

While the form of this service was usually dictated by local custom, prayers for such occasions have been published by Baptists from time to time. In a modern version, published in *Praise God*, compiled by Alec Gilmore, Edward Smalley and Michael Walker (1981), the parents promise that they will bring their child up 'in the spirit of the gospel'. The child is named. The members of the congregation affirm that they will 'always stand by him in friendship'. Finally, the child is solemnly blessed. It is a sign of the ecumenical times that this particular service of dedication is remarkably like a liturgy of infant baptism in other churches – without, of course, the administration of the sacrament.

While Baptists have thus been moving closer to paedobaptists, some paedobaptists have been questioning the practice of widespread infant baptism. In the years since the Second World War, increasing numbers of Anglicans have argued that it is inappropriate for parents who have little contact with the church to make promises about the Christian upbringing of their children, and some parish priests began offering them services of blessing and thanksgiving instead. Chelmsford was the first diocese in England to adopt this practice officially in 1968.

In these years, too, the churching of women* fell into disuse. Prayer book language about 'the great pain and peril of childbirth' and the somewhat gloomy character of the rite seemed depressing on what

should be a joyful occasion. There was an obvious need for the church to make provision for an expression of thanksgiving when children were born.

To meet these pastoral requirements the Church of England's Liturgical Commission included in the Alternative Service Book 1980 a 'Thanksgiving for the Birth of a Child'.

The rite is designed to be inserted into the normal Sunday worship of the congregation. The underlying note is one of joy and gratitude not only for the birth of the child but also for the family's share in God's creative activity. The parents pray together, 'Make us patient and understanding, that our child may always be sure of our love.' Psalm 100 is recited ('Know that the Lord he is God: it is he who has made us and we are his'). Mark 10.13–16 is read ('Let the children come to me'). Various prayers are said for the child and the family, and the rite concludes with a solemn blessing pronounced over the child.

Although this rite was provided for the pastoral circumstances just described, its liturgical status is one of looking forward to the later initiation of the child in the church. This comes out clearly in one of the final prayers said by the whole congregation: 'God our Father, we pray for this child, that in due time he may be received by baptism into the family of your church, and become an inheritor of your kingdom; through Jesus Christ our Lord. Amen.'

What it does in effect is to reintroduce the catechumenate* into the Anglican Church. If the baptism, confirmation and first communion of these children is postponed until later years, then their relationship to the Christian community is one of 'learners' or 'hearers' – catechumens who are being prepared for their initiation into the church.

J. D. Crichton, *Christian Celebration: the Sacraments*, 1973, pp.40–64; R. C. D. Jasper (ed), *The Alternative Service Book 1980: A Commentary*, 1980, pp.99–104; Michael Walker, *Infant Dedication*, 1981.

JOHN GUNSTONE

Blessing of a Marriage

The gradual secularization of Western Europe and North America has produced two major problems for the churches' practice of marriage. The first arises in countries where a civil ceremony of marriage is either obligatory regardless of whether a church service is to follow (e.g. France), and in areas where the civil ceremony is slowly taking over as the norm as a result of the churches' receding influence over people even for 'rites of passage'. A further variant of this tendency arises when the couple come to a firm Christian commitment after their marriage in law, and wish to ritualize this faith. The official Roman Catholic and Reformed provision is that of a full-blown marriage service, with consent, blessing, and (where appropriate) eucharist. However, several provinces of the Anglican communion have issued official services for the 'Benediction of Married Persons' (Scottish Prayer Book, 1929), which vary somewhat from one province to another. The Scottish example opens with a short exhortation, on the indissolubility of marriage, the consent of the partners (passively given, i.e. not the 'active' vow), followed by the *preces* and marriage prayers from the second part of the full marriage rite.

The second problem, that of marriage after divorce, has been increasingly dealt with in a similar way by various Anglican provinces, namely, a service of blessing at some time following the civil ceremony. But both the context and the form differ. For example, some dioceses of the Church of England have forbidden music, and other expressions of joyful liturgy, in order to prevent the service resembling the full marriage liturgy; other dioceses permit a celebration of the eucharist, which is particularly appropriate when the couple have a serious Christian faith. The forms of prayer may resemble the Scottish order of 1929, or else that of South Africa (1954), which has no form of consent, but an acknowledgement of marriage by law, by each of the partners. These rites show the apparent conflict between the Christian ideal of life-long commitment, and the easy way in which civil ceremonies can be arranged. The American Book of Common Prayer has forms for the Celebration of Christian Marriage (the full rite) as well as the Blessing (after a civil ceremony), but this latter is normally used when the couple have undergone the civil rite by choice (or, previously, through lack of conscious

Christian conviction), since the full marriage rite is usually permitted when one (or both) of the partners has been divorced and the previous partner is still living. The Church of England, unique in the Anglican Communion for being established by law, has wrestled with divorce and second marriage for several years. The 1978 Report, 'Marriage and the Church's Task', recommended that services of blessing should cease, and that the full service should be permitted, with a new preface to the marriage liturgy. However, after synodical debate, and widespread dissension, a set of 'Services of Prayer and Dedication after Civil Marriage' was produced by the Liturgical Commission (1984), which can be used in conjunction with the eucharist; which may include a penitential section (cf. Orthodox practice); but which begin with a statement to the effect that the service is not a marriage. Such a compromise may commend itself to indissolubilists and others, but it is becoming apparent that the Church of England is slowly following other Provinces of the Anglican Communion in making the double provision of full marriage and blessing of marriage, to meet increasingly varied circumstances. To refuse a full service because of a divorce but to allow such a second-class rite is, in the eyes of many, unsatisfactory, particularly in view of Roman Catholic, Lutheran, and Reformed Church procedures, which may permit the full marriage liturgy.

Kenneth Stevenson, *Nuptial Blessing: A Study of Christian Marriage Rites*, 1982.

KENNETH STEVENSON

Blind People and Worship

Corporate worship is an activity in which people who are visually handicapped in every degree should be encouraged to participate in a meaningful way to the fullest possible extent. In one respect, lack of sight can actually be an advantage for personal devotion, because it removes some of the superficial hindrances – the distractions caused by other people and the vagaries of officiants. Lack of sight does not of itself make for better concentration on God, but it can function in just the same way as shutting the eyes in prayer. Nor does blindness seem to diminish the aura of ancient and hallowed buildings. The effectiveness of music and the words of the liturgy are if anything heightened. The unique smell of a church at harvest festival and the smell of incense for those accustomed to it retain their powerful evocations.

The experience of *koinonia* need not and should not be decreased by lack of sight. Blind people are as capable of creating friendships, acquaintanceships and enjoying good company as anybody else. The nexus of relationships within a congregation should therefore be of immense supportive value. If it is not so, there is cause for serious questioning. The kiss of peace (*see* **Gestures** 8) is a detail of the service of especial value; and it should not be forgotten that there is a wide range of practical activities in which a blind person may become involved. There is no intrinsic reason why a blind person should not serve at the altar, sing in the choir, read a lection or prayers, become a church officer – just as there have been a great many effective blind clergymen and church organists.

It is of course the duty of a congregation to ensure that blind and other handicapped people are able to reach and enter the building where services are held. The vast increase in the volume of traffic makes the problems of mobility horrendous, even for the small minority with modern aids like guide dogs and the long cane. Besides, 80% of blind people are elderly.

The largest single practical difficulty for the blind participating in worship is the availability – or rather, non-availability – of reading material in raised type. Some of the earliest efforts to produce books in Braille were motivated by the desire to enable blind people to read the scriptures for themselves. Until recently the standard English braille code included abbreviations for God, Lord, Jesus and Christ. In regular production today are the AV, RV, RSV, NEB New Testament, the Greek New Testament and the Hebrew Old Testament, the last named being produced by the Jewish Braille authorities. Other versions in whole or part have been produced in small numbers. The impetus to produce a variety of hymnals and psalters in Braille has come not least from the needs of blind musicians. The whole of the Book of Common Prayer has long been available, many of the services being edited in such a way as to facilitate their use in conducting or follow-

ing public worship.

At the time of Vatican II, a bi-lingual Sunday missal was in course of production with the Ordinary in one Braille volume with a slot in its cover into which the Proper for each Sunday might be placed. The English rite replacing the missal is available in Braille.

The Anglican Alternative Service Book is presenting a formidable problem. It is a very large book with its own psalter and a wealth of lections and many alternatives within particular services. A number of specific ASB offices are in course of production, but Braille production availability is severely limited, and a further difficulty is of course the great bulkiness of Braille. An officiant, who knows exactly which psalms, lessons and prayers he will need, can take the appropriate volumes along with him to church, but a layperson does not have this advantage.

I know of a blind Roman Catholic priest who has found a novel way round the whole problem of reading-material in church. He pre-records all the liturgical material he will need, and speaks the words aloud as he hears them through an ear-plug.

Within the past few decades, some welcome attention has been given to the needs of a very large group of people previously neglected, the partially-sighted. There is an ever-increasing number of books available in large print; for example, the Rite A Communion Service of the ASB. With present-day printing technology, it ought to be practicable completely to satisfy the requirements of this sector of worshippers.

STEWART LAWTON

Books, Liturgical

Liturgical books are those used in the performance of church services. Both in manuscript and printed form they are an essential source of information for the worshipping practice of any group of believers.

1. *The Early Church.* Since liturgical prayer was largely extempore until the early third century, the only books required were rolls of the scriptures. In time, however, there were produced the church orders, a series of documents, claiming apostolic authority, which contained both liturgical prescriptions and also rules for the life of the congregation. The earliest extant example is the *Didache* or *Teaching of the Twelve Apostles*, probably a product of the second century. There followed the *Apostolic Tradition* of Hippolytus, *c*.217, the *Didascalia*, *c*.250, the *Apostolic Church Order*, *c*.250, the *Apostolic Constitutions*, *c*.375, and the *Testament of Our Lord*, *c*.400.

In addition to these general handbooks, individual bishops made their own compilations, e.g. the prayer book of Serapion of Thmuis, *c*.350, containing prayers for the eucharist*, baptism*, ordination*, the blessing of oils and a commendation of the dead. With the elaboration of the liturgy and the acceptance of stereotyped forms, numerous service books eventually became necessary.

EDITOR

2. *Orthodox.* (More properly, Byzantine.) The service books at present in use in the Byzantine rite are as follows:

(*a*) *The Euchologion* (Greek, 'book of prayers') contains those parts of the sacraments and other services, together with many occasional offices and blessings, which are required by the officiating ministers (bishop, priest and deacon). It exists in two forms, in addition to which excerpts from it are often printed separately, individually or in combination.

The Great Euchologion (Greek, *euchologion to mega*) normally contains:

(i) The fixed parts, or ordinary, of vespers, matins, the eucharistic liturgy, and the liturgy of the presanctified, the priest's part being given in full, and those of deacon, reader and singers usually in an abbreviated form.

(ii) The six remaining sacraments, namely: baptism, with a number of related offices; chrismation or confirmation (which forms an integral part of the baptismal rites); ordination; confession; marriage; and the anointing of the sick. A more complete text of these is provided in most editions, the deacon's, reader's and singers' parts not being so readily available elsewhere as those of the services in the preceding group.

(iii) Other occasional offices, some of which in the West would be called sacramentals (although the Byzantine books do not distinguish liturgically between sacraments and sacramentals so rigidly as do those of the West), such as the various services connected with monastic profession, the consecration of a church, the greater and lesser blessing of holy water,

and so forth; and others such as the various rites connected with the burial of the dead.

(iv) A large number of offices for the particular blessing of persons and things.

The Small Euchologion (Greek, *mikron euchologion*, or *agiasmatarion*, 'book of blessings') omits the whole of the first group of services listed above, and also those rites, such as ordination and the consecration of a church, which appertain specifically to the bishop; it contains the five remaining sacraments, the funeral offices, and those occasional offices and blessings most commonly required. Some editions do add the priest's part of the major daily offices and the liturgy.

The Liturgikon (Greek, 'book of the liturgy') or *Hieratikon* or *Hierotelestikon* (Greek, 'book for the priest') is an altar book, containing the priest's, and in some editions also the deacon's, part at vespers, matins and the liturgy, together with related supplementary matter, the extent and arrangement of which differ from one edition to another.

The Archieratikon (Greek, 'book for the bishop') corresponds to the Western pontifical, and contains services and blessings either reserved to or most commonly performed by the bishop. Some editions use *Hieratikon* as the title of this book and not of that considered in the preceding note.

The next group of books, seven in number, is concerned principally, although not exclusively, with the divine office.

(*b*) *The Horologion* (Greek, 'book of hours') is a book for the use of readers and singers, just as the *Euchologion* is for the use of priest and deacon. Its fuller form, the *Great Horologion* (Greek, *horologion to mega*) includes:

(i) The ordinary, or fixed part, of the daily offices, namely, nocturns, matins, the lesser hours (prime, terce, sext, none), vespers and compline (*see* **Canonical Hours**); together with graces before and after meals. The reader's and singers' parts are given in full; most of the priest's and deacon's parts is omitted.

(ii) A list of feasts and saints' days throughout the year, for each of which a short account of the feast or the life of the saint is given, together with certain of the principal anthems appointed for the day.

(iii) A similar section, covering Sundays and movable feasts, within the periods of the *Triodion* and *Pentekostarion* (*see below*).

(iv) The common principal anthems for the days of the week.

(v) A miscellany of other services related to the divine office and in frequent use.

All the lesser hours can be recited in full from the *Great Horologion*. But a number of other books are required for vespers and mattins, books containing the proper texts which change from day to day. These volumes contain the material of the three cycles which together constitute the Byzantine liturgical year: (i) the weekly cycle, contained in the *Oktoechos*; (ii) the annual cycle of movable feasts, contained in the *Triodion* and *Pentekostarion*; (iii) the annual cycle of fixed feasts, contained in the *Menaia*.

(*c*) *The Oktoechos* (Greek, 'book of the eight tones'), also known as the *Parakletike* (Greek, 'book of supplication'), contains the variable parts of the daily offices through the week. Eight series of offices are provided, one for each of the eight tones of Byzantine chant *, and each series comprises seven sets of services, one for each day of the week. The eight tones are used in sequence, week by week, through the year, beginning with the first tone on the Sunday after Easter. The texts contained in the *Oktoechos* are combined, when appropriate, with those for fixed feasts contained in the *Menaia*. The *Oktoechos* is used in Lent only on Saturdays and Sundays, and it is not used at all from the Saturday preceding Psalm Sunday until the Sunday after Pentecost, any material from it which is used during these seasons being repeated in full in the proper seasonal books. An edition of the *Oktoechos* for Sundays only also exists.

(*d*) *The Triodion* (Greek, 'book of the three odes', from the circumstance that for most days it provides only three proper odes or canticles for matins) contains the propers for Lent.

(*e*) *The Pentekostarion* (Greek, 'book of the fifty days') contains the services proper to Eastertide and Pentecost.

(*f*) *The Menaia* (Greek, 'books of the months') contain the propers of fixed feasts throughout the year; most editions are divided into twelve volumes, one for each month. Various combinations of excerpts from the *Menaia* are also published.

(*g*) *The Eirmologion* (Greek, 'book of the *eirmoi*') contains the texts of the anthems

known as *eirmoi* which are sung at the beginnings of the odes or canticles of matins. The major books listed above commonly give only the opening words of these, assuming, apparently, that the reader will know them by heart; hence the need for the *Eirmologion*.

The next group of books comprises three volumes, the *Evangelion*, the *Apostolos*, and the *Psalterion*.

(*h*) *The Evangelion* (Greek, 'book of the gospels') contains the text of the four gospels; in some editions the text is printed continuously, the lessons to be read on particular days being noted in the margins, or in some similar way, while in others the text is arranged in the order required for liturgical use, the latter being the more common arrangement. The *evangelion* is treated with great reverence: it is usually bound in a cover decorated with silver or gold, often indeed actually made of silver or gold; when not in use it is usually kept on the altar; it is carried in procession and venerated by the congregation when there is a gospel lesson at matins, and on certain other occasions.

(*i*) *The Apostolos* (Greek, 'book of the apostle') contains the lessons from the Acts of the Apostles and the epistles, together with the *prokeimena* or graduals which are sung before the epistle at the liturgy, and the alleluias which are sung after it.

(*j*) *The Psalterion* (Greek, 'book of psalms') contains the psalms, arranged according to their normal liturgical use, together with the necessary canticles from the OT and NT.

The lessons from the OT are normally included in the appropriate choir book for the day in question – *Triodion*, *Pentekostarion*, or *Menaion*; some editions, however, do include a separate book containing them.

(*k*) *The Synaxarion* (Greek, 'book of the assembly') or *Menologion* (Greek, 'book of remembrance') contains brief lives of the saints, and brief accounts of the mysteries of redemption celebrated on particular days, and is an exact counterpart of the Western martyrology (*see* 3[2] below).

(*l*) *The Typikon* (Greek, 'book of the ordinances') corresponds to the Western *ordo* (in the older sense of a permanent book, not the more recent one of an annual one), and contains the rules and rubrics governing the celebration of services throughout the year. The history of the *Typikon* is extremely involved: that now in use represents a crystallization of liturgical practice in the high Middle Ages, and includes elements of two originally very distinct liturgical traditions within the Byzantine rite, the 'monastic' (*see* **Divine Office, The**) and the 'cathedral' (*see* **Cathedral Office**), which were fused during that period; the Greek-speaking churches now follow a redaction of this *Typikon* dating from no earlier than 1888, and many aspects of modern Russian usage do not antedate the seventeenth century.

From the preceding remarks on the *Typikon* the reader will realize that the Byzantine rite liturgical books described here embody an order of service which is essentially mediaeval, although many of its parts are very much older. It will also have been noticed, however, that whereas in the West the whole division and arrangement of the service books was changed in the mediaeval period, in the Byzantine East the old division and arrangement of the books was retained, notwithstanding the considerable changes of content. There is unfortunately no book in any Western language which deals in detail with either the pre-mediaeval or the post-mediaeval books.

W. JARDINE GRISBROOKE

3. *Mediaeval and Roman Catholic*

(1) *Mediaeval*. This section is concerned with the books used in liturgical worship during the Middle Ages, a period running roughly from the sixth to the thirteenth centuries. Today, the books used for worship in the Roman rite may be numbered as seven: the missal, the breviary, the gradual, the antiphonal, the pontifical, the ritual and the martyrology. In mediaeval times this was not so. The books used in worship were many and complex. C. Vogel has counted as many as a hundred. The reasons for this number and diversity are to be sought in the facts of history. The Middle Ages knew no principles of uniformity in matters liturgical, despite the attempts of pope and emperor. Each ecclesiastical province, each diocese, each monastery had its own liturgical books and rites. Before the thirteenth century, and even as late as the *incunabula* of the fifteenth century, this diversity was widespread. A further reason for this is to be found in the

fact that each minister or celebrant had his own book, and often enough a special book for each rite or ceremony. In the following pages we can treat only the main liturgical books of the period. This may be done under two headings: the mass and the divine office.

(*a*) *The mass*

(i) *The sacramentary.* This was the celebrant's book. It contained all the texts needed for the celebration of the eucharist, the administration of the sacraments, the formularies of blessing, the rites of ordination. Its history is obscure, but it would seem that from the sixth century onwards the compilation of a sacramentary was part and parcel of a bishop's charge. Already in the times of Augustine collections of euchological formularies were being drawn up in Africa and authorized for official use by the local bishop's synod. This was a counter-measure to the many such productions emanating from heretical sects. The sacramentary was preceded by small collections of euchological texts, to which the name *libelli missarum* has been given. The earliest collection of such books would seem to have been gathered together to form the well-known sacramentary preserved in the chapter library of Verona, the *Sacramentarium Veronense*. Other official sacramentaries have come down to us under the names of Gelasius and Gregory the Great. By the thirteenth century each see, each church, each monastery had its own collection of sacramentaries, until the process ended with the production of the missal.

(ii) *The antiphonale missarum.* In origin this book developed from the antiphonal. This latter was a book containing all the sung portions of both the office and the mass. In time the collection became voluminous and the portions were divided into two distinct parts. The material to be used in celebrating the eucharist was called the *antiphonale missarum* or the *graduale*. Ehrensberger divides the book used at mass into *gradualia*, *troparia* and *rotuli paschales*. Bannister added a further division into *kyrialia* and *sequentiaria*. Historically such divisions are justified. Manuscripts of these books are rare, and their contents are found in the graduals.

(iii) *The lectionary.* This book contained the epistles and gospels read at mass. It is found in several forms during its history. Its most perfect form is the *lectionarium missae* containing in full the liturgical pericopes read at mass throughout the liturgical year. In origin this book consisted of a list of references to the Bible. Each reference began with the first and last words of the passage to be read. Such lists were known by different names: *capitulare epistolarum* or *evangeliorum*; *comes* or *liber comitis* or *comicus*. Over the past sixty years the Roman lectionary system has been studied by such scholars as Beissel, Godu, Frere, Hesbert, Klauser, Wilmart, Chavasse, and Gamber.

(iv) *The missal.* This is a book which resulted from the fusion of the above three distinct volumes into one. This fusion, however, was gradual. Its history is not clear, but the book itself appears in MSS from the end of the tenth to the middle of the thirteenth centuries. The evolution seems to have begun with small collections of complete mass formularies within the compass of one volume. This type of book seems to have been a link between the sacramentary and the later *missale plenum*. The Vatican library contains some forty interesting examples.

(*b*) *The divine office*

(i) *The psalter.* At the origins of Christian worship the Bible itself was sufficient for the essential prayer of the church. Once the period of improvisation was over, and the liturgy was celebrated within the bounds of set forms, various books for use in the celebration of the divine office came into being. One of the earliest books to be formed was the psalter. This was a distribution of the psalms for liturgical use over the period of a week or according to feasts. Little by little these psalters attracted additions. From the twelfth century onwards, antiphons and versicles are found written in the margins or between the lines of the psalms. Later other elements of the office were added: invitatories, responds, the opening words of hymns, etc. By the fourteenth century it became the practice to group certain psalms according to the offices celebrated during the day or the week. Thus evolved the liturgical psalter described by V. Leroquais and P. Salmon.

(ii) *The antiphonal.* This book contained the antiphons and responds of the divine office. There are two types, a monastic type, easily recognized by the number of responds

for the celebration of matins (twelve), and the Roman type, containing only nine responds. Normally this book contains the chant for the antiphons and responds, but there are exceptions.

(iii) *The hymnal*. The collection of hymns, used at the celebration of the office, was often combined with the psalter, but there are many MSS which contain the hymns alone.

(iv) *The breviary*. Like the missal, the breviary is the result of the fusion into one volume of the above elements. Like the missal also it was the product of an evolution. Towards the eighth/ninth centuries, the collects used at the office became separated from the sacramentaries, and formed a book of their own, called a *collectarium*. From the eleventh century onwards other elements of the office were added to this book: the calendar, the antiphons, responds, hymns. Later still a description of the office and its celebration was added under the title *Breviarium sive ordo officiorum per totam anni decursionem*. It was only a step to the formation of the breviary. The result of this evolution, and the fusion of four or five distinct books into one volume, was a shortening of the elements of the office, hence the name *breviarium*. The biblical and patristic lessons were no longer read from the Bible or the great tomes of the patristic authors. This was one of the results of the reform begun during the eleventh and twelfth centuries, and ended with that of the office of the Curia under Innocent III. The composition of these breviaries, especially those of the eleventh to twelfth centuries, is highly diverse, and often runs into several volumes.

HENRY ASHWORTH OSB

(2) *Roman Catholic*. By the end of the Middle Ages both liturgical observance and the liturgical books were in a state of disarray. Reform had become necessary; the Council of Trent decreed it and committed the task to the papacy. A small commission, of whose work little is known, produced the liturgical books that were in use until recently. The *Missale Romanum*, 1570, was substantially the same as the first printed missal of 1474, containing the Roman rite as celebrated in the papal chapel in the thirteenth century and as propagated throughout Europe by the Franciscans. Like the *missalia plenaria* of the earlier Middle Ages, it contained the order of mass, the propers* and the lessons to be read at the eucharist. It was prefaced by a long document, *Ritus Servandus*, giving minute directions about the celebration of the mass.

The *Breviarium Romanum*, 1568, giving the offices of the night and day (matins, lauds, prime, terce, sext, none, vespers, and compline – *see* **Canonical Hours**), represented a conservative reform. The offices were long and the form monastic.

To these must be added the *Pontificale Romanum*, 1596, giving the rites celebrated only by a bishop, and the *Rituale Romanum*, 1614, for the administration of baptism, marriage and a great variety of other rites.

Apart from the breviary, which received a newly arranged psalter in 1911, these books remained substantially the same throughout the centuries. New feasts required new propers and there were one or two revisions, notably that of the liturgy of Holy Week in 1955.

The reform of the liturgy decreed by the Second Vatican Council (1963–1965) necessitated a complete revision of all the liturgical books. At the time of writing they are:

Missale Romanum, 1970, containing the order of mass with the four eucharistic prayers, the prefaces (82) and the collects with their corresponding prayers over the offerings and after communion and the entrance and communion verses.

Lectionarium, 1969, containing the course of scripture readings for Sundays (three-year cycle) and weekdays with the responsorial psalms and other texts used in the ministry of the word.

The *Breviary*, now called *The Liturgy of the Hours* (English edition, *The Divine Office*), 1971, is a radical revision of the divine office and is intended for use both by the pastoral clergy and the people.

The *Pontificale Romanum* underwent partial revision in 1961 and further revisions in 1968, 1972 (the rites of ordination) and 1977 (the Dedication of Church).

The radical revision of the *Rituale Romanum* has now been completed. The principal rites are: Baptism (1969), Marriage (1969), Confirmation (1971), Adult Christian Initiation (1972), Pastoral Care and Anointing of the Sick (1972), Penance (1973), Funeral Rites (1969). The

revision of other rites was completed in 1984 with the section *De Benedictionibus*.

Other books used in the Roman rite are the *Martyrology* (last edition, 1956), a list, with brief biographies, of the saints recognized by the Roman Catholic Church; the *Graduale Romanum* (1907, revised edition 1974), giving the plainchant propers for the eucharist for the year, and the *Antiphonale* (*Ordo Cantus Officii*, 1983) giving the plainchant texts for the hours of the divine office. The *Caeremoniale Episcoporum* (1600) contains the rubrical directives for episcopal ceremonies and and has now been revised (1984).

J. D. CRICHTON

4. *Anglican*. The book with the best claim to be called the first Anglican service book is the *Litany* of 1544, which was published under the auspices of 'the King's Majesty and his clergy'. It was followed by *The King's Primer* (1545), *The Book of Homilies* (1547), and *The Order of the Communion* (1548). Each of these, however, presupposed the continuance of the traditional Latin services, and the first book to provide a complete range of reformed services in English was the BCP of 1549. This was a translation and abridgement of the Sarum rite with a strong admixture of Reformed ideas, owing much to the services of the continental Reformers, notably Luther and Bucer. It covers the ground formerly occupied by the breviary, the missal, the manual, and the processional, and was supplemented in 1550 by a set of ordination services, replacing the pontifical. The saying of the daily office requires in addition the use of a Bible, as the psalms and lessons are not printed in full. The other services are self-contained. A music edition by John Marbeck appeared in 1550, as did a French translation for use in the Channel Islands and a very inaccurate translation into Latin.

A revised version was issued in 1552, of a much more definitely Reformed character, though the main outlines of 1549 are retained. It was followed by a similarly reformed *Primer*, but the two books had a life of only a few months before the Roman allegiance was restored under Mary.

On Elizabeth I's accession the book of 1552 was reissued with minor alterations designed to make it slightly less Protestant. The Edwardine *Primer* reappeared, together with three new books of devotion which attempted to reintroduce traditional forms (*Primer*, 1559; *Orarium*, 1560; *Preces Privatae*, 1564). A new Latin translation of the BCP appeared in 1560, followed by a more accurate rendering in 1571; and a Welsh translation was issued in 1567. A second *Book of Homilies* followed in 1563. From 1578 onwards unofficial editions appeared, conforming the book to Puritan ideas.

The accession of James I resulted in further minor changes, this time with an eye to the Puritans. This version appeared in Irish in 1608. Charles I commissioned a book of devotions for the ladies of the court from John Cosin, who took the *Orarium* of 1560 as his model. In 1637 a prayer book was printed for use in Scotland, which reintroduced many of the ideas of 1549 that had been discarded in 1552. Not surprisingly, the book proved completely unacceptable. In 1645 the BCP was banned and was only restored with the return of Charles II in 1660. Despite vigorous demands for revision from both wings of the church, Laudian and Puritan, the book eventually annexed to the Act of Uniformity of 1662 was substantially the book of 1552 with minor ceremonial additions. There were, however, numerous small improvements in the text, and some additional services.

It will be convenient at this point to list the contents of the book, which remained almost unchanged for 300 years. After three prefaces, tables of psalms and lessons, and much calendrical matter, the services included are:

Morning and evening prayer
The litany, prayers, and thanksgivings
Collects, epistles and gospels
Holy communion
Baptism (public, private, and for those of riper years)
Catechism and confirmation
Matrimony
Visitation and communion of the sick
Burial of the dead
Churching of women
Commination
The psalms
Ordination service (deacons, priests and bishops)
Forms of prayer for use at sea
State services

The Psalter, either in the translation of the Great Bible (Coverdale) or in metrical form (Sternhold and Hopkins), had often been bound up with the BCP, but now became an integral part of it; and the same is true of the ordinal. The state services added in 1662 were withdrawn in 1859; an accession service was a normal part of the book from Queen Anne onwards. The Thirty-Nine Articles, though customarily printed at the end of the book, have never formed part of it. There has never been an official music edition; pointed psalters, chant-books and hymnals have been left to private enterprise, though the metrical psalter of Tate and Brady (1696) was so widely used in the eighteenth century that it acquired a virtually official status.

The 1662 BCP was translated into French (1662), Greek and Welsh (both 1665), and Latin (1670). By 1985 it had been translated into 210 languages. Editions of the book for use in Ireland from 1666 onwards contained supplementary services such as consecration of churches and visitation of prisoners. The disestablished Episcopalians in Scotland produced a series of 'wee bookies' containing a communion service based on primitive liturgies, which reached its definitive form in the communion office of 1764. This was taken as a model by the infant Protestant Episcopal Church of the USA, which produced an entire prayer book in 1789. During the eighteenth century various bodies in the process of secession from the Church of England made their own revisions of the prayer book, notably the Nonjurors, the Unitarians, and the Methodists. The disestablishment of the Irish Church in 1871 led to the issue of a conservative revision in 1877, while the Americans revised their own book in 1892.

From the beginning of the twentieth century revision took different forms. In England it was unhappily seen as a means of enforcing uniformity, especially upon Anglo-Catholics. Others, especially overseas, saw it as an opportunity of 'enrichment', usually from mediaeval sources. A considerable encouragement was given to the process of revision by the Lambeth Conference in 1908. This was soon reflected by draft proposals in Scotland, Canada, and South Africa, and later in the USA and Ireland. Each of these drafts is closely related to the others and to the English book of 1928, the product of twenty years' drafting. The latter book, intended as an alternative to 1662, was rejected by Parliament, though it subsequently came into wide, if unofficial, use. It departed sufficiently from the doctrinal standards of the Thirty-Nine Articles to alarm the Evangelicals, but without appealing to many Anglo-Catholics. In other parts of the world there was no need for parliamentary sanction, and the revisions duly appeared in their final forms as follows: 1922, Canada; 1926, Ireland; 1928, America; 1929, Scotland and South Africa. Of these, the first two are Evangelical in churchmanship, the others Anglo-Catholic. The South African is perhaps the most thorough and satisfactory.

In 1947 the Archbishops of Canterbury and York issued an abridged version of the prayer book incorporating the more popular proposals of 1928. These were reintroduced in 1966 in a modified form entitled Alternative Services: First Series. Interest in liturgy had become much keener since the Second World War, and in 1955 the Archbishops set up a Liturgical Commission to prepare new alternative services. The pace quickened: 1959 saw the adoption of new revisions in Canada, Japan, and the West Indies, and 1960 in the Church of India, Pakistan, Burma, and Ceylon. In the 1960s Scotland, Ireland and America resumed the work of revision; Wales, Australia and New Zealand entered the field for the first time. Experimentation was also proceeding in many other countries.

The process of revision now took on a new form: services were published separately in booklets, so that they could be further revised before being collected into a book. The presuppositions of the revisers were also different: it was no longer a case of simply revising the BCP, or even of looking back to 1549 or the mediaeval Roman rite. Instead, they took as their model the liturgies of the early centuries, notably the *Apostolic Tradition of Hippolytus*.

In England the first services to be issued bore the title Alternative Services: Second Series (1966–71). A further change occurred in the later 1960s, when it was decided that all future services should be written in modern English. These services appeared as Third Series (1973–78), and were gathered

together in The Alternative Service Book 1980, which was authorized for ten years. Its contents are:

- Calendrical tables
- Morning and evening prayer
- Prayers for various occasions (including the Litany)
- Holy communion (Rite A, modern English; Rite B, traditional)
- Thanksgiving for the birth of a child
- Baptism
- Confirmation
- Marriage
- Funeral services
- Ordination
- Collects, epistles, and gospels
- Lectionary tables
- The psalter (a new translation by D. L. Frost and A. A. Macintosh).

A fourth difference in the situation was that since the passing of the Doctrine and Worship Measure 1974, these services did not have to be submitted to Parliament. The legal status of the BCP remained unchanged, though its use has diminished greatly.

Similar processes were in operation throughout the Anglican Communion, resulting in the production of complete books in Australia (1978), the USA (1979), and Ireland (1984). Canada and Wales produced books containing holy communion and the daily office in 1984; seasonal services were authorized in 1985. Elsewhere revision had not in 1984 covered the full range of BCP services. The use of modern English has become universal.

G. J. CUMING

5. *Baptist*. The use of liturgical books was regarded by John Smyth, the founder of the General Baptists, as 'the invention of the man of sin'. It was incompatible with the spiritual worship of the NT proceeding from the heart. The Separatists rejected not only prescribed liturgies but also the use of books of any kind in worship. As books were excluded prayers could not be said or praises sung by all together. During the course of the seventeenth century, the singing of metrical psalms, paraphrases, and hymns was introduced, and by the eighteenth century congregational singing had become general among Baptists. Many collections of praise material were made by individuals, the most notable of which, after revision by a committee of ministers, was published in 1858 under the title *Psalms and Hymns*. The publication of *The Baptist Church Hymnal* (1900, revised 1933) was a landmark, for in addition to hymns and metrical psalms, it contained the traditional canticles, a selection of prose psalms for chanting, and anthems. *The Baptist Hymn Book* (1962) is now widely used throughout Britain and by English speaking Baptists overseas. It contains hymns, canticles, prose psalms, a few prayers, and passages of scripture for alternate reading. Responsive readings are also a feature of American hymnals. It should be understood that the hymnal is *the* liturgical book of the Baptists, in comparison with which all other service-books are of secondary importance. Concerning the latter, there are three facts to be emphasized. First, since each Baptist church is autonomous there is no prescribed liturgy, and a service book may be used much, occasionally, little, or not at all. Secondly, the service books have been prepared for the pulpit, not the pew; they are manuals for ministers, not congregational prayer books. Thirdly, they have been compiled by individual initiative, not by representatives commissioned by the denomination. In Britain, a small book of services for special occasions was compiled by Dr M. E. Aubrey, General Secretary of the Baptist Union (*A Minister's Manual*, 1927). The current service book, in widespread use throughout Britain, is a comprehensive book of common order (Ernest A. Payne and Stephen F. Winward, *Orders and Prayers for Church Worship*, 1960, revised 1965, adapted for use in the USA by James W. Cox under the title *Minister's Worship Manual*, 1969). A second comprehensive service book has been produced in the USA (John Skoglund, *A Manual of Worship*, 1968). While these, together with the service books of other communions, are now used by many ministers and lay preachers, the hymnal is the only liturgical book used by the congregation in all Baptist churches.

See also **Baptist Worship**

S. F. WINWARD

6. *Christian Church*. In its century and a half of history the Christian Church (Dis-

ciples of Christ) has made the congregation, with its minister and elders, responsible for ordering worship. One result of this policy has been to avoid the publication of official liturgical books. Not until 1953, with the publication of *Christian Worship: A Service Book*, did the denomination produce an authorized book, and this was for voluntary use only. This volume was largely the work of Professor G. Edwin Osborn (1897–1965), who for a third of a century was the denomination's acknowledged authority in liturgics. Educated at the University of Edinburgh, Osborn was an advocate of a psychological basis for worship. He represented a liberal attitude, holding that a service should be planned by the minister around a theme that he had chosen.

The book included recommended liturgies for the several rites of the church, a lectionary and some 400 pages of biblical materials and prayers for use by ministers and congregations. Although the book enjoyed only modest sales, it remained in print for some two decades and greatly influenced Disciple liturgical practice. Prior to the publication of this volume there were other books of lesser quality developed by pastors and published for wider use. A new Disciple service book will likely appear about 1990 following the publishing and trial use of a series of provisional texts.

Throughout their history Disciples have published hymnals. A hymnal first published by Alexander Campbell in 1834 was in widespread use throughout the several decades that followed. Other hymnals were developed under unauthorized auspices, including *Hymns of the United Church* co-edited by C. C. Morrison, editor of *The Christian Century*, and published in 1924.

In 1941 a hymnal entitled *Christian Worship: A Hymnal*, was published by the denomination's publishing house in co-operation with the publishers for the American Baptist Convention. In 1970 a successor, *Hymnbook for Christian Worship*, was published in similar fashion. Both books are representative of mainstream Protestant hymnals. They contain large collections of hymns from a wide range of Christian experience, with a strong emphasis upon nineteenth-century religious music. The 1970 book has reduced the number of revival songs and increased the number of modern hymns. Both books contain collections of prayers and scripture readings for congregational use; and they both contain small collections of service music.

KEITH WATKINS

7. *Congregationalist*. Since the first Congregationalists believed in free prayers, not in a liturgy, there are no early Congregational prayer books. There is, however, an influential manual for ministers in the *Westminster Directory for Public Worship* (1644), which was the joint work of Presbyterians and Congregationalists. This became the standard for English-speaking Calvinist churches (Congregational, Baptist, and Presbyterian) for 250 years.

In the nineteenth century and after, some influential Congregational ministers compiled their own service-books. The two most famous were John Hunter's *Devotional Services for Public Worship* (1882) and W. E. Orchard's *Divine Service* (1919), the former being a liturgical expression of the social gospel, the latter being more traditional and Catholic in character.

The twentieth century sees the publication of denominational service books. In England the first was *The Book of Congregational Worship* (1920), strongly imitative of the BCP. No attempt was made to return to the biblical or Reformation sources of worship. The same is even more decidedly true of its successor, *A Manual for Ministers* (1936). An important but unofficial service book which did return to the scriptures and original Calvinism was *A Book of Public Worship Compiled for the Use of Congregationalists* (1948) by John Huxtable, John Marsh, Romilly Micklem, and James Todd. A companion volume was the latter's *Prayers and Services for Christian Festivals* (1951). 1959 saw the publication of another official English Congregational manual of worship, *A Book of Services and Prayers*, the chairman of the compilers being W. Gordon Robinson. The eucharistic theology shows a notable advance from the book of 1920 by the following of the traditional structure of the Western prayer of consecration*, with the addition of an epiclesis. The considerable impact of both the ecumenical movement and of modern liturgical studies is evidenced in the last production of English Congregationalism before union with the English Presbyterians. It is entitled *An*

Order of Public Worship (1970). It clearly intends a eucharistic shape to every Lord's Day service. Since the union, the United Reformed Church* has produced its own *Book of Services* (1980), which is notable for being the first 'official' Congregational/Presbyterian service book in Britain to have all its services in modern English.

On the American side two important denominational service books have appeared. *A Book of Worship for Free Churches* (1948) was prepared under the direction of the General Council of the Congregational Christian Churches, Boynton Merrill being the chairman of the compilers. It has many alternative orders, uses ecumenical resources, and stresses the importance of symbolism.

The United Church of Christ, which came into being with the union of the Congregational Christian Churches and the Evangelical and Reformed Church in 1950, necessitated the provision of new orders of worship. The new commission on worship, under the leadership of Louis H. Gunnemann, produced as its first fruits *The Lord's Day Service* (1964). Two years later the commission published *Services of Word and Sacrament*, and the two orders have exactly the same structure stressing the unity of word and sacrament, but the first uses traditional and the second contemporary language. Recognizing the transitional character of modern liturgical productions, the commission has committed its successive works to paperback publication, thus combining realism with modesty and tentativeness.

Modern Congregational liturgical books seem to be based upon five liturgical principles: 1. the reaffirmation of the biblical basis and content of Christian worship; 2. the importance of claiming our ecumenical inheritance; 3. the combination of a firm order of liturgy with a place for free prayers and silent prayer; 4. the provision of many alternatives to provide variety and flexibility within order; and 5. the inclusion of both classical and contemporary prayers.

There are three current hymn books in use. The English Congregational hymnal is *Congregational Praise* (*see* E. R. Routley and K. L. Parry, *Companion to Congregational Praise*, 1953). This is still in use in the United Reformed Church, together with a supplement entitled *New Church Praise* (1975). The United Church of Christ in the USA has compiled a new hymnal, but the pre-union hymnals are still being used. The ex-Congregationalists use *The Pilgrim Hymnal*, while former members of the Evangelical and Reformed Church use *The Hymnal Containing Complete Orders of Worship* (1941).

See also **Congregationalist Worship.**

HORTON DAVIES

8. *Jehovah's Witnesses.* Jehovah's Witnesses are a world-wide congregation of Bible students. All of their meetings, whether conducted in Kingdom Halls or in private homes, focus primarily on the Bible as the book of instruction.

The Watch Tower Bible and Tract Society, the legal corporation of Jehovah's Witnesses, has, since its inception one hundred years ago, always been active in the production and distribution of Bibles. Starting in 1896 it published in English Rotherham's New Testament and by the early 1940s was printing both the King James and the American Standard versions of the Bible.

In 1950 the Society released the first volume of the *New World Translation*, namely the Christian Greek Scriptures, the basic Greek text used being that by Westcott and Hort. By 1960, the five volumes of the Hebrew Scriptures were completed, the Masoretic Hebrew text used for the preparation being R. Kittel's *Biblia Hebraica.* In 1961, the *New World Translation of the Holy Scriptures* was published in one volume.

In the years following a number of revised editions have been produced culminating in the *New World Translation Reference Bible*, released in 1984. This contains extensive marginal and footnote references, a word index and appendix material. This translation has to date been distributed in over 40,000,000 copies and appears in seven major languages and in part in three others.

The Kingdom Interlinear Translation of the Greek Scriptures, featuring beneath the Greek text by Westcott and Hort a word-for-word translation into English, is also used extensively by Jehovah's Witnesses.

Weekly meetings held at Kingdom Halls of Jehovah's Witnesses are opened and closed with song and prayer. The songs and

their music have been written by Jehovah's Witnesses and published in *Sing Praises to Jehovah*. Prayers offered on behalf of the congregation are never read but spoken from the heart.

The Watchtower, a twice-monthly magazine, is now published in 103 languages (simultaneously, as to contents, in 24 languages) in an average printing each issue of 11,150,000. As its name implies, this magazine keeps watch on world events as they fulfil Bible prophecy and a regular weekly study is conducted by each congregation on a scriptural theme featured in this publication.

Awake!, a companion twice-monthly magazine, reports the news, tells about people in other lands, examines religion and science, and shows how to cope with today's problems. The magazine circulates in 54 languages with an average printing each issue of 9,800,000.

The Truth That Leads to Eternal Life, a 192–page book, is a foremost Bible study aid produced by Jehovah's Witnesses. With good reason it appears in *The Guinness Book of Records*, as 105,316,837 copies have already been printed in 115 languages since its first appearance in 1968.

DAVID SIBREY

9. *Lutheran*

(1) *Europe*. Lutheran liturgical books have their starting point in two orders of service outlined by Luther, the *Formula Missae* of 1523 and the *Deutsche Messe* (German mass) of 1526. These in turn followed the pattern of the Roman mass, which was altered to follow the perspectives of the Reformation.

(i) *Germany*. Because of the territorial divisions of Lutheranism, there was no single service book used by all the German-speaking Lutheran churches in common, as was the case with Luther's translation of the Bible, his catechism and his hymns. Indeed, appeals to article VII of the Augsburg Confession even prevented energetic efforts at such a book. Nevertheless, a series of common liturgical features are to be found within the various 'church orders' that appeared. The North German orders, in which Luther's friend Johannes Bugenhagen played a substantial part, come close to the type of the *Deutsche Messe*. Their freedom in shaping the eucharist is striking. Similar influence was exercised by the Brandenburg–Nuremberg church order of 1533, which continued the conservative line prefigured in the *Formula Missae*. In South-West German Lutheranism, a liturgy going back to the mediaeval Dominican pattern was used.

The Reformation orders of service were preserved down to the period of pietism, when the traditional liturgical forms rapidly began to break up. Their place was taken by private forms of service, newly-constructed artificial orders in the spirit of rationalism. A restoration counter-movement began in the nineteenth century. In Prussia, where in 1817 a union had been brought about between the Lutherans (numerically, by far in the majority) and the Reformed, a 'church order' (with fundamentally a Lutheran structure) worked out by King Friedrich Wilhelm III was introduced. The great Lutheran churches of Bavaria, Hanover, Mecklenburg and Saxony similarly took upon themselves regulative orders, which were based on the sixteenth-century forms of service. They also set the pattern for the smaller district churches. The formation of the United Evangelical Lutheran Church of Germany (VELKD) in 1948 led to the creation of a great four-volume work which for the first time in the history of German Lutheranism provided a common basis for liturgical action. The main liturgy has the structure of the 'evangelical mass', from which the sacramental part can be excluded. Lutheran churches which belong to the United Evangelical Church also have the possibility, after the new service book of 1959, of using the main Lutheran liturgy as well as the preaching service and the eucharist following the Reformed pattern. So far, the separation of the organizations of the Lutheran churches in East and West Germany has not led to any sacrifice of liturgical uniformity.

In many places, the demand for new, contemporary forms of service alongside those forms of service shaped by traditional patterns has led to modern attempts at liturgies. Such experiments are not, however, given fixed forms in service books. Suggestions and models are published in 'work books', which do not have any official standing. The tendency to avoid the constricting pressures of a service book is

at present stronger than ever.

(ii) *Northern Europe*. The *Swedish* service books similarly begin from Luther's reform of the mass. However, from 1560 onwards, a predilection for richer liturgical forms is perceptible, though intensive efforts to restore the liturgy of the ancient church (Liturgy of King Johann III) were rejected as being too 'catholic'. With the service book of 1693, the particularism of the episcopal sees was broken and a national church uniformity was introduced throughout Sweden, with the full support of Lutheran orthodoxy. Orders of service maintained a much purer form than in Germany through the period of the Enlightenment. The church books of the nineteenth century, stamped with the spirit of the age, were replaced by the new service book of 1942. This is characterized by a far-reaching reform of the lectionary of the ancient church.

In 1968 a new liturgical commission was appointed. As a result of its work and with the general approval of the General Church Council of the Church of Sweden a tentative order was given to the local congregations to be used on a voluntary basis. In 1982 a new voluntary order for baptism, confirmation etc., was published. A revision of all these will be acted upon by the General Church Council in 1986.

The new liturgical book of the Church of Sweden which relates to present day ecumenical developments in the field can be characterized in terms of liturgical models and orders where different groups of ordained and lay people are invited to play their role in the liturgy. There is also a certain amount of liturgical freedom, e.g. the opening part of the service and the general intercession.

In 1969 another commission was appointed to prepare a new hymnal. In 1976 and in 1982 books were published with new hymns. These included new hymns and melodies as well as new translations and revisions of existing chorals in the present hymnal. The General Church Council is expected to accept a hymnal in 1986 in which the first 325 hymns are common to all Christian denominations in Sweden. The second part of the hymnal with approximately 340 hymns will consist of hymns more exclusively connected with the tradition of the Church of Sweden. It will also include some 40 hymns from the Psalter with new melodies and refrains to be sung by the congregation.

Until the separation of Finland from the Swedish communion of churches in 1809, the *Finnish* liturgy was closely connected with developments in Sweden. After two service books of 1886 and 1913, a new liturgy was adopted in 1969.

Bugenhagen was also an influence on the *Danish* mass of 1539. Even now, the 'Church Ritual' of 1685 is the basis of the Danish liturgy. An 'Experimental Book of Ritual' which appeared in 1963 is intended once again to make greater room for sung liturgical prose. This 'Experimental Book of Ritual' has been discontinued and no new proposals have been made.

The most recent order of the *Norwegian* church, which received its church ritual in 1683, is the Norwegian mass of 1920. Since 1969, a new experimental service book has been introduced, which seeks to pioneer new liturgical music.

(iii) *The rest of Europe*. The minority Lutheran churches have mostly adopted new service books since the Second World War, following the line laid down in the great book of the VELKD (e.g. France 1953, Czechoslovakia 1954, Poland 1955).

E. J. R. H. S. VON SICARD

(2) *United States*. Lutheran settlers brought with them their own vernacular liturgies, effectively keeping Lutheran communities separated by language. Liturgical progress in American churches has paralleled the spread of English as the Lutheran common language. The *Church Book*, 1868, not only was one of the first Lutheran books in English, it also marked a restoration of Reformation fullness of form already heralded by the work of the patriarch, Henry Melchior Muhlenberg, in 1748. This restoration phase was given decisive form in the *Common Service*, 1888, later included in the *Common Service Book*, 1917. Over the subsequent decades the *Common Service* became the standard of virtually all English-speaking Lutherans, being included, for example, in the *Lutheran Hymnary* (Norwegian heritage), 1913; *The Hymnal and Order of Service* (Swedish heritage), 1925; *American Lutheran Hymnal* (German heritage), 1930; and the *Lutheran Hymnal* (Lutheran Church-Missouri Synod), 1941. The *Service Book and*

Hymnal, 1958, marked in its liturgy both the culmination of the restoration phase and an opening towards ecumenical consensus. The *Lutheran Book of Worship*, 1978, puts the Lutheran churches in the midst of contemporary liturgical convergence. Though it participated with the other churches in preparation of the 1978 book, the Lutheran Church–Missouri Synod did not accept the manuscript, publishing instead its own version, *Lutheran Worship*, in 1982.

EUGENE BRAND

10. *Methodist*. The first Methodist liturgical book, as distinct from collections of prayers and hymns, was *The Sunday Service of the Methodists in America, With Other Occasional Services*, 1784, an abridgment, with some amendments, mostly of a Puritan character, of the BCP, 1662, of the Church of England. There were many subsequent editions, two at least for Methodists in the USA, one for Methodists in His Majesty's Dominions, and the rest simply for Methodists. The Americans did not view it with much favour and soon discarded it, but they incorporated some parts of it in their *Discipline* under the title 'Sacramental Services, etc.'; the title was subsequently changed to 'The Ritual'. There were extensive revisions in 1864, 1916 and 1932 in the Methodist Episcopal Church and from 1854 to 1870 and in 1910 in the Methodist Episcopal Church South. The *Methodist Hymnal*, 1935, incorporated some orders of service for optional use which were not part of 'The Ritual' but had come to be printed with 'The Ritual' in the *Discipline*. *The Book of Worship for Church and Home*, 1944, was an innovation, and contained 'The Ritual' and much else, though many people in the pew used only the material in the *Methodist Hymnal*. All these books were revised in 1964 and *The Book of Worship for Church and Home*, 1964, included orders and offices for the official rites of the church and all the other liturgical material, except hymns, which were needed in this church. It has now united under the title of the United Methodist Church with the Evangelical United Brethren, whose *Book of Ritual*, 1959, is recognized together with the books previously mentioned.

The currents of reform following Vatican II gave impetus for the revision of all the Methodist rites. This has led to the *Supplemental Worship Resources*, of which fifteen volumes have been published, most of which contain commentaries as well as rites. These volumes include the eucharist (1972, revised 1980, 1984), all the other rites, plus the lectionary and calendar, and services for the Christmas and Easter cycles. *An Ordinal* was published in 1980. Five of the basic services were issued in 1980 as *We Gather Together*, made part of the official 'Ritual' in revised versions in 1984, and appear in *The Book of Services* in 1985. The services approved in 1964 remain in use but have been largely replaced by the reformed rites.

In England *The Sunday Service* went through many editions until 1910. Between 1839 and 1881 a shorter version, containing only certain services, *Order of Administration of the Sacraments*, also went through many editions. There were revisions in 1846 and 1864. The Wesleyan conference of 1882 produced a modified version of it known as *The Book of Public Prayers and Services*, which was intended to safeguard the principles of evangelical Protestantism; at several points, however, it restored portions of the BCP which Wesley had omitted. It is curious that this also had a shorter version with the same title as its predecessor, *Order of Administration of the Sacraments*, and that *The Sunday Service* continued to be published for many years after it had been officially superseded. The non-Wesleyan branches of Methodism also produced service-books, which were very much simpler and less Anglican than the Wesleyan books and also were probably much less used.

After the union of the Wesleyan Methodists, the Primitive Methodists and the United Methodists in Britain in 1932, the conference in 1936 published *The Book of Offices*, being the orders of service authorized for use in the Methodist Church, together with *The Order for Morning Prayer*. This book, though it had the characteristically liberal Protestant tone of that period, was still recognizably indebted to the BCP. A supplementary book, *Divine Worship*, 1935, was little used.

The British Conference, after a series of experimental services, produced a new official book in 1975, *The Methodist Service Book*, which reflects the insights of the Liturgical Movement. This contains Entry

into the Church (baptism and confirmation), The Sunday Service (which is a full service including the Lord's Supper), The Sunday Service without the Lord's Supper, appendices for use with these services, the 1936 Lord's Supper, Collects, Lessons, and Psalms (the lessons based on *The Calendar and Lectionary*, 1967, of the Joint Liturgical Group), Covenant Service, Marriage, Burial or Cremation, Ordination of Ministers also called Presbyters. A reprinting of 1984 also contains recognition and commissioning services of local preachers, class leaders, and workers with children and young people.

Liturgical books do not have the same binding authority in Methodism which they have in some other churches. The services in them are authorized and generally followed (at ordinations invariably); but other forms are not prohibited. An unofficial British book by Neil Dixon, *Companion to the Lectionary, 3, A New Collection of Prayers*, 1983, provides materials particularly useful at non-eucharistic services. It has often been said that the true liturgy of Methodism is to be found in its hymns, and this is reflected by the fact that its hymn books are authorized by its Conferences. The Wesleys published many hymn books; the definitive edition was that of 1780. British Methodism currently uses *Hymns and Psalms*, 1983.

There are many Methodist churches in other parts of the world, but they all stem originally from either British or American Methodism, and their service books are usually adaptations, sometimes indeed abbreviations, of the English or American books, often translated into other languages.

A. RAYMOND GEORGE

11. *Old Catholic*. Each of the Old Catholic churches belonging to the Utrecht Union has its own liturgical books. The *jus liturgicum* (i.e. the right of ordering the liturgy in the church) belongs to the bishops of each church; they also have the duty of supervising the versions of the liturgical books.

The basis of the liturgical books of the Old Catholic churches is the books of the Roman Catholic rite. As the liturgy has long been celebrated in the vernacular, these books have had to be translated into various languages. Sometimes they are almost literal translations; sometimes they are free revisions. Corresponding to the geographical spread of the Old Catholic church, there are liturgical books in the following languages: German for Germany, Austria and the German-speaking parts of Switzerland; French for the French-speaking part of Switzerland and France; Italian, Croatian, Dutch, Polish (and also English for the Polish National Church in the USA and Canada), and Czech.

The following is a list of the more important liturgical books of the Old Catholic churches.

(*a*) Altar books and mass books for the congregation: Germany has the *Altarbuch für die Feier der heiligen Eucharistie im Katholischen Bistum der Alt-Katholiken in Deutschland*, Bonn 1959; *Eucharistiegebete*, 1979; *Die Feier des Gottesdienstes*, 1983; Austria has the *Altkatholisches Altar-Buch*, Vienna 1933. For the ordinary of the mass it has now been replaced by the *Ordnung des Heiligen Amtes der Gemeinde*; the proper is still to come. The volume *Das heilige Amt für die Gemeinde, II Ordnung*, provides alternative texts for the eucharistic prayer as experimental forms.

Switzerland has the *Messliturgie der Christkatholischen Kirche der Schweiz*, Bern [2]1905. The French edition (1910 is its most recent date) is at present out of print. In 1971 a completely revised text of the ordinary of the mass was published (*Nouvel Ordinaire de la Messe*); a new proper will follow. Italy has the *Messalino e piccolo Catechismo, Chiesa Cattolica Antica*, no date.

Holland has the *Misboek ten dienste van de Oud-Katholieke Kerk van Nederland*, 1909. The edition in a small format for the congregation last appeared in 1960 in a fourth edition (with some alterations); in addition a *Tweede Misorde* (second order) appeared in 1970. The order of mass for the Polish National Catholic Church is to be found in *A Book of Devotions and Prayers according to the use of the Polish National Church in Polish and English*, Scranton, Pa. 1951.

(*b*) *Books of ritual*, containing the rites for the celebration of the sacraments, burials, blessings, etc., are as follows: *Katholisches Rituale der alt-katholischen Kirche des Deutschen Reiches*, Bonn 1876, abbreviated edition 1933. For baptism there is now *Die Feier der Taufe*, 1983, and for burial *Die Feier der Bestattung*, 1985. A

thorough revision is planned. *Das österreichische Rituale* of 1929 is out of print; a new edition is being prepared. There was a completely revised second edition of the *Rituale der Christkatholischen Kirche der Schweiz*, Bern 1940. For the Netherlands, *Gebed en Sacrament* has gone through a number of editions since 1935; it also contains private devotions and the order of the mass. *Rytual Kosciola Polskokatolickiego* for the Polish Catholic Church appeared in Warsaw in 1961. It also contains the Holy Week liturgy and a number of benedictions, liturgies and hymns.

(*c*) *Prayer books* for congregational use corresponding approximately to the English BCP usually contain the order of the mass, morning and evening prayer and the sacraments, as well as private prayers, especially for the sick; some also have a hymn book. One is the *Katholisches Gebet- und Gesangbuch für die Alt-Katholiken in Deutschland*, Bonn ²1965. It also contains the special liturgies for Good Friday and Easter Even. A new book, *Dein Antlitz Suche ich: Gebetbuch des Katholischen Bistums der Alt Katholischen Kirche für Christen heute*, was published at Easter, 1985. *Unser Beten* is the prayer book for the Old Catholic Church of Austria, Vienna ²1962. The *Gebetbuch der Christkatholischen Kirche der Schweiz*, Allschwil ¹¹1968, is bound up with a hymn book (see [*d*] below); it also contains all the propers of the mass. *Prières liturgiques en usage dans l'Eglise Catholique-Chrétienne de la Suisse* appeared in a considerably altered new version in 1971. For Holland *see* (*b*) above, *Gebed en Sacrament*. For the Polish National Catholic Church *see* (*a*) above, *A Book of Devotions* . . . and (*b*) *Rytual* . . .

(*d*) *Hymn books*. These contain truly liturgical hymns and above all the congregational hymns which are much loved in Old Catholic churches.

For Germany, *see* (*c*) above. A new hymn book was published in the autumn of 1985. The *Gesangbuch der Christkatholischen Kirche der Schweiz* is combined with the prayer book (*see* [*c*] above). A new and enlarged edition of the French hymn book is in preparation. There are three hymn books for the church of the Netherlands: *Misgezangen* (mass hymns), new edition, 1949; *Vesperboek*, several editions since 1909; *Gezangboek ten dienste van de Oud-Katholieke Kerk*, enlarged edition, 1942. In 1970 a second hymnal was published, *Gezang en Liturgie* (Hymns and Liturgy).

(*e*) *The rites for the consecration of priests* (major and minor orders) were produced in German at the request of the Conference of Old Catholic Bishops in a free rendering that followed the *Pontificale Romanum*, Bern 1899. This was translated into Dutch in 1900 and Polish (in *Rytual* . . .), *see* (*b*) above. In addition there are formulae for the consecration of a bishop and for the consecration of churches, altars and bells.

S. KRAFT/C. TOL

12. *Pentecostal*. E. Leonard called attention to the oral, non-literary character of classical Pentecostalism (*L'illumisme dans un protestantisme de constitution récente*, 1953, p.99). Since classical Pentecostalism (*see* **Pentecostal Worship**) represents a preliterary culture whose tools of socialization are the story, the parable, a witness, a prophecy, a song, and face-to-face encounter, since the Pentecostal ethos is experience-oriented and leader-dominated, since their liturgical presuppositions are the actuality and immediacy of God's presence ('He is real; the really real'), and since all is under the guidance and prompting of the Holy Spirit, there are many classical Pentecostals who look upon a written liturgy and liturgical paraphernalia as a quenching of the Spirit. However, in South Africa the Apostolic Jerusalem Church in Sabbath has taken over the office of bishop together with copes, capes, mitres, acolytes or deacons. In Chile certain denominations have developed a ritual of entrance for the pastor. 'Like the bishop who enters only after the ceremony has begun, he (the pastor) comes with hat on head and a cape on his shoulders, three councillors following him, one carrying a Bible. When they reach the platform, an elder takes the hat, one the cape, and the third hands the Bible to the bishop, who then takes his seat' (C. Lalive d'Epinay, *Haven of the Masses*, 1969, p.52). Though such rituals might never be reduced to print – indeed to do so might in some cases be a scandal – yet rubrical observance might be as rigorous as in any of the high liturgical churches.

Some of the tendencies towards ritual are motivated by desire for social respectability. In South America norms of social ac-

ceptability are determined by the mores of Catholic practice. To disassociate their churches from the image of the culturally disinherited, Pentecostal churches conform to the socio-cultural patterns of the more respectable churches, i.e. the liturgical practices of Catholicism.

Those churches which have lost some of their prophetic character and become more or less centralized and bureaucratized also tend to move away from the oral and non-literary culture of classical Pentecostalism. These groups have published manuals with ceremonies for the reception of members, Lord's Supper, baptism, marriage, burial, dedication of churches and children (*Discipline of Pentecostal Holiness Church*, 1961; *Ministers' Manual*, 1965). When these manuals are used it is as a servant rather than a master. An Assemblies of God pastor wrote: 'I believe that the Holy Spirit should be able to break in at any time he chooses. When we lose this – we've lost everything' (F. Masserano, *A Study of Worship Forms in the Assemblies of God Denomination*, 1966).

Classical Pentecostals are not at their best when composing liturgical texts, even in those churches which have moved beyond an oral, pre-literary culture to a literary culture. Their liturgical experience is, even in these cases, determined by their pre-literary origins. This can be deceptive. A classical Pentecostal eucharistic service the author attended in Minneapolis, Minnesota, was a liturgical success; but if it were reduced to the printed page it would look impoverished. Also, the rite is not understandable apart from spirituality of which it is an expression.

Neo-Pentecostals tend to follow the liturgical books of their own churches but with a freedom which allows for the exercise of charismatic gifts. In some Lutheran Neo-Pentecostal groups (e.g. Arnold Bittlinger, Schloss Craheim, Germany; Paul Anderson, Trinity Lutheran Church, San Pedro, California), the charismatic element has been integrated into the total Lutheran approach. Instead of an aggressive self-conscious Pentecostal message, there is the quiet availability of the Pentecostal dimension within the Lutheran framework. Roman Catholic charismatics follow the liturgical order with greater fidelity than the underground churches, but with moments within the eucharistic action for community participation through the exercise of the gifts.

The weaknesses of the classical Pentecostal liturgical practice (e.g. excessive subjectivism, restricted theological horizon, ritualization of impoverished patterns, want of theological penetration) indicate that for the liturgical churches to abandon their tradition of printed texts would be an ill-advised move. But the strengths of the Pentecostal tradition would indicate that to concentrate on a purely literary tradition is to ignore those elements of the non-rational, pre-literary in the theological and liturgical traditions of the early church (O. Cullmann, *Early Christian Worship*, 1953, p.20; E. Schweizer, *Church Order in the New Testament*, 1961, p.221) and also to ignore the experience orientation of much of contemporary culture with its sensitivity sessions, T-groups, drug addiction, hippy movement, and participatory theatre. The classical Pentecostals have been especially productive and successful in creating new worship forms. A Negro preacher from the Dominican Republic sang his worship service to a Chilean congregation. It was a free rhythmed spontaneous composition of high musical quality (film *Gloria a Dios, Pfingstkirchen in Chile*, Zweites Deutsche Fernsehen, directed by Fritz Puhl). From the Pentecostals the historic churches can learn how to maintain a more immediate contact between cultural patterns and liturgical forms, a contact which is established in an oral, pre-literary mode. What Ernst Troeltsch wrote of the social ethics of the churches is in a measure also true in the area of liturgical renewal:

> It is the lower classes which do the really creative work, forming communities on a genuinely religious basis. They alone unite imagination and simplicity of feeling with a non-reflective habit of mind, a primitive energy, and an urgent sense of need. On such a foundation alone is it possible to build up an unconditional authoritative faith in a divine revelation with simplicity of surrender and unshaken certainty. (*The Social Teaching of the Christian Churches*, ET 1931, I, p.44).

Though classical Pentecostalism can no longer be identified without qualification with the lower strata, it is from this level that its liturgical creativity still comes.

For bibliography *see* **Pentecostal Worship**.

KILIAN MCDONNELL

13. *Plymouth Brethren.* The Brethren have no liturgical books in the ordinary sense. Traditionally they interpret the freedom of the Spirit as ruling out such 'aids' to public worship. If this interpretation were pressed to its logical conclusion, it would rule out the use of hymn books, but in fact liberal use is made of hymn books in their worship. The selection of appropriate hymns for various services, and especially for the successive stages of the communion service, will sometimes be regarded as a mark of spiritual intelligence.

Among the Exclusive Brethren the standard hymn book since 1856 has been *Hymns for the Little Flock*, compiled in that year by G. V. Wigram, revised in 1881 by J. N. Darby and subsequently issued in several further revisions for the use of the various Exclusive bodies. In the body led by the late James Taylor, Jr, successive revisions (by T. H. Reynolds in 1903, James Taylor, Sr, in 1932 and A. E. Myles in 1951) have increasingly made this collection a handbook to the liturgy (*see* **Liturgies** 13). It accurately reflects some notable features of this body's doctrine and practice, as in the avoidance of any reference to the eternity of Christ's relation as Son to the Father and in the absence of any note of confession of sin (which is not, however, a sign of antinomianism).

Among the Open Brethren a variety of hymn books is in use. The most widely used in Great Britain and Ireland are *The Believer's Hymn Book* (1884; enlarged with a supplement, 1959), *Hymns of Light and Love* (1900), *Hymns for Christian Worship and Service* (1909) and, surpassing all others, *Christian Worship*, edited by B. H. Mudditt (1976). Some of their churches prefer to use interdenominational collections, such as *Christian Praise* (1957) or *Hymns of Faith* (1964). To the latter of these the Brethren at Mitchley Hill Chapel, Sanderstead, Surrey, have provided an excellent supplement of hymns specially suitable for use at the communion service.

Apart from its use as the basis for expository ministry, the Bible serves in some degree as a liturgical book. At the communion service in particular, one or another of the worshippers may read (with or without brief comment) a scripture bearing on the purpose of the meeting – for example, a suitable passage from the NT or a 'messianic' psalm or prophecy from the OT calculated to promote the spirit of worship and anamnesis. As with the selection of suitable hymns, use and wont have established a feeling for what scripture lessons are appropriate for this purpose, so that the reading of passages that are deemed inappropriate may be put down to lack of spiritual intelligence. Departure from the accepted though unwritten liturgical pattern may be the result of inexperience or of mature and deliberate breaking with tradition.

F. F. BRUCE

14. *Reformed.* The Protestant Reformation brought changes in service books for use in worship as in other things. The replacement of Latin by the vernacular was a far-reaching change adopted by all the reformers, which enabled the worshipper to understand the service. But on other points the reformers adopted differing policies. In the Book of Common Prayer (BCP) the text had to be strictly adhered to. But in other books there were specific points where variation was permitted. Thus in Calvin's *Forme des prieres* (1542) one rubric says, 'on use de cette action de graces ou semblable', and in the Scottish *Book of Common Order* (*BCO*) 1564, at a few places the rubrics permit the minister to pray 'either in these words following or the like in effect'. Another change was that the books were used by all the worshippers. Indeed in the case of the *BCO* an Act of Assembly of 26 December 1564 ordered 'every minister, exhorter and reader to possess a copy' and use it, and an Act of Parliament of 1579 decreed that every person of a certain rank and class had to have copy. Possession of a copy by the worshipper was required because it contained metrical psalms for singing. Calvin's *La Forme* of 1542 contained thirty-five psalms with music and others were added in later editions. The *BCO* of 1564 for the first time provided metrical versions of all the psalms. How widely used the various editions of the *BCO* were is shown by the condition of most surviving copies, the beginning and the end being usually defective, leaves missing or heavily finger-marked and dirty.

Out of the many Reformed liturgical

books that have been produced, the following deserve special mention. The story begins with Zwingli, who produced two forms, both for the Lord's Supper. The first in 1523, *De Canone Missae Epicheiresis*, was an attack on the canon of the mass and indicated his ideas for the service. The second, two years later, entitled *Action oder Bruch des Nachtmals*, was more radical, but it became the guiding rule for Zwinglian worship. Next to be noted is Farel's *La manyere et fasson qu'on tient es lieux que Dieu de sa grace a visites*, dated 1533, prepared for the use in Strasbourg of the Zwinglian Reformed congregation. This was Zwinglian in tone and had little influence on other rites, though Calvin adopted the marriage rite almost as it stood.

Strasbourg had already seen the important first reformed German mass, arranged by Diebold Schwartz in 1524, and frequently revised, more and more under the influence of Bucer. When John Calvin came to Strasbourg in 1538 he made a Latin version of the Schwartz form; this was later translated into French as *La manyere de faire prieres aux eglises francoyses* and used by the Strasbourg French congregation. A later edition was printed in Geneva in 1542. This contained thirty-five psalms with melody, the creed, the Lord's Prayer, and an order of service for Sunday morning with the addition necessary when the eucharist was celebrated, the marriage service, and a section for the visitation of the sick. Some revisions of this were issued in succeeding years. A Latin translation was issued in Geneva in 1552, and one in English, by William Huycke, in London in 1550. Other editions continued to appear, a very important one being that printed in Geneva in 1556, under the title. *The Forme of Prayers and ministration of the sacraments as used in the English Congregation at Geneva.*

This was John Knox's *Genevan Service Book*. There was also a Latin translation, *Ratio et Forma*. An edition similar to that of 1556, but containing additional prayers and the Genevan Confession of Faith, was issued in Geneva in 1561. The next edition takes us to Scotland where in 1562 Robert Lekprewick printed *The Forme of Prayers and Ministration of the Sacraments* at the order of the General Assembly, which gave him a grant towards his expenses. This was adopted for use in the Church of Scotland under the title *The Book of Common Order*.

La Forme des prieres continued to exert great influence both in Switzerland and in France. Many of the Swiss Cantons, such as Geneva, Vaud and Neuchâtel produced their own books, based on the great original though with many local accents. A notable attempt at revision was that of Jean-Frédéric Osterwald, who published a liturgy in 1713 which showed the influence of the BCP, but had little influence on further Swiss books, except that of Vaud in 1725, but, translated and revised, it became the book of the Huguenot congregation in Charleston, South Carolina, 1853. Recent Swiss revisions include those of Vaud (1945) and Geneva (1946).

In France liturgical books were issued from time to time, and there were many attempts to revise and enrich the content. One important attempt was that of Eugène Bersier who in 1876 issued a *Projet de revision* and in 1888 a liturgy. Here was evidenced a moving towards a new spirit of worship. Its influence is seen in the recent *Liturgie de l'Église Réformée de France* of 1963, the result of the prolonged work of a commission de liturgie.

The German and Dutch Reformed Churches gave much attention to the problems of the liturgy, and issued various service books. The majority of the German Reformed churches joined with Lutheran churches in 1817. But in the Dutch Reformed Church there was a liturgical revival with the foundation in 1920 of the *Liturgische Kring* and in 1938 of the *Kring Eeredienst* which published its *Kanselboek* in 1944.

Now we return to consider the liturgical books of the churches which came to be known as Presbyterian. The original of these was the *BCO*, popularly known as the psalm book. From 1564 to 1644 fully seventy editions appeared. The contents of these editions varied very considerably, but usually included the calendar; the psalter with music; scripture songs or hymns, i.e., metrical versions of the ten commandments, the Lord's Prayer and the Veni Creator, etc.; the catechism (Calvin's up to 1611, the Palatinate or Heidelberg in 1615); the order of baptism, the Lord's Supper, marriage, visitation of the sick, the order of burial. Much other material appeared in some edi-

tions. This book was widely used, though not without some criticism at times, but its use ceased in 1645, when the General Assembly adopted the *Westminster Directory*.

The *Directory* was not a liturgical book. It did not provide prayers or forms of prayer, but detailed subjects for prayer. It completely superseded the *BCO*, but itself soon came to be much neglected, and worship reached a low level. But by the end of the eighteenth century many ministers grew tired of the baldness and poverty of the services, and not a few published orders especially for holy communion. The Church Service Society of the Church of Scotland was formed in 1865 and its influence, especially through the issue of *Euchologion*, gradually led to much improvement. Other societies, with the same intention, were formed in the United Presbyterian and Free Churches in Scotland, and they also published service books. The United Free Church after 1900 followed the same course, leading to the issue in 1928 of the *Book of Common Order* (1928). Similar movements were taking place within the Church of Scotland, an influential book, *Prayers for Divine Service*, appearing in 1923, revised in 1929. The reunited Church produced the *Book of Common Order* (1940). This book has greatly influenced the books of other Presbyterian churches throughout the world. These churches, in England, Canada, Australia, New Zealand and South Africa, have all issued service books and have all revised them. In the USA three Presbyterian churches produced their own books, but have recently joined in the publication of a new book for all – *The Worship-Book* (Philadelphia 1970). The now-reunited Presbyterian Church (USA) together with the Cumberland Presbyterian Church has begun to publish a series of Supplemental Liturgical Resources, of which the first is *The Service for the Lord's Day* (1984). These recent books express an 'ecumenical consensus', the fruit of ecumenical liturgical scholarship. There is sensitive use of modern language and a careful avoidance of 'sexist' language. The Scottish *Book of Common Order* (1979) has some orders in modern language, and shows a similar influence of the ecumenical consensus.

See also **Presbyterian Worship**.

JOHN A. LAMB/JAMES A. WHYTE

15. *Seventh-day Adventist*. The Seventh-day Adventist Church, in the tradition of Evangelical Protestantism, does not use special liturgical books for its worship services. Various publications are drawn upon for guidance in worship, but they are not authorized or used as service books.

The early leaders of the Seventh-day Adventist Church emphasized the blessedness of genuine worship, as opposed to what they called the evil of formal worship. Adventists still generally keep to the relative informality of early years and do not worship according to a prescribed ritual with fixed words and formalized prayers. In recent years form consciousness in the regular services for worship has become more pronounced. *The Seventh-day Adventist Church Manual* (1981) states: 'We do not prescribe a set form or order for public worship' (p.110). Nevertheless, the *Manual* does suggest a longer and shorter order of worship and offers considerable guidance regarding the Sabbath worship service.

The Church Hymnal (USA, Australia, etc.) and the *New Advent Hymnal* (Britain, some West African countries) are the two most widely used hymn books in English-speaking Adventist churches. *The Church Hymnal* also contains a selection of responsive scriptural readings. In 1985 the General Conference issued a new hymnal, *The Seventh-day Adventist Hymnal*. This will in due course replace *The Church Hymnal*. It incorporates more recent hymns and enlarges the worship aids section (scripture readings, calls to worship, words of assurance, benedictions, etc.). A series of special devotional readings is prepared annually for use in all Seventh-day Adventist churches around the world during the yearly Week of Prayer in November.

The Manual for Ministers contains suggested services and prescribes certain ritual forms for special occasions, such as ordinations, burials, church dedications and marriage ceremonies. In addition, various Seventh-day Adventist publishing houses issue every year quite a number of new books and inspirational readings for private and corporate devotions.

B. B. BEACH

J. S. Andrews, 'Brethren Hymnology', *Evangelical Quarterly* 28, 1956, pp. 208–29; J. C. Bowmer, *The Sacrament of the Lord's*

Supper in Early Methodism, 1951; F. E. Brightman, *The English Rite*, 1915, 2 vols., esp. pp. xlix–ccxxx (Anglican); C. O. Buchanan, *Modern Anglican Liturgies 1958–1968*, 1968; *Further Anglican Liturgies 1968–1975*, 1975; *Later Anglican Liturgies 1975–1984*, 1984; Horton Davies, *The Worship of the English Puritans* 1948; *Worship and Theology in England, 1900–1965*, 1965, ch.x; Jean Deshusses, *Le Sacramentaire Grégorien. Ses principales formes d'après les plus anciens manuscrits*, 1971–1982; K. Gamber, *Codices Liturgici Latini Antiquiores*, 1963; A. R. George, 'The People called Methodist – 4. The Means of Grace' in *A History of the Methodist Church in Great Britain* Vol. 1, ed R. E. Davies and G. Rupp, 1965, pp. 259–73; N. B. Harmon, Jr, *The Rites and Ritual of Episcopal Methodism*, 1926; M. J. Hatchett, *Commentary on the American Prayer Book*, 1979; R. C. D. Jasper (ed), *The Alternative Service Book 1980: A Commentary*, 1980; W. K. Lowther Clarke (ed), *Liturgy and Worship*, 1932; A. G. Matthews, 'Puritan Worship' in *Christian Worship*, ed N. Micklem, 1935, reissued 1955; L. C. Mohlberg (ed), *Gelasian Sacramentary*, 1960; *Verona (Leonine) Sacramentary*, 1956; Pierre Salmon, *Les Manuscrits liturgiques latins de la Bibliothèque Vaticane*, I, II, 1968, 1969; Cyrille Vogel, *Introduction aux Sources de l'Histoire du Culte Chrétien au Moyen Age, 1965;* B. J. Wigan, *The Liturgy in English*, 1964 (Anglican).

Bowing

see **Gestures** 2

Buddhist Worship

Buddhist worship is a peculiarly delicate topic, in a religion or ethic which has been called atheistic and appears to emphasize meditation rather than prayer. Buddhism began as a reform movement within Hinduism; and its religious objects may be compared with those which feature in Hindu worship*. Some of the Hindu gods remain in Buddhism, so that it is not atheistic but perhaps 'transtheistic', since the gods Indra and Brahmā which figure in Buddhist texts are subordinate to the Buddha. To this day many, perhaps all, Buddhist temples in Sri Lanka have images of at least two Hindu gods, usually Vishnu and Indra (Sakka), though they are often behind curtains. But Kataragama (or Skanda), second son of the great Hindu deity Shiva, is the most popular god of the Hindus of Sri Lanka and his temples are visited by Buddhists to pay reverence and make vows.

In Buddhism it is the Buddha or Buddhas who are pre-eminent, even in the conservative Theravāda Buddhism of South-East Asia. The gods exist, as part of the world of beings, above most men except monks, but the Buddha is supreme, 'the teacher of gods and men' and the 'god above the gods', as the texts call him. Although in monkish theory the Buddha was a man, who is now dead, and only one in a series of Buddhas, yet in practice from olden times till now he is the supreme object of worship. It was the first lay convert, therefore, about 500–400 BC, who is said to have invoked the Threefold Refuge, or the Three Jewels, which are still the daily expression of Theravāda Buddhist devotion: 'I go to the Buddha for refuge, I go to the Doctrine (*dharma*) for refuge, I go to the Order (*sangha*) for refuge.'

The earliest centres of Buddhist devotion were probably small *stūpas*, relic-holders, containing some fragment of the Buddha's body or an object associated with him or his disciples. Already at the cremation of Gautama the Buddha, eight cities are said to have shared his relics. Buddhism was established in Sri Lanka by the arrival of the collar-bone and begging-bowl of the Buddha, and a shoot of the Bo-tree under which he had been enlightened. Relics not only show the teacher to have been historical, but even more convey his power. All great temples claim some outstanding relic, and one was brought to England in 1964 by the Prime Minister of Sri Lanka to hallow a new Buddhist temple in Chiswick. In Sri Lanka the relic-holders have developed into dome-shaped buildings, *dāgobas*, which are called pagodas in Burma and beyond. Some great *dāgobas* are over a hundred feet high and made of brick. The relic is enshrined in the depths, but unseen by most visitors who lay their gifts of flowers, incense and money in small shrine rooms full of images. Burmese pagodas and Thai wats have spires above the images and wide courtyards for worshippers.

Images are of the Buddha in various postures, meditating, teaching or passing

into ultimate Nirvāna. In making the images, great care is devoted to painting in the eyes, a dangerous operation which reveals the power of the being represented. In front of these images, monks and laymen meditate and repeat sacred texts from the extensive Buddhist scriptures. But prayers are also offered. One widely known prayer in Sri Lanka, in the Pāli liturgical language, is used daily at the Temple of the Tooth, the greatest relic in the town of Kandy: 'Forgive me my transgression committed through carelessness by body, word or thought, O Tathāgata [Buddha] of great wisdom' (R. F. Gombrich, *Precept and Practice*, 1971, p.140). The significance of such a prayer is that it not only reveals religious worship, but contains an appeal to cancel sin which in theory might be held to depend on the individual's own efforts in conquering Karma.

Although there have been and will be other Buddhas, yet Theravāda texts say that there can only be one Buddha in this present long world-eon, and in practice he holds the centre of worship in monotheistic fashion. In Northern Mahāyāna Buddhism, however, in Tibet, China, Japan, Korea and Vietnam, there are countless Buddhas and Bodhisattvas, 'beings of enlightenment', to whom men pray for help and salvation. Amitābha or Amida, Buddha of 'infinite light', rules in the Buddha-fields or Western Paradise to which he guides the faithful over the sea of sorrows. Avalokita, who 'looks down', becomes Kwanyin and Kwannon in China and Japan, not a goddess but a gracious Bodhisattva who 'hears the cry' and gives children. Maitreya, the Buddha to come, is the fat jolly figure depicted with money-bags and giving fortune.

Tibet has been noted for its prayer and praising wheels, prayer flags, prayer walls, and common invocation: *Om mani padme hum*, 'Hail to the jewel in the lotus', the doctrine in the scripture. In China and Japan, the Pure Land schools repeat the names of Amida endlessly on great rosaries and their prayer is adoration rather than petition. In Japan also, great Buddhist temples were built for regular congregational worship comparable to that of Western religions.

Much Buddhist worship is individual and occasional, with invocations at home and visits to pagodas when time permits. But great festivals are held on anniversaries of events in the lives of the Buddha or Buddhas, and at ancient national ceremonies such as the famous Perahera festival in Sri Lanka in August, where processions of four gods join up with that of the sacred Tooth. There are also important feasts for the dead, to ensure their rest and blessing, since although Nirvāna is the goal, it is far distant. In China, where many temples have been destroyed or turned into museums, ceremonies for the departed remain and Buddhist texts are used.

The Sangha, the church and monastic order, is not a priesthood, though monks have been teachers and leaders of the religion in Theravāda lands. In Mahāyāna countries there are Buddhist priests, often married, who officiate in temples, while monks may also participate or meditate and teach in monasteries. But for monks and laity Buddhism is not merely an ethic but a religion of devotion and salvation.

Mahāyāna Buddhism in Japan encouraged communal worship, especially in Amidist buildings where worshippers bow to the west to Amida in his Pure Land, while altars, images, hangings and lamps glitter with gold. Colossal ancient bronze images of Daibutsu, 'great Buddha', such as Amida at Kamakura and Roshana at Nara, receive worship from endless pilgrimages. Modern movements, Buddhist and Shinto, give prominence to communal worship and work. Soka Gakkai, 'creative-value study society', a powerful religious and political movement of the forceful Nichiren school of Japanese Buddhism, has a great worship hall at the foot of Mount Fuji which is claimed to be larger than St Peter's in Rome. Rissho-koseikai, 'society for establishing righteous and friendly association', another modern Nichiren sect, celebrates festivals with great processions and has huge buildings in Tokyo. In its Great Sacred Hall: 'at noon a sonorous gong from the chancel area sounds, and everyone immediately orients himself towards the altar and image, whereupon the entire membership chants the sacred formula, *Namu Myōhō Renge-kyō* (Hail to the Lotus sutra), in unison with hundreds of other voices, for three or four minutes. Then there is a brief silence while all prostrate themselves facing the altar. The ritual

ends with expression of gratitude to Mr Niwano, the founder and leader. Finally all sing together the theme hymn, to the accompaniment of the great pipe organ' (K. J. Dale, *Circle of Harmony*, 1975, p.39). Mr Niwano is one of the few non-Christians to have received the prestigious annual Templeton prize for Progress in Religion, and his movement is notable for both religious and social works.

C. Blacker, *The Catalpa Bow*, 1975; J. Blofeld, *Beyond the Gods, Taoist and Buddhist Mysticism*, 1974; J. Bunnag, *Buddhist Monk, Buddhist Layman*, 1973; H. Hoffmann, *The Religions of Tibet*, 1961; T. Ling, *The Buddha's Philosophy of Man*, 1981; E. G. Parrinder, *Worship in the World's Religions*, [2]1974; M. E. Spiro, *Buddhism and Society*, 1971.

GEOFFREY PARRINDER

Burial

The solemn interment of the dead is a practice found in almost all the great religions. Christian funeral rites express the church's care for the departed, its belief in the resurrection and its reverence for the body as sharing in redemption.

1. *The Early Church*. Funeral rites consisted of five main items, of which certain were in pointed contrast to contemporary pagan customs. (*a*) Prayer in the house – the corpse was washed and anointed and swathed in white linen to the accompaniment of prayers. (*b*) Procession – whereas the Romans chose night for interment because of a belief that a funeral was of evil omen, the Christians chose the daytime, and, wearing white garments, sang psalms of hope and alleluias of victory. Palm leaves were carried, together with lights, and incense was burned – all expressing the idea of triumph over death. (*c*) Office – a short service of praise and thanksgiving, around the body, including Bible readings and psalms. (*d*) Eucharist – the celebration expressed the belief in the communion that still exists between the living and the dead. The kiss of peace (*see* **Gestures** 8) was given to the corpse. (*e*) Interment – the corpse was placed in the grave with feet towards the east as a sign of hope in the coming of the Sun of Righteousness (*see* **Orientation**).

An agape (*see* **Love Feast**) often followed, and on the third, ninth and fortieth days afterwards friends and relatives met to join in psalms, hymns and prayers. The procedure was not immediately stereotyped and differences are to be noted depending upon whether the procession went to the church or directly from the house to the cemetery. The whole was characterized by the note of peace and hope, confidence in the felicity of the departed and the certainty that death had erected no real barrier.

EDITOR

2. *Orthodox*. Deceased members of the Orthodox Church are buried according to several different liturgical offices. These are: the Order for the Burial of a Lay Person, the Order for the Burial of a Child (usually seven years old or less), and the Order for the Burial of a Priest (used for bishops as well, with other ranks of clergy being buried according to the order for lay persons). Special Paschal variations in the offices are applied during Easter Week.

The principal differences between these offices are found in the texts of their prayers and hymns. The burial of a priest is considerably more elaborate than the other rites. It includes five epistle and five gospel readings as well as a much greater volume of hymnography (a full *kontakion* of twenty-four stanzas is but one example).

The full funeral liturgy in each of the orders of service mentioned above (none of which in present practice requires the celebration of the eucharist) consists of three parts. The first is a brief service celebrated at the home of the deceased (or frequently at a 'funeral home'), before bringing the body of the deceased to the church. The second is celebrated in the church. The third is celebrated in conjunction with the interment and takes place at the graveside. All three parts are joined together in the basic form of an ancient funeral procession. This union is effected by the singing at appropriate intervals and places – at the beginning of each segment of the service as well as during each of the transfers of the body of the deceased – of a liturgical adaptation of the angelic *Trisagion**: 'Holy God! Holy and Mighty! Holy and Immortal! Have mercy on us!' Each part also includes at least one recitation of the ancient prayer for the dead: 'O God of spirits and of all flesh, who has trampled down

death and overthrown the devil, and given life to thy world . . .' This prayer, addressed to Christ, is but one of many elements which transform the age-old funeral procession into a pilgrimage and journey with Christ, in Christ and to Christ: an entrance, as the service will manifest, into the Sabbath rest of the Lord.

Once the deceased is brought into the church, the coffin bearing the remains is usually opened and the body is situated so that it faces the altar. When the burial service for a priest is to be conducted, the deceased priest (or bishop) is clothed in his full eucharistic vestments*. He holds a cross in his hand and the gospel book rests on his chest. His face is to be covered with the same veil used to cover the eucharistic gifts at the divine liturgy. Many meanings are attached to this covering of the face. Obviously, such a practice draws attention to the priesthood, the ministry belonging to Jesus Christ – the ministry of his altar, gospel and cross, rather than to the person of the sacramentally ordained priest who, like all others, is 'unworthy to draw near or to serve' the King of Glory.

The celebrant priest stands in the centre of the church behind the head of the deceased. He is vested in the stole and chasuble, and, in some traditions, he carries a candle in his left hand. With his right hand he swings the censer almost continuously, censing and blessing the body of the deceased many times.

The service in church, like all Orthodox worship, is chanted melodiously and responsorially as a liturgy of priest and people together. It follows the form of matins, the Matins of Great and Holy Saturday* in particular. For the one who has died, this day is a personal Holy Saturday, a personal entrance into Christ's Sabbath rest and entombment, into Christ's 'trampling down death by death'. Psalm 119, the great messianic psalm chanted over the icon of the entombed Christ during the Matins of Holy Saturday, occupies nearly the entire initial portion of the service. This psalm delights in the law of God and praises the victorious Messiah who fulfils it. In him is health, joy and life. As the troparia which follow the psalm are sung, the priest, following the pattern of Great Saturday Matins, censes the whole church while carrying a candle: 'The light shines in the darkness, and the darkness has not overcome it' (John 1.5).

Blessed art thou, O Lord, teach me thy statutes.
The choir of the saints have found the fountain of life,
and the door of paradise.
May I also find the way through repentance.
I am a lost sheep. Call me, O Saviour, and save me.

Gradually, a penitential element begins to emerge in the service, a more sombre and pedagogical tone whose origins may be attributed to the influence of monasticism on Orthodox worship. The penitential Psalm 51 is followed by the chanting of a lengthy intercessory hymn patterned after the biblical canticles and composed of nine odes. Then the poetical stanzas of John Damascene along with the Beatitudes and accompanying hymns are sung:

What earthly sweetness remains unmixed with grief?
What glory stands immutable on earth?
All things are but shadows most feeble . . .
Yet one moment only, and death shall supplant them all . . . (Tone 1)

I weep and I lament, when I contemplate death,
and behold our beauty fashioned after the image of God,
lying in the tomb disfigured, dishonoured, bereft of form . . . (Tone 8)

The theme unifying this particular layer of the service is clear. A lesson is being given to the living. Death comes to everyone and destroys everything. Where are riches, and power and glory? Where are the kinsmen and friends? Those present at the service are summoned to arouse themselves, to repent before it is too late, to call upon the Theotokos and all the martyrs and saints for help.

The final portion of the service in church is inaugurated by the *prokeimenon*: those selected verses which introduce the readings from the scripture.

Blessed is the way in which you shall walk today, O soul; for a place of rest is prepared for you.

The theme here is joy in Christ. The 'place of rest' is the blessed Sabbath in Christ, 'a

place of brightness, a place of refreshment, a place of repose, where all sickness, sorrow and sighing have fled away . . .' (prayer for the departed). The epistle reading is I Thess. 4.13–17, where St Paul urges us not to sorrow as others do who have no hope. 'For since we believe that Jesus died and rose again, even so, through Jesus, God will bring with him those who have fallen asleep.' The gospel reading, John 5.24–30, also proclaims the good news about Christ's resurrection. Christ has destroyed the power of death. Those who die may hear his voice and believe, and pass from death to eternal life.

During the singing of numerous dismissal hymns, the people in the church come to the dead to exchange a final kiss of peace. The priest and singers go before the coffin, now usually closed, and lead a procession from the church to the site of interment.

At the graveside the service is again brief and simple. Several hymns and prayers from the service in church are repeated. The priest sprinkles earth in a crosswise fashion over the coffin of the deceased while saying the words: 'The earth is the Lord's and the fullness thereof; the universe and all that dwells therein (Ps. 24.1).' He blesses the grave with holy water and pronounces the dismissal. After a special intonation by the priest everyone sings two words which for many are synonymous with all prayer for the dead in Orthodox worship: *Memory Eternal*. Humanly, it is a tradition of long standing to perpetuate the memory of the departed through prayer and good works in their name. Eternal memory, however, belongs only to God. It is one of his many gifts to us in Christ. Eternal memory is Christ keeping present and therefore alive in the memory of God all those who are asleep in his body, the church. 'For you have died, and your life is hid with Christ in God. When Christ who is our life appears, then you also will appear with him in glory' (Col. 3.3–4).

PAUL LAZOR

3. *Mediaeval and Roman Catholic*. This topic requires a threefold division: the Middle Ages, the *Rituale Romanum* of 1614 and the 1969 *Ordo Exequiarum*.

(*a*) *The Middle Ages*. In the early Middle Ages the funeral liturgy consisted essentially of the preparation of the body for burial, accompanied by psalms and prayers, the procession with the body from home to church, a period of prayer for the dead person which might include the eucharist*, and finally the procession from the church to the grave and the interment. By this time the ancient custom of continuous psalmody for the dead person had become ritualized in the form of the office of the dead, consisting of vespers, matins and lauds (*see* **Canonical Hours**). This office was sung daily in addition to the normal office of the day. The word *Dirige*, beginning the first antiphon of matins, gives us the English 'dirge'.

Later the preparation of the body for burial is accomplished in private, without liturgical accompaniment, and the eucharist becomes a normal part of the funeral liturgy. It is followed by responsories, prayers of absolution and the incensation and aspersion of the corpse. These rites indicate an increased stress on need for forgiveness and fear of judgment, and also the value attached to the priest's prayer of absolution, an extension of his power to absolve the living.

These developments find excellent expression in the *Dies irae* chant, composed in the twelfth or thirteenth century, and they modify somewhat the atmosphere of joy and hope so characteristic of the ancient funeral liturgy, which looked forward to the resurrection of the body and entrance into God's kingdom. The mediaeval liturgy is conscious rather of sin and death, purgatory and judgment, thinking of the soul's destiny rather than the body's.

(*b*) *The* Rituale Romanum *of 1614*. Our sources for the mediaeval burial rites are mainly monastic, but the Roman ritual's burial rite is a simplified version of the mediaeval one, designed for use in parishes. While permitting local adaptation it remains the first official and universal funeral rite.

It begins with the processional transfer of the body from home to church, accompanied with psalmody. After the reception of the body into church the office of the dead follows, in whole or in part, though it is acknowledged that circumstances may prevent this. Mass is followed by a single absolution, after which the body is taken out to burial, the traditional antiphons *In paradisum* and *Chorus angelorum* being sung. Interment is preceded by the canticle* *Benedictus*, versicles and a prayer.

The rite retains some of the best of the ancient burial chants and prayers which stress welcome into paradise and bodily resurrection, yet the mediaeval emphasis on the need for the forgiveness and fear of judgment remains.

(*c*) *The* Ordo Exequiarum *of 1969*. The Second Vatican Council's Liturgy Constitution called for the revision of funeral rites to express the Paschal character of Christian death, while taking account of local customs. Accordingly, the new funeral rite envisages three types of service, the traditional one with prayers at home, in church and at the graveside, a second form in the cemetery chapel and at the graveside, more in line with German custom, and a third form taking place entirely in the home, in acordance with conditions in Africa and elsewhere. The rite is extremely flexible, with great scope for local variations.

Provision is made for funeral vigil in the home, and it is no longer presumed that the eucharist will always be celebrated as part of the burial rite. The absolution after mass is transformed into a final farewell to the deceased. There is a wide choice of readings, prayers and chants, prayers for the mourners are included, and the whole rite expressed Christian hope in our share in Christ's resurrection and enjoyment of God's presence in his kingdom.

It may be noted that cremation* has been permitted for Roman Catholics since 1963.

BRIAN NEWNS

4. *Anglican*. In mediaeval England, burial rites had two distinguishing features, their complicated and drawn-out structure and their purgatorial theology. Thus when Cranmer put the service into English in 1549 he simplified its structure and assimilated material from the previous vespers and matins into the 'office'. The rite began with the churchyard procession, and this 'office' in church might come before or after the committal. Finally came proper introit, collect, epistle and gospel for the (presumably optional) eucharist. In doctrine, cautious petitions for the departed were retained, but with the excision of mass-sacrifice (let alone the earlier confiscation of chantries) votive masses* for the dead ceased. The atmosphere now reflected a new emphasis on rest in Christ and resurrection to life. The service was generally directed to giving hope to the living, rather than seeking deliverance from sufferings for the departed.

1552 worked out the logic of 1549 more exactly. The service was further truncated, and was performed wholly at the graveside. The procession to the grave led almost immediately to the committal, and to an 'office' consisting solely of the reading from I Cor. 15, lesser litany, Lord's Prayer and two other prayers, one of which was the 1549 eucharistic collect (there was now no eucharist). Petitions for the departed disappeared. For the living there was prayer that they should be joined with the departed in the general resurrection to life. (The 1552 communion service dropped all mention of the departed.) Petitions for the departed (though perhaps theoretically a possible private practice) were now contrary to the policy of the Church of England for public worship. They escaped condemnation in the 1571 Articles, but the Homily on Prayer discountenanced them as lacking commandment in scripture, and as devoid of rationale once purgatory is rejected.

The 1552 rite, revived in 1559, remained unchanged till 1645 (though the 1637 Scottish eucharist reintroduced remembrance of the departed). Then the Puritan *Westminster Directory of Public Worship* forbade all burial services, and bodies were to be interred without ceremony, prayer, scripture or preaching.

At the 1661 Savoy Conference the Puritans objected that the 1552 rite was too assured about the state of the departed. They gained the addition of a 'the' to the committal – thus giving to the living hope not specifically of the deceased person's resurrection to life, but more objectively in *the* (general) resurrection of all at the last day. A new rubric disallowed use of the rite over the unbaptized, the excommunicate and suicides.

Other additions were made. The service could now be read in church and psalmody preceded the reading of I Cor. 15 straight after the procession. The committal followed, and the 1552 'office' (except the reading, but including 'The Grace . . . etc.') completed the service.

The last hundred and fifty years have seen great changes in the ecclesiastical and social context within which burials are conducted, and the following in particular

have inevitably affected the liturgical evolution not only in England, but also in the Anglican Communion around the world.

First, the gulf between church and society has broadened visibly and continues to do so. Yet the great bulk of society still expects a Christian burial, and this has set up a tension for the church (and particularly for the Church of England).

Secondly, the church building has been slowly but surely set aside from the majority of funerals in England. Until the second part of the last century parish churches generally had their own churchyards attached, and the committal would take place under the walls of the church building. Then, as churchyards filled and were closed under the pressures of fast-increasing population, corporation cemeteries, divorced from the churches and boasting their own chapels, slowly took their place. In recent decades these in turn have given way to crematoria, and cremation* appears to be the almost invariable future practice. Curiously, in a crematorium chapel, the 1662 sequence can once again be followed, as the 'committal' can come naturally before the prayers, which is difficult when a service is split between church and graveside. However, the practice of cremation calls in question the suitability of a committal 'to the ground' and 'earth to earth'. The wording has to be amended.

Thirdly, the practice of the last century has seen a growing flexibility introduced. Clergy who have treated the requirements of the Act of Uniformity fairly loosely in their Sunday services are hardly likely to take it very seriously in the cemetery or crematorium chapel on a weekday. The pastoral situation has often cried out for more relevant liturgical material (e.g. at the funeral of a child). And liturgical revision has inevitably followed what was already being done without controversy. Thus the 1928 rite (since 1966 authorized as the Church of England's Series 1 rite) provided other psalms, alternative readings, prayers for the bereaved and other occasional material. Overseas revisions have gone the same way, and there is often renewed provision for communion services at funerals.

Fourthly, there has been a reintroduction of petitions for the departed. Partly this arose through the doctrinal convictions of the 'Catholic Revivalists' of the last century, partly through a growing national sentiment (e.g. in the First World War) that wished to say *something* about the departed, while being hesitant to state they were undoubtedly in bliss. The petitions have usually had a rationale which excluded belief in purgatory, and with that exclusion have some show of primitive, and possibly even Anglican, precedent. In Scotland, America and other 'Catholic' provinces the reintroduction has usually gone unchallenged. But Evangelicals have always contested the move. Thus the Church of England's Series 1 rite only just secured the requisite two-thirds majority in the House of Laity in 1966, and the Liturgical Commission's Series 2 rite (which also raised the problem of petitions for the *un*faithful departed) was never put to the final vote in the same House in 1968–9. The dialogue necessitated by such controversies led to a more satisfactory 'remembrance' of the departed in Series 2 communion. In January 1971 the Archbishops' Commission on Christian Doctrine published their Report *Prayer and the Departed*. The intention of the recommendation here was to produce cautious and unitive proposals in which the whole Church of England could agree. When the Liturgical Commission came to draft intercessions about the departed in the communion service, and particularly the Series 3 funeral rites, the proposals of this report were followed at the doctrinally sensitive points.

Fifthly, liturgy for 'funerals' (this term is replacing 'burial' as the rites are used so much for cremation) has reflected changes in other liturgical forms. Three of these which particularly touch English-language rites are worth mention: the change to addressing God as 'you' instead of 'thou'; the return to hardback liturgical books (which bind funeral services in with other rites); and the accelerating move to 'inclusive' language*. The first of these is general in the English-speaking world, but often older rites are preferred in times of transition for an event at which many present are elderly. The second of these is particularly to be found in the richer nations, and the best-known books are in America (1979), Australia (1978), England (1980), and Canada (1985). (The Irish Book of 1984 does not include funeral services.)

The books enable a wide and flexible provision to be made for burial or cremation, for adults or children, for prayers the night before a funeral, for the interment of ashes, for a wide choice of occasional prayers covering many pastoral situations, and for pastoral ministry around and after the time of death. The American rites have a strong element of petitions for the departed, which the Australian rites scrupulously avoid. The English pattern is to 'entrust' the departed to God's mercy. The third tendency, towards 'inclusive' language, does not bear heavily upon funerals, but affects the use of the pronoun 'he' in rubrics, now that women, whether ordained or not, are conducting many funerals, the use of 'man' 'men' in a generic sense, and sometimes the way in which the masculinity of God is mentioned or evaded.

Lastly, with the secularizing of society in the Western nations, there have come signs that secular forms of disposal of corpses are slowly growing, and the trend will probably accelerate in the coming years. Whilst this may deprive the church of such evangelistic opportunities as funerals for all and sundry give, yet it may also clarify the purpose of a specifically Christian funeral, and enable the hope of glory through Christ's resurrection to stand out strikingly when the church does conduct its rites.

C. O. BUCHANAN

5. *Baptist*. No common practice prevails in Baptist memorial, including burial, services. Local custom usually dictates the time, place and form. Also, Baptist services tend to be similar to those in the other Free Churches.

Generally the service is in two parts: the first in the church or funeral chapel and the second at the graveside or crematorium (*see also* **Cremation**). An ordained minister generally conducts the service, but if no ordained minister is available a lay minister, designated by the congregation, may conduct the service.

The service at the church or funeral chapel begins with the minister reading a number of suitable scriptural texts, followed by a hymn, choral or solo musical number. After a prayer the scripture lessons are read. These may be followed with the *Gloria Patri*, a doxology or a hymn of affirmation. The minister then usually interprets a scripture passage dealing with Christ's victory over death which is followed by a prayer and a blessing. Occasionally a eulogy will be included.

The service of committal at the grave or crematorium begins after the people have assembled, with several scripture sentences followed by the words of committal, a prayer and benediction.

Increasingly Baptists, along with others, are moving away from the 'funeral' service with the body present to memorial services in which family and friends gather to remember with thanksgiving the life of the one who has departed. For such a service the setting may be a home with an informal service of readings, prayers and words of remembrance. Or a more formal service is held as part of the regular Lord's Day service and incorporated as an act of thanksgiving and remembrance for 'the saint (or saints) who from their labours rest'. When such a service is held, then a family memorial usually takes place at the time of death. Suggested memorial and burial services as well as worship materials can be found in E. A. Payne and S. F. Winward, *Orders and Prayers for Church Worship*, 1965 and J. E. Skoglund, *A Manual of Worship*, 1968.

Present-day Baptists generally have no special places of burial such as 'Baptist cemeteries'. They generally use the common grounds provided by the community or a burial association.

JOHN E. SKOGLUND

6. *Christian Church*. The burial practice of the Christian Church (Disciples of Christ) tends to be similar to that of other Free Churches. Because the denomination has no officially prescribed service book, Disciple funeral practice varies somewhat from congregation to congregation. Although the Christian Church has no normative theological statement, Disciples seem to hold few peculiar beliefs concerning death and resurrection, the purpose of the funeral or the disposition of the body.

Disciple funeral practice normally includes three moments. First is an informal visit by the pastor and perhaps lay elders to the home of the bereaved for the reading of the Bible, prayer and initial grief counselling.

The second moment is the funeral itself which is held either at the church building

or at the mortuary. The funeral service usually has a strong positive character which acknowledges grief and which focusses on the presence and power of God.

The service typically includes a call to worship, prayers, a brief biographical sketch of the deceased, readings from the Bible, a homily which interprets the meaning of death and life in the light of the gospel, and instrumental and vocal music. The congregation seldom participates verbally in the service; even the music is customarily handled by instrumentalist and vocalist(s). If the body is absent because of cremation*, donation for medical or scientific use, or for some other reason, a memorial service similar in content to the funeral service is usually held.

The third moment is a brief service at the grave, usually comprised of scripture, committal (which sometimes includes the sprinkling of earth on the casket) and prayer. Ordinarily the congregation provides a meal (or similar service) for the bereaved family.

RONALD J. ALLEN

7. *Congregationalist*. In their earliest days the Independents had deep doubts about the propriety of burial services, partly because they led to superstition and partly because they were the occasion of hypocritical eulogies.

In modern days these dangers are overcome by services that avoid elaborate eulogies, or, in many cases, have no eulogy at all, and by keeping strictly to the biblical promises. The emphasis in 'burial' services (English) or 'funeral' services (American) is on scriptural readings and prayers that reiterate the promises of the risen Christ, the enduring covenant love of the divine Father, and the comfort of Christian friends in the hope of the gospel, with a solemn reminder of the transitoriness and accountability of human life.

According to the English Congregational service book, *A Book of Services and Prayers* (1959), provision is made for three separate but related burial services. There is first a short, simple, and intimate family service in the home. This consists of the reading of declarations of notable divine promises and affirmations of faith from the scriptures, including Ps. 23, and of prayers for faith and hope and comfort, concluding with the Lord's Prayer. The minister usually offers one or more extempore prayers.

The second service, no longer restricted to family and close friends, but now including former associates in many walks of life, takes place either at the church or cemetery chapel. It may well include a hymn (frequently the favourite hymn of the deceased), and a short address, especially if the deceased were a pillar of the church and community. It will include scripture lessons and prayers which will normally include thanksgiving for our hope and assurance of eternal life through the gospel; a prayer of grateful memories; supplication for the mourners; and a petition for grace to live the life of faith.

The third service is held either at the graveside or in the crematorium. The form of committal is that of the BCP: 'For as much as it hath pleased Almighty God of his great mercy to take unto himself the soul of our dear *brother* here departed, we therefore commit *his* body to the ground: earth to earth, ashes to ashes, dust to dust; in sure and certain hope of resurrection to everlasting life through our Lord Jesus Christ . . .' At a cremation the wording of the committal is changed to read, 'we therefore commit *his* body to the elements . . .'

The same service book also provides two very moving alternatives for use on special occasions. The one is for the burial of a child. The other is 'A Service for use in Circumstances of Deep Distress', including the burial of a suicide.

The burial services in the United Reformed Church's* *Book of Services* (1980) are not materially different. The book contains a Service before a Funeral, which can take place in the home or elsewhere and consists mainly of readings and psalms; a Funeral Service, which covers both the full service at a crematorium and a church service followed by committal; a Funeral Service for a Child; and a new Service for the Burial and Scattering of Ashes.

The funeral services of the United Church of Christ in the USA are similar in character, with the notable difference of often including a eulogy of the deceased.

HORTON DAVIES

8. *Jehovah's Witnesses.* Funeral services conducted by Jehovah's Witnesses are designed to give scriptural comfort to the bereaved. At the same time, the speaker in outlining the condition of the dead explains the Bible's hope, the resurrection.

The funeral discourse opens with prayer and sometimes a song, concluding likewise. The speaker, usually one of the local elders, will also mention certain aspects of the life of the deceased so that each occasion is a very personal one.

The Bible's teaching of the resurrection is a precious one to Jehovah's Witnesses. They understand that 'since death is through a man, resurrection of the dead is also through a man. For just as in Adam all are dying, so also in the Christ all will be made alive' (I Cor. 15.21, 22). Death resulting from the sin of the first human pair, Adam and Eve, is lovingly cancelled out by the sacrifice of the perfect human life of Jesus Christ (John 11.24, 25).

The Bible clearly teaches that the human soul is mortal. Nowhere does it link the word 'immortality' with 'soul'. It follows that death is the cessation of life. The Hebrew *sheol* and the Greek *hades*, usually translated as 'hell', mean simply the common grave of mankind. The words carry no thought of torment at all but that of inactivity at death. The Greek word *gehenna* in its twelve appearances in the Greek scriptures refers to the deep, narrow valley of Hinnom lying to the south and south-west of Jerusalem. It was never a symbol of everlasting conscious torment, but rather one of complete destruction (Matt. 10.28; Luke 12.4, 5). As the words 'purgatory' and 'limbo' do not appear in any translation of the Bible, Jehovah's Witnesses dismiss the religious traditions taught regarding them.

The choice of cremation* or burial is a personal one to be decided in the light of local customs and requirements. No special 'consecrated' burial grounds are used.

DAVID SIBREY

9. *Lutheran.* Luther and the Reformers had more criticisms to make of the Roman Catholic rite of burial than of any of the other traditional offices of the church. As early as the writing 'To the Christian Nobility of the German Nation' (1520; *Martin Luthers Werke*, Weimar, 1883ff. = WA 6,444f.; LW 44,180f.). Luther vigorously attacked masses for the dead and vigils. In a late writing, a collection of Christian hymns for funerals, he regards vigils, requiems, funeral pomp and purgatory as 'popish abominations' which must be completely rejected because they contradict scripture, especially in the fact that their help is enlisted to influence the fate of the dead (1542; WA 35,478; LW 53,325–331; cf. Apolog. der Conf. Aug. 24, 89ff.). On the Reformed side this radical rejection of traditional rites meant that for a long time burial was left to the personal initiative of the members of the family, the guilds or the authorities; the church did not co-operate. The same tendency can also be found, to begin with, in Lutheran areas. But very soon a criticism of this attitude makes itself felt: having laid aside 'superstitious pomp of the dead', people treat them 'quite bestially' (Strasbourg 1533). However, for some decades there is no liturgical formulary to lay down the details of a funeral. Luther produced manuals for baptism* and marriage*, but no order for funeral services; he was content – as has been said – to publish a few German and Latin chorales for this purpose. He did propose, in the same preface, that funerals should be conducted with decorum, and even with 'splendour' and processions, in order to defy death and praise the resurrection. But the lack of an order of service authorized by Luther is presumably the reason why there is a confusing number and variety of forms and orders for burial in individual Lutheran churches and areas. This position has only been changed in the last few decades.

Nevertheless, some common principles and even some basic structures for funerals can be found in the sixteenth century. According to Luther, a funeral should serve to 'strengthen our faith and encourage the people to true devotion. For it is right and fitting that a funeral should be performed honourably, to the praise and honour of the joyful article of our faith, the resurrection of the dead' (WA 35,479; LW 53,326). Accordingly, from now on (*a*) the focal point is no longer to be the dead body but faith in the resurrection, which is to be expressed in hymn, prayer and sermon. In addition, (*b*) even in early times, burial was regarded as an act of love by the congregation towards the dead person and the family. 'For the dead are still our brothers,

and have not fallen from our community by death; we still remain members of a single body'; therefore it is one of the duties of 'civic neighbourliness' to accompany the dead to the grave (Church order of Schwäbisch Hall 1526; Richter I, 47). Finally, (*c*) burial is to remind us of our own deaths and to cause us to lead an appropriate way of life (for these three points see Württemberg 1536; Richter I, 273).

Traditional features retained are the ringing of the church bells, either at the moment of death or at the burial, and the procession to the grave. The church ordinances of the sixteenth century prohibit 'secret burials'. Pastor, verger, teacher, school children and as far as possible one person from each house in the community are to join the family in accompanying the body to the grave, usually in a prescribed order. On the way to and at the grave, hymns are to be sung by the congregation or at least by the children, 'not mourning hymns nor sorrowful, but comforting hymns about the forgiveness of sins, rest, sleep, the life and resurrection of departed Christians' (Luther, WA 35,478f.; LW 53,326). It seems that at the beginning people were content simply to sing hymns at the burial. This expressed the fact that it was the congregation that bore the body to the grave and confessed its faith in the resurrection. Prayers and a sermon were added relatively soon; there is not always explicit mention of either, but in the course of time they will have become the rule, though with exceptions.

According to Schulz, some forty-five funeral prayers have been preserved from the sixteenth century; they have a christological basis and express faith in the resurrection, ask for a strengthening of faith in earthly life and give thanks for the life of the departed. At first there are only hints of a prayer for the departed at the burial itself (e.g. Württemberg 1536, Richter I, 273); they occur occasionally later (e.g. Hessen 1566 and 1574; Sehling 8, 336 and 450). The coffin or body is at first lowered into the grave to the singing of a hymn. Only later are affirmations made, e.g. 'Earth thou art . . .' (following Gen. 3.19; Dessau 1532, Sehling 1.2, 541), Rev. 14.13 (Pfalz-Neuburg 1543, Sehling 13, 90) or, as earth is thrown three times: 'Of dust thou art made and to dust must thou return. May the Lord Jesus Christ raise thy body and soul (!) that thou mayest rise again with the righteous on the Last Day. Amen' (Waldeck 1556; Richter II, 171).

To begin with, a sermon was only preached in the case of people of standing (princes and other notables), usually not at the burial itself but as a memorial sermon some time afterwards. Generally speaking, if there was a sermon at all, short admonitions were thought to be sufficient, often in connection with the readings I Thess. 4.13–18 and John 11.21–27. In the course of time the sermon became an essential part of the funeral; thus the *Kursächsische Kirchenordnung* of 1580 contains four funeral sermons, two each for adults and young people, which are to be read in the church after the burial (Sehling I, 1, 371ff.). At this particular point, however, ominous differences arise at an early stage. According to the *Wittenberger Kirchenordnung* of 1533, 'common people' are to be buried without bells, 'citizens of middle degree' with the singing of school children and 'honourable people' with a procession and the sound of the great bells (Sehling I, 1, 195). As early as 1540 it is mentioned on many occasions that differing fees are exacted for the different forms of funeral. This is related above all to the sermon: 'funeral sermons' or 'eulogies' are delivered only on the payment of an appropriate fee; otherwise, people have to be content with a brief 'dismissal' or a mere 'blessing'. This shameful classification of funerals lasted right down to the beginning of our century; it involved not only the sermon, but the whole of the funeral.

Leaving aside new hymns and prayers for funerals, the structure of the funeral service hardly altered over the next two centuries, down to the time of the Enlightenment. This was not, however, the case with funeral sermons, where they were required and given. In the sixteenth century the preaching was predominantly biblical and christological, but in the seventeenth century a strong personal element was added, among other things by the inclusion of a *curriculum vitae*; at the same time, funeral sermons took on a learned tone, used allegory and often occupied an intolerable amount of time. A eulogy of the dead person took precedence over what were originally the main themes of funeral sermons

(the proclamation of the last things, preparation for a happy death) (E. Winkler). At the time of the Enlightenment the biblical orientation of the funeral sermon disappeared still more; at its centre stood the life of the dead person and the parting from him, both presented in the Baroque and sentimental style of the time.

In many places in Germany there was no funeral sermon at all. This was connected with an extremely strange development. Silent 'interments', once provided for suicides, notorious sinners, etc. took the place of public funerals. It became the custom to inter the dead at a late hour of the evening or at midnight, by torchlight, with only family and friends present, and usually without any participation by the pastor. The place of the funeral sermon was taken by the 'eulogy' of a friend at the graveside. The funeral service of the congregation in many cases, particularly in towns, became a family gathering. In addition, under the influence of the numerous private forms of service published and used, the hymns, prayers and words of committal were adapted to the language of the time. For example, one committal takes the following form: 'Take this body, mother earth, into thy protection under the oversight of almighty God! The day will surely come again when death must return even this its prey' (1802, according to P. Graff, II, 275).

Contradictory intentions arise with the movement for liturgical reform in the middle of the nineteenth century. Using portions of church orders from the sixteenth century, W. Löhe and others propose complete funeral services for the first time; their characteristics are that a number of passages are proposed as readings, and a large number of collects and prayers, especially the committal from King Edward VI's prayer book of 1552 (with a few alterations), are suggested. Most local churches in Germany and the *Common Service Book* in America shaped their funeral services along these lines about 1900. Usually the funeral begins – often after a biblical sentence – with Ps. 130 or another psalm; one or two lessons, for which a number of passages are suggested, are followed by the sermon (which has become a permanent feature), sometimes by the *Nunc Dimittis* and a prayer, for which a few models are provided. At the graveside, the coffin is lowered with the committal from the prayer book, occasionally (as in Prussia, 1895) with the additional words: 'From the earth thou art taken, to the earth thou shalt return. Jesus Christ, our Redeemer, will raise you on the Last Day.' Here, too, a lesson and prayers are provided for. The service can begin at the grave and be continued in the church (or cemetery chapel) or vice versa. There is singing by the congregation or a choir at appropriate places.

Some private forms of service have had an influence on the further shaping of the funeral by providing 'different psalms, scripture readings (sometimes made up of isolated verses from the Bible) and prayers depending on the life, status, age and sex of the dead person. Newer official forms, which have appeared since 1960, take up this suggestion; they offer a considerable number of introit psalms, readings, prayers, hymns and committal prayers to suit individual cases. The prayers aim at a modern form of expression, without always being successful. One leading funeral service is that in the *Agende für Evangelisch-Lutherische Kirchen und Gemeinden* (III, 1964, pp.155–222). First of all it has the ordinary forms for different places: (*a*) house of mourning or undertaker's chapel (greeting, collect, hymn, invitation to proceed to the cemetery); (*b*) cemetery chapel or church (introit hymn, biblical sentence, Ps. 130 or another, scriptural reading, hymn, sermon, possibly with *curriculum vitae*, hymn, prayer, invitation to proceed to the grave with Ps. 121.8); (*c*) at the grave (hymn, greeting, biblical sentence, committal ['Since it has pleased almighty God to call from this life our *brother* N, we lay *his* body in God's earth, that *he* may become again the earth from which *he* is taken: earth to earth, ashes to ashes, dust to dust. We commend our *brother* N into God's hand. Jesus Christ will raise *him* on the last day. May he be gracious to *him* in judgment and assist *him* to his everlasting kingdom'], scripture reading I Cor. 15.42–44, 55–57; I Thess. 4.13–18; Rom. 14.7–9 or Rev. 21.1–5a, possibly an anthem; Lord's Prayer, a collect, possible Apostles' Creed, hymn and trinitarian blessing); the forms also contain suggestions for cremation and the committal of ashes. This is followed by a proper of about ten psalms, thirty readings (all

from the New Testament) and about the same number of prayers, mostly with indications of individual usage.

The *Lutheran Book of Worship* (US and Canada 1978) introduces a funeral rite which is the fruit of Lutheran reflection on current ecumenical liturgical proposals. The rite in the church is essentially the service of the word from the eucharist. The full eucharist may be celebrated. The rite may be preceded by a reception of the casket and the use of a pall* (with baptismal reference). It is concluded by a commemoration in the church, which restores the primitive Lutheran willingness to pray for the deceased, and by a procession to the grave and a burial rite.

A. NIEBERGALL/GORDON LATHROP

10. *Methodist.* John Wesley, in the Preface attached to some copies of *The Sunday Service of the Methodists*, 1784, said that he had omitted some sentences in the office for the burial of the dead. He had in fact omitted Ps. 39, the committal, and the prayer 'Almighty God, with whom we live, etc.' These changes were largely in harmony with Puritan objections. In other respects Wesley followed almost exactly the 1662 BCP of the Church of England. Methodist funerals were marked by a strong note of joy, as was shown by the use of such hymns as:

Rejoice for a brother deceased,
Our loss is his infinite gain.

In the following century these omitted passages were for the most part restored, often with some alterations, in the service books, both in America and in Britain. In England, Methodists in country districts are often buried in the Anglican parish churchyard, and the service was thus the Anglican service performed by an Anglican clergyman until a change in the law in 1880 made it permissible for burials to take place in such churchyards without the Church of England service and thus by a Nonconformist minister.

In the present century there have been further changes. Major reforms occurred in American Methodist practice with the publication of *A Service of Death and Resurrection* in 1979 of which the basic service became a part of *The Book of Services* (1985). The 1979 volume stresses the paschal character of Christian burial and includes an optional eucharistic rite. Additional resources for the death of a child, untimely death, and the death of a non-Christian are provided. The British form is in *The Methodist Service Book*, 1975. Both the American and the British forms have sentences, prayers (an addition to Anglican use), psalm(s), lesson(s), optional sermon, prayers to conclude the service in church (an addition; the old custom was that the service had prayers only at the graveside). The British service has a further new feature designed to make the service in church more complete, namely a commendation of the deceased to God's mercy and wisdom. This was suggested by a similar Anglican proposal. Both services have the optional use of the Apostles' Creed, but at different points. At the grave or in the crematorium (*see also* **Cremation**), both services have sentences, committal (both services have variant forms to provide for different circumstances), Rev. 14.13, prayers. Both services have unambiguous prayers for the dead; they are, however, optional. Funerals are much influenced by local customs. In practice the whole of the first part of the service is sometimes said in the home rather than the church.

A. RAYMOND GEORGE

11. *Old Catholic.* Rites for the burial of the dead differ in detail in the Old Catholic churches, and in addition, liturgical practice is influenced by regional and local customs. Nevertheless, some common features can be established. These, in essentials, are: blessing of the corpse and the grave, the recitation of appropriate psalms, intercessions for the dead and the bereaved, thanksgiving for God's grace towards the dead and through them to us. A eucharist often accompanies the funeral. All Souls' Day* (2 November) is celebrated as a day of remembrance for all the departed.

As an example, we give a brief description of the form of funeral to be found in the Old Catholic Church of Germany.

The burial service commences with a prayer and a Bible reading. This is followed by the address (homily) and the remembrance of baptism, at which point the coffin is besprinkled and a somewhat longer prayer is said. The congregation then moves to the graveside which is first blessed. After

a prayer the priest throws the first handful of earth into the grave and makes the sign of the cross over it. Intercessions, the Lord's Prayer, thanksgiving and benediction follow. The new order (1985) is noteworthy for the number of alternatives provided. Cremations* follow the same basic pattern. The texts provided for use at the graveside are, however, omitted, but they can be used later when the urn containing the ashes is placed to rest.

In the Old Catholic Church in the Netherlands, it is in some places the custom to have a prayer-meeting with scripture reading, prayers and hymns selected by the officiating clergyman, on the eve of the burial. The official rite is made up of the requiem mass* and burial prayers. The requiem mass is an almost literal translation from the Roman missal. As it was forbidden in the Netherlands to practise the Old Catholic faith openly between the beginning of the Reformation and 1800, and as it was only possible to do so secretly and in hidden churches, the different elements of the funeral are still gathered up into one continuous whole: bringing the body to the church, prayers in connection with the absolution after the mass and the ritual in the burial ground. This is usually said in the church building after the requiem mass (in former times, more often in the home of the dead person). After a month and after a year (and, if required, monthly and annually), the departed is remembered during the mass.

S. KRAFT/C. TOL

12. *Plymouth Brethren.* There is no distinctive order for the burial of the dead among the Brethren. Frequently, when members of the fellowship die, a service is held at their home or at the meeting-place which they attended, before the departure of the funeral procession for the ceremony, and a short committal service is held at the graveside. These services may be conducted by elders of the church or by friends or family who are able to say what is appropriate for such an occasion. At these services emphasis is customarily laid on the faith in which the departed lived and died, and reference will be made to features of their Christian life, service and witness which can be commended as an example to others. It will be made clear that their friends' assurance of their eternal bliss is based not on their record or merit but on the faithfulness of God, in whom they had put their trust. Sometimes one or two suitable hymns of confidence and hope will be sung. Scriptures read will probably make mention of the immediate and present well-being of departed believers as being 'absent from the body and at home with the Lord' (II Cor. 5.8) and of the coming day of resurrection and reunion at the Second Advent. Prayers for the dead are never heard, for it is not doubted that the dead in Christ do rest in peace; interesting situations arise, however, when an informal service is conducted jointly by (say) the vicar of the parish and a member of the Brethren; it is not unknown for the former to pray for the soul of the departed and the latter (presumably for the sake of Christian unity) to add a loud Amen.

Where the deceased has lived to a good age, or has been released from long illness and pain, this atmosphere of confidence and hope can make a burial service a remarkably joyful occasion. The confidence and hope will still be present, but the feeling and language will be different, at the burial of a child or young person, or of someone whose life has been tragically or suddenly cut short; yet the comfort of the scriptures will send the mourners away greatly strengthened in heart. Where the departed person is a known unbeliever, the character of the service will be perceptibly modified, but it will be emphasized that the only hope for eternal life lies in the Saviour who died and rose again.

In some areas (e.g. in the north of Scotland) it is taken for granted that a funeral service will be the occasion for a full-blown proclamation of the gospel, but this is not confined to one denomination.

Cremation* is still probably exceptional, but is less unacceptable than it used to be.

F. F. BRUCE

13. *Reformed.* In the early Reformed Church the procedure at burial was influenced by the mediaeval background and reaction against it so that in some places no service was held at the grave. This appears to have been the practice at Strasbourg to, at least, 1533, when at the first Synod of Strasbourg the *Kirchenpfleger* protested against the custom for its irreverence, citing

the OT patriarchs and early Christian usage (*Arch. S. Thos*, 45.1, fol.87). It was ordered that a pastor should be present at burial, but no order for burial was drawn up until 1537. It consisted of scripture reading, exhortation, silent or free prayer, collect and almsgiving (Hubert, *Die stras. lit. Ordnungen*, pp. 128–130).

This would have been Bucer's practice, and he makes similar provision in the *Consultatio* he prepared for Cologne in 1543 (*Con.* fol.ccxliv). Calvin would have known it, but no such provision is made in either his Strasbourg or Genevan liturgies (*Op.* vi, 172–208). The Genevan *Ordonnances ecclesiastiques* (1541) simply say:

> The dead are to be buried decently in the place appointed. The attendance and company are left to each man's discretion. It will be good that the carriers be warned by us to discourage all superstitions contrary to the Word of God . . .

Calvin approved an 'appropriate sermon' being given 'in the churchyard' (*Letter to Farel*, 1543), and considered 'the Spirit no less attentive to the burial rites . . . than to the chief mysteries of the Faith' (*Inst.* III. xxv.8), so his practice may not have been so severe as in the *Ordonannces* but have approximated to Pullain's *Liturgia Sacra*:

> The corpse shall be carried by trusty men from the city to the cemetery. The whole church shall follow with great modesty, the pastor or other minister leading. When it is come to the place where the body is to be placed in the ground, a brief address concerning death and the resurrection of the dead is given, with commendation of the deceased, if he has any virtues from which to edify the church. Prayer shall be made for the church that as God gives us this transient life so we may pass through death into his Kingdom, and that he will raise all through Christ at the last day to immortality. The people shall be dismissed with an admonition that they give an offering for the relief of the poor.

The *Form of Prayers* (1556) of the English congregation in Geneva ordered:

> The corpse is reverently brought to the grave, accompanied with the congregation, without any further ceremonies, which being buried, the minister goeth to the church, if it be not far off, and maketh some comfortable exhortation to the people, touching death and resurrection.

This was incorporated into the Scottish *Book of Common Order* (*BCO*, 1564), adding after 'minister' the words 'if he be present and required'. This leaves the question of a service open, as had the first *Book of Discipline* in 1560, although the General Assembly in 1562 had enacted:

> That one uniform order shall be taken or kept in ministration of the Sacraments, and solemnization of the Marriages and Burial of the Dead, according to the Kirk of Geneva.

Funeral services were not uncommon in Scotland, although in some places there were none, until with the growth of Brownism the Glasgow Assembly in 1638 decided 'to discharge funeral sermons, as savouring of superstition'. In England, the BCP contained a burial office, but among the Puritans there is evidence for 'sermon' only or 'singing of a psalm' only, and no service at all.

The debate on burial in the Westminster Assembly shows the Scots to be opposed to 'sermons', but that the opinion of the divines was that there should be liberty concerning whether 'something might be said at the very interment of the body' and that the clause 'without any ceremony' did not prevent a minister 'at putting the body in the ground' saying, 'We commit the body to the ground, etc.' (Lightfoot, *Works*, xiii, p.340). The text of the *Westminster Directory of Public Worship* adopts the extreme Puritan position, but tries to keep open the door for the 'positive' approach demanded by Palmer, Whitaker and Marshall:

> When any person departeth this life, let the dead body, upon the day of burial, be decently attended from the house to the place appointed for public burial, and there immediately interred, without any ceremony . . .
>
> For that, praying, reading both in going to, and at the grave, have been grossly abused, are no way beneficial to the dead, and have proved many ways hurtful to the living, therefore let all such things be laid aside.

> Howbeit, we judge it very convenient, that the Christian friends, which accompany the dead body to the place appointed for public burial, do apply themselves to meditations and conferences suitable to the occasion; and that the minister, as upon other occasions, so at this time, if he be present, may put them in remembrance of their duty.

This, together with the triumph of Independency during the Commonwealth, resulted in a position where it was possible to write in 1867 of Scotland (equally true of Ireland and England):

> In many, if not most, parts of the country, the religious observance at present consists of prayer alone ... the solemn reading of the pure Word of God, without which no Protestant Service is true to its character, or complete – is generally omitted ... The religious Service at funerals ... is, as a general rule, confined to the house of mourning, except on the occasion of the death of ministers, and of others who have filled positions of special prominence, when sometimes a Service is held at the Church or the place of interment.

In the renewal of English rites the main influence was the Church Service Society, who in the first edition of *Euchologion* (1867) included a 'Manual for the Burial of the Dead' based on the American 'Manual of Devotional Services' and the Dutch and German Reformed rites.

American Presbyterianism followed the 1788 revision of the *Westminster Directory of Public Worship*, and, if anything, this was even more deficient than the original. Indeed, the deficiency of this aspect of the church's ministry to people was one of the factors leading to liturgical renewal, which resulted in the formation of a Church Society, on the Scottish model, in 1897, and eventually to the *Book of Common Worship* (*BCW*) in 1906, which was revised in 1932 and 1946. In the last and the *Book of Common Worship: Proposed Services* (1966), which after an experimental period were finalized in *The Worshipbook* (1977) prepared by a joint Committee of the Cumberland Presbyterian Church, the Presbyterian Church in the United States, and the United Presbyterian Church in the United States of America, the influence of the Scottish *BCO* (1940) is evident.

Modern Rites (*a*) *English.* An examination of modern Reformed burial rites in Scotland, England, Ireland, Wales, Canada, Australia and South Africa reveals a common structure and content, and that they have all been much influenced by the *Euchologion* and the BCP. All provide for two services, one in church or home, and the other at the graveside. While there are variations in details, the general order of the former is scripture sentences, invocation, psalm, scripture readings, address, prayers of adoration, confession, thanksgiving, supplication, intercession and commemoration of saints, hymn and benediction. At the graveside the order is scripture sentences, committal, prayers and benediction. The prayers are drawn from the Reformers, the BCP, *Euchologion*, Dutch, German, Scottish, English and American sources.

(*b*) *American.* The rite used in the United Presbyterian Church in the USA and the Presbyterian Church in the US (Southern) provides for two services – one for use in the church, and one for the committal service. No provision is made for worship in the home, though doubtless in practice one was customary. Each is entitled 'Witness to the Resurrection'. The church service consists of scripture sentences, prayer, OT and NT lections with a prayer, hymn, sermon (optional), Apostles' Creed, prayer of thanksgiving and intercession, hymn and benediction. The committal service is brief, consisting of scripture sentences, committal, prayer, Lord's Prayer and benediction.

(*c*) *French.* Taking the liturgies of France, Geneva and Vaud as representative of French rites, the *Liturgie de L'Église de Genève* and *Liturgie de L'Église Nationale Évangélique Réformée du Canton de Vaud* provide for two services as in the English rites and are similar to them in content. The church or home service is invocation and introduction, scripture texts and psalm, prayer before Bible reading, scripture reading, address, prayer after address and benediction. At the graveside the order is invocation and committal, scripture reading, prayer, conclusion (scripture sentences of exhortation) and benediction.

On the other hand, the *Liturgie de L'Ég-*

lise Réformée de France provides for three services – home (*levée de corps*), church (*service principal*) and cemetery. The first consists of invocation, declaration (*accueil*), Apostles' Creed, prayer, psalm, scripture reading, address or meditation, chant, prayer, Lord's Prayer and benediction. The third is introduction, prayer, scripture sentences of exhortation and benediction.

(*d*) *German*. These rites retain many of the exhortations of the Reformation era against 'abuses' and emphasize the necessity for 'absolute simplicity and common decency'. Structurally they do not differ greatly from the English and French rites, but lay a greater stress on the necessity for 'sermon'. Basic to them all is à Lasco's *Forma ac Ratio*, the Palatinate order for the preaching of the word of God at burial, and the Zurich order for burial (1529).

The prayers in the French and German rites are drawn from Strasbourg (1537), Calvin, BCP (1549, 1552), à Lasco, Micronius, Pullain, Cassell (1657) and St Gallen (1699), adding in the case of the German rites Zurich (1529, 1626) and Pfalz (1563), and of the French Neuchâtel (1713).

(*e*) *Others*. As Reformed rites belong to the one family, they contain many common features. The Dutch rites remain closely related to à Lasco and Pullain. The Hungarian and Czechoslovak rites are akin to the German, as are the Waldensian and Belgian to the French. The Portuguese and Brazilian rites (through American influence) and the Spanish (through Irish) have much in common with the English.

In all these rites the centrality of the life, death and resurrection of Christ is basic. The Strasbourg order (1537) declared: 'It is our task at burial to comfort each other in the Lord and to encourage to Christian endeavour.' All give adequate expression to this. On the other hand, one point appears to receive inadequate expression. With Paul and the Fathers, Calvin could write 'baptism is the seal of our future resurrection (Col. 2.12); no less does the sacred Supper invite us to confidence in it' (*Inst.* III.xxxv.8). Few, if any, of the rites include a specific reference to this.

In all these rites a large selection of lections is provided, some of them numbering over seventy. While recognition must be given to the fullness of scriptural teaching, surely for liturgical purposes this could be reduced considerably.

JOHN M. BARKLEY

14. *Seventh-day Adventist*. The burial service of the Seventh-day Adventist Church does not differ a great deal in its forms from that of most Protestant churches. Since interment customs vary from country to country, there are naturally also some variations in Adventist burial rites in different parts of the world; there are, however, also many constants. It is the generally accepted practice for SDA ministers to charge no fee for conducting funerals. They co-operate closely with the funeral director and endeavour to meet the wishes of the sorrowing family in making arrangements for the funeral service at the home, the funeral parlour or the church.

The doctrinal basis for the SDA funeral service is conditionalism, that is, the belief that immortality or everlasting life is the gift of God through faith in Christ. As conditionalists, Adventists believe that the Bible teaches that man rests in the grave until the resurrection and they therefore consider as unscriptural the doctrine of immortal-soulism, according to which man was created with a soul that has a separate, indefeasibly immortal existence, apart from the body.

A typical church funeral service is opened by a hymn followed by a brief prayer. Then a suitable collection of scriptural passages may be read, taking into consideration the age, life and experience of the deceased. As a rule, the reading includes such Bible passages as Ps. 90.1–4, 10, 12; Job 14.1, 2, 14, 15; I Cor. 15.51, 57. Then a short obituary sketch presenting the life of the deceased is read. There follows a brief homily, not a long doctrinal sermon on the state of the dead, pointing the bereaved to the glorious hope of the resurrection and underlining the power of Christ to deliver from sin and conquer death by bestowing immortality upon the righteous at his second coming – the blessed hope of all ages.

After the homily or address a prayer follows, making thanksgiving for all that God's goodness has done for the departed, for the assurance of the resurrection's restoration, praying for the finishing of the gospel work on earth, and remembering the dear ones left to mourn. Another song may

be sung at this point in the service, which closes with the benediction.

At the graveside a quartet or some other group may sing, and as the casket rests above the grave, or is being lowered into the earth, the minister reads appropriate scriptural passages, such as John 11.25; Rev. 1.17,18; 14.13; 21.3–5; I Thess. 4.13–18.

In some countries the minister or funeral director drops a little earth or flower petals on the casket as the minister repeats the liturgical committal. If a hymn is sung at the graveside it is usually sung at this point. A closing prayer follows together with the benediction.

B. B. BEACH

S. Benko, *The Meaning of Sanctorum Communio*, 1964; B. Bürkli, *Im Herrn entschlafen. Eine historisch-pastoral theologische Studie zur Liturgie des Sterbens und des Begräbnisses*, 1969; J. Calvin, *Institutes* III, xxv, 5–8; G. Cope (ed), *Dying, Death and Disposal*, 1970 (a treatment of pastoral, architectural and theological problems arising in connection with funerary practice today); O. Cullmann, *Immortality of the Soul or Resurrection of the Dead?*, 1958; J. Dowdall, 'The Liturgy of the Dead', *Studies in Pastoral Liturgy*, I, ed P. Murray, 1964; L. E. Froom, *The Conditionalist Faith of our Fathers*, 1966 (Seventh-day Adventist); P. Graff, *Geschichte der Auflösung der alten gottesdienstlichen Formen in der evangelischen Kirche Deutschlands*, [2] 1937, I, pp. 345–372; II, 272–279; M. Gy, OP, 'La Mort du Chrétien', *L'Église en Prière*, ed A. G. Martimort, 1965; M. J. Hatchett, *Commentary on the American Prayer Book*, 1979; R. C. D. Jasper (ed), *The Alternative Service Book 1980: A Commentary*, 1980; B. Jordahn, *Das kirchliche Begräbnis. Grundlegung und Gestaltung*, 1949; T. Kliefoth, *Liturgische Abhandlungen*, I and II, 1869; M. Luther, *Werke*, Weimar 1883ff.; *La Maison Dieu*, 101; *Manual for Ministers*, 1977 (Seventh-day Adventist); H. Maser, *Die Bestattung*, 1964; W. D. Maxwell, *John Knox's Genevan Service Book*, 1931; R. Mehl, *Notre vie et notre mort*, 1953; K. F. Müller and W. Blankenburg (eds), *Leiturgia. Handbuch des evangelischen Gottesdienstes* (6: Begräbnis, etc.), 1952; *The Prayer Book of Edward VI* (Everyman or other editions; there exists no collection of later Anglican funerary rites); A. L. Richter, *Die evangelischen Kirchenordnungen des 16. Jahrhunderts*, 2 vols, 1846; G. Rietschel-P. Graff. *Lehrbuch der Liturgik*, [2] 1951, pp.764–788; M. Righetti, *Storia Liturgica*, II, [2] 1955; G. Rowell, *The Liturgy of Christian Burial*, 1977; F. Schulz, 'Die Begräbnisgebete des 16. und 17. Jahrhunderts', *Jahrbuch für Liturgie und Hymnologie*, XI, 1966, 00.1–44; E. Sehling, *Die evangelischen Kirchenordnungen des XVI Jahrhunderts*, 14 vols, 1962ff.; *Services Funèbres*, 1963 (Reformed); John E. Skoglund, *A Manual of Worship*, 1968 (Baptist); E. Winkler, *Die Leichenpredigt im deutschen Luthertum bis Spener*, 1967.

Byzantine Chant

The Eastern Orthodox Churches owe allegiance to the four ancient Patriarchates of Jerusalem, Antioch, Alexandria and Constantinople. Together they form what is known as the Holy Oriental Orthodox Catholic Apostolic Church, to give it its full title. There are also a number of smaller groups, known as Uniate Churches, which, while belonging liturgically and culturally to Eastern Christendom, are in full communion with the See of Rome. Of the many ancient liturgies used in the East, the one that has prevailed among both Orthodox and Uniates is that of the Patriarchate of Jerusalem, which exists in a longer form for special days, the Liturgy of St Basil, and in a shorter form for all the rest of the year, the Liturgy of St John Chrysostom. Originally in Greek, the liturgy has been translated over the centuries into many Eastern languages, and, at the present day, into a number of Western languages as well, including English. The best-known of these are Church Slavonic, Arabic, Armenian, Coptic, Georgian and Ukrainian. The music, though it may sound very different in the various churches and cultures, is mainly derived from the music of the Byzantine–Greek rite. The term Byzantine comes from Byzantium, the name of the ancient site that became Constantinople, the Istanbul of modern times. It was the centre of the Eastern Christian Roman Empire from the beginning of the fourth century until the Ottoman conquest of 1453. The full repertory of chants used

in mediaeval times by the Greek Orthodox Church exists in manuscript with two systems of musical notation, and can therefore be studied in depth, like the Gregorian chant* of Western Christianity. The two systems of notation are the *ekphonetic* system, an aide-mémoire for the chants of the lectionary, and a *melodic* system for all the other kinds of chant, syllabic, formulaic or florid.

Byzantine chant recognizes a modal system of eight modes, the *Octoechos*, which has its counterpart in the West. The modes of the *Octoechos* are used in rotation over a period of eight weeks. The numbering differs from that of the Western system: the authentic modes, 1, 2, 3 and 4 end on D, E, F and G and the plagal modes, numbering 5, 6, 7 and 8, also end on D, E, F end G.

All Eastern rite services are sung throughout: a said liturgy is an impossibility. The Council of Laodicea (367) ruled that the people should have no vocal part to play in the services, so as to safeguard the purity of the chant: only the clergy, the cantor* and the trained choir are permitted to perform, and so the chant is divided between these three participants in the form of a lively and moving dialogue. The Council of Laodicea also ruled that musical instruments were to be banned from the services; bells, however, did not classify as such. One typical feature of Byzantine chant, which is unisonic, is the addition of an *ison*, or bass drone, introduced in accordance with strict rules of performance. The *ison* serves to keep the pitch and also adds an element of rudimentary harmony with strikingly beautiful effect.

Some splendid recordings are at present available, notably those from Mount Athos. They are ample proof, if such were needed, that the time-honoured tradition of Byzantine chant is still as fresh and impressive as ever.

Egon Wellesz, *Eastern Elements in Western Chant*, [2]1967; *A History of Byzantine Music and Hymnography*, [3]1963.

MARY BERRY

Byzantine Worship

see **Orthodox Worship**

Calendar

The calendar or liturgical year is the list of commemorations observed throughout the Christian year. It combines complexity of detail with a simple fundamental underlying structure. It consists of two parts, called the temporale and the sanctorale. The temporale, a word indicating the passage of time, is a series of christological festivals, based upon the two great independent festivals of Easter and Christmas. The sanctorale, as its name indicates, is concerned with the celebration of the feasts of individual saints. The pattern of the temporale varies from year to year depending upon the day of the week on which Christmas falls and the date of Easter. The feasts of individual saints are fixed upon certain dates in the calendar year. The fitting together of the temporale and the sanctorale is of necessity therefore somewhat different each year, and is governed by carefully evolved sets of rules which enable the pattern for each particular year to be worked out.

The evolution of the calendar into its present form or forms is a story of development from original simplicity to later complexity. In pre-Nicene times the emphasis was on Sunday* as the day for commemorating salvation in Christ in worship in the weekly memorial of the resurrection. The only real festal observances were Easter*, and to a lesser extent Pentecost*, and their celebration consisted quite simply of a special vigil* plus the observance of the day itself. Easter was and is the Christian Passover and Pentecost, which by the first century in some parts of Judaism had come to commemorate the giving of the law, became the celebration of the outpouring of the Spirit; the significance of this theological parallel should be noted.

From the fourth century onwards the system began to grow more complicated. One of the oldest developments was that of Holy Week*, which received a great impetus from the example of the Jerusalem church, where it became the custom to commemorate the events of Holy Week and Easter at the supposed original locations where these had taken place as well as at appropriate times. By the end of the fourth century Jerusalem had become a great centre of pilgrimage and returning pilgrims,

notable among whom was the Spanish nun Egeria, took these liturgical practices with them back to their own churches; identity of place was of course not possible, but identity of time was. Thus Palm Sunday*, Maundy Thursday*, Good Friday* and Easter Day itself became separate liturgical events, though Easter always retained through its vigil a sense of being a complete celebration of the whole of the paschal mystery, a relic of the time when it was.

The calendar came to adopt the chronology given in the Acts of the Apostles, and so Pentecost, the commemoration of the giving of the Spirit, was seen in relation to Easter as part of one sequence of events, with the Ascension* being celebrated on the Thursday ten days before Pentecost. In the West the first Sunday after Pentecost is designated Trinity Sunday*, which may be seen as a kind of liturgical and theological summary of all that has been commemorated in the Easter-Pentecost season. It originated in the tenth century and was finally adopted by Rome in the fourteenth. It happens that in the Sarum tradition subsequent Sundays were named 'after Trinity', rather than the more usual designation of 'after Pentecost', and this arrangement was adopted by the (Anglican) Books of Common Prayer. In this, on the whole, they have not been followed by modern Anglican revisions.

Independent of, and prior to, the Jerusalem inspired celebration of Holy Week, the observance of the pre-Easter period of Lent* developed. This originated from the proximate period of preparation of candidates for baptism* at the following Easter. Along side these at a later date would be penitents observing Lent in preparation for readmission to communion at Easter. From this it developed into a general penitential season preparatory for the celebration of the coming Easter while, with the decline in adult baptisms consequent upon the growth of infant baptisms, it lost its association with baptismal preparation. Initially somewhat variable in length, it settled at forty days, partly by devotional indentification with Jesus' forty days fasting and temptation in the wilderness, beginning on Ash Wednesday* and Holy Week became integrated into it as the last week of Lent. By a further process of elaboration Lent developed its own pre-lenten preparatory season of two and a half weeks starting on Septuagesima (*see* **Quinquagesima**). Thus that large section of the calendar deriving from Easter, the whole of the period from Septuagesima to Trinity Sunday, was complete.

The Christmas*-Epiphany* cycle has a quite different origin, being a Christianization of pagan mid-winter festivals. The reasons for the celebration of two feasts separated by twelve days are complex, but the end product of this is concentration on the birth of Jesus on Christmas Day and the visit of the magi and the baptism of Jesus, in West and East respectively, at Epiphany. Epiphany means 'manifestation', and both epiphany themes concern the showing forth of God in Christ, which theme continues to be observed on succeeding Sundays.

By analogy with Lent, Christmas acquired its own preparatory season of Advent*. This originated in Gaul, and eventually settled at being a period of up to four weeks, having four Sundays. Its theological themes are preparation for the coming of Christ, both in his incarnation and in his second coming at the end of time, with the concomitant subjects of death, judgment, heaven and hell.

Thus the pattern of the temporale is completed and in broad outline has altered little for more than a thousand years. The Christmas and Easter cycles have remained throughout essentially independent of each other with, for example, the themes of creation and the fall being considered on Septuagesima and Sexagesima respectively. It should be noted that the weekly Sunday celebration remains one of its important concepts.

The sanctorale has its origin in the early Christian custom of celebrating the eucharist at the tombs of martyrs and confessors. In pagan Rome the tombs of the dead were visited on their birthdays and a meal held there in their honour. It was a small step from this to celebrating the eucharist at the tomb of a martyr (on the anniversary of death, being the heavenly birthday). From the fourth century onwards basilicas were erected over the tombs of the martyrs or the celebration moved into the local church, in order to accommodate the much larger number of people attending, but still in each place it was essentially a list of local

saints that was being observed. But as time went on much cross borrowing took place, with the calendars of the major sees acquiring pre-eminence. To these lists the biblical saints and the apostles tended to be added, the dates in their cases usually deriving from the date of the dedication of one of the early church buildings put up in their honour or some other similar reason.

The tendency over the course of time, in the West in particular, was for the sanctorale to grow at the expense of the temporale, and by the period immediately prior to the Reformation this had become quite excessive, a problem exacerbated by the growth of the celebration of octaves (i.e. celebrating the feast again eight days later, or even continuously throughout the period) as well as by the multiplication of saints' days themselves, whose celebration frequently displaced that of the ordinary Sunday liturgy. This was compounded in the pre-Reformation church by two other practices, namely the cult of relics and the invocation of saints (*see* **Saints, Cult of the**).

In the Roman liturgical reforms following the Council of Trent the sanctorale was very substantially cut down, but it subsequently grew again. In the post-Vatican II reforms the primacy of the temporale, with particular emphasis on the Sunday, was restored. The sanctorale was reduced to 7 solemnities (including feasts of the Blessed Virgin Mary), 25 feasts, of which Lawrence is the only non-biblical saint, and 150 memorials, which latter only involve the use of an additional collect with the temporale propers, and of these 92 are optional. There remain permission and some provision for additional local usage.

In the Anglican tradition, the Book of Common Prayer made liturgical provision for about twenty biblical saints' days (red letter days, so called because their titles were actually printed in red ink in the calendars in some early printings of the prayer book). Other saints' days (black letter saints) remained in the calendar, but without liturgical provision, probably for secular calendrical reasons. Modern Anglican calendars have tended to enrich themselves, in a rather informal and *ad hoc* way, with fairly firm suggestions as to the differing degrees of importance of different catagories of observances; it may be doubted whether that much liturgical use is made of many of these provisions.

On the whole Reformed and Free Churches have not observed the sanctorale to any extent.

Both Reformation era and recent revisions of the temporale have been much less drastic. The temporale emerged from the Counter Reformation in the Roman Church virtually unchanged. In the post-Vatican II Roman Church the temporale has been clearly delineated into two parts, that part of it associated with the great feasts of Easter (the Gesimas are suppressed) and Christmas, and the rest of the year, the latter beginning after Epiphany and resuming after Pentecost. The importance of all Sundays is stressed. In the Anglican tradition the Book of Common Prayer took over the temporale in its Sarum version virtually unchanged. Historically Reformed and Free Churches have tended not to observe the calendar at all, but have instead put great stress on the Sunday (reinterpreted as the sabbath) as the Lord's Day.

In recent years interest in observing the calendar has revived in Reformed and Free Churches, and in England, combined with Anglicans in the Joint Liturgical Group, it has lead to a recasting of the temporale in order to integrate the Christmas and Easter cycle of feasts theologically into one continuous series of commemorations. The major change involved is starting the annual cycle nine Sundays before Christmas in order to have sufficient time to accommodate what it was desired to commemorate before Christmas, beginning with creation, the fall, Old Testament themes and leading up to John the Baptist and the annunciation immediately before Christmas itself.

The great advantage of using the calendar to guide liturgical celebration over the year is that proper attention can be given to all aspects of the mystery of salvation in worship in a balanced way. A possible disadvantage, perhaps, is a tendency for it to make liturgy over didactic.

A. Adam, *The Liturgical Year*, 1981; G. Dix, *The Shape of the Liturgy*, [2]1945; W. H. Frere, *Studies in Early Roman Liturgy: I. The Kalendar*, 1930; Joint Liturgical Group, *The Calendar and Lectionary: A Reconsideration*, 1967; C. Jones, G.

Wainwright and E. Yarnold (eds), *The Study of Liturgy*, 1978, Part 2, Section VI, 'The Calendar'; A. A. McArthur, *The Evolution of the Christian Year*, 1953; M. Perham, *The Communion of Saints*, 1980; W. Vos and G. Wainwright (eds), *Liturgical Time*, 1982.

R. F. BUXTON

Camp Meeting

The origin of the camp meeting lies in the American frontier around 1800. People travelled several miles to reach the place where the preaching took place. They could not leave early enough to return home the same night. Therefore they brought their equipment for camping on the spot. The preaching was soul-searching. People were faced with a choice between God and the devil. Terrible was the description of hell, when a sinner was 'sinking into the liquid, boiling waves of hell, and accursed sinners of Tyre and Sidon, and Sodom and Gomorrah sprang to the right and left and made way for him to pass them and fall lower down even to the deepest cavern in the flaming abyss. Here his consciousness like a never-dying worm stings him and forever gnaws his soul . . . Now through the blazing flames of hell he sees that heaven he has lost . . . In those pure regions he sees his father, or mother, his sisters or brothers, or those persons who sat under the same means of grace with him, and whom he derided as fools, fanatics, and hypocrites' (J. C. Brauer, *Protestantism in America*, 1965, p. 107). Such preaching led to highly emotional results. Men and women began to cry for mercy. Turning and twisting, wringing their hands, beating their breasts, they struggled to be released from sin and to experience the new birth in Christ.

The camp meeting matched the needs of the frontier: an un- or even anti-intellectual preaching, a personal decision on things which were controllable (sinners were swearing, drinking and dancing; saints abstained from such things; there was no middle way), the possibility of leaving the isolation of everyday life and enjoying fellowship with a crowd.

In the middle of the last century the mainline churches abandoned the camp meeting. Some Christians, longing for revival, gathered together and revived the old customs, which eventually gave birth to the Holiness denominations, with their tangible experience of sanctification, including 'holy laughter', 'holy barking' and 'holy jerks'. At the beginning of the twentieth century the Holiness denominations became more fashionable. The camp meeting tradition was then taken up by the Pentecostal movement.

Today the camp meeting has lost its cruder sides. It is a place where one lives as the forefathers did, assembles around a fire, sleeps in country houses or tents, far away from the jungles of modern cities.

The future of the camp meeting can be just this (or – what is not excluded – a re-awakening of the former emotionalism). But it could also be an exercise in using leisure time intelligently, rediscovering those parts of the person which are suppressed in today's society, through relationship with other persons and nature, through a growing awareness of intuition, through means of art and meditation.

W. J. Hollenweger, *Handbuch der Pfingstbewegung* (02a.02.001), 1965/1967; W. L. Sperry, *Religion in America*, 1948.

W. J. HOLLENWEGER

Candle Service, Moravian

Like the slightly more elaborate Christingle Service*, the Moravian Candle Service now widely used at Christmas in the European and North American Moravian churches had its origin in a children's service held on Christmas Eve 1747 at Marienborn, Germany. During this service the minister gave each child a lighted wax taper tied with a red ribbon to symbolize 'the flame of love in the heart of Christ which kindles an answering flame in the hearts of children'.

This service became very popular in Moravian churches all over Europe and spread from there to North America. An account of the service is given in the diary of the Moravian congregation in Bethlehem, Pennsylvania, for the year 1756 which describes how 'each child received a wax candle, lighted while stanzas of hymns were being sung, and before one was aware of it more than 250 candles were ablaze, producing a charming effect. Finally the children were dismissed with the wish that their hearts might burn as brightly toward

the Child Jesus, as now the candles burned. Then they went happily homeward with the burning candles in their hands.'

In the North American churches the Candle Service usually takes the form of a love feast in which the children are served with milk and a biscuit. The candles, hand made from beeswax, are distributed during the singing of the traditional Christmas candle hymn,

Morning star, O cheering sight!
Ere thou cam'st how dark earth's night!

which is sometimes sung antiphonally.

See Plate 22.

J. H. FOY

Plate 22 Receiving candles at a Moravian Candle Service

Candlemas

see **Mariological Feasts**

Candles, Lamps and Lights

The use of the term 'lights' in Christian worship refers to the use of candles and lamps not only for the purpose of illumination but also for liturgical observance. The history of the use of such lights is complicated and somewhat obscure. There is some difference of opinion as to how far Christian usage was influenced by the use of such lights in the worship of the Jewish Temple and synagogue.

The reference to the 'many lights' in Acts 20.8 at the celebration of the eucharist at Troas probably implies no precise liturgical use, since this observance was at midnight. The reference to the seven lamps of fire in Rev. 4.5 probably reflects an apocalyptic vision of the heavenly temple rather than current Christian practice. Also the argument that such lights are derived from their use in Christian worship in the catacombs during the early centuries is no longer regarded as valid, and the use of the catacombs for public worship in times of persecution was not normal; they were too confined and too well-known to the Roman authorities.

Tertullian (*c.* AD 200) inveighs against 'the useless lighting of lamps at noonday' (*Apol.* 46); but he is probably referring to their use in pagan worship if we consider his words in their context.

It is most likely that the lighting of candles and lamps in Christian worship is bound up with the vigil* service that was held on the Saturday night–Sunday morning, and to which the reference in Acts 20.8 may be early evidence, if it preceded the mass held at dawn. The kindling of light at this service, although probably originally entirely functional, became a liturgical celebration of which the lighting of the Paschal candle* is a traditional continuance.

By the fourth century, both lamps and candles were in normal use in Christian worship. The Spanish Christian poet, Prudentius (*c.* 348), in his hymn *Inventor rutili*, says: 'The lamps hang by flexible cords and shine over the ceilings to which they are fixed, and the flame, fed by floating wicks, casts its light through clear glass. You would believe that the heavens were adorned with the twin constellation of the Wain' (*Cath.* V.141 ff.). A similar kind of testimony comes to us from Italy in the poems of Paulinus of Nola about the same date. The *Liber Pontificalis* tells of lamps of gold given by Constantine the Great to burn before the altars of the Roman basilicas erected by him. Lamps burnt before the shrine of St Peter, a custom which has

continued to the present day not only at Rome but before the shrine of St Francis at Assisi. In the fourth and fifth centuries, the *Liber Pontificalis* records the gifts of bronze and silver candlesticks as well as crowns and candelabra given by Popes Damasus, Innocent I and Celestine. While some of these were utilitarian, the suspension of lamps in the form of dolphins from the corners and under the canopy of the altar (*see* **Altar**) must clearly have had a votive and honorific significance.

For over a thousand years it was not the normal custom to stand candlesticks on the altar. Indeed, there is little explicit evidence for this arrangement until the twelfth century. The evidence of Pope Innocent III (*c.* 1198) in his *De Sacro Mysterio* is the most important. In the earlier usage it was the custom to carry lights and incense* before the bishop and his assistants at the entry for the mass; and some commentators have derived this from secular custom in which the emperor and other persons of note had such ceremonies accorded them. The bishop came to be regarded as a civil dignitary from the fourth century. *Ordo Romanus Primus*, an eighth-century document, but which reflects the customs of the papal mass in the time of Pope Gregory the Great (d. 604), shows that the papal cortege was preceded by seven acolytes* with candlesticks which were set down round the altar and not on it during the mass.

As we have indicated, it is not until the second part of the Middle Ages that the placing of candlesticks on the altar commences; but there was no invariable rule about this matter, and mediaeval paintings and illuminated MSS of the fourteenth and fifteenth centuries often depict the mass in progress with no candlesticks on the altar. What was regarded as of importance from the thirteenth century was the holding of a lighted torch or candle by the parish clerk or one of the assistant ministers at the elevation of the host (*see* **Gestures** 4).

Until the sixteenth century there was considerable latitude and freedom of action in the Latin West as to how candles were employed in the mass and in the choir offices, and there were variations as to the number of candlesticks placed on the altar in the later Middle Ages. Until recently it was the custom of the Roman Catholic Church to require six lights on the altar at high mass and seven when a bishop sings such a mass. This requirement was first laid down in the *Caerimoniale Episcoporum* of 1600 and there is no explicit evidence for this arrangement before its mention by Burchard and the writers of the Counter-Reformation. In France until the nineteeth century, modern Roman Catholic ceremonial both in regard to lights and other customs was widely disregarded. A point that should be noted is that candlesticks were not left on the altar as a permanent form of decoration but were only placed there at the time of liturgy.

According to the General Instruction attached to the *Ordo Missae* of 1970, candles are used either on or near the altar 'to indicate the various degrees of solemnity', but they must not impede the people's view of the altar or anything placed on it. The *Caerimoniale Episcoporum* of 1984 authorizes the carrying of up to seven candles in procession for a pontifical mass, though two are sufficient. These are then placed near but not on the altar during the celebration.

In the Church of England in the nineteenth century there was considerable litigation and dispute as to the legality of the use of lights at the eucharist. But since the Restoration under Charles II there is continuous evidence for their use and some of our cathedrals and greater churches possess altar candlesticks belonging to the seventeenth century. Upholders of Anglican tradition point to the injunction of Edward VI in 1547 referring to the retention of 'two lights upon the high altar, before the sacrament, which for the signification that Christ is the very true light of the world, they shall suffer to remain still'. There is also evidence that during the reign of Elizabeth I not only were candlesticks in use in the Queen's Chapel but 'in many cathedral churches, besides the chapels of divers noblemen' according to Bishop Cosin in his *Notes on the Book of Common Prayer* (*c.* 1640).

A matter that has also been disputed is the question of a continuous light burning before an aumbry* or tabernacle* containing the reserved sacrament. While reservation* can claim a very high antiquity, the custom of a perpetual light can only be found in the later Middle Ages. In 1240,

Walter de Cantilupe, Bishop of Worcester, ordered that 'a lamp must burn day and night before the eucharist'. There is little evidence earlier than this time.

In the Eastern Orthodox Church it is customary to have a seven-branched candlestick standing on the altar; and the bishop blesses the people during the liturgy holding the *dikiri* and the *trikiri* (a two-branched and three-branched candlestick) in either hand.

D. R. Dendy, *The Use of Lights in Christian Worship*, 1959; L. Hertling and E. Kirschbaum, *The Roman Catacombs and their Martyrs*, 1960; A. A. King and C. E. Pocknee, *Eucharistic Reservation in the Western Church*, 1965; V. Staley (ed), *Hierurgia Anglicana*, pt.I, 1902.

C. E. POCKNEE/G. D. W. RANDALL

Canon

The Greek word *kanon* means a rule or measuring rod; it came to be applied to the consecration prayer in the eucharistic rite of the West. In some early sacramentary manuscripts the word appears in the heading above the *Sursum corda* – *incipit canon actionis* – indicating that the text from this point was fixed. The word then came to be used for the whole prayer. As early as Justin Martyr (*c.* AD 150) this prayer was not regarded as fixed, for at this point the president prayed 'as he was able'. By the time of Hippolytus of Rome (*c.* AD 217) it would appear that a text existed, but was still not regarded as definitive: it was simply a model to be used as required. The precise origins of the Western canon remain obscure: but the basic elements must have existed by the late fourth century, for Ambrose in *De Sacramentis* (*c.* AD 378) quoted portions of a eucharistic canon which is found in its entirety in manuscripts of the sixth century. The texts of the canon as they appear in the Gelasian and Gregorian sacramentaries of the seventh century remained basically the same until the revisions of the twentieth century.

A noteworthy characteristic of the Roman canon was its small amount of variation throughout the church's year. In this respect it resembled the eucharistic prayer or anaphora* of the Eastern liturgies rather than the canon of the non-Roman Western or Gallican rites, which was simply a collection of constantly changing elements. The Roman canon was a combination of short prayers lacking any real cohesion; its pattern would suggest that at an early stage in its history the text suffered some dislocation. Its elements were as follows:

Introductory dialogue – *Sursum corda*
Preface, culminating in *Sanctus* and *Benedictus*
A plea for the acceptance of the offerings
Prayer for the living and departed
Prayer of offering
Narrative of the institution
Anamnesis – oblation
Prayer for acceptance and fruitful reception
Prayer for the living and departed
Two doxologies

At the Reformation the abolition of the canon was almost an article of faith with the Reformers except for Cranmer. In nearly all Reformed rites it was normally reduced to the narrative of the institution with the possible addition of a prayer for worthy reception. But in the 1549 Anglican prayer book Cranmer retained the main elements of the Roman canon. In 1552, however, these were divided into three distinct prayers at different points in the rite – the prayer for the church militant, the severely truncated prayer of consecration ending with the narrative of the institution, and the prayer of oblation following communion and the Lord's Prayer. Today there has been a general movement among both Catholic and Reformed Churches to recover in their revised rites a primitive trinitarian pattern of canon, in which God is blessed or thanked for his mighty acts of creation, redemption and sanctification, the total redemptive activity of Christ is 're-membered' and proclaimed, and the Holy Spirit is invoked to unite and strengthen the communicants.

J. M. Barkley, *The Worship of the Reformed Church*, 1966; B. Botte, *Le Canon de la Messe*, 1935; F. E. Brightman, *The English Rite*, 1915; R. C. D. Jasper and G. J. Cuming, *Prayers of the Eucharist Early and Reformed*, 1980; C. Jones, G. Wainwright and E. Yarnold (eds), *The Study of Liturgy*, 1978; W. S. Porter, *The Gallican Rite*, 1958; L. D. Reed, *The Lutheran Liturgy*, 1947; C.

Vagaggini, *The Canon of the Mass and Liturgical Reform*, 1967

R. C. D. JASPER

Canonical Hours

The *canonicae horae* are the times of daily prayer laid down in the Roman Catholic breviary, or the comparable hours of the Eastern churches and, hence, the services appointed to be recited at these times. (*See also* **Divine Office, The**.) The seven hours officially appointed in the Western church are matins and lauds (reckoned as one hour), prime, terce, sext, none, vespers and compline. This rota of prayer was already complete in the West probably by the end of the fifth century, but the structure and content of the hours were modified by later reforms of the breviary, notably by the Council of Trent, which led to the issue of the *Breviarium Romanum* in Rome in 1568 under Pius V, by Benedict XIV and by Pius X (1911).

In his Tract No. 75 'On the Roman Breviary', published in 1835–36, J. H. Newman asserted that 'the Jewish observance of the third, sixth, and ninth hours for prayer, was continued by the inspired founders of the Christian church' (*Tracts for the Times*, III, [2] 1837, Tract 75, p.3). He proceeded: 'Such was the apostolic worship as far as scripture happens to have preserved it . . . in subsequent times the hours of prayer were gradually developed from the three, or (with midnight) the four seasons, above enumerated, to seven, viz. by the addition of prime (the first hour), vespers (the evening), and compline (bedtime); according to the words of the psalm, "Seven times a day do I praise thee . . ."' (ibid., p.4).

The origin of the canonical hours, however, is not so simple as Newman supposed. Newman relied on scripture to prove that the Jews observed the third, sixth and ninth hours for prayer. He cited Daniel who prayed three times a day (Dan. 6.10); at the third hour the Holy Spirit descended at Pentecost (Acts 2.15), at the sixth hour Peter 'went up upon the housetop to pray' (Acts 10.9), and at the ninth hour 'Peter and John went up together into the temple' being 'the hour of prayer' (Acts 3.1). Tertullian had already noted these biblical references, but wisely contented himself with the remark, 'these facts are simply stated without any command about the practice' (*De Orat*. XXV).

A more modern approach to the subject is reflected by Mgr Pierre Salmon who, while recognizing the NT teaching, reiterated by Tertullian, Cyprian and Clement of Alexandria, that the whole Christian life should be one of prayer, sees the origin of the canonical hours in the Roman division of the day into four 'hours' (*prima, tertia, sexta* and *nona*) and the night into four 'watches' – the first in the evening, the second at midnight, the third at cock-crow and the fourth at dawn (P. Salmon, 'La prière des heures' in *L'Église en Prière: Introduction à la Liturgie*, ed A. G. Martimort, [3] 1965, p.814). The present writer had already drawn attention in 1944 to the fact that Tertullian called the third, sixth and ninth hours 'these common hours, which mark the intervals of the day' (*De Orat*. XXV; cf. *De Jejun*. X); that they were publicly announced (Varro, *De Ling. Lat*. vi. 89); and that it would be natural for Christians to adopt them as hours of prayer, hallowed as they were for them by the events connected with the crucifixion (C. W. Dugmore, *The Influence of the Synagogue upon the Divine Office*, 1944, pp.66f., repr. Alcuin Club Collections, XLV, 1964). The *Apostolic Tradition* of Hippolytus of Rome (*c*. AD 215), indeed, was already urging prayer at home or 'if thou art elsewhere' at these hours for this specific reason (*Ap. Trad*. XXXVI. 2–6, ed Gregory Dix, reissued with corrections and preface by H. Chadwick, 1968, pp.62–64). Lechner rightly regarded the prayers at terce, sext and none in the second century as 'private daily practice', but, like Salmon, he thought the night office and the prayer at dawn were also private-prayer hours (Ludwig Eisenhofer-Joseph Lechner, *The Liturgy of the Roman Rite*, ET edited by H. E. Winstone, 1961, pp.438f.). Salmon noted that Tertullian described the (older) morning and evening prayers as *legitimae orationes* (Salmon, op.cit., p.815; cf. C. W. Dugmore, op.cit., pp.47, 60) but failed to give the context or to point out that the prayers at dawn and at dusk (*ingressu lucis et noctis*) derive, through the hours of prayer in the Synagogue, from the hours of sacrifice in the Jerusalem Temple. Tertullian was supporting the new rota of private prayer at the third, sixth and ninth hours, introduced

by the ascetics in North Africa – but these must, he said, be in addition to the regular hours of public prayer, on Sundays and weekdays, *quae sine admonitione debentur ingressu lucis et noctis* (*De Orat.* xxv; cf. Cyprian, *De Orat. Domin.* xxxv). The morning prayers, consisting of the four elements of synagogue worship (namely prayer, psalmody, scripture lections, and a sermon expounding the lections), formed the first part of the Sabbath and Sunday service of the eucharist. The evening prayers were probably conducted on the same plan, without the sermon, as in the synagogue. We have the evidence of Hippolytus that the *missa catechumenorum* (as this part of the service was later called) was used on weekdays (*Ap. Trad.* xxxi. 2; xxxv. 2), but nothing is said about public assembly in the evening: the *lucernarium* of the Ethiopic version and the *Testamentum Domini* (Dix-Chadwick, op.cit., pp.49–52) clearly belongs to a service preceding the agape (*see* **Love Feast**) or eucharist*, and was, therefore, originally not a daily service.

Among the canonical hours, lauds (or matins) and vespers are the ancient prayers of the church, said at dawn and at sunset. Terce, sext and none have no basis in Jewish usage, except that none (3 p.m.) was the hour at which the 'evening sacrifice' was offered in the Herodian Temple (cf. Acts 3.1). There is no evidence of Jewish worship, either in temple or synagogue, at noon (the sixth hour) and the prescription that Christians should say the Lord's Prayer thrice daily (*Didache* viii. 3) makes no mention of the time of prayer. The hours of terce, sext and none were first observed as times of private prayer by the specially devout (the ascetics) and later were incorporated with the older lauds/matins and vespers into the cycle of daily prayer developed by the monks. Jerome wrote in the fourth century, in a letter to the virgin Eustochium: 'Prayers, as everyone knows, ought to be said at the third, sixth and ninth hours, at dawn and at evening' (*Ep.* xxii. 37). Cassian tells us that it was at Bethlehem (where Jerome ruled the men's monastery from *c.* 386) that prime was introduced, at the first hour, to put an end to the laxity of the monks *c.* 382 (Cassian, *De Coenob. Instit.* iii. 4). Compline, consisting of Ps. 90, is mentioned by Basil, but was probably not introduced to the West as part of the regular cycle of daily prayer before Benedict (P. Batiffol, *History of the Roman Breviary*, ET 1912 by A.M.Y. Baylay, p.28). Thus the 'seven times a day do I praise thee' referred to by Newman were complete.

It has been noted above that the earliest Christian daily public prayer was at dawn and at sunset (*ingressu lucis et noctis*, to use Tertullian's phrase), and that these times of prayer were basic to the canonical hours observed by the ascetics and the later monks. There is no problem concerning the evening prayer (vespers), but the relationship between matins and the nocturnal offices has been the subject of much discussion among liturgical scholars. Mgr Salmon has remarked that 'it is difficult to know what were the night offices' (op.cit., p.816). Anton Baumstark, the author of a famous study entitled *Comparative Liturgy* (revised by B. Botte, ET by F. L. Cross, 1958) maintained in his *Nocturna Laus* (ed Odilo Heiming, 1957) that the Christian nocturnal hours of prayer were modelled on those of the Graeco-Roman world – the Dionysian rites (*Nyktelia, Nyktophylaxia*), the *Bacchanalia*, known at Rome about 168 BC, the *Pannychis* of the cult of Aphrodite, and so forth. In his view the Christians imitated, or took over, non-Christian custom, and the origin of the nocturnal hours is to be found in the early Christian night-time vigils. But there is no evidence of any nightly vigil, except the Easter vigil*, before the time of Tertullian and Cyprian. Baumstark was apparently not acquainted with the work of J. M. Hanssen (*Nature et Genèse de l'Office des Matines*, Analecta Gregoriana, LVII [Series Facultatis Theologicae, Sect. A No. 7], Rome 1952), who rightly saw that the dawn office is the oldest (though he did not trace its origin to Temple and synagogue) and rejected the hypothesis of an origin derived from pagan nocturnal acts of worship. Hanssen argued critically, with reference to the various liturgical texts, the case for the three possible hypotheses concerning the origin of matins. He utterly rejected, first, the theory that it was partly a nocturnal and partly a dawn office, on the grounds that the 'midnight office' was purely a later monastic invention (despite Paul and Silas, Acts 16.25); secondly, the theory that matins resulted from the juxtaposition of two offices (nocturns and lauds), previously

recited separately, the one in the night and the other at dawn. He concluded that matins as it was later known was the result of the amplification of the primitive matins, or lauds, augmented by the addition of a pre-matins, or prime. The use of the psalms is the key. The recitation of one or more chosen psalms and the recitation of the psalter itself are two totally different modes of psalmody: the first characterizes a well-defined office to be celebrated at a precise hour, the second provides the means of occupying piously a more or less long space of time, such as was the vigil. The office of matins consisted of specified psalms, hymns and prayers. The earliest documents mention Pss. 50; 66; 117; and especially Pss. 148–150, called *laudes*.

The first text which describes in any detail a regular cycle of prayer comparable to the later canonical hours is to be found in the journal of a woman pilgrim, named Egeria (or Etheria), who visited Jerusalem about 385–88. In the *Peregrinatio Egeriae* there is a description of a service at the tenth hour ('called here [Jerusalem] *licinicon*, which we [in the West] call *lucernare*') and another at dawn. The services of the hours are obviously of a monastic nature, attended by ascetics and nuns, but at the evening and morning services (vespers and matins) the laity were also present in the church of the Anastasis.

But it was in the monasteries that the hours found their natural home. Some Eastern features were introduced at Milan by Ambrose and in Gaul by John Cassian, who had spent the early years of his life in a monastery at Bethlehem and had studied the monastic systems of Egypt. But the greatest influence on the development of monasticism in the West was Benedict of Nursia, who was probably the first to give a permanent place in the hours to compline (*completorium*), as a last office in the evening before retiring to rest. According to Professor David Knowles, at Monte Cassino in St Benedict's day the following would seem to have been the skeleton timetable.

In winter, from 1 November

2.00 a.m.	rise for nocturns (the modern matins)
2.10–3.30	nocturns
3.30–5.00	reading
5.00–5.45	lauds
5.45–8.15	reading, including prime (20 mins.)
8.15–2.30	work, broken by terce, sext and none (10 mins. each)
2.30–3.15	dinner
3.15–4.15	reading
4.15–4.45	vespers, collation (reading), compline
5.15	in bed

In summer, say from 30 June

1.00–2.00 a.m.	nocturns
2.15–3.00	lauds
3.00–4.30	reading
4.30–9.15	prime and work
9.30–11.30	reading
11.45–12.30	dinner
12.30–2.00	siesta
2.00–6.30	work
6.30–7.00	vespers
7.00–7.30	supper and collation
7.30–8.00	compline and bed

The most remarkable thing, to us in the twentieth century, about this daily programme is the early rising and early end of the day, but in central Italy darkness fell about 5 p.m. at the winter solstice and about 7.45 p.m. at midsummer. (I wish to thank Prof. Knowles for permission to reproduce these tables and facts from his *Christian Monasticism* [World Christian Library], 1969, pp.213f.) Candles* or olive oil lamps would suffice for reciting the hours at the beginning of the day and for reading, but work could only be done in daylight, and if the day began at 1 or 2 a.m. it was reasonable to retire at nightfall. In more northern climes the hours of daylight were different and five centuries after St Benedict the *horarium* of the English monastery of Christ Church, Canterbury, began in winter at 2.30 a.m. and ended at 6.30 p.m., but the scheme drawn up by Lanfranc differed greatly from that of St Benedict. 'Of the time, roughly fourteen hours, available after the hours of sleep, meals and toilet have been deducted, no less than eight are occupied in religious services in church, while reading has less than three hours and work three at most . . . What, we may ask, had made the change? Above all, two weighty additions. The first was the two masses daily attended by the whole community – perhaps three, if the priest's pri-

vate mass was taken out of reading or work time. The second was the large quantity of psalms, prayers, litanies and minor offices. Besides these, both office and mass had been lengthened by the chant*, which was now far more elaborate than in St Benedict's day' (ibid., pp.218–20).

In the later Middle Ages the divine office became so elaborate that reform of it was almost continuous from the time of Gregory VII to the Council of Trent. The Gregorian Reform and the twelfth-century Renaissance did not immediately produce changes in the *Ordo Romanus* of the office, which Gregory VII confirmed against those who wished to reduce the psalmody of mattins to three psalms. Indeed, he extended to all Christendom the obligation of observing the festivals of martyr popes and, while he ordered that on Easter Day and the six weekdays following, as on Pentecost and the six days following, the nocturnal office should have only three psalms, three lessons and three responds, for the rest of the year, the nocturnal office for festivals was to have nine psalms, nine lessons and nine responds; the ferial office twelve, three and three; and the Sunday office eighteen, nine and nine. Gregory VII suppressed the Mozarabic rites in favour of the *Ordo Romanus* – an illustration of the Holy See's new interest in the canonical hours, which was part of the progressive assertion of the Roman primacy in the field of liturgy, as elsewhere. Attempts by the clergy, through laziness, to reduce the office to one nocturn of three psalms and three lessons were thwarted by Gregory VII. But the offices were too long for the changed circumstances of the twelfth century, when travel became more frequent, many beneficed clerks frequented the universities and non-residence increased. Thus the *modernum officium*, used by the pope and the curia in the papal chapel, came into use during the twelfth century. This modified the calendar, abbreviated the lectionary and adopted the monastic hymnal (which had been gradually making its way into the monastic hours, despite Roman disapproval, since the time of Ambrose). It also added the *Quincunque vult*, the daily office of the Blessed Virgin Mary (a brief office in honour of the Virgin modelled on the divine office and containing the usual canonical hours) and the office of the dead (*see* **Burial** 3) as supplements to the canonical office, together with commemorations (*Memoriae*) of the saints, always comprising an antiphon, versicle and response, appended to lauds and vespers.

The *modernum officium* was shorter than the old *Ordo Romanus* and it was adopted by the Franciscans in 1223, but they needed an office still shorter; thus, their general, Haymo of Faversham, undertook a revision of the *Breviarium Romanae Curiae* which was approved by Gregory IX in 1241. Already in 1227 a Council of Trier obliged all priests to possess a breviary which would permit them to recite the hours when travelling. The Franciscans, because of their itinerant and apostolic way of life, could not always recite the solemn office in choir: they often had to recite it privately. Thus, in the thirteenth century a profound change occurred, not so much in the structure of the canonical hours as in the manner of their observance. The scripture lessons were further reduced, the number of festivals was increased; the Franciscans did not celebrate the double office still maintained in the Roman basilicas, but recited only the office of the festival, omitting that of the day. Thus the recitation of the breviary office became a succession of festival observances, and the old office of the day or season fell largely into disuse. This, in turn, resulted in the introduction of lessons from mythical and spurious 'lives' of the saints. By the fifteenth century the structure of the earlier canonical hours, based on regular recital of the psalms and scripture lections, had become so overlaid by later accretions that council after council vied with one another 'in deploring the coldness with which the clergy perform their duty of reciting the canonical office, even in choir' (P. Batiffol, *History of the Roman Breviary*, ET 1912, p.173). The offices were now almost entirely the concern of the clergy and there was little attendance by the laity, except at matins sung before mass and vespers on Sundays and festivals. It is interesting to observe here the continuity of tradition, despite all the mediaeval changes, with the observance of the hours of morning and evening (originally sunrise and sunset) by the laity in the early church. We noted above that these hours of prayer, taken over by the church from the synagogue, were observed in the

period before Tertullian in North Africa and Hippolytus in Rome, as well as in Jerusalem in the late fourth century. They were destined to survive the sixteenth century Reformation.

By the sixteenth century the *modernum officium*, with its complicated service due to the multiplication of festivals, the frequent recitation of the office of the Blessed Virgin Mary and of that of the dead, and of the gradual and penitential psalms, was felt to be burdensome, unedifying and far removed from the canonical hours of the early church as they had been enshrined in the old *Ordo Romanus*. Two attempts to remedy the situation were made under Clement VII (1523–34). He first approved the plan of Carafa, General of the Theatine Order and later Pope Paul IV, to revise the office and also the missal for the use of his order. Nothing came of this. More important, in 1529 Clement issued a commission to Cardinal Francisco de Quiñones, General of the Franciscans, to prepare a new breviary which would simplify the divine office by a return to the practice of the fathers of the church and so attract the clergy to discharge their canonical duty of reciting it (as laid down by Innocent III in 1215). Quiñones's *Breviarium Romanum nuper reformatum* was published in 1535 (modern ed by J. Wickham Legg, 1888). 'The reform was drastic: antiphons, responds, chapters and preces are abolished. The psalter is redistributed, three psalms being assigned to each office throughout the week, except in so far that the *Venite* is added at matins, and the Old Testament canticle of each day serves as the third psalm in lauds' (F. E. Brightman, *The English Rite*, 1915, I, xxvi, where further details of the reform may be found). In July 1535 the Sorbonne condemned these innovations and Cardinal Quiñones produced a further revision in July 1536 (*The Second Recension of the Quignon Breviary*, 1908). This restored the antiphons to the psalms in all the offices, and some other features which had become traditional, but it was abandoned by the Council of Trent and suppressed by Paul IV in 1558. Eventually a new reformed breviary was issued by Pius V by the bull *Quod a nobis* of 15 July 1568, which abolished that of Quiñones and all other Roman breviaries of less than 200 years' standing.

Meanwhile, reform of the canonical hours which comprised the breviary had been urged by Hermann von Wied, archbishop-elector of Cologne, in 1536. By 1543 he had become a Lutheran; he invited Martin Bucer from Strasbourg, Philip Melanchthon from Wittenberg and others to help in carrying through his reform. The resulting church order, in which Bucer was mainly responsible for the liturgical parts, was issued in a Latin version, known as the *Simplex ac pia deliberatio* in 1545 (ET entitled *A Simple and Religious Consultation* published in 1547 and 1548). This made use of several Lutheran German church orders, but chiefly Osiander's Brandenburg-Nuremberg order of 1533.

Since Thomas Cranmer was certainly in Nuremberg in 1532, where he married Margaret, niece of Osiander's wife, it is inconceivable that he was unaware of the existence and content of the last-named church order. It does not follow from his contacts with Lutherans that he himself became a Lutheran, either now or later. The important point in the present context is that he was acquainted with the Lutheran revisions of the canonical hours to form two vernacular services of morning and evening prayer. Within the year he became Archbishop of Canterbury (30 March 1533).

There is in the British Museum a manuscript (MS Royal, 7.B.iv) which contains two draft schemes for the reform of the Latin daily office (best edition in J. Wickham Legg, *Cranmer's Liturgical Projects*, I, 1915). 'The handwriting of a part of the manuscript is that of Cranmer's secretary, Ralph Morice. The additions and corrections are in Cranmer's own hand. The manuscript undoubtedly once belonged to Cranmer. We need not hesitate in attributing the authorship of these schemes to him' (E. C. Ratcliff, 'The Liturgical Work of Archbishop Cranmer', *Journal of Ecclesiastical History*, 7 [1956], p.190). As Ratcliff pointed out (ibid., p.194), Cranmer had the choice of two methods of revision. Either he could follow Quiñones and preserve the traditional cycle of eight canonical hours of the breviary, or he could follow the Lutheran church orders and reduce the daily services to two. In the British Museum MS, scheme I is Lutheran in type: scheme II is Quiñonian. Since the later BCP is closer to scheme I, in the matter of two

daily services (mattins and evensong), the monthly recitation of the psalms and the system of lessons, Gasquet and Bishop concluded that this scheme was nearer in date to the BCP and that scheme II was earlier. This theory was accepted by Frere and Brightman, but C. H. Smyth and E. C. Ratcliff have concluded that the reverse is the truth. In Ratcliff's words: 'Scheme I, therefore, may be assigned to 1538, the year in which Thomas Cromwell was conducting Henry VIII's last and abortive negotiations with the Lutherans . . . scheme II, on the other hand, belongs to the period between 1543 and 1546 when, more conservative ideas having regained ascendancy, Cranmer was obliged to conform his liturgical projects with the prevailing mood' (ibid.). Both schemes were in Latin and, therefore, could only concern the clergy. In the next reign, when a vernacular BCP became possible, an English translation of scheme I provided the basis for mattins and evensong.

The prayer book of 1549 and the services of mattins and evensong which it contained were, nevertheless, no mere English reproduction of a Lutheran liturgical book or rite. The preface to the BCP was modelled on that of Quiñones's *Breviarium Romanum nuper reformatum* (1535), but the order for mattins and evensong was derived directly from the Sarum breviary. Cranmer's innate conservatism, as also his creative skill, may be seen in the fact that, while the Lutheran church order of Calenberg-Göttingen (1542) provided an ingenious fusion of the old services of matins and lauds for use on Sundays and festivals, Cranmer drew upon matins, lauds and prime for his English mattins, and where the Lutheran order depended on vespers alone, Cranmer no less ingeniously fused vespers and compline to form his English evensong. Thus the two offices retained by the English church represented in their contents five out of the eight mediaeval offices. The result was as follows:

English Mattins

Lord's Prayer Versicles Gloria (Alleluia) Venite Psalms with Gloria Lesson from OT Te Deum	From Sarum Matins
Lesson from NT Benedictus	From Sarum Lauds
Kyrie Creed Lord's Prayer	From Sarum Prime
Preces Collect for the Day Collect for Peace	From Sarum Lauds
Collect for Grace	From Sarum Prime

English Evensong

Lord's Prayer Versicles Gloria (Alleluia) Psalms with Gloria Lesson from OT Magnificat	From Sarum Evensong
Lesson from NT Nunc Dimittis	From Sarum Compline
Kyrie Creed Lord's Prayer Preces Collect for the Day Collect for Peace	From Sarum Evensong
Collect for Aid	From Sarum Compline

The sixteenth-century Englishman was not entirely unfamiliar with regular liturgical prayer. For a hundred years the educated layman had been accustomed to use the psalms, prayers and litanies* of the Prymer, and the early years of the sixteenth century saw the publication of various Prymers in English. Now the Tudor Englishman had a more truly catholic as well as more scriptural form of liturgical service for use on Sundays and weekdays. For the clergy there was provided a less complicated and more easily discharged form of daily devotion, much more suited to the needs of the parish priest now that monastic communities had ceased to exist. Moreover, the congregational services held in the early church at dawn and at dusk were restored to the laity as mattins and evensong, while the terce, sext and none of the ascetics, together with the night offices of the later monks, ceased with their demise. Quite naturally, they were revived in the Anglican Communion with the re-establishment of religious orders in the nineteenth and twentieth centuries. But for four centuries

the mattins and evensong of the 1549 BCP (with small additions in the revisions of 1552 and 1662) remained the chief services on Sundays and festivals in the English-speaking world, since weekly communion was almost unknown before the Evangelical and Tractarian revivals of the nineteenth century.

Attempts at further reform of the prayer book in the eighteenth and nineteenth centuries concentrated mainly on the communion office, and although they bore fruit outside the Church of England they had little impact within it (*see* A. Elliott Peaston, *The Prayer Book Reform Movement in the XVIIIth Century*, 1940; R. C. D. Jasper, *Prayer Book Revision in England 1800–1900*, 1954). The proposed prayer book of 1928 which was rejected by Parliament made only minor alterations in mattins and evensong, apart from a revised lectionary* and calendar* (for details see W. K. Lowther Clarke, *The Prayer Book of 1928 Reconsidered*, 1943). Between 1929 and 1965 the climate of opinion in Parliament and in the country underwent a change and the Prayer Book (Alternative and Other Services) Measure 1965 was passed by Parliament, received the Royal Assent in March 1965, and came into force on 1 May 1966. Under the provisions of this Measure, morning and evening prayer in Alternative Services: First Series were authorized for permissive use in the Church of England for seven years from 10 June 1966. These were basically 1662 with the amendments and additions proposed in 1928, together with a new 'Table of Psalms' for Sundays and certain other days and ordering the holy scriptures to be read either in accordance with the lectionary of 1871, or that of 1922 (as revised in 1928), or that revised by the Convocations of Canterbury and York and authorized by them in May 1961. Alternative Services: Second Series, which began 'The Order for Morning Prayer, commonly called Mattins' – similarly 'Evensong' – at 'O Lord, open thou our lips', making the introductory scriptural sentences and penitential introduction voluntary, even on Sundays, was authorized for experimental use for three years from 16 February 1968. The Second Series (Revised) 'Morning and Evening Prayer' was laid before the new General Synod of the Church of England in November 1970 and was approved in February 1971 for experimental use for four years from 28 November 1971. This departs still further from the BCP, both in the penitential introduction by providing alternative forms, and in the services themselves, by introducing as alternative canticles at mattins, a shortened form of *Benedicite, Salvator Mundi*, and *Gloria in Excelsis*, and at evensong Psalm 134, 'Hail, gladdening Light', 'Great and wonderful' (Rev. 15.3b–4) and 'Worthy art thou' (Rev. 4.11; etc.). Provision is thus made both for Sunday and weekday use of the daily offices, and an alternative lectionary is provided for weekdays.

The canonical hours in the Orthodox Church are virtually the same as in the Latin rite of the old *Ordo Romanus*. There are eight hours, beginning with vespers, since the day starts at sundown as among the Jews (Gen. 1.5; Lev. 23.5; cf. II Cor. 11.25). They are vespers (*esperinos*), compline (*mikron apodeipnon*), matins (*mesonuktikon*), lauds (*orthros*), together with the minor hours (*mikrai horai*) of prime, terce, sext, and none. During certain periods of fasting each of the hours is followed by an intermediate office, or inter-hour (*mesorion*). The offices consist principally of liturgical compositions – hymns and chanted prayers – but the whole psalter is read each week, divided into twenty parts (*kathismata*), each comprising seven or eight psalms. These services are to be found in the *Horologion*, which corresponds to the *Breviarium* of the Western (Latin) Church.

The discussions in the Second Vatican Council reflected a widespread desire for the reform of the Roman breviary. The breviary had its roots in the monastic choral office and the Council had no intention of rejecting this tradition. At the same time it was desired to make it easier to pray at least some of the canonical hours with a congregation in church. Thus, in 1965, over eighty experts from various parts of the world, divided into twelve study groups, began working on the revision of the Latin Roman breviary. The *editio typica* prepared under the presidency of A. Martimort and ready for press in 1970 received the approval of Pope Paul VI on 1 November 1970 in his Apostolic Constitution *Laudis canticum*. The four-volume

Liturgia horarum juxta ritum romanum appeared in 1972, and in 1974 an English version appeared, in three volumes, under the title *The Divine Office*: The Liturgy of the Hours according to the Roman Rite as renewed by Decree of the Second Vatican Council and promulgated by the authority of Pope Paul VI. The general structure of the new office presents us with two major hours: morning prayer (lauds) and evening prayer (vespers); an office of readings (matins) which may be said at whatever time of the day is found most suitable, or as a vigil; a midday prayer (little hour); a night prayer (compline). In the words of the Constitution on the Liturgy (art.89a): 'Lauds as morning prayer and vespers as evening prayer are the two hinges on which the daily office turns: hence they are to be considered as the chief hours and are to be celebrated as such.' As we have seen, this return to the usage of the early church, together with the participation of the laity, was achieved by Cranmer for the Church of England in 1549. As in the morning and evening prayers of the Anglican Alternative Services: Second Series, in the new arrangement of the breviary the day begins with 'O Lord open my lips': in the evening prayer, the office starts with the second suffrage of the Anglican office – 'O God, come to my assistance. Lord, make haste to help me.' This is followed in the morning by Ps. 94 and then a hymn, which is always found at the beginning of the other hours. Among the other principal changes are the redistribution of the psalms over a four-week period; the psalter includes fourteen new biblical canticles for the morning office and seven from the NT (Paul or the Apocalypse) for the evening office; the short lections of each hour are much more varied than in the past; the intercessory aspect of prayer, restored to morning and evening prayer, permits the expression of the needs of the church and of the world in the chief prayers of the daily office. Times of silence are indicated in the actual structure of the hours. In the rite different texts for terce, sext and none are not given, but only a *Midday Prayer*. In the *editio typica* provision is made for those who want to say only one hour and for those who want to say all three of the little hours. The common offices and prayer for the dead conclude the main book, but there are supplements containing the propers* of the seasonal cycles and those of saints' days.

After further revision by the Liturgical Commission of the Church of England and prolonged debate in its General Synod, The Alternative Service Book 1980: Services authorized for use in the Church of England in conjunction with the Book of Common Prayer was issued under the terms of the Worship and Doctrine Measure, 1975, from which such services now derive their legal status. The ASB, as it is generally called, is intended to supplement the Book of Common Prayer, not to supersede it. So far as morning and evening prayer are concerned, a longer form and a shorter form are provided, both including the alternative canticles of Second Series (Revised). Either form may be used on Sundays or weekdays, but the full form is recommended for use on Sundays. The prayer book version of the canticles is provided as an alternative to the modern version, together with prayers for various occasions and new tables of psalms and lections from scripture.

The Alternative Prayer Book 1984 of the Church of Ireland was published in September 1984 and officially inaugurated, in the presence of the entire episcopate of the Church of Ireland, at a service in Armagh Cathedral on St Luke's Day, 18 October 1984.

C. W. DUGMORE

Canticles

From the Latin *canticulum*, a little song. Canticles are songs from the Bible other than from the Book of Psalms. The four canticles most used in Christian worship are the *Benedictus* (Luke 1.68–79) (not to be confused with the *Benedictus qui venit*, which in most eucharistic liturgies follows the *Sanctus**) the *Benedicite* (vv. 35–66a of the Song of the Three Holy Children in the Apocrypha), the *Nunc Dimittis* (Luke 2.29–32) and the *Magnificat* (Luke 1.46–55). The title is also applied to the *Te Deum* and, in the Roman Breviary, to several songs derived from the OT, namely, two songs of Moses (Ex. 15.1–18; Deut. 32.1–43); the song of Hannah (I Sam. 2.1–10); of Isaiah (Isa. 12); of Hezekiah (Isa. 38.10–20); and of Habbakuk (Hab. 3.2–19).

EDITOR

Cantor

The person, clerical or lay, who sets the pitch and leads the singing – especially unaccompanied singing. In synagogue worship the cantor is a minister of considerable importance and the office existed early in both Eastern and Western Christendom. With the elaboration of psalmody and its accompanying antiphons in the monastic and cathedral services of the mediaeval West, the cantor became essential for the proper performance of the liturgy and offices. Elaborate rules were laid down to govern the number of cantors proper to the various feasts and seasons. The titles of precentor and succentor borne by clergymen in cathedral and collegiate churches are derived from the term, as is the custom of describing the northern side of the choir as 'cantoris'.

P. HINCHLIFF

Carol

In common use, the name given to a type of simple, traditional, essentially rhythmic song, particularly one whose words concern the nativity. Obscure in origin, the term has been conclusively traced only so far as the Old French form *carole*; but ultimate derivations have been claimed from the Latin *corolla*, Greek *choros*, and even *kyrie eleison*. Continental equivalents of the Christmas carol are the French *Noël* and German *Wiegenlied*.

In England, from their first appearance in the fourteenth century, carols were marked by a characteristic refrain or burden intended for dancing. The opening words of one of the earliest surviving burdens (c. 1350) describe the singers joining hands in a ring-dance: 'Honnd by honnd we schulle us take ...' Early use (1470) of the term carol for 'a ring of standing stones' (OED) reflects this implicit meaning. There is thus a clear distinction between a carol and a Christmas hymn.

During the fifteenth century, the carol developed as an art-form, both words and music being produced at the hands of learned ecclesiastics, not semi-literate minstrels. Preserved in manuscript form rather than by popular tradition, the 'art-carol' of the fifteenth century differed from the 'folk-carol' in a number of respects. First, its text had a highly organized fixed form closely related to the stanza-pattern of the French *virelai* and the Italian *ballata*. Secondly, it was not necessarily composed in the vernacular; many surviving examples are in Latin while others are *macaronic* – having alternate lines in English and Latin throughout. Thirdly, unlike the folk-carol sung by a soloist or a chorus in unison, the art-carol was set for a group of singers in two or three contrapuntal parts. However, such sophisticated examples retained the pronouncedly rhythmic character of the popular carol – though their association with physical movement was likely to have been limited to processional use. In recent years a full study of the fifteenth-century art-carol has been made (*see* bibliography); but the most familiar ancient carols in modern use are folk-carols, handed down by oral tradition until their collection and publication after 1820.

The mediaeval carol may be seen as the result of a desire to introduce a more jovial element into particular acts of worship – both in and out of church – than the sober traditional melodies of plainchant could afford. The Christmas crib* introduced by St Francis of Assisi, and the miracle and mystery plays of the thirteenth century, forecast that desire, doubtless later providing some of the first occasions for carol-singing.

The great age of the English carol was the fifteenth century – the age of humanism and the emergence of the ballad. Subjects treated include many beside the nativity. Some are purely secular – the *Agincourt Song* is an example. Others are intended to celebrate particular seasons of the year, particularly from Advent to Candlemas. A third type retells in many-versed form a Christian legend (*The Cherry Tree*) or propounds a homily (*Remember, O thou man*). Akin, though hardly to be considered a true carol, is the *Wassail Song* – pagan in origin, but made respectable by its commendation of the virtue of hospitality.

The impact of the Reformation and the consequent growth of Puritanism in this country changed the nature of the English carol, without causing its disappearance. After the ban imposed upon Christmas festivity during the Commonwealth was lifted, the singing of folk-carols was revived,

to last in dwindling popularity throughout the eighteenth century.

In 1822, two amateurs independently remarked the imminent disappearance of the carol; and each attempted to 'rescue from oblivion some carol melodies which in a few years will be heard no more'. William Hone's article *Christmas Carols* and Davies Gilbert's *Some Ancient Christmas Carols* were the first printed collections of modern times. Their appearance heralded the rebirth of carol-singing. Other more important collections were to follow: W. Sandys, *Christmas Carols, Ancient & Modern* (1833); E. F. Rimbault, *Little Book of Carols* (1846); Neale and Helmore, *Carols for Christmastide* (1853) and *Carols for Eastertide* (1854); and Edmund Sedding, *Ancient Christmas Carols* (1864) marked the first stage. Stainer and Bramley, *Christmas Carols New and Old* (1871), brought the carol into every pew.

During the last quarter of the nineteenth century a flood of so-called carols issued from the pens of an army of would-be composers, some of whose effusions are still unfortunately current. A first attempt at redress came with G. R. Woodward's *Cowley Carol Book* (1901); and in 1928 the appearance of the *Oxford Book of Carols*, edited by Percy Dearmer, R. Vaughan Williams and Martin Shaw, presented a model carol collection of authentic character. Since that book became available, popular standards of taste and awareness have been strengthened, and carols have recovered something of the health and vitality which was theirs during the fifteenth century. Modern composers have shown that they are able to present the simplicity, strength and honesty requisite in a true carol; but the modern commercialization of Christmas has also encouraged the production of a repertoire of spurious carols of a type as sickly, sentimental and inappropriate as anything produced during the decadence of a century ago.

P. Dearmer, Preface to *The Oxford Book of Carols*, 1928; R. L. Greene, *Early English Carols*, 1953; E. Routley, *The English Carol*, 1958; J. Stevens, *Medieval Carols: Musica Britannica*, Vol. IV, 1952.

BERNARR RAINBOW

Cassock

see **Vestments** 2(*b*)

Catechesis

see **Catechumen**

Catechism

Catechisms of a primitive kind existed in the later Middle Ages, and their contents usually consisted of material on the creed, the sacraments, the virtues and vices and the seven capital sins. With the coming of the Reformation, more complete ones appeared, of which the first were those of Martin Luther. Largely in response to these St Peter Canisius wrote two, one for adults and one for younger people. After that catechisms, usually in question and answer form, proliferated in great numbers. In some countries each diocese or province had its own catechism. A catechism was appended to the First and Second Book of Common Prayer, completed in 1604, for the Church of England. The Roman Catholic recusants produced their own books: the Douai Catechism, a shorter version of it, and in the eighteenth century *An Abridgment of Christian Doctrine*, the first known edition of which is of the year 1772. Upon this was based *A Catechism of Christian Doctrine*, often known as the 'Penny Catechism' which, however, in the nineteenth century was extensively rewritten and added to. Until recently it remained the only quasi-official catechism for Roman Catholics in England. Though still in use, the changes in catechetics have rendered it largely obsolete and other means of handing on the faith are being used.

Nowadays, catechisms do seem to be a distinctively Roman Catholic form of teaching. There are a number of modern ones, a good example being Herbert McCabe, *The Teaching of the Catholic Faith. A New Catechism of Christian Doctrine*, 1985. Though in question and answer form, the answers are not intended to be memorized. *See also* John A. Hardon, *The Catholic Catechism*, 1975; Anthony Wilhelm, *Christ among Us: A Modern Presentation of the Catholic Faith for Adults*; and *A New Catechism: The Catholic Faith for Adults*, 1967, which is a translation with supplement of the famous Dutch catechism.

J. D. CRICHTON

Catechist

The name given in the early church to a teacher of catechumens*. Since the restoration of the catechumenate in the Roman Catholic Church the name is used in its original sense as the instructor of those approaching the church, especially but by no means exclusively in 'missionary' lands. Catechists now exist in England and the USA and in all countries where the rite of the Christian Initiation of Adults is in use. As with other 'auxiliary ministers' (*see* **Lay Ministries**), they may also be commissioned to perform other duties, such as taking a service of the word, or administering communion from the reserved sacrament.

In some parts of the Anglican Church, particularly in Africa, the name is used to denote a lay person licensed to take services, teach and preach, particularly where there is no ordained clergyman. It is virtually indistinguishable from lay preacher* and has, perhaps, been adopted because of its etymological associations with catechumen, catechesis etc. It is thought to be a somewhat more responsible position than that of lay reader*but is probably less widely used than it was in the nineteenth and early twentieth centuries.

J. D. CRICHTON/P. HINCHLIFF

Catechumen, Catechumenate

An organized preparation for baptism* came into being in the second century. Under the heading of the Two Ways the *Didache*, a Syrian document, included moral teaching to be given to catechumens. Justin Martyr in Rome briefly alluded to a moral and doctrinal preparation, which included also prayers and fasting. Tertullian in Carthage mentioned frequent praying, fasts and all night vigils* before baptism. Much fuller information is given in Hippolytus' *Apostolic Tradition*, where the catechumenate, or period of preparation, is divided into two parts, the long-term preparation, lasting up to three years, when the candidates were trained in Christian doctrine and morals, and the final intensive preparation, when those accepted for baptism were exorcised daily, fasted on the two days before Easter, kept an all-night vigil consisting in the reading of scripture and instruction, and were finally baptized on Easter morning. A very thorough preparation such as this was possible during the age of persecution when inquiries were comparatively few.

After the peace of the church, however, converts were so numerous that this long and meticulous preparation could not be maintained. Much valuable information concerning the catechumenate in this period is found scattered among the writings of Augustine, in the sermons of Ambrose on the sacraments, in John the Deacon's letter to Senarius, the Pilgrimage of Egeria and the catechetical lectures of Cyril of Jerusalem. Those catechumens who wished for baptism and were approved by the church were enrolled at the beginning of Lent, during which they met frequently for prayer, exorcism* and instruction (catechesis), being taught the creed* (*traditio symboli*), and repeating it from memory (*redditio symboli*) shortly before their baptism at Easter. Catechumens who were taken ill could be baptized in haste. Although they attended the first part of the eucharist, they were dismissed before the eucharist proper began, never being allowed to see the communion of the faithful until they were themselves eligible by baptism to communicate.

As infant baptism prevailed the long term preparation necessarily disappeared. All the time that infants were reserved for baptism at Easter or Pentecost they were enrolled as catechumens half way through Lent and were brought to a number of scrutinies which consisted in prayer and exorcism, instruction being now out of the question. But when in the late Middle Ages it was deemed necessary to baptize all infants within a week of birth for fear that they might die unbaptized and consequently be deprived of salvation, the ceremonies of the catechumenate became compressed into a rite, based on the old order for the making of a catechumen, which took place at the church door immediately before baptism. In England this practice is seen in the Latin Sarum manual and in the first English prayer book of 1549. In response to Bucer's criticism, this rite at the church door was abolished in 1552, everything henceforward taking place around the font.

In the Roman Catholic Church the catechumenate was restored in 1972 by the Order of the Christian Initiation of Adults, which was made obligatory (except in cases

of emergency) for all adults seeking baptism. After a period of instruction the catechumen is enrolled in a special ceremony, usually at the beginning of Lent*. There ensues a series of services during which the catechumen is initiated into the life of the church, including scrutinies, the giving of the creed and the Lord's Prayer. The final stage is reached in the Paschal vigil*, when the catechumens are baptized, confirmed and allowed to receive communion for the first time. Its use has now become very widespread, not only in 'missionary' countries, but also in Europe and other parts of the world.

J. D. Crichton, *Christian Celebration: The Sacraments*, 1975; J. D. C. Fisher, *Christian Initiation: Baptism in the Medieval West*, 1965; A. Schmemann, *Of Water and the Spirit*, 1976; E. C. Whitaker, *Documents of the Baptismal Liturgy*, 1960; E. Yarnold, *The Awe-Inspiring Rites of Initiation*, 1971.

J. D. CRICHTON/J. D. C. FISHER

Cathedra

From Greek, meaning 'a thing sat upon', with particular reference to the official seat or throne of the bishop. Hence the church in which this seat is placed is known as the cathedral church. This is undoubtedly the oldest insignia of a bishop's authority, and some centuries before bishops assumed the wearing of mitres, rings or even the carrying of pastoral staves and croziers, they were enseated in their throne or cathedra on the day of their consecration to the episcopate as the sign that they were invested with authority to preside over the church in their diocese. Thus the writer of the fourth-century *Apostolic Constitutions* (8.5) says: 'And early in the morning let him be placed in this throne in a place set apart for him among the bishops, they all giving him the kiss in the Lord.'

In the earlier centuries the bishop's throne was normally placed in the centre of the apse* behind the altar; on either side there were lesser seats for his presbyters. It was from this seat that the bishop presided at the eucharist and also preached the sermon. Such an arrangement may still be seen at St Clement, Rome.

In the later Middle Ages the consecration of a bishop tended to take place in the church of the archbishop or metropolitan, and thus the enseatment of the new bishop in his own cathedral took place in a separate ceremony on another day. The lawyers discovered that by this means they could ask for two fees in connection with the consecration and enthronement of a new bishop.

In northern Europe in the later Middle Ages the east ends of cathedral churches were developed into a series of chapels and so the bishop's cathedra had to be brought round to one side of the sanctuary* before the high altar, but the idea that this throne was always on the north side is not correct. The mediaeval thrones at Exeter and Durham are both on the south. In Norwich Cathedral we can see the restored bishop's throne today behind the altar (*see* Plate 23).

Plate 23 The restored bishop's cathedra or throne behind the high altar, Norwich cathedral, England

In East Syria an entirely different arrangement prevailed, where the bishop's throne was placed half-way down the nave inside a horseshoe-shaped chancel facing east. Thus the bishop sat in his cathedra with his back to the congregation and his presbyters on either side. This arrangement was the apsidal arrangement in reverse. In the first part of the East Syrian liturgy the bishop sat facing east; but at the offertory* he advanced to the altar with his assistants and stood facing east as the altar was right against the east wall.

DACL, III, 19–75; XV, 1866–1884; F. Van der Meer and C. Mohrmann, *Atlas of the Early Christian World*, 1958; G. Randall, *Church Furnishing and Decoration in England and Wales*, 1980.

C. E. POCKNEE/G. D. W. RANDALL

Cathedral

The principal church of a diocese, containing the bishop's seat or throne (*see* **Cathedra**), the symbol of his authority. This was originally at the east end behind the high altar, facing west; during and since the Middle Ages it has usually been set on the north or south side of the sanctuary*. The day to day management of the cathedral was vested in a chapter of clergy, called canons since they lived by a common rule. Together with other clergy, singing men and boys, lay officials and servants, they formed a resident community, with living quarters, library, school, guest house, etc. Of the 17 mediaeval cathedrals in England 8 were monastic communities (all but one Benedictine) ruled by an abbot; 9 had chapters of secular priests under a dean.

The characteristic architecture of a cathedral in the West is continuous with the basilica* of Roman times. The sanctuary or choir* at the east end was frequently separated from the nave* by a solid screen*. The baptistery* was at the west end, often in a separate building (*see* Plate 19). This basic shape was sustained through rebuilding or extension, which had to accommodate 1. elaborate shrines for the relics of saints (usually beyond the high altar at the east end), and circulation space for the multitude of pilgrims; 2. extra altars for private masses by the clergy, including (fourteenth century onwards) chantry* chapels for masses for the dead. The nave was used for a variety of secular activities.

At the Reformation in England the monastic cathedrals were given new statutes, and 6 new cathedrals were created out of former abbeys, following the dissolution of the monasteries. The shrines were destroyed.

The cathedrals had long been places of elaborate regular worship, centred on the divine office*, and after the Reformation this choral tradition continued (following the Book of Common Prayer). But by the end of the eighteenth century the life of the English cathedrals was at a low ebb. They continued to be very wealthy institutions, until an Act of 1836 annexed much cathedral property and revenues to the Ecclesiastical Commissioners, for the benefit of the non-cathedral clergy of the church. During the following century 20 new dioceses were created in the Church of England, the cathedrals of which consist of 2 former collegiate churches, 3 new buildings, and the rest converted parish churches. The restored Roman Catholic Church has also built cathedrals, beginning with Birmingham in 1840. Architecturally both Churches have remained faithful to the basilica tradition, except for the Roman Catholic cathedrals of Liverpool and Clifton (Bristol), where the high altar is near the centre of a round or polygonal area (cf. St Mary's Roman Catholic Cathedral, San Francisco).

The purpose of a cathedral has been the subject of lively debate during the last one hundred years or so. The primary functions continue, of 1. being the appropriate place for episcopal services, such as ordinations, and for diocesan celebrations; 2. a place for the regular offering of elaborate and beautiful choral worship, using a professional choir* and organ*. Apart from the services many people continue to come into the cathedrals to pray. 3. Down to the twentieth century the tradition continued in many cathedrals of theological learning, and the writing of books by deans and canons relatively free of other duties. Today the centres of theological scholarship are in the universities. But there are still seminaries or theological colleges attached to cathedrals, and a new development in some has been the provision of lectures and adult edu-

cation programmes. 4. Another ancient function of cathedrals which is as lively as ever today is the patronage of the arts. The mediaeval cathedrals are buildings of astonishing aesthetic excellence, and great expenditure of care and money today goes into their renovation and repair. In addition, cathedrals old and new continue to commission and install modern works of religious art, in sculpture, painting and stained glass. Many cathedrals provide temporary exhibitions of works of art, or 'treasuries' of historical objects of beauty. Most cathedrals are also used for music festivals and concerts, and dramatic productions. 5. In a secular age of easy travel, the great cathedrals are now more thronged with tourists than they once were with mediaeval pilgrims. To people of little or no commitment to the Christian faith, they resonate with a sense of history and the roots of European culture, and they communicate to many visitors a deep feeling of inarticulate wonder. Chapters are aware of a problem as to how best to respond, especially under the extreme pressure of numbers, and are experimenting with skilfully written guide books, acts of recollection and prayer at certain hours, and the provision of visitors' chaplains and counselling services. 6. Cathedrals are now called upon to provide a very wide variety of services and special occasions of worship, attended (in these ecumenical days) by Christians of all denominations. Civic services and services for the High Court Judges and the legal profession have a very long history. Other examples are carol services for special groups, all-night vigils for peace, youth festivals, special worship on national occasions. The question is how to infuse 'folk religion' with authentic Christian proclamation. 7. Lastly, there is the area of activity, not easy to define with any precision, which arises from the fact that the dean and one or two residentiary canons are (or should be) sufficiently free of diocesan or parochial duties to undertake pioneer work in secular society, or to develop a specialized piece of mission or ministry. This is sometimes centred in the cathedral building itself, with public dialogue or group discussion of contemporary questions of social ethics or human need. Or a cathedral dignitary may be invited to fulful a public role in the city. For example, in the early 1970s three English cathedral deans were acting as chairmen of Community Relations Councils, dealing with contentious issues of racial discrimination in the urban areas round the cathedral.

G. Cope (ed), *Cathedral and Mission*, 1969; J. G. Davies and B. S. Moss (eds), *The Cathedral and the Arts*, 1976.

BASIL S. MOSS

Cathedral Office

In recent years liturgical scholars have become increasingly interested in an important aspect of liturgical history in the late patristic and early mediaeval periods: the disappearance, more or less complete over a large part of Christendom, and everywhere to some extent, of what is for convenience called the 'cathedral office', the regular public services of the church, other than the eucharist* itself, in their original form, and the forms which developed from it, and their replacement by other forms which originated in the private worship of monastic communities in the fourth century.

The original public worship of the church, apart from the eucharist, comprised only two regular gatherings, evening and morning – vespers and matins; on the eves of Sundays and great feasts a third, a vigil* or night office, was added. But the same fourth century which saw the definitive establishment of this pattern – derived ultimately from the synagogue, and in respect of the vigil from the Paschal vigil* of the early church – saw also the growth of the movement which was destined to overthrow it, organized cenobitic monasticism. In a very short time monastic ideals and spirituality were dominant, and it was inevitable that the consequent monasticizing of the church's life should extend to its worship. From the beginning the monastic movement had developed a way of worship of its own, which was naturally very different from the public worship of 'secular' churches. In some places, where monastic establishments were attached at an early stage to the public churches, a liturgical compromise grew up between the old way – the 'cathedral office' – and the new way of the monks. The latter was marked, first, by an increase in the number of daily services

from two or three to seven or eight (*see* **Canonical Hours**), and second, the structuring of these services round the continuous reading of the scriptures in a given period, and the continuous recitation of the psalter in another given period (in most places, a week), together with the virtual elimination of most other elements of public prayer. Ultimately the monastic round and structure of the office conquered nearly everywhere. In some places the cathedral office disappeared almost completely: at Rome, for example, where monastic clergy were early placed in charge of the great basilicas, the disappearance was so fast and so complete that so far it has proved impossible to reconstruct the Roman cathedral office at all with any certainty, although it is possible, by applying the principles of comparative liturgics, to arrive at some approximation to it. The Roman breviary offices until their recent revision were purely monastic in structure and content, and the differences between the 'monastic' and 'secular' breviaries were no more than minor variations within one essentially monastic rite. The recently revised Roman offices still retain a basically, albeit modified, monastic structure and disposition, although so far as detail is concerned many of their provisions reflect the beginnings of a welcome shift in the cathedral direction. Elsewhere in the West, elements of the cathedral office survived, and continue to survive, at Milan, and to a much greater extent in the books, although less in actual use, at Toledo. In the East the Chaldean rite preserves more of the structure and content of its original cathedral office than does any other rite in Christendom; the Byzantine rite has preserved far more elements of its cathedral rite than has its Roman counterpart – the persistence of these side by side with the monastic elements is the principal cause of the often excessive length of Byzantine services. (An essentially cathedral office survived at Constantinople, although with some monastic additions, down to the Latin conquest in 1204.)

The principle of *lectio continua* (continuous reading of the scriptures and recitation of the psalter, with little reference to the church's year), which makes the divine office less an act of liturgical worship in the strict sense than a corporate occasion of individual meditation, has dominated attempts at reform or renewal of the office in the West from the early Middle Ages to the present day. In England, Cranmer may have reduced the number of daily services to two in the BCP, but the structure and content of those two services are based on a purely monastic *concept* of the office; and this is true, to a large extent, of the *Daily Office* published by the (English) interdenominational Joint Liturgical Group, as well as of the offices in the ASB (1980) of the Church of England. It does not seem to have occurred to the authors of these and similar attempts at producing a divine office suitable for modern use that the fundamental principle on which their work is based is itself highly questionable both theologically and pastorally, and is itself part and parcel of a spirituality which, whatever its virtues (and they are many), no longer provides a viable foundation for public devotion. Such a foundation can only be found in a return to the principles of the cathedral office, and an imaginative application of them to the contemporary situation, by which a form of divine office may be produced which is truly integrated with the eucharist, with the church's year, and with the pattern of everyday life.

Some attempts at moving in this direction have been made, notably in the United States in the work of Professor W. Storey, and more officially in some of the provisions of the new American BCP (1979), but these are only a beginning, welcome though they be.

A. Baumstark, *Comparative Liturgy*, 1958; W. C. Bishop, *The Mozarabic and Ambrosian Rites*, 1924, chs. III and IV; P. F. Bradshaw, *Daily Prayer in the Early Church*, 1981; J. Casper, 'La prière des heures canoniales dans les rites orientaux', in *La Maison Dieu*, 21, 1950; W. J. Grisbrooke, Part II, Ch. V, 'The Divine Office', section 2, 'The Formative Period: Cathedral and Monastic Offices', C. Jones, G. Wainwright and E. Yarnold (eds), *The Study of Liturgy*, 1978; 'A Contemporary Liturgical Problem: The Divine Office and Public Worship', *Studia Liturgica*, 8, 3 (1971–2) and 9, 1–3 (1973); J. A. Jungmann, *Pastoral Liturgy*, 1962, pp.105–62; J. Mateos, 'Les différentes espèces de vigiles dans le rite chaldéen', *Orientalia Christiana Periodica*,

27 (1961); *Lelya-Sapra: Essai d'interpretation des matines chaldéennes*, 1959; 'Les matines chaldéennes, maronites et syriennes', *OCP*, 26 (1960); 'L'office paroissial du matin et du soir dans le rite chaldéen', *LMD* 64 (1960); 'L'office divin chez les chaldéens', Mgr Cassien and B. Botte, *La Prière des Heures*, 1963; 'Quelques problèmes de l'orthros byzantin', *Proche-Orient Chrétien*, 11 (1961); *Le Typicon de la Grande Église*, 2 vols, 1962–3; 'La Vigile Cathédrale chez Egérie', *OCP*, 27 (1961); W. Storey, 'The Liturgy of the Hours: Principles and Practice', *Worship*, 46 (1972); 'Parish Worship: The Liturgy of the Hours', *Worship*, 49 (1975); 'The Liturgy of the Hours: Cathedral versus Monastery', *Worship*, 50 (1976); 'The Hours for the People', *Liturgy*, 18 (1973); and a number of forms of office compiled or edited by W. Storey, and published by the Notre Dame, Indiana, University Press; O. Strunk, 'The Byzantine Office at Haghia Sophia', *Dumbarton Oaks Papers*, 9–10 (1955–6); G. Winkler, 'Über die Kathedralvesper in den verschiedenen Riten des Ostens und Westens', *Archiv für Liturgiewissenschaft*, 16 (1974).

W. JARDINE GRISBROOKE

Celebrant

The principal minister at the eucharist. Originally Christian worship, like its synagogue equivalent, was probably directed by a liturgical president and there is some evidence to suggest that in the early church the celebrant was actually called 'the president'. When the office of bishop* was fully developed, he was the normal celebrant at the eucharist for so long as it was possible for the greater part of the Christian community in each city to worship as a single congregation. Presbyters* later became the normal celebrant at the eucharist. By an ironical twist in the meaning of the terms, the bishop when present was said to 'preside' but not to 'celebrate', i.e. the bishop sat in his throne and performed certain actions such as blessings, but a priest at the altar actually celebrated. For various reasons it became the custom, in the mediaeval West, for the number of celebrations to be multiplied and for the celebrant to recite almost the whole of the service himself. In the East this has never happened and there are certain parts of the rite that can only be recited by another minister, e.g. a deacon*. The Liturgical Movement* has tended to revive the practice of participation by several ministers (ordained or lay) in the taking of the service, and there is a new interest in 'concelebration'* (several clergymen sharing together as joint celebrants). The position of the celebrant (whether he should face east, west or south) has also attracted a good deal of attention (*see* **Postures** 1, 2). In most churches the celebrant is required to be an ordained person, but the Congregationalist tradition maintains the rights of laymen to preside at the eucharist and in the Methodist Church it is possible for a layman to be specially authorized to celebrate the sacraments.

G. Dix, *The Shape of the Liturgy*, 1945; A. A. King, *Concelebration in the Christian Church*, 1966; B. Minchin, *Every Man in his Ministry*, 1960.

P. HINCHLIFF

Censer

see **Thurible**

Centralized Building

By the central type of architecture no one uniform plan is indicated but the general principle of eurhythmic disposition around a central vertical axis. The buildings for liturgical use to which this classification applies did not develop from the basilica* but existed side by side and independently from the beginnings of Christian architecture. Centralized buildings are of three types: 1. martyria*; 2. baptisteries*; 3. congregational churches.

See also **Architectural Setting.**

EDITOR

Ceremonial

According to strict ecclesiastical usage, ceremonial refers to the prescribed and formal actions that constitute worship. It is therefore to be distinguished from ritual*, which refers to the prescribed form of words. Hence the use of incense falls within the category of ceremonial, while the canon is within that of ritual. However, the two terms are often used interchangeably and this may lead to some confusion. The Royal Commission, which was established in 1867 to inquire into the differences of ceremonial practice in the Church of England, was

known as the Ritual Commission and within its purview it included vestments*, incense* and lights (*see* **Candles, Lamps and Lights**). In fact, vestments are neither an essential part of ceremonial nor of ritual but are rather to be classified as ornaments, while lights may be no more than a necessary source of illumination. Lights only come under ceremonial when their use is an integral part of the service, as, for example, at *Tenebrae**.

If this strict sense of ceremonial is adhered to, it includes such actions as the kiss of peace, the fraction*, elevation, the pouring of water in baptism, the laying on of hands in ordination, etc.

See also **Gestures**.

EDITOR

Chairman of District

In the Methodist Church circuits, which are under a superintendent*, are grouped in districts under a chairman who presides over the district synod and may exercise certain pastoral and disciplinary functions in relation to other ministers. No special liturgical position is reserved to him though, in practice, he may officiate at ordinations. In America the corresponding office is that of the superintendent of the district under the bishop.

P. HINCHLIFF

Chaldean Church

see **East Syrian Worship**

Chalice and Paten

Chalice. The term is an anglicized form of the Latin *calix*, meaning cup. The vessel used by Jesus for the wine at the institution of the eucharist may reasonably be supposed to have been one of the ordinary two handled cups of that period. The cathedral at Valencia, Spain, has in its treasury what has been claimed to be this identical cup. It is a circular cup nearly four inches in diameter, hollowed out from a single brown sardonyx, with a plain stone moulding round the lip. Its style shows it to be of antique Roman origin. While it is not actually impossible that this vessel was used at the Last Supper, modern archaeologists feel that the evidence does not satisfy all the requirements of historical criticism.

In tracing the history of the use of the chalice in Western Christendom and its evolution, two historical facts need to be borne in mind: 1. the recognition of Christianity by the Emperor Constantine the Great in the early fourth century; 2. the gradual withdrawal of the chalice from the laity, begun in the twelfth century, which was officially confirmed by the Council of Constance in 1415.

Chalices of precious metal were not unknown in the early days of the church, nor were cups made from large jewels that had been hollowed out. But cups of glass and base metal such as pewter or lead were also used. The official recognition of Christianity gave a considerable impetus to the use of chalices of gold and silver decorated with precious stones. But Boniface, the English missionary to Germany, was not unfamiliar with wooden chalices in the eighth century. Among religious communities there were ascetic objections to the use of any appearance of luxury in worship which chalices of precious metal encouraged.

Prior to the withdrawal of the cup from the laity in the West, two kinds of chalices were in common use at the eucharist, the chalice used by the celebrant* on the altar for the consecration, and the ministerial chalice used for the communion of the congregation, known as the *scyphus*. The latter was furnished with two handles for convenience when carrying (*see* Plate 24). The ministerial chalice was filled with wine at the time of the offertory* and held by one of the deacons or acolytes. In *Ordo Romanus Primus* we are told, 'when . . . the lay folk are to be communicated, the archdeacon pours a little of the consecrated chalice into the ministerial chalice, the contents of which are supplied by the offering of the faithful'. It was the teaching of the church in the earlier centuries that the addition of a small quantity of the consecrated species to another chalice was enough to extend the virtue of consecration to the whole contents of the second chalice. The consecration chalice was usually smaller than the ministerial chalice. In the larger churches several ministerial chalices were used at one eucharist.

The communicants imbibed the consecrated wine through a gold or silver tube or reed known by a variety of names such as *fistula, pipa* or *calamus*, rather like the modern lemonade straw in form. As late as

Plate 24 The Gourdon chalice and paten, gold and enamel, *c.*527, France

1269 an inventory of St Paul's Cathedral mentions 'two calami'. The pope at Rome still receives the chalice in this manner. The reception of both sacred species by the congregation was made standing and not kneeling. After the twelfth century with the withdrawal of the cup from the laity the chalice became smaller, since only the celebrant communicated from it; and it assumed the form with which we are now familiar, being composed of three distinct parts or members, the bowl, the knop, and the foot (*see* Plate 25).

The Reformation brought about the restoration of the chalice to the laity in the Church of England. The late mediaeval form of chalice was then found to be too small and was replaced by the 'fayre', 'decent' or 'comely' communion cup, a vessel of German form, but lacking the grace of the pre-Reformation chalice. In some instances the foot and knop of a pre-Reformation vessel were brazed to a new and larger bowl. But in the seventeenth and eighteenth centuries some magnificent cups of silver-gilt were produced in England. Under Archbishop Laud in the middle of the seventeenth century a number of chalices based on a modified form of the pre-Reformation chalice were brought into use.

Plate 25 A modern chalice and paten

Since the Oxford Movement in the nineteenth century, there has been the tendency, as in other matters, to revert to pre-Reformation forms of the chalice.

In the Roman Catholic Church in the seventeenth and eighteenth centuries the design of the chalice was considerably affected by the liberal art of the Renaissance. The chalice tended to assume a greater height and the bowl passed from a conical to a bell-shaped form and the decoration assumed secularized motifs.

In Eastern Christendom, where the chalice has never been withdrawn from the laity, it has remained larger in form. In the Eastern Orthodox rite communicants are given both species together, the bishop or priest dipping the consecrated bread into the chalice and then conveying the bread thus intincted on a spoon into the mouth of the communicant.

Paten. According to tradition, the church of St Lorenzo, Genoa, possesses the dish used by Jesus at the Last Supper for the consecrated bread. It is a shallow glass bowl, hexagonal in form, with two small handles, deep green in colour and was at one time thought to be an emerald. As with the chalice, it is much more likely that Jesus used an ordinary domestic vessel of the time.

Furthermore, as with the chalice, it is likely that the paten may have had more than one form and use for many centuries: 1. the dish or paten used by the celebrant at the altar; 2. the ministerial paten for use in distributing the consecrated species. It should be understood that throughout the whole of Christendom for the first millennium the use of leavened bread was more usual. Only in the Latin West did wafer-

bread gradually replace leavened bread from the end of the ninth century onwards. Consequently the ministerial paten, used probably for collecting the offerings of bread from the people, and subsequently used also for the administration of the consecrated loaves, was more like the modern tea-tray in form, being made of gold or silver and decorated round its borders with precious stones and filigree design.

The consecrating paten was circular in form and this remained in use after the introduction of wafer-bread in the West. The later mediaeval forms usually fitted into the top of the chalice bowl by having a 'well' sunk in them.

In the post-Reformation era in England, when leavened bread was reintroduced the cover of the communion cup often served as a paten when reversed. It was usually surmounted by a disc on which the date was frequently engraved. Towards the end of the eighteenth century the paten took the form of a circular dish of considerable size known as a 'tazza' standing on a raised foot. The Eastern Orthodox rite employs a paten of this type. With a revived use of wafer-bread, under the second phase of the Oxford Movement and the Catholic Revival in the nineteenth century, the late mediaeval form of paten has also been reintroduced.

J. Gilchrist, *Anglican Church Plate*, 1967; J. A. Jungmann, *The Mass of the Roman Rite*, 2 vols, 1951, 1955; E. Mercenier, *La Prière des Églises de Rite Byzantin*, I, 1947; C. Oman, *English Medieval Base Metal Church Plate*, 1964; W. W. Watts, *A Catalogue of Chalices*, 1922.

C. E. POCKNEE

Chancel

The term chancel is derived from the Latin *cancellus* or balustrade and originally referred to that part of a church which was reserved for the officiating clergy and was divided from the rest of the building by low screens. In this sense it was synonymous with the first meaning of the word sanctuary*.

In the mediaeval two-room plan (*see* **Architectural Setting**), chancel continued to be used of the whole space east of the nave*, demarcated by the chancel screen*, but now it was understood to comprise two sections: the sanctuary, in its second sense, i.e. the limited area immediately around the altar, and the space between it and the screen.

In popular parlance, the intervening area from the chancel steps up to but not including the sanctuary is often called the chancel, and therefore corresponds to the restricted sense of choir*. As with the term sanctuary, this dual usage can lead to ambiguity, since the same word refers both to the whole of an area and to a subdivision of the same area.

EDITOR

Chant, Byzantine

see **Byzantine Chant**

Chant, Gregorian

see **Gregorian Chant**

Chantry

Derived via Old French from the Latin *cantare*, to sing, a chantry was an endowment for the maintenance of a priest to chant masses for the soul of the founder. The term was then applied to the chapel, containing an altar and sometimes a tomb, where the service was conducted.

From the early Middle Ages, but increasingly in the fourteenth and fifteenth centuries, large numbers of these chapels were erected inside existing churches and cathedrals as self-contained units. Though suppressed at the Reformation, many of the structures have survived and are often of great beauty e.g. Prince Arthur's chantry in Worcester cathedral or the magnificent Beauchamp chapel in St John, Devizes, Wiltshire.

G. H. Cook, *Medieval Chantries and Chantry Chapels*, 1947.

EDITOR

Chants

For the purpose of this article chanting may be defined as the recitation of prose – as opposed to verse – to a melodic formula. Thus, the rhythm of chanting reflects the irregular stresses of speech rather than the regular rhythmic flow of simple melody. The prose psalms provide the main occasion

for congregational chanting today, but different systems have been employed for chanting the psalms over the centuries.

Throughout the Middle Ages the psalms were chanted in unison to a series of short plainsong melodies known as tones (*see* **Psalm-Tones**).

As their technical competence increased, composers began to 'harmonize' the psalm tones by adding parts for higher and lower voices above and below the original plainsong. These ornamental versions, known as *faux-bourdons*, were sung alternately verse by verse with the unison tones.

From these faux-bourdon settings emerged the Anglican chant. One of the earliest surviving examples of the Anglican chant is given below. Dating from the sixteenth century and sometimes attributed to Adrian Batten, its tenor part comprises the first psalm-tone:

Several other early examples to be found in most modern chant books similarly include one of the tones in their tenor parts.

During the Commonwealth, psalm-chanting was suppressed in England and thus tradition was broken. Efforts to revive the choral service at the Restoration (1660) encouraged the writing of new Anglican chants, both 'single' and 'double', in which the melodic interest of the treble part – rather than the presence of a psalm-tone in the tenor – became the main feature. Because of their own independent rhythmic character, such chants lent themselves less readily to the prose of the psalms; and it has frequently been remarked that 'tuneful' chants, with melodies designed for boys' voices, tend to discourage congregational participation. These characteristics were to be responsible for later attempts to supplant the Anglican chant.

Until the nineteenth century, the psalms were customarily chanted *extempore* from the prayer book – the length of the recitation in each half-verse being decided according to the 'Rule of Three and Five', whereby the third and fifth syllable from the end of each half-verse were made to correspond with a change of note in the chant. The standard of chanting, even in cathedrals, was therefore extremely haphazard. Pointed psalters were prepared in an attempt to achieve unanimity, the first example to appear being J. E. Dibb's *Key to Chanting* (1831). It was followed by those of Janes (1837), Stimpson (1840), S. S. Wesley (1843), and Hullah (1844); but the age of congregational chanting of the prose psalms cannot be said to have begun until the publication of Mercer's *Church Psalter and Hymn Book* (1854).

Dissatisfaction with the 'jaunty' character of the Anglican chant led to various attempts to re-introduce the use of Gregorian tones to the Anglican service (*see also* **Gregorian Chant**). The first plainsong psalter with English text was *Laudes Diurnae*, produced by a leading Tractarian, Frederick Oakeley, and his organist Richard Redhead, in 1843. In spite of its faulty pointing the book enjoyed considerable use among Tractarians, until the appearance of Thomas Helmore's more practical *Psalter Noted* in 1849. Thereafter, the use of 'Gregorians' for the psalms tended to be regarded as the prerogative of High Anglicans.

More recently, continuing dissatisfaction with the Anglican chant led to the introduction of other less four-square melodies. First came the 'Gelineau' settings originally produced for Roman Catholic use in France in 1953 by Joseph Gelineau, SJ. Here new translations from the Hebrew provided regularly stressed prose versions married to simple new tunes. Next followed new sets of simplified plainchant and simple unison chants such as those of Gregory Murray in *English Praise*, and Colin Mawbey's more extended versions for the responsorial psalms. David Frost's new translation of the psalter in the ASB (1980) is pointed for Anglican chants. But most congregations still find themselves at a disadvantage in singing the prose psalms. Experiments in simplified plainchant seem to be called for and some religious communities have already risen to this challenge by providing local versions of their own.

P. le Huray, *Music and the Reformation in England*, 1967; C. H. Phillips, *The Singing Church*, rev ed 1968; N. Temperley, *The Music of the English Parish Church*, 1979.

BERNARR RAINBOW

Chants of the Proper of the Mass

The chants of the mass fall into two categories: 1. those of the ordinary*, with texts that are fixed – *Kyrie**, *Gloria*, *Credo*, *Sanctus** (with *Benedictus*), *Agnus Dei**; 2. those of the proper*, with texts that change from one mass to another – Introit, Gradual, Alleluia, Tract, Sequence, Offertory, Communion. The function of each of these chants determines the form of the music. The Introit and the Communion, for example, both accompany processions. The Introit accompanies the celebrant and his retinue as they enter the church and advance towards the altar. The Communion accompanies the procession of the faithful to receive holy communion towards the end of mass. In either case the chant takes the form of an antiphon*, sung with one or more verses of a processional psalm. For many centuries only one verse of the psalm was sung at the Introit and the antiphon was repeated after the *Gloria Patri*, which is a doxology* sung normally at the end of every psalm. Recently attempts have been made to restore the singing of several verses, the antiphon being repeated between them. In the course of time the Communion psalm also came to be omitted: eventually nothing was left but the antiphon, which was sung on its own. Here, too, there has been a move to re-introduce the missing psalm verses, so that the Communion chant can now last for the entire duration of the communion of the faithful.

The Gradual was originally a psalm sung by a solo cantor* to which the congregation, as described by Augustine (fourth century) originally responded with a brief interjection, such as Alleluia, or a verse from the psalm itself. During the second half of the fifth century the Gradual assumed its present form: a respond for the choir, made up of one or two verses, followed by a solo florid verse for the cantor. At present it is recommended that the respond be sung again by the choir at the conclusion of the verse, giving an overall form of ABA. The usual form of the Alleluia is AABA, with the Alleluia and its *jubilus* (wordless vocalization on the last syllable) sung first by the cantors, then repeated by the choir. This is followed by a solo verse, and the alleluia is repeated after the verse. Both the Gradual and the Alleluia are chants of meditation and they follow the first and second readings (from the Old Testament and the Epistles). In Paschaltide two Alleluias with their respective verses are sung, the first one replacing the Gradual after the first reading.

During the season of Lent a Tract replaces the Alleluia. The Tract is either part of a psalm or, more rarely, a complete psalm, sung straight through without antiphon or response. The melodies of Tracts are extremely old and venerable monuments of the chant of the Latin church. They may be sung with the verses alternating between the two halves of the choir, or between two solo cantors.

The Sequence was a new form of chant that grew out of the Alleluia and was associated with it. It was an addition, of either melody, or text, or both. One suggestion as to its origin is that it came about because of the difficulty of memorizing the florid vocalizations of the Alleluia. It is said to owe much to Notker Balbulus, a monk of St Gall in Switzerland (*c*.840–912), whose master instructed him to set every note of the *jubilus* to a separate syllable; this shows that Notker did not invent the form. Sequences became extremely popular during the Middle Ages. Many were written in rhyming verse. The Council of Trent discarded all but a handful of them. The modern Roman *Graduale* has retained four: *Lauda Sion* (for Corpus Christi), *Stabat Mater* (for the Seven Dolours of the Blessed Virgin Mary), *Veni, Sancte Spiritus* (for Pentecost) and *Victimae paschali laudes* (for Easter). The Benedictines have retained a proper Sequence in honour of St Benedict: *Laeta dies*. The best-known of all Sequences, the *Dies irae* (from the Requiem Mass) no longer figures in the repertory of proper chants for the mass: it is at present sung as a hymn during the Office of the Dead.

One of the most interesting of all the chants of the proper is the Offertory. This was originally a psalm sung antiphonally by the two halves of the choir. In its present form it is a fully developed semi-florid chant, more suitable for a solo cantor than for the choir. The chants of the Offertory are the only ones that repeat words or phrases; this may be due to the fact that the chant would have continued until a sign was given by the celebrant for the cantors to

cease. In 1935 Carolus Ott published a collection of Offertories with their full complement of verses and more recently Solesmes has published *Offertoires Neumés* (1978), which shows the original notation of these chants. Other modern editions of the chants of the proper include the new *Graduale Romanum* (Solesmes 1974) and the *Graduale Triplex* (Solesmes 1979). The *Triplex* gives the original notation from two schools of early notation above and below the square notation.

MARY BERRY

Chapel

From the *cappella* or cloak of St Martin, the term was applied to the sanctuary in which it was preserved and ultimately to any building for worship not being a church. It is now used of: 1. public places of worship in many Christian traditions; 2. a private place of worship, as in a college or school, or belonging to an individual, in which case it is known as a proprietary chapel; 3. part of a large church or cathedral with its own separate altar.

EDITOR

Charismatic Movement

see **Pentecostal Worship**

Chasuble

see **Vestments** 1(*f*)

Children, Blessing of

see **Blessing of Children**

Children and Worship

The place of children in Christian worship was not originally a matter requiring self-conscious reflection. Though the Jewish boy entered upon his religious responsibilities at the age of thirteen years, he belonged to the covenant people of God by birth, received the seal of circumcision, and had his part to play in the central Passover observance. The movement of the church into the Gentile world seems to have relied heavily upon the adherence of households which could, in some sense, be viewed as religious units. A worship that was in crucial respects domestic comprehended the child without searching question.

Yet the shift from 'domestic' to 'public' worship in the early Christian centuries did not basically disturb the inherited situation. A 'Christian' empire and, later, 'Christian' nations simply threw on to a wider canvas that community dimension which encompassed the child and which the near-universal practice of infant baptism forcefully portrayed. In the Eastern Orthodox Churches infants received baptism*, chrism, and communion*. In the Roman Catholic Church the increasing separation of (infant) baptism and (child) confirmation* delayed the reception of communion but did not materially affect the place of children at masses at which, in any event, the laity generally did not communicate. It was the Reformation that sowed the first seeds of change.

Two key factors presaged the future. The one was the translation of Bible and liturgy into the language of the people. The other was the according of a controlling place in worship to the word. The result was a shift in emphasis from seeing to hearing and an allied concern with intelligibility and understanding. Yet where the Reformation posed questions most acutely it also provided the apparently satisfactory answers. Without ceasing to be public, worship once again became domestic. The church became a community of families, with each *paterfamilias* a high priest presiding over daily family worship. That fact ensured that, in however restricted a way, children found their natural place in worship, a place where they were indeed 'at home'.

The Industrial Revolution signalled the breakdown of the family as an economic unit, and the consequent social upheaval began the long process that was to erode domestic worship and eventually throw back upon the local congregation controlling responsibility for the spiritual life and worship of the Christian child. The Sunday School, created to minister to the children of the socially deprived and the spiritually dispossessed, lay ready to hand to be used and adapted, as the church picked up responsibilities for nurture and worship surrendered by the Christian family. The stage was set for children at worship to emerge as a distinctive phenomenon posing special questions and problems.

Yet, because the Sunday School

Movement visibly and institutionally dominated the church's approach to its children, the questions were framed first of all and most of all in educational rather than liturgical terms. Throughout most of the modern period the instructional model of education held sway. In the post-war period, however, there occurred a decisive shift to an understanding of education in terms of exposure to experience, eliciting of discovery, learning by doing. To strike such notes was inevitably to challenge the educational suitability for the child of the inherited patterns of corporate worship.

Hand in hand with the educational revolution and in part prompting and empowering it went the insights of developmental psychology. The dynamics of human growth and development seemed startlingly to have been laid bare. The child was to be seen not so much as an adult in the making, half-formed and incomplete, but as, at every stage, a person with particular capacities, receptivity and readiness. To insert children into a worship frame designed for adults could be adjudged the short road to the destruction of their spiritual potentialities. To deluge them unselectively with the whole range of biblical material would arguably ensure a mishearing and distorted reception incapable of later correction.

Given this combination of new insights and pressures, fresh perspectives on the place of children in worship irresistibly began to impose themselves. As domestic worship faltered and died, public worship inherited the spiritual and nurturing roles that the Christian home bequeathed. Yet, in the dying, domestic worship achieved its own measure of immortality by imparting to its churchly legatee a subtly-shaped self-understanding. The Free Churches in particular began to view themselves after the model of the Christian family and their worship as family worship. Inevitably, the model that controlled was not that of the post-Reformation family social unit but that of the modern nuclear family where, in substantial measure, the child was king. It was a small step from seeking worship within which the child found and could find a place to conforming worship to what were judged to be the educational requirements and capacities of the child. Where the liturgical inheritance was least ordered that step could most easily be taken.

Against such a background it is not surprising to find a wide diversity of post-war liturgical provision for children. In the Roman Catholic Church there is official authorization for children's masses with specially provided eucharistic prayers. In the Anglican Church, where the parish communion movement made eucharistic liturgy dominant, children are widely encouraged to be present at communion to receive a blessing. The children of the unconfirmed may find place within the corporate worship provided by periodic family services of a non-eucharistic character. In the Free Churches, morning worship is characteristically marked by the presence of children at its opening and/or its close and by their withdrawal into peer groups while the word is proclaimed. Yet amid this diversity of practice certain constant notes are being sounded. Among them are participation, informality, activity, education.

It may well be concluded that at this protracted feast theology has been the absent guest. Certain it is that unresolved theological issues of substance lurk behind the uncertainty of liturgical developments. If the corporate worship of the people of God is in its normative fullness the liturgy of word and sacrament, on what grounds are the children of the church to be offered something different or something less? If the word of God is focally concerned with the mediation of an encounter between God and his people, on what grounds should the children of the church be removed from the possibility of that encounter or offered merely the illustrated moralism of many a children's address? If the sacrament moves to its normative completion in communion, on what grounds should the children of the church be excluded from this burning heart of worship or offered at its climax a substitute blessing? If corporate worship engages the deep places of the heart and lures and menaces the human will, on what grounds should the children of the church be debarred from exposure to that engagement or denied the possibility of appropriate responses to its claim? To such theological questions, liturgical practice always advances implicit, if unrecognized, answers.

Explicit framing of such answers will necessarily be bound up with judgments

about the meaning and interrelationship of baptism and confirmation as these bear on 'membership' of the church of God, about the frequency or infrequency of the celebration of the sacrament, about the place, dominating or otherwise, accorded to the proclamation of the word. Divergent Christian traditions at all these points remain.

Yet compass bearings on the shape of the future may perhaps be glimpsed. The liturgical assembly is a primary vehicle of Christian formation. For Christian formation involves entry into the overarching tradition of the one church of God, a living tradition normatively focussed in the Bible and providing the determinative script for the liturgical drama. To maximize experience of the full corporate worship of God's people is to initiate the child into the freedom of that new world of God that the tradition bears, to expose the child to that gracious pressure of the presence of God that the tradition mediates, to prompt the child to those developing responses that the tradition claims. If such an understanding of the liturgical assembly is not to suffer distortion, then the scriptural image of the church as the 'household of faith' must be allowed to correct the more popular image of the church as 'family'.

Yet, given the demise of domestic worship, some measure of withdrawal from the full range of public worship may be necessary, so that the child may gain an overview of the tradition and a familiarity with its native tongue. Such preparation will serve Christian formation provided only that it is from first to last governed by the imperatives of the liturgy, that it reflects the liturgical handling of the tradition, and that it is not prey to conflicting models of learning. When the child moves at last to full liturgical participation, he must be able to come not as an intruder in a strange land with an alien tongue but as an heir claiming an inheritance the contours of which have been long familiar and hauntingly experienced.

British Council of Churches, *The Child in the Church*, 1976; *Understanding Christian Nurture*, 1981; Catholic Truth Society, *Directory on Children's Masses*, 1974; R. C. D. Jasper (ed), *Worship and the Child*, 1975.

NEVILLE CLARK

Choir (Architectural)

Originally that part of the church which contained the clergy, i.e. it referred to the chancel* or the sanctuary* as a whole, situated at the east end of the building. A church therefore had two interrelated parts, the choir and the nave*.

In the mediaeval plan these two were separated to form two rooms (*see* **Architectural Setting**) and the choir itself was further subdivided into the sanctuary, containing the altar, and the place of the clergy, the term choir now being restricted to the latter. So what was once a designation of the whole came to be applied to a part of the whole. The size of the choir, in the narrower sense, was much increased and often equalled in length a half or two-thirds of the nave. This enlargement was to provide space, particularly in monastic establishments, for the staff of clerics. So a tripartite division was created, consisting of: 1. the nave, which constituted one room; 2. the choir, with 3. the altar precincts together forming the second room.

An exception to this separation of the laity from the altar, common to most European countries, is to be noted in Spain. There the short eastern apse containing the altar was retained, and the choir or *coro*, enclosed on the north, west and south sides, was placed at the west end of the nave. The laity therefore had their place between the sanctuary and the choir and were not separated from the former by the latter.

After the Reformation the choir was used in England for the celebration of the eucharist, the communicants coming from the nave to gather round the altar*, which was brought forward from the east wall. By the nineteenth century this practice had tended to lapse and the choir was pressed into use for the singers. Two men in particular were responsible for this innovation, J. Jebb and W. F. Hook, who adopted the expedient in the newly built parish church of Leeds immediately after its consecration in 1841. They placed the musical choir*, robed in surplices, in the architectural choir, and this practice has become widespread in all denominations. As a tradition it has not had a very long history, and at the present day many question the rightness of this separation of the congregation from the altar.

G. W. O. Addleshaw and F. Etchells, *The Architectural Setting of Anglican Worship*, 1948.

EDITOR

Choir (Dance)

Sometimes designated rhythmic, motion or movement choir, a dance choir is a group of 8 to 15 people, who exercise a ministry of dance. This special ministry, which has developed out of the increasing interest in liturgical dance, can be analysed in relation to its objects. It can be directed to

1. Its own members, in that seeking together to know what worship through symbolic movement is, they develop an embodied spirituality.

2. The congregation of which it is a part. In this respect a dance choir has a fivefold function: first, it may enrich a service, the grace of bodies in motion being a channel for the worship of all present in a way similar to the beauty of an anthem sung by a choir. Second, it may interpret through bodily movement the meaning of what is taking place (e.g. a baptism) or is being said or sung (e.g. by incarnating the words of hymns). Third, it may provide a seasonal note (e.g. expressing the joy of Easter). Fourth, it may be a source of instruction, as when a dance drama is presented with themes from the Old and New Testaments (*see* Plate 26). Fifth, it may exercise a leadership role encouraging the congregation by visible example in new ways of worship.

3. Other congregations who may invite it to visit them – in this respect its ministry is an extension to others outside the immediate locality of that which it is already exercising in its own church.

4. The aged and infirm and those unable to attend services in a church building – worship can be enriched in old people's homes, geriatric wards, etc. by means of

Plate 26 Stretching of hands and arms in worship from *Creation*, danced at the opening of the WCC Assembly, Vancouver 1983

liturgical dance.

5. Those who wish to learn something of the gospel; the choir will be using dance as a teaching medium e.g. in Sunday School, as part of parish mission, etc.

The setting up of a dance choir requires careful attention to detail. Initially the support of the local priest or minister is essential. There must too be a willingness on the part of all would-be participants to be involved regularly in long hours of rehearsal. There has to be a leader, with some aptitude for choreography. Then resources have to be built up: tapes, books, etc. Finances have to be carefully controlled; costumes will need to be designed and made; consideration of the space available must precede every presentation.

See also **Dance, Liturgical**

J. G. Davies, *Liturgical Dance*, 1984, pp.196–206; M. P. Fisk, *The Art of the Rythmic Choir. Worship through Symbolic Movement*, 1950; M. F. Taylor, *Considerations for Starting and Stretching a Sacred Dance Choir*, 1978; M. C. Yates, *Financing a Sacred Dance Choir*, 1981.

EDITOR

Choir (Musical)

The presence of a white-robed assembly of the sons of Kohath 'cunning in song' is the subject of frequent reference in Old Testament accounts of worship both before and after the dedication of Solomon's Temple. Under Asaph, Heman and Jeduthun the Temple choir was divided into sections which undertook their ministry 'by course'. The tradition was preserved until the destruction of the Temple in AD 70, at which time Rabbi Joshua ben Hananiah, a member of the Temple Levitical choir, recorded that the Temple choristers were accustomed to sing as a body both in the Temple itself and in the synagogue. Thus may be traced the pre-Christian ancestry of those choirs which formed a constant element in Christian worship once the days of active persecution were over. A concrete link between the two traditions is provided by the psalms and by the antiphonal mode of singing which they suggest. Another is found in the insistence, both in Judaism and the early Christian church, that skill and training were requisite in those to whom was entrusted the ministry of song. The Council of Laodicea (*c.* 360) even forbade all others to sing in church beside the canonical singers. That inflexibility was not, happily, to survive; but the need to ensure the worthiness of the music offered in worship which it emphasized is noteworthy.

With the evolution of the Gregorian repertory, by the year 600 clear principles had emerged governing the respective contributions of choir and people in the music of the liturgy. The congregation was given simple melodies and refrains within their competence to perform; the choir was allotted more elaborate melodies, some of which called for skilled solo cantors*. The same principle was to govern the situation as the art of musical composition developed to make available the splendid polyphony of the fifteenth and sixteenth centuries as an accessory to heighten worship – so long as trained singers competent to perform such music were available.

It is a fallacy that at the Reformation choirs were abolished, so as to allow the people themselves to sing. This was by no means the case. Luther certainly introduced the chorale with the intention of encouraging the congregation to take an active musical part in the service; but his musical understanding prevented him from robbing the Reformed service of those devotional elements which a trained choir could provide. Calvin, too, introduced the metrical psalm* as the people's song; but though his fear of a possible abuse of music's emotional power made him destroy the organs at Geneva, Calvin yet preserved, even developed, the choir as an agent to lead corporate singing. We thus find that, after the Reformation, Protestant choirs assumed a new role. In addition to their former function as performers of music beyond the capacity of the general congregation, they were now required to lead the voices of the people. That situation still exists today – the relative importance attached to one or other aspect varying according to the liturgical ideal observed.

In English cathedrals the choirs are endowed. Thus, apart from an interruption during the Commonwealth (1649–1660), choral services of some elaboration and competence have been performed there

daily since their foundation. In English parochial churches, during the seventeenth and eighteenth centuries, the custom arose of introducing 'cock and hen' choirs of men and women into west-gallery singing pews. In urban churches at this time a choir was often provided by charity children – pupils from the local charity school. The result was seldom devotional; and in neither case was it usual to find congregational singing stimulated by the development. As a result, with the growth of the Oxford Movement, consistent attempts were made from 1839 onward to introduce surpliced choirs of men and boys into Anglican churches. The avowed intention was to encourage the people to take up again their responsibility as a *singing* congregation; to provide a choir which should lead the people in singing the psalms and chanting their responses, and where possible to add the singing of a simple anthem as a stimulus to devotion. The eventual success of this movement to develop surpliced parochial choirs provided the Anglican church with a feature unique in Christendom.

Like any other institution, the parochial choir proved capable of misuse. And before the end of the nineteenth century, many instances occurred where, perhaps through the use of unworthy music, or because the choir was allowed to monopolize the service, the original role of the parochial choir was forgotten. Under the leadership of the Royal School of Church Music, the situation improved during the present century. But since the passing of the Prayer Book (Alternative and Other Services) Measure by the Church Assembly in 1965, the introduction of alternative forms of service has left the liturgy in a state of permanent flux, confronting church musicians with conditions comparable with those at the Reformation. Current admission of types of music falling far short of norms established by the Royal School of Church Music before mid-century exposes today's dilemma: how to distinguish between the acceptable and unacceptable, bearing in mind the need to offer music relevant to modern congregations while preserving from past tradition what is permanently valuable. There seems little doubt that the Tractarian ideal of the parochial church choir has already become a victim of the search for an acceptable answer. How far present trends risk sacrificing the dignity of worship remains to be seen.

L. Dakers, *Church Music at the Crossroads*, 1969; S. Nicholson, *Quires and Places where they Sing*, 1942; C. H. Phillips, *The Singing Church*, rev ed 1968; B. Rainbow, *The Choral Revival in the Anglican Church*, 1970; E. A. Wienandt, *Choral Music of the Church*, 1965.

BERNARR RAINBOW

Choir (Sign Language)

A sign language choir is one which is composed of deaf people who use signs in synchronization with the beat of music which is sung by a congregation in the normal way. Such people are usually profoundly deaf and have been so since birth or infancy. Many of them have never heard music or certainly cannot do so now.

There is not a sign-per-word match for hymns, choruses etc. but mimed action can be used when a conventional sign is not available. (*See* Plate 27.) The first thing to do in training such a choir is to consider what is the overall message of the hymn. Is it, for example, a hymn of praise, or a prayer or meditation? A hymn such as 'Immortal, invisible, God only wise' conveys in both words and music the majesty and omnipotence of God. Bearing in mind that the deaf choir members will hear nothing of the music, the sign language they use will convey this majesty with more sweeping hand movements and with facial expressions of awe.

'When I survey the wondrous Cross' is a hymn which gives tremendous scope for sign language to *re*-present the picture of the crucifixion. Choir members can gaze with awe and expressions of unworthiness as moving hands depict 'his head', 'his hands' and 'his (crossed) feet'. Such a hymn would be signed with great reverence and dignity. In contrast a gospel chorus can be signed with swaying movements of the body and elation both in facial expression and hand movements.

The British Deaf Choir was founded in 1972 for a special event in Westminster Abbey. It was not envisaged then that the whole idea would be so attractive to deaf people that it would spread throughout the

kingdom until, at the present time, there are 25 or more deaf choirs. The International Year of Disabled People (IYDP) gave a boost to this when it was realized that handicapped people should be given the opportunity to lead in worship instead of being just passive members of a congregation. At first it was considered that conductors of deaf choirs must themselves be hearing people who could both hear the organ and use sign language fluently (in order to effect the vital synchronizing process). It is now realized that a totally deaf person can conduct such a choir provided a hearing person gives a visual clue about the timing of the music.

Undoubtedly deaf sign language choirs are here to stay. They bring joy to both deaf and hearing congregations and can be an excellent means of uniting both.

Plate 27 A Signing Choir at a service for the deaf

See also **Deaf People and Worship; Handicapped People and Worship.**

B. M. SUTCLIFFE

Chrism

see **Chrismatory**

Chrismatory

A metal receptacle or casket of precious metal, such as silver, but more frequently of latten or brass, designed to hold the three sacramental oils that have been in use since at least the second century: 1. the oil of the catechumens*, for the pre-baptismal rites; 2. the oil for the sick used in the anointing of the infirm. Both of these were composed of olive oil. But the chrismatory gets its name from 3. the third oil, chrism, which was rather a cream or ointment composed of olive oil and balm, and used in the rite

of confirmation* and in the anointing of sovereigns at their coronation. All three oils were blessed by the bishop on Maundy Thursday*.

See also **Unction.**

J. Gilchrist, *Anglican Church Plate*, 1967.

C. E. POCKNEE

Christian Church (Disciples of Christ) Worship

The Christian Church (Disciples of Christ) began in the USA in the early nineteenth century when a loose alliance of independent congregations was drawn together by the leadership of Barton W. Stone (1772–1844), Thomas Campbell (1763–1854), his son Alexander Campbell (1788–1866), and other frontier preachers. This movement now includes three American denominations – Christian Church (Disciples of Christ), the Churches of Christ (using only vocal music), and the Christian Churches (affiliated with the North American Christian Convention) – and denominations in other countries. Worship in all of these denominations is characterized by these practices: 1. the regular act of congregational worship, celebrated each Sunday, is a service that includes preaching and the Lord's Supper; 2. their liturgical practice is in the family of Reformed-type worship, as distinguished from the modified-mass type or the Spirit-filled type; 3. they have entrusted the care of congregations and administration of the sacraments to local elders who ordinarily have not studied theology nor receive salary for their ecclesiastical work; 4. baptism is by complete immersion or submersion and limited to those old enough to answer for themselves; 5. the normal practice has been to use extempore prayer even for the eucharistic prayers.

This liturgical practice emerged in one of the most interesting periods of American intellectual life. Beginning in New England in the early eighteenth century, and spreading through the populated eastern seaboard, a powerful surge of religious revival transformed the American spirit, effectively severing its ties with Europe and the scholasticism of the Middle Ages. Under the most eminent of its theologians, Jonathan Edwards, this Great Awakening re-established a passionate Calvinist theology and created a new social striving for the creation of the Kingdom of God in North America. The American Revolution and Jeffersonian republicanism both resulted.

One last episode in the Great Awakening was the Kentucky Revival of 1800–01. The celebration of the Lord's Supper proved to be one of the chief stimulants of glossolalia and related phenomena. One reporter stated: 'The greatest work was on sacramental occasions.' With the dying of revivalism, the new frontier churches – notably Baptist and Methodist – came to depend more upon preaching services than upon the Lord's Supper as the focus for Sunday worship.

In contrast, the newly emerging Disciples of Christ built their congregational life around the Lord's Supper as the major act of worship. Furthermore, they avoided the emotionalism that had been associated with the revival. Indeed, their approach to things increasingly emphasized reason in religion. In this way they were very much like the anti-revival party during the eighteenth-century awakening, a party made up mostly of 'old side' Presbyterians and Episcopalians. Yet their liturgical practice differed from others of the enlightenment, especially Episcopalians. Like most other Protestants on the frontier, Disciples rejected the use of imposed liturgies. Instead, following the lead of Alexander Campbell, they sought to find a basis for their worship, and everything else in church life, in the 'clear' teaching of the NT. This principle had two implications: everything should be discarded from faith and practice which 'is not found written in the New Testament of the Lord and Saviour', and 'whatever is there enjoined' is to be believed and practised. In order to further the study of scripture by the people, Alexander Campbell prepared a modern speech translation of the NT, first published in 1826 under the title *The Living Oracles*. Probably the best English version then available, it was used widely by Disciple preachers through much of the nineteenth century and was in many congregations the one translation generally read and studied.

Their examination of the scriptures led them to conclude that the Lord's Supper* is the significant act of Christian public worship. Their restorationist approach to

the Bible led to a tendency towards legalism, that is towards the tendency to minister communion because Christ commanded it. Yet, their understanding of the meaning of 'the breaking of bread' suggests a more profound grasp of this sacrament. When each Disciple receives the bread and cup, Campbell wrote, Christ says to him, 'For *you* my body was wounded; for *you* my life was taken.' When he receives these elements, the Disciple says, 'Lord I believe it. My life sprung from thy suffering; my joy from thy sorrows; and my hope of glory everlasting from thy humiliation and abasement even to death.'

Interpretation of the meaning of the Lord's Supper has moved in two directions since that time. Formal theological discourse has tended towards commemoration, with very little effort to explain that term. Under the influence of liberal theology, especially in the first third of the twentieth century, this interpretation was drained of the content suggested by related terms in NT Greek. Despite this academic thinning out of meaning, a second trend persisted, the insistence that 'Christ is the unseen host at this table'. Consequently, the piety of church people and the devotional homilies at the table have maintained a seriousness of tone that is felt rather than defined. A theology of the eucharist based on these sources would be closer to Calvin than to Zwingli.

In the twentieth century three reform movements have affected the shape and sense of Disciple worship. The first revolved around G. Edwin Osborn (1897–1965), for long a Professor of Worship at Phillips University in Oklahoma. His doctoral dissertation granted by the University of Edinburgh in 1935 dealt with the psychology of Christian public worship. His work culminated in *Christian Worship: A Service Book*, published in 1953, where he presented a rationale and materials for worship that are biblically rich and ecumenical.

During this same period the Disciples shared with most branches of American Protestantism the trend towards aestheticism in worship. One evidence was the erection of Romanesque and Gothic churches, with the largest number built after 1925, especially under the influence of A. F. Wickes (1880–1958), for a long time architectural consultant to the denomination.

The second influence began when William Robinson (1888–1963), British Disciple theologian, came to teach at Christian Theological Seminary in Indianapolis. He helped a new generation of students discover what had become obscured during the previous decades – that the Lord's Supper is the very principle of Sunday worship rather than something added on. He opened the doorway to serious theological engagement with classical Christian theology, especially as represented by P. T. Forsyth. Similar lessons have been learned by the Disciples in their extensive activities in ecumenical and union negotiations, most notably the Consultation on Church Union.

The third influence upon Disciple worship is this church's participation in the ecumenical movement, and especially the liturgical aspects of this movement. (*See also* **Ecumenical Worship**.) For example, Disciple scholars have been active leaders in the Consultation on Church Union and its commission on worship, as well as in bilateral conversations between their church and the Roman Catholic Church. The modern consensus on worship, especially as it has developed among scholars of the Roman Catholic, Lutheran, Reformed, Anglican, and Methodist traditions, has shaped most recent Disciple writings on worship and promises to be the major factor in revising Disciple liturgical books.

In recent service books, such as the Episcopal Book of Common Prayer (1979), and in some of the recent ecumenical discussions of the eucharistic prayer, there is growing interest in recovering simplicity and extempore dimensions of this central prayer of the church. Thus, the experience of the Christian Church (Disciples of Christ) will be useful to the church at large; for Disciples are the one Protestant denomination experienced in the practice of extempore prayer in a service of preaching and the Lord's Supper, administered every Sunday.

See also **Books, Liturgical** 6; **Liturgies** 6.

Alexander Campbell, *The Christian System*, 1843; W. E. Garrison and A. T. DeGroot,

The Disciples of Christ: A History, 1948; G. Edwin Osborn, *The Glory of Christian Worship*, 1959; William E. Tucker and Lester G. McAllister, *Journey in Faith: A History of the Christian Church (Disciples of Christ)*, 1975; Keith Watkins, *The Breaking of Bread*, 1966; *The Feast of Joy*, 1977.

KEITH WATKINS

Christingle

Although little is known about the development of the Moravian Christingle, it had its origin in a children's service held on Christmas Eve 1747 in Marienborn, Germany. At this time a group of Moravians occupied the castle there and they and their families customarily met for devotions in one of its rooms.

On Christmas Eve 1747, Bishop John de Watteville conducted a service for the children belonging to this group, their elders also being present. As befitted the occasion the service was very free from formality. Christmas hymns were sung, some of them antiphonally by the Bishop and the children, some as solos, and some by the whole group. Christmas poems, composed by the children, were recited by them. Then Bishop de Watteville spoke to the children of the unspeakable happiness which is ours through the Saviour's birth, and how his coming 'has kindled in each happy little heart a flame which keeps ever burning to His joy and our happiness, for an impressive memorial of which each child shall now have a little lighted wax candle with a red ribbon, which was done accordingly and occasioned in great and small a happy children's joy'.

This 'Candle Service'* as it came to be called, became very popular in Moravian Churches throughout the world. But in Great Britain, probably around the end of the nineteenth century, the candle tied with a red ribbon was replaced by a 'Christingle'. The name probably derives from the German, 'Christ-engel' (Christ Angel), or 'Christ-kindl' (Christ Child).

The Christingle consists of an orange, in the top of which a small hole has been bored. A cleansed goose quill, from which the feathered portion has been removed, is wrapped in a white paper frill and inserted in the hole. The protruding end of the quill is cut into half a dozen sharp 'points', to which are affixed blanched almonds, raisins and small jellied sweets of different colours. A small Christmas tree candle is pushed down into the heart of the goose quill to complete the Christingle. (*See* Plate 28.)

Plate 28 Advent Star and Christingle

In the symbolism of the Christingle the orange is the world; the white paper frill represents purity; the nuts, raisins and sweets God's good gifts to his children; and the lighted candle stands for Christ, the light of the world.

Christingles are used in the Christingle service held in all Moravian Churches in Britain on the Sunday nearest to Christmas Day, or on Christmas Eve. Children participate as they did at Marienborn and the climax of the service comes as each child is given a lighted Christingle. At this point the church lights are extinguished and by the twinkling flames of the Christingle candles the children sing the traditional Christingle hymn:

Morning star, O cheering sight!
Ere thou cam'st how dark earth's night!
Jesus mine,
In me shine;
Fill my heart with light divine.

or a more modern children's hymn such as:

Jesus bids us shine with a pure, clear light,
Like a little candle burning in the night . . .

In recent years, the custom of holding Christingle services at Christmas time has spread to churches of other traditions.

J. H. FOY

Christmas

In Egypt in 1996 BC the calendar recorded the winter solstice as being on 6 January, but by the time Alexandria was founded in 331 BC the inaccuracy of the calendar meant that the solstice was on 25 December. The dates of the Christian festivals of Christmas and Epiphany* are both linked with the winter solstice, transmuted celebrations of the pagan world. It is at Rome in the early fourth century that we find firm evidence of the celebration of Christmas. In the year 274, the emperor Aurelian introduced in the imperial capital the festival of the Invincible Sun, *Natalis Solis Invicti*, on 25 December. At some point before 336 the church must have established on this date the commemoration of the incarnation, the birth of the Son of Righteousness.

The evidence for this is contained in a martyrology written by Philocalus in 354 giving two lists of anniversaries, the one detailing the burial days of Roman bishops and the other those of martyrs. He based this work on and added to a list whose latest date was 335. Both lists are set out in the order of the months, and it is highly significant that the opening date in the first is 27 December, and in the second 25 December, where the entry makes reference to the nativity. From this it is possible to conclude that by 336 Christmas was in existence in Rome, and was the beginning of the liturgical year. Some scholars have argued that the identification of 25 December as the date of the birth of Christ predates this winter festival of the sun, and originates in circumstances unlikely to be influenced by it. It can be noted that both Hippolytus and Tertullian identify the date of the crucifixion as 25 March; if one then adopts that as the date of the conception of Jesus as well, 25 December becomes the date of his birth. Be that as it may, there seems no doubt that the Christianization of the pagan festival of the sun gave the celebration of Christmas on that date an enormous boost even if it was not the original reason for it; the existence of an earlier tradition of celebrating the birth of Christ on this date would have made the transition even easier.

By tradition, the Christmas season is regarded as consisting of twelve days, and ends with the Epiphany. The liturgies of this period are woven around the infancy narratives from the gospels of Matthew and Luke, together with all those passages that were seen to anticipate the incarnation in the Old Testament and expound its significance in the New. It remains the most widely observed of all Christian feasts, perhaps because this festival combines human need for a party to enliven the gloom of midwinter, the natural human response to childbirth, and the message of 'Immanuel' – 'God with us'. It was a stroke of sheer pastoral genius to Christianize the pagan midwinter festival in this way. The midnight eucharist of Christmas is probably the most commonly attended of all liturgical observances.

J. Gunstone, *Christmas and Epiphany*, 1967. *See also* bibliography under **Calendar.**

R. F. BUXTON

Christmas Crib

A crib, derived from the Latin *corbis* a basket, is a container for animal fodder, and a manger (French *manger*) equally designates a trough in a stable. It was in such a receptacle that the new-born Jesus was placed according to Luke's account of the infancy (2.7 where *phatne*, manger, derives from *pateomai*, to eat). A Christmas crib is a model of the manger which St Francis of Assisi is thought to have been the first to make in 1223. The term is now used in a general sense to refer not only to the manger itself but also to the entire scene including Mary and Joseph, ox and ass, and possibly shepherds and wise men. The number of figures can be multiplied indefinitely as in the Neapolitan crib on display in the church of SS. Cosmas and Damian in Rome. Provençal *santons* include all manner of characters – a fisherman, a poacher, a simpleton, etc. – who come to pay their respects to the saviour. It is customary in Roman Catholic and many Anglican churches to place a crib in the building on Christmas Eve, leaving it until the octave day of the Epiphany*.

EDITOR

Church of Jesus Christ of Latter-Day Saints Worship

Popularly known as the Mormons, the Church of Jesus Christ of Latter-Day Saints was formally incorporated on 6 April 1830 under the direction of Joseph Smith, Jr, its first prophet and president. It followed over a decade of personal search and revelation which began when Joseph was a boy in his fourteenth year. Confused by the state of revivalism which permeated the area in which he lived, he was inspired by a New Testament verse to ask of God which was the true church, and the one he should join. In answer to his prayer, he claimed that he was visited by two heavenly beings, who presented themselves as God the Father, and his Son, Jesus Christ. He was told to join none of the churches then in existence, but that he would become an instrument through which the Lord's true church would be restored to the earth.

Worship in the church is centred around the weekly Sacrament Meeting, held each Sunday, and which forms one third of a three-hour meeting, divided into three approximately equal separate portions. Since the church is founded on a principle of continuous revelation, there are no recitative prayers nor worship, except the prayer to bless the sacrament before it is passed among the members, which is taken from *The Book of Mormon*.

Since the church is also organized locally by a lay administration, there is no single person responsible for preaching and teaching. This is carried out by assignment to the members, who may speak for ten to fifteen minutes on any subject of their choice.

All other meetings, which are for special groups of members such as women, youth, children, adult Sunday School classes, are conducted by local members who use course materials provided centrally by the church. All meetings are opened and closed with prayer, and usually a hymn.

The regular pattern of Sunday worship may then be summarized as follows:

1. First Hour: sacrament meeting (on the first Sunday in each month there is a testimony meeting). All members attend to partake of bread and water in remembrance of Christ's sacrifice. This is followed by inspirational talks. On testimony days members are encouraged to bear their individual witness to the truth of the gospel.

2. Second Hour: Sunday School divided into those aged 3 to 12 and seniors.

3. Third Hour: religious instruction with those present divided into three groups – (i) priesthood, all males over 12 (ii) young women, aged 12 to 18 (iii) relief society, all women over 18.

Worthy male members of the church are ordained to the priesthood, that is are given authority to act in God's name when carrying out the duties pertaining to that priesthood. Blessing of the sick, blessing of infants (there is no infant baptism), ordination of other men, a blessing (or 'setting apart') before taking on a calling, such as a mission, and any other like duties are all done on an inspirational basis – there is no set liturgy, other than to declare that the blessing is in the name of Jesus Christ and offered by a holder of his holy priesthood. An exception to this is baptism (by immersion), which, like the rest is performed in the name of Christ, but has a set form ('[Name of candidate], having been com-

missioned of Jesus Christ, I baptize you in the name of the Father, the Son and the Holy Ghost. Amen').

The lack of 'set form' and written prayers within the church is intentional, to encourage the members to become more spiritually aware, and to rely on the personal revelation to which they are entitled. The only undisputed written works in constant use are those of the prophets, the Bible, *The Book of Mormon* (1830) and *Doctrine and Covenants* (1835).

This 'reliance on the Spirit' is demonstrated by the once monthly fast meeting, which replaces the sacrament meeting on the first Sunday of each month. Members are encouraged to abstain from food and drink for twenty-four hours, at the conclusion of which is a testimony meeting. This may open with the blessing of infants and/or confirmation (the giving of the gift of the Holy Spirit). Each member, as prompted, then may rise and witness to the truth of the gospel as they understand it, and give relevant experiences to uplift those present.

G. B. Hinckley, *Truth Restored*, 1969; B. R. McConkie, *Mormon Doctrine*, 1958.

ROSEMARIE A. LOFT

Church Modes

During the eighth or ninth century the melodies of the Western chant repertory came to be classified according to a system of eight modes comparable to that already practised in Eastern Christianity. The Western system post-dated by many centuries the bulk of these melodies, which had already existed in a living oral tradition, obeying its own rules of melodic structure as regards opening phrases, passages of recitation on pre-selected degrees of the scale, and typical cadences. In dealing with this ancient repertory, the new Carolingian modal theory achieved a brilliant synthesis, though the musical facts occasionally belie the logic of such systematization.

The eight modes may be reduced to four, as each pair shares a portion of the same complete modal scale and returns to the same final, or 'home' note. Using the white notes of the piano to illustrate the modal scales, the four finals are d, e, f and g. These explanations can be made clear in the simple diagram below which will avoid the misleading, if picturesque, Greek names, such as Dorian, Lydian, Phrygian, given in the textbooks and in use for many years.

Mode		*Final* (or 'home' note)	*Range*	*Dominant* (or reciting note)
I	1	d	d–d′	a
	2	d	A–a	f
II	3	e	e–e′	c′
	4	e	B–b	a
III	5	f	f–f′	c′
	6	f	c–c′	a
IV	7	g	g–g′	d′
	8	g	d–d′	c′

The even-numbered modes start a fourth below the odd ones. Their dominants are a third below those of the odd modes, but it will be seen that the dominant of Mode 3 is not the normal fifth note of the scale (as in the modern major and minor scales): it is a semitone higher, c′, not b. The reason for this is because b was found to be an unsatisfactory note for recitation because in the mediaeval scale this note could be sung either as a b natural or a b flat. So the reciting note came to be raised to the more stable c′. By analogy, in Mode 4 the g was raised to a. In Mode 8 the reciting note is again c′, not b, because of the instability of the b.

The mediaeval modal system, like its more ancient ancestor, is both more complex and more subtle than our modern system of two modes, major and minor, which superseded it from about the seventeenth century. Much of the beauty of the chant is due to its ancient modality. The melodies gravitate around other notes of the scale than the customary major and minor tonics: semitones are found in unexpected places, and leading-notes have little or no part to play. All this contributes to the extraordinary richness and variety of

the music. Modal writing was not extinguished by the appearance of the modern scale system, but lived on to give welcome variety and contrast to diatonic melody and harmony. It is used in such great works as Bach's B Minor and Beethoven's D Major Masses, and in a large number of sacred works from the eighteenth century to the present day.

Mary Berry, *Plainchant for Everyone*, 1979; Michel Huglo, *Les Tonaires*, 1971.

MARY BERRY

Church of South India Worship

The Church of South India (CSI) is a union of Anglicans, Presbyterians, Congregationalists and Methodists which was inaugurated in 1947. Initially it was assumed that its congregations would continue to use the service books to which they were accustomed before union, with occasional united worship as directed by Synod. The rite of ordination, prepared before union and inspired mainly by Anglican models in its first edition, was alone obligatory on the whole church.

At an early date, however, the need was felt for new forms to be used when the heirs of the different heritages met together for worship. Priority was given to orders for the Lord's Supper* and confirmation*. The ready acceptance of these prompted the production of others covering all the normal requirements of worship. These were each revised after a period of experimental use before being brought together in *The Book of Common Worship Supplement* (1967). Though the old service-books, not least Anglican BCP, are still in use, it is increasingly regarded as old-fashioned to adhere to these pre-union traditions.

The Synod Liturgy Committee, though indebted in its compilations to the rites of the uniting churches, has eschewed any mere amalgam of them. Its intention has been threefold: to return in some measure to the classical heritage of liturgy (here it has been guided by studies emanating from the Liturgical Movement*); to give value to the insights of the Reformation which were the common heritage of the uniting churches; to take account of South India's own cultural *milieu* and to produce forms of worship which, while treasuring the church's universal legacy of worship, would nevertheless be expressive of India's own religious genius and relevant to the needs of her people.

This third intention may not always be apparent in English, the *lingua franca* which had to be used for the original compositions. In fact the Indian ethos of CSI worship can only be fully appreciated where hymns composed by Indian poets in Tamil, Telugu, Malayalam or Canarese are sung to Carnatic *ragas*, and psalms, canticles, the *Gloria in excelsis*, *Sanctus*, etc. are rendered poetically and sung in the same way. Such Indian musical settings are still in an experimental stage, but are becoming increasingly popular.

Points of particular interest in the several orders are:

1. *The Lord's Supper or holy eucharist.* This is on the classical pattern with a preparatory section of adoration and confession, a liturgy of the word and a liturgy of the sacrament. Variability of collects, lections and prefaces, derived from the ancient Western and the Anglican traditions, has been retained. The greeting of peace in its Kerala Syrian form of handclasp (*see* **Gestures** 8) may be passed throughout the congregation at the point before the offertory*. Responses derived from the Eastern liturgies are said or sung after the narrative of institution and the anamnesis. The offertory sentences and the epiclesis (which is of a Hippolytean rather than later Eastern type) both stress the theme of congregational corporateness and Christian unity. As in all CSI worship, value is given to congregational participation.

2. *Morning and evening worship.* Three alternative orders are specified: (*a*) Ante-communion* with adaptations for non-eucharistic worship. (*b*) An order modelled on Anglican mattins and evensong. In this the *Trisagion**, or *Kauma*, to give it its Syrian name, may be said or sung as an initial adoration of the Trinity. The *Benedictus* comes between OT and NT lections as belonging between the Testaments, and the *Te Deum* after the NT lection as expressive of the faith of the church which has heard the gospel. The canticles* traditionally linked with mattins and evensong respectively may be sung at either of them. More elasticity

than in the Anglican tradition is permitted in the concluding prayers. (*c*) A simpler and 'freer' order with 'responsive readings' of scriptural verses and permission to sing either hymns, psalms or canticles between the lections, but with some encouragement to use at the discretion of the minister liturgical pericopae from the other orders.

3. *Baptism and confirmation.* Appropriately in a church which is in a 'missionary situation', priority in the printed text is given to baptism of believers, with infant baptism taking second place. Baptism by immersion is encouraged, though not obligatory. The fiction of adult promises made 'in the name of the child' in infant baptism has been abandoned in favour of promises made by parents (and godparents if any) to bring up the child in the Christian way. The proleptic character of baptism and of the Christian life as 'becoming what we are' appears in the post-baptismal prayers. Some thought has been given to the relation between baptism and confirmation. There is stress in confirmation on the fulfilment of baptism in repentance, profession of faith and self-dedication on the part of the candidates. One petition in the confirmation prayer (which closely follows the Roman/Anglican model) sums up the meaning of confirmation: 'Establish them in faith . . . by the Holy Spirit . . .', that is, the Spirit is already present and operative in the life of the baptized; but confirmation, which is the occasion for public commitment to the Christian faith and life, is a prayer for and effective sign of the operation of the Spirit in a new way. In baptism there is a brief reception by the congregation of the newly baptized. In confirmation the act of reception is highlighted, and the greeting of peace is given to the newly-confirmed for the first time. There is provision in the rubrics for baptism, confirmation and first communion to be linked closely together if desired, as in the ancient tradition of Christian initiation.

4. *The ordinal.* The radical revision of 1957 was much indebted to the ordinal of the Church of Scotland. At the same time it was warmly commended at its publication by the Anglican liturgist, E. C. Ratcliff, as a model for future revision of ordination services. Some significant amendments were made in it in the ordinal produced in 1965 for the proposed united church in Nigeria. The churches of North India and Pakistan, where union was inaugurated in 1970, have for an experimental period adopted the CSI rites of eucharist and ordination.

5. *The lectionary and calendar* have, both in daily Bible readings and propers for Sundays and special days, implemented a simplification of the structure of the Christian year, as suggested by A. A. McArthur in *The Evolution of the Christian Year* (1953). Collects and lections have been chosen with a theme for the day in mind.

The Church of South India Book of Common Worship, 1963; *BCW* Supplement, 1967; T. S. Garrett, *Worship in the Church of South India*, [2]1965; E. C. Ratcliff, 'The Ordinal of the Church of South India', *Theology*, January 1960.

T. S. GARRETT

Churches of Christ Worship

see **Christian Church Worship**

Churching of Women

The title of the Sarum 'Order for the Purification of a Woman after Childbirth before the Door of the Church' sufficiently indicates the purpose of the rite. Its scriptural authority is to be found in Lev. 12, according to which a woman who has given birth is unclean, and must not 'come into the sanctuary' until she has made a burnt offering and a sin offering, which she brings to the door of the tent of meeting. Luke 2.22 provides an example of compliance with these regulations by the parents of Jesus. The Sarum service was brief, consisting of the lesser litany and Lord's Prayer, Pss. 121 and 128, the *preces* also used in marriage, and a collect; the priest then sprinkled the woman with holy water and led her into church, and the mass followed. The collect gives thanks for deliverance from the dangers of childbirth, and prays that the woman may finish her temporal course faithfully and attain eternal life. A rubric defines the purpose of purification as enabling the woman to enter the church to give thanks. According to ancient custom the woman wore a veil.

The 1549 'Order of the Purification of Women' follows the mediaeval service quite closely. It is to be held 'nigh unto the quire door' (i.e. the chancel screen). There is no suggestion of ritual impurity barring the woman from entering the church. The priest's opening address states that baptism of the child has already taken place, and puts the emphasis on thanksgiving for safe delivery. Psalm 128 is omitted and the collect is freely paraphrased. The woman is bidden to offer the chrysom (the white robe given to the baby at baptism) and 'other accustomed offerings'. If the holy communion is to follow, it is fitting that she should communicate.

The 1552 BCP reflects the change of emphasis by a change of title to 'The Thanksgiving of Women after Childbirth, commonly called the Churching of Women'. The service is now to be held 'nigh unto the place where the table standeth'. The only other alteration is the removal of the reference to the chrysom, which was no longer given in baptism.

During the seventeenth century, the custom of wearing a veil came under heavy fire from the Puritans, and in many churches special churching-pews were provided in the nave. Laudian bishops in their visitation articles insisted on the retention of the veil and also on the service being said at the altar rail. A rubric proposed in the 'Durham Book' directed that the woman should come 'a month after her delivery . . . decently veiled', but in the 1662 BCP this was toned down to 'at the usual time after her delivery . . . decently apparelled', while the place was to be 'as hath been accustomed, or as the Ordinary shall direct'. Psalm 116 with vv. 14–17 omitted was substituted at the suggestion of Robert Sanderson, with Ps. 127 as an alternative.

In the proposed book of 1928 the presence of the woman's husband was encouraged; and a blessing and two optional prayers were added, one dealing with the child's upbringing, the other for use when the child had died.

The service was obsolescent: the ASB contains a form of Thanksgiving for the Birth of a Child which fulfils the purpose of the old service, but without any suggestion of the necessity of purification. It envisages the presence of the whole family. A similar form is to be found in the American BCP of 1979.

There is no separate form in the new Roman rite, but baptism includes prayers and a blessing at the end of the service, which makes an adequate substitute. The father is given equal importance with the mother.

G. W. O. Addleshaw and F. Etchells, *Architectural Setting of Anglican Worship*, 1948, pp.84–6; F. E. Brightman, *The English Rite*, 1915, I, pp.cxxviii, clxiv, ccxxii; II, pp.880–5; A. J. Collins, *Manuale Sarum*, 1960, pp.43f.; R. C. D. Jasper (ed), *The Alternative Service Book 1980: A Commentary*, 1980, pp.99–104; M. J. Hatchett, *Commentary on the American Prayer Book*, 1979, pp.441–7; William Maskell, *Monumenta Ritualia Ecclesiae Anglicanae*, I, 1846, pp.37f.

G. J. CUMING

Ciborium

This term is thought to be derived from the Greek *kiborion*, which originally meant the hollow seed-case of the Egyptian water-lily, and the term came to be applied to a drinking-cup because of its resemblance to the seed-case. The use of the word ciborium now applies to two distinct objects in ecclesiastical usage: 1. a canopy of stone, wood or metal supported on four columns over an altar*; in several Roman basilicas* there are ciboria of Cosmati work of the twelfth and thirteenth centuries (*see* Plate 1). 2. a chalice-like (*see* **Chalice**) vessel with a cover for holding a large number of wafer-breads. The latter must have developed from a pyx* with a stem and foot and this could only have happened when wafer-breads finally replaced the use of leavened bread in the West after the twelfth century. The term was also applied to a little canopy on four columns standing on the altar under which the metal pyx or ciborium containing the reserved sacrament stood. In England some splendid examples of a flat chalice-like vessel with a cover all in silver-gilt and known as the bread cup appeared during the time of the Caroline divines in the middle of the seventeenth century. While the metal ciborium has usually been of silver or silver-gilt, examples of such vessels completely decorated with coloured ena-

mels are known, such as the thirteenth-century Kennet ciborium.

R. Beny and P. Gunn, *The Churches of Rome*, 1981; J. Gilchrist, *Anglican Church Plate*, 1967; A. A. King and C. E. Pocknee, *Eucharistic Reservation in the Western Church*, 1965; C. E. Pocknee, *The Christian Altar*, 1963.

C. E. POCKNEE/G. D. W. RANDALL

Class Leader

The class leader is a layman given special pastoral responsibility within the Methodist societies established by John Wesley. One of Wesley's problems was the provision of proper continuing care and discipline for his converts. Part of his solution was to group them in 'classes' under a leader who was responsible for instructing them, developing their devotional life and seeing that they maintained the high moral standards required of all members of the societies. Members of the classes also contributed one penny a week to the funds of the society. At one time the office of class leader was generally regarded as one of great importance and influence. It is still a real ministry in some parts of Methodism, though in others the class system seems to have become vestigial.

P. HINCHLIFF

Collect

1. A prayer of a distinctive stereotyped form, peculiar to the Western liturgies, although with certain parallels in the Eastern rites, with which the president closes a unit of liturgical worship, or some part of such a unit; 2. one such prayer in particular, namely, that referring to the mystery or person commemorated on a given day, which closes the entrance rite in the eucharistic liturgy; 3. derivatively, any other prayer written in the same form; 4. derivatively again, the term may for convenience be applied to modern prayers marked by a deliberate theological structure and a careful attention to form and brevity, although the form and structure may vary considerably from those of the classical collect.

In the Roman rite the prayer cited in definition 2 above is called simply *oratio* – 'the prayer'. In some ancient Western liturgical books, however, it is called *collectio, collecta,* or *ad collectam*, whence the English name is derived. The meaning of the Latin is not certain: it means literally 'assembly', but it may refer either to a prayer in which preceding devotional themes are assembled, or to a prayer – such as that in definition 2 – which is spoken when the congregation is assembled. These interpretations, however, are complementary, for both throw light on the function of the prayer. In the historic Western liturgies collects are normally preceded, directly or indirectly, by a mutual greeting of president and people and a bidding to prayer, to emphasize the nature of the collect as a solemn summary by the president of the corporate prayer of the assembly. (In the Roman *Ordo Missae* of 1969, the removal of the greeting to the very beginning of the entrance rite tends, especially when the celebrant's extempore introduction which follows it is too general or extended, to obscure the greeting's connection with prayer altogether.)

Ancient examples of the collect after the entrance, of which many survive to this day in the Roman rite, exhibit an all but unvarying structure: 1. an address to God the Father; 2. a reference to some divine attribute or act as a ground for prayer; 3. the prayer proper, short, simple and definite; 4. a concluding doxology, offering the prayer to the Father through the Son and in the Holy Spirit. They also follow a distinctive literary pattern, following the rules of late classical Latin artistic prose. The collects of the Hispano-Gallican rites exhibit much more variation, and are often both theologically and stylistically excessively complicated. Other prayers of the collect type in the historic Western rites, such as those which close the offertory (in the Roman rite called *secreta* or *super oblata** and the communion (in the Roman rite called *postcommunio*), exhibit a theological and literary pattern similar, although with differences according to their function, to those of the collects proper.

The translation of a prayer of this type from Latin into the vernacular presents a considerable problem; the most successful solution of it so far, in its own day, was that of Cranmer in the collects of the BCP. The attempts of modern liturgical revisers to translate or compose collects in a more

informal style, supposedly more appropriate and intelligible today, have so far (with a few outstanding exceptions) been markedly less successful than those of their sixteenth-century predecessors, and it must be queried whether it is in fact possible to produce prayers of this kind without obeying the conventional rules for their formulations or at least without seeking out alternative rules and adhering to them.

B. Bruylants, *Les oraisons du missel romain, texte et histoire*, two vols, 1952; J. A. Jungmann, *The Mass of the Roman Rite*, 1, 1951, pp.359–90; G. G. Willis, *Further Essays in Early Roman Liturgy*, 1968, pp.89–131.

W. JARDINE GRISBROOKE

Colours, Liturgical

The association of particular colours with seasonal worship and personal commemoration has developed for several reasons – some psychological and some historical. It seems 'natural', for instance, to associate red with blood, yellow with energy, white with purity, gold with festivity, purple with dignity, green with growth, light blue with hope, dark blue, violet and black with despair and mourning, and drab earth colours with burial.

The use of colours in connection with Christian worship has had a varied history. For the first millennium the colour of vestments* and hangings was without liturgical significance and, save for a preference for white robes, did not differ from what was customary among the Roman middle and upper classes of the empire and of its Byzantine continuation.

Although liturgical vesture remained the same in form as civilian dress, the indications are that the clergy reserved special 'suits' of alb and chasuble for use in church, and also that increasingly these vestments were of white material only. Jerome, in argument with Pelagius (*c.*415), asks what objection could be made if bishop, priest, deacon and the rest of the clergy appeared at the administration of the sacrifice in white array (*candida veste processerit*). Pseudo-Alcuin in the tenth or eleventh century writes only of white vestments and mentions red stripes on those of the deacons.

Not until the twelfth century is there evidence of correlation between significant colours and the seasonal feasts and fasts of the church's year and the various classes of saints, etc., in the calendar. The Augustinian canons at Jerusalem prepared the first known sequence of liturgical colours and, somewhat surprisingly, this proposed the use of black for Christmas and for festivals of the Blessed Virgin Mary, and blue for Epiphany and Ascension. Presumably the growing wealth of the church had permitted the use of a wider variety and richness of textiles for vestments, hangings and accessories and, understandably, their colours came to be associated with the developed mediaeval system of annual liturgical observances. At first such sequences were local and informal: they were unavoidably restricted to wealthy cathedrals and abbeys and to rich collegiate and parish churches. A common practice was to wear the newest or most magnificent vestments – virtually irrespective of colour – on the great festivals and to use the older ones on other occasions. Gradually, however, a generally accepted pattern of colour association emerged in the mediaeval West: Innocent III (1198–1216) outlined the Roman rule based on white for feasts, red for martyrs, black for penitential seasons and green at other times.

A general rule was not formally defined in rubric until 1570 in the reformed missal under Pius V: in brief, the type of sequence which eventually emerged was as follows:

Advent to Christmas Eve	Violet/Blue/Black
Christmas to Epiphany	White/Gold
Sundays after Epiphany	Green
Septuagesima to Ash Wednesday	Violet/Blue/Black
Throughout Lent	Veiling of colours
Passion Sunday to Easter Eve	Red/Rose
Easter	White/Gold
Pentecost	Red
Trinity	White/Gold
Sundays after Trinity	Green
Ordinary weekdays	Green
Blessed Virgin Mary	White/Red
Apostles, evangelists, martyrs	Red
Saints other than martyrs	White/Yellow

Baptism/confirmation	White/Red
Ordination/marriage	White
Funeral	Violet/Blue/Black
Dedication of a church	White

As the above list indicates, there was latitude in the choice of liturgical colours, especially in the 'mourning' range of violet, dark blue and black: further, distinctions were made in the various shades of red, and in pre-Reformation England, green and yellow were regarded as interchangeable. Regional variation persisted and other colours altogether were sometimes employed, e.g. the brick-red of Sarum for the Sundays after Epiphany. Latin names in mediaeval inventories include *albus* and *candidus* for white, *rubeus, sub-rubeus* and *coccineus* for various shades of red (including rose), *purpureus* for red-purple and *violaceus* for blue-purple, *viridis* for green and *croceus* for yellow.

The Eastern Orthodox churches use coloured materials in great variety and Eastern churches in communion with the Roman Catholic Church broadly follow the Western customs; they do not, however, regard themselves as bound so strictly to adhere to a colour sequence as did the Roman Catholic Church in the period preceding Vatican II.

The liturgical colours were primarily to be seen in the material of the chasubles and copes and that of altar cloths and textile hangings. The colours were also used in the embellishment of the vestments – orphreys and apparels – and in the material or decoration of the stole and maniple. In this connection it may be noted that the colour of the stole and maniple generally accorded with that of the orphreys and apparels and contrasted with the predominant colour of the chasuble. This custom has been contradicted by the recent practice which is concerned to make everything 'match'.

It is interesting to note that the English Lenten vestments were for the most part white (often with a limited amount of red decoration), and that those of passiontide, including Palm Sunday and Good Friday, were red.

Many of the Lenten entries include veils* and other hangings which were used to cover all pictures and images, and on fast days to curtain off the high altar. The purpose of these hangings was to some extent contradicted when themselves they came to be 'steyned', i.e. painted, with symbols and scenes of the passion. Modern practice is to shroud the coloured adornments of a church with a Lenten array of buff-coloured material sparsely embroidered with red emblems.

In the sixteenth century the Reformed Churches generally rejected colour as an adjunct to worship. Where the Calvinist or the Puritan spirit prevailed, all vestments and coloured textiles were abrogated and the ministers were content merely with a black preaching gown worn over dark civilian clothes. Among other Protestants (especially Lutherans and Anglicans), in sectors where it has been customary to retain or to re-introduce some or all of the traditional vestments and hangings, it has also been usual to observe the 1570 Roman Catholic colour sequence so far as this was possible.

A rubric in the 1549 BCP of the Church of England ordered that the parish priest should wear 'a white albe plain, with a vestment or cope', and Canon XXIV (1603–4), based also on the *Advertisements* (1566), curiously ordered that the principal minister at the eucharist in cathedrals and collegiate churches should wear a coloured cope over a plain alb. This perverse practice became quite widespread in the seventeenth century among the so-called Laudian school and, in the early eighteenth century, the high churchmen among the Non-jurors restored the eucharistic vestments in the contemporary Roman Catholic style and sometimes took the liberty of interpreting 'cope' as 'chasuble'. Only in this tenuous way was regard for liturgical colour maintained in the Established Church, for the majority of the clergy obeyed Canon LVIII which prescribed surplice and academic hood or black scarf for the eucharist; there were, however, some clergy who continued to wear a black gown for the celebration as well as for preaching and singing the choir offices until the end of the seventeenth century.

The Catholic sacramental revivalism of the Oxford Movement and the romantic Gothic revivalism of the Cambridge Ecclesiologists converged in the middle of the nineteenth century to focus attention upon

Anglican ceremonial, and hence to advocacy of the eucharistic vestments and the liturgical colours for renewed use in the Church of England.

The result of this stimulus was twofold. On the one hand, Evangelicals denounced the neo-mediaevalism as 'popery' and refused to wear liturgical vestments other than those prescribed by Canon LVIII, namely surplice and academic hood or black scarf. On the other hand, to meet the growing demand of the high-churchmen of the Church of England and of the clergy of the Roman Catholic Church, Victorian commercial interests were mobilized to supply full sets of vestments and hangings in the 'correct' liturgical colours. It is stated by several writers on the subject that complete standardization of the colours in the Roman Catholic Church was not attempted until the nineteenth century, and this, presumably, is an allusion to the persistence of local uses in France until this time, and to the growing commercial pressures for mass-produced correctness.

Eventually, all but the most extreme of the low-church Evangelicals adopted the strange compromise of wearing a seasonally coloured stole over a surplice for the eucharist, while a different compromise (though with some historical justification) in the form of a complete set of all-white linen vestments was accepted by moderate churchmen.

As a result of the influence of the Liturgical Movement*, radical changes are taking place in the design and decoration of vestments and the liturgical use of colours. In general it is recognized that there is historical and psychological virtue in the traditional seasonal colours – provided that they are interpreted in terms of mood rather than in conformity to a rigid system of rules. Thus, it is reasonable in penitential periods to use drab materials in the violet-brown-grey range (though avoiding black), to use red-purples and gold to express majesty and high-priesthood, challenging reds for leaders and martyrs, green and yellow to signify renewal, and to employ white and gold (with the whole palette, if desired) for festivals.

In the Roman Catholic Church the post-Vatican II *Ordo Missae* (1969) generally reaffirmed current practice: white for Easter, Christmas, feasts of Christ (other than the Passion), of Mary, of angels and of saints (not martyrs), All Saints, John Baptist, John Evangelist, Chair of Peter and Conversion of Paul; red for Passion and Palm Sundays, Good Friday, Pentecost, feasts of the Passion of Christ and of martyrs; violet for Advent and Lent and possibly for funeral masses in place of black; rose for Gaudete Sunday (Advent III) and Laetare Sunday (Lent IV); green at other times, It is also recommended that on special occasions more solemn vestments may be used, even if not of the colour of the day.

The combination of a whole range of new materials and colours, together with a fresh understanding of the emotional effect of colours, their optical relationships and their design possibilities, permits a renewed approach to all aspects of their use in worship. For example, especially in new churches, it is possible to integrate all the coloured items – vestments, hangings, carpets, glass, furnishings, timber and other structural materials and finishes – into a total liturgical environment: even in existing churches much can be done to create a meaningful sense of seasonal colour and to refrain from a sterile following of what commercial church furnishers may insist is correct.

J. Braun, *Die liturgische Gewandung im Occident und Orient nach Ursprung und Entwicklung, Verwendung und Symbolik*, 1907; P. Dearmer, *The Ornaments of the Ministers*, 1908/1920; W. H. St J. Hope and E. G. C. F. Atchley, *English Liturgical Colours*, 1918; J. W. Legg, *Notes on the History of Liturgical Colours*, 1882; L. J. Mayo, *A History of Ecclesiastical Dress*, 1984; C. E. Pocknee, *Liturgical Vesture*, 1960.

GILBERT COPE

Commination

In pre-Reformation times, after sext on Ash Wednesday* a sermon was preached and the imposition of ashes* followed. The rite consisted of the seven penitential psalms (6, 32, 38, 51, 102, 130 and 143), *preces*, seven collects for penitence and forgiveness, and a solemn absolution; the blessing of the ashes was accompanied by two more collects*, and the ashes were applied to the foreheads of the penitents with the words

'Remember, O man, that thou art ashes, and unto ashes shalt thou return'; further antiphons and collects then led into mass.

This ceremony (and by implication the rite accompanying it) was abolished by the Council in January 1548, and there is no reference to ashes in the BCP of 1549. Indeed, the name 'Ash Wednesday' is eliminated from the BCP of 1552. The occasion is put to a rather different purpose. After mattins, the people are summoned by the ringing of a bell, and the litany is said, in accordance with the injunctions of 1547, 'in the midst of the church . . . before High Mass'. A completely new section follows, which gives the service its name 'commination' (*Oxford English Dictionary*: 'a threatening of punishment'). The priest goes into the pulpit and reads 'a declaration of scripture' consisting chiefly of 'the general sentences of God's cursing against impenitent sinners' (Deut. 27.15–25). This is meant to take the place of the primitive discipline of open penance, and was probably suggested by the mediaeval rite called the greater excommunication, a denunciation of sinners read three or four times a year. It is followed by a long catena of scriptural texts on judgment and repentance woven together into a continuous sermon.

The priest then returns to the midst of the church, and the rest of the service (described in the title as 'certain prayers') is an abridgement of the Sarum rite, shorn of course of its ceremony. The BCP retains only one of the penitential psalms (Ps. 51), the *preces*, the first collect, a collect made up of phrases from four of the Sarum prayers, and one of the antiphons, which leads into the introit psalm (Ps. 6) of holy communion.

The title 'A Commination against Sinners' dates from 1552, and in 1662 Bishop Wren added to it the explanatory phrase 'or Denouncing of God's Anger and Judgments'. The connection with Ash Wednesday, severed in the 1552 BCP, was maintained in practice throughout the sixteenth century, and was restored in 1662, with provision for use 'at other times, as the Ordinary shall appoint'. By then the service seems to have become separated from the holy communion, and a blessing was added at the end.

Modern revisions have tried various expedients to keep the service in use. England 1928 substitutes censures based on the Decalogue and abbreviates the catena; Scotland 1929 has the Decalogue itself and the Lucan Beatitudes (6.20–26), while omitting the catena altogether. America 1928 omits the whole of the first part; England 1966, First Series, the whole of the second. Only in India, where penitential discipline is still in force, does Deut. 27 survive; and even here the catena is shortened.

The ASB has no equivalent to this service. The blessing of ashes on Ash Wednesday has been widely revived in England, and in 1985 a form was produced by the Liturgical Commission. It owes something to the American form of 1979.

American BCP, pp.264–9; F. E. Brightman, *The English Rite*, 1915, I, pp.cxxix, clxiv, ccxxii; II, pp.886–901; A. J. Collins, *Manuale Sarum*, 1960, pp.9–12; M. J. Hatchett, *Commentary on the American Prayer Book*, 1979, pp.218–22.

G. J. CUMING

Commixture

The commixture is the placing of a particle of the consecrated host in the chalice* after the fraction* at the eucharist*. The origins of this ceremonial act are complex. It appears to have derived from the *fermentum*. This was a fragment of bread consecrated at an episcopal celebration and taken to a church where a presbyter was presiding, it being added to the chalice after the fraction as a symbol of unity. This custom died out in the East, probably in the fourth century, but continued in Rome until the eighth or ninth. At that period there was also current the practice of sanctifying extra chalices by adding a piece of the already consecrated host. It would appear that the *fermentum* was transformed into the commixture under this influence. The commixture was further affected by a Syrian symbolic interpretation, to the effect that the words of consecration represent the death of Christ and so the separation of his body and blood, while the bringing together of these two through the commixture shows forth his resurrection. Hence in the Liturgy of St James it is called the *henosis*, i.e. union, while in that of St Chrysostom it is accompanied by the words: 'The fullness of

the Holy Spirit' – the Spirit being regarded as the agent of the resurrection.

J. A. Jungmann, *The Mass of the Roman Rite*, rev ed 1959, pp.475–9.

EDITOR

Common of Saints

Unlike a proper*, which is that service that is proper to a particular day, season or person, the Common of Saints is a form that may be used appropriately on many occasions throughout the church's year. The only differentiating factor is the name and designation of the person being commemorated, there being a standard collect and series of readings. The American Episcopal BCP (1979) allows the use of the Common for numerous commemorations, including Ember* and Rogation Days*. It also provides for six categories of persons, namely martyrs, missionaries, pastors, theologians or teachers, monastics or any saints without a proper. The ASB likewise has six but substitutes bishops for pastors.

EDITOR

Communion

1. The partaking of the consecrated elements at the eucharist*, whereby there is a communion or participation (*koinonia*) in Christ and in him with all the members of the congregation. Methods of partaking and of distribution as well as posture have varied throughout the ages and from church to church.

In the patristic period the worshippers received the bread in their hands but do not appear to have touched the chalice*. Cyril, or John, of Jerusalem describes the fourth-century practice when he says: 'As you approach then, come not with your wrists extended or your fingers open, but make of your left hand a kind of throne by placing it under your right which is about to receive the King, and in the hollow of your hand receive the body of Christ, replying Amen. Carefully hallow your eyes with the touch of the holy body, and then partake of it, seeing to it that you lose no particle . . . Then, after the communion of Christ's body, approach also the cup of his blood, not stretching forth your hands, but bending forward in attitude of adoration and reverence, and saying Amen, be hallowed as well by the reception of the blood of Christ. And while the moisture thereof is still on your lips, touch it with your hands and hallow both your eyes and brow and other senses' (*Catech.* 5.21 f.).

Before the end of the sixth century women were forbidden to receive the bread on the naked hand and the *Ordo Romanus VI* (? *c.* 900) only allows this for bishops, priests and deacons, apparently from a desire to protect that which is holy from profane or superstitious uses. This practice was also required by the 1549 BCP but was thereafter omitted. By the thirteenth century communicating under the species of wine had almost universally disappeared in the West, probably to avoid the risk of spilling. Objections to this were raised by the Hussites in Bohemia, and the Reformers insisted that communion in both kinds alone had scriptural warrant. In the Roman Church since Vatican II communion from the cup for the laity has become very widely used. The somewhat detailed instructions on the matter that came after the Council have now been made more flexible and there is no reason why communion in both kinds should not be given in every church. The only requirement is that it should be done reverently. The institution of lay ministers, both men and women, for the distribution of the eucharist has greatly facilitated the practice.

Another method of partaking is by intinction*, i.e. the bread is dipped in the wine so that the two kinds can be administered conjointly. This became popular in the seventh century but was condemned in the West in the thirteenth; it is now permitted in the Roman Catholic Church, and also communion through a reed. In Orthodox churches it is the almost universal practice to partake from a spoon containing the bread sprinkled with a few drops of wine. Today this method is sometimes used in the USA for hygienic reasons. Similar motives have also led to the use in many non-episcopal churches of small individual cups.

Distribution of communion has also varied. In the early church the worshippers came up to a balustrade demarcating the sanctuary* and this has continued to be the practice in many churches, e.g. Anglican, Orthodox and Roman. An alternative method is to bring the elements to the communicants. This change was instituted

by the English Puritans who then influenced Congregationalists, Methodists and Presbyterians. Some Presbyterians, however, particularly in Holland and Westphalia, leave their seats and sit around a table in the nave or sanctuary.

This last statement indicates that for these Christians the posture for communion is sitting. However, in the early church it was usual to stand, and this is still the norm in many Reformed congregations in Alsace, France and Switzerland. Reception kneeling only gained ascendance gradually in the Roman Church between the eleventh and the sixteenth century and remains usual as well as among Anglicans.

2. Communion can also be a translation of the Latin word *communio* which denotes a psalm sung during communion. According to Cyril, Ps. 34 was sung at Jerusalem in the fourth century, and both the *Apostolic Constitutions* and Augustine refer to the practice. The psalm is sometimes replaced by a communion hymn at the present day.

See also **Chants of the Proper of the Mass; Music in the Mass of the Roman Rite**

EDITOR

Communion Table

This term has been preferred to the term altar* by those churches that have sprung out of the Protestant Reformation in the sixteenth century. The Reformers were anxious to play down or remove altogether the catholic emphasis on the sacrifice of the mass performed by the priest, and to balance or replace it by underlining the corporate aspect of fellowship at the Lord's Table. So, for example, in the 1559 prayer book it was decreed that at communion time the holy table should be so placed within the chancel that the minister might conveniently be heard and the communicants conveniently communicate, though later Laudian piety preferred the table to stand altar-wise in the sanctuary behind altar rails*.

Seventeenth-century Puritan arrangements with the table standing permanently in the body of the chancel may still be seen at Deerhurst and Hailes, Glos., and Langley, Salop. In the Church of Scotland, in English and Welsh Nonconformist churches generally, and in a few eighteenth-century Anglican churches, the table stands in front of the pulpit and is frequently flanked by chairs for the minister and the elders or deacons. This last custom symbolizes the belief that celebration is a corporate activity, though presided over by the minister, and seats are also provided behind the table in some modern Anglican churches. That this is a variation on ancient practice may be seen by reference to the stone benches for presbyters in the apses of some of the oldest churches in Rome and at St Irene, Constantinople.

In the BCP the usual term is the Lord's Table, and the ASB uses 'holy table', but in common parlance in the Church of England the term altar is in frequent use.

G. W. O. Addleshaw and F. Etchells, *The Architectural Setting of Anglican Worship*, 1948; K. Lindley, *Chapels and Meeting Houses*, 1969; G. Randall, *Church Furniture and Decoration in England and Wales*, 1980.

G. D. W. RANDALL

Community and Worship

In early Christianity worship was in general intended for the faithful. Nevertheless, already in the earliest liturgical regulations we find an unexpected preoccupation with the outsider, the 'idiotes' (1 Cor. 14.24, 25). If the guidelines in 1 Cor. 12.7, where it is stated that the charismata should be *pros to sympheron* (useful), are applicable also to the whole of the liturgy, then we might ask: Useful for whom? For the fellowship of the believers or for society at large? The answer 'for both' does not help in those cases where there is conflict (or thought to be conflict) between the two groups of people.

We find the same uncertainty today. It is not quite sure for whom worship is intended. Is it for the baptized, the initiated, the committed? Such an understanding is usually rejected at least in theory by most European established churches. They believe in public worship, which is to be conducted for and on behalf of the whole of society. This has led the Anglican, Roman Catholic and European mainline churches to adapt their liturgies to so-called modern man. In general the public has not reacted favourably to these changes. It seems that the outsiders want the church to remain a guardian of the values *and* forms of the past.

Most Non-conformist churches, on the

other hand, have developed two types of worship: one for the initiated, the other for the non-committed. This distinction is developed in an exemplary way in the Salvation Army: holiness meetings on Sunday mornings for the salvationists, evangelistic meetings in the evening for the sinners. In churches where the borderline between outsiders and insiders is not as clear as in the Salvation Army this distinction is not helpful. Most evangelistic meetings (which are intended for the non-committed) are frequented by committed Christians, and most services which are intended for the committed are also frequented by outsiders when there is a confirmation, a baptism, a wedding or another family event which makes opting out of a religious service difficult.

One way forward might be to invite outsiders and non-Christians to participate in the process of preparing specific experimental liturgies. About half of the preparation group for such experimental forms of worship* services should be insiders and the other half outsiders, the criterion for the latter being that they have not been to church for at least two years. This forces the insiders to articulate their belief and the outsiders their scepticism in everyday language, because this is the only language they have in common. In the cases where a common liturgy emerges, it proves to be highly satisfying for those who are engaged in the process. The value for those who are invited as guests to the celebration of these liturgies (in this case they were the outsiders, notwithstanding their long standing in the church) depends on how well they know the creators of the liturgy and how much credit they are prepared to give them – an observation which shows that in a pastoral context the terms 'committed/uncommitted' have a marginal theological connotation. They resemble much more the generally observable psychological categories used to describe relationships between insiders and outsiders. Therefore it would seem right and proper that in the church cultural, theological and religious outsiders should receive preferential treatment. That means that worship cannot be geared totally to the needs of the insiders. But they hire and pay their liturgical president, they decide on the shape of the liturgy on the basis of their needs and tastes. That is why Paul's admonition to take the reaction of the outsider seriously is as important as it is generally ignored in liturgical discussions.

W. J. HOLLENWEGER

Compline

see **Canonical Hours**

Concelebration

A form of rite in which several bishops or presbyters jointly celebrate the eucharist* or other sacrament.

At the close of the first century, Clement of Rome had described the organic yet hierarchical nature of the church celebrating the eucharist, each order (bishop*, presbyters*, deacons*, laity) with its own contribution or place. At the beginning of the second century, Ignatius of Antioch had insisted on the unity of the eucharist: one celebration at one altar* presided over by one bishop with his 'presbyterium', or college of presbyters, and the deacons. A century later we have explicit directions for the participation by presbyters in the bishop's eucharist at Rome in the *Apostolic Tradition* of Hippolytus: the deacons present the oblations* over which the whole presbyterium extends hands, while the bishop alone gives thanks. Just a few years later, from a very different community in Syria, the *Didascalia* has a bishop welcoming a visiting colleague by inviting him not only to preach but also to say the eucharistic prayer, or at the very least to pronounce the words over the cup. In this way both the unity of the sacrament and communion of faith and ministry were expressed. As yet there could be no question of joint recitation, as celebrants still improvised.

Even when texts were fixed, from the fourth century, this mode of concelebration did not change. Both Cyril of Jerusalem and Pseudo-Dionysius the Areopagite describe presbyters celebrating with the bishop, and as late as the Council of Constantinople (680) and the Photian Synod (880) Latin legates were invited to concelebrate with the Greeks without knowing enough of the langugage to recite the anaphora*. But already by the eighth century a different practice was developing at Rome. While *Ordo I* directs the concelebrating bishops and priests to bow their heads during the

pope's recitation of the canon*, *Ordo III* has the cardinal priests recite the canon together with the pope, while each holds bread in his hands.

In the West, the diffusion of the church in rural areas and the development of 'private mass' led to the abandonment of the tradition of only one celebration. Traces of the older custom survived here and there only on Maundy Thursday* at the blessing of oils during the canon, and in the ordination mass of priests and bishops (at least according to the Pontificals of the twelfth and thirteenth centuries). According to their rubrics, all the concelebrants recited *sotto voce* all the prayers from the offertory* onwards, or even, in some cases, from the beginning of mass, including the choir chants. At communion*, however, they received kneeling and in one kind only, like the rest of the congregation. St Thomas Aquinas (d.1274) testifies that the practice was disappearing in his time, but justifies concelebration theologically on the grounds of the unity of all the priesthood in Christ.

A great variety of traditions has survived in the Eastern churches. With the East Syrians, Copts and Ethiopians, the presiding bishop asks one of the presbyters to recite the anaphora; the other presbyters flank him without making any active contribution. The West Syrians and Ethiopians on certain occasions have synchronized celebrations by several priests who consecrate simultaneously, sometimes at the same altar. In the Byzantine rite, the bishop remains the principal celebrant. In the Russian church the concelebrants recite together the most important parts of the anaphora, including the words of institution and the epiclesis, though this seems to be due to Western influences in the seventeenth century. Similar practices are to be found among the Greek Catholics, the Maronites and the Uniate Copts. But in the rest of the Orthodox churches the current practice is to share out only the 'ekphoneses' (vocalized conclusions of the otherwise silent anaphora) and other prayers outside the anaphora, but this too seems to be a relatively late development.

In Roman Catholicism, the twentieth century Liturgical Movement* led in some quarters to the demand for a revival of concelebration, at least as an alternative to the entrenched practice of multiple 'private' masses. In 1956 Pius XII ruled that 'in the proper sense of the term' concelebration meant the recitation by all the concelebrants of the words of institution, all else was only 'ceremonial' concelebration; and it was in the light of this judgment that the Second Vatican Council discussed the question, decided upon a restoration, and commissioned the composition of a new rite, which was issued in 1965. In the discussions and in the ensuing rite restored emphasis is given to the organic yet hierarchical nature of the church, to the unity of the eucharist, and to the collegiate character of the ministry.

According to this restored rite, it is the prerogative of the bishop to preside over his own presbyterium (or a representative part of it) as principal celebrant, thus manifesting the original unity of the local church. In cathedral liturgies, stational celebrations at deanery level and major diocesan gatherings, this is now general. In the absence of the bishop, the presidency could be said to be collective: any priest can take the role of principal celebrant. However, it is required that this essentially collegial ministry be represented by a single person who alone pronounces the greetings, dialogues, blessings and presidential prayers. The participation of the remaining concelebrants could in principle be expressed in various ways. According to this rite it is expressed in both word and gesture as follows: all sing or recite in unison the core of the eucharistic prayer (first epiclesis, words of institution, anamnesis, second epiclesis) and the concluding doxology, with the principal celebrant's voice prevailing. The intercessions of the anaphora may be allocated to individual concelebrants. The concelebrants gather round the altar after the preparation of the gifts, taking care not to obscure the view of the congregation. During the first epiclesis, they extend their hand(s), palm downwards, over or towards the elements (as indicated by Hippolytus), and during the words of institution they (may) extend their right hands towards the elements, this time palm upwards in an indicative sense. After each elevation they bow profoundly. At communion they receive in both kinds according to a variety of methods, being served by bishop or

deacon, passing the vessels among themselves, or serving themselves directly from the altar. Any of the concelebrants may give the homily, proclaim the gospel in the absence of a deacon, distribute communion. All wear the usual mass vestments*, but for a sufficient reason may adopt simply an alb and stole.

Not all have been happy with the form of concelebration adopted, feeling that the unity of eucharist and priesthood is expressed only at the cost of separating the 'power' of consecration from the role of presidency and unduly isolating the role of 'co-consecrating' presbyters from the rest of the celebrating church. For this reason many presbyters prefer to join the celebration as members of the congregation.

It should be pointed out that the current attitude of the Roman Catholic Church is not simply permissive but positively encourages concelebration 'whenever pastoral needs or other reasonable motives do not prevent it'. This is in line with the stated preference of the Second Vatican Council in its constitution on the liturgy for 'celebration in common rather than by an individual and quasi-privately'. Thus, in the revised rites for the other sacraments a form of concelebration is now encouraged, in which Pius XII's distinction between 'sacramental' and 'ceremonial' concelebration is much less clear cut. Not only in the ordination of bishops and presbyters do other members of the respective order (as in Hippolytus' rite of the third century) lay hands on the candidate together with the ordaining bishop, but in the rite of confirmation, too, presbyters who have a special pastoral relationship with the candidates may actually confer the sacrament along with the bishop; and in the rites of baptism, anointing of the sick, and the reconciliation of several penitents, several priests may share the texts and secondary rituals between them and baptize, anoint or absolve concurrently within the one corporate celebration.

In the Church of England, cases of concelebration have been known since the 1920s, but the practice has grown in recent years. Many simply follow the Roman guidelines, while others find them theologically unsatisfactory and would prefer to adopt the older or 'Eastern' form, which they feel would accord better with the rubrics of ASB 1980. In 1982 the Liturgical Commission issued a booklet on the question, *Concelebration in the Eucharist*, but declined to offer specific guidelines.

See also **Celebrant**.

P. Jounel, *La Concélébration*, 1966; A. A. King, *Concelebration in the Christian Church*, 1966; B. Neunheuser et al., *Théologie et pratique de la concélébration*, 1967; *Missale Romanum*, 1970, ET *Roman Missal*, 1975.

C. J. WALSH

Confession

see **Prayer** 2

Confirmation

The earliest attestation of the ceremony which ultimately came to be called 'confirmation' (Lat *confirmatio*, Gk, *bebaiōsis*) is to be found in the baptismal rites of Hippolytus' *Apostolic Tradition* (AD 215) and Tertullian's treatise *De Baptismo* (AD 198). Both works attest a ceremony after baptism* consisting of a prayer said by the bishop with his hands extended over the candidates, the anointing of the candidates on the forehead, the imposition of the hand on the head of each, and the sign of the cross (*see* **Gestures**) on the forehead. The precise manner and order in which these elements were combined varied in the subsequent development and they did not always appear in their entirety. Thus according to the *Ordo Romanus XI* of the late sixth century 'the pontiff makes a prayer over them . . . and when the prayer has been said he makes the sign of the cross with his thumb in chrism on the forehead of each one, saying, "In the name of the Father and the Son and the Holy Spirit. Peace be to thee".' On the eve of the Reformation, the Sarum manual and the Roman pontifical differed from this only in so far as the formula which accompanied the anointing had grown longer and the Roman rite specifically preserves a mention of the extension of the bishop's hands over the candidates as he prays for the sevenfold gifts of the Spirit. The BCP has abandoned the anointing and the sign of the cross but preserves the imposition of the hand, in the belief that this accords better with the example of the apostles, and has provided a

new formula, 'Defend O Lord . . .', to accompany it. The BCP order retains also the prayer for the sevenfold gifts of the Spirit from the Sarum rite, but does not provide any more than the Sarum rite for the extension of the bishop's hands over the candidates while it is said. This prayer is broadly the same as that which appears in the early sixth-century Gelasian Sacramentary and has formed a constant feature of the Roman rite ever since that date. It is believed to be first attested by Ambrose in his treatise *De Sacramentis*, and is almost certainly quoted by some of his Roman contemporaries.

Originally no distinction was made between infants and adults in the use of this post-baptismal ceremony. When infants were baptized they were also anointed and hands were laid on them. But the requirement of the Roman and African churches that the anointing and imposition of the hand must be reserved to the bishop came to result in their separation from baptism, for infants and adults alike. In cases of emergency baptism, administered by a priest, or when bishops were no longer able to preside over all baptisms, the post-baptismal ceremony was inevitably delayed until the candidates could appear before a bishop. This separation between baptism and confirmation, which was originally imposed on the church by practical necessity, came ultimately to be regarded as the normal practice, and led to a situation in which baptism was thought to be appropriate to infancy and confirmation to later years.

Although in the Roman rite this ceremony was associated with the gift of the Holy Spirit, it is not clear that this was the case with the other rites of the Latin West. These provide for a simple post-baptismal anointing of the forehead, which in Gaul and Spain was performed by the priest who baptized, with oil which had been consecrated by the bishop. But in rites which were unaffected by Roman influence there is nothing to indicate that the bestowal of the Spirit was understood to be the purpose of the anointing.

In the early Syrian church no post-baptismal ceremony corresponding to the Western anointing and imposition of the hand intervened between the baptismal washing and the holy communion*. Although some scholars have claimed that the pre-baptismal anointing in this rite must therefore have been for the bestowal of the Spirit, it seems more probable that this anointing served the same apotropaic purpose as it did in the West and that the Syrian church recognized no sign other than water by which the Spirit was imparted in Christian initiation. If this is correct, it carries with it the important implication that a second sign other than water in Christian initiation was not a matter of universal observance in the early church.

The earliest Syrian attestations of a post-baptismal anointing are to be found in the *Apostolic Constitutions* (*c.*AD 375) and the *Catecheses* of Cyril of Jerusalem, and these most probably represent an importation from the churches of the West. By degrees this anointing after baptism was adopted throughout the churches of the East, where it is now accepted as a sacrament, although the Nestorian rite to this day has no such anointing. The rite consists of a chrismation made in the sign of the cross to the forehead and other parts of the body, but not the imposition of the hand. The formula varies, but the formula of the ancient Byzantine rite is still used in the Orthodox Church, 'The seal of the gift of the Holy Spirit'. This chrismation is performed by the priest who baptizes and is administered to infants as well as adults.

1. *Meaning*. The significance of this post-baptismal ceremony is a matter of controversy. According to the Council of Trent, confirmation is one of seven sacraments instituted by Christ. Until recently, Roman Catholic theologians defined the matter of the sacrament variously as chrism, the imposition of the hand, or the combination of both. The form used throughout the Roman Catholic Church was as follows: *I sign thee with the sign of the cross, and I confirm thee with the chrism of salvation, in the name of the Father and of the Son and of the Holy Spirit. Amen.* A distinction was commonly made between the grace of baptism and that of confirmation: in baptism the Holy Spirit is given for pardon and new birth, in confirmation for strength to preach the gospel and to live the adult Christian life. Such a distinction does not seem tenable in the context of infant confirmation, and appears to have originated in the Middle Ages as a ration-

alization of the situation when baptism was administered in infancy and confirmation in later years. However in 1971, as a consequence of the Second Vatican Council the Roman Catholic Church replaced the mediaeval rite with a new one. Confirmation is conferred after the Ministry of the Word, usually in the eucharist. After a renewal of baptismal promises, the bishop lays hands (i.e. holds his hands) over all at once, while he says the ancient prayer for the sevenfold gifts of the Spirit. However according to the Apostolic Constitution on the Sacrament of Confirmation delivered in 1971 by Pope Paul VI, this 'does not belong to the essence of the sacramental rite, but contributes to the integral perfection of that rite'. The sacrament itself is then performed by an anointing on the forehead, which is identified with the laying on of the *hand*, and the form *Accipe Signaculum Doni Spiritus Sancti*, of which the official English translation is 'N, be sealed with the gift of the Holy Spirit'. Apart from the word *Accipe* the Latin text is a translation of the ancient formula of the Byzantine rite. The meaning of the rite may be discerned from the rite itself and from the Apostolic Constitution of 1971: some Roman Catholic commentators have difficulty in discerning any gift in confirmation more than is already conveyed in baptism.

A. J. Mason, followed by Dom G. Dix and Fr L. S. Thornton, has argued that baptism and confirmation make up one sacrament consisting of two signs, each one conveying its own distinctive grace. In baptism the Holy Spirit operates from the outside to convey pardon and new birth; in confirmation the gift of the indwelling Spirit is bestowed.

The BCP states that *It is certain by God's Word, that children which are baptized, dying before they commit actual sin, are undoubtedly saved*, and this appears to imply the view that confirmation is not necessary to salvation. Consistently with this, the Thirty-Nine Articles distinguish confirmation and other ceremonies 'commonly called sacraments' from baptism and holy communion, which are 'sacraments of the gospel'. Since confirmation is not regarded as a sacrament in the strict sense by the Church of England, its form and matter are not defined: but the laying on of hands with prayer are commonly regarded as its necessary features. While the Church of England has retained inflexibly the ancient rule that only bishops may confirm, the Church of Rome permits bishops to delegate this function on appropriate occasions: and as we have seen, the priest is the normal minister of the sacrament in the Eastern churches.

2. *Origins*. In the Middle Ages the origin of confirmation was variously traced to the action of our Lord laying his hands on children (Mark 10.16), or in breathing on the apostles (John 20.22) or to his teaching after the resurrection of 'the things pertaining to the kingdom of God' (Acts 1.3). An alternative to these speculations was the view that confirmation was exemplified, if not instituted, by the apostles when they laid hands on the baptized and the Spirit came upon them (Acts 8.15; 19.6). These passages in Acts had been cited by Irenaeus and Tertullian and others of the fathers to show that the apostles regularly laid hands on their converts for the bestowal of the Spirit. But this interpretation has been contested by leaders of the continental Reformation and at the present day notably by G. W. H. Lampe, who claim that the events recounted in the Acts are not to be understood as normative: and the evidence of the Syrian rite to which we have referred above suggests that in fact it was not normative.

The ablutionary customs of the ancient world called for the use of oil as well as water in bathing, and it has therefore been suggested that confirmation may have originated in the oil which would commonly have been used after the baptismal bath. Passages in the NT which have been thought to refer to the use of oil or chrism in initiation include II Cor. 1.21 and I John 2.20,27; but the anointing to which these texts refer may be nothing more than a metaphor for the gift of the Holy Spirit in baptism.

Another explanation for the origin of confirmation has been sought in the complexity of the Gnostic and mystery religions in which candidates proceeded from one stage in initiation to higher and more advanced stages.

While some of these accounts of the origins of confirmation may seem more prob-

able than others, their variety indicates that there is no certainty on the point, which remains a matter for speculation.

3. *The age of confirmation.* The practice of infant confirmation did not entirely disappear until the end of the Middle Ages, so that it was still possible in 1533 for the Princess Elizabeth to be baptized and confirmed at the age of three days. Nevertheless, over the previous centuries a number of circumstances led to the situation in which confirmation came to be reserved to the 'years of discretion'. First, the difficulty of obtaining confirmation and the sense that baptism itself conveyed the grace of the Holy Spirit and all that was necessary for salvation (which few mediaeval theologians denied) led to a general neglect of confirmation and a disposition to delay it indefinitely. This neglect was then countered by the teaching that confirmation was necessary in order to become fully Christian, and by the regulation which in England originated with Archbishop Peckham in the thirteenth century, which laid down that no one should be admitted to holy communion until he had been confirmed. Although a number of continental and English councils laid down that children must be confirmed by the age of two, three, or seven, the result of the process was that the age of seven or more became established as the normal age for confirmation. At the same time a theology of baptism and confirmation had been developing to match the facts of the changed situation, teaching that baptism restores innocence and gives new birth and that confirmation gives the strength to live the Christian life and to preach to others. It was in the light of this that the Catechism of the Council of Trent (1566) laid down seven to twelve years old as the appropriate age for confirmation, and preferred the latter. Since then pastoral considerations have led the Roman Catholic Church to admit children to holy communion some years before their confirmation. However, since 1971 it has been made clear that the normal sacramental progress of the Christian begins at baptism and continues with confirmation and only then with the eucharist, although exception may be made to this if there should be good pastoral reason for admitting to the eucharist people of mature age (i.e. sixteen or seventeen) who have not yet been confirmed.

In the Church of England today the most suitable age for confirmation is a matter of debate. To some it is determined by the fact that the laying on of hands is associated with the re-affirmation of baptismal vows, which suggests that confirmation should be deferred to an age when candidates can speak from personal conviction. On the other hand, those who regard confirmation as a source of sacramental grace argue for an earlier age. The school-leaving age and modern insights into child psychology are other factors in the debate.

The Reformers regard confirmation as an 'idle ceremony'. In their experience it was administered with oil (which they sometimes chose to call 'grease'), and thus appeared to have no foundation in scripture. Moreover, as we have noted above, many of the Reformers did not accept that the imposition of the apostles' hands described in Acts was to be taken as an example which the church must necessarily follow. In their view the NT gives no indication that confirmation can be traced to the institution of Christ, nor indeed says anything at all about confirmation. They regarded baptism as the one sacrament of initiation and resented the teaching that before confirmation a man was only half a Christian. At the same time, they perceived the value of an occasion when the child baptized in infancy might make a public profession of his baptismal faith in later years. This matched their convictions about the importance of individual faith and the need to answer the Anabaptists who criticized the practice of infant baptism; and it was supported by their mistaken belief that Christians in the primitive church commonly made such a declaration when they reached maturity. From these premises there developed in the Reformed churches a rite of 'confirmation' of which the principal element was an examination of the candidates and a declaration of their Christian commitment: and this was followed by the imposition of the pastor's hands, which was understood as a blessing. In the late Middle Ages it had already been required that parents and godparents should teach their children such elements of the faith as the *Paternoster, Ave Maria,* and *Credo*, and from this the Reformers quickly developed the system of preparation for confirmation

in classes and by catechisms.

Although Calvin would have been content to see the 'restoration' of the laying on of hands when children made a personal confession of faith, on condition that it was understood as a blessing, he did not provide or practise such a rite himself. The churches of the Reformed tradition have varied, some observing a confirmation of this kind and others not. Today, in response to pastoral needs, many churches which formerly had no rite of confirmation have now adopted one, which is often associated with admission to holy communion. Thus the Methodist Church has provided a service of 'Public Reception into Full Membership, or Confirmation'. Services of this kind provide a form of commitment to the Christian faith and life, followed by the laying on of hands in blessing performed by the local minister, and often include a prayer for the strengthening of the Holy Spirit. Sometimes they also provide that the minister or some other member of the church shall extend 'the right hand of fellowship' to the new member.

4. *Recent Anglican rites.* The ASB provides that ideally adult baptism shall be followed immediately by confirmation, and it follows the BCP in providing an order of confirmation 'for those who are already baptized'. The rite is the same in each case. After the renewal of baptismal vows, the bishop extends his hands over all the candidates while he says the prayer for the sevenfold gifts of the Spirit. This has been a little amended, and the central petition is 'Let your Holy Spirit rest on them' (see Isa. 11.2, RSV). Then the bishop lays his hand on the head of each one in turn saying 'Confirm, O Lord, your servant N with your Holy Spirit'. Finally the congregation joins in saying the form 'Defend, O Lord, your servant . . .' which in the BCP rite was the form said by the bishop at the laying on of his hand. It is allowed that oil may be used at the imposition of the hand. The BCP and the Thirty-Nine Articles continue to be the norm of doctrine in the Church of England, and these observances must therefore be understood in the light of BCP and the Articles.

The Book of Common Prayer of 1979 of the Episcopal Church in the USA provides only one order of baptism, for use with infants and adults alike. Baptism in water is followed immediately by a ceremony consisting of the imposition of the hand, marking the sign of the cross on the forehead of the candidate, using chrism if desired, with the form 'N, you are sealed with the Holy Spirit in Baptism and marked as Christ's own for ever.' Both priests and bishops perform this ceremony, over infants and adults. Although the ceremony is mandatory, and appears to correspond with the imposition of the hand and chrismation of the early rites, which developed into confirmation, it is not called confirmation, it is not mentioned in the catechism as a necessary part of initiation, and no particular meaning is assigned to it. In the American book, confirmation appears as a pastoral office. It is for mature people, and consists of a renewal of baptismal vows followed by the laying on of hands by the bishop. It is described in the catechism as a rite which has evolved in the church under the guidance of the Spirit, it is not necessary in the same way that baptism is necessary, and in it we receive strength from the Holy Spirit through prayer and the laying on of hands by a bishop.

5. *The word confirmation.* To many people today the word connotes the fact that candidates confirm their baptismal vows at confirmation. This interpretation of the word dates only from the Reformation and takes no account of such prayer-book expressions as 'to be confirmed by the bishop', which go back to a higher antiquity. The words *confirmatio, confirmare* began to be used of the post-baptismal anointing or hand-laying in the early fifth century in the sense that the bishop then ratified or completed what had been begun in baptism. At a later stage, when the church had accepted the doctrine that this rite supplied strength for the adult Christian life, it was natural that the word *confirmation* came to be understood as 'strengthening'.

For confirmation in the Orthodox rite *see* **Baptism** 2.

A. D'Ales, *De Baptismo et Confirmatione*, 1927; J. D. Crichton, *Christian Celebration: The Sacraments*, [2]1980; J. D. C. Fisher, *Christian Initiation. Baptism in the Medieval West*, 1965; *Christian Initiation. The Reformation Period,* 1970; *Confirmation Then and Now*, 1978; P. J. Jagger, *Christian In-*

itiation, 1552–*1969*, 1970; G. W. H. Lampe, *The Seal of the Spirit*, 1951; T. A. Marsh, *Gift of Community, Baptism and Confirmation*, 1984; A. J. Mason, *The Relation of Confirmation to Baptism*, 1893; L. L. Mitchell, *Baptismal Anointing*, 1966; B. Neunheuser, *Baptism and Confirmation*, ET 1964; S. L. Ollard (ed), *Confirmation or the Laying on of Hands*, 1926; E. C. Whitaker, *Documents of the Baptismal Liturgy*, [2]1970; *The Baptismal Liturgy*, [2]1981; J. Ysebaert, *Greek Baptismal Terminology*, 1962.

E. C. WHITAKER

Congregationalist Worship

The earliest worship of the English Congregationalists had affinities with Presbyterianism and with the Society of Friends. It was both biblical in seeking precedents for all its ordinances and for their content and also charismatic in stressing the role of the Holy Spirit in worship. Had it been biblically-based alone, it would have been indistinguishable from the liturgies of the Presbyterian churches, as in Calvin's *La Forme des Prières* or in John Knox's *Genevan Service Book*. Had it been simply Spirit-led, without a consistently biblical basis, it could easily have led to the silent worship of the Quakers. Like Presbyterian worship*, early Congregationalist worship insisted upon six ordinances; prayer; praise; preaching; baptism and the Lord's Supper; catechizing; and the exercise of discipline. Its single important difference from the Presbyterians was in the demand that public prayer, following Rom. 8.26,27, should be 'not in any *prescribed* form of prayer, or *studied* liturgie, but in such manner as the Spirit of grace and of prayer who teacheth all the people of God, what and how to pray . . . helpeth our infirmities, we having respect therein to the necessities of the people, the estate of the times, and the work of Christ in our hands' (John Cotton, *The Way of the Churches of Christ in New England*, 1645, p. 65).

This distinctive emphasis on free prayer was supported by six arguments. The reliance upon liturgy would deprive minister and people of the capacity to pray in their own thoughts and words. It was also argued that set forms could not meet the varied needs of differing congregations and occasions. Further, the implication that God could only be worshipped properly in a set liturgy was idolatry, in that it equated the liturgy with the Bible and infringed Christian liberty. Yet again, the constant use of set prayers would lead to the familiarity that breeds contempt or heedlessness. John Owen, the Puritan Vice-Chancellor of Oxford, accused the imposers of liturgies of bringing persecution into the church – 'Fire and faggot into the Christian religion'. Finally, and most compellingly, the point was made that read prayers utterly contradicted the appropriate approach to a heavenly Father by his children, especially as he had promised to help the infirmities of his children by the Holy Spirit. Liturgies or set forms must be abandoned like crutches that God's people may walk in the power of faith. So persuasively were these arguments presented by the small number of Independent ministers (the earlier name for Congregationalists) at the Westminster Assembly of Divines called to provide a national settlement of religion in the Cromwellian era that they compelled the Presbyterians to drop their demand for a more biblically-based Genevan type liturgy and instead provided a manual or *Directory for the Public Worship of God Throughout the Three Kingdoms* (1644).

The importance of this manual of worship, prescribing the order of the items in public worship, but not the words which are to be used, is that it has provided the standard shape of worship for the Calvinistic churches (Presbyterian and Congregational, as well as that of the Particular Baptists) in the English-speaking world for approximately two hundred and fifty years.

The other pioneering contribution made to worship by Congregationalism came from the pen of Isaac Watts; the Baptist Benjamin Keach had preceded him in time, but not in quality. Watts, in *The Psalms of David imitated in the Language of the New Testament*, made the transition from the old covenant to the new, teaching 'my author to speak like a Christian'. It was then only a short step to the hymn of Christian experience; Watts took this in *Hymns and Spiritual Songs*. His most famous paraphrase is of Ps. 90: 'Our God, our help in ages past' and his most famous hymn is 'When I survey the wondrous cross'.

The strength of the Congregationalist and Puritan tradition in worship was

fourfold. 1. Its biblical and revelational emphasis gave it an august objectivity, unchallenged until the arrival of the eighteenth-century Deists and the nineteenth-century historical critics of the Bible. 2. Its second quality was its relevance to life, for this worship held in simple scrubbed meeting-houses was the incentive to, never the substitute for, civic duty, and the exercise of ecclesiastical discipline guarded against unworthy recipients of the Lord's Supper. Also, special days of thanksgiving and humiliation, and the keeping of spiritual diaries as moral ledger books, as well as the practice of family and private prayer daily, all kept morality rooted in devotion. 3. This worship also had the merit of flexibility, spontaneity and warmth. 4. Finally, on the positive side, any tendency to eccentricity or subjectivity due to the absence of a set liturgy was corrected by the biblical authority of the worship, the unity of Calvinistic theology which controlled it, and the standard shape of worship provided by the *Westminster Directory*.

It did, as its later history was to prove, have serious weaknesses. These included the absence of creeds for which covenants were not wholly a satisfactory substitute; the disuse of the red-letter days of the Christian year; the infrequent celebration of the Lord's Supper; the excessive didacticism of the pastoral prayers and prolix sermons; and the depreciation of symbolism and colour in art and architecture, and of ceremony in worship.

In time the Puritan and classical heritage was dissolved through rationalism, moralism, and pietism, and activism replaced adoration, while the warm-hearted fellowship replaced the theocratic community. There ensued a serious revaluation of the tradition in the late nineteenth and early twentieth centuries. The trend was away from spontaneous to pre-composed prayers, and from the combination of forms of prayer and free prayer to the adoption of liturgies. What individual congregations or their ministers of a 'high church' outlook did in the nineteenth century became a permissive option for all congregations in the twentieth century. By 1920 the Congregational Union of England and Wales had published its own denominational service book, *The Book of Congregational Worship*, the work of a committee that included the theologian P. T. Forsyth. It was a portent of the future, but is now seldom used in the United Reformed Church* in the United Kingdom, which has its own modern-language *Book of Services* (1980). In the USA the Congregational churches produced in 1948 an important book, *A Book of Worship for Free Churches*. The wheel had come full circle. A denomination that had originated in North America because of the dissatisfaction of the Puritans with a nationally-imposed liturgy (BCP) was now seeking to unify its people in a liturgy that expressed the ecumenical insights of the century.

See also **Books, Liturgical** 7; **Liturgies** 7.

Horton Davies, *The Worship of the English Puritans*, 1948; *Worship and Theology in England, 1900–1965*, 1965, ch.X; A. G. Matthews, 'Puritan Worship', Nathaniel Micklem (ed), *Christian Worship*, 1935; Bryan D. Spinks, *Freedom or Order? The Eucharistic Liturgy in English Congregationalism 1645–1980*, 1984.

HORTON DAVIES

Consecration of Bishops

see **Cathedra; Ordination**

Consecration of Churches

The consecration of churches is the act of solemnly dedicating them to God for the purposes of worship.

Solomon's dedication of the Temple (I Kings 8.63) provided the model for the consecration of churches by Christians, but no special rite was at first devised. The dedication of the cathedral of Tyre in 314, described by Eusebius, simply involved the celebration of the eucharist. As late as the sixth century the saying of mass was still regarded as the essential element and so the Leonine Sacramentary (*c*.540) has only a proper collect, *oratio super oblata*, preface* and post-communion. The first special feature to be introduced was the deposition of relics which were brought into the new building and enclosed in the altar* immediately before the mass. A second feature, which was adopted in the eighth century, consisted of lustrations. This practice of sprinkling buildings with holy water had been used in relation to pagan temples converted for use as churches and thence

became an element in the rite of consecration of a new building. So by the eighth and ninth centuries the Roman form of consecration consisted of the following: 1. the carrying of the relics in procession; 2. the entrance of the bishop and his party to prepare the mortar for sealing the altar stone and to wash the altar with exorcized water; 3. the temporary withdrawal of the clergy; 4. a second entrance, followed by the anointing of the altar and the deposition of the relics; 5. the blessing of the entire building; 6. the mass. The model of this rite is that of a funeral, the central idea being that the tomb-altar of the saint, represented by his relics, is prepared and he is conveyed to it and buried within it.

The Gallican model was based upon a different rationale, that of baptism* and confirmation*, the church being washed and anointed. The main elements of this form are to be found in the Angoulême Sacramentary (*c*.800), the material probably dating from the eighth century. They are: 1. arrival of the clergy; 2. blessing of a mixture of wine and water; 3. *asperges** of the whole church and then of the altar; 4. the anointing of the altar and then of the whole building; 5. the blessing of the altar linen and vessels; 6. withdrawal to fetch the relics; 7. return and placing of the relics in the altar; 8. the mass. *Ordo* XLI (775–800) adds a further feature to this sequence, the alphabet ceremony which took place immediately upon the first entrance of the clergy. This consists of inscribing the alphabet twice along the lines of a St Andrew's cross traced on the pavement in ashes or sand. In this way the building was claimed for Christ, represented by the initial of *Christus* in Greek.

The mediaeval Western rite was the result of the fusion, in the tenth century, of these Roman and Gallican forms. The prominence given by the former to the deposition was retained, but the washing and anointing and alphabet ceremony were preserved from the latter. This rite, with some minor modifications such as the inclusion of the seven penitential psalms (i.e. Pss. 6, 32, 38, 51, 102, 130 and 143), persisted within Roman Catholicism into the latter half of the twentieth century, since the revision of 1961 was largely an abbreviation and simplification by the removal of doublets. However in 1977 there was issued *Ordo Dedicationis Ecclesiae et Altaris*. This is divided into three parts and the dedication, which previously preceded the mass, has now been brought completely within its framework. The new structure is as follows: I. 1. solemn entry; 2. hallowing of walls with blessed water – a Gallican feature; 3. ministry of word; 4. bishop's homily; 5. creed. II. 1. litany of saints; 2. deposition of relics *under* not *in* the altar – these relics have to be of such a size as to suggest at least that they are those of a human body; this means deposition is likely to become very rare; 3. prayer of dedication; 4. anointing of altar and walls; 5. incensing of altar and walls; 6. lighting of candles. III. 1. presentation of gifts; 2. eucharistic prayer and special preface; 3. communion; 4. inauguration of chapel of reservation; 5. blessing and dismissal.

The deposition of relics is a common feature in Eastern Orthodox rites, e.g. in the Byzantine and Syrian. But the focal point is the solemn consecration of the altar, which is washed and anointed and the *antimension* is laid on it – a square of linen or silk with relics inserted in one corner. Even the aspersion of the walls and their anointing with oil are to be understood as an extension of what is done to the altar. A circuit of the exterior, a series of litanies, the blessing and censing of the iconostasis* and finally the celebration of the eucharist bring the rite to its conclusion and reveal certain parallels with Gallican customs.

Consecration rites were not an immediate concern of the Reformers. The number of churches existing in England in the sixteenth century was ample, and so the question of a form of dedication scarcely arose. Similarly in Germany, it was not until after the Thirty Years' War that new Lutheran churches were built in any quantity. The Puritans rejected all idea of consecrating buildings, partly because they would not countenance the continuation of any mediaeval practice and partly because they could find no reference to consecrated buildings in the NT. It was not until 1620 that the first Anglican rite was produced by Bishop Andrews and this consisted of a perambulation with appropriate prayers at each stopping place – baptistery*, pulpit*, lectern*, etc. – followed by morning prayer and the eucharist, the general concept being that consecration is effected by use. In 1662

and 1663 the convocations discussed the provision of an official form, but none was ever promulgated with authority, and to the present day, in England, there are only diocesan uses, often based on rites by Bishop Wordsworth of 1887 and 1898. Other provinces of the Anglican Communion, however, have authorized forms, frequently included in their prayer books. In 1666 an Irish rite was promulgated; in 1799 one was approved in the USA, and there exist similar orders for South Africa, Canada and Scotland.

The orders in use in Lutheran churches are noticeable for their simplicity. One example will suffice as an illustration. The rite published by the United Evangelical Church in Germany in 1952 consists of four parts: 1. The bishop, clergy, elders, confirmation candidates, builders, etc. all gather in the building that has been in use for worship prior to the erection of the new church. A short service takes place, with address and prayers. 2. Procession to the new building to the singing of hymns and blowing of trumpets. One of the confirmation candidates carries the key, while the clergy bear Bible, vessels, etc. A hymn is sung before the door, which is eventually opened. 3. After an introit psalm or hymn, there is prayer and short address, the Lord's Prayer and consecration formula. The vessels, etc. have prayers said over them. 4. The main Sunday service follows, frequently with communion.

Reformed practice is not markedly different. So the consecration service of the French Reformed Church (1955) opens with a procession in which are carried a Bible, the baptismal bowl, the paten and chalice. During the ensuing prayers and lessons, the Bible is placed on the lectern, the bowl on the table, etc. and the whole culminates in a celebration of the eucharist.

Other churches, which have no authorized service books, have a number of models suggested. *The Call to Worship* (1956) includes a possible dedication rite for the Baptists. The service begins at the church door which is ceremonially opened. The minister proceeds to the pulpit and leads the congregation in an act of dedication of the church and people to God. A prayer for the dedication of the baptistery is also included, and there is provision for a lesson, hymn and sermon. According to a Congregational form (*Services and Prayers*, 1959), the presiding minister knocks on the door and, to the accompaniment of verses from the psalms and followed by the choir and congregation, takes his place. Lessons from the OT and NT follow and then the act of dedication which is concluded with a blessing. In the Methodist book for optional use (*Divine Worship*, 1935) there is a form for the dedication of churches which may be adapted for use on anniversaries – it consists of prayers, lections, hymns, sermon and an act of dedication.

At the present day it is particularly the rationale of consecration that needs further exploration and analysis rather than the exact forms it may take. In the past there have been three ways in which consecration has been understood to be effected. First, by the provision of relics (the Roman form) – but this cannot be regarded as a *sine qua non* of Christian worship, since this was celebrated for decades before any relics existed and is performed to this day in houses, in the open air, etc., apart from any relics of a saint. Second, by being baptized and confirmed – but to treat a building as a human being is hardly more than a pious fiction. Thirdly, by use – but if this were correct the regular celebration of the eucharist in places other than churches would consecrate these too.

Basically, consecration is thanksgiving. The rendering of thanks to God upon the opening of a new church is natural and right: this is its consecration. The result is that its God-relatedness is acknowledged, its function is declared and it is dedicated as an instrument of the mission of God. Indeed within Roman Catholicism, 'dedication' is now the most favoured term referring to buildings for permanent use for worship, and 'blessing' is restricted to more temporary accommodation.

See also **Dedication** 1.

J. D. Crichton, *The Dedication of a Church*, 1980; J. G. Davies, *The Secular Use of Church Buildings*, 1968; R. W. Muncey, *A History of the Consecration of Churches and Churchyards*, 1930; G. G. Willis, *Further Essays in Early Roman Liturgy*, 1968.

EDITOR

Consecration, Prayer of

One of the many names of the eucharistic prayer or anaphora*; its currency in English-speaking countries is due to the use of 'Prayer of Consecration' as the title of this prayer in the English BCP of 1662, following the Scottish Book of Common Prayer of 1637. The use is now decreasing, due no doubt to its abandonment in the ASB and other revised liturgies.

W. JARDINE GRISBROOKE

Cope

see **Vestments** 2(*a*)

Coptic Worship

The three cycles, daily, weekly and yearly. are an important feature of Coptic worship. During the first thousand years of Christianity, the weekly and yearly cycles were blended together and then the daily office was overlaid, until a complex was created within which the overall pattern is difficult to discern.

The oldest cycle is the weekly one, which from the very beginning of Christianity has centred on the liturgical celebration of Sunday. Later, perhaps in the third century, Wednesdays and Fridays were added as station days or fasting days. In fact, it was in Egypt that Wednesday was first singled out as the day on which Judas Iscariot's betrayal of Jesus is remembered and Friday as the day on which the crucifixion is commemorated. The weekly celebration of Sunday as Easter Day seems to have died out very early, perhaps around or some time before the date of the composition of the *Apostolic Tradition* of Hippolytus, when an annual feast of Easter*, preceded by a period of Lent*, seems to have been taking place. Nevertheless, the fact remains that every Sunday throughout the year at dawn, before the main eucharistic celebration of the week takes place, the gospel reading consists of part of the account of the resurrection. Sunday also clearly remains a day of celebration of the joy of Easter, and cannot be designated a day of fasting.

The daily cycle was the last of the three to be formulated, and seems to have been the product of the Pachomian monasteries, where the daily office (*see* **Canonical Hours**) may have been in use in much the same form as that in which we have it today. The daily cycle appoints prayers to be said at dawn and then at 9.00 a.m., 12.00 a.m., 3.00 p.m., 5.00 p.m. and 6.00 p.m. (that is, the first, third, sixth, ninth, eleventh and twelfth hours). The present daily office may be seen as a collection of the main celebrations included in the weekly and yearly cycles: the resurrection of Christ is celebrated at dawn, the coming of the Holy Spirit upon the apostles at 9.00 a.m., the crucifixion at noon and the death and burial of Christ at 3.00 p.m. These are followed by the two evening hours, and the midnight prayer, which seems to have been added later, as there is no record of it before the fourth century.

Historically, no link has been established between the daily office and the celebration of the eucharist, but in modern times, whenever a eucharistic celebration takes place, the daily office is said first. The Coptic celebration of the eucharist on Sundays begins with vespers on Saturday evening, which is followed by the midnight office. In most parish churches today, these two services of prayer have in fact been joined together. Matins is said on Sunday morning immediately before the liturgy, and has become part of the eucharistic celebration. Both vespers and matins are traditionally known in Coptic and Arabic as 'the raising of incense', since incense* is offered at the beginning of every litany. The highly symbolic meaning of the incense can be seen in Coptic hymns, where the censer is seen to be a symbol of the Virgin Mary, the coal a symbol of the humanity of Christ and the fire his divinity. This image of fire united to the coal is used by Cyril of Alexandria as a type of the mystery of the incarnation. The incense is then seen as the fragrance of the life of Christ offered to God the Father on behalf of the church. This accompanies the litanies to signify that the life of Christ mediates between us and God.

The Coptic Church has retained until the present time the prayer of general absolution at the end of both vespers and matins. This same prayer is also used for absolution at private confession, a fact which has caused many questions to be raised regarding the practice of private confession in the Coptic Church. It is known that it was abandoned in the Middle

Ages and not restored until the present Coptic revival, which gathered momentum in the 1940s.

The Coptic Church at the present time uses three liturgies, those of St Basil, St Gregory of Nazianzus and St Cyril of Alexandria, which was originally known as the liturgy of St Mark. St Basil's liturgy, being the shortest, has become the one most commonly used in modern times. Many parishes still have the liturgy of St Gregory from Easter to Pentecost, and the liturgy of St Cyril during Lent, but this is not an absolute rule.

The Coptic liturgy differs from the Byzantine liturgy (*see* **Liturgies** 2) in three significant features:

1. All the prayers said by the celebrant are recited aloud and followed by responses sung by both the deacon and the congregations.

2. The whole celebration takes place inside the sanctuary, and the doors of the sanctuary remain open throughout.

3. The readings consist of five lessons: the Pauline and Catholic epistles, the Acts of the Apostles, a reading from the lives of the saints (the Synaxarion) and the gospel.

The three Coptic liturgies contain almost identical intercessions for peace, the clergy and the meetings of the church.

Baptismal and other sacramental rites resemble those of the Greek Orthodox Church (*see* **Baptism** 2; **Burial** 2; **Marriage** 2; **Ordination** 2). Baptism begins with exorcisms* which assume that the candidates are converts from idolatry, and anointing. Four lessons follow, as in the liturgy, further anointings, and the actual baptism, for which the positive form 'I baptize thee . . .' is used, as in the West; and finally chrismation for the gift of the Spirit with the chrism consecrated by the patriarch. Unction* of the sick calls for the lighting of seven lamps by seven priests if available. It is often administered as a public healing service on the Friday before Palm Sunday. Funeral offices, varying for adults, children, clergy and monastics, each consist of a psalm, epistle, gospel, and prayers. Holy Week* is marked by long readings from the OT and NT, terminating with the Apocalypse and Gospel of John on Easter Eve. An impressive ceremony is the procession of the entombment on Good Friday afternoon. Water is blessed at the Epiphany and there are foot-washing ceremonies on Maundy Thursday and the feast of St Peter and St Paul. The temporale is arranged by the ancient Egyptian calendar, with twelve thirty-day months beginning on 29 August and five or six extra days at the end.

A traditional (mediaeval) Coptic church has a solid sanctuary screen*, with a central door flanked by windows and side doors, and lighter screens to mark off the choir* and the men's and women's sections of the nave*. But the latter divisions are now omitted in modern churches, and often removed from old ones. Music has been preserved by oral tradition, but is now also studied formally. The blind are often trained as church singers and ordained as deacons.

A. Abdallah, 'L'Ordinamento Liturgico di Gabriele V', *Studia Orientalia Christiana*, 1962; O. H. E. Burmester, 'The Canonical Hours of the Coptic Church', *Orientalia Christiana Periodica*, 1936; *The Egyptian or Coptic Church. A Detailed Description of her Liturgical Services*, 1967; John, Marquis of Bute, *The Coptic Morning Service of the Lord's Day*, ET 1882; A. Veilleux, 'La Liturgie dans le Cénobitisme Pachomien au quatrième siècle', *Studia Anselmiana 57*, 1968; G. Viaud, *La Liturgie des Coptes d'Egypte*, 1978; L. Villecourt, 'Les Observances Liturgiques et la Discipline du Jeûne dans l'Eglise Copte', *Le Muséon* 36, 1923, pp.149–92; 37, 1924, pp.201–82; 38, 1925, pp.261–320.

GEORGE BEBAWI

Corporal

A piece of linen measuring about twenty inches square which is spread in the middle of the altar-top before or at the time of the offertory* (Latin *corpus*, body, referring to the sacramental context). The correct material is linen of good quality, rather than lawn trimmed with lace. The BCP in the rubric* after the administration of holy communion expects that there will be a second corporal to be used to cover the chalice* and paten* if they still contain the remains of the consecrated elements of bread and wine and this custom is still normally followed in the ASB rite, although there is no rubric to direct it. These two

corporals are derived from the one very large cloth, known as the *palla corporalis*, which in the earlier centuries was used as a corporal and drawn up over the chalice.

Plate 29 Two corporals, one beneath and one covering the chalice

Our present custom of having this cloth divided into two parts belongs to the Gothic or late mediaeval period. When the corporals are not in use they are kept in a case known as a burse. *See* Plate 29.

P. Dearmer, *The Linen Ornaments of the Church*, 1929; C. E. Pocknee (ed), *The Parson's Handbook*, rev ed 1965.

C. E. POCKNEE/G. D. W. RANDALL

Corpus Christi

The observance on the Thursday after Trinity Sunday* of a commemoration of and thanksgiving for the eucharist*. It was established by Rome in the thirteenth century, following the advocacy of Juliana of Liège, and became universal in the West in the fourteenth century, the service of the day being composed by St Thomas Aquinas who also wrote some of the hymns associated with the feast. Following mass, a common form of observing the feast is by a procession of the eucharistic host in a monstrance*, an indication of the eucharistic doctrine and devotion of the period in which the feast originated. There is no particular reason for its observance on this day, apart from a desire to find a Thursday outside the period of Lent, Eastertide and Pentecost, and the question could be raised as to whether its observance does not unduly distract from both the celebration of the institution of the eucharist on Maundy Thursday* and the paschal context of the events the eucharist commemorates. No doubt because of its mediaeval origin and the customs associated with it, it has never been observed in Protestantism.

The name of the feast, Corpus Christi, is perhaps too an unconscious reflection of the era in which it originated, for in the elevations in the eucharist and in the extra-liturgical cultus of the sacrament, it was always the bread (the body) that received much the greater emphasis, probably for the entirely practical reason that this is what could actually be held up for people to gaze upon, particularly in the form of a circular wafer as came to be the practice. Its title in the modern Roman rite, *Corpus et Sanguis*, the body and blood, can probably be seen as a corrective to this.

N. Mitchell, *Cult and Controversy: The Worship of the Eucharist Outside Mass*, 1982.

R. F. BUXTON

Covenant Service

The covenant service is, at present, mainly a special Methodist service, usually held on the first Sunday of the year, at which church members rededicate themselves to God.

1. *Beginnings of the custom.* John Wesley held the first formal covenant service in London on 11 August 1755. He knew the idea of covenanting with God from OT literature (*see* II Kings 23), Anglican devotional writing on baptism*, confirmation* and communion*, and the devotional writings of Puritans and later Free Churchmen (notably Philip Doddridge). He transformed a custom of private devotion into a corporate renewal of dedication.

2. *Development of the custom.* Introduced by Wesley at main centres of his work (London, Dublin, Bristol, Newcastle), the service spread throughout early Methodism. It was held in London during Wesley's annual visitation around the New Year. Many other societies imitated this, and the covenant service thus came to seem almost essentially a New Year observance.

Apparently, Wesley usually linked the service with the communion. This his unordained helpers could not do, but the combination of covenant and communion service became general when the Methodists, after Wesley's death, came to hold their own communions regularly.

The service was most widely observed by Wesleyan Methodists, less regularly in the smaller Methodist denominations (Methodist New Connexion, Primitive Methodism, Bible Christians, United Methodist Free Churches, United Methodism). It is now almost universal in British and related Methodist churches and districts. It is known, but apparently little used, in American and cognate branches of Methodism. Charles Wesley wrote a hymn for the covenant service, 'Come, let us use the grace divine', now incorporated into the official liturgy. Participation, originally limited to Methodists in good standing, is now (in Britain) open to all Christians, as is communion.

Other traditions have shown interest in the covenant service. It has been adapted for use in the Church of South India, and for special occasions in the Church of England. It is also an honoured tradition in Baptist churches. It has suggested a model for the initiation of closer relationships between churches.

3. *Content and form of the service in Methodism.* Wesley's own service (published 1780) consisted of a long exhortation to make an explicit covenant with God (derived from *Vindiciae Pietatis*, 1663, by the Puritain Richard Alleine), followed by a lengthy prayer of self-dedication composed by Joseph Alleine. The communion apparently went on from the prayer of humble access. Wesleyan Methodism used this service, with only two major revisions (1879, 1897) until Methodist union (1932). Private individuals made unofficial revisions: J. A. MacDonald, 1883; anonymous minister in Eccles, 1884; G. B. Robson, *c.*1922. The smaller Methodist denominations each produced one or more forms of the service. After Methodist union, a form based on that of G. B. Robson was prepared for the *Book of Offices* (1936). A further revision, influenced by the CSI version, appears in *The Methodist Service Book* (1975, pp.D1–D11). Within the new standard eucharistic order, there are special forms of adoration (the work of the economic Trinity as the source of Christian life); of confession (failure to fulfil our part of the covenant) and absolution (I John 1.5–9); a proper collect; lessons: Jer. 31.31–5, Heb. 12.22–25[a], John 15.1–8; sermon; (dismissal); short exposition of the covenant of grace; Wesley's hymn; invitation to accept anew the yoke of Christ's obedience; and the covenant prayer, the former part said by the celebrant, the second by all: 'I am no longer my own, but yours. Put me to what you will . . . And now, glorious and blessed God, Father, Son, and Holy Spirit, you are mine and I am yours . . . Our Father . . .' The eucharist continues from the peace.

4. *Covenant service among Baptists.* In many Baptists churches the covenant is read out either at a service before the celebration of the Lord's Supper* or at the time of the Supper itself. Each congregation has its own form of covenant and when new members are welcomed, they are often asked to sign it. A service of covenant renewal at New Year is quite common.

5. *Ecumenical interest of the covenant service.* The interest lies in the unusually distinct emphasis on Christian self-dedication, congregationally expressed. No other act of worship regularly observed in any tradition does this in the same way (the nearest equivalent is the renewal of baptismal vows*, included in the Easter vigil* service of the Roman Catholic and other churches). The pursuit of complete dedication to God in the strength of Christ's incarnation and passion and in the power of the Holy Spirit is a concept shared by the great confessions, and sufficiently central to the faith to serve as a major theme of common devotion.

6. *Some questions of principle on the covenant service.* The reluctance of some Methodists to take part in the service has raised the questions whether its delineation of the Christian life is too intense for regular repetition, or too demanding for most Christians, and therefore whether or not it should be a principal act of worship for the whole church. Various occasions for it have been suggested: the New Year (to consecrate a natural unit of human life), early September (to hallow a new Methodist church year), or Easter (to show our

common dependence on the Risen Christ). The existing forms of the service have been accused of being wrongly introspective and centred on the worshippers, of paying inadequate attention to the resurrection and the Holy Spirit, and of saying too little of the maturity and liberty promised to the children of God. The custom of renewing the covenant has in itself been deprecated as tending to overshadow sacramental Christian initiation and to usurp the function of the eucharist in the constant renewal of the Christian life, and as being inconsistent with the uniqueness of Christ's mediation of the New Covenant. These serious issues, still under discussion, will doubtless affect the future development of the covenant service.

D. H. Tripp, *The Renewal of the Covenant in the Methodist Tradition*, 1969.

DAVID TRIPP

Credo

see **Creed, Creeds; Music in the Mass of the Roman Rite; Ordinary**

Creed, Creeds

In the earliest Christian church, candidates for baptism were required to confess their personal belief ('I believe') in the presence of the congregation. The earliest confessions of belief were short and simple: e.g. 'Jesus is Lord' (I Cor. 12.3) or 'I believe that Jesus Christ is the Son of God' (Acts 8.37, RV margin only). Eventually such simple baptismal creeds developed into the confession which we know as the Apostles' Creed. Later, another kind of creed, the conciliar creed ('We believe') was promulgated with the authority of a council; its purpose was to define the true faith as over against the teaching of heretics. The Nicene Creed (now usually regarded as a product of the Council of Constantinople in 381, but expressing the faith of the preceding Council of Nicaea in 325) is the most important and best known of the conciliar creeds of the patristic age. Its use at the eucharist appears to have been introduced by Peter the Fuller at Antioch in 473 to emphasize the adherence of the Monophysites to Nicaea as opposed, by them, to Chalcedon. In the early sixth century its use spread to Constantinople and it was adopted in Spain by the third Council of Toledo in 589 as a test for Arians, being recited before the fraction*; in the Mozarabic rite it still retains this unusual position. It was later favoured by Charlemagne but was not accepted in Rome until 1014 by Benedict VIII under the influence of the Emperor Henry II.

But besides these two credal types there was a third form of confessional utterance, namely the credal hymn. Examples are, in the opinion of the majority of NT scholars, to be found in the NT, and at least some of these date from the apostolic period. The best known is Phil. 2.6–11, in which the pre-existence of Christ with God, his taking the form of man (and a slave at that), his death on the cross and his exaltation and universal lordship, are quoted by Paul as if from a liturgical setting which would be well known to the recipients of his letter. Other examples might be I Tim. 3.16; Eph. 4.4–10; and the doxologies in the Apocalypse. Oscar Cullmann writes: 'The need to confess one's faith according to a fixed text manifested itself in every gathering of the community. The believer wants to confess with the brethren before God what unites them before him. It was so already in the worship of the Synagogue, where in pronouncing the Shema, one confessed with all Israel that Yahweh is One. The confession of faith is pronounced within the liturgy at every divine service of the primitive Christian community.' Even more cogently Cullmann might have pointed to the recital of the *Heilsgeschichte* in the liturgy of the Temple (e.g. Pss. 105, 106 and many others).

This credal recital of God's saving acts is indeed an on-going characteristic of biblical-Christian liturgical worship. It arises naturally from the character of the faith as *historical*; it is a spontaneous thanksgiving for the salvation which God has wrought. Thus, many of the hymns which are most popular among Christian congregations today are those which embody the great themes of the proclamation of God's action in Christ 'for us men and for our salvation'. For example, 'At the name of Jesus' is a hymnal paraphrase and exposition of Phil. 2.6–11, and there are countless other examples in the hymn books of all the churches. And, of course, in the main tradition of Christendom the recitation of the ancient creeds, whether said or sung, is a

normal ingredient of liturgical worship. The choral singing of the Nicene Creed, set to the music of Merbecke in the sixteenth century and by many other composers right down to Beaumont in our own times, bears witness to the continuing 'need to confess one's faith according to a fixed text' in liturgical worship.

O. Cullmann, *The Earliest Christian Confessions*, ET 1949; J. N. D. Kelly, *Early Christian Creeds* [3]1972; John H. Leith, *Creeds of the Churches*, [3]1982; 'Creeds', *NDCT*, 1983; R. P. Martin, *Carmen Christi: Philippians ii. 5–11 in Recent Interpretation and in the Setting of Early Christian Worship*, 1967; J. T. Sanders, *The New Testament Christological Hymns: their Historical Religious Background*, 1971, which takes the view, not universally accepted, that the NT hymns are modelled on pre-Christian Gnostic forms.

ALAN RICHARDSON

Cremation

The past century has seen in urban Western societies the growth of cremation as a hygienic and space-conserving process for disposal of the bodily remains of the dead. It reflects also the growing mobility of the population, when a family grave in a local churchyard has ceased to be a loved focus for the testifying to the continuity, unity and identity of a local family, and instead has become the occasion of guilt and financial cost as relatives hundreds of miles away still feel some obligations towards the upkeep of the grave. The crematorium has released both ground space and guilt. The churches generally opposed the use of cremation when it was first allowed by civil authorities, but they have at different speeds come to terms with the practice, the last of all being the Roman Catholic Church which has only approved cremation in the post-Vatican II years.

For the liturgical implications of cremation, *see* **Burial** 4. Crematorium chapels are used in two ways: either for the whole funeral rite, including ministry of the word, prayers and committal; or solely for the committal, after the service has been held in a church. In the first case the traditional graveside order can be followed, with prayers following the committal, but in the second the prayers have to come at the service in church, and the committal has minimum liturgical material around it. Many urban crematoria in England have a very tight timetable, with services being held every thirty minutes or so, and thus the use of hymns, preaching, etc. is strictly limited. In some areas the clergy observe 'crematorium weeks', in which they officiate by rota for a week every few months, being hired by the undertakers for the cremation of the unchurched. Such a background and context puts severe difficulty in the way of a true proclamation of Christ's victory over the grave.

In some cases, cremation is followed by a later interment (or scattering) of the ashes. While there is a tidy sense of the final disposal of the remains by this means, if the cremation itself is not felt as final by relatives, then the extra period of waiting for the final disposal may be emotionally counter-productive.

In the Church of England's Alternative Service Book 1980, the word 'funeral' is used instead of 'burial' just because of the frequency of cremation. The opening notes provide for alterations when cremation is used, and a separate rite is included for the interment of the ashes. A similar provision is made in the Australian Prayer Book (1978), but the American Book of Common Prayer (1979) rather quaintly provides all its funerary rites without regard to cremation, save for one passing mention in the notes. That mention was itself novel in the American rites.

The rites of the various churches are usually subject to slight variation to meet the particular characteristics of crematoria services. A body which is to be buried may be committed 'to the ground', with the phrase 'earth to earth' also added. At a crematorium the alternatives are 'to the flames', 'to be cremated', 'to the elements' or suchlike, and 'earth to earth' is omitted though 'ashes to ashes, dust to dust' may still be applicable. The Roman Catholic texts make no such concession to cremation, but the rites of the Church of England, the Methodist Church in Great Britain, the United Reformed Church in England and Wales and the Church of Scotland do make provision for varying the standard texts of the committal, and of its accompanying prayers, from those used at burials.

The Christian hope of the resurrection of the body has never been closely linked to the preservation of mortal remains, though they are always treated as deserving of great respect. Persons who have died through explosion or fire have the same hope as those whose bodies are buried. But the crematorium does offer a way of disposal with a nod to the Christian church in passing, and that seems to correspond to the position of millions in post-Christian societies. The difficulty lies in getting the destruction-line process to exhibit Christian truth in its fullness.

N. Autton (ed), *Funerals and Ministry to the Bereaved: A Handbook of Funeral Practices and Procedures*, 1985; G. Cope (ed), *Dying, Death and Disposal*, 1970.

C. O. BUCHANAN

Cross, Crucifix

The history of the use and development of this emblem in Christian worship is a long and complicated one. There was considerable reluctance to depict the crucifixion of Christ in the earlier centuries as that event was regarded by the early Christians from the side of Easter* Day rather than Good Friday*.

The complete absence of the depiction of the crucifixion in the paintings of the Roman catacombs, and even as late as the fifth-century mosaics at Ravenna, should be noted. The cross was certainly used as a decorative symbol of triumph, as we can see in the mosaic in the saucer of the apse of S. Apollinare in Classe, Ravenna. The earliest depictions of the cross with a figure are far from realistic and Christ is frequently shown with a diadem on his head and vested in the kingly *colobium*. His eyes are open and his arms outstretched (*see* Plate 30).

It is not until we come to the twelfth and thirteenth centuries under the impetus of the Franciscans, when the cultus of the passion was greatly developed, that the realistic crucifixes (i.e. a cross bearing a figure of the suffering Christ) begin to appear, but this development does not reach its zenith until the fifteenth century in such works as those of Matthias Grünewald (d. 1528). (*See* Plate 31.)

Processional crosses can be found as early as the fourth century, but the altar

Plate 30 Thirteenth-century crucifix with crowned and vested figure

cross was introduced much later. In the Middle Ages altars in England seldom had a cross standing upon them since the Crucified was depicted in the middle of the reredos* although the ivory Bury St Edmunds cross, now in the Metropolitan Museum of Art in New York, is thought to have been made for an altar. In the case of free-standing altars the processional cross was sometimes placed in a socket behind the altar and examples of these survive at St David's Cathedral, Wales, and Lamport, Northants. But towering crucifixes standing on a shelf behind the altar are a product of the Counter-Reformation in the Roman Catholic Church.

DACL, III, cols 3045–3131; C. E. Pocknee, *Cross and Crucifix*, 1962.

C. E. POCKNEE/G. D. W. RANDALL

Plate 31 Grünewald crucifixion, Isenheim altar, Colmar, France

Cross, Sign of

see **Gestures** 3

Crucifer

The person who carries the processional cross on liturgical or ceremonial occasions.

P. HINCHLIFF

Crucifix

see **Cross**

Cruet

Derived from the mediaeval French *cruette*, meaning 'little jug'. A pair of such vessels is used to contain the wine and water for the eucharist; while they are now usually made of glass, sometimes with a lip or mounting of precious metal, they were anciently made of base metal such as pewter, or else of silver or silver-gilt. Some very handsome examples of silver-gilt 'flagons' for holding the wine and water were made during the seventeenth and eighteenth centuries for the churches in the City of London and elsewhere.

J. Gilchrist, *Anglican Church Plate*, 1967.

C. E. POCKNEE

Cult, Cultus

Like the French *culte*, cult and cultus designate an act of religious worship. They can also refer to the veneration of the Virgin Mary and in particular it is usual to speak of the cult of the saints (*see* **Saints, Cult of the**).

From the strictly etymological point of view the terms suggest a certain understand-

ing of worship which is open to question; *colere* means to till the ground and hence to take care of or attend to, the aim of the action being the production of some benefit by the object of attention. From 'giving attention to' via 'paying respect to', it was no great step to 'honouring' and finally to 'worshipping'. Cultus is therefore a cultivation of the gods, a cherishing of them, seeing to their needs. It is both a bestowing of labour on them and a manifestation of regard towards them. There is then more than a hint of doing something to obtain a favour, as in the phrase 'to cultivate someone's acquaintance'. In this sense cultus stems from the human side, whereas Christian worship has been regarded as deriving from the side of God. He it is who through the Son has provided the form and matter of worship which is essentially eucharistic, i.e. a thanksgiving for what God has done – it is a meeting, not an occasion for cajoling.

EDITOR

Culture and Worship

Patterns of culture, such as language, ritual, art-forms, design and architecture, structures of time, are in their use and development very much concerned with how we understand ourselves in relation to our environment, personal and impersonal. These patterns can help our growth in relationship. They can also inhibit and block growth.

Language is a fundamental means of communication. It can both imply and interpret action. It cannot be divorced from action. Yet, as a medium of rational analysis, with its tendency to separate reason and exalt it above the other human faculties, language can inhibit or prevent fully integrated action. Ritual*, by stylizing and objectifying basic actions, events and relationships, serves to give them continuity, validity and authority: so with the cosmic myths enacted in ritual drama; the theatre; ritual connected with such basic functions as sex, eating and washing; and worship. But ritual can also become an end in itself, a means of escape. Art makes present, and apprehensible, aspects of reality which may not otherwise be apparent, or cannot be conveyed adequately through other media. Hence the great part played by art in the religious life. Art can also merely imitate, photograph-like, confirming perhaps a traditional pattern or approach to a thing, yet giving no deeper insight into its reality. Buildings, in their design and in the symbolism of their architecture, may express the intention of drawing people together for a specific activity, where a certain level of community and communication is assumed. So with buildings for worship. But they may also inhibit or prevent communication by confining people within separate and self-contained areas. Time can be the sphere of creative activity and so of freedom and hope. Yet if it is seen as a sort of exhaustible capital which is always running out, it again can inhibit and produce anxiety. 'Time is short', 'There is no time left for this', 'We must hurry'. The past may condition and limit us, the future may threaten.

We make various judgments as to the value of our environment and the patterns through which we relate to it. First, that the environment as it now stands is the only given frame of reference within which we discover our place: reality does not extend beyond this. Secondly, that such an environment proves inadequate, deceptive and imprisoning: we must be enabled to stand outside it if we are to see more deeply into reality. Thirdly, that this environment does provide the framework within which we must live. But it has definite limitations. So there is the continuing need for ecstasy (standing outside) and transformation.

Patterns of culture, therefore, can be either creative, or divisive and limiting. They are for the development of understanding and communication. They provide necessary safeguards and frameworks within which we grow in relationship and knowledge. They help us to position ourselves in relation to our environment and so reach some idea of our identity, some sense of security. As such they are creative. But these patterns can also limit or prevent understanding and communication. They can divide people through lack of creative interchange between them: undoubtedly this is reinforced by the analytical, compartmentalizing tendency of classical, Western culture, with its stress on the rational. They can become negative safeguards, shields behind which we hide to avoid the pain of exposure to other viewpoints and apprehensions of reality, and the discovery of our own weaknesses. We come to find

security and identity in the patterns of culture, rather than in the growth towards deeper understanding and communication for which they provide the framework. As such they are divisive and limiting.

These patterns, therefore, do play a significant part in the forming of relationships, primarily between persons, but also between us and our total environment. Since reality is many-levelled, different patterns of culture can be complementary. They can also, as we have seen, become limiting and divisive. At those points we need to think again.

Christian worship expresses our response to God as Being of the highest worth and value, the source of our understanding of worth and value. It therefore focusses our deepest hopes about relationship, with our fellow human beings and with the environment in which we live and work. Worship has to do with a growing in discernment, and with communication, in the context of our being met and addressed by God. Patterns of culture within worship (language, ritual, art, the design and symbolism of the building) should always serve this primary end. The degree to which all this is formally structured, liturgically, will vary as between different tranditions. But the fact that liturgical worship, as a structured ritual, is formative of our growth in understanding and in living the faith, argues strongly for some discipline of continuity and regularity in its practice.

Worship has three fundamental dimensions. First, the work of God in Christ towards man and creation, revealed finally and most completely in the ministry, death and resurrection of Jesus Christ: this is an action of total self-giving, reaching out in relationship towards man and creation. Secondly, the life of the church as embodying within itself God's action. Thirdly, the life of the church as representative of the world, where God is active in creation and redemption, and as pointing to this action.

The central act of Christian worship is the eucharist*. Through breaking and sharing in the word, and in bread and wine, we offer ourselves to be taken and transformed by God's self-giving in Christ, through death to resurrection. In this sacrament the church, by its response, is drawn into God's action: and through the church, all creation. How is this so? In the ministry of the word God communicates his purpose to us and challenges us to respond. Here it is primarily through language that we attempt to understand, make present, and respond to the communication of God. In the ministry of the sacrament this divine activity of self-giving communication, and our response, is confirmed and fully realized. The bread and wine represent Christ's life offered completely for us and, through his self-giving on the cross, transformed into the new life of the resurrection: the bread and wine become the resurrection body and blood of Christ. But they also represent our lives – our work, our culture – and the life of creation: we offer this in self-giving to God, for ourselves and all creation – but only through Christ. By sharing in Christ's body and blood, that is, his life, we and all that we offer are drawn into this life and so into deeper understanding and communication with one another. We become what we eat and drink.

There are in the eucharist two levels of action. On the one hand it is a thanksgiving for, and celebration of, God's finished work in creation and redemption. The offering of bread and wine affirms and celebrates our community, our culture and our environment in so far as they realize God's self-giving love. But it is also a penitential action in which we confess our brokenness and division and that of the world for which we offer. Through the eucharistic action, the fullness of God's work, which is far from being realized in the church's life or that of the rest of the world, is made present: this stands over against our failure to realize self-giving love, not least in the patterns of culture which divide us and prevent understanding and communication.

So the eucharistic action is ecstatic and transforming, breaking through all the attitudes, the patterns, and images of ourselves, other persons, and the environment which divide and limit us. If culture plays a part in the formation of humanity, Christian worship, especially its central act the eucharist, is a drama of transformation through union with Christ. Here we move through what can be celebrated of culture and community, through penitence for our common failures and brokenness, to the reshaping and transformation of all that we do and are.

There is naturally a strong formation

element in worship, since it involves cultural patterns within which our response to God, and so a transforming encounter between God and humanity, can take place. Hence the need for a regular, structured pattern of worship, as well as acts of worship more tied to particular situations and cultural patterns. The most pressing problem with regard to such regular, public worship is to determine a recognizable common culture and to provide adequate patterns for response, understanding and communication in worship.

Worship is a human activity in response to God and in relationship with him. But the eucharist is primarily the action of God, though made present through our responsive action. This places a big question mark over our concern as to how we worship, and what cultural patterns are most adequate and relevant for contemporary worship. All liturgical revision must be seen in the context of the God–mankind relationship, in which we respond to and realize the action of God. This action is both within and beyond time. Therefore worship can never become a mere cultural activity within time, conditioned by this or any other cultural patterns.

Worship, because it is both ecstatic and transforming, and also celebratory, is open to two dangers. First, it can become an ecstatic activity of the church, divorced from the life and concerns of the world. The church before the fourth century suffered from this. Admittedly it was in an underground situation. But also, to judge from its penitential discipline, it seems in great part to have viewed itself as the redeemed community which has nothing more to do with the world. Secondly, through its effort to meet, work through and transform the life of the world, the church can become accommodated to this life and conditioned by cultural patterns so that it loses the ecstatic and transforming power which flows from God as he meets and addresses us. The church of the fourth century and following, after Christianity had become the recognized religion of the state, by no means avoided this danger. To keep the necessary balance in its worship, both affirming and yet standing over against culture, is a task which the church has always been hard put to realize.

What of culture and worship today? We note that in the face of great change and upheaval, and the breaking up of previously stable and more homogeneous cultures, there is a deep-seated anxiety among many people which shows itself in a desire for security and settlement. Liturgy-wise a familiar plea is 'Let's stop chopping and changing and tinkering, and let's work for a while with the orders of service we now have (whether ASB, Series 3, Sunday Service or BCP).' The anxiety shows itself, too, in forms of fundamentalism, (not only within Christian belief), a looking for clear-cut, black-and-white positions. There is also, more positively, a growing concern, in the face of a culture dominated by technology and the 'scientific' approach to human issues and their solutions, to work at and rediscover the primacy of personal relationship at both one-to-one and corporate levels. This I believe reflects, very often, a new yearning for the rediscovery of God at the centre and heart of all our activity. The church, in meeting and responding to this situation, has itself to work at rediscovering the essential fullness of Christian belief and practice. Its worship must be open to meet and to offer the anxiety: to maintain within its drama the vital tension between stability and change, priestly and prophetic: to hold before us the primacy of the personal as we celebrate the coming of the word made flesh: to nurture and shape a faith which questions and explores. Above all its worship must, through all our anxieties and hopes, continually bring us back to the central truths of Christian belief, which are about God as Creator and Redeemer, about incarnation, cross and resurrection.

R. Pannikar, *Worship and Secular Man*, 1977.

PAUL FISHER

Daily Office

see **Canonical Hours; Divine Office, The**

Dalmatic

see **Vestments** 1(*g*)

Dance, Liturgical

Dance, as a form of religious worship, would seem to be universal both in time and

space. Depicted in Stone Age cave paintings, it is still a feature of the observances of most of the world's major religions. The Jewish *Hasidim* dance with scrolls of the law; the Whirling Dervishes have a rotating step as their principal spiritual exercise; Hindu temple dancing has an unbroken history of centuries; it can be witnessed at Buddhist and Shinto shrines and within Christianity it is becoming a feature of many services, not only among the Pentecostals but also within the historic churches. It is not surprising in view of this intimate link between dance and devotion that according to many religions dance was both instituted by the gods and is an activity in which they themselves engage – such beliefs were shared, for example, by the Greeks and Romans and are embodied in Hindu thought in the person of Shiva or Naṭarāja, the Lord of the Dance, while in Christian thought dance is a symbol of heavenly bliss (*see* Plate 32). To dance is then to commune with heavenly beings. But liturgical dance covers a variety of forms and is understood to fulfil a host of functions.

When the dance is mimetic, it can narrate the stories of the gods and the history of a tribe or nation or people. It can constitute

Plate 32 The Heavenly Dance. Angels circling Mary at her coronation, from a painting by Sandro Botticelli in the Uffizi, Florence

a plea for success in hunting, for victory in war, for good weather and a plentiful harvest. When it is non-representational, it may express thanksgiving; it may be a way of welcoming a deity, a form of homage, of honouring, of offering. It can be a voiceless prayer. It can accompany and provide an interpretation in bodily terms of rites of passage, such as initiation ceremonies, weddings and funerals. It can sound a festive note, as in a processional dance; it can foster fellowship, as in a circle or ring dance.

The attitude of Christians to liturgical dance, and indeed to dance in any form, has been ambivalent. It was roundly condemned in the patristic era, although some did take place in church buildings, particularly at martyrs' shrines. It was condemned, despite the positive assessment of it in the Old Testament, because it had become a degraded pastime which was as much repudiated by educated pagans of the time as it was by the church fathers. Moreover it was a feature of the pagan cults, of Jewish celebrations and of certain heretical sects and the church wished to distance itself from all these. So favourable an understanding of the physical aspect of human nature was also questioned when, under the influence especially of Neo-Platonism, a spirituality was encouraged that was largely anti-body.

Throughout the Middle Ages dancing in churches was a very frequent occurrence, and while it was usually of a social rather than a religious nature there is evidence that the great festivals were marked by it. The churches of the Reformation were not well disposed to the practice, but the Puritans, despite their reputation as kill-joys, were prepared to allow it as long as it was not mixed and, in the words of Philip Stubbes, 'it is done to the setting forth of God his glory (as the dances used in former ages did) to draw others to piety . . . and to praise and rejoice in God, to recreate the mind oppressed with some great toil or labour, take in true virtue and godliness.' This view was shared by the Shakers (*see* **Shaker Worship**) of the late eighteenth and early nineteenth centuries whose services consisted entirely of dancing and who put forth a series of arguments in its defence – arguments that in the main are still valid. So they contended: 1. It is a gift of the Holy Spirit and is not to be neglected. 2. It is in accordance with Old Testament precedent. 3. It is a 'natural impulse of joy' suitable for the last days in which we live. 4. Indeed Jeremiah (31.13) foretold that this form of worship would be restored to the people of God when the eschaton came. 5. We are like the prodigal son whose return to his father's house was celebrated with music and dancing (Luke 15.21). 6. Worship should not be passive but active and this means that not only the tongue and the vocal chords but the whole body should be dedicated to the praise of God. 7. Congregational dancing both expresses and renders more profound that unity which should characterize God's people. 8. Such dancing allows for the recognition and consecration of natural aptitudes and it affirms the equality of the sexes. 9. The movements enable the worshippers to enter into the spirit of the sentiments expressed in the songs. 10. Christians, being pilgrims towards the heavenly Jerusalem, may by means of a processional dance recall both the liberation from the bondage of Egypt and the way of the cross and join with the heavenly hosts in a triumphant campaign against the forces of evil.

However, as the teaching of Descartes began to be absorbed, his emphasis upon the intellectual to the detriment of the physical encouraged most people to disdain dancing and this negative approach culminated in the Victorian period when it was dismissed as frivolous, inconsistent with the work ethic and certainly to be kept apart from any religious observance.

The present century has witnessed a considerable change of view. This is due to the pioneering efforts of certain gifted individuals – Isadora Duncan, Ruth St Denis, Ted Shawn, Martha Graham, Mary Wigman and Doris Humphrey – who rehabilitated dance as an art and stressed its expressional aspect rather than its potential for story telling. This is something very different from the degraded displays against which the fathers fulminated. Indeed many of these dancers were themselves concerned about the relation of their art to religion. Isadora Duncan held that dance can be a form of worship (*see* Fig. 21); Ruth St Denis shared the same conviction and her husband Ted Shawn created a complete dance service as long ago as 1917. From then on, and especially after the end of

World War II, dancing in church has been more and more widely practised, as evidenced, for example, by the danced mass at the opening of the Metropolitan Cathedral of Christ the King in Liverpool in 1967 or the dancing of the Lord's Prayer at a gathering of the Life and Peace Conference in Uppsala cathedral in 1983. Further encouragement has come from the founding of the Sacred Dance Guild in the USA in 1958 and of the Christian Dance Fellowship of Australia in 1978. Dance choirs* are now being introduced into many churches side by side with singing choirs*. Liturgical dance has come to stay and the direction of the psalmist is once again being observed: 'Praise him with timbrel and dance' (Ps. 150.4).

Fig. 21 Isadora Duncan, from a drawing by Gordon Craig

Christian liturgical dance as it is now conceived can either take the form of story telling or of expressional movement. As narrative it may accompany biblical readings, both illustrating and supplementing them: it can replace a sermon; it can be a proclamation of the gospel: it can be a commentary on prayers, psalms, hymns and carols. It is a way of exploring physically the meaning of stories, such as the resurrection of Jesus or the parable of the talents. When it is expressional, dance can give bodily shape to gratitude and to joy; it can promote participation and *shalom*; it enables worship to be offered by each person in his or her totality; it can be an act of worship in itself, being sacramental in character in that it unifies the physical and spiritual aspects of human nature; it encourages creativity; it gives scope for enrichment; it allows greater diversity; it can present a challenge.

Doug Adams, *Congregational Dance in Christian Worship*, 1980; N. Challingsworth, *Liturgical Dance Movement. A Practical Guide*, 1982; J. G. Davies, *Liturgical Dance. An Historical, Theological and Practical Handbook*, 1984; C. DeSola, *The Spirit Moves. A Handbook of Dance and Prayer*, 1977; A. Long, *Praise Him in the Dance*, 1976; A. Ortegel, *A Dancing People*, 1978; M. F. Taylor, *A Time to Dance, Symbolic Movement in Worship*, 1976.

EDITOR

Deacon

The office of deacon is frequently mentioned in the NT though there is no evidence at all to support the tradition that the seven, whose appointment is described in Acts 6, were deacons. The tradition was strong enough, however, to persist over many centuries and to create the feeling that seven was the proper number of deacons, and in Rome the order was for a long time restricted to that number. In the NT the deacon was a minister associated with prebysters* and bishops* in the ministry of the local church. They appear in much the same sort of position in the writings of the apostolic fathers. A little later there seems to have been some tension and jealousy between the orders of presbyters and deacons. Deacons are always formally reckoned as the third order and below the presbyters. On the other hand, they were a full-time and professional ministry, with clear liturgical and administrative functions at a time when the presbyters were hardly more than an advisory board. In Rome, especially, the deacons were of considerable importance and were often chosen to occupy the episcopal throne. Evidence for the importance of the deacon is to be found in the leading part played by Felicissimus in the opposition to Cyprian at Carthage, and the schism of Hippolytus may have

been partly a result of presbyteral jealousy of the deacon's growing importance. As presbyters gained a new position as the normal minister in charge of particular districts and congregations, the balance began to swing the other way. In the Middle Ages the parish priest became the local embodiment of the church's life, while the diaconate lost most of its real functions. In the early church the deacon had often exercised real power as the officer responsible for poor relief and, therefore, for administering the church's property. He had also possessed a prominent liturgical role, reading the lessons and especially the gospel, distributing the elements at the eucharist, directing the prayers of the congregation, generally maintaining order in the services, and assisting at baptism. By the end of the mediaeval period in the West the office of archdeacon, representing the deacon's administrative function, was almost invariably occupied by a priest. The vestigial liturgical functions, chiefly reading the gospel, were also normally performed by a priest. In the modern Anglican and Roman Catholic Churches the diaconate has become a grade through which a candidate for priest's orders passes for a brief period before being ordained to the higher grade. In the Eastern Churches the deacons have remained a quite distinct order with a liturgical function proper to them alone.

Since the Second Vatican Council the Roman Catholic Church has permitted older married men to be made deacon and has thus gone some way towards restoring a permanent diaconate. These deacons may preach, instruct, baptize, take the sacrament to the sick and read the gospel at the eucharist. A significant number have been ordained in recent years.

In the Anglican Church in Canada, the United States, Kenya, Uganda, New Zealand and Hong Kong, women have been admitted to the diaconate. The question of the ordination of women to the diaconate in the Church of England is at present under consideration. Women who have been made deacons are not to be confused with deaconesses*.

John Calvin included the office of deacon (together with pastors, doctors, and elders) in the fourfold ministry which he believed to be most consonant with the pattern of the apostolic church. In the Reformed tradition the deacon remains the officer charged with the care of the sick and the poor. It is a pastoral, charitable and administrative, rather than a liturgical, office. Congregational churches also use the title but the deacon has a role in the celebration of the eucharist and distributes the elements. In Baptist churches, deacons may be either male or female and many are ordained. They have a responsibility for the spiritual welfare of a congregation; they assist in visiting, in taking communion to the ill and infirm; they provide pulpit supplies, administer the welfare fund and assist the pastor in the planning of worship.

H. W. Beyer, *TDNT*, II, pp.88–93; L. Vischer (ed), *The Ministry of Deacons*, 1965.

P. HINCHLIFF

Deaconess

In the fourth century the general and informal ministry and service of women in the Christian community seems to have been formalized in the office of deaconess. Before that there are many references to the service and devotion of widows and virgins and other Christian women without necessarily implying that they comprised a special order of ministry. By the fourth century, however, the deaconess's duties and functions were clearly defined. She performed many of the duties of a deacon* in relation to the care of the sick and the poor, the maintenance of order in church and, particularly, assisting at the baptism of adult women. The office disappeared by the Middle Ages, but has been revived since about the middle of the nineteenth century in the German Lutheran, Anglican, Methodist and Presbyterian Churches. Her duties are usually to act as a general pastoral assistant in the parish or congregation. How far the deaconess is a 'minister' in any technical sense is usually far from clear and in the Anglican Church, for instance, there is considerable disagreement about whether a deaconess can properly be described as part of the 'ordained ministry' or not. A distinction is made in those provinces in which women are ordained to the diaconate and priesthood between women who are deacons and deaconesses.

Methodist deaconesses are sometimes in

pastoral charge of congregations and are authorized to administer the sacraments.

Orders of deaconesses are to be found in several European Baptist Unions. In Germany they perform many services, but particularly exercise a ministry in hospitals and homes for the aged. In America they are usually lay persons and serve in conjunction with the deacons; often there is a single board of deacons which includes both men and women and then the term deaconess tends to be dropped. One of their primary responsibilities is preparing the table for the Lord's Supper.

The Church of England, *The Ministry of Deacons and Deaconesses*, 1977; J. G. Davies, 'Deacon, Deaconess and the Minor Orders in the Patristic Period', *JEH* xiv (1963), pp.1–15; J. Grierson, *The Deaconess*, 1981; C. H. Turner, 'Ministries of Women in the Primitive Church', *Catholic and Apostolic*, 1931, pp.328–43.

P. HINCHLIFF

Deaf Choir

see **Choir (Sign Language)**

Deaf People and Worship

There is no single uniform category to which all deaf people belong; indeed depending upon the character of their hearing defect and at what stage in their life it began, they may be classified in three groups.

1. Those born profoundly deaf, or who have become so before learning to speak naturally. Most of these are unfamiliar with their native language, never having heard it. It is consequently extremely difficult for them to learn to articulate with ease or with normal pronunciation. Understanding by means of lip-reading is too laborious, and impossible for the majority of them, and following a printed text gives little pleasure. Worship, therefore, to be visible and meaningful, must be conducted through gestures, signs, mime and finger-spelling. The meaning of hymns and prayers can also be expressed in this way by the persons, deaf or hearing, who share in leading the worship. It is essential that the person who has the ministry of interpretation should be within easy range of vision so that deaf worshippers are not distracted from their main devotional purpose by having to concentrate over much on the medium of communication.

2. Those who have become severely deaf early in life after learning to speak naturally. These people have a working knowledge of their native tongue and can express themselves in ordinary language forms. Unlike those in the first category, they seldom have difficulty in reading and so it is important to make available to them printed forms so they can follow the order of service. Those who cannot benefit from hearing aids will also rely on sign language in the company of deaf friends and at times of worship. In addition, the use of visual aids, such as overhead projectors, is to be commended. Choirs rendering hymns eloquently in sign language are also being more and more recognized as a positive assistance in worshipping together (*see* **Choir (Sign Language)** and Plate 27).

3. The hard of hearing and the partially hearing. Many of the hard of hearing have become so late in life and are therefore either too old or do not wish to learn sign language. Indeed, since most of their friends can speak and hear there seems little point in doing so. Unfortunately, in many cases hearing aids provide only limited help whereas the problems of the partially hearing can normally be overcome by using them. However most of those in this third category would benefit greatly if an induction loop system was installed in church buildings, enabling them to hear with enhanced clarity what is said or sung. Making this provision should be a top priority for all congregations.

A congregation of deaf people is often made up of persons from each of the three categories mentioned above so a wide range of needs has to be met in services specifically for the deaf. Much tact and understanding must be exercised by those who wish to work with them. Failure to appreciate their difficulties – their lack of understanding through being unable to hear, their embarrassment, their tension even – can often lead to unnecessary suffering. Continual experimentation in ways to overcome the barrier created by this handicap is clearly required.

See also **Handicapped People and Worship**.

C. E. DE C. CHITTTENDEN

Dedication

Dedication is the act of formally making over something or somebody to another, and in Christian usage the other is God. Dedication is related to five liturgical acts.

1. The term has been used interchangeably with consecration, and so to describe the dedication of a church is to outline the rite of consecration (*see* **Consecration of Churches**). A distinction is, however, made in modern English law between the two, dedication being a simple blessing while consecration is regarded as separating the building for ever from unhallowed uses. This differentiation has little or no basis in Christian usage or theological thought.

2. The dedication of a church also refers to the name given to a particular building, e.g. St Paul's or St Mary's. Strictly speaking the church is dedicated to God in honour of a saint or a divine mystery.

3. A dedication festival is the annual commemoration of the day of a church's consecration and is therefore to be distinguished from the patronal festival which is in honour of the patron saint. The first observance of such a feast is recorded by the fourth-century pilgrim Egeria, who describes the practice at Jerusalem in connection with the Church of the Resurrection and the Martyrion. According to her this takes place on the same day as the dedication of the Jerusalem Temple by Solomon and it would appear to have been observed on 23 September.

The dedication festivals of the four main Roman basilicas were included in the general ecclesiastical calendar: the Lateran (9 November), St Peter and St Paul (18 November), Santa Maria Maggiore (5 August). Gregory the Great ordered the conversion of heathen festivals connected with temples in England into dedication festivals.

In 1536 the English Convocation fixed the first Sunday in October as the universal date. The Scottish and American prayer books provide for the festival, and the 1928 book does also, with the directive that, if the day of consecration is not known, the feast may be observed on the first Sunday in October.

4. Dedication is also used of the blessing or offering of liturgical objects to God. So the Church of Scotland has a series of forms for the dedication of an altar, the font, etc.

5. In churches which do not practise infant baptism*, a service of dedication of the child is sometimes held at which the child receives a Christian name.

EDITOR

Dedication Festival

see **Dedication** 3

Devotions

see **Benediction**; **Exposition**; **Forty Hours' Devotion**; **Reservation**; **Rosary**; **Sacred Heart**; **Stations of the Cross**; **Veneration of the Cross**

Diptychs

The name is derived from a hinged board, on the two wings of which were anciently written the names of persons, both living and departed, for whom the prayers of the church were specifically desired in the offering of the eucharistic sacrifice.

The diptychs (*see* **Anaphora** 9) appear to go back to the reading by a deacon* of the names of those who had brought an offering of bread for the eucharist. Once the custom of making an offering as an act of prayer or thanksgiving on behalf of other individuals was established (which had certainly occurred by the middle of the third century), their names also, by a natural development, were read together with, and in the same way as, those of the offerers themselves. Originally, such vicarious offerings appear to have been made only, or at least normally, on behalf of the departed; hence there was added to the existing list of the names of the (living) offerers a second list containing the names of the (departed) beneficiaries of the offerings. It was not long before a further development took place – that of making offerings for other people still living: early examples of this include the provision of the ancient Roman rite that godparents should offer for their godchildren while the latter are still catechumens*. Except in cases of this kind, however, for which special provision was made, the names of the living beneficiaries of the offerings appear not to have been read separately, but to have been added to the list of the offerers. Another slightly later development was the addition of yet another list, containing the names –

sometimes only the classes – of martyrs (and then other saints as well) for whom it was desired to give thanks, separately from the rest of the departed. The diptychs, then, may be defined for practical purposes as 'intercessions for, or commemorations of, specified persons, living and departed, by name, offered in close and intimate connection with the offering of the eucharist itself'; the name 'diptychs' should not be interpreted too literally, as there are often sub-divisions within the basic divisions of living and departed – the Roman diptychs in the early Middle Ages, for example, may on certain occasions have comprised up to seven lists of names. The actual place in the eucharist at which the diptychs are read in the historic liturgies varies: this variation, indeed, is one of the principal structural distinctions between the eucharistic prayers of different traditions. In the Eastern liturgies of the Antiochene family (including the Byzantine, commonly called 'the Orthodox liturgy') they are placed in the second part of the prayer, after the consecration; in those of the Alexandrine family they are placed in the first part of the prayer, before the consecration; in the West, the historic Roman canon divides the diptychs – the diptych of the living occurs in the former part of the prayer, and that of the dead in the latter part; the ancient Hispano-Gallican liturgies of the West placed the diptychs before the eucharistic prayer, after the offertory*. Some scholars have said that this was their original position in the Roman rite as well, but the evidence which is cited in favour of this assertion does not, when closely examined, support it.

In the East the diptychs very early came to be expanded into a more general intercession (or they may have been combined with an already existing intercession, and the consequent combination expanded); in the West, except for certain isolated instances, they retained their original character more closely. In East and West alike the practice, dating from the early Middle Ages, of reciting the greater part of the eucharistic prayer in secret inevitably diminished the pastoral effectiveness of diptychs recited in the course of it, and other provision was made to supplement them, e.g. in the Byzantine East in the prothesis* and at the great entrance*, and in the West during the Middle Ages, in the bidding of the bedes (*see* **Bidding Prayer**). In the Byzantine East the practice of submitting a list of names of those for whom prayer is desired, together with the offering of bread, is still very much alive. The theological rationale of the diptychs, and any other intercession, in the eucharistic prayer is briefly discussed in connection with the anaphora.

W. Jardine Grisbrooke, 'Intercession at the Eucharist', *Studia Liturgica*, V, 1, 1966, pp.20–44; ibid., V.2, 1966, pp.87–103. For a detailed study of the Roman diptychs, *see* J. A. Jungmann, *The Mass of the Roman Rite*, II, 1955, pp.152–87, 237–59. For the Byzantine diptychs, see C. Kucharek, *The Byzantine-Slav Liturgy of St John Chrysostom*, 1971, pp.518–27, 624–42.

W. JARDINE GRISBROOKE

Directions, Liturgical

Directions have always been important for human beings. Jews pray towards Jerusalem; Muslims face towards Mecca; Christians build their churches with the sanctuaries at the east end. Moreover, while nowadays few believe that God dwells in the upper atmosphere, height is everywhere taken to symbolize that which is more important and indeed the upward direction is interpreted as Godward, while downwards is the direction of the grave and even of hell itself. The east, where the sun rises, has often been referred to Christ, symbolized as the dayspring from on high, while the west, where the sun sets into darkness, has been interpreted as the realm of Satan. So in the patristic period, to give one example of the liturgical use of these directions, candidates for baptism faced west to renounce the devil and east to recite the creed.

See also **Orientation**.

EDITOR

Disciples of Christ Worship

see **Christian Church Worship**

Dismissal

The act of sending forth the worshippers at the end of a service. In the early church, the catchumens* were dismissed after the ministry of the word. By the third century, a prayer for those being dismissed was inserted at the beginning of the community prayer. Then in the next century, they were

allowed to stay until the completion of that part of the prayer of the church which was on their behalf. With the disappearance of the catechumenate, the need for these dismissals ceased, but they still survive in the Byzantine rite.

At the conclusion of the whole service, there was a further act of dismissal of the faithful. The Roman form was terse, namely *Ite missa est* (hence the name mass), to which was added an introduction and a response: *Dominus vobiscum* – *Deo gratias*. The Gallican formula, however, seems to have *Benedicamus Domino*. From the eleventh century both were used, the Roman when there was a *Gloria* and the Gallican on other occasions. At the present day several new formulae are in use to emphasize that the Christians' duty is in the world and that worship is not an isolated incident.

J. A. Jungmann, *The Mass of the Roman Rite*, rev ed 1959, pp.301–4, 535–58.

EDITOR

Disposal of Eucharistic Remains

During the patristic period there was universal agreement that the consecrated elements at the eucharist* should be treated with reverence. As early as Tertullian we read: 'We feel pained should any wine or bread, even though our own, be cast upon the ground' (*de Cor.* 3). What was left after communion* was carried into the sacristy* at the conclusion of the service. There the remains were kept for at least one day following a precept of the Mosaic law in relation to the disposal of certain sacrifices (Lev. 7.16). They were then consumed by the priests or, in certain areas, burned, again following Jewish practice (Lev. 7.17), or given, in Evagrius' phrase, to 'uncorrupted boys' (*Hist. eccl.* 4.36). The practice of having the ablutions* immediately after communion meant that in the West the consumption of the remains eventually took place in the church itself before the end of the mass.

In the Eastern Orthodox churches the early practice has continued, i.e. consumption at the table of oblation in a side chamber or sacristy close to the high altar after the service, except when a deacon* is assisting in which case disposal is prior to the final dismissal. The Anglican custom is similar to the mediaeval and modern Roman practice, i.e. what is left is eaten and drunk immediately after all have communicated, but both the BCP of the Episcopal Church (1979) and the ASB (1980) allow consumption either at the end of the distribution or after the service. In the Lutheran churches the elements remaining are often stored with those that are to serve for future celebrations, but sometimes they are thrown away. The Reformed practice is not uniform, but the bread is sometimes burned. Among Methodists the wine is returned to the bottle and the bread put out for birds or otherwise thrown away.

W. Lockton, *The Treatment of the Remains at the Eucharist after Holy Communion and the Time of the Ablutions*, 1920.

EDITOR

Divine Office, The

The canonical hours* of the Western church together make up the Divine Office. These little services grew up from earliest times and their broad outline was described in the sixth century by St Benedict in his *Rule*. The Day Hours are seven in number and are celebrated at roughly three-hourly intervals from dawn to dusk: lauds at daybreak, prime at 6.00 a.m., terce at 9.00 a.m., sext at mid-day, none at 3.00 p.m., vespers at sunset (about 6.00 p.m.) and compline before retiring to bed. The Night Office of vigils, also called matins, or the Office of Readings, is traditionally divided into three nocturns. All the services of the Divine Office are based on psalmody*, combined with scripture readings and commentaries, hymns, antiphons* and responsories*. The music may be found in a service book known as an *Antiphonale*. Since the Second Vatican Council the Divine Office (*Liturgia Horarum*) has undergone radical revision and has been much abbreviated. Today it is commonly recited in the vernacular and one has to travel far to hear the ancient traditional offices still celebrated in Latin and in Gregorian chant*.

Over the centuries many composers have set parts of the Divine Office to music in the style of their own period. One of the parts most frequently set is the solemn *Magnificat*, which is the high point at vespers. England can boast of some

splendid Tudor settings of the *Magnificat*, particularly those of the *Eton Choir Book*. Any present-day concert-goer will be familiar with Monteverdi's *1610 Vespers*. Another part of the Divine Office which has lent itself to elaborate polyphonic settings is the service of matins and lauds for the last three days of Holy Week*. This is the service known as *Tenebrae**, taking its title from the splendid responsory *Tenebrae factae sunt* ('There was darkness when they crucified Jesus') which is sung during Good Friday matins. The Spanish composer Victoria wrote magnificent settings of the *Tenebrae* responsories in his masterpiece *Officium Hebdomadae Sanctae* (1585). The lessons of the first nocturn of each day are taken from the *Lamentations of Jeremiah*. Palestrina composed several settings of these, as did Tallis and Victoria. The traditional monophonic settings of all these texts are among the finest in the whole corpus of Gregorian chant.

Dom Timothy Fry (ed), *The Rule of St Benedict*, 1981; S. van Dijk and J. Hazelden Walker, *The Origins of the Modern Roman Liturgy*, 1960.

MARY BERRY

Doxology

An ascription of praise (Greek *doxologia*, lit. 'words of glory'), usually trinitarian in form, and often beginning with, or including, the word 'glory'.

1. The 'lesser doxology' is composed of the two verses commonly added, in most Christian liturgies, to the end of psalms and canticles: 'Glory be to the Father, and to the Son, and to the Holy Spirit; as it was in the beginning, is now, and ever shall be, world without end. Amen.' In the Eastern liturgies the second verse usually runs: 'both now, and for ever, and world without end. Amen.' (The Greek and Latin phrase commonly translated 'world without end' literally reads 'to the ages of ages', i.e. 'for ever and ever'.)

2. The 'greater doxology' is the hymn *Glory to God in the highest*, which exists in a number of versions, and dates from at latest the third quarter of the fourth century. In the fifth-century Codex Alexandrinus it is entitled 'morning hymn', and it features as such in the divine office of a number of the historic liturgies, notably the Byzantine rite, in which it is the climax of the morning office of *orthros* or matins (*see* **Canonical Hours**).

The use of this hymn at the eucharist is peculiar to the West. By the beginning of the sixth century it had already an established place in the mass at Rome, although only when a bishop was the president; not till the eleventh century was the present rule finally settled, by which it is used at all masses on Sundays and feasts, although this had already been the custom in many places for some centuries. In the Roman rite, and in other historic Western rites when it has been used at the mass, as well as in the Lutheran liturgy and in a number of recent revisions of the eucharistic liturgy in various denominations, the *Gloria* has always been sung after the entrance and before the collect* of the day, as a preparatory hymn of praise and prayer, for which use it is particularly well suited; its transference to a position after the communion is a peculiarity of the BCP and liturgies derived from it.

3. 'The great doxology' is also a title commonly used to denote the doxology at the end of the eucharistic prayer (*see* **Anaphora** 10).

4. A trinitarian conclusion to a prayer – e.g. a collect – is referred to as its doxology.

J. A. Jungmann, *The Mass of the Roman Rite*, I, 1951, pp.346–59.

W. JARDINE GRISBROOKE

Drama and Worship

1. *History*. The roots of theatre are in religious ritual; and the history of the theatre is a history of its growth over against worship. Mimetic magic, in which reality was thought to be directly affected by the action of the rite, became make-believe – in Aristotle's words, a play is 'an imitation of an action, and not the action itself'. By this definition the culture of Greece in the fifth century BC produced the first theatre out of the cults of Dionysus; a drama played on hallowed ground, but not in temples; and by actors, not priests. Thus drama may be seen as a prodigal child of worship – which could explain the often uneasy relationship between the two.

Theologians have often given the drama a rough ride (and not only Christians;

Julian the Apostate exhorted followers of Mithras to avoid the theatres), but the impulse to share in make-believe proved difficult to eradicate. Tertullian in *Of Public Shows* (*c*. 200), condemns the Roman theatre with his customary reserve: '. . . the devil raised the tragic actor up on his buskins, since "no man can add one cubit to his stature" and he wants to make Christ a liar . . . The Author of Truth hates whatever is untrue, in his sight everything fabricated is corrupt'. Yet in the same work he suggests that the mass and the life of discipleship are themselves 'the spectacles fit for Christians' and that drama may be seen there.

In mediaeval times this advice was heeded. Liturgy was the seed-bed for Christian drama. The Easter trope *Quem quaeritis*, based on the angelic conversations at Christ's tomb, marks the development of characterization within the liturgy, as priests 'played' angels and women in dialogue. Later texts include 'stage directions' for what has become a piece of ritual drama. From these beginnings the mediaeval mystery plays flowered. The development of vernacular drama and secular themes was not perceived as a threat by the church, and indeed the vernacular theatre grew within the twelfth century shift in devotion to the humanity and suffering of Christ. From the later twelfth century the 'Feasts of Fools' or 'Feasts of Asses' saw the burlesquing of the ritual itself, within the churches: an extraordinary contradiction of Tertullian's views. Yet although the mystery cycles gradually went the way of the Greek plays, out of the churches, the drama nevertheless enjoyed the blessing of the church until the Reformation. Despite this, Britain produced no one to compare with the Spanish priest/playwright Calderon (d.1681), whose play *el gran teatro del mundo* explicitly developed the theme of the world as a stage, and the theatre as a metaphor for creation. In Britain the professional theatre grew away from a church which increasingly distrusted the body and movement, and whose liturgy became increasingly cerebral. This division of church and theatre was sealed by the Puritan condemnation of all theatre and the closing of the theatres in 1642. When the theatre returned with the monarchy in 1660, links with worship were severed completely.

2. *Present practice.* The director Peter Brook in his seminal book *The Empty Space* (1968) distinguished several genres of theatre; among them the Deadly, the Rough, the Holy. Each of these may be seen in current attempts to use drama in worship.

(*a*) *Deadly.* Deadly theatre, deadly worship, is that which is bad, counterfeit, false. A legacy of the division between church and theatre has been that people who manage worship, and who genuinely want to experiment creatively, have tried to staple bits of 'drama' on to their work, in place of sermons, or readings. This has been done in the hope of 'brightening it up' or of 'attracting the young'. Looking for models of drama, their eye has fallen on the commercial West End stage, and so Agatha Christie and Terence Rattigan inspire religious drama, some twenty or thirty years after the best of secular culture moved elsewhere. The relationship between church and professional theatre illustrates the problem. *Murder in the Cathedral* was the last great play on a Christian theme which reflected the church's own beliefs. Christians have commissioned plays since (Edward Bond's *Narrow Road to the Deep North*) and Christian themes have been used (John Arden's *The Business of Good Government*, Dennis Potter's *Son of Man*), but these have quite properly reflected the views of their authors, and there is no longer a major Christian playwright writing in English. Consequently those Christians who want to retain the 'look' and style of the commercial theatre in their worship have had to resort to pastiche and nostalgia, and it is this, the very worst of 'amateur theatricals', which represents drama in many churches today. The basis of mutual respect and shared belief between theatre and church, which inspired the best religious drama of the past, has simply vanished.

(*b*) *Rough.* In Brook's words, it is always the popular theatre that saves the day. Burlesque, direct humour, physical contact is central to drama, and this is the level at which it was condemned by the Fathers. Nevertheless, the only successful religious theatre of the last twenty years (the musicals *Jesus Christ Superstar* and *Godspell*, and the English National Theatre's 'Mystery Cycle') operated at this exuberant level. And at the same level the drama now operates in the

churches. By a curious irony, it is those in the evangelical tradition, the descendants of the Puritans, who have pioneered the use of rough drama in worship. The rediscovery of the body by evangelical Christians is a fruit of the charismatic renewal, and it is charismatic communities which have produced the leading Christian performance groups such as the Fisherfolk and Riding Lights. The style of these groups is simple and direct, drawing more from the circus and music-hall than the mainstream theatre. Equipment is simple – a few battered props, or none at all, with the actors using their own bodies to produce Jonah's whale, or Jesus' tomb. Scripts are home-made. Because of its simplicity this style of performance breaks away from the need to seem 'professional', while still giving scope for the exercise of ingenuity and skill. And like the mediaeval drama, it is as effective in the street as in the church. It is usually seen in worship as a reinforcement of the ministry of the word – obedient to the almost universal commandment, 'Thou shalt not laugh after the offertory'.

(*c*) *Holy*. Within the churches drama is used to make people think, or to make them laugh. But it is possible for the theatre to touch and move people at the most profound and serious level. The realm of what Brook called holy theatre is that of worship itself; and although the secular theatre may want rituals, it may seem that the church has little to learn in this area. Yet at a time when modern liturgy is accused of shallowness and heartiness, the leaders of the theatre's avant-garde (Brook, the Pole Jerzy Grotowski, his disciple Eugenio Barba) have turned to a disciplined use of performance as a spiritual way. Here it is not the audience who are the focus, but the performers themselves, who try to share themselves honestly, free of false pretence, through make-believe. There are lessons here, both for those who lead worship and also for small groups of worshippers who want to grow together through their worship. The techniques of performance here overlap with those of modern spiritual direction and of humanistic psychology – for example, using physical exercises to release inhibition and unlock creative and expressive energy; or the disciplined use of the imagination through guided fantasy or role-playing. These methods are not new; Pope John Paul II, when Bishop of Krakow, improvised many rituals, gatherings and pilgrimages, inspired by his own early training as an actor. These kinds of imaginative experiment represent the latest incarnation of the basic impulse behind both religious drama and worship – to be present honestly before God, in a situation which is inevitably artificial and structured.

3. *Conclusion*. Make-believe or imagination is a commodity which has been undervalued. As the churches wake up to the drama after a long sleep, so also theology begins to pay attention to the power of narrative and of myth, and to the extraordinary religious power of stories and myths which are honestly accepted as such. This sympathy on the part of theology has a counterpart in the early Middle Ages, when theologians such as Amalarius of Metz saw great potential in allegorical and dramatic interpretations of the rituals of the mass. From that sympathetic atmosphere the great mediaeval miracle cycles grew. And the impulse to play, to perform, to celebrate, has not been lost since. Worshippers are now rediscovering it. The theatre has always existed to take that impulse and to discipline it. When make-believe is integrated into worship, the result is more than 'drama'. In Grotowski's words, 'all the elements of a certain type of theatre are present: contacts, impulses, movements, improvisations, sounds, music, space. There is also an aspiration to go beyond the mode of communication used in everyday life. But we are not seeking to create characters as in a play. We are ourselves. Is this theatre? Or is it something else?'

History: Francis Edwards, *Ritual and Drama; the Medieval Theatre*, 1976; Phyllis Hartnoll, *A Concise History of the Theatre*, 1968; Richard Schechner and Mady Schuman (eds), *Ritual, Play and Performance*, 1976; Victor Turner, *From Ritual to Theatre*, 1982; William Tydeman, *The Theatre in the Middle Ages*, 1978. Rough theatre: Patricia Beall, *The Folk Arts in God's Family*, 1984; Paul Burbridge and Murray Watts, *Lightning Sketches*, 1981; *Time to Act*, 1979. Holy theatre: Eugenio Barba, *The Floating Islands*, 1979; John Heilpern, *The Conference of the Birds*, 1977; James Roose-Evans, *Experimental Theatre*, [3]1984.

PAUL BAYES

Dry Mass

see **Ante-communion**

East Syrian Worship

1. *Historical.* The East Syrian Church (known to many as the Nestorian or Chaldean church) is the Syrian Church of Antioch as it developed east of the frontiers of the Roman-Byzantine empire. Its centre was Nisibis, but its distinctiveness as a tradition could be dated from the Synod of Beth Lapat in AD 484, when this church recognized Theodore of Mopsuestia as its official teacher, i.e. his teachings were to be the standard by which the faith of other churches was to be tested. During the seventh and later centuries this church spread to Turkestan (now in the Central Asian republics of the USSR) with bishops in Samarkand, Tashkent, Karakoram and also in Tibet as well as in China and India. Today this church, except a part now in the Roman Catholic communion, is limited to small pockets in USA, Iraq, Iran and India.

2. *Liturgical books.* The main eucharistic liturgies are three, which go by the names of (*a*) Addai and Mari, (*b*) Theodore of Mopsuestia and (*c*) Nestorius. In addition to various lectionaries (one for the gospels, a second for the apostle Paul and the *qaryana* which contains the first two lessons for the liturgical office, from the OT and the Acts), they have the *turgame*, which are homilies on the lessons in the form of hymns to be chanted with the aid of the psalter (*Dawida*), consecration of an altar (without chrism), prayers for ferial days, rites of marriage, the ordination manual, etc. The offices are chanted with the aid of the psalter (*Dawida*), the *hudra*, which contains the propers of the office, antiphons, hymns and prayers, the *gazza*, which contains the offices for the feasts of our Lord and the saints (except those that fall on Sundays), and other books for the choirs.

3. *The eucharistic liturgy.* What has astonished many liturgists about the liturgy of Addai and Mari is the absence of the words of institution; this is not unusual in the West Syrian* tradition either. (The two other Chaldean anaphorae* do have the words of institution.) This is shocking only to those who believe that the recital of the words of institution effect the consecration. There is a form of the Liturgy of the Presanctified (*see* **Presanctified Mass**) for use on Good Friday.

The Liturgy of the Catechumens begins with the *Trisagion**, which is followed by the lections: one from the OT, and a second from either the OT or the Acts of the Apostles. These are supposed to be read from the *bema*, the raised platform in the centre of the church. After the first two lections, as the priest leaves the *bema* to ascend the altar, the *turgama* or the homiletic hymn for the day is sung, interpreting the main point of the lection from the Pauline epistles which follows it. The *turgama* of the gospel comes next, followed by the gospel itself.

The Liturgy of the Faithful begins with a litany of intercession much as in the Byzantine liturgy. The diptychs* after the creed and the *lavabo** are also in the form of litanies. Mary is commemorated thus: 'For the memorial of Lady Mary the holy virgin who bare Christ our Lord and our Saviour.' The 318 fathers of Nicaea are commemorated, and among the other fathers are mentioned both Theodore and Diodore as well as Nestorius, Flavian, Ambrose and Meletius. Emperor Constantine, his mother Helena, and later Byzantine emperors like Constans and Theodosius are also commemorated.

Even when the words of institution are missing, the epiclesis of the Holy Spirit upon the offering is given in full.

There is a second *lavabo* before the fraction* and consignation. The priest censes his hands after the *lavabo* before proceeding to the fraction. The Lord's Prayer precedes the elevation and communion. The deacon who read the epistle is to administer the body from the paten and the deacon who gave the peace to administer the blood from the chalice.

The eucharist is called the *kudasha* or sanctification; the liturgical language is Eastern Syriac, though the vernacular is used in most churches today. Leavened bread is used and communion is generally now in both kinds by intinction.

4. *Offices.* The canonical offices are mainly three: *lelya* (nocturns), *sapra* (matins)

and *ramsha* (vespers) (*see* **Canonical Hours**).

5. *Other liturgies.* The baptismal liturgy is modelled on the eucharistic liturgy, with a pre-anaphora and anaphora for the consecration of the water with the chrism. Confirmation does not exist as a separate rite. Neither penance nor the sacrament of confession is used in this tradition. The anointing of the sick was also unknown until it was borrowed from the West in the sixteenth century. The marriage liturgy includes crowning and common drinking of wine from the same cup, but it is doubtful whether the East Syrians regarded marriage as a sacrament. The ordination practices are similar to those of other Eastern churches.

The text of Addai and Mari is given in ET in F. E. Brightman and C. E. Hammond, *Liturgies Eastern and Western*, I, 1896, pp.247–305; G. P. Badger, *The Nestorians and Their Rituals*, 2 vols, 1852; H. W. Codrington, *Studies of the Syrian Liturgies*, 1952.

PAULOS GREGORIOS

East, Turning

see **Posture** 5

Easter

The Pasch, the Christian Passover, the transformation of the Jewish Passover, was the great festival of redemption, and was a unitive commemoration of the cross* and the resurrection. In the fourth century there was a process of evolution, and with the development of Good Friday* as we know it, the Pasch became limited to the theme of the resurrection. So Easter emerged in our understanding of the term.

The Gospel narratives make it abundantly clear that there was no coincidence in the fact that the passion and victory of the Lord took place at the season of the Passover. He chose the place and time of crisis, and with this in his heart he went up to the Holy City. The secrecy of the arrangements for the Last Supper indicates his intense desire to hold this meal with his disciples. The synoptic narrative in its various forms plainly states that the meal was the Passover. Therefore the Jewish day which began at sunset on Thursday was 15 Nisan. It began with the Passover, and before that day had ended at sunset on Friday the Messiah was dead. The Passover commemorated with joyfulness and thanksgiving the central event of the old covenant, the deliverance from Egypt. But in his cross and resurrection, the central events of the new covenant, the Lord Jesus Christ was to accomplish a new and supreme deliverance for all mankind, the redemption from sin and death. The cross and resurrection, seen as a unity, constituted the new exodus.

The Lord had foretold his passion and triumph and, within the context of these events, the Last Supper was of immense significance. The Pasch, which was the interpretation of the exodus, became on this most sacred night the interpretation of what was now at hand – the entering of the Lord into his kingdom through the gate of suffering and death. This Pasch therefore stands as the decisive frontier between, on the one side, the Jewish Passover of the old covenant and, on the other, both the annual Christian Pasch and the weekly celebration of the Christian eucharist*. It is essential to remember that the annual and weekly Christian commemorations were related in the closest possible way. It was a perfectly natural development that the Christian 'Passover' should be an all-night festival, and that it should be divorced from the Jewish liturgical year, that is, from 15 Nisan, though how early this divorce was made is still a matter of debate, some scholars arguing that in its very earliest years the primitive Christian community would have continued to celebrate Passover in accordance with the Jewish calendar. Certainly some Asian churches continued to do this in the second century and beyond, which gave rise to the Quartodeciman controversy (the Pasch actually being celebrated on 14 Nisan in these communities) with the rest of the church which was celebrating Pasch on the weekly liturgical day of the church, the Sunday, the day of the resurrection. The Christian Pasch thus came to begin on the Saturday evening, that is at the commencement of the primitive Sunday, and it culminated at the resurrection dawn with the sacraments of baptism and the eucharist. For it was in the light of the victory of the Lord's Day that the church looked upon the cross. The weekly Lord's Day (*see* **Sunday**) was very like the annual Pasch, for the eucharist was a memorial, not of the death alone, but of the death and the triumph.

The evidence of the third century enables us to see in the baptism at cockrow, followed at once by the eucharist, the culmination of the Pasch, that is the rejoicing in the resurrection. So also in the preliminary fast of the Pasch, which normally extended over the Friday as well as the Saturday from the late second century onwards, the dominant note must have been the passion. But the vigil contained the hope of the resurrection, and there would be no rigid distinction. The unity of the passion and victory was what the whole celebration of the Pasch conveyed. The great redeeming action into the benefits of which the candidates were baptized at dawn was the action of the cross and the resurrection. Baptism* took place at the point where the sternness of the fast and vigil yielded to the rejoicing of that hour in which, according to tradition, the Lord rose triumphant over death, and into the joy of which the sorrow of the cross was merged. The sacrament of baptism led at once to the first communion* of the newly baptized. It is to be remembered that the sacrament of the Lord's Supper was essentially a recalling before God of the redeeming work of the Lord in his death and resurrection. This fundamental unity of conception must be grasped so that we may understand the full significance both of the primitive Sunday eucharist and the primitive Pasch.

When Holy Week* developed from the late fourth century onwards, the Easter vigil and eucharist service still retained something of the feel of the original unitive paschal celebration. This great service has four parts which traditionally follow one another in the following order: the lighting of the new fire * and blessing of the paschal candle* together with the singing of the Easter song of praise, the Exultet, the vigil itself, the baptismal liturgy and the Easter eucharist.

The fire and candle ceremonies may well be a combination of material from two sources, a special adaptation for Easter of the usual lighting of the evening candle, the *lucernare*, and a pagan spring festival of lighting a fire to greet the returning light of the new year, possibly Irish in origin, the former being Eastern and general and the latter peculiarly Western. The East lights the vesper light before the beginning of the service and further lights between vigil and eucharist as a theophany, a symbol of God's manifestation.

The West solemnly blesses light as paschal. The Exultet, with its theme of the triumph of Christ over darkness, dates from the seventh century in its present form, and probably originates from north Italy in the fifth. The paschal candle having been lit outside the building, possibly from an actual fire, or at least in the main entrance, it is then carried in procession into the church and set up in the sanctuary. This first part of the service in the West is the least primitive part of the rite and, since its prefix to the vigil, forms a celebratory introduction to the latter.

The vigil is a series of lessons, interspersed with psalms and prayers. Originally it lasted the whole night through from the previous evening to the baptismal and eucharistic liturgies at dawn, so a considerable amount of material was needed for it. The lessons are all drawn from the Old Testament and traditionally there were twelve of them, though recent revisions have tended to reduce their number (the modern Roman rite has seven, and even some of these may be omitted). However, too much shortening and the whole idea of vigil with its sense of expectant waiting will be lost. (*See also* **Paschal Vigil**.)

Whether it is appropriate to have the blessing of the candle before the vigil can perhaps be questioned, in spite of the age of this tradition; after all is not the point of the vigil to await the resurrection, which the paschal candle symbolizes? The service of light could perhaps more logically follow the vigil, and precede the eucharistic readings including the Easter gospel, as the newly proposed Church of England services suggest; this serves to heighten the symbolism of the new light of Easter emerging from the surrounding darkness after the period of waiting and watching (the vigil), though the darkness of the vigil can never be total for some light will be needed to read the vigil lessons by, and even more if there is to be congregational singing.

The baptismal liturgy is a reminder of the era when this was *the* time for baptisms. If an actual baptism, or confirmation*, is fairly rare at the Easter vigil now, it has become the custom for all present to make

a solemn renewal of their baptismal vows*, and modern revisions make provision for this. It is to the Roman revision of the vigil rite in 1951 that we owe this valuable liturgical innovation.

The Easter eucharist itself is the culmination of the rite, is particularly joyful in character, and should anticipate the spirit of the whole of the great fifty days of Eastertide.

Another more difficult problem from a practical point of view is that of timing. It is highly undesirable that the eucharist be celebrated earlier than dawn on Easter Day itself (the resurrection was revealed to the disciples in the dawn, not the middle of the night!) yet an all-night vigil is hardly practical for most people nowadays. Perhaps one solution is to split the service into two parts, with the service of light, vigil and renewal of baptismal vows on the Saturday evening, leaving the eucharist until the Sunday morning.

Reception of communion has always been of obligation at Easter and, in the centuries when lay communion was very rare, it may have been the only occasion of the year when many people actually received communion. The Book of Common Prayer orders that communion be received three times a year, of which Easter is to be one. In an age when the majority of Christians receive communion frequently these provisions seem quaint, but they do underline the supreme importance of Easter in Christian faith and liturgical celebration, and it always needs to be celebrated in ways that will make this as fully apparent as possible to all worshippers.

K. W. Stevenson, 'The Ceremonies of Light – Their Shape and Function in the Paschal Vigil Liturgy', *Ephemerides Liturgicae* 99 (1985), 2, pp.170–85. *See also* bibliographies under **Holy Week**.

R. F. BUXTON

Easter Garden or Sepulchre

The Easter Garden is a model of the holy sepulchre used in the Holy Week* services. Its origins are uncertain; it may have arisen, as did the Christmas crib*, as a more or less spontaneous act of devotion during the early part of the Middle Ages. It took the form of a simple walled recess, a tomb, a vaulted enclosure, a chapel or a temporary structure. On Good Friday*, after vespers, it was the practice to place a cross in the sepulchre to represent the burial of Christ and a candle was lit in front of the shrine. In the thirteenth century, in England and Normandy alone, one of three hosts consecrated at the mass on Maundy Thursday* was also placed in the sepulchre. On Easter Day the cross and/or host was removed to represent the resurrection.

EDITOR

Easter Vigil

see **Paschal Vigil**

Eastward Position

see **Posture** 1

Ecumenical Worship

A convenient phrase to describe types of worship which have evolved as a consequence of the ecumenical movement. That movement, developing gradually throughout this century, has taken many forms, international, national and local, and, throughout its history of drawing together previously separated Christians, common prayer has played a central role. Some of the pioneering experiences were in the context of the World Student Christian Federation (founded 1895), with its early involvement of Eastern Orthodox, as well as Anglicans and Protestants. From the time of the Edinburgh World Missionary Conference in 1910, corporate prayer which involved Christians from widely diverse backgrounds was assumed to be an essential ingredient of such gatherings. Out of Edinburgh 1910 developed the other two organized strands of the ecumenical movement, Life and Work (founded 1926 at Stockholm) and Faith and Order (Lausanne 1927). All three strands eventually merged into the World Council of Churches, and it is in this context that the development of ecumenical worship can be most visibly traced, though of course the experience of shared worship was also widely spread into thousands of local scenes in which the ecumenical fellowship found expression.

Surveying the whole story so far, ecumenical worship may be conveniently classified as 1. comparative and parallel and 2. creative and convergent, though both types are likely to continue to co-exist since

the ecumenical experience is to some extent known afresh in every generation.

1. *Comparative and parallel.* At the Second World Conference on Faith and Order at Edinburgh in 1937 it was perceived that one of the grounds for separation and misunderstanding between the churches was in their 'ways of worship'. Consequently, an international study commission was set up, under the chairmanship of Dr Gerardus van der Leeuw of the Netherlands, to study that subject thoroughly in preparation for the Third World Conference. Its report (delayed by the war) was published in 1951 and consisted primarily of a series of expositions of worship and the understanding of it by well-qualified scholars of the main Christian traditions, Roman Catholic, Orthodox, Anglican and various Protestant traditions including Quakers. This 'comparative ecclesiology' inevitably characterized the earlier phases of the ecumenical movement, for many of the participants were meeting for the first time a living exposition of liturgical life and devotion which was quite unfamiliar. Some of them had already met as students in national or international gatherings of the SCM, where it had become a matter of policy to confront each other with acts of worship (including the Orthodox Holy Liturgy) in which both a unity in Christ and a separation into 'churches' were paradoxically experienced. (This inevitably raised the question of intercommunion*.)

A consequence of this approach to worship was the danger that it might become too much a spectacle, an event at which one was either self-consciously demonstrating 'how we do things in our tradition' or a spectator assessing someone else's 'performance' – a danger only avoided by being aware of it. There was a large area in which un-selfconscious sharing was possible, including hymnody and the classic expressions of diverse piety. Quite early on in the World Student Christian Federation, two publications made this kind of sharing available on a wide scale, *Cantate Domino* (1924), a collection of hymns, and *Venite Adoremus* (1935), a collection of forms of service from various confessions. The former, in a revision of 1980, is still in use at ecumenical gatherings, so that it begins to bridge the gap between the 'comparative' and the 'creative' by being in itself something of a common possession.

Meanwhile, a somewhat hybrid type of worship has also grown up and is frequently met, on occasions both large and small, which is dominated by the desire to be 'representative' of many traditions within the same occasion. Inevitably this means snippets from different sources and voices with many accents in many tongues from speakers of different colours and styles. But with experience something more satisfying emerges, as self-consciousness diminishes and a style of praising God is discovered which increasingly belongs to none and yet to all. As the 1952 *Report on Ways of Worship* concluded: 'Liturgy ... is not something prepared and made by man, as a scientific text book, or even as a novel or a poem is made ... Liturgical renewal is neither emendation nor creation, but an attempt to enter or re-enter the liturgy which has been alive ever since the first liturgy of the Upper Room, from which springs all our sacramental worship, and the synagogue services which are the origin of our preaching-centered worship ... liturgical experiments are attempts to decide where we stand in the Church of God, and what, being where we are, we have to do.'

2. *Creative and convergent.* It may thus be clear that 'ecumenical worship' can not avoid moving from a sharing of unfamiliar ways into a discovery that something new has grown in the process. This has many affinities with the Liturgical Movement* which has itself been ecumenical. The latter half of this century is witnessing much mutual enrichment between the churches and a re-discovery of common origins in liturgy and worship as in other aspects of theology.

More recently, the scene has grown more vivid and complex through the contributions of Christians in Asia, Africa, the Caribbean, Latin America and those affected by the Pentecostal and Charismatic movements (*see* **Pentecostal Worship**). All this is most clearly visible in the Assemblies of the World Council of Churches, especially at Nairobi (1975) and Vancouver (1983).

The most arresting evidence of convergence is in the Faith and Order studies (inheriting those already mentioned) on

Baptism, Eucharist and Ministry. At a meeting of the Faith and Order Commission at Lima (Peru) in 1982 the solid theological consensus on the doctrine of the eucharist was given liturgical expression in a widely agreed text, which was again used as a central act of worship at the Vancouver Assembly, when the Archbishop of Canterbury was the presiding minister. Such a eucharist well exemplifies the paradox of 'ecumenical worship' – it still symbolizes more than it can effect. It is still impossible for Catholics and Orthodox to participate in full eucharistic communion with other Christians in the ecumenical movement, yet they are able today to profess a common faith in a way inconceivable fifty years ago.

See also **Love Feast**.

The History of the Ecumenical Movement, I, ed R. Rouse and S. C. Neil 1950, II, ed H. E. Fey 1970; *The Eucharistic Liturgy*, WCC 1983.

OLIVER TOMKINS

Elder

Etymologically the word is simply the Anglo-Saxon equivalent of presbyter*, though for some curious reason the two terms are thought of as being quite different. Presbyter almost always means an ordained minister: elder refers to an office in the Reformed tradition which is usually described as 'lay' (though there has at times been considerable controversy over whether an elder is ordained or lay). Calvin distinguished between the minister of word and sacrament and the kind of elder who had no such responsibility but was associated with others in the government of the church. This distinction between presbyter/minister and elder has been retained in almost all churches of the Calvinist, Reformed or Presbyterian tradition. The elders belong to the board or session which governs the local congregation. They may have a certain pastoral responsibility for a part of the community and may sit or stand round the minister when he performs his liturgical functions. Representative elders will also be chosen to participate in the higher courts of the church.

J. H. S. Burleigh, *A Church History of Scotland*, 1960; J. Calvin, *Institutes of the Christian Religion*, IV, iii; G. Donaldson, *The Scottish Reformation*, 1960.

P. HINCHLIFF

Elevation

see **Gestures** 4

Ember Days

The designation refers to four groups of three days each in the church's year, ember being either a corruption of the Latin *quatuor tempora* (four seasons) or of the Old English *ymbren* (recurring or periodic). Probably originating in Roman agricultural festivals connected with seedtime, harvest and the vintage, they formed part of the ecclesiastical calendar from at least the fifth century and by *c*. 1100 they were the Wednesdays, Fridays and Saturdays following the first Sunday in Lent, Pentecost, 14 September (Holy Cross Day) and 13 December (St Lucy's Day).

Like Lent*, Ember Days were times of spiritual renewal, with an emphasis upon prayer, fasting and almsgiving and so, while they continued to have an association with the crops, they were also linked with ordination which calls for the united prayer of the whole community and presupposes its spiritual renewal. In adapting these special days of prayer to modern circumstances the Roman Catholic Church has emphasized the importance of taking local conditions into account. According to the *Calendarium Romanum* of 1969, they must be related to different cultures in different parts of the world. Local conferences of bishops are to set aside certain days in the year for prayer for the harvest and for human labour. In England these days are observed in May and September and special mass texts have been provided.

The Church of England has preserved the link with ordination and in the ASB it is stated that 'on these days prayer is offered for all who serve the church in its various ministries, both clerical and lay, and for all who are to be ordained or commissioned to those ministries'. While the mediaeval days are listed, it is also permitted to bishops to observe Ember Days whenever they choose to direct. The BCP of the American Episcopal Church (1979) regards them as 'commemorations' when the common of saints* is to be used.

EDITOR

Enarxis

The name commonly given to the preparatory office of prayer and praise which precedes the liturgy of the word and the eucharist in the Byzantine rite (Greek 'opening' or 'beginning'). It comprises an opening blessing of the Trinity, three litanies* (the first a general intercession, the second and third very brief) each concluding with a collect-like prayer, and three anthems* (one after each litany) which vary somewhat according to the day, and are usually psalms or based on psalms, with additional material proper to the feast or season. The regulations concerning the use of these anthems vary somewhat from one Orthodox national church to another; the concluding prayers of the litanies have since the later Middle Ages, and probably since a much earlier date, been said secretly, except for their concluding doxologies*, a practice which deprives the two lesser litanies of their rationale, their function being simply to act as an introduction to the prayer.

It is difficult to be precise about the origins and antiquity of the enarxis, or of its several parts, the history of which is complicated and disparate. There appears to be no evidence for any part of it in the fifth century, although the greater litany, the first of the three, may well already have been in existence, and used in another place: such would seem to be the conclusion to be drawn from Pope Gelasius' imitation of it, and use of that imitation, at Rome (*see* ***Kyrie***; **Litany**), as well as from other fragmentary evidence. The enarxis certainly existed, in some places and in something like its present form, by the end of the eighth century, while elsewhere it did not attain its full development until as late as the twelfth century. For a considerable period after it came into existence there were many days on which it was omitted, and there are still a few – those when the liturgy is (in theory, and in recent years increasingly in practice) celebrated in the evening, and is therefore combined with vespers (*see* **Canonical Hours**). Nor is it easy to determine how it was originally used, although there are strong indications that it may well have been a stational or processional rite: it certainly was not sung, as it is today, with the celebrant already in the sanctuary before the actual entrance rite, now called the 'little entrance'*, which follows it.

See also **Liturgies** 2.

H. Holloway, *A Study of the Byzantine Liturgy*, 1933, ch. 11; C. Kucharek, *The Byzantine-Slav Liturgy of St John Chrysostom*, 1971, pp.337–80; J. Mateos, *La Célébration de la Parole dans la Liturgie Byzantine*, 1971, pp.27–68.

W. JARDINE GRISBROOKE

Enthronement of Bishops

see **Cathedra**

Entrance, Great

The name now given to the procession of the ministers bringing the gifts of bread and wine to the altar at the beginning of the eucharist proper in the Byzantine rite, together with the rites and ceremonies before and after it. The celebrant* and deacon* go to the prothesis* on the north of the sanctuary*, take up the paten and chalice*, and preceded by acolytes* bearing tapers (and, according to the customs of some of the Orthodox national churches, cross and censer also), leave through the north door of the screen*, proceed down the north aisle and up the nave* (but in most Slav churches this longer procession is omitted) and, after certain intercessory commemorations before the holy doors (the central doors of the screen), re-enter the sanctuary through these doors, and place the gifts on the altar.

See also **Liturgies** 2.

H. Holloway, *A Study of the Byzantine Liturgy*, 1933, pp.76–79; C. Kucharek, *The Byzantine-Slav Liturgy of St John Chrysostom*, 1971, pp.477–503; A. Schmemann, *The World as Sacrament*, 1966, pp.39–42; R. F. Taft, *The Great Entrance*, [2]1978 (the definitive study of the subject).

W. JARDINE GRISBROOKE

Entrance, Little

The name now given to the entrance of the ministers with the book of the gospels at the beginning of the synaxis* or liturgy of the word in the Byzantine rite. Originally the beginning of the service, and therefore a real entrance of the ministers through the church and into the sanctuary*, the prefixing to it of the enarxis* has reduced it to a purely decorative ceremony: the

celebrant*, already in the sanctuary, together with the deacon*, who takes up the book of the gospels, already on the altar, and the acolytes* bearing tapers, leaves the sanctuary through the north door of the screen*, and re-enters it almost immediately through the central doors, the deacon carrying the book of the gospels before him, and replacing it on the altar.

Inevitably, the ceremony having lost its purpose, far-fetched 'symbolic' meanings have been invented to explain it, despite the fact that they in no way correspond either to the action itself, or to the texts which accompany and follow it.

See also **Liturgies** 2.

H. Holloway, *A Study of the Byzantine Liturgy*, 1933, pp.56–59; C. Kucharek, *The Byzantine-Slav Liturgy of St John Chrysostom*, 1971, pp.381–6; J. Mateos, *La Célébration de la Parole dans la Liturgie Byzantine*, 1971, pp.71–90, 123–6; A. Schmemann, *The World as Sacrament*, 1966, pp.35–37.

W. JARDINE GRISBROOKE

Epiclesis

see **Anaphora** 8

Epiphany

The origin of the feast of the Epiphany lies in the Eastern celebration of the incarnation, and its fundamental concern is the epiphany, or theophany, the manifestation, the revelation of God to the world in Jesus Christ.

The date for this feast in the East is 6 January, possibly because this was the original date of the winter solstice in the East, possibly too because it was the pagan festival of the birth of a god. Certainly, as with Christmas* in the West, this was the Christianizing of an existing celebration.

It seems clear from the evidence that originally the Eastern epiphany on 6 January celebrated two things, the birth of Christ (all aspects of it including the visit of the magi), and the baptism of Jesus, and that this remained the case until the late fourth century. Evidence that this was so in Egypt in the period 380–400 comes from John Cassian's *Conferences*, and up to 385 in Antioch from a sermon preached there by John Chrysostom at Whitsun 386, where he makes reference to the Epiphany as the first of the Christmas festivals, commemorating the appearance of God on earth. But by 380 sermons preached by Gregory of Nazianzus in Constantinople make it clear that Christmas was being celebrated there on 25 December. No doubt this was a copying of the Western celebration of Christmas on that date, by then established for half a century or so, and this spread rapidly all over the East in the last quarter of the fourth century. So the incarnation was detached from the baptism in liturgical celebration, with all aspects of the former, including the visit of the magi, being celebrated on 25 December, leaving the original united feast of the Epiphany to commemorate subsequently only the baptism of Christ.

However when the borrowing took place in the other direction, and the West acquired a feast of the Epiphany on 6 January, it did not adopt the Eastern commemoration of the baptism. Instead it separated a part of the Christmas story off for celebration on that date, namely the visit of the magi, and this has been what the West has celebrated at Epiphany ever since.

Nevertheless, in the modern West, the celebration of Christmas Day now totally overshadows 6 January, and Christmas itself is in practice a united feast covering all aspects of the stories surrounding the birth of Jesus including the visit of the magi. In contrast, the Eastern theme of the baptism of Jesus has never been prominent in the West until very recent times. But the traditional Western sequence of gospel readings at the eucharist for the Sundays after the Epiphany is a series of passages that may be said to demonstrate the manifestation of God in Christ, the first two in the series being the story of Christ's visit to the temple in Jerusalem as a boy of twelve years of age and the miracle of turning water into wine at the marriage at Cana in Galilee.

In the liturgical revisions of the last twenty years the West has built the theme of the baptism of Jesus into its Epiphanytide celebrations in the choice of gospels provided for the first Sunday after the Epiphany, in the modern Roman rite, in the proposals of the Joint Liturgical Group, in service books of churches that have largely adopted these proposals, in-

cluding the British Methodist and United Reformed Churches, and in modern Anglican revisions including those of Australia, England and the USA. Thus perhaps it may be said that in this respect the West has finally caught up with the East after a gap of 1600 years. In these modern revisions subsequent Sundays appoint a variety of gospel passages that continue the Epiphany theme in a broad way, as did the traditional series of Epiphanytide Western Sunday gospels.

See also **Calendar**.

J. Gunstone, *Christmas and Epiphany*, 1967.

R. F. BUXTON

Epistle

The term in its strict sense refers to the liturgical reading in the eucharistic celebration of a pericope from any of the NT Epistles, although the term was formerly applied to the first reading of the eucharistic celebration where only two readings (the other being the Gospel) are proclaimed. In such a case it may in fact be from any scriptural source other than the Gospels.

The former Roman Lectionary has only one reading before the Gospel. For this it drew upon the Pauline Epistles for the Sundays throughout the year, except for Paschaltide, when I John, I Peter and James were used. The OT was used for Lenten weekdays and for some of the commons of saints.

The current Roman Lectionary ([2]1981) has three readings on Sundays and major feasts, the Epistle being the second. On Sundays the Epistle is unrelated to the other readings, pursuing the continuous reading of the Pauline Epistles, with James and Hebrews, in a three-year cycle. I Peter, I John and the Apocalypse are read during Paschaltide. On weekdays the first reading alternates every few weeks between OT and NT books, in a two-year cycle.

The Church of England's Alternative Service Book (1980) also has three readings for the eucharist on Sundays and major feasts, but arranged in a two-year cycle. For the nine Sundays before Christmas the Epistle is chosen to fit the first reading from the OT, and from Christmas to Pentecost it is selected to accord with the Gospel. For the rest of the year the Epistle itself governs the choice of OT reading and Gospel, and is itself chosen to illuminate the time of the church, on pilgrimage from Pentecost to Parousia.

At morning and evening prayer the second reading is taken from the NT, so that at each service either a Gospel or another NT book is read. The two-year cycle means that the whole of the New Testament is read in two years.

J. A. Jungmann, *The Mass of the Roman Rite*, rev ed 1959; M. Righetti, *Storia Liturgica* III, [3]1966.

BRIAN NEWNS

Ethiopian Worship

1. *Historical.* The Orthodox Church in Ethiopia was organized by Frumentius in the decade immediately following the council of Nicaea (AD 325). According to Rufinus' narrative, Frumentius was from Syrian Tyre, and must have had his early education in the Syrian Church. He was consecrated bishop by Athanasius of Alexandria (*c.* AD 340), and brought the Alexandrian or Coptic tradition of faith and worship to Ethiopia.

On the foundation of this fully formed Nicene tradition as interpreted by the Church of Alexandria, the nine Syrian monks who came to Ethiopia at the end of the fifth century built a liturgical structure derived from the Coptic * and Syrian * Orthodox traditions which had rejected the Council of Chalcedon (451). During the sixth century the monastic movement spread throughout the country and propagated the faith of the 'Nine Saints'.

A great revival of the Ethiopian Church took place in the fifteenth century under king Zara Yaeqob (1434–68). Many liturgical and theological books were translated from Coptic or Arabic. The sixteenth century Portuguese missions and later Protestant missions have made the Ethiopian Church somewhat hostile towards Western churches.

In 1959, as a result of the efforts of Emperor Haile Selassie, the Ethiopian Church became autocephalous under Patriarch Baselius, after being for some sixteen centuries an integral part of the see of St Mark in Alexandria. The emperor introduced the use of the vernacular * (Amharic) in a few churches, but most parishes still worship in the ancient classical language (*ge'ez*).

2. *Liturgical books*. The main sources for Ethiopic worship are *Sunodos* (Apostolic Canons), *Mets'hafe–Kidan* (The Testament of our Lord), *Didaskalia*, *Feteha Negest* (Nomocanon), *Ser'at-we-tezaz* (Ordinances and Instructions), *Mets'hafe Bahr'i* (The Book of Nature), *Te'aqebe Mestir* (Stewardship of the Mystery). The seventeenth-century liturgical revision resulted in four major liturgical books: *Mets'hafe Qeddase* (Missal), *Mets'hafe Nuzaze* (Manual of Penitence), *Mets'hafe Taklil* (Matrimony) and *Mets'hafe Qandil* (Manual of Unction of the Sick). The missal has two parts, one containing sixteen to twenty anaphorae (*Qeddase*) and another with the psalmody for the eucharist (*Zemmare*), often chanted by choirs specially trained.

In addition there are four books for the canonical daily offices: 1. *Deggwa*, or the antiphonal chants for the whole liturgical year except Lent; 2. *Tsomedeggwa*, containing chants for Lent, but not for Holy Week; 3. *Mawase'et*, an alternate form, less frequently used, of the daily offices; 4. *Me'eraf*, the common order for the daily office.

One could also mention paraliturgical works produced in the monasteries like *Wuddase Mariam* (Praises of Mary) and *Anqetse-Berhan* (Gate of Light).

3. *Eucharistic anaphorae**. Twenty different anaphorae are known, under the names: 1. The Apostles; 2. Our Lord Jesus Christ; 3. Our Lady Mary (by Cyriacus or Qirqos); 4. St Dioscurus; 5. St John Chrysostom; 6. St John the Evangelist; 7. St James the Brother of our Lord; 8. The Hosanna – Liturgy of St Gregory; 9. The Christmas Liturgy of St Gregory; 10. The Anaphora of our Lady Mary by St Gregory; 11. Another Anaphora of our Lady by St Gregory; 12. The 318 Orthodox Fathers of Nicaea; 13. St Basil; 14. St Athanasius; 15. St Epiphanius; 16. The longer St Cyril; 17. The shorter St Cyril; 18. St James of Sarug; 19. St Mark; and 20. Yet another Anaphora of our Lady Mary. Marcos Daoud, the Egyptian layman who was the first director of the Theological School in Addis Ababa, published in 1954 an English version of the pre-anaphora and fourteen anaphorae (Apostles; Our Lord; St John the Evangelist; St Mary; The 318 Fathers; St Athanasius; St Basil; St Gregory; St Epiphanius; St John Chrysostom; St Cyril; St James of Sarug; St Dioscurus and St Gregory II). The Ethiopic and Amharic texts of these also have been published. Many of the anaphorae indicate a Syrian origin, possibly in the Syrian monastery of the Skete in Egypt. The Liturgy of St Mark is not widely used in Ethiopia; only three of the Ethiopic anaphorae are found in the Coptic Church of Egypt (Cyril, Gregory and Basil). There is no reason to believe therefore that the Ethiopian Church simply copied the Egyptian liturgical practice. Elements of Coptic, Syrian and Byzantine liturgical practices are seen in the Ethiopian tradition, but the latter has a personality of its own.

4. *Structure of eucharistic liturgy*. The Ethiopic liturgy has two main parts: 1. the pre-anaphora, common to all the anaphorae; 2. the anaphora proper. The pre-anaphora, which is unusually long, consists of six psalms (Pss. 25; 61; 102; 103; 130; 131), prayers for the cleansing of the celebrants and the vessels, prayers of vesting, the prothesis of the elements (ending with Ps. 117), the enarxis* (the prayers of the oblation, the prayers of the 'wrappings', the prayers for absolution and a long litany of intercession), and then the liturgy of the catechumens (censing of the elements, prayers of intercession for the living and the departed, censing of the priests and people, the three lections from Pauline epistles, Catholic epistles and Acts, the *Trisagion** addressed to Christ and embellished with incarnational epithets; prayers of the gospel, the chanting of an antiphon from the psalms, the blessing of the four quarters of the world, the censing of the gospel, and then the reading of the gospel and a sermon). The pre-anaphora concludes with a long litany of intercession for the church, the catechumens and the people, especially the poor, the dismissal of the catechumens, a creed or confession of faith in the mystery of the Holy Trinity, in the full deity and humanity of Christ, in the goodness of all that is created, about the undefiled nature of marriage and childbirth, a repudiation of circumcision, etc., followed by the *lavabo**, the prayer of salutation and the kiss of peace.

The Ethiopic anaphorae vary considerably in structure. The basic structure is: 1. eucharistic thanksgiving, parallel to the Western canon* up to the words of institu-

tion; 2. prayers of intercession and conclusion of the thanksgiving prayer; 3. *Sanctus* (which is missing in one or two anaphorae); 4. institution narrative (replaced by a prayer in James of Sarug); 5. anamnesis, epiclesis; 6. fraction* and commixture*; 7. Our Father and continuation prayer; 8. inclination of the head and prayer of penitence before communion; 9. elevation of the body and blood for adoration; 10. the communion, during which Ps. 150 is chanted; 11. post-communion thanksgiving and a special prayer called the 'Pilot of the Soul' and 12. the benediction and dismissal with the imposition of the hands of the priest.

5. *Hymnody and music.* Syro-Byzantine and Coptic musical elements must have come to Eithopia as early as the fifth century. But it was Yared, a disciple of the nine Syrian saints who came in the sixth century, who is the father of the distinctive Ethiopian hymnody and musicology. He is regarded by Ethiopian tradition as the author of all the divine offices, and of the system of Ethiopian chant called *zema*, with its three different chants: *ge'ez, 'ezl* and *araraye*. Yared is also credited with being the author of the Ethiopian musical notation system, which uses letters of the alphabet written above syllables to indicate the note.

6. *Liturgical year.* The Ethiopian Church follows the Julian calendar. The year is divided into thirteen months – twelve of thirty days each and one of five or six days. The year commences on 1 Maskaram which corresponds to 11 or 12 September in the Gregorian calendar. The year is seven or eight years behind the Western year (AD 1986 would be 1978 or 79 in the Ethiopian calendar). The major feasts are 1. the nine feasts of our Lord – incarnation, passion, resurrection, appearance to Thomas, ascension, Pentecost, transfiguration, epiphany-baptism, and the miracle of Cana; 2. six secondary feasts – exaltation of the cross, circumcision of the Lord, feeding of five thousand, presentation in the Temple, invention of the cross, and sojourn of Jesus in Egypt; 3. the thirty-two Marian feasts established in the fifteenth century by king Zara Yaeqob; 4. the fifty main feasts of the saints, of the OT and NT, universal and national, including the archangels Michael, Gabriel, and Raphael.

There is also the special peculiarity of the Ethiopian Church – the liturgical *month*, with its eighteen monthly commemorations, four for our Lord, six for Mary and eight for other saints.

7. *Fasting.* The following fasts are observed very strictly in Ethiopia: The great Lent fast (fifty-five days preceding Easter); Advent fast (forty days); the fast of the apostles (from the day after Pentecost till the feast of the Apostles); the fast of Mary; the fast of Nineveh; and Wednesday and Friday each week.

8. *Daily offices.* Forms of the daily offices (*see* **Canonical Hours**), of Ethiopian origin, follow the traditional structure used in all ancient churches. There are forms of vigil (*Wazema*); offices for Sunday (*Mawaddes*); offices for special feasts of saints (*Kestat'aryam*); offices for Lent (*Zaatswam*); daily matins (*Sebhate-nage zazawoter*) and matins for principal feasts (*Sebhate-nage za-ba'alat 'abiyan*). Each office consists of: 1. scriptural praises – the 150 psalms and 15 biblical hymns of the OT and NT; 2. special prayers for the feasts or for seasons; 3. poetic or hymnic elements (*qene*); 4. readings from the scriptures; 5. prayers and invocations.

The main manual for the daily offices is the *Me'eraf*, which has been studied in detail by Bernard Velat in the *Patrologia Orientalis*, XXXIII (1966).

Marcos Daoud, *The Liturgy of the Ethiopian Church* (text of pre-anaphora and fourteen anaphorae in English), 1954; E. Hammerschmidt, *Studies in the Ethiopic Anaphoras*, 1961; S. Mercer, *The Ethiopic Liturgy*, 1915; Bernard Velat, *Études sur le Me'eraf, Common de l'office divin Ethiopien, Patrologia Orientalis* XXXIII, 1966.

PAULOS GREGORIOS

Eucharist

Since the beginning of the second century the term has been used as one of the titles for that rite which is at the heart of Christian worship and which derives its existence from the Last Supper of Jesus with his disciples before his crucifixion. The word comes from the Greek *eucharistia*, 'thanksgiving', and refers to the characteristic prayer-pattern or 'grace' used by Jews before eating or drinking anything, in which they blessed or thanked God, remembering,

confessing, and proclaiming what he had done for his people. Such would have been the forms used by Jesus himself at the Last Supper, and they constitute the source of the eucharistic prayer in later Christian rites.

It is generally agreed by New Testament scholars that the earliest Christian eucharists were in fact complete meals shared together by the local Christian community (*see* **New Testament Worship**). In this corporate act done in remembrance of Christ and in thanksgiving for what God had done through him, his followers experienced the presence of their risen Lord as a living reality, uniting into one body the individuals gathered there, and they looked forward in hope to the final consummation of God's kingdom and the fulfilment of the messianic banquet, of which their meal was a foretaste.

This situation, however, did not last, and before the end of the first century it was already running into difficulties: in a Gentile environment the sacred nature of the meal could easily be lost in the festal atmosphere surrounding it, and anti-social behaviour could emerge, as appears to have been the case at Corinth (*see* I Cor. 11.17f.); periods of persecution and Roman legislation against meetings of clubs could also make it difficult to maintain a full evening assembly; and there were also no doubt practical catering difficulties. It is not so surprising, therefore, that in our earliest full account of eucharistic practice outside the New Testament, given by Justin Martyr at Rome in the middle of the second century, a dramatic transformation has taken place. The eucharistic action (the taking of bread and wine, saying the eucharistic prayer over them, breaking the bread, and distributing both) has now become separated from a meal. It is an early morning service instead of a Sunday evening assembly, and has been prefixed with a synagogue-style liturgy of the word and prayers.

Nevertheless, the eucharist continued to be seen as the corporate action of the local Christian community in which all were involved; and considerable importance was attached to the bread and wine being taken to those unable to be present at the rite, so that they might continue to be able to share in it in some way. Alongside this emphasis on the meal-event as the means by which Christ's presence was experienced, however, there was also a growing emphasis on the food, the bread and wine themselves, as the *locus* of this presence, and consequently on consecration as the means by which this was effected. This developed even more strongly in the period after the conversion of Constantine in the fourth century, when there was a great increase in church membership, and the consciousness of the local church as a tight-knit community began to decline.

This influx of new converts had other effects on the nature of the eucharistic celebration. Because of the fact that many of them had only a limited grasp of the Christian faith and were inclined towards irreverent behaviour at the eucharist, the bishops and clergy began to stress the need for a proper disposition in approaching the sacred mysteries. Unfortunately, far from encouraging a more reverent attitude when receiving communion, it had the opposite effect and discouraged them from the reception of communion altogether, as people judged themselves to be unworthy to be communicants.

Thus, by the end of the Middle Ages the majority of people made their communion no more than about once or twice a year, and attended the service without receiving the sacrament on other occasions. This in turn encouraged the eucharist to be seen not as a meal, not as heavenly food or the medicine of immortality, as formerly, but principally as an object of devotion: the rite had in effect been transformed into a visually dramatic ceremony by which, it was thought, the bread and wine became Christ's body and blood through the action of the priest on behalf of the people, to be worshipped from afar but not approached; and Christ's sacrifice of himself was offered to the Father so that the benefits of his passion might be appropriated by those for whom it was offered, whether present or absent.

The sixteenth-century Reformation in the West sought to restore the eucharist to what was thought to be its New Testament form and purpose – the eating of bread and drinking of wine in thankful remembrance of Christ's death. The Reformers rejected the notion that Christ was in any sense offered in the eucharist; and most, except

for Lutherans and some Anglicans, rejected the idea that any transformation took place in the bread and wine themselves, and generally thought instead that Christ was present only to the worthy communicant through the reception of the elements. All were agreed that there could be no celebration of the eucharist unless a substantial number of the congregation received communion with the minister, and most would have desired to have made it a regular weekly service. However, since they continued to stress the need for worthy reception, they were in general unable to persuade the laity to receive communion much more often than the few times a year to which they had previously been accustomed. Thus eucharistic celebrations tended to become infrequent events in most reformed churches, and were reduced to little more than an 'extra' for the specially devout.

The Liturgical Movement* in the twentieth century has tried to restore the eucharist to the place which it had in early Christian practice, as the central service of the church every Sunday, and as a corporate celebration by the congregation rather than merely an opportunity for individuals to receive communion. In this there has been considerable – if far from complete – success. In some places experiments have also been made in integrating the eucharistic action with a full meal once again.

See also **Anaphora**; **Canon**; **Communion**; **Entrance, Great**; **Entrance, Little**; **Eucharistic Sacrifice**; **Exposition**; **Fraction**; **Gestures**; **Intercommunion**; ***Kyrie***; ***Lavabo***; **Liturgies**; **Love Feast**; **Oblation**; **Offertory**; **Presanctified Mass**; **Proper**; **Prothesis**; ***Sanctus***; **Synaxis**; **Votive Mass**; **Words of Administration**.

Donald Bridge and David Phypers, *The Meal that Unites?*, 1981; L. Bouyer, *Eucharist: Theology and Spirituality of the Eucharistic Prayer*, 1968; Y. Brilioth, *Eucharistic Faith and Practice: Evangelical and Catholic*, 1930; G. J. Cuming, *He Gave Thanks: An Introduction to the Eucharistic Prayer*, 1981; J. G. Davies, 'The Introduction of the Numinous into the Liturgy: an historical note', *Studia Liturgia* 8, 1971/2, pp.216–223; Lucien Deiss, *It's the Lord's Supper: Eucharist of Christians*, 1980; G. Dix, *The Shape of the Liturgy*, 1945; David Gregg, *Anamnesis in the Eucharist*, 1976; R. P. C. Hanson, *Eucharistic Offering in the Early Church*, 1979; T. Klauser, *A Short History of the Western Liturgy*, 1969; G. A. Michell, *Landmarks in Liturgy*, 1961; Nathan Mitchell, *Cult and Controversy: The Worship of the Eucharist Outside Mass*, 1982; Geoffrey Wainwright, *Eucharist and Eschatology*, 1971; Rowan Williams, *Eucharistic Sacrifice – the Roots of a Metaphor*, 1982.

PAUL F. BRADSHAW

Eucharistic Prayer

see **Anaphora**

Eucharistic Sacrifice

The way in which eucharistic liturgies expressed themselves in sacrificial terms does not appear to have been questioned in the West until the Reformation, and there has been no comparable controversy in the East which has had any major liturgical consequences. Thus, the eucharistic liturgies of the mediaeval East and West are rich (but often imprecise) in their use of sacrificial metaphors. For example, the *Didache* (ch. 14) describes the eucharist* on three occasions as a sacrifice, in the context of right relationships in the Christian community. However, when the later texts begin to appear, sacrifice and offering are variously treated in the anaphora*. One strand (represented by Hippolytus' *Apostolic Tradition*, and the classical texts of Basil of Caesarea, John Chrysostom, and James) use an offering-verb in the present-tense, in conjunction with the anamnesis ('remembering . . ., we offer'); and Basil, Chrysostom and James also use offering language at the epiclesis and the intercession. Another strand (represented by the old Syriac tradition of Addai and Mari, and the Syrian Jacobite and Maronite anaphoras) are more imprecise still, and while they may not use an offering-verb at all in conjunction with the anamnesis, they will still have one at the epiclesis and/or intercession; sacrifice and eucharist are not closely identified. Yet another strand 'offers' the eucharistic sacrifice in the preface and uses a past-tense verb of offering in the anamnesis (Greek Mark and Coptic Cyril; compare Serapion). (There is a complication in the Basil tradition, in that the early Coptic fragment has the Egyptian past-tense verb at the an-

amnesis; the later Alexandrian version follows, in this regard, Chrysostom and James; but the later Byzantine version adds an offering of praise in the preface in terms similar to Greek Mark.)

In the West, the Roman canon*, which may be distantly related to the anaphora in Hippolytus' *Apostolic Tradition*, opts for a series of sacrificial formulae which dominate the whole prayer, whereas in all the Eastern prayers, offering is but one ingredient among many (e.g. salvation-history, epiclesis, kingdom, intercession). The ancient Gallican and Visigothic anaphoras use strong sacrificial language at times, but within an anaphora made up of variable parts; many of these texts reflect a confidence in the use of typological formulae in eucharistic sacrifice from the Old Testament, but they are often off-set by an insistance on the unique character of the work of Christ. In the Mediaeval West, however, the development of offertory prayers (e.g. the 'Orate, fratres'), together with the increase in the number of private masses, served to strengthen even more the sacrificial character of the eucharist; many of these prayers (which Gregory Dix called 'Stratum 3', along with other private prayers in the mass) had rich sacrificial images and meanings. In the East, no such emphasis on offertory is to be found, for the ceremony of the Great Entrance*, while impressive and rich in symbolism, is a solemn transfer of the gifts from the prothesis to the throne (or altar), and no more.

At the Reformation, the liturgical projects of Luther, Zwingli, Calvin, Cranmer, and others either reduced considerably or eliminated altogether any prayers which implied eucharistic sacrifice, except in referring to the unique work of Christ and the self-offering of the worshippers. However, so embedded was the offertory as a preparatory act with symbolic overtones, that some rites (mainly Anglican) began to build upon the preparation of the gifts as a means of reintroducing what had been lost; the Scottish Episcopal rites of 1637 and 1764 are key-points in this regard, the rite of 1764 even introducing words of oblation into the anamnesis, 'these gifts, which we now offer unto thee'. The recovery of eucharistic hymnody through the Wesleys, the Tractarian Movement, and the revival of eucharistic worship, with its emphasis on the offertory procession earlier this century have all served to bring back the symbolism of offering, in different ways, though Reformation self-consciousness lingers, as instanced by the controversy in the Church of England over the words 'we offer this bread and this cup' in the draft Series 2 Communion rite in 1966.

The Roman Missal of 1970 keeps many of the traditional Western emphases, but the new eucharistic prayers (2, 3, and 4) deal with sacrifice in a more imprecise and Eastern way, and the offertory prayers are simpler in their language. Non-Roman rites, by contrast, tend to have a formal offertory, but tend also to handle sacrifice in the anaphora with a certain circumspection. (Compare the 1982 Lima Liturgy with the 1952 South India Liturgy.) Contemporary eucharistic theology finds sacrifice only as a result of more central themes such as memorial, kingdom, supper, reconciliation, and the self-offering of the faithful in the service of its Lord. Old controversies are seen more as differences of emphasis, as renewal in eucharistic worship and life becomes more and more an ecumenical exercise.

Texts in R. C. D. Jasper and G. J. Cuming (eds), *The Prayers of the Eucharist Early and Reformed*, 1980, and M. Thurian and G. Wainwright (eds), *Baptism and Eucharist – Ecumenical Convergence in Celebration*, 1983. For studies of texts and theological implications, see Kenneth Stevenson, *Eucharist and Offering: a Liturgical Study*, 1986; see also Stevenson, '"Anaphora Offering" – some observations on Eastern Eucharistic Prayers', *Ephemerides Liturgicae* 94, 1980, pp.209–228; and 'Eucharistic Offering: does research into origins make any difference?', *Studia Liturgica* 15, 1982/3, pp.22–37.

KENNETH STEVENSON

Evensong

see **Canonical Hours**

Exorcism, Exorcist

The practice of exorcism depends on the belief that persons and things may be subject to evil or diabolic power, and that this power may be driven out through the words and actions of the exorcism rite. The ancient Assyrians, Babylonians and Egyp-

tians practised exorcism, and it is also found in late Judaism, cf. Tobit 6.8; 8.2; Mark 9.38; Luke 11.19; Acts 19.13. The Gospels mention Jesus exorcizing on numerous occasions; he gave his disciples power to exorcize, cf. Matt. 10.1, and we find Paul exorcizing in Christ's name in Acts 16.18.

In the Christian church the power to exorcize was initially seen as a charismatic gift. This view survived in the East until the end of the fourth century at least, but in Rome in the middle of the third century the exorcistate is listed as one of the minor orders. This was the case until recently in the Roman Catholic Church, whose clerics received the order of exorcist on their way to the priesthood, without, however, exercising this order.

Exorcism played an important part in the preparation of catechumens* for baptism*, besides being used to assist those thought to be possessed by the devil. The water, salt and oil used in the rites of exorcism came to be exorcized themselves, before they were blessed. The rites of exorcism varied greatly in length and content. They usually involved prayers, commands to the devil to leave the afflicted person, and the imposition of the exorcist's hands on the person. Signs of the cross and anointing with oil were also sometimes used, as was aspersion with blessed water, and the imposition of the exorcist's stole.

The Roman Catholic Church's new rite for the Christian Initiation of Adults (1972) has omitted the exorcisms presented in the previous rite, which directly addressed the devil or evil spirit. Instead it has three exorcisms, used in three successive services or scrutinies, which ask God to free the catechumen from the spirit of evil or falsehood. In addition there is an optional exorcism in the entrance rite to the catechumenate, which may be used where the false worship of spiritual powers flourishes, involving magic or calling on ghosts. Minor exorcisms, prayers for the deliverance of the catechumens from evil and sin, also feature in the celebrations of the word of God held during the catechumenate.

The rite for the baptism of infants contains only one exorcism, for which there is a choice of two prayers. Both of these refer to Satan or 'the devil'; the first prays that the child be set free from original sin, and the second that he be brought out of the power of darkness.

All of these prayers are to be distinguished from traditional exorcisms which address the devil directly. These are addressed to God and do not really differ from other prayers. Even when the devil is mentioned in them, the prominence is no longer given to him but rather to God and his saving work. This trend is confirmed by the abandonment of the old practice of exorcising material things before blessing them. The exorcising of people troubled by the devil seems to have virtually disappeared.

The Orthodox Church uses exorcism in preparation for baptism and where diabolic possession is suspected. In the Church of England's baptismal rite the pre-baptismal exorcism, retained in the first BCP of 1549, was omitted in the 1552 BCP in response to Bucer's criticism that it implied all unbaptized persons were demoniacs. No other exorcisms were included in the BCP, yet the practice survived, for in 1604 Canon 72 forbade Anglican clergy to exorcize without episcopal permission. Exorcism is uncommon in the Church of England today.

---

1. Texts: L. C. Mohiberg (ed), *Liber Sacramentorum Romanae Ecclesiae* (*Gelasian Sacramentary*), 1960; *Rituale Romanum*, 1614, *Titulus XII*; C. Vogel (ed), *Le Pontifical Romano-Germanique du dixième siecle*, 11, 1963; *The Rites of the Catholic Church*, 1976. 2. Studies: J. Forcet, 'Exorcisme', *DTC*, V, cols, 1762–80; C. Harris, 'Visitation of the Sick', *Liturgy and Worship*, ed W. K. Lowther Clarke, 1932; C. Jones, G. Wainwright and E. Yarnold (eds), *The Study of Liturgy*, 1978, pp.79–146; A. G. Martimort (ed), *Introduction to the Liturgy*, 1968; F. Procter and W. H. Frere, *The History of the Book of Common Prayer*, 1901; M. Righetti, *Storia Liturgica*, IV, [2]1959.

BRIAN NEWNS

Experimental Forms of Worship

I recall once when I was at Green Lake, Wisconsin, for a conference, and we had a folk singing in the lobby. Christians were gathering together singing for joy. We sang 'We Shall Overcome', a song that expresses the hope which is part of God's *shalom*. Then we sang about God's

drowning the Egyptians, 'Pharaoh's Army Got Drowned', and 'He's Got the Whole World in His Hands'. These songs were very good theology. Then someone said, 'Oh-oh! Time for the worship service.' We all filed out over to the vesper circle, the organ came in with its tremolo, and we sang some songs about our own souls. That was supposed to be 'worship'. But it wasn't!

That is how the Baptist theologian Harvey Cox describes in his *God's Revolution and Man's Responsibility* (1969, p.84) an experience which most Christians have had. There are everyday experiences which have a dimension of worship, and formal worship services which appear very ordinary and boring. Yet it is not true that worship is out of favour. What is out is the present way of conducting worship. Worship has ceased to be *une expérience*, as the French understand the word, i.e. an experience which includes the risk of an experiment. That is what is meant by experimental forms of worship. But this is in fact a pleonasm. Worship is either experimental (in the sense of being a real experience and in the sense that in this experiment one never knows what is coming next) or it is not worship at all. The reason for this is that in worship one expects God himself to act. And who can pretend to prejudge his actions? 'Worship is an activity freely undertaken, but its outcome is by no means known in advance' (J. G. Davies).

That worship is not rejected can be seen from the fact that even today secular forms of celebration are continually being invented (*see* **Secularization and Worship**). In an enquiry which was made in the autumn of 1968 among the personnel of the Ecumenical Centre in Geneva it became evident that in principle even the critical observers still expected something from the weekly worship service. 'I keep hoping for something better', said one. And another one was 'sad and sometimes irritated because of the verbal impotence'. People asked for fellowship. They wanted to learn to pray, 'but then scarcely anyone knows how to pray in this day and age, and the clergy are as weak in this as anyone'. We have forgotten how to pray! Responsive prayers are 'almost never true reflections of our lives', particularly if they must be read at breath-taking speed. So the prayers on paper prevent the prayers of heart and body, in which one could find and articulate one's own job, sorrows, joys and faith (or the faith of one's church). So the questions remain: How can we pray together without trying to teach each other theology? How can there be an intensive silence full of content from which well up intercession, praise, celebration and mutual care? People ask – according to this enquiry – for intelligible, interpretative information. They are looking for mutual help and tolerence. There was no question of secularism breaking into the Ecumenical Centre, of the rejection of the gospel, although many of the staff do not attend worship.

Many other enquiries produce similar results. Section V of the WCC's Assembly at Uppsala (so far the only section at a WCC Assembly which examined worship as a topic) had the task of dealing with worship in a secular age, but it camouflaged the problem by the alliteration: 'Worship, for a Christian, is not a problem but a privilege' (*Drafts for Sections*, p.97). The hiatus between secular and sacred liturgies – it proposed – should be overcome by education. People should be adapted, conditioned and shaped for the liturgy of the church, so that the church does not need to change. The document adopted at Uppsala was no better than the draft, except that it proposed a Faith and Order Consultation on 'Worship in a Secular Age'. The *status quaestionis* was formulated by Lukas Vischer as follows:

> The main questions were how to worship and how to worship together. The present generation, however, is less concerned with modes and ways. It rather raises the more radical question as to whether it is possible at all. How can we, as men, speak of God and, even more difficult, speak to God? How can we meaningfully pray? All forms of worship are equally challenged by these questions and in the face of these new challenges it is clear that the differences between the various traditions cannot claim more than secondary importance (*Worship and Secularization*, p.1).

Indeed, one can go a step further, saying that in worship the difference between those who are commonly called believers and

those who are commonly called unbelievers is secondary. This lesson I learnt from a group of agnostic nuclear researchers. They wanted to organize a worship service. The topics which were proposed to them (Faith and Technology, Art and Technology, etc.) did not interest them. They concentrated on one question, saying: 'We do not believe in God. But we want you to teach us to pray.' These are the people who pray, even when they believe they do not believe. Research into popular unbelief in Birmingham has resulted in similar conclusions. Most of these unbelievers have very vague or no ideas about God – but they pray privately and in secret. One may rightly ask: What has happened to public prayer in the Christian liturgy, that it cannot welcome these unbelievers who cannot square their ideology with their prayer? (*See* **Community and Worship**.)

It seems that the Indian theologian Raymond Panikkar has hit the nail on the head when he describes the societal function of worship like this: 'Only worship can prevent secularization from becoming inhuman, and only secularization can save worship from being meaningless.' 'Probably one of the reasons (effect or cause, I leave it open) of the crisis of the United Nations organization is that it could not or did not know how to develop a really common and thus universal and meaningful liturgy, cult, worship' (*Worship and Secularization*, pp.28, 53). And the German theologian Will Adam, in describing Jesus' practice of worship, came to the conclusion that he not only broke the social and political taboos of his time, but violated – in order to do the will of God – what at that time people considered to be the will of God. In celebrating communion with people who were excluded from communion, he defined what he considered to be worship. That is experimental worship in the truest sense! Adam even thinks that worship was the most efficient instrument for mission, because it celebrated the overcoming of segregation (between slaves and free people, rich and poor, men and women), which in their society was considered impossible, immoral or both. Nobody can measure the power worship could regain, if we were to take up once more this original experimental dimension, which at the moment we have frozen with memories of past experiences.

New forms of worship do not need to justify themselves any more. They are not the hobby of liturgical playboys. But if they relate mainly to jazz attractions as the worms on the church extension hook to draw the fish into the empty ecclesiastical aquarium, then they are just brushed-up varieties of worship, which are wrongly understood as Christian duty or religious matinees, instead of being the worship 'which the world needs as badly as its daily bread' (Adam), 'the reasonable worship' (Paul).

The question is not to change instruments and words, although this is in many cases necessary and overdue. The question is, how to celebrate communion in the face of the real segregations of this world, how to celebrate hope amid despair, instead of creating artificial barriers by confessional frontiers and then trying to overcome them by so-called intercommunion.

Such a celebration cannot happen unless liturgy becomes an event of the whole people of God and even of those who believe they do not believe. The methods and tools for this 'liturgical alphabetization' of the people of God cannot be described in detail here. They can probably be transmitted by literature only very incompletely, just as one cannot learn to make a film or to produce a play by reading a book on film-making or play-producing.

Some theological colleges incorporate courses on the technique of such services into their pastoral training. There are two main models for creating such services. 1. The liturgist (clergy or lay) devises a liturgy with 'windows', i.e. with spaces in the liturgy for spontaneous responses, questions, contributions from the congregation in words, song or dance. An example is the Roman mass in Latin American basic communities; the liturgy is 'opened up' to congregational participation for personal and political comments, testimonies, prayers and thanksgivings. 2. The liturgist works with a representative group of people. About half should come from the worshipping congregation, the other half from non-churchgoing members of the same geographical area (*see* **Community and Worship**). This latter point is very important because it opens up a dialogue

between churchgoers and non-churchgoers; because these non-churchgoers will invite their friends and relatives to a service in which they contribute, the worshipping congregation will become more representative of the whole population.

When one works according to model 2, it is important first to discuss and then formulate a mutually acceptable topic. People have to be helped to concentrate on those issues which really preoccupy them and not on those which they think the church will be interested in. Then one has to find out what gifts in liturgy, music, language and dance the people present can contribute to the worship. The topic is then broken down into sub-topics and distributed to subgroups along the lines of the available gifts. Finally the liturgical expert has to help the participants towards an emerging worship which is not just a kind of religious variety programme but a worship which grows into a liturgy with its inner drama. While it is important in this process that his liturgical expertise is fed into the process, it is equally vital that the group leader does not dominate the process. In no case should he have a completed liturgy up his sleeve in case the group feels unable to create its own. This attitude kills the creativity of the group. One has to trust that they will eventually produce something. In a case of conflict between the liturgical expert and the participants it is more important to follow the people's ideas than the rules of liturgical expertise.

Liturgies where the whole people of God shared their Christian and non-Christian traditions including their personal and collective sufferings and joys, were tried out at the World Mission Conference of the WCC at Bangkok (1971/72) and later boldly explored at the Full Assembly of the WCC at Nairobi (1975) and Vancouver (1983) as well as at the biennial German Evangelical Kirchentage. The celebration for the conferment of the Certificate of Theology at the University of Birmingham (which was created mainly for the many black pastors in England) is – in spite of its formal setting and preparation – becoming an experimental worship service in the way defined above, as the congregation is invited to join in with prayer, song and dance and particularly as the conflicting ideas on Christianity and culture are unashamedly shared around the communion table. Police commissioner and black revolutionary pastor, Anglican bishop and Senior Apostle of the Cherubim and Seraphim Society, university dons and worker pastors, men and women, black and white are able to celebrate and disagree together.

A great wealth of liturgies, new music, songs and hymns is being created and published all over the world. Musical elements from Latin America, black and charismatic traditions blend with the chanson tradition of Western and Eastern Europe, where the new Christian song is playing an increasingly important part. *Music from Taizé* (1983) is a good guide for the expert and the beginner.

Experimental worship as a free-for-all is a misunderstanding which is as common as it is wrong. Participation by the worshippers demands a framework, a set of rules. It demands as in play 'a balance between freedom and rules' (J. G. Davies). Rightly Davies and Killinger stress the parallels between play and worship. Liturgy is in fact 'the playing of the church' (Rahner). 'A properly conceived liturgical opportunity in the contemporary church should offer the worshipper a chance to play the fool without actually saying so in so many words' (Killinger). That is why laughter, dance*, the body, and touching are being rediscovered as elements of liturgy, including the laying on of hands for the sick in a public service. If we abstain from touching each other we may never be touched by God. If that means taking risks, so be it. The trouble with most of Christianity is that it has 'destroyed our power to touch and experience the sacred through limited and controlled transgression' (Richard Coe, *The Vision of Jean Genet*, 1968, pp.37f).

The following example of an experimental service is already dated and has its weaknesses, e.g. it does not contain enough of the 'bodily' (although there is some of it) and hardly any 'laughter'-elements. But then it was a service for Thanksgiving Day in Geneva, the nearest celebration in Switzerland to the British and American Remembrance Day. To experiment with such public, holy and highly emotional liturgies takes as much courage as those responsible for organizing the service after the Falkland war needed when they

transformed a Victory Service into a Repentance Service.

As is the custom on a Swiss Thanksgiving Day, the parishioners wore black at the Sunday morning service. But what a strange smell in the church! Surely, it was the smell of freshly-brewed coffee? And there were present Italian and Spanish waiters, greeting everyone as they came into the church and offering them a cup of hot coffee.

During the prelude, the *Kyrie* from the *Misa Criolla*, Italian and Spanish waiters, some Swiss participants and a pastor processed through the church. They were carrying bread and wine for the Lord's Supper, but also a big bag of coffee beans, which was emptied on the altar. Then the foreigners led the service in Italian and Spanish, sometimes with a translation for the Swiss congregation.

First came the *coffee*. Every person received a little bag of coffee. The Spanish layman explained to the congregation how much the Brazilian coffee worker was earning for his work; only enough to feed himself and his family during eight months, even if the harvest is good. For the rest of the year he must suffer from hunger. He only survives by begging and by taking odd jobs.

The bread: an Italian read the famous story by Ignazio Silone of the picture of the Lord's Supper. The Christ in the picture of the eucharist in the church at Fontamara has a piece of wheat-bread in his hand, not maize-bread such as the poor farmers of Southern Italy have to eat. Maize-bread is for the farmers, for the pig and goats. But Christ has a real piece of bread and says: this – the wheat-bread – this is my body. The one who has wheat-bread has me, he has God. The one who does not eat it, is like the pigs and the goats. And the Italian finished: how could we help thinking of wheat-bread, when we work day and night to produce the wheat-bread of the rich but never eat it?

A Spanish worker told the story of the Roman Catholic Bishop of Cuernavaca in Mexico. He had removed all the images of saints from the church, except one of Mary, pointing to the Crucified. Even the tabernacle was removed. In its place a table was brought into the church for the actual celebration of the eucharist, as in Zwingli's liturgy. The body of the Lord is present in Cuernavaca, when the people of God celebrate the Lord's Supper, when the believers are *sola gratia* transformed into the body of the Lord.

The Bishop of Cuernavaca trains the workers and Indians, so that they can understand the revolutionary undertones of the Lord's Supper. That is why they go to their directors and landowners and talk with them about the Lord's Supper: 'How is it that we are equal partners at the Lord's table, but not at the conference table?'

'*The cup* is the new covenant' (Luke 22.20), the new covenant which the Father has created through his Son between himself and men and between men of all classes and nations. The Swiss parishioner who introduced the cup, mentioned the eucharistic hymn by J. C. Lavater which the congregation had just sung. J. C. Lavater knew what he was doing, when he made the new covenant the topic of his eucharistic hymn. He was pastor at St Peter's in Zürich during the French occupation of Switzerland. Lavater had the courage to live the new covenant, because he believed in it. He had to pay for his belief with his own life. He tried to protect a fellow citizen who was persecuted by a French soldier. The bullet which should have hit his fellow-citizen killed him.

Sermon. The pastor preached for five minutes (in a Reformed service!) in French (which was the common language) on Levi. But not many words were necessary after the congregation had introduced themselves and their foreign fellow human beings into the right context. Levi was an outsider in his society. But when Jesus came to him, he organized a feast for his friends and neighbours with Jesus at the centre. The text does not say that Jesus preached at this feast, but he was the occasion for the feast. Such a feast, the pastor said, we are going to celebrate now.

During the distribution of the Lord's Supper the congregation received cards. They were invited to answer the question: what can we do so that the Brazilians may receive more money for their coffee, so that the people from Southern Italy can eat enough bread, so that the outsiders in our society (both Swiss and foreigners) are not put aside? What are the things in our world which the Lord's Supper changes? The comments of the congregation (published

later in the church bulletin) were resumed in the final prayer, a real 'collect' and not the usual pre-written prayer which goes by the name of collect. About half of the people did not react to the question given them, but expressed their thoughts on this form of the Lord's Supper. One woman wrote: 'During the whole week we have to hear these foreign languages. Why should they bother us again in church?' Others confessed that for the first time in their life they had experienced the real presence of the Lord. A Spaniard wrote in impossible Spanish orthography: 'I thank the Lord for the privilege of celebrating the Lord's Supper with my Swiss brethren.'

Harvey Cox, *The Feast of Fools: A Theological Essay on Festivity and Fantasy*, 1969; J. G. Davies, *New Perspectives on Worship Today*, 1978; W. J. Hollenweger, *Conflict in Corinth*, 1983; John Killinger, *Leave it to the Spirit. A Handbook for Experimental Worship*, 1971 (many examples); WCC, *Risk* V, no.1, 1969; Wiebe Vos (ed), *Worship and Secularization*, 1970.

W. J. HOLLENWEGER

Exposition

The earliest form of exposing the sacrament to the people was, from the fourth century at least, at the invitation to communion*. Until the thirteenth century this was the only point in the Western eucharist* that the people were invited to gaze on the elements and reverence them. But from *c.*1200, beginning in Paris, the elements were also elevated after the words of institution in the canon*, and this soon became in effect the ritual climax of the mass, and in many ways a substitute for communion for a people deprived of aural and sacramental participation. It is recorded that people went from church to church to witness elevations, fought each other for better vantage points, and beseeched the priest to prolong the moment.

But exposition probably had other sources besides this, such as the custom of showing the elements to the dying, seemingly as a visual substitute for viaticum*, and above all in the development of the feast of Corpus Christi* and its procession in the late thirteenth and early fourteenth centuries. Not until the close of the fourteenth century do we find evidence for the exposition of the sacrament independently of the liturgy in a monstrance*, and this may well have derived from the German manner of reservation in a 'sacrament-house', which often had a glass window or open grille enabling the sacrament to be seen at all times. In the fourteenth century prominent churchmen and theologians like Nicholas of Cusa and Jean Gerson expressed serious reservations about these forms of extra-liturgical exposition, and provincial councils and synods warned repeatedly against excesses.

With the Counter Reformation, it became most popular in the two forms known as Benediction* and Forty Hours Devotion*, and in the Baroque and subsequent periods, the principal altars of churches were designed in such a way that a 'throne' for the monstrance, high above the tabernacle*, often came to dominate the interior. Although in this period exposition was subjected to canonical regulation, it was not until the mid-twentieth century that the Roman authorities definitively accepted it into the official books of the liturgy.

In 1973 the Roman Ritual provided for the first time official guidelines for all forms of exposition and devotion to the eucharist, all of which, it insists, must be seen in clear and proper relation to the mass. They derive from it, must be in harmony with it, and should lead the faithful back to it. 'They prolong the union with Christ which the faithful have reached in communion, and invite us to the spiritual union with him which culminates in sacramental communion.' The arrangement and conduct of exposition should carefully exclude 'anything which might obscure the principal desire of Christ in instituting the eucharist, namely to be with us as food, medicine, comfort'. Accordingly, the celebration of mass during exposition is forbidden, a single genuflexion is made before the exposed sacrament, the monstrance should normally stand on the altar table itself rather than on a distant pedestal, and the same number of candles are deployed as at mass. The host used should have been consecrated at the most recent mass in the church.

During the exposition there should be prayers, songs and readings; a homily may be given, and periods of silent prayer should be observed. Part of the liturgy of the hours

may be celebrated. Exposition concludes with benediction. The normal minister is a priest or deacon, but in their absence an acolyte*, special minister of the eucharist or specially designated religious may expose the sacrament but not make the concluding blessing with it. Priests and deacons wear an alb (or surplice) with stole, and for the concluding benediction a cope and humeral veil (*see also* **Vestments**).

Roman Ritual: *Worship of the Eucharist*, 1973; N. Mitchell, *Cult and Controversy: The Worship of the Eucharist outside Mass*, 1982.

C. J. WALSH

Extempore Prayer

Spontaneous prayer composed at the time of utterance, though possibly with some preparation. The NT implies (e.g. I Cor. 14) that the ability thus to pray is a gift of God. In the early church the eucharistic prayer was often thus composed by those competent to do so, but according to a fixed pattern. The clearest example is in the *Apostolic Tradition* of Hippolytus, X: 'Let each one pray according to his own ability.' But in course of time the formulae became fixed, and the invention of printing favoured uniformity. In traditional liturgies only a few parts survived where some spontaneity was permitted, e.g. the insertion of names into intercessions.

After the Reformation in England, whereas all Puritans disapproved of the imposition of conformity to the BCP, some favoured the production of Puritan liturgies, but others were opposed to all set forms, and conducted a considerable polemic against them. Some even argued that the Lord's Prayer was given only as a model, and was not intended for actual repetition. The objection to read prayers was based on Rom. 8.26; the promised help of the Holy Spirit was to be obtained at the moment of utterance. It was also thought that set prayers could not meet the varying needs of congregations, that they quenched a gift of God, and that their use was hypocritical and insincere. In reply it was pointed out that not all ministers have the gift of extempore prayer, that it is not always easy for a congregation to follow extempore prayer, and that many extempore prayers are florid and ostentatious. This controversy, which incidentally has somewhat distorted the meaning of the word 'liturgical', often taken to mean 'fixed, stereotyped', has never been entirely resolved in the English Free Churches and in the Church of Scotland. Apart from the Society of Friends, they have now not merely directories, but liturgical books, whether official, as among Presbyterians and Methodists, or unofficial, as among Congregationalists and Baptists; yet these books are guides, not rigidly binding. Many ministers judiciously alternate both methods. It is also possible to combine the two methods as by writing a prayer suitable to a particular occasion, or by composing as one utters it a prayer which nevertheless follows a fixed pattern as in the early church. Probably on the whole extempore prayer is declining in Free Churches. Pentecostal churches, however, make extensive use of free prayer in their services. (*See* **Pentecostal Worship**.) Similarly, in the mainstream churches of all denominations those who are influenced by the charismatic movement use free prayer. Sometimes this occurs in the course of charismatic prayer meetings; sometimes it influences the style of regular services of worship. Sometimes people pray collectively, which is called praying in concert. The leader invites the assembly to pray for a certain person or cause, and everyone prays audibly but quietly in his or her own way. The muttered words are said to be like the sound of a power house.

Meanwhile, quite apart from this, the churches with more traditional liturgies are rapidly adopting more flexible methods, especially in the intercessions of the eucharist. The English Anglican BCP of 1928 had a rubric: 'Note: that subject to any direction which the Bishop may give, the Minister may, at his discretion, after the conclusion of Morning or Evening Prayer, or of any Service contained in this Book, offer prayer in his own words.' New Roman Catholic services often have many permitted alternatives and often the rubrics attached to homilies contain the phrase 'or in like words'. These are similar tendencies and may encourage extempore prayer.

See also **Books, Liturgical; Prayer Meeting**.

A. RAYMOND GEORGE

Family Services

'Family Services' are a relatively recent phenomenon in the churches of the Western Protestant tradition, and they can best be defined by looking at the two areas of liturgical life which have suffered most over the past fifty years. The first is the decline of worship at home, and the second is the decline of the non-eucharistic service, which used to draw into church many people who were not communicants, but who wanted 'something' to feed their spiritual life (e.g. Anglican evensong). Many reasons can be given for both these declines, negative (domestic piety) as well as positive (revival of eucharistic worship).

In Anglicanism, the office (at least on a Sunday) was for a long time a 'popular' service, in that it was never allowed to become the exclusive property of the clergy. Despite the decreasing congregations at evensong over the years in parish churches on Sunday nights, there is still a lingering tradition that the office belongs to the whole people of God. In Britain, the provisions of the Joint Liturgical Group (*The Daily Office* [1] 1968 and [2] 1978) are a good example of the way the traditional office of the Anglican/Methodist traditions has been made more simple, and more flexible, for many different uses, including in the home. The new *Roman Catholic Daily Office* (ET 1974, 3 vols) is a bold revision, partly intended to popularize the office among lay people; the abbreviated single-volume *Morning and Evening Prayer* is used by many clergy and laity (including those outside the Roman Catholic Church), partly because of its relative simplicity when compared with the JLG *Daily Office* (everything is printed out in full, so that the reader needs no lectionaries and psalters), and partly because of its richness (many antiphons, and litanies of intercession). In the USA, the *Lutheran Book of Worship* (1978) contains several different forms of worship for daily use, including morning and evening prayer, and these are described as 'suitable for family or small group devotion'. The Episcopal Book of Common Prayer (1979) revises the traditional hours and makes them more flexible and variable, but also adds a whole section entitled 'Daily Devotions for Individuals and Families', which follow the structure of the more normal offices, but are simpler, and consist of a short portion of psalmody, and short reading, with provision for hymnody as well, and concluded by prayer. These are really 'little hours' for modern (rapid) use. The Episcopal Church, always the liturgical pioneer, also provides for festal services at home in its *Book of Occasional Services* (1979); these include lighting the Advent wreath, blessing homes at Epiphany, blessing food and homes at Easter.

In a completely different ethos, many extended families and communities have developed their own styles of daily prayer, which vary from those which are easily adapted for use with children, to those exclusively for adults. The form and structure of all these services (at their best) embodies a good balance of praise, word, and prayer; and they show signs of tiredness when one of these ingredients dominates to the exclusion of another, or when the service is unduly rushed or unduly prolonged. They increasingly meet the needs of married ordinands, who would prefer to worship as a family, or (with their colleagues) later in the morning, since the monastic pattern of daily office mixes strangely with their domestic situations. All these developments demonstrate that the liturgy of the hours is alive and vibrant, largely thanks to the effect of historical research into the origins of the office, and to the way in which different groups of people have responded to a society that has changed a great deal.

The other type of Family Service meets an altogether different need, namely that of the large number of people on the fringes of Christianity, who are either non-communicants, or who have lapsed from regular worship in church. Churches with a more set liturgical tradition have tried to avoid the pitfalls of the 'hymn-sandwich', so that Anglicans have generally used either the office or the first part of the eucharist (synaxis*) as the framework within which to operate on this front. Lutherans generally use the synaxis also, exploring new musical possibilities.

In many local churches, of whatever denomination, these Family Services occur once a month, and are occasions when the Sunday clubs and youth groups are present throughout the main act of worship, instead of going out half way through (or coming

in at the offertory, in a eucharist). Often uniformed organizations parade on these Sundays; and invitations are sent out to the parents of children and teenagers involved in these various groups. Thus, the local church may be considerably fuller than on a normal Sunday. Liturgies for these occasions can be specially prepared around a particular theme. As with the previous type of family worship, a good balance is sought between praise, word, and prayer; some leaders of these services allow them to degenerate into a kind of entertainment, with a compère, instead of being good and viable acts of worship, with a sensitive president, and other ministers, who may represent the leaders of the groups involved. The more people involved in planning and presenting such services, the greater the need for co-operation, good relationships, and rehearsal. Some congregations prepare their own liturgical anthology, containing different songs, prayers, responses etc.; some even include activities and notes for Bible study and group discussion on the service sheet, so that the family service is seen to be closely linked to the education programme of the church. Again, there are pitfalls. One of these centres upon the catechetical function of such liturgies: they are there to help people worship, not primarily to teach them, so that the congregation should not walk out of the service asking one another 'what have I learned?' Catechumenal liturgy in the early centuries was distinct from training/education, though worship and education do overlap. Nevertheless, the folk who come along only to these services (and never darken the door on other occasions) need to be fed spiritually, and one of these areas of growth is the capacity to pray and enjoy God's company. Furthermore, many congregations draw their adult confirmation candidates largely from family services. An underlying principle in compiling these services (which have possibilities far beyond even the most experimental eucharist) is that the liturgy is the educational matrix of the church. Another pitfall is the relationship between these services and the eucharist. The Catholic tradition has always maintained that the eucharist* itself is the only family service; such a stance has a great deal to commend it, but in many congregations, it ignores local history and church life. Many people may attend a eucharist, intermittently, but feel cut off at the moment of communion*, because all they can digest is a word liturgy. On the other hand, some churches include an adapted eucharist in their monthly family service, perhaps two or three times each year, with a narrator (acting like a patristic deacon*), as well as president. These occasions can become more familiar if the word services include liturgical material such as the preface and *Sanctus*.

Many hidden reasons inhibit people from coming to church regularly, and the family service frequently is an effective vehicle for bringing them along. Nonetheless, clergy can be overprotective about the sacraments, and John Wesley's much-acclaimed description of the eucharist as 'a converting ordinance' is a necessary corrective for leaders of worship who want to wait until everyone is ready.

John C. A. Barrett, *Family Worship*, 1982; Richard More, *Freedom in a Framework*, 1975; Michael Perry (ed), *The Family Service Book*, 1985; Kenneth Stevenson, *Family Services*, 1981.

KENNETH STEVENSON

Fan

The use of liturgical fans was at one time very widespread. In a rubric found before the eucharistic prayer in the eighth book of *The Apostolic Constitutions* (fifth century), their use is ordered thus: 'Let two deacons on either side of the altar hold a fan of thin tissues, or of peacock's feathers, and let them gently ward off the small flying creatures, so that they may not approach the cups.'

In the Latin West fans were undoubtedly employed for a similar purpose, as we can see from the rubrics in the liturgical rites of the Dominicans and the Cluniacs. In the present Eastern Orthodox liturgy, fans are waved over the elements during the recitation of the Nicene Creed and at the commencement of the anaphora* or eucharistic prayer. These fans now have a symbolic meaning, since they have a six-winged cherub depicted on them, whence the name hexapterigon (six-winged). They are carried in processions by deacons*, acolytes* and choir-boys on either side of the book of the gospels or at the great

entrance* of the offerings of bread and wine.

F. E. Brightman, *Liturgies Eastern and Western, I: Eastern Liturgies*, 1896; S. Salaville, *An Introduction to the Study of Eastern Liturgies*, 1938.

C.E POCKNEE

Fast Days

Fasting is recommended by the scriptures and practised by the church as a means of atoning for sin and commending individuals and their prayers to God. Hence the fast days of the Christian calendar and their connection with times of prayer, such as Lent*and Ember days* and the eves of great feasts.

See also **Ethiopian Worship** 7; **Good Friday**.

J. CONNELLY

Feminist Liturgical Movement, The

A product of the increasing dissatisfaction of women with existing worship, both in form and content. This dissatisfaction goes beyond the question of inclusive language* for existing texts. It points to an increasing recognition that women have been left out of the religious tradition. Their history has not been remembered; their pain and hope have not been lifted up as a context for religious experience and celebration. This impels them to create new symbols and stories to express their experience.

Feminism in liturgy crosses religious traditions and takes several organizational forms. As increasing numbers of women attended theological schools and were ordained to the ministry in the 1970s, especially in North America, denominational or interdenominational gatherings of such women would be expressed by the creation of a feminist liturgy. New hymns, reworkings of the creed and litanies of remembrance of foremothers in biblical, Christian and feminist history were some of the elements of such liturgies.

Jewish women in North America in this same period also began a drive for greater rabbinical education. Recognizing the androcentric character of the key Jewish rites of circumcision, bar mitzvah and the hallowing of study, such women began to write new rituals, such as the initiation of a female infant into the covenant, and to develop feminist communities for study and prayer. New Seder celebrations were written to remember Jewish women's history and to mourn their exclusion from Jewish memory.

Some women concluded from these explorations that the Jewish and Christian traditions were incapable of really including women. They began to revive or develop religious expressions focussed on goddesses. Reinterpreting ancient traditions of magic and witchcraft as a feminist and nature religion, they gathered in small communities or 'covens' for worship. Seasonal observances and rituals which celebrated women's bodily experiences characterized such gatherings. Such goddess worshippers have developed not only in North America, but in Britain and northern Europe as well.

Feminist liturgy has developed particularly among Roman Catholic women. In 1975, Catholic women in the United States organized the Women's Ordination Conference to promote women in the priestly ministry. Local groups affiliated with this movement spread throughout the country. A similar organization in Canada was developed a few years later. In Britain, the Catholic Women's Network was organized in 1984. Feminist liturgy was a usual feature of the gatherings of such groups.

By 1980, the opposition of the Vatican to the participation of women in ministry, even in such minor roles as altar server, convinced many of these women that ordination should no longer be their major focus, although it would remain a long-term goal. For the present, they should concentrate on renewal of ministry and church. Increasingly, this took the form of small groups of women who gathered for regular worship in house churches*. This became an arena for free liturgical experimentation.

Larger networks of such women in particular cities, such as Boston and Chicago, sponsored more occasional liturgies, usually on a monthly basis. Existing women's religious communities, such as the Grail, in Loveland, Ohio, or new groups, such as WATER (Women's Alliance for Theology, Ethics and Ritual) in Washington, DC, undertook to provide resources for such feminist liturgies. New songs, prayers, litanies and symbolic actions circulated from group to group and were collected in *ad hoc* hymnals and worship books. Some of

this material has appeared in published form.

In 1983, in Chicago, a coalition of Catholic feminist groups sponsored a conference titled *Woman Church Speaks* which signalled the formal break with the earlier focus on ordination in favour of feminist communities for worship and ministry. Themes for the conference, organized under the three headings of 'spirituality', 'sexuality' and 'survival', indicated the broad social, personal and spiritual concerns of the movement, ranging from questions such as the feminization of poverty to wholistic health. Feminist liturgical communities were understood, not as an isolated religious experience, but as the way of experiencing and celebrating liturgically the whole of women's lives in a struggle for personal meaning and social justice.

The feminist liturgical movement is ecumenical, not only drawing in a broad spectrum of Catholic and Protestant women, but also reaching out to similar movements among Jewish and neo-pagan women. In the summer of 1983, a dialogue between religious feminism in these three contexts was held at the Grail, in Loveland, Ohio. Liturgical expressions drawn from the three traditions were shared. It has become common at such gatherings of Christian women that ideas drawn from feminist Judaism or the Goddess movement might also be employed in liturgy.

Most of the Christian women, however, intend to stay affiliated with their denominational church traditions. They wish to promote free communities of celebration and renewal of ministry, where ideas can be tested experimentally and, from that context, fed back into more traditional church gatherings open to such developments. Their relationship to existing churches is dialectical rather than rejectionist.

Yet these women are cognizant of the radicality of their project. Such a liturgical movement goes beyond conventional church renewal on the basis of established sources. Seeing these sources themselves as patriarchal, shaped by the exclusion of women, such groups see themselves as reaching back to lost options before the rise of patriarchy and, perhaps, being the harbingers of, if not a new religion, at least a new *midrash* or 'third covenant' that will decisively transform the existing religious traditions.

Linda Clark et al, *Image Breaking, Image Making: A Handbook for Creative Worship for Women in the Christian Tradition*, 1980; Susannah Heschel, *On Being a Jewish Feminist*, 1983; Starhawk, *The Spiral Dance: The Rebirth of the Ancient Religion of the Goddess*, 1979; Rosemary Ruether, *Women-church: The Theology and Praxis of Feminist Liturgical Communities*, 1986; Arlene Swidler, *Sistercelebrations*, 1974.

ROSEMARY R. RUETHER

Ferial

Christians, like the Jews, designated the days of the week by numbers, not by names. A day was called a *feria* (without the meaning of a day of rest or a feast). Sunday was the first day, *feria prima*, but from earliest times it was called the 'day of the Lord', *dies dominica* (cf. Rev. 1.7). Saturday, the seventh day, was called the Sabbath, *Sabbatum*.

In Christian usage, ferial is opposed to dominical. A *feria* or a ferial day is a weekday to which no solemnity or feast is assigned. Some ferial days have a special place in the calendar, namely the weekdays of Lent*, 17 to 24 December, the Ember* and Rogation Days*; but most ferial days are an extension of the preceding Sunday. As Sunday is the weekly commemoration of the resurrection, the ferial days make the week a reflection of the Easter octave. 'Ferial', therefore, is not essentially a synonym for penitential or sorrowful.

J. CONNELLY

Font

A receptacle to hold water for the administration of baptism*, the term deriving from the Latin *fons* meaning 'a spring of water'.

A sufficient number of datable fonts, from the beginning of the third century onwards, is now known to allow the determination of the historical sequence of their shapes. The most primitive form was the quadrilateral; this was succeeded by the hexagon, octagon and the cruciform. Round or oval fonts were next adopted and finally, in the sixth century, the quatrefoil. Apart from the hexagon and octagon in Italy and France, no one shape seems to have been preferred in any one area, although it is possible to affirm that the

Plate 33 'Quatrefoil font', Stobi, Yugoslavia

cruciform and quatrefoil (*see* Plate 33) were Eastern creations and were thence introduced into North Africa.

Each and every one of these shapes had its own ideological content, the form being a symbol to convey some aspect of the meaning of baptism. The initial adoption of the quadrilateral, which is the design of the first extant font from Dura Europos, is explicable on the grounds that it is similar to a sarcophagus; i.e., since in baptism the believer is buried with Christ, the font was made to look like a coffin. So Ambrose refers to 'the font, whose appearance is somewhat like that of a tomb in shape'. Numerology provides the clue to the meaning of hexagon and octagon: six refers to the death of Christ on the sixth day of the week and eight to his resurrection (cf. Rom. 6.4). So fonts were shaped in the same way and with the same intention as the baptistery*, and various combinations were possible. As the candidate entered an octagonal building, he was buoyed with hope in the resurrection of Christ; as he entered the hexagonal font, he knew he was to die with Christ, but as he left the font and stood once more in the eight-sided room he also knew he was to walk in newness of life. Alternatively, as he entered an hexagonal building, he knew that the baptismal death awaited him, but as he entered the octagonal font he knew that this was the means of rising again.

The round font, as the circular baptistery, introduces a different aspect of baptism, namely that of rebirth (cf. John 3.3ff.), and so this type of font was regarded as a womb whereby the children of God are regenerated and have the church as their mother. The cruciform font, on the other hand, together with the quatrefoil which is no more than a variant, connects once more with the idea of death. So according to John Chrysostom: 'Baptism is a cross. What the cross was to Christ and what his burial was, that baptism was to us.'

One further feature of the arrangement of the font has a bearing upon the meaning of the rite and that is the steps with which many were provided, anything from one to four. Their main purpose was not to allow easy access but to emphasize the fact of descent. So Cyril of Jerusalem, or his successor John, comments: 'You descended three times into the water, and ascended again; here also covertly pointing by a figure to the three days' burial of Christ.'

All these fonts were more frequently placed in a decorative setting, with mosaics

on the dome, walls and floors, than they were decorated themselves. Some of them, however, were ornamented, either with simple geometrical patterns, as the one at Timgad, or with a multitude of symbols, as the one at Kélibia. The latter depicts an ark, stressing salvation in the church, fish, based on the *ichthus* symbol of Christ (the initials of the Greek word stand for Jesus Christ, Son of God, Saviour), and a cross, affirming that by baptism we share in the victorious death of Christ.

The fonts themselves not only provide evidence of the early Christian understanding of baptism; they also give a clue to the actual method used. Strictly speak, there are four principal methods of baptizing: 1. submersion, when the candidate goes completely below the surface of the water; 2. immersion, when the head is dipped, with or without the candidate standing in the water; 3. affusion, when water is poured over the head; 4. aspersion, when water is sprinkled on the head. However, method 2 is now rarely used, and the term immersion normally denotes 1. If the dimensions of all the early Christian fonts known are examined, it is evident that the great majority of them were not capable of being used for submersion; in only a few would this have been possible. Hence if baptismal practice were uniform, then it must have been either by immersion or affusion; even in this case the parallelism with burial would not have been lost, since the essential feature of this was the casting of a handful of earth upon the corpse, and affusion does no more than reproduce this action.

From the mediaeval period a vast number of fonts have survived, and they are so plentiful and diverse that an exact typology is not easy. However, it is possible to make certain general statements which may be taken as usually valid despite exceptions. In the eleventh and twelfth centuries the tub-font was prevalent and this consisted of an unmounted bowl resting on the ground. Overlapping this in the twelfth century and continuing through the thirteenth, a mounted type came into use and was polypod in form, i.e. the bowl was supported on four or more legs. This was superseded in the fourteenth century by a monopod, i.e. the receptacle was held up on a single central shaft. This last type was

Plate 34 Font, Stottesdon, England

tripartite and consisted of bowl, pedestal and base (*see* Plate 34) but there had existed previously a bipartite form which derived from the tub-font. Many examples of the tub have a band or cable-moulding around the middle; a tightening of this girdle contracts the tub in the centre and both elongates it and makes it assume the appearance of a cup – hence the appearance of the bipartite chalice.

This evolution is explicable in the light of two factors. First, the universal practice of infant baptism required the raising of the font so that the celebrant could handle the children with greater ease. Second, submersion had now become the norm and so the bowls had to be fairly large and, if they were to be at a convenient level, supports were required. Nevertheless submersion did not continue in all countries, being eventually replaced by affusion. In France affusion appears to have been widespread by the fourteenth century, in Italy by the fifteenth, but in England it was not adopted until after the Reformation. Where this was the practice, a second receptacle was required to catch the drops of consecrated water that dripped from the children's heads; hence the presence of secondary bowls by the side of a number of mediaeval fonts. Hence also the appearance of font covers to prevent the consecrated water from being stolen for the purposes of magic and witchcraft. The earliest covers were

simply flat lids, but their decorative possibilities were soon appreciated and the result, from the fourteenth century, was the towering tabernacles of open-tracery work.

Mediaeval fonts were covered with sculptural ornament and the subjects chosen naturally refer to baptism. Scenes from the life of Christ were not infrequent, in particular his nativity, baptism, crucifixion and resurrection, each therefore affirming either baptismal rebirth or co-death and co-resurrection. But one of the most dominant themes of the early mediaeval iconography of baptism was not so much death as the struggle against and destruction of the devil and his minions, hence the host of bas-reliefs depicting the powers of evil as toads, serpents, dragons or griffins. In the fifteenth and sixteenth centuries there was a decline in the artistic merit of these decorations, at the same time as the cult of the saints was reaching its zenith. The result of this was the representation of the saints and/or of scenes from their lives, they being regarded as protectors and intercessors, their names given in baptism to the children, whose patrons and models they thereby became.

From the Reformation to the eighteenth century, the history of the font is relatively uninteresting. There were two main types, either those designed on traditional lines and perpetuating the general features of the fifteenth-century examples, or those of Renaissance pattern, which were usually like vases on slender pillars, the diminutive bowl marking the final discontinuance of submersion (*see* Plate 35). The chief decoration was realistic cherubic heads, disposed around the rim; only rarely were any of the subjects of the mediaeval iconography reproduced. Among the Calvinists, basins were general, while among Roman Catholics a divided font bowl came into use, one part holding the consecrated water and the other collecting the drops from the children's heads. With the Gothic Revival, octagonal fonts of the decorated period were introduced into church after church, often dispossessing the ancient ones *in situ*. In both Greek and Russian Orthodox churches, despite an increase in adult baptisms which is leading to new forms, most fonts are portable and are kept in the sacristy, when not in use. They are chalice-shaped, sufficiently large for infant submersion and are usually of bronze or silver-coloured metal.

Plate 35 Font, Ruabon, Wales

In the West the present century has witnessed the production of a large number of fonts (*see* Plate 36), some of which are no more than bizarre, but the majority are sufficiently similar to those of the mediaeval period to allow them to be classified in the same way. So there are unmounted fonts, consisting of either tanks or different forms

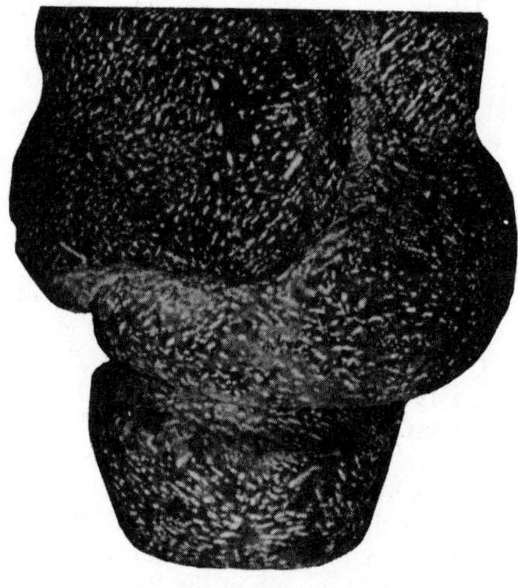

Plate 36 Font, Audincourt, France

of the tub-font standing on the ground. There are also mounted ones, both monopods and polypods, but their decorative treatment is almost nil. The result is that few really convey the meaning of baptism. Perhaps the time has come when the refined austerity that characterizes so many of them should give way to a little more boldness in experiment and symbolic representation, in the light of what has previously been achieved.

S. Bedard, *The Symbolism of the Baptismal Font in Early Christian Thought*, 1951; F. Bond, *Fonts and Font Covers*, 1908; J. G. Davies, *The Architectural Setting of Baptism*, 1962.

EDITOR

Foot-Washing

see **Liturgies** 15; **Maundy Thursday**

Forty Hours Devotion

Also known by its Italian name *Quarant' Ore*, this was a Roman Catholic devotion in which the reserved sacrament was exposed for a continuous period of about forty hours, with the faithful praying before it in relays throughout.

The remote origins of the devotion may have been in the very popular mediaeval custom of keeping watch from Good Friday evening to Easter morning at the 'sepulchre'* in which first the cross and later the eucharistic elements were 'buried'. Its immediate origins, however, were in sixteenth century Milan as an intensive form of prayer during a national crisis. Soon this was organized in all the churches of the city in rotation. As early as 1534 St Antony Mary Zaccaria was propagating the devotion further afield, and in 1550 St Philip Neri introduced it to the churches of Rome. In 1539 Paul III gave approval to it as a form of reparation in time of severe social tension; in 1560 Pius V related it to Christ's forty-day fast and to the ancient Christian ideal of uninterrupted prayer. Clement XII in 1731 issued regulations for its conduct in the diocese of Rome, and these were widely adopted elsewhere. These show that the emphasis was by now less on reparation and more on piety towards the sacrament itself. The devotion was to open and close with a votive mass* of the blessed sacrament, and on the second day a mass of peace was to be celebrated at a separate altar in the church. The 1917 *Code of Canon Law* ordered it to be held annually in all churches where the sacrament was regularly reserved.

The recently revised *Roman Ritual* makes no explicit mention of the devotion. It recommends that an 'extended period of exposition' should be observed each year in churches where the sacrament is regularly reserved, provided that suitable numbers can be present. It need no longer be strictly continuous, and indeed must be interrupted if mass is to be celebrated in the church or if the number of worshippers cannot be sustained (e.g. during the night). Otherwise the normal regulations for exposition* and benediction* apply.

Roman Ritual: *Worship of the Eucharist*, 1973; J. A. Jungmann, *Pastoral Liturgy*, 1962; N. Mitchell, *Cult and Controversy: The Worship of the Eucharist outside Mass*, 1982.

C. J WALSH

Fraction

The ceremonial breaking of the eucharistic bread for distribution. It derives from Christ's own action at the Last Supper (Matt. 26.26) and was a sufficiently striking element to make 'the breaking of bread' (Acts 2.42) a title for the eucharist.

In all non-Byzantine Eastern rites and in all non-Roman Western rites, the fraction

takes place before the Lord's Prayer. In the Roman mass, since Gregory the Great, it is performed after the Lord's Prayer, as in the Byzantine rite. The rubric in the Roman mass requires the host to be broken into three, and one particle is then placed in the chalice* at the commixture*. The Mozarabic rite prescribes an elaborate ceremonial, the host being broken into nine, and seven of these pieces being arranged in the shape of a cross.

The 1662 BCP, in order to emphasize that the fraction is in imitation of Jesus' action at the Last Supper, requires it to take place during the consecration prayer at the words 'he brake', and this is also the practice in the Coptic and Abyssinian rites.

Originally the fraction was entirely utilitarian and so Augustine refers to the bread being 'broken small for distribution' (*Ep.* 149.16). It soon attracted a symbolic interpretation, Paul paving the way with his argument for unity on the grounds that the communicants have all partaken of the fragments broken from a single loaf (I Cor. 10.17) – so it was a sign of the gathering into one of the children of God (cf. *Didache*, 9.4). Later it was thought to symbolize the death of Christ, although this is in contradiction to John 19.36. The Stowe missal accompanies it with a quotation from Luke 24.35 to the effect that the Lord is known in the breaking of the bread.

EDITOR

Frontal

In the earlier centuries the altar was enveloped in a silk cloth on all sides (*see* **Altar Hangings**). But in the second part of the Middle Ages, when altars came to be placed against screens or walls, the cloth had to be adapted to meet this changed setting of the altar. Thus only that side of the altar which was visible to the congregation came to have a flat silk or brocade cloth hung in front of it; this is what is termed the 'frontal' and in the Latin *antependium*. The frontal is suspended on legs that project from the altar. Over the top of the altar there is hung another strip of silk attached to a coarse linen cloth and this has a fringe running along its length and is termed the *frontlet*, sometimes miscalled the 'superfrontal'. Frontals are often made in various colours to agree with the liturgical colour of the season of the church's year. Where an altar is free standing and visible on both sides two 'frontals' are necessary if the throw-over type of cloth is not adopted. *See* Plate 2.

Examples of precious metal frontals were not unknown in the Middle Ages; and we may see an outstanding example still in use at the Church of St Ambrose in Milan by a ninth-century goldsmith.

The practical details for the making of altar frontals and other hangings are given in: C. E. Pocknee, *The Parson's Handbook*, rev ed 1965, and The Warham Guild, *The Warham Guild Handbook*, rev ed 1963.

Modern altars are frequently designed not to be vested, and that this was sometimes also the custom of the early church may be seen in a detail of the mid-fifth century cupola mosaic in the Baptistery of the Orthodox, Ravenna.

C. E. POCKNEE/G. D. W. RANDALL

Funeral

see **Burial**; **Cremation**

Furnishings

see **Altar Hangings**; **Baldachin**; **Corporal**; **Frontal**; **Pall**; **Purificator**; **Riddel**; **Veil**

Furniture

see **Altar**; **Altar Rails**; **Ambo**; **Aumbry**; **Cathedra**; **Ciborium**; **Communion Table**; **Cross**; **Font**; **Iconostasis**; **Lectern**; **Monstrance**; **Pew**; **Piscina**; **Pulpit**; **Pyx**; **Reredos**; **Rostrum**; **Screen**; **Tabernacle**

Gallery

A platform or balcony projecting from the interior wall of a building. Such galleries were not uncommon over the aisles in pagan basilicas and were included in the fourth-century Christian basilica* as well as in the centralized architecture of the East (*see* **Centralized Building**). They served a twofold purpose: 1. They provided space for the worshippers where the nave was largely occupied by the clergy for the performance of the liturgy and 2. they enabled the women, in the East, to be segregated from the men.

In the large churches of the Middle Ages, particularly cathedrals, the gallery persisted as the triforium, which allowed for circulation and for extra accommodation at the great festivals.

In post-Reformation churches galleries were often erected at the west end for the singers. In auditory churches, galleries, occupying three sides, enabled large numbers of worshippers to have places as close as possible to the minister. So-called Free Church architecture has made great use of this feature. It has one drawback, however, and that is its tendency to divide the congregation to such an extent that its unity and sense of corporateness is impaired.

EDITOR

Genuflexion

see **Gestures** 2

Gestures

Liturgical gestures are stylized forms of natural movements of the limbs, especially the hands, in the context of corporate worship (*see* **Movements in Worship**). These movements are basically instinctive in character and constitute an important non-verbal mode of communication. The invention of written language eventually made possible the separation of words and gesture and, thus, in religious terms, the differentiation between ritual* and ceremonial*, i.e. the written text of the liturgy and the accompanying gestures and movements.

Protestant rejection of liturgical gesture is based on the association of the gestures with doctrines which are held to be objectionable, e.g. the elevation of the eucharistic elements associated with the theory of transubstantiation and with the eastward position (*see* **Posture** 1).

The significance of liturgical gestures is to be understood mainly in terms of the conversion of personal relationships into directional movements. Thus upward and downward movements can express feelings and beliefs about the relationship between God and humanity, while horizontal movements – towards-self and away-from-self – can be employed to communicate social inter-personal relationships (*see* **Directions, Liturgical**). Significantly, the Eastern Orthodox name for the central part of the eucharist is anaphora* – the Greek word for 'lifting up' or 'offering' (Heb. 7.27). Correspondingly, the kiss of peace is a ritual gesture in which the emphasis is upon the human personal relationships within a Christian community.

1. *Beating the breast.* Smiting the chest with the hand is an expression of grief (Nahum 2.7) and so of sorrow or penitence for sin. In the parable of the Pharisee and the Publican, it is the latter who beats his breast and says: 'God be merciful to me a sinner' (Luke 18.13). In Christian liturgical practice this gesture became the accompaniment of confessions of sin, especially during the preparation before the mass at the words *mea culpa*.

2. *Bending the knee and bowing the head.* These are both expressions of reverence. The first gesture, which can also be called genuflexion, recalls Phil. 2.10: 'at the name of Jesus every knee shall bow'. It is usually associated with the *incarnatus* of the Nicene Creed (from the eleventh century) and with reverence for the Blessed Sacrament (from the fourteenth century). It derives from civil recognition of imperial officials in antiquity. In the Roman Catholic Church it is also commonly used as a reverence towards prelates and crucifixes, as is also the bowing of the head. In the mediaeval period it became customary to incline the head at the *Gloria Patri*, at the name of the Holy Spirit in the Nicene Creed and at the *Sanctus*.

3. *Cross, sign of.* One of the earliest references to signing with the cross is found at the end of the second century in some words of Tertullian: 'at every forward step and movement, at every going in and out, when we put on our clothes and shoes . . . in all the ordinary actions of everyday life, we trace the sign [of the cross]' (*de Cor. Mil.* 3). It is impossible to know whether such continuous domestic self-crossing was ever generally observed, but as a liturgical gesture it certainly became customary and eventually was prescribed as a regular ceremonial gesture at many points in the whole cultus.

A sacramental interpretation is clearly expressed by Augustine (354–430): 'Unless the sign of the cross is made on the foreheads of the faithful, as on the water itself wherewith they are regenerated, or on the oil with which they are anointed with chrism, or on the sacrifice with which they are nourished, none of these things is duly performed' (*Tract.* cxviii *in Joan.* xix 24). Augustine's view of the need for the sign of the cross in the 'due performance' of sacramental acts prevailed in the mediaeval church, and by the eighth century it was customary to incise crosses on altars and

churches at the places where they had been manually anointed with the sign of the cross in the course of their consecration*.

Thus, signing with the cross became an integral part of the *ex opere operato* sacramental theory of the mediaeval church and, as such, was rejected by Protestant reformers.

Signing with the cross is still extensively used in this sense in the Roman Catholic Church, but in the Anglican BCP it is ordered only in baptism* and there merely as a custom which 'is no part of the substance of the sacrament' but which may be accounted 'a lawful outward ceremony and honourable badge, whereby the person who has been baptized is dedicated to the service of him that dies upon the Cross' (Canon XXX, 1603).

The first prayer book of Edward VI (1549) included two signings in the great eucharistic prayer, but these were omitted in 1552 and the sign of the cross has never been re-introduced into any other authorized BCP of the Church of England.

It should be noted that the sign of the cross may be made on or over both persons and things, that it may be single or multiple, and that it may be self-administered or directed towards others. Further, this gesture may take several different forms: originally it seems to have been restricted to the forehead and made with the thumb of the right hand. Subsequently (probably at the time of the Arian controversy), the signing became associated with the Trinitarian formula and the crossing was extended from forehead to heart and across the upper chest – now from left to right in the West and from right to left in the East. Alternatively, a number of small thumb-crossings may be made at various parts of the body, customarily as acts of anointing in the course of rites of initiation or sickness. Self-crossing is common in association with the reading of the gospel, and also at the words 'resurrection of the body' in the creed with the implication 'this, my body'.

4. *Elevation*. This gesture is made in the Roman Catholic Church when the 'celebrant' of the mass raises the host so high that all present may look upon it. The origin and significance of this important act are complex matters and, perhaps more than any other liturgical gesture, it serves to focus attention upon a syndrome of essential differences between Catholics and Protestants, in the matter of sacramental theology.

The elevation itself was first formally recognized in 1210 when the Bishop of Paris ordered that before the 'consecration' the bread should not be held more than breast-high, and only after the words 'This is my body' should the host be raised high enough for everyone to see.

The theological arguments of the previous centuries had largely turned upon eucharistic change, and involved the concept of a 'consecration-moment' when the offered bread and wine were so transformed through the words of the priest that the real presence of Christ was an event to be recognized. The faithful had been taught that not only was the 'substance' of the bread and wine changed into the 'substance' of the body and blood of Christ, but that the whole Christ, *totus Christus*, was present on the altar – concealed under the appearance of the bread and wine. The sacrament came to be regarded as so holy that it might not readily be received in hands or mouth, so that, correspondingly, for the faithful, it was all-important to *see* the host. The popular impatience to see led to premature reverence when the priest took the bread and cup into his hands *prior* to the 'consecration', and for this reason it was ordered that the elevation should be a distinct gesture indicating to all the achievement of the real presence and the moment for appropriate reverence.

The eucharistic participation of the congregation consisted in observing with adoration the 'realization' of Christ in their midst and, therefore, it became more important to 'see' *him* in the transubstantiated bread and wine than to eat and drink *them* at the communion.

Other factors in the mainstream emphasis on elevation were the proto-Reformation challenges to the feudal structure and ostentatious wealth of the church from the Albigenses, who virtually denied the hierarchy and the sacraments, and the Cathari, who advocated a church of primitive poverty in which the eucharistic body was accepted as pure bread, *purum panem*. Thus, by emphasizing the real presence of Christ in the cultus, the hierarchy defended its own status and, at the same time, defended a

particular theory of eucharistic change against what was judged to be heresy. Essentially the same challenges and reaction reached a climax three centuries later at the Reformation and led to the rejection of any elevation in the Protestant churches. Even the 1549 **BCP** directs that the words of the Last Supper are to be said 'without any elevation, or shewing the sacrament to the people'.

The elevation itself is an extension of a modest 'raising' (anaphora) of the sacramental elements as the eucharistic president takes the bread and the cup into his hands when he repeats the corresponding words of the institution narrative. Whether or not it is justifiable to develop this ancient custom into a distinct theological gesture is clearly dependent upon particular theories of how 'consecration' is achieved and how the eucharistic presence of Christ is envisaged.

Prior to the eleventh century the church had not concerned itself with speculation about a precise moment when 'consecration' took place, but, during the thirteenth century, the elevation having been established, a natural ceremonial consequence was that reverence should be expressed by bowing or kneeling and subsequently by prostration and genuflexion, by censings, and by ringing of bells. However, the desire to see waned and it became customary to kneel with bowed head at the elevation. A temporary revival of looking occurred after 1907 when Pius X granted an indulgence to all who said 'My Lord and my God' while contemplating the host, but this practice was officially renounced in 1925.

Current celebration of the mass in the vernacular* from the basilican position (*see* **Posture** 2) itself tends to reduce the original significance of the elevation and to reproduce the situation of the first millennium of eucharistic worship when such a gesture and the accompanying reverences were entirely unknown.

5. *Elevation, little.* The so-called little (minor or lesser) elevation is a gesture of raising both host and chalice* at the end of the canon*, after the words *per quem haec omnia, Domine, semper bona creas, sanctificas, vivificas, benedicis et praestas nobis* (through whom, O Lord, all these gifts are ever created as good, sanctified, vivified, blessed and bestowed upon us). Having said this, the priest then uncovers the chalice and takes it into his left hand and makes a threefold sign of the cross over it with the host held in his right hand, saying 'through him +, with him +, and in him+', and continuing with two more signings between the chalice and his breast 'is to thee God the Father +, Almighty, in the unity of the Holy + Spirit', and at this point elevating host and chalice, and concluding 'all honour and glory, world without end'.

The paragraph appears to be a twofold doxology*, the former part referring to divine creativity mediated through Christ as Logos, while the latter is a declaration of praise being offered through Christ 'present' in the bread and wine. The words '*all* these gifts . . .' are really a vestige of a much earlier prayer associated with the custom of 'eucharistizing' other produce (water, milk, honey, oil, cheese, fruits, seeds, wine and bread) at this point in the mass.

The close association of other 'good gifts' with this elevation of the bread and cup has a certain symbolic value, but in the new *Ordo Missae* (1969) it has been minimized and would generally pass unnoticed in the recitation of the words: 'We hope to enjoy for ever the vision of your glory through Christ our Lord, from whom all good things come. Through him, with him, in him, in the unity of the Holy Spirit [*little elevation*], all honour is yours, almighty Father, for ever and ever.'

The little elevation in the Roman Catholic rite corresponds to a similar ceremony in the Eastern liturgies: the priest within the sanctuary says a secret prayer recognizing the invisible presence of Christ and, as he reaches for the holy bread, the deacon (outside the sanctuary doors) says 'Let us give heed', and then the priest elevates the host and says 'Holy things to holy people'.

6. *Manual acts.* The designation refers to the gestures executed by the president during the recitation of the prayer of consecration at the eucharist. In the 1549 **BCP** the priest was required to take the bread and the cup at the appropriate words in the institution narrative, but there was no reference to a fraction*. In 1552 all mention of manual acts was omitted, to be reinserted in 1662 when the fraction was also required at the words 'he brake it'. The **ASB** has restored the fraction to its original place immediately before communion but

specifies nothing else, apart from declaring in its preliminary notes that 'the president may use traditional manual acts during the eucharistic prayers'. The BCP of the Episcopal Church of the USA specifically directs the celebrant to hold or lay a hand on first the bread and then the cup.

7. *Imposition of hands*. The gesture of laying hands upon (or over) a person or a thing has the multiple significance of blessing, setting apart, consecrating, commissioning, absolving, healing, confirming, declaring, ordaining, and other associated ideas. Underlying the liturgical act is the notion of the transmission of power, *mana*, authority, spiritual grace, etc., from one specially endowed or recognized person in a community to others. Such channelling of unseen 'charisma' is thought of as being achieved through the physical action of touching with the hands – a visible gesture which can also serve to establish the concept of continuity of role in a sequence of persons, e.g. the apostolic succession.

There are descriptions of laying on of hands in a number of biblical passages – both in the sense of blessing, ordaining or healing and in the sense of setting apart for sacrifice – and these form the basis of the liturgical practices of imposition which developed in the church (e.g. Gen. 48; Acts 8.19; 13.3; I Tim. 4.14; Mark 6.5; 16.18; etc.).

Laying on of hands is often closely associated with anointing with oil and, in this way, the spiritual purposes of ordination*, consecration and unction* receive additional visible expression. In the Christian cultus, oil has become a symbol of the gifts of the Holy Spirit – the 'Giver of Life' – and is so used in some rites of baptism*, confirmation* and ordination along with the imposition of hands. Such ceremonies still form part of the liturgical practice of the Roman Catholic and Eastern Orthodox Churches, but Protestants generally have discontinued the use of unction, while laying on of hands survives only in those Reformed churches where episcopal ordination is the rule.

In the rites of initiation in the early church, water baptism was always accompanied by anointing and invocation of the Holy Spirit and, through this sacramental gesture, the candidate was incorporated into the 'royal priesthood' (I Peter 2.9; cf. Rev. 5.10) and proceeded to participate in the eucharist. These ceremonies are kept together in the Eastern Orthodox rite of infant baptism without any specific laying on of hands by the priest. In the West, however, the imposition of hands (with anointing) developed as the rite of confirmation and, since the late Middle Ages, in the Roman Catholic Church the sacrament is administered by a bishop anointing the forehead, signing with a cross and extending his hands over the candidate's head. In the Church of England the bishop lays his hands on the head of each candidate but there is no anointing.

Laying on of hands is also an essential ceremony in the rites of episcopal ordination. In the Anglican Church, for example, in the 'making' of a deacon the bishop lays his hands on the head of the kneeling ordinand; in the ordering of priests, not only the bishop but other priests present collectively lay their hands on the head of the deacon; at the consecration of a bishop, the archbishop and other bishops lay their hands on the head of the elected priest. Similar ceremonies accompany the rites of other episcopally ordered communions.

8. *Kiss of peace and the pax*. As a liturgical gesture, the kiss (actual or token) is a mutual salutation of participants in the Western eucharist: it is now initiated by the president shortly before the communion and, in one form or another, the greeting is exchanged by some or all of those present as a sign of fellowship.

In the NT there are a number of references to a kiss of greeting, e.g. a 'holy kiss' (Rom. 16.16, etc.), and the linking of the gesture with 'peace' occurs thus: 'Greet one another with a kiss of love. Peace to you all who belong to Christ' (I Peter 5.14). Liturgically, the gesture accompanies the pax: *Priest*: The peace of the Lord be always with you; *People*: And with thy spirit. According to Hippolytus a liturgical kiss was given at the conclusion of the initiation rite (thus signifying membership in Christ), and also to a newly consecrated bishop.

It seems probable that the eucharistic kiss originally concluded the synaxis* and then, in the light of the command of Jesus to make peace before bringing a gift to the altar (Matt. 5.23f.), became more closely associated with the offertory*. In the second century, Justin Martyr writes in the *Apo-*

logy: 'At the conclusion of the prayers we greet one another with a kiss. Then bread and a chalice containing wine mixed with water are presented to the one presiding over the brethren.' In all Eastern Orthodox rites the kiss remains in this position, but in the Latin rite by the beginning of the fifth century it had been moved to the end of the canon, and was subsequently moved into the midst of the communion ritual.

In the first English liturgy, 1549, the pax remained in a comparable position but without rubrics concerning the kiss: the pax disappeared in the 1552 prayer book but has since been re-inserted in several revisions in English. In the 1967 Series 2 holy communion of the Church of England, the pax appears as an optional salutation at the end of what is called 'The Preparation of the People' and immediately before the placing of the bread and wine on the table: thus, although no rubrics are provided concerning a ceremonial kiss, the opportunity is provided at the original place in the liturgy, namely the offertory (even though this word is not used). In the 1971 Series 3, the pax is made mandatory in the same position, namely, at the beginning of 'The Communion' and immediately before 'The taking of the Bread and Wine': again no suggestion is made concerning any gesture which might accompany the salutation. Similar provision is made in other recent rites, and in some there is a rubric indicating how the gesture may be made; e.g. immediately before the offertory of bread, wine and alms the Church of South India has: 'The "Peace" may be given here. The giver places his right palm against the right palm of the receiver, and each closes his left hand over the other's right hand . . . The Presbyter gives the Peace to those ministering with him, and these in turn give it to the congregation . . .'

With few exceptions the liturgical kiss has ceased to be a literal touching with the lips of one person by another, and the gesture may be a light embrace, a hand-clasp or a bow. Again the kiss may be restricted to the sanctuary, or it may be general throughout the congregation. In the latter case, the eucharistic president may initiate a kiss which passes in hierarchical order down through the clergy to the laity or, alternatively, each member of the congregation may simultaneously salute his immediate neighbour. The form of the salutation depends much on what kind of greeting is customary on civil occasions in any community: thus, among East Syrians each person clasps the hand of his neighbour and kisses him, while Armenians merely bow. In the Roman Catholic Church since 1969 the kiss is not limited to a formal 'continental' embrace between the clergy and only at high mass: it is not given on Maundy Thursday, Good Friday or Holy Saturday nor in masses for the dead.

J. Benthall and T. Polhemus (eds), *The Body as a Medium of Expression*, 1975; E. Beresford-Cooke, *The Sign of the Cross in Western Liturgies*, 1907; F. Cabrol, *Liturgical Prayer*, 1922; J. G. Davies, *Liturgical Dance*, 1984, ch.7; G. Dix, *The Shape of the Liturgy*, [2]1945; A. Fortescue and J. B. O'Connell, *The Ceremonies of the Roman Rite*, 1917/37; J. A. Jungmann, *The Mass of the Roman Rite*, rev ed 1959; *Public Worship*, 1957; C. E. Pocknee, *Cross and Crucifix*, 1962.

GILBERT COPE

Girdle

see **Vestments** 1(*c*)

Gloria

see **Doxology**; **Music in the Mass of the Roman Rite**; **Ordinary**

Good Friday

In the earliest period of the church's life there was a definite feeling that the only real time for general Christian fasting was in the period immediately preceding the great annual festival of the Pasch, commemorating the death and resurrection of the Lord. Later, when the general custom of a Friday fast arose, it led naturally to the fast on the Friday before the Pasch being integrally linked with the Saturday of the Paschal fast. This may be regarded as the root of the Good Friday of the late fourth century.

At Jerusalem late in the fourth century it was beginning to be light on Good Friday when, following services throughout Thursday night, the procession from Gethsemane reached the city. At the Sanctuary of the Cross the entire narrative of the trial before Pilate was read and soon

after, still before sunrise, all went to pray at the column where Jesus was scourged. After the people had rested in their homes they returned to the Sanctuary of the Cross. A casket containing a relic which was believed to be wood from the cross was placed on a linen covered table in front of the bishop. The people filed past, bowing, touching the cross and the title with their foreheads and their eyes, and kissing the wood. At noon they assembled in the open courtyard of the Sanctuary, and from that hour until three o'clock the time was entirely occupied with lessons about the passion, from the psalms and the prophets, the Epistles or Acts and the Gospels, prayers suitable to the day being said between the lessons. At three o'clock the passage from St John's Gospel about the death of the Lord on Calvary was read, and soon after the service ended. In the evening the story of the burial was read in the Anastasis, the Sanctuary of the Resurrection, and a vigil was maintained there throughout the night by all who were able to sustain it. A great crowd took part, although some did not begin their watch until midnight.

It was the development of Holy Week* at Jerusalem in the late fourth century which transformed the Friday of the Paschal fast into Good Friday as we understand it. The full growth of Good Friday meant that the commemoration of the passion was detached from the unitive Pasch, which eventually came to designate the resurrection alone. But time was required for the evolution of Good Friday and Easter to become the clear pattern for Christendom.

The classical Western liturgy for Good Friday is part simplification and part elaboration, that has evolved through time, of the fourth-century Jerusalem ceremonies, inspired by the same spiritual approach, with the addition of the reception of communion reserved from Maundy Thursday*. In its current form it is made up of three parts, namely liturgy of the word, veneration of the cross*, and the reception of communion. The liturgy of the word itself consists of three parts, an introduction, the reading of the Johannine passion preceded by the fourth servant song from Second Isaiah and a passage from the Letter to the Hebrews, followed by intercessions. These latter are called the solemn prayers. They consist of a series of biddings each followed by silent prayer and a collect. They are very ancient in form, probably following the pattern of the early Roman intercessions in the eucharist, alone surviving on this day. Thus the ministry of the word on Good Friday has the form of a eucharistic synaxis* in its barest early simplicity; there is provision for preaching after the reading of the passion if desired. What has been heard in the word is then responded to in symbolic action in the veneration of the cross. The precise manner of doing this can vary according to local custom, but typically a cross or crucifix will be brought into the church, accompanied perhaps by a formula such as 'Behold, the wood of the cross'; then the worshippers may approach the cross, bowing or genuflecting towards it or kissing it, or a combination of these gestures*, while suitable chants are sung.

The reception of holy communion from the reserved sacrament is the one part of the rite that owes nothing to the liturgy and spirituality of fourth-century Jerusalem, but to a desire that arose in the late seventh or early eighth century at Rome to receive communion on this day when by very strong tradition the eucharist was not celebrated. It could be argued that communion at this rite detracts from its powerful bareness and simplicity, with its note of desolation as well as the victory of the cross, and from the Easter liturgy and communion to which celebration of the passion and death of Christ looks forward. Perhaps the early instinct that on this day the eucharist should not be celebrated nor communion received was the right one, and we should return to it. Neither the Visigothic, nor the Mozarabic nor the old pre-Charlemagne Gallican rite contain any such provision.

An interesting variant proposed by the Church of England Liturgical Commission is putting the intercessions after the veneration, thus making them a response to both word and symbolic action. This has long been the order in the Ambrosian rite at Milan.

Protestant churches have on the whole not used this classical liturgy, but services more attuned to their own traditions of worship where they have observed the day at all. One exceedingly popular service is,

or used to be, the Three Hours Devotion*, a service consisting of a series of addresses, usually based on the seven words from the cross, intermingled with readings, prayer, silence, psalmody and hymns, in whatever combination is chosen by the person conducting the service. It is ironic that this service, so widespread in Protestant churches, was invented by seventeenth-century Peruvian Jesuits.

A well-known Catholic devotion, not limited to Good Friday, but particularly appropriate to it, is the Stations of the Cross*. These are late mediaeval in origin, and were popularized by the Franciscans, and are a classic example of popular representational piety.

For bibliography *see under* **Holy Week**.

R. F. BUXTON

Gospel

The reading of a passage from one of the four canonical Gospels concludes and forms the climax of the liturgy of the word which precedes the eucharist proper. The Gospel reading is surrounded with much greater ceremony than the other readings; since the fourth century it has been reserved to the deacon*. It is customary for all to stand while the Gospel is read. The Gospel book itself is venerated as a symbol of Christ; before the reading of the Gospel the book is carried in procession to the lectern*, accompanied by lights and incense*.

As with the other readings, there are basically two systems for determining the choice of texts to be read. Either a Gospel is read more or less continuously, or else pericopes particularly appropriate to the occasion are chosen. Examples of the second system abounded in the traditional Roman Lectionary as contained in the Roman Missal, but the remains of an ancient system of continuous reading could also be discerned.

The present Roman Lectionary (*Ordo Lectionum Missae:* ET = *The Lectionary*) with its three-year Sunday cycle, devotes a year to the continous reading of each of the Synoptic Gospels, John's Gospel occupying its traditional place in Lent and Paschaltide annually, in both the Sunday and weekday cycles. In year two, the brevity of Mark is supplemented by the reading of John 6. The weekday lectionary covers all four Gospels every year; in addition a wide choice of Gospels is provided for votive masses* and the commons of saints*. In the current second edition of the Lectionary (1981), all the saints' days have been provided with proper Gospels for use instead of weekday readings if desired.

The Church of England's Alternative Service Book (1980) adopts for the eucharist the system of 'controlling readings' originally drawn up by the Joint Liturgical Group, published in R. C. D. Jasper (ed), *The Calendar and the Lectionary*, 1967. This means that for the nine Sundays before Christmas the choice of Gospel is determined by the first or Old Testament reading. Then from Christmas to Easter the Gospel becomes the controlling reading and gives a more or less chronological account of Christ's life and ministry. From Easter to Pentecost it is still the Gospel which is dominant, in one year giving the resurrection appearances and in the other the 'I am' passages from John's Gospel. For the rest of the year the Gospel is chosen to fit the second, New Testament reading. This lectionary adopts a two-year cycle.

Gospels are read as the second reading at either morning or evening prayer on most days of the year, so that the four Gospels are read in their entirety at these services in the course of the year. The Roman Catholic weekday lectionary has been adopted for celebrations of the eucharist on weekdays.

J. A. Jungmann, *The Mass of the Roman Rite*, rev ed 1959; R. C. D. Jasper (ed), *The Alternative Service Book: A Commentary*, 1980; M. Righetti, *Storia Liturgica*, III, [3]1966.

BRIAN NEWNS

Grace

From the Latin *gratia* in the sense of gratefulness, grace is used of an expression of thanks at the beginning and end of a meal. The custom was followed by Jesus (John 6.11) and by the apostles (Acts 27.35). Fixed forms were devised for monasteries, colleges and schools. The Roman breviary contains a *Benedictio Mensae*.

Grace also designates II Cor. 13.14 which is often used as a prayer. It is found *c*.375 before the *Sursum corda* in the *Apostolic Constitutions* (8.12) but this does not seem

to have influenced its later employment as a conclusion to a service. This was first added in 'The Litany used in the Queen's chapel' of 1559 whence it found its way into the Elizabethan BCP and became a normal termination of morning and evening prayer.

EDITOR

Gradual

see **Chants of the Proper of the Mass; Music in the Mass of the Roman Rite**

Gregorian Chant

The traditional monophonic music of Western Christianity has often been inaccurately described as 1. *Cantus Romanus* (Roman chant); 2. *Cantus planus* (plainchant or plainsong); 3. *Cantus Gregorianus* (Gregorian chant). The term 'Roman chant' is misleading, as there exists another repertoire that goes by the name of 'Old Roman chant' and which is distinct from what we now know as 'Gregorian chant'. The term *Cantus planus* was used in the thirteenth century to distinguish the traditional chant from the various kinds of measured music and polyphony that had come into being. The more familiar term Gregorian chant refers back to the legend which attributes the composition of the whole of the basic repertoire to St Gregory the Great (*c.*540–604), under divine inspiration. Gregory may indeed have had some part in the codification of the chants of the mass in the *Antiphonale Missarum* that bears his name and perhaps in the organization of a *Schola cantorum*, but there is no certain knowledge about the extent of his activities, and his writings rarely mention music. Scholars are divided on the subject of the origins of the so-called Gregorian chant. Its early sources clearly lay, not only in Rome, but also in such centres as St Gall, Einsiedeln, Metz, Chartres, Laon, etc. One widely-held theory is that at some stage – possibly around the year 700 – an earlier form of the chant repertoire, stemming from Rome, underwent a fundamental revision somewhere in Gaul, returning to Rome in its new guise, thereafter being recognized as the standard chant for the whole of Western Christendom. It is remarkable to find that, with few exceptions (such as the Diocese of Milan, which had its own distinct repertoire known as Ambrosian chant), all the earliest manuscripts with musical notation (tenth to eleventh centuries) bear witness to a quite extraordinary uniformity. One single vigorous tradition is to be found everywhere, from the British Isles to Switzerland and from south of the Alps to the Pyrenees.

The repertoire remained substantially intact, the melodies substantially unchanged until the later years of the sixteenth century. From this time on the melodies suffered mutilation and distortion at the hands of successive editors, imbued with notions of classical Latin but ignorant of the principles underlying the word-setting of the traditional chant. They took upon themselves to change the placement of the text, to bring it into line with their Renaissance theories of Latin prosody. They also drastically reduced the number of notes in the florid chants. This refurbished repertoire, that would have been unrecognizable to the early chant composers, was published in the official service books of the church and used from the end of the sixteenth century to the beginning of the twentieth. Towards the middle of the nineteenth century, however, a group of monks from the Abbey of Solesmes in France undertook the arduous task of preparing new editions of the service books based on the scholarly comparative study of large numbers of the earliest manuscripts with musical notation.

The principal service books in use today are largely the work of the monks of Solesmes. The *Graduale* contains the music of the mass, with the melodies restored to their original shape, and the *Antiphonale* contains the music of the divine office*, with the exception of the chants used during the night office (matins). These books contain the largest assemblage of monophonic music in existence, totalling about 3000 melodies for cantors, choirs, and congregations, and 'recitatives' for priests, and cover every phase of the church's worship from baptism to the blessing of aircraft. Gregorian chant – to use the now generally accepted term – is spiritually, aesthetically, and practically the ideal kind of church music – truly sung-prayer and prayer-song.

Willi Apel, *Gregorian Chant*, [3]1966; G. B. Baroffio, 'Die liturgischen Gesänge im Abendland: ambrosianische Liturgie', *Ge-*

schichte der katholischen Kirchenmusik, i, ed K. G. Fellerer, 1972; Helmut Hucke, 'Gregorian and Old Roman chant', *The New Grove Dictionary of Music and Musicians*, 1980.

MARY BERRY

Handicapped People and Worship

When worship is conceived to be exclusively spiritual and spiritual is understood to be the equivalent of cerebral or mental, then no great problems are involved in devising forms believed to be suitable for handicapped people. The physically handicapped e.g. the paralysed, can just as well listen and read as the able-bodied. The blind (*see* **Blind People and Worship**) can equally participate as long as the trouble has been taken to provide Braille versions of hymn and prayer books. The deaf may be assisted by an efficient hearing-aid system – although in how many churches are these currently provided? However, when the dumb are concerned, and especially the deaf and dumb, the barrier to corporate worship erected by sensory deprivation is great and can only be partially breached by means of sign language (*see* **Deaf People and Worship**). Indeed those in this condition who wish to take part in acts of worship call in question its interpretation as essentially a verbal activity. They compel recognition that worship should be an offering of the total self and that this includes the physical as well as the mental. Awareness of this can lead to acceptance of the importance of movement-prayers* which, especially for the dumb but also for everyone, may replace verbal utterances completely. *See also* **Choir (Sign Language)**. Liturgical dance* is another form of worship open to the handicapped and even to the physically handicapped – devotional dances for those confined to wheel chairs are perfectly feasible. *See* Plate 37.

Unfortunately, many Christian congregations are not remarkable for including the disabled in the category of those they welcome to their services, as distinct from the alternative of tolerating them. This is to be guilty of 'handicappism', a pernicious attitude which some American writers are now ranking with racism and sexism as three of the major evils afflicting human kind. Handicappism is that frame of mind that looks down on people with mental, emotional and/or physical disadvantages and promotes in them feelings of isolation and inferiority. Rather 'esteem' should characterize the approach, i.e. not only love, affection and care but everything that is the opposite of fussing over the disabled as poor things needing pity. Forms of service that do not meet the needs of those with deficiencies manifest both a lack of esteem and an implicit and often unsuspected handicappism. Despite the devoted work of specialized chaplains (to the blind, the deaf, etc.), the churches in general have not been remarkable for facing the issues involved and devising means of drawing the handicapped out of their imposed isolation into the worship of the body of Christians – special services are one thing; regular participation is another.

———

J. G. Davies, *Liturgical Dance*, 1984; K. Hill, *Dance for the Physically Disabled*, 1976; *Is Our Theology Disabled? A Symposium on Theology and Persons with Handicapping Conditions*, 1982.

EDITOR

Harvest Thanksgiving

Although the OT prescribes a feast to celebrate the first fruits of the harvest (Pentecost), and another to celebrate the ingathering of the threshing floor and the winepress (Tabernacles: Ex. 23.16; Deut. 16.9, 13), the church does not appear to have observed any such festivals until relatively recent times. The Ember Days* of June, September, and December were agricultural in origin and very probably related to the pagan observances of Rome at the time of sowing and the harvests of corn and wine; but in Christian liturgy these have always been observed as fasts. However, Lammas (loaf mass: 1 August) has been observed in England from Saxon times and throughout the Middle Ages with the blessing of bread made from the first ripe corn.

The harvest home was a secular, weekday, observance, but it is to be noted that since the Reformation, in a period when people made their communion only a few times in the year, 'afore and after harvest' was one of the occasions prescribed

Plate 37 Handicapped children at the Victoria Special School, Northfield, Birmingham

by George Herbert and others for the purpose. In 1843 when the Revd R. S. Hawker, Vicar of Morwenstow in Cornwall, revived the Lammas custom (on the first Sunday of October) and used bread made from the first ripe corn for the bread of the sacrament, it was partly his purpose to redeem the secular character of the harvest home.

In the BCP, as in the mediaeval Latin books, no mention is made of Harvest Thanksgiving. A special prayer of thanksgiving for an abundant harvest was first officially provided, for use after the General Thanksgiving, in 1796. Similar provision was made at intervals for the next fifty years, whenever the abundance of the harvest seemed to justify it. This led to the belief that such an observance should be made regularly. It was about this period that most of the popular harvest thanksgiving hymns were written, and in 1862 Convocation made official provision for the occasion with proper psalms, readings, and prayers. In America similar provision had been made since 1790, and the Irish followed in 1877. Today the festival is recognized and provided for in the ASB and other books of the Anglican Communion, and in the Roman Catholic Missal.

G. Harford and M. Stevenson (eds), *The Prayer Book Dictionary*, 1912. For Ember Days *see* G. G. Willis, *Essays in Early*

Roman Liturgy, 1964. For R. S. Hawker, *see* Piers Brendon, *Hawker of Morwenstow*, 1975.

E. C. WHITAKER

Hindu Worship

Hinduism is a complex term invented by the West to indicate the majority religion of the Indian sub-continent, but this is a vast area of great religious diversity in which many kinds of worship are practised. There are ancient models, with elaborate scriptural directions, but restricted today to comparatively small circles, and great popular festivals and pilgrimages which attract millions.

The most revered texts are the Vedas ('knowledge'), which were compiled from about 3000 years ago but not written down for many centuries. The most important is the Rig Veda ('praise'), composed of 1028 hymns to the gods of the Aryan tribes of North India. The three other Vedas are the *Sāma* ('chant'), *Yajur* ('sacrifice') and *Atharva*, named after a priest. The Vedas are followed by a series of Brāhmanas, which explain the hymns and their ritual for Brahmin priests, and by philosophical deductions in the Upanishads, which are the 'Veda's end', Ved-ānta.

Vedic religion was priestly and public and it concerned the worship of the gods (*devas*, related to Latin *deus*). These are chiefly ritual and sky gods and nearly all male. Agni (like Latin *ignis*), the god of fire and messenger to the gods, has nearly a quarter of the hymns. Soma, a fermented drink for libations, also has many hymns in the Rig Veda and much of the Sāma Veda. A third most prominent god was Indra, who combined the functions of storm and national warrior deity. There were countless lesser divinities addressed in hymns and sacrifices, but many of these are long forgotten or survive in little-understood texts since the Vedic form of the Sanskrit language has long been obsolete.

The Rig Veda names eight kinds of priest, and in later times double this number might be required. Sacrifices were performed in the open on a brick altar but not in a temple. They centred upon the sacred fire and libation, and other materials were offered, of butter, milk, wine and animal flesh. Priests recited Vedic formulae and these verses were regarded as having sacred and magical power, so that on the one hand Brahmin priests were masters of magic utterance, and on the other the sacred word or power was developed in philosophy to the supreme power of the universe, the cosmic soul or Absolute. There were also great communal sacrifices, royal consecrations and a Horse Sacrifice (*Ashvamedha*) by which kings strengthened and extended their territory.

The chief survivals of Vedic religion today, among high caste Hindus only, are found in marriage and ancestral ceremonies. When a household is established at a wedding the sacred fire is kindled, which is not used for domestic purposes and should never go out, and here three times a day Five Great Sacrifices should be offered. These are to the gods or Supreme Being, the ancestors, living beings including animals, the poor, and wise men through hearing the Vedas. The most elaborate offerings are those made to the ancestors, who receive food and water every day, and gifts of rice-balls (*pinda*) in an open place at each new moon in a Shrāddha ('faithful') ceremony. This begins after the cremation of the dead, and is held to nourish the departed so that they can bless their descendants. This domestic religion is performed by the householder, who has been initiated previously by the conferment of the sacred thread in adolescence which makes him 'twice born'. He also received at that time the sacred verse (*mantra*) which all high caste Hindus recite daily in all rituals: 'Let us meditate on the glorious light of the Sun, may he inspire our minds.'

Most Indians are not high caste males, and even among the latter, many of the Vedic rites have disappeared and popular gods have replaced Aryan deities. Vishnu, Shiva and the Goddess, with hosts of lesser divinities, are the modern objects of worship. Vishnu is for millions the only god, but his transcendental beneficence is coloured by his Avatars (*avatāra*, descent, 'incarnation') who are glamorous personifications. The two most popular Avatars are Krishna, the herdsman and lover, and Rāma, the noble epic king. Shiva is also regarded as the supreme and only real god by his millions of devotees, and many scriptures sing of him in monotheistic terms. His mixed character makes him at once the Lord of the Dance and the Great

Ascetic and Yogi, a god of death and destruction and also a gracious teacher who appears in visions to his worshippers. Shiva is the Great God (*Mahā-dev*) whose spouse is the Great Goddess (*Mahā-devī*), known to her followers by various names: Shakti, Durgā, Kālī. In the latter form she is the destroyer-goddess who at Calcutta (*Kālī-ghat*, 'Kālī's steps') and in the region still receives animal sacrifices, practices which most Hindus now find abhorrent. Other very popular gods are the elephant-headed Ganesha, son of Shiva and the Goddess, who brings good luck, and Lakshmi the wife of Vishnu, who is celebrated every New Year. To all of these deities offerings and prayers are made at home and in public.

India is noted for its countless temples, many of them in the south of great beauty and covered with lavish stone sculpture which surpasses even that of Gothic cathedrals (*see* Fig. 22). Many northern temples

Fig. 22 Temple of Brihadishvara, Tanjore

were destroyed by Muslim iconoclasts. Temples are not built for regular congregational services but contain a central sanctuary, usually small, surrounded by courtyards and walls which contain great decorated gateways and pillars, and there are large water tanks for ritual washing. Temple worship is the concern of priests whose rites are not normally observed by the laity. Images and symbols are bathed and anointed, to the accompaniment of repeated texts. In home worship also, images of Krishna and other gods are similarly dressed and washed, and receive food, flowers and incense. Laymen crowd to the temple for special occasions, and notably the annual festivals when temple images are taken to a river and bathed, being drawn in temple cars like the Juggernaut (*Jagan-nātha*, 'world-lord', a title of Krishna).

Other annual festivals mark ancient rites: Holi in the spring as a fertility ritual, Dashara in the autumn celebrating both Kālī and Rāma where carnival processions provide entertainment, and Dīvālī for Lakshmi at the New Year. Many temples are famous places of pilgrimage connected with stories of the gods, and Benares (Varanasi, or Kashi) is the holiest city of all, with rather dilapidated shrines but of antique sanctity, where cremations take place and many holy men come to die. There are also occasional pilgrimage festivals, especially Kumbha Mela ('pitcher fair'), held every twelve years or so, at which millions of people and many holy men attend.

M. Dhavamony, *Love of God according to Śaiva Siddhānta*, 1971; W. D. O'Flaherty, *Hindu Myths*, 1975; F. Hardy, *Viraha-bhakti*, 1983; K. Klostermaier, *Hindu and Christian in Vrindaban*, 1970; G. Michell, *The Hindu Temple*, 1977; R. B. Pandey, *Hindu Samskāras*, [2]1969; E. G. Parrinder, *Avatar and Incarnation*, [2]1982; M. Singer (ed), *Krishna: Myths, Rites and Attitudes*, 1966; L. P. Vidyarthi, *The Sacred Complex in Hindu Gaya*, 1961.

GEOFFREY PARRINDER

Holy Days

see **All Saints**; **All Souls**; **Ember Days**; **Fast Days**; **Ferial**; **Rogation Days**; **Saints' Days**

Holy Saturday

In the primitive church the great festival of the Pasch (Easter) began on the Saturday evening and continued through the night, the fast lasting until midnight or dawn. Although the unity of the cross and resurrection would be more important than differences of emphasis, the cross would be the great motif of the vigil and the resurrection of

the vigil's end, with the sacrament of baptism*, followed by the eucharist*, celebrated at the point where the one yielded to the other. It was inevitable that the evolution of the Pasch into Good Friday* and Easter Day* should modify the place of Saturday in Holy Week*, turning it into an essentially aliturgical day, a period of waiting between the sorrowful commemoration of the passion on Good Friday and the joyful celebration of the resurrection on Easter Day.

By a process of liturgical corruption it became the custom in the Latin rite to celebrate the Pascal vigil* service during the day on Saturday, but the vigil was restored to its proper place in the Latin rite following the Holy Week reforms of 1955, anticipated by the renewal of the vigil in 1951. A vigil service commencing on the Saturday evening is not a Holy Saturday liturgy, but part of the Easter Day liturgy itself.

For bibliography *see* under **Holy Week**

R. F. BUXTON

Holy Week

When Egeria made her pilgrimage to the Holy Land towards the end of the fourth century, the complex structure of Holy Week services at Jerusalem was clearly something new in the church's worship. There is no evidence elsewhere at the time for anything of this nature. The week before the Pasch had held a unique position in the Christian year since the middle of the previous century, but there is nothing to suggest that observances on the lines of this rich development existed before the latter part of the fourth century. Now for the first time Palm Sunday* and Good Friday* make their appearance. The essential feature was the attempt to link the culminating events of the ministry with the days of their occurrence and the places where they happened. Jerusalem was the one location where the process of change could go forward quite naturally. The essential conservatism of Christian worship makes it most unlikely that important transformations will originate in a region or period which, in respect of the particular matter, is a liturgical vacuum. In Constantinople or Carthage or Rome a development of this nature would not have evolution but revolution. It was otherwise in Jerusalem. In and around the city were the sacred sites themselves. With the ending of persecution and the erection of sanctuaries on the holy places, pilgrims were arriving from every quarter of the Christian world and ascetics were coming to stay in Jerusalem. Thus, for the enrichment of its worship, the church of Jerusalem doubtless evolved the structure of these services in the third quarter of the fourth century.

Holy Week at Jerusalem was intimately and topographically related to the sanctuaries of the holy places. It was entirely natural in the environment. Egeria described the customs in detail because they were novel. There was necessarily some modification in the details of the celebrations as they spread beyond Jerusalem, for complete realism was possible only in the Holy City. It must be emphasized how powerfully the dynamism of this profound innovation surged throughout the Christian world. The pulsation of that movement has never ceased to throb with energy through all the Christian centuries. For it is this idea of liturgical realism, this idea that the life of Christ is manifested to the worshipper in the liturgical year, which has not only transformed Holy Week but has also been the motive power behind the mature growth of the Christian year as a whole. Important though the influence of Jerusalem was here, the rapidity with which the rest of the church adopted it shows that it was psychologically and spiritually ready to make this fundamental change in its approach to its worship.

In the general celebration of Holy Week, four great services highlight the main events being celebrated, namely those of Palm Sunday, Maundy Thursday*, Good Friday and Easter*. For the rest of the week the normal round of eucharist and office, with appropriate lessons and other seasonal material, supplies the fare.

Along with much else, the churches of the Reformation largely abolished the special liturgies of Holy Week, and often the observance of the week itself. The Book of Common Prayer retained the week in outline but liturgical provision was limited to the normal services of morning and evening prayer and holy communion with appropriate lections. In recent decades many Anglicans have found this inadequate, and

there has been much borrowing and adaptation of material from the Latin rite, itself radically revised and purified from 1955 onwards. Both the Joint Liturgical Group and the Church of England Liturgical Commission have produced sets of proposed services for Holy Week. The spread of traditional and modified forms of Holy Week observance across ecclesiastical boundaries is one of the fruits of the present ecumenical age.

The way Holy Week liturgy has developed down the centuries illustrates three types of liturgical piety, which may be called respectively 'unitive', 'rememorative' and 'representational'. The primitive paschal vigil* and eucharist in which all aspects of the mystery of redemption through the death and resurrection of Christ are celebrated in one rite was a unitive celebration. The developed classical Holy Week rites that owed so much to fourth century Jerusalem were essentially rememorative, each part of the total mystery of salvation being celebrated separately at an appropriate time, but still through a mixture of word, ceremony and symbol with no attempt being made to portray literally or act out the events themselves. When the latter stage of development occurs liturgy becomes representational, though by and large Holy Week rites have stayed rememorative, with representational elements being confined to a small number of subsidiary ceremonies that have tended to be both local and ephemeral. The modern Roman rites and those suggested by the Joint Liturgical Group and the Church of England Liturgical Commission are essentially rememorative in character.

Church of England Liturgical Commission, *Lent, Holy Week, Easter*, GS643 1984; J. D. Crichton, *The Liturgy of the Holy War*, 1971; J. G. Davies, *Holy Week: A Short History*, 1963; R. Greenacre, *The Sacrament of Easter*, 1965; Joint Liturgical Group, *Holy Week Services*, 1983; C. P. M. Jones (ed), *A Manual for Holy Week*, 1967; K. W. Stevenson, 'On Keeping Holy Week', *Theology*, Vol 89, No 725, Jan 1986; J. W. Tyrer, *Historical Survey of Holy Week*, 1932; J. Wilkinson, *Egeria's Travels*, 1981.

See also bibliography under **Calendar**

R. F. BUXTON

Hood

see **Vestments** 2(*d*)

Hour Services

see **Canonical Hours**

House Churches

During the second half of the twentieth century, the house church has emerged as an important expression of religious life. Behind this phenomenon is a longing to recapture the essence of the early church in the days before Christianity became institutionalized. The house is the church – the people who come to it are a closely related family or fellowship; religion and liturgical expression are spontaneous and essentially relevant to every aspect of daily life.

In the Anglican church, a forward-looking experiment was successfully carried out in the 1950s by the Reverend E. W. Southcott at Halton, Leeds, England. He had the vision of a church that was more than an institution used for convenience, spasmodically or out of a sense of duty; he knew that it should be an integral part of the life of the community, and that the worship of the people must be meaningful in daily life. And so meetings in homes were arranged as an extension of the services of the church. These included Bible study meetings, which served as missionary enterprise, as well as meetings when committed members of the congregation celebrated the eucharist. Halton was a large parish, one third of it being a working-class area. The success of the experiment is indicated by the title of Southcott's book, *The Parish Comes Alive* (1956).

The idea was little developed by other Anglicans in England. However, during the 1960s and 1970s home meetings for Bible study became a popular practice. The idea of the house church might have ended with the experience at Halton, but for a spiritual phenomenon which emerged and escalated into an international religious movement of some significance. During the 1960s charismatic renewal spread through all the Protestant denominations, and even aroused interest in the Roman Catholic Church.

Various religious expressions resulted, one of them being a movement which can loosely be termed house churches. There is

an important difference between these and the house churches established by E. W. Southcott. The latter were an enrichment of liturgical and pastoral life; the former are independent groups of churches set up in place of established denominations, although those involved are anxious to avoid the accusation of forming yet another new denomination. Basically, there are three types of this latter-day house church.

1. That which has developed from the influence of an independent Pentecostal church in the village of South Chard, Dorset, England, whose founders were a married couple formerly belonging to a Christian Brethren Assembly. This church has attracted visitors from far and wide, both individuals and groups, who wish to imitate the fellowship at South Chard. Its Elders visit each new group that is formed to encourage its progress.

2. That which has developed from the work of one man, G. W. North, a lay preacher of an independent Baptist tradition, and which stands firmly in the tradition of the Holiness movement. Each group is autonomous, being linked with other groups and with the founder informally. G. W. North visits each only when he is invited.

3. That which has evolved through the efforts of a group of men, all of whom were involved in charismatic renewal, led by two brothers, Bryn and Keri Jones. Currently, this is the largest and most rapidly expanding of the three types. Among their enterprises, they operate a publishing house under the name of Harvestime.

The Harvestime churches have a firm hierarchical system of authority. Each individual is under the authority of the Elders of the group, each group is linked to the others through a chain of Elders and Apostles which refer ultimately to the headquarters in Bradford, England. Divine election is claimed for each Apostle and Elder, and a clear anti-clerical position is maintained. Most of these groups have around 200 members, and so they have outgrown the houses in which they began. Many now meet in schools, and some have bought disused churches.

Of remarkable significance is the sociological composition of house churches. Such groups tend to appeal to the middle-class professional. In the pioneer period of their formation, they had great appeal for young married couples, and in their early years they had very few members who were over forty.

Each of the three types has developed its own life-style and liturgy. Basically, each sees itself as returning to the early Christian fellowships depicted in Acts. Each offers an alternative way of life to existing society, providing meetings for prayers, Bible study, worship, leisure activities, self-help groups and in many cases a residential community life. Obviously each type has its characteristic differences which mirror the aims and spiritual heritage of the founders, and the circumstances which have moulded development and progress. It is in the liturgical expression of worship that these differences become apparent.

The three types of house church have very different forms of worship. South Chard, the first to emerge in the early 1950s, has a traditional Pentecostal form of worship, but with distinctive characteristics, the most obvious being the practice of singing a hymn, a chorus or even one line over and over again. Tambourines and hand clapping are much in evidence, as in classic Pentecostal worship.

None of the three types has a set order of service, except in so far as the first hour is occupied by worship, and the second hour or longer by a sermon, with a brief time of worship to close.

The Chard fellowships are unmistakable, with their loud, repetitive singing. The meetings of the North fellowships are quieter, with the leader playing an all-important part, both in leading the worship and delivering the sermon. Music is provided by piano and guitars. The singing is mostly from *Redemption Hymnal* (the Pentecostal hymn book also used by both other types of house church), and also from a collection of Wesley hymns, *Hymns of Eternal Truth*, compiled by G. W. North, whose length and solemnity typify the nature of the worship. There is a strong emphasis on personal holiness, and the exuberance of the other two types is lacking.

The character of the Harvestime meetings, in contrast to the other two types, is symbolized by the spontaneous singing, led by a group of men with the backing of piano, drums, cymbals, violins, guitars,

flutes and even harps. Any who wish to do so may lead the singing, and often this is done by different people each week. The music gives a quality to the worship which is most attractive, and provides an informality not found in traditional church music. Many of the songs have a rhythm reminiscent of Jewish folk songs. A feature of the Harvestime churches is the constant stream of new hymns and choruses which are composed. Each yearly conference has produced a new pamphlet of hymns. This reflects the leaders' concern that the movement will not stagnate nor develop traditions, but will continue to represent the ongoing activity of the Spirit of God among his people.

The differences in the three types of house church reflect the differences in the underlying vision of each. The South Chard groups set out to establish what they term 'body ministry' in the context of Christian worship. This means that anyone in the congregation is free to contribute to the public ministry in any of its forms, so that any individual may preach, pray, lead the singing or minister in one of the Pentecostal gifts such as prophecy or healing. The North groups are concerned with the personal holiness of the individual, whereas the Harvestime churches see themselves as an eschatological grouping of God's people. As the last days draw near, God is calling out his people into a fellowship.

All three types of house church, therefore, provide an alternative to the traditional church, both in ways of worship and in a total way of life, and clearly indicate the desire to establish an alternative society.

See also **Pentecostal Worship** 3.

Horton Davies, *Worship and Theology in England*, V, 1965, pp.323–27; Joyce V. Thurman, *New Wineskins*, 1982; A. Walker, *Restoring the Kingdom: the Radical Christianity of the House Church Movement*, 1985.

JOYCE V. THURMAN

Humeral Veil

see **Vestments** 2(*j*)

Hymns

1. *Latin.* In his commentary on Ps. 148.14, Augustine described a hymn as 'the praise of God in song', adding that praise of God that is not sung is not a hymn. Ambrose (339–97) is named as the real father of Latin hymnody and four hymns are attributed to him by Augustine: *Aeterne rerum conditor*, *Deus creator omnium*, *Iam surgit hora tertia* and *Veni redemptor omnium*. These early hymns with their simple iambic metre were easy to understand, to remember and to sing. Tradition has it that these and other hymns were sung by the people in Ambrose's church in Milan during the long night vigils. The names of other early Christian poets are associated with hymn-writing and they include Caelius Sedulius (*c*.450) famous for his Christmas and Epiphany hymns (*A solis ortus cardine* and *Hostis Herodes impie*), and Venantius Fortunatus (530–609), author of a fine hymn in honour of the cross (*Vexilla Regis*). The best-known of all Latin hymns, the *Veni creator spiritus*, has been attributed to Hrabanus Maurus (776 or 784–856), though his authorship is disputed by scholars.

About 350 hymn texts, ranging in date from the fourth century to the twentieth, occur in the various hours of the divine office*. Few hymn melodies, however, are to be found before the eleventh century. St Benedict (*c*.480–*c*.550) made provision in his *Rule* for a hymn (which he termed 'the Ambrosian') to be sung by his monks at each hour of the divine office. The Roman Church did not admit them into the secular office until the twelfth century on account of the prejudice against importing other than biblical words into the liturgy, and even more because the form was used by heretics for propaganda purposes. Indeed, the psalms had in earlier centuries been regarded as hymns and tradition links the great Hallel group (113–118), which was recited or sung at the principal Jewish festivals, with the hymn sung at the Last Supper by Jesus and his disciples.

Polyphonic settings (*see* **Polyphony**) of the Latin metrical hymns began in the thirteenth century and were contributed by such great church composers as Dunstable, Dufay, Josquin des Prez, Tallis and Byrd. Palestrina published a fine collection of 79 hymns, mostly for vespers, founded on the chant melodies. Many of the Renaissance settings were intended for *alternatim* performance, one verse in chant followed by the next in polyphony, and so on. The *Liber Hymnarius* (Solesmes, 1983) is an

up-dated edition of the main Latin hymn repertory.

MARY BERRY

2. *Vernacular* Perhaps the first appearance of vernacular hymns came with the Italian *Laudi Spirituali*, introduced as part of the revivalist apparatus of the Franciscan movement in the thirteenth century, to grow in number and popularity over the next four centuries. Hymn-singing in the vernacular also formed a feature of the worship of the Bohemian Brethren led by John Huss early in the fifteenth century. With the Lutheran and Calvinist reforms of a century later, and the translation of the liturgy itself, new types of vernacular song were introduced – to exert lasting influence upon congregational music. The Lutheran *chorale*, epitomized in *Ein' Feste Burg* and the *Passion Chorale*, provided a melodic line of great strength familiar today in four-square Bach-type harmonized form. Once evolved, the Lutheran chorale book was to be preserved in its integrity, no new tunes being added. Succeeding generations of Lutherans thus inherited an unvarying repertoire of congregational song. In Geneva, Calvin introduced the metrical psalm*, which was a verse translation by Marot and Bèze of the prose psalter. Sung in unison to subtly rhythmic melodies largely composed by Goudimel and Bourgeois, the Genevan model was to be adopted in Dutch, Scottish and English churches.

Metrical psalmody thus became for two centuries the staple of congregational music in England – at first in the *Whole Book of Psalms* of Sternhold and Hopkins (1562) and subsequently in the *New Version* of Tate and Brady (1696). Both collections included a few supplementary hymns; and the appearance of Wither's *Hymnes and Songs of the Church* (1623) and Bishop Ken's *Morning, Evening and Midnight Hymns* (1674) indicates that hymn singing was not dead in England at this time. The signal for its revival was the publication of John and Charles Wesley's *Hymns and Sacred Poems* (1739). Thereafter, Wesleyan congregations soon become noted for the fervour of their hymn singing; while Anglican bishops remonstrated with their clergy upon the neglected and apathetic state of parochial psalmody.

Under the influence of the Oxford Movement, efforts were made after 1833 to restore to the Anglican service something of its lost dignity; and although the hymn was at first regarded by Tractarians as too reminiscent of Nonconformity to receive approval, under J. M. Neale's leadership that view changed with the appearance of the *Hymnal Noted* (1851), a collection of Latin hymns in translation associated with their plain-song tunes. Less 'advanced' churchmen adopted other collections – such as Havergal's *Old Church Psalmody* (1847) and Gauntlett's *Hymn and Tune Book* (1852) – while Maurice's *Choral Harmony* (1854) introduced the German chorale to English congregations.

All these trends were to merge with the appearance of *Hymns, Ancient and Modern* in 1861. Remarkable for its eclecticism, the new book assembled examples of plainsong, psalm-tune, chorale and old church-tune, adding to the traditional element some new tunes of a distinctive type by Dykes, Ouseley and Monk. During the remainder of the nineteenth century *Hymns, A & M* in successive editions was almost to attain the status of an official Anglican hymnal. Later reaction against the quality of some of the words and music in that book, however, was to produce the *English Hymnal* (1906) and *Songs of Praise* (1926), both of which sought to provide a less emotional tone.

The first authorized modern hymnal for Roman Catholic use in England was the *Westminster Hymnal* (1912). Important collections issued for Nonconformist use include *Wesley's Hymns* (1877), the *Congregational Church Hymnal* (1887), the *Baptist Church Hymnal* (1900) and the *Methodist Hymn Book* (1933) with its supplement *Hymns and Songs* (1969).

The task of bringing existing hymnals up to date has been regularly undertaken. *A Hundred Hymns for Today*, a supplement to *Hymns, A & M*, was published in 1969, and *English Praise*, a supplement to the *English Hymnal*, in 1975. Most recent among complete revisions of earlier collections are the *New Catholic Hymnal* (1971); *Hymns and Psalms. A Methodist and Ecumenical Hymn Book* (1983); and the *New Standard Edition, Hymns A & M* (1983). In every case the editors have had to prune drastically while trying to preserve 'old favourites' and the genuinely worthwhile.

The *Cambridge Hymnal* (1967) was a new collection designed 'to produce a fitting expression of Christian thought and feeling in the twentieth century'. The same ideal has prompted the publication of a number of hymnals in the USA, where a sense of propriety and traditional values is often very marked. This trend is well illustrated in *American Hymns, Old and New* (1980), and the role of the hymn in the liturgy is carefully considered in M. J. Hatchett, *A Manual for Clergy and Church Musicians* (1980).

At another (and very different) level, the pop hymn movement begun with Geoffrey Beaumont's 'Chesterton' in 1955 seems to have demonstrated clearly enough the need for new words rather than new tunes. Sydney Carter's 'Lord of the Dance', set to an old Shaker* melody, showed how quickly a new text could spread in the wake of liturgical experiment. One wonders if this hymn will be seen as the modern congregation's vocal apogee, much as Vaughan Williams' 'For all the saints' represented a new peak following its introduction in 1904.

See also **Indigenization**.

BERNARR RAINBOW

P. Dearmer, *Songs of Praise Discussed*, 1952; W. H. Frere, Preface to *Hymns, A & M, Historical Edition*, 1909; Maurice Frost, *Historical Companion to Hymns Ancient and Modern*, 1962; John Julian, *Dictionary of Hymnology*, ²1985; K. L. Parry and E. Routley, *Companion to Congregational Praise*, 1953; E. Routley, *Hymns and Human Life*, 1959.

Icon

see **Iconostasis**; **Orthodox Worship**

Iconostasis

The term is Greek in origin, and means, literally, 'picture-stand'; it refers to the screen* separating the altar* in Eastern Orthodox churches from the nave* where the main body of the worshippers are assembled. The history of the development of this type of screen has, until recently, been misunderstood by writers in Western Christendom; it has been mistakenly assumed that this kind of screen, entirely covered with icons or pictures and made of wood, has always been a prominent feature of the Eastern Orthodox rite. But this is a telescoping of the historical development of the screen in the Orthodox or Byzantine liturgy.

In the earlier centuries the screen in the Orthodox rite was made of stone or marble (*see* Plate 38) and it differed little from the type of screen still to be found in some of the older Roman basilicas, e.g. Santa Maria in Cosmedin. At first, at Constantinople, pictures were hung on the altar screen on festivals and these were rather like large medallions made of mosaic or painted with a brush; but they were comparatively small. As time went on these began to multiply and they tended to become a more permanent feature of the screen in the Byzantine rite.

The solid wooden screen or iconostasis proper, with gates and completely covered with large pictures or icons, appears to be a

Plate 38 Sixth-century Byzantine screen and altar, Archaeological Museum, Athens

development in Russia in the late fourteenth and early fifteenth centuries under Theophanes the Greek and the Russian Andrei Rublëv; under them the Byzantine screen was raised in height so that it completely hid the altar from the congregation. With this action, the icons themselves were increased in size from half-length to full-length figures. The fact that these later screens are of wood rather than stone indicates that they are Russian in origin, since that country is a land of vast forests, whereas the stone screen with carved panels and columns was a feature of Byzantium and the eastern Mediterranean area.

The usual explanation of the solid iconostasis is that it veils heaven from earth, the altar being heaven and the saints who are depicted on the screen the mediators between the church on earth and the church in heaven. When the celebrant speaks from the altar obscured by the screen it is as the voice of God speaking to his people on earth. When the gates are opened and the ministers come forth from the altar to the people at the reading of the gospel and the giving of holy communion, it is like the incarnation when Christ came forth from heaven to earth for the salvation of the human race.

In lesser Eastern churches, such as the Armenian and the Coptic, the iconostasis is not employed, but at certain points in the liturgy a veil or curtain may be drawn across the sanctuary.

The term iconostasis is sometimes used for chancel* screens in the Western church, especially those with Byzantine affinities and on which figures of saints stand, e.g. St Mark's Venice.

See also **Orthodox Worship**

L. Ouspensky, 'The Problem of the Iconostasis', *St Vladimir's Seminary Quarterly*, 8.4, 1964, pp.186–218; L. Ouspensky and V. Lossky, *The Meaning of Icons*, 1982; C. E. Pocknee, *The Christian Altar*, 1963.

C. E. POCKNEE/G. D. W. RANDALL

Immaculate Conception

see **Mariological Feasts**

Imposition of Hands

see **Gestures** 7

Incense

The term is used of a number of woods and resins which, when heated or burned, give off a fragrant smell; 'frank' or pure incense, otherwise known as *olibanum*, is the solidified resin of trees belonging to certain species of *Boswellia*.

The use of incense in divine worship appears to be of great antiquity and is exceedingly widespread. In the pre-Christian cultures of the Middle East and the Mediterranean, seven religious uses of it may be distinguished: as a sacrifice to the god or gods; as a sacrifice to the shades of a deceased human being or beings; as a symbol of honour to a living person or persons; as a demonifuge, to drive away evil spirits, whether from the living or from the departed; as a means of purification or healing (a use not always to be distinguished from the preceding); as a festive accompaniment for processions and similar ceremonies; simply to create a worshipful atmosphere. It was also used on non-cultic as well as cultic occasions for practical purposes; but there is no evidence for, and considerable evidence against, the theory that this is the origin of its religious use.

During the first three centuries of the Christian era there was no ceremonial use of incense in the church's worship, and many writers of this period refer to it, as to most other practices of other religions, in terms of disapprobation. It is not difficult to account for this attitude; on the one hand incense was inevitably associated in the Christian mind with its use in the emperor-worship test; it was also used in the ceremonies of what the Christian regarded as false religions.

Christian writers of the fourth and fifth centuries modify this disapprobation; they condemn only the sacrificial use of incense. And, indeed, from the middle of the fourth century the honorific use of it spread rapidly in the Christian church. By the sixth century there are clear cases of the use of incense as a sacrificial offering, in the sense of an act of adoration in return for which divine blessings are asked, a use which persists to this day in most of the Eastern liturgies. In the West this sacrificial interpretation has almost completely disappeared since the early Middle Ages, being

replaced by the offering of incense not in itself, but simply as a symbol of prayer. The use of incense in one way or another has been common to all the historic liturgies since the beginning of the sixth century at the latest, and in most places it is probably at least a century older.

1. *Incense at the eucharist**. The earliest use of incense at the eucharist was honorific: it was borne before the celebrant* at the entrance, and before the book of the gospels before the reading of the gospel. The use of incense in the entrance procession gave rise in the mediaeval West to a censing of the altar* on arrival, a sacrificial or devotional censing, to which was commonly added an honorific censing of the celebrant, and sometimes of others as well. A censing of the altar, or of the book of the gospels on it, came commonly to be prefixed to the bearing of incense in the gospel procession, and in many places a censing of the ministers and the choir was added after the reading of the gospel. From the tenth century a sacrificial or devotional censing was added after the offertory*, often with a censing of ministers, choir and people as well. From the thirteenth century, in many places, with the introduction of elevations of host and chalice at the consecration, censing came to be added at this point, as an act of adoration. The detailed arrangements of the censing at any of these points in the service varied widely. According to the revised Roman Missal of 1970, incense, when it is used at all, is used in the entrance procession, to cense the altar after the entrance, in the gospel procession and during the reading of the gospel; after the offertory, to cense the offerings, the altar, the ministers and the people; and at the elevation of the host and chalice at the consecration.

In the Byzantine, as in most other Eastern rites, the eucharist is never celebrated without incense. According to current Byzantine usage, the celebrant or the deacon censes the altar, the offerings on the prothesis*, the icons, and the people, before the commencement of the service; further censing, the extent and detailed arrangement of which varies from place to place, takes place before the gospel; before, during and after the offertory or great entrance*; after the consecration; and after the communion.

2. *Incense at the divine office**. Incense is used at the major offices in all the historic rites (in the Roman rite only on Sundays and festivals, in the Eastern rites normally daily). The most characteristic use is a devotional – in origin, and still in some rites, sacrificial – one which is probably a conscious imitation of Jewish Temple practice, at the principal morning and evening offices (in the Roman rite at the *Te Deum* at matins, or the office of readings which has replaced it in the modern rite, the *Benedictus* at lauds or morning prayer, and the *Magnificat* at vespers or evening prayer; in practice the ceremonial accompaniments of the revised offices vary considerably from place to place). The origin of this use is almost certainly to be traced to the reference to incense in the classic evening psalm, 140 (141).

3. *Incense at other services*. The use of incense in the Eastern rites is extensive, being prescribed in most of them for all major, and many minor, services. Its use in the West is more restricted: its use at funerals (with what original significance is not easy precisely to determine) appears to have been the origin of its use at the consecration of an altar (having been used in the procession of relics to be sealed in the altar), and its use on this occasion is possibly itself the origin of other censings of the altar; its use in other processions may also derive from its funeral use, but may be of independent origin; its use, with holy water, at many blessings may originally have been demonifugal.

4. *Incense outside the historic rites*. The non-ceremonial – and occasionally ceremonial – use of incense was common in the Church of England during the seventeenth century; it disappeared in the eighteenth century, to be revived in the later nineteenth century, together with so many other traditional practices, under the influence of the Tractarian movement, in a considerable number of churches. Those Anglican churches which use incense today usually follow the Roman use of it. Incense is also used in a very small number of churches of other Reformed traditions.

E. G. C. F. Atchley, *A History of the Use of Incense in Divine Worship*, 1909.

W. JARDINE GRISBROOKE

Inclusive Language

The question of inclusive language in liturgy and biblical translation has been a subject of considerable controversy in the English-speaking church. The issue has been raised in connection with other languages as well. In the United States and also in Canada, where feminism has been advanced in the churches and theological seminaries and where increasing numbers of women are being ordained to the ministry, there has been particular attention to this issue. The definition of inclusive language depends on a perception of current English usage as characterized by androcentrism. The male is taken to be the normative human person; i.e., the word 'man' connotes both the male and the human being as such. Male pronouns are used as generic pronouns. The term 'woman' and female pronouns are never used as generic references for human being, but are exclusive to females. This pattern of grammar is not a linguistic accident. It has developed under the influence of a patriarchal social order in which the male head of family was regarded legally as the representative human person, while women and other dependents could not represent themselves, but were included under the male head of family.

This patriarchal social pattern is further reflected in theological language by referring to the community of Christians as 'brothers', and, in relation to God, as 'sons', while God is imaged in terms of male leadership roles, such as father, Lord and king. Male generic language renders women invisible as autonomous persons, and conveys the implicit message that women are secondary and dependent beings whose relationship to males is analogous to the relationship of human creatures to God. This pattern of male generic language has today come to be recognized as incompatible with the equal dignity of female and male as human persons.

The corrections of male generic language can be done either by using neutral generics, such as 'person' rather than 'man', or by adding words that connote the female counterpart to the male term, such as 'brothers and sisters' rather than 'brothers'. Avoidance of male generic pronouns can be done by repeating the noun, or using either 'he or she' or 'them' in place of the generic 'he'. The objections to this have often been the sense of awkwardness of style, due to the lack of an inclusive third person singular pronoun in English. However, in liturgical usage, this awkwardness can often be avoided by substituting first and second person pronouns, 'we' and 'you' or 'thou', in places where such direct address is appropriately the language of the prayer.

Such rewriting of the language of hymns, readings and liturgical prayers has often been done on a local basis by church groups concerned about the issue. The most ambitious effort at developing inclusive language for church use has been the *Inclusive Language Lectionary* mandated by the Division of Education and Ministry of the National Council of Churches of Christ in the USA. Since 1980, a three-year cycle of lectionary readings in inclusive language has been in preparation for use by the member churches.

The committee of the *Inclusive Language Lectionary* has undertaken to provide inclusive terms, not only for human beings, but also for God. Theologically, the committee understands its mandate for such inclusive language for God as based on the fundamental affirmations that God is, by nature, beyond gender, and that all images for God derived from gender roles are metaphorical, not literal. To use exclusively male metaphors for God implies either that God is literally male or that males alone are the appropriate human images for God. Such an assertion implies that women are not truly theomorphic; that is, do not possess the image of God. If women are truly equivalent with men as images of God, then metaphors for God drawn from female roles should be as appropriate as metaphors drawn from male roles.

Consequently, the *Inclusive Language Lectionary* adds the word 'mother' to that of 'father' as a metaphor for God's parental relationship to humanity. It also substitutes neutral generic terms, such as 'sovereign' or 'ruler', for male leadership roles, such as 'Lord' or 'king'. In relation to christology, the committee uses male nouns and pronouns for Jesus Christ's historical humanity, but substitutes inclusive terms for the divine word or second person of the Trinity manifest in him, such as 'child of God' for 'son of God'. The term 'son of man' as a

messianic title has been replaced by the term 'the Human One', as a translation of the Hebrew term *ben Adam*, a term which, although male generic in form, means simply 'a human being'.

These changes of language, not only for humans, but also for God and Christ, have provoked profound anxiety and animosity among church members, as well as church leaders. Clearly, inclusive language is not simply an academic matter, but strikes deeply at people's emotional feelings about their sexual and social identity. Although inclusive language is sometimes decried as 'trivial', the depths of emotion stirred up by this question suggests that the implications are complex and far-reaching.

Part of the anxiety comes simply from the sense of being deprived of familiar language which has acquired great emotional resonance through usage in prayer and worship. For many, the word itself is the bearer of the reality to which it points. To have the words 'father' and 'Lord' vanish from public worship, to be replaced by 'father and mother' and 'sovereign', is experienced as a literal loss of the familiar divine presence for an alien divinity. For some, underlying this sense of the loss of familiar language is a deeper association of male generic language with social and cosmic order, and a fear that all right order is upset if male and female stand on the same plane socially and as metaphors for the divine. Thus, the question of inclusive language points to profound connections between language and experience of reality, which have only begun to be explored.

An Inclusive Language Lectionary: Readings for Year A, 1983; *Readings for Year B*, 1984; Barbara A. Withers (ed), *Language and the Church*, 1984.

ROSEMARY R. RUETHER

Indigenization

To say that something is indigenous is to affirm that it has been produced naturally in a country or that it is native to a particular land. An indigenous liturgy would therefore be an act of worship which is at home within a country, possibly created there or certainly having affinity with its cultural forms. In the early centuries of the church indigenous liturgies were produced throughout the Roman Empire, the use of the vernacular* in different areas, e.g. of Coptic in Egypt, being but one aspect of this positive process. With the expansion of Christianity outside the Mediterranean basin, the tendency was to export the existing liturgical forms which thus became something of an intrusion within the many countries to which the gospel spread. Native cultural forms were deliberately rejected as 'pagan' and Western European orders of service were transplanted without modification. Awareness that the church with its worship was being regarded as something foreign rather than native to the country in which it sought to be domiciled has led to a demand for indigenization.

At first indigenization was conceived in terms of *adaptation*, i.e. the Western forms continued with some adjustment to local customs. In time it was realized that this was insufficient and that the attempt had to be made to achieve *incarnation*, i.e. to create a truly native expression of Christianity which would be indigenous in the proper sense in that it would be 'of the country'. The tendency has been to consider indigenization from a Western-centred perspective so that it has been regarded as a process to be encouraged 'overseas'. Little note has been taken of the fact that with the immense transformation from an agricultural to a scientific society a similar creative effort is required in Europe and North America.

A survey of indigenization on a global scale is beyond the scope of this present volume and a general discussion in theoretical terms would be misplaced because indigenization is concerned with praxis. To limit the material and at the same time to make it specific, data will be presented from four main areas: Africa, India, Latin America and South East Asia. Even within these vast regions further restriction has been necessary, but it is hoped that the following sections will serve a useful purpose in illustrating the problems involved and different ways of approaching them.

EDITOR

1. *Africa*. In Black Africa south of the Sahara, the area considered in this article, indigenization is closely related to inculturation, incarnation and contextualization. Inculturation is the process of incarnating the Good News in a particular

cultural context. More specifically, it is a process by which people of a particular culture become able to live, celebrate and communicate their Christian faith and their experience of the Paschal mystery in the terms (linguistic, symbolic, social) that make most sense and better convey life and truth in their social and cultural environment. This is quite different from adaptation. The Catholic bishops of Africa stated in 1977: 'The Bishops of Africa and Madagascar consider as being completely out-of-date the so-called theology of adaptation. In its stead, they adopt the theology of incarnation.'

Evangelization and liturgy have gone through three stages in Africa:

Transplantation (or translation): imposing Western expressions of Christianity without modifications.

Adaptation: introducing Western expressions of Christianity with some adjustment to local culture.

Incarnation (inculturation in the best sense of the term): creating truly African expressions of Christianity.

An important turning point in the indigenization of Catholic worship was the promulgation of the *Constitution on the Sacred Liturgy* on 4 December 1963. Since then Catholic worship and liturgy in Africa have undergone dramatic changes. The highest Catholic leadership has spoken strongly on the importance and necessity of indigenization, inculturation and incarnation. In 1969 Pope Paul VI stressed: 'You Africans are from now on your own missionaries. That is to say, you Africans must continue to build the church in this continent . . . You may and you must have an African Christianity.' In his three visits to Africa Pope John Paul II insisted on the supreme importance of inculturation to make the church's teaching and rituals meaningful.

The ideal or goal is clear. Alex Chima of Malawi emphasizes giving the whole liturgy an 'African face and flesh', while Bishop Peter Sarpong of Ghana describes the integration of religion and life in Africa:

> To the African religion is like the skin that you carry along with you wherever you are, not like the cloth that you wear now and discard the next moment . . . His role in worship is active and meaningful. He knows what to do, when and how to do it, with whom and where to do it – without being prompted. For him, worship is not a dreary duty to be gone through and quickly finished with . . . Therefore, the African sings, drums, dances when the need arises, even talks and converses, but he also prays reverently. He takes part in worship with his body and soul, mind, and conscience – his whole being.

But the present reality is quite different. The situation in most parts of Africa seems to show that inculturation is more at the level of *talking about* liturgy than *doing* liturgy. Much liturgy and worship in Africa is still a prefabricated, Western liturgy far from having African 'flesh and blood'. Elochukwu Uzukwu of Nigeria makes a very important distinction between 'adaptation' and 'genuine and systematic creativity'. The former (still predominant in Africa) is a matter of throwing a few African cultural elements into a liturgy that still remains Roman and Western. The latter is to give the whole liturgy an African face and flesh, even if this means reshuffling some of the structural elements of the Mass.

(*a*) *Examples of systematic liturgical creativity in Africa*

(*i*) *Zaire rite for the mass*. This complete eucharistic rite was introduced in 1972 and approved by the Sacred Congregation for Divine Worship on an experimental basis. It is certainly the most successful attempt at genuine 'inculturation'. It follows the traditional order of the mass except that the penitential rite is after the gospel. This prayer uses many features from African tradition. These include an invocation of the saints and of the ancestors 'who have served God with a good conscience'; there are many gestures such as the whole community raising up hands during the prayers and everyone bowing heads and crossing arms on their breast during the penitential rite; and concrete imagery taken from real life, rather than abstract imagery. Sin is described as 'the insect that sticks on to our skin and sucks our lifeblood'. The Word is the one through whom God has created 'our river the Zaire, our forests, our rivers, our lakes'. Drums or gongs are

beaten at particular moments during the celebration (e.g. during the consecration) and during the *Gloria* there is a dance led by the main celebrant. The celebration concludes with a final dance out of the church. Traditional style vestments and headdresses are worn.

(ii) *The mass in Yaounde*. The mass in Ndzon Melen parish in Yaounde, Cameroon (begun in 1969) is an open-air eucharistic celebration based on a traditional neighbourhood assembly of the Beti ethnic group. Emphasis is put on the penitential rite and on colour (red for joy), singing, dancing, clapping, incense and processions. The special African flavour comes from the spontaneity and movement.

(*iii*) *Proposed African eucharistic prayers*. Several of these from various regions – Kenya, Nigeria, Tanzania and Uganda – have been submitted to the respective Bishops' Conferences. The texts include all the liturgical elements deemed to be essential, combined with certain rituals of traditional African worship and African values. So, for example, an all African canon composed by Aylward Shorter at the AMECEA Pastoral Institute (now in Kenya) uses images from the prayers of the Shona of Zimbabwe, the Ga of Ghana and the Dinka of Sudan.

African values portrayed are life, fecundity, the ancestors (the 'living dead'), blood-pact of brotherhood, medicine and kinship. Certain Christian traditional concepts are 'translated' into African values, e.g. the Holy Spirit becomes the 'Spirit-medicine of life' and covenant becomes 'pact of blood brotherhood'. The prayer is styled in short phases, typical of African ritual formulae, and special emphasis is placed on the efficacy of the spoken word.

(*iv*) *Baptismal ritual in Bukina Faso*. Encouraged by the West African Bishops' Commission on Catechesis and Liturgy, research was done among the Mossi Ethnic Group in their language More. Regarding Christian initiation proper, instead of the traditional school-type catechism, an orientation towards the family circle is preferred. Emphasis on the vital element – life being at the centre of the African perception of the universe – demands that the process of being born into the Christian community and of participating in Christ's life should highlight the role of the family or lineage (ecclesial community) and of parents (god parents). The link with the family ancestors (the saints) is stressed – the chief ancestor and the key person in the ceremony being Christ himself.

(*b*) *Other examples of inculturation in African worship*

(*i*) Many themes of African traditional religions and African cultural values are expressed in contemporary African prayers. The language and references to God in these prayers are vivid, concrete and down to earth. God is described as 'Source of All Life', 'Eternal Chief', 'Nursing Mother', 'Piler of Rocks Into Towering Mountains', 'Rain', and 'Sun'. God the Father is the 'Great Elder', Jesus Christ is the 'Elder Brother' and 'Chief Medicine Man' and the Holy Spirit is the 'Unsurpassed Great Spirit'. The communion of saints is very real and the canonized saints are Christian ancestors. Great importance is given to clan and family ancestors (the living-dead).

(*ii*) Substituting the word 'food' for 'bread' in the *Our Father*, since many African languages do not have a word for bread.

(*iii*) Vestments following local traditions and customs, e.g. since the leopard skin is the symbol of royalty among the Wasukuma Ethnic Group in Tanzania, vestments include a leopard skin cope, chasuble and tabernacle cover.

(*iv*) In some Catholic masses the exchange of peace takes place at the end of the penitential rite. This symbolizes the bonding of the community before they hear the Word of God not as individuals but as a faith community. African symbols that are used in the exchange of peace in different reconciliation services are: special tuft of grass (Masai Ethnic Group); green leaf or '*isale*' (Chagga Ethnic Group); eating or drinking from the same bowl or calabash.

(*v*) Sitting during the reading of the gospel. In the African tradition when a powerful chief sent his messengers to each village, the villagers would sit in an open area. The messenger would stand in their midst and announce the chief's news. So too with the gospel.

(*vi*) Since clapping is an integral part of giving thanks the congregation claps during the thanksgiving song after communion.

(*c*) *Paraliturgical services including sacraments*

(*i*) *Christian marriage*. Integrating the basic elements of consent in the traditional marriage ritual into the Christian sacrament of marriage. In Zaire research and discussion is taking place on how to incorporate the stages of traditional or customary African marriage into the church sacrament.

(*ii*) *Ministry of healing*. The official Catholic Church still feels uneasy about the ministry of healing despite its clear evangelical basis. Some paraliturgical services take into account the African anthropology of sickness and suffering. The Wednesday Healing Prayer Services at Nnewi have been acclaimed as one of the significant pastoral accomplishments in Onitsha Diocese, Nigeria. Healing by prayer has made its impact in Abidjan, Yaounde, Kinshasa, Lusaka and Nairobi. In healing and other inculturation areas the Catholic Church can learn a great deal from the experience of the African Independent Churches.

(*iii*) *Christian paraliturgical services* to celebrate the circumcision rite (with special blessings).

(*d*) *Architecture and Art*

Church buildings are now being designed with respect for local materials and forms. The parish church at Bujora, Tanzania, for example, has the shape of a Sukuma round house. Both painters and sculptors are playing their part too in developing an authentic African Christianity by depicting a 'Black Christ'. Since faith can be communicated through images, this African Christ affirms the incarnation of God, i.e. his becoming human for the people of Africa.

What about the future? The sheer size and diversity of Africa presents exciting but demanding challenges for the indigenization of liturgy and worship. The over 50 African countries include over 7,000 distinct languages. Tanzania alone has 120 ethnic groups each with its own distinct language, customs and traditions.

Tony Barrett, *The Church in Turkana*, 1977; Alex Chima, 'Africanizing the Liturgy – Where Are We Twenty Years After Vatican II?', *AFER*, 1983; Joseph Healey, *A Fifth Gospel*, 1981; Brian Hearne (ed), *An African Christmas?*, 1983; *Living Worship in Africa Today*, 1980; E. Fashole Luke (ed), *Christianity in Independent Africa*, 1978; Aylward Shorter, *African Culture and the Christian Church*, 1973; 'Liturgical Creativity in East Africa', *AFER*, 1971; Elochukwu Uzukwu, *Liturgy: Truly Christian, Truly African*, 1982.

JOSEPH G. HEALEY

2. *India*. Hinduism, the oldest living tradition in the world and the native religion of most Indians today, has developed possibly the richest and most diversified forms of worship among all the religious traditions of the world. Even today the magnificent temple feasts, the immense processions, the activities in innumerable places of pilgrimage and the regular public and domestic rituals and devotions shape the personal and social life of Indians to a degree probably unknown anywhere else. (*See* **Hindu Worship**.)

Christianity reached India in many forms and from many sources. Scholars still dispute the claims of the Thomas Christians of South India to have had Thomas, one of the twelve apostles, as their founder. They retained throughout the centuries an ancient Eastern Christian form of worship (*korban*) and still use Old Syriac as their liturgical language. For many centuries they maintained contacts with the Nestorian Christians of Asia Minor. The Thomas Christians never felt any need to indigenize their worship further: many would have considered it a sacrilege, to suggest changing or tampering with, a liturgy which had been instituted by an apostle of Jesus. Although living in a (mostly) Malayalam speaking community, sharing its language and culture (including the caste-structure), they never translated their liturgy and preserved it unchanged throughout the centuries. (*See* **Mar Thoma Church Worship.**) Indian society, divided as it is into a great number of fairly isolated communities, apparently accepted the community of Christians with its own customs and its own forms of worship without much questioning. It enjoyed the protection of some local rulers and the respect of other communities. Since it did not engage in proselytizing it never felt any need to make its worship more accessible to members of Hindu communities.

The Portuguese, who first made contacts with local Christians in Kerala and were welcomed as fellow Christians, soon

pursued a policy of conquest and colonization. The territories they acquired were to be transformed into replicas of the motherland. Portuguese was the official language in Goa, Diu and Damān – the Latin liturgy of the Roman Church the only form of worship officially tolerated. Hindus had to be converted or to leave the Portuguese territories. The Portuguese made efforts to convert the – in their opinion heretical – Thomas Christians to their Roman Catholic faith and to make them give up their Syriac liturgy for the Latin rite. While they succeeded in breaking up the unity of the Old Indian Church, Roman instructions allowed the neo-converts to retain their Syriac form of worship. The Portuguese demanded that their converts from Hinduism and Islam accept not only their faith but also their language, their names and their culture. They razed Hindu temples and outlawed Hindu forms of worship. They succeeded in forming a tightly-knit Christian community with its own identity, which felt completely at home with Latin liturgy and Portuguese popular piety, the feasts and saints of the Roman calendar, and was proud of its European standards. For centuries the laws regulating the contact between Catholics and non-Catholics were very strict. Goanese Christians were not allowed to participate in any form of non-Christian worship, to read Hindu religious literature or to visit Hindu shrines. Children were brought up in the belief that Hindus worshipped the devil, that it was pleasing to God to desecrate Hindu images, that strict adherence to the command of their clergy was the only way to save their souls. No less a person than St Francis Xavier had written to Rome from India: 'The invocations of the pagans are hateful to God, since all their gods are devils.'

The consolidation and expansion of the *padroado* coincided with the time of the Counter Reformation and the growing role of the Inquisition. The Patriarchate of the East was no less zealous in enforcing the law of Rome than its counterparts in the West. Increasingly Christianity was identified with a following to the letter of the instructions of the Roman Pope. Worship in India had to be an exact replica of worship in Rome: cathedrals, Latin, canons, rituals.

Among the thousands of Jesuit missionaries who strictly adhered to this pattern during the first two centuries of Jesuit missions in India there is one exception: Roberto de Nobili's lonely and short-lived experiment in indigenization. An Italian nobleman, he adopted the life-style of local brahmins in Madurai, studied Tamil and Sanskrit, had contacts with knowledgeable pandits and aimed at creating a community of Christian brahmins, who should continue to follow their traditions with the exception of those elements which were incompatible with Christian faith. We do not know whether and to what degree de Nobili indigenized the celebration of the eucharist. Rivalry and jealousies among fellow-missionaries brought this first major accommodation to a sudden end. Vatican authorities repeatedly issued over the centuries diplomatically wise and otherwise totally pointless directives concerning the indigenization of worship not only in India but all over Asia.

Towards the beginning of the eighteenth century the first Protestant missionaries appeared in India. The Dutch began mission work in South India. Some of these early Dutch missionaries compiled important and largely objective information on the local forms of Hinduism which they studied with the help of brahmins. Since the emphasis of Protestantism has always been on scripture, their major efforts went into the direction of translations of the scriptures into Indian languages. Pioneering work on a large scale was done by the Englishman J. Carey and his co-workers in Serampore around the turn of the nineteenth century. Within a few decades major portions of the Bible had been translated into many of the main languages of India. This led to an indigenization of worship at least to the extent that the readings and prayers of congregational services were in indigenous languages. While the text of hymns sung by Christian congregations was translated into Indian languages, the tunes were taken over unchanged from their German, Italian, English etc. sources. Only after gifted Indian Christians like Krishna Pillai, Narayan Vaman Tilak and Moses Walsalam had started to compose Indian Christian songs with Indian tunes did the church in India give up its prejudice against Indian music, which was thought to be inextricably linked with Hinduism. The adaptation of elements of Hindu worship,

of Hindu symbols and gestures was another matter. Some early missionary chapels exhibit a felicitous blend of Indian architectural elements with the requirements of Christian communal worship, quite in contrast to the nineteenth-century neo-gothic monstrosities in most major cities.

Under the expansion and consolidation of British colonial rule the question of indigenization of Christian worship hardly arose. Most missionaries and indigenous clergy had as low an opinion of Hinduism as most of the British officials, and considered it their task to modernize, westernize, anglicize India. Native reform-movements like the Brahmo Samāj seemed to prove them right: the future belonged to the West; a modern India would be a Christian India. Individuals who thought otherwise were not totally absent: persons like Sundar Singh and Brahmabāndhav Upādhyāya, Indian Christians who pleaded for Hindu-Christianity and who retained a living connection with their Indian past, or Jack Winslow, an Anglican missionary, who founded the Krista-Seva Ashram in Pune in the conviction that Christianity could not become acceptable to Hindu India if it did not cultivate the contemplative life.

Mahatma Gandhi, while basically sympathetic to Christianity, criticized its foreign, colonial character in India. Independence in 1947 also ended a chapter in the history of Indian Christianity.

Christianity was looked upon by many Hindus as a remnant of colonialism which ought to be eliminated. Indian Christians felt uncomfortable in their newly independent homeland. Some independent churches were formed. Some rethinking began among missionaries as well as among Indian Christians. The association with a foreign power suddenly ceased to be of advantage. The Indian government demanded 'indigenization'. Its first phase took place in the form of appointing Indians to positions of responsibility in the churches. The winds of liturgical experimentation and renewal which began to blow in Europe in the 1950s eventually also reached India. Sensitive men like Abbé Monchanin and Dom Le Saux, the founders of Saccidananda-ashram in South India, or Fathers Antoine and Fallon, the founders of Sántisadan in Calcutta, began introducing Hindu symbols and gestures into worship. Father George Proksch successfully transformed Indian folk-dance into a liturgical dance-drama which was well-received by Indian as well as by Western audiences.

The Second Vatican Council officially opened the door for the indigenization of worship: 'Whatever good lies latent in the religious rites and cultures of diverse peoples, is not only to be saved from destruction but is also to be healed, ennobled and perfected...' If this could be understood as a call to indigenize worship the response has been less than universal and not entirely enthusiastic. While individuals and a few institutions went ahead with adopting some elements of Hindu worship (e.g. readings from Hindu scriptures together with Bible readings, squatting instead of standing, *namaste* instead of kiss of peace, *capattis* for bread, *ăratī*-ceremonies, etc.) the Indian Catholic Church as a whole is very reluctant to 'hinduize' its worship. Many argue that the Christian meaning of worship cannot be replaced; that Hinduism itself has many different forms of worship; that a taking over of elements of Hindu worship would blur the distinction between Hinduism and Christianity.

The All India Seminar 'Church in India Today' in 1969 had a lively workshop on worship but came to few conclusions and resolutions. In the Protestant Churches the situation is comparable: while the Barthian stance which was adopted under Krämer's influence in Tambaram 1938 can be said to have been abandoned, the openness for indigenization in worship varies greatly from one place to the other. Experimental centres like Murray Rogers' Jyotiniketan and the revived ecumenical Kristasevashram have incorporated numerous indigenous elements into their worship. Others insist that Christian worship must be kept distinctly biblical/Christian. While architectural models for churches in post-independence India borrow increasingly from indigenous examples, the content of worship – excepting perhaps marginalia like the use of Indian oil-lamps, garland, prostration – shows little signs of indigenization.

The Church of South India has recently come out with recommendations to retain everything of spiritual value in its Indian

heritage and to strive to express the universal Christian message in Indian cultural garb. It also encouraged its members to celebrate the Indian national (Hindu) festivals and experts at the Bangalore United Theological College were experimenting with Christian celebrations of Divali, Dassarah, Pongal and Onam.

By way of conclusion one can state that while immense progress has been made in the area of indigenization of Christian worship in India, the aim has hardly been achieved: much more theological reflection is required to deal with the many open problems in this area, much emotional resistance has to be overcome among ministers and congregations alike, much more importance overall has to be given in the Indian churches to the recognition of the intrinsic spiritual value of the Indian heritage as a whole.

Kees Abel, 'Non-Christian Revelation and Christian Worship', G. Gispert-Sauch (ed), *God's Word Among Men*, 1973, pp.257–303; N. Abeyasingha, *A Theological Evaluation of Non-Christian Rites*, 1979; Swami Abhishiktananda, *Towards the Renewal of the Indian Church*, 1970; M. Amaladoss, 'Adaptation in Liturgy and the Problem of Meaning', *God's Word Among Men*, pp. 305–324; C. F. Hallencreutz, *New Approaches to Men of Other Faiths*, 1969; I. Hirudayam, *Christianity and Tamil Culture*, 1977; J. S. M. Hooper, *Bible Translation in India, Pakistan, Ceylon*, 1963; S. Neill, *A History of Christianity in India: The Beginnings to AD 1707*, 1984; E. Rao, 'The Indianization of the Catholic Church', *The Illustrated Weekly of India*, 28 Dec. 1969, pp.20–22; A. Soares, 'Foreign Missions in India', ibid., pp.23–25; K. N. Sahay, 'Indigenization of Christianity in India', *Man in India* 61/1 (March 1981), pp.17–36.

KLAUS KLOSTERMAIER

3. *Latin America*. 'Even in the liturgy, the church has no wish to impose a rigid uniformity in matters which do not implicate the faith or the good of the whole community; rather does she respect and foster the genius and talents of the various races and peoples. Anything in these peoples' way of life which is not indissolubly bound up with superstition and error she studies with sympathy, and, if possible, preserves intact. Sometimes in fact she admits such things into the liturgy itself, so long as they harmonize with its true and authentic spirit' (Article 37 of the Vatican II Constitution on the Sacred Liturgy).

The renewal of the pastoral ministry in Latin America – made possible by Vatican II, brought about by the liberating Second General Conference of the Latin American Episcopate of Medellín 1968, and confirmed by the Third General Conference of Puebla 1979 – has involved the liturgy and worship of the church. The official policy has been one of adaptation (see the Final Document of Puebla 899, 926, 940) or even 'indigenization'. But what is the meaning of adaptation or indigenization in the context of the Latin American reality? If these words are meant to indicate that the liturgical life of the church should *belong* to the people and should meet their real spiritual and moral needs and aspirations, then not only the cultural aspects of their life and history must be taken into account but also their social and political consciousness. In the Latin American countries 'the pain that is felt at the wretchedness of the poor and the atrocities to which they are subjected, but also the love of God that burns especially in those who have given their lives out of love for their brothers and sisters, have become a fire that consumes – and fuses – the disparate elements of our Latin American reality and our Latin American history. From this action – which is only apparently destructive, inasmuch as in it a basically creative work is also being accomplished – there is emerging the "gold refined by fire" (Rev. 3.18) of a new spirituality' (Gustavo Gutiérrez, *We Drink from Our Own Wells*, 1984, pp.25f.). This spirituality expresses the experience of suffering and oppression of the poor, the affirmation of their right to live, their longing and struggle for a world of justice and peace; it is the spirituality of the church of the poor, the *Iglesia popular*.

The various types of *Comunidades Cristianas de Base* (basic Christian communities), that during the past twenty years have come into existence in Brazil, El Salvador, Nicaragua and other countries, are the places where this new spirituality has become a style of life. Contrary to what is sometimes suggested, the growing commitment of Christians to the popular movement did not imply a reduction of the

Gospel to the political realm. At the International Ecumenical Congress of Theology in Sao Paulo 1980 it was clearly stated that the basic ecclesial communities form an integral part of the 'irruption of the poor' into the historical process of Latin America, but do not constitute a movement or political power parallel to the popular organizations. Their task is to exercise among the poor a liberating ministry: 'The church redeems the people's symbols of hope, manipulated for centuries by the system of domination. The church celebrates the presence of the God of life in the people's struggles for a more just and human life. The church encounters the God of the poor by confronting the idols of oppression. The church receives the kingdom as a free gift of the Father in the building of brotherhood and the solidarity of all oppressed classes and races, humiliated by this anti-kingdom of discrimination, violence, and death that is the dominant capitalist system' (Sergio Torres and John Eagleson, *The Challenge of Basic Christian Communities*, p.235).

It should be stressed that the spiritual fecundity of the church of the common people is essentially a *communal* affair. Although outstanding individuals such as Julia Esquivel, Ernesto Cardenal, Helder Camara or Luis Espinal have made important contributions, many liturgical texts have come into existence spontaneously and their authors remain anonymous. They are characterized by a very direct and intimate relationship with Jesus, who shares the pain and suffering of the people, by a simplicity that never becomes superficial, by a deep love of life and, in spite of all the misery and senseless bloodshed, a joyful affirmation of the goodness of creation. A moving example of this is the creed from the well-known Nicaraguan *Misa Campesina* (Peasant Mass):

I believe, Lord, firmly
that from your fertile mind
this whole world was born;
that from your artist's hand,
as a primitivist painter,
all beauty flowered forth.
The stars and the moon,
houses, lagoons,
the little boats that sail
down the river to the sea,
the immense coffee fields,
and the white cotton plantations,
and the forests
mutilated by the criminal axe.

I believe in you,
architect, engineer,
artisan and carpenter,
mason and builder,
Creator of mind,
of music and the winds,
of peace and love,
I believe in you.

In many of the basic ecclesial communities the interpretation of the Bible by the common people themselves is a new and exciting phenomenon in the history of the Latin American church. But, together with the sharing of the word of God, it is the eucharist, or the supper of the Lord, that holds the central place. In the eucharist, Christ is felt to be present both as the suffering servant and as the risen Saviour who gives life out of death. The celebration of the eucharist is not an evasion of the harsh reality of daily life; on the contrary, it is very close to the experiences of suffering and hope in the community. As an anticipation of the kingdom of God, the eucharist strengthens the congregation in the struggle against the injustice of the present order.

The confidential and very direct relationship to God is nowhere better expressed than in the prayers. Gutiérrez rightly remarks: 'The present is also a *time of prayer*. Anyone who is in contact with base-level ecclesial communities can attest that there is a great deal of intense and hope-filled prayer going on in Latin America today' (op. cit., p.22). In these prayers we find a deep trust in the love of God, a profound confidence in his wisdom, but also expressions of utter despair and bitter accusations. In their denunciation of injustice people recognize themselves directly in certain parts of the Bible such as the Psalms and Lamentations; in a meditation from the basic communities of Lins (Brazil), for example, there are passages from Lamentations next to the description of present needs, such as hunger, illness, and shortage of regular jobs. There is no separation between 'the life of prayer' and the concerete, material needs of the people. The way these two dimensions are interrelated is very clearly put into words by Luis

Espinal, as he prayed: 'Lord of mystery, let us feel your presence at the heart of life; we desire to find you in the depths of everyday things.'

Luis Espinal was a priest who was murdered in Bolivia. He is by no means the only one who died for the cause of the common people as a martyr. During the terror and repression of the 1970s the church in Latin America has become a church of martyrs. In the community of believers there is a deep awareness of this saddening, but at the same time joyful fact. The day Archbishop Oscar Romero was murdered, for instance, is commemorated every year all over Latin America. It is not too much to say that the need to stay in communion with the martyrs belongs to the characteristics of worship in Latin America today. Often the martyrs are remembered in a litany of names; after every name the congregation responds by saying 'present', 'they are among us'. In this way the celebration of the presence of the martyrs functions as a stimulus not to resign but to continue the struggle. It is an impressive expression of the faith that death does not have the final word in history. As a celebration of the final victory of life over death it 'actualizes' the event of Easter, and leads to a deeper understanding of the Lord's cross and resurrection.

In addition to books mentioned in the text, *see* Ernesto Cardenal, *The Gospel in Solentiname*, 4 vols, ET 1976–1982; Pastoral Team of Bambamarca, *Vamos Caminando: A Peruvian Catechism*, ET 1985.

THEO WITVLIET

4. *South-East Asia.* Earliest records of indigenous Christian Worship in South-East Asia come from the Nestorian Churches of India, Ceylon, Indo-China and China, in the sixth and seventh centuries (e.g. the Syriac Liturgy of Addai and Mari, and canticles such as the Hymn to the Trinity – Chinese *Gloria in excelsis* – from Dunhuang, China). Four centuries of Roman Catholic presence in China bore fruit in the seventeenth century, in the work of Ricci and fellow Jesuits, utilizing Confucian terms in liturgy and Bible, and adapting such ceremonies as those honouring ancestors. But few other consistent attempts at indigenization can be discerned, even though quite drastic adaptations in Christian practice and worship have been imposed by persecution or cultural domination. Japanese Christians, following proscription in the seventeenth century, were able in the following centuries to retain only a simple baptismal order and prayers. On the other hand, the numbers of Filipinos seeking baptism in the late sixteenth and early seventeenth centuries were so large that even traditional instruction in the Lord's Prayer, *Ave* and *Credo* was often waived.

In the early decades of this century, indigenous forms of worship appeared in only a few countries. In the Philippine Independent Church, Aglipay and de los Reyes, with strongly nationalist concerns, introduced Unitarian and native Filipino content to traditional Roman Catholic forms (*Filipino Missal, Filipino Ritual*). Ceylon saw creative work in indigenous Christian architecture (e.g. Trinity College, Kandy) sometimes as an integral part of a larger recovery of Christian community in residential ashrams (Christaseva, near Jaffna) which would later provide the impetus for indigenous liturgies (Devasarana, near Kurunegala). The unique role of Bible study in Japanese Protestant churches led to many forms of Christian fellowship and publication and, notably, to the very simple Bible services which characterize the Mukyokai (Non-church) movement. In other countries, exceptional church leaders and missionaries such as Cheng Ching-Yi, Lebbe, Reichelt (in China), Kim Jai-Joon, Song Chang-Un (in Korea) and Mulia, Liemena, Schuurman (in Indonesia), entered into the life and culture of their people and in the 1940s called upon the church to reflect this life in new liturgical forms. Additional impetus came in the years immediately following World War II, as many Asian churches found themselves within newly independent nations and now members of a world-wide ecumenical family which valued the unique contributions and setting of each. The principle outcome would long remain, though, in the area of hymnology. Possibly the earliest modern Christian hymnal appeared in Japan (1874), already containing 76 Japanese hymns influenced by classical haiku and tanka poetry. By comparison the *Union Hymnal* in China (1936) would have 62 Chinese

hymns (out of 512), but there, as in almost every country of the region, the post-war period has seen the growth of many larger collections of indigenous hymns. Often, as in the Philippines, these are now in most major languages of the particular country. A major step was taken in the preparation of ecumenical hymnals for Asian Churches; one originally under the direction of D. T. Niles (*CCA Hymnal*, 1964, 1974) and the other compiled by I-To Loh (*New Songs of Asian Cities*, 1972).

It is perhaps inevitable that creative response in liturgy and worship to the challenges of traditional, or rapidly changing Asian contexts, is more apparent in those sections of the church working on the frontiers of mission – in lay-fellowships, urban mission projects, ecumenical centres, ashrams, people's movements, youth groups. Where such challenges are *not* recognized, new hymns, liturgies and symbolism may be devised – as in the 1965 Experimental Liturgy, or the 1976 Common Prayer liturgies (both for South-East Asia) – but these will not have organic relationship with the life and culture of a people, nor embody their contemporary experience of God in their own context. In what follows, an introduction will be given to the indigenization of worship in response both to experienced tradition and to contemporary social change, country by country.

In culturally rich, socially turbulent Indonesia, special occasional liturgies have emerged, especially since the 1960s, in Roman Catholic churches of West Java, Flores, Timor, Kalimantan, and Bali. Along with gamelan accompaniments to the mass and original compositions, traditional dance, drama and symbolism have been used both on Christian holy days and in presenting the gospel, and new liturgies have been devised for such culturally important events as birth, marriage and selamatan. Similar developments, utilizing local dramatic and symbolic arts and in dialogue with traditional meditation and thought-forms, have occurred in some Protestant churches of West and Central Java, and Bali, sometimes through a conscious attempt to relate Christian faith and worship to the whole person-in-culture.

However, the vast majority of Christians and congregations remain untouched. Protestants adhere closely to patterns still recognizably Dutch Reformed, despite the occasional Indonesian hymn. Among Roman Catholics, little creative change has occurred since the post-Vatican II vernacular* mass, although the books of liturgical prayers now prepared in some dioceses may lead to this. Some ecumenical institutes, lay centres and movements, however, are developing worship-forms shaped by more urgent human issues and expressing the secular experience of Christians engaged in urban mission, development motivation, inter-faith co-operation or social justice issues. In recent years, important resources have emerged from such Protestant centres as the Malang Lay Centre, and Duta Wacana Seminary, and Catholic institutes in Jogjakarta, Jakarta and Flores.

The experience of Sri Lanka since the 1950s shows more fully the sources and development of contextualized worship. The sequence begins in the recognition both of Sinhalese culture and of the life-situation of urban and rural masses, leading to the growth of many experimental Christian communities and movements. From this a body of indigenous liturgy has emerged, shaped by Sri Lankan society and culture. The seminal work was done in the Anglican diocese of Kurunegala, where in the mid-1950s Bishop Lakdasa de Mel introduced Sinhalese prose-chants, dance and folk-music, in addition to the indigenous architecture, arts and seating-mats already used at Christaseva.

From 1957, Yohan Devananda's small ashram (Devasarana Aramaya) began to evolve contemporary indigenous offices which included free prayer, silence, readings from the *Dhammapada* and contemporary sources, and the offering of flowers and lights. From long studies of the eucharist and growing involvements in village development, the central emphasis came to be on the worship of the cosmic Christ. This was later embodied in the New World Liturgy, which draws also on Buddhist and Marxist sources to express strong social and indigenizing concern. The work of Devasarana and other para-church groups was encouraged by Bishop Lakshman Wickremasinghe, who developed de Mel's measures and added regular readings from the classics of Sri Lanka's principal re-

ligions. He also gave particular support to the Christian Workers' Fellowship, whose common life has been characterized since 1960 by the weekly Workers' Mass. The fellowship is committed to being a part of Sri Lanka's working-class movement and to foster contemporary understanding of the gospel in the context of the country's predominantly Buddhist cultural heritage and of proletarian socialist ideology. Drawing on Orthodox and contemporary liturgies and experience at Devasarana, the mass utilizes indigenous dress, symbols and vessels along with dance, prostration and music, including conch and drum (*see* Plate 39). Many indigenous prayers, chants and lyrics, batik vestments, liturgies and local ceremonial have been devised for the mass, but most noteworthy are the motifs and themes shaping the liturgy. These are strongly emancipatory, focussing on biblical visions of a just society. The liturgy is sometimes preceded by a procession in which the Workers' Litany is sung to a Buddhist pilgrim chant. The mass is usually held in a secular building, in the open air, or in workers' homes – all settings where the regular attendance of many non-Christians, including Buddhist clergy, is natural. Sometimes church buildings are also used.

In recent years other liturgies have been developed: the fellowship meal, which includes the lighting of the lamp (from Hindu tradition); Vandana (orders for daily worship), which include cleansings, offerings of flowers, light and incense, and meditation; special liturgies for Holy Week and Easter (with vigils *, the stripping of the altar *, veneration of the cross * and festivals of light and of water) and for baptism, repentance, marriage and death. A unique liturgical development now comes full circle in the incorporation of many elements from the Workers' Mass in the *Holy Eucharist – a Liturgy for Sri Lanka* of the Church of Ceylon (1983).

Compared to this there have been few other attempts in indigenous liturgy, apart from some innovations by Bishop Leo Nanayakkara, in Badulla Diocese, and the low-profile work of such centres as Satyodaya (Kandy), the Centre for Society and

Plate 39 Workers' Mass, Christian Workers' Fellowship, Sri Lanka – Procession

Religion (Colombo) and groups of the SCM.

In Japan the recent decades have seen some modest steps towards indigenization within the institutional church. Roman Catholic liturgical hymns now include some Japanese melodies based on Gregorian models, and special collections of 'prayers for the faithful' (Seisho to Tenrei) are available for use during the eucharist. In some dioceses, Christian rituals for the New Year have been devised to include acts of penitence, stripping and reconstruction of the altar, and the use of New Year psalms. In Iwate Prefecture, J. Schmidlin has produced widely-used booklets in which indigenous symbols replace culturally-confined terminology (Benedictions, 37 Psalms, Prayers for use by Non-Christians, Liturgy for the Deceased, Mass for the New Year). Traditional verse-forms such as haiku and tanka – from a growing body of Christian poets (including Fujii Takeshi and Takeda Tetsuzo) – have provided resources for worship in a number of Catholic and Protestant churches. Special worship services are also enriched by the work of artists in painting, ikebana and sculpture.

Protestant worship has generally been little influenced by liturgical movements, retaining as central the long evangelical sermon. But many new ministries and movements, beyond the local church, have provided the setting for creative contextualization. In industrial evangelism, lay academies, peace movements, ministries to day-labourers, minorities and other deprived groups, a wide variety of ecumenical and contextual services and prayer rallies have emerged. In restaurants or lay institutes, down-town centres, on campus, in the street, and in numbers of house churches, Christian response to urgent social and religious issues (in Japan, Korea, and Asia-wide) have been expressed in contemporary litanies, biblical meditation and study and protest songs.

In the Philippines, one of the most sustained endeavours to foster indigenous liturgy and music has been made in the Asian Institute for Liturgy and Music (Manila), in the production of an impressive collection of Filipino melodies (by, for example, Feliciano, Pajaro and Dadap) and lyrics (by Sanchez, Feliciano, Rigos and Aguila). The New Filipino Hymnology Movement within the Roman Catholic Church (led by Eduardo Hontiveras) has produced a widely-used body of Filipino hymns along with Filipino settings for the mass. The fullest worship manual prepared for Protestant use – Lydia Niguidula's *Celebration. A Sourcebook for Christian Worship* – contains forms for a wide range of occasions, including agape meals and house churches, but especially Filipino elements appear only in the liturgies for weddings, vigils (at death), thanksgivings (fiestas) and covenant services*.

Similarly, the regular courses and conferences on inculturation and indigenization, such as the summer schools of the East Asia Pastoral Institute, produce much valuable material but few specifically Filipino forms.

Once again it is in new centres and movements which have grown in response to changed social and cultural situations that the fullest contextualization of worship and liturgy has occurred. In the last twenty years, new traditions of ecumenical prayer services, protest liturgies and masses have been forged – to intercede for prisoners or oppressed workers, to commence or conclude rallies or marches, or to celebrate solidarity across denominational and social barriers. Not only the quantity of such innovative liturgies but the new forms themselves have to be taken seriously. New elements incorporated include stories and testimonies, poems, statements, dramatic action and corporate reflection, while new content, expressing suffering and aspiration, is given to traditional elements; in acts of contrition, readings, responses, homily, antiphons, prayers of the faithful and procession.

Something of the quality of such socially aware liturgy can be found in innumerable local congregations and groups, in fellowships like the Wednesday Forum, or in the widespread basic Christian communities. Centres such as the Institute for Religion and Culture issue regular calendar-kits for seasonal and occasional liturgies which bring vividly together Bible, prayer and contemporary situation.

In South Korea also, the present experience of Christians, striving to maintain witness to the whole gospel, has shaped most of the creative worship in recent

decades. For although there has been continued work in liturgical revision (of e.g. the Anglican prayer book), little that is specifically Korean can be discerned in this work. In other services of more traditional form, a small number of congregations have initiated a thanksgiving service on the Korean moon festival, using folk-drama and traditional labour songs.

But it is in the context of long continued struggles for democratic government, social justice and human rights that contextual worship forms have emerged. Sustained series of more informal prayer services have become a tradition, being held weekly since 1971 in the Protestant Christian building, Seoul, and monthly since 1974 in Myong Dong and Wonju cathedrals. These are explicitly prayer services for prisoners, their families, and for specific victims of injustice. The Protestant groups, up to 300 strong, vary in length from one hour to three days; their services have included homilies, overnight fasts, direct supplication and sometimes become an enforced sit-in when the interceders have given food to their police guards! The cathedral prayer services have also celebrated mass with specific intentions for prisoners and victims, or have been the occasion for ecumenical declarations and petitions (again often ending in arrests). But the songs, litanies, statements and poems of a prophetic gospel can be heard in local churches, teahouse fellowships, seminaries and lay-centres also.

In China, the experience of the Cultural Revolution has brought a major transition in the form and role of Christian churches, although this was not immediately obvious in patterns of worship. The few churches still open in the late 1960s were often bereft of symbolism, windows, books and much of their furniture; and services held, as in the North Shanghai Catholic Church in 1967, might include (under compulsion) readings from Mao's writings. Yet throughout the 1960s and 1970s a steadily growing number of home-gatherings preserved Christian worship and the life and identity of the church. In house, hall or out-of-doors, the informal services would include – as they still do – Bible reading and lengthy sermons, 'home-made' songs, testimonies and responses. In many, extemporary prayer may predominate, while in others, healing or silence, Bible study or the celebration of communion provide the main focus. Such worship, functioning at least partly underground until 1979, now supplements that of the more than 2,000 open churches. In these, if Catholic, the mass is celebrated in pre-Vatican II form with traditional congregational litanies in Chinese accompanying the Latin mass of priest and choir. Protestant churches have restored much of the former evangelical tradition in apparently Western form, but a degree of indigenous character can be discerned in the simplicity of language and prayer-form, the use of Chinese hymns and – despite some features continuing from particular traditions – the evolution of flexible, post-denominational orders of worship. As in Catholic worship, however, the influence of post-1950 liturgical developments is yet to be felt.

Only exceptional congregations in (Asian) overseas Chinese churches *do* show such influence. Once again it is in para-church groups or lay movements that genuinely indigenous/contextual elements can be found: in new workers' congregations of the Christian Industrial Committee in Hong Kong, or the weekly services of fasting and prayer on behalf of prisoners and their families in many cities in Taiwan. New hymns, by John Cheng and Kao Chun Ming, have also emerged in such settings.

The rich and growing resources of contextual theology and Christian writing in Asian countries will surely nurture the future worship and liturgy of creative and prophetic fellowships throughout the region.

Yohan Devananda, *If They Had Met*, 1967; John Fleming, *Some Asian Orders of Worship*, 1965; Raymond Fung, *Households of God on China's Soil*, 1982; Takenaka Masao, *Creation and Redemption through Japanese Art*, 1966; Ron O'Grady and T. K. Thomas, *Your Kingdom Come*, 1980; *Living in Christ with People*, 1981; Worship Handbooks published for the Fifth, Sixth and Seventh Assemblies, Christian Conference of Asia, 1973, 1977, 1981.

JOHN C. ENGLAND

Institution Narrative

see **Anaphora** 6; **Canon**

Insufflation

Having the precedent in John 20.22, the church used insufflation to signify the conferring of the Holy Spirit, and also the expulsion of the evil spirit. This ceremony, however, is found not in the rites of ordination* but in those of baptism*, where it occurs among the preliminaries in Hippolytus' *Apostolic Tradition*, when the bishop exorcized the candidates, breathed on their faces and sealed them with the sign of the cross (*see* **Gestures** 3), in symbolic fashion expelling the evil spirits and barring the door against their return. Cyril of Jerusalem too said that exorcisms*, infusing fear by a divine breath, made the evil spirit flee. Infants, said Augustine, are exorcized and breathed upon to show that they are delivered from the power of darkness and transferred to the kingdom of Christ. Quodvultdeus explained that it was not the person created by God that was breathed upon but he who holds in his power all who are born in sin.

According to Gennadius of Marseilles, exorcism with insufflation was an ecclesiastical custom universally observed. Other authorities who mentioned it are John the Deacon of Rome (but not the Gelasian Sacramentary or *Ordo Romanus XI*), Isidore of Seville, Hildephonsus of Toledo, the Mozarabic *Liber Ordinum*, the Gallican Bobbio Missal, and in Germany Alcuin, *Ordo Romanus L* and the Sacramentary of Fulda.

The Latin rite of baptism known to the Reformers began with a breathing on the child's face, together with the words, 'Depart from him, unclean spirit, and make room for the Holy Spirit, the Comforter.' In his first *Taufbüchlein*, Luther retained the ceremony while translating the formula into German; three years later he abolished the ceremony but kept the formula. The first services of baptism in the vernacular used in Strasbourg and Zurich included the insufflation; but Bucer and Zwingli subsequently abolished it. There was no insufflation in Calvin's Genevan or Knox's Scottish rite. In England the prayer book of 1549 ordered the priest to look upon, as opposed to breathe upon, the child, as he said a prayer of exorcism. Thus among the Reformed churches Luther's view prevailed that insufflation was an unnecessary outward ceremony. It did, however, survive in the Roman Catholic Church until the revision of 1969.

Insufflation for the purpose of exorcism accompanied the renunciation of Satan in the Byzantine and Coptic rites and the *Effeta* in the Ambrosian Manual.

In the Gregorian Sacramentary, Sarum Manual, the mediaeval rites of Gaul, Spain and Germany, and in the Jacobite and Maronite rites, the officiant breathed on the water in the font while reciting the prayer for its consecration. This symbolized the entry of the Holy Spirit into the water, as a result of which the ensuing baptism was a regeneration by water and the Spirit and not a merely physical washing. Timothy of Alexandria and the Coptic rite supply evidence of a breathing on the candidates at the anointing with chrism which concluded the rite of baptism, and which had the purpose of imparting the Holy Spirit to them.

H. Denzinger, *Ritus Orientalium*, 1863; J. D. C. Fisher, *Christian Initiation: The Reformation Period*, 1969; E. C. Whitaker, *Documents of the Baptismal Liturgy*, 1960.

J. D. C. FISHER

Intercession

Intercessory prayer has from the very beginning been given a prominent place in Christian worship. Its earliest formal embodiment in the liturgy appears to have been in the common prayers which concluded the synaxis*, to which reference is made in the first detailed outline of the eucharistic liturgy, that in the *First Apology* of Justin Martyr; the forms which these prayers have taken in the principal historic rites are briefly considered in the article just cited.

Intercessions in the eucharist proper appear to have been a slightly later development, although it is not possible to assert this categorically; while no conclusion can be drawn from a possibly ambiguous phrase in Justin Martyr, and there are certainly no intercessions in the eucharistic prayer contained in the *Apostolic Tradition* of Hippolytus of Rome, the earliest text of such a prayer which is known to survive, all other ancient liturgies, and those of the historic rites following them, include an intercessory element either in the

eucharistic prayer itself (the most common place) or in close connection with it. Assuming that these intercessions are no original part of the earliest forms of the prayer (but it must be remembered that there are intercessory elements in some of the Jewish *berakoth* from which the Christian prayers originated), it is most likely that they originate in the diptychs*, especially as in some eucharistic prayers, most notably the historic Roman canon, they retain a marked diptychal formulation. The theological rationale of intercessions in the eucharistic prayer is briefly considered in the article anaphora*.

From the last quarter of the fourth century at the latest, intercessory prayers have been included in the divine office*, their form and content, as well as their prominence, varying considerably from one historic rite to another. A similar considerable variation is to be found in the treatment of the intercessions in the liturgies compiled during and after the Reformation and their later revisions, both in eucharistic and in non-eucharistic services.

Contemporary liturgical revision displays a marked trend towards restoring the intercession of the synaxis where this has been dropped over the centuries, and with it, in some circles, to the suppression of any intercessory element in the eucharist proper; the latter tendency appears to owe more to liturgical archaeologizing than to serious theological consideration. A further contemporary trend is towards a more free and flexible form of intercession than has been customary for at least sixteen centuries, a change the advantages of which are obvious and valuable, but the disadvantages of which are all too obvious when the writer and reader of the prayers are evidently not equal to their task. Whatever the degree of flexibility provided within a given form, however, most modern liturgies at least offer several alternative forms, a very welcome provision.

See also **Prayer** 3.

W. Jardine Grisbrooke, 'Intercession at the Eucharist', *Studia Liturgica*, IV, 1965, pp.129–55; ibid., V, 1966, pp.20–44, 87–103, and works therein cited; C. Jones, G. Wainwright and E. Yarnold (eds), *The Study of Liturgy*, 1978, using the index under 'Intercession'; for the intercessions of the Roman rite, *see* G. G. Willis, *Essays in Early Roman Liturgy*, 1964, pp.3–48.

W. JARDINE GRISBROOKE

Intercommunion

The word is a late-comer to the Christian vocabulary. For the greater part of church history, Christians have been either in communion with their fellow Christians or else in schism. The term intercommunion has developed to describe an intermediate stage, but one of such complexity that it will be necessary here to survey: 1. the use of terms; 2. the nature of the problem and questions involved in its solution; 3. the current situation.

1. *The use of terms.* Far the most comprehensive treatment of the whole subject was by an international theological commission set up by the Faith and Order Commission of the World Council of Churches in preparation for the Lund Conference in 1952. Its report makes clear that terminology is affected by the ecclesiological assumptions, and indeed by the language, of the speaker, e.g., there is no word in Greek or any of the Slavonic languages which corresponds to the term 'intercommunion' and the idea has no place in Orthodox thought; in German, the Lutheran term for the sacrament of communion is *Abendmahl*, so that *Abendsmahlgemeinschaft* is the nearest equivalent to intercommunion, though by no means a synonym. However, since the ecumenical discussion has been largely conducted in the English-speaking world, the following definitions have been drawn from the principal Church of England report, *Intercommunion Today* (1968), and a Roman Catholic statement of the Ecumenical Commission of England and Wales (1969).

Intercommunion is a general term to describe the various ways in which members of another church may be admitted to holy communion in one's own church or of receiving it in a church other than one's own. If both are permitted, this constitutes reciprocal intercommunion. Inter-celebration signifies that the presiding ministers are also mutually acceptable. (For the meaning of church in this context, see 2 below.)

But various other terms enter into the discussion:

(*a*) Full communion is a relationship of

sharing in the eucharist between churches which recognize each other's faith and ministry, e.g., the relationship not only between the various Provinces of the Anglican Communion, but also between most of them and the Old Catholics by terms of the Bonn Agreement of 1931 (establishing what at that stage was referred to as 'intercommunion').

(*b*) Organic union is a relationship of full communion between Christians in the same area, e.g., a nation, and the term is relevant to this discussion for reasons given below in 2 (*a*).

(*c*) Open communion is a relationship in which the communicants of other churches are invited to receive communion in one's own, though the terms of invitation may vary. See 3 below.

(*d*) Free communion is a term sometimes used to describe the widest form of 'open communion', an invitation 'to all who love the Lord Jesus'.

(*e*) Admission to communion in special cases is to be distinguished from 'intercommunion' in that it is related only to exceptional circumstances (e.g., dangerous illness, distance from one's own communion, mixed marriages).

(*f*) Eucharistic hospitality is sometimes used to describe this situation. In Orthodox Churches such exceptions are said to be 'on grounds of economy'.

2. *The nature of the problem.* 'Intercommunion' arises from attempts to deal with a theological anomaly. Christians widely believe, as they profess faith 'in One, Holy Catholic and Apostolic Church', that the People of God is in some sense indestructibly one; baptism in the three-fold name is a visible sign of the given unity. But as a fact of history, this one church is divided into 'churches', denominations, confessions or communions, 'separated brethren', ecclesial bodies – the variety of terms signifies the variety of doctrines about the nature of the church and the kind of manifest unity which it should have. *Intercommunion* relates the unity which is sought to the eucharist which is the divinely instituted sign of a common life in Christ.

The ecumenical movement, by drawing Christians into personal relationship, has given urgency and poignancy to the situation. The experience of being excluded from communion fellowship with brothers and sisters in Christ can be distressing, especially for those who have no tradition of 'non-communicating attendances' at the eucharist.

It has also identified some questions involved in its solution.

(*a*) *The relation between intercommunion and organic union.* Three views may be distinguished:

(i) Organic union and eucharistic communion are coterminous, therefore 'intercommunion' with those outside that fellowship is not admissible. This is, in general, the view of the Orthodox Churches and the Roman Catholic Church.

(ii) The unity constituted by common baptism and the faith it implies is not so negated by the existence of separate churches as altogether to exclude eucharistic sharing as a *means* towards the visible union of all Christians. This is the general view of the churches deriving from the Reformation.

(iii) An intermediate position would see that the divisions between Christians are normally a barrier to communion but that in contexts specifically seeking visible unity, eucharistic sharing has a place. This is the view of many Anglicans and Lutherans, and some Roman Catholics.

(*b*) *Intercommunion and agreement in doctrine.* Some hold that doctrinal agreement needs to be complete for communion to be possible, but those who allow that intercommunion has a role as a means to full unity stress that growth in doctrinal agreement should be a precondition; especially so in Lutheran-Reformed relations.

(*c*) *Intercommunion and church order.* Some churches restrict intercommunion to those who share certain features of the ministry, e.g. relations between Anglicans and some other episcopal churches. Between Catholics and Orthodox, certain provision for 'special cases' of admission to communion is based on a common acceptance of valid orders.

3. *The current situation.* Since intercommunion signifies a relationship between separated churches, it has acquired a particular acuteness in the ecumenical movement. Since ecumenism is a movement, those relationships undergo continuous change. After some seventy years of increasingly close fellowship, of which the

last twenty have explicitly involved Roman Catholicism, a complex pattern has evolved. With misleading brevity, it may be summarized thus:

(*a*) The Orthodox and Oriental Churches on the whole adhere to the classical position of regarding other Christians as being either in communion or schism. No official statements envisage intercommunion, though these churches are in constant touch with one another and with other Christians in the ecumenical movement's search for full communion in faith and order.

(*b*) The Roman Catholic Church takes a similar stance, though in regard to the Eastern Churches there are reciprocal understandings on admission to the sacraments in exceptional circumstances which do not apply to other Christians (cf. *Orientalium Ecclesiarum*, pp. 26f.). Certain other exceptions may be considered in a variety of pastoral situations, at episcopal discretion.

(*c*) The Lutheran, Reformed, Methodist, Baptist, Disciples and other Protestant Churches on the whole have maintained a relationship of open communion, though in some cases (e.g. between Lutherans and Reformed in Europe) the matter is affected by older traditions of discipline in doctrinal and eucharistic standards. In contemporary ecumenical relationships, however, intercommunion is generally acceptable as a means towards more visible unity.

(*d*) The Churches of the Anglican Communion, characterized by a common inheritance both Catholic and Reformed, have in successive Lambeth Conferences moved from a restriction of intercommunion only with churches also possessing the 'historic episcopate' towards a more general open communion, welcoming baptized communicants of other trinitarian Churches (e.g. resolution 45, Lambeth 1968 or Canon B.15A of the Church of England, 1972), though different Provinces vary in the terms upon which intercommunion is encouraged and its relationship to plans for achieving organic union; e.g., in the United States an agreement in 1982 between the Episcopal Church and three Lutheran bodies there permitted 'interim eucharistic sharing' and occasional common joint celebration as a stage towards full communion.

See also **Ecumenical Worship**.

Ecumenical: *Intercommunion*, 1952 (report of a Theological Commission of Faith and Order); Reports of the World Conferences on Faith and Order, esp. Lund (1952) and Montreal (1963). Anglican: *Intercommunion Today*, 1968 (report of an Archbishops' Commission) and its sequel *Reciprocal Intercommunion*, 1973; Roman Catholic: *Documents of the Second Vatican Council*; the Decrees *de Ecumenismo* and *Orientalium Ecclesiarum* (1964) and the *Ecumenical Directory* (1967) of the Secretariat for Promoting Christian Unity and consequent documents.

OLIVER TOMKINS

Inter-Faith Worship

As members of the world's religions increasingly meet in everyday life and for dialogue and joint action, occasions arise when there is a desire to pray together. In recent years a growing number of 'inter-faith' services have been arranged, but some believers are hesitant about this practice.

Often the occasions have been personal or informal, e.g. prayers for an invalid, for the blessing of a marriage, at a funeral. The first organized attempt of members of several religions to share in prayer together seems to have been at the World Parliament of Religions in 1893, when each morning began with silence and the saying together of the Lord's Prayer. The opening and closing sessions included some hymns, such as 'Lead, Kindly Light'. Already in the Brahmo Samaj, Hindu Reformers such as Ram Mohun Roy and Keshub Chandra Sen had added readings from the scriptures of the world to the reading of Hindu texts. In the 1920s Mahatma Gandhi included hymns and readings from many traditions at the ashram's evening prayers. In some Christian ashrams in India, Hindu scriptures were sometimes read and some missionary colleges broadened their daily worship to encourage participation by Hindu and Muslim students.

In Britain, Unitarians were probably the first to include in their services readings from other scriptures as well as from the Bible. Will Hayes, for example, as early as 1924 published *After the Great Companions*. At the 1924 Religions of Empire Conference there were no devotional times, although the Revd Tyssul Davies independently arranged an inter-faith gathering at

the Theistic Church. At the 1936 World Congress of Faiths there were some readings from the sacred scriptures and most members of the Congress accepted invitations to attend Anglican services at St Paul's Cathedral and at Canterbury Cathedral. One of the first large public services in which people of several faiths took part was the memorial service for Sir Francis Younghusband, the founder of the World Congress of Faiths, held at St Martin-in-the-Fields in 1942. On the occasion of the Coronation of Queen Elizabeth II, the World Congress of Faiths arranged a special service of prayer for people of all faiths and subsequently for several years arranged an annual All Faiths' service. (*See* Plate 40.)

In 1965 an inter-faith service was held at St Mary-le-Bow to mark the opening of the Commonwealth Arts Festival. In the following year a similar occasion was arranged for Commonwealth Day at St Martin-in-the-Fields. Because of some protests about the use of a church for this, for a few years the ceremony was held at the Guildhall, a neutral building, but now an Observance for Commonwealth Day is held each year at Westminister Abbey. Organized local services have become increasingly common, often linked to the Week of Prayer for World Peace. An inter-faith civic service held in Wolverhampton in 1978, at the wish of the Mayor, caught the public attention. School assemblies are a particular issue, but partly because of the presence in Britain of children of many faiths and because of new approaches to religious education, some now have an inter-faith character. (*See* **School Worship**.)

International inter-religious conferences will often include devotional times led in turn by members of different religions and some joint ceremony at the end. The 1984 Congress of the International Association of Religious Freedom, held in Tokyo, for example, had daily devotions, each led by a different tradition in which sometimes a member of another religion was asked to participate. The closing ceremony, in which representatives of all religions took part, included a flower communion and an affirmation of allegiance to the church universal 'which recognizes in all prophets a harmony, in all scriptures a unity, and through all dispensations a continuity'.

Plate 40 One of the first All Faiths' services to be held in Britain, during the 1946 Annual Conference of the World Congress of Faiths. A Jew, a Buddhist, a Christian and a Muslim lead the service.

Inter-faith services may be of several types. They may be personal and informal or large and carefully planned. They may be the regular acts of worship of a community at which guests of other faiths are present. This may demand some explanation or modification of the rite or perhaps an invitation to a visitor to speak or read. They may be an act of witness to human rights, consisting of a series of readings or songs from different religions – the 'serial multi-faith service', as it is sometimes called. They may be planned as a unity with members of different religions sharing together in prayer, silence, the singing of hymns, some symbolic action, such as the passing of lights or a flower communion, or in a common act of witness. They will vary depending on the intentions and assumptions of the organizers, be they Baha'is, Unitarians, Theosophists, Sufis, Christians or members of a Community Relations Council or United Nations Association.

Theological hesitations about participating in inter-faith worship have been voiced by some Christians.

1. Some doubt whether it is the same God who is worshipped in all traditions. Some forms of Buddhism are not theistic and some Christians consider forms of Hinduism to be idolatrous. 'When Christian worship is addressed to the God revealed in the saving work of the Lord Jesus Christ and through the personal operation of the Holy Spirit, it is not easy to apply the word with any meaning to other expressions of communion with God' (from a comment on the Archbishops' Consultants report on *Interfaith Services and Worship*). This relates to the understanding that Christian worship is always 'through Jesus Christ Our Lord'. Sometimes this objection is eased by avoiding the word 'worship' or 'service'. Defenders of these services stress that the Ultimate Divine Mystery transcends all our understanding or descriptions. According to Bishop George Appleton, in a sermon to the World Congress of Faiths in King's College Chapel, London, 1970: 'We stand in worship before the Mystery of the final Reality to whom or to which we give different names, so great and deep and eternal that we can never fully understand or grasp the mystery of His Being.'

2. They fear syncretism, which implies watering down or mixing of religions. This would be rejected by believers of most religions, although some believe there is an underlying unity of religion. Organizers of inter-faith services usually insist that participants must remain loyal to their own tradition but that as children of the One God, there are values such as justice, peace and the sanctity of life which are held in common.

3. They are anxious lest the apparent equality of religions weakens Christian witness to the uniqueness of Jesus Christ. This reflects sharp differences among Christians as to their theological evaluation of other faiths and their understanding of mission. Is God's saving activity found exclusively in the church or in all the religious traditions of humankind?

Orthodox Jews and Muslims also have hesitations. While no one suggests that inter-faith worship should replace the traditional liturgies of religious communities, the occasions when people of different faiths meet in God's presence, whether for prayer of a personal nature, or to witness to shared ideals or to dedicate work undertaken together, seem likely to increase. Maybe where words divide, shared silence can unite.

Peter R. Akehurst and R. W. F. Wootton, *Inter-Faith Worship?*, 1977; Marcus Braybrooke (ed), *Inter-Faith Worship*, 1974; BCC, *Can We Pray Together?: Guidelines on Worship in a Multi-Faith Society*, 1983.

MARCUS BRAYBROOKE

Intinction

From the Latin *intingo*, I dip in, intinction is the action of dipping the bread into the wine at the eucharist so that the two kinds can be administered conjointly. This is the practice of the Eastern Orthodox Churches, and was introduced into the West for reasons of expediency in the eleventh century. It was, however, condemned by the Council of Clermont in 1095, while continuing in England until forbidden by the Council of London in 1175. Today it is sometimes practised in the USA for hygienic reasons.

Reservation* of the intincted host was common in the later Middle Ages and is still practised in some Anglican churches.

EDITOR

Introit

see **Chants of the Proper of the Mass; Music in the Mass of the Roman Rite**

Invocation

A calling upon God or the saints in prayer or attestation. So the epiclesis (*see* **Anaphora** 8) is an invocation of God to send down the Holy Spirit. Prayers before sermons, calling on God to assist the preacher in declaring his word, are similarly invocations.

EDITOR

Islamic Worship

The Muslim's concept of worship is *'ibādat* or 'service' rendered to God by man, the *'abd* or 'servant' of God. *'Ibādat* is traditionally coupled with *mu'āmalāt* or 'works', in order to stress the Islamic view that spiritual and secular duties, duties to God and duties to one's fellow men, belong together.

The duties of worship are summed up in the 'five pillars of the faith': 1. confession of the unity of God and prophethood of Muḥammad (*shahādat*); 2. ritual prayer (*ṣalāt*); 3. almsgiving (*zakāt*); 4. fasting (*ṣawm*); 5. pilgrimage (*ḥajj*). These are all obligatory (*wājib*) on the capable adult believer, and all have a communal dimension. There are also many additional duties recommended (*sunnat* or *mandūb*) for the believer; these may have a more individualistic flavour, such as intercessory or supplicatory prayer (*du'ā'*) or free-will almsgiving (*adaqāt*).

The central act of Muslims' worship is the ritual prayer. This is offered five times a day by the orthodox Muslim: between dawn and sunrise; after noon; before sunset; after sunset; when night has fallen. These prayers may be offered anywhere, although it is recommended for men that they should be offered in the mosque (women are permitted, though not recommended, to use the mosque). On Friday the midday prayers should be congregational prayers in the mosque, with a sermon preached in addition. The basic furniture of the mosque is simply a niche (*miḥrāb*), directed towards Mecca, the direction (*qiblah*) of all Islamic prayer, and a pulpit or ladder (*minbar*) from which the sermon is preached; small mosques may have nothing more than an indication of the *qiblah*.

The words used in the call-to-prayer (*adhān*), given by the muezzin (*mu'adhdhin*) from the minaret, if there is one, or from the entrance to the mosque, include, with various repetitions: 'God is most great . . . I bear witness that there is no god but God . . . I bear witness that Muḥammad is the prophet of God . . . Come to prayer! . . . Come to the good! . . . (in the early morning) Prayer is better than sleep! . . .' Only in Turkey have reforms ever been attempted to use a vernacular for these formulae; otherwise Arabic, the language of Qur'ānic revelation, is used all over the Muslim world for the call-to-prayer and for the liturgical service of *ṣalāt* which follows. After ritual ablution (*wuḍū'*) of the face, hands and feet (assuming that the body and clothes of the worshipper are already clean), the worshippers line up behind the *imām* who is chosen to lead the prayers by virtue of his learning or seniority; everyone joins in the prayers both physically and verbally. They stand and recite the prayer of intention (*niyah*) that they may be sincere. With their open palms by their ears and held facing forwards they say, 'God is most great' (this prayer is called the *takbīr*). Standing with downcast eyes and hands folded, they pray a prayer of praise called the *subḥān*, and then the first *sūrah* of the Qur'ān followed by at least one long or two short verses from elsewhere in the Qur'ān. While bowing from the waist, with hands on the knees, they repeat the *takbīr* with another prayer of praise (*tasbīḥ*). Everyone then stands erect, with arms at the side, and after the *imām* has said, 'God hears him who praises him', they reply 'Lord, Thou art praised' (if one is alone one recites both sentences). With knees, nose and forehead touching the ground in full prostration the *takbīr* and *tasbīḥ* are repeated; sitting back on the heels with hands on the thighs the worshipper again offers the *takbīr* before renewed prostration and *tasbīḥ*. After repeating this rite (from the Qur'ān recitation to the prostration) one or more times (depending on the time of day), the liturgy concludes with the worshipper kneeling and offering prayers of blessing upon the prophet and upon God's righteous servants. Finally the 'peace' (*salām*) is said first to the right and then to the left.

With the completion of this rite of *ṣalāt* the worshipper may go on to offer further more intimate prayers of 'secret whisperings' or 'supplication' (*munājāt* or *du'ā'*); these are offered in a kneeling position with the open palms held together facing the neck. There is a very rich devotional literature in Islam containing such prayers selected from the Qur'ān, the biography of the prophet and the traditional *Ḥadīth* literature of the prophet and the early community of Muslims. To this has been added a wealth of prayers and poetry attributed to famous mystics of Islam, many of whom asserted their influence over their followers by prescribing particular forms of supererogatory prayer. An excellent analysis of their prayer manuals is Constance Padwick, *Muslim Devotions*, 1961.

A famous treatise on the external and the internal aspects of *ṣalāt* and *du'ā'* is the book on worship in the *Iḥyā'* of al-Ghazālī, translated as *Worship in Islam* by E. E. Calverley, 1925 and as *Inner Dimensions* of *Islamic Worship* by Muhtar Holland, 1983.

Special acts of worship are associated with annual feast days. Since the lunar year is followed, dates must be calculated from tables such as those in G. S. P. Freeman-Grenville, *The Muslim and Christian Calendars*, 1963, but easy reference may be made to the *Calendar of Religious Festivals* published annually by the Commission for Racial Equality. The chief festivals are *'Īd al-Fiṭr* at the end of the month of fasting and *'Īd al-Aḍḥā* during the month of pilgrimage. Descriptions of these occasions could be found in T. P. Hughes, *A Dictionary of Islam*, 1885, and further details of the pilgrimage to Mecca are given in A. Kamal, *The Sacred Journey*, 1961, in the *Autobiography of Malcolm X*, 1964, and in Guellouz/Arkoun, *Pélérinage à la Mecque*, Paris 1977 (with photos).

The discipline and the rhythm of Islamic worship has been a unifying and appealing factor in Islamic history. Without any dependence upon a 'clergy' (which does not properly exist in Islam), the individual, the group or the whole 'people' have demonstrated a pattern of response to God and communion with God which has commended itself to increasing numbers, especially in Asia and Africa. While other aspects of Islamic jurisprudence have undergone modernization, the 'five pillars' remain intact in theory and also in the practice of many Muslims. Few Muslim parents would neglect to instruct their children in matters of worship. A moving personal reflection, 'A Muslim Experience of Prayer' by Mohamed Talbi, is found in *Encounter*, April 1977 (Piazza S. Apollinare, 49, Rome, Italy). A more dogmatic analysis is found in Mustafa Ahmed al-Zara, 'The Islamic Concept of Worship', in Khurshid Ahmad, *Islam – Its Meaning and Message*, 1976.

J. TAYLOR

Jacobite Church

see **West Syrian Worship**

Jehovah's Witnesses Worship

Jehovah's Witnesses are a body of ministers commissioned to preach the end of the present system of things and to proclaim the incoming Kingdom of Jehovah God as the only rightful government of the world. Jesus Christ, God's only-begotten Son, is the one anointed by God as ruler of the Kingdom (John 3.16). Before being born on earth as a man, Jesus had been in heaven as a mighty spirit person and Jehovah's Witnesses acknowledge him as their Leader, Ransomer and now reigning King (John 17.5; Matt. 23.10; 20.28; Rev. 17.14; 19.11–16).

Jehovah's Witnesses are monotheistic, worshipping only the true God, the Creator, Jehovah. They do not acknowledge a Trinity as that word does not appear in any translation of the Bible, and the teachings and creeds that proclaim it are part of tradition that has built up over the centuries. Jehovah's Witnesses follow the clear statement of Jesus Christ, namely: 'It is Jehovah your God you must worship, and it is to him alone you must render sacred service' (Matt. 4.10; Deut. 6.13).

True worship of the Creator embraces every phase of an individual's life. As the apostle Paul wrote: 'Whether you are eating or drinking or doing anything else, do all things for God's glory' (I Cor. 10.31). Jehovah's Witnesses seek to be conscientious in all they do, to be honest and law-abiding. They acknowledge worldly governments as 'superior authorities' permitted by God to exercise authority. But

such authority is relative, and when a conflict of loyalties arises, Jehovah's Witnesses follow the Christian precept, 'We must obey God as ruler rather than men' (Acts 5.29). For this reason Jehovah's Witnesses are conscientious objectors in times of worldly conflict, adopting a course of strict neutrality in all political matters. As a consequence they have suffered at the hands of totalitarian governments as, for example, in Germany where during the course of the Nazi rule some 10,000 Witnesses were imprisoned and together received sentences totalling 20,000 years. One out of every two German Witnesses was imprisoned and one in four lost his life. (*See* C. E. King, *The Nazi State and the New Religions: Five Case Studies in Non-Conformity*.)

Even in more liberal lands, Jehovah's Witnesses have had to fight for their rights of conscience and to preach the good news. But their actions have led to the safeguarding of freedom of speech and religion as the following demonstrates:

> Through almost constant litigation [Jehovah's Witnesses] have made possible an ever-increasing list of precedents concerning the application of the Fourteenth Amendment to freedom of speech and religion . . . And so, a body of precedent crystallizing rules regarding the limits of encroachment by the States has been developing. To this development Jehovah's Witnesses have contributed the most, both in quantity and in significance (*Bill of Rights Review*, The American Bar Association, 1942).

Around the world thousands of Kingdom Halls are used by the 47,869 congregations of Jehovah's Witnesses. These halls are modest buildings suitable for gatherings of people to receive Bible instruction. Each week there is a public talk usually given by one of the local elders, a congregation study of a Bible theme as featured in *The Watchtower*, a Theocratic Ministry School programme to provide training in public speaking, and a Service Meeting where practical suggestions relating to the Christian ministry and everyday life are considered. In addition, smaller discussion groups are held in private homes as local centres for Christian instruction. Larger meeting halls, known as Assembly Halls, are also a feature of the meetings of Jehovah's Witnesses where many congregations can gather together twice a year for Christian fellowship and instruction. In addition, national and international conventions are arranged annually.

The spiritual oversight of the congregations is entrusted to appointed elders (*episkopos*) and ministerial servants (*diakonos*) who are appointed specifically to each congregation. The scriptural requirements set out at I Tim. 3.1–10 and Titus 1.5–9 are strictly adhered to. The scriptural standards for Christian overseers are admittedly high, but the responsibility for taking the lead in Jehovah's worship and in being exemplary in Christian conduct is great (Heb. 13.7; I Peter 5.1–3).

The worldwide report prepared by Jehovah's Witnesses for the year 1984 reveals the following: a total of 2,842,531 active ministers (100,000 of them in the British Isles), a 7.1% increase worldwide over the previous year, preaching in 203 countries. 179,421 adults were baptized during the year. A grand total of 505,588,037 hours were spent in active preaching and 2,047,113 Bible studies were conducted in the homes of interested people, usually on a weekly basis.

See also **Books, Liturgical** 8; **Liturgies** 8.

DAVID SIBREY

Jewish Worship

If the Psalter is the hymn book of the Second Temple, Dan. 6.11 and Ps. 55.18 attest thrice-daily Jewish private prayer outside the Temple; not only scripture, but Apocrypha, Pseudepigrapha, Scrolls and Josephus provide numerous instances of specific Jewish prayers in Second Temple times. Public reading and interpretation of the scriptures was widespread at least by late Second Temple times, and to this institution we owe the rich literature of Greek as well as Aramaic translations and paraphrases.

Yet it is not until the time of Gamaliel II (*c.* AD 100) that we find an attempt to regulate the structure, content and to a lesser extent the wording of prayer. The rabbis speak of prayer as the service of the heart (*avoda shebalev*), emphasizing the inwardness which is of its essence. They admired the 'pious men of old' who spent a silent hour before prayer focussing their minds on holy things; later Jewish usage

sets the devotional atmosphere by the recitation of psalms prior to the main prayers.

Three sections of the Pentateuch (Deut. 6.4–9; 11.12–21; Num. 15.37–41) form even today the central reading of the morning and evening orders of service. They declare God's unity (*Sh'ma Israel* – 'Hear, Israel, the Lord our God, the Lord is one') and the duty to love him and to follow his commandments. Before and after these readings God is praised as the Master of the Universe 'who creates the light' (morning prayer); 'who lets the night follow the day' (evening prayer); who gave his Torah to Israel as a sign of his love, and who is the Redeemer of his people in past and future.

The morning, afternoon and evening orders of prayer focus on the *tefilla* (prayer *par excellence*) for which the pattern was set under Gamaliel's guidance. Its originally eighteen, now nineteen, blessings (the prayer is sometimes called *sh'mone esre*, meaning 18) open with praise of God and conclude with thanksgiving and prayers for peace; a central section on weekdays includes petitions for the granting of discernment, forgiveness, health and material well-being, as well as the fulfilment of messianic hopes, and on Sabbaths and festivals substitutes for the petitions prayers appropriate for the day. Gamaliel and his colleagues sought a link between prayer and Temple service; not only does the Jew say prayers turning in the direction of Jerusalem, but prayer times were fixed to correspond with the Temple procedure. On Sabbath, New Moon and festivals, when extra sacrifices used to be offered, an additional prayer (*mussaf*) is said.

Readings from the Torah (Five Books of Moses) and the Prophets feature in the Synagogue service on Monday and Thursday mornings (no three days should pass without a Torah reading) and on Sabbaths and festivals. The present lectionary incorporates an annual reading of the whole of the Pentateuch, though well into Talmudic times three or seven year cycles were common.

Gamaliel knew that fixed words of prayer might undermine spontaneity; he aimed to set basic contents rather than wording, using fixed formulae only for 'beginnings' or 'endings' of blessings. He and his contemporaries encouraged spontaneous and occasional prayer as well as fixed orders of service. One of their most beautiful creations is the programme of *berachot* (blessings), on the basis of the 'Blessed art thou, O Lord . . .' formula (cf. Ps. 119.12) in which the *tefilla* also is couched. These blessings are said on occasions when one derives enjoyment or inspiration from God's world, as for instance when eating, drinking, hearing thunder, seeing beautiful things, or smelling the fragrance of flowers; through these short, simple prayers the most humble Jew learns to appreciate the blessings he daily receives from God. The Talmud records many examples of private, spontaneous prayer, often enough opening with the formula 'our Father in heaven' or 'may it be thy will, my God and God of my fathers . . .' Further contributions to the liturgy have come through processional litanies, such as the Temple 'Hosannahs', through the *hekhalot* literature, incorporating early Jewish mysticism, and through the prayers of the House of Study (including the *Kaddish*).

After the framework of the liturgy had been settled, poets strove to express the religious message of the festivals and other special days of the Jewish calendar in lyrical form (*piyyutim*). Some of their creations, as those of Eleazar Kalir (sixth century?), were widely acclaimed and adopted into the prayer-book. Mediaeval Spanish poets such as Solomon ibn Gabirol, Judah Halevy and Abraham ibn Ezra combined mastery of language and beauty of verse-form with deep spiritual thought.

Though prayers were not written down in earliest times, the continuing spread of Jewish communities in the Diaspora and the wealth of new liturgical compositions made it necessary to give guidance on the form and contents of the prayers; much of this is to be found in the Talmud itself. The first known prayer books were compiled in the Babylonian academies in the ninth and tenth centuries; they are compendia of the devotions and rules for all days of the year and for occasions like birth, marriage and mourning.

Though the Jews who lived for centuries in Mediterranean countries (Sephardim) differed in some customs from the Jews of Central and Northern Europe (Ashkenazim), the main prayers and the essential mode of worship, being rooted in the Talmud, differed little. Only non-statutory additions, such as the *piyyutim*, vary substan-

tially by place of origin. A great unifying force for Jewish worship is the calendar, common to Jews throughout the world.

Mystics, such as the sixteenth-century Isaac Luria at Safed, introduced new elements into their devotions, and these were popularized with the spread of mysticism among wider circles of the Jewish population in Europe (seventeenth century onwards), above all through the Hassidic movement.

Prayers in the synagogue are led by a reader (*hazzan*). The reader, though sometimes a minister with pastoral responsibilities, need be neither priest nor rabbi; any competent male of thirteen or over who is acceptable to the congregation may lead prayer. Sermons – in orthodox synagogues almost the only part of the service in the vernacular – are the prerogative of the rabbi.

The desire to modernize the synagogue service was felt strongly in the nineteenth century, at the time when the mediaeval isolation of the Jews had finally come to an end. In many communities the knowledge of Hebrew had declined and translations of the texts have found their way into the prayer books. The traditional prayers were revised and cleared of obscurities and grammatical errors (Heidenheim). To enhance the beauty of the service, greater care was taken with the vocal part, in particular recitations by the reader who is now often supported by a choir. In orthodox synagogues the use of musical instruments on Sabbaths and festivals is not permitted, but in reform synagogues the organ and other instruments are used and many composers such as Bloch and Milhaud have made settings of the synagogue services. In reform and liberal synagogues the overall length of the service has been reduced; also, contrary to traditional usage, women sit together with men and take an active part in the conduct of the service.

Orthodox synagogues expect both men and married women to cover their heads at prayer; men wear the fringed *Tallit* (cf. Num. 15.38) at morning prayer each day and the *tefillin* (cf. Ex. 13.16) on weekday mornings only. Progressive synagogues vary both with regard to adoption of these practices and with regard to differentation between the sexes.

Talmud, especially *Berachot*, *Megillah*, *Tamid*; Orthodox, Conservative, Reform and Liberal Prayer Books (numerous translations and editions); N. H. Glatzer, *Language of Faith*, 1967 (a selection of Jewish prayers of all times); Joseph Heinemann, *Prayer in the Period of the Tannaim and the Amoraim* (Hebrew, with English summary), 1964; A. Z. Idelsohn, *Jewish Liturgy and its Development*, 1967; Louis Jacobs, *Jewish Prayer*, 1956; Abraham E. Millgram, *Jewish Worship*, 1971; David de Sola Pool, *The Kaddish*, 1964. *The Penguin Book of Hebrew Verse* (T. Carmi, 1981) contains a useful selection of liturgical poetry.

NORMAN SOLOMON

Kiss of Peace

see **Gestures** 8

Kneeling

see **Posture** 3

Kyrie

The invocation *Kyrie eleison* (Greek, 'Lord have mercy') is found in nearly all the historic liturgies, in many of them in the original Greek, whatever the language of the rest of the service, and appears to have been derived both from Jewish and from pagan liturgical formularies. The first definite evidence of its use as the response to the petitions of a litany* comes from fourth-century Jerusalem and Antioch, whence both the litany form itself and this response rapidly spread to all parts of the Christian world.

At Rome an intercessory litany of this type was inserted after the introit of the mass in the fifth century, probably during the pontificate of Gelasius (492–6), who was responsible for considerable changes in the Roman liturgy; texts of this and related litanies survive. At the time of Gregory the Great (590–604), and possibly at his instigation, the petitions of this litany were omitted on ordinary days, the responses being sung alone, as precatory acclamations. By the end of the eighth century the litany had disappeared altogether, and the acclamations were arranged in a way which remained fixed for over eleven hundred years – *Kyrie eleison* three times, the variant

Christe eleison three times, and finally *Kyrie eleison* again three times. During the Middle Ages, many of the numerous local variants of the Roman rite took to 'farcing' the *Kyries* on feasts – phrases appropriate to the day were inserted between '*Kyrie*' or '*Christe*' and '*eleison*'. In the revised *Ordo Missae* of 1969, the same order is retained, on those occasions when the *Kyrie* is ordered to be used, but the threefold form has been replaced by a responsorial twofold one (although the threefold form may be used if the musical setting at a sung mass requires it). The *Kyrie-Christe-Kyrie* alternation has often been explained in a trinitarian way, the prayer being said to be addressed first to the Father, then to the Son, then to the Holy Spirit. This is historically incorrect: there is no question but that the whole prayer was originally addressed to the Son.

Kyrie eleison is still the most common response to litanies in the Eastern rites, although the acclamation alone, in variously numbered groups, is found in them also; the ninefold and sixfold Roman forms, with other variants, are found also in many reformed liturgies in the West.

See also **Music in the Mass of the Roman Rite; Ordinary**

J. A. Jungmann, *The Mass of the Roman Rite*, I, 1951, pp.333–46. For Gelasius' litany *see* G. G. Willis, *Essays in Early Roman Liturgy*, 1964, pp.21–25.

W. JARDINE GRISBROOKE

Laity and Worship

While the New Testament clearly expects that all believers (i.e. the *laos* or people of God) will actively participate in worship (with some cultural reservations about the role of women) most churches had, by mediaeval times, reduced the laity (i.e. the non-ordained) – who now very rarely communicated at the mass – to the role of passive spectators, while the clergy offered worship in languages like Latin and Old Slavonic which the common people could not understand, and in styles which seemed to emphasize a fundamental division between bishops, priests and laity. Church architecture also increasingly separated the people from even seeing many ceremonies, with screens to fence off the high altar and the sanctuary from the nave where the laity huddled at the back or followed other occupations. (Perhaps the 'new' Coventry cathedral is the last of the old-fashioned cathedrals.)

The Reformation, of course, did much to bring laity back into active worship, especially in the more radical sects. To have the Bible and various liturgies in the vernacular started a true revolution in worship, which is only now having its profound effects in many Roman Catholic churches, after the recent changes associated with the Second Vatican Council. The Reformers laid great emphasis on preaching and on a solemn participation in holy communion, after careful preparation. Nevertheless, much Protestant worship, up to the present day, has also been infected by an overwhelming tendency to regard worship as the work of the pastor (and perhaps of the choir) with the majority of the laity having very little to do but sing a few hymns and listen in a prayerful and attentive way.

The last fifty years have seen great changes, and a recovery in very many churches and denominations of all kinds of a true spirit of participation in Christian worship. (Most Orthodox and Coptic churches still keep to a variety of very traditional and 'timeless' rituals and – some of them – to ancient languages: they would nevertheless claim that their laity are deeply incorporated in these styles of worship: a controversial point.) In both Catholic and Protestant churches, and in all kinds of informal Christian groups, worship is now developed as the work of the whole people of God. Lay people help with praises and intercessions, with the administration of the sacraments, and with sermons and all kinds of Christian learning. They help design Sunday worship and major church festivals, they join in all kinds of religious music and drama and dance. They pass the peace, they criticize the pastor's teaching and suggest topics for study.

This welcome ferment in Christian worship, in which radical clergy and laity are often opposed by more conservative clergy and very conservative laity, has produced some weighty problems.

1. Even if theologically it is accepted that worship must be an offering of all the people, there are still many historical and

psychological pressures to make lay people regard worship as overwhelmingly the responsibility of the clergy. The attitude is often, 'It's their job: they are the experts.' It is important to learn the ways in which some Roman Catholic and Evangelical churches encourage ordinary lay people – not just teachers and professional people – to take leadership at Sunday services.

2. Christians are still unsure, and sometimes bitterly divided, about problems of indigenizing worship today, how to and whether to adapt it to fit into the cultural styles of many lay people. In particular young people (so numerous in the populations of Third World countries) and working-class people, almost everywhere, find it very difficult to join in traditional church language or music or learning styles. Yet popular church worship is often adjudged as banal and 'unmysterious'. Almost all churches now find it difficult to deal with the great traditions of Christian worship. They are often captive to or contemptuous of their history (even the history of the nineteenth century) instead of learning to use and to profit from their rich traditions as they rightly look to the future.

3. The eucharist, or mass, or holy communion, has rightly come to the forefront of much Christian worship in recent years. Yet it is often the symbol of *disunity* for many laity, especially when marriage partners or friends are from different denominations. (This is a scandal which some church leaders seem to live with all too easily.)

4. Allied to this is, of course, the plain fact that some Roman Catholics and 'high' Anglicans hold that bishops and priests are sacramentally different from lay people, and that they alone may offer absolution and consecrate the elements at the eucharist. Some such churches are nevertheless very successful in involving lay people actively in worship: others still perpetuate a kind of two-grade, shepherd/sheep differentiation within the whole people of God.

5. Many lay people protest (or quietly accept) that Sunday worship does not speak helpfully about their responsibilities on Monday mornings, or for that matter on Saturday evenings. Those laity who engage in useful church work (the choir, the altar guild, the Sunday school, the stewardship campaign) are affirmed and honoured; those whose ministries for the Lord take them away from the local parish are neglected in the prayers and ceremonies and teaching. Few denominations have any regular rituals to affirm that all God's people, irrespective of their occupation or sex or age or anything else, are called to discipleship. Orders of worship like the Methodist covenant service* and the Iona Community's service of profession of faith are worth study as admirable examples of what may be attempted here.

6. Everywhere, especially in urban areas, and including the great new cities of the Third World, lay people, especially men, are giving up regular Sunday worship (and this includes many Roman Catholics). There are now many who claim to be Christians, but hold quite sincerely that church worship is optional. They cannot be answered by simple charges of 'disloyalty'.

7. Many would contend that a church that does not evangelize is not a true church, but numerous congregations, both Protestant and Catholic, find great difficulty in welcoming 'outsiders'. Here North American congregations, of all kinds, have much to teach Europeans about making strangers feel at ease, without pestering them. Some local churches in Britain and Europe, perhaps unconsciously, give so strongly an impression of being a 'club' of worshippers – often with mysterious prayer books and unexplained rituals – that it is very difficult for visitors to feel that they are welcome.

8. In past centuries, and in both Protestant and Catholic traditions, the laity have considered even public worship as very largely an individual affair. It is an opportunity to stand or kneel before God, to say private prayers. In many churches today there is a much stronger emphasis on the communal aspects of Christians worshipping together, often symbolized by the passing of the Peace at the eucharist. Yet there are very often tensions between laity on these two different attitudes to worship, which are not always resolved by careful teaching and discussion.

Indeed it may be said that the *art* of Christian worship, which monks and nuns and clergy have in their own ways developed and patiently practised over the centuries, is still something which many laity feel

is beyond them, 'not their cup of tea'. A certain number of lay people gladly and profitably join in these special and traditional styles of worship: others find them less helpful, and often long for liturgies and rituals and celebrations which will fulfil for them what mattins and evensong and compline offer to more churchly people.

D. Clark, *The Liberation of the Church*, 1984; J. G. Davies, *Every Day God*, 1973; D. Forrester and D. Murray (eds), *Studies in the History of Worship in Scotland*, 1984; H. E. Horn, *The Christian in Modern Style*, 1968; M. McCauley, *On the Run*, 1974; M. H. Taylor, *Variations on a Theme*, 1973; T. Ware, *The Orthodox Church*, 1963.

MARK GIBBS

Lammas

see **Harvest Thanksgiving**

Lamps

see **Candles, Lamps and Lights**

Language, Inclusive

see **Inclusive Language**

Last Gospel

The reading of the Johannine prologue (John 1.1–14) at the end of mass only became general with the *Missale Romanum* of Pius V, published in 1570. It was suppressed in 1964 as part of the reform of the rite of mass for which Vatican II legislated. In the Middle Ages this gospel was considered to have miraculous efficacy when read; it was used as a blessing for fine weather and was read over the sick. The 1614 *Rituale Romanum* concludes the rite for the visitation of the sick with the reading of this gospel.

It is first found as the conclusion of the mass in the Dominican Mass Ordinary of 1256. It was said in the sacristy* by the priest as he took off his vestments*, or later. From the Dominicans the custom passed to the Armenians, who retained it even after the schism of 1380. At the end of the Middle Ages the last gospel was read, like the gospel of the mass, at the north end of the altar, and the people often joined in its recitation.

Originally it seems likely that the Johannine prologue was read as a blessing; it came of course immediately after the blessing at the end of mass. As time went on, however, the content of this pericope came to be emphasized for its own sake. This trend clearly predominated once it became customary to read as the last gospel the gospel of a second mass formulary merely commemorated in the mass of the day, a practice found from the fifteenth century which originated in the 'dry' mass (*see* **Ante-communion**).

J. A. Jungmann, *The Mass of the Roman Rite*, new rev ed 1959; A. G. Martimort (ed), *Introduction to the Liturgy*, 1968; M. Righetti, *Storia Liturgica*, III, [3]1966.

BRIAN NEWNS

Last Rites

The liturgical acts that are celebrated for the dying: confession (when possible), absolution*, unction* (if appropriate) and communion (viaticum*).

Lauds

see **Canonical Hours**

Lavabo

Lavabo is the first word of Ps. 26.6: 'I will wash my hands in innocency' – the verse which is recited at the ceremonial washing of the hands in the eucharist. From the patristic period this washing usually accompanied the offertory*. Cyril of Jerusalem is the first witness, although it was probably practised long before his day. According to him, it is essentially symbolic: 'We do not set out for church with defiled bodies' (*Mystag.* 5.2). In the *Apostolic Constitutions* (8.11f.) the sequence is pax, handwashing, offertory and *Sursum corda.* So the action was not a cleansing of the hands after the reception of the gifts.

In the Ethiopic rite, the priest does not dry his fingers but sprinkles the remaining drops towards the people with a warning that only the pure should approach. The emphasis therefore is not upon hygiene but upon purity symbolized by the ceremonial cleansing.

In the Middle Ages in the Roman rite the symbolism was subordinated to the cleansing – an unusual reversal, since the general rule was for utilitarian actions to be given a symbolic meaning – and the *lavabo* was transferred to a position after the reception of the gifts and the censing. The

ancient position is retained only in the Carthusian rite.

Since Carolingian times a preliminary washing of the hands has accompanied the vesting and a similar practice is found in some manuscripts of the Liturgy of St Chrysostom, but it would be incorrect to apply the term *lavabo* to this.

J. A. Jungmann, *The Mass of the Roman Rite*, new rev ed 1959, pp.349–52.

EDITOR

Law and Worship

The influence of *civil law* on worship has been varied, and mostly indirect. In virtually every country public worship, in so far as it may impinge on human rights, liberties and law and order, is subject to the law of the land concerning such matters. At certain times and in certain places, especially under totalitarian regimes, public worship has been restricted or even banned altogether, e.g. in the USSR after the 1918 revolution, Mexico in the 1930s, China during the Cultural Revolution. The promulgation of the Creed of Nicaea under Constantine, and the Old Believers schism in seventeenth-century Russia, are examples of church/state relations influencing liturgy. In Western Christendom public worship, at least of the dominant religious groups, has usually enjoyed the protection of the law. Where the church has been established such protection has often been accompanied by a measure of state control. The history of liturgy in the Church of England may illustrate this.

The early liturgical reforms of Cranmer, Archbishop of Canterbury, were carried out in close collaboration with King Henry VIII, and sometimes at his instigation. The further reforms under Edward VI were carried out by royal rather than church authority. The prayer books of 1549 and 1552, both composed by Cranmer, were accompanied by Acts of Uniformity, imposing severe penalties on those who refused to use them. During the Rebellion the Book of Common Prayer was forbidden in cathedrals and churches, while after the Restoration the BCP of 1662 was also accompanied by an Act of Uniformity. The theological differences between these three prayer books were occasioned as much by changes in royal or political preference as by church authority. Later modifications made to the Act of Uniformity all required Parliamentary sanction. In 1928 a crisis was reached when Parliament refused to authorize a very modest revision of the 1662 prayer book, even though that revision had full ecclesiastical authority and approval. In response the bishops took the technically unlawful step of authorizing the contents of the 1928 book by those who wished to use it, or parts of it. It was not until 1974, with the passing of the Church of England (Worship and Doctrine) Measure, that Parliament transferred authority in liturgical matters to the General Synod, but even then making legal requirement that the BCP was to be permanently available.

The influence of *canon law* on church authority has naturally been much stronger. In both Western and Eastern catholicism, and in some Protestant churches, public worship has been almost totally governed by such ecclesiastical law, since liturgy is almost by definition the corporate, even official, worship of the Christian community. As such it has been generally welcomed by lay people, since it protects them from the vagaries and prejudices of individual priests or pastors. However the Liturgical Movement* of this century has ushered in a period of liturgical experimentation, leading to officially revised liturgies in most churches of the West. In the Roman Catholic Church this has been imposed by central authority, driving some to an unlawful use of the old Latin mass. More recently Pope John Paul II has licensed the Latin mass for an occasional use more frequent than before, but still very restricted. In the Church of England an Alternative Service Book was authorized by Synod in 1980 after a long procedure in various committees, and indeed after prolonged and detailed debate in full Synod. The influence of such committee work, together with the attempt to provide for the conflicting views of the various parties in the Church of England, has in the view of many had an adverse effect on the alternative book, both in style and content. In 1979 a massive petition was presented to the Synod for a 'continued and loving' use of the Book of Common Prayer and the Authorized Version of the Bible, claiming that this was of popular and not merely ecclesiastical concern. However, attempts to

push through legislation along these lines in parliament failed.

On the whole the revised liturgies have now won wide acceptance, and a recognition that on balance the result has been gain. The dilemma remains that, at a time of rapid change and development in all aspects of life and thought, when liturgical flexibility would seem to be appropriate, the legally authorized use of set patterns of worship may prove a strait-jacket against much needed further development in worship. Perhaps a resolution may lie in the combination of an imaginative use of the new official liturgies with further experimentation in the realm of para-liturgies and the worship of small groups or house churches.

In the Eastern Orthodox Churches the liturgy has been governed by an almost exclusive appeal to ancient tradition expressing itself in ecclesiastical law and custom, with the result that there have been virtually no changes in the text of the Orthodox liturgies.

T. G. A. BAKER

Lay Ministries

The Constitution on the Liturgy of Vatican II detailed a number of ministries in the celebration of the eucharist* which include that of servers*, lectors* and members of the choir*, all of whom 'exercise a genuine liturgical function' (no.29). Paul VI extended this notion with the statement in *Immensae caritatis* of 1973 that laymen and laywomen might assist the celebrant in the giving of holy communion. Such ministers may also take the reserved sacrament to the sick, the housebound and the dying. This practice is now very widespread. They are called 'extraordinary' ministers or 'special' or 'auxiliary' ministers, the last two terms being the ones that are favoured. These are selected by the parish clergy, are given appropriate instruction and then are commissioned by the local bishop or his delegate.

Various reasons were given for the institution of these ministries: the need to assist the celebrant in the distribution of holy communion when there is a very large number of communicants, the need to give the sacrament more frequently to the sick and the housebound in parishes and other places where they are very numerous, and to provide holy communion for the people in those places where there is no ordained minister.

In addition to their purely liturgical function, they are recommended to visit the sick, to keep them in touch with the life of the parish community and to provide such spiritual help as may be necessary.

Auxiliary ministers are commissioned for a given space of time. They renew their commitment of service every Maundy Thursday and in the event of their leaving the parish they are given a certificate to authenticate their ministry if their services are required in their new parish.

Administration of Communion and Viaticum to the Sick by a Special Minister, 1978; *Handbook for Special Ministers of Communion*, 1982, with extracts from *Immensae caritatis* and the text of the liturgy for the commissioning.

J. D. CRICHTON

Lay Preacher

This is often a term used simply to describe a lay person who takes services and preaches when there is no minister. In some Baptist, Congregational and Presbyterian churches, however, lay preachers are formally recognized and authorized, after receiving the necessary training, and are often responsible for maintaining services in small congregations who could not support a full-time minister.

P. HINCHLIFF

Lay Reader

see **Reader**

Laying on of Hands

see **Gestures** 7

Lectern

A bookrest for public reading. It can be a separate structure or it can be attached to the pulpit* as it usually is in Nonconformist churches. In the Church of England after the Reformation a reading desk was normally provided, sometimes attached to the pulpit, often with two book ledges, one facing across the church on which the Book of Common Prayer rested, the other facing west for the Bible.

However, lecterns are frequently distinct pieces of furniture. The most ambitious type is the ambo*, which is really a reading

Plate 41 Modern lectern designed by Colin Shrewring

platform, a feature of the early church which persisted into the Middle Ages in Italy. In the high Middle Ages lecterns stood in the chancel* for the reading of the gospel during the eucharist, and the mediaeval eagles and pelicans, made either of wood or latten, were provided for this purpose, being moved to the nave* after the Reformation in England for the reading of the lessons at morning and evening prayer. But the oldest examples in England, where no early ambo has survived, are of stone, either freestanding, as a Crowle, Worcestershire, *c.* 1200, or built into the chancel north wall as at Etwall, Derbyshire, thirteenth century.

At the end of the Middle Ages lecterns were sometimes used for the epistle as well as the gospel and examples are found with a double desk that revolves on the column, e.g. at Shipdham, Norfolk, in wood, and King's College, Cambridge, in latten.

It seems that in general only wealthy churches could afford separate lecterns before the Reformation. This remained broadly true even up to the nineteenth century, and most seventeenth- and eighteenth-century lecterns in England stand in cathedrals or college chapels. The eagle and desk-top types have remained the most popular up to the present day (*see* Plate 41), though in a desire to be different there have been occasional exceptions such as the angel in Worcester Cathedral.

G. W. O. Addleshaw and F. Etchells, *The Architectural Setting of Anglican Worship*, 1948; J. C. Cox and A. Harvey, *English Church Furniture*, 1907; G. Randall, *Church Furnishing and Decoration in England and Wales*, 1980.

G. D. W. RANDALL

Lectionary

The term is employed in both a wider and a narrower sense. In the wider sense it denotes an ordered system of selected readings ('pericopes') appointed for liturgical use on specific occasions in the church year, thus presupposing a calendar, while in the narrower sense it is used to designate a MS (especially in Greek) with the pericopes thus used written out in full. Lectionaries in this latter sense provide important evidence for the history of the NT text.

The concept of the lectionary in the wider sense evidently goes back to the synagogue, which also had fixed readings from the OT appointed for the Jewish feasts, with pericopes chosen on the principle of *lectio continua* (*l.c.*) for ordinary Sabbaths. But the extent to which the church took over the synagogue system for its OT lessons is unclear, except for Ex. 12, which was used at the Jewish Passover and also for the Christian 'Pasch' (better: 'Passa', so J. Jeremias), as evidenced both in Rome *c.* 200 and among the Quartodecimans (Melito, *c.* 180). The church added gospels and apostolic writings to the OT readings (Justin Martyr, *I Apol.* 67). It has been suggested that the gospel materials were designed for lectionary use in their preliterary stage, and that the

evangelists arranged the pericopes in the order in which they were already used liturgically in the course of the year (P. Carrington), but this theory has found little acceptance. The notes in early manuscripts, αρχ and τελ, denoting the beginning and end of the pericopes, and the assignations of these pericopes to particular days in the church year in marginal notes are indicative only of the later liturgical use of the written gospels, not of their pre-literary use. Specially selected lessons were appointed at first only for Passa and Pentecost*, then for other feasts and fasts of the Easter* and Christmas* cycles and Ember days* and martyrs' days as the calendar grew. For ordinary Sundays the principle of *l.c.* was used, a book being selected apparently at local discretion and read in successive pericopes until it was finished. Thus in pre-Nicene times there was a more or less fixed lectionary only for major feast days.

During this period there were several lessons, both OT and NT, interspersed with psalms (*see below*). Later, the use of three lessons (OT, epistle or other apostolic writing, gospel) was widely standardized (Armenian, Mozarabic, Milanese, Gallican), but at Constantinople (fifth century) and Rome (from sixth century) the lessons were increasingly reduced to two, which eventually became the norm in both East and West. Usually the two lessons were an epistle and gospel, but sometimes it is the OT lesson rather than the apostolic lesson that survived (e.g. especially in Lent in *Missale Romanum. Missale Romanum* occasionally preserved a multiplicity of OT and NT lessons (e.g. in Lenten Embertide).

In the West, Alcuin standardized the mass lectionary from existing local provisions (Roman for the gospels, Gallican for the epistles), though the provisions were never quite complete (last Sundays in Epiphany and Pentecost), the combinations of lessons were largely fortuitous, and only the debris of the earlier *l.c.* survived (as can often be seen in the epistles of the Pentecost season). Sarum, the Lutheran orders, BCP and *Missale Romanum* represent variations and successive modifications of Alcuin's standardization.

Modern dissatisfaction with the traditional eucharistic lectionary arises from: 1. the minimal use of the OT; 2. the haphazard selections for Sundays on which there is no major feast; 3. the non-use of many significant parts of scripture; 4. lack of interconnection between the pericopes on any given occasion.

To meet these difficulties new lectionaries have been compiled on the following principles: 1. A two- or three-year cycle. Two-year: German Lutheran 1896; Church of England Alternative Service Book (ASB) 1980 and the English Free Churches; three year: Roman Catholic *Ordo Lectionum Missae* (second edition) 1981 followed by the Episcopal and several other churches in North America, and by some Anglican churches in other countries; 2. OT lesson additional to or alternative to epistle; 3. more *l.c.* in ordinary time; the designation of one lesson, usually the gospel, as the controlling lesson for the day, the other lessons being selected to go with it, a principle in conflict with that of *l.c.* and more pedagogical than kerygmatic (ASB).

In the breviary of the West, *l.c.* was featured in one office only, namely nocturns or matins, the scripture readings of the day hours being only a short text (*capitulum*). At nocturns lessons were read in threes or groups of three (cf. the tenuous survival in the popular Christmas service of nine lessons and carols). Non-canonical ecclesiastical writings were used. As the preface to the BCP complains, this system had broken down completely in the later Middle Ages. Following Quiñones, Cranmer sought to restore the ancient *l.c.*, with an OT and NT lesson at his two daily offices, and based his lectionary on the civil calendar. The traditional reading of Isaiah in Advent was preserved by beginning that book on 28 November. Recent Anglican revisions of Cranmer have reverted to the church year as the basis, shortened the lessons (especially the Episcopal Church in the USA) and restored other traditional features, e.g. the beginning of the Pentateuch in pre-Lent.

At mass, the standardized Western lectionary provided psalms* for the introit, gradual, offertory* and communion*, the gradual being the most ancient. In the Middle Ages the psalms were drastically reduced in length as the music became more elaborate but in the Roman Catholic lectionary of 1969 ([2] 1981) and in the missal of 1970 a responsorial psalm was restored. At the Reformation the Lutheran orders retained the traditional introits and

graduals, but dropped the offertories and communions. Cranmer provided a new introit for each mass (1549), comprising a whole psalm. His principle of selection, except for major feasts, is obscure, but was seemingly governed by considerations of length. The introits were dropped in 1552. Psalmody at the eucharist is being recovered in current Anglican revisions of the eucharist lectionary, the attempt being made to fit the psalmody to the season, to the lessons, or to both.

For his two offices Cranmer provided (1549) a monthly course of continuous recitation of the psalter, following the civil calendar. In 1552 this system was interrupted by the provision of proper psalms (as also lessons) for 'diverse feasts and fasts'. Cranmer's system has been widely replaced in Anglican revisions by a selection of special psalms for each Sunday and major feast, and in some cases (American BCP 1979 and ASB 1980) by a complete system of daily selections based on the church calendar. In Lutheranism the daily offices have never been widely used, although the American *Lutheran Book of Worship* (1982) provides a daily lectionary of psalms and lessons.

N. M. Denis-Boulet, *The Christian Calendar*, 1960; R. C. D. Jasper (ed), *The Calendar and the Lectionary*, 1967; A. A. McArthur, *The Evolution of the Christian Year*, 1959; Standing Liturgical Commission of the Episcopal Church in the USA, *The Church Year*, 1970.

See also bibliography under **Sermon**.

R. H. FULLER

Lector

The second of the traditional minor orders after the acolyte*, his function was originally to read liturgical portions of scripture at the eucharist, especially the OT lesson, but also the epistle and in some cases even the gospel. The order of lector continues to exist in both the Roman Catholic and the Eastern Churches, but has tended to be absorbed by the major orders. In the Roman Catholic Church since 1972 a layman may be trained for and instituted to the office of lector so that he may read in church and give instruction. Since the Liturgical Movement* it has become common in all churches for lay people to read the lections in services without any formal licensing being required.

See also **Reader**.

P. HINCHLIFF

Lent

The English word 'Lent' means 'Spring', but this does not express the significance of the six-week period of spiritual discipline before Easter* as conveyed by the 40 days of the Greek *tessaracoste* or the Latin *quadragesima* (the latter has given its name to the first Sunday in Lent). Its origin probably lies in the formal and final period of preparation of candidates for baptism* at Easter, with which those undergoing penance* rapidly became associated. With the atrophy of both of these it became transformed into a period of general devotional preparation for Easter for all.

Originally it was somewhat variable in length, but six weeks seems to have been the norm in many places from the fourth century onwards, with Quadragesima (Lat 'forty days') marking its commencement. When the desire arose to keep the Lenten fast as a strict 40 days, and equally to exclude the Sundays from this total on the traditional grounds that Sunday was never a fast day, it was apparent that the weekdays of the six weeks before Easter only provided 36 days, so Lent became extended for four days prior to Quadragesima to make up the total and therefore now started on Ash Wednesday*.

Various liturgical observances grew up associated with Lent. One of the first of these was the scrutinies, services concerned with the examination of and praying for the candidates preparing for baptism. When Lent was no longer associated with baptismal preparation, these no longer took place, being specific to the needs of the baptismal candidates rather than to the season itself, though the modern Roman rite for the Christian Initiation of Adults attempts to revive them.

Within the city of Rome the custom of the stational masses was emphasized in Lent, that is, the principal mass on a particular day, often presided over by the Pope as Bishop of Rome, was celebrated in a particular church, and always the same one on the same day; on certain days the Pope would ride to the stational church in solemn procession. The listing of these stations

survived into the 1570 missal. The custom of stational masses was observed in other cities as well, the bishop going round to the various churches in turn. The modern Roman missal merely commends the custom of stational liturgy in Lent in general and very vague terms, as though wanting to preserve a tradition about the possible observance of which in the modern world it was by no means sure.

But the main liturgical provision for Lent consists of the ordinary liturgy provided with appropriate lessons* and propers*, and with furnishings, vestments* and music suitable for the penitential nature of the season. Many churches and congregations will supplement this with a variety of provisions, special services, series of addresses, study groups and so forth. In recent years support for special observance of Lent has probably been in something of a decline.

The traditional lenten mass lections in the Latin rite reflect the needs of the catechumenate*, to which material suited to the reconciliation of penitents and the more generally penitential nature of the season was added later, and the modern Roman mass lectionary has preserved a lot of this arrangement.

R. Greenacre, *The Sacrament of Easter*, 1965; J. Gunstone, *The Liturgy of Penance*, 1966.

See also under **Calendar**.

R. F. BUXTON

Lesson

The term refers generally to liturgical readings from the scriptures or elsewhere. Apart from the occasional reading from the *Acta* of the martyrs in Africa, Gaul and Milan in patristic times, readings at the eucharist* have always been scriptural. In the divine office*, in the office of readings, there are, however, patristic and hagiographic readings. Here we are concerned only with OT readings in the eucharist and with scriptural readings in the office.

1. *The eucharist*. The church inherited the OT readings from the synagogue service (*see* **Jewish Worship**), supplementing them with NT ones. The East Syrian (*see* **East Syrian Worship**) liturgy accordingly still has lessons from the law and the prophets preceding the epistle and gospel. In the Roman liturgy, the OT readings survived only on Lenten ferias, vigils and in the commons of saints.

The Roman Lectionary ([2] 1981) has restored the OT lesson on Sundays as the first reading, except in Paschaltide when Acts is read. On Sundays through the year the lesson is chosen to accord with the gospel; during Advent Isaiah is prominent, while in Lent passages covering the main stages of the history of salvation are read. The lessons are spread over a three-year cycle, include the principal passages of the OT and in relation with the gospels manifest the harmony between the two Testaments.

On the weekdays of Advent and Lent an OT reading precedes the gospel; during the rest of the year, apart from Paschaltide, the OT lessons alternate every few weeks with NT epistles, over a two-year cycle.

The Church of England Alternative Service Book (1980) has also restored the Old Testament reading as the first of three. During the nine Sundays before Christmas it is this reading which determines the choice of the accompanying epistle and gospel. It is selected to trace during this pre-Christmas season the story of the creation, the fall and the beginnings of God's work of salvation leading up to the incarnation of his Son. For the rest of the year the Old Testament reading is chosen to accord with the gospel (Christmas to Pentecost) and with the epistle (Sundays after Pentecost).

2. *The divine office*. The traditional Roman Office was monastic rather than popular in form, with lessons only in the night hour of matins. The other hours had only a *capitulum*, a brief extract from scripture. The system of lessons went back to the seventh or eighth centuries and once covered most of the Bible, but gradual abbreviation over the centuries meant that much came to be omitted.

The post-conciliar Roman Office (1971), or Liturgy of the Hours, was intended to have a two-year cycle of readings from scripture, covering the whole of the Bible, apart from the gospels. Regrettably this was abandoned to keep the size and cost of the books within bounds, so there remains a one-year cycle covering half the scriptures, Old Testament and New being read alternately. At morning and evening prayer a longer reading may replace the brief extract given, particularly in public celebration.

Cardinal Quiñones' reformed breviary (1535), eventually rejected by Rome, influenced Cranmer, whose office lectionary has OT lessons morning and evening, with readings from the gospels and Acts in the morning and from the other NT books in the evening. Unlike the Roman system which began at Septuagesima, Cranmer's lectionary followed the civil year, covering the OT once and the NT three times annually. Cranmer's lectionary has been greatly revised since.

The Church of England's Alternative Service Book (1980) provides Old Testament readings as the first reading for morning and evening prayer based on a two-year cycle. The second reading is from the New Testament so that the gospel is read at morning prayer, with a non-gospel New Testament second reading at evening prayer, or vice versa.

See also **Lectionary**.

Breviarium Romanum; W. K. Lowther Clarke, 'The Lectionary', *Liturgy and Worship*, 1932, pp.296–301; R. C. D. Jasper (ed), *The Daily Office*, 1969; J. A. Jungmann, *The Mass of the Roman Rite*, new rev ed 1959; *Missale Romanum*; *Ordo Lectionum Missae*, ²1981 (ET: *Roman Lectionary*); F. Proctor and W. H. Frere, *The Book of Common Prayer*, rev ed 1901; M. Righetti, *Storia Liturgica*, IV, ²1956; S. P. Salmon, *The Breviary through the Centuries*, 1962.

BRIAN NEWNS

Liberal Catholic Church Worship

The Liberal Catholic Church originated in a mission of the Old Catholic Church of Holland to England in 1908, led by Bishop Arnold Harris Mathew, a former Roman Catholic priest. He carried with him the apostolic succession which it is generally agreed that the Dutch Old Catholic Church had inherited from the eighteenth-century Bishop Dominique Marie Varlet, a missionary bishop of the Roman Church.

In England Bishop Mathew found that his mission did not prosper, but in 1913 it was joined by a young man named James Ingall Wedgwood who had been studying for Anglican orders in York. Wedgwood had, after attending a lecture by Mrs Annie Besant, become deeply interested in theosophical ideas. After it became clear that those ideas were not acceptable in a postulant for Anglican orders, he joined Mathew's movement which then numbered about half a dozen adherents, and which seemed to give him a freedom of interpretation which he could not find in other churches. In 1913 he was ordained priest by Bishop Mathew and subsequently became bishop and, partly by his powerful personality and partly by his interpretation of doctrines, soon transformed the mission, which began to grow and flourish. Regular services were held in an oratory in London, and Bishop Wedgwood toured the country lecturing. He also embarked on missionary visits all over the world.

The Liberal Catholic Church was soon established in every continent and was particularly strong in Australia and Holland. It now has 41 bishops in various countries, who together compose the General Episcopal Synod, with a Presiding Bishop as its head. The General Episcopal Synod is the governing body of the church and meets about every five years to discuss changes in worship and teaching. There are now 13 Provinces of the church, each governed by a Regionary Bishop. Membership of the church is estimated to be between 10,000 and 12,000.

The Liberal Catholic Church may be distinguished from older churches in two particular ways. First of all it has retained the full Tridentine mass, with its stately ritual undiminished but purified of all that was unworthy of Christian worship and incompatible with the teaching of Christ. In the course of a lengthy visit to Sydney, Australia, Bishop Wedgwood consecrated as bishop Charles Webster Leadbeater, a former Anglican priest and an influential theosophical teacher who, in 1920, published *The Science of the Sacraments*, a book which set out in a vivid and compelling way what he saw as the objective reality of worship. Together, in 1917 and 1918, Wedgwood and he composed a completely new Liberal Catholic liturgy. To this, Bishop Wedgwood brought his particular gift of liturgical English, while simplifying some of the more involved practices of the Tridentine liturgy. The two bishops were also anxious to make the tone of the new liturgy more joyful than its predecessors, and rid it of expressions of fear and abasement which impaired the old

rite. It was first published in 1919 and revised in editions of 1924, 1942, 1957 and 1983.

In using the pattern of the Tridentine mass the Liberal Catholic Church applied to it the teaching of Bishop Wedgwood, who insisted on the fullest participation of clergy and congregation in the understanding of the real and inner meaning of every word and every action. The Liberal Catholic Church accepts that the rite has a language of its own which cannot be expressed fully in words alone and that, in performing it, the worshippers are able to draw upon a life and power which are of inestimable value. The church accepts the inner reality of what is created by the words and actions of the mass. It also accepts, as a fact, the doctrine of transubstantiation as the centre of its worship. The reality of an angelic hierarchy is important to most Liberal Catholics as an adjunct to their worship.

The second way in which The Liberal Catholic Church differs from older churches is in its belief that man is not merely in the image of God but is of the same essence as God, and that the universe and mankind have come from and are maintained by an overflowing of the love of God. It is therefore easier for a Liberal Catholic to accept that God is present in the consecrated host, since he is indeed present in all things and all beings, but clearly his presence is more particular and more immediate where the words of institution have been pronounced.

For most Liberal Catholics there can be no eternal damnation and no inherited original sin such as the older churches preach. Sin there obviously is, since man is in an imperfect state, immersed in matter. But the world is an incarnation of God, and the incarnation in Palestine was an image of the eternal incarnation and one of the overflowing of divine love which will lead all mankind back to God. The cycle of involution and evolution which leads eventually to divinity demands a period far longer than a single life span. Many Liberal Catholics therefore have accepted the idea of reincarnation in some form or other as a means of gathering experience and transforming the soul into a perfect man.

All this is not by any means unique. It has been taught by many of the great fathers of the church, Origen, Pseudo-Dionysius the Areopagite, Meister Eckhart, as well as isolated thinkers such as John Scotus Erigena. But it does not find any scope in the teaching of St Thomas Aquinas which is the basis of all Roman Catholic doctrine and, to some extent, of Anglican doctrine too.

Liberal Catholics recite the Nicene Creed, but they claim the necessary right to interpret it in the light of all the great philosophical teaching which has been given over the centuries, particularly in the first millenium after the death of Jesus. Such teaching is a part of the Catholic Church, but Liberal Catholics insist on absolute individual freedom in the interpretation of doctrine. Their priests are unsalaried but they are under an obligation to follow the authorized form of the liturgy.

I. S. Cooper, *Ceremonies of the Liberal Catholic Rite*, [2]1964; C. W. Leadbeater, *The Science of the Sacraments*, [2]1929; *The Liturgy of the Liberal Catholic Church*, [5]1983; F. W. Pigott, *The Parting of the Ways*, 1927; E. S. Taylor, *The Liberal Catholic Church – What is It?*, [2]1978; J. I. Wedgwood, *The Presence of Christ in the Holy Communion*, 1928.

ERIC S. TAYLOR

Liberation and Worship

Since about 1970, when new ways of doing theology began to develop in different parts of the world, the theme of 'liberation' has occupied a predominant place in theological discussions. The meaning of the word is of course dependent on the particular contexts in which it is used: while Latin American theologians are committed to the liberation of the people from dependency and economic exploitation, Black Theology aims at liberation from racial oppression. It is, however, important to notice that the one meaning does not necessarily exclude the other. In all these forms of 'contextual' theology liberation is essentially a comprehensive concept that expresses the totality of God's saving action in history. It is understood to be an inclusive, all-embracing process that covers every dimension of human life.

It is true that, over against the dualism and idealism of more traditional forms of theology, liberation theology strongly emphasizes the political, social and economic aspects of the process of liberation.

Especially in Latin American theology the primacy of praxis – the praxis of liberation that *precedes* theological reflection – was mainly explained in terms of political struggle. But it should be recognized that in recent years the cultural and spiritual dimension of 'the praxis of liberation' has received far more attention. Undoubtedly this is due to the incisive as well as subtle contributions of the Asians in the ecumenical debate of third-world theologians in the last ten years. In the methodology of liberation theology not only the political commitment to the struggle of the oppressed, but also liturgy and worship are now seen as necessary preconditions for the doing of theology. This insight comes out very clearly in the important final statement of the Fifth International Conference of the Ecumenical Association of Third World Theologians (EATWOT), New Delhi, 1981, where the praxis that precedes theological reflection is not only understood as action, but also as contemplation: 'Action in service of the people is necessary for genuine theological reflection, but equally necessary is silent contemplation. To be committed to the people's struggle for social justice and to contemplate God within this involvement – both form the essential matrix of theology. Without this prayerful contemplation, God's face is only partially seen and God's word only partially heard within our participation in God's liberating and fulfilling action in history' (Virginia Fabella and Sergio Torres [eds], *Irruption of the Poor*, 1983, p.198). But in the missionary churches of the third world (and not only there!) Christian worship has been and still is an ambivalent phenomenon, to say the least. Whatever its liberative potential might be, it cannot be denied that it has contributed to deprive people of their culture and identity by imposing liturgical forms from the outside. So, if the liturgical life of the Christian congregations should really be liberative, the first priority is to restore the people's sense of dignity and identity by recognizing the legitimacy of *contextual* forms of worship whereby elements of the indigenous culture are incorporated in the liturgy. In countries of Asia and Africa traditional music, dances, symbols, festivities are more and more being used in order to create a new spirituality that really belongs to the people (*see* **Indigenization**).

It should, however, be remembered that in the context of the third world culture and religion are invariably intertwined. Sri Lankan theologian Tissa Balasuriya, for instance, argues: 'Symbolism and symbolic rites in other religions – ablutions, lights, simple white attire, flowers – are often more related to the sociocultural milieu than to religious beliefs as such and are easily adaptable to the Christian liturgy. Such an adaptation would be especially meaningful to Asians: it would unite their traditional social values with Christian values' (*Planetary Theology*, 1984, 247). Therefore, 'adaptation' or 'indigenization' in practice always means the integration of elements of other religious traditions in the liturgical life of the church. Asian and African theologians and church leaders are inclined to recognize and respect the fact that Christianity has no monopoly on liberative spirituality. Without denying the centrality of the Christ, the essential question for them is not whether expressions of spirituality are exclusively Christian, but whether they serve and celebrate the God of life or the idols of death.

As we have seen, the New Delhi statement considers 'prayerful contemplation' just as important as 'action in service of the people' in the life of the church. But how are these two related? We are misunderstanding the meaning of the text when we see them, as is usual, as distinct moments or alternative practices. Among liberation theologians of different continents there is a growing awareness that it is vitally important to overcome the dualisms of contemplation and action, prayer and struggle, faith and life, spirituality and material needs. In this respect Nicolas Berdyaev's famous dictum, that while the problem of my own bread is a material question, the problem of my neighbour's bread is a spiritual one, summarizes very well what is meant here. The former moderator of the World Council of Churches' Central Committee, M. M. Thomas, who often quoted the Russian philosopher, spoke about the need for a 'spirituality for combat' (the expression comes from David Jenkins) in his report for the Fifth Assembly in Nairobi, 1975: 'The rediscovery of the Bible and the Liturgy are basic here. In this context, the Orthodox concept and practice of *theosis*, and the centrality of the eucharist as the celebration of a humanity in community with transfigured nature, society, and cosmos, need

to be redefined and reaffirmed in relation to the spirituality of contemporary struggles for the defence of the *humanum* and the unity of mankind. Let us not forget that our struggle is not merely against others but also against ourselves, not against flesh and blood, but against the false spiritualities of the idolatry of race, nation, and class, and of the self-righteousness of ideals which reinforce collective structures of inhumanity and oppression' (M. M. Thomas, *Towards a Theology of Contemporary Ecumenism*, 1978).

M. M. Thomas seems to imply that the celebration of the eucharist as a messianic reality can help the Christian community and individual believers to discern and to fight the 'false spiritualities' of collective structures of injustice. Liturgical celebration, then, is the place *par excellence* where a creative tension develops between history and eschatology, particularity and unversality. The eucharist, as an anticipation of messianic life, is not an evasion from the conflicts of daily life, but the spiritual force that challenges the idolatry of historical pessimism and cynicism.

It should, however, be very clear that this can only be the case when the Christian community is *really* involved in the struggles of the oppressed. Celebrating the eucharist can only be a liberating event when it takes place among and with the victims and the little ones, for they are the bearers of the messianic hope of the kingdom. Consequently, 'spirituality *for* combat' is only possible as spirituality *in* combat and *of* combat. Spirituality is not merely a distinct moment within the struggle for liberation, but the experience itself of the encounter of Jesus Christ, the crucified and resurrected, in the midst of the hardships and trials, the hopes and joys of the common people.

These insights into the interrelatedness of spirituality and commitment, which developed almost simultaneously in various contexts, constitute no idle theory. The small basic Christian communities that are mushrooming not only in Latin America but also in many other countries in the world are, although certainly not exclusively, the places where mutual reinforcement of contemplation and action can be observed. Having learned from the experiences of the basic ecclesial communities in Brazil, Leonardo Boff refuses to distinguish the mystique of the experience of God from the process of liberation; in order to express the bond between mystic and political struggle he uses the term *contemplativus in liberatione*.

In the same line it must be stressed that the old saying *ora et labora* should not be interpreted in a dualistic way as if labour has nothing to do with spirituality. It is, for instance, important to realize that the bread that is offered in the eucharist is *real* bread, the product of collective human labour. Bread is fruit of the earth, wine is fruit of the vine; in this respect they are the gift of creation. But the wheat and vine have been worked by the people to become bread and wine, and in this respect they are the product of the way human labour is organized. In a world in which the means of production are in the hands of the happy few, the breaking and sharing of bread are the visible sign of what all the participants want to realize: a world in which hunger and poverty are eliminated. As long, however, as we live in a world in which the basic material needs of most of the people cannot be fulfilled, the breaking of bread – pre-eminently the symbol of life itself – is a sign of repentance and conversion. Therefore, the eucharistic celebration as an act of thanksgiving and offering 'is a constant challenge in the search for appropriate relationships in social economic and political life (Matt. 5.23f.; I Cor. 10.16f.; I Cor. 11.20–22; Gal. 3.28). All kinds of injustice, racism, separation and lack of freedom are radically challenged when we share in the body and blood of Christ' (Agreed statement on *Baptism, Eucharist and Ministry*, World Council of Churches 1982, 14). As a sign of communion (*koinonia*) and service (*diakonia*) the breaking of bread means a commitment for liberative action against the destructive powers of death and oppression.

In the same way it can be said that The Lord's Prayer's 'give us this day our daily bread' is a plea and a commitment to make life possible for *all*. In 'The Lord's Prayer from Guatemala' Julia Esquivel has expressed this in an impressive way:

> Let the bread of your word and the bread of education

come into our huts made of cane stalks and straw,
into our cardboard shacks, and let us carry them
in our knapsacks as we travel through life.

The bread of land titles for all campesinos,
the bread of a place to live
for all those in the slums of Guatemala City,
the bread of milk for all children under two years of age
who suffer malnutrition and hunger,
the bread of medical assistance
for those in the countryside,
the bread of land
for the thousands of landless campesinos
who live subjugated to the interests
and whims of the landowners
on large farms in the high plains,
on the coast . . . invaded by the transnational corporations and the generals.

This 'translation' of the Lord's Prayer in the context of Guatemala is very typical of the free, creative way in which the biblical and ecclesiastical traditions are being actualized in order to communicate and celebrate the liberating message of the gospel in specific situations of poverty and oppression. Especially the Old Testament – the story of Exodus, the words of the prophets, Psalms and Lamentations – is an inexhaustible source of inspiration for the worship and liturgy of the basic Christian communities.

Sometimes, however, the use of the Bible and ecclesial tradition is severely questioned. This is the case, for instance, with feminist liturgy in the USA, where the 'Woman Church' expresses herself in a way that challenges the traditional systems of the hierarchical-patriarchal culture of the church. The need is felt for a radically new spirituality that enables women to express their personal and collective experiences and to reinforce their solidarity towards each other (*see* **Feminist Liturgical Movement**).

In view of the confusing variety of liberating experiments that are going on everywhere on the field of liturgical renewal, it is impossible to make any general, conclusive remarks. But one cannot avoid the impression that in the final analysis it is not the liturgical text itself, however forceful its content might be, but the *context* in which it is used, that decides whether or not worship is a liberating event. If the following of Jesus leads to *real* participation in the struggles against oppression and destitution, then words, rites and symbols that seem to have lost their vitality long ago regain a new spiritual force that is an indispensable element in any liberation process.

H. Assmann, *Practical Theology of Liberation*, 1975; T. Balasuriya, *The Eucharist and Human Liberation*, 1979; J. G. Davies, *New Perspectives on Worship Today*, 1978; Theo Witvliet, *A Place in the Sun: An Introduction to Liberation Theology in the Third World*, 1985.

THEO WITVLIET

Lights

see **Candles, Lamps and Lights**

Litany

'A litany is a form of prayer in which fixed responses are made by the people to short biddings or petitions said or sung by deacon, priest, or cantors' (E. C. Ratcliff). Most litanies are precatory, although litanies of adoration or thanksgiving are not unknown; most precatory litanies are either in whole or in part intercessory.

Some early forms of the litany in Christian worship are reminiscent of pagan formularies: 'We need not, therefore, conclude with some scholars that the Christian litany is borrowed from pagan usage; but it is nevertheless reasonable to think it an adaptation to a new purpose of a form which was traditionally associated with prayer and devotion, and which in the directness and simplicity of its address was intrinsically appropriate to that purpose' (Ratcliff).

The first definite evidence of the use of litanies in Christian worship suggests that the litany originated at Antioch in the second half of the fourth century; by the end of the century a litanic form of intercession was in use at Jerusalem; from Syria the litany travelled to Constantinople, and thence (apparently) it spread rapidly throughout the East. Whether the im-

portation of the litany to the West was originally directly from Syria, or whether it was from Constantinople, is a question which cannot be definitively answered.

Constantinople certainly took to the litany more thoroughly and more enthusiastically than any other of the great liturgical centres, and to this day it is prominent and frequent in the services of the Byzantine rite. (The litanies of the Byzantine rite are called by various names: *ektené* and *synapté* are the most common, and strictly refer to different kinds of litany – they still do in Greek usage, but Slav usage confuses them, or rather their translations. Some particular forms of these litanies have alternative names proper to themselves, and there are others which are known only by their own proper names, e.g. the *lité*, for which see below. It is better when writing in English to use 'litany' as a general term for all of them, to avoid needless complication.) The *lesser litany*, a short form of general content, is the normal introduction to any formal prayer by the celebrant, corresponding in function to the mutual greeting and bidding to prayer in the Western rites; the *greater litany*, a more extended form, containing a number of intercessory biddings, occurs with variations in a number of services, commonly near the beginning, in what was originally a 'preparatory' or sometimes a 'processional' context. These litanies are mainly composed of biddings; other litanies of the same type are the *morning litany* at matins and the *evening litany* at vespers, and the litanies preceding the prayer over the offerings and the Lord's Prayer at the eucharistic liturgy. The *litany of fervent prayer*, so called because the response to each petition (and in this case most are direct petitions, not biddings) is tripled, is the main intercessory litany of the Byzantine rite, coming at the end of the liturgy of the word before the eucharist, and as the intercession at matins and vespers (*see* **Canonical Hours**). Other litanies are those for the catechumens after the liturgy of the word, the proper litanies of the baptismal and marriage liturgies, the greater and lesser litanies for the departed, and the processional festal litany (*lité*) at vespers, which in addition to intercessions includes a lengthy commemoration of the saints.

The earliest surviving text of a Western litany is that of the *Deprecatio Gelasii*, a Roman litany of the late fifth century, which bears a close relationship both in form and in content to the Byzantine litanies, and was almost certainly inserted between the entrance chant and the collect of the day in the Roman mass by Pope Gelasius (492–6), whose name it bears, replacing the older intercessory biddings and prayers after the readings and sermon. Related texts are found in non-Roman Western rites; one of them continued to be used at Milan on Sundays in Lent, at the same point in the mass.

At Rome this litany was already beginning to fall into disuse in the late sixth century (*see* ***Kyrie***), and later litanies in the Roman rite and its variants differ considerably from it both in form and in use. The latter difference is marked by the change of name: Gelasius' litany was called a *deprecatio*, that is, an intercession without further qualification; *litania*, from which 'litany' is derived, and which is the name used for its successor, signifies either a penitential observance, or a procession, or, ultimately, a penitential procession, and is clearly connected with a particular use of this type of litany on the three days preceding Ascension Day, known as the rogations, from which use the combination of penitence and intercession found in the later Roman litany originates.

This rogation litany, commonly called, from one of its parts, the litany of the saints, may be divided into six sections: 1. the introductory *kyrie* and invocations of the Persons of the Trinity; 2. the invocations of the saints; 3. the deprecations, or supplications for deliverance; 4. the obsecrations or appeals for deliverance by virtue of events in Christ's redemptive life; 5. the intercessions; 6. a concluding invocation of Christ as the Lamb of God; a number of other prayers, of Gallican origin, with the Lord's Prayer and a concluding collect or collects, the set differing somewhat from time to time and place to place, are added to these six sections of the litany proper (this litany has been simplified and abbreviated in recent years, and the Gallican additions removed, but its structure otherwise remains basically the same). Different though this form of the litany is from the type to which the Byzantine litanies and

the *Deprecatio Gelasii* belong, it appears nevertheless to have originated, as they did, in Antiochene Syria, and to have been imported to the West in the seventh century, probably during the pontificate of Sergius I (687–701), who was himself of Antiochene descent (*see* ***Agnus Dei***).

In mediaeval England the litany was sung on the rogation days*, and also daily in Lent and in many places in procession every Sunday before the parish mass. It is hardly a coincidence that Cranmer provided in the BCP what is probably the best-known, and certainly the finest, litany to be found in any of the liturgies of the Reformation, the structure of it based on that of the Roman litany, but the contents showing the influence of Luther's litany of 1529, as well as of the Byzantine greater litany, while from 1549 onward all invocations of the saints were omitted. Cranmer's one departure from the Roman structure is in his treatment of the deprecations and obsecrations, where he combines several of the original petitions in each one of his.

A good many litanies have been produced in the course of recent liturgical revision. Lack of space precludes us from considering them all: a few examples must suffice. A litany based on Byzantine models which first appeared in the Scots BCP of 1929 re-appeared as an alternative form of the synaxis* intercession in the Scots Liturgy of 1970, in a revised form in that of 1977 (although not in that of 1982, in which, however, two other litanic forms were among the three provided), and in the Church of England's Alternative Services Series 2 communion service of 1967. The Church of England's ASB includes a revised form of the BCP litany, and a proper litany, adapted from it, for ordinations; the second alternative form of intercession in its Rite A communion service is also a litany, apparently influenced both by that of the BCP and by the Scots litany mentioned above. The revised American BCP provides a number of litanies: 'The Great Litany', a revision of that of the BCP; proper litanies for the alternative rite for evening prayer (Byzantine-based), for ordinations, for the commendation of the dying, for the burial of the dead, and at the dedication of a church already in use; and in Rite II for the holy eucharist three of the six forms of intercession are litanies, two of them following a Byzantine-inspired structure. The quality of these American litanies is high. The most notable use of the litanic form in the revised services of the Roman rite is in the *preces* which have replaced the former suffrages* at morning prayer or lauds and evening prayer or vespers; there are also others, notably in the rite for the Christian Initiation of Adults, as well as the revised general litany referred to above. The liturgy of the Communauté de Taizé makes extensive use of litanies: four of the five forms of intercession at the eucharist are litanies (of a Byzantine/Gelasian type), while proper litanies, varying with the day or season, are provided at the morning and evening offices: these show great imagination and sensitivity in both form and content. The Taizé litanies, indeed, are perhaps the best of the many modern forms, both as liturgy and as literature.

Of all forms of public prayer, the litany is perhaps the most flexible and the most conducive, when used competently, to effective congregational participation in the liturgy.

P. de Clerck, *La 'Prière Universelle' dans les liturgies anciennes*, 1977; W. Jardine Grisbrooke, 'Intercession at the Eucharist', *Studia Liturgica*, IV, 3, 1965, pp.129–55; C. Jones, G. Wainwright and E. Yarnold (eds), *The Study of Liturgy*, 1978, using the index under 'litanies'; E. C. Ratcliff, 'The Choir Offices: The Litany', W. K. Lowther Clarke (ed), *Liturgy and Worship*, 1932, pp.282–7. For the *Deprecatio Gelasii*: J. A. Jungmann, *The Mass of the Roman Rite*, 1955, I, pp.333–46; G. G. Willis, *Essays in Early Roman Liturgy*, 1964, pp.1–4. For the litanies in the Byzantine eucharistic liturgy: C. Kucharek, *The Byzantine-Slav Liturgy of St John Chrysostom*, 1971, pp.342–64, 446–57; J. Mateos, *La Célébration de la Parole dans la Liturgie Byzantine*, 1971, pp.28–33, 148–73; R. F. Taft, *The Great Entrance*, 1975, pp.311–73.

W. JARDINE GRISBROOKE

Liturgical Movement, The

This present century has seen an extraordinary recovery and renewal by the Christian church of its worship and the understanding of that worship as central to its life and work. The name usually given to the means

by which this recovery and renewal has been brought about is the Liturgical Movement. Its origins are to be found in the Roman Catholic Church in France during the nineteenth century. In the year 1832, Dom Prosper Guéranger refounded the Benedictine Abbey of Solesmes as a monastery dedicated especially to the study and recovery of the authentic Gregorian Chant* and the church's liturgical heritage generally. Solesmes became a centre of liturgical worship and life, and its publication *L'Année Liturgique*, the first issue of which appeared in 1841, had a wide influence. The works of Guéranger and the Solesmes monks awakened a new interest in the liturgy. It was a springboard for a revival by the Benedictines of their traditional concern for the liturgy which eventually placed the monks among the pioneers of the Liturgical Movement, and it spurred an investigation into the origins and history of the liturgy in which such scholars as Cabrol and Batiffol provided the foundation for present-day liturgiological study. Guéranger's work has been adversely criticized as being too narrowly mediaeval, too limited in pastoral concern, and too archaeological. While this criticism may be right from our present point of view, Guéranger's work must be seen in the setting of the church of his day in order to be evaluated justly. Guéranger and the monks of Solesmes were not alone in their mediaevalism. Their contemporaries were discovering the Middle Ages, and to many these times were the ideal ages, in which had been all that was right and good. This was the time of the Gothic revival, of romanticism in art and literature. To men of the church, the Middle Ages appeared to be the epitome of Christian life, to be indeed the Christian Ages. In them was to be found an ideal of worship and church life which must be recovered in order to release the church of their own time from its lassitude and sterility. Guéranger was able to recall men in the church of his time to an interest and concern for the liturgy as something to be prayed and lived, and it is interesting to note that most of the major points which the Liturgical Movement has made in recent times were in some way anticipated by Guéranger. He must justly be called the precursor of the Liturgical Movement.

However, the Liturgical Movement itself began to get under way in the opening years of the present century. In 1903, Pope Pius X issued a *Motu Proprio* on church music. He saw in the active participation of the faithful in the liturgy the source of the renewal of the Christian spirit, and called for more active participation in the worship of the church. A few years later the same pope called for a more frequent reception of holy communion. In 1909, a Catholic conference was held in Malines in Belgium; it is this conference which was probably the real inauguration of the Liturgical Movement. The conference saw the liturgy as the fundamental means of the instruction of the people in the Christian faith and life. An active participation by the people in the liturgy was the best means of nourishing and deepening the spiritual life. The conference called for a translation of the Roman missal into the vernacular* so that it could more readily serve as the main manual of devotion for the church. It called for a centring of the Christian life in the liturgy of the church, the restoration of Gregorian Chant as a means of helping participation, and it asked for retreats for church people to be held in centres of liturgical worship and life. The outstanding leader in the conference was Dom Lambert Beauduin, of Mont César in Louvain. His book, *La Piété de l'Église*, published in 1914, contained ideas which became fundamental principles in the Liturgical Movement, and is still necessary reading if the purpose of the movement is to be understood. Beauduin saw that a better understanding of the incarnation and its meaning would lead to a deeper understanding and appreciation of the dignity of human life and all life. He pointed out that an understanding of the nature of the church as the body of Christ would enable the development of a deeper sense of community in both worship and life, and he emphasized that an understanding of the sacrifice of Christ would result in the living out of the eucharistic sacrifice by the people of God and the offering of their lives along with the offering of Christ. Worship, Beauduin stressed, was the common action of the people of the church, an action which involved them all in a sharing in the saving work of Christ in and for the world. The orientation of the Liturgical Movement during these early years was deeply pastoral. While it is not anti-traditionalist and

aimed at renewal rather than revolution, it was concerned with the present situation in the church and how that situation might be changed to bring about a better future. It thus sought to reach the ordinary church people rather than the theologian and the intellectual. It sought to recall the members of the church to an active involvement in the liturgy of the church. That liturgy was not to be a resuscitation of the past, nor something to be merely seen and heard, but a living worship in which the whole church should take part actively and with understanding, and the wellspring of a renewal of Christian life and mission. In these years the principal organ of the movement was *Les Questions Liturgiques*, later entitled *Les Questions Liturgiques et Paroissiales*, and then returning to its original designation. It was particularly the eucharist which the leaders of the movement saw as the central act of Christian worship, and it was an active participation in this on the part of the 'people in the pews' which the first stage of the Liturgical Movement sought in every way to encourage. The movement sometimes ran counter to the established ideas and practices of the church of the time; hence it aroused considerable opposition. Despite this, the movement began to spread and to become more and more an influence in the thinking and acting of the Roman Catholic Church, especially at the parish level.

In the years between the two world wars, the focus of leadership in the movement shifted from Belgium to Germany, and the second phase in its development got under way. The ideas of worship which the Liturgical Movement actively propagated had come under criticism as being too radical, too much a departure from the tradition of the church. Some felt that the movement was too modernist, and lacked a sound basis in the theology of the Roman Catholic Church, indeed was contrary to it. There was some justification for the criticisms, given the official patterns of worship and the Ultramontane theology in the early decades of this century; further, the earlier phase of the movement had been more concerned with the immediate pastoral needs of the church than with the production of an apologetic for its position. In the second phase of the development of the Liturgical Movement the emphasis was reversed. The work of building a sound theology of worship was spearheaded by the Rhineland Abbey of Maria Laach. The Abbot Ildefons Herwegen and Dom Odo Casel pioneered in this work, and the publication *Ecclesia Orans*, begun in 1918, enjoyed wide circulation and was an important means of dissemination of the new theology. Soon other theologians and church historians were turning their attention to the study of the liturgy. The result has been the production over the past half-century of a huge literature on Christian worship which has not only provided a deep knowledge and understanding of the origins and development of the liturgy, but has also opened up liturgical theology as an important field of theological studies. The list of contributors to this development is too long to give in full; we mention Josef Jungmann, Jean Daniélou, and Louis Bouyer as outstanding. Neither the historical nor the theological investigation shows signs of flagging at the present time; rather, both will doubtless increase in scope as the liturgy is seen in relationship to modern social sciences, psychology, and the like. While Maria Laach spoke primarily to the expert, the Canons of Klosterneuberg, and especially Pius Parsch, gave the same ideas a more popular expression. Klosterneuberg also turned to a study of the biblical basis of the liturgy, and inaugurated a biblical movement which has spread widely in the Roman Catholic Church, made important contributions to biblical theology and hermeneutics, and has served as a link between Roman Catholics and the Ecumenical Movement. In the period immediately before the Second World War and during the early war years the Liturgical Movement was spreading widely outside Europe. By the late 1920s, St John's Abbey in Collegeville, Minnesota, was becoming, under the leadership of Dom Virgil Michel, a major centre of the movement in the USA. The Abbey's periodical *Orate Fratres* (later named *Worship*) was addressed especially to the parish clergy and the laity, and became one of the most important means of spreading the movement in America. The Abbey also published a large selection of tracts and service leaflets which have found their way into churches and homes throughout the USA. Liturgical conferences began to be

held and were well attended by clergy and laity. A Liturgical Arts Society was organized to find ways of improving the standards and craftsmanship of church art and architecture and for encouraging contemporary expression in liturgical art. Its journal *Liturgical Arts Quarterly* has become one of the finest reviews of the building and decorative arts. By 1940 a series of annual Liturgical Weeks was begun, and these have trained many for the liturgical apostolate and have taken on ecumenical significance. The Liturgical Movement in the USA has always tended to be less strongly intellectual in its appeal than it was in Europe. It took the form of a more grass-roots movement in the Roman Catholic Church. Liturgical theology was by no means neglected, but in the USA especially the Liturgical Movement and the rediscovery of the role of the laity (*see* **Laity and Worship**) were strongly interlinked.

By the end of the Second World War, the movement had spread widely in the Low Countries, Germany and France. The Centre de Pastorale Liturgique had been founded in Paris in 1940, and its principal publication *La Maison-Dieu* combined the emphases of Maria Laach and Klosterneuberg and went beyond them. In North America generally the movement was affecting deeply the patterns of worship, and bringing about many changes in them. The church in Asia and Africa in the postwar years was faced with the challenge of nascent nationalisms and the resurgent indigenous religions. The Liturgical Movement was beginning to assist the church in searching for expressions of worship and art drawn from the local cultures, and it was in these lands that the missionary implications of a liturgical renewal were being explored. The movement was less widespread in Southern Europe and in the British Isles, and its influence had hardly begun to be felt in large parts of South America and in some parts of South East Asia. But the Litùrgical Movement had become a force to be reckoned with in the Roman Catholic Church. It could not be overlooked or disregarded as something passing and unimportant. It was producing a growing revival of worship, and was a major source of the growing ferment within the Roman Catholic Church which resulted eventually in the summoning of Vatican II. The official framework of the liturgy was proving too restrictive and out-dated to meet the needs of the church in the postwar secular society. Demands for reforms in the liturgy were being made from all parts in the Roman Catholic Church and were constantly becoming more insistent. The attempt to carry out in practice the principles which the Liturgical Movement had widely disseminated led to experimentation and to a search for new expressions of worship which would have more meaning for people in the present day. These often began to outrun the official liturgical rules of the church. Some members of the hierarchy, as in the Low Countries, sought to give leadership and encouraged the experimentation; others adopted a negative and restrictive posture and attempted to restrain or forbid it. The situation in respect to the liturgy was tending to become chaotic, and considerable controversy was being aroused by well-meant, but misguided, efforts at liturgical reform.

Concrete evidence that Rome was now at last prepared to give official recognition to the liturgical renewal and to implement at least some of its demands, while placing a guiding and restraining hand on the more radical tendencies, came in the promulgation by Pius XII in the year 1947 of the encyclical *Mediator Dei et Hominum*. This document has been regarded by some as the charter of the Liturgical Movement, and as endorsement of it. The pope praised the liturgy and emphasized that its celebration should be the work of the whole church. He expressed the desire that the faithful should be able to participate fully in the liturgy with understanding, and that they should take an active part in the services. He recalled the church to the need to live the liturgical life which was renewed and strengthened by the liturgy. This encyclical was the first papal encyclical to be devoted wholly to a discussion of the church's liturgy. Positive steps were taken to implement the encyclical in 1951 by the restoration of the Paschal vigil*, and four years later by the decree *Maxima Redemptionis* followed by the *Instructio* reforming and restoring the whole Holy Week* celebration. The intention was a recovery of an important part of the tradition which had been lost. As the Paschal mystery was the centre of the

liturgical life of the church, so the annual celebration of that mystery should be the centre of the liturgical year. At the same time, the restoration was intensely pastoral in outlook. The restoration of the major rites to evening hours made possible an attendance on the part of working people, and the provision of an up-dated and reformed liturgy for the rites made a more active participation in them possible. Other reforms followed. The pope sought to meet the need of people living in the industrial-urban complex by relaxing the rigour of the eucharistic fast and by permitting evening celebrations of mass. The rubrics* governing the conduct of the services were simplified, and a new codification of them undertaken. Pius XII issued another encyclical, *De musica sacra*, in 1955, which laid down guidelines and rules for increased participation of the faithful in the rites of the church. Further indications of reforms to come were given in the pope's address to a congress meeting in Assisi in 1956. Some of the reforms which were undertaken during the pontificate of Pius XII were completed and promulgated by his successor John XXIII, including the new rubrics and the revision of a part of the Roman Pontifical.

But it was in Vatican II that the work of the Liturgical Movement bore fruit, and the extent to which it had aroused the church became fully apparent. There was no doubt from the beginning of the Council that the assembled council fathers had every intention of making the liturgy more responsive to the needs of the contemporary church. A schema had been prepared after some discussion by a representative group, and this was submitted to the Council. Between 22 October and 13 November 1962, the Council devoted fifteen sessions to debate on the proposed constitution, and its text was approved in principle. But the discussion continued and many amendments and additions were proposed. Finally the Constitution *De sacra liturgia* was passed by an overwhelming majority in 1963. It was promulgated by Paul VI on 4 December 1963, the first Constitution to be published by Vatican II. The Constitution on the Sacred Liturgy contains what is probably one of the best and clearest statements of the theology of the liturgy, its meaning and its function in the life of the church which has as yet been made, a statement which is in its approach thoroughly biblical, patristic and eirenical. At the same time it is a statement which exhibits an intense pastoral awareness of and concern for the needs of the church and its mission in the present-day world. The Constitution unleashes the liturgy, so to speak, and allows it to become the living service of the Christian community in a way which has not been possible since the beginning of the Middle Ages. Of special significance for the Roman Catholic Church was the opening of the gate for the use of the vernacular* tongues in the rites of the church. The Constitution might also be said to be the best and most concise statement of the principles and objectives of the Liturgical Movement. Entirely ecumenical in its scope and significance, the Constitution on the Liturgy must be given thorough study by anyone who wishes to understand the liturgy and the importance of the liturgical renewal of the whole Christian Church. Immediate steps were taken to implement the Constitution. Large parts of the Roman rite, and especially that for the celebration of the eucharist, were issued in the vernaculars of the different peoples of the church, and were received with enthusiasm. The rites themselves have been thoroughly revised and updated and the whole series of new *ordines* were issued, the principal ones being: 1968, Holy Order; Rite of Funerals: 1969, Infant Baptism; Lectionary; Marriage: 1970, Missal: 1971, Confirmation: 1972, Christian Initiation of Adults; Lesser Ministries; Pastoral Care and Anointing of the Sick: 1973, Penance: 1977, Order for the Dedication of a Church and Altar. All these, with the exception of the last, are to be found translated into English in *The Rites of the Catholic Church*, 1976. The result of this is that the worship of the Roman Catholic Church is changing and developing in a truly thrilling manner. It is too soon to judge objectively the full impact of Vatican II upon the liturgical life of the Roman Catholic Church. At the present time that life is being revolutionized. The reforms in the liturgy made as a result of Vatican II have been so sweeping and so many that it will take a number of years for them to be assimilated and their significance realized. The work of the Liturgical Movement by no means ended with the publication of the Constitution on the

Liturgy and the *ordines*; rather, Vatican II opened the door to new opportunities. The movement in the Roman Communion today is part of the vanguard of the ferment in that church which has not been allayed; if anything, it is increasing. We may predict that in the immediate future the activities of the Liturgical Movement will be chiefly along two lines: 1. leadership and encouragement in still more spontaneity and freedom in worship and in finding new and contemporary ways of expressing that worship; 2. leadership in the re-thinking and renewal of mission and Christian action as necessary parts of liturgical renewal, as part of the service which the church offers to God.

But the Liturgical Movement has not been confined to the Roman Communion. Although it first got under way in that church, it has spread particularly during the past thirty years or so to almost every part of the church, and has made an impact upon the worship of most of the Christian communions. At the present time the Liturgical Movement may fairly be said to be part of the Ecumenical Movement, and it is proving more and more instrumental in drawing together the different Christian traditions of worship. In Anglicanism, the preliminary work carried out by Guéranger was in many ways parallel by the activities of the ritualist wing of the Tractarian Movement. There was much common ground between the French Catholics of the persuasion of Guéranger and the tractarian Anglicans. Both emphasized the centrality of the eucharistic worship in the life of the church, and both were inspired by that worship to self-sacrificing service to the people of God. The Anglicans, like Guéranger and his associates, were unable to get behind the mediaeval church and accepted it as their ideal. But they did succeed in provoking interest in the liturgy and discussion of it, even if some of it was of a controversial nature. There was evidence on all sides of a growing dissatisfaction with the limitations of the normative Anglican patterns of worship and with the restrictions and limitations of the 1662 BCP. This dissatisfaction was not limited to England. Anglican liturgical scholars of the stature of W. H. Frere, Bishop Parsons, and Howard Baldwin St George both prepared the way for the spate of BCP revision which swept the Anglican Communion in the late 1920s and made permanent contributions to the rediscovery of the liturgical tradition. But these revisions proved to be a kind of watershed. It was after them that the Liturgical Movement began to influence Anglicanism more and more widely. If there is any one thing to which we might point as the real beginning of the Liturgical Movement in the Anglican Communion, it is to the publication in 1935 of the book *Liturgy and Society* by Father Gabriel Hebert of the Kelham Fathers. A movement to restore the parish eucharist as the common central act of parish worship got under way, and its effects are to be seen in the ever-increasing number of Anglican parishes where this has taken place. In the USA, the Associated Parishes came into being in 1946 to further the movement's objectives and to implement them in parish worship. A few years later in England the Parish and People movement began its work with the same objectives. The Anglican Liturgical Movement has also produced a large literature, which has influenced the thinking of leaders in the movement in the Roman Communion, just as the works of Roman Catholic scholars greatly influenced Anglican thinking. We can mention here but a few of the most outstanding Anglican contributors to liturgical knowledge: Dom Gregory Dix, E. C. Ratcliff, Massey E. Shepherd, H. B. Porter and J. G. Davies. There was a ferment in Anglicanism which in many ways was very like that in the Roman Communion, which aroused the churches of the Anglican Communion to the realization that the BCP was not the final expression of liturgical worship and needed to be revised and changed, and which was deeply concerned with renewal of worship in the ordinary parishes as part of the much-needed renewal of Christian life and mission.

The extent to which the Liturgical Movement has become grounded in Anglicanism can be gauged from the number of revisions of the BCP completed in many parts of the world, e.g. Australia 1978, USA 1979, England 1980 (*see* **Revisions, Liturgical**). These new books, intended to embody the accepted insights of the Liturgical Movement, were the end product of intensive study. So, for example, before issuing the final versions, the Standing

Liturgical Commission of the Protestant Episcopal Church in the USA published some two dozen prayer book studies and the Liturgical Commission of the Church of England produced Alternative Services in three series. The resulting services have not commended themselves to all; opposition has been vigorously expressed, but then liturgical tradition is always conservative. For many, however, these new patterns, whatever their weaknesses (less than admirable style, etc.), are providing an opportunity for liturgical renewal. Indeed, within Anglicanism, as a consequence of this exercise, evangelicals and catholics are converging, although they have not yet reached full conjunction; there is, too, a greater emphasis upon the practice and understanding of worship rather than upon further discussions of its forms.

Among Christians of the Reformed and other traditions also the Liturgical Movement has come of age. The Reformed churches have also had their liturgical pioneers. In the latter part of the past century Eugène Bersier of Paris emphasized the centrality of the worship of the church in Christian life and the need for the Reformed churches to recover liturgical worship. In the liturgy which he produced may be seen the understanding of the worship of the church as a fully corporate action, and a balance between the word and sacraments which was uncharacteristic of Protestant worship in his time. In Scotland, we may point to the work of the Church Service Society and its *Euchologion*, which was certainly one of the major influences behind the present liturgical renewal in the Scottish church and that church's excellent liturgies, which in so many respects incorporate the insights of the Liturgical Movement. But probably the extent to which the Liturgical Movement has gained ground in the Protestant traditions may be seen in the liturgy of the Church of South India, in which a number of these traditions, including the Anglican, have been brought together and submitted to the normative tradition of the scriptures and the early church which underlies them all. Yet the liturgy of the Church of South India is not an essay in liturgical archaeology; it is a restatement of the essential Christian tradition of worship in a liturgy which is immediately relevant to the life of Christians in South India. The work of the Church of South India has influenced practically all liturgical revision in the Protestant churches, and it is recognized also as an influence upon Vatican II. Or again, we may point to the thrilling work of the Taizé Community, with its emphasis upon the living of a common liturgical life of worship and mission, its deep ecumenical understanding and outreach, and the contributions of such writers as Max Thurian. The Taizé liturgy is undoubtedly among the very finest expressions of the principles of the Liturgical Movement. Yet it is fully ecumenical, and is an excellent illustration of a liturgy which can at one and the same time stand squarely in both the Reformed and Catholic traditions. The same awakening and ferment as that within Roman Catholicism and Anglicanism is today evident in Protestantism, and is bringing all parts of the church to a new willingness to submit to self and mutual criticism and to learn from each other. For the churches of the Protestant tradition as well as those of the Catholic, this is meaning a deep renewal of worship and rediscovery of the liturgy. Of special significance for the future is the growing tendency to search for liturgical expressions which will transcend and draw together the different Christian traditions. In this connection we may mention the new ecumenical texts for the creeds, Lord's Prayer, and other common parts of the liturgy, which will undoubtedly serve to make our worship more truly common, the proposals of the Conference on Christian Union in the USA, the work of the Joint Liturgical Group in Great Britain, the establishment of such societies as the Societas Liturgica, and centres for the study of the liturgy on an ecumenical basis. The church as a whole is finding in the Liturgical Movement a new frontier on which, in the words of H. G. Hageman (*Studia Liturgica*, II, 4), 'all the churches, regardless of the rigidity of their liturgical traditions, now find themselves. In the common exploration of what is for all of us, in one way or another, new material, we are bound to reach easier ecumenical conversation. I do not know where these new agreements may take us; I would be suspicious of any attempt to overplay their importance. But the fact remains that

the liturgy is the most fruitful area for ecumenical exploration. If that face is recognized, and, in the best sense of the word, exploited, we shall know what the next step may be.'

The continuing Liturgical Movement is part of the reawakening of the church. It seeks a recovery of those norms of liturgical worship of the Bible and the early church which lie behind Reformation divisions and mediaeval distortions, and which are fundamental to Christian liturgy in every time and place. It aims, however, not at an attempt to resuscitate the liturgy of the early church in the twentieth century, but at the restatement of the fundamentals in forms and expressions which can enable the liturgy to be the living prayer and work of the church today.

J.-J. von Allmen, *Worship, its Theology and Practice*, 1965; W. Bardin, 'Phases of the Liturgical Movement', *Studies in Pastoral Liturgy*, II, 1961; L. Beauduin, *Liturgy the Life of the Church*, [2]1929; L. Bouyer, *Liturgical Piety*, 1950 (also published as *Liturgy and Life*, 1958); *Rite and Man*, 1963; O. Casel, *The Mystery of Christian Worship and Other Writings*, 1962; I. H. Dalmais, *Introduction to the Liturgy*, 1961; J. D. Crichton, *The Church's Worship*, 1964; *Changes in the Liturgy*, 1965; J. D. Crichton, H. Winstone, J. Ainslie (eds), *English Catholic Worship*, 1979; J. G. Davies, *Worship and Mission*, 1966; J. Jungmann, *Pastoral Liturgy*, 1962; E. B. Koenker, *The Liturgical Renaissance in the Roman Catholic Church*, 1954; A. G. Martimort (ed), *The Church at Prayer*, ET 1966; B. Morris (ed), *Ritual Murder*, 1980; J. A. T. Robinson, *Liturgy Coming to Life*, 1963; O. Rousseau, *The Progress of the Liturgy*, 1951; A Shands, *The Liturgical Movement and the Local Church*, 1965; M. H. Shepherd, *Liturgy and Education*, 1965; K. Stevenson (ed), *Liturgy Reshaped*, 1982; B. Wicker, *Culture and Liturgy*, 1963; H. Winstone (ed), *Pastoral Liturgy*, 1975. Periodicals and Series: *Ecumenical Studies in Worship*; *Studies in Pastoral Liturgy*; *Studia Liturgica*.

H. ELLSWORTH CHANDLEE

Liturgical Revision

see **Revisions, Liturgical**

Liturgies

In the singular the word 'liturgy' denotes an act of worship, more specifically the eucharist*. Derived from the Greek *leitourgia*, it was used in Hellenistic Greek of an act of public service. In the NT it is employed of an act of service or ministry (e.g. Phil. 2.30). In time it was confined in Christian usage to the idea of service to God and finally, since worship was regarded as the supreme service to God, it was applied to the eucharist. Consequently to study liturgies is to examine the forms which the eucharistic rite has taken throughout the centuries.

1. *Patristic*. The NT does not provide a detailed description of the worship of the early church. Because worship was a regular element in the lives of the first Christians, a great deal was taken for granted. Our knowledge of this period is therefore restricted (*see* **New Testament Worship**). It is clear, however, that the eucharist was of great importance, in virtue of Jesus' institution at the Last Supper. His followers continued to partake of bread and wine 'in remembrance of him'. Whether the Last Supper was actually the passover meal or not, it was associated with passover ideas, and it must also be seen in connection with the other references to meals in the gospels – particularly the feeding of the five thousand, to which John attached eucharistic teaching. These NT passages would appear to have been influenced by current liturgical practice in the areas in which they were written; and books such as Hebrews and Revelation clearly indicate a knowledge of the eucharist. However, the tendency to read liturgy into every page of the NT must be treated with reserve.

The early Christian eucharist followed the pattern of the Last Supper. Bread was taken, blessed, broken and distributed before a meal; and wine was taken, blessed and distributed after it. For the Jew, thanksgiving and blessing were synonymous, and bread and wine were blessed when God was thanked over them for his mighty acts of creation and redemption. When Paul wrote his first letter to the Corinthians the eucharist and the meal were apparently still together; but at some early date, precisely when is unknown, the meal

disappeared and the rites over bread and wine were brought together and became a single entity.

Forms of thanksgiving used over bread and wine which date from the late first or early second century appear in the *Didache*. Scholars differ as to whether they all apply to the eucharist, but as forms of thanksgiving they may well indicate the kind of prayer which was used at the eucharist. The first writer to give a detailed account of the liturgy is Justin Martyr in his *Apology to the Emperor Antoninus Pius,* written in Rome *c.* AD 150; this is supplemented by further information in his *Dialogue* with the Jew Trypho. The eucharist was celebrated every Sunday. It began with a synagogue type of service – scripture reading, a sermon by the president, and intercessions concluded by the kiss of peace. Bread and a cup of wine and water were then brought to the president, who said a prayer of thanksgiving over them; the congregation said Amen*. After the administration, there was a collection for the needy and the deacons* took the sacrament to those who were absent. The prayer of thanksgiving was trinitarian in form and extempore: it referred to God's activities of creation and redemption, the bread and wine was described as a memorial of the passion, and there was an odd passage on 'the prayer of the word which is from him', which might apply to Jesus at the Last Supper or to the Logos. Like the *Didache*, Justin also referred to the eucharist as a sacrifice, quoting Malachi 1.11.

Some sixty years later Rome also provided the first eucharistic text to be discovered. The presbyter, Hippolytus, wrote the *Apostolic Tradition* as a guide to church life in the early third century; in describing the consecration of a bishop, he set out the text of the eucharistic prayer. It was neat and compact, and followed the lines described by Justin. The original Greek text has never been found, and we have to rely on an early fifth-century Latin version, together with Coptic, Arabic and Ethiopian translations: and many scholars argued that the text has suffered changes in the process of transmission. But basically it was a prayer of thanksgiving for creation and redemption, an offering of the bread and cup in memory of Christ's death and resurrection, and a prayer for the gift of the Spirit on the communicants – a primitive form of epiclesis (*see* **Anaphora** 8). Clearly this was not *the* Roman rite of the time, but simply a pattern which could be followed; later its influence was felt, not in Rome and the West, but in Egypt and Syria in the East, and not least in the Ethiopic liturgies.

Much of the liturgical material from the East during the second and third centuries is unreliable, for it derives from Gnostic sects. With strange beliefs about creation, the incarnation and the atonement, their prayers do not follow the lines of Justin and Hippolytus: but one interesting feature was a primitive form of invocation, which became an important element in eucharistic prayers of the East by the middle of the fourth century.

Two centres which were influential in the East were Egypt and Antioch. From Egypt in the fourth century comes the prayer book of Bishop Serapion of Thmuis (*c.* AD 350), a private and untidy collection containing all the main elements of the eucharistic rite. Noteworthy features in its eucharistic prayer were the absence of the phrase 'Do this in remembrance of me' and the presence of two invocations – one before and one after the institution narrative. The second more explicit invocation invoked the Logos and not the Spirit, and it was characteristically Eastern in that it prayed for the consecration of the elements. The prayer ended with intercessions, which probably came during the third or fourth century in both East and West. Serapion was the precursor of the Alexandrine Greek Liturgy of St Mark, from which in its turn came the Coptic Liturgy of St Mark or St Cyril.

From Antioch in the later fourth century came the so-called Clementine Liturgy in the eighth book of the *Apostolic Constitutions*. It agreed with the descriptions of the rite given in Chrysostom, and textually it owed much to Hippolytus. Its preface was very long; the institution narrative was introduced by the Eastern form 'in the night in which he was delivered up'; the anamnesis (*see* **Anaphora** 7) included the second coming; the epiclesis was of the developed Eastern type; and it was followed by intercessions. From this rite developed the Liturgy of St James and the West Syrian family of rites, and ultimately the orthodox rites of St Basil and St John Chrysostom.

One further Eastern rite to be mentioned is that of SS Addai and Mari from Edessa in East Syria. It was written in Syriac and it lay outside the main influences of Greek-speaking Christendom. The extant text is very late and corrupt, but it may well point to the existence of an independent liturgical tradition as ancient as the third century. The main part of the eucharistic prayer is addressed to Christ, and it contains no institution narrative; the epiclesis is of the Hippolytean type. Its users finally became Nestorians, and the rite came to be known as the Nestorian Liturgy.

Just as there were families of rites in the East, so there were families in the West. There was, for example, a North African family. Unfortunately no liturgical texts or treatises survive from this area: and the only evidence is references in the writings of Tertullian, Cyprian, Augustine and Optatus. It would seem, however, that there was borrowing from both East and West. So some churches used an epiclesis and some did not. On the other hand the kiss of peace (*see* **Gestures** 8) was in the Roman position before communion, not before the anaphora. At some stage freedom of experiment must have been excessive, for the Council of Carthage (397) and the First Council of Milevis (402) forbade uncontrolled freedom and insisted that all prayers should be officially approved.

In Rome the development of the rite was obscure. After Hippolytus there was a gap of some 150 years about which we know almost nothing. The first solid piece of evidence comes from the end of the fourth century with *De Sacramentis*, the lectures of Ambrose of Milan to the newly baptized. Here he made numerous quotations from a eucharistic text which later appeared in its entirety in the Gelasian Sacramentary. Its original form is unknown, but the disjointed text in the Sacramentary makes it clear that it has undergone revision. Ambrose also wrote of the eucharist in another treatise, *De Mysteriis*, and it would appear that in his time Milan used a rite which was fundamentally Roman. It followed the family pattern, but with significant features: intercessions came before the institution narrative, which was introduced in the characteristic Western manner – *Qui pridie*; consecration was effected, not by an epiclesis but by Jesus' own words in the institution narrative; and the Lord's Prayer had now found a place in the rite after the canon.

Other parts of the church in the West would also appear to have enjoyed an independent liturgical life in the early centuries, and the later evidence of what are known as the Gallican family of rites would suggest this; but of their origins virtually nothing is known.

It remains to note a few general developments, particularly in the East. First there was in the fourth century a growing attitude of awe towards the sacrament. Cyril of Jerusalem spoke of the 'holy and most dread sacrifice'; and Chrysostom and Theodore of Mopsuestia used similar language. Furthermore, with the imperial toleration and then the imperial establishment of Christianity, worship became more public and formal. So there developed a growing separation between clergy and laity: the corporate aspect of the eucharist faded; non-communicating attendance by the laity grew; the priest celebrated on behalf of the laity; and the most significant parts of the rite were withdrawn from their sight and hearing. In the West, however, changes were less serious. Gradually the canon came to be recited silently, and non-communicating attendance grew: but the priest remained in sight of the people, and no significant changes in dress or ceremonial occurred until after Gregory the Great.

R. C. D. JASPER

2. *Orthodox*. More correctly, Byzantine: what is commonly called the Orthodox liturgy, because by the historical and geographical accidents of subsequent Christian divisions it has come to be that in practice, is the liturgy of the Byzantine rite; that is, the liturgy of those churches which follow the order of service of the patriarchal see of Constantinople or Byzantium. The word 'liturgy' is normally used in the Byzantine rite only of the eucharistic liturgy, and not of the whole of formal public worship as it is in the West.

In the Eastern Orthodox Church today (as in those churches of the Byzantine rite in communion with Rome) the holy eucharist is celebrated according to three liturgies. The Liturgy of St James the Brother of the Lord is now used only on the feast of that saint in certain places, al-

though the number of such places has tended to increase somewhat in recent years. The historic liturgy of the Church of Jerusalem, and in its essentials the oldest of the three, it differs considerably from the other two, although its main parts, such as the eucharistic prayer or anaphora*, follow the same structure. The Liturgy of St Basil the Great, the anaphora of which, at least, was written by the father whose name it bears (on the basis of an older form which has in recent years been distinguished), is used on the eves of Christmas* and the Epiphany*, on the feast of St Basil (1 January), on the Sundays of Lent* (except Palm Sunday*), and on the Thursday and Saturday of Holy Week*. The Liturgy of St John Chrysostom (which appears to have little to do with St John Chrysostom, the ascription to him not being found until at least three hundred years after his death) is now the normal form: it is celebrated on all other days except those on which Byzantine liturgical law forbids the celebration of the eucharist altogether (*see* **Presanctified Mass**). The liturgies of St Basil and St John Chrysostom are identical in their order; they differ only in the texts of the principal prayers, those of the Liturgy of St Basil being much longer and fuller. They may therefore be considered together; further consideration of the Liturgy of St James must perforce be omitted.

Four principal divisions of the liturgy may be distinguished: 1. the preparation of the bread and wine, or prothesis*, which is performed privately before the service; 2. the introductory office of prayer and praise, or enarxis*; 3. the synaxis*, or liturgy of the word, or liturgy of the catechumens; 4. the eucharist proper, or liturgy of the faithful. A full account of the prothesis, and of its history, is given in a separate article.

The *enarxis* is also considered in a separate article, but a summary of its order and contents here may be useful: (*a*) opening blessing of the Trinity, by the celebrant; (*b*) the first (or greater) litany* by the deacon, with responses by the people (in most churches in practice these and other responses are sung by the choir), and a concluding prayer (now said, as are most such prayers, silently, apart from its doxology) by the celebrant; (*c*) the first anthem (variable, usually a psalm, or based on a psalm); (*d*) the second (short) litany, with its concluding prayer; (*e*) the second anthem; (*f*) the third (short) litany, with its concluding prayer. The enarxis is now sung with the celebrant standing in the sanctuary before the holy doors: originally it was certainly sung with all the ministers outside the sanctuary, and possibly in the narthex*, or in procession; the present usage completely changes the character and function of the entrance rite of the synaxis which follows.

The *synaxis* comprises three parts: (*a*) the entrance rite; (*b*) the readings from the scriptures; (*c*) the common prayers of the church.

The entrance rite commences with the entrance with the book of the gospels, commonly called the little entrance*; further details will be found in the article devoted to it. It is followed by censing, during which anthems proper to the day (*troparia*) are sung: the original entrance chant has been shortened to a single verse sung between the last anthem of the enarxis and these *troparia*. The latter are followed by the hymn called the *Trisagion**, corresponding here to the *Gloria in excelsis* (*see* **Doxology**) in the Roman rite, and a lengthy prayer by the celebrant taking up the theme of this hymn (corresponding in function to the collect* of the Roman rite), which is now said silently, and often before the hymn itself during the *troparia*.

The readings from the scriptures comprise: (i) the *prokeimenon*, part of a psalm, corresponding to the Roman gradual or responsorial psalm (the OT lesson, to which it was originally a response, has long since disappeared); (ii) the epistle; (iii) the alleluia (a verse or verses from the psalms, with the response 'Alleluia'); (iv) the gospel. The sermon, if there is one, should follow the gospel, but is often postponed to a later point – in Greek churches before the communion (a practice comparable to the Italian *fervorino*), and in Russian churches to the end of the whole service.

The common prayers of the church comprise three litanies: (i) the litany of fervent prayer, so called from its tripled response, and essentially a litany for the living, although a petition for the departed has been added to it; (ii) the litany for the departed (often sung only when there are particular departed persons to be prayed for); (iii) the litany for the catechumens*. They end with the dismissal of the cate-

chumens. In Russian churches all these litanies, together with the dismissal, are used, even when there are no catechumens; in Greek churches, on the other hand, they are commonly all omitted. The prayers which conclude each of the litanies are in most churches said silently, apart from their doxologies.

The eucharist proper commences after the dismissal of the catechumens, and comprises seven parts: (*a*) the first part of the preparation of the offerers, or 'prayers of the faithful'; (*b*) the great entrance* or entrance with the offerings; (*c*) the second part of the preparation of the offerers (the kiss of peace and the creed); (*d*) the eucharistic prayer or anaphora*; (*e*) the breaking of the bread; (*f*) the communion; (*g*) the conclusion.

The 'prayers of the faithful' (which should not be confused, in the Byzantine or any other historic liturgy, with the common prayers of the church closing the synaxis) consist of two litanies introducing prayers (now said silently) of preparation for the offering of the eucharist.

The great entrance comprises five acts, the first four of which are covered by the singing of the almost invariable offertory chant, the 'hymn of the cherubim' (*cherubikon*): (i) a long secret private preparatory prayer of the priest, a typical 'apologetic' interpolation of the early Middle Ages; (ii) censing of the altar, prothesis, and the whole church and congregation; (iii) the actual 'entrance' itself, in the midst of which the *cherubikon* is interrupted for certain intercessory commemorations related to the diptychs*; (iv) censing of the offerings now placed on the altar; (v) a litany leading to a prayer over the offerings, the latter exactly parallel to the Roman *super oblata**, but now in practice said secretly under cover of the litany.

The second part of the preparation of the offerers consists of the kiss of peace (which is no longer passed throughout the congregation, and is therefore omitted in practice unless several priests are present), the Niceno-Constantinopolitan Creed, and a brief exhortation by the deacon to reverence and awe in the offering of the eucharistic sacrifice which is about to take place.

The eucharistic prayer or anaphora is of the Antiochene pattern; it is difficult for anyone not well acquainted with the Byzantine liturgy to follow it in a contemporary celebration, due to the long standing custom, still all but universal, by which the celebrant says the greater part of it secretly (*see* **Silent Prayer**), while the congregational or choral responses are extended to cover his praying. Its order is: (i) Introductory dialogue, of the universal pattern with certain minor elaborations. (ii) Preface, or first part of the thanksgiving, basically a brief and simple thanksgiving for creation and redemption in general terms, expanded at some time in the Middle Ages by trinitarian interpolations which confuse the theme. Each of the two liturgies has its own form, as it has for every part of the prayer, but apart from this the preface, like the rest, is invariable. The preface is now said secretly, while the choir sings the last response of the introductory dialogue; the last clause is sung aloud, to provide a cue for the *Sanctus*. (iii) *Sanctus* and *Benedictus*, sung by the choir; the text is identical with that (of the Latin text) of the Roman rite, except that it reads 'Lord of Hosts' instead of 'Lord God of Hosts'. (iv) *Post-sanctus*, being a continuation of the thanksgiving, said secretly while the choir sings the *Sanctus*. In the Liturgy of St John Chrysostom a brief thanksgiving for the first coming of Christ, introducing the narrative of the institution; in the Liturgy of St Basil an extended and detailed thanksgiving for the whole history of creation and redemption, one of the finest examples of theological writing in the whole corpus of Christian liturgical literature, concluding with the introduction to the institution narrative. (v) Narrative of the institution. The actual words of institution are sung, each of the two sentences being followed by the response 'Amen' by the choir. (vi) Anamnesis, normal in structure and content (*see* **Anaphora** 7); said secretly under cover of the prolonged closing 'Amen' of the institution narrative, apart from the penultimate clause, which serves as the cue for a choral response which now covers the epiclesis. (vii) Epiclesis, of a normal descendant type in both structure and content. (viii) Diptychs: commemoration of the saints, said secretly apart from one clause, which introduces an anthem, in honour of the Mother of God, which now covers the secret recitation of the next two sections. (ix) Diptychs:

commemoration of the departed. (x) Diptychs: commemoration of the living (one clause, that for the bishop, sung aloud). This commemoration is expanded, as in most eastern rites, into a general intercession. (xi) Doxology and final Amen (aloud).

The breaking of the bread comprises (i) a blessing of the people by the priest (many Western rites once had a corresponding blessing, which is in origin a preparation for communion); (ii) a litany, similar to that after the great entrance, leading to the Lord's Prayer; (iii) the breaking of the bread, with various secondary ceremonies, such as an elevation and a commixture, preceded by the original invitation to communion and its response, now purely formal, and covered by the communion hymn of the day, now thus used as a fraction hymn.

The communion comprises (i) the communion of the ministers; (ii) the invitation to communion, to which the choir respond with Ps. 117 (118).26–27; (iii) preparatory prayers, said aloud, a mediaeval interpolation; (iv) the communion of the people, during which the choir sing appointed anthems; (v) the blessing after communion; (vi) the first postcommunion anthem. Communion is given in both kinds, administered together with a spoon, the bread having been placed in the chalice after the communion of the ministers; in the accompanying formula the communicant is referred to by name.

The conclusion comprises: (i) the second post-communion anthem; (ii) a brief litany of thanksgiving, leading to the post-communion prayer (the latter said secretly); (iii) the prayer over the people, or prayer outside the chancel, the original form of blessing; (iv) the dismissal anthem, properly Ps. 33 (34) but now usually abbreviated; (v) the blessing and dismissal, with various responses, all of mediaeval origin.

The Byzantine eucharistic liturgy is unsurpassed in Christendom for clarity and coherence both of liturgical structure and of theological content – virtues which, unfortunately, are to some extent compromised by the combination of mediaeval interpolations and alterations and the current manner of celebration; there is no rite which would benefit more from a comparatively small and conservative measure of informed and intelligent reform.

See also **Orthodox Worship**.

W. JARDINE GRISBROOKE

3. *Mediaeval and Roman Catholic*

(*a*) *Mediaeval liturgies*. The Celtic liturgy, of which little is known before it had received Roman interpolations, was by the time of the Norman Conquest (1066) confined to Scotland and Ireland. It was probably of Gallican origin, and the lingering Celtic practices were suppressed in Scotland by St Margaret in 1069 and in Ireland in the twelfth century.

The Roman rite was introduced into England by the missionaries of St Augustine (d.605) and the main structure continued throughout the Middle Ages.

After the Conquest, the building of churches, cathedrals and abbeys on a grand scale involved the compilation of a series of liturgical books of what came to be called different uses or even rites, although all were of the Roman rite.

There were extensive borrowings from the books in the Duchy of Normandy, and the process was completed by the thirteenth century. It is impossible to identify any specific 'ancestors' for the English uses, except, probably, Rouen for that of Hereford.

The structure was the same in each of them, but the prayers often differed, especially the preparatory prayers and those at the offertory and before communion.

By the time of the Reformation only three of the uses remained, since those of Bangor and Lincoln were virtually Sarum: Sarum, York and Hereford. All the others had adopted the Sarum liturgy, which became a model for the greater part of England and also for Scotland and Ireland. York had resolutely refused to give up its local use, but over the century many Sarum interpolations were accepted by Hereford.

The elaborate ceremonial of the 'Illustrious Church of Sarum' contrasted vividly with the comparative simplicity of liturgical worship in Rome.

The compiler of this English use could not have been St Osmund (d.1099), although he may have laid a simple foundation. It is much too elaborate for his period. It was in all probability Richard Poore, Dean and Bishop (1217–28) of Salisbury, in whose time the cathedral was moved from

Old Sarum into the city.

The last Sarum missal was printed in 1557 in the reign of Queen Mary.

In all the countries of Europe, diocesan missals appeared in the course of the Middle Ages, but, like the English service-books, they were variants of the Roman rite, with a choice of prayers.

(*b*) *Liturgy of Trent*. The fathers of the Council of Trent (1545–63) requested the pope to reform the liturgy, as it varied in almost every diocese. The new missal was completed under Pius V in 1570 to be an exemplar for all churches, and the mass was to be followed for all time. (It was not until 1964 that it was superseded and then again in 1970.) An exception had been made for those churches and religious orders which could show a distinctive use for at least two hundred years. All of them, however, were variants of the Roman rite, with the exception of the Mozarabic in a few churches in Toledo and that of Milan (Ambrosian), if a Gallican origin is maintained.

A few Marian priests in hiding continued their Sarum, York or Hereford mass, but the 'missioners' who came to England in the time of Elizabeth I followed the new Tridentine missal. Ancient sources had been studied in its production, but it preserved without change or verification the elements added in the Franco-German period to the original form of the Roman mass. The number of the feasts of saints was diminished and only four sequences were admitted. Unnecessary accretions were eliminated, such as the added words (tropes) in the *Kyrie** and the Marian farcing in the *Gloria in excelsis*. The time was unpropitious to reintroduce communion under both kinds. In order to answer difficulties in the celebration of mass, Sixtus V in 1588 founded the Congregation of Rites, but it could not change existing rubrics* or the text of the prayers. An epoch of stability followed.

It is a mistake to think that this was a virtually silent mass. The rubrics ordered three voices: heard by the faithful, heard by those near to the celebrant, and silent, as in the canon. Above all, the epistle and gospel, the word of God, were for the benefit of the people and were to be read or sung in a clear and distinct voice. There was no justification for the subdeacon to chant the epistle in the sanctuary with his back to the congregation. True, the gospel was read in the vernacular* in the pulpit before the sermon, but this was extra-liturgical, not part of the mass.

There were four revisions of the Tridentine liturgy, but the changes brought little modification of the text. The reform of Pius X (1911) affected the calendar: so that 'the very ancient masses of Sundays throughout the year and of the week days, especially in Lent, might be restored to their proper place'. Clement XI (1721–24) had decreed that the preface of the Holy Trinity should be said on Sundays and Leo XIII (1878–1903) added the prayers after low mass. In 1953, the Liturgical Congress of Lugano discussed revolutionary changes in the mass, with the intention of simplifying the rite, removing what was redundant and giving the faithful a more active part in the liturgy. At that time, some alterations appeared possible, but not the abandonment of the rite which had served the Western Church since the sixteenth century and the substitution of the vernacular for the Latin. A new Easter vigil appeared under Pius XII in 1951, with a change in all the offices of Holy Week in 1956.

The result of the debate on the liturgy in the Second Vatican Council (1962), which had been called by John XXIII, left no doubt that the changes would exceed mere alterations in the Tridentine mass.

(*c*) *Post-conciliar liturgies*. The aim of the post-conciliar commission was to produce a liturgy which should make the mass more alive and meaningful. Life was very different from 1570.

The priest should lead the community in worship, but the congregation must take a more intelligent and active part. 'Participation' is the key-note of the new liturgy, and, in order to effect this, the mass is said in the vernacular, although Latin is not altogether suppressed.

An 'interim' liturgy was ordered as from Advent Sunday 1964, with the people reciting the *Gloria in excelsis* and the creed, as well as responses and the variable 'chants' of the mass. Instructions were given as to when the faithful should stand, sit or kneel. The psalm 'Judge me, O God' in the preparatory prayers and the last gospel* at the end of the mass were suppressed. The prayers of the faithful, general petitions linking the world with the eucharist, were

introduced after the creed. The prayer after the offertory*, known hitherto as the 'secret', was said aloud and rightly renamed the prayer over the offerings (gifts). The Roman canon* or eucharistic prayer, unaltered (with the exception of two phrases) since the sixth century, remained the same, although said aloud and with the final doxology in a more solemn form, with the people responding amen. Three new eucharistic prayers, bringing fresh expression of the role of the Holy Spirit, were introduced in 1969. After the consecration, at the words 'mystery of faith', a choice of four acclamations by the faithful was introduced. Before the communion of the priest, 'Lord, I am not worthy' was said by all. The communicant replied 'Amen' after the words of administration: The body of Christ. Finally, the dismissal was transferred until after the blessing.

The ceremonial* of the mass had been greatly reduced, as had the signs of the cross and genuflections (*see* **Gestures**). The commission regulated also the rite of the concelebration*and, for certain occasions, the administration of communion under both kinds. The number of communicants in large churches would make the giving of the chalice at all times very difficult.

The final and normative order of the mass was first said in France, Italy and Spain on Advent Sunday in 1969 and in Great Britain on the first Sunday in Lent 1970. Rome had conceded that its use was not compulsory for two years, but it was largely adopted. The various changes in the 'interim' rite have been retained in the new liturgy.

Incense* may be used whether the mass is sung or said. The mass begins with an entrance song, which may be either the old introit or a hymn. Then, after a greeting of the people, there is a penitential act with a shortened confession in which the faithful join with the priest. 'Lord have mercy' and 'Glory be to God on high' are followed by the first of the presidential prayers, the collect, of which there is never more than one.

The liturgy of the word, since the Council, has a more vital role. The pope has said that 'the treasury of the written word of God should be more generously distributed'. A third lesson, from the OT, is provided for Sundays and feasts, and a new lectionary has been compiled. The four sequences or hymns before the gospel have been retained, but only those of Easter and Pentecost are obligatory. The creed and the prayers of the faithful follow.

The offertory procession, at the beginning of the eucharist liturgy, linking the gifts of bread and wine with the giving of money, is encouraged where possible. The prayers at the offertory are shorter and have been modelled on the prayer spoken by the father of the family at the beginning of a formal Jewish meal.

Some eighty new prefaces have been added as well as two more eucharistic prayers for masses of reconciliation and three for masses with children. The Roman canon, as an alternative to the three eucharistic prayers, has been retained, with a few minor alterations. The list of saints before and after the consecration may be considerably shortened, and what may be called the three false conclusions in the canon suppressed. An acclamation by the faithful has been introduced after the words 'mystery of faith', as in the other prayers. This acclamation highlights Paul in his First Letter to the Christians of Corinth (I Cor. 11.26).

The central and vital part of the canon, including the words of consecration, may be sung, as well as the final doxology. The prayer following the Our Father has been simplified and changed at the end, with an acclamation of faith in the glorified Christ.

The 'sign of peace and mutual love', usually a handshake, is given before communion. The consecrated bread is broken at the threefold *Agnus Dei*. After communion, a silence for thanksgiving is prescribed. Notices are given before the blessing. The ablutions* may be taken after mass.

The calendar has been simplified. The masses of the three Sundays before Lent have been suppressed. There are fewer feasts of saints, and very many of the commemorations are optional. John the Deacon (872) in his assessment of the work of St Gregory could be writing of the new mass: 'leaving out much, changing little, adding something for the exposition of the lessons of the Gospel'.

See also **Roman Catholic Worship**.

J. D. CRICHTON

4. *Anglican.* The roots of Anglican eucharistic liturgy lie in the reforming work of Cranmer in the reign of Edward VI (1547–53). By 1547 he had already come to strong convictions about the *desiderata*, and when Edward, a minor, inherited the throne, Cranmer's Protestantism in theology was reflected in the Council of which he was a member, and the opportunity came to reform the liturgy.

Cranmer's main aims were: a wholly vernacular* liturgy, a simplification of ceremonies, participation by the people (including receiving communion regularly and in both kinds), and elimination of transubstantiation, mass-sacrifice, and other unreformed doctrines. His purpose was far more to write a liturgy embodying receptionism than to revive patristic usage. It was not that he lacked scholarship or materials – rather he was not interested in copying patristic use for its own sake anyway. Certainly his developed liturgy was *sui generis* and unlike any earlier production.

Reform came by stages – a method advertised in advance in the Royal Proclamation prefixed to *The Order of the Communion* of 1548. In 1547 the epistle and gospel had been read in English. Now this brief insert into the mass came as the first new eucharistic work in Cranmer's planned programme. Written in English, it implemented reception in both kinds by being inserted after the priest's communion in the mass. It contained a long exhortation to worthy reception, a short exhortation, confession, absolution, 'comfortable words', and the famous 'prayer of humble access' leading into communion in both kinds. A blessing followed, and if the wine were insufficient more was to be consecrated.

In the 1549 BCP the whole service was in English. The mass-plus-*Order* shape was followed closely, but the contents were subtly changed. The ante-communion* merely lost the priest's preparation and the gradual chant. It gained a sermon or homily after the creed, and the 1548 long exhortation followed that. The offertory* – consisting of a collecting of money – concluded the ante-communion. The worshippers left their places to put their alms in a box near the screen, and intending communicants proceeded on to the choir or chancel.

The elements were then made ready and the cunningly altered canon* ensued. The Roman intercessions remained, but only prayers, not oblations*, were offered. The saints were honoured, but not expected to help. Prayer was made for the departed, now grouped with the living. The intercessions broke off, and the sacramental theme began, abruptly. God was invoked as having given his Son to make on the cross 'a full, perfect, and sufficient sacrifice, oblation and satisfaction' for sins – words serving devotional, didactic and polemical purposes. The *quam oblationem* petition then asked God to bless and sanctify the gifts by his 'Holy Spirit and word'. This is sometimes called an epiclesis (*see* **Anaphora** 8), but occupied the Western position and owed little or nothing to Eastern models. The institution narrative had two manual acts but no other ceremonial. But the anamnesis was the key to Cranmer's step by step reform. The old canon responded to the command 'Do this in remembrance' with 'we offer a pure victim'. Cranmer removed this oblationary terminology, but left the response unexplained. It read 'we ... celebrate and make ... the memorial which thy Son hath willed us to make'. In brief, whatever he meant, we mean! The canon continued with self-oblation, petition for fruitful reception, some wisps of the old canon and a doxology*. After it came the Lord's Prayer, the peace, and the whole 1548 *Order* from the short exhortation to communion (including the priest's). After a brief post-communion, rubrics* ordered 'something more larger and thicker' than wafers, to be divided during distribution. Further consecration was lacking.

Reactions to this service merely paved the way for the next round, which may have been already in preparation. Implementation came in 1552. Now the shape was altered, slightly in the ante-communion, drastically around the anamnesis (*see* **Anaphora** 7). To the question, 'What do we do in response to our Lord's command?' the 1552 *Order* answered, 'We eat bread and drink wine'. This was incorporated after the institution narrative not by mere verbal assertion, but by *actual eating and drinking*. New words of administration reflected not new doctrine but the new 'anamnesis' role of communion – 'Take and eat this in remembrance ...'. The 1552 *Order* left no

break between reading the Lord's command and obeying it, the table was in the midst and the distribution was immediate.

Further consequences followed. Sacramentally speaking, nothing preceded reception. There was no trace of consecration, whether name or thing. The elements were not mentioned rubrically till distribution, and the minister took the remains home. The *quam oblationem* petition located consecration in reception, and this is the logic of the whole rite. Further consecration was thus impossible.

The promoted administration squeezed considerable 1549 material out of its place. The end of the 1549 canon became an alternative post-communion 'prayer of oblation' (still, oddly, asking for fruitful reception). The Lord's Prayer opened the post-communion. The peace was lost, and the 1548 *Order* began the sacramental half of the service. Cranmer hit on the happy transition from the fourth 'comfortable word' to 'lift up your hearts', but this excluded 'humble access' from the sequence. It, however, replaced the 1549 intercessions after the *Sanctus**. As these had lost their connection with the 'oblations' they no longer belonged in the canon, and went more naturally (and perhaps primitively) at the end of the ante-communion. Thus they were read each week, even when there was no communion. The saints and the departed disappeared and the intercessions were explicitly labelled for the 'church militant here on earth'. Inserting 'humble access' after the *Sanctus* has been thought to break up the canon, but to Cranmer there was a gaping hole there, and a subjective approach to the table suited the progress of the service, to a single climax in reception, far better than the 1549 intercessions could do. Thus the 1552 'canon' was merely the 'one oblation' paragraph, the receptionist *quam oblationem*, and the institution narrative ending in the administration. The post-communion included *Gloria in excelsis*, and the rubrics ordered bread 'usual to be eaten'.

Mary brought back the mass, but Elizabeth in 1559 revived the 1552 *Order*, though she clumsily prefixed 1549 words of administration to the 1552 ones. Jewel's controversy with Harding made it policy to assert that the dominical words in the narrative of institution consecrated the elements, and a Puritan, Robert Johnson, was imprisoned in 1574 for omitting a 'further consecration'. The 1604 canons underlined this new policy.

The ill-fated 1637 Scottish rite was a half-reversion to 1549. After the *Sanctus* 'humble access' fell out, and the 'one oblation' paragraph followed immediately. The 1549 *quam oblationem* returned, manual acts were reintroduced, the 1549 anamnesis dislodged the administration, and the 1552 'prayer of oblation' followed as in 1549. The Lord's Prayer and 'humble access' intervened before communion, but the rest of the 1549 *Order* held its 1552 position. The canon was now called 'the prayer of consecration', and rubrics ordered both further consecration and consumption of consecrated remains.

The 1662 Restoration liturgy kept the 1552 text and structure, but firmly clamped the 1637 'consecration' rubrics upon it. Cranmer's words were to enact Jewel's theology! A discreet (non-petitionary) mention of the departed came into the intercessions, and an amen concluded the 'prayer of consecration'. As, under Laud's influence, tables had already returned to the east wall of the chancel, a break between the institution narrative and distribution had arisen. Thus the amen merely regularized a *de facto* departure from the continuity which Cranmer had planned.

The 1662 *Order* still remains today the official service of the Church of England and of many other Anglican provinces. However, many provinces have superseded it, and most have at least some alternative. Its use is now more deeply entrenched in vernacular languages (in, say, Africa) than it is in English-speaking communities. These latter show impatience at its antique (but majestic) language, its unique shape, and (sometimes) its Cranmerian theology. It is consequently disappearing from use.

Early variants occurred in eighteenth-century Scotland. A scholarly theory that the *Apostolic Constitutions* were really apostolic led to changes from 1637 to 1764. The 1637 *quam oblationem* was moved to the Eastern position and made into a full-blown epiclesis. The 1549/1637 anamnesis now had an explicit oblation of the elements attached. The intercessions were moved to the end of the canon. Finally, the whole 1548 *Order* returned to its 1549 position. The 1928 Scottish rite descends from 1764.

The same text was taken to America by Samuel Seabury in 1784, was crossed with the 1662 rite over there, and a hybrid rite emerged in 1790. The 1790 rite lay behind American (and Brazilian) use in 1928 and into the 1960s, though many other influences have been at work since.

In the early twentieth century the Universities' Mission to Central Africa and Korean mission fields went over to near-Roman rites (usually only available then in vernacular tongues). An Eastern-type epiclesis also had its advocates again, and was not only retained in the Scottish and American rites when they were revised, but was also introduced in South Africa (1924), England (1927–8), and in the 1930s in Ceylon, China, Madagascar and elsewhere. Anglo-Catholics led all these revisions, seeking a more primitive pattern for the canon, petitions for the departed, and some form of Godward 'memorial' in the anamnesis. They were divided, however, about the propriety, wording and position of the epiclesis. In England the 1927–8 rite created grave suspicions among Protestants for these very reasons, but it was finally defeated over the (not strictly liturgical) question of reservation.

In the late 1940s India experimented with a 1928-type rite, and Japan and the West Indies followed in the 1950s on a more 1549-cum-Roman basis. The 1959 Canadian rite stood between 1662 and the Indian rite.

The 1960s brought a new era. Experimental revision started all round the Anglican Communion. G. Dix's *The Shape of the Liturgy* (1945) had focussed attention on the *action* and less on the *words*. The first result of this had been the ecumenical South India liturgy of 1950; its principles, embodied in the 1958 Lambeth Report, were worked out for Anglicans in *A Liturgy for Africa* (1964) and in various other rites of the 1960s. New features were: penitence (and the *Gloria in excelsis*) at the beginning; a fuller ministry of the word, including the OT; the creed following the sermon; responsive forms of intercession; an embryonic restoration of the peace; and a sacramental action more or less following Dix's 'four-action shape'. Within this the eucharistic prayer recovered its traditional length and shape, but it was the whole prayer which consecrated rather than simply the narrative of institution. While the cross was usually emphasized in the prayer, the other 'mighty works' of God were set alongside it; congregational acclamations were added to it; and the first awareness of drafting problems in relation to the anamnesis – should it include an oblation of the elements to God? – was experienced.

Parallel with these African and Asian developments, the Church of England in 1967 authorized its Series 2 rite, which had been drafted by the Liturgical Commission independent of revision processes elsewhere, and another independent initiative came in the American *Prayer Book Studies XVII* (1967). However, with regard to language, all the new rites of the 1960s were quickly swallowed up in a new move – the change from 'thou' to 'you'. This started with rites in New Zealand and Australia in 1966, and from 1968 onwards hardly any drafting anywhere was done in the old style. Accompanying this change, Series 2 communion was revised and enriched in several ways with biblical material, and was published in 1971 as Series 3, authorized in the Church of England from 1973. This started to have influence in other parts of the world, either by direct importing or by large-scale borrowing (as, for instance, in the Church of North India, 1973). In the American Episcopal Church the new rites, published as experimental drafts in 1970, not only addressed God as 'you', but also offered great choice of alternative forms of intercession and several eucharistic prayers. There was even a skeletal 'structure outline' of a rite with freedom to create local and *ad hoc* wording (and mention of an agape). In 1976 the drafts became a whole hardback book, and in 1979 this replaced 1928 as the Book of Common Prayer. Not only were all the propers now between one set of covers, but language had moved on again, and the inclusive style – i.e. that which does not appear to refer only to males – took over. Others have followed this style since, though the Church of England's rites did not do so in 1980.

In so far as common trends can be discerned in the contents of the modern rites, it is clear that the needs of a main service parish communion have been paramount. There is increased congregational participation, stronger emphasis upon the corporate and ecclesial significance of the

rite, and a persistent note of joy and celebration. At the same time, even the most daring rites are theologically conservative, and often stand in theological tension with the speculative formulation of each decade's more liberal theologians.

Definitive books for modern liturgy have followed in places other than America: Australia (1978), England (ASB 1980), Ireland (1984), Canada (1985) and so on. In these certain nods towards the older traditions were made – 'thou' form rites were revamped and placed alongside 'you' form ones (in Wales the 1984 book actually made the 'thou' form rite the definitive one), or 1662 appears in 'you' form language (as in both Australia and England). New experimental booklets were authorized in less rich provinces, and some new drafting was done in Spanish, Swahili, Korean and other vernacular tongues. The overall structure of the rites varied very little, but growing flexibility and provision of alternatives and of room for extemporization meant that tremendous variation between actual celebrations from one area to another, and even from one parish to another, would be experienced. The opportunities for local innovation and creativity are now considerable, and the liturgy can therefore be adapted to local contexts and resources. This liberty would also allow for true cultural indigenization*, though the general impression in the Anglican communion is that the more daring adaptations occur in the more Westernized parts of the communion, and a more cautious usage is found in the developing countries. The liberty which now exists also poses questions about Anglican liturgical identity which are not easy to answer.

See also **Anglican Worship**.

C. O. BUCHANAN

5. *Baptist*. While most Baptists would affirm their worship as 'eucharistic' in the sense that it is a time of thanksgiving, they would not use the term 'eucharist' to describe it. Likewise, they generally do not use terms like 'sacrament' or 'holy communion'. They rather prefer the 'Lord's Supper'*, or the 'breaking of bread' or the 'memorial meal' to designate the central act of Christian worship.

The Lord's Supper is understood as anamnesis (*see* **Anaphora** 7). The Lord's death is remembered and re-enacted as a memorial 'until he comes'. The bread and wine are symbols of the body and blood of Jesus Christ. The presence of the Lord is a spiritual presence.

Baptists, though having a high regard for the Lord's Supper, do not observe it with great frequency. Daily communion is not practised by Baptists. Weekly communion is only rarely observed, and then usually by congregations which have had some contact with the contemporary movement for liturgical renewal. The general practice among Baptist churches is monthly communion, usually on the first Sunday of the month. Baptist churches in some places observe only four communion Sundays a year.

The administrator of the communion is generally an ordained minister, but if no ordained person is available the congregation may designate a lay person as the administrator. Deacons assist in the services. They serve the elements, pass the peace, and lead in the prayers. The service is generally conducted from behind the table, the minister facing the congregation.

Communion* is in two kinds. Formerly a common loaf was broken and distributed to each communicant and a common cup was passed among the congregation. Today communion wafers or small bits of bread and individual cups are in general use, although in some places the common loaf and cup are being reintroduced. Communion is generally received in the pews. The bread is eaten at the same time by the minister and congregation as the minister says: 'Jesus said, "Take eat; this is my body which is broken for you. Do this in remembrance of me."' The cup is drunk simultaneously as the minister says: 'Jesus said, "Drink of it, all of you; for this is my blood of the covenant, which is poured out from many for the forgiveness of sins."'

Communion among the early Baptists was generally reserved for those who were members in good standing of the local congregation or who were members of other Baptist congregations in good standing. That meant that only those who had been baptized 'on profession of faith' as believers were to be communicants. In many places the practice was to hold two services on a communion Sunday. The first, including the sermon, would be for all who

came; the second was only for those who were entitled to receive communion. In recent decades this practice has been greatly modified. While some churches still practise 'closed communion', most Baptist churches issue a general invitation to 'all who believe in Christ and who are in love and fellowship with your neighbours' to partake in the service. The service of word and table is one, and all, including those who do not communicate, remain.

Each congregation determines the structure of its worship. Thus no one service would be considered typical, but with modifications the following would find acceptance in many Baptist churches.

THE SERVICE FOR THE LORD'S DAY
(with the Lord's Supper)

Affirmation of purpose and entry of scriptures
Adoration
  Scripture sentences
  Hymn
  Prayer
  Ascription
Confession
  Call
  Prayer
  Assurance of forgiveness
  Praise: *Gloria patri, Gloria in excelsis*, or hymn

Ministry of the Word

Scripture lessons
Prayer of illumination
Sermon
Affirmation of faith or church covenant

Ministry of the Table

Offertory: gifts, bread and wine, and self
Prayer of dedication
Invitation to communion
Affirmation of unity and peace
  Scripture sentence
  Right hand of fellowship (the peace)
Words of institution
Prayer of thanksgiving
Prayer for the presence of the Holy Spirit
Lord's Prayer
Breaking and distribution of the bread
Eating of the bread
Pouring and distribution of the wine
Drinking the wine
Agnus Dei
Prayers of petition and intercession

Dismissal

Hymn
Benediction

The service generally includes several hymns, an anthem and service music. A choir is used to assist in the service and to offer the special music.

See also **Baptist Worship**.

JOHN E. SKOGLUND

6. *Christian Church* (*Disciples of Christ*). From its earliest days, in the early nineteenth century, the Christian Church (Disciples of Christ) has combined two principles bearing upon the order of worship. First, the regular service of worship has included preaching and the 'breaking of bread'. Second, this church has entrusted decisions about the order and words of the liturgy to each congregation. Although there has been considerable similarity among congregations, it must be said that the practice is neither common order nor common prayer.

The first exposition of this practice was developed by Alexander Campbell (1788–1866) in his writings during the third and fourth decades of the century. After observing that the NT, in contrast to the OT, gives no formal requirements for worship, Campbell concluded that Christians have reached the 'manhood of the religious world', and are therefore 'permitted to exercise their reason, and to act from the principles infused into their minds from the development of the divine philanthropy'. He affirmed that the weekly observance of the Lord's Supper on the Lord's Day is commanded but that the rules are not. Accounts of that period indicate that a typical service began with readings from scripture interspersed with hymns. There followed brief extempore prayers over bread and wine with the distribution of each. Impromptu exhortations or preaching, spiritual songs, and a collection concluded the service.

During the period from 1880 to 1920 this combination of elements was gradually formalized in general practice: opening praise, scripture lessons, pastoral prayer, communion, offering and sermon. The position of the sermon is a vestige of earlier practice when the congregation always ministered the Lord's Supper whether there

was a preacher or not. Communion was ordinarily conducted with these sub-sections: a brief homily on the meaning of the act, an extempore prayer over the loaf by one elder, a second prayer over the cup by a second elder, and distribution of both to the congregation. An invitation to confess faith in Christ was regularly extended following the sermon. A number of private service books was published during this time giving suggestions for pastors for the construction of their services.

Not until after the Second World War did Disciple congregations in large numbers develop an order of worship more closely parallel to that followed in other denominations. By transposing communion and sermon, they overcame their one major disparate practice. By 'enriching' the service with devotional elements previously not used they developed a tone to their services increasingly like that of other denominations.

The use of extempore prayer at the communion table has continued with little change, illustrating positive and negative values in such a practice. Ordinarily these prayers have referred specifically to the bread and the cup and have given thanks for Jesus who gave himself for our sins. Frequently there have been requests for the Holy Spirit to come and for our sins to be forgiven. A common element has been a vow that Disciples will give their lives now to greater service to God. The use of extempore prayers at the table makes possible a directness and immediacy that is rarely present in the language of prescribed eucharistic prayers. At the same time, this practice opens the way for unevenness and irregularity.

Disciples, despite a long-time tendency towards legalism, have never raised questions about the validity of the Lord's Supper, about the 'form' and 'matter' of the eucharist. Consequently, the varied theological content of the eucharistic prayer has not raised for them the problems that would arise in other portions of the church. Adequacy of the rite has been gauged by different criteria: Is the table spread in remembrance of Christ? Has the conducting of the service been according to the congregation's unwritten standards or expectations? Does the combination of music, word, and act communicate a sense of divine presence? On every Sunday the entire congregation present communicates and in this way affirms the integrity of the rite.

See also **Christian Church Worship**.

KEITH WATKINS

7. *Congregationalist*. There is no single official Congregational liturgy. None the less the structure, order, and content of Congregational services of word and sacrament do not differ greatly between Britain and the USA (for the sources of these services *see* **Books, Liturgical** 7).

The nearest approach to an archetypal Congregational liturgy, and one which unites the largest number of Congregationalists in the world, is the first recommended service in *Services of Word and Sacrament*, first published in 1966 by the United Church of Christ. It is archetypal yet not monopolistic, since alternatives are provided. It is a firm guide to worship with a coherent theology and careful order, but welcomes the supplementary use of free prayer, silent prayer, and bidding prayers, as long as they do not break the basic order and progression of the service.

The service has two parts, which correspond to the origin of Christian worship in the synagogue and the upper room. The first part is essentially a service of the word; the second part is essentially the service of the Holy Supper or eucharist. The first part consists of praise, prayers, the reading and exposition of scripture, an affirmation of faith, and the response of the people in the offertory – the climax of the service of the word and the beginning of the service of the Lord's Supper.

The second part of the service recalls not only in words, but also in symbolic and prophetic acts, the four actions of the Lord who *took* the bread and wine, *blessed* them by prayer, *broke* or poured them, and *gave* them to his disciples, as the anticipation of his sacrifice on the cross and of his messianic banquet in eternity.

The aims of the entire service are: to stress the unity of word and sacrament; to offset an overly introspective and penitential character in historic Western worship by accenting the elements of adoration and joyful gratitude and the presence of the risen Christ; to make the central eucharistic actions plain; and, finally, to

emphasize that the true consecrator is the Holy Spirit. These are not, of course, uniquely Congregational or even Reformed contributions to liturgical theology – they are the common gains of the liturgical and ecumenical movements of our days.

In two respects only has this liturgy made a distinctive contribution, and these are worthy of elaboration. The peril of the exclusively retrospective gaze and of a theological memorialism are minimized by beginning the eucharistic part of the service with Luke's account of the risen Saviour breaking bread with his disciples. Since the Pauline account of the Holy Supper in I Corinthians is by far the commoner usage as a warrant in our tradition, this feature is genuinely innovative.

The second innovation, for which the Church of South India (*see* **Church of South India Worship**) provides a partial precedent, was to provide some new responses for the people in the great prayer of consecration. The most significant response, after the anamnesis and epiclesis (*see* **Anaphora**), affirms the priesthood of all God's people, in the following words of oblation: 'Here we offer ourselves in obedience to Thee, through the perfect offering of thy Son Jesus Christ, giving Thee thanks that Thou has called us to be a royal priesthood, a holy nation, thine own people . . .' The distinctive Congregational witness has not been lost, but rather recovered in this rich rite which won the approval of the late E. C. Ratcliff as having recovered 'the spirit and emphasis of the Early Church'.

There have been two significant changes incorporated in the more recent Congregational communion services in both Britain and the USA. One has been the increasing appropriation of the historic structure and wording of the consecration prayer of the Western tradition, including the salutation, the *Sursum corda*, the *Sanctus*, the anamnesis, and the oblation.

A second change has been towards a deeper sense of the real presence in the sacrament as evidenced by the requirement of an epiclesis, in contrast to earlier eucharistic theologies which were virtualist at best and memorialist at worst. The evidence for this claim can be found in the most recent service books of the United Reformed Church* in the United Kingdom and the United Church of Christ in the USA.

The theology of the first and second communion orders of *A Manual for Ministers* (1936) is clearly memorialist. Four of the five communion orders in *A Book of Public Worship Compiled for the Use of Congregationalists* (1948) have an explicit epiclesis, and a fifth has an implicit doctrine of the real presence. Both communion orders in *A Book of Services and Prayers* (1959) have an explicit epiclesis, as does the revised edition of 1969. The Order of Worship in the United Reformed Church's *Book of Services* (1980) contains three eucharistic prayers, all of which have an explicit epiclesis.

In the American Congregational publication, *A Book of Worship for Free Churches* (1948), two communion orders include an ambiguous epiclesis in the words: 'We humbly beseech thee to grant thy Holy Spirit and to sanctify this bread and wine, which now we offer unto thee; that they may become unto us symbols of the body that was broken and of the blood that was shed for us . . .' (pp. 108, 115–6). On the other hand, the two communion orders of the United Church of Christ published in *Services of Word and Sacrament* (1966) include the following epiclesis: 'Bless and sanctify by thy Holy Spirit both us and these thy gifts of bread and wine that in this holy communion of the body and blood of Christ we may be made one with him and he with us . . .'

HORTON DAVIES

8. *Jehovah's Witnesses.* During a simple ceremony, Jesus Christ used wine and unleavened bread as symbols of his human life to be sacrificed for mankind. When instituting this ceremony, he said: 'Keep doing this in remembrance of me' (Luke 22.19).

Jesus specifically introduced his congregation to the 'new covenant' (Luke 22.20) and it is a remnant of this 'little flock', revealed in scripture to number 144,000 (Rev. 14.1–5), that is seen to partake of the bread and wine in these 'last days' (Luke 12.32; II Tim. 3.1). These ones, to be resurrected to heavenly life with Christ Jesus as priests of God, are destined to rule with him as kings for the millenial reign, during which time the earth will be

restored to its original paradisal condition (Rev. 5.9, 10).

Following the pattern Jesus set, Jehovah's Witnesses annually meet on the commemorative day, according to the Jewish calendar Nisan 14, to commemorate his death. Accordingly, on 15 April 1984, 7,416,974 individuals met with Jehovah's Witnesses world-wide. Of this number, 2,842,531 were active Witnesses. Only 9,081 partook of the emblematic bread and wine.

For the millions of others who attend this annual memorial celebration, the hope they entertain is that of living through the conclusion of the present world order into a cleansed earth with the prospect of everlasting life under God's kingdom (Matt. 24.3; 25.31–34).

DAVID SIBREY

9. *Lutheran*. At the time of the Reformation (from *c*. 1517–), liturgical reform among Lutherans had a twofold motivation: theological and didactic. There was no attempt to break the mould of Western Catholic tradition nor to return to liturgical practices of the primitive church. The inherited rites were judged theologically by the Reformation norm: justification by grace through faith. Neither the Roman canon nor offertory prayers were acceptable because their emphasis on sacrifice suggested that the mass is primarily the congregation's service of God. Lutherans insisted on the opposite, that the mass is primarily God's work among the congregation. The need to release people from mediaeval superstition and expose them to the teaching of the gospel was met by a strong emphasis on preaching and by the use of the vernacular in the liturgy. Preaching was accorded sacramental status as the living voice of the gospel: Christ present and active.

Martin Luther turned his hand to liturgical reform reluctantly, being forced by what he considered ill-advised attempts of others. Because of his prestige, his two major reforms of the mass were widely imitated. The first, *Formula missae et communionis* (*FM*, 1523), was a Latin rite which provided for vernacular hymns and sermons. Only minor changes were made in the *missa catechumenorum*. The sermon might come either before the introit or following the creed. The excision of offertory* and most of the canon* resulted in the following order for the *missa fidelium*: preface, words of institution (sung), *Sanctus* (with elevation), Our Father (omitting doxology), pax (interpreted as a public absolution), communion in both kinds (with *Agnus Dei*), collect, *Benedicamus* (replacing *Ite missa est*), Aaronic blessing*. Compared with other Reformation rites the *FM* is conservative, but Luther cut out the heart of the mediaeval mass, i.e. the offertory and canon.

Though he realized its inevitability, Luther took the step towards the vernacular* with reservations. The Latin rite was imbedded in his piety and he loved its music dearly. He insisted that a German rite must be supplied with 'German music'; he viewed with horror attempts to fit the heavy accents of modern languages to the fluid grace of plainsong. But the pastoral need triumphed and the *Deutsche Messe* (*DM*) was published in 1526. (English versions of *FM* and *DM* are in *Luther's Works*, vol 53, American edition, 1965. Original texts are in the Weimar edition: *FM*, vol 12; *DM*, vol 19.) It was designed especially for village churches and the unlettered majority. It was not intended to supplant the Latin mass in city churches or schools. (Portions of the Latin rite survived in parts of Germany into the eighteenth century.)

The basic structure of the *DM* is traditional, though greatly simplified. The prose texts of the ordinary were put in metrical paraphrase and assigned to the congregation. The popularity of this practice estranged large portions of Continental Lutheranism from the ancient mass texts. Again the *missa fidelium* is most altered: paraphrased Our Father, exhortation to communicants, words of institution and communion. There was an abortive attempt to divide the words of institution and distribute each element after its appropriate blessing. But the *DM* provided the people with a rite admirably suited to their needs and ability. The post-communion collect is one of Luther's finest prayers.

The Lutheran Reformation in Germany was scattered geographically. Since there was no unified church structure, there could be no liturgical equivalent of the BCP. Instead there was a proliferation of local *Kirchenordnungen*, most of whose liturgies were modelled after Luther. These church

orders fall into two major groups: the Brandenburg-Nürnberg type (*FM* as model) and the Bugenhagen type (*DM* as model) (original texts in E. Sehling (ed), *Die Evangelischen Kirchenordnungen des XVI. Jahrhunderts*, vols. 1–13, 16, 19). Johann Bugenhagen was one of Luther's emissaries to churches accepting the Reformation stance, and was responsible for the rites of many churches in Northern Germany and the Church of Denmark (1537). Liturgical development in Norway was tied to that in Denmark.

The Swedish liturgical tradition begins with the vernacular rite (1531) of Olavus Petri which follows the *FM* structure. The *Church Order* (1571) of Laurentius Petri was a revision which restored Latin texts in certain parts. After several abortive attempts at both left and right wing reform, the *Prayer Book* of 1614 was authorized. It followed the 1531 rite and established the *FM* tradition for the following three centuries.

By the eighteenth century, Lutherans were firmly established on the eastern seaboard of North America. Their worship reflected the languages and traditions of their various motherlands. But Henry Melchior Muhlenberg, patriarch of American Lutheranism, dreamed of the day when these groups could be united and have a common rite. Towards that end he produced a communion liturgy based upon several German models which was remarkable for its Reformation fullness. This German rite, together with English orders for baptism and marriage (from the BCP), constituted the first American liturgy. The first Lutheran communion service in English was not published until the mid-nineteenth century.

Generally, however, the eighteenth century was a time of liturgical decline affecting Lutheran churches everywhere. Pietism, with its anti-liturgical bias, and rationalism, which had little place for cultic action, took their toll. Liturgies were rationalized (employing deistic expressions), then psychologized as a passion for relevance set in. But by the mid-nineteenth century a neo-orthodox movement brought with it the glimmer of liturgical renewal. Wilhelm Löhe, a leader in establishing a female diaconate in the Bavarian church, joined other voices calling for a churchly and sacramental revival which would return the church to its own rich tradition. Because of his connection with mission pastors on the American frontier for whom he prepared a liturgy, Löhe's work was more directly influential there than in Germany.

The ecumenical Liturgical Movement* of the late nineteenth and early twentieth centuries resulted in various 'high church movements' throughout Lutheranism. But its enduring contribution was to stimulate a recovery of pre-eighteenth-century fullness. The various national and provincial churches on the Continent produced service books which re-established contact with their own Reformation traditions. Several groups in the USA began work on a Common Service which would exemplify the consensus of the 'best liturgies of the sixteenth century'. This setting formed the nucleus of the complete *Common Service Book* (with hymnal) of 1917. Subsequently the Common Service was incorporated into other North American service-books and became the common rite for a majority of English-speaking Lutherans.

As a result of early development and the impetus of the Second World War, the post-war years were marked by greater Lutheran unification and inter-Lutheran co-operation. *The Liturgy of the Church of Sweden* had already appeared in 1942, 1955 saw the publication of *Agenda 1* for the Lutheran Churches of Germany. *The Service Book and Hymnal* for about two-thirds of the Lutherans in North America appeared in 1958. Australian Lutherans brought out their *Orders of Service* in 1966, and in 1970 the *High Mass* for the Church of Norway was published. Lutheran churches in Africa, Asia and Latin America which were born in missionary movements tend to use liturgical books that mirror traditions of the sending churches. All these books mark the culmination of a long period of recovery of the Reformation tradition. They also symbolize the high degree of uniformity within major geographical areas and among them. Without its having been imposed by ecclesiastical authority, and allowing for different linguistic traditions, world Lutheranism has achieved a remarkable liturgical consensus.

The more recent liturgical books of the Lutheran communion reflect the growing consensus among the confessional

groupings of churches triggered by the liturgical reforms following Vatican II and the progress made in ecumenical dialogue. One example is the *Lutheran Book of Worship*, 1978, published by churches in North America following a ten year period of trial-use publications. Other examples are *Evangélikus Énekeskönyv*, 1982, of the church in Hungary and *Liturgie des dimanches et fêtes*, 1983, of the Lutheran churches in France. Studies toward new books and trial-use services are being produced in Sweden and Finland. The German churches are issuing supplementary materials to the earlier *Agende*. Liturgical work in Africa, Asia and Latin America tends to focus on issues of contextualization. Through its secretariat on worship, the Lutheran World Federation provides links between these various efforts.

Having reclaimed their liturgical identity, Lutherans are now stepping forward creatively beyond their Reformation tradition. By reintroducing fuller eucharistic prayers and, in some instances, more elaborated offertory sections, the eucharistic rites of the new books exhibit the convergence in structure and texts characteristic of the contemporary ecumenical scene. This is also true of new forms of baptism, ordination, the divine office, and the occasional services.

See also **Lutheran Worship.**

EUGENE BRAND

10. *Methodist.* Methodist communion liturgies are based on John Wesley's revision of the 1662 BCP rite as published in his *Sunday Service of the Methodists in North America* in 1784. As Wesley said, it was 'a liturgy little differing from that of the church of England'. Wesley is correct in saying that he made 'little alteration' in the book as a whole and especially with regard to the communion service. Most of the holy days were omitted, the word 'priest' was translated as 'elder' throughout, and the pronouns of the prayer of absolution changed from 'you' to 'us'. Service music was not expected and it was indicated that the *Gloria in excelsis* and the *Sanctus* were to be recited. Wesley expected that hymns would be sung and he and his brother, Charles, wrote 165 eucharistic hymns. A few changes were made in the rubrics, while the Nicene Creed, exhortations, and second post-communion prayer were dropped. One collect for the king was eliminated and the other changed to pray for 'the Supreme Rulers of these United States'. Only one word was omitted in the prayer of consecration, a redundant 'one'. Before the final blessing a significant new rubric appeared: 'Then the Elder, if he sees it expedient, may put up an Extempore Prayer.'

Wesley, it soon proved, was a poor judge of the old 'poor sheep in the wilderness' to whom the *Sunday Service* was directed. The year after his death in 1791 his book was drastically abbreviated to thirty-seven pages of 'Sacramental Services, &c.' in the 1792 *Discipline*. The people of the frontier had little learning and less love of what seemed to them overly formal types of worship. 'The Order for the Administration of the Lord's Supper' was drastically abbreviated, the whole synaxis* disappeared along with the prayer for the church, the comfortable words, the *Sursum corda*, and all proper prefaces. The collect for purity took the place formerly held by the *Sursum corda*. It was even provided that 'if the elder be straitened for time, he may omit any part of the service except the prayer of Consecration'. Actually, the Lord's Supper usually followed a preaching service, so a service of the word could be presumed. And few words in the eucharistic portion had been changed, perhaps none of the theological significance.

Only small changes were made in the next half century. In 1844 the Methodist Episcopal Church underwent a major split on the question of slavery, the Methodist Episcopal Church, South, and the Methodist Episcopal Church emerging. An earlier split had produced the Methodist Protestant Church in 1830 which published a communion service in 1831, a curiously scrambled version of the 1792 service. Changes in the communion service appeared in the *Discipline*, published every four years by each of the three main branches of Methodism.

The most important of these changes are mentioned here. The Southern Church remained the most conservative and made minor changes, none of great theological consequence, from what was left of the 1662 BCP rite. The Methodist Episcopal Church was less reluctant to change. Many minor changes appeared, especially in 1864 and

1916. The invention of pasteurized grape juice and the temperance movement became apparent in 1876 when 'unfermented juice of the grape' was first recommended in the rubrics (wine had always been used previously). The most important changes occurred in 1932 when a synaxis was recovered. The liberal theology of the time made some radical changes in the prayer of consecration and the prayer of humble access. With the reunion of Methodism in 1939 both the then current Northern and Southern services appeared in *The Methodist Hymnal*, though liturgically and theologically they had become distinct; the Northern service was more traditional liturgically and the Southern more traditional theologically. Both services were in the first (1944) *Book of Worship*.

A major revision occurred in the 1964 *Book of Worship*. The 1964 rite came just before the Post-Vatican II reforms and various factors led to the appearance of 'The Sacrament of the Lord's Supper' in 1972. Unexpectedly popular, it has largely replaced the traditional rite. Minor revisions were made in 1980 and 1984, and in 1984 the new rite became part of the official 'Ritual' in addition to the 1964 rite.

The reformed rite is in contemporary and inclusive language*. No longer is it simply a revision within the Anglican–Methodist traditions but establishes contact with the eucharist of Hippolytus as well as worldwide ecumenical developments. The three-fold lections are recovered, as well as a full eucharistic prayer on the Antiochene model. *At the Lord's Table* (1981) provides a collection of 22 eucharistic prayers for general, seasonal, and occasional use.

The communion rites of the black churches have been among the more conservative. The African Methodist Episcopal Church and the Christian Methodist Episcopal Church have retained essentially the 1792 service. Both also contain rubrics for the benefit of those who have scruples about kneeling, similar to those the two large white churches introduced during the nineteenth century but later removed.

In Britain Wesley's *Sunday Service* went through many editions, and then was succeeded by other books in the various branches into which Methodism became divided. After the union of 1932 came *The Book of Offices*, 1936. Then, after experimental drafts, came *The Methodist Service Book*, 1975. This book, much influenced by the liturgical movement, marks a return from the traditional Anglican–Methodist style to a more primitive pattern. The main service is called 'The Sunday Service' and the first general direction says 'The worship of the Church is the offering of praise and prayer in which God's Word is read and preached, and in its fullness it includes the Lord's Supper, or Holy Communion.' The service has the features which are common to most modern liturgies, e.g. three lessons, the intercessions in the form of a litany, a four-action shape for the Lord's Supper, with a prayer of thanksgiving which includes the mighty acts of God in creation and redemption in a long common preface. Special features are the placing of the Lord's prayer after the intercessions, and of the Nicene Creed between the peace and the setting of the table.

A further notable feature is an outline, somewhat in the manner of a directory, for 'The Sunday Service without the Lord's Supper'. This contains a prayer of thanksgiving and dedication for such occasions, which might be termed a 'dry anaphora'. Four others are provided in an appendix.

These services all address God as 'you', but the 1936 Holy Communion is also printed in *The Methodist Service Book*, 1975.

JAMES F. WHITE

11. *Old Catholic*. In the Old Catholic churches of the Utrecht Union, the celebration of the eucharist stands at the centre of liturgical life. Alongside that, however, the greatest emphasis is also placed on the proclamation of the word of God in the reading of scripture and in preaching. The celebration of the mass must therefore be supported by the two pillars of the service of the word of God and the liturgy of the sacrament.

In the Old Catholic churches, the whole service has for a long time (in some cases for almost a hundred years) been celebrated in the vernacular*. Some of these churches have been content with an accurate translation of the Latin text with very few deviations; this has been the case in the Netherlands and in the Polish National Catholic Church in the USA and in Poland.

Elsewhere, however, the Roman model has been treated with rather more freedom, and this has led to some theologically significant alterations; this has been the case above all in Switzerland, but the same thing has also happened in Germany and Austria. Nevertheless, even here the structure of the Roman mass remains clearly recognizable. It should be noted that the basis for the Old Catholic forms of mass is the *Missale Romanum* in its old form, as laid down by Pius V in 1570, and not the liturgy as revised after Vatican II. It can be seen, however, that some alterations were made to Old Catholic liturgies at an early stage which have only been introduced in the Roman Catholic church in the last few years (for the texts and books used today for celebrating mass in the Old Catholic churches *see* **Books, Liturgical** 11).

New ways of structuring the liturgy are still being investigated in the Old Catholic churches today. The Old Catholics of Germany received a new missal in 1959. In 1979 there was published a collection of nine eucharistic prayers, including a translation of the Taizé and modern Church of England canons, while in 1983 a new ordinary of the mass was issued with emphasis upon congregational participation. In Austria and Switzerland, attempts are being made with new formulae, especially for the canon of the mass. Even in the Church of the Netherlands, which until recently has been very conservative in liturgical matters, an experiment is now under way with a new 'second order of the mass'.

It is impossible here to indicate all the differences and peculiarities of the Old Catholic liturgies. The following are the most important points:

Service of the Word of God. In the German and Swiss liturgies the selection of biblical readings has been considerably increased. In Switzerland and in Germany there are now three readings (OT, epistle and gospel) for each mass in a three-year cycle; in Germany there are two (OT or epistle and gospel) in a four-year cycle.

*Creed**. The Western addition *filioque* is omitted, with particular concern for the close relationships with the Orthodox church.

Prayer of the Faithful. As in the revised Roman liturgy, the general intercessions, which had vanished from the Roman mass on every day except Good Friday, have been restored before the offertory.

*Offertory**. The prayers of the old Roman missal imply an anticipation of the epiclesis (*see* **Anaphora** 8) and consecration, elements which only belong in the canon. Even the notion of an offering of the as yet unconsecrated gifts (*'Suscipe ... hanc immaculatam hostiam, quam ... offero tibi'*) is rejected. The offertory prayers are therefore rightly limited, in one part of the Old Catholic liturgies, to the notions of the preparation of the gifts and thanksgiving.

*Prefaces**. The number of variable prefaces has been considerably increased in Old Catholic missals. The Altar Book of the Old Catholic Church of Germany (1959) contains 19 prefaces (Netherland 15, Austria 14).

*Canon**. The link between the *Sanctus* and the canon in Austria (second order) and in the Swiss outline of 1971 is made by a *Vere Sanctus* prayer on the Gallican pattern, as in the second and third formulations of the eucharistic prayer in the Roman *Ordo Missae* of 1969.

It is in the old Swiss liturgy that the canon has undergone the most significant transformation. Whereas in the Roman canon the account of the institution occupies the central place, here it is brought quite close to the beginning. The words of institution are followed by the anamnesis and the 'sacrificial prayer' (*Unde et memores*), which closes with a petition for a blessed communion (*Supplices te rogamus*). The 'remembrance of the saints' (*Communicantes*), the prayer for the dead (*Memento etiam*) and for the living (*Memento, Domine*) are brought together into a group.

In the Swiss canon, all expressions are avoided which might suggest that the eucharistic sacrifice was a repetition of the sacrifice of the cross or an offering by the priest. On the other hand, the position of Christ as the one high priest is strongly stressed (*see* Bishop Herzog in *IKZ*, 1911, pp.340ff. and Küry, *Die altkatholische Kirche*, pp.190–200).

Epiclesis. The Swiss liturgy has an explicit invocation of the Holy Spirit, *before* the institution, as in some of the oldest Egyptian liturgies and in the new texts of the Roman canon. This has partially been taken over into the German liturgy (first order) and the

Austrian missal of 1933. On the other hand, in the second Austrian order and the new Swiss order of 1971, the epiclesis follows the account of the institution as in present-day Eastern liturgies. This is also the case in the 'second order' of the Church of the Netherlands, which closely follows the eucharistic prayer of Hippolytus, and also in various new Old Catholic eucharistic prayers.

Lord's Prayer. In missals in German and French, the Lord's Prayer now appears in the agreed ecumenical text, which also contains the doxology as in the the Anglican order of the holy communion.

Breaking of the Bread. According to the German rite of 1959 (second order), this takes place during the singing of the *Agnus Dei.* Instead of the usual sequence of Lord's Prayer, breaking of the bread, the peace, *Agnus Dei*, we have here *Agnus Dei* with breaking of the bread, the peace, Lord's Prayer. All may exchange a sign of peace.

*Communion**. Whereas earlier the faithful only received communion on a few days in the year, it is now usually given at every mass and indeed in both forms, sometimes also by intinction*.

S. KRAFT/C. TOL

12. *Pentecostal.* In open-air meetings, worship and evangelistic services, black and white Pentecostal denominations follow the pattern of different Protestant traditions. In certain North American white Pentecostal denominations written liturgies have been developed along Protestant lines. Third World 'non-white indigenous churches' sometimes developed a liturgy which is similar to a high Anglican service. This is particularly true for certain groups of the Aladura Churches in West Africa. However, this Anglican liturgy is enriched with African elements. The most interesting liturgies in Pentecostalism are those of the eucharistic service, which is celebrated in British Pentecostal churches usually once a week, and in most of the other Pentecostal churches once a month. The eucharistic service has created some difficult problems for Pentecostals. Donald Gee (1891–1966), a British Pentecostal leader, warned against those Pentecostals who want the eucharist to be wholly unstructured. The result of this, he said, 'is to produce meetings so stereotyped that, for all their boasted freedom, they become more barren than the very liturgical services they deprecate – and with less aesthetic appeal' (*Study Hour* 5/2, 15 February 1946, p.2).

How is the problem solved? On the one hand a minority of Pentecostal churches use written liturgies as indicated above. In the majority of Pentecostal churches, on the other hand, an 'oral liturgy' is followed which consists of the classical liturgical elements: invocation, *Kyrie**, confession, *Gloria in excelsis*, eucharistic canon* and blessing. Yet these parts are never so named and for most observers not recognizable as such, since the elements which structure the different parts of the service are the so-called choruses, i.e. short spontaneous songs, known by heart by the whole congregation. Some of the key choruses indicate the transition from one part of the service to the next. They are intoned either by the minister (*see* **Ordination 12**) or by members of the congregation. Key choruses vary from one congregation to another, yet everyone in the congregation understands them as signals. During the time of participation of the whole congregation, if someone sings a song of praise in the *Kyrie* part, or gives a prophecy in the invocation part, he will be corrected either by the pastor, or by an elder, or if he persists, by the immediate and spontaneous singing of the whole congregation. Most Pentecostals are not aware of the liturgical function of these choruses, yet they are clearly observable.

The Pentecostals thus demonstrate that the alternative to a written liturgy is not chaos, but a flexible oral tradition, which allows for variation within the framework of the whole liturgical structure, similar to the possibilities of variation in a jam session of jazz musicians (*see* **Spirituals**).

For bibliography *see* **Pentecostal Worship**.

W. J. HOLLENWEGER

13. *Plymouth Brethren.* The Brethren's most distinctive meeting is the communion service normally held every Sunday morning. The communion table* is frequently placed in the centre, with the congregation seated in rows round three or four sides of it; where it is not convenient to rearrange the seating, the table will be left in front.

The first part of the service is devoted to

suitable hymns, prayers of thanksgiving and scripture readings, introduced or carried through by various members. Then the thanksgiving for the bread is followed by its distribution from hand to hand, each communicant breaking off a small piece and eating it. (The bread is usually an entire loaf, which may be broken in two before distribution.) The thanksgiving for the cup is followed by the passing of the common cup from hand to hand, each communicant drinking a little from it. The wine may be fermented or unfermented according to local preference. It is normally senior members of the church who give thanks for the bread and the cup. In the Exclusive tradition the same brother will give thanks for both elements on any one occasion, breaking the bread in two and pouring the wine into the cup before distribution. The practice of Open Brethren is more variable. Open Brethren customarily welcome all Christians present to communicate, in accordance with the Brethren's original policy.

The communion is followed either immediately or after some further exercises by the offering. Those who regard the offering as an integral part of the worship take it up in close proximity to the eucharist.

In many places the eucharist is followed by a short period of expository ministry; elsewhere this may be given in a separate service preceding the communion service.

Where the modern charismatic movement has exercised some influence there can be greater flexibility and spontaneity. Audible participation by women (except in congregational singing) is still exceptional, although their equal share in the common priesthood of believers is recognized in theory.

Among Exclusive Brethren of the late James Taylor's connection the liturgy is much more uniform. R. C. Walls, writing in *Theology* 60, 1957, pp.265f., 'A Visit to the Brethren – A Lesson in Liturgy', indicates the trinitarian sequence which would have been followed at that time in almost any of their assemblies throughout the world on any Sunday morning. An introductory hymn to the Holy Spirit was followed by a prayer of thanksgiving addressed to him and a lesson from Ephesians. The Son then became the focus of devotion in the eucharists which was accompanied by a long anamnesis (*see* **Anaphora** 7) or thanksgiving for his person and work from his incarnation through his passion, triumph and present high-priestly ministry and abiding presence to his parousia. This part of the service was concluded with a hymn of praise to the Son and a reading from the gospels. Then the worshippers claimed access to the Father, to whom a hymn of praise was sung, and after further devotions and silent intervals the service ended with a hymn to the Trinity. (Since then, the eucharist has been moved right to the beginning of the service.)

F. F. BRUCE

14. *Reformed.* Although the Reformed churches have been accused of neglecting the eucharist, their liturgies all stress its importance. The Reformers were unanimous in their aim to provide liturgies suitable to the new views on religion. Thus Zwingli produced two books entitled *De Canone Missae Epicheiresis* (1523) and *Action oder Bruch des Nachtmals* (1525). These were derived from the mass, but with all accretions removed. He provided separate orders for the ordinary preaching service without communion, and for the eucharist, which he regarded as another form of preaching. The order of the eucharist is simple – exhortation and fencing of the table, Lord's Prayer, prayer of humble access, the words of institution, fraction, communion first of the ministers and then of the people, a psalm (said, not sung), post-communion prayer and dismissal. There is no consecration prayer and no intercession. Celebration was only four times in the year. This rite had little influence on later developments.

Another rite with little influence was Farel's *La manyere et fasson* (Neuchâtel 1533), the first liturgy of the Reformed churches. The eucharist contains a long exhortation, Lord's Prayer, Apostles' Creed, institution narrative, the communion of all, post-communion prayer and dismissal.

The rite of John Calvin, *La forme des prières* (1542), was of much greater importance. It was derived from the Strasbourg Reformed German rite of Diebold Schwartz, which was derived from the mass. It was greatly simplified through the in-

fluence of Bucer. For Calvin the correct procedure was a preaching service followed by the eucharist. The full order was as follows: scripture sentence, confession of sins, metrical psalm (sung), prayer for illumination, lesson, sermon; intercessions, Lord's Prayer (an uninspiring paraphrase), preparation of elements, Apostles' Creed, words of institution, exhortation, consecration prayer, fraction and delivery (during communion, psalm sung or read or scripture lesson), read post-communion prayer, Aaronic blessing.

This form was somewhat bare, but Calvin was prevented from carrying out all his desires. Thus he regarded weekly communion as scriptural, and therefore essential, but the Genevan magistrates allowed it only quarterly. However, the form has had great influence on all succeeding Reformed liturgies. Of these there were many varieties in the Reformed churches in Switzerland, France, Holland and elsewhere. From time to time suggestions for revision were made, and of these two may be noticed.

In 1713, Jean-Frédéric Osterwald published a liturgy. He had already expressed an aversion from Calvinism and his good opinion of Anglicanism, but his proposals, influenced by these feelings, were too radical for general acceptance. The revision proposals of Eugène Bersier (1874) had more influence. He desired to give the eucharist 'the central place which is its due in Christian worship' and thus to 'return to the true primitive teaching of our Reformed Church'. The eucharist was to follow (as if not an essential part of) the morning service. The minister, after dismissing those who were not to communicate, descends from the pulpit and, standing before the table, addresses the people who group themselves as near the table as possible. Then he goes behind the table, uncovers the bread and wine, and prays. *Sursum corda* and the consecration prayer follow. 'It is verily right, just and salutary . . .' The prayer includes *Sanctus* and *Hosanna* and words suited to the season of the Christian year. There is an epiclesis, followed by the words of institution, fraction, Lord's Prayer, the distribution, thanksgiving and dismissal. Much of this has been found acceptable in France, and the liturgy of 1958 follows many points of this form. The consecration prayer includes thanksgiving, *Sanctus*, epiclesis, Lord's Prayer, Apostles' Creed, words of institution, followed by communion, thanksgiving and blessing. A revision of 1963 has a new eucharistic prayer, which shows some dependence on the liturgy of the Church of South India (*see* **Church of South India Worship**).

The Reformed rites of some other countries have been of interest. Several of the Swiss cantons, such as Vaud (1940), Geneva (1946) and Bern (1955), have issued revised liturgies, influenced both by the earlier Reformed rites and by the classic forms. In Germany and Holland there has been much liturgical work. The two Dutch groups, *Liturgische Kring* and *Kring Eeredienst*, have been specially active, and the *Kanselboek* (1949) and *Dienstboek* (1955) express concern for congregational participation in responses and allow many alternatives.

The Genevan rite of 1556, known as *John Knox's Genevan Service Book*, was the first Reformed rite in English. It was adopted, with only slight changes, by the Church of Scotland in 1562 under the title, *The Forme of Prayers and Ministration of the Sacrament*. In 1564 it became *The Form of Prayers or Book of Common Order*, but with some additions, especially in the completion of the metrical psalter. The full eucharistic order here was as follows: confession of sins and prayer for pardon, metrical psalm, prayer for illumination, lesson, sermon, thanksgiving and intercession, Lord's Prayer, Apostles' Creed, offertory, words of institution (i.e., the warrant), exhortation, consecration prayer (including adoration, thanksgiving for creation and redemption, anamnesis and doxology), fraction and delivery (minister's communion followed by the people's), post-communion thanksgiving, Ps. 103, Aaronic or apostolic blessing. This form lacks an epiclesis, but contemporary evidence shows that one was included in the consecration and was regarded by many as essential. This form remained generally in Scottish use from 1564, many editions being published. Some editions were printed in England or on the Continent for the use of English Puritans. *The Book of Common Order* was superseded by the *Westminster Directory* in 1645.

The *Directory*, as a compromise between the Independents and the Scottish and

English Presbyterians, was rather unsatisfactory, but it remained and indeed still remains an authority for public worship. There are no prayers, but only lists of subjects for prayer. The eucharistic order is little changed, but an epiclesis is now prescribed. During the eighteenth century the standard of worship in Scotland, as elsewhere, fell very low, with the loss of the Creed, Lord's Prayer, *Gloria Patri*, and the people's amen.

By the opening of the nineteenth century some ministers had begun to publish books of their own. In 1867 the Church Service Society was formed, and soon published *Euchologion*, a service book which was revised in many editions, the tenth being published in 1919. The Order for Communion combined Catholic elements in a Reformed framework, and though there was some development of these elements in subsequent editions, the framework remained unmistakably Reformed. Following the service of the word, and the prayer after the sermon, came an exhortation (fencing), the words of institution as warrant, an address, the Nicene Creed (in earlier editions, the Apostles'), *Agnus Dei*, prayer of access, *Sursum corda*, thanksgiving, anamnesis, *Sanctus*, epiclesis, Lord's Prayer, fraction, distribution, pax, exhortation, thanksgiving and self-dedication, intercession for the church, thanksgiving for the church triumphant, hymn, benediction.

The communion service in *Euchologion* lies behind subsequent services, notably *Prayers for Divine Service* (1923) and *The Book of Common Order* (1940). The United Free Church of Scotland in 1928 issued its *Book of Common Order*, which was the fruit of a similar liturgical movement. Its influence is seen in one of the Orders in *The Book of Common Order* (1940). That book contained five communion orders, of different lengths and for different occasions, including one for 'A Second Table' which proposed the distribution of elements already consecrated. The book had wide influence on other Presbyterian service books, in England, Wales, Ireland, Canada, Australia and elsewhere. It represented a particular ideal of worship, but never its general practice in Scotland, though it influenced that practice considerably.

The Committee on Public Worship and Aids to Devotion of the Church of Scotland issued *The Book of Common Order* (1979), which contains three communion orders, including one in modern English. The main innovation here is that in all three it is proposed that the words of institution be read as part of the prayer, rather than as a warrant. The General Assembly in 1980 made it clear 'that their use as a warrant continues to be normal usage in the Church of Scotland'.

The Book of Common Order (1979) contains the outline (and nothing more) of a service 'when the Lord's Supper is not celebrated'. This is considered as an exception: the norm proposed is communion every Sunday. Communion is celebrated more frequently than formerly in many parishes, but the general practice of the church remains very far from what is suggested in the service book.

Here the Scottish book is following *The Worshipbook* (1970), prepared by a joint committee of three Presbyterian churches (two of which have now united) in the USA. Here 'The Service for the Lord's Day' is the communion service, and the service 'when the Lord's Supper is omitted' is treated as an exception. The book employs 'the straightforward use of words and language in current contemporary use', and therefore the words of some new translations have been employed for scriptural quotations. The 'Liturgy of the Word' includes confession of sin, declaration of pardon, prayer for illumination, lessons, sermon with ascription, Nicene Creed (using 'we'). The 'Liturgy of the Faithful' includes intercessions, pax, the offering, invitation to the table, thanksgiving (with *Sursum corda*, the seasonal preface, *Tersanctus*, Lord's Prayer), fraction, distribution, post-communion prayer, hymn, benediction. Supplemental liturgical resources are being added, and the hymnbook has been designed to reinforce the liturgical order. (*See* **Presbyterian Worship**.)

All Presbyterian books are for voluntary use, and even where used there are many variations introduced by individual ministers. In many places books are not used at all, but the prejudice against 'read prayers' is no longer general. It is in the sacraments and ordinances of the church that the books have had most influence. Many or most Reformed churches now have stand-

ing committees charged with the study of worship and the preparation of forms for specific occasions. The study has become ecumenical, and those involved claim that an 'ecumenical consensus' is emerging. At the same time there is much experiment by those who wish to find forms that will be less traditional and more related to the modern world.

See also **Reformed Worship**.

J. A. LAMB / JAMES A. WHYTE

15. *Seventh-day Adventist*. In the Seventh-day Adventist Church the communion service includes the ordinance of foot-washing or humility and the Lord's Supper. Adventists believe that in washing his disciples' feet Christ instituted a consecrated ordinance, a religious service with a promise of blessedness (John 13.14–17). It is a memorial of Christ's act of self-abasement and a symbol or type of higher cleansing. Like early church fathers such as Origen, pioneer Adventists considered foot-washing a spiritual experience and a symbol of humility. It was sometimes referred to as Christ's 'least commandment' (*Day-Star*, 7.8, 18 August 1845). While baptism is a symbol of justification once and for all, the daily experience of sanctification is represented by foot-washing. 'This ordinance is Christ's appointed preparation for the sacramental service' (E. G. White, *The Desire of Ages*, 1946, p.650). For this reason Adventists often call this ordinance the 'preparatory service'. It is a time for self-examination, confession of sin and reconciling of differences. Two emblems are used: water, symbol of cleansing, and towel, symbol of service. Some regard the ordinance of humility as a 'miniature baptism' (*see* John 13.10).

Adventist churches have a communion table*, not an altar*. The Lord's Supper is not a mystery but a memorial, not a sacrifice but a sacred service. Its theme is salvation through the sacrifice of Christ on Calvary. It is a memorial of the deliverance from the power of sin and as such is a continual reminder of the atonement. It also has an eschatological orientation pointing forward to the parousia and is designed to keep this hope vivid (Matt. 26.29; I Cor. 11.26).

Adventists believe in the real spiritual presence of Christ at the supper, but not in the elements as such. 'As faith contemplates our Lord's great sacrifice, the soul assimilates the spiritual life of Christ ... The Service forms a living connection by which the believer is bound up with Christ' (White, op.cit., p.661).

In most Adventist churches the communion service is held once a quarter. In early Adventist history the Lord's Supper was a regular part of the 'quarterly meeting'. While other aspects of this meeting have largely faded away, communion is still sometimes called in Adventist parlance the 'quarterly service'.

The opening service may be as usual for divine worship, but the sermon is limited to 10–15 minutes and deals with some aspect of the communion service. The congregation then separates for the ordinance of humility, the men in one place and the women in another. Hymns may occasionally be sung during its progress.

After the foot-washing, the congregation reassembles for the Lord's Supper. The minister and elder (or elders) take their places by the table on which the deaconesses* have previously placed the unleavened bread and unfermented wine, covered by a white linen cloth (*see* 1 Cor. 5.7, 8). After a hymn the minister (in some churches the deaconesses) removes and folds the linen covering. Then he reads I Cor. 11.23, 24 or a parallel passage from the gospels, after which the blessing of God is asked on the emblem of the bread, representing the body of Christ, while the whole congregation kneels (in some churches only the officiating minister and elders kneel, while the congregation remains seated with bowed heads). Following the breaking of the bread by the officiating minister, the deacons* serve the congregation and, after returning, the minister serves them; then in turn one of the deacons, taking the plate, serves the minister. All are seated and silent prayer is offered while they partake of the bread together.

The minister then reads 1 Cor. 11.25, 26 or a similar passage from the gospels. The blessing is asked on the emblem of the wine, representing the shed blood of Christ, and the deacons serve the congregation following a similar procedure as with the bread. For health reasons the recommended and prevailing practice in Seventh-Day Adventist churches is to use small, indi-

vidual communion cups.

The remaining emblems are recovered and after the service the deaconesses clear the table and the deacons dispose of any bread or wine left over, by burning the bread and pouring out the wine.

In the Seventh-day Adventist Church only ordained ministers or ordained local church elders may conduct the communion service. Adventist practice 'open communion', believing that Christ's own example forbids exclusiveness at his table (*see* Matt. 26.21–25).

B. B. BEACH

K. Amon, 'Das eucharistische Hochgebet in den altkatholischen Kirchen des deutschen Sprachgebiets', *Liturgisches Jahrbuch* 18, 1968; A. Baumstark, *Comparative Liturgy*, 1958; F. E. Brightman, *Liturgies Eastern and Western*, 1896; Yngve Brilioth, *Eucharistic Faith and Practice*, 1930; R. Bruinsma, 'Christ's Commandment of Humility', *The Ministry*, July 1966, pp.24–6 (Seventh-day Adventist); C. O. Buchanan (ed), *The Development of the New Eucharistic Prayers of the Church of England*, 1979; *Eucharistic Liturgies of Edward VI*, 1983; *Modern Anglican Liturgies 1958–68*, 1968; *Further Anglican Liturgies 1968–75*, 1975; *Latest Anglican Liturgies 1975–1984*, 1985; *What did Cranmer think he was doing?*, [2]1982; R. H. Connolly, *The Liturgical Homilies of Narsai*, 1909; J. D. Crichton, *The Church's Worship: Considerations on the Liturgical Constitution of the Second Vatican Council*, 1964; G. J. Cuming, *He Gave Thanks: An Introduction to the Eucharistic Prayer*, 1981; *Hippolytus: A Text for Students*, [3]1984; *A History of Anglican Liturgy*, [2]1982; G. Dix, *The Shape of the Liturgy*, [2]1945; Paul Graff, *Geschichte des Auflösung der alten gottesdienstlichen Formen in der Evangelischen Kirche Deutschlands*, 2 vols. 1921, 1939; A. Hänggi and I. Pahl, *Prex Eucharistiea*, 1968; M. J. Hatchett, *Commentary on the American Prayer Book*, 1979; H. Holloway, *A Study of the Byzantine Liturgy*, 1933; R. C. D. Jasper and G. J. Cuming, *Prayers of the Eucharist Early and Reformed*, 1980; C. Jones, G. Wainwright and E. Yarnold (eds), *The Study of Liturgy*, 1978; J. Jungmann, *The Mass of the Roman Rite*, 2 vols, 1951–55; T. Klauser, *A Short History of the Western Liturgy*, 1969; C. Kucharek, *The Byzantine–Slav Liturgy of St John Chrysostom*, 1971; U. Küry, *Die altkatholische Kirche* (Kirchen der Welt, Band III), 1966; M. Luther, 'Liturgy and Hymns', *Works*, vol 53, 1965; *Manual for Ministers* (Seventh-day Adventists), 1977; C. F. D. Moule, *Worship in the New Testament*, [2]1983; Don F. Neufeld (ed), 'Lord's Supper', 'Foot Washing', *Seventh-day Adventist Encyclopaedia*, 1966, pp.414–6, 720–2; Ernest A. Payne and Stephen F. Winward, *Orders and Prayers for Church Worship*, 1960 (Baptist); N. F. Pease, *And Worship Him*, 1967, pp. 76–8 (Seventh-day Adventist); K. Pursch, 'Das Opfermahl und die Neuordnung seiner Gestalt', *IKZ* 46, 1956; K. Pursch, 'Die Probleme des Offertoriums und Versuche zu ihrer Lösung', *IKZ* 46, 1956; Luther D. Reed, *The Lutheran Liturgy*, rev ed 1959; A. E. Rüthy, 'Bemerkungen und Erwägungen zu den altkatholischen Liturgien', a series of articles in *IKZ* 47–60, 1957–70; S. Salaville, *Introduction to the Study of Eastern Liturgies*, 1938; Emil Schling (ed), *Die Evangelischen Kirchenordnungen des 16. Jahrhunderts*, vols. 1–5, 1902–1913; vols 6 and 11, 1955–1961; *Seventh-day Adventist Church Manual*, 1981, pp.115–21; L. Sheppard (ed), *True Worship*, 1963; John E. Skoglund, *A Manual of Worship*, 1968 (Baptist); J. H. Srawley, *The Early History of the Liturgy*, 1947; R. F. Taft, *The Liturgy of the Great Church*, Dumbarton Oaks Papers 34–35, 1980–81; James F. White, *Sacraments as God's Self Giving*, 1983; *John Wesley's Sunday Service*, 1984; B. J. Wigan (ed), *Liturgy in English*, 1964 (this contains virtually all Anglican eucharistic texts from 1549 to 1960); L. Winterswyl, 'Das eucharistische Hochgebet der altkatholischen Liturgien', *IKZ* 24, 1934.

Local Preacher

An office (open to both men and women in the Methodist Church) instituted by John Wesley to provide, as the name implies, a local ministry to supplement that of the few itinerant ordained clergymen who joined his movement initially. The ministry is a 'part-time' one, being exercised normally by a layman with a secular job. A local preacher regularly conducts Sunday worship and appears on the preaching plan. He does not normally celebrate the eucharist*, though there are cases where a layman may be specially authorized by Conference to do so

if a congregation might otherwise be almost totally deprived of the sacrament. Baptism* may also be administered by a local preacher or other layman in very exceptional circumstances.

P. HINCHLIFF

Lord's Prayer, The

Not surprisingly, the Lord's Prayer has come to be used universally and frequently in liturgical worship. It was not always so, however; its use at the eucharist*, for example, does not antedate the middle of the fourth century at the earliest, being first clearly attested in the *Mystagogical Catecheses* of Cyril of Jerusalem. From John Chrysostom onwards, liturgical commentators in the East witness to its use after the eucharistic prayer (*see* **Anaphora**) as a preparation for communion*; Augustine and Ambrose presuppose its use at the same place and for the same purpose in the West at about the same time. Since about 400 it has been so used in all the historic liturgies, and in many others as well; it is only in some of the post-Reformation Protestant rites that it has been removed from this position and function, and placed elsewhere. Early commentators stress its suitability for this purpose, laying emphasis on the petitions for the forgiveness of sins and, above all, for daily – or, rather, arguing from the alternative reading, heavenly – bread: Ambrose advocates frequent communion on the ground of the relationship between the two texts.

In most of the historic rites the Lord's Prayer is placed after the breaking of the bread which follows the eucharistic prayer; in the two most widespread of them, however, the Roman and the Byzantine, it precedes the breaking of the bread, the Roman usage in this respect being probably a Byzantine importation.

The use of the Lord's Prayer in a quasi-liturgical context outside the eucharistic liturgy probably antedates its use in the latter; certain early writers prescribe it as the essential prayer to be used by the faithful at set hours of prayer. Its use in the divine office*, which is universal in the historic rites as well as in most of the post-Reformation liturgies, presumably originates in this prescription.

In English-speaking countries, efforts have been made to substitute a 'modern' translation of the Lord's Prayer for the 'traditional' one, which, with minor variations, has been universally used since the sixteenth century. The form produced by the International Consultation on English Texts (ICET) at one time seemed likely to win widespread support, but in fact its success has turned out to be very limited, even in those churches which have happily adopted other ICET texts: the Roman Catholic Church has so far retained the 'traditional' text, albeit with the ICET doxology at mass, an inconsistent and inelegant compromise; other churches (e.g. the Church of England in the ASB) have adopted texts based on that of ICET, but differing from it in various ways, thus frustrating the aim of establishing a new common text; and often (as in the ASB and the new American BCP) even where one of these has been provided, permission has had to be given to substitute the 'traditional' text where it is desired. In so far as the latter is the one prayer-text known by heart by large numbers of those who still know any prayer at all by heart, there appear to be major difficulties in the way of establishing any alternative version.

C. Jones, G. Wainwright and E. Yarnold (eds), *The Study of Liturgy*, 1978, using the index under 'Lord's Prayer'; J. A. Jungmann, *The Mass of the Roman Rite*, II, 1955, pp.277–93; C. Kucharek, *The Byzantine–Slav Liturgy of St John Chrysostom*, 1971, pp.653–7.

W. JARDINE GRISBROOKE

Lord's Supper, The

1. This title was used in the patristic period of the Last Supper, e.g. by Hippolytus.

2. It was also employed by Paul (I Cor. 11.20) of the central act of Christian worship, which when he was writing would appear to have consisted of a repetition of the Last Supper in its entirety, i.e. blessing, breaking and distribution of bread, followed by a meal and concluded with the blessing and distribution of wine.

3. In the fourth century, it was the practice on Maundy Thursday*, in commemoration of the institution of the sacrament on that day, to combine the agape or love feast* with the eucharist, and this, too, was known as the Lord's Supper.

4. The separation of eucharist and agape

and the discontinuance of the latter led to the title Lord's Supper being applied to the sacrament alone. This use was widespread in the Middle Ages and the Catechism of Trent endorsed it. The Reformers favoured the title because of its scriptural basis and so, e.g. in the 1549 BCP, the service is headed: 'The Supper of the Lorde and the Holy Communion, commonly called the Masse'.

EDITOR

Love Feast

There is little doubt that a common meal with at least semi-liturgical features was regularly held by Christians shortly after the death of Jesus, or that it combined observances which were later separated to become on the one hand the agape or love feast, and on the other the eucharist* or holy communion*. Such meals were a common feature both of pagan and of Jewish circles, and regulations for that observed by the Qumran sect are found in their *Manual of Discipline*. Dom Gregory Dix makes a strong case for the Christian meal being a variant of a typical *chaburah* or formal fellowship meal of pious Jewish friends. The early Christians seem to have met for this purpose weekly on the evening of 'the Lord's Day'. The term 'Lord's Supper'* may well have been applied both to the occasion as a whole and also to its major components, the meal itself and the liturgical commemoration of the Lord's living presence which accompanied it. Both agape and embryonic eucharist emphasized the fact that his followers constituted a community in spiritual fellowship both with each other and with their risen Lord. Associated with the meal was the distribution of food to the needy, especially widows. The technical term eventually reserved for the meal among the Greek-speaking Christians was agape, literally 'a love'. In other words it was an occasion for the display and growth of God-centred Christian love as opposed to merely human eros or philia. Among the Latin-speaking Christians this became caritas, 'charity', a word whose meaning degenerated (as did the love feast itself) from an expression of the purest of emotions to the social activities which normally demonstrated that emotion, but which could too easily be divorced from it and be regarded as self-sufficient.

Unambiguous evidence about the love feast in the NT is scanty. It is quite clear, however, that throughout his ministry Jesus stressed the importance both of meals in general, especially the evening meal, or supper, and the banquet with invited guests – a favourite symbol of his messiahship. He taught his disciples to pray for food. He was even chided for his emphasis upon eating and drinking (Matt. 11.18f.; cf. 9.10–15). Not only the apostles but two anonymous followers who met the risen Lord on the road to Emmaus were apparently familiar with some idiosyncrasy in his prayer and breaking of bread at such meals (Luke 24.30f.). At one of his last recorded appearances he presided over a meal with seven disciples by the Sea of Galilee, a meal climaxed by a threefold emphasis alike upon agape and upon the pastoral feeding of the Christian flock (John 21.1–17). The 'breaking of bread' was linked with the sharing of goods and temple worship as a distinctive feature of the earliest church (Acts 2.41–47).

In Paul's classic description of the eucharist in I Cor. 11.17–34, a common meal either precedes or is inseparably linked with a more liturgical celebration. Paul's words show, however, that already abuses were creeping in, the table-fellowship occasionally being marred by examples of gluttony and drunkenness. The same was true a generation or two later when Jude wrote – the only undoubted use of the term agape (in the plural) in the NT: 'These men are a blot on your love feasts, where they eat and drink without reverence' (v.12, NEB). Without a familiar background of Jewish piety in the *chaburah* such meals could easily become assimilated to the less restrained pagan banquets, and joy in the fellowship of the risen Lord and his followers could deteriorate into unbridled joy in food and wine, with an emphasis upon variety and luxury such as encouraged gluttony, pride and selfishness. It is sadly clear that this indeed happened, even during the apostolic age, and apparently formed the chief reason for separating the liturgical celebration of a commemorative token meal (the eucharist) from a genuine meal (the agape). Overlapping and some mutual influence continued, however. The need was constantly felt to urge moderation even in the separated agape, which gradually developed its

own distinctive rituals, differing from area to area.

The *Didache* preserves the prayers associated with the Eastern agape early in the second century, probably in Syria. It contains groups of prayers to be used by the presiding minister before and after the meal, together with congregational responses, which rang the changes on the theme of 'To thee be glory for ever', the final petition being the Aramaic *Maranatha*, 'Our Lord, come!' Tertullian's *Apology* (*c.* AD 197) reveals the rite as it was practised in Carthage and probably in Rome – a genuine meal, to which the poor were invited, begun and ended with prayer. The meal was followed with scripture reading, spiritual discourse, the singing of hymns, and apparently an opportunity for individual testimonies of some kind. The *Apostolic Tradition* of Hippolytus shows that in Rome by the third century the agape was celebrated in private homes, guests being invited by the host, though a minister was always present to 'say grace' and to offer a spiritual exhortation. The guests were urged to 'eat sufficiently, but so that there may remain something over that your host may send it to whomsoever he wills, as the superfluity of the saints, and he [to whom it is sent] may rejoice with what is left over' (Dix). The guests were also urged to pray for their host. Strong evidence exists that the agape gradually came to be assimilated with pagan funeral banquets, which were thus transformed both into occasions for feeding the poor and into symbolic representations of the messianic banquet, a foretaste of the joys of heaven. Conciliar rulings show that from the fourth century onwards the possibility and actuality of abuse, combining with a more formal approach to church life, had steadily undermined the ancient fellowship meal, at least as an official element in Western worship. In the Eastern church the agape lingered on for two or three centuries more.

By the eighth century the agape seems to have been almost universally defunct apart from vestigial remains whose origins were forgotten and occasional survivals in out-of-the-way sects. Vestiges are probably to be seen in the offertory for the poor at holy communion, in the distributions to the poor on Maundy Thursday*, and (in Eastern Churches only) in the distribution of pieces of unconsecrated bread after the eucharist. One example of what appears to be a genuine survival (albeit indirect) is to be found among the Christians of St Thomas in Southern India. Another was probably among the Paulicians of Armenia, who may in turn have sown some of the seed which eventually led to the revival of the love feast among the Moravians (*see* **Moravian Worship**).

Along with the Protestant Reformation went a somewhat self-conscious attempt among several pietistic sects to reproduce the actual customs as well as the spirit of the primitive church. Although the details and the dimensions of this process are difficult to recover, it appears that this imitation of the early church combined with the vestigial remains of the agape to foster the modern love feast in some western European communities such as the Mennonites, the German Baptist Brethren (or 'Dunkers'), and the Moravians, frequently allied with the kiss of peace and the ceremonial washing of feet. Encouraged by Pietism, the love feast flourished especially during the eighteenth century in Germany and the Netherlands, and was imported to America by the more zealous (and therefore the more persecuted) members of those bodies.

Although the ancient agape thus survived or was revived during modern times in various small sects, the mainstream denominations were hardly affected until John Wesley introduced it to his societies. In his own search for spiritual renewal by means of imitating primitive Christianity, Wesley was greatly impressed by the Moravian love feast as he experienced it both as a missionary in Georgia and as a pilgrim to Herrnhut in Germany. In 1738 he transplanted it to British soil. Convinced as he was of the stabilizing and stimulating power of Christian fellowship, he moulded the love feast into a climactic concentration of the more subdued fellowship of the band meeting and (later) the class meeting. The love feast became the occasion par excellence when after the symbolic sharing of a token family meal the assembled members of several classes and possibly of several societies would take turns in testifying to their Christian experience as they were so moved by the Holy Spirit. New converts especially were encouraged to speak of the change wrought in them, and their testi-

monies frequently led to further conversions. Charles Wesley put his genius to work in composing special hymns for these occasions, though strangely enough there was never a distinct love feast collection. At first Methodist love feasts were held monthly, but after a time this gave place to a quarterly, and later still to an annual, celebration, which thus tended to become the more momentous. Enthusiastic Methodists assembling from a wide area rarely failed to experience a spiritual blessing, and the love feast became one of the more exciting events in the Methodist year, to which the general public sought entry, out of curiosity if not always from spiritual expectancy. The fact that these were private gatherings, to which admittance was secured by the possession of a current class ticket or a special note from the itinerant preacher, encouraged scurrilous rumours about immoral practices, though these were readily refuted as without foundation.

When Methodists emigrated they took with them (among other practices) their love feast, so that the Methodist variant became familiar in many parts of the British Commonwealth, as in America. The British offshoots of Wesley's Methodism also adapted the observance. During the nineteenth century, however, with the growing church-consciousness of the Methodist societies, and a consequent lessening of the emphasis upon the conversion experience, as also upon the class meeting and the prayer meeting, the spiritual testimonies at the love feasts lost much of their colourful spontaneity, while the more liturgical element was not by itself sufficient to retain popular adherence. Throughout World Methodism the love feast died out except for a few local survivals and an annual observance in some Methodist Conferences.

During the middle years of the twentieth century there was a revival of interest in and practice of the love feast, both aspects linked closely with the ecumenical movement (*see* **Ecumenical Worship**). The eucharist had proved the greatest symbol of Christian unity on the theoretical level but of disunity on the practical level. Many Christians were therefore grasping at straws, sacramental substitutes which might afford visible proof to the world that divided denominations were in fact one in spirit, even in a symbolic meal akin to the Lord's Supper, and indeed a collateral descendant from the same primitive stock. Thus there was a period of experimentation with interdenominational fellowship in another symbolic commemorative meal which because of a different theological focus and comparative disuse had not become so hedged around with inhibitions and prohibitions.

In *Christian Worship* (1961) T. S. Garrett had spoken of modern revivals of the love feast such as 'the parish breakfast following the parish communion', including a Cambridge college occasion when the breaking of pieces from a loaf was accompanied by the recital of a passage from the *Didache*. He also told of Christian festivals in Tamil villages, historically linked with non-Christian festivities, yet in fact called 'love feasts' and having genuine spiritual links with the primitive agape (p.43). It was also realized that in a sense the 'faith tea' of British churches and the 'covered dish supper' or 'home-coming' meal of American churches might similarly be regarded as modern forms of the love feast.

Sporadic or regular celebrations of love feasts as occasions for Christian fellowship continue to appear, not only among Moravians and Methodists, but even Baptists – like that introduced on 24 May 1984, in a congregation founded by Charles Haddon Spurgeon, East Hill Baptist Church, London. In Highland United Methodist Church, Raleigh, North Carolina, 1980 witnessed the beginning of a Christmas Eve Love Feast, when spoken testimonies were replaced by the coming forward of individuals for silent prayer at the altar, while the congregation sang Christmas carols. This observance was grafted on to the former tradition of an annual candle lighting service, very happily so in view of the fact that the early agape was normally an evening meal, frequently associated with the ceremonial bringing in of lamps and a special thanksgiving to God as the creator of light.

Much more self-conscious revivals took place a generation ago, however, having an avowedly ecumenical intention. After lengthy preparations the two denominations represented in the parish of Hilgay, Norfolk, England – Anglicans and

Methodists – came together on Maundy Thursday, 1949, and again on Wednesday in Holy Week, 1951, to celebrate a love feast combining liturgical elements deliberately representing churches both Eastern and Western, both primitive and modern. The issue was taken up by the Friends of Reunion, and discussed in successive issues of their *Bulletin*, attracting correspondence from many parts of the world. The instigator, the Revd Ian Thomson, claimed that this was 'a serious attempt to break a deadlock that has long existed between separated churches'.

The Ecumenical Institute organized at the Chateau de Bossey in Switzerland by the World Council of Churches for years treated the last meal of its course there as an agape, when the participants were urged 'to express, by a symbolical act, the reality of our unity'. A revival of the agape in Holland linked Catholics and Protestants in a joint search for unity. From the initial gathering attended by 800 people of all ages and denominations in The Hague, on the Friday evening before Pentecost in 1961, the movement spread to other places. This 'pre-eucharistic' meal, emphasizing the desire and need for fuller Christian unity around the Lord's table, aroused such enthusiasm that in 1965 the bishops of Holland found it necessary to issue directives about such 'agape celebrations'. They spoke thus: 'The conscious intention of the agape celebration is to act in the service of that unity of which the eucharist is the decisive sign and the highest sacramental expression.'

It may well be that this enthusiasm for the agape as a possible means for breaking an impasse in interdenominational relations played a significant part in fostering the new spirit of resolve and expectancy in the church universal. Certainly a new ecumenical generation has arisen which has little time for substitutes, but confidently envisages genuine intercommunion* this century. The greater cause, however, was surely the ebullient churchmanship of Pope John XXIII and his summoning in 1963 of the Second Vatican Council. In true succession to this was the revision of the constitution of the World Council of Churches at Nairobi in 1975, which insisted that its first function was 'to call the churches to the goal of visible unity in one faith and in one eucharistic fellowship expressed in worship and common life in Christ, and to advance towards that unity in order that the world may believe'. Another major step along this road was the important document, *Baptism, Eucharist, and Ministry*, prepared by the Council's Commission on Faith and Order, meeting in Lima, Peru, and presented in 1983 to the World Council of Churches at its meeting in Toronto. One of the participants, Professor J. Robert Nelson, reported at Emory University, shortly after his return, that whereas at most ecumenical conferences the delegates had often 'felt most divided at worship', on this occasion 'the throngs of people manifested an almost palpaple oneness', and that no other session could equal 'the doxological ecstasy which caught up the three thousand or more who celebrated the Holy Communion according to the new 'Lima Liturgy', over which the Archbishop of Canterbury presided.'

In a climate so positive in its surge towards intercommunion, it is clearly very unlikely that the love feast will any longer be stressed in ecumenical circles, even as a major catalyst of Christian unity. Nevertheless it may well prove an auxiliary means of making visible our increasing Christian love for those in other denominations. This was expressly the design of what was probably the first Moravian–Methodist love feast to be held since that well-known occasion on 1 January 1739, in Fetter Lane, London, described in John Wesley's *Journal*, which lasted about six hours, and ended with a united chorus of *Te Deum Laudamus*. In Bethlehem, Pennsylvania, Moravians and Methodists met in a joint conference to celebrate the bicentennial of American Methodism, and the spiritual highlight was a love feast in the Central Moravian Church on 26 October 1984. Bishops and other officials of both churches, together with about three hundred members of both communions from all over the United States, ceremonially drank cups of coffee and ate sweet buns brought down the aisles by white-robed Moravian ladies, while a united choir, supported by organist and trumpets, accompanied the congregation or choir in fifteen hymns and anthems drawn from various denominations, but especially their joint treasures, including, of course, the traditional grace

by John Cennick (successively a Methodist and a Moravian), and too frequently attributed to Wesley, 'Be present at our table, Lord.'

For this kind of agape, a genuine expression of Christian love in a symbolic meal, without the gluttony and pride which ruined it for the early church, and without the modern tinsel glitter of an artificial ecumenical tokenism, there is surely a place today in at least some Christian communities.

Frank Baker, *Methodism and the Love-Feast*, 1957; G. A. Buttrick et al., 'The Agape', *IDB*, 1, p.53; R. Lee Cole, *Love-Feasts*, 1916; W. K. Lowther Clarke and Charles Harris, *Liturgy and Worship*, 1932; Dom Gregory Dix, *The Shape of the Liturgy*, 1945; J. F. Keating, *The Agape and the Eucharist in the Early Church*, 1911; Anders Nygren, *Agape and Eros*,1953; G. I. F. Thomson, *An Experiment in Worship*; *One in Christ*, II.1, 1966.

FRANK BAKER

Low Sunday

The English designation for the Sunday after Easter*, by a kind of anticlimactic contrast with Easter Day? In the Latin tradition its name is *Dominica in Albis*, a reference to the custom of the newly baptized continuing to wear their baptismal robes on the seven days after Easter, finishing with this day.

R. F. BUXTON

Lutheran Worship

The Augsburg Confession (1530) sets the tone for the Lutheran Reformation and clearly indicates that the protest is theological. Structures and tradition of the church are valued though they are attacked where authoritarianism has perverted them. The Augsburg Confession purports to be the authentic voice of Western Catholicism, repeatedly citing the church fathers to register its point. Lutheran reformers harboured no romantic notion of re-establishing the primitive church and were, therefore, conservative in liturgical reform.

> Our churches are falsely accused of abolishing the mass. Actually, the mass is retained among us and is celebrated with the greatest reverence. Almost all the customary ceremonies are also retained . . . the mass among us is supported by the example of the church as seen from the scriptures and the fathers . . . (*Augsburg Confession*, 24).

When the protest did not register and Rome severed ecclesial ties, liturgical reform became a necessity. Because of its prestige, Luther's own work was widely imitated. He purged the inherited rites ruthlessly where in his view they reflected an antibiblical theology, but was remarkably conservative in matters of ceremony. Biblical preaching was restored to the mass and also included in matins and vespers (*see* **Canonical Hours**). The fundamental emphasis on preaching grew out of both polemical and didactic concerns: it would free the people from ecclesiastical bondage and teach them the basis of the faith. The same pastoral concern led to vernacular* services.

Lutheran churches share this common liturgical orientation, but have developed three families of rites: Germanic, Scandinavian, North American. (Lutherans in eastern Europe and South America are Germanic in orientation; Australian Lutheranism combines Germanic and North American influences; Lutheran churches of Africa and Asia combine all three influences.)

All the sixteenth-century German *Kirchenordnungen* show their affinity to 'justification by grace through faith', the synoptic theology of the Lutheran protest. The Roman canon* and offertory* were cut out and, unfortunately, nothing replaced them. Thus the words of institution, stripped of their context of prayer, gained unprecedented prominence which was intended to enhance their proclamatory function. Instead, 'consecration piety' was reinforced and Lutheranism was kept tied to the mediaeval ethos of the awesome and dread presence. Disputes with the Swiss reformers made such piety even more tenacious.

In spite of heroic efforts to restore frequent communion among the people and thus balance sermon and sacrament, old habits prevailed. Awe of the presence and the need for solemn self-preparation, the individualism resulting from an almost exclusive emphasis on the forgiveness of sins as chief fruit of the sacrament and the

strong stress on the importance of preaching all contributed to infrequent celebrations. This did not result, as it did in England, in the ascendency of mattins. Lutherans used ante-communion* (*missa catechumenorum*) as their preaching service with the result that, in spite of the infrequency of the eucharist, their devotion remained orientated to the mass.

Dominance of proclamation produced glorious results in church music. Such giants as Heinrich Schütz and J. S. Bach used music in the exposition of the scriptures. Though their music is not liturgical in the usual sense, neither is it autonomous as masses of Mozart and Beethoven tend to be. It was related to lessons and sermon rather than the ordinary. From the beginning Lutherans fostered the use of vernacular hymns*, giving impetus to the chorale tradition. These hymns, in turn, generated a superb body of organ literature based on their melodies. Music is one key to the liturgical ethos of the Lutheran churches.

Scandinavian Lutheranism parallels the German development to a great degree. Denmark, especially, has a similar tradition. Norway, long under Danish rule, was late in developing its own style of life. But Norwegian worship bears the imprint of an intense pietism and tends, accordingly, to be individualistic in mood.

The Church of Sweden made the Reformation transition structurally intact. Because Roman influence virtually disappeared and Calvinistic influence was never significant, the Swedish church has been comparatively free of theological strife. Structurally, Swedish liturgies resemble the German. But in such matters as ceremony and vestments there has been more continuity with Western Catholic tradition. Even so, the Swedish Reformation could not restore frequent communion, and it also became a preaching church.

North American Lutheranism became the heir to the various European traditions. Since their arrival, the numerous immigrant groups have been engaged in the process of merging into one Lutheran tradition which is at home in the new world. This has required learning a new, common language, confronting a Protestantism of Anglo-Saxon origins with its different theological mentality, and adjusting to being a minority among Christians.

American Lutheran liturgies have followed the Reformation models in matters of structure, but have adopted the verbal habits of the BCP. Their musical practice has absorbed the Anglo-American tradition of hymnody and other conventions typical of American Protestantism. Ceremony and vestments have increasingly reflected the influence of the Episcopal Church, the Swedish heritage, and the catholicizing tendencies of the Liturgical Movement*.

The Liturgical Movement has influenced all branches of Lutheranism. Primarily it resulted in a recovery of the fullness of the sixteenth-century heritage after 150 years of decline. New service books in the decade after the Second World War demonstrate this. Since then a more ecumenical mood has developed as the result of increased knowledge of the pre-mediaeval church and the conviction that liturgical renewal cannot take place in isolation.

More recently, Lutherans have been challenged by Vatican II Roman Catholicism. A reformed Roman Church forces Lutherans to ask whether their protest has registered at last and, if so, whether the time for reconciliation has come. The spirit of rapprochement is strongest, at least on a practical level, in North America. The new American Lutheran rite (1978) for holy communion bears striking parallels to the new Roman mass (1969) and also the eucharist of the (pan-Protestant) Consultation on Church Union (1968). But similar observations are increasingly possible in other parts of the world, too.

Liturgical renewal among Lutherans shares goals similar to those of other communions: restoration of significant practices of mainstream Western Catholicism, expressing the interrelation of worship and mission, recovering the spirit of joy and celebration in the eucharist, grasping the mystery that God's work is always incarnate in human work. But in all this there is a sustained commitment to proclamation as the living voice of God among his people and a pardonable pride in a rich musical heritage to be shared with others.

Peter Brunner, *Worship in the Name of Jesus*, 1968; F. Kalb, *The Theology of Worship in Seventeenth-Century Luther-*

anism, 1965; Vilmos Vajta, *Luther on Worship*, 1958.

EUGENE BRAND

Maniple

see **Vestments** 1(*e*)

Mar Thoma Church Worship

The Mar Thoma Church is unique in the sense that it is at once Eastern and Reformed. This church still maintains aspects of its Eastern Orthodox heritage, but has undergone a thorough reformation along the lines of the English and Continental Reformations.

The church claims historical continuity with the ancient church supposed to have been established by the apostle Thomas in the first century. The Reformation of the nineteenth century, which originated this church as an independent unit, distinct from the Syrian Orthodox Church of which it formed part before that time, was ostensibly an effort to restore the purity of faith and practice of the original apostolic church which had been corrupted by the Syrian Orthodox.

The liturgical tradition of the Mar Thoma Church thus follows very much the patterns set by the Syrian Orthodox tradition. (*See also* **East Syrian Worship; West Syrian Worship**.) There have been several revisions of the prayers, especially in the eucharistic liturgy, to eliminate certain supposedly wrong teachings, e.g. 1. to take out all intercessions to the saints or the Blessed Virgin Mary since Christ is the only mediator; 2. to take out all prayers for the departed, since there is no biblical teaching that tells us that the dead will be benefited by our prayers; 3. to take out elements in the liturgical prayers which over-emphasize the sacrificial element in the eucharist; 4. to revise prayers which may seem to imply a doctrine of transubstantiation of the bread and wine into the body and blood of our Lord; 5. to revise texts which over-emphasize the powers of the priesthood.

In these reforms the Mar Thomas Church was guided especially by the pattern of the English Reformation as the Church Missionary Society had interpreted it. As in the English BCP, sometimes two alternative versions are given of prayers, one of which has a 'high' theology of the sacrament, whereas the second may reflect a 'low' view. In the revisions, the basic allusions of the Orthodox text have been maintained wherever possible. For example, the opening words of the public celebration of the eucharistic liturgy in the Orthodox and Mar Thoma texts are: *Orthodox* – 'Mary who brought Thee forth and John who baptized Thee – these are intercessors on our behalf before Thee – Have mercy upon us.' *Mar Thoma* – 'Our Lord Jesus Christ who took flesh from Holy Mary and received Baptism from John, pour forth Thy blessing upon us.'

The introduction by the Metropolitan Yuhanon Mar Thoma, Head of the Mar Thoma Church, to the finally revised (1954) text of the eucharistic liturgy, gives these basic principles of the revision: 1. removal of all prayers addressed to the saints; 2. removal of all prayers for the departed; 3. removal of the prayer (at the time of communion): 'Thee I hold, who holdest the bounds of the world; Thee I grasp, who orderest the depths; Thee, O God, do I place in my mouth . . .'; 4. change of the prayer 'we offer thee this bloodless sacrifice for thy Holy Church throughout the world . . .' to read 'We offer this prayer . . . for the Church'; 5. change of the prayer 'we offer this living sacrifice' to read 'we offer this sacrifice of grace, peace and praise'; 6. removal of the statement 'this eucharist is . . . sacrifice and praise'; 7. removal of the declaration that the Holy Spirit sanctifies the censer; 8. omission of the rubric about blessing the censer; 9. alteration of the epiclesis, giving freedom to say '(may the Holy Spirit sanctify it) to be the body of Christ' or 'to be the fellowship of the Body of Christ'; 10. insistence on communion in both kinds separately; 11. abolition of auricular confession to the priest; 12. prohibition of the celebration of the eucharist when there is no one beside the priest to communicate.

Changes along similar lines were made in all the forms of prayer and administration of sacraments. Since the revision has not yet been carried out in a thorough manner, elements of the Orthodox tradition now co-exist with definite Reformation features.

In the canonical offices, the use of incense has been largely discontinued. The prayers for the offering of incense are retained;

however, the word 'incense' is replaced by the word 'service' or 'prayers'. The typical Syrian Orthodox pattern of *proemion* (introductory doxology) followed by a *sedra* (long meditative prayer) is retained, but the invariable reference to the departed at the conclusion of the *sedra* is either omitted or replaced by reference to 'all believing members of the church'.

The Mar Thoma Church remains Eastern in not adding the *fiilioque* to the Nicene Creed, in insisting on the celibacy of bishops, in vestments and church utensils, in full congregational participation in worship, in the use of the mother tongue in worship, in adding 'O Christ, who was crucified for us, have mercy upon us' in the *Trisagion* and in many other respects.

At the same time there has been a liberal acceptance of and accommodation to Western Protestant or Evangelical forms of worship. The prayer meeting finds a place in the constitution, and each parish is divided into regional groups which meet together for informal group prayer. The eucharistic service is not obligatory on all Sundays, and quite often the priest or presbyter presides over a meeting around the preached word and prayer alone.

Hymns from the Anglican, Presbyterian, Lutheran, Methodist, Baptist and other books are found in the manuals of worship and are frequently used, either in English or in Malayalam. Several litanies and collects have also been similarly adopted.

The traditional seven canonical offices have been reduced to two (morning and evening), following the Reformers at this point. A form for compline has, however, been retained. There are special offices for Sundays and certain feast days, but different forms for the different days of the week are no longer in use.

A special feast called 'Community Day' (*Samudayadinam*) has been added, and a special form of service provided for the day, which coincides with the feast of St Thomas. A special offering is taken on this day for the central treasury of the church.

PAULOS GREGORIOS

Mariological Feasts

The Christian church has always held Mary the Virgin in special honour. The church's calendar* shows clearly the place Mary has in the liturgy, while private devotions as well as the work of artists and poets show the place she has in the minds and thoughts of individuals.

From early times Mary was honoured with the title 'Mother of God', which emphasized the status she enjoyed by virtue of her Son. In addition, however, the continuing devotion of the church to her person over the centuries led to her being given such titles as 'sinless' and 'immaculate'. Consequently two elements may be traced in the feasts in her honour, the vocational and the personal. The Immaculate Conception, for instance, may well be called a personal feast, while the Annunciation is rather to be regarded as a vocational one. These vocational, mother-and-son, feasts are, in a way, twofold celebrations and they become feasts of the mother or the son according to where the emphasis is put. Thus the Annunciation, Lady Day in England, is renamed in the new Roman calendar 'The Annunciation of the Lord' (by the angel to the mother). The octave day of Christmas has for centuries been called the Feast of the Circumcision, but originally it was a day in honour of the mother of God and in the new calendar it is now called 'The Solemnity of Holy Mary, Mother of God'.

The oldest feasts of Mary have a local connection with the church at Jerusalem. They also came into being largely because of the christological controversies of the early church. As the true humanity of Christ (as well as his divinity) came to be stated in clearer and more emphatic terms, the reality of the status of the Mother of God came to be better appreciated and underlined by feasts in its honour.

The feasts of the Purification, the Annunciation, the Birth and Assumption seem to be the oldest Marian feasts and to have been of Byzantine origin. They are recorded in the Gelasian Sacramentary, and so must have been known at Rome in the seventh or eighth century. To these, very many other feasts, especially of local usage, have been added over the centuries. Only a brief mention of the principal feasts is here possible.

The dogma of the *Immaculate Conception* was not defined until 1854, but the feast is very old. A feast was certainly observed in the East in the seventh century, and spread from there to Naples, Ireland, England and

so to the continent. It gained a measure of universal observance through the breviary of Pius V, and became a feast of the highest rank for the whole Roman Catholic Church after 1854. Its date is 8 December.

The *Birthday* of the Blessed Virgin, 8 September, is a very old feast – in origin as much a feast of her parents, Joachim and Anne, as of Mary. No reason can be given for the choice of date.

The *Annunciation* celebrates the incident related in Luke 1.26–38. It is recalled, in the framework of the Advent liturgy, on 20 December. But from quite early times it was given a special day of its own – 25 March in the Western calendar. The hymn *Ave maris stella* is said to have been first used as a hymn for this feast.

The *Visitation* (Luke 1.39–55) is recalled in the Advent liturgy on 21 December. There is an old Eastern feast on 2 July. The Western feast is probably not connected with the Eastern one and dates from the Middle Ages. The new Roman calendar has transferred it from 2 July to 31 May.

The *Purification* of the Blessed Virgin (2 February), as it has long been called by the Western church, is observed in the East as a feast of the Saviour. In the new calendar it is called the 'Presentation of the Lord'. Both names are derived from Luke 2.22. The real significance of the feast is the meeting (*hypapante*) of the old dispensation and the new, of Simeon and Jesus. The day is also known as *Candlemas*, for candles are blessed for liturgical use and also distributed to the faithful on this day. It also marks the end of the Christmas cycle and, through the candles, emphasizes the 'light' motif of the Christmas feasts: 'a light for revelation to the Gentiles, and for glory to thy people Israel'.

The *Assumption* of Mary, 15 August, commemorates her death. It also celebrates her entrance into heaven. The dogma was not defined until 1950, but the feast is one of the earliest Marian ones.

Other Mariological feasts have a local origin or are a development, often devotional and subjective, of one of the earlier feasts. The feasts listed above are christocentric and celebrate Mary's unique honour of being the mother of God and mother of man's Redeemer.

J. CONNELLY

Marriage

According to Western Christian thought, but not according to Eastern Orthodox thinking (*see below*), the actual ministers of marriage are the bride and groom who marry each other; and so the liturgical act is not of the essence of marriage and is rather a blessing additional to the primary entering into a contract in front of witnesses.

1. *The Early Church*. A clear distinction was drawn between the betrothal or engagement and the nuptials or marriage ceremony proper, although the former was considered to be as binding as the latter. There remains no full description of the primitive rite, but from scattered allusions it may in part be reconstructed and it can be seen to consist of practices current in paganism.

(*a*) *Betrothal*. According to Ignatius, this must take place with the bishop's cognizance (*ad Poly*. 5). It involved the giving of *arrhae* or earnest money as a pledge that the marriage would eventually take place. Next a ring was given, used for the sealing of household effects, to indicate that the future wife would be in charge of the home. A dowry was then promised and the woman was veiled – the veil being part of the engaged or married woman's normal dress. The couple's hands were joined and a kiss was exchanged (Tertullian, *Apol*. 6; *de Virg. Vel*. 11). In the course of time some of these elements were transferred to the marriage ceremony itself.

(*b*) *Nuptials*. According to Tertullian this included the celebration of the eucharist and a blessing (*ad Ux*. 2.6). From later writers we learn that in the East the man was given a crown, according to Chrysostom 'as a symbol of victory, indicating that he approaches the marriage bed unconquered by pleasure' (*Hom.in I Tim*. 9). An agape or love feast* usually followed.

EDITOR

2. *Orthodox*. The rite used by the Orthodox Church has a long and complex history. It achieved something near its present form only in the seventeenth century, and slight differences may still be observed between Slavic and Greek usages. Originally, no separate marriage ritual existed. Prayers and a blessing for marriage were pro-

nounced by the bishop during the context of a celebration of the holy eucharist. Despite its gradual development and eventual detachment from the eucharistic celebration, the Orthodox marriage rite to this day retains a basic shape and order as well as many particular features taken from the eucharist. This demonstrates that it continues to derive its meaning from that great 'sacrament of sacraments'.

The marriage rite is made up of two parts: the betrothal and crowning. Although they may be performed separately, they are usually done together. The betrothal is celebrated in the vestibule or near the entrance to the nave of the church. The crowning is performed in the centre of the church. The priest is vested in the stole and chasuble, and the couple, standing behind him, hold lighted candles.

The betrothal ceremony is the Orthodox Church's liturgical embodiment of marriage as it has been publicly performed in the natural order since ancient times. A man and a woman are naturally attracted to each other, 'for it is not good that the man should be alone' (Gen. 2.18). They come to love each other and desire to be together as a family. By a public promise and the exchange of rings they make their fidelity and unity known and recognized in a formal way. In these ancient forms the church sees something good, something desired by God and awaiting salvation and fulfilment in his kingdom. When placed within a Christian, liturgical context, the pledge and the exchange of rings may be compared to the bread and wine of the eucharistic offering. They, too, anticipate being offered, sanctified and transformed into that consummate reality of marriage, family and home: the nuptial union between Christ, the bridegroom and head, and the church, his beloved bride and body. 'For this reason a man shall leave his father and mother and be joined to his wife, and the two shall become one. This is a great mystery, and I take it to mean Christ and the church' (from the epistle read during the rite of matrimony, Eph. 5.20–33).

This offering to God and eschatological direction of the marital union takes the form of a procession (a liturgical form which runs throughout the service). The priest, as the celebrant of the sacrament, leads the couple to a table or lectern located either in the centre of the church or, in some traditions, near the holy doors to the sanctuary. The gospel book and other items needed for the service are placed on the table. During the procession the priest and singers chant verses from Ps. 128, a psalm chanted by the Hebrew people as they ascended the steps to God's dwelling place, the temple in Jerusalem.

From the centre of the assembled congregation the priest inaugurates the rite of crowning by proclaiming the destination of all the church's offertory processions: 'Blessed is the Kingdom of the Father, and of the Son, and of the Holy Spirit, now and ever, and unto ages of ages.' This exclamation, taken from the eucharistic rite, is followed by the ancient 'catholic collection' of petitions: the Great Litany. The priest then chants the three great prayers of the sacrament of matrimony. These prayers, the oldest of which is the third, dating from about the eighth century, are cosmic in character. God created a man to be king of all creation. With the woman whom God created as his companion, he was to increase and multiply, ruling and caring for the whole earth. The prayers have a distinct historical dimension. They place the names of the couple being sacramentally united at the end of a long list of other holy couples who preceded them, who are remembered in the church as having prepared the way for the first coming of Christ, who built up the church, and who anticipated his second and glorious coming. These prayers also contain a particular ecclesiological emphasis. In the words of John Chrysostom, the family is a 'small church'. According to the prayers, the newly-married couple, like the great church itself, in 'having sufficiency in all things', is to 'abound in every work that is good and acceptable to Thee . . .' and 'give in turn to those in need'. The whole scope and agenda for sacramental marriage, seen in the light of the mysterious union between Christ and his church, is set forth in these prayers.

These and other prayers also emphasize the normally inseparable connection between marriage and the begetting of children. 'That [the Lord] will grant them chastity, and of the fruit of the womb as is expedient for them ... fair children ... offspring in number like unto full ears of grain . . .' The gift of children is seen as one

of the greatest of God's blessings, and the 'expedient' number is to be understood soteriologically: as an element in the couple's 'working out their salvation' (Phil. 2.12) with the help of God and the guidance of their pastors in the church.

The three great prayers are followed logically by that sacramental act which, as it were, seals them, i.e., manifests their implantation and realization in the life of the couple – in their oneness of heart and mind, body and spirit. This act is the crowning. 'The servant of God N is crowned unto the handmaiden of God N, in the name of the Father, and of the Son, and of the Holy Spirit.' Crowns or wreaths are placed on the head of the husband first, then the wife. This liturgical order maintains that essential hierarchy in love found in the Holy Trinity, the church and in all of creation, for 'the head of every man is Christ, the head of a woman is her husband, and the head of Christ is God' (I Cor. 11.3). After the epistle, the gospel is read (John 2.1–11). The presence of Jesus Christ at the wedding in Cana and his miraculous changing of water into wine comprise the first sign of his impending kingdom, 'and his disciples believed on him'. Remembering this event, the prayers of the marriage rite stress the abiding presence, through the Holy Spirit, of Christ's power to transform and save now: 'As Thou wast present there, be Thou also present here, with Thine invisible protection. Bless this marriage . . .'

After the gospel and the Lord's Prayer, the priest blesses a common cup of wine and offers it to the couple. They each drink from it three times, manifesting that in their marriage, as from one cup, they share always and totally a uniquely given and divine destiny (in earlier times this common cup was smashed after its use in the wedding).

As a concluding action to the service, the priest joins the right hands of the couple and leads them three times in a procession around the table. During the procession, the singers chant these hymns:

Rejoice, O Isaiah! A virgin is with child, and shall bear a son, Emmanuel: he is both God and man . . .
O holy martyrs, who fought the good fight and have received your crowns . . .
Glory to Thee, O Christ God, the apostles' boast, the martyrs' joy, whose preaching was the consubstantial Trinity.

The procession forms a circle which reveals the eternal character of marriage in Christ (no prayers in the Orthodox service speak of the husband and wife parting at death), a unity transcending all pledges and contracts. The hymns emphasize the vocation of Christian marriage as a martyria, a sacrifice, a witness in this world to Christ, his gospel and cross, his kingdom, and his unity with the Father and the Spirit in the Trinity. The crowns point to a victory yet to be achieved. When the 'Isaiah dance', as this procession is sometimes called, concludes, the priest removes the crowns and pronounces the dismissal to end the service.

The Orthodox Church has a separate marriage rite which is used when both parties are entering into a second or third marriage (fourth marriages are not allowed). It is similar to the normal marriage rite in most ways. The main difference is in the several distinctly penitential prayers which are added to the betrothal service. In tolerating second and even third marriages, the Orthodox Church directs its efforts towards the salvation of the persons involved. The Church may not 'allow' that which Christ himself forbids, but the Church, like Christ, may extend mercy to those who repent: who have suffered the tragic consequences of a broken marriage or who cannot bear the loneliness of widowhood. The normal marriage rite is used when both spouses are Orthodox as well as when a 'mixed' marriage occurs, i.e., a marriage involving an Orthodox and a non-Orthodox Christian.

PAUL LAZOR

3. *Mediaeval and Roman Catholic*. The marriage liturgy to be found in the early sacramentaries (*Veron*., *Gelas*. and *Greg*.) was never obligatory and it was not until the social order had broken down (seventh to eighth century) that the church felt it necessary to take cognizance of the matrimonial consent and the conditions attaching to it. This was necessary to protect freedom of consent and to prevent clandestinity. Hence the rite of marriage *in facie ecclesiae*, which meant, literally, at the doors of the church. This is first recorded in Normandy in the early twelfth century.

The minister addressed the couple and inquired about the consent. The bride was 'given away', the scrip of the dowry was read, the ring was blessed and put on the right hand of the bride, the bridegroom gave some pieces of gold or silver (according to his wealth) and the priest concluded the rite with a blessing. If there was to be a wedding mass, the spouses (with their party) entered the church, carrying candles. They made an offering at the offertory*, there was the recital of the nuptial blessing (the text being that of the sacramentaries), and at this date and until much later, while the prayer was said, the veil was laid on the head of the bride and on the shoulders of the bridegroom. Thus was preserved the ancient rite of *velatio* which, according to some modern authorities, derives not from the ancient Roman *flammeum* but from the Christian rite of the *velatio virginis*. No formula is supplied in the Norman books, but in other mediaeval French rituals formulae very much like those of the Sarum rite are to be found.

It is there, however, that the origins of the Sarum rite of marriage are to be found, a rite that was retained by the Roman Catholic Church in England after the Reformation and with a few modifications (e.g. the omission of the blessing of the ring) by the Church of England. It is worth noting that in mediaeval England the text of the wedding mass was not used; it was replaced with that of the Holy Trinity, often used in England for joyful occasions.

The rite of the Roman Ritual of 1614 derives from the mediaeval one described above but, as its rubrics remark, since there are many local customs in the celebration of marriage, those countries and regions which have local rites may continue to use them. This is the explanation of the brevity and sheer starkness of the Roman rite of that time. In fact, in Europe there has always been a variety of marriage rites though in the nineteenth century there was a tendency to uniformity.

In recent years, with a developing theology of marriage, it was felt that a more adequate rite was needed. This appeared in 1969. It assumes (but does not order) that marriage is to take place at mass and appoints that it should take place after the ministry of the word where now other sacramental rites like confirmation* and ordination* are administered. The celebrant greets the couple who are seated in the sanctuary. After the homily he questions them about their willingness to undertake the obligations of marriage and their freedom. It is noteworthy that the English civil form declaring freedom and the matrimonial consent that follows has been incorporated into the rite for use in England. The form of consent has retained most of the phrases of the Sarum rite and these have now become part of the official Roman rite of marriage. After the blessing of the ring (or rings) the bride's is put on her finger with a new formula expressing love and fidelity (the one for the giving of gold and silver has been omitted as being archaic and obscure). In *all* weddings the nuptial blessing is given in one of the three forms that are provided. Bride and bridegroom may receive communion* in both kinds if they so wish. The mass (or service) ends with blessings for the bride and bridegroom and for all present.

If there is no mass, the marriage service must be celebrated with a ministry of the word (lessons from the lectionary), including a homily, which may never be omitted. In the case of marriages between Catholics and non-Christians certain adaptations (given in the official texts) are to be made.

Three mass formulae for weddings are provided in the *Missale Romanum* of 1970 with a rich collection of prayers, prefaces and insertions into the eucharistic prayers.

J. D. CRICHTON

4. *Anglican*. The marriage service is probably closer to its mediaeval predecessor, and has changed less in the ensuing four hundred years, than any other in the BCP. The obvious example of this is the vernacular form of vows, which is found in the Sarum and York manuals in almost exactly the same words that are used today. Cranmer keeps the traditional division into two parts (*sponsalia* and *nuptiae*), but allows the espousals to take place in the body of the church, marking the beginning of the second part by the customary procession to the altar.

The service begins with a long address, expanded from the mediaeval 'banns' with material that was evidently traditional, since Chaucer uses it in *The Parson's Tale*

(1387), and much of it is found in the Cologne *Encheiridion* (1538). Marriage was instituted by God in paradise, adorned and beautified by Christ at Cana, and commended by Paul in the Epistle to the Hebrews; it must not be entered upon for the wrong reasons; the right reasons are the procreation of children, continence, and 'mutual society, help and comfort'. The third 'cause' is stressed throughout the service: the mediaeval promise to love, honour, hold, and keep becomes love, *comfort*, honour, and keep; and the vows now include the duty 'to love and to cherish'.

The introduction of Matt. 19.6 ('those whom God hath joined . . .') and the subsequent declaration of marriage are German customs derived from Luther. The possibility that the woman may be past childbirth is covered by the suggestion of Ps. 67 as an alternative to the traditional Ps. 128 and a rubric before the collect for fruitfulness. This latter reveals a change of emphasis in the second part of the service, which was originally the blessing of the bride. Now there are prayers that 'they may *both* be fruitful' (instead of 'that she may be . . .'), and that 'this man may love his wife' (compare the interpretation of the ring as a token of the '*covenant* betwixt them made'). The attributes of Christian married life include 'quietness, sobriety, and peace' and 'holy love'.

In 1552 the only change of importance was the omission of the 'tokens of spousage' (gold and silver, often bracelets), whose place was taken by the priest's and clerk's fees. The tokens, however, continued to be brought in the North of England well into the seventeenth century. Surprisingly enough, the ring is retained. This became one of the major grievances of the Puritans, on a par with the surplice, the sign of the cross in baptism, and kneeling at the communion. They also objected to the phrase 'with my body I thee worship', but neither objection was successful in 1662.

In 1928 the phrasing of 'the causes for which matrimony was ordained' was modified to suit a more refined taste. The bride was no longer required to promise to obey her husband; and instead of endowing her with all his worldly goods, he was to share them with her. The Puritan criticism of 'worship' was at last met by substituting 'honour'. The prayers in the second part were shortened, chiefly by leaving out allusions to OT figures. No blessing of the ring was provided, though this was done in most other contemporary revisions. The omission was made good in Alternative Services, First Series (1966). A eucharistic proper was appointed in which divine love was the chief theme ('Love one another as I have loved you'). The American revision of 1929 omits the second part of the service altogether; the Scottish and South African books provide a form for blessing a civil marriage.

In the ASB the conservative character of the service is maintained by the retention of the BCP vows almost untouched, but contemporary thinking about marriage has been recognized by the complementary, rather than subordinate, status given to the bride, and by incorporating into the preface such insights as the relational value of sex, the importance of family life, and the role of marriage as a cohesive element in society. It is made clear that the couple, not the priest, are ministers of the sacrament: the role of the priest is to pronounce the church's blessing on the couple. The 1662 prayers are replaced by new ones, and a number of additional prayers are provided.

The American BCP service has similar features, though the language is more conventional.

Forms for blessing a civil marriage are to be found in the American BCP, and were authorized in England in 1985.

G. J. CUMING

5. *Baptist*. Baptists are found in many parts of the world, but in no country do they have a prescribed marriage service. These two facts taken together account for a wide diversity of practice. Marriage may be solemnized in a home, or in a church, in a civic hall, or in a registry office. In Britain, since the marriage act of 1863, after the civil preliminaries, it is customary for the ceremony to take place in a Baptist place of worship registered for marriages. The practice of blessing in church a marriage already contracted in a civil registry office, while much less frequent, is on the increase. Civil marriage is obligatory in many countries, but in the USA, where Baptists are most numerous, the church marriage ceremony is recognized by the state. Two

convictions are common to Baptists – marriage is not a sacrament of the church, but a divine institution for mankind; believers should enter the marriage covenant in the presence of God and with prayer for his blessing. The persistent opposition of the early Baptists to marriages outside their own communion has disappeared, but unions between believers and unbelievers are still discouraged. A marriage service in church usually includes the singing of hymns, the reading of scriptures, a message, and extempore or free prayer. The three main parts of the service are the introduction, the covenant, and the word. The ministry of the word sometimes precedes, but more usually follows the marriage covenant. The introduction commonly includes a hymn, a statement of the purposes of marriage, a declaration by the couple that they know of no legal impediment, and a prayer. The marriage covenant is made by the exchange of promises, the joining of hands, and the giving and receiving of a ring or rings. In Baptist manuals, the actual wording of the promises has been profoundly influenced by the service books of other communions, especially by the BCP. The ceremony concludes with the declaration that the couple are now husband and wife, and a blessing. Then the scriptures are read, there is usually a short sermon or address, and prayer(s) for the divine blessing on the marriage contracted. The service ends with a hymn and the benediction. Marriages take place usually on weekdays, occasionally on Sundays in the context of the congregation at worship, rarely at the Lord's Supper.

S. F. WINWARD

6. *Christian Church* (*Disciples of Christ*). Because the Christian Church (Disciples of Christ) has no normative theological statement and no officially prescribed service book, the conduct of the marriage service varies from congregation to congregation.

Most Disciples see marriage as a covenantal relationship. Divorce is never an impediment to church membership and only occasionally an issue in holding church office.

For a generation, following its publication in 1953, the most widely used liturgical resource was G. Edwin Osborn (ed), *Christian Worship: A Service Book*, which contains two marriage rites: one adapted from a service of Horace Bushnell and another from the Book of Common Prayer. Neither rite reflects peculiarly Disciple convictions.

As the use of Osborn's service book has declined in the latter years of the twentieth century, Disciple marriage services have become even more eclectic and are often drawn from rites issued by other denominations and commercial publishing houses.

Disciple marriage services tend to include a formal entry, a statement of the purpose of the occasion, a declaration of readiness to enter into the marriage covenant on the part of the bride and groom, readings from the Bible, a brief homily, the exchange of vows and rings, a prayer of blessing, a declaration of marriage and music (instrumental and vocal). Some services include the Lord's Supper and other symbolic actions like the lighting of a 'unity candle' which represents the union of two lives becoming one.

Marriage practices which reflect patriarchal society, such as the 'giving away' of the bride, are frequently replaced by practices more reflective of the movement toward equality between women and men, such as the blessing of the marriage by family, friends and sometimes children.

RONALD J. ALLEN

7. *Congregationalist*. Traditionally there have been two reasons for Christian marriage. The first is for the avoidance of concupiscence (or, in Pauline words, the choice is 'to marry or burn'). The second is for the procreation and upbringing of children. The third emphasis was added by the Puritan predecessors of the modern Congregationalists: for companionship through life. This also has biblical authority, for God is said to have created Eve for Adam 'because it is not good for man to be alone'. This is the dominant emphasis in modern Congregational marriage services, often called 'solemnizations of marriage' because they are regarded as ecclesiastical blessings of civil covenants, and in no sense as sacraments. In common with other Christians, Congregationalists recall that Jesus hallowed marriage by his presence at the marriage at Cana in Galilee, and that Paul used marriage as an analogy of the intimate relationship of Christ to his church.

Though there is no single, exclusive and official form of marriage service for Congregationalists, the many services from which a minister can select have a common lineage and common characteristics. If the English Free Churches have borrowed any single ordinance from the Church of England, it is surely the service of holy matrimony. The ceremonies of the giving away of the bride by her father and the giving and receiving of rings, as well as the very words of the solemn promises which bride and groom make to each other in plighting their troth, are all borrowed from the BCP. The exact words are used in *A Book of Public Worship for the Use of Congregationalists*, 1948, p. 174, and there is a revised version in *A Book of Services and Prayers*, 1959, p. 67. Similarly, the marriage service in the United Reformed Church's* *Book of Services* of 1980 is modelled on the service in the Anglican ASB, 1980.

The essentials of a Congregational marriage service comprise: reminders of the purposes of Christian marriage in an opening exhortation and in NT lessons; the charge that any impediments to the marriage be openly declared; the affirmations of mutual loyalty made by groom and bride; the mutual pledging of their troth and the exchange of rings; the minister's pronouncement in the triune name of God that bride and groom are married; and prayers and hymns for the keeping of the promises made and for the building of a Christian home, with the divine assistance, concluding with the Lord's Prayer and the blessing. Occasionally the service includes a celebration of holy communion in which the bride and groom are the sole communicants, but this is very infrequent.

HORTON DAVIES

8. *Jehovah's Witness*. Marriage is a divine institution, authorized and established by Jehovah God in Eden. There he made male and female and ordained marriage as a proper arrangement for the multiplication of the human family. The first human wedding was performed by Jehovah, as described at Gen. 2.22–24.

Marriage was designed to form a permanent bond of union between a man and a woman that they might be mutually helpful to each other. Living together in love and confidence, they could enjoy great happiness. By creating the woman from man's rib she became man's closest fleshly relative on earth, his own flesh (Gen. 2.21). As Jesus pointed out, it was not Adam but God who said: 'That is why a man will leave his father and his mother and he must stick to his wife and they must become one flesh.' The wording of this text makes it evident that monogamy was the original standard for marriage in the eyes of Jehovah God (Matt. 19.4–6).

A marriage is a time for celebration. The Bible abounds with examples of such happy occasions and Jesus himself graced a marriage feast in Cana of Galilee where he performed his first miracle, turning water into wine (John 2.1–11).

Moral cleanliness and fidelity in the marriage bond are emphasized throughout the Christian Greek scriptures. Paul wrote: 'Let marriage be honorable among all, and the marriage bed be without defilement, for God will judge fornicators and adulterers' (Heb. 13.4). He also counselled mutual respect between husband and wife in the payment of the marriage due (1 Cor. 7.1–5). To marry 'only in the Lord' is likewise a matter of apostolic admonition, in harmony with the practice of ancient worshippers of Jehovah in marrying only those who were likewise true worshippers (I Cor. 7.39).

The Bible nowhere records requirements of a religious ceremony for a marriage. At a Kingdom Hall of Jehovah's Witnesses one of the elders well known to the bride and bridegroom may be asked to conduct the service which will consist of song and prayer and a talk lasting for approximately twenty minutes in which the speaker will outline the privileges and obligations of marriage and speak personally to the couple. The legal requirements must be met for the marriage to be recognized in accordance with state regulations and in harmony with Romans 13.

The Bible allows for a course of celibacy if chosen by a Christian but it does not make it a mandatory pursuit. Such enforced celibacy was spoken of by Paul as a sign of a falling away from the true faith (I Tim. 4.1, 3). Some of the apostles were married and the qualifications for overseers and ministerial servants in the Christian congregation stipulate that if the candidates are married, they may have only one wife (1 Tim. 3.1, 2, 12; Titus 1.5, 6).

Jesus stated the principle governing the Christian congregation regarding divorce, namely that the only grounds could be *porneia*. This Greek word embraces fornication, adultery and other sexual perversions. If a Christian were to divorce on grounds other than *porneia* then the divorce, although legal, would not be a scriptural one and scripturally the individuals concerned would not be free to remarry (Matt. 19.3–9).

DAVID SIBREY

9. *Lutheran*. On the eve of the Reformation, and indeed throughout the sixteenth century, marriage law and forms of marriage were still developing. At this time we find the precepts or customs of Roman, Germanic, canon and imperial law, according to which the mutual agreement of the nuptial pair is the foundation of their marriage (*consensus facit nuptias*); certain degrees of relationship are given as hindrances to marriage, and to a limited extent it is presupposed that the marriage will be held in public. The involvement of the church authorities in the ceremony (namely, the publication of banns, the wedding itself as the questioning of the nuptial pair before the congregation, and the nuptial mass) will also have been a widespread custom. At the beginning of the sixteenth century, there can be no question of rules which embraced every detail. Responsible authorities, and later both the Roman Catholic and Protestant churches, fought passionately against *clandestina sponsalia* or *matrimonia*, 'secret marriages' or 'hedge marriages', but they were still permissible under the systems of law mentioned above, as they rested on the principle of *consensus facit nuptias*. Despite prohibitions by the church, lay marriage continued for a very long time. There is no mistaking a certain emancipation movement, which not only grants the female partner in the marriage a greater degree of independence but represents a move towards a greater freedom in the formation of individual modes of living. At the same time, the sources continually lament the detrimental effect this has on the sphere of sexual morality; official ordinances seek to rectify this situation even before the Reformation, and still more after it.

In view of this situation, during the sixteenth century, marriage in church becomes increasingly important on both the Roman Catholic and the Protestant side; towards the end of the century it acquires an unprecedented significance on the Roman Catholic side in canon law as a result of the Tridentine *tametsi* and a growing place in civil law on the Protestant side with the rise of regional churches.

Over against Roman Catholic tradition, all Reformation churches are agreed that the conception of marriage as a sacrament and obligatory celibacy are not in accordance either with scripture or with the original Christian tradition. It thereby follows that the association of marriage with the eucharist in a nuptial mass comes to be rejected, and permission for priests, monks and nuns to marry to be passionately required. Virginity is no longer regarded as a merit; marriage is seen as a state or calling in which everyone should and must prove himself or herself as a Christian. This fundamentally different conception, reached from a new interpretation of the testimony of scripture, did not exclude the adoption of features of Roman Catholic marriage where they did not conflict with the Reformers' scriptural norm; instead of marriage being linked with the mass, scriptural statements about marriage were given a greater place in the service.

The history of Lutheran marriage ordinances is further complicated because in the centres of the Lutheran Reformation (Wittenberg, Strasbourg, Nuremberg, etc.) marriage formulae from the liturgies of the respective Roman Catholic dioceses (Brandenburg, Magdeburg, Mainz, etc.) were often taken over. There were also certain differences in the legal conceptions of marriage in the different areas – at any rate, different terms were used.

There is a report of a first 'priest's marriage' from Augsburg in 1523; as the priest concerned was refused entry into church, he had his betrothal, or marriage, confirmed by an already married priest in the presence of 32 witnesses at a marriage feast in an inn. He and his bride made a mutual declaration that they took each other in marriage (E. Sehling, *Die evangelischen Kirchenordnungen des XVI Jahrhunderts*, XII, pp.33f.). The first Reformation marriage formula comes from the year 1524; in its original version it is most probably from the city pastor of Wittenberg, Johannes

Bugenhagen. After a brief address, based essentially on the relevant statements of Gen. 1–3, the nuptial pair are asked: 'N, will you take N to be your wedded wife (wedded husband) according to God's ordinance?' etc. After the exchange of rings ('a sign of betrothal'), the pastor says: 'So I give you both in wedlock before the face of God and our Lord Jesus Christ and before this congregation in the name of the Father, the Son and the Holy Spirit. God our Father and our Lord Jesus Christ be with you. Be fruitful and increase the world.' Principal additions to other versions of this formula are the declarations in Matt. 19.6 and NT readings. The formula spread very rapidly, especially in South Germany. However, in Strasbourg, in the same year 1524, another form of marriage arose (printed in 1525) which largely followed the diocesan liturgy of 1513. It was more extensive than the Wittenberg formula and regarded the 'blessing of the marriage' as 'confirmation'. The Strasbourg order also had a significant influence on the marriage formulae of South German Lutheranism.

It is Luther's *Traubüchlein* (Little Wedding Book) of 1529 (WA 300, III, pp.74–80; LW 53, pp.111–15), however, that had the greatest significance. Here Luther principally follows the order already existing in Wittenberg, but in some places he also takes up Roman Catholic formulae and the tradition of the early church. The service consists of three parts: public announcement, betrothal and blessing. The publication of the banns, which is also a public summons to prayer for the couple, is first followed by the 'betrothal' (*copulatio*) in front of the church door ('bridal door'). The questions run: 'Hans, will you have Greta as your wedded wife? Greta, will you have Hans as your wedded husband?' After the exchange of rings, joining of right hands and the pronunciation of Matt. 19.6b (in the present tense), the pastor says: 'Seeing that Hans N and Greta N seek each other in marriage and acknowledge the same publicly before God and the world, and have given each other hands and rings of betrothal, I pronounce them joined in marriage in the name of the Father, the Son and the Holy Spirit, Amen.' The 'confirmation' in the church itself, presumably only on the day after the betrothal, essentially consists of scripture reading and prayer. The first lesson, Gen. 2.18, 21–24, is a kind of word of institution. The following three lessons are addressed directly to the bridal pair: 'Because you have both entered into the state of marriage in God's name, hear . . .' The lessons themselves present a systematic approach: Eph. 5.25, 29, 22–24 (God's commandment), Gen. 3.16–19 (the cross) and Gen. 1.27, 28–31 (consolation), together with Prov. 18.22. At the end there follows a prayer taken over from earlier examples, which the pastor is to say over the bridal pair with hands raised: 'Lord God, who has created man and woman and hast ordained the state of marriage, who hast blessed them with the fruit of the body and hast designated therein the sacrament of thy Son Jesus Christ and the church, his bride . . . We pray that thou wilt not allow thy creation (foundation), ordinance and blessing to go astray or to perish in us, but wilt graciously preserve it in us . . .'

In the 'Preface' to this order Luther describes the purpose and conception of the marriage rite that he proposes. He feels it necessary to compose the *Traubüchlein* because of widespread uncertainty and confusion, and in order to educate the people. In Luther's view, marriage is a matter which falls within the competence of the authorities, especially as 'weddings and the state of marriage are a worldly concern', though at the same time marriage is a 'divine state' as well. Luther does not hold that the order he proposes is in any way obligatory; it is there in case a pastor is asked for it – a further indication that final regulations are still to come and that Luther neither wants to stand in the way of the tradition where it does not conflict with the word of God, nor seeks to create new law. Nevertheless, his order of marriage does have a legal character: anyone who submits to it has (after the preceding betrothal in the family circle) fulfilled all the necessary legal conditions for a valid marriage. That Luther felt it necessary to compose the *Traubüchlein* for pastoral reasons also is clear from the writing 'Marriage Matters' (1530, WA 30, III, pp.205f.; LW 46, pp.265ff.) and countless other statements on the questions of marriage, betrothal and divorce.

Luther's *Traubüchlein* has influenced almost all forms or church ordinances and

liturgies in North and Central Germany. There are, however, numerous alterations, expansions and re-arrangements. To the scripture readings provided by Luther with which the ceremony now usually begins are sometimes added Matt. 19.3–9; John 2.1–11, etc. The questions are expanded, partly following the Strasbourg order of 1530: 'N, do you acknowledge before this Christian congregation that you have taken (and take) N as your wedded wife (husband) and promise to love her (him) as your spouse in the Lord and with the help of God never to leave her (him)?' As in the Brandenburg-Nuremberg order of 1533, a declaration by the nuptial pair can also take the place of a question: 'I N take thee N as my wedded spouse and plight thee my troth.' The question can be omitted altogether, as in the Augsburg order of 1527 and the Hessen order of 1539. As far as the betrothal formula is concerned, in North Germany Luther's vow is almost always used which 'pronounces' or 'makes' the nuptial pair man and wife. Instead of this, the Strasbourg and Brandenburg–Nuremberg orders have: 'The obligation of marriage, which you have commended to each other before God and his congregation, I confirm at the behest of the Christian congregation in the name of the Father etc.' There is a controversy as to whether there is a material difference between 'pronounce' (constitutive) and 'confirm' (declaratory); towards the end of the sixteenth and in the seventeenth century, there was a clear tendency to see church marriage as the constitutive act, whereas earlier betrothal had had this function. Matthew 19.6, in the present or the perfect, is almost always used in connection with the act of marriage proper. The usual benediction is that of Luther, occasionally in conjunction with a prayer from Hessen dated 1539. A wedding sermon, whether free or with a liturgical formulation, found its way into the service, as did choir and congregational singing (Pss. 128, 127, *Te Deum*, etc.) or organ music and more elaborate forms. In some places the service was spread over two successive days, first of all the wedding ceremony with questions and 'saying together' or 'confirming'; the following day the entry into the church with sermon and blessing, in some places still called the 'nuptial mass' or 'nuptial office'. With increasing frequency the ceremony was concluded with the Aaronic blessing*.

In the sixteenth century, church weddings were still voluntary acts almost everywhere; as before, there were lay weddings. However, there was an increasing recognition that marriage 'is very useful for the improvement of the church' (Württemberg 1553), that the state of marriage is hallowed not only by faith and trust in the word but also by a ceremony which needs particular conditions and has particular consequences. Among the conditions are often to be found a catechetical examination of the nuptial pair, fulfilment of the requirements of the 'marriage ordinances' that arose everywhere, the strict prohibition of secret betrothals and pre-marital intercourse and the introduction of ecclesiastical and civil penalties for 'fallen couples' ('church discipline'). The ceremony, at first a proclamation and act of blessing, acquired increasing legal significance. Towards the end of the sixteenth century official certificates were required, and the authorities stated that no one was legally married without a ceremony in church. The betrothal questions become more imperative: the nuptial pair promise ('swear', Hamburg 1726) love, faithfulness, support to each other in good and bad times, 'until death do you part'; the formula of marriage becomes weightier: '. . . in God's stead . . ., as an ordained servant of the church of Jesus Christ . . .'

The strong influence of the ecclesiastical lawyer J. H. Boehmer (d.1749) led to the view that the marriage ceremony, or more accurately the affirmative answers to the marriage questions as a public declaration of the *consensus matrimonialis* and their public confirmation by the pastor, represented the legitimate conclusion of a marriage. Church marriage thus becomes a legal act which the church performs for the state: 'A fully valid marriage is brought about by the marriage ceremony of the church' (*Allgemeines Preussiches Landrecht*, 1794). While in this way the marriage ceremony acquired a clear legal significance, during the Enlightenment it increasingly lost its ecclesiastical character. The service became a family celebration. In many places the tradition was given up in favour of a sentimental, verbose loquaciousness; the address to the bridal couple stood in the foreground. Proposals to this effect are to be found in the private liturgies which now

appear, but they also occur in official liturgies as well. The traditional formula is expanded at Württemberg 1809 as follows: 'God's peace be with you. May your hearts and lives be dedicated to him. May your home be a dwelling of contentment, love and blessing. May each of your days until you go down to the grave be a new testimony to the grace of the eternal Father, who rules over you.'

It is a mark of the nineteenth century in Germany that in the West an obligatory civil marriage was introduced, in 1848 by the Civil Code in many districts, and in 1875 by national law. The churches at first fought bitterly before accepting the new situation ('Throne and altar'), without of course fundamentally altering the marriage formulae and without being able to solve the problem of the 'double' marriage, the official act and the church ceremony. The local liturgies which arose about 1900 provide either the scriptural readings from Luther's *Traubüchlein* or a formulated address in the form of a biblical paraphrase; the questions are presented in the traditional, verbose form, and the traditional expression 'pronounce' is used in the formula of betrothal. Some private liturgies are freer. Some of them understand marriage as 'ordination to the priesthood of the home' (J. Smend).

The marriage rite of the *Common Service Book* (US 1917) follows the English-speaking Lutheran pattern of borrowing some wording and the use of both questions and vows from the English prayer book tradition, while setting these in an essentially continental context. At the entrance to the chancel an invocation and scripture reading (from Luther's list) are followed by the prayer book questions, but in the same form for both man and woman, without 'obey' and 'serve' for the woman. Then before the altar the couple exchange vows, in a simpler form than in the prayer book: 'I N take thee N to my wedded wife/husband and pledge thee my troth till death do us part.' Then follows an exchange of rings, a 'pronouncement', a blessing, a prayer and benediction. The *Service Book and Hymnal* (1958) follows essentially this same pattern but it adds the full text of the prayer book vows, still without 'obey': 'for better, for worse, for richer, for poorer, in sickness and in health, to love and to cherish . . .'

It is only the marriage forms that have been produced in the last decades, above all the *Agende für Evangelisch-Lutherische Kirchen und Gemeinden* (1964, III, pp.139–54), that draw the consequences from the introduction of obligatory civil marriage. Now the marriage ceremony is regarded as being the concern of the congregation. Accordingly, on the analogy of a congregational service it is introduced with a biblical greeting, prayer or psalm, and then followed by the wedding sermon. The scripture readings provided are those from Luther's *Traubüchlein*. The questions now run: 'N, will you love and honour this N, born N, whom God entrusts to you, as your wife, and live a married life with her according to God's command and promise, in good and in bad days, until death parts you? Your answer should be, "Yes, with God's help."' The question to the wife takes the same form. There follow the exchange of rings, the joining of right hands, Matt. 19.6b and the Lord's Prayer. A new principle is that the marriage formula is to be understood as a consequence of the preceding prayer of intercession for the nuptial pair. The first formula runs: 'God the Father, Son and Holy Spirit bless your marriage. May he enlighten you by his word and fill you with his grace, so that you may remain in his community and reach everlasting life.' The second formula comes from pre-Reformation times: 'The blessing of the triune God be upon you and remain with you now and always.' A general prayer brings the ceremony to an end.

The marriage rite of the *Lutheran Book of Worship* (US and Canada 1978) makes significant changes in this pattern. The rite may be inserted within a celebration of holy communion. After the entrance and an opening prayer (using the image of Cana), a scripture reading and a sermon follow. A brief exhortation leads to the exchange of vows and rings. The prayer book tradition of both questions and vows has disappeared. The pronouncement says that the man and woman have made themselves husband and wife. Blessings and prayers follow with the option that the exchange of peace may then lead to the celebration of holy communion, with clear direction that the communion itself is to be congregational and not limited to the couple. These changes follow the pattern,

generally found in the *Lutheran Book of Worship*, of attempting to relate Lutheran liturgical tradition to ecumenically shared liturgical experience and scholarship.

A. NIEBERGALL/GORDON LATHROP

10. *Methodist.* The basis for Methodist marriage services is in John Wesley's edition of the 1662 BCP which appeared in 1784 as *The Sunday Service of the Methodists in North America.* Wesley's editing of the wedding service was relatively minor. For unexplained reasons he dropped the giving away of the bride. He also changed the phrase 'plight thee my troth' to 'plight thee my Faith', omitted the rubrics on impediments and receiving communion, removed any reference to the giving of the ring (perhaps in deference to Puritan practice), and dropped out the psalms and exhortation (probably for sake of brevity). In 1792 American Methodists abbreviated the service further, deleting the list of the ends of marriage and omitting the versicles and the prayer for childbearing.

The subsequent development of the service, both in Britain and in America, shows remarkable conservatism, though this may be natural in a service which is rooted in the structures of society itself. In America, the banns were dropped by the Methodist Episcopal Church South (MECS) in 1854 and in the Methodist Episcopal Church (MEC) in 1864, but the giving away of the woman was restored in MEC in 1916. The promise on the woman's part to obey was dropped as early as 1864 in the northern church and in 1910 in the second vows of the southern church. In 1864 MEC and in 1866 MECS restored the giving of the ring. Eventually all but one of the concluding prayers were omitted except for the Lord's Prayer.

Major reforms have occurred in the American rite with the publication in 1979 of *A Service of Christian Marriage*, also included in *The Book of Services*, 1985. Movements for social justice are reflected in changes in wording and actions (such as omission of the giving away of the bride). The service is intended to be a full service for a worshipping congregation and includes the service of the word between the betrothal vows and the espousal vows. Provision is made for celebration of the eucharist. Additional provisions are made for blessing of a civil marriage, celebration of the anniversaries of a marriage, and renewal of wedding vows.

In general the black Methodist churches have preserved conservative versions of the 1792 service, especially the African Methodist Episcopal Church which retained the banns and concluding prayers. The Christian Methodist Episcopal Church was more prone to brevity and dropped the second vows, though adding an optional ring ceremony.

In Britain the current use is in *The Methodist Service Book*, 1975. The order is: declaration of purpose, the declarations which the parties are required by law to make, collect for purity, confession of sin (sometimes omitted), the ministry of the word, the questions leading to the words 'I will', the giving of the bride (optional), the vows, the giving of the ring(s), the pronouncement of the marriage and a blessing, the intercession, the Lord's Prayer. If the Lord's Supper does not follow, there is a new thanksgiving, based on Jewish models, leading to the *Sanctus*.

JAMES F. WHITE

11. *Old Catholic.* In the period after the Council of Trent, the view became widespread in the doctrine and practice of the Roman Catholic Church that it is the bridal couple themselves who mutually celebrate the sacrament of marriage. This view is also held to some degree in the Old Catholic Church. Alongside, however, and with even greater emphasis, the church teaches that according to an earlier and more correct view, the sacrament is bestowed by the priest through blessing and the laying on of hands; this is the case above all in the Netherlands, but also in the Polish National Catholic Church, in whose catechism it is said, 'The *priest* is the minister of the sacrament of matrimony' (Scranton, Pa. 1962, Question 410).

The Old Catholic churches in common recognize civil betrothal as a legitimate contract of marriage, but this has no sacramental dimension.

The marriage rite takes different forms in individual churches. Everywhere, however, it is composed of the same elements: address, repetition of the word 'Yes', blessing and giving of the rings, mutual joining of

hands, blessing of the bridal couple, the Lord's Prayer and other prayers. The ceremony often, though not always, takes place within the framework of a nuptial mass.

In the Old Catholic Church of the Netherlands, there are two different forms of marriage:

(*a*) The sacrament of the blessing of the church. This sacrament is administered when two Old Catholics, or an Old Catholic and a Roman Catholic, get married. Since 1968 this has also been the case if the partner who is not an Old Catholic is a baptized and communicant member of a Protestant church and accepts this sacramental form of blessing. The formulary is taken from the *Rituale Romanum*, but is fairly freely revised.

(*b*) A non-sacramental form of blessing. Here there is no question of a lesser blessing – this is up to God alone – but this rite seeks to meet with the conviction of the partner who is not an Old Catholic if the latter is not a communicant member of any denomination, yet wants to place his marriage under God's blessing. It is a fairly simple form, consisting of readings (Ps. 121 and Eph. 5.22–33), some prayers, and a concluding blessing.

S. KRAFT/C. TOL

12. *Plymouth Brethren*. The marriage service among the Open Brethren closely resembles the order followed in other Free Churches. Some variations arise, as in other denominations, because of differences in national law. In England, where a church building must be registered for the solemnization of matrimony, the person who conducts the marriage ceremony does not need to be specially licensed; what is important is the presence of a member of the local registrar's staff or of a member of the church recognized by the Registrar-General as custodian of the church's marriage register. In Scotland, where the place of the ceremony need not be registered, the person conducting the ceremony must be registered for that purpose by the Registrar-General for Scotland. Normally one responsible member of each Open Brethren congregation is so registered. It is his responsibility to see that the marriage certificate is duly completed by the bridal couple and the witnesses, signed by himself and delivered to the local registrar. As a matter of convenience, an office in Glasgow serves as a clearing-house for communication between the local churches throughout Scotland and the Registrar-General.

The service takes the usual form: introductory words setting forth the divine institution and purpose of marriage and its indissoluble bond, so that the bridal couple and the congregation may understand clearly what Christian marriage involves by way of blessing and responsibility; then the mutual plighting of troth (for which national law may stipulate a minimum form of words), made while the couple clasp each other by the right hand and followed by the giving of the wedding ring. After pronouncing the couple to be husband and wife, the person conducting the ceremony prays for God's blessing on their marriage, and either he or someone else gives a short address appropriate to the occasion. Two or three suitable hymns are usually sung in the course of the service.

Among the Exclusive Brethren it has been customary for the legal part of the marriage to be performed in the registrar's office. This is followed by a service of prayer, thanksgiving and exhortation in the meeting room or other suitable place, which may well be combined with the wedding breakfast. In their way of life there is no line of demarcation between religious and social activities, just as there was none in the early church.

There is no uniform ruling among Brethren on the admission of divorced (more especially, of divorced and remarried) persons to church fellowship. The importance of maintaining Christian standards is recognized by all, but charity is recognized as one of those standards, so that in some places a less rigorist and in others a more rigorist attitude is taken up on this issue. A common attitude would admit them to church fellowship but not to public ministry in the church.

F. F. BRUCE

13. *Reformed*. All Reformed communions rejected the mediaeval idea that marriage is a sacrament, yet held high views of its importance. According to them the essence of marriage lies in the mutual declaration and promise of fidelity before witnesses, the consequence being that the 'pronouncing-together' by the minister was only a con-

firmation of the marriage. Yet marriage services appeared in all the service books. Many changes have taken place from time to time, though there is a clear ancestral line through them all, since they were derived ultimately from the form of Farel.

Farel's *La manière et fasson*, first printed in 1533, was adopted by Calvin in his *La forme des prières* (1542) and in the *Forme of Prayer and Ministration of the Sacraments* (1558, 1561), followed by Knox's *Genevan Service Book* (1556). *The Form of Prayers and Ministration of the Sacraments* (1562) came from the Genevan *Forme of Prayer* with only few changes. This was followed by the *Forme of Prayers* of 1564/5, printed in Edinburgh, which came to be known as *The Book of Common Order* (*BCO*), of which fully seventy editions appeared before 1645. Throughout these the marriage service remained practically the same. The *Westminster Directory* (1644/5) made little change in the order though no prayers were printed. These books have greatly influenced the many service books issued by English-speaking Presbyterians throughout the world.

Similarly, the French and Swiss (Vaud, Geneva, Neuchâtel, etc.) Reformed service books were derived from Farel through Calvin.

In Calvin's service the first requirement is the proclamation of banns of marriage, though this was a pre-Reformation custom (as in Sarum). Banns were to be read on 'three several days'; in practice these would normally be Sundays or preaching days during the week, the point being that intimation should be made when the largest proportion of the parishioners would be present in church. The marriage was normally to take place in church before the sermon on Sunday. But later, at least in Scotland, Sunday marriages were prohibited to prevent 'riotous profanation' of the day (cf. *Westminster Directory*). Modern service books do not usually specify any particular day.

The service opens with an exhortation based on scripture, preceded in continental books and in modern English forms by the words, 'Our help is in the name of the Lord . . .' The exhortation is long in early books (*BCO* has some 600 words), but much shorter in modern books. The couple are then challenged to confess any impediment, and the same challenge is made to the congregation. If none is alleged, the minister says, 'Forasmuch as no man speaketh against this thing, you, N, shall protest here before God and his holy congregation, that you have taken and are now content to have N here present for your lawful wife, promising to keep her . . .' The answer is, 'Even so I take her before God and in the presence of this holy congregation.' The woman is addressed similarly and gives the same reply. (In some forms the two parties say the words of promise, either by repeating them after the minister, or by memory, or by reading them from a book or card.) The minister then addresses the people on the duties of marriage, reading from Matt. 19. The service ends with the blessing. In the early forms there is no declaration that the parties are married. The ring is not mentioned in early forms. But its use was widely customary, though the *Westminster Directory* says the two parties join the right hands during the vows, 'with no further ceremony'. This has been regarded as prohibition of the ring.

Two other points must be made. First, in some modern continental forms (e.g. Geneva 1946 and Paris 1963) there are two alternative addresses after the vows, the first being the more instructive, and the second the more intimate in nature. Secondly, some modern books (e.g. *BCO*, 1940, but *not* 1979) contain not only the marriage service but also a form for 'The Blessing of a Civil Marriage' or 'Recognition of a Marriage' (*Worshipbook*, 1970). Modern language is now used in some marriage services, but less theological work seems to have been done on this than on the other services of the church.

J. A. LAMB/JAMES A. WHYTE

14. *Seventh-day Adventist*. While attributing no sacramental value to the marriage relationship, Seventh-day Adventists believe that marriage, a divine institution established by God himself prior to the fall of man, is the foundation of human society and was designed to be a blessing to mankind. True affection between man and woman is thus ordained by God. 'Central to God's holy plan was the creation of beings made in His image who would multiply and replenish the earth, and live together in purity, harmony, and happiness'

(*Seventh-day Adventist Church Manual*, 1981, p.265). Thus marriage and the family relationship should be the means for ennobling both partners and facilitating the development of mature, unselfish characters in the home. The marriage relationship is highly exalted in scripture, where it is used to represent God's relationship to his people, to symbolize the union between Christ and his church, and thus typify the union of humanity with divinity.

Monogamy (e.g. Gen. 2.21–24; Matt. 19.5) has ever been God's ideal plan, and any existing polygamous situations were simply tolerated. In the light of God's plan that man should have only one living wife, today when the gospel message in certain countries reaches a man living in a state of polygamy, he is upon conversion required to put away all his wives save one before he is eligible for baptism and membership in the SDA Church. In such cases proper provision is required to be made for the future support of the wives put away and of their children, and for their protection from disgrace (*see* General Conference *Working Policy*, 1968, pp.48, 49).

In harmony with Christ's statement in Matt. 19.3–6, Seventh-day Adventists believe that the marriage relationship is to be indissoluble. The only scriptural ground for divorce is unfaithfulness to the marriage vow, and this rule is to be followed by the church, whether or not the state or prevailing custom allow larger liberty. In the case of adultery and in the event that reconciliation is not effected, 'the innocent spouse has the biblical right to secure a divorce, and also to remarry. A spouse found guilty of adultery by the church shall be subject to church discipline . . . [He] has not the moral right to marry another while the innocent spouse still lives and remains unmarried and chaste; should he or she do so, he or she, if a member, shall be disfellowshipped' (*Church Manual*, pp.267, 268).

In the SDA Church only ordained ministers (*see* **Ordination** 14) are authorized to perform the marriage ceremony. Since laws regarding marriage vary a great deal from country to country, the role played by the minister also takes on different forms. In countries where marriage is legally regarded as a state responsibility and purely civil contract, the SDA minister conducts a marriage service that takes the form of a nuptial blessing. Being a world-wide church, the SDA Church has 'no prescribed nuptial liturgy that must be followed' (*Manual for Ministers*, 1977, p.122). Though customs vary in different countries, there are some well-defined principles adhered to by Adventists. The marriage of believers with unbelievers is expressly contrary to the teachings of the church. Relative simplicity and dignity in decorations and arrangements are recommended and ostentatious display in dress and ceremony should be avoided.

A typical Adventist marriage ceremony would include the wedding march, sermonette, musical item, charge, vows, prayer, and benediction. The *Manual for Ministers* contains suggestions for sermonettes, charges and vows, providing for variation and allowing the minister to choose the form best suited for the occasion. In all cases, however, the ceremony must be kept strictly within the legal requirements.

B. B. BEACH

F. E. Brightman, *The English Rite*, 1915, I, pp.cxxiv, cxxv, clxiii, clxiii, clxiv, ccxx; II, pp.800–17; J. D. Crichton, *Christian Celebration: The Sacraments*, 1973, pp.114–36; A. J. Collins, *Manuale Sarum*, 1960, pp.44–59; *Constitution, Bylaws and Working Policy of the General Conference of Seventh-day Adventists*, 1968; H. A. Dombois and F. K. Schumann, *Familienrechtsreform. Dokumente und Abhandlungen*, 1955; H. A. Dombois and F. K. Schumann, *Weltliche und kirchliche Eheschliessung. Beiträge zur Frage des Eheschliessungsrechtes*, 1953; P. Graff, *Geschichte der Auflösung der alten gottesdienstlichen Formen in der evangelischen Kirche Deutschlands*, [2]1937, I, pp.331–54; II, pp.260–72; M. J. Hatchett, *Commentary on the American Prayer Book*, 1979, pp.427–40; Clifford Howell, SJ, *Companion to the New Order of Marriage*, 1970; R. C. D. Jasper (ed), *The Alternative Service Book 1980: A Commentary*, 1980, pp.120–31; T. Kliefoth, *Liturgische Abhandlungen*, 1986, I, p.1; U. Küry, *Die altkatholische Kirche* (Die Kirchen der Welt, III), 1966, pp.212–14; M. Luther, *Werke*, Weimar edn 1883ff. (WA), 30, III; C. Mahrenholz, *Die Neuordung der Trauung*, 1959; A. G. Martimort, *L'Eglise en Prière*,

III, 1984; William Maskell, *Monumenta Ritualia Ecclesiae Anglicanae*, 1846, I, pp.42–64; A. Niebergall, 'Geschichte der evangelischen Trauung in Hessen, Teil I', *Jahrbuch der hessischen kirchengeschichtlichen Vereinigung*, 21, 1970; A. L. Richter, *Die evangelischen Kirchenordnungen des 16. Jahrhunderts*, 2 vols, 1846; G. Rietschel-P. Graff, *Lehrbuch der Liturgik*, [2] 1951, pp.701–56; M. Righetti, *La Storia Liturgica*, 1959, IV, pp.455–72; A. Rinkel, 'Ehe und Sakrament', *Internationale Kirchliche Zeitschrift*, 31, 1941, pp.1–28; E. Schillebeeckx, *Marriage, Secular Reality and Saving Mystery*, 1965; E. Sehling, *Die evangelischen Kirchenordnungen des XVI Jahrhunderts*, 14 vols, 1902ff; K. Stevenson, *Nuptial Blessing. A Study of Christian Marriage Rites*, Alcuin Club 64, 1982.

Marriage, Blessing of a

see **Blessing of a Marriage**

Martyrium

A building enshrining the tomb and/or relics of a martyr. The forms adopted by the church were those already in use for pagan tombs. Almost invariably roofed with a dome to symbolize heaven, martyria could be, depending upon local customs and prototypes, cuboid, circular, cruciform, octagonal or triconch, or they could combine more than one of these plans, e.g. Church No. 8, Bin Bir Kilisse, which unites the cross with the eight-sided figure (*see* Fig. 23).

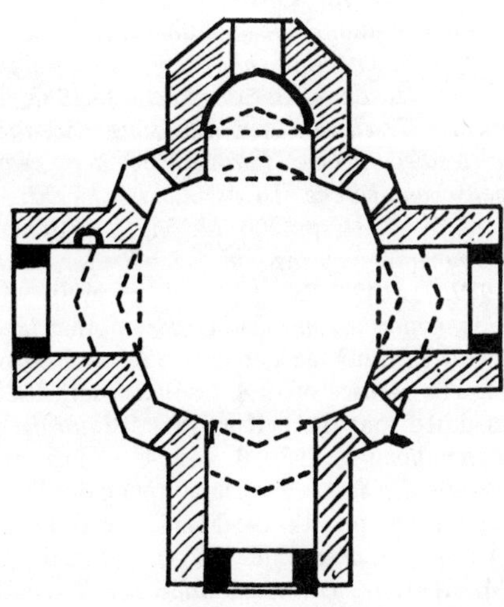

Fig. 23 Church No. 8, Bin Bir Kilisse, Turkey

A. Grabar, *Martyrium. Recherches sur le culte des reliques religieux et l'art chrétien antique*, 2 vols, 1946.

EDITOR

Mass, High

The term 'high' translates the Latin *sollemnis*, and *Missa sollemnis* (or even *sacra sollemnia*) meant a sung mass at which the deacon* and subdeacon* assisted the celebrant* and performed certain duties that belonged to them alone. Thus it was the deacon who sang the gospel, the subdeacon who sang the epistle, as well as other lessons if there was no lector*. In addition, the deacon was the immediate minister of the priest, pouring the wine into the chalice* at the offertory* and covering and uncovering the chalice during the canon*. The subdeacon poured the water with which the wine is mingled. The subdeacon held the paten in a humeral veil (*see* **Vestments** 2[*j*]) from the offertory until the end of the Lord's Prayer. This observance, which had its origin in the papal liturgy when the bread was brought to the altar on large platters at the offertory, which were then held by the subdeacons until just before communion, has now been abolished. At the end of mass the deacon sang the dismissal (*Ite, missa est*) before the celebrant gave the blessing.

The ceremonial of high mass was somewhat complicated not only in the sanctuary*, where the deacon and subdeacon had to make their movements in concert with acolytes*, thurifer* and master of ceremonies, but also in the total organization of the rite. Thus the choir sang the Introit, the Gradual, the Alleluia and its verse (in Lent replaced by the Tract), the Offertory verse and the Communion verse, and the people were supposed to sing the *Kyries*, the *Gloria in excelsis*, the *Sanctus*, the *Benedictus* (until recently sung *after* the consecration) and the *Agnus Dei* (*see* **Chants of the Proper of the Mass**). In fact in most places the choir sang all these too. Before a high mass on Sundays there was the rite of the *asperges**, although celebrant, ministers, servers and, where there was a surpliced choir, the choir had already made their solemn entry. In addition, the cele-

brant was required to say the prayers of preparation with the ministers in a low voice and to read everything that was sung by anyone else. In cathedrals and parish churches where the gospel was read out in English after its singing in Latin, the gospel was thus recited three times in one mass.

Incense* was used (and might only be used at sung masses); the altar was censed after the prayers of preparation and at the offertory, the gospel book before the singing of the gospel and the celebrant on all three occasions. In addition, the ministers and servers were censed at the offertory and the people on the latter occasion only. The blessed sacrament was censed at the two elevations of the consecrated bread and wine.

The whole of this ceremonial was controlled by a rigid corpus of rubrics*, elaborated by the ceremonialists whose practical regulations sometimes acquired the force of law.

Its origins are to be found in the Gregorian tradition (the 'Gregorian' sacramentary and the *Ordo Romanus Primus*) of the seventh century, with the elaborations and adaptations of the *Ordines* and pontificals of the following centuries. The 'Gregorian' sacramentary and the *Ordo Romanus Primus* give the ceremonial of the mass when the pope celebrated. North of the Alps this had to be adapted to the conditions of an episcopal celebration and it was the episcopal high mass which, in spite of accretions, gave the best picture of the Roman mass of the seventh century. Then, with the multiplication of churches within a city and outside it, with the spread of monasticism, it was necessary to arrange the rite for celebration by the simple priest. It was shorn of certain ceremonies proper to a bishop (thus the priest did not use a throne but a seat at the side of the sanctuary), and so we get by the thirteenth century the rite known in English-speaking lands as 'high mass'. In spite of the ever increasing prevalence of low mass*, at least the ceremonialists regarded high mass as the typical rite of the Roman Catholic Church. It had the advantage of indicating that the mass is celebrated not by one man, the priest, but by a community, even if by the eighth century this community had become almost entirely clericalized. The Carolingian reform of the ninth century made attempts to keep a community spirit alive by enjoining on the people the duty of singing the *Kyries*, the *Gloria*, etc., but apparently without great success. The ceremonial of high mass, as it was known until recently, was finally fixed and imposed as of obligation on the whole church of the Roman rite by the corpus of rubrics called *Ritus servandus* which was inserted into the missal of Pope Pius V in 1570.

The term 'high mass' and much of its ceremonial is now obsolescent or obsolete. The *Ordo Missae* of 1969 has brought a great flexibility to the celebration of the mass. Singing may and should take place at every kind of mass, incense may or may not be used at will, the ceremonial is much simplified (the order of subdeacon has been abolished), but above all, the emphasis is put on the worshipping community and their part in the celebration is considerable. The people are required to sing or say those parts of the rite that properly belong to them, the celebrant never says anything read, said or sung by anyone else, and lay readers for the first and second lessons are allowed and recommended. The celebration of mass in its simplest or more elaborate form is now once more a paradigm of the Christian community, the church.

J. D. Crichton, *A Short History of the Mass*, 1983; J. A. Jungmann, *The Mass of the Roman Rite*, 1961; J. B. O'Connell, *The Celebration of Mass*, III, 1945.

J. D. CRICHTON

Mass, Low

The low mass (also called in some languages and places the 'said mass' or the 'read mass' or even 'private mass') is, ceremonially speaking, one that is celebrated by a priest with single server*. In practice, for a variety of reasons, it was for hundreds of years the form of mass with which lay people were most familiar. It was celebrated without song, with a minimum of ceremonial, and the celebrant* faced eastwards (*see* **Posture** 1). The rubrics of the Pius V missal (1570) assumed that the people would be on their knees throughout, occupied with their own devotions and hearing only occasional phrases from the celebrant. On Sundays in parish churches, its rigours were somewhat reduced by the reading of the epistle and gospel in the people's tongue after they had

been read in Latin and (usually) by the sermon. In some places vernacular hymns* were allowed to form an accompaniment of the rite, notably in Germany. From the eighteenth century, a style of mass that came to be called the *Betsingmesse* (prayer-and-song-mass) was introduced. Here the sung texts were paraphrases (more or less close) of the mass texts and were sung while the Latin text was being read by the celebrant. It was a way of securing some popular participation and became common in the church after the Second World War until the liturgical reform of Vatican II.

The rite of low mass, which the rubrics of the Pius V missal seem to have regarded as typical, is the result of a long development. The classical Roman mass of the seventh century (*see* **Mass, High**) was a community celebration. But with the spread of monasticism, the custom of private masses in chapels for special 'intentions' began to come in, and as Christianity spread into the rural parts of Europe, it became impossible to celebrate the mass in country churches with all the ceremonial of the papal-episcopal rite. The sung parts of the mass (introits, etc.) seem to have been omitted, but the priest himself said all the rest, the collect, the epistle, the gospel, etc., and the single minister or server responded for the people. With the changing habits and organization of the papal curia which gave employment to a considerable number of clerics, mostly priests, and with the rise of the new religious orders like the Dominicans and Franciscans who were clerks (in holy orders), the custom of low masses became ever more prevalent. Concelebration*, apart from ordinations, was unknown. When in the thirteenth century the Franciscans adopted the papal-curial liturgy and penetrated into every corner of Europe, the Roman rite of low mass became very common. They took over from the Roman books certain prayers provided for the devotion of the priest at the offertory and before communion, and a selection of these prayers was included in the missal of Pius V and made a matter of obligation.

For this kind of celebration a single book was needed, for it was manifestly impossible for a man to take around with him a small library consisting of sacramentary, collectary, epistle and gospel book and gradual. This the monks had provided by the eleventh century with the so-called *Missale Plenum*, which contained *all* the texts of the mass whether sung by others or said by the priest. It was this book, reformed in the sixteenth century, that became the *Missale Romanum* and that was the official mass book of the Roman Church until 1969.

Like the term 'high mass', the term 'low mass' is now practically obsolete. The thinking of the *Ordo Missae* of 1969 moves in a quite different direction. It emphasizes the community participation of the people and admits singing at any and every kind of celebration. It does indeed envisage the 'private' mass (a term now frowned on) and provides an order for a priest who has to celebrate in the absence of people. The ritual is slightly adapted, though he is still required to say the entrance text and the communion verse. The server has to make the responses of the people.

J. B. O'Connell, *The Celebration of Mass*, II, 1942.

See also bibliography under **Mass, High**.

J. D. CRICHTON

Matins

see **Canonical Hours.**

Mattins

The name commonly given to morning prayer in the Church of England.

See also **Canonical Hours**.

Maundy Thursday

Maundy Thursday, the Thursday in Holy Week*, is a day of great liturgical complexity, with three quite distinct acts of liturgical celebration.

The first, and possibly the oldest, is the public reconciliation of penitents, prior to their readmission to communion at Eastertide. It takes place during a special mass. Because of changes in pastoral practice this is now redundant and can be regarded as having fallen into disuse, and the modern Roman rite makes no provision for it. The services of penance now being used in the Roman Catholic Church and elsewhere can be regarded as distant descendants of this ancient Maundy Thursday rite.

The second is the chrism mass, the occasion at which oils are blessed by the bishop in his cathedral for subsequent use in

baptism, confirmation, ordination and anointing of the sick (*see* **Unction**). With this has become associated in the modern Roman rite the corporate renewal of priestly vows; this is a specific post-Vatican II invention, also copied in some Anglican dioceses.

The third is the evening mass giving thanks for the institution of the eucharist, regarded by the modern Roman rite as the start of the Triduum, the three great days of the paschal celebration. It is this service alone that will take place in parish churches, and which the ordinary worshipper will regard as the service for this day. As well as lections and propers appropriate to the day, two special ceremonies have become associated with it. The first of these is the washing of feet, a rite also found in some baptismal liturgies, notably in the early Milanese rite as described by Ambrose. It is possible that this was originally seen as being part of the symbolic and sacramental cleansing, and then later as an imitation of the humility of Christ, derived from the example in John 13. It is a ceremony that in the Maundy Thursday liturgy goes back to at least the seventh century, but its appropriateness as a symbol of humble service, in a modern Western society at least, may be questioned. In the modern world hosts do not have servants to wash the feet of their guests, nor do guests wash their feet on arrival anyway. Its symbolism is therefore no longer really apparent, and it becomes a rather forced and artificial archaism.

The second ceremony is the reservation of the sacrament and procession to the altar of repose. The purpose behind this is in origin strictly utilitarian. Originally neither was the eucharist celebrated nor communion received between the eucharist of Maundy Thursday and that of Easter Day, and when the desire arose to receive communion at the liturgy of Good Friday* the custom of not celebrating on Good Friday proved too strong to be reversed, and so the sacrament was reserved from the Maundy Thursday for use at the Good Friday liturgy, a development originating in the late seventh or early eighth century in Rome (an example of a comparative rarity, a liturgical innovation originating in the conservative Church of Rome!). At first this was done in a plain and unceremonious manner, the actual place of reservation being a vestry. At a later period the sacrament was carried ceremoniously to a side altar, called for this purpose 'the altar of repose', which was often elaborately decorated with many lights and flowers, and a watch kept before it, the symbolism of this being going with Jesus to Gethsemane and watching with him there.

Following this the main altar is stripped (*see* **Altar, Stripping of**) and all the furnishings removed from the church so that it is bereft of decoration for Good Friday. This custom seems to have originated in seventh-century Spain and is also attested in several eighth-century Roman *ordines*, and the fact that the altar was washed (*see* **Altar, Washing of**) as well as stripped betrays its utilitarian origin, namely to give the church building a good clean up before Easter Day. But the bareness came to symbolize the desolation of the passion, and it is this that no doubt keeps the custom alive. It should be noted that only the ornaments and decorations were originally removed; essential items of furniture such as the cross remained in place.

All these ceremonies are ancient, but none go back further than the late patristic period. In recent years it has been suggested that Maundy Thursday is an appropriate occasion to remember that the eucharist was instituted within the context of a meal, and therefore to reunite a meal with the eucharist. The recent Church of England Liturgical Commission Report makes suggestions as to how this might be done.

The title Maundy Thursday derives through the Old French *mandé* from the Latin *mandatum novum*, 'a new commandment' (John 13.34), associated with the ceremonial foot-washing part of the rite. The English distribution of Maundy money by the sovereign is a vestigial trace of this.

For bibliography *see* under **Holy Week**.

R. F. BUXTON

Media, Worship on the

The impact of the explosive growth of modern media on Christian worship has hardly begun to be assimilated. It is only in very recent times that the churches have had to expose their long liturgical traditions to the possibilities and limitations of mass communication.

The first broadcast religious talk in the

United Kingdom was a Christmas Eve address by the Rector of Whitechapel in 1922, for the newly founded British Broadcasting Company. From 1924 regular services of worship began to be broadcast over the air. Radio services were either direct relays from churches, modified to suit an audience made up of people from different religious backgrounds, or specially created acts of worship from studios.

In 1928 an enthusiastic listener won a campaign for a daily act of worship on the radio. This Daily Service was a simple liturgy made up of a Bible reading, a hymn and a psalm framed by a sequence of newly written and traditional prayers. *New Every Morning* was published first in 1936 as an accompanying service book. Eventually the BBC also produced its own *BBC Hymn Book*. The Daily Service was intentionally non-denominational. It was the first religious service created by the media and it is still offered today.

Radio has developed into a cheap, flexible and durable world-wide communications system. The smallest and most remote communities are within reach of radio transmitters. Christian evangelists and missionaries use radio to spread the gospel to the unconverted, to build up Christian community and to offer Christian insights to society as a whole. Radio is a medium for preaching, teaching and prophecy.

Religious services began on television in the 1940s in the USA and on the continent of Europe. The mass was televised regularly in Canada and France in the years after the war. The first televised service in the United Kingdom was on Christmas Day 1949. At first there were very few direct relays from churches because of the scarcity of outside broadcasting equipment and the very high cost of television lighting and communications. For some years the choice of churches for such relays depended on their proximity to the locations of sporting events televised the day before. Generally speaking, television was felt to be more of an entertainment medium than radio, and, therefore, rather less suitable for conveying worship than radio had proved itself to be.

Today both the BBC and the IBA transmit some form of Christian worship on television on Sunday mornings. There are direct relays from churches and live or recorded studio services. In recent years the BBC has evolved a form of worship, *This Is The Day*, designed to enable viewers to participate directly in a television liturgy of their own, rather than to watch passively a service created and conducted elsewhere (*see* Plate 42). Such innovations indicate a recognition of the transforming effect of television on all human culture. The verbal basis of much Western culture is being amplified and altered by the growth of visually-based methods of communication. Through modern satellite systems live sound and television pictures can be flashed instantaneously from one part of the globe to another.

The expansion and proliferation of modern media may well bring about long-term effects on our awareness of ourselves, not only in relation to one another, but as free and responsible agents before God. It has been argued, most notably by the Catholic philosopher of media, Marshall McLuhan, that television is creating a new sense of universal community, a 'global village'. If this is true it has profound implications for Christian liturgy and worship. Religion is already perceived, by television viewers, as a distinctive human phenomenon with particular and observable effects in a complex and divided world. It is impossible to ignore the plurality of faiths. These factors may well have a double and apparently contradictory effect on the evolution of television and radio worship. On the one hand it may well drive the churches and the broadcasters to preserve and cherish the distinctiveness of their particular traditions. On the other hand it may give rise to further experiments and innovations which cross the barriers of different faiths.

One important factor influencing worship on the media is the political relationship between the churches, the broadcasting organizations and the state. There are a number of different ways in which Christian worship finds its way into radio and television schedules, and these different arrangements influence the forms of worship offered and the ways in which it is received.

The broadcasting and televising of acts of worship is commonplace in countries where religion is practised freely. In many countries radio and television are state-owned and controlled. The established

Plate 42 This is The Day. This shot of receding television sets is used in the programme to signify the way in which viewers are linked in an unseen community.

church, if there is one, or the major denominations, offer suitable services for transmission, often on some cost-sharing basis. The degree of editorial involvement on the part of the state-run television or radio organization varies. So does the enthusiasm, creativity and commitment of the churches. But on the whole the churches retain the initiative in worship on the media, and create the editorial policy. This means that they are likely to think of radio and television worship as an extension of what happens in a local congregation. Services are designed to reach out to lapsed or incapacitated church members.

In contrast, some religious bodies, especially in the USA, run their own television and radio stations. They offer, not only worship, but a full range of pastoral, teaching and inspirational programmes, often supplemented by 'family' entertainment bought in from other networks. They obviously retain full editorial control over the material they produce.

Other religious organizations buy airtime on commercial networks. Here they are under pressure to maximize audiences. Their approach is often dominated by evangelistic and didactic motives. What they offer as worship has to compete as entertainment. New viewers are constantly required, not only as members of the worshipping community, but to provide financial backing for the operation. 'Electronic churches' or 'churches of the air' are an expanding sector within the media industry.

Mainstream churches, in the US and elsewhere, tend to distance themselves from

this kind of operation and to doubt whether such an approach is credible in religious terms.

Worship on the media in the United Kingdom takes place against a very different background. The BBC and the IBA are largely independent of government control. Independent television and radio are financed by advertising, the BBC by a television licence fee. Both organizations, however, are committed to what is known as public service broadcasting. This is an ethical and practical commitment to use the media to educate and inform as well as to entertain, and to give due attention to the interests of minorities. Religious broadcasting is usually understood as part of this commitment. The initiative and responsibility for the production of worship programmes lies with the broadcasters rather than with the churches.

This arrangement has exposed over the years the deep inherent tensions of worship on the media. It has also fostered a tradition of creative innovation both in radio and television.

The tensions, and innovatory potential, were there from the beginning. John Reith, the first Director-General of the BBC, wanted the best in Christian worship to be reflected in the then new medium of radio. He believed in the Christian basis of British culture and was impatient both with doctrinal controversy and with the scandal of Christian division. His own robust Christian commitment was itself divisive. Some saw in radio a marvellous opportunity for the spread of the gospel; others were hostile, fearing the spread of a bland and unhistorical 'BBC religion'. There was also a fear that broadcast worship would lead to a decline in church-going; steps were taken in the early years to make sure that broadcast services avoided the times when most congregations could be expected to be gathered.

In spite of early doubts it is now clear that radio and more recently television have become in their own ways guardians and custodians of Christian tradition. They allow millions to participate in the great religious events of state. They set before hundreds of thousands the scriptures and sacraments, the prayers and preaching, the liturgy and hymnody of the Christian past. There can be little doubt that Choral Evensong, broadcast regularly on Radio 3, has helped to maintain the excellence of English cathedral music. At the same time television and radio have provided ecumenical opportunities. Long running series such as *Sunday Half-Hour* and *Songs of Praise* have kept the common theology of popular hymns in circulation in a society not notable for its theological literacy.

Like all transmitters of tradition, however, television and radio also modify and transform what they hand on. In two important ways they simultaneously enhance and inhibit the experience of Christian worship.

The first way in which they do this concerns the mystery at the heart of worship and the means by which the holy is apprehended. Television and radio have access to the best means of apprehension: the best music, the best architecture, the best preachers, the best liturgy. Yet all these put together do not necessarily convey anything more than a splendid aural or visual event.

There are a number of reasons for this. First, the presence of microphones, cameras and television lights makes congregations self-conscious, except on those unusual occasions when a service is conducted at night and in the dark. Second, both radio and television have their own built-in limitations. Radio can only transmit sound. There is a positive gain in this, for radio can be powerfully evocative in its own unique way. But the one thing radio cannot endure for long is silence. Silence on radio comes without interpretation. It is heard as emptiness, coldness, non-communication, even technical error. So one of the aspects of worship which is becoming increasingly important to modern believers, and which is attached particularly to the sense of mystery, is lost on radio.

Television has different gains and losses. Television is good at conveying spectacle, event, human reaction and those forms of ritual where people are the focus of attention. Religious ritual, however, uses prescribed human words and actions to signify what is beyond itself. Without the implicit understanding of what lies beyond the rite worship is incomprehensible. By simply showing what happens in a church service television can easily miss the entire point. What interests the camera distracts from the invisible God.

So, in their different ways, what radio and television are usually thought to be good at can easily work against the listener's or viewer's apprehension of divine mystery.

The second way in which the media simultaneously enhance and inhibit the experience of worship concerns the individual's relationship with other worshippers. Television and radio make worship accessible to those who are unable or unwilling to go to church. At the same time they undermine the widely-held belief that Christian worship is, in essence, an activity of a community gathered in a particular place at a particular time. If that belief is true, however wide the media extend the experience of worship the individual viewer or listener can never be part of a genuine Christian community. This is most clear in sacramental worship. No listener or viewer can be baptized over the air or receive holy communion. The church's great acts of incorporation leave the home-bound viewer isolated and uninvolved.

Real participation and fellowship appear to be insurmountable problems in media worship. The barrier of the set or screen inhibits some of the key communicative aspects of worship at the same time as it widens the circle of those who can see and hear.

In spite of these limitations some religious broadcasters believe that there are strong theological reasons for refusing to limit authentic community worship to the gathered church. The church proclaims its faith in the communion of saints and holds that the living and the departed are united in worship across the barriers of space and time. At the height of the eucharist all who stand before God, whether in earth or heaven, are invoked to join in the chorus of human praise. In the same way television and radio can link separated and isolated listeners and viewers in a common experience of prayer and worship which transcends their physical aloneness.

It is such a belief that has sustained radio's Daily Service from the early days of broadcasting to the present time, and which continues to motivate such innovations as television's *This Is The Day*.

Marshall McLuhan, *Understanding Media*, 1964; Colin Morris, *God-in-a-Box*, 1984; Kenneth M. Wolfe, *The Churches and the British Broadcasting Corporation 1922–1956*, 1984.

ANGELA TILBY

Methodist Worship

1. *Britain*. John Wesley, a presbyter of the Church of England, intended his preachers and his people to follow his own example by attending 'the Church Service', i.e. the services of the parish churches of the Church of England; they were to be supplemented, not superseded, by simple Methodist preaching services at 5 a.m. and 5 p.m. The Methodists were increasingly reluctant to attend the parish churches where indeed they were not always welcomed and, though the custom of attending the parish churches lingered for a long time in country districts, they increasingly established in their chapels a complete pattern of their own Sunday services which, after the Plan of Pacification in 1795 included in nearly all places the Lord's Supper from time to time. From this pattern the preaching service at 5 a.m. eventually disappeared, as did evensong in the afternoon; but evening services, usually at 6 p.m. or 6.30 p.m. became very popular. The morning service, usually at 10.30 a.m. or 11 a.m., replaced attendance at the parish church for morning prayer, litany*, and ante-communion*. In a few chapels in England and a larger number overseas this morning service consisted of morning prayer, either from the BCP or from Wesley's version of it in *The Sunday Service*, together with hymns and sermon. But in most churches the service was a simpler preaching service, though not quite as simple as the supplementary 5 a.m. preaching service had been. It consisted of hymns, lessons, extempore prayers and sermon, though occasionally with traces of morning prayer such as a psalm before the OT lesson. The evening service almost always took this simpler form.

The holy communion was usually observed monthly in towns, quarterly in villages, after the morning or evening preaching service. For that service a liturgical book was generally used, at least in the Wesleyan chapels, as also for occasional offices. In the preaching services, liturgical books (*see* **Books, Liturgical** 10) were little used except where the custom was retained

of saying morning prayer, often called 'the liturgical service'.

These services were enriched, as Methodist worship still is, by the use of hymns*, especially those of Charles Wesley, which are in some sense the 'liturgy' of Methodism.

To these services were added not only such 'instituted' means of grace as scripture reading, prayer (private, family, public) and fasting, but also 'prudential' means such as the love feast*, the watch-night*, the covenant service*, and the distinctive Methodist forms of fellowship meeting; society meeting, class meeting, band meeting. Some of these survive, and they have given a distinctive tone of fellowship to all Methodist worship. There was also open-air preaching. The pattern of Sunday during most of Methodist history also included morning and afternoon sessions of the Sunday school, which in various ways involved many people.

The main pattern still remains, but in recent decades fresh tendencies have appeared. The afternoon session of the Sunday school is tending to disappear, and the morning session is combined with the morning service under such titles as junior church. The children attend the earlier part of the service, and then depart to their own session; but from time to time, usually monthly, the children remain throughout for what is called 'Family Service'* or 'All-age worship'. The morning service has acquired a greater prominence; the evening service has a declining attendance, and will probably take more experimental forms.

The British Conference, after various experimental drafts, authorized *The Methodist Service Book*, 1975. This gives to the main service the heading 'The Sunday Service', a revival of Wesley's title. This seeks to establish, primarily at morning services, a flexible structure, combining fixed and free elements, which may be used whether or not the service culminates in the Lord's Supper. The structure of the preaching service is as follows: hymn, collect for purity, confession of sin, declaration of forgiveness, collect, OT lesson or epistle or both, hymn, gospel, sermon, intercessions, Lord's Prayer. When there is no communion, a prayer of thanksgiving for creation and redemption and of dedication is to be said before or after the intercessions. Other forms may be substituted for all the prayers except the Lord's Prayer.

The structure of the Lord's Supper, which immediately follows the preaching service, is as follows: peace, (sometimes the Nicene Creed,) hymn, the setting of the table, the thanksgiving, the breaking of the bread, (sometimes the prayer of humble access,) the sharing of the bread and wine, final prayer, hymn, blessing, dismissal. The thanksgiving includes the dialogue, long preface with recital of the mighty acts of God, *Sanctus**, *Benedictus qui venit*, words of institution, acclamation, anamnesis, modified forms of oblation and epiclesis, prayers for benefits of communion, doxology*.

A. RAYMOND GEORGE

2. *USA*. The forms of worship used in American Methodism reflect in many ways the social and cultural situations of American Methodists. These forms of worship often have had more in common with those of other American denominations than with English precedents.

John Wesley remained a priest of the Church of England throughout his lifetime, highly esteeming and utilizing the BCP even while supplementing it with other forms. In 1784 he sent his followers in the newly independent USA a book of over three hundred pages, entitled *The Sunday Service of the Methodists in North America with Other Occasional Services*. It was his revision and abridgement of the 1662 BCP, not too different from that adopted a few years later by the new Protestant Episcopal Church. Perhaps even more significant, Wesley sent over at the same time a hymn book.

Wesley was, it turned out, a poor judge of the American situation. Though the *Sunday Service* was reprinted in 1786 and 1790, it hardly survived Wesley as far as American usage was concerned. One year after Wesley's death, *The Sunday Service* was replaced by thirty-seven pages of 'Sacramental Services, &c.' in the 1792 *Discipline*. Gone were morning and evening prayer, the psalms, litany, and the collects, epistles, and gospels for the Lord's Supper. Orders remained for both sacraments, weddings, funerals, and the forms for the ordination of deacons, elders, and bishops. These services appeared thenceforth in the *Dis-*

ciplines. After the split of 1844 the Methodist Episcopal Church renamed this section of the *Discipline* 'The Ritual' (1848). The Methodist Episcopal Church, South, dropped the term 'Sacramental Services, &c.' in 1854 in favour of no title and adopted the term 'The Ritual' in 1870. Both churches eventually added services for the reception of new members and various dedications.

'The Ritual', however, was only used on those occasions when the sacraments or occasional offices were celebrated. Methodist worship tended to centre upon preaching services. This is especially the case in the evangelization of the West, a process largely contributing to the rapid growth of Methodism from a small sect to the largest Protestant church in America during the nineteenth century. Bishop Francis Asbury (the American John Wesley) and many of his preachers were men of the frontier, preaching and organizing societies wherever they could gather a few individuals. In such frontier situations, worship usually consisted of fervent preaching and hymn-singing. Since many of the frontier people were illiterate, a type of hymn involving considerable repetition evolved. These so-called 'gospel songs' were often testimonials to the worshipper's conversion experience.

At yearly intervals, camp meetings* were held in which crowds assembled from considerable distances to hear evangelistic preaching. At times the services developed highly emotional reactions. After several days, the camp meeting ended with separate communion services conducted by the various denominations sponsoring the session. In the second third of the nineteenth century, the revival system spread similar techniques to the churches on the more sedate eastern coast, utilizing such practices as preaching for conversions, the sawdust trail, the mourner's bench, and protracted meetings. Much of the historic content and forms of Christian worship were bypassed in favour of a pragmatic spirit that pointed to results calculated in the number of converts.

The period from 1920 to 1970, on the other hand, has been the era of middle-class respectability due to the upward social mobility of most Methodists. A second Gothic revival occurred in Methodism prompted by denominational executives. Choral music, sometimes of high quality, came to be a normal part of worship, often while congregational singing declined. Orders of worship began to appear in *The Methodist Hymnal* in 1905. In 1944 the Methodist Church published its first *Book of Worship* and another one followed twenty years later.

Beginning about 1966, another tendency appeared in the growth of experimentation with the forms of worship and a refusal to believe that recovery of past forms was the answer to making worship authentic and relevant. Many innovators have looked to new communications media as indicating directions that worship might move, especially in adding non-verbal forms of worship.

In general, the black Methodist churches have been less attracted by the forms of respectability. Their worship has often retained the spontaneity, rhythmic music, and high degree of participation characteristic of the revival system.

The 1970s and 80s saw heavy impact of the post-Vatican II reforms. Most noticeable of these have been widespread adoption of the Methodist-COCU version of the ecumenical lectionary and (eventually) the *Common Lectionary* (in 1985) by about half of Methodist congregations. This has had profound influence on the ordering of worship and fuller observance of the church year. All of the rites have been reformed and published in various volumes of the *Supplemental Worship Resources* plus *An Ordinal*. All are characterized by the move to contemporary and inclusive language*. The process of initiation has undergone major rethinking with attendant reforms. The eucharist and all other rites have moved in an ecumenical direction. Sacramental worship has become more prominent although the service of the word remains the usual Sunday service in most congregations.

The Book of Worship, 1964; William F. Dunkle, Jr and Joseph D. Quilliam, Jr (eds), *Companion to the Book of Worship*, 1970; H. Grady Hardin, Joseph D. Quillian, Jr, James F. White, *The Celebration of the Gospel*, 1964; *The Methodist Hymnal*, 1964; *Seasons of the Gospel*, 1979; *Word and Table*, 1980.

JAMES F. WHITE

Metrical Psalms

The ancestor of the modern hymnal was the metrical psalter, comprising versifications of the psalms with simple strophic tunes designed to fit the metres employed. Perhaps the most familiar example of a metrical psalm is the version of the hundredth psalm in which the original prose, 'O be joyful in the Lord, all ye lands', has become 'All people that on earth do dwell'. Included in almost every modern hymnal, and hence usually thought of as a hymn, those words first appeared in *Fourscore and Seven Psalms of David* published in Geneva in 1561. The tune always associated with them is from the still earlier *Genevan Psalter* of 1551. Thus, both words and music take us back to the same source – the English Protestant exiles who fled to Geneva in 1553 to escape persecution under Queen Mary at home.

First given a formal place in Protestant worship by Calvin, the metrical psalm owed its origin, not to him, but to Clement Marot, a poet at the court of Francis I who had begun to translate the psalms into French verse in 1533. Marot's versions soon began to enjoy great popularity at the Catholic court; but they were quickly taken up in Protestant circles, first by the Huguenots and later by Calvin for use among his 'little flock'.

By coincidence, shortly after Marot had begun to produce his versified psalms, Thomas Sternhold started upon a similar task at the court of Edward VI; and some time before his death in 1549 nineteen of his metrical psalms were published under the title *Certaine Psalmes . . . drawen into Englishe metre*. To that nucleus, John Hopkins added several versifications in 1551, certain of the English exiles in Geneva completing the translation of the psalter between 1556 and 1562. The complete version of the metrical psalter thus produced was first published in the latter year – four years after the accession of Elizabeth I – under the title *The Whole Booke of Psalmes, collected into Englysh metre by T. Starnhold, I. Hopkins and others* . . . The book contained, in addition, a few hymns, metrical versions of the canticles, and a selection of tunes, some of which were drawn from the *Genevan Psalter*. Under the Royal Injunctions of 1559, a hymn was allowed to be sung 'in the beginning or at the end of Common Prayer'; thus legally sanctioned, *The Whole Book of Psalms* became recognized as the chief song book for Anglican worship. Commonly bound up with the Bible and the BCP, the collection begun by Sternhold and Hopkins (and invariably referred to by those names) held that authorized position until a *New Version* was published in 1696.

The work of Nahum Tate, the Poet Laureate, and Dr Nicholas Brady, the *New Version* was designed to supplant the 'scandalous doggerel' of Sternhold and Hopkins. It was to become the source of many of the hymns in current use, including 'As pants the hart' – the metrical version of Ps. 42. Authorized for use in churches by an Order in Council of William III, 'Tate and Brady' yet never superseded 'Sternhold and Hopkins', the two collections serving side by side until the advent of the hymn book (*see* **Hymns** 2) ousted them both during the nineteenth century. The best of the contents of both Old and New Versions were then incorporated into the new hymnals where they still serve, together with the fine old tunes originally associated with them.

M. Frost, *English and Scottish Psalm and Hymn Tunes*, 1953; J. Julian, Preface to *Hymns Ancient and Modern, Historical Edition*, 1909; R. R. Terry, *Calvin's First Psalter*, 1932.

BERNARR RAINBOW

Mission and Worship

The contemporary development of the doctrine of mission has inevitably raised the question of its relationship to worship. This relationship may be examined in three complementary ways: 1. The precise nature of the relationship may be considered. 2. Specific acts of worship, e.g. the eucharist, may be interpreted in terms of mission. 3. Particular elements in the cultus, e.g. prayer, may be given a missionary dimension. An examination of worship and mission under each of these three heads will illustrate the scope of this subject.

1. A contrast has to be noted between the OT understanding of Israel's vocation and the role that worship has to play within that vocation, and the NT understanding of the vocation of the church and the role that

worship has to play within that vocation. Briefly put, Israel's vocation is to be a holy people (Lev. 19.2), i.e. a people whose life is patterned after the very being of its holy God. In so far as this is achieved, Israel then becomes a 'light to the Gentiles'; it is a witness before the nations to Yahweh in order that the nations themselves may come to acknowledge his universal lordship. The function of worship in relation to this vocation is to enable Israel to be holy; it is a means of sanctification for the Chosen People, who are set apart for the worship of Yahweh (Ex. 19.6). The Temple cultus is both the guarantee of the purity of Yahwism and the centre to which the nations are to come (Isa. 2.2f.). It will be noticed that Israel's vocation is interpreted centripetally; Israel is not sent to the nations; instead they are to come to it, attracted by its life and worship. In exact conformity with this, Israelite worship is understood centripetally; it has its true centre in a single place, namely the Jerusalem Temple, and it is to this that all the nations are to come.

The NT presents the antithesis to this view, in that this centripetal attitude is replaced by a centrifugal one. The church's vocation is to go out; it is to participate in the divine mission (Matt. 28.19; John 20.21; Acts 1.8). It is to join in God's action in the world as he continues his movement of humanization, assisting man towards that maturity or fullness that is embodied in Christ. The function of worship in relation to this vocation is to celebrate God's action in the world and 'so to proclaim the Lord's death until he come' (I Cor. 11.26), this being involved in the eating of the bread and the drinking of the wine at the eucharist*. Thus, as the church's vocation is interpreted centrifugally, so is its worship; it does not have a centre in a single place; anywhere is the place of encounter with God in the context of everyday life, and in so far as any temple continues to exist, this is not a building of stone but a community living in the world (II Cor. 6.16). Hence the OT is consistent in understanding both the vocation and the worship of Israel centripetally, while the NT is equally consistent but understands both the vocation and worship of the church centrifugally.

To these concepts must be added a third, namely the contrast between the general understanding of Christians today of their vocation and worship and that which we have just examined in the NT. As a consequence of the great missionary awakening of the eighteenth and nineteenth centuries, many Christians now understand the vocation of the church centrifugally, but they still persist in viewing their cultic acts centripetally. They thus give up the logical consistency that is to be found in both the OT and NT, and attempt to combine the NT centrifugal concept of vocation with the OT centripetal concept of worship in terms of ingathering. Hence the relationship of worship and mission has for decades been defined in terms of gathering and sending. The idea of gathering and sending was prominent in Germany missiological thought at the end of the last century and it is often re-presented at the present day. According to this, worship is an occasion for the gathering together of the Christian community in order that its members may be strengthened to engage in mission. So cultic acts and missionary activity can be compared to breathing in and breathing out, which are both necessary for life, and hence both worship and mission – gathering and sending – are essential for the church. The analogy is a plausible one, but is it accurate? In effect it merely associates centripetalism – breathing in – with centrifugalism – breathing out – and therefore fails to resolve the basic tension between them. Moreover, it involves the idea that cultic acts are interruptions in the church's participation in mission. When the church ceases its centrifugal action in mission, for however brief the periods may be, in order to engage in centripetal actions or worship, it is no longer being missionary during those cultic acts – in terms of the analogy, one is breathing either in or out; one cannot do the two at once. Whereas if mission and worship are to be truly united, the cultic assembly must be understood within the context of mission; the coming together takes place in mission and it is not preparatory to mission. The church is the church when it is participating in the mission of God; if it is to fulfil its role constantly, it cannot disengage itself from mission in cultic activity. The church services then must not be conceived as halting places on the way nor as iron rations; they are an essential part of being

on the way. So while the gathering and sending analogy does point to a relationship, it is not a relationship of unity, and this is precisely what has to be rediscovered if we are to be true to the NT. Worship then is not a means to mission; nor is it a preparation for mission, since we worship in mission. The inadequacy of the analogy should become more apparent, as we examine what worship means from a centrifugal or missionary perspective.

Worship, as presented in the NT, is the joyful celebration of life in the world; it is the response of man to what God has done and is doing in history. Two examples will serve to illustrate this.

In Luke 17, Jesus is met by ten lepers who ask him to have mercy on them. He accedes to their request and they are made whole. One of them, a Samaritan, recognizes in this the act of God and accordingly he worships – 'praising God with a loud voice, he fell on his face at Jesus' feet, giving him thanks' (17.16). The man does not draw apart from the world in order to worship; the basis of his act of worship is his response to God's action in the world – his restoration to wholeness by Christ – and this takes the form of expressing thanks and giving praise. The Lord's Supper* itself, throughout the apostolic age, was also essentially a secular act, since it was an everyday meal, although one which, while not ceasing to be a source of physical nourishment, was at the same time a vehicle of worship. So it can be said that in the NT worship was not defined in terms of what happened at a certain time when and at a certain place where Christians assembled. What happened on those occasions was understood within the context of response to God in their total existence.

Here we have worship interpreted from a centrifugal position. Just as the world is the sphere of mission, so it is of worship which is to be offered in terms of the Christians' total existence. The church of the apostolic age does not withdraw from mission to engage in cultic acts which prepare it for mission; it never ceases to be in mission in the secular world whether it is preaching, serving or worshipping. There can therefore be no great single centre of worship corresponding to the Jerusalem Temple.

2. The two chief Christian liturgical acts, baptism* and the eucharist, can themselves be understood in terms of mission. It is possible to indicate this by a series of theses which, in a full treatment, would require considerable expansion:

(*a*) Baptism is ordination to the royal priesthood and acceptance into the covenant, both priesthood and covenant being understood in terms of mission. The eucharist renews both the ordination and the covenant.

(*b*) Baptism, with its pattern of life and death, initiates us into mission. The eucharist re-establishes us in this pattern.

(*c*) Baptism includes us in the obedience of Christ and so in his mission. The eucharist renews our commitment to God and so to mission.

(*d*) Baptism is an eschatological sacrament and so is the eucharist; both are intimately related in this sense to mission.

3. Of the many specific elements that make up an act of worship, two may be selected to demonstrate their necessary missionary dimension, namely prayer and the dismissal*.

According to Karl Barth, Christ's 'earthly mission was accepted through his prayers as well as by his preaching and his mighty works'. This means that prayer is a part of mission. Prayer is not something separate from mission nor is it the cause of mission. When the church prays, as when Christ prayed in Galilee, it is engaged in mission; it participates in the divine action for the world. So in Eph. 6.18, prayer is referred to in the context of the weapons of warfare against the alien powers that threaten to dominate men and from which they are to be liberated through mission. Prayer is therefore one aspect of the total missionary outreach.

Next, the dismissal. Although it is now customary to conclude every service with a blessing*, in the early church the dismissal did not take this form and was very brief. Indeed it is or should be an echo of the missionary command in Matt. 28. Any and every service is most fittingly brought to an end by a dismissal which expresses this outgoing to the world at large. It is therefore not a cosy rounding-off of a cultic act but part of the sending of God's servants in mission.

Within the NT there is a continual emphasis upon the unity of worship and mission. Not only does Paul describe

mission in cultic terms and cultic acts in terms of mission (cf. Rom. 12.1; II Cor. 2.15; Phil. 2.17), but the life and work of Jesus are similarly spoken of in terms both of mission and of worship (John 6.51, 57; 12.49; Heb. 3.1). It is this relationship of unity that is gradually being rediscovered at the present day.

Simon Barrington-Ward, 'Theology of Mission', *NDCT*; W. Bühlmann, *God's Chosen People*, 1982; J. G. Davies, *Worship and Mission*, 1966; D. Senior and C. Stuhlmueller, *The Biblical Foundations for Mission*, 1983.

EDITOR

Mitre

see **Vestments** 2(*k*)

Mixed Chalice

The reference is to the mingling of water and wine in the cup at the eucharist. This was the invariable practice of the early church (cf. Justin, *Apol.* I, 65, 67; Cyprian, *Ep.* 63.13) and was probably what Jesus himself did at the Last Supper, since it was usual for the Jews to mix water with their wine. All the ancient liturgies either contain a direction for the mixing or refer to it in the prayers, e.g. in the *Apostolic Constitutions* (8.12), reading the words of institution, the priest says: 'Likewise also mixing the cup of wine and water and blessing it, he gave it to them.'

Various symbolic meanings have been attached to this. Some have seen it as a sign of the union of the people with Christ, others of the issue of water and blood from his side on the cross, and others again of the union of the two natures in Christ. This latter interpretation has led the Armenians to reject the practice because it conflicts with their monophysitism, i.e. belief in the one nature of Christ.

It was rejected, too, at the Reformation by Luther, who regarded it as symbolizing an impossible participation of the human with the pure work of God. Churches in the Calvinist tradition, e.g. the Church of Scotland and the Reformed Church of France, do not practise it. The 1549 BCP ordered it, but the rubric* was omitted in 1552. It is customary in the Episcopal Church of Scotland, but was expressly forbidden by canon 37 of the Church of Ireland. It is widespread, but not universal, in the Anglican Communion, having been declared legal in a judgment in the case of the Bishop of Lincoln (1891). The BCP of the Episcopal Church (1979) states: 'it is customary to add a little water to the wine'.

In the Liturgy of St Chrysostom *hot* water is added to the chalice at the commixture*. The origins of this are unknown, but it appears to have been established from at least the sixth century. This *zeon* or living water, as it is called, is said to symbolize the fervency of faith and the descent of the Holy Spirit.

EDITOR

Monstrance

A vessel designed for the purpose of showing the consecrated host to the people came into use from the thirteenth century in the Latin West as a result of the increased cultus of the reserved sacrament that arose in the later Middle Ages. No such cultus has ever existed in the Eastern Orthodox Church or the lesser Eastern Churches. The earliest forms of the monstrance were pyxes* standing upon a stem and foot with openings or fenestrations on the sides of the pyx as in the thirteenth-century example preserved in the Church of St Quentin, Hasselt, Limburg. The next stage was to replace the metal sides with a cylinder of glass (*see* Plate 43); then finally it assumed the form of a circular window surrounded by a silver or gold frame with rays. The ceremonies associated with the use of the monstrance arose in the Low Countries and Germany, first in connection with the Feast of Corpus Christi*, but in the Counter-Reformation era the exposition of the host became very much more frequent (*see* **Benediction; Exposition**).

The monstrance and its associated ceremonies have come into use in the Church of England since the Catholic revival, but liturgical reforms now taking place in the Roman Catholic Church are tending to discourage this type of devotion to the blessed sacrament.

A. A. King and C. E. Pocknee, *Eucharistic Reservation in the Western Church*, 1965.

C. E. POCKNEE

Moravian Worship

Moravian worship cannot properly be understood or evaluated without some introduc-

Plate 43 The Belem monstrace, Lisbon, Portugal

tion, however brief, to the history of the church itself.

The Moravian Church came into being in the kingdom of Bohemia (now part of Czechoslovakia) in the year 1457. It consisted at first of a small group of men and women who lived in brotherly fellowship according to the principles of the Sermon on the Mount. They called themselves 'The Unity of Brethren', or in Latin, *Unitas Fratrum*, which is the official name of the Moravian Church. In 1467 they established their own ministry with episcopal orders and withdrew from the Church of Rome.

In 1620 Protestantism was overthrown in Bohemia and the *Unitas Fratrum* ceased to exist as an organized body. But about a century later some survivors from the old *Unitas* fled into Saxony and were allowed to settle on the estates of a Lutheran nobleman, Count Nicolaus Ludwig von Zinzendorf. Other religious refugees joined them and together they founded a new community called Herrnhut. This diverse and often disunited group experienced a 'second Pentecost' at a celebration of the Lord's Supper on 13 August 1727, which marks the birth of the renewed Moravian Church.

One direct result of this renewal was a burning desire to carry the gospel wherever Christ should call, and it was in fulfilment of this task that the renewed church became established in the eighteenth and nineteenth centuries in England, North, Central and South America, the Caribbean, Africa and India.

Moravian worship as it is practised today contains active elements from these three periods of the Church's history – the ancient church, the renewed church and the missionary church.

In the ancient *Unitas Fratrum*, in sharp contrast to the Roman Church, worship was Bible-centred and congregation-orientated. To provide for this, the first hymn book of the *Unitas Fratrum* was published in 1501 and was followed a few years later by a translation of the Bible into the Czech language, the Kralitz Bible. The services in this early period were extremely simple and consisted of the singing of a hymn or hymns, a threefold reading of psalm, gospel and epistle, and a sermon. 'Free' prayer was linked with the Bible reading and the sermon, but from about 1566 onwards Luther's 'German litany' was introduced into the Moravian hymn book. A liturgy retaining elements from these early sources is still used in parts of the Moravian Church.

In the renewed church some of the forms of worship from the ancient *Unitas* were taken over and adapted, but other distinctive services developed to meet particular needs. Of these the following are of special interest in that they are still in use:

1. The love feast*. The 'agape' of apostolic times was part of the common meal which ended with the Lord's Supper. The spontaneous revival of this custom in the renewed Moravian Church of Herrnhut followed the rich experiences of unity and fellowship in the historic communion service on 13 August 1727. At the close of this service many members were loath to leave the church but continued in prayer, in religious conversation and hymn singing. Hearing of this Count Zinzendorf sent food to the church – 'in order for them to stay undisturbed together'. From this the love feast grew into a recognized service expressing in a special way the fellowship of each member with his brethren and sisters. The Moravian love feast today consists of the singing of hymns and an informal discourse by the minister on the life and work of the church, during which a simple meal is served and partaken of together.

2. The use in public and private worship of the Moravian 'Daily Texts' or 'Watchwords'. Soon after the renewal of the church, the Herrnhut elders went each morning from house to house giving a scriptural 'watchword' for the day as a guide to meditation and conduct. Count Zinzendorf selected these texts and later added to them a few lines from hymns in current use. In 1730 a collection of these 'watchwords' was printed in advance for the year 1731. Moravian family worship usually consists of the reading of the texts for the day followed by Bible reading and prayer. The 'text book' is printed in twenty-six languages with a circulation of over a million copies. It is frequently used in public worship especially in the love feast, which closes with a short homily on the NT text for that particular day.

In the missionary period, with the granting to the provinces and mission fields of the Moravian Church of a greater measure of autonomy, coupled with a diminution in the control and influence formerly exercised by Herrnhut, each province has tended to develop worship forms and usages to suit its own needs. But in the Moravian Church throughout the world there is still a recognizable basic pattern of worship which owes something to the two earlier periods of the ancient and the renewed church. The chief characteristics of this basic pattern are:

1. The use in public worship of liturgical forms of service, and of 'free' services comprising hymns, 'free' prayer, scripture reading(s) and a sermon.

2. Regular observance of the Lord's Supper in which common features are the distribution of the elements to the congregation during the singing of hymns, partaking of the elements together, and the conclusion of the service with a so-called 'covenant hymn' during which the members of the congregation exchange the right hand of fellowship with each other in token of the renewal of their 'covenant' of love and service with Christ and with one another.

3. The use of the love feast as a preparation for the Lord's Supper, or to mark some special church gathering, festival or anniversary.

Congregational singing has always played a major part in Moravian worship. It is therefore not surprising that the Moravian Church has produced down the centuries many famous hymn writers, including Michael Weisse, Count Zinzendorf, John Cennick and James Montgomery, whose works are to be found in most Protestant hymn books (*see* **Hymns** 2), and 1975 saw the publication of a new music edition of the Moravian Hymn Book of the British Province.

J. T. and K. G. Hamilton, *History of the Moravian Church*, 1967; J. E. Hutton, *A History of the Moravian Church*, 1909; A. J. Lewis, *Zinzendorf, The Ecumenical Pioneer*, 1962.

J. H. FOY

Mormon Worship

see **Church of Jesus Christ of Latter Day Saints Worship**

Motet

From the thirteenth century to the eighteenth the motet (from French *mot* = word), which arose as a trope, or insertion, in the liturgy, was one of the most significant forms of polyphonic music (*see* **Polyphony**). The mediaeval motet and its allied forms cover a huge quantity of music, little of which in modern times is sung in church, but which can be fairly frequently heard in the concert hall, on the radio and

on gramophone records, performed by specialist vocal groups. The characteristic features of the early motet may be summarized as follows: the lowest voice (tenor) carried the chant, usually cut up and arranged in a series of recurring rhythmic patterns; above this voice there were one, two or three additional parts with texts that paraphrased the text of the tenor, as may be seen in the following example:

1. In saeculum saeculi, Artifex saeculi, etc.

2. In saeculum saeculi, supra mulieres, etc.

3. IN SAECULUM (this was the chant itself, known as the *cantus firmus*).

The added parts normally moved more quickly than the *cantus firmus*. Each part was independent, so that if, in fact, one or other of the upper parts was omitted or sung alone, the music still made sense; but the fragmented chant in the tenor, deprived of its flowing phrase and rhythm, by itself would not.

Polytextuality enabled the clerical poet-musicians to make a kind of musical mosaic in this way, but one that, as prayer, could only be appreciated to the full by the singers. This inherently attractive scheme became corrupted by the use of polylingual texts, sometimes of purely secular origin; thus, a French *chanson* might be in the top part with the Latin liturgical texts beneath it. Among the many developments in succeeding centuries the most important, at the start of the fifteenth century, was the replacement of the chant by a freely-invented melodic line, combined with a contrapuntal treatment in which the parts were equally dependent on one another, often imitating one another's phrases and none being *primus inter pares*.

The motet was usually an extra-liturgical piece, that is, it had no necessary place in mass or vespers. The liturgy, strictly speaking, required that if a motet used the text (or a part) of the offertory, for example, the latter had still to be sung in chant in its usual place in the mass before the motet was introduced. But in the second half of the fifteenth century there was a return to a more strictly liturgical use of the genre, with texts drawn from the ordinary* of the mass or from the various chants of the divine office*.

Perhaps the greatest composer of motets in the late fifteenth and early sixteenth century was Josquin des Prez. He was followed by a pleiad of outstanding Renaissance composers: de Monte, Lassus, Palestrina, Giovanni Gabrieli, Morales, Victoria, and the English William Byrd and Peter Philips.

Settings of the proper of the mass have been called motets, for example those in Byrd's *Gradualia*, his greatest work; but in this case they should properly bear their liturgical titles. Palestrina, to give another example, set the offertory texts for the whole of the church's year and they are published under that title.

The later history of the motet includes the works of Alessandro Grandi, in Italy, the *Grands Motets* of Du Mont and Lalande and the *Petits Motets* of Nivers and Clérambault in France; the classical motets of Michael Haydn and Mozart; Gounod's *Motets solennels*, and the *20 motets* of Saint-Saëns.

John Caldwell, *Medieval Music*, 1978.

MARY BERRY

Movement-Prayer

A movement-prayer is a response to God – it may be a supplication, an act of praise or thanksgiving – which involves physical actions (*see* Plate 44). The action either embodies the meaning of what is said, i.e. it incarnates the words, or it replaces verbal utterance entirely so that the movement is itself the prayer. The sign of the cross (*see* **Gestures** 3) is one such movement-prayer of long use in the Christian church.

Since prayer* is a communing with God, it should be an offering of our total selves as beings with unified spiritual and bodily aspects. Through physical movements we can reinforce or complement verbal utterances. So we may say with the psalmist as we kneel: 'Let us worship and bow down' (Ps. 95.6). The posture adjustment is then itself worship. Moreover to adopt a posture (*see* **Movements in Worship**) is to encourage the condition expressed by it; when one assumes a posture of humility, by kneeling or prostrating oneself, one's sense of humility declared verbally is fostered. Attitudes are in this way strengthened by bodily expression; movements quicken feelings. Even when devotion is dormant, it can be evoked by physical activity. This is all the

Plate 44 'Give us this day our daily bread.' Students of the Department of Theology, University of Birmingham.

more important because prayer is not just the uttering of words; it involves feelings, and sometimes, as with Jesus in the Garden of Gethsemane, feelings at their most intense. But feelings are inseparable from the bodily aspect of human nature. Indeed movements increase sensitivity; they are a medium of expression and should be the partner of vocal prayer. The authors of the Armenian liturgy were well aware of this. At the 'inclination', when the people bow in adoration, the priest is directed to pray that the Holy Spirit may 'keep them entire and stamp upon their hearts the posture of their bodies'.

Movement-prayer is important in order to protect the reality of worship so that there should be an agreement between what is said and what is done. To say Psalm 47 motionless is to create a disease, since verse 1 bids us clap our hands and verse 7 tells us to sing praises. To rejoice, exult and shout (Zeph. 3.14) while sitting flopped in a pew produces a conflict between voice and posture. Similarly, to pray 'Your kingdom come' while in a sedentary posture is to suggest that little can be done about it, whereas standing with arms raised and extended forwards declares that those praying can and will be agents of its advent. To do this in unison is at the same time to make the prayer itself truly corporate. Movement-prayer assists people not just to know about prayer but to experience praying together.

J. G. Davies, *Liturgical Dance*, 1984; M. E. Moynahan, *Embodied Prayer* (4 tapes), 1980.

EDITOR

Movements in Worship

Because human beings are not discarnate spirits but bodies, their acts of religious devotion frequently take the form of physical movements. Islamic worship*, for example, consists of a series of gestures and postures. Christian worship similarly, from its earliest days, has included standing, sitting and kneeling, as well as walking in processions and other activities. Contemporary studies of human physical be-

haviour have led to a more or less precise vocabulary for categorizing movements and these are obviously relevant to the analysis and understanding of liturgy. The main categories are as follows:

1. *Gesture*. This refers to the movement of a part of the body as distinct from the whole. Wagging the fingers, shaking the fist, stamping the feet – these are gestures*.

2. *Posture*. This denotes the position and carriage of the limbs and indeed of the entire body when in a state of immobility. Under posture, then, are to be grouped a long list of words that designate total body shape. A person is said to be standing, sitting, squatting, crouching, kneeling – these are all postures*.

3. *Posture adjustment*. This refers to the act whereby one changes one's body shape. I am standing (posture) and I then lie down on my back (posture adjustment) and so become supine (posture).

4. *Locomotion*. As its etymology indicates, this involves motion from one place (*loco*) to another. A procession* around the altar is one form of locomotion. It refers therefore not to movement on the spot but through space. In the horizontal plane one runs or marches, while in the vertical it is possible to jump or hop.

Because human beings are not just bodies but have a spiritual aspect to their nature, all these movements have been invested with meaning. The Bible in particular uses psychological concepts to characterize bodily parts and movements, e.g. the arm signifies strength and salvation; kneeling is a posture of penitence and humility; skipping expresses joy. It is consequently possible to formulate a movement vocabulary comprising a list of movements with definitions of their meanings. This, then, can serve as a tool to interpret liturgical actions and as an encouragement of their use in relation to movement-prayers*, psalms*, hymns* and carols*.

J. G. Davies, *Liturgical Dance*, 1984; W. Lamb, *Posture and Gesture*, 1965; W. Lamb and E. Watson, *Body Code*, 1979.

EDITOR

Music

see **Anthem, Antiphon; Byzantine Chant; Canticles; Carol; Chants; Chants of the Proper of the Mass; Choir (Musical); Church Modes; Divine Office; Gregorian Chant; Hymns; Metrical Psalms; Motet; Music in the Mass of the Roman Rite; Music, Modern; Music as Worship; Notation and Rhythm; Office Hymn; Organ; Polyphony; Psalmody; Psalm-Tones; Responsorial Psalmody and Responsories; Spirituals**

Music in the Mass of the Roman Rite

The mass*, or eucharist*, is the central act of worship of the Christian church. The mass of the Roman rite is that form of the service proper to Western Christianity. It is derived structurally from the papal mass of the early seventh century. Apart from the chanted readings and the celebrant's prayers the music of the mass falls into two categories known as the proper* and the ordinary*. Full musical settings of the texts of the proper and the ordinary in Gregorian chant* may be found in the *Graduale Romanum*. The chants of the proper* have texts drawn mainly from the Bible (in particular from the psalms) and they differ from day to day and from feast to feast. They are five in number for each day: 1. the Introit, or entrance chant; 2. the Gradual; 3. the Alleluia (replaced by a Tract in seasons of penance, such as Lent, and followed occasionally by a Sequence); 4. the Offertory, sung during the procession to the altar with the gifts, and 5. the Communion, sung during the distribution of holy communion. The chants of the ordinary have fixed texts, the same at all masses. They, too, are five in number: 1. *Kyrie**; 2. *Gloria*; 3. *Credo*; 4. *Sanctus** (with *Benedictus*); and 5. *Agnus Dei**. The *Gloria* and the *Credo* are sung on Sundays and on certain feast days only. The texts of the ordinary are the ones that have been commonly set by composers of polyphony from mediaeval times to the present day, though certain pieces of the proper have also occasionally been set, either for voices or for the organ*. Some of the finest music for the mass was composed by the great European masters of the sixteenth and early seventeenth centuries.

The Tridentine *Missale Romanum* of 1570 is frequently spoken of as if it were a creation of the Council of Trent as a result of proceedings concerning it in the session presided over by Pope Pius V. In fact, as Dom David Knowles has pointed out, it

was in all essentials a replica of the Roman missal of 1474, and that, in its turn, followed the practice of the church in the reign of Innocent II which derived from the usage of Gregory the Great and his successors in the seventh century. The 1570 missal was, therefore, essentially traditional, more so, some scholars think, than the reformed missal published in 1971. The modern *Missa normativa* of Pope Paul VI is now the official mass of the whole Roman Church and is usually celebrated in the vernacular* of each country. Special permission can still be obtained for the occasional celebration of the old Tridentine mass. It is, however, important to realize that the present *Missa normativa* was first formulated in Latin and may therefore be freely and legitimately celebrated in that ancient and universal tongue. It is, in fact, celebrated regularly in Latin in a number of churches. When this is the case, 'the treasury of sacred music', as Pope Paul VI has called it, dating from the earliest centuries of the chant to the present day, is always available to choirs and congregations competent to do justice to it. Indeed, it would be a major loss if a repertoire of such immense cultural and spiritual value were to be permanently deprived of its *raison d'être* and merely relegated to the concert hall. On the other hand, there is no reason why, for example, Latin chants and Latin polyphony should not be combined with English readings and English prayers in a single celebration. Furthermore, the permission, widely interpreted as an injunction, to celebrate in the vernacular has opened up endless possibilities for the composition of new musical settings of the texts of both proper and ordinary, in English and in other modern languages. Moreover, there is no law forbidding anyone to make adaptations to English words of the sacred music of earlier centuries, including the music that is our closest living link with the church of the apostles: Gregorian chant.

C. Jones, G. Wainwright and E. Yarnold (eds), *The Study of Liturgy*, 1978; Josef Jungmann, *The Early Liturgy*, reissued 1976; Ferdinand Haberl, *Das Kyriale Romanum*, 1975; *Das Graduale Romanum*, 1976.

MARY BERRY

Music, Modern

A vague term used to denote the music of the present century, or its antecedents in the romantic movement, or even – colloquially – the popular music of the day. In the later nineteenth century the Austro-German tradition, and its means of structuring music through tonality or key relationships, was extended by composers within it and challenged by those from outside. Particularly crucial was the work of Arnold Schoenberg (1874–1951) and his pupils Anton Webern (1883–1945) and Alban Berg (1885–1935). They have been called the Second Viennese School – a misleading title, since the tradition was continuous, even though Schoenberg's development of twelve-note technique appeared revolutionary at the time. Claude Debussy (1862–1918, France), Bela Bartok (1881–1945, Hungary), Igor Stravinsky (1882–1971, Russia), and Charles Ives (1874–1954, USA) must also be included among the major innovators of the first half of this century.

After the Second World War there emerged a generation less radical than some of their elders and often showing humanitarian or specifically religious commitment: Olivier Messiaen (1908– , France), Luigi Dallapiccola (1904–1975, Italy), Michael Tippett (1905–) and Benjamin Britten (1913–1976, England), and Hans Werner Henze (1926– , Germany). There is a breadth of popular appeal in much of the work of Aaron Copland (1900– , USA) and Dmitry Shostakovich (1906–1975, Russia). John Cage (1912– , USA) is the pioneer of the musical avant-garde, where some of the later work of Karlheinz Stockhausen (1928– , Germany) also belongs. A technological paradise for music, with major facilities for electronic composition, the *Institut de Recherche et de Coordination Acoustique/Musique* was opened in Paris in 1976 by composer-conductor Pierre Boulez (1925–).

The twentieth century is the age of jazz, which has grown rapidly from Afro-American folk music into an improvizing art of great virtuosity and international acclaim, documented through recordings. The 1960s saw a flowering of pop, or rock, and the importance of groups such as The Beatles became recognized by critics and historians

as well as fans. The range of musical experience is now greater than ever, thanks to recording techniques and broadcasting media: electronic resources, including computer control, are increasingly involved.

These heterogeneous developments have resulted in a fragmentation of musical society with separate publics for jazz, folk, early music, orchestral, or avant-garde. The notion of a common musical language was difficult to sustain in the 1960s, but by the 1980s composers were becoming more aware of the needs of the listener and different musical categories were made to interact. One example is the *Sinfonia* (1968/9) by Luciano Berio (1925– , Italy), an orchestral work using the Swingle Singers and quoting many other composers including Mahler: another is *St Thomas Wake: Foxtrot for Orchestra on a Pavan by John Bull* (1969) by Peter Maxwell Davies (1934– , England).

The use of contemporary music in church has always presented problems, which reflect wider debates. On the purely practical level, church choirs find the rhythms and harmonies of Stravinsky difficult to master and congregations may not always respond to the visionary intensity of Messiaen's organ cycles. Stockhausen's *Gesang der Jünglinge*, for electronic tape, was written in 1956 for a large cathedral but is not often heard in such places. There is a wide gap between current musical thinking and the opportunites the church affords, even literally in economic terms. Some composers have specialized in liturgical music and churches have commissioned works from living composers. Much of this is of local interest compared with the inspiring concert works to sacred texts, such as Stravinsky's *Symphony of Psalms* (1930), *Canticum Sacrum* (1955) and *Threni* (1957/8); Britten's *War Requiem* (1961); Tippett's *The Vision of St Augustine* (1963/5); and the *St Luke Passion* (1963–5) by Krzystof Penderecki (1933– , Poland), which combines monody, choral polyphony and avant-garde orchestral effects.

Some composers, like Britten and Lennox Berkeley (1903– , England), have written church music in an existing tradition which respects the formalities of public worship. Of the previous generation Herbert Howells (1892–1983) was notable for services, anthems and organ music. But in the search for a means of direct communication, the church has turned enviously to the success of folk groups and ephemeral popular music of any kind. This do-it-yourself situation can only be regarded as transitional, perhaps a challenge to the future where an experimental attitude is healthier than the formulae of the past. But ultimately it is no substitute for bringing the finest composers into contact with the churches to transmit, as in the past, their message through music to the world.

William W. Austin, *Music in the Twentieth Century*, 1966; P. Griffiths, *A Concise History of Modern Music*, 1978; Charles Hamm, *Music in the New World*, 1983; P. Hardy and D. Laing, *The Encyclopaedia of Rock*, I–III, 1976; E. Routley, *The Church and Music*, 1967; S. Sadie (ed), *The New Grove Dictionary of Music and Musicians*, 1980; Eric Salzman, *Twentieth-Century Music – An Introduction*, 1967; Gunther Schuller, *Early Jazz*, I, 1968, II (forthcoming); H. H. Stuckenschmidt, *Twentieth-Century Music*, 1969.

PETER DICKINSON

Music as Worship

For most primitive peoples the origin of life is a sound; it was God's hum, shout, croak or gibber that stirred creation within the void. That there are physiological reasons for this age-old, widespread belief may be implicit in the cry of the newborn babe who, separated from the mother as he struggles into an alien world, yells for mammalian security, yearning to be again part of Nature, mother of all creation. Physiological factors may be linked with philosophical 'laws' in that the mathematical principles by which sound operates are a microcosm of those that control the universe. In this sense music springs simultaneously from our emotional instincts and from the extra-sensory harmony that, in Sir Thomas Browne's phrase, 'intellectually sounds in the mind of God'. No wonder music and the numinous have always been inseparable.

The music of primitive peoples does not exist in itself but is usually ancillary to action. Music and dance ritually succour, and hopefully control, the seasonal processes of the earth; the gods are appeased

in the interests of practical efficacy. Hunting songs are acts of worship in that they invoke the gods' help in securing a desired end; even play songs call on metaphysical sanctions to ensure success, either of the community or, less commonly, of the individual. Primitive man does not distinguish between the sacral and the expedient. His music is religious in being concerned with origins, but is practical 'music of necessity' in fulfilling social and therapeutic needs.

With the great – sophisticated rather than primitive – oriental cultures, Indian, Asiatic and Chinese, the purpose of most music is religious in that it seeks, in accord with inherited beliefs, to release men and women from the burden and contagion of the world, absorbing rather than asserting the mind and flesh. Christian Europe in its mediaeval heyday accepted this legacy from the East, though in the West a dichotomy emerges between music for worship and the secular act of dance. Of course mediaeval people danced, like any others; but they regarded dance as suspect in being, like life itself, essentially ephemeral. This became patent when literate Western man wanted to preserve his artefacts in some form of notation. 'Worldly' dance music was seldom thus perpetuated; 'heavenly' plainsong, on the other hand, became, as the doctrinal music of the Roman Church, a written as well as aurally transmitted Law springing from the Sacred Word. 'Serious' mediaeval music was affiliated to the Latin liturgy. Conceived as monody, as were oriental musics, plainsong aurally incarnates God's unity, carrying both singer and auditor 'beyond' the self, into communion with the One: as does also the quasi-secular monody of the troubadours as they celebrate a woman who is also an Eternal Beloved. Even when mediaeval composers write polyphonically, in two, three or very occasionally in four parts, they evade harmonic progression, subsuming everything into the plainchant's inexorable law. *Cantus firmus* technique, as the term implies, was based on the 'firm song' which was God's undeviating gift to faltering men. Structural principles in mediaeval music demonstrate how music had nothing to do with human expressivity but was regarded as a branch of theology, astronomy and mathematics.

With Europe's slow efflorescence into the Renaissance, religious duty merges into social life. The metaphysical heritage of Christianity is not substantially weakened, but it comes to terms with man's awareness of his temporal mind and senses. Thus for William Byrd, greatest English composer of Shakespeare's day, the divine music was manifest in his Latin and English motets and masses for voices, while the civic music was manifest in his madrigals and instrumental music for strings and keyboards. That the two genres are now interdependent is evident in sixteenth-century polyphonic technique itself: for although the free-flowing lines are as atemporal as plainsong, the effect of the 'many voices' when sung together depends on the harmonies the lines create at consecutive 'moments in time'. Vocal rhythm and dance metre co-exist. Despite the meta-physical nature of the melodies, dance comes into its physical own as a formalizing principle, being an order men make as they tread the earth they live on. The ticking of time's clock is essential to the effect and this, of its nature, tends to emphasize flesh at the expense of spirit.

It is not therefore surprising that with the advance of European humanism into the periods we call Baroque, the numinous went underground. Opera – an imitation of actions considered worth imitating precisely because they are human – literally took the centre of the stage. At the beginning of the seventeenth century Monteverdi composed music in what he called the 'old practice', adhering to the simultaneously divine and civic techniques of the Renaissance. More significantly, he explored in his 'new practice' music's power to emulate and sublimate human voices speaking in the throes of passion, relating these expressive accents to the gestures of dancing bodies. By the time we reach the High Baroque such expressive accents and physical gestures have been stabilized into a code of manners and morals. Handel's operas and oratorios embody a scheme of melodic, rhythmic, harmonic and tonal relationships which auralize ideals of human behaviour in a civilized community. Though Handel is a great composer because he exhibits so profound an awareness of the difficulty and complexity of such ideals, he is a humanitarian rather than a religious artist – and most so in his most popular work, *Messiah*,

which offered to the rising middle class a compendium of moral and civic virtues, based on New Testament ethics rather than on Old Testament theology. Though the work has moments of sublime transcendence, they are an overflow of man's humanity rather than of God's will; and the fact that Handel's contemporary Bach *is* a religious composer in the sense that Handel is not, does not affect this historical evolution. Even in his own day Bach was considered anachronistic. Nowadays we recognize in the B Minor Mass some of the most 'numinous' music in European tradition, miraculously reconciling the operatic passions of his day with the 'eternal' unity of contrapuntal science and a quasi-magical numerology. Given the temper of his time, however, we can understand why the burgomasters who employed Bach considered him inferior to Telemann.

With the next great watershed in European music, that of the Viennese classics, the new, democratic world hinted at by Handel comes to fruition. No longer is a law imposed from above, whether by God or the state, for if every one is potentially equal in the sight of God music must become a search for an individual's own identity, before he or she can be responsible for other people. Haydn, first of the Viennese masters, belonged to the old world in being a countryman reared as a pious Roman Catholic. Yet although throughout his long life he made music for the liturgy of his church, he inevitably modified that faith-affirming music in the light of the sonata principle which was his first love, and which he did more than anyone to establish. *The Creation*, the work in which his church music culminates, is not a Catholic mass but a post-Handelian oratorio dedicated to ethical enlightenment, spelling out verbally what had been implicit in the evolving cycle of his symphonies and string quartets, which are a voyage of discovery in the interests not of the numinous, but of human self-fulfilment and social amelioration here and now, in a rapidly changing world. The dawn of Light in *The Creation* is paralled by the marvellous aspiring opening of the Quartet in B flat from Opus 76. The 'Sunrise' it celebrates is in the natural world, over the hill: but also in the hearts of those who hoped to create a new society.

Significantly Haydn, without renouncing his Catholicism, espoused the fashionably ethical religion of Free Masonry, having been introduced to it by Mozart who, as opera composer, said that he 'deemed nothing human alien' to him. Yet Mozart's late instrumental works, complementing the humanely Shakespearean plenitude of his mature operas, reveal that an inner voyage of discovery may entail a renewal of the mystical sense. The Masonic works of Mozart's last years breathe an ethereal radiance that 'transcends' their death-haunted qualities. If the divertimento-like String Quintet in E flat K 614 sounds superficially like social persiflage, it would also divert a company of angels, and is light years from being music to eat or chatter to. The rediscovery of the numinous through *self*-discovery reaches its apex in late Beethoven who, having in his middle years encompassed the fiercest degree of duality in music, found serenity within the Promethean fire itself. Like Kant, Beethoven learned that 'we live in an Invisible Church; God's Kingdom is in ourselves'. In his last Piano Sonata, Opus 111, 'shipwrack' – to quote Hopkins – 'becomes a harvest, tempest carries the grain'. This sonata opens with an introduction that reinterprets the grandeur of the old heroic overture in introspective terms; embarks on a divisive conflict between the contradictory principles of dualistic sonata and monistic fugue; and in a sublime coda reconciles the opposites of the Blakean Tyger and Lamb so that conflict may flower, in the Arietta, into a song melody that proliferates into divisions on a ground. The sonata is a retrospect of Beethoven's lifelong experience, and the celestial peace it wins to is a new kind of religious affirmation, discovered within the psyche. Though Beethoven's *Missa Solemnis*, composed at the same time as the sonata, makes this affirmation within the framework of the Christian church, it is not formally doctrinal and is far too long and too difficult for liturgical use. Yet no more numinous music has been created than the Benedictus of the *Missa Solemnis*, wherein the 'still, small voice' rings, for those who have ears to hear, in Beethoven's deaf ears.

Of his *Missa Solemnis* Beethoven memorably remarked: 'He who truly understands this music will be freed thereby from all the miseries of the world.' He was right (the rub being in that 'truly'); and it might

be fair to say that Beethoven's *Missa Solemnis* and his late string quartets are creations that may numinously serve as a substitute for orthodox religious experience. Their significance is the more potent in that most of the major composers of the nineteenth century were, in a world increasingly mercantile, agnostic. Schubert, uncommitted to his Catholicism, lived on his nerves and senses, intermittently glimpsing intimations of immortality; Brahms, of sturdy Protestant stock, was stoic rather than Christian. Berlioz was a visionary rather than a man of faith; Verdi, a Catholic by upbringing rather than inclination, rooted his theatrical art in the desperate realities of post-lapsarian human nature. Only Bruckner was by temperament mystical, his Catholicism renewed in quasi-mediaeval innocence: though the fact that his most significant music is symphonic, owing as much to 'dualistic' Beethoven as to 'monistic' Bach, points to an element of ambiguity within his faith. Moreover Bruckner was obsessed no less by the New Master, Wagner: which makes sense if we remember that although Wagner's deification of the self was in one sense the twilight of European humanism, he too achieved transcendence *through* self-discovery, notably in *Tristan* and *Parsifal*, the latter described by the composer as re-created ritual and myth. Wagner's successor Schoenberg reaffirms transcendence in a Christian Hebraic context, especially in his opera *Moses and Aaron*. Schoenberg's pupil Webern, who was something of a scholar in the field of mediaeval music, reinstates the mathematical certitudes that lie 'behind' the numinous. Later Webern disciples, serializing rhythm and dynamics as well as pitch, further relate musical structure to the concepts of mediaeval and oriental alchemy and mathematics.

There is thus some evidence that music as worship may be re-emerging in the twentieth century: not merely in obvious areas like the neo-primitive fertility rites of Stravinsky and the Roman-Catholic-Indian-Peruvian quasi-liturgical works of Messiaen, but also in music-theatre pieces such as Stockhausen's *Stimmung*, wherein the performers seek magically to 'tune to the universe', creating not a concert but a ritual act in which the audience participates. Though such esoteric phenomena may have little sociological significance, we should remember that the audience for the later Stockhausen overlaps with that for 'progressive' pop; and that most pop musics reinvoke the tribal gods. Throughout the century, indeed, black, originally African jazz has reintroduced music as orgiastic ritual to the inhabitants of white industrial cities. Over the next half-century music may be increasingly reoperative as worship, effecting a religious commitment beyond the confines of an Established church.

Jan Chiapusso, *Bach's World*, 1965; R. A. Leaver, *The Liturgy and Music*, 1976; Wilfrid Mellers, *Bach and the Dance of God*, 1981; *Beethoven and the Voice of God*, 1984; Dane Rudhyar, *The Magic of Tone and the Art of Music*, 1982; Hermann Scherchen, *The Nature of Music*, 1950; Herbert Whone, *The Hidden Face of Music*, 1950; Victor Zuckerkandl, *Sound and Symbol*, 1956; *Man the Musician*, 1973.

WILFRID MELLERS

Narthex

The porch or vestibule in the Hellenistic basilica*, closed to the exterior but opening into the nave*, It was the place where people waited before services, and from which the Great Entrance*, in its original form, began.

EDITOR

Nave

The body of a church, usually separated from the aisles* or wings by pillars. The term derives from the Latin *navis* meaning a 'ship'. This comparison of a church building to a ship was made at an early date, so the *Apostolic Constitution* (*c*.375) says: 'When thou callest an assembly of the church as one that is the commander of a great ship, appoint the assemblies to be made with all possible skill, charging the deacons as mariners to prepare places for the brethren as for passengers, with all due care and decency. And first, let the building be long, with its head to the east, with its vestries on both sides at the east end, and so it will be like a ship. In the middle let the bishop's throne be placed, and on each side of him let the presbytery sit down; and let the deacons stand near at hand, in close and

small girt garments, for they are like the mariners and managers of a ship: with regard to these, let the laity sit on the other side, with all quietness and good order. And let the women sit by themselves, they also keeping silence. In the middle let the reader stand upon some high place' (2.57).

In certain areas during the patristic period the nave was kept free from the laity who were confined to the aisles, either because the altar was placed there, as in North Africa, or because, as in Syria, it was occupied by a large semi-circular construction containing the bishop's throne and seats for the presbyters.

In the Middle Ages, churches were widely used for secular activities, the nave in particular being the scene of dancing, eating, drinking, plays, etc.

EDITOR

Nestorian Church

see **East Syrian Worship**

New Fire

The lighting and the blessing of the 'new fire' takes place at the opening of the Paschal vigil*.

Fire was a most important element to primitive peoples as the source of warmth and light. No doubt under the symbolism of Christ as the 'light of the world' the church devised a rite for the creation of light to mark the beginning of the Easter* festival. In fifth-century Jerusalem (and perhaps earlier) the bishop went into the church of the Anastasis, kindled new fire (though we do not know how) and from this his own candle* and the candles of his ministers were lighted. They then went to the people, who lighted theirs, all entered the church, and the vigil of Easter began. There is a close parallel to this in the liturgy of the *Liber Ordinum* of the Spanish church. In both places the light was kindled in secret and it was under Irish influence that a fire was lighted outside the church, a custom said to derive from St Patrick. This usage infiltrated into Gaul in the eighth century but was unknown to the Roman liturgy until the twelfth century.

Roman usage was in fact quite different. Light from the church lamps was preserved from Good Friday* (later from Maundy Thursday*) until the beginning of the vigil on Saturday. From the lamps two 'torches' were lit, solely, it would seem, for the purpose of giving enough light to read the lections. Later in the service all the candles and lamps of the church were lit. The Roman use probably recalls the Jewish custom of the lighting of the lamps on the eve of Sabbath, a custom that was taken over by the Christians, as is attested by Hippolytus in his *Apostolic Tradition* (ed G. Dix, XXVI, 18–27, 1937, pp.50–51). This in turn gave rise to the *Lucernarium*, still preserved in the Ambrosian rite and of which there are echoes in Roman vespers.

Even in the Gallican tradition the significance of the new fire is to be found in light rather than heat. But to understand its use at all, it is necessary to give the background of the whole liturgy of Good Friday and Holy Saturday. The church celebrates the Passover of the Lord in which he suffers, dies and rises again. In the phrase of Tertullian, Good Friday is the day *ubi ablatus est sponsus*: the bride (the church) is bereft of her bridegroom. The church as it were dies and has to be brought back to life again. This is done in symbol through fire and light, and the lighting of the new fire at the beginning of the Paschal vigil is the first sign that the church is returning to life. The new fire thus had to be kindled from a virgin flame, struck from a kindling stone and steel. Or, as one of the prayers of blessing had it in the rite before 1951 when it was suppressed, Christ is the corner stone which, struck by the rod of the cross, sends forth the light of the Holy Spirit.

However, as the order of the service indicates to this day, the new fire is in fact lighted before the service proper begins and in some places is a great bonfire. It is on account of this that the rite has to take place outside the church; since there are practical difficulties in city and town churches, the procedure may be considerably modified. Once the fire is lit, the celebrant with ministers and servers comes to the place of the fire and after a short address giving the sense of the whole Vigil, blesses the fire with a single prayer. Then, from the fire, light is taken for the lighting of the Paschal candle*. This now becomes the centre of interest, for it is the candle that is the symbol of the Risen Christ. The fire having served its purpose is left to die out.

In many parts of Europe in former ages and perhaps even now, not only were all

the lights in church extinguished, but the all-important hearth-fire was allowed to die. From the new fire or the candle people took light with which to re-kindle their fires at home. It is an interesting example of how the liturgy could influence social customs outside the church and in the life of the people.

M. Andrieu, *Les Ordines Romani du Haut-Moyen Age*, III, pp.277–97, 311–29; H. Leclercq, 'Pâques', *DACL*, XIII, 2, cols 1559–71; 'Semaine saint', id., XV, 1, cols 1151–1185; *New Catholic Encyclopaedia*, 1967, 5, p.10, 'Easter Vigil'; M. Righetti, *Manuale di Storia Liturgica*, [2]1955, II, pp.185–88.

J. D. CRICHTON

New Testament Worship

The word 'worship' basically expresses the general idea of offering to God adoration and service; the concept can be extended to include offering prayers to God including petition and intercession, and it can also refer to obedient listening to God speaking. If we take the concept in the narrower sense, we discover with some surprise that the NT scarcely ever uses the basic vocabulary (words such as *leitourgeo*, *sebomai*, *latreuo* and *proskuneo*) with reference to what went on when Christians gathered together as the *ekklesia*. This vocabulary is used to refer to the activities of pagans (Acts 17.23), to the reaction by pagans to Christian meetings (I Cor. 14.25), to the activities of the Jews in temple and synagogue, to the adoration offered to God and the Lamb in the visions of heaven in Rev., and to the obeisance offered to Jesus during his lifetime. It can also be used of the total attitude of Christians to God (Rom. 12.1), and it is assumed that the followers of Jesus will worship God (John 4.20–24). Only very rarely is the language applied to Christian meetings, notably in Heb. 13.15f. and 1 Peter 2.5, where the sacrifices offered by Christians are said to consist in doing good to one another and offering praise to God. We are thus compelled to the conclusion that the early Christians did not think of their meetings as being specifically or exclusively for the purpose of worshipping God or Jesus, even though activities that we would associate with worship took place in them; only in the broad sense that all of the Christian's actions should be regarded as worshipful can we categorize Christian meetings thus.

Since, however, this article is intended to discuss the communal meetings of Christians for what is popularly summed up in this way as 'worship', we must ask what went on in them. There is general agreement that their form was partly shaped by their environment. One important influence was that of the synagogue with its regular weekly programme of readings from the scriptures, accompanied, where possible, by some kind of expository teaching, and set in a context of prayer and confession. By contrast, the temple did not contribute decisively to the content of Christian meetings, although the idea of the church as a company of people constituting a new temple is attested widely in the NT and found expression in the belief that God was in their midst. Greater significance should be given than is sometimes done to the influence of the domestic religion of the Jews – the gathering together of the family or of religious 'fraternities' of various kinds at table for ordinary meals, to celebrate the beginning of the sabbath, and to hold the passover meal. Nor should we forget the importance of meals, particularly after sacrifices, in the Hellenistic world.

Against this background it emerges that an important structural element in early Christian meetings was the gathering for fellowship at table, centred on a meal. The early church believed that it was patterning itself on the example of Jesus; whatever the precise history of the tradition, from an early date Christians were gathering together, probably weekly, for a meeting which involved a common meal in the course of which they remembered the death of Jesus by partaking of bread and a cup on the pattern of the Last Supper. This action had the effect of 'proclaiming the Lord's death' (I Cor. 11.26) and it was accompanied by prayers of thanksgiving which no doubt were not merely for the food but above all for what it symbolized. This celebration set the pattern for the three activities which are implicit in the Christian gatherings – the proclamation of salvation as God's word to his people along with appropriate teaching, the offering of prayers and praises as their words to him, and the constitution of the church as his people in fellowship with him and with one

another. For Paul the controlling factor in church meetings is 'edification', the building up of God's people in faith and love.

From I Cor. we get fuller details of what happened. It is reasonable to assume from I Cor. 16.1 that church gatherings were held weekly. They were held in the homes of the wealthier members of the congregation who had the resources to accommodate the church. Whatever role was occupied at this stage by persons holding any kind of 'official' status, all members of the church were free to take part and to exercise whatever gifts of the Spirit might be conferred on them: thus different people might participate with a psalm, a piece of teaching, a revelation, a 'tongue' or an interpretation of what was said in tongues. Women took part in praying and prophesying, although Paul laid down some requirements about their hairstyle and forbade them to talk in church in a way that showed insubordination to their husbands. The teaching included the reading of passages from the scriptures and also from writings by leading Christians. The rite of baptism was practised at appropriate times. Various passages in the Epistles where Paul tells us how he prayed for his friends give indications of the language of prayer, and the fact that he asked his friends to pray for him suggests that intercession took place in Christian meetings. There does not appear to have been any fixed order for the various parts of the service, and Paul's appeal for things to be done 'decently and in order' was a step towards a more orderly procedure.

The picture in Acts is not dissimilar. It is disputed whether Acts 2.42 is an 'order of service' or a list of things that the Christians did on various occasions, but we can at least conclude that it mentions the kind of things that happened in Christian meetings. Luke here claims to be describing the early days of the church in Jerusalem, but the description need not be confined to that period. There is reference to the teaching of the apostles, to fellowship (which may mean sharing together on a spiritual or material level), to the breaking of bread (Luke's name for the Lord's Supper, or for an equivalent celebration – opinion is divided whether there were significantly different forms of the rite) and to prayers. It is notable that Luke also refers to the provision of food for the poor by the church: social care and spiritual fellowship could not be separated. We also hear in Acts of meetings at which prayer together (sometimes apparently in unison) was the main feature, and these meetings could last well into the night; this may have been partly because slaves and other workers might not be free until late in the evening, but the practice of prayer by night was well known in the ancient world. Paul is also depicted as preaching until a late hour on the first day of the week and joining in the breaking of bread at Troas.

The Pastoral Epistles reflect a situation in which the activity of the church was becoming more organized and formal with the passage of time and the need for consolidation. Yet even here we hear of prophetic utterances given to the congregations. A major emphasis is on the appointment of elders/bishops* and deacons* in the local churches, but the description of the qualifications of the former emphasizes their ability to teach. The public reading of scripture, preaching and teaching are important, and the men in the church take part in prayer; the restricted place allotted to women to take part may be due to local problems.

I Peter paints a rich picture of the congregation as the people of God, inheriting the role of Israel and forming a priestly people to offer spiritual sacrifices to God, apparently by declaring his wonderful deeds. Spiritual gifts are to be exercised in the congregation, and these are understood to consist in the ability to speak the oracles of God and to render service.

Not much can be gleaned about Christian meetings from the Johannine writings, but we do learn of groups of Christians meeting in houses and being served by groups of travelling brothers who acted as teachers.

The traditional elements of worship that have survived from the early days include some Aramaic words addressed to God and the Lord's Prayer*, but for the most part the traditional material consists of baptismal and catechetical instruction and various confessional elements in which early Christians joyfully celebrated the drama of salvation.

It is thus the concept of teaching which seems to be most prominent in the glimpses that the NT affords us of early Christian meetings. The primary movement is from

God to man as through prophets and other individuals gifted by the Spirit he conveys his word to the congregation. At the same time the church meeting is the occasion for response to God expressed in prayers and acts of praise, often of a spontaneous nature. At this stage there was no fixed 'liturgy' that was followed in detail, but there was a constitutive pattern of God's word being given to the congregation and their response being made to God, the whole taking place in an atmosphere of fellowship between God and his people.

R. Banks, *Paul's Idea of Community*, 1980; G. Delling, *Worship in the New Testament*, 1962; F. Hahn, *The Worship of the Early Church*, 1973; R. P. Martin, *Worship in the Early Church*, [2]1974; *The Worship of God*, 1982; C. F. D. Moule, *The Birth of the New Testament*, [3]1981.

I. HOWARD MARSHALL

Nocturns

see **Canonical Hours**

None

see **Canonical Hours**

Noonday Prayer

The title of a short service for midday included in the BCP (1979) of the American Episcopal Church. It consists of psalms and prayers and is loosely similar to sext, the fifth of the canonical hours*, which it may be said to replace for general use.

EDITOR

Notation and Rhythm

The precise date of the invention of a system of musical notation in the West is unclear. Isidore, Archbishop of Seville (*c.*560–636) claimed that in his day music was taught and passed on orally, for there was no way of setting down audible sounds on the parchment. The invention and dissemination of a system of neum notation was therefore a major event, the importance of which cannot be overestimated. The term 'neum' (or 'neume') appears to be derived from a Greek word meaning a sign, or a gesture. If a singer traces in the air with his hand the movement of his voice it is conceivable that the pen of a scribe might trace the movement of the singer's hand on his parchment, noting down a kind of musical graph to indicate the flow of the melody. It is just possible that some such form of neum notation was already known to the Synod of Cloveshoe (747) and also to Charlemagne, legislating for the programme of studies in his schools. However, the earliest surviving neum notation would appear to be that of Engyldeo of St Emmeram, Regensburg, dating from 817–34.

Fully notated service books began to appear around the year 900. Various schools of neum notation arose, some of them inter-related, and each devising ways of indicating pitch, rhythm and to a lesser extent expression. Before staff lines were invented the earliest manuscripts with notation were written in what musicologists call *campo aperto* ('in an open field'), meaning without precise indications of pitch. Later, heighted neums were used, which were placed relatively higher or lower, as if on an invisible stave. But as the chant repertoire had in any case to be learned by heart pitch imprecision was not an inconvenience: the notated service books would probably have been intended, first and foremost, as works of reference, not books from which the choir-members were expected to sight-read the melodies.

The rhythmic indications of the early manuscripts with notation are now gradually revealing their secrets. Sometimes the shapes of the signs themselves are modified to show length or brevity, emphasis or lightness. At other times a different sign altogether may be used by the scribe for the same reasons: a dot, for example, may replace a short horizontal or oblique line to indicate extreme brevity. Sometimes an extra sign is attached to a note to indicate emphasis or length. Letters may be inserted to indicate pitch, rhythm or expression: for example, 'l', *levate*, for a note of higher pitch than expected; 'c' *celeriter*, meaning lightly, quickly; 't', *trahere*: hold back, slow down. But all the early schools of notation, whether or not they use one or more of these devices, follow another principle, unknown to present-day musicians accustomed only to modern staff-notation: the principle of *coupure*. This is an ingenious way of showing length by the separation of the notational elements and was first described by Dom Eugène Cardine in 1957.

The 4-lined stave came into general use

in about the twelfth century, by which time the numerous rhythmic and expressional indications of the earlier manuscripts were fast disappearing from the copies made of them. The traditional manner of performance appears to have been gradually losing ground and finally lost, particularly with the rise of measured music and the slowing down of the chant. Notation itself became thicker and heavier and by the thirteenth century was developing into what is known as 'square notation' (or, in Germany and the Low Countries, the so-called 'Hufnagel-schrift') similar to that of the modern service books. At the present day there is a considerable area of disagreement as to the 'correct' interpretation of the rhythm of the chant. Perhaps, before attempting to tackle this problem with a choir of singers, the choirmaster should stop and ask himself which period of the chant he wishes to reconstruct and interpret? Is he aiming at re-discovering how it was sung when it first became visible in the early neum notation? This notation does, indeed, represent the chant when it was still a living oral tradition. On the other hand, he might be wishing to intersperse a recital of thirteenth-century motets* with suitably related chants, or it might be a Palestrina mass, with the propers (*see* **Chants of the Proper of the Mass**) sung to the chant. In these cases it would be necessary to find out, as far as possible, which version of the chant to use and what style of performance would be historically suitable in the thirteenth century or in the sixteenth. For there is plenty of evidence to show that the chant was performed in very different ways at different periods of its long existence.

Dom Eugene Cardine, *Gregorian Semiology*, 1982; Solange Corbin, *Die Neumen*, 1977.

MARY BERRY

Oblation

A synonym for 'offering', derived from the Latin *oblatio*; like the latter it may refer either to an act of offering, or to the thing offered. Four different Christian uses of the term may be distinguished: 1. the self-offering of Christ in the Last Supper* and on the cross for the redemption of the world: 2. the celebration of the eucharist* as an anamnesis* of this self-offering; 3. its application to the material elements of bread and wine with which this anamnesis is made, according to Christ's command; 4. its application to the dispositions of the worshippers which are externalized by 2 and 3.

Other uses, such as the application of the term to monetary offerings in general, would seem to fall outside the legitimate Christian usage of the term. In the Christian dispensation the only offering or oblation which may strictly be so described without qualification is that of Christ himself, the only oblation which is intrinsically acceptable. Its application to the eucharist, which is ancient, and universal until the period of the Reformation, depends upon the doctrine that what the church does in the eucharist is, in virtue of the divine command, and by divine grace, identified with the self-oblation of Christ; its application to the eucharistic elements is further dependent upon that identification, which was anciently and universally held to be effected by the identification of the bread and wine with Christ's body and blood; its application to the dispositions of the worshippers is equally dependent upon it, in that they can only offer themselves *in Christ*, into whose self-offering they are assimilated by participation in the celebration of the eucharist.

The Protestant Reformers denied the legitimacy of describing the eucharist, and *a fortiori* the eucharistic elements, as an oblation, on the ground that to do so denigrated from the uniqueness of Christ's offering, an objection based on a misunderstanding of the doctrine involved, as well as on *a priori* grounds derived from their novel doctrine of justification and grace. Some of them, however, were still prepared to apply it, with qualification, to the dispositions of the worshippers – an application which, outside the context of its application to the celebration of the eucharist itself, would seem to merit their condemnation of the latter.

No other individual issue has so divided Western Christendom since the sixteenth century as the oblatory concept of the eucharist. In recent years, however, there has been a considerable softening of attitudes and drawing together on this subject;

at the same time, there has been an increase of emphasis on the offering of the material elements of bread and wine as symbols on the one hand of the natural order, and on the other of the lives and labours of the worshippers, in a way which, valuable as these concepts are in themselves, has tended towards an implicit doctrine of the possibility of oblation other than, or in addition to, that of Christ. Only the doctrine of the identification of the oblation of the church, and of the individual member of it, with the oblation of Christ in the celebration of the eucharist as the divinely-appointed anamnesis of the latter is able to safeguard the uniqueness of Christ's oblation on the one hand, and provide for man's desire and need to offer all that he is and has to God on the other.

W. Jardine Grisbrooke, 'Oblation at the Eucharist', *Studia Liturgica*, III, 4, 1964, pp.227–39; ibid., IV, 1, 1965, pp.37–55, and the works therein cited. Still the most useful survey of eucharistic doctrine is D. Stone's monumental two-volume *A History of the Doctrine of the Holy Eucharist*, 1909.

W. JARDINE GRISBROOKE

Octave

The celebration of a feast again on the eighth day after the feast itself, the day itself being reckoned as the first day, or continuously throughout the eight-day period. It is a custom that has virtually disappeared from modern liturgy.

R. F. BUXTON

Offertory

The name given to the oblation rites which come at the beginning of the liturgy of the eucharist* (as distinguished from the liturgy of the word). The motif of oblation* runs throughout the eucharist, but the offertory is specifically concerned with oblation. The theme of the offertory is that the church must provide the elements for the sacrificial meal. The elements of bread and wine are presented, prepared and formally offered by the presiding priest, who then prays over them. These elements are to be transformed into the one gift that pleases God during the eucharistic prayer which follows the offertory, though their transformation is curiously anticipated, particularly in the Roman offertory. Still, Roman Catholic theologians hold that the offertory is not essential to the sacrifice. However, though the offertory may not be theologically essential, some presentation, preparation and perhaps formal offering of the elements, no matter how simple, seems practically indispensable. It is this presentation, preparation and formal offering of the elements which might be called the function of the offertory and which offers us insight as to the nature of the offertory. The offertory is that part of the eucharistic liturgy which is concerned with the fitting oblation of the elements to God for their consecration.

The theme of offering gifts is as old as religion, and the ancient cults and folk practices were a providential preparation for the Christian offering of gifts for the eucharistic sacrifice and the service of the poor and the otherwise needy. There is reason to believe that the early church had an understanding of the eucharist as a corporate action, with each rank having its special task in relationship to the offering of the gifts. Writing as early as the autumn of AD 96, Clement of Rome reminds the church at Corinth that Christ is the 'high priest of our oblations' (*I Cor.* 36.1) and that he 'commanded us to celebrate oblations and liturgies' (*I Cor.* 40.2). Clement continues: 'Unto the high priest (bishop) his special liturgies have been appointed, and to the priests their special place assigned, and on the levites (deacons) their special ministry; the layman is bound by the ordinances for the laity. Let each of you, brethren, make eucharist to God according to his own order, keeping a good conscience and not transgressing the appointed rule of his own liturgy' (*I Cor.* 40.5–41.1). That Clement was talking about the oblational aspects of liturgy is indicated further on in the letter where he says that it is the bishop's office to 'offer the gifts' (*I Cor.* 44.4). We might conclude from this that every rank in the church has its role to play in the offering of the gifts. This implies that the layman, too, has a role, though his role is in no way spelled out by Clement.

Justin Martyr, in the early years of the second century, is the first to give explicit evidence about the offertory. In the first and fuller reference in his *Apology* (ch.65), he gives the following order of service: the prayers are concluded; the kiss of peace (*see*

Gestures 8) is given; bread and wine are presented to the one who presides over the assembly; he takes them and over them he pronounces the thanksgiving. Justin, in his *Dialogue with Trypho* (9–13), also seems to reject all oblation of things which might be used for sustenance. But this is in reality a rejection of the material sacrifices of creatures as practised by Jews and pagans. His ideal is the *oblatio rationabilis*, the spiritual sacrifice, which the Greek philosophers declared to be the only veneration worthy of God. He sees that there is no longer any room for bloody sacrifices since the Logos himself, Jesus Christ, is the victim of the spiritual sacrifice which is the eucharist. But emphasis on the spiritual sacrifice gives way to a re-statement of the importance of the material and material sacrifices in the face of Gnosticism in the latter part of the second century. Irenaeus leads the battle against those who would spiritualize the Christian sacrifice out of existence.

The *Apostolic Tradition* of Hippolytus (AD 215–217) offers two descriptions of the eucharistic order of service. In the first account we find one item to add to Justin's description, namely, the deacons* are expressly mentioned as offering the oblation. The second account, which is an account of the eucharist in conjunction with baptism*, does add something further. On this occasion, milk, honey and water are added to the usual oblations of bread and wine, and these are received by the newly baptized at communion before the consecrated wine. Interestingly, the catechumen* is earlier told to bring some offering for the eucharist which will follow his baptism. Hippolytus' accounts therefore give some confirmation to what is much earlier suggested by Clement as to the participation of deacons and laymen in the offertory rite. In North Africa in the same century we have the witness of both Tertullian and Cyprian to lay participation in offering the elements, though the precise time when these elements were presented (before the mass began or at the offertory) is not indicated.

In the fourth and fifth centuries, after peace had come to the church, there was a great growth of the liturgy. In the East during the fourth century, the laity provided the elements for the sacrifice, though, except in the Egyptian rite, the exact time of their offering is not known. It is also generally agreed that during this century whatever presentation of the gifts at the offertory there had ever been in the East died out, and with the beginning of the fifth century we have the evidence of Theodore of Mopsuestia (in his *Catechesis*) that the offertory was moving in the direction of a 'processional' rite as opposed to the Roman 'oblational' rite. The East now substitutes the great entrance* for the simpler presentation, preparation and offering of the elements, and the participation of the laity and even the meaning of oblation is more and more obscured in the representational rite of the Byzantine liturgy. The evidence from the West during this two-century middle period is sparse indeed. Except for passing references in Spain and Milan which indicate that the laity in those cities provided the oblations according to a certain ritual, the only important Western evidence we have is from North Africa where Augustine reports that the laity actually offered the elements at the offertory.

If there was ever a real offertory procession of the laity, it occurred during the following centuries at the papal stational liturgy in the city of Rome. *Ordo Romanus Primus* describes in detail the action, but instead of the laity coming up to the altar to hand in their offerings, the pope and his assistants go down to the laity to take up those gifts to be used for the sacrifice and for the needs of the church and those who were in the care of the church. It seems that the formalization of the people's offertory in the Roman stational liturgy dealt the death blow to a sense of liturgical role which until that time the laity had understood themselves as having. During this same period the Gallican rite developed an approach to the offertory which was in spirit closer to the later Eastern practice. Duchesne, describing the Gallican rite in *Christian Worship*, [6]1931, p.203, states categorically that 'the offering by the people at this point in the mass (i.e. the offertory) is a ceremony of Roman origin, and is incompatible with that of the *processio oblationis*, a custom common to the Gallican and Oriental rite'. Before passing on to the post-developmental period, it is important to note that the secret prayers which we find in the Roman sacramentaries

of this period, particularly the Leonine and the Gregorian, reflect a highly developed theology of the offerings as oblations (*see* **Silent Prayer**). One can learn a great deal about the theology of the offertory by a study of these prayers, many of which are still to be found in the Roman missal.

By the year AD 800, the eucharistic liturgy of the Western church, like that of the East, had become more or less uniform and established. Substantially the liturgies of both East and West manifested no important change after this date, though the actual offertory rite was considerably modified in the West, particularly by the addition of prayers full of Gallican symbolism and piety to accompany the simple actions. All of this was made uniform and unchangeable in the West with the publication of the Roman missal in its first edition in 1474. So it remained until the 1969 missal of Pope Paul VI. In this missal the prayers are considerably simplified or omitted. The offertory is once again restored to a relatively simple, straightforward rite. The gifts are brought up. Bread is offered to the accompaniment of a modified OT blessing. Wine with a little water is taken and similarly offered to the accompaniment of a similar blessing. After hand-washing and an invitation to the gathering to pray that the sacrifice may be acceptable to God, an invitation which evokes a proper corporate response, the ancient secret prayer, renamed the 'prayer over the gifts' (*see* ***Super Oblata***), is spoken by the presiding priest. And so ends the present offertory of the Roman mass.

One might argue that even greater simplification would make the offertory rite more effective. More importantly, there is still a great need to find a way to re-awaken in the laity a sense of their having a proper liturgy – probably in connection with the offertory – and a heightened sense of the social needs of less fortunate brethren.

However, in a climate of liturgical experimentation and assumed liturgical freedom, in which the offertory is often minimized, it is important to point out that the offertory oblation forms the link between the order of creation and the order of redemption. Minimizing the offertory separates these orders and tends to detach the eucharist from the created and human order. This, of course, is an aberration which can only result in serious theological problems in the long term.

See also **Chants of the Proper of the Mass; Music in the Mass of the Roman Rite**.

C. Buchanan, *The End of the Offertory – An Anglican Study*, 1978; A. Clark, 'The Function of the Offertory Rite in the Mass', *Ephem. Liturg.* 64 (1950), pp.309–344; G. Dix, *The Shape of the Liturgy*, [2]1945; A. Hamman, *Vie Liturgique et Vie Sociale*, 1968; J. A. Jungmann, *The Mass of the Roman Rite*, rev ed 1959.

THOMAS PHELAN

Office Hymn

A hymn appointed for use at the hour services (*see* **Canonical Hours**). They were omitted from the BCP for lack of English versions, but many have now been translated and find their place in Anglican hymnals. A custom had arisen in some churches of singing such a hymn after the first lesson and before the *Magnificat* at evensong.

EDITOR

Old Catholic Worship

Of the Old Catholic churches, linked together in 1889 in the Union of Utrecht, the church in the Netherlands is by far the oldest. This church was a continuation of the church for which Willibrord was consecrated first archbishop of Utrecht in Rome, in 695, and after the period of the Reformation, which was extremely difficult, it was involved in an increasingly sharp conflict with Rome in the seventeenth century. In 1703, the archbishop Peter Codde was suspended by Pope Clement XI. From that time onward the episcopal succession was continued in the church as the 'Roman Catholic Church of the old episcopal clergy'. As this was a split for reasons of canon law and not because of dogmatic differences, there was a continual hope that the difficulties might be resolved. During the early period of the split, the old Roman post-Tridentine liturgy was adhered to almost completely.

There was an important turn of the tide after 1870. Vatican I and the development of Old Catholic movements outside the Netherlands not only caused the 'Old Episcopal' clergy to call themselves increasingly 'Old Catholics'; it also induced

them to be more closely connected in theological thinking as well. This led to the Union of Utrecht in 1889. The influence of the German and Swiss sister churches was also felt in the liturgy through the spread of the idea of community, the introduction of the vernacular, the rejection of private masses and the renewal of the liturgy. Thus several new liturgical books came out, especially in the period between 1900 and 1910, taking the place of the old Roman formularies (*see* **Books, Liturgical** 11).

Compared to the Old Catholic reforms abroad, those in the Netherlands were on the whole less radical. For instance, in the translation of the liturgy of the mass and especially of the canon dating from 1909, there were very few departures from the Roman missal. The cycle of saints' days was far less restricted than elsewhere. After the Second World War, the voices clamouring for a renewal of the liturgy grew louder and louder. In 1960 a revised liturgy of the mass did in fact come out, but as research had not yet been completed, the alterations were still fairly limited. Under the influence of very lively liturgical renewal movements in the Netherlands, both among Roman Catholics and among Protestants, the desire for radical changes has grown very strongly since. What is specifically aimed at is directness, greater transparency and ecumenical openness. This desire for radically revised formularies has by no means been fulfilled yet. In 1968 there appeared an alternative 'Second Order of the Mass', and here and there new formularies for the administration of the sacraments have been tried out. It looks as if tangible results in the shape of official formularies may be expected.

In the Old Catholic churches which separated from Rome because of their rejection of the Vatican dogmas of 1870 (above all in Germany, Austria and Switzerland), powerful reform movements soon became evident, in contrast to the situation in the Netherlands. As a result of their separation from Rome, these churches gained the freedom to carry out reforms which had long been desired in progressive Catholic circles. In those parts of Switzerland and South Germany which had belonged to the See of Constance until 1814 or 1821, the ground for liturgical reform had been prepared by the activity of the Vicar General (later vicegerent of the See), I. H. von Wessenberg. His German ritual served as a model for Old Catholic rituals, and the tradition of German vespers still lives on in the Old Catholic congregations in Switzerland. In Austria, the church reforms of Emperor Joseph II (1741–1790) had a wide influence.

Soon after 1870 the liturgical books were produced in German and French editions. The editors were not, however, content with a translation of the Latin books, as in the Netherlands, but worked over them more freely. Of course, all Old Catholic liturgies are descended from the Roman liturgy, like those of the Anglican and Lutheran churches, though like them they differ to a greater or lesser degree from their ancestor.

A considerable part in the reform of the liturgy was played by Eduard Herzog (1841–1924), the first bishop of the Christian Catholic (Old Catholic) Church of Switzerland, and Adolf Thürlings (1844–1915), Professor of Liturgy in the Christian Catholic theological faculty in Bern (Switzerland), who was also a distinguished musicologist. In the Polish Old Catholic Church in the USA and Canada (founded in 1897), as in Poland itself, the liturgy was translated into Polish, but the translation strictly followed the Roman rite. In America, English has been used to an increasing extent alongside Polish.

In the Old Catholic churches, some of the manifestations of so-called vulgar Catholicism have been rejected, e.g. pilgrimages*, reverencing of images, indulgences, the cult of the Sacred Heart*, and so on. The liturgy is meant to be celebrated in a clear and pure form, bringing the christological element, in particular, to the fore. Thus the Old Catholic churches play a lively part in the liturgical renewal that is taking place in both Roman Catholic and Protestant churches.

For Old Catholicism with particular reference to worship, *see*: K. Algermissen, *Konfessionkunde*, [8]1969; P. Fox, *The Polish National Catholic Church*; U. Kunz, *Viele Glieder – ein Leib*, 1953 (and especially P. Pfister, 'Die altkatholische Kirche'); U. Küry, *Die altkatholische Kirche* (in *Die Kirchen der Welt*, III), 1966; C. B. Moss, *The Old Catholic Movement*, [2]1964; A. E. Rüthy, 'The Place of the Old Catholic

Church in the Liturgical Scene', *Studia Liturgica,* II, 1963, pp.66f.; F. Siegmund-Schultze (ed), *Ekklesia,* III: *Die altkatholische Kirche*, 1935.

S. KRAFT/C. TOL

Old Testament Worship

The Hebrew scriptures accumulated for some thousand years and reflect rather haphazardly the practices of worship from various localities and from the successive forms of the society. The Pentateuch is especially complex. It offers an amalgam of widely differing practices, and attributes most of it to the legislation of Moses. One can trace here, for example, how in the later monarchy all sanctuaries but Jerusalem were suppressed, and how the festivals were changed in various periods.

Early lists of pilgrimage festivals (Ex. 23.14–17; 34.18–23) do not mention Passover (presumably because it was observed at home), but tell of three annual festivals: Unleavened Bread, Weeks (or Harvest), and Ingathering. The week of Unleavened Bread, in March–April, saw the presentation at the sanctuary of the first cuttings of the barley harvest and first-born animals; the ban on leaven would originally emphasize a fresh start. With this week later texts (Deut. 16) join the Passover, which had become a centralized public observance under the later kings (II Kings 23.21–3), a dramatic re-living of the night of the Exodus (Ex. 12). Seven weeks later fell the festival of Weeks (Pentecost), also called Harvest as linked with the offering of the first cuttings of the wheat. While information on these festivals is sparse, the third to be listed, Ingathering (later Tabernacles) is the one which usually features in OT narratives. It fell in September/October when the long summer drought should end and all harvested produce be gathered in to shelter. With the beginning of rain, the annual cycle of agriculture could commence. Most earnest, then, at this festival were prayers for rain, and much of the liturgy was in effect a statement of faith in the creator's power and will to replenish his creatures.

This chief festival of old Israel is illumined by various texts, such as the story of its first occurrence in Solomon's temple (I Kings 8) or the prophecy of its celebration by all nations, with emphasis on God's kingship and gift of rain (Zech. 14.16–17). But it is the psalms above all which enable us to appreciate the experience of the ancient pilgrims. Using psalms linked with the festival by Jewish tradition or by the logic of their contents, the Norwegian Sigmund Mowinckel found the key to the riches of this chief season of Israelite worship in a series of studies from 1921. His fruitful work has been developed by other scholars, although there remain others who have little sympathy for it.

We should think of an extended holy season in the period of the monarchy, forerunner of the present Jewish New Year, Atonement and Tabernacles. The main themes are eloquently expressed in the psalms. There is the pilgrimage itself, like a thirsty traveller's approach to a spring. There is repentance and cleansing, the cry from 'out of the depths' and the answer of 'plenteous redemption'. There is the consecration of the Davidic king, preparing him to mediate God's rule, and perhaps using rites symbolic of humility and conquest 'by the name of the Lord'. There is the dramatization of the creator's universal supremacy, his renewed conquest of chaos. He re-enters his temple, the festal gospel is proclaimed, 'The Lord reigns!', and all participate in the triumph with prostrations, praises, songs and dances.

God, as present, speaks; through psalmists and prophets his words of poetry decree order, life, destiny, promise, warning. And while he thus 'is near', 'letting himself be found', intercessors pray for the needy and oppressed and the gospel is confronted with the reality of many ills. As well as this dialogue of God and corporate people, there are spaces during the days and nights of the festival for individuals to approach the temple or holy men with their personal needs and to bring offerings in testimony to past mercies. There is also the theme of the holy city itself, centre of God's work, mother of all peoples, source of the river of life. Not least, there is the benediction and departure, the pilgrims carrying the touch of life wherever they tread. They go out replenished: 'We have feasted on the abundance of thy house; with thee is the fountain of life; in thy light have we seen light.'

There are many aspects of this worship which invite further study, such as revela-

tion, sacrifice, prophecy, praise. But not least remarkable is the role of the arts. The festival rang with *poetry*, whether uttered on behalf of congregation or God. The words of the liturgy thus danced with rhythm and sound-play and glowed with bright images. Wedded to the poetry was *music*, the voices of many lively instruments, male and female singers, soloists and choirs, completed with congregational responses. It was seen as inspired, indeed a form of prophecy, and yet performed for the Lord, in concert with a heavenly and universal music. Its percussive style leads us to another sister art, *dancing*. To 'rejoice before the Lord' meant self-evidently to dance. Led by the king and lithe specialists, the dancing of all the worshippers helped them to enter into the festal gospel and to express joy and praise. Indeed it was a communion with God, himself rejoicing. (*See* Fig.24).

The joy was the climax of the festal 'story', the eternal events now 'done'; hence *drama* was of the very essence of the worship. Just as we still see the Passover as the re-enacting of the Exodus in which all take part, so the autumn festival distilled the story from the deepest human experience and drew all the worshippers into its enactment. It was the story of life's origin and destiny and the triumph over evil and death – in short it was the story of the kingdom of God. It was a sacrament, for in this enactment appointed by God, so the worshippers believed, he came and his triumph was all about them.

The poetry, music, dance and drama happened in a prepared place, the contribution of *architecture*. The compact city of Jerusalem nestling in the mountains, its spring and water channels, its processional way, its ring of walls, its complex gateways, its courts, trees, temple, fine works of

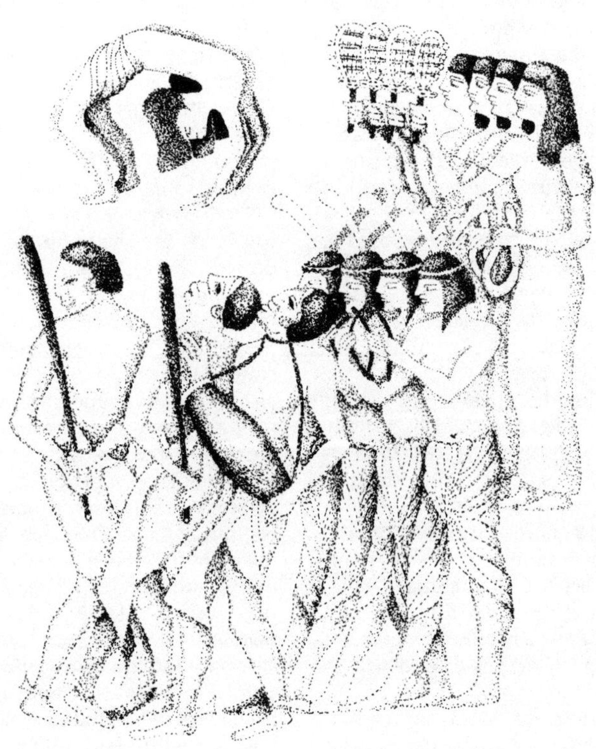

Fig. 24 Dancers and singers from an Egyptian festal procession. The figures are selected from reliefs at Luxor depicting processional scenes from the Opet festival of the god Amun, which have resemblances to David's procession with the ark in II Sam. 6.

bronze, gold, wood and stone – all this work of builders and craftsmen served to shape the festal experience. Here was acknowledged 'the city of God', 'the house of the Lord', the symbol of heaven, the awesome place where the being and action of God were known. And here, year by year, through the ministry of all the arts, the worshippers were formed and renewed in faith and hope.

J. H. Eaton, *Festal Drama in Deutero-Isaiah*, 1979; *Vision in Worship*, 1981; *The Psalms Come Alive*, 1984; H.-J. Kraus, *Worship in Israel*, 1966; S. Mowinckel, *The Psalms in Israel's Worship*, 1962; H. Ringgren, *Sacrifice in the Bible*, 1962; H. H. Rowley, *Worship in Ancient Israel*, 1967.

J. H. EATON

Open-Air Meeting

The tradition of the open-air meeting was common in Europe among the persecuted minorities of the Middle Ages (Hussites, Waldensians). It was also used by popular preachers like Bernard of Clairvaux and Francis of Assisi. Later the French Protestants held their meetings in woods and fields (*L'église du désert*). In another form this tradition was taken up by Fox, Wesley, the Salvation Army, the Pentecostals in Latin America and many African churches (*see* **Liturgies** 12). The latter three added to the oral methodology of communication the tradition of folk music. So, the Salvation Army used the folk music of the turn of the century (brass-band!). By now this has become traditional in the Salvation Army, although some attempts are made to use today's folk music.

Of great importance are the open-air meetings of the OT prophets. They did not preach from a pulpit, nor did they usually interpret a written text, though they related themselves critically *and* positively to the tradition of their listeners. They had to formulate their message in short, easily memorized sentences and parables, not unlike the modern commercial spots on television, but very different from today's sermons. The same method was used by Jesus and the apostles. This form of concentrated communication was forgotten in the mainline churches for many centuries. It was replaced by the sermon, which has no precedent in biblical tradition, but has its roots in the cultural background of the early church and the Reformation.

Roughly speaking there are two types of open-air meetings today:

1. *The public religious mass meeting*. With the invention of high-powered loudspeaker systems, it has become possible to address thousands of people in the open air. Billy Graham and the German Kirchentag, Martin Luther King and ecumenical youth gatherings at Taizé, Roman Catholic congresses and ecumenical festivals are public demonstrations which seek to strengthen certain (evangelical, catholic, ecumenical, or pentecostal) beliefs among their followers and friends. In the case of the German Kirchentag this public propaganda is corrected and deepened by controversial public debates and small discussion groups on political, ecological and theological issues.

2. *The open-air meeting as an encounter with the world* is in certain cultures one of the best schools for the humanization of man. Every one – not only the pastor – who has the courage and the gift can speak. The speakers realize themselves as persons who have something worthwhile to contribute, a tremendous process of experiencing the value of the human person. One must have seen these people, reduced to silence by political and religious powers through centuries, suddenly discovering that they have something to say, although they do not have much formal education. For this process it is not of the first importance for them to use the ready-made language of their tradition. The main thing is that they discover the possibility of standing up and speaking. In a more sophisticated stage the open-air meeting could offer the chance to rediscover the proclamation of the gospel in the world's agenda, i.e. a proclamation which does not protect itself from any criticism by basing itself on a biblical text; by confining itself to biblical thought patterns and to a religious public which agrees with the preacher's basic assumptions; and by shutting itself in a church building, where counter-arguments are rarely allowed and never expected. Thus, this preaching could be more biblical than the usual sermon, not by basing itself *expressis verbis* on a biblical text, but by risking the biblical method of proclamation, which begins with the listener's questions,

with his concrete situation, and accepts his interruptions as a vital means of communicating the gospel.

———

W. J. Hollenweger, *Evangelism Today*, 1976.

W. J. HOLLENWEGER

Ordinary

A term of the Roman rite which has had three different, although related, meanings: 1. the unvarying parts of the mass; 2. those unvarying parts of the mass which are rendered chorally, and which compose the 'mass' as a musical work, namely, the *Kyrie**, *Gloria in excelsis*, *Credo*, *Sanctus** with *Benedictus*, and *Agnus Dei**; 3. the unvarying parts of the mass up to the secret prayer or *super oblata**, a usage followed in the page headings of the Roman missal of 1570, but abandoned in the *Ordo Missae* of 1969.

W. JARDINE GRISBROOKE

Ordination

Ordination is the act of conferring holy orders and so admitting a candidate into the ministry of the church. Strictly speaking only presbyters* or priests undergo ordination, and it is customary to refer to the consecration of bishops*, to the making of deacons*, and to the admitting of readers*, etc., to the lesser ministries. The central element in ordination is the laying on of hands with prayer, and various NT passages are regarded as the basis for this practice (Acts 6.1–6; 13.1–3; 20.28; I Tim. 4.14; 5.22; II Tim. 1.6).

1. *The Early Church*

(*a*) *Bishops*. They were elected by the people and consecrated by a fellow bishop laying his hands upon them and uttering prayers in the presence of other bishops and the local Christian community. After being saluted with the kiss of peace (*see* **Gestures** 8), the new bishop presided at the eucharist, occupying the cathedra*, so consecration can be described as 'being placed in the cathedra'. Consecration rites were not greatly elaborated, but by the fourth century deacons held a gospel book over the candidate's head (*Apost. Const.* 8.4) and one of the other bishops present is instructed to 'elevate the sacrifice upon the hands of him that is consecrated' – possibly in imitation of the consecration of the Jewish high priest (Lev. 8.27).

(*b*) *Presbyters*. They were ordained by the laying on of hands with prayer, of both the local bishop and other presbyters.

(*c*) *Deacons*. The bishop alone laid his hands upon them with prayer.

EDITOR

2. *Orthodox*. Holy orders, i.e., the sacramentally ordained ministries of bishop, priest and deacon, belong to the essential theological structure of the Orthodox Church, to the fundamental realization of the church in space and time as the body and bride of Christ. These ministries are neither mere administrative positions, filled by properly trained professionals, nor ranks in a power structure. They are neither submerged within nor standing over and above the church. They are not to be confused with personal charisms or the bequeathing of ontological distinction to those ordained. They are the christologically rooted teaching, pastoral and priestly ministries established by God and inspired by his Spirit in the church, for the church and, as the liturgical rites amply demonstrate, received always by the church. Simply stated, they belong to the very life and being of the church. 'The bishop is in the church, and the church is in the bishop . . .', said Cyprian of Carthage (d. 258). As such, ordinations to these offices are always performed in the context and at the altar of the sacrament of the church's very life and being: the holy eucharist.

Only certain canonically qualified and appropriately prepared males may be ordained to the offices of bishop, priest and deacon in the Orthodox Church (cf. I Tim. 3 and Titus 1.5–9). From the earliest times the image of marriage and family has been seen as particularly adequate to describe the place and functions of the ordained ministers in the church. A church which has lost its bishop is referred to in the ancient canons (Chalcedon 25) as a 'widowed' church. Ordinations to the episcopate, priesthood and diaconate are treated liturgically and canonically in a way very similar to marriages. All are ordained for particular churches and communities (never 'at large'), and at his consecration (during the consecration prayer itself) a bishop is given the title of his church's city and place. Ordinations to the priesthood and diaconate include liturgical actions and hymns

used in the Orthodox sacrament of holy matrimony (*see* **Marriage** 2). The ordinands are led three times in procession around the altar table. Ideally, this should be the altar table of the church community in which they should serve and remain throughout their ministry. All these references indicate that when an ordination takes place, a marriage is being realized anew and celebrated: the marriage between Christ and his church. As Father Thomas Hopko puts it, the man ordained to the sacramental priesthood in the Orthodox Church 'presents the image and images the presence' of Christ himself, as bridegroom, head and shepherd, to his beloved bride and body: a particular, local church.

Bishops, priests and deacons are ordained at different points in the order of the eucharistic celebration. The location in the order is important in that it discloses the particular nature of each office's function in the church. Bishops are consecrated in a three-part ceremony which precedes, takes place during and follows the divine eucharistic liturgy. Prior to the vigil service on the evening before his consecration, the candidate is brought before all (or as many as possible of) the other bishops of the territorial church of which he is a member. A liturgical enactment of his election to the episcopate is conducted entirely by the bishops. He is informed of his election and must express openly his acceptance of it. On the day of his consecration, prior to the synaxis* for the divine liturgy, the bishop-elect is brought before all the bishops for the rite of his confession of faith. Clad in the vestments* of a priest, he is led by the chief administrators of his future diocese (a senior priest and a deacon) to the centre of the church, where he stands on a special ecclesiastical carpet. The carpet bears the image of an eagle standing erect with its wings outspread. Under its feet is a walled city. The scene of the bishop-elect standing on the carpet and gradually moving up from the feet to the head of the eagle, as the rubrics direct, serves to manifest something of the meaning of the episcopal office. Not only is the bishop an 'overseer' (as the Greek *episkopos* indicates) looking down on his flock; he is also its head and must elevate the flock to its vocation as a 'holy nation', the presence in this world of a kingdom 'not of this world'.

The bishop-elect is now questioned by the senior bishop of the synod. He is again asked about his willingness to accept consecration to the episcopal office and in more detail about the content of his beliefs. He responds with three separate confessions of faith. First he recites aloud the Niceno-Constantinopolitan Creed. Then he gives a second, more detailed confession regarding especially the Holy Trinity and the incarnation of our Lord Jesus Christ. Lastly, he expresses his obedience to the canons, regulations and traditions of the church.

These simple liturgical actions of election, presentation and confession of faith deal with the content of apostolic succession: that which awaits final validation and sealing through the laying on of hands in the rite of ordination. Apostolic succession and validity of ordination are issues whose true meaning is discovered only in the context of the unity of the episcopate and the perpetuation in and through this unity of the apostolic faith, the 'faith which was once for all delivered to the saints' (Jude 3). Apostolic succession and validity depend not only on a laying on of hands, but on a fully recognized identity between the faith 'believed everywhere, always and by everyone' (St Vincent of Lérins) and the faith publicly confessed by the bishop-elect of the local church at the time of his consecration to the episcopate.

The consecration of the new bishop takes place after all the bishops enter the sanctuary (the little entrance*) during the divine liturgy and the *Trisagion** is sung. At one time this was the actual beginning of the eucharistic celebration. His consecration at this point in the service, immediately before the liturgy of the word, indicates that the bishop is the chief teacher and preacher, as well as sacramental officer and pastor in the local church. After the other bishops receive him into the sanctuary, the bishop-elect kneels directly in front of the altar. The bishops hold an open gospel book with the print facing down over his head; they also lay their right hands on his head. The senior bishop then chants the prayer common to all ordinations (with the appropriate variations for each office): 'The grace divine, which always heals that which is infirm, and completes that which is lacking, through the laying on of hands elevates you, Archimandrite N, duly elected, to be the

bishop of N. Let us pray for him, that the grace of the holy Spirit may come upon him.' Following this and other prayers for the new bishop, which ask God to 'make this man ... a true shepherd ... a leader ... reprover ... teacher ... lamp ... and perfector of the souls entrusted to his care', the other bishops vest him in all his episcopal vestments. As each vestment is put on, all the clergy and people in turn exclaim: '*Axios*' (He is worthy). When the eucharistic liturgy has concluded, the new bishop is brought before the senior bishop in the centre of the church. The senior bishop presents him with an episcopal staff and exhorts him to use it to 'support the obedient' and 'correct the wayward'.

Similar ceremonies, less elaborate than the one celebrated for the consecration of a bishop, are used for the ordination of priests and deacons. A priest is ordained directly before the anaphora * and immediately after the eucharistic offertory procession (great entrance *). This *kairos* draws attention to the fact that the central function of the priestly ministry is to offer, i.e., to manifest the presence and action in the priestly community of Christ himself: '... our high priest ... the Offerer and the Offered, the Receiver and the One who distributes Himself ...' (Offertory Prayer). The ordinand himself, walking in the offertory procession with a eucharistic veil draped over his head, is brought before the doors of the sanctuary as an 'acceptable' offering.

Deacons are ordained immediately after the anaphora but before the distribution of holy communion. This *kairos* points to the ancient understanding (cf. Acts 6.2) that the primary task of the deacon is to be a servant, to conduct works of charity and social welfare, to 'serve tables', 'to administer the spotless sacraments' and thus to be a holy witness like the first deacon and martyr, Stephen (Prayer of Ordination).

Before a man to be ordained either priest or deacon is led to the ordaining bishop in the sanctuary, the deacons (or subdeacons) accompanying him exclaim three times: 'Command!' This signifies that the moment has arrived for everyone involved in the ceremony to give his full consent. The first 'Command' is addressed to the ordinand, the second to the people, and the third to the ordaining hierarch. Only after all parties concur does the ordination proceed.

As the clergy and singers in turn chant the wedding hymns mentioned earlier, the ordinand bows before the altar and is led in procession three times around the altar table, kissing its corners as he goes. The procession, forming a ring, manifests the eternal and all-embracing character of the marital union between Christ and the church, realized anew in the impending ordination. The kissing is an expression of fidelity to the altar table, to the gospel and cross which rest on it; to the sacraments which are celebrated on it. After the procession, the ordinand kneels on his right knee at the front (right) corner of the altar table. The bishop, who has been sitting on a chair to the left side, rises and, laying his hands on the ordinand, chants the appointed prayers of ordination. These prayers urge a new priest to 'proclaim the Gospel ... minister the word ... offer spiritual gifts and sacrifices, and ... renew the people through the laver of regeneration'.

When the prayers of ordination are completed, the new priest or deacon rises. The bishop takes him to the ambo * before all the people and clothes him in the vestments appropriate to his office. Here, too, the clergy and people in turn chant: '*Axios!*'

A new deacon is given a liturgical fan * with which he slowly fans the consecrated eucharistic gifts until the time of their distribution. A new priest is summoned near the altar table by the bishop and given, usually on a small paten, a portion of the eucharistic bread after its consecration during the anaphora. The bishop instructs him to 'receive this pledge and preserve it whole and unharmed until your last breath ...' The consecrated particle is returned to the bishop's paten at the time of holy communion, and all the clergy partake of it.

Other 'minor' orders, the ranks of subdeacon * and reader *, also exist in the Orthodox Church. The rituals which set apart men for these offices take place in the centre of the church before the beginning of the divine liturgy. The bishop lays his hands on the candidate and reads the appointed prayers of ordination. A reader is also tonsured and is required to read a segment from the NT Epistles which the bishop randomly selects. Both readers and subdeacons are finally vested in a dalmatic (*see*

Vestments 1[*g*]), with the subdeacon receiving an orarion as well.

All clerical orders in the Orthodox Church involve specific, non-interchangeable ministries. Priests may not serve liturgically as deacons, etc. No one, however, may be consecrated a bishop without having been ordained, on separate occasions, to all other orders. No one may be ordained a priest without having first been a deacon, etc. Since the sixth century, candidates for the episcopate have been selected exclusively from the ranks of professed celibates or widowers. Married men may be candidates for the offices of priest and deacon, but no one already ordained a priest or deacon may marry.

PAUL LAZOR

3. *Mediaeval and Roman Catholic.* The sober rites of the Roman tradition underwent a considerable change in the ninth and tenth centuries when certain observances, deriving from Gallican and German sources, were added to them to give a rather different picture to holy orders. These observances are found in the Roman-German pontifical (tenth century) which made its way to Rome in the eleventh century and became part of the tradition. By way of the pontifical of Durandus of Mende (d. 1298), who made further additions, they came to form the rite of the Roman pontifical of 1485 which in turn was substantially the pontifical of 1596. These new rites consisted principally of anointings (of the head for a bishop, of the hands for a priest) and of the *porrectio instrumentorum*, the handing over of the symbols of office. The intention was to explicate the meaning of the various orders, but in the process the emphasis was somewhat changed. For instance, the handing of chalice* and paten to the priest heavily emphasized that his chief duty was to offer sacrifice. On the other hand, the delivery of the gospel book to the deacon underlined that he was a minister of the word. What was more important is that the *porrectio* overshadowed the ancient rite of the laying on of hands (which always remained) and was generally thought to be necessary for validity. This was corrected by Pius XII, who in the Apostolic Constitution *Sacramentum Ordinis* of 1948 laid down that the laying-on of hands for the three orders of the episcopate, the presbyterate and the diaconate, with certain formulae in the ordination prayers, was all that was necessary for validity.

The minor orders of doorkeeper, reader*, exorcist* and acolyte* with the ceremony of tonsure before them and the subdiaconate (until 1207 ranking as a minor order) also underwent development. These officers were from the third century appointed by a simple blessing with the delivery of the symbols of office. Now the formulae were elaborated and the rites expanded. There was an address, the delivery of the symbol of office with a formula and two prayers of blessing.

That part of the *Pontificale Romanum* containing the liturgy of ordination to the episcopate, the presbyterate and the diaconate was revised in 1968 and the liturgy of tonsure, the four minor orders and the subdiaconate in 1972 when it appeared that the subdiaconate had been suppressed and the minor orders (now called lesser ministries) reduced to two, reader and acolyte.

The pattern of the services for all three major orders is the same: they are conferred within the eucharist, after the gospel and homily; there follow the questions, prayer (litany of saints), the laying-on of hands (in silence), the prayer of ordination and the delivery of the symbols of office.

For the ordination of a presbyter* the bishop lays hands on the candidate first and then all the presbyters present do likewise; the anointing of the hands has been retained with a different formula, charging the presbyter to serve God's people and to offer the eucharist. The paten and chalice and the bread and wine to be used at the eucharist are then delivered to him with a new formula indicating that they are the offerings of the people to be used in the mass.

The texts of the prayers of ordination for diaconate and presbyterate remain those of the (early) Roman tradition, that for the presbyterate being slightly shortened. Noteworthy in the rite for the 'Ordination' (*sic*) of a bishop* are that the consecrator and then the assistant consecrators lay hands on him, the book of the gospels is placed on his head and held over it during the consecration prayer by two deacons and the principal part of the prayer is said by all the consecrators together. It is a true concelebration*. The anointing of the head

remains as well as the delivery of the gospel book (now in first place), the ring and the staff or crozier. The consecrator puts the mitre on the candidate without formula. The whole service has been much simplified. The prayer of ordination (or consecration) is that found in the (Latin) Verona fragment of the *Apostolic Tradition* of Hippolytus, very slightly revised.

Like the major orders, the lesser ministries are conferred after the gospel and the homily (or during a service of the word). There is an invitatory, a prayer and the delivery of the symbol of office. Tonsure is replaced by a service of 'Admission to the Clerical State'. The candidates are questioned, admitted by the bishop to the clergy, there are prayers of intercession and the final prayer of the bishop.

J. D. CRICHTON

4. *Anglican*. Services of ordination did not appear in the 1549 BCP but were published independently in March 1550. In 1552 they were revised and annexed to the second BCP. A third edition appeared in 1559, again as a separate document, and finally a fourth edition was annexed to the BCP of 1662.

In the Preface to the 1550 Ordinal, Cranmer and the Reformers stated their intention of continuing the threefold order of bishops*, priests (*see* **Presbyter**) and deacons* which had existed since apostolic times; they made no provision for the subdiaconate and other minor orders. In an attempt to simplify the obscurities of the mediaeval Roman rite they retained the eucharist* as the frame for ordination and emphasized the essential elements as expressed in the NT and by the early church, namely prayer and the imposition of hands. Thus the basic pattern of the rites in the Roman Pontifical was followed, but a number of individual features were changed, and the influence of Bucer's tract *De Ordinatione* was recognizable. The anointing of bishops and priests and the formal vesting of all three orders was abolished. The delivery of the instruments (*porrectio instrumentorum*) was retained in the case of priests, but the staff was the sole insignia delivered to the bishop. A Bible instead of the gospels was laid on the bishop's neck, a Bible was delivered to priests, and the NT instead of the Gospels was delivered to deacons. While it was undoubtedly right for the Reformers to avoid the traditional multiplied and diffused acts of ordination and to concentrate on the central imposition of hands with prayer, it would seem that they were misled over the relation between the form and the matter. Not only did the traditional eucharistic pattern of prayer introduced by the *Sursum corda* disappear, but the ordination prayers which were used were separated from the imposition of hands, and the latter were accompanied by imperative formulae addressed to the candidates and authorizing them to execute the functions of the order which they were receiving.

In 1552 further mediaeval elements in the rites disappeared. Bishops were no longer invested with the pastoral staff, and the Bible was not laid on their necks but handed to them, although the formulae which had accompanied these two ceremonies in 1550 were retained. The delivery of the instruments was also modified for priests: they too received only the Bible, the delivery of the chalice and the bread being omitted. In 1559 and 1662 no further basic changes were made, but in 1662 an addition was inserted in the formulae accompanying the imposition of hands in the case of bishops and priests. A specific reference was made to the order being conferred, 'for the office and work of a bishop' and 'for the office and work of a priest', thereby meeting the Puritan argument that from the similarity of the earlier formulae there had been no clear distinction between the episcopate and the priesthood.

Throughout the Anglican Communion the 1662 rites have continued with little change until the twentieth century. One improvement was made in the Scottish prayer book of 1929 and in the proposed English prayer book of 1928. A eucharistic type of ordination prayer introduced by the *Sursum corda* was inserted before the imposition of hands in the rite for deacons, while the existing prayers for bishops and priests were remodelled to conform to the same pattern. But the most thorough revision appeared in the Ordinal of the Church of South India in 1958. Here the rites for all three orders followed the same pattern within the framework of the eucharist. Candidates were first presented to the congregation, and the latter was

required to express approval or disapproval. Then followed the ministry of the word; the examination; silent prayer and *Veni creator Spiritus*; the solemn ordination prayer itself, during which the imposition of hands occurred; the giving of the Bible (and staff to bishops); and a declaration of ordination. The eucharist then continued, beginning at the intercession. Thus form and matter were once again closely related. This Ordinal met with widespread approval and provided a valuable model for other revisions, such as West Africa 1965–66, Anglican-Methodist in England 1968, and America 1970–77. The Anglican-Methodist Ordinal was of particular interest, for it was the immediate precusor of the new Anglican Ordinal in the Alternative Service Book 1980. It varied little in structure or content from the South Indian rite, except that the ministry of the word preceded the presentation, and the declaration of ordination and the presentation of staff to bishops were omitted. Furthermore, all three orders were 'ordained', and bishops were no longer 'consecrated'.

The Ordinal in ASB 1980 makes the following important modifications of the Anglican-Methodist Ordinal – a new opening collect; an Old Testament reading and psalm for each order; a statement of the office and work of each order before the declaration; the restoration of the Litany in conformity with long tradition; and in the case of bishops it is 'ordination or consecration'. The services for deacons and priests are set out both separately and in combined form, and the whole Ordinal is in 'you' language. The Methodists produced their own revision of the Anglican-Methodist Ordinal in 1975 which differs in a number of ways from ASB 1980. Every effort has been made in ASB to provide a set of services which would not only place no obstacle in the way of Roman Catholic recognition of Anglican orders but also give consideration to the views of the Free Churches on the ministry.

R. C. D. JASPER

5. *Baptist.* Baptist ordination is primarily for ministry in a local congregation; therefore, the service of ordination is a service of a local congregation, generally the one to which the ordinand will minister. When a congregation determines that one of its members is to be ordained, it sends out a call to other nearby congregations that a council meet to examine the candidate's qualifications for the ministry. While such a council is not required by strict Baptist polity, it represents symbolically the unity of the Baptist churches as well as the fact that ordination is mutually recognized by other churches than the one actually doing the ordaining.

The service of ordination is generally held at a time when representatives of other churches in the area can attend. It is set within a full service of worship (for the outline of the Lord's Day service *see* **Liturgies** 5). The act of ordination takes place as part of the offertory*. As the gifts and the bread and wine are brought to the table, the moderator or a deacon presents the ordinand to the congregation with the recommendation of the council that the church proceed with the ordination. After receiving vows from the ordinand, the presiding minister declares that the ordinand has responded faithfully to the call to the set-apart ministry and is fit through preparation to be ordained at this time. After a blessing upon the ordinand, clergy and in many cases representative laity are invited to lay hands on the ordinand for the prayer of ordination. After the prayer charges are given to both the candidate and the church, and the newly-ordained minister is given the right hand of fellowship into the ordained ministry. To symbolize the minister's role as a preacher of the word a Bible is presented to the newly-ordained minister. As a first act of ministry the new minister is invited to preside over the Lord's Supper and pronounce the benediction. Complete Baptist services of ordination can be found in E. A. Payne and S. F. Winward, *Orders and Prayers for Church Worship*, 1965 and J. E. Skoglund, *A Manual of Worship*, 1968.

Baptists ordain women as well as men. Women serve as pastors, missionaries and denominational executives. The act of ordination is not seen as the conferring of some special grace, but rather the recognition of graces already received. Ordination is a recognition on the part of a congregation of a person's call and fitness for special ministries. In essence the ordained minister is set apart by the congregation to minister in special ways, but

what the ordained person does can also be done by a lay person, provided such a one is designated by the congregation for such service. This process is called licensing and is used when no ordained minister is available or when there is need for the extension of ministry to other areas.

Many Baptist churches ordain deacons*. They serve the Lord's Supper, visit the sick and infirm, carry responsibility along with the pastor for the spiritual well-being of the congregation and assist the pastor in whatever ways the congregation may so designate. Ordained deacons continue to be members of the laity. Services for the ordination of deacons can be found in the manuals listed above. Missionaries and other special service workers who retain lay status are commissioned.

Exceptions to local church ordination can be found among some European Baptist bodies (as e.g. the Swedish Baptist Union). Both the ordination of pastors and the commissioning of missionaries is done at the annual conference of the Union.

JOHN E. SKOGLUND

6. *Christian Church (Disciples of Christ)*. The Christian Church (Disciples of Christ) is like other churches in that it sets people apart for the office of ministry by an act of prayer and laying on of hands. Where it has differed from many has been in its understanding of the persons who should receive this rite of the church. From their studies of the NT, Disciple leaders in the early nineteenth century derived three ministerial offices. Evangelists were itinerant proclaimers of the gospel whose chief work was to found and organize churches. Elders* were mature men, resident in the community, who would be elected by members of the local church and ordained by them for the overseeing of the church's life. Although they held secular employment, they were to preach – if possessing the necessary skill – and administer baptism and the Lord's Supper, the latter every week. Deacons* were also local men and their service was limited to matters more temporal than preaching and praying.

During the course of the last third of the nineteenth century and the first half of the twentieth, Disciples developed an educated, salaried ministry. Until the 1960s such ministers would ordinarily preside over the Sunday service and would preach. Always a part of that service, however, was the Lord's Supper and invariably elders (as described in the above paragraph) would preside over that portion of the service. They offered the eucharistic prayer while the minister sat near the pulpit. In later years the minister came to share in this service at the table – delivering a brief meditation before the prayer and reciting the words of institution after the prayers.

It is normal practice for such a minister to be ordained. Elders from several congregations, and a small group of other ministers, lay their hands on the ordinand's head while a prayer of dedication and invocation is offered by one of them. There is divided opinion among Disciples concerning the ordination of the elders. Before the rise of the office of minister, the elders in a congregation were ordained because they were understood to be fulfilling the ministerial functions of teaching and overseeing. In some congregations this practice of ordaining elders continues unabated. In others, however, the service of prayer and laying on of hands has been replaced by installation into a functional office.

Until the mid-twentieth century, only men became elders, deacons, and ministers. In part, this pattern simply continued the long-standing practice of most churches and of secular culture. It was reinforced by the dominance of male leadership in biblical literature. Apparently Disciples overlooked Romans 16.1 where Phoebe is called *diakonos*. Although women regularly served as missionaries and directors of Christian education, they usually were not ordained. By mid-century, however, a rapidly growing number of women were ordained into the ministry of word and sacrament. Late in this same period, women were also elected into the eldership and diaconate.

It is not yet clear what will happen to the Disciple elder in the coming decades. The current trend seems to be in the direction of continued diminution of this office with the result that ordination would be increasingly inappropriate. This trend continues even though there is growing interest in some quarters of the church for a ministry that is not dependent upon the church for livelihood.

At the present time there is no official definition of ordination. There would be

widespread agreement to the definition that ordination is a corporate act by the church in which it appoints certain persons to the work of public ministry. Ministers, as distinguished from elders, are ordained, usually after graduation from seminary.

KEITH WATKINS

7. *Congregationalist.* The classical Congregational theory and practice of ordination is described in *The Savoy Declaration* of 1658:

> The way appointed by Christ for the calling of any person, fitted and gifted by the Holy Ghost, unto the Office of Pastor, Teacher, or Elder in a Church, is that he be chosen there unto by the common suffrage of the Church itself, and solemnly set apart by fasting and prayer, with Imposition of Hands of the Eldership of that Church . . .

If exception was taken to the laying on of hands, it could be omitted.

Congregational ordination today is not materially different, except that it is more liable to be preceded by feasting than fasting, and that the moderator of a province (in Britain) or a conference minister (in America) will represent the wider fellowship of Congregational churches. Essentially though, the service is still the solemn recognition that the ordinand has been called by God to the ministry and that he (or she) has the necessary gifts and grace, and is now by the invocation of the Holy Spirit and the laying on of hands set apart for this ministry and invited to be pastor of this local fellowship and congregation of Christ.

The order of service for the ordination of a minister in *A Book of Services and Prayers* (1959) for the use of English Congregationalists will be taken as the model.

The service in the United Reformed Church's* *Book of Services* (1980) differs in slight particulars, and in its order (the addresses are generally brought forward to an earlier point in the service), but not in general ethos. That book also contains an order of service for the Ordination and Induction of Elders.

After an introduction of sentences of scripture and an invocatory prayer, followed by the reading of appropriate lessons from both Testaments, the presiding minister summarizes the foundation and duties of the church and ministry. Then he calls upon the secretary of the local church to record the steps that have led the congregation to the issuing of the invitation to the ordinand to be their minister. The ordinand is then called upon to make a statement expounding 'his Christian experience; his assurance of his call by God to the holy ministry; (and) his Christian belief' (ibid., p. 93). Thereupon the ordinand is required to confess his belief in the Holy Trinity, the lordship of Christ, in the scriptures as containing 'all doctrine required for eternal salvation through faith in Jesus Christ', and to give assurance he is truly called to the ministry, and to promise that he will fulfil the pastoral office with all fidelity. The presiding minister then asks the members of the local church to stand in silent prayer in token that they receive the ordinand as their minister.

After the singing of a hymn of the Holy Spirit or the *Veni Creator*, the ordination prayer follows. During the saying of this prayer ministers and church representatives lay their hands upon the head of the ordinand, while the presiding minister prays for the continuance of the gifts of the Holy Spirit, and for the welfare of pastor and flock, ending with the Lord's Prayer said by all. The presiding minister then says in the name of Christ and of the churches of the Congregational faith and order, 'We declare you to be ordained to this ministry of the gospel in the church of Christ, and to be appointed pastor of this church and congregation.' The minister is then given a Bible as token of his privilege and duty to preach God's word, and he receives the right hand of fellowship from representatives of the local and wider churches.

It is then customary for two invited ministers to preach, one of them reminding the congregation of its privileges and duties, and the other reminding the minister of his. Sometimes a single address covers both aspects. The newly-ordained minister gives the final blessing to the congregation. The custom in the USA is not materially different. However, ordination within the United Reformed Church* in the United Kingdom now always includes a statement concerning the nature, faith and order of that church, and the questions to the minister-elect are based upon that statement.

HORTON DAVIES

8. *Jehovah's Witnesses*. In sending his Son to earth Jehovah gave us a perfect model to follow (I Peter 2.21). Jesus called certain individuals to come and be his followers (Matt. 9.9; John 1.43). He trained them in the ministry and sent them forth to do the same work he was doing (Matt. 10.1–11.1; Luke 4.43). Later he sent seventy others to share in declaring the good news concerning God's kingdom (Luke 10.1, 8–11). They were to represent the Most High God, as do all others who respond to Jesus' invitation to 'come be my follower' (Luke 18.22). All who respond to the divine commission to preach the good news of the kingdom make disciples (Matt. 24.14; 28.19, 20).

The baptism (*see* **Baptism** 8) of an individual in water as a symbol of dedication to Jehovah constitutes the ordination of that person as one of God's ministers.

Jehovah's Witnesses take their ministry seriously and their calling from house to house is virtually their trademark in many lands. This primitive method of preaching was the one used by Jesus and his apostles and enables the good news of the kingdom to reach millions of people. The good results obtained over the years give evidence of Jehovah's approval and blessing (Acts 20.18, 20, 21).

Aside from house-to-house witnessing, Jehovah's Witnesses preach on the streets and in market places, in fact wherever people are to be found. Informal conversations often spark interest which can then be developed. Return visits are made when interest is manifested, and conducting Bible studies in the homes of the people is part of the regular activity of Jehovah's Witnesses world-wide. At these studies it is possible for questions to be asked and answered from the scriptures to the satisfaction of the individual householder.

The Watch Tower Bible School of Gilead, established in 1942, has thus far graduated over 6,000 missionaries for assignments all over the world. So as to equip overseers (elders) to provide better spiritual supervision in the congregations, a special Kingdom Ministry School was inaugurated in 1959 in all countries. Updated refresher courses are provided from time to time. The Watch Tower Society also operates Pioneer Service Schools for the training of full-time pioneer ministers, of whom there are now well over 250,000 world-wide. In addition, in order to help many illiterate people to take in Bible knowledge effectively, Jehovah's Witnesses have set up reading classes in a number of countries and taught many thousands to read and write.

Before being publicly identified as one of Jehovah's Witnesses each individual must measure up to the moral requirements expected of a Christian and be free from involvement in the political affairs of the world. He must, of course, know and believe the basic teachings of the scriptures so that, when asked questions, he will answer in harmony with the Bible (I Peter 3.15).

Jehovah's Witnesses concentrate on building up men, women and children spiritually by instruction in the Bible. Among them there is no class distinction or racial discrimination. Those who are elders or ministerial servants are but part of the congregation in which 'all are brothers' (Matt. 23.8). This 'entire association of your brothers in the world' constitutes the world-wide preaching organization of Jehovah's Witnesses today (I Peter 5.9).

DAVID SIBREY

9. *Lutheran*. The Reformation led to a complete change in the understanding of the ordained ministry. Luther denied the traditional view of the priestly office as having a sacrificial and mediatorial character. He turned against the idea of the clerics as a separate order from that of the laity and the idea of the transfer from the ordinator to the ordinand of a *character indelebilis* which was supposed to give him a sacramental character and enable him to perform the right sacrifice when celebrating the eucharist (*Werke*, Weimar, 1883ff. = WA 6,562, 567; 12,172,190).

As a support for this view of the ordained ministry, he referred to the biblical office, which he considered instituted by Christ when he chose his apostles and sent them out to preach. The apostles in turn sent others, thus continuing the office. Luther could find no support for the idea that the apostles had transferred the office to an order of bishops* (*episkopoi*) separated from the elders (*presbyteroi*, *see* **Presbyter**) (WA 40, 59; cf. 16, 33). So since a special office of bishop did not exist in NT times,

there can be no fundamental division between bishops and priests, and hence a non-episcopal church cannot be considered less apostolic than one which has the office of bishop. The arrangement may serve the church for practical reasons. According to the Lutheran Confessions, therefore, no other authority was vested in the bishop except to ordain, and this authority was not by virtue of any inherent power in the bishop, but was entrusted to him by the church (WA 6,407). The authority to proclaim the word, administer the sacraments and the power of the keys belongs to everyone ordained, as a trust given for reasons of order by the church. Ordination provides for orderliness but does not constitute an 'order'. This development was dictated by the 'enthusiasts' who claimed only an inner and immediate call from the Holy Spirit (WA 30,519,524; 31,211; 32,483).

Basically every Christian is in baptism ordained priest (priesthood of all believers) with the duty to proclaim the word to those around him. (WA, 8,423; 11,413). According to Lutheran teaching the main emphasis lies on *ministerium verbi divini*, in which the office is subordinate to the word. 'The ministry of the word makes ministers, not ministers the ministry' (WA, 6,566; 8,422).

Ordination bestows the office of a public servant of God in his church (WA 38,228; 15,721). The office belongs to the church and ordination to it is to be administered by regularly constituted authorities of the church. It is a function, not a rank of the church.

Necessary to ordination are:

1. The assertion of an inner conviction that God has called a person to the ministry of the gospel.

2. A public confession of evangelical faith with a pledge of loyalty to the revealed truth and the confession of the church.

3. A specific and regular call received and accepted (WA 11,40ff.; 12,169ff.).

4. A readiness to give unconditional devotion to the work of the Lord.

The rite. In view of the doctrine outlined above the first change in the Lutheran ordination ritual was the exclusion of anointing, considered to be an expression of the new character in traditional teaching. In 1535 Luther produced a Rite for Ordination, the basic core of which is an emphasis on the Word of God and Prayer, which has been the base for the rites of most Lutheran churches (WA 38,401ff.). From it two types of order have developed. The first kept closer to Luther's own formula, as in *Kirkeordinansen* of 1539 for Denmark and Norway and in the German and North American formulae of the 1970s and 1980s. In the second type, as in *Kyrkoordningen* of 1571 for Sweden and Finland and more recent forms in these churches and their sister churches in Tanzania and Namibia, additions have been made which derive from mediaeval ordination rites. These consist for the most part of extra liturgical traditions such as *investiture* – clothing in official vestments, *porrectio instrumentorum* – Bible and chalice with prescribed formulae, the ordinand's confession of faith, 'priestly oath' and *pax*.

To the one ordained is given both authority and assurance as the instrument of the Holy Spirit in the performance of his duties. The laying on of hands, not instituted by Christ but from the old dispensation, is not decreed as necessary. It is, however, considered symbolically valuable as an expression of the church's interest and intercession. (*See* **Gestures** 7.)

Elements included in the rite of ordination:

1. Confirm the call to a specific task in the church's ministry.

2. Commit to the ordinand the office of public ministry of word and sacrament.

3. Pledge the ordinand to faithful service.

4. Invoke the Holy Spirit on the ordinand.

5. Mark the apostolicity of the office by the laying on of hands.

The order for ordination includes distinctive propers*, the formal presentation of the candidate, reciting the approving actions of the church, a series of pertinent questions calling for answers by the ordinand to bind the ordinand to the confession of the church and a life consonant therewith, the laying on of hands, and the commissioning followed by appropriate prayers. An admonition to the congregation assembled is also included.

The fact that ordination is a responsibility of the church at large is seen in the liturgy by the fact that:

1. It is performed by the appointed head

of the church or his appointee.

2. Ordained ministers representing the church at large participate especially in the laying on of hands.

3. It takes place in the context of the main service of the church.

4. Candidates are presented as approved by the regularly constituted council of the church.

In Africa and Europe ordination takes place in the diocesan cathedral, while in Asia and North America some churches ordain in connection with the synodical conventions while others ordain in the congregation where the ordained is to serve.

E. J. R. H. S. VON SICARD

10. *Methodist*. John Wesley in *The Sunday Service*, 1784, in general copied the ordinal of the 1662 BCP of the Church of England, but used the names superintendants* (sic), elders*, and deacons*. There were, however, several changes, of which the most important were the omissions both of John 20.23 in the formula for ordaining an elder and of the gospel containing it in the form for ordaining a superintendant. Coke, a presbyter of the Church of England whom Wesley had set apart as a superintendant, took this book to America, and it passed into the Ritual in the American *Discipline*, where it underwent various changes. 'The form of Ordaining of a Superintendant' has become 'The Order for the Consecration of Bishops'. The word 'bishop' goes back to 1792. There has been much discussion about the difference between ordination and consecration, but it is difficult to attach much significance to it. The phrase 'Receive the Holy Ghost' is replaced by 'The Lord pour upon thee the Holy Spirit', a change which was effected (except for the change of 'Ghost') in 1792 for elders, though not till later for bishops. The terms 'epistle' and 'gospel' are retained, but there is no mention of the rest of the communion service.

In 1980, the United Methodist Church adopted 'for official alternate use' (in addition to the rites in the 1964 *Book of Worship*), a completely new volume, *An Ordinal*. The new volume contains a rite for the ordination of deacons and elders at the same occasion plus separate rites for the ordination of deacons, elders, and consecration of bishops. The new rites reflect the recent reforms of Roman Catholics and Anglicans, especially in stressing the ordination prayer as invocation of the Holy Spirit, increasing the role of the congregation, downplaying subsidiary ceremonies, and placing ordination in the context of the eucharist. Contemporary and inclusive language is used throughout the services.

In British Methodism the services of 1784 continued to be printed in the subsequent editions of *The Sunday Service*, very curiously because the British ministry is not divided into superintendants (though the word is used), elders and deacons, and ordination services with the imposition of hands were not often held until the Wesleyan Conference adopted the practice in 1836. But in the edition of 1846 and subsequent editions the three ordinations were replaced by the 'Form for Ordaining Candidates for the Ministry in the Wesleyan-Methodist Connexion', which contained features from all three. This was not greatly altered in the revision of 1882, nor indeed in that of 1936 after the union, though the services of the non-Wesleyan churches had been very much simpler. *The Methodist Service Book*, 1975, is in current use. The President of the Conference or his representative presides, assisted by other ordained Ministers; a lay person usually reads one of the lessons. The service is set in the context of holy communion. After the Creed come the presentation (with acclamation 'They are worthy'), homily and examination, silent prayer with concluding collect, 'Come, Holy Ghost, our souls inspire', the ordination prayer, the Lord's Prayer, presentation of a Bible, declaration about authority to preach and administer the sacraments and homily. This service shows considerable changes, the chief of which is that the ordination is not effected by a formula addressed to the candidate but by the ordination prayer, during which hands are laid on the head of the ordinand with the words 'Father, send the Holy Spirit upon N, for the office and work of a Minister in the Church of God'.

There are also American services for the consecration of diaconal ministers, for licensing persons to preach, and for admission of ministerial candidates to membership in an annual conference. The British *Book of Offices*, 1936, had a service

for the ordination of deaconesses*, which continued in use until admission to the order was suspended, pending reconsideration of the nature of diaconal ministry.

A. RAYMOND GEORGE

11. *Old Catholic.* The Old Catholic churches of the Utrecht Union have always attached the utmost importance to maintaining the apostolic succession. This holds even for the earlier of them, the Old Catholic Church of the Netherlands, which, despite its separation from Rome since the beginning of the eighteenth century, has succeeded in maintaining canonically valid episcopal orders. As a result, the Old Catholic churches which arose in protest against the papal dogmas of 1870 were able to carry on the apostolic succession. The validity of Old Catholic episcopal orders has always been recognized, even by Rome.

Because they possess the apostolic succession, the Old Catholic churches have a validly ordained clergy at all stages: the lower orders, the diaconate, priesthood and episcopate. Although the traditional system of lower orders (door-keepers, lectors, exorcists, acolytes) has been felt to be problematical for some time, so far it has been kept on in the Old Catholic churches, with an eye to the mother church of Rome. But now that the problem of these lower orders has been recognized in the Roman church within the framework of liturgical renewal, and a new church order has been sought, the question is being re-examined.

Until recently, the rites of consecration were derived from the *Pontificale Romanum*, having been produced in 1899 in German by order of the Old Catholic Bishop's Conference, and then translated into other languages (*see* **Books, Liturgical** 11). The International Old Catholic Liturgical Commission has now published new rites for the ordination of deacons (and deaconesses) and priests, and for the consecration of bishops, which were confirmed by the International Bishop's Conference in September 1985. The new rites are based on those of the ancient church, and draw the whole congregation into the prayers and ceremonies taking place. Thus the congregation says, after the candidate has been presented, 'He shall be a deacon (priest/bishop) to the honour of God and for service in the church of God.'

All ordinations take place within the mass, but at different points. 'Clothing in the spiritual state' comes first for the lower orders. Candidates are dressed in a white surplice. There is no tonsure. The lower orders are bestowed in accordance with the traditional rites. The office of exorcist*, which is no longer held actively, is now interpreted as the entrusting of the duty of pastoral care. It is still an open question whether the subdiaconate (*see* **Subdeacon**) is to be included among the lower or the higher orders.

The most important elements of the rites of consecration are: presentation of the ordinands, address by the bishop (instruction on the meaning and the duties of the order to be bestowed), handing over the *instrumenta* (i.e. the vessels and books necessary for exercising the office in question), the prayer of consecration, and dressing in the garments proper to each order. From the consecration of subdeacons upwards, the litany is added, and from the diaconate upwards the invocation of the Holy Spirit; with priests, the hands are anointed and with bishops, the head. At the consecration of priests, hands are laid on the candidate by the bishop and the other priests present, the Apostles' Creed is recited and a promise of obedience is made to the bishop; at the consecration of bishops there is an examination of faith and the handing over of insignia (cross, staff, ring and mitre). Newly ordained deacons assist during the celebration of the eucharist which follows; newly ordained priests concelebrate with the bishop; and a newly consecrated bishop takes charge of the celebration of the eucharist after the offertory. Two other bishops, at least, should assist at the consecration of the bishop, and should lay hands on the bishop with the bishop who consecrates him.

The forms of address and prayers are not translated from the Latin completely literally, but have been reshaped in a form that has strongly biblical colouring.

S. KRAFT/C. TOL

12. *Pentecostal.* In younger Pentecostal churches ordination is not the initiation into the ministry but its acknowledgment by the church. A young Pentecostal, therefore, begins (with or without Bible school education) to preach, to lead services, to pray

with the sick *before* his ordination. If the church recognizes in him the gifts of a preacher he will *then* be ordained. This pattern is particularly common in Africa, Latin America and Indonesia, but it was also the rule in USA and Europe thirty years ago. With the establishment of Bible schools this pattern begins to be changed towards a system which approaches that of the main-line Protestant churches. The liturgical formulae for ordination vary. In the Iglesia Metodista Pentecostal the bishop and the superintendents ordain pastors and deaconesses according to the Methodist ordination liturgy, including laying on of hands. The only difference from a Methodist ordination service is the highly intense participation of the whole congregation by loud Hallelujahs, shoutings and singing. After the ordination there is the 'kiss of peace' among all the pastors, from which the deaconesses are not excepted!

The special gifts for which the congregation tests the candidate for the ministry are not in the first place those of intellect and education – although formal Bible school or theological education are beginning to play a greater part in European and North American Pentecostal denominations. Rather they search to learn whether the future minister is able to lead the Pentecostal liturgy by his sensitivity and his musical ability to intone a chorus (*see* **Liturgies** 12), so that chaos *and* cold stiffness are alike avoided, and further whether he is a man who is able to articulate what his people feel, what they fear and what they rejoice about.

For bibliography *see* **Pentecostal Worship**.

W. J. HOLLENWEGER

13. *Reformed.* The Reformed Church holds itself to be part of the one, holy, catholic and apostolic church. John Knox said it was:

> a part of that holy Kirk universal, which is grounded upon the doctrine of the prophets and apostles, having the same antiquity that the Kirk of the Apostles has as concerning doctrine, prayers, administration of sacraments and all things requisite to a particular Kirk (Knox, *Works*, VI, p.492).

On the basis of the NT (Acts 20.17–35; I Tim. 4.14; Titus 1.5–7; I Peter 5.1–4; etc.) and also of the *communior sententia*, found in Aquinas and the scholastics, that the highest order of the Christian ministry is the presbyterate and that the bishop is only a presbyter who has been given the episcopal office (Barkley in *The Newman*, IV, 3, pp. 115–31), the Reformed Church accepts the original identity of presbyter and bishop. Presbyterianism means government by presbyters (not presbyteries), just as episcopacy means government by bishops. Ordination is an act of God through presbyters, constitutionally associated, within the people of God. In the words of the Provincial Assembly of London, who carried on the work of the Westminster Assembly,

> The power of ordination of ministers exercised for these many hundred years by bishops did belong to them as presbyters and not as bishops (*Jus Divinum Ministerii Evangelici*, II, 20, 33).

The procedure for ordination in the Genevan *Ecclesiastical Ordinances* (1541) was:

> It will be good in this connection to follow the order of the ancient Church, for it is the only practice which is shown us in Scripture. The order is that ministers first elect such as ought to hold office; afterwards that he be presented to the Council; and if he is found worthy the Council receive and accept him, giving him certification to produce finally to the people when he preaches, in order that he be received by the common consent of the company of the faithful . . . As to the manner of introducing him, it is good to use the imposition of hands, which ceremony was observed by the apostles and then in the ancient Church, providing that it take place without superstition and without offence. But because there has been much superstition in the past and scandal might result, it is better to abstain from it because of the infirmity of the times (*Corpus Reformatorum*, X, 15).

These regulations cover (*a*) the election and examination, and (*b*) the act of ordination. The former varied in different places. For example, in the English congregation in Geneva, the congregation nominated several candidates to the

ministers and elders, who examined them as to their life and education. The one approved was made known to the congregation, and time provided for them to enquire as to his fitness and character. If nothing was charged against him, a day was appointed for his ordination. The same procedure, in broad outline, was followed in France and Scotland.

One of the essential elements in ordination is the 'call'. As the Genevan *Ordinances* put it, 'No one ought to intrude himself into this office without a call'. This emphasis is found in Zwingli (*CR*, IV, 425), Calvin (*Inst.* IV, iii, 10), the second *Helvetic* (18) and *Gallican* (31) *Confessions*, as well as in Holland (G. Brandt, *The Reformation in the Low Countries*, 1720, I, p.318). In Scotland, however, they preferred to speak of a double call: 'called of God and duly elected by men'. The 'call' of the people was seen as confirming the inward 'call' of God. The Holy Spirit works not only in the aspirant, but also in the electors.

With regard to the ordination, it was by prayer with the laying on of hands in Zurich (H. A. Daniel, *Codex Liturgicus*, III, 1851, 234). This is also true of the first and second *Helvetic Confessions* (H. A. Niemeyer, *Collectio Confessionum*, 1840, pp.110, 119, 507), of Calvin in Strasbourg, John a'Lasco in Frankfurt (*Forma ac Ratio*, 1556), Valerand Pullain (*Liturgia sacra*, 1551) and in France (J. Quick, *Synodicon*, 1692, I, 3, 62). On the other hand, in Geneva and Holland (Brandt, I, p.319) the laying on of hands would appear to be an open question. The Scottish first *Book of Discipline* (Knox, *Works*, II, 193) contains wording similar to that in the Genevan *Ordinances*, but this may only refer to those who had formerly been priests in the mediaeval church. In 1566, the Scottish assembly approved the second *Helvetic Confession*, and in 1581 adopted the second *Book of Discipline* (III, 6), both of which prescribe the laying on of hands. It also was the practice of the English Puritans, as the 1586, 1587, and 1602 editions of the *Form of Prayers* show. In all these rites the essence of ordination is prayer (cf. L. Duchesne, *Christian Worship*, [6]1931, p.377).

Calvin's ordination service is based on the practice of the early church rather than the mediaeval ordinals, but the liturgical sections do not appear to go farther back than himself or perhaps Bucer.

In the Scottish *Book of Common Order* (1564) the service is headed *The Form and Order of the Election of the Superintendent which may serve in election of all the Ministers*. It is really the form, drawn up by John Knox in 1560, largely based upon a'Lasco, for the admission of John Spottiswood as Superintendent for the Lothians (*BCO*, ed Sprott, pp.20–7).

After a sermon which, as with Calvin, dealt with the office and nature of the ministry, the people were asked if they accepted the minister and would 'obey him as Christ's Minister'. Then a series of questions was put to the minister-elect, and after satisfactory answers had been given the people were again asked whether they would receive him. A short exhortation 'to the nobility' followed, and then came the ordination prayer ending with the Lord's Prayer. After this the ministers and elders gave the right hand of fellowship. A benediction followed, and then an exhortation to the minister, the final direction being 'Sing the 23rd Psalm'.

Spottiswood was in Anglican orders, so there is no reference to the laying on of hands. The same applied to priests of the mediaeval church. They were admitted, not ordained.

Ordination was a catholic rite, not merely an admission to the ministry of a particular church. The people were given a place in the choice of the ordinand, but he was ordained by those already holding the office. His commission was not from the people, but from God through presbyters, lawfully associated, within the people of God.

In 1570 and 1620 further ordinals were produced in Scotland, and both make prayer and laying on of hands the main portions of the ceremony (*Miscellany of the Wodrow Society*, 1844, pp.597ff.). In 1645, the Westminster *Form of Presbyterial Church Government* was adopted, and it remains the basic document to the present day in English-speaking Presbyterianism. It states:

> No man ought to take upon him the office of a minister of the word without a lawful calling . . .
>
> Every minister of the word is to be ordained by imposition of hands and

prayer, with fasting, by those preaching presbyters to whom it doth belong.

It then sets out *The Directory for the Ordination of Ministers*. The structure of the service is:

Sermon 'concerning the office and duty of ministers of Christ'.
Questions to ordinand concerning his faith in Christ, the truth of reformed religion, etc.
Questions to people 'concerning their willingness to receive and acknowledge him as the minister of Christ' . . . 'to obey him . . .', 'and to maintain, encourage, and assist him in all the parts of his office'.
Prayer of ordination with laying on of hands.
Charge to minister and people.
Prayer 'commending both him and his flock to the grace of God'.
Psalm.
Dismissal with a blessing (XIX 5–9).

These works contain the basic principles which govern all modern rites.

Following the Westminster Assembly, owing to the rise of Independency and Brownism there was a period of liturgical decadence. Renewal came with the founding of the Church Service Society in 1865. It published the second edition of its *Euchologion* in 1869. This included an introductory article (pp.294–303) on the ordination service, a table of scripture lessons 'proper for the Service preceding the Ordination of Ministers and their Induction to Office' and 'portions of psalms proper to be sung' (p.317), as well as a text for the rite (pp.303–316).

The liturgical sources for the prayers in this rite are Calvin, Knox, the *Westminster Directory*, and the *Provisional Liturgy* of the German Reformed Church in America, 1850 (*Euchologion*, ed Sprott, p.431).

In the *Euchologion*, ordination is treated as an ordinance following the liturgy of the word, and this is still the practice in some places. On the other hand, Scotland, Ireland, England-Wales, Canada, Geneva and Vaud see the rite as a unity and set out the service as consisting of both the liturgy of the word and ordination. All include the order for ordination of ministers in their service book, except the Church of Scotland and the United Church of Canada, where it is published in a separate ordinal. The latter was also true in America, but in *The Worshipbook* (1970) it has been re-introduced (pp.89–95). From the standpoint of Reformed theology the ordination prayer is open to criticism in that it makes no specific reference to ordination to the ministry of the word and sacraments or to the laying on of hands. As a result of the *Euchologion* in Scotland, Osterwald in Switzerland, van Dyke in America, Bersier in France, van der Leeuw in Holland, and Albertz in Germany, all modern rites show traces of a more careful handling of the theological implications of ordination. As the various rites, whether in English, French, or German, follow a common pattern it is unnecessary to deal with them in detail.

The Church of Scotland produced an *Ordinal and Service Book for use in the Courts of the Church* in 1931, with revisions in 1954 and 1962. It provides a full service, 'which in most Presbyteries is followed very closely'. In the ordination service proper the following elements are mandatory: the preamble concerning the faith of the church, the prescribed questions to the ordinand, ordination by prayer with the laying on of hands, the signing of the formula, and the declaration. This service, and in particular its ordination prayer, has been influential beyond the bounds of the Church of Scotland, for example, in the Ordinals of the Church of South India (*see* **Church of South India Worship**) and the Church of North India.

Because of the close family ties of all these rites, only a few comments are necessary:

(*a*) The lections set forth the biblical basis for the ministry.

(*b*) In the Presbyterian church in Canada a statement on the ministry may be read instead of the sermon.

(*c*) The prescribed questions differ in each church because they are drawn up by the various assemblies. They always cover: 'call of God', belief in the fundamental doctrines of the Christian faith, acceptance of scripture, obedience 'in the Lord' to the church, and fidelity as a minister of Jesus Christ.

(*d*) Some rites, for example, the Scottish, have the *Sursum corda* before the ordination prayer. Basically all are thanks-

givings with an epiclesis and the laying on of hands. Though the words vary they are all identical in substance.

(*e*) Some churches, for example, Scotland, provide a charge which may be read.

The most significant change in recent years with regard to ordination within the Reformed Churches is the decision of the National Synod of the Reformed Church of France at Dourdan in May 1984. This church has devoted much attention for a decade to the diversification of ministries within the church. Discussing the question of the recognition of ministries in the church, the National Synod decided to abandon the term ordination and replace it by a 'Liturgy of Recognition of Ministries', which will be equally applied, with the necessary adjustments, both to the general ministries (such as pastors, elders, deacons) and to the local ones (such as catechists). The main argument for the decision was that the church is 'the people of God', and that the limiting of the use of the term 'ordination' to ministers, elders and deacons was 'a form of clericalism, separating them from the remaining people of God'. While the term ordination is to be abandoned, it is essential to recognize that the 'setting apart' of pastors, etc. will continue, using different terminology.

On this two things may be said. 1. During the discussion the Synod was aware that its approach was at variance with the view set out in the Faith and Order Lima document, *Baptism, Eucharist, and Ministry*, but 'deemed that being faithful to the Reformed insights concerning the ministries would bring a useful contribution to the ecumenical dialogue.' 2. It is too early yet to assess the effect of the decision of the French Reformed Church on the Leuenberg Talks for the co-ordination of Lutheran/Reformed relations, as they have not yet discussed 'Ministry and Ordination'.

In the Reformed Church, the rite of ordination is an ordinance of the word and always takes place within the setting of public worship, thus placing the holy ministry within the context of the sovereign grace of the Lord Jesus Christ, sole king and head of the church. All ministry is ultimately his ministry within the life of his body. The holy ministry is of divine institution and derivation, renewed in every age by Jesus Christ through the creative power of the Holy Spirit, acting through his church when it is faithful to its apostolic institution, practice and doctrine.

JOHN M. BARKLEY

14. *Seventh-Day Adventist*. In the Seventh-day Adventist Church ordination is the liturgical act by which a member of the church is set apart by prayer and the laying on of hands for a special function of service in the church and is authorized to perform this function.

In the very early days of the SDAC there appears to have been little need for ordaining new ministers, because congregations were small and most of the ministers had already been ordained in the churches of their former membership. However, as the need for some clear form of church organization arose, and in order to avoid any tendency towards want of method or lack of co-operation by self-appointed preachers, the leaders of the movement began to practise ordination in the early 1850s. It was not instituted to build up a religious hierarchy or to exalt a clergy to a place of special privilege, but rather to provide for proper church order as the ordained individual receives new responsibilities and consecrates his life to God, the special service of the church, and to the world.

The SDAC ordains three categories of church workers: (*a*) ministers, (*b*) local church elders and (*c*) deacons.

Ordained ministers are full-time, salaried workers of the church, who have completed the requisite academic and theological studies prescribed by the church. Candidates for ministerial ordination have for the most part served as licensed ministers for a minimum of four years (including a two-year ministerial internship). Customarily they are married men; however, marriage is not a prerequisite for ordination. Though the church has taken no stand against the ordination of women, in practice only men have been ordained so far. The General Conference *Working Policy* outlines a careful procedure for authorizing ordination. The usual process is for local conference (or mission) and Union committees to suggest ordinands to the committee on credentials and licences at the triennial conference (or mission) session, on whose favourable report the

session delegates make the final decision. Before ordination is carried out, a careful interview of the candidate is held, usually in the presence of his wife. It is conducted by ordained ministers only. There must be evidence of the person's divine call before the church sets him apart by ordination. Seventh-day Adventists reject as without biblical foundation the concept of 'apostolic succession', seeing little guarantee in the physical act of imposition itself. The laying on of hands *per se* adds no new grace or virtual qualification. By this act the church sets its seal upon the work of God.

The ordination service is one of the most solemn of all services of the church. It usually takes place on a Sabbath (Saturday) afternoon and is conducted with a view to exalting the office of the ministry in the eyes of the people and solemnizing the call in the heart of the candidate. For this service all ordained ministers present, if feasible, are invited on to the rostrum. Three ministers are chosen to take the three leading parts in the service: the *ordination prayer*, the *charge*, the *welcome*.

After a brief sermon on the high calling and responsibility of the ministry, followed by the presentation of the candidate, the ministers, with the candidate in the centre of the group, kneel for the ordination prayer, while the congregation remains seated with bowed heads. When in the prayer mention is made of the laying on of hands, those kneeling near the candidate place a hand upon his head, continuing thus until the close of the prayer.

Rising from prayer, all the ministers stand while the charge is given. It is largely in the language of scripture, including such passages as Ezek. 33.7–9, 11; Acts 20.28; I Tim. 4.12–16; II Tim. 2.3, 4, 24; 4.1–5; I Peter 5.2–4. Following the charge, words of welcome are spoken, usually by the conference president.

Local church elders* and deacons* are laymen elected by the local church they serve, in contrast to the ordained minister who serves the world-wide church. Local elders and deacons are usually ordained in a simple ceremony during the divine service on Sabbath, with an ordained minister in charge. After reading a few appropriate passages of scripture (e.g., I Tim. 3.1–7 for elders, and I Tim. 3.8–13 for deacons), the candidate and minister kneel for the consecration prayer and the laying on of hands. After the prayer, the minister clasps the candidate's hand with a word of blessing. A local elder need not be reordained upon re-election by the same congregation or another local church, or if subsequently elected as a deacon. Likewise a deacon is not reordained; however, if he is elected as an elder, he must be ordained as an elder, since this is an office of a higher degree.

In ordaining ministers, elders and deacons Seventh-day Adventists believe they are operating in harmony with the NT custom of having apostles and evangelists (itinerant ministry) to look after the general interests of the church as a whole, elders ('presbyters' or 'bishops') looking after the spiritual welfare, and deacons after the more temporal interests, of their local congregation.

B. B. BEACH

J. J. van Allmen, 'Ministry and Ordination according to Reformed Theology', *SJT*, 1972; John M. Barkley, 'The Meaning of Ordination', *SJT*, 1956; P. Bradshaw, *The American Ordinal: Its History and Development*, 1971; F. E. Brightman, *The English Rite*, 2 vols, 1915; Raymond Brown, *Priest and Bishop*, 1970; W. Brunnotte, *Das geistliche Sinn bei Luther*, 1959; Church of South India, *The Book of Common Worship*, 1963; *Constitution, Bylaws and Working policy of the General Conference of Seventh-day Adventists*, 1984; J. D. Crichton, *Christian Celebration: The Sacraments*, 1973, pp.137–67; P. Edwall, E. Hayman and W. D. Maxwell (eds), *Ways of Worship:* Report of a theological commission of Faith and Order, 1951; W. K. Firminger, 'The Ordinal', *Liturgy and Worship*, ed W. K. Lowther Clarke and C. Harris, 1932; T. F. Gulixson, 'The Ministry', *What Lutherans are Thinking* ed E. C. Fendt, 1947; G. D. Henderson, *Church and Ministry*, 1951; Winthrop S. Hudson and Norman H. Maring, *A Baptist Manual of Polity and Practice*, 1963; B. A. van Kleef, *Gescyedenis van de Oud-Katholieke Kerk Van Nederland*, 2nd edn 1953; U. Küry, *Die altkatholische Kirche* (*Die Kirchen der Welt*), 1966; N. Lindroth, *En bok om Kyrkans ämbete*, 1951; M. Luther, *Ordinationsformular*, WA 38, 401ff.; *Manual for Ministers*, 1977 (Seventh-day Adventist); A. G. Martimort, *L'Eglise en Prière*, III, 1984;

W. D. Maxwell, *John Knox's Genevan Service Book*, 1931; N. Mitchell, *Mission and Ministry*, 1982; Don F. Neufeld (ed), *Seventh-day Adventist Encyclopaedia*, 1966, pp.925ff.; A. Nygren, *This is the Church*, 1952; H. B. Parker, Jr, *The Ordination Prayers of the Ancient Western Churches*, 1967; David Power, *Ministers of Christ and his Church*, 1969; *The Christian Priest: Elder and Prophet*, 1973; F. Proctor and W. H. Frere, *A New History of the Book of Common Prayer*, 1949; F. C. Ratcliff, 'The Ordinal of the Church of South India', *Theology*, 63, January 1960; *Report on Anglican-Methodist Unity: The Ordinal*, 1968; E. Schillebeeckx, *The Church with a Human Face*, 1985; *The Standing Liturgical Committee of Protestant Episcopal Church in USA* (*Prayer Book Studies No 20*), 1970; V. Vajta, *Luther on Worship: An Interpretation*, 1958.

Ordination of Women

The rites of ordination for women have been similar to those for men, varying according to the office and according to the particular church tradition rather than to the gender of the ordinand (*see* **Ordination**). Thus, for example, the ordination of a woman as an evangelist, deacon*, priest (*see* **Presbyter**), pastor or bishop* would be the same as that of a man. The only separate rites would be those developed for such female ministries as deaconess* and abbess which are not usually considered ordained offices. An obvious exception to this is that contemporary services of ordination have had to use inclusive language* in services where women and men are being ordained, and to use female pronouns when there is a single female candidate.

The central issue is not what rite a particular church body will use to admit a woman to priesthood or ministry, but whether women are capable of receiving ordination to ministry in the church. The participation of women in the ministry of the church has been a matter of debate since NT times and the question of their ordination has been an important point in the wider debate over whether the subordination of women is ordained by God, or part of the fallen order of creation which was overcome in Jesus Christ. The debate over the ordination of women may be most clearly discerned in the life of the church at moments when women are exercising ministries in the church and some church authorities are opposing this practice. There are still traces of such a situation in NT times, and this same situation exists today in ecumenical discussions of ministry between churches who do and who do not ordain women. The discussions appeal to scripture and historical precedent in church traditions, but they open up a wide variety of continuing theological issues that are the subject of research at the present time.

In the Hebrew scriptures the role of woman as priest is resisted because of its association with the rival religion of Asherah. Women could become prophets through whom God spoke, but their primary role was as mother (Joel 2.28; II Kings 22.14–20). In the temple and later in the synagogue women were not allowed to provide leadership in worship or the teaching of scripture. In the NT women were welcomed as followers by Jesus and they were not only included as equals in the earliest congregations, but also became local leaders and travelling evangelists. Yet by the end of the NT period two different and contradictory trajectories of women's roles developed. The Pastoral Epistles limited women's teaching role (I Tim. 2.11–13), while at the same time the Fourth Gospel placed women on an equal level with men as witnesses to Christ (John 4.1–42).

We cannot speak of the exclusion of women as priests in the NT because this model of ministry does not yet exist in that period. Rather the royal priesthood applies to *all* members of the new people who live by the mercy of God, as signified by baptism in the death of Jesus Christ (I Peter 2.9). Baptism, not circumcision, is the sign of Christ's calling to service for both women and men. In baptism all put on Christ (Gal. 3.27–28). All receive the same gifts of the one Spirit (I Cor. 12; 13; Col. 3.9–11). Ordination as the laying on of hands was not practised in the Pauline churches in regard to the role of president and deacon. In the Palestinian churches ordination was practised in setting apart the presbyter or elder. There is no clear consensus on how many of these functions of ministry were performed by women, but it is possible to discern some of the roles they played in the earliest congregations.

In these congregations religious and cultural patriarchal patterns were replaced by a community in which privileged religious, class and gender roles were abolished. There is no reason to assume that women were excluded from the leadership of the house churches or from presiding at worship, especially when the assembly was held in their home (Col. 4.15). The 'household codes' in Ephesians and the Pastoral Epistles seem to reflect a later patriarchal reaction to just such leadership by women, by seeking to re-establish an order of subordination (Eph. 5.21–6.9). Paul explicitly mentions women as his missionary co-workers, using the same terms for women and men in this regard: 'co-worker' (Prisca), 'brother/sister' (Apphia), and 'apostle' (Junia). In Rom. 16.1f. Phoebe is called not only *diakonos* (minister, missionary, servant), but also *prostatis* (leading officer, president, governor, superintendent). In comparison to the ministry of deaconess in the later church, their ministry was not limited to ministry with women nor to specific gender roles and functions. Yet the words of Paul in I Cor. 11.2–16 indicate the continuing tension with the surrounding cultural norms as Paul allows women to prophesy, but says that they should cover their heads. His appeal to a revealed hierarchy of God-Christ-man-woman opens up the way for further injunctions to subordination for the sake of church order (I Cor. 14.33b–36).

Much of this appeal to hierarchy as divine order was a response to conflicting views of other Christian groups such as the Montanists and Gnostics. Prophets played a prominent role in the early Christian community and Paul takes for granted that women will act as prophets communicating divine oracles in the Christian assembly. He only insists that they do not overstep the gender differences between women and men (I Cor. 12.2–16). In the second century the Montanists continued this prophetic ministry and appealed to Gal. 3.28 as the basis for their inclusion of women as leading prophets who converted, baptized and celebrated the eucharist. Some of the Gnostic groups were open to woman's participation because of their inclusion of male and female cosmic principles or archetypes. In the second and third centuries the leadership of women within the Christian community was a very live and controversial issue in which both sides appealed to apostolic tradition to make their point. The various third- and fourth-century church orders reflect the continuing patriarchal reaction against female leadership. Women are acknowledged as disciples, but they were not appointed by Jesus to teach and proclaim Christ. As the early, more charismatic role of widow was suppressed, the Eastern Church developed the role of deaconess as a ministry of women with women (*Didascalia Apostolorum*).

Gradually the Christian ministry replaced the old Roman priesthood as the clergy of the established religion of the empire and a hierarchy of order emerged. By the fourth century a new priestly cast had reassimilated the OT images of temple priesthood with taboos against women in the sanctuary. In the mediaeval period canon law forbade women the priesthood on the grounds that the female was unfit to represent Christ. At the same time women were forbidden to exercise authority as preachers, although both queens and abbesses were invested with the juridical authority of bishops.

The Reformation did not remove either of these patriarchal attitudes towards women as priests or teachers. In fact it took away the only other option besides marriage that had been open to women with spiritual gifts for ministry, the life of service as a nun. Women were to be partners with clergy in their ministry, but they were to exercise their gifts through marriage and family. The apostolic injunction that 'women shall keep silence' was understood by both Calvin and Luther as excluding women from preaching office. This exclusion was occasionally modified by left-wing sectarians. For example, Baptist women occupied pulpits in England in the mid-seventeenth century and Quakers defended the right of women to preach. In the left-wing tradition the charisma of ordination was a gift of the Holy Spirit for prophecy. It was not until the nineteenth century, however, that this charismatic view of ministry was joined with liberal theology and biblical exegesis to provide a basis for return to the full participation of women in the ministries of the church. This view held that there is a created equality of all persons, and salvation is a restoration of this

original order. The use of historical criticism in biblical exegesis led to the relativizing of texts used to exclude women from preaching.

Today conservative Protestant churches with a charismatic view of ministry have combined this with a literal interpretation of the Bible. For instance the Southern Baptist Convention in the U S voted in 1984 to deny women ordination on the basis of the order of authority, and the submission required by God because man was created first and woman fell first (I Tim. 2.12f). They join other conservative Protestant groups, as well as Roman Catholic and Orthodox churches, in excluding women from ordination. In 1975 a World Council of Churches survey showed that over a third of the 295 member churches ordained women. The increasing experience of churches who do include women in all forms of ministry is leading to new questions about necessary changes in church life and attitude in order to place women as pastors, as well as questions about mutual recognition of ministries among churches who hold such different theological views.

Many aspects of classical theology are being re-thought as a basis for understanding ordination. For instance, some argue that a woman cannot represent Christ as priest if the maleness of Christ was a historical given which must not be lost in the representation. Others argue that the living Christ who is present in the eucharist assembly is eschatological and risen, and thus beyond the male emphasis. Still others argue that the point of the incarnation is not maleness, but humanness, and that any child of God through faith and baptism may represent Christ. Problems of language, imagery and symbols of God in worship and theology are immediately raised when women are able to image God as well as men. The ecclesiastical understanding of hierarchy as sacred order within the life of the church continues to be called into question by those who see in that co-equal order, an actual practice of subordination in the ranks of clergy and laity. The nature of ordination itself is being reexamined today as some theologians investigate, not whether women, but whether anyone should be ordained in a manner which excludes others from recognition of their gifts for ministry in the body of Christ.

Baptism, Eucharist and Ministry, Faith and Order Paper 111, 1982; *Concerning Ordination of Women*, WCC 1964; V. Elizondo and N. Greinacher (eds), *Women in a Men's Church, Concilium* 134, 1980; E. Schüssler Fiorenza, *In Memory of Her*, 1984; P. Jewett, *The Ordination of Women*, 1980; J. Morris, *The Lady Was a Bishop*, 1973; C. Parvey (ed), *The Community of Women and Men in the Church*, 1983; *Ordination of Women in Ecumenical Perspective*, Faith and Order Paper 105 with bibliography, 1980; I. Ramig, *The Exclusion of Women from the Priesthood*, 1975; R. Ruether and E. McLaughlin, *Women of Spirit: Female Leadership in the Jewish and Christian Traditions*, 1979; K. Stendahl, *The Bible and the Role of Women*, 1966.

L.M. RUSSELL

Organ

A keyboard instrument, which can be traced back to the ancient Greeks, in which wind is blown through pipes by mechanical action or, in modern imitations, tone is produced electronically. Pipe organs vary in size from the mediaeval portative, which can be carried about, to modern giants with four, or more, manuals (keyboards) and pedals. The tone of the instrument is varied by the use of different ranks of pipes brought into action by the player through controls called stops. A medium-sized church organ is likely to have three manuals: swell, great and choir. The first of these gets its name through the practice of enclosing its pipes in a box with shutters, so that the swell pedal controls crescendo and diminuendo. Alternative, or further, manuals to be found are: positive, solo and echo. The pedal keyboard is a separate division of the instrument requiring a foot technique only otherwise found in the pedal harpsichord, now obsolete.

The compass of an organ manual is normally five octaves (sixty-one notes), or slightly less, and of the pedals two and a half octaves (thirty-two notes) or a few less. Some organ pipes play at unison, or piano pitch, whereas others sound an octave lower or one, two, or more octaves higher, with various fractions of an octave also available. As a result the instrument has a wider compass than a piano, or even the whole orchestra. The characteristic tone of the organ comes from diapason or principal

Plate 45 Organ, The Lyons Concert Hall, York University, England

stops, but flutes and string-toned stops are common, as well as a variety of reeds based on wind and brass instruments. High-pitched stops, called mixtures, reinforce the upper frequencies to create a brilliant sound of high definition.

The glory of the organ is its association with Bach in the Baroque era. The magnificence of his organ music, and that of some of his contemporaries, has caused twentieth-century organ builders to re-create the finest features of the Baroque organ, which had been a lost art. Many composers before Bach made contributions to the literature of the instrument: outstanding among these is Buxtehude, and later on Handel wrote his concertos. The changing ideals of romantic composers are reflected in the works of Mendelssohn, Schumann and Liszt. Cesar Franck and Max Reger wrote extensively for the organ, and many twentieth-century composers have written for the instrument at a time of transition. The only major modern composer to specialize in the organ has been Olivier Messiaen, whose innovations have revealed new possibilities to later generations. Avant-garde examples include György Ligeti's *Volumina* and Mauricio Kagel's *Fantasia for Organ with Obbligati*, which requires an electronic tape. The portative organ and the harmonium have been revived by modern composers, and the electronic organ has a life of its own in certain works of Stockhausen, quite apart from extensive use in jazz and pop (rock) music.

Organs and church choirs* have long been adjuncts to Christian worship, although the Puritans in England and America distrusted music in church and organs were even destroyed during the English civil war. This was a temporary setback following the golden age of Elizabethan music; it was succeeded by the Restoration era of Purcell and Blow, both of whom were organists at Westminster Abbey. From the sixteenth to eighteenth centuries much concerted music was written for church use (e.g. Bach's cantatas) with an essential part for the organ. Throughout this period and up to the present day the English cathedral tradition has concerned choir and organ, and most British (and some American) composers have written for these resources. Apart from recital music, such as the Preludes and Fugues of Bach, or the Chorales of Franck, there is a quantity of organ music from all periods designed for liturgical use, often based on hymn tunes, the mass, or passages of scripture.

In times of economic stringency churches find organs an expensive luxury, as a large instrument requires skilled and continuous maintenance, not to mention periodic rebuilding. As a result, small churches have had recourse to cheap electronic organs which, although they have been improving in quality, rarely give satisfaction to musicians. A parallel development among organ builders has been the revival of the chamber organ, a small instrument of almost domestic size consisting of four or five ranks of pipes only, with one or two manuals and pedals. The modern trend in organ building is to retain all features of the historic instrument so that the music of all periods can be performed, and the varying demands of church use be met. After a century of attempting to imitate the orch-

estra the organ has rediscovered its heritage.

See Plate 45.

William Leslie Sumner, *The Organ, Its Evolution, Principles of Construction and Use*, [4]1973; Peter Williams, *A New History of the Organ: from the Greeks to the Present Day*, 1980.

PETER DICKINSON

Orientation

The siting of a building so that its sanctuary* points to the east (Lat *oriens*) ultimately derives from the early Christian practice of facing the east for prayer. In Judaism, prayer was offered towards the Temple at Jerusalem as the place of the presence of God; the Christian eastward direction could well have begun in conscious contrast to the Jewish custom, but it would also have been influenced by the general pagan understanding of the time that the east is the direction in which the good divine powers are to be found, a view originally connected with sun worship. Moreover, the NT itself suggests that the *parousia* of Christ will be from the east (Matt. 24.27), and since the ascension is a type of the second coming – he 'shall so come in like manner as you beheld him going into heaven' (Acts 1.11) – this, too, was envisaged as taking place in an eastward direction. As primitive Christian prayer was directed towards Christ and particularly towards the coming Christ, it was quite natural for orientation to be adopted.

Patristic teaching on the subject also referred to Jesus as 'the dayspring from on high' (Luke 1.78; cf. Clement of Alexandria, *Strom* 7.7) and suggested that in praying to the east the soul is hoping for restoration to its ancient home in Paradise through Christ the Second Adam (Basil, *de Spir. Sanct*. 27).

The Constantinian buildings, however, had their sanctuary at the west end. It is difficult to decide which of three possible explanations of this is correct. It may have been that the direction reflected Constantine's continued devotion to the Unconquered Sun. Again, since the president at the eucharist, adopting the basilican position (*see* **Posture** 2), faced the congregation across the altar, to have the sanctuary at the west end meant that he and his assistant clergy did in fact look towards the east. Finally, it could be that Constantine and his architects understood their buildings as types of the Jerusalem Temple, of which the holy of holies was itself at the west end (I Kings 6).

From the middle of the fourth century the practice of locating the sanctuary at the east end was adopted and became all but universal, but without complete accuracy in every case; so in Rome St Maria Maggiore is north-west, but both St Sabina and St Agnese are south-east. Throughout the centuries since there has been a basic preference for the east–west orientation, and we find Durandus of Mende (1285–96) listing eight reasons for this: 1. 'The east is the image of Christ who, like the rising sun lighteth every man that cometh into the world.' 2. 'Our souls be thereby taught to turn themselves to the things that are most desirable.' 3. 'Because those who praise God ought not to turn their backs on him.' 4. 'To show that we seek our country.' 5. 'Christ is the true east.' 6. 'Christians look towards Paradise from whence man has been excluded.' 7. 'Christ on the cross looked towards the east, he ascended thither and will come again from that direction.' 8. 'Daniel prayed towards the temple when he was in captivity' (*Rat. div. off.* 5.2.57).

Nevertheless, despite this array of allegory and symbolism, orientation has never been considered absolutely essential and many churches have been built regardless of it to accommodate them to the site available. Certainly in the twentieth century many modern churches neglect it entirely, the primary consideration having been how best to arrange the building in a given confined area.

EDITOR

Orthodox Worship

When an Anglican cleric asked Patriarch Aleksii of Moscow to define the Russian Orthodox Church in a phrase, he received the answer, 'It is the church which celebrates the divine liturgy.' This was in the 1950s. But it was not an equivocal answer conditioned merely by Soviet circumstances. The patriarch spoke out of an age-old

tradition, and his words could have been echoed by any of his predecessors. They are words which point to the centrality of worship, above all of eucharistic worship, in the life of the Orthodox Church. For it is in the eucharist that she most fully confirms her identity, integrity and her vocation.

Although this confirmation is at all times new, the Orthodox have never striven to be innovative in the making of it. In modern times the (Western) Liturgical Movement* has often fostered deeper understanding of liturgical practice in the Orthodox milieu. But it has never prompted the re-ordering of services. Indeed, the order of this church's elaborate services has remained exceptionally constant over the last millenium or more. Even the steady modification (usually amplification) of detail gradually ceased to be of serious import after the fifteenth century. The largely Byzantine ritual of the Orthodox Church can thus provide the outsider with ample scope for archaeological research. By contrast, the average Orthodox sees it as nothing other than the norm, available for worship, rather than for study or delight.

Worship is conducted by the body of the church. And while Orthodox worship is necessarily personal, it is never individualistic. Prayers are almost invariably couched in the first person plural; and the principal services are arranged for a single occasion, so that the whole community may gather, rather than spread throughout the day. Indeed, no altar table may be used more than once a day for the celebration of the eucharist; nor may any one cleric celebrate it more frequently than that.

The community gathers the more easily and more organically since seating is generally eschewed. Provision is made for the elderly and the ailing, but the central area of the church building is left unencumbered by pews or seats. Worshippers are thus not segregated from each other, nor are they immobilized. Their normal position at prayer in any case is upright. At the same time absence of pews also makes it easier for worshippers to practice prostrations as particular devotions demand. Such prostrations are more frequent in penitential seasons. At the other end of the scale, neither kneeling nor prostrations are permitted in the joyful weeks which follow Easter. By the same token, the first ecumenical council (325) also prohibited kneeling on each and every Sunday.

The human body is equally involved in various other ways. The clergy and (less frequently) the laity will engage in symbolic processions in or around the church. In Holy Week*, for example, the burial of Christ or the arrival of the myrrh-bearing women at his tomb are marked in this way. But many a week-day service will involve less elaborate processions, especially into and out of the sanctuary area. These gain the greater prominence since the sanctuary is screened behind its iconostasis*: the area within represents the heavenly realm, with the throne of God (a free-standing altar table) at its centre. The carrying of the censer, gospel book or eucharistic vessels in processions such as these adds silent and symbolic drama to them.

In general, however, the significance of particular actions is expressed in words. These words are usually sung or chanted. Regional tradition determines whether the music (invariably unaccompanied) is performed by a choir or by the people as a whole. In either case, services involve a dialogue between the people and the celebrant* or celebrants of the day. The celebrants have distinct and well-established roles to play; but the concelebration* of priests and deacons with their bishop is natural and normal. At the same time, no eucharistic worship should take place in the absence of laity, else the celebrating body is incomplete. Never was there a question of celebrating private masses.

The worshipper participates orally or, at least, aurally; and in either case positively. Silence on the part of most worshippers should not be taken to imply private and separate devotions. On the contrary it could be argued that those who are freed from the obligation to sing are the better placed to participate prayerfully in the service as it unfolds, to 'stand aright' and to 'stand in awe' as the text of the Liturgy prescribes.

There is also an olfactory dimension to the worship. Incense* is frequently used, as it has been through much of the Byzantine rite's history. It is offered by the clergy before sacred objects such as icons. It is also offered before the worshippers, since each is made in the image and likeness of God.

The icons provide yet another dimension. These should be distributed on the icon-

ostasis and throughout the church in such a way as to communicate a coherent account of the divine economy. Thus they express and enhance the symbolic value of the structure itself. But they also provide access to that which is represented on them, they are loci of devotion. The simplest form of devotion involves the kissing of an icon and the lighting of a candle by its side.

The stands on which single icons are displayed will usually be covered with material. Its colour will vary with the season, as will that of vestments*. Thus the solemn tones of Lent* will be replaced at Eastertide with the most radiant colours available. For this transformation a particular moment is set aside, which immediately precedes the first reading of the paschal gospel and its presentation of the angel at the tomb with his raiment 'white as snow'. The significance of all the various feasts and phases of the church's year is thus determined and enhanced.

The liturgical calendar is regulated by several interrelated, yet independent cycles. Only in a monastic context is the calendar likely to be kept in all its mediaeval fullness and complexity. But the monastic system was early assimilated and variously adapted by the parishes. A weekly cycle centred on the Lord's day is matched by a daily cycle (vespers and matins most prominent within it). The original Lord's day, the day of resurrection, is at the heart of the church's annual cycle – some of it mobile, since its pattern is determined by the varying dates of Easter, some of it shaped by reference to dates which are permanently fixed.

The church 'which celebrates the divine liturgy' necessarily seeks to involve her members to the fullest possible degree in that celebration. The eucharist is enacted for communicants, not spectators. All who are baptized and chrismated are bidden to the feast. Since baptism* and chrismation are likely to be administered early in the first year of a person's life, babes in arms are regular communicants, being full members of the church. They receive the sacred elements by intinction* from a spoon, as do the laity at large. That which they receive is acknowledged to be the very Body and the Blood of Christ.

But the consequent generation of awe (together with a demanding penitential code) led to an early decrease in the frequency of adult lay communion. From the fourth century down to modern times communion for most adults was limited to a few occasions per annum, or even to one. The twentieth century has seen a gradual, as yet only partial, restitution of the primitive practice which seems to have linked attendance at a eucharistic celebration with communion.

Nevertheless, however partial this restitution, the principle remains unchallenged: all who belong should seek communion. Thus they would participate not only in that which is already given. They would anticipate that which is to be. For there is an eschatological dimension in this worship: and even that which brings fulfilment in the present yet points beyond itself, and certainly beyond all ritual and rubrics, to a timeless consummation. Hence the post-communion prayer with its petition 'that we partake of thee more fully in that day of thy kingdom which shall have no night'.

N. Cabasilas, *A Commentary on the Divine Liturgy*, 1960; C. Kucharek, *The Byzantine-Slav Liturgy of St John Chrysostom*, 1971; S. Salaville, *An Introduction to the Study of Eastern Liturgies*, 1938; A. Schmemann, *An Introduction to Liturgical Theology*, 1966; *The World as Sacrament*, 1966.

SERGEI HACKEL

Pall

1. The term is applied to any cloth or covering that envelops or covers some object. The cloth of silk which in the earlier centuries completely enveloped the altar*, and which was revived in the Church of England in the seventeenth century, was sometimes termed 'altar-pall' (*see* **Altar Hangings**).

2. It is also used for the cloth of velvet or damask that envelops a coffin when it stands in church at a funeral service. This should reach almost to the ground and cover the bier or trestles as well as the coffin. Most parish churches had such a pall until the middle of the last century and it covered the coffin of all parishioners, rich and poor alike, without distinction.

3. The term is also sometimes applied to the cloth that is hung from the desk of the pulpit*. At the Reformation period, only persons who had a doctor's degree were

permitted to have such a cloth displayed when they preached, and preachers who were merely masters or bachelors of arts had no such cloth.

C. E. Pocknee (ed), *The Parson's Handbook*, 1965; The Warham Guild, *The Warham Guild Handbook*, rev ed 1963.

C. E. POCKNEE

Palm Sunday

The origin of Palm Sunday is to be found at Jerusalem in the latter part of the fourth century. On the Sunday with which the Great Week, i.e. Holy Week*, began, the people went to the Mount of Olives in the early afternoon. About five o'clock the gospel passage telling of the triumphal entry was read, and there was a procession by foot from the summit of the Mount of Olives into the city, children also sharing in the celebration and all carrying branches of palm or olive. In the course of time the observance spread from Jerusalem, being adopted in Spain in the fifth century, Gaul in the seventh, Britain in the early eighth, and by conservative Rome in the twelfth century. The blessing and distribution of palms, procession and reading of the palm gospel remain prescribed in the Roman rite, and are frequently observed in Anglicanism, and are now provided for in the proposed Church of England services.

In the Latin rite the specific palm ceremonies became attached to the beginning of the mass of the Sunday, whose theme was the passion, and included as its gospel the whole of the passion according to Matthew. Thus the palm ceremonies became attached to a eucharist with an essentially different theme. If Holy Week is to be celebrated as an entity, with each event in the last week of Jesus' life commemorated on the appropriate day, and this is the logic of the way of celebrating Holy Week that the whole church adopted from fourth-century Jerusalem, this is misconceived (as well as being burdensome in practice). Such is the force of conservatism in liturgical tradition, however, that it has been retained in modern Western revisions, Roman, Anglican and the Joint Liturgical Group suggestions, with a sole reading of the palm gospel as the gospel of the eucharist itself as no more than a permitted alternative, one that is however frequently exercised in practise.

For bibliography *see* under **Calendar**; **Holy Week**.

R. F. BUXTON

Papal Rites

With the revision of the liturgy of the Roman Catholic Church, following Vatican II, the papal mass does not now differ from that at which any other bishop presides. Moreover the vestments that were peculiar to the pope (such as the *falda* or white skirt and the *fanon* or double cape of white silk) are no longer worn. The last pope to have a coronation at his installation was Paul VI in 1963 and he subsequently gave away the papal tiara. The ceremonies that are still proper to the pope are the Consistories, in which cardinals are created, the blessing of *palliums* (*see* **Vestments** 2[g]) – given to archbishops throughout the world on their appointment – and the Canonization of Saints. The simplified rites by which the pope is installed and buried are familiar on account of television coverage in recent years, and the visits of John Paul II to many countries have afforded the opportunity for large numbers of people to see, possibly for the first time, a papal mass.

ANTONY HOWE

Pasch

see **Easter**

Paschal Candle

The lighting of a large and special candle on its own stand or candlestick forms one of the ceremonies in the vigil service on the eve of Easter (*see* **Paschal Vigil**), all candles* and lamps having been extinguished on Maundy Thursday*. The rekindling of fire and light, including the lighting of the Paschal candle, symbolize the triumph of the resurrection over darkness and sin (*see also* **New Fire**). The lighting of the Paschal candle is accompanied by the singing of a special chant known as the *Praeconium* or *Exultet* sung by the deacon from the ambo* by the side of which stands the Paschal candlestick. In the words of the *Exultet* there are allusions to the Passover and the crossing of the Red Sea which are

types foreshadowing the new Passover effected by Christ's cross and resurrection. It is not possible to say with certainty when and where these ceremonies originated, though it may have been in Northern Italy in the fourth century. By the seventh century they were in use in the presbyteral churches of Rome, though they only entered the papal rite in the eleventh century. Jerome in the fourth century complained about the deacon's hyperbole of language as he chanted the *Praeconium*. Also the hymn *Inventor rutili*, composed by Prudentius in the same century, was sung during the Easter vigil service; its allusions leave little doubt about the rekindling of fire and light. In the older Roman and Italian basilicas the Paschal candlestick was of marble or porphyry decorated with tesselated inlay and it stood as a permanent feature either on one side of the chancel* or even part-way down the nave*. Several examples in Cosmati work of the twelfth and thirteenth centuries may still be seen in Rome, e.g. at St Clement and St Mary-in-Cosmedin. The idea that this candlestick could only stand immediately on the north side of the altar* is a late mediaeval innovation.

The Paschal candle is now in use from the eve of Easter until Whitsunday*. In some examples the candle was on a pan or dish suspended by chains instead of on a stand. In the late English mediaeval rites this candle assumed enormous proportions, that at Salisbury Cathedral being thirty-six feet (eleven metres) high, while that at Westminster Abbey weighed three hundredweight (740 kilograms).

Sometimes five grains of incense are inserted in the candle, signifying the five wounds of Christ. In the Roman rite of 1970 it is set up on its candlestick after the procession of the *Lumen Christi* at the beginning of vigil and is taken from there to be plunged into the baptismal water during the prayer of blessing. The date of the year may be inscribed on its length.

D. R. Dendy, *The Use of Lights in Christian Worship*, 1959; H. J. Feasey, *Ancient English Holy Week Ceremonial*, 1897; A. G. Martimort (ed), *L'Eglise en Prière*, IV, 1983; J. W. Tyrer, *Historical Survey of Holy Week*, 1932.

G. D. W. RANDALL/J. D. CRICHTON

Paschal Vigil

The celebration of the Pasch, the passion, death and resurrection of the Lord, on the Saturday night and Sunday morning of Easter*, is the church's oldest liturgical observance with the sole exception of the weekend vigil* that was celebrated in NT times and from which the Paschal vigil itself is derived.

The church was conscious that it owed its existence to the saving events of the cross and the resurrection, and there was a vivid sense of the presence of the Lord who was with his people in and through the celebration of these events and who would come again in glory to complete the work of his redemption. The Paschal celebration therefore was not a mere recalling of the past events; it made the power of those events present to the worshippers, who could thus make a renewed encounter with their Lord. The first-century vigil centred upon the eucharist, the Passover meal of the Lord, but by the second century, baptism*, by which new members were added to the church, was celebrated as part of the Paschal vigil. Possibly the Jewish observance of the lighting of the lamps on the eve of the sabbath influenced the Christian liturgy and so we get the third element, light. In the Johannine tradition, Christ is the light of the world, and out of these two elements, Jewish and Christian, the church gradually evolved the symbolism of the candle which in the fourth century became the centre of interest of the first part of the rite (*see* **Pascal Candle**). But the Christian vigil had always included the celebration of God's saving deeds in the word of the scriptures, and with the development of the catechumenate*, the word-service came to be regarded as the last instruction of the candidates before their baptism. Thus by the end of the fourth century all the elements of the vigil celebration had been assembled, and light, word, water and the bread and wine of the eucharist all became efficacious symbols conveying the power of the redeeming Christ to the gathered assembly.

The Paschal vigil was the total and unitive celebration of the redeeming work of Christ, and until the end of the third century, Good Friday* (except in Asia, where Christians kept the vigil on 14 Nisan instead of the Saturday/Sunday, hence their name

Quartodecimans) was observed only by a solemn fast, and Maundy Thursday* became a separate celebration only when the historicization of the liturgy was well under way in the fifth century. Yet, the sense of a unitive celebration of Christ's redeeming work was retained for centuries, and it was not until the seventh century, when the hour of the vigil began to be anticipated, that a tendency set in to break up the pattern. All during the early Middle Ages the vigil was celebrated earlier, until by the late Middle Ages it was celebrated in the morning of Holy Saturday*. This was the position consecrated by the missal of Pius V (1570) which *ordered* that the service (hardly any longer to be called a vigil) was not to be celebrated *after* mid-day on Saturday. Yet, with astonishing fidelity, the church retained all the ancient rites and texts (though with some strange accretions) and still sang of the 'holy night' when Christ liberated man from sin. With the gathering momentum of the Liturgical Movement*, this anomaly became increasingly obvious and intolerable. In response to requests, Pius XII in 1951 restored the proper hour of the vigil celebration and partly revised the rites and texts. This restoration was at first experimental only, and the definitive reform of the whole of the Holy Week* liturgy came in 1955. Since then there has been a further revision in the direction of simplicity, and it is this revision that will be described now.

The church is in darkness and the new fire* is lighted. From this light is taken to the Paschal candle. This may be simply lighted and then carried into and through the church by a deacon who sings three times 'Christ our light', the third time in the sanctuary*. Meanwhile the people's candles are lighted from the Paschal candle. There follows the Easter proclamation (*Exultet*) in which the saving events of the OT and NT are recalled. The word-service now begins, and there are readings from the OT (five, to be used at choice, are provided) and the NT (the epistle). Before the epistle, the *Gloria* is intoned and the bells* rung, heralding the arrival of Easter. The gospel and the homily follow, and after these the blessing of the baptismal water and baptism itself if there are candidates. If there are no baptisms, the formula of blessing is shorter. There follows the renewal of baptismal promises and the sprinkling of the people with the newly blessed water. The mass then continues as usual.

Two special observances may be noted. 1. The Paschal candle may be marked by the Alpha and Omega, the sign of the cross and the year of salvation, thus indicating that Christ the redeemer is present among his people. Five incense grains may be inserted into the candle with a formula which interprets the gesture: 'May Christ by his glorious wounds preserve and guard us.' 2. After the epistle the Alleluia*, suppressed at the beginning of Lent, is now solemnly intoned.

J. D. Crichton, 'The Feast of Easter', *A Catholic Dictionary of Theology* ed J. Crehan and H. F. Davis, 1967, pp.202–4; *The Liturgy of Holy Week*, 1983, pp.69–90; J. G. Davies, *Holy Week*, 1963; A. Allan McArthur, *The Evolution of the Christian Year*, 1953, pp.77–139; H. A. P. Schmidt, *Hebdomada Santa*, 1956, II, ii, pp.808–77.

J. D. CRICHTON

Pastoral Care and Worship

Pastoral care may be broadly defined as activity undertaken by representative Christians which is directed towards the elimination of sin and sorrow and the presentation of all people perfect in Christ to God. Its primary constituent functions are those of healing, sustaining, reconciling and guiding.

Like worship, pastoral care has been an integral part of the life of the church since its earliest beginnings, although its forms and methods have changed and evolved. In the present century psychological insights and techniques have been particularly influential and pastoral counselling as a specialized activity has threatened to become the dominant model for pastoral care, especially in the Reformed Churches of North America and to a lesser degree in Britain.

It can rightly be assumed that there should be a close relationship between worship and pastoral care. Regrettably, this relationship has been little explored in recent times despite the similarities and common aims these activities share. Both of them edify and build up the Christian community, help to form Christian identity and are involved in the process of personal transformation. Many significant themes

such as guilt, grace, reconciliation, dialogue, communication, new beginnings and healing are shared by worship and pastoral care. The term 'pastoral office', used by some to denote rites such as marriages and funerals, points up the fact that liturgical acts are often occasioned by pastoral needs. They make explicit in a symbolic way the theological realities of the pastoral situation. Both pastoral care and worship focus on relationships between people and between people and God. The Reformed tradition's inclusion of worship and pastoral care under the general area of practical theology highlights the practical, action-oriented nature of both. Finally, in most Christian denominations the pastoral role is almost invariably linked with liturgical functions, a relationship made explicit in the rite of ordination.

The common concerns and features of worship and pastoral care can lead to a temptation to reduce the one to the other so that pastoral care is seen only as a subordinate tool of worship or *vice versa*. It is, however, more appropriate that their distinctiveness and relative autonomy as well as their close relationship should be preserved. If it is recognized that worship has a pastoral care dimension and pastoral care has a liturgical dimension but that each is irreducibly distinct, then each can offer the other vital, complementary, critical and corrective functions. Pastoral care can be seen as the context, content and consequence of worship in the pastoral fellowship which is the church. While the primary aim of worship is to give praise and thanks to God, it also has pastoral effects in terms of building up human fellowship, creating personal wholeness and integrity and in making the liberation of the gospel a contemporary reality.

Worship provides a critique of some aspects of pastoral care. Its corporate aspect counteracts a tendency to individualism in the latter, particularly when it has been modelled on counselling. The intensely private aspect of pastoral care is rightly questioned by the public nature of worship. Pastoral care tends towards being a-historical and untheological, absolutizing the significance of the present moment and accepting uncritically insights and values from the secular world at the expense of those to be found in the Christian tradition. Worship ensures that all Christian activity is seen in the light of the history of the Christian community and as a participation in the redeeming work of Christ. The rhythm and positive affirmations of worship provide a corrective to pastoral care understood as problem-centred crisis ministry and incipient professionalism is relativized by the mutuality of worship. Most fundamentally, worship recalls pastoral care to the truth that ultimately it is God who cares for people and that pastoral care is participation in that divine care.

Pastoral care offers a reciprocal critique of worship. Its human and contemporary concerns question rigidity and antiquarianism in liturgy. It invites worship to take into account and be relevant to human needs and prevents worship becoming narrowly centred on the church. Practical ethical questions emerging from pastoral care remind worshippers that they remain firmly in a world of suffering and contradiction. This counteracts liturgical escapism. Where worship may seem impersonal and non-specific, the concrete and personal emphases of pastoral care form a counterbalance. Pastoral care summons worship to take living people seriously and to situate itself within God's overall purpose of making and keeping human life human in the world. It is a forceful reminder that the sacrifice of praise is not simply or even primarily a matter of correctly ordered liturgy in the classic mode but also of honouring God by practical co-operation with his will so that the kingdom may become a reality in human lives.

Pastoral situations frequently occasion liturgical rites. All acts of worship have pastoral implications and effects. Thus poor worship can vitiate pastoral action while good worship can enhance it. The eucharist helps the Christian fellowship to grow together in grace and to be formed into the image of Christ. Baptisms, confirmations, marriages and funerals occur at naturally important transition points in the lives of individuals and communities and can be educative, formative, supportive and indeed reconciliatory. The sacrament of penance is integrally linked to the pastoral task of reconciliation and rites like anointing and the laying on of hands relate closely to the healing aspect of pastoral care. Ordination affirms the close relationship between

liturgical and pastoral roles in ministry while the recitation of daily offices allows the opportunity for pastoral intercession and the nurture of pastoral care itself.

Before the Reformation, J. A. Jungmann asserts, public corporate worship was the main tool of pastoral care and this remains the case in the Roman and Anglo-Catholic traditions where administration of the sacraments lies at the centre of the pastoral office. In the Protestant tradition the close link between worship and pastoral care has been less coherently preserved. Detailed reconsideration of the relationship is now overdue and it should form an important task for liturgists and pastoral theologians, as well as for those who embody liturgical and pastoral roles in themselves by virtue of their office in local Christian communities.

W. A. Clebsch and C. R. Jaekle, *Pastoral Care in Historical Perspective*, 1975; D. B. Forrester, J. I. C. MacDonald and G. Tellini, *Encounter With God*, 1983; J. A. Jungmann, *Pastoral Liturgy*, 1962; T. C. Oden, *Pastoral Theology*, 1983; B. Reed, *The Dynamics of Religion*, 1978; W. H. Willimon, *Worship as Pastoral Care*, 1979.

STEPHEN PATTISON

Paten

see **Chalice and Paten**

Patronal Festival

see **Dedication** 3

Pax, Peace

see **Gestures** 8

Penance

That repentance is an imperative of the gospel is clear (Mark 1.14, 15) but in the course of history it has taken different forms. In the early second century there were those who were reluctant to admit repentance after baptism* but by the beginning of the third century there was some mitigation. Those guilty of very serious sins (principally, it would seem, apostasy, homicide and adultery) might present themselves to a bishop, make an avowal of their sins to him and receive from him counsel and accept the discipline of penance which lasted for a long time, sometimes for life. The last period of penance took place during Lent* and in the Roman rite that season was much marked by the need to prepare penitents for the reconciliation which took place on Maundy Thursday*.

By the sixth century the system had broken down because even shorter periods of penance made the daily life of ordinary Christians all but impossible. A development came in the seventh century, it would seem from Ireland where the organization of the church was monastic. The regular avowal of faults in 'chapter' moved easily into an avowal of sin. The Penitentials of Irish, Anglo-Saxon and even of Byzantine provenance began to appear and gave rise to what is known as 'tariffed penance' (the punishment was made to fit the crime, often murder, violence and rape). At first the 'penance' had to be performed before absolution, but gradually the absolution came to be given before the penance had been performed. Thus by the twelfth century the practice of private penance was the norm, at least for those who wished to avail themselves of it and they were few. The order had become repentance, confession of sins, absolution and penance. This was the system that was imposed on the Western church by the Fourth Lateran Council in 1215 which decreed that all Christians should present themselves to their parish priest at least once a year at about the time of Easter. In the sixteenth century the Council of Trent brought some order to the system which has lasted until the present day.

Against the background of its theology of the liturgy (it is public and communal) the Second Vatican Council in its Constitution on the Liturgy (no.72) decreed that 'The rite and formula for the sacrament of penance are to be revised so that they more clearly express both the nature and the effects of the sacrament'. Accordingly the Order of Penance appeared in 1973. It has changed a number of emphases. Its Pastoral Instruction has much to say about reconciliation, reconciliation with God and reconciliation between human beings. There are signs in the document that the Order might well have been called the Order of Reconciliation and the sacrament is frequently so named nowadays. In the same line the Instruction also emphasizes the 'social dimension' of sin and the corresponding need for reconciliation in society. It insists much less on a detailed accounting

of sins (though confession of sin remains) and much more on *metanoia* which in the view of the Instruction demands a real conversion of life. So that both private penance and the communal nature of the sacrament may be expressed adequately the Order provides three services of penance.

1. Individual penance: a penitent approaches a priest in some private place ('confessional rooms' are now in use where the penitent can enter into dialogue with the confessor and receive counsel in suitable surroundings) and after a brief reading from scripture he (or she) gives an account of his (her) condition, confesses whatever is sinful, makes an expression (in words) of repentance and seeks reconciliation. The confessor gives such counsel as may be necessary and then pronounces the formula of absolution. The rite concludes with a brief thanksgiving.

2. The second rite is a Bible Service*. There are readings from scripture, hymns, prayers and homily, all leading to an examination of conscience and to an arousal of repentance. After this there is private confession and reconciliation and the service concludes with prayers and hymns of thanksgiving.

3. The third is the rite of General Reconciliation and Absolution which takes the same form as 2 but concludes with a prayer of absolution, of some length, which finishes with the formula 'I absolve you . . .'.

This form may be used in certain circumstances, e.g. when there is imminent danger to life, when there is a very great number of penitents and a sufficient number of confessors is not available, but penitents are required to present themselves within reasonable time to a confessor for a personal avowal of sins.

J. D. Crichton, *The Ministry of Reconciliation*, 1974; *Christian Celebration: The Sacraments*, [2]1980, pp.210–46; H. Dunne, 'The Sacrament of Penance in the Eastern Churches', *Doctrine and Life*, Supplement, January–February 1977; Monica Hellwig, *Sign of Reconciliation and Conversion. The Sacrament of Penance for our Times*, 1982; R. C. Mortimer, *The Origins of Private Penance in the Western Church*, 1939; *The Rite of Penance* (ET of the Order of Penance), 1976; C. Vogel, *La Discipline pénitentielle en Gaule des origines à la fin du VIIIe siècle*, 1952.

J. D. CRICHTON

Pentecost

The day of Pentecost, commonly called Whitsunday, was a unitive festival commemorating both the ascension of Jesus and the descent of the Holy Spirit. In the course of the fourth century it was resolved into two commemorations corresponding to the distinct parts of the primitive celebration, the institution of Ascension Day* in the later part of the century resulting in the limitation of Pentecost to the second theme.

The Greek word Pentecost refers to the fiftieth day, defining the time after the season of the Pasch when Pentecost, one of the pilgrim festivals of the old covenant, celebrated the wheat harvest. In the Old Testament itself this agricultural festival is not identified with the law giving on Mount Sinai. If the identification had been made in Judaism as a whole by the time of the gospel, and it had certainly been made by some groups in Judaism by this time, it would be profoundly significant that on the day of Pentecost the disciples experienced the dynamic power of the Holy Spirit. In that case the event, in the particular sense of the occasion as well as in the general sense of the revelation given, would be the action of the divine purpose. As the old covenant, ratified in the Exodus which the Passover commemorated, was completed on Mount Sinai, so the new covenant, ratified in the events which the Christian Pasch commemorated, the cross and the resurrection, was completed on the festival of Pentecost when the power of the Holy Spirit came upon the disciples. Pentecost was the birthday of the church as the New Israel of God. The link between the law-giving and the descent of the Holy Spirit was appreciated by Augustine and Leo the Great. When Paul made his contrast between the law and the Spirit, he may have written in the context of a liturgical connection between the Pentecost of the old covenant and that of the new. It is possible he regarded the law-giving, the consecration of the Old Israel, as the work of the Spirit within the time of the old covenant. His emphatic rejection of the legalism of rabbinic Judaism from which he had been de-

livered by the gospel does not invalidate the comparison which gives point and relevance to the contrast.

At the beginning of the third century Tertullian refers to the day of Pentecost in terms which are consistent with a unitive commemoration, but the evidence does not permit a precise statement. Eusebius, describing the death of the Emperor Constantine in 337, makes specific reference to the festival as the occasion of the ascension of Jesus and the descent of the Holy Spirit. It is unmistakably clear that Ascension Day was not in existence at this time. On the contrary, the liturgical commemoration of the ascension on the day of Pentecost must have been so familiar to Eusebius that he forgets the book of Acts and identifies the event historically with that day. In view of the direct evidence, it cannot be doubted that early in the fourth century the day of Pentecost was a unitive festival, commemorating both the ascension of Jesus and the descent of the Holy Spirit.

Towards the end of the fourth century at Jerusalem, according to Egeria's description, there was a procession on the fiftieth day after Easter to the traditional site of the event of Pentecost, the Church on Mount Zion, where, at 9 a.m., a service was held in the course of which the passage was read concerning the descent of the Holy Spirit. This was a commemoration in the Jerusalem fashion at the proper place and time. Just after midday the people gathered at the sanctuary on the traditional site of the ascension, and the passages about the ascension from the gospel and Acts were read. A great candlelight procession came to the city in the darkness, and it was eventually about midnight when the people returned to their homes. This is the early unitive Pentecost, commemorated, in the way worship was now celebrated in the Holy City, with careful attention to the symbolism of the sacred sites.

In the early period of the church the term Pentecost does not simply indicate the fiftieth day as such, but frequently refers to the entire period of fifty days which would begin with the day of the Pasch. This season, our Eastertide, was regarded as a time of joy and triumph. As every Lord's Day was a commemoration of the glory of the divine kingdom in the resurrection of Christ, so the fifty days of Pentecost echoed to the same trumpet note of victory. Kneeling in prayer and fasting were forbidden on Sundays, and this privilege applied also to the great fifty days.

Apart from appropriate lections and prayers, which since the late fourth century have been concerned exclusively with the descent of the Holy Spirit, there are no particular liturgical ceremonies associated with the day, apart from the fact that the Paschal candle* will be lit at ordinary services for the last time on this day. Thereafter it will be moved from the sanctuary to the baptistery and lit during baptisms, when it serves as a reminder of the Easter significance of all baptisms, that is all are being baptized into the death and resurrection of Christ.

J. Gunstone, *The Feast of Pentecost*, 1967; A. A. McArthur, *The Evolution of the Christian Year*, 1953.

See also under **Calendar**.

R. F. BUXTON

Pentecostal Worship

The term covers four distinct forms of worship: 1. Worship in black Pentecostal churches; 2. Worship in white Pentecostal churches; 3. Worship in charismatic prayer groups and communities within traditional churches; 4. Worship in non-white indigenous churches.

1. Most Pentecostal historians trace the history of their churches back to a revival in Los Angeles (1906) under the leadership of black ecumenist William J. Seymour (1870–1922). Worship during this revival was characterized by its inter-racial, intercultural and inter-class nature. White bishops and black workers, men and women, Asians and Mexicans, white professors and black laundry women were equals, a view that was considered un-Christian and immoral in the USA. No wonder that the religious and secular press could not understand the revolutionary nature of this Pentecostal worship and took refuge in ridicule: 'What good can come from a self-appointed Negro prophet?'

The characteristics of this worship were: oral nature of liturgy; narrative character of theology and witness; maximum participation at the levels of reflection, prayer and decision-making and therefore a form of community which is reconciliatory; in-

clusion of dreams and visions into personal and public forms of worship which function as a kind of icon; understanding of the body/mind relationship which is informed by experiences of correspondence between body and mind, characteristically expressed in dance, speaking in tongues and laying on of hands for the sick. It was this type of worship which was responsible for the phenomenal growth of Pentecostalism amongst the black population and the working classes, both in the West and in the Third World, and not its specific doctrine on Spirit baptism.

2. Forced by public opinion which despised the developing Pentecostal churches because of their lowly black origins, the emerging Pentecostal church bureaucracy soon tamed the revival of Los Angeles. Pentecostal churches segregated into black and white organizations just as most of the other churches had done and many, but by no means all, of the original ingredients of black worship were lost. The well-known upward social mobility of white Pentecostals brought them into contact with evangelical and fundamentalist educational institutions. Today the development of an evangelical Pentecostal theology and of written liturgies is in full swing in European and American Pentecostal churches. Where Pentecostalism has become a middle-class church it follows the pattern of mainline protestant liturgies with some 'Pentecostal additions', such as Pentecostal hymns and choruses. Where Pentecostalism has moved into the upper part of the middle class and beyond, it adopts patterns of the third form considered below. In the rare cases where it continues to minister among the 'oral masses' of the population (e.g. in the Soviet Union) it retains much of its original worship patterns.

3. Very soon after the emergence of the Pentecostal Movement at the beginning of this century, small charismatic groups appeared in most European mainline churches. These early beginnings never developed substantially and are neglected by most historians, although they provide good examples of combining elements of the worship in black Pentecostal churches with their traditional liturgies. Particularly important in this respect were the Anglican priest Alexander A. Boddy (1854–1930), the French Reformed pastor Louis Dallière and the German Lutheran pastor Jonathan Paul (1853–1931).

Most historians, however, date the beginning of the Charismatic Movement in the early 1960s in the USA. Charismatic worship was first heavily influenced by that in the white Pentecostal churches because they were not only the midwives but also the teachers of the first charismatic leaders. After the initial honeymoon of Pentecostals and Charismatics, the latter found a way to integrate the practice of speaking in tongues, visions and laying on of hands into the framework of their traditional liturgy. Most successful in this were the Roman Catholic groups as the mass seems to be particularly suitable for receiving this kind of congregational participation into its liturgy.

Originally many of the charismatic prayer groups were ecumenical. So far they are (or were) the only worldwide grass-roots movement of any size where Catholics and Evangelicals meet regularly. This was of particular importance in Ireland, Italy, the USA and France. However, these ecumenical services (masses, prayer meetings) were met by the suspicion of the church hierarchy because of their uncontrollable grass-root ecumenism which by-passed the theological controversies with common prayer meetings and shared eucharists.

At the present time worship in the Charismatic Movement polarizes into two opposite factions:

(*a*) There are charismatic groups who regress more and more to their original denominational worship because they want to prove that they are not trouble-makers but loyal members of their respective churches.

(*b*) There are other charismatic groups which develop into independent congregations called House Churches* in the UK and Independent Churches in the USA. Their worship resembles that of the white Pentecostal churches.

4. Liturgically the most interesting and numerically the most important group is the non-white Indigenous Churches in the Third World (for statistics see D. Barratt, *World Christian Encyclopaedia*, 1983) such as the Zionists in South Africa, the Aladura Churches in West Africa, the Kimbanguists in Zaïre, the Christian Guru Churches in

India, and many independent Pentecostal churches in the Caribbean and in Africa. It has been convincingly argued that this diverse group of churches can in fact be treated as one group. Whether they should be counted amongst the Pentecostal churches is still controversial, but the phenomenological parallels with original black Pentecostalism and many historical links with early Pentecostal missionaries make it possible to list them under Pentecostalism.

In addition to the features of black Pentecostal worship listed above there is a recognition of elements of their pre-Christian cultures as gifts of the Holy Spirit (such as dancing, pilgrimages, conversation with ancestors, washing, precognition and telepathy). That is why some observers consider their worship to be syncretistic. Such an overall judgment is highly questionable. It is necessary to examine and evaluate each liturgy on its own merit. In any case these are not more syncretistic than any European or American liturgy.

Some scholars emphasize the political character of these oral liturgies in that they awaken confidence, make people feel accepted and loved and strengthen trust in their inborn indigenous gifts. Thus they unfreeze liturgical, theological and socio-political formulae and replace imported ideologies by the political alphabetization of the whole people of God, practised and learned within the framework of an oral liturgy. That this type of worship is in danger of becoming enslaved by the limitations of its cultural context, should not be denied. That is why this type of worship needs the inspiration and criticism of the whole ecumenical church as badly as any other liturgy. For political and cultural reasons this dialogue does not yet take place at a sufficiently sophisticated level. At the present time it is even difficult (but not impossible) for Pentecostals of all four types to worship together.

Arnold Bittlinger (ed), *The Church is Charismatic. The WCC and the Charismatic Renewal*, 1981; Luther P. Gerlach and Virginia Hine, *People, Power, Change. Movements of Social Transformation*, 1970; W. J. Hollenweger, *The Pentecostals*, 1972; *Pentecost Between Black and White. Five Case Studies on Pentecost and Politics*, 1974; Charles Edwin Jones, *A Guide to the Study of the Pentecostal Movement*, ATLA Bibliography Series no. 6, 2 vols, 1983; David Martin and Peter Mullen (eds), *Strange Gifts? A Guide to Charismatic Renewal*, 1984; Kilian McDonnell (ed), *Presence, Power, Praise. Documents on the Charismatic Renewal*, 3 vols, 1980; Harold W. Turner, *Religious Innovation in Africa*, 1979; William Wedenoja, 'Modernization and the Pentecostal Movement in Jamaica', Stephen D. Glazier (ed), *Perspectives on Pentecostalism: Case Studies from the Caribbean and Latin America*, 1980.

W. J. HOLLENWEGER

Petition

see **Prayer** 3

Pew

Seating in the naves* of churches was practically unknown for many centuries, as worshippers normally stood during the liturgy as they do in Eastern Orthodox churches today, though sometimes there were stone ledges round the wall of the church or round the bases of arcade pillars. In Northern Europe seating was gradually introduced in naves from the thirteenth century, but most of the mediaeval examples in England belong to the fifteenth and sixteenth centuries, when the wood-carver's craft reached its zenith as we can see in East Anglia and the West Country. These late mediaeval benches or pews are nearly always constructed in 'islands', leaving room around them for ordered movement.

After the Reformation, when for the first time all churches were provided with seating, pews were often given high backs and sides to exclude draughts and to provide seclusion. Carving became increasingly rare and most box-pews are made of plain but comely wainscot oak. Many pews were rented by individual families, thus providing an additional source of income for the church, but it was customary to have some free seats for the poor. Seating was arranged to face the pulpit*, and in crowded churches part of the chancel*, too, was sometimes pewed, the occupants necessarily sitting with their backs to the communion table, though generally in Anglican churches the chancel was kept for

holy communion, and the nave for morning and evening Prayer. Galleries* were sometimes installed, especially during the eighteenth century, and the west gallery was often occupied by the singers together with the instrumentalists or the organ. By the sanctuary*, low *houseling benches* were sometimes provided for communicants.

In the Middle Ages wealthy families generally sat in their own private chantry* chapels, but after the dissolution of the chantries it became customary for them to build specially imposing and sequestered pews with an excellent view of the pulpit. Squires' pews sometimes took the form of galleries, as at Stapleford, Leicestershire, 1783, and their Scottish equivalents, called lairds' lofts, can be highly elaborate, as at Kilbirnie, Ayrshire, early eighteenth century.

Nonconformist arrangements were generally similar to those in Anglican and Presbyterian churches, and the only radically different tradition is that of the Quaker Meeting House, where the seating faces inwards to the centre of the room, there being neither altar* nor pulpit (*see* **Quaker Worship**).

In Victorian times much earlier seating was done away with on various pretexts in Anglican schemes so as to make the altar rather than the pulpit the chief focus of the church. Modern seating arrangements are generally more flexible and comfortable than any of their predecessors, though they rarely look happy in old buildings. There is no doubt that the oldest churches look better as they were intended, without any permanent nave seating at all, and where the seating in such a church is not historically or aesthetically important it would often bring new life to the building to replace it with simple stacking chairs which can be arranged as required for liturgical or compatible secular activities, and otherwise recreate the nave space which has been lost since the fifteenth century.

G. W. O. Addleshaw and F. Etchells, *The Architectural Setting of Anglican Worship*, 1948; K. Lindley, *Chapels and Meeting Houses*, 1969; G. Randall, *Church Furnishing and Decoration in England and Wales*, 1980.

G. D. W. RANDALL

Pilgrimages

Christian tradition has always regarded pilgrimage as a way of life, the believer's earthly existence seen as a continuing journey towards a heavenly goal. But from the earliest centuries Christians have also localized the habit of pilgrimage, and shrines and holy places have provided the focus for devout journeys capable of being accomplished in this life. As early as the mid-second century AD we begin to hear of commemorations at the tombs of martyrs who had fallen victim to Roman persecution: such gatherings were occasions of local pilgrimages. It was, though, the emergence of the Holy Land at the centre of the Christian stage, in the course of the fourth century, which provided the real stimulus for the development of pilgrimage. The church buildings of the Roman Emperor Constantine and his successors in Jerusalem and the surrounding regions were the setting for gatherings of Christian travellers from east and west, as far afield as Italy, Gaul, Spain, even Britain – and it is to surviving accounts of pilgrims from these Western areas, like that of the Galician pilgrim Egeria (who was in Jerusalem in the 380s), that we owe our knowledge of Holy Land pilgrimage. It was a mixture of historical tourism and devout piety, grounded in a predominantly literal reading of the scriptures, which encouraged at the holy places a detailed re-creation of the biblical past. The pilgrim's objective was not only to be present at these significant places, but to see there – with the aid of the 'eyes of faith' – the events of the Bible unfolding before him. The arrival of the pilgrims also stimulated the development of a liturgy which answered to their particular view of the holy places: from the fourth century onwards the Jerusalem church 'pioneered' the annual cycle of worship (which subsequently spread to the church at large), re-enacting the historical progress of Christ's birth, ministry, death, and resurrection. Pilgrims enthusiastically participated in this liturgy, moving among the holy places and re-living the sacred history *in situ*. Through the centuries the *imitatio Christi* became more precise, as tradition added to the details of Christ's life on earth: the exact route, for example, which he followed from Pilate's headquarters to his crucifixion, and hence the

liturgical stations of the cross*.

The pilgrim's positive desire to re-live the Bible was often accompanied by, or the product of, social uprooting and the rejection of the secular world. The distant journey to holy places could be seen as part of the process of ascetic withdrawal, the pilgrim enduring the discomforts and hazards of long-distance travel, even on foot, as a spiritual exercise, praying at shrines *en route* and Bible always to hand. On the main pilgrim routes, and at the holy places themselves, local churches set up hostels (*xenodochia*) to provide Christian hospitality for these devout travellers who might otherwise be subject to the temptations of more worldly establishments. The chief exemplars of world rejection were the desert monks of Egypt and Syria, and these holy men came increasingly to form part of the itinerary of visitors to the Holy Land in search of spiritual edification as well as the visual realization of Christian history.

Such was the persistence of the Holy Land pilgrimage that it survived the coming of the Arabs in the seventh century, as it has survived more recent political and ecclesiastical divisions. The individual enterprises of the early church were to become formalized into the mass pilgrimages of the high Middle Ages, characterized by rituals such as the taking of the pilgrim's vow and the wearing of a distinctive 'uniform'.

The special place of the Holy Land in the history of pilgrimages should not be allowed to detract from the proliferation of other cult centres, and other reasons for undertaking such journeys. Wherever the tombs of saints and martyrs were honoured, wherever fragments of their remains signalled a saintly presence, pilgrims are to be found (*see also* **Saints, Cult of the**). Certain centres came to transcend all the rest: the churches of apostles and martyrs in Rome were transformed from local shrines in the early church to become the focal point of Western Christendom; they were followed by other great shrines like Santiago de Compostella and Canterbury, and the routes along which the pilgrims travelled were elaborately organized for the reception of the devout on the move. In ages when medicine was rudimentary and suspect, the shrines of saints were accorded special esteem as sources of miraculous cures, and from the fifth century onwards such cures were often systematically recorded and publicized, thus attracting ever more travellers in search of relief. Moreover, as the saints were intercessors for men before the judgment of God, so pilgrimage to their shrines was associated with forgiveness of sins, and an act of penitence. The voluntary quest for remission came to be overshadowed by the imposition of pilgrimages to distant shrines as a penance for offences committed, an enforced exile for the condemned criminal which rid the community of him for a long period under the pretext of his seeking absolution: tradition recounts how criminals were miraculously released from their chains as they fulfilled their pilgrimages at saints' tombs. The connexion of pilgrimage and penitence lay behind the church's practice of granting 'indulgences', by which pilgrims who made the journey to certain designated shrines earned for themselves remission of the punishment due to them for their sins – and for the favoured shrines much fame and prosperity. The wholesale granting of pilgrim indulgences can be traced to the example set by the Crusades; for it was Pope Urban II, in proclaiming the first Crusade at Clermont in 1095, who announced 'remission of the entire penance for sins' for those who took up arms and set out for Jerusalem.

By the last quarter of the twelfth century a formal rite for taking the cross had been devised. This had developed out of an earlier ceremony for blessing the insignia of pilgrims, namely the scrip and the staff. These formulae have been preserved in various mediaeval manuals and they also found a place in the *Pontificale Romanum*. This liturgical action, prior to setting out, was balanced, as it were, upon arrival at the shrine by further devotional practices: indeed each pilgrimage culminated in a mini-pilgrimage in and around the sacred site(s). There was a perambulation from altar to altar, with prayers, veneration of relics, lighting of candles and presentation of votive offerings. The returning pilgrims then obtained further tokens as evidence of having completed their devotional task, e.g. a shell at Compostella and a palm at Jerusalem.

The Reformers were unanimous in their condemnation of pilgrimages which they regarded as issuing in superstition and idol-

atry. Nevertheless in the present century many Protestants have once again begun to undertake them, a form of devotion which has indeed never been intermitted within the Roman Catholic Church.

R. B. Brooke and C. N. L. Brooke, *Popular Religion in the Middle Ages*, 1984; J. A. Brundage, 'Cruce Signari: The Rite for Taking the Cross in England', *Traditio*, xxiii, 1966, pp.289–310; R. C. Finucane, *Miracles and Pilgrims: Popular Beliefs in Medieval England*, 1977; E. D. Hunt, *Holy Land Pilgrimage in the Later Roman Empire AD 312–460*, 1982; J. Sumption, *Pilgrimage: An Image of Mediaeval Religion*, 1975; V. and E. Turner, *Image and Pilgrimage in Christian Culture*, 1978; J. Wilkinson, *Jerusalem Pilgrims before the Crusades*, 1977; *Egeria's Travels*, [2]1981.

E. D. HUNT

Piscina

A Latin word, meaning literally 'fish-pond' or 'fish-tank'. The term was probably transferred to the baptismal font*, since the fish was one of the symbols of Christ in primitive Christianity. Tertullian, writing at the end of the second century in his treatise *De Baptismo* (ch. 1), says, 'We, being little fishes, as Jesus Christ is our great Fish, begin our life in the water, and only while we abide in the water are we safe and sound.' Examples are known of the fish being depicted inside the basin of the primitive font, e.g. the one in Kélibia, North Africa.

But the term piscina came to assume another meaning in the Middle Ages, and it was applied to a shallow saucer-like basin in a niche in the wall of the south side of an altar*. This basin has a drain attached to it leading into the earth. This arrangement was also termed *lavacrum* and *sacrarium*. The purpose of this type of piscina has been disputed. But as early as the ninth century Pope Leo IV ordered that a receptacle was to be provided near the altar for the disposal of the water that had been used in the ablutions* of the hands and the chalice. Until the end of the twelfth century there was a single drain and piscina attached to any altar; from then on until about the middle of the fourteenth century we get examples of the double piscina, e.g. in Exeter Cathedral, England. It is supposed that one drain was used for the ablutions from the chalice and the other for that of the hands. In the fifteenth century there was a reversion to the single piscina.

F. Bond, *The Chancel of English Churches*, 1916; J. G. Davies, *The Architectural Setting of Baptism*, 1962; G. Randall, *Church Furnishing and Decoration in England and Wales*, 1980.

C. E. POCKNEE/G. D. W. RANDALL

Plymouth Brethren Worship

The Plymouth Brethren are so called by others – not by themselves – from the fact that their first congregation in England was established at Plymouth, about 1831. They called one another 'brethren', and when they moved into neighbouring areas they were referred to as 'the brethren from Plymouth' or Plymouth Brethren. Their movement began in Dublin some years earlier, when a few young men came together to take the Lord's Supper informally in an attempt to surmount the denominational barriers which otherwise would have prevented their intercommunion and in the hope that they might thus recapture the simplicity of apostolic times. When they were joined by John Nelson Darby (1800–82), a priest of the Church of Ireland, he quickly dominated the group by his powerful personality and forceful ecclesiology, which aimed at reconstituting the faithful remnant of the end-time. During a visit to Francis William Newman at Oxford in 1830, Darby influenced some other young men there, especially Benjamin Wills Newton (1807–99), Fellow of Exeter College, who returned to his native Plymouth the following year and founded the Brethren congregation in that city. Darby then carried his teaching to the Continent, especially to French Switzerland, where his followers are known to this day as Darbistes. On his return to the British Isles his imperious pressing of an exclusive church doctrine and polity occasioned a cleavage (1848), those who followed his lead being thereafter referred to as Exclusive Brethren and the others, by contrast, Open Brethren.

The Open Brethren, because of their evangelistic energy, were profoundly influenced by the Revival of 1858–60. In some parts of the UK (e.g. north-east Scotland) there were formed, as a result of that re-

vival, independent congregations which were soon attracted into the Brethren orbit; elsewhere their ethos was recognizably modified by the revival. One symptom of this was the widespread use of the term 'Gospel Hall' to denote their meeting-places (nowadays 'Evangelical Church' is becoming increasingly popular). Among Exclusive Brethren places of worship were more commonly and modestly called 'The Room' or 'The Meeting Room'. The initiated can usually tell from the phraseology on the notice-board which group of Brethren worships in the building.

The Exclusive principle of church fellowship has been summed up in the title of one of J. N. Darby's treatises: 'Separation from evil God's principle of unity' – the separation in question being understood in terms of the Darbyite exegesis of II Tim. 2.19–21, in which the 'great house' is the sum total of Christendom. By contrast, Open Brethren have generally preferred, with Anthony Norris Groves (1795–1853), to accept 'recognition of Christ alone in my brother, as the Alpha and Omega of terms of communion'. Groves, who has been called the archetypal Open Brother, declared in a letter to Darby in 1836, regarding certain Christians who seemed to him in some respects to be following the wrong path: 'I would infinitely rather bear with all their evils, than separate from their good.' Groves was also the Brethren's first foreign missionary; he led a pioneer band to Baghdad in 1829 and spent the last twenty years of his life in India. The missionary work which he initiated is carried on today by over 1000 missionaries in all five continents, especially in India, Central Africa and South America; this enterprise is commonly designated 'Christian Mission in Many Lands' and its records are published in the monthly periodicals *Echoes of Service*, Bath, England and *The Fields*, New York. Other pioneer Brethren missionaries were the two Scots, Frederick Stanley Arnot (1858–1914), the first European to explore Katanga, and Dan Crawford (1870–1926), who opened up to Western knowledge other uncharted areas of Central Africa.

Groves's brother-in-law, George Müller (1805–98), was the Prussian-born founder of the Bristol orphanage which bears his name. Along with Henry Craik (1805–66), a St Andrews graduate and Hebrew scholar, he was joint pastor of Bethesda Chapel, Bristol, which took a foremost part in resisting the authoritarian demands of J. N. Darby in 1848 and thus became, among Darby's followers, a by-word for all that is ecclesiastically reprehensible. The Exclusive adoption of separation as the principle of unity, when pressed to its logical conclusion, has led to a diversity of Exclusive divisions, the most 'exclusive' of which is that led until his death (in 1970) by James Taylor, Jr, of New York. (Since his death it has tended to disintegrate; the group which regards itself as in the main succession is led by J. H. Symington.) Some Exclusive groups, however, are 'exclusive' only in name, in the sense that they stem from the Darbyite side of the 1848 cleavage, but in practice they are as evangelically cooperative as the Open Brethren.

The Brethren accept the doctrines of the historic creeds, except that the Taylorite Exclusives have manifested an Apollinarian tendency and, since about 1929, have denied the eternity of Christ's relation as Son to the Father – this relation, they hold, started with the incarnation, although they believe in his eternal pre-existence. The Brethren are evangelical in doctrine and practice, leaning for the most part towards Calvinism rather than Arminianism. Their most distinctive feature is that (like the Friends) they reject all differentiation between clergy and laity. While several of their members are set apart for an evangelistic, teaching or pastoral ministry, this gives them no special status. They do (unlike the Friends) administer the sacraments of baptism and the Lord's Supper (*see* **Baptism** 13; **Liturgies** 13). In polity the Open Brethren are uncompromisingly congregational, their churches being administered by elders; the Exclusive Brethren have centralized control, most stringent of all in the late James Taylor's connection.

The Open Brethren participate freely in interdenominational evangelical activity, e.g. in the Evangelical Alliance, the Inter-Varsity Christian Fellowship, etc. Their closest affinities in England are with evangelical Anglicans. In Great Britain and Ireland the Brethren's numbers are estimated at about 100,000, of whom perhaps two-thirds are Open Brethren.

The Open Brethren's interests are served

by several periodicals (none of which is under ecclesiastical control), e.g. *The Harvester* (monthly) and *Christian Brethren Review* (occasional).

See also **Books, Liturgical** 13; **Liturgies** 13.

F. R. Coad, *A History of the Brethren Movement*, 1968; P. E. Cousins, *The Brethren*, 1982; D. J. Ellis and W. W. Gasque (eds), *In God's Community*, 1978; H. L. Ellison, *The Household Church*, 1979; R. H. McLaren, *The Triple Tradition: The Origin and Development of the Open Brethren in North America*, 1982; H. H. Rowdon, *The Origins of the Brethren*, 1967; W. T. Stunt (ed), *Turning the World Upside Down: A Century of Missionary Endeavour*, 1972; B. R. Wilson (ed), *Patterns of Sectarianism*, 1967.

F. F. BRUCE

Polyphony

Polyphony (from Greek *polyphonia* = that which has many voices) is the technical term for music having two or more individual parts intended to be heard simultaneously, as opposed to monophony, where one part only is sung by one or more voices. There are many theories as to how polyphony came to be introduced, in about the ninth century or earlier, in church music. It is thought to have existed already in a primitive form in secular music. It might have been suggested by chants that lay too high for basses at times and too low for tenors at other times. The earliest polyphony appears to have consisted in adding a part which moved in parallel fifths or fourths with the given part – a phrase of chant. Another very ancient form of polyphony, which one can still hear in Eastern Orthodox music, was the accompaniment of the traditional chant by a bass drone. In the ninth century these two systems were combined, and it was only a step from such a combination to discover how to give greater independence to the parts by the systematic use of contrary motion.

These simple beginnings gave place to various kinds of innovations, such as the transference of the *Cantus firmus* from the top to the lowest part, where it was known as the tenor, or 'holding part', above which one or more voices indulged in long florid passages called melismas. The chant itself, in the lowest voice, was put into long notes and lost its character altogether. The increasing complexity, rhythmically and melodically, of these developments made the notating of precise time values an urgent necessity in order that several voices might sing together in a disciplined way. Measured music thus became totally distinct from the chant, which, when sung on its own, was characterized by its highly complex freedom and flow of phrase and rhythm. Gregorian chant* found its architectural counterpart in the churches of the Romanesque period; the measured music of polyphony in the cathedrals of the Gothic period, those mounting prayers in stone and glass that, from about 1180 to 1250, were constructed by the genius of Germany, England, Spain and pre-eminently France, with Notre-Dame Cathedral in Paris and Notre-Dame at Chartres as prime centres of highly sophisticated musical composition and performance. Two great masters of the period have been associated by historians with Paris: Léonin (*c.*1162–90) and his pupil Pérotin (*fl.c.*1200), perhaps the first composer to write for three and four voices in a truly contrapuntal style.

Succeeding centuries were to witness the further development of polyphony, ever enriching the 'treasury of sacred music', until it reached perhaps its highest point in the hands of the composers of the high Renaissance. This greatest epoch of polyphonic liturgical music came to an end with the first decade of the seventeenth century.

MARY BERRY

Posture

A physical position which is stationary, e.g. standing (erect) or lying (recumbent). Postures are not therefore to be included among movements in worship*, although where there is posture adjustment there is mobility, i.e. to turn to the east is to execute a posture adjustment relating to directions*. Both postures and their adjustments express meanings and so an understanding of them is a necessary part of interpreting liturgical activity as a whole.

1. *Eastward position*. This term is used to describe the posture of the eucharistic president when he stands before the altar with his back to the people: in church buildings which are literally 'orientated'

(*see* **Orientation**) so that the altar is at the eastern end, the priest also is literally eastward-facing, but the term is generally used irrespective of compass direction.

2. *Westward position*. This term (identical with basilican position) is used when the liturgical president faces the people across the communion table or altar, no account being taken of actual direction. The first churches to be built under Constantine were in the form of a modified basilica* with the apse* at the western end, thus enabling the bishop and presbyters to face eastwards over the altar. In the middle of the fourth century the orientation was reversed so that the altar in the apse was at the eastern end, with the consequence that the people faced eastwards and the clergy westwards. In order that they too might face the east (and for other reasons), the clergy in the West eventually abandoned the basilican position in most church buildings and assumed places to the west of the altar. Thus, the eastward position was the norm in the Middle Ages and remained so in the Roman Catholic Church until the second half of the twentieth century. In the mediaeval period, when altars came to be placed very close to the east wall and to be furnished with hangings, pictures or more permanent structures, it became impossible to take the basilican position which (with very few exceptions) had been the norm in the early church.

The Reformed Churches generally reverted to the original disposition of ministers facing the people across the holy table at the eucharist, but deliberately ignored questions of solar orientation in the building. When existing mediaeval churches continued to be used, the Calvinists usually set up a wooden table in the nave on a north-south axis, whereas Lutherans and Anglicans retained the traditional orientation. Characteristically the English church proceeded by way of compromise: at first the 1549 BCP ordered the priest to stand 'afore the middle of the Altar' i.e. in the middle of the long side of the wooden table which replaced the fixed stone altar; then, when this was set up 'table-wise' in the chancel or the nave, the minister faced south in accordance with the rubric of the 1552/1662 BCP 'The Priest standing to the north side of the Table . . .'. When, subsequently, in the seventeenth century, the table was returned to its former position 'altar-wise' along the east wall, this rubric was interpreted by some as requiring the minister to stand at the north *end* (or short side) of the table in order to avoid the eastward position, while others faced east but stood at the northern end of the west side. The inherent ambiguity of the rubric was recognized in the 1637 Scottish prayer book and the presbyter was ordered to stand 'at the north side or end' of the table. The option was tacitly accepted in the Church of England, though the 'north end' eventually became a token of evangelicalism while the middle eastward position (Roman Catholic) came to be favoured by the Oxford Movement. Anglican concern was really that superstition should be avoided and that the manual acts of the priest should not be concealed from the people, hence the 1552/1662 rubric before the consecration prayer which reads: 'When the Priest standing before the Table hath so ordered the Bread and Wine before the people that he may with the more readiness and decency break the Bread before the people and take the Cup in his hands . . .'

All these ambiguities and awkwardnesses are obviated when, as under the influence of the Liturgical Movement*, a return is made to the westward position: and, since this basilican position is acceptable to virtually all sectors of the church, the ecumenical advantage also is considerable.

3. *Kneeling*. In the early church there was for a time a class of penitents who were permitted to be present only for the synaxis*: they knelt at the west end of the nave and were known as *genuflectentes*. Originally, then, kneeling was not a common posture for prayer of all kinds as it has become in the Roman Catholic and Anglican churches. The primitive posture for prayer was standing (often with arms outstretched – as in the catacomb paintings), and this is still the custom in the Eastern Orthodox churches: in contrast, in most Protestant churches sitting is the preferred posture.

The change from standing to kneeling in the West came about through the omission of a command to rise after a short period appointed for silent kneeling prayer. It became customary in many liturgies after the *Gloria in excelsis* to call the people to prayer with the word *Oremus* and then to

summon them to kneel with the words *Flectamus genua* for private devotions; this was then followed by the invitation to stand, *Levate*, for the succeeding collective prayers. By the twelfth century the period for silent prayer had been eliminated and, as the command to stand was no longer given, the people were left kneeling for the collects. From this beginning the penitential posture spread to other parts of the service – at first in the Latin rite and thence into the English rites. Thus in the 1662 BCP the faithful are ordered to kneel from the opening Lord's Prayer and collect, through the ten commandments, collects and epistle, and to stand only for the gospel and the creed; it is also common for the people to kneel from the offertory onwards through the communion to the blessing since there is no rubric ordering them to stand – not even for the *Gloria in excelsis*!

However, in order to guard against a mistaken inference from the requirement to kneel to receive the sacrament, there was inserted in the 1552 BCP a Declaration on Kneeling. This statement, which was printed without the authority of Parliament, was to the effect that kneeling did not imply the 'real and essential' presence of Christ, and that no adoration was intended but, rather, that kneeling signified the humility and worthy reception of 'the benefits of Christ'. The 'rubric' was omitted in the 1559 edition, but was re-inserted in the 1662 BCP with the alteration of 'real and essential' to 'corporeal' in order to avoid gross superstition and yet to maintain the reality of the sacramental presence. In the nineteenth century it was customary to print rubrics* in red and, in order to indicate that this 'declaration' was not technically a 'rubric', it was printed in black; perversely it became known as the Black Rubric.

Under the influence of the Liturgical Movement the custom has become widespread of standing to receive the sacrament. The ASB in its notes to the Order for Communion states that local custom may be followed, but it also emphasizes that 'the Eucharistic Prayer is a single prayer, the unity of which may be obscured by changes of position in the course of it'.

There is much to be said, in principle, for kneeling only for penitential prayer and for either standing or sitting at other points in the liturgical action – standing for praise in fellowship and sitting to listen to readings, sermons, notices, lengthy musical renderings and for meditation. It is to be remembered, first, that for more than a millennium in Christian churches there were seats only for the officiating ministers and for the aged and the disabled ('the weak must go to the wall', i.e. to the seats by the wall); secondly, that 'Let us pray' is not the same as 'Let us kneel', and thirdly, that crouching between seats is not kneeling.

4. *Sitting*. Liturgical sitting was originally the prerogative of the bishop (or his deputy) who at the eucharist was the enthroned president ('one who sits before'), and of the senior members of the congregation – the presbyters – who had their seats alongside him around the apse. No other seats were provided in churches, except for the elderly and infirm, until monastic choir stalls with misericord seats made their appearance. In the mediaeval period, in line with increased seating on secular public occasions, some additional seating was provided in church buildings in the form of backless benches (from the twelfth century onwards). But not until the period of the Reformation (with long sermons) and the Counter-Reformation (with long musical settings) did extensive lay seating become general. Eventually, what was once only a convenience came to be regarded as a necessity and, correspondingly, there occurred the curious liturgical inversion which gave the clergy little opportunity to sit down and the laity no occasion to stand up – except for the singing of popular hymns.

Sitting, like standing or kneeling, should really be reappraised as a positive liturgical posture. The clergy, who have usurped much of the liturgy of the laity, need to sit down more frequently or for longer periods in the course of the action, and so enable the latter to rise to their own liturgical occasions: in this way the people will be less inclined to remain seated in order to 'hear mass' or to 'listen to the word' in a negative manner, but will sit down for definite liturgical reasons.

5. *Standing*. The erect position, according to the Old Testament, is that adopted by priests when exercising their

ministry (Deut. 18.5). At the present day, with a growing recovery of the idea of the common priesthood of all Christians, many who are not ordained assume this posture during the prayer of consecration at the eucharist and for the act of communion. Standing was also for many centuries the position for prayer, following Old Testament and Jewish practice (e.g. I Sam. 1.26), and the many depictions of the *orans* in the catacombs and on sarcophagi show how normal this was (*see* Fig. 25), except during penitential seasons such as Lent when the more humble, suppliant posture of kneeling was adopted. Standing also indicates readiness to hear and obey (Ezek. 2.1) and so is the position for the hearers of the gospel when it is read aloud at the Lord's Supper.

Fig. 25 *Orans* from the catacomb of Priscilla

Posture adjustment, as previously stated, refers to a change of body position and the one most significant for worship is turning east. From the second century it became customary to turn in this direction when praying because, according to Clement of Alexandria: 'the east is an image of the day of birth', while other writers suggest that the rebirth of the soul through the Second Adam will be associated with Paradise 'eastward in Eden'. Such interpretations of orientated prayer are linked with the custom at the beginning of the initiation ceremonies for the candidate to turn first westwards to renounce Satan and then eastwards to profess Christ. A similar symbolic movement was adopted in the Church of England in the seventeenth century, and since then eastward turning has been common for every liturgical recitation of a creed. In the mediaeval West it was customary for the whole congregation to turn eastwards (i.e. altar-wards) at the *Gloria Patri* and the *Gloria in excelsis*. As with most liturgical gestures, this posture also has been discontinued by many Protestants, especially when, in non-orientated buildings, ministers and elders face the rest of the congregation throughout corporate worship.

J. G. Davies, *Liturgical Dance*, 1984, ch. 7; W. Lamb and E. Watson, *Body Code. The Meaning in Movement*, 1979.

GILBERT COPE

Praise

see **Prayer** 4

Prayer

Prayer is the generic term for all aspects of humanity's conscious relationship to God, as in 'the life of prayer'. As such it has been held to include liturgical worship, meditation and individual prayer, as well as such other religious duties as fasting and almsgiving. In a more specific sense, it denotes that part of humanity's relationship which consists of mental and verbal fellowship with God. The word can also refer, in the plural or with the indefinite article, to forms of words addressed to God.

Current writing about prayer is generally concerned to direct attention more to the second sense than to the third, and most of all to the first sense given. There is a widespread quest for forms of contemplation and meditation which attach less importance to the recitation of forms of words. Of late there has also been a growing quest for forms of the spiritual life which do not seem to involve emphasis on withdrawal from secular concerns so much as the discovery of the presence of God within the concerns of daily living. Those who are concerned with specific acts of

prayer and times of prayer have therefore to discover a way in which these can form a framework for the constant practice of the presence of God.

The traditional divisions of prayer into adoration or praise, thanksgiving, confession and petition or supplication are relevant to all kinds of spirituality whether they involve specific acts of prayer or not, because they describe essential components of man's relationship to God. This is due to the fact that forms of prayer have been considerably moulded by theological considerations; since prayer is the expression of humanity's relationship to God, the content of it is closely linked with the nature of that relationship as human kind has discovered it, and the present discussion of prayer results directly from theological questionings. Forms of prayer which have traditionally been valued now raise very serious questions about how God is conceived and how, if at all, he is thought of as intervening in the life of the world.

1. *Adoration.* This aspect of prayer consists in the contemplation and worship of God as he is in himself. It is the word that most accurately describes the prayers of the mystics, and consists in focussing on and celebrating the qualities of the Godhead as they have been revealed to and experienced by the believer. The forms under which such prayer has occurred are many and various; the vision of heaven recorded in Isa. 6 appears to include an intense visual experience of God, and many of those who have been best known for their constant adoration of God, and who are classified as mystics, have experienced visions of God which have given rise to intense adoration. Much adoration has also included intense emotional expression, with extensive use of erotic imagery as the believer has contemplated with joy the deeply intimate relationship between God and the soul.

Others have been led to adoration by the contemplation of the world around them. The word adoration connotes a 'resting' in the presence of God, and of the forms of prayer described here is the least tied to verbal forms of expression. As such it has a strong contemporary appeal to those who are disillusioned with institutional religion and seek a spirituality which would involve the contemplation of the timeless qualities of God, such as truth, beauty, love and faithfulness. The parallels between the adoration of the mystics and the experiences of many who have used the techniques of Eastern religions or hallucinogenic drugs are easy to draw.

The church's attitude to adoration, especially as practised by the mystics, has been characterized by a certain ambivalence. On the one hand it has been said that God is to be adored, and indeed the traditional picture of heaven includes the constant adoration of God by the angels and the saints. On the other hand it has been suspected, by some because of the quality of freedom from restraint which characterizes much mystical adoration, and by others for a certain 'other-worldly' sense which pervades adoration. On the whole the tendency has been to commend for most believers the practice of a much more disciplined variety which is tied to more verbal forms of expression and is in fact a combination of praise and thanksgiving related both to the biblical account of God and to the specific experiences of the believer. Adoration remains, however, that which is thought by many to be the highest form of prayer, and the canons of most eucharistic liturgies begin with the *Sanctus* (Holy, holy, holy), the song of heaven recorded in Isaiah's vision.

2. *Confession.* The acknowledgment by believers of their sin. This occurs under three chief forms, general, personal and sacramental.

General confessions are characteristic of most liturgies. They occur extensively in the Bible (e.g. Ps. 51) and consist of the acknowledgment by the believing community of its unrighteousness before God and of its need of his forgiveness. The forms of such confessions vary greatly, but generally include an expression of sorrow for past transgression, a petition for God's forgiveness and, in some cases, the expression of resolve to amend. Under the influence of the Reformation many of the expressions of sorrow were highly elaborate, and there is a tendency at the present time to modify both the tone and the length of such general confessions.

Personal confession after self-examination has always been a feature of Christian private prayer, and in the past some elabor-

ate lists have been provided of questions with which believers are asked to face themselves at the end of the day or at least as part of their preparation for receiving holy communion. With the questioning of ethical theories which relied heavily on rules there has also come a questioning of this kind of approach to self-examination. Once again, the extensive discussion about God is raising questions that have implications for self-examination; the issue is whether the shortcomings we need to confess actually consist in the breaking of a series of small rules.

Sacramental confessions, or confession before a priest, is a practice enjoined on Orthodox and Roman Catholics, but optional in the Anglican churches and some Protestant denominations. In some cases this form of confession is undertaken at regular intervals as a discipline, and in others as a means of quieting a conscience which is burdened with guilt for some specific offence, though Roman Catholics hold that mortal sin can only be forgiven by this means.

3. *Petition*. This aspect of prayer, known also as supplication or, when it is on behalf of others, intercession, has always been part of prayer, and indeed may be the most common and instinctual prayer which men and women offer. It is the asking of God for something which is desired. There are records of people of all religions and civilizations asking their gods for rain, for success in war, for the healing of the sick, for the blessing of a new ruler and indeed for the satisfaction of just about every conceivable need. It is in some way or other an almost invariable part of liturgical worship, and some liturgical acts are devoted almost entirely to petitionary prayer, e.g. the litany*.

There has been a tendency among teachers of the devotional life to regard petitionary prayer as the 'lowest' form of prayer, as something which ought not to occupy too large a place in the life of prayer. This is largely because it is seen as that part of prayer which gives the most opportunity for selfish asking in one's own interest. It remains true, however, that this most basic form of prayer occupies a large place in the life of praying people. It occurs in the psalms, and formed a part of Jesus' prayers recorded in the gospels, as well as seeming to be a feature of some of the healing miracles. He prayed on behalf of the disciples and, in the Garden of Gethsemane, is recorded as asking that the cup of suffering might pass from him.

Petitionary prayer, probably more than any other form of prayer, has been affected by secular patterns of thinking, and the question of whether and how God answers prayer presents an inescapable dilemma. On the one hand, the abandonment of petitionary prayer altogether would seem to deny a basic part of prayer and also to deny to God the power to change and overrule events. On the other hand a *deus ex machina* God, who in response to individual requests does things which would not otherwise happen, becomes less credible as more and more of the life of the world is brought under control or at any rate explained. Various solutions to this dilemma are offered: it is suggested that prayer has its primary effect in attuning the mind of the one who prays to the will of God, increasing and focussing concern in a way which could be effective, without the need of miraculous divine interventions. Jesus' prayer in Gethsemane is cited as an example of the way in which all petitionary prayer has to be modified by the petition 'Thy will be done', and thus negative 'answers' have to be expected.

What does need to be pointed out, however, is that prayer in the biblical tradition has always been presented as an activity which did not limit the freedom of God, that is to say it was not a mechanical magical procedure which was designed to produce automatic effects; rather it appears to be thought of as communication between the believer and God which accepts the liberty and integrity of both. There can be no doubt that petitionary prayer more than any other depends upon the view of God which undergirds it.

4. *Praise*. The outward expression of the believer's worship and adoration of God, in words, music and ceremonial. The focus of praise is not only upon God himself, as in adoration, but above all on his mighty acts in nature and history. Hymns and acts of praise are a common feature of all liturgy, and frequently the distinction between it and adoration on the one hand and thanksgiving on the other is not clear-cut.

A feature of praise in the Christian tradition, but going back to pre-Christian times, is the recital of the great deeds of God in the past. The reading of the gospel in the liturgy is, for example, answered with the response 'Praise (or thanks) be to thee, O Christ', and the ancient hymn of praise *Te Deum Laudamus* (fifth century) begins with the adoration of God but includes the recollection of the work of Christ as the basis of the praise that is being offered ('When thou tookest upon thee to deliver man, thou didst not abhor the virgin's womb; When thou hadst overcome the sharpness of death thou didst open the kingdom of heaven to all believers').

In being invited to share in the offering of praise, believers are asked to share in the life of the whole community of believers through the ages and to join in the praise they gave for their deliverance. They are responding to their own prayer in the Lord's Prayer, 'Hallowed be thy name', by participating in the hallowing of God for that which he has done for the world and for mankind.

5. *Thanksgiving*. A feature of prayer both public and private is that the believers are invited to offer thanks to God for their personal experiences of his goodness. It is natural that it should be closely linked to praise, as in the General Thanksgiving in the BCP, where thanks for God's 'loving-kindness to us and to all men' passes on to a recollection of 'his inestimable love in the redemption of the world by our Lord Jesus Christ'. The specific need for thanksgiving, however, is part of what is involved in the believers' relating what they know of God to their experience in daily living. Once again there are problems about the listing of their experiences at the hand of God, and difficulties about the extent to which, in a secular age, it is appropriate to thank God for things which can be otherwise explained. The possibility of thanksgiving, however, is available if the model of a personal relationship with God can be rediscovered in a contemporary form.

For liturgical prayers, see ***Agnus Dei***; **Anaphora**; **Collect**; **Doxology**; **Extempore Prayer**; **Intercession**; ***Kyrie***; **Litany**; **Lord's Prayer, The**; **Ordinary**; **Preface**; **Proper**; ***Sanctus***; **Silent Prayer**; **Suffrages**; ***Super Oblata***; ***Trisagion***.

The spiritual tradition: L. A. Bouyer, *A History of Christian Spirituality*, 3 vols, 1982; M. Gibbard, *Guides to Hidden Springs*, 1979; *Twentieth-Century Men of Prayer*, 1974; J. R. H. Moorman, *The Anglican Spiritual Tradition*, 1983; R. Williams, *The Wound of Knowledge*, 1979; Theological approaches: P. Baelz, *Does God Answer Prayer?*, 1982; *Prayer and Providence*, 1968; D. W. Hardy and D. F. Ford, *Jubilate, Theology in Praise*, 1984; The practice of prayer: G. Appleton, *The Practice of Prayer*, 1980; A. Bloom, *Living Prayer*, 1980; R. Harries, *Turning to Prayer*, 1978; K. Leech, *True Prayer*, 1980; H. A. Williams, *Becoming What I Am*, 1977.

PETER SELBY

Prayer Meeting

An informal meeting, usually additional to the regular worship of the church, at which those who are present offer spontaneous vocal prayers. Scriptural warrant for such meetings may be found in such passages as Acts 4.24ff.; I Cor. 14; they have sometimes been described as 'the liturgy of the Holy Ghost'.

The English Puritans, in addition to the use of extempore prayer by the minister in the regular services, sometimes held meetings, usually on weekdays, at which members, often without a minister, themselves prayed aloud; and some element of spontaneous prayer often formed a part of the church meeting of the Independents. The Sunday 'meetings for worship' of the Society of Friends still contain this element, interwoven with silence and exhortation (*see* **Quaker Worship**).

Pietism and the evangelical revival gave a fresh impetus to spontaneous prayer, and this no doubt formed a large ingredient in the various kinds of fellowship meeting in early Methodism. In some places, meetings for prayer with appointed leaders were planned as carefully as preaching services. The actual term 'prayer meeting' came into regular use in evangelical circles in the early part of the nineteenth century. A fresh impetus came from the camp meetings* which the Primitive Methodists adopted from America, for, while some preached, they were supported by others in praying bands. In some parts of England the custom became widespread, especially in Methodism, whereby almost every Sunday even-

ing, except when the Lord's Supper was observed, the more devout members of the congregation stayed to a prayer meeting after the service. At such an 'after-meeting', as it was sometimes called, fresh converts were made welcome, and the young could listen to the prayers of others and make their own first efforts at praying aloud spontaneously. Individuals would also strike up well-known hymns and choruses in which the others would join. Sometimes the prayers would have an ecstatic, affectionate quality usually more characteristic of mental than of vocal prayer.

Such meetings, whether on Sundays or on weekdays, were indeed prominent in all the Free Churches. They were also widespread in Evangelical Anglicanism, though naturally not in such close connection with the services of the church. They were also held in undenominational gatherings and conferences of evangelical societies, and were often called for special purposes, as to support evangelistic campaigns.

In recent years in many churches prayer meetings, especially those closely linked with the services of the church, have tended to die out. One reason is that intense fervour was difficult to maintain, and some members of congregations, lacking fresh inspiration, tended, perhaps unconsciously, to repeat the prayers which they had uttered on previous occasions, so that the meetings lost their spontaneity. The practice has recently grown in some churches of inviting members of the congregation to suggest topics at the time of the intercession, and this could develop into a kind of prayer meeting. This is perhaps the most suitable form for such congregational participation in close association with the regular worship of the church.

Where religious fervour continues or revives, prayer meetings of the older pattern still flourish. They are often used extensively in preparation for or support of evangelistic campaigns. Moreover in the classic Pentecostalist churches the main service of worship has some of the characteristics of a prayer meeting (*see* **Pentecostal Worship**). In churches of all denominations those who are influenced by Neo-Pentecostalism or the Charismatic Movement often hold prayer meetings. These may include the offering of spontaneous prayer both individually and collectively, the singing of choruses, and the exercise of such gifts of the Spirit as glossolalia and prophecy.

P. R. Akehurst, *Praying Aloud Together*, 1972; C. O. Buchanan, *Encountering Charismatic Worship*, 1977; J. Gunstone, *The Charismatic Prayer Meeting*, 1975.

A. RAYMOND GEORGE

Preface

A name, originally proper to the Roman rite, for the thanksgiving which opens the eucharistic prayer or anaphora*. The Latin *praefatio* in this context does not mean a preliminary, but a proclamation. In the ancient Gallican liturgy the word *praefatio* was used differently, of a descriptive invitation or bidding to prayer.

J. A. Jungmann, *The Mass of the Roman Rite*, II, 1955, pp.115–28.

W. JARDINE GRISBROOKE

Presanctified Mass

Mass or liturgy of the presanctified (i.e. 'of the previously consecrated') is a form of service prescribed in the historic rites for use on certain days when the eucharist is not celebrated, but when it is at the same time necessary or desirable to make provision for communion.

In the early church the eucharist was held to be a festive act, by definition, and it was therefore not celebrated, even when it came generally to be celebrated on weekdays as well as Sundays, on days of penitence. From a very early period, however, daily communion was common, being normally made at home from the reserved sacrament taken from church by the worshippers on the previous Sunday; and when more frequent celebration of the eucharist became widespread after the peace of the church in the fourth century, the desire to provide a public opportunity for the reception of communion on the days when it was, for liturgical reasons, not celebrated, became increasingly felt, even with the decline in frequency of communion which set in at this time. This was the origin of the mass or liturgy of the presanctified. For reasons of space consideration of the service today must be restricted to the provision for it in the two most widespread of the historic rites, the Byzantine and the Roman.

In the Byzantine rite the eucharist is not

celebrated on any day in Lent other than Sundays and Saturdays (which like Sundays are not fast days) and the feast of the Annunciation if it falls in the season. On other days the liturgy of the presanctified is used; today there is no communion at all on Good Friday, but this is a mediaeval innovation, the liturgy of the presanctified having originally been used on that day like all other Lenten weekdays. As in theory it is not permitted on fast days to take any food until after vespers, the office for communion from the reserved sacrament is attached to that office, which exhibits certain variants from its normal order, and this combination forms the liturgy of the presanctified. Today it is celebrated in most churches only on Wednesdays and Fridays, and except in the increasing but still small number of churches to which liturgical reform is beginning to penetrate, it is celebrated by anticipation in the morning, which renders much of the text of the service inappropriate.

The reserved sacrament is prepared for communion during the recitation of the psalms of the day in vespers; it is taken from the tabernacle on the altar to the prothesis* table, where wine and water are also poured into a chalice. Vespers is cut short at the lessons, after which the altar, and then the whole church and congregation, are solemnly censed, to the singing of Ps. 140 (141). The second part of the service is composed almost entirely of extracts from the eucharistic liturgy: 1. the litanies which close the synaxis* and open the eucharist proper, with special closing collects; 2. the great entrance*, in an especially solemn form, with a proper anthem, as it is a procession with the consecrated, instead of the unconsecrated, gifts; 3. the Lord's Prayer, with the litany which usually introduces it, slightly modified; 4. the elevation of the gifts, the fraction*, and the placing of the particles of the broken bread in the (unconsecrated) chalice, the contents of which were anciently regarded, in East and West alike, as consecrated by this commixture*; 5. communion*; 6. the normal concluding rites, although with certain proper texts. For further details of these parts of the normal liturgy, *see* **Liturgies** 2.

In the Roman rite, the mass of the presanctified (no longer called by that name since 1955) is celebrated on only one day in the year – Good Friday. For this reason the service exhibits a number of striking features peculiar to that day, such as the veneration of the cross*, but in essence, like the Byzantine service, it is simply part of a normal service followed by communion from the reserved sacrament – the first part of the Roman service being not vespers as in the Byzantine rite, but the pre-eucharistic synaxis, in an unusually primitive and simple form, and concluding after the readings with the full ancient Roman synaxis intercession, somewhat adapted to modern use. (The veneration of the cross is interpolated between the intercession and the communion.) The communion rite is extremely simple: the sacrament reserved overnight from the mass of the Last Supper on Maundy Thursday* is brought in by the deacon (or priest himself if there be no deacon) accompanied by two acolytes*, in silence: even the three antiphons* which in 1955 had replaced the hymn *Vexilla Regis* have now disappeared. The Lord's Prayer, with other normal devotions preparatory to communion, is recited; the communion follows, and the service is concluded with a post-communion prayer and a prayer over the people.

Since 1955 the Roman mass of the presanctified, which like its Byzantine counterpart was for many centuries anticipated in the morning, has again been celebrated at its proper hour – in this case, three o'clock in the afternoon. It has undergone a number of minor changes since its first introduction, which appears to have been not later than the sixth century (the opinion of some writers that it is of later date is based on a misreading of the evidence; the communion is absent from the Good Friday service in the earliest *papal* books of the urban Roman rite because the papal service was held in the morning, while the *parochial* books include it, the parochial services being held in the afternoon, and many people no doubt going to both).

What is in fact a presanctified mass, although again it is not called by that name, is now provided for in the Roman rite for use on occasions when public worship is desired but owing to the absence of a priest the eucharist itself cannot be celebrated. It comprises a normal liturgy of the word, with only slight adaptations, and a simple communion service very like that on Good

Friday, communion being given by a deacon or an authorized lay minister.

W. JARDINE GRISBROOKE

Presbyter

The term is derived from the Greek word meaning elder*, and appears to be used in the NT as interchangeable with the word *episcopos*, from which bishop* is derived. It is notorious that there are widely differing views of the way in which the early ministry of the church developed. One view, held by a good many authorities, is that in each Christian centre there was a college of presbyter-bishops from among whom the monarchical bishop emerged in due course. Whatever may be the truth of the matter, it is clear that by the second century the presbyters formed an advisory body associated with the bishop in the pastoral and administrative work of his office and also associated with him (by their physical presence round him) in his liturgical functions. In the third century the presbyter began to be the person to whom the bishop delegated the responsibility for the pastoral oversight of an area and the duty of presiding at celebrations of the eucharist. In due course the mediaeval concept of the parish priest developed, the man who was almost the personification of the church in the local community, who baptized and said mass and performed all other Christian rites except confirmation and ordination. The English word 'priest', like its equivalents in most Germanic languages, is derived from 'presbyter' and not from the Greek or Latin terms for priesthood. (The Greek and Latin terms are hardly ever used for the Christian ministry in the early church, and then of bishops rather than of presbyters. Thus Cyprian uses *sacerdos* to mean bishop, not presbyter.) After the Reformation, Anglican and some Lutheran churches retained 'priest' for the second order of the ministry, though it became more usual for churches of the Reformation to use the term 'presbyter' or the vaguer term 'minister' to describe the person normally responsible for the preaching of the word and the administration of the sacraments. In most modern schemes for a reunion of the churches, 'presbyter' rather than 'priest' is used for the order next below that of bishop.

In the Anglican Church in Canada, the United States, Kenya, Uganda, New Zealand and Hong Kong, women are now ordained to the priesthood. Other provinces have accepted the principle of the ordination of women* but have not yet acted upon it.

G. B. Henderson, *Presbyterianism*, 1954; C. Howard, *The Ordination of Women to the Priesthood: Further Report*, 1984; A. Piolante, P. Siffrin and E. Josi in *Enciclopedia Cattolica*, IX, cols 1961–4; D. N. Power, *Ministers of Christ and his Church*, 1969; B. H. Streeter, *The Primitive Church*, 1929.

P. HINCHLIFF

Presbyterian Worship

The Presbyterian Churches are that part of the world-wide Reformed family which has its roots in the Scottish (and, to a lesser extent, the English) Reformation. From the beginning they included some whose native language was not English but Gaelic or Welsh, and today include many whose language is Kikuyu or Korean or any of a hundred others. In such a group there is wide diversity of practice, especially as younger churches seek to indigenize their worship, but the older churches, notably the Church of Scotland (the only Presbyterian church which is a National Church) and the recently reunited Presbyterian Church (USA), exercise considerable influence. The fastest-growing churches are in Africa and the Far East, notably in Korea, but their influence on worship has yet to be felt.

Presbyterian worship was never bound to a fixed liturgy. John Knox's book, which became the *Book of Common Order* (1564), allowed the minister either to use the prayer provided or pray 'as the spirite of God shall move his harte'. The struggle against an imposed liturgy led to a reaction against all read prayer. (Even the Lord's Prayer ceased to be used.) The *Westminster Directory* (1644) was not a liturgy, although its directions are so detailed that it could be used as one, but became the 'standard' for worship.

The evidence for Presbyterian worship from the seventeenth century on is not found in service books but in the accounts of interested observers and participants, and in the attempts of church courts to regulate worship. The sermon, God's word to man, is at the heart of such worship. Prayer,

man's word to God, was often not less scriptural, since its sources were in the psalms and the New Testament. The cast of the Presbyterian mind is didactic, and in worship this meant wordiness. If some observers were charmed by the biblical simplicity and solemnity of Presbyterian worship (not least, the infrequent communion services, with the long tables set for the communicants), others were repelled by its bareness and verbosity.

The experience of Scots in the Colonies, who felt the lack of a book which could be used in the absence of a minister (as Anglicans could use the BCP) helped to fuel the movement for the renewal of worship; but the Romantic movement, the influence of Tractarianism, and the defection of middle- and upper-class Presbyterians to a more genteel episcopacy, all played their part. The movement for the 'renascence of worship' took parallel forms in the main Presbyterian churches, in America and elsewhere, and resulted in the issue of service books, first by worship societies, later by official church committees. (*See* **Books, Liturgical** 14; **Liturgies** 14.)

The changes which have come, first through Catholic enrichment, later through ecumenical influence, have meant the ironing-out of many Presbyterian idiosyncrasies. The Scots at the Reformation resolutely rejected the Christian year as tending to superstition, refusing not only saints' days but also dominical feasts. The return of the Christian year to Presbyterian worship was marked by *Prayers for the Christian Year* (1935). A lectionary, which had been rejected by the Reformers as 'skipping and divagating from place to place', was recommended in *Prayers for Divine Service* (1923) and all books thereafter, *lectio continua* having long since ceased. The 'fencing of the tables' – words of warning and of invitation before communion – was a feature of all Reformed liturgies, but came to be much abused, to the discouragement of communicants. With the abandonment of the long tables in the nineteenth century it became less appropriate. There is a fine example, with echoes of the 1644 *Directory* in *Common Worship* (1905), of the Presbyterian Church in the USA, and a similar, in an Alternative Service, in *The Book of Common Order* (1940). The only trace in more modern books is in the 'words of invitation' sometimes used.

In the above matters the books probably express, though they may have influenced, changes in popular practice. However, modern Presbyterian service books are misunderstood if they are read as reflecting the *actual* worship of the church. That is not their intention. They are instruments of change, attempts to 'improve' worship. Since their use is optional, their influence is gradual, but can be considerable. *The Book of Common Order* (1940), distributed free to every ministerial candidate, had enormous influence, not only in Scotland but in all the churches. The Australian book of 1956 acknowledges that 'every book published since bears evidence of its influence'. Yet there were not many congregations in Scotland where the full 1940 communion service was used. *The Book of Common Order* (1979) puts the narrative of institution within the eucharistic prayer in all three orders. That this is an innovation and not current practice was made clear in a Deliverance of the General Assembly in 1980. 'The General Assembly regret that in *The Book of Common Order* (1979) the use of the words of institution as part of the eucharistic prayer is preferred: and wish to make it clear that their use as a warrant continues to be normal usage in the Church of Scotland.' Since, however, the book continues to circulate, and a deliverance of the General Assembly is soon forgotten, the innovation quickly becomes invested with authority.

The above innovation clearly derives from the 'ecumenical consensus' which is the main influence in liturgical change in the late twentieth century. So also does the determination of both the Scottish *Book of Common Order* (1979) and the American *Worshipbook* (1970) to present the communion service as the normal service for the Lord's Day, and the service without communion as an exception. The eucharist was the normal service for the Lord's Day in the early church. It is so in other communions today, where regular weekly communion is now encouraged. The Presbyterian tradition, however, was of infrequent communion. In the *First Book of Discipline* (1560) four times a year were thought sufficient, because instruction and discipline had to go before. The *Directory*

(1644) said 'frequently', but left it to each congregation, and infrequency remained the general custom. Custom may change, given good reason. The discipline of communion is much slackened, and more frequent celebration is now common. But if the new books succeed in making weekly communion the actual practice of the Presbyterian churches, they will have achieved a change more radical than any that has gone before.

Because Presbyterian worship has never been bound to a fixed liturgy, and ministers enjoy considerable freedom in the ordering of worship, the liturgical movement has not been the only influence for change. Its theological conscience and liturgical gravity are often in competition with more populist tendencies of gimmickry and sentimentality. Against these it stands as an austere corrective. It may well preserve into the next phase of its history at least one characteristic of the Presbyterian tradition – its seriousness.

See also **United Reformed Church Worship**.

JAMES A. WHYTE

Priest

see **Presbyter**

Prime

see **Canonical Hours**

Procession

A planned movement of a group of people from one place to another for some specific religious purpose, often to the accompaniment of singing and music. It may be a self-contained, independent act, e.g. a Rogationtide* procession around the fields, or an act within a service, e.g. an offertory* procession at the eucharist. Early evidence for processions is found in the *Pilgrimage of Egeria* (late fourth century) which describes the pilgrimages* to the sacred sites in Jerusalem during the rites of Holy Week. A valuable Western source is *Ordo Romanus Primus*, which describes the seventh century pontifical stational masses of Rome. In the later Middle Ages material for various occasions was collected from such books as the *Missal*, the *Ritual* and the *Pontifical* to form the *Processional*.

A procession could be held for various reasons. It could be an act of Christian witness, an act of penitence or praise, or an act of supplication. Some processions served more than one purpose. The St Mark's Day procession, instituted in Rome in the sixth century, was an act of Christian witness on the same day as the old pagan festival of the Robigalia, when the gods were asked to preserve the crops from mildew; but it was also used as an act of supplication similar to the Rogationtide procession, at which litanies* were sung, praying for God's blessing on the crops. Again, the Corpus Christi* procession, instituted in the thirteenth century in honour of the blessed sacrament, was combined in Germany with a supplication for God's protection on the countryside. Other processions were held in connection with pilgrimages to shrines, or the transference of relics to a new home, or the dedication of a new church. On such occasions full use was made of external aids to excite devotion – incense*, lights, banners, relics and rich vestments*. Sometimes processions invited more than simply walking: special steps and choreography were involved, and the act almost became a religious dance.

Other processions were integral to particular rites: the procession to the font at baptism; the procession of the bridal party to the altar at matrimony; the procession to the grave at burial; the procession before the eucharist; or the gospel and offertory processions (the lesser and greater entrance). The Reformers in general protested against abuses connected with processions and abandoned, not only the processions themselves, but also – with the exception of Luther and Cranmer – the litanies associated with them. Cranmer and Henry VIII apparently contemplated a new English *Processional*, but the project came to nothing. By a royal injunction of 1545 Cranmer's litany of 1544 became the sole procession in England; and by the royal injunctions of 1547, even the litany could only be used kneeling in church. After a temporary reprieve under Queen Mary, processions were again suppressed under Elizabeth in 1559 except those of Rogationtide. The 1662 BCP, however, sanctioned processions occurring within rites – namely in baptism, matrimony and burial; and such processions are assumed, though not specifically mentioned, in the Alter-

native Service Book 1980. These, with the gospel and offertory processions at the eucharist, are found in whole or in part in the Roman, Orthodox, Anglican and in some Reformed Churches: and their use is still spreading. The rites of Holy Week* provide a striking illustration. South Africa, for example, provides for processions in its services for Palm Sunday, Maundy Thursday, Good Friday, and the Easter Vigil; while the interdenominational Joint Liturgical Group in England also makes similar provision in its services for Palm Sunday and the Easter vigil. A Presbyterian member of that Group also makes the point in one of its reports that the West has something to learn about processions from the Little Entrance* and the Great Entrance* of the Orthodox Church (*Getting the Liturgy Right*, p. 59). The public procession as an act of Christian witness or as a pilgrimage has also revived – note the Roman processions on the feast of Corpus Christi, the Whitsuntide processions in the north of England, and the ecumenical processions of witness on Good Friday.

M. Andrieu, *Les Ordines Romani du Haut Moyen Age*, 5 vols, 1931–61; F. E. Brightman, *The English Rite*, 2 vols, 1915; J. G. Davies (ed), *Worship and Dance*, 1975; C. Dunlop, *Processions*, 1932; W. H. Frere, *The Principles of Religious Ceremonial*, 1906; M. J. Hatchett, *Commentary on the American Prayer Book*, 1979; W. G. Henderson, *Processionale ad usum Sarum*, 1882; R. C. D. Jasper (ed), *Getting the Liturgy Right*, 1982; J. A. Jungmann, *The Mass of the Roman Rite*, 1951, 1959; *La Maison Dieu*, no.43,1955.

R. C. D. JASPER

Prone

see **Bidding Prayer**

Proper

A term of the Roman mass (although applicable to other rites also), having two different but related meanings: 1. those parts of the service which vary according to the day or season; 2. those variable parts of the service which are rendered chorally, principally composed of psalmody, and comprising the Introit or entrance chant (in the 1969 *Ordo Missae* 'entrance antiphon'), the Gradual or responsorial psalm (formerly – and still when there are only two readings – sung after the epistle, but since 1969 before it and after the OT reading when there are three readings), the Alleluia (sung between the epistle and the gospel), the Offertory chant, and the Communion chant. Derivatively, the term may be used of those parts of any service which vary according to the day or season.

See also **Chants of the Proper of the Mass.**

W. JARDINE GRISBROOKE

Prothesis

The name prothesis (Greek 'preparation') is used in the Byzantine rite (commonly referred to as the Orthodox* liturgy) to designate three different but related things: 1. the rite of preparation before the divine liturgy or eucharist; 2. the chamber to the north of the sanctuary in which the greater part of this rite takes place; 3. the table in that chamber on which the elements, usually referred to in the Byzantine rite as the gifts, are prepared.

The rite of preparation currently in use is elaborate, and falls into two principal parts, the preparation of the ministers and the preparation of the gifts. The former comprises three acts: 1. introductory prayers which are recited by the celebrant and deacon together outside the gates of the sanctuary, with the veneration of the principal images on the iconostasis* or sanctuary screen; 2. the vesting of the ministers, the putting on of each garment being accompanied by the recitation of a supposedly appropriate verse from the psalms or some other part of the OT; 3. a washing of their hands by the ministers, with the recitation of Ps. 25 (26).6–12. The second and third of these properly take place in the chamber called the *diakonikon* (Greek lit. 'deaconry', commonly translated 'vestry') on the south of the sanctuary, corresponding to the prothesis on the north, but not every church today has such a chamber, and where it is absent the vesting and washing often take place in the sanctuary itself.

The preparation of the gifts opens with the recitation of an anthem about the passion, after which it falls into four distinguishable parts: 1. the preparation of the bread; 2. the preparation of the chalice; 3. commemorative and intercessory prayers, a

kind of anticipated diptychs*; and 4. veiling and censing of the prepared gifts. The preparation of the bread, which varies somewhat in detail from one Orthodox national church to another, consists principally in the cutting out of a square from a pure wheaten leavened loaf (the square being called the 'lamb', an exact counterpart of the Western 'host'), and placing it on the paten, to the accompaniment of a number of scriptural formulae which relate the cutting of the loaf in a highly literal way to the wounding of our Lord in the passion. The preparation of the chalice is much simpler: it consists simply of blessing wine and water, and pouring them into the chalice. There follows a lengthy and involved commemoration of the saints, and of the living and departed for whom the prayers of the church at the eucharist are particularly desired; a small particle of bread is taken from the loaf or loaves at the mention of each name or group of names, and placed upon the paten beside the 'lamb', theoretically in an intricately specified order. The commemorations completed, the celebrant blesses incense, covers the vessels with their veils, censing each veil as he does so, and saying appointed formulae, including Ps. 92 (93). He then censes the gifts thus prepared and covered, and says a concluding general prayer, after which he or the deacon censes the altar, the sanctuary, and finally the whole church and congregation.

This rite of preparation has undergone a long development, and the greater part of it dates from a comparatively late period. The preparation of the ministers is entirely absent from the earliest surviving texts, and does not arrive at something like its present form until the thirteenth century; the earliest evidence for the washing of the ministers' hands at this point is in a printed edition of 1526. As for the preparation of the gifts, until the ninth century it was done with the utmost simplicity, with a single prayer; as late as the middle of the eleventh century there are still texts in which it has developed no further; not until the late twelfth century is there definitive evidence for more intricate ceremonial at it, and even then this was performed in silence, with a single prayer before and after; something resembling the present form is found in a text of 1225. The pseudodiptychs first appear in the twelfth century, and become longer and more elaborate during the course of the later Middle Ages, finally achieving their present form (apart from a few minor details) in 1600. The whole rite, in its present form, is an outstanding example of the mediaeval tendency to confuse the essentials of liturgical action by superimposing on them a mass of secondary, and often theologically inappropriate, detail.

On the other hand, the prothesis still makes provision for the ancient custom of individual offering of the bread and wine for the eucharist, lost for centuries in the West, a provision still largely made use of by the faithful, and unless and until the restoration of the diptychs in the anaphora* to their pristine integrity is accomplished, the lengthy intercessory commemorations in the prothesis are necessary in this connection.

H. Holloway, *A Study of the Byzantine Liturgy*, 1933, ch. I; C. Kucharek, *The Byzantine–Slav Liturgy of St John Chrysostom*, 1971, pp. 254–324.

W. JARDINE GRISBROOKE

Psalmody

From the earliest times the Christian community sang the psalms following the practice of the synagogue. During the first centuries, when the practice was passing from the synagogue to the church, various methods of psalmody (from Greek *psalmodia* = singing to the accompaniment of a stringed instrument) involving a solo cantor* and a (usually unlettered) group appear to have been customary. The group might, for instance, repeat each verse after the soloist. Or he might intone each opening phrase for them to finish. The group might repeat the first verse as a refrain after each succeeding verse, or it might interject a short response such as 'Alleluia' after each of the soloist's verses. A more experienced group would learn to alternate with the cantor, singing the second half of each verse. Finally, if the group happened to be a trained monastic choir, the two halves of the choir would alternate, with each side taking one whole verse of the psalm, singing antiphonally.

We learn from the fathers of the church how psalmody spread over the Christian

world. Eusebius (*c*.260–*c*.340), Bishop of Caesarea, paints a vivid picture of the result: 'The command to sing psalms in the name of the Lord was obeyed by everyone in every place: for the command to sing is in force in all churches which exist among the nations, not only the Greeks but also the barbarians throughout the whole world, and in towns, villages and in the fields.' Tertullian (*c*.160–*c*.220) speaks of the use of psalms at household prayer and exhorts married Christians to emulate each other in psalm singing.

It is certain that all the people took part in psalm singing in the fourth century when Christians were free of persecution. Certain of the fathers forbade women to take part but others, in the next century, gave grudging permission, since if they were not allowed to sing they might gossip during the services. Monks, nuns and members of the clergy had to commit the whole psalter to memory: Jerome told the nuns at Jerusalem that no sister might remain if she did not know the psalms. Enthusiasm for the psalms followed from the realization that the psalter – as still today – was, in the words of Athanasius (*c*.296–373), 'a book that includes the whole life of man, all conditions of the mind and all movements of thought'.

Psalmody pervades the whole of Christian worship. In the *Rule of St Benedict* the founder of Western monasticism divided up the 150 psalms over the various services of the divine office so that the entire psalter would be recited in the space of one week. Psalmody is also at the heart of the music of the mass: the great majority of texts used for the propers are taken from the psalms. (*See also* **Music in the Mass of the Roman Rite**.)

With the coming of the Reformation, psalmody began to be practised by the laity in the various modern languages of Europe. Protestant metrical psalms* in rhyming verse were a feature of the life and worship of the sixteenth century, especially in France with the work of Clément Marot and Loys Bourgeois. In England the metrical psalter of Sternhold and Hopkins became standard after 1562. Choral psalmody became popular in England with the rise of parish choirs towards the end of the seventeenth century, and although it has suffered a decline in recent years, psalmody sung to Anglican chants is still to be heard, expertly rendered by specialist choirs, in cathedrals and in college chapels.

MARY BERRY

Psalm-Tones

The eight tones, or 'tunes', used in the singing of the psalms are related to each of the eight church modes* defined by mediaeval musical theory. A psalm-tone amounts to a neat little musical form made up of two phrases that balance each other, as can be seen in the following diagram:

PHRASE ONE

Intonation – recitation – mediant cadence

PHRASE TWO

more recitation and final cadence

The first half of each psalm verse corresponds to phrase one and the second half to phrase two. The intonation (two or three notes) leads to the reciting note – on the dominant of the mode – and it is this note which carries the bulk of the recitation, ending with the mediant, or half-way cadence. The second half usually starts immediately on the reciting note and ends with the final cadence. There may be quite a choice of final cadences, or 'differences', as they are called: Tone 1, for example, has ten differences. The choice of difference depends on the melody of the antiphon* – or short refrain – sung before and after the psalm.

One constant feature of psalmody is the considerable pause between phrase one and phrase two, but not between consecutive verses. The reason for this *pausa conveniens* is to allow the singers to meditate upon the meaning of the words of each verse half-way through, and since the Hebrew poetry of the psalms uses the device of parallelism this is a good place to think about what has just been sung and what is about to be sung: 'Praise him, sun and moon' – (pause) – 'praise him, all ye stars and light.' Another feature is that the intonation is only used for the first verse of a psalm, the others beginning straight away on the reciting note. However, in the case of the New Testament canticles* (*Benedictus*, *Magnificat* and *Nunc dimittis*)

every verse begins with the intonation, in order to give greater solemnity to the chant, and on major festivals a particularly elaborate version of the psalm-tone is used.

In addition to the eight psalm-tones corresponding to the eight modes several other tones are used in psalmody. One is the beautiful *Tonus Peregrinus* (the 'wandering' tone) which has two reciting notes, the second, after the mediant cadence, lying a second lower than the first. It is traditionally associated with Ps. 113 (114) *In exitu Israel* ('When Israel went out of Egypt'). Bach uses this tone, in its Lutheran form, at a high pitch on the oboes in the sixth verse of his Latin setting of the *Magnificat*. The other tones are used most effectively, with some variations such as the introduction of chromatic notes, in all but one of the five psalms of Monteverdi's *Vespers* of 1610. They exert a stabilizing influence, especially in the decorative florid passages in one part or another. Mozart makes effective quotations of the first tone on the oboes in his fine *Masonic Funeral March* (K477) for small orchestra.

Other special psalm-tones are the hauntingly beautiful *Tonus Irregularis* and the straightforward *Tonus In Directum*. These psalm-tones, as well as the usual eight, can be found in the *Antiphonale Monasticum* (Desclée 1934).

During the fifteenth and sixteenth centuries it was a favourite practice of composers to set alternate verses of the canticles of lauds, vespers and compline (*see* **Divine Office, The**) either for organ or for choral performance, in alternation with the other verses, which would be sung to the chant.

The codification of the psalm-tones as they appear in the *Antiphonale* today dates from about the eleventh century. The notable resemblance between the first psalm-tone and the *Tonus Peregrinus* and the tones of Jewish psalmody discloses a link with the practice of the synagogue.

MARY BERRY

Pulpit

In the early church it was customary for the bishop to preach the sermon from his cathedra * behind the altar. The early Christian ambo * looks like a pulpit but its main purpose was the reading of the gospel at the eucharist, and pulpits are essentially a mediaeval invention. Abbot Samson of Bury St Edmunds had one made in the late twelfth century so that he could preach to the people in English, and thirteenth century examples still exist in Italy, but none surviving in England is older than about 1400. They do not become frequent until c. 1450–1540 along with nave seating, although it is possible that British evidence has been distorted by the almost total destruction of the Friars' churches.

A few pulpits were made in England in the second half of the sixteenth century, but under Edward VI and Elizabeth I preachers had to be licensed, and it was not until a canon of James I in 1604 ordered that a pulpit should be placed in every parish church that they became standard pieces of church furniture.

In the seventeenth and eighteenth centuries it was common in England to have pulpit and reading desk combined in a single structure called a two-decker, or to incorporate the clerk's pew at the base to make a three-decker, with the reading desk in the middle and the pulpit proper as the top stage, generally surmounted by a tester or sounding-board. These sometimes stood in the centre of the nave at the east end; alternatively they were attached to one of the nave pillars, as their Baroque contemporaries were in Roman Catholic countries, or, in the case of an aisleless church, to the nave wall.

The standard Anglican position today is at one side of the east end of the nave. This became the fashion in Victorian times. At the same time it became fashionable in the Church of Scotland and the Nonconformist churches of England and Wales to make the pulpit the focal point of the interior, often placing it against the wall opposite the entrance. In these churches there is usually no separate reading desk, and unless there is holy communion the whole service is conducted from the pulpit.

G. W. O. Addleshaw and F. Etchells, *The Architectural Setting of Anglican Worship*, 1948; K. Lindley, *Chapels and Meeting Houses*, 1969; G. Randall, *Church Furnishing and Decoration in England and Wales*, 1980.

G. D. W. RANDALL

Purification

see **Mariological Feasts**

Purificator

A towel or napkin that is used to dry the chalice* and other vessels after the consumption of the remains of the consecrated elements at the eucharist when the ablutions* are taken. Another towel is also used for drying the hands of the celebrant* and this is termed the *lavabo** cloth. This cloth is somewhat larger than the purificator.

P. Dearmer, *The Linen Ornaments of the Church*, [2]1950; C. E. Pocknee (ed), *The Parson's Handbook*, 1965; The Warham Guild, *The Warham Guild Handbook*, rev ed 1963.

C. E. POCKNEE

Pyx

Also spelt pix. A receptacle used chiefly for housing the consecrated elements of bread, and sometimes wine, when reserved outside the time of the celebration of the liturgy. The custom is of very high antiquity, being mentioned by Justin Martyr (*Apol.* I. 65.) about AD 150. This reservation* was chiefly for the sick and those prevented from attending the Sunday eucharist. Also, it was the custom during the first three centuries to permit the faithful to take away from the Sunday eucharist portions of the consecrated bread in order to communicate themselves at home during the week. For this purpose, little boxes of wood, ivory or metal with a cord that could be suspended round the neck were in use. These were known as *arcae* or *arculae*; examples have been found on the breasts of the deceased buried in the Vatican catacombs during the second and third centuries. This custom led to the abuse of the *arcae* and their contents as a charm or talisman, so it was discontinued.

From the fourth century the reserved sacrament was kept in the church or its sacristy*. But not until the ninth century were precise regulations issued regarding the kind of receptacle to be used for this purpose. Pyxes or containers of ivory and precious metal as well as latten and brass were in use; not infrequently the metal ones were decorated with coloured enamels.

In the second part of the Middle Ages in the Latin West, with the development of the cultus of devotions to the reserved sacrament, pyxes displaying the skill of the silversmith and craftsman came into use. Such pyxes were mounted on a stem and foot (*see* Plate 46). A particular form of pyx that has excited antiquarian interest since the last century is that which came into use in England and France in the later Middle Ages, when the blessed sacrament was reserved in a vessel suspended by a chain over the high altar. Sometimes this pyx was contained in a steeple-like tower; in other instances it was suspended under a trumpet-shaped canopy of silk or fabric. A modern

Plate 46 Fourteenth-century Italian standing pyx, silver-gilt and enamel, Victoria and Albert Museum, London

revival of this custom is to be seen in Gloucester and Ely Cathedrals. This whole arrangement including the canopy is frequently referred to as a 'hanging pyx'. A particular form of metal pyx associated with this method of reservation was that made like a dove into which the consecrated hosts were placed by lifting a lid on the back of the 'dove'.

Since the revival of continuous reservation in the Church of England and the churches of the Anglican Communion in the nineteenth century, the use of a pyx has been revived. When a priest takes the holy communion reserved to a sick person it is usually in a circular silver pyx suspended round his neck by a cord. Another form of this receptacle is the so-called 'double-pyx' containing two sections, one for the element of bread, and the other for the consecrated wine.

W. H. Freestone, *The Sacrament Reserved*, 1917; A. A. King and C. E. Pocknee, *Eucharistic Reservation in the Western Church*, 1965; C. E. Pocknee, *The Christian Altar*, 1963.

C. E. POCKNEE

Quadragesima

see **Lent**

Quaker Worship

Ecumenical discussion recognizes the existence of three broad types of worship, often referred to as 'altar-centred', 'pulpit-centred' and 'waiting upon the Spirit'. Traditional Quaker worship, with its abandonment of prearranged form, ordained ministry, and sacraments, is then seen as the extreme example of this third type. Its true character is positively determined, however, by the full seriousness with which it witnesses to the reality behind the words 'Where two or three are gathered together in my name, there am I in the midst.' It is thus the central activity of a fellowship committed to the discerning and 'answering' of him who, as 'the light that enlightens every man, coming into the world', is a hidden presence in every situation and relationship. Such a group seeks to *offer*, in attentive and expectant waiting, its present experiences, needs, confessions, thanksgivings and intercessions. It *awaits* a word, expressed either 'inwardly' or in such spoken words as the Spirit may prompt in any person present. Such words may include prayer, exhortation, reflection upon experience, exposition of a biblical passage or theme. The keynote of Quaker worship is, therefore, not the quest for mystical absorption, nor preoccupation with individual meditation and private devotions. It is, rather, the profoundly simple intention, by a gathered group, of opening itself to the presence of Christ, to the implications of the discovery that Christ's presence in the Spirit requires no other mediation and is that by which isolation is overcome and communion is experienced.

Inseparable from this conception of worship is a no less profoundly simple conception of ministry. Worship is both nourished by ministry and issues in ministry. The form this ministry takes, whether in word or in action, will depend for each individual upon personal gifts, responsibilities and opportunities. But ministry is seen as a function, not a profession; for Quakers the difference between cleric and layman is irrelevant. All Christ's followers, men and women equally, are 'ordained' and, in the Spirit, have access to gifts and graces sufficient for their several needs.

This richly varied and fully shared ministry is directed towards the needs of the world, either indirectly, by the building up of the life of the worshipping community, or directly, through the rendering of service by the community corporately or by any member of it. As the members become sensitized in this corporate life, through worship and faithful caring for one another, they become painfully aware of areas of darkness and oppression, both in and among themselves and also in the world around them. These are seen as areas in which the strivings of the Spirit of God in human life are being ignored or withstood. In relation to them, individuals or groups may find themselves 'under concern' to bear witness and to accept obligations, so that liberation and true community may be more truly known and more widely shared.

The early Quaker attitude to the sacraments expressed the conviction that no external rite could effect spiritual change

and that clerical celebration was a limitation upon the 'priesthood of all believers'. Quakers regarded 'water baptism' as merely diverting attention from the reality of 'baptism in the Spirit'. They understood themselves to be obeying Christ's command 'Do this in remembrance of me' whenever, in everyday life, they took food and drink. They supported their convictions regarding worship and sacraments biblically and theologically by reference 1. to the 'New Covenant' whereby, with the coming of Christ, all ceremonial and 'typical' forms of worship were abrogated, and 2. to the 'offices of Christ' as prophet, priest and king, exercised in the gathered, worshipping group in such wise that silent, attentive and expectant waiting was the sole appropriate response. Their eucharist was inward: 'Behold, I stand at the door and knock; if any man open the door, I will come in and sup with him.'

The mode of worship so far described has continued, from the seventeenth century, to be practised in Britain, in overseas areas where Quaker groups have close links with Britain (e.g. Australia and New Zealand), on the continent of Europe, in Canada and in parts of the USA. In other parts of the USA, and in areas of Asia, Africa and Latin America influenced by Quaker evangelical missionary activity, a form of worship is practised similar to that of most Protestant 'Free Churches', and pastoral leadership is generally accepted. Rather less than half the total membership of the Society of Friends now worships in the traditional manner described above. The four World Conferences of Friends held since 1920 have made possible a growth of understanding among Friends of the psychological, theological and historical grounds of their diversities, and have encouraged mutual openness and appreciation as well as a desire to rediscover, in appropriate contemporary forms, the experience which gave birth, in seventeenth-century England, to the mode of worship here delineated.

Both for the Society of Friends and for the Christian church as a whole, this mode of worship today raises far-reaching questions. If it is not, as early Friends claimed, the *only* form of worship appropriate to the new covenant dispensation, what is it? Is it simply a mode which appeals to certain temperaments? Or is it an emphasis – even an exaggeration – justified so long as it is balanced or offset by other emphases? Or is it possible that it represents an essential ingredient or dimension of worship which, historically, found separate expression in conscious opposition to others? To express the matter otherwise, is it possible to think that, with other forms, it points beyond itself and them towards an understanding of the fullness of worship appropriate to today?

The Reports on Worship adopted by the World Faith and Order Conference (Montreal) 1963 and the British Faith and Order Conference (Nottingham) 1964, and the Fourth Assembly of the World Council of Churches (Uppsala) 1968, emphasized the need to go beyond all our inherited and traditional patterns of worship. They also recognized the obstacles posed for many of our contemporaries by the prescribed forms of ecclesiastical ritual, embodying traditional formulations of doctrine. They also deplored the gulf which appears to many to separate worship from responsible life in the world. Is it inconceivable that a mode of worship which minimizes ritual, requires no doctrinal affirmations but, instead, strongly requires the full and equal responsible participation of every worshipper, issuing directly in his service in and to the world, may have a contribution to make far greater than might be inferred from the fewness of those who, for more than three centuries, have practised it?

Robert Barclay, *An Apology for the True Christian Divinity . . .*, 1675, Propositions xi, xii, xiii; H. Brinton, *Creative Worship*, 1931; *Christian Faith and Practice in the Experience of the Society of Friends*, 1960, chs 3, 4, 5, 7; T. Canby Jones, 'Worship as Experienced', *Quaker Religious Thought*, 15, 2 (Winter 73–74), pp.17–40; George Fox, 'Concerning Silent Meetings', *Gospel Truth Demonstrated*, 1657, p.103; T. F. Green, *Preparation for Worship*, 1952; T. Edmund Harvey, *Silence and Worship: A Study in Quaker Experience*, 1923; L. V. Hodgkin, *Silent Worship, the Way of Wonder*, 1919; George Keith, *The Benefit, Advantage and Glory of Silent Meetings*, 1670; James Nayler, 'Concerning Worship', *Collected Works*, 1656, pp.272ff.; Isaac Penington, 'Concerning the Worship of the Living

God', *Works*, 1681, Part I, pp.350ff.; 'A Brief Account of the Ground of Our Worship', *Works*, Part II, pp.258ff.; 'A Few Words concerning the Worship which our God Hath Taught Us', *Works*, Part II, pp.374ff.; 'A Brief Account concerning Silent Meetings, the Nature, Use, Intent and Benefit of them', *Works*, Part II, pp.256ff.; D. V. Steere, *Where Words Come from*, 1955; John Woolman, *Journal and Essays* (1772), ed A. M. Gummere, 1922, pp.508ff.; John Woolman, 'On Silent Worship', *Works*, [2] 1775.

M. A. CREASEY

Quinquagesima

The name denotes the Sunday preceding Lent, being 50 days before Easter. Similar names became attached to the Sunday before that, Sexagesima, and before that, Septuagesima, the names meaning 'sixtieth' and 'seventieth' respectively, though they are clearly not these precise numbers of days before Easter. These three Sundays emerged as a preparatory cycle for Lent itself in the West from the middle of the fifth century onwards and were established at Rome before the end of the sixth century which, through the spread of the Roman rite, ensured their eventual acceptance throughout the West and, at the Reformation, into the Book of Common Prayer. As Septuagesima was the Sunday that thus came to mark the beginning of the approach to Easter, it became the custom to celebrate the doctrine of the beginning of things, namely creation, on this day, with appropriate lections.

The 'Gesimas' have been abolished in the modern Roman rite. The names have been abolished in the Church of England, though, following the Joint Liturgical Group calendar which it has largely adopted, it still has a nine Sunday pre-Easter period, naming these three Sundays prosaically as the ninth, eighth and seventh Sundays before Easter respectively, thus creating a numerical parallel with its arrangements for the period prior to Christmas.

R. F. BUXTON

Rastafarian Worship

Rastafarian worship has to be understood against the background of more than three hundred years of slavery, racism and colonial exploitation in Jamaica. It is a relatively new expression of the folk culture of the mass of ex-Africans who are struggling to survive the harsh reality of life and recover their human identity in a hostile environment. The movement came into being in the 1930s. When in November 1930 Ras Tafari was crowned as the Emperor of Ethiopia, Haile Selassie I, King of Kings, Lord of Lords and the conquering Lion of the Tribe of Judah, some people in the shanty towns of Kingston and other places remembered the words spoken by the great black leader Marcus Garvey in 1916, before he left Jamaica for his campaign among the black masses in the United States: 'Look to Africa, when a black king shall be crowned, for the day of deliverance is near.' On the streetcorners of Kingston preachers like Leonard Howell, Joseph Hibbert and H. Archibald Dunckley proclaimed that Ras Tafari Haile Selassie I of Ethiopia was the living God, and they found several passages of their King James Bible as proof of their faith, such as Ps.68, 31: 'Princes shall come out of Egypt, and Ethiopia shall stretch forth her hands unto God', or Rev. 2. 2–5: 'Weep not; behold, the lion of the Tribe of Judah, the root of David, hath prevailed to open the book, and to loose the seven seals thereof.' Although frequently harassed by the police, the movement grew steadily. It was, however, not before the 1970s that Rastafari became widely known outside Jamaica, thanks to the popularity of reggae-musicians Bob Marley, Peter Tosh and others who transmit their Rastafarian philosophy and life-style through their singing and dancing. Nowadays Rastafarian beliefs and rituals are found and practised all over the Caribbean, whereas those black Caribbeans that are oppressed by racism and unemployment in the United States and Western European countries find comfort and a sense of dignity in the acceptance of the Rastafarian faith.

The movement does not have generally accepted leaders, a headquarters, official regulations or teachings; and 'to attempt to understand Rastafari in terms of its institutions is to miss its very essence, which is fluid and personal rather than institutional' (The Catholic Commission for Racial Justice). It is difficult, therefore, to say

something definite about worship. Practices may differ from place to place, and from person to person. There are, however, four basic 'doctrines' that most Rastafarians subscribe to:

1. *Ras Tafari is the living God.* Although Jah – the Rastas' word for God, probably an abbreviation of Jehova or Jahweh – is in many ways similar to the God of the Christian tradition, he is seen as black. In Rastafarian worship the Bible holds a central place, but the scriptures need a careful reinterpretation because, originally written in Amharic (the official language of Ethiopia), they have been distorted by European translators. The Rastafarians maintain that the people of Israel were in fact a black nation, and that they themselves, in exile in Jamaica and dispersed, are a remnant of the Israelites, the true people of God. Jah Rastafari is the same as Jesus, whose divinity is not in any sense denied, and he is the *living* God, the God of life, not of death – Rastafarians reject the idea of a 'pie in the sky' life after death, and they avoid funerals. The Rastafarians were not shocked by the death of Haile Selassie, because, being a real messiah in the flesh until August 1975, his presence in the spiritual body since his death is with them in all they do.

2. *Ethiopia is the black man's home.* Ethiopia is the oldest independent country in Africa, a country that was never colonized. It is the land of freedom in the religious imagination of the Rastafarians, and in fact the proper name for Africa, the original Eden and, therefore, at the same time the promised land. It is understandable that the Rastafarians welcomed the establishment of the Ethiopian Orthodox Church in Jamaica in 1968. Although many participated and still participate in the liturgy and worship of this church (which also has branches in the Sudan, New York, Jerusalem, London and other places), the relationship has never been without tensions. The Ethiopian Orthodox Church holds Haile Selassie in respect as a God-serving Christian, but denies his divinity. On the other hand, many Rastafarians are disappointed with this church because they consider its beliefs and practices too Christian and too formal.

3. *Repatriation is the way of redemption for the black man. It has been foretold and will occur shortly.* When Haile Selassie visited Jamaica in 1966, he is supposed to have spoken about 'liberation before repatriation'. In earlier times Rastafarians in Jamaica were patiently waiting for their eventual return to Africa. Nowadays there is, according to Barrett, a strong tendency to be politically alert and involve themselves in all political enterprises aimed at liberating black people in Jamaica and abroad.

4. *The ways of the white man are evil, especially for the black.* To the Rastas the Western, white civilization is decadent and corrupt. This 'system', however, is doomed, because, according to Rev. 17, 'Babylon' must fall. Many reggae songs express the idea that, when these apocalyptic events take place, liberation from the suffering caused by injustice and deprivation will finally come.

The Rastafarians regularly hold meetings and spiritual gatherings. The most important convention is called *Nyabingi*, the first of which took place in March 1958. According to Barrett a typical monthly meeting often begins in the early evening and 'will last for the entire night with dancing, smoking, and eating. First the group recites Ps. 133: 'Behold, how good and how pleasant it is for brethren to dwell together in unity!', followed by the Rastafarian prayer and various scriptures and comments, and ends with the Rastafarian national anthem. Following this, the drummers and singers will participate for hours of jollification' (*The Rastafarians*, p.120f.). It should, however, be remembered that the Rastafarians worship Jah essentially through their way of life. In opposition to the world of Babylon, they try to stay close to nature and to honour in this way their creator. In creating their own language, in wearing 'dreadlocks' (uncombed and uncut hair), in eating I-tal (vital, total) food, unprocessed, unspoiled and unrefined, in smoking ganga (marijuana), the holy herb, Rastafarians perform their daily liturgy and worship. In this way they feel in accordance with the divine order of things, as documented in the ancient scriptures. In the same way the rhythm, drive and gestures of their music-making and dancing evoke the power and beauty of creation, and so songs and poems function as a celebration of life and a

denial of the power of injustice and oppression.

Leonard E. Barrett, *The Rastafarians*, 1977; Sebastian Clarke, *Jah Music*, 1980; Tracy Nicholas and Bill Sparrow, *Rastafari*, 1979; Ernest Cashmore, *Rastaman*, 1979; The Catholic Commission for Racial Justice, *Rastafarians in Jamaica and Britain*, January 1982.

THEO WITVLIET

Reader

Etymologically, reader is simply the English translation of 'lector'*, one of the minor orders of the ministry or, according to contemporary Roman Catholic usage, a 'lesser ministry'. In the Church of Scotland after the Reformation readers acted as assistants to parish ministers and in a number of cases were given full pastoral responsibility for a parish. They were authorized to *read* the prayers, the lessons from scripture and a homily and, after 1572, to perform baptisms and marriages. In the Church of Scotland at the present time readers are nominated by presbyteries and authorized to conduct services when there is no minister. In the Anglican Church lay men (and, more recently, lay women) have been licensed as lay readers since 1866. They may take services and preach and may be authorized to administer the chalice*.

P. HINCHLIFF

Reformed Worship

The origins of Reformed worship in the strictly Calvinistic sense are to be found in Strasbourg, where in St John's chapel below the high altar of the cathedral the first German mass, translated and modified by the ex-Dominican Diebold Schwarz, was celebrated in 1524. It was simply the Latin eucharist translated into plain homely German designed to express the new spirit, while retaining as far as possible the old familiar things. The ceremonial, e.g., was not appreciably altered – that is to say the action itself looked much the same as before. The words also were not much changed, except unobtrusively to remove from the canon* (the consecration prayer) phrases which seemed to confirm the Roman doctrine of the sacrifice of the mass as a repetition of what took place on Calvary. The really far-reaching change, however, was to say the whole service in a clear audible voice and in the vernacular* tongue. Low mass* had been the popular form of service for a considerable period before the Reformation, and this meant that the old service had been said in Latin and also inaudibly. Now, for the first time, the people both heard the words and understood them, while at one stroke the old secret prayers disappeared and the central rite stood clear of its mediaeval accretions. It was in fact very similar to the new liturgical revolution which has taken place in the Roman Catholic Church during the last few years, even in some respects perhaps less radical.

During the next five years the reforms were carried farther (and independently) in Strasbourg. German metrical psalms and hymns were introduced to enable the people to take an active part in the worship, and more than one observer remarked that the church was full of the people's song. The Apostles' Creed, as simpler, is offered as an alternative to the Nicene; the lectionaries are abandoned, and the epistle and gospel read in course and at greater length; sermons are preached at every service; and the ceremonial is much reduced. The ancient basilican posture of the celebrant, when he stood behind the holy table facing the people, replaces the eastward position (*see* **Posture** 1, 2) and the holy table itself, now no longer called the altar* is moved forward in the sanctuary* to be nearer to the people.

From 1530 onwards Bucer's influence became dominant and the reforms more radical. Choices were offered in the prayers, necessitating departure from the old text; each successive variant was more verbose and didactic. The responses of course had long ago disappeared from the people's usage, but now they were excised from the text. Sermons were very long, an hour or so in length, and the abandonment of the old lectionary which could have been profitably revised was a loss, as in fact reading the scriptures in course is unworkable for weekly worship. The eucharistic vestments now gave way to cassock and bands, black gown and scarf (or tippet), formerly the outdoor and preaching garments of the clergy (*see* **Vestments**). The *Orate fratres*, a

bidding to prayer where no prayer then existed, was expanded into a long didactic exhortation and fencing of the table; and such exhortations became a feature – in truth, a somewhat tedious feature – of every subsequent Reformed liturgy. A central and important reform was the restoration of weekly communion, to replace the yearly communion of the mediaeval church. This became a primary principle of nearly all the Reformers (Zwingli, e.g., was an exception), though it was not always successfully given effect to. In Strasbourg there were weekly celebrations in the cathedral and monthly celebrations in the parish churches. When holy communion was not celebrated, all except that immediately pertaining to communion was retained, the eucharist thus remained the norm of worship, and in the BCP later issued it was described as ante-communion. Communion was received standing. It will be seen that to give effect to such reforms as we have mentioned, service books became necessary for the people's use, and these were prepared and issued. Such books were unknown in the mediaeval church (there were rare exceptions); thus the people's prayer books were an invention of the Reformers, and were in use thereafter in every Reformed church, though abandoned by some in the seventeenth century.

This was the situation when Calvin came to Strasbourg late in 1538, exiled from Geneva because of differences with the magistracy. Bucer and other Reformers there welcomed him (after a while Bucer even found this somewhat reserved young man a charming wife) and gave him charge of the small congregation of French exiles in the city. The condition was that the same form of worship as used in the German churches be adopted and holy communion be celebrated once a month. This was very congenial to Calvin, and as he did not speak German he had prepared a Latin translation of the German service book, then cast it into French. He made minor changes, such as substituting a metrical decalogue (divided into two tables by a collect) for the *Kyries* and the *Gloria in excelsis*.

Persuaded upon urgent invitation of the magistrates to return to Geneva in 1541 he took this book with him for use there. By this time it included an order for holy baptism, directions for the ordination of ministers, and other occasional offices, and metrical psalms were gradually added to it as they became available. Entitled *La Forme de Prières*, it became the standard of Reformed worship among Calvinists everywhere. During Mary's reign it was translated into English, slightly revised, and used in the Congregation of Marian exiles in Geneva, of which such men as John Knox and Whittinghouse were ministers. Thus after Mary's death it was taken back to Britain to be used in Scotland and among many Puritans in England. In 1560 it became the official service book of the Church of Scotland, passing through over sixty editions between 1564 and 1638, variously known as the *Forme of Prayers*, the *Book of Common Order* and the *Psalm Book*, and later nicknamed Knox's Liturgy. In England it was generally known as the *Forme of Prayers*, 'the Waldgrave Liturgy', the 'Middleburg Liturgy', the 'Genevan Form', etc. The last editions known were printed in London in 1641, 1642 and 1644 for submission to Parliament and the Westminster Divines.

None, I think, would now hold the liturgical quality of this book or advocate it for present-day use. But it presented certain principles of enduring value, many of which have been forgotten by subsequent generations, including our own. For example, it presupposed the Lord's Supper* as the normative worship of the church, desired frequent communion, weekly to be preferred. Calvin declared infrequent communion to be 'an invention of the devil' and held that 'once a week at the very least the Lord's Supper should be celebrated in the Christian Congregation'. This he made clear upon his first visit to Geneva, fought for it all his life, and declared that 'our practice is defection' because his purpose was not achieved, 'owing to ignorance' and other conservative opposition. The Sunday worship, even if there was no communion, was always based upon the eucharist.

One may summarize the Calvinistic rite as follows. It contained no order for daily prayer, though daily services took place, chiefly of a didactic nature with prayers added; and family prayers were also encouraged in the homes at a later period. The Sunday service consisted of (in this order): scripture sentence, Ps. 124.8; confession of sins, with scriptural words of pardon or

absolution; the commandments sung in metre with Greek *Kyries* after each, the two tables divided by a collect for grace to keep God's law; a collect for illumination; scripture reading, and sermon; collection of alms; intercessions and Lord's Prayer (sometimes in a long paraphrase); Apostles' Creed in metre; metrical psalm; Aaronic blessing. In addition, as we learn from contemporary descriptions, one or two other metrical psalms were inserted at what were considered to be appropriate points. When holy communion was celebrated, the Lord's Prayer and blessing were omitted from the above and the prayer of consecration (*see* **Anaphora**) followed the creed and was completed by the Lord's Prayer. Then followed the words of institution, the fraction*, the celebrant's communion, and the delivery to the people who came forward to the holy table standing to receive in both kinds, during which a psalm was sung or the scriptures read. The service concluded with a brief post-communion thanksgiving, the *Nunc dimittis* in metre and the Aaronic blessing. Originally, Calvin's service was conducted from the communion table, with readings and sermon from the pulpit. Later, the whole service gravitated to the pulpit as any understanding of liturgical appropriateness disappeared, as it did also for a time in Anglican practice. The Christian year was followed widely in its main feasts, but not in detail.

See also **Books, Liturgical** 14; **Liturgies** 14.

Strasbourg liturgies; F. Hubert, *Die Strassburger liturgischen Ordnungen im Zeitalter der Reformation*, 1920; for genealogy of *Form of Prayers* and text in use in Scotland, *see* W. D. Maxwell, *Genevan Service Book*, 1931, reprinted 1965, and for English translations of two Strasbourgian liturgies, *see* W. D. Maxwell, *An Outline of Christian Worship*, 1936 (both of these books contain extensive additional bibliography); Calvin's liturgy will be found in Calvin's *Opera*; William Cowan has given in the papers of the Edinburgh Bibliographical Society (X, 1913) a *Bibliography of the Book of Common Order*, and a large number of Puritan liturgies of the period have been collected in Hall, *Reliquiae Liturgicae*, 1847, and *Fragmenta Liturgicae*, 1848. *See also* W. D. Maxwell, *The Book of Common Prayer and the Worship of the Non-Anglican Churches* (Dr Williams' Lecture, 1949).

WILLIAM D. MAXWELL

Remembrance Sunday

The cessation of hostilities in World War I took place at 11 a.m. on 11 November 1918. This came to be observed in participating countries annually at the same time on the same day, and was known as Armistice Day. Commemoration was observed at War Memorials, with the laying of wreaths and a two minutes' silence. In 1946, after World War II, the fallen of both wars were commemorated; and in some countries the observance was later transferred to a Sunday, e.g. in Britain to the Sunday nearest 11 November, and in Germany to the last Sunday but one before the end of the Church's year – roughly a week later; in America, however, it remains on 11 November, which is observed in many states as a legal holiday.

In all countries the commemoration is marked by national and civic ceremonies rather than by special church services. In England, however, the Archbishop of Canterbury consulted the leaders of other churches and of the British Legion in 1968; and as a result an ecumenical form of service was produced on the fiftieth anniversary of the first Armistice Day, which could be used either at a war memorial or in church. The commemoration primarily involves organizations such as the British Legion and the American War Veterans and their campaigns for the relief of ex-servicemen and their families. With the passage of time general interest in the actual observance of the day has tended to decline, and the two minutes' silence is by no means universally observed, although considerable sums of money are still collected for the service charities.

R. C. D. JASPER

Renewal of Baptismal Vows

see **Baptismal Vows, Renewal of**

Requiem Mass

A mass offered for the repose (*requiem*) of the dead. It is often a part of the burial* service and may also be celebrated on the anniversary of a death.

EDITOR

Reredos

Strictly speaking, a reredos is a decorated wall or screen rising from ground level behind an altar, while a retable stands on the back of the table or on a pedestal behind it, but in common use the term reredos is used for both (*see* Plate 2). It was usual in the Middle Ages for the central figure to be a crucifix, though towards the end of that period the custom of commissioning a painted altarpiece on canvas or panel led to a much wider variety of subject matter, and by this time a cross* or a crucifix normally stood on the altar. In Belgium, Germany, Italy and Spain in particular, altarpieces may be seen by some of the greatest artists of their day (*see* Plate 31). In some instances a fabric hanging of embroidery or tapestry was preferred to stone or wood, and this idea has recently been revived: there are well-known examples in Coventry Cathedral, by Graham Sutherland, and Chichester Cathedral, by John Piper, both of the 1960s.

In cathedrals and larger churches where there was a solid screen behind the high altar in the late Middle Ages, e.g. Winchester Cathedral, the panel immediately above the altar was treated like a reredos in a parish church with more detailed and refined carving (*see* **Screen**).

In the Baroque era in France, Italy, Southern Germany, Austria and Spain there was a great development of the reredos into a vast altarpiece with dramatic details, e.g. in the church of St Ignatius, Rome. But in England the altarpieces designed by Wren and Hawksmoor seldom attained such proportions, although rising well behind the altar since they often had panels on which the Lord's Prayer and the ten commandments were inscribed.

The current return to the westward position (*see* **Posture** 2) of the celebrant at the eucharist has made retables impractical in modern churches, and the practice of central altars, as in the Metropolitan Cathedral in Liverpool, England, implies the omission of reredos and retable alike.

C. E. Pocknee, *The Christian Altar*, 1963; G. Randall, *Church Furnishing and Decoration in England and Wales*, 1980.

G. D. W. RANDALL

Reservation

In the earliest description of the eucharist to come down to us, Justin Martyr (*c.* 155) tells how at the end of the Sunday celebration deacons took the eucharistic elements to those who were unable to be present (presumably including the sick). In the third century Tertullian, Hippolytus, Novatian and Cyprian all testify to the practice of taking the eucharist home from the Sunday liturgy to communicate oneself on weekdays when there was no liturgical assembly, and where no doubt it would be available for the use of the sick and the dying. The practice declined considerably after the fourth century as the eucharist came to be celebrated daily, at least in the cities, to meet the pastoral needs of an expanding urban community. But that it still survived into seventh-century England can be seen from the writings of Bede. It seems that the sacrament must have been reserved in both kinds, at least in some places, since the sick were often given communion by intinction*. The practice is not heard of in the West after the twelfth century.

Alongside domestic reservation, the sacrament was also reserved in churches for viaticum* (and at Rome for inclusion as *sancta* in the next celebration of the pope's mass). From the ninth century it became general. At first it had been in a simple box (*capsa*), then in a more elaborate pyx*, casket or 'propitiatory', usually kept in the sacristy. But in the early Middle Ages the place of reservation came closer to the altar. The Fourth Lateran Council (1215) required the sacrament to be kept in safe custody under lock and key, but did not specify a method. In England and France a hanging pyx (sometimes in the form of a dove) was often used; in Scotland, Scandinavia, Portugal and parts of Italy it was more often an aumbry* (wall-cupboard); in Germany and the Low Countries most commonly a sacrament-house (elaborate free-standing tower) (*see* Plate 47).

There is little evidence of any devotional cult of the eucharistic elements outside the liturgy before Carolingian times. But within the celebration gestures of reverence and adoration began to appear at the invitation to communion ('Holy things for holy people') from the fourth century in the East,

Plate 47 Sacrament house, St Pierre, Louvain, Belgium

also in the Gallican and Ambrosian rites in the West, and at the elevation which concluded the Canon at Rome (seventh century). The eucharistic controversies of the ninth century in the West, and the triumph of the realist school of interpretation, did not lead immediately to the extra-liturgical veneration of the elements, but did hasten a number of developments which indicated a new type of eucharistic piety and a shift of interest and emphasis from the dynamic to the static presence of Christ. Thus, alongside communion given directly into the mouth, unleavened bread, the progressive distancing of the laity from the chalice, the giving of communion after or outside mass, private masses and the intrusion of private devotions into the mass liturgy, we also find instances of consecrated hosts being sealed into altars in the manner of relics.

But it seems to have been in the communion of the sick that special signs of reverence to the reserved sacrament first appeared (*see* **Sick, Visitation of the**). In England, the tenth century *Regularis Concordia* describes a solemn procession to the sick with the reserved sacrament, and a century later Lanfranc's *Monastic Constitutions* prescribe incensations, genuflexions, and a perpetually burning lamp. The same two sources enable us to see the evolution of the traditional Palm Sunday procession into a solemn procession with the sacrament, and the gestures of reverence previously accorded to cult objects like the cross and the gospel-book are now transferred to the eucharistic elements. At the same time a comparable development took place all over Europe in the burial originally of a cross but now of the eucharistic host in the Easter sepulchre* on Good Friday to be solemnly brought forth on Easter morning. In all these trends, the sacrament could be seen less as something to be eaten and drunk, more as a cult object to be venerated for its own sake outside the context of the mass.

Further theological controversies in the eleventh and twelfth centuries about the nature of eucharistic change and the moment of consecration seem to have led directly to the custom of elevating the elements after the words of institution in the canon of the mass (first decreed by Eudes de Sully, Archbishop of Paris,

c. 1200?). From this developed in turn the devotion of exposition*.

Devotional 'visits' to the reserved sacrament seem to have originated in the priest's private salutation of the elements before communion (eleventh century), which the people subsequently adopted as a greeting of the Lord after the introduction of the new elevation (early thirteenth century), and was then extended to periods of adoration outside the liturgical celebration, probably by religious communities and contemplatives (thirteenth century, e.g. in England, the *Ancrene Riwle*).

After the Council of Trent (mid-sixteenth century), the sacrament was increasingly reserved in a fixed tabernacle* placed on the altar itself. This innovation has been attributed to the reforming Italian bishops Matteo Giberti (d. 1543) and especially St Charles Borromeo (d. 1584). The Roman rite of 1614 encouraged this development, but at least in major churches the altar in question would not have been the principal altar. It was only Baroque piety and architecture which finally installed the tabernacle at the centre of the principal altar and made it the pre-eminent visual focus of the whole building. (So much did the tabernacle become wedded to the altar that from the seventeenth century onwards even side-altars were each designed with an integral tabernacle even though few of them could ever have been used.)

In the recently revised Roman rite it is stressed that 'the primary and original reason for the reservation of the eucharist outside mass is the administration of viaticum. The secondary reasons are the giving of communion and adoration of the Lord present in the sacrament.' Because of the nature and dynamics of the eucharistic celebration, the sacrament should no longer be reserved on an altar where mass is celebrated but, if possible, in a chapel or area apart, suitable for private adoration and prayer. The tabernacle should be solid, fixed and opaque, and there should normally be only one in a church, covered by a veil or otherwise suitably decorated, and indicated by a lamp.

While communion may be given outside mass for good reasons and according to a new special rite, it should normally not be distributed from the tabernacle during mass. The Council of Trent had called for communion as the normal conclusion of the eucharistic sacrifice for all the faithful, and since the eighteenth century various popes, the Sacred Congregation of Rites, the Second Vatican Council and the revised liturgical books have all insisted that the congregation should receive elements consecrated during the same celebration, and not on some previous occasion. The more prevalent custom now is for members of the congregation to place their altar breads in a ciborium* as they enter the church, and for these to be brought up with the wine and the collection at the 'presentation of gifts' (formerly 'offertory'), and for only a small number of consecrated hosts to be kept in the tabernacle, strictly as a 'reserve' or 'float'. In this way the integral connection between the people's offerings and communion has finally been restored.

The one occasion in the year in the Roman rite when communion is universally and mandatorily given outside the celebration of mass is on Good Friday*, when the solemn afternoon liturgy concludes with a communion service with bread consecrated at the mass of the Lord's Supper the previous evening and reserved overnight at a separate 'altar of repose' where the faithful watched in prayer until midnight. This practice, formerly known as the 'mass of the presanctified' (*see* **Presanctified Mass**) is much more widespread in the Byzantine, Maronite and Syrian Catholic traditions. It originated probably in Antioch, and is best known in the Byzantine rite where during Lent the full eucharist is celebrated only on Saturdays and Sundays; on other days the reserved sacrament is brought in solemn procession to the altar during vespers and is distributed after veneration and after a portion has been mixed with a chalice of unconsecrated wine (*see* **Orthodox Worship**). But apart from the reverence shown to the reserved sacrament during this liturgy and during communion of the sick, the sacrament is otherwise kept without ceremony and inaccessible to the faithful in an annexe of the sanctuary, usually in the care of deacons. The marks of reverence which in the West are shown to the reserved sacrament tend rather to be addressed to the altar itself and to the icons. The Copts and Ethiopians generally do not practise reservation at all.

In the Church of England, reservation (in an aumbry) is fairly widely practised, but despite attempts in the 1928 prayer book it was nowhere acknowledged or provided for canonically or rubrically until the alternative *Services for the Sick*, 1980, and the *Lent, Holy Week, Easter* report of the Liturgical Commission, 1984. In *Services for the Sick*, besides the traditional celebration at the bedside, provision is made for what is termed 'communion by extension', whereby previously consecrated elements are taken to the sick 'as soon as it is conveniently possible' by priest, deacon or duly authorized person, and ministered to them with the customary formulae after a statement that the church 'has taken this bread and wine and given thanks according to the Lord's command. We now share together in the communion of his body and blood.' The proposed Holy Week services permit reservation of the sacrament from Maundy Thursday's celebration for communion on Good Friday, and direct that it 'be kept in a safe and seemly place'.

P. Browe, *Die Verehrung der Eucharistie*, 1933, 1967; W. Freestone, *The Sacrament Reserved*, 1917; A. A. King and C. E. Pocknee, *Eucharistic Reservation in the Western Church*, 1965; N. Mitchell, *Cult and Controversy: The Worship of the Eucharist outside Mass*, 1982; O. Nussbaum, *Die Aufbewahrung der Eucharistie*, 1979; Roman Ritual: *Worship of the Eucharist*, 1973.

C. J. WALSH

Responsorial Psalmody, Responsories

Both these terms involve the repetition of a word or a phrase by the congregation or the main body of singers. In responsorial psalmody the verses of a psalm are sung by a solo cantor in alternation with a brief response by the congregation. This form of psalmody differs from antiphonal psalmody (*see* **Antiphon**) of a later date and was adopted from the Jewish liturgy. In the simplest cases the refrain can be as short as 'Alleluia', or 'Amen'. A familiar example is Ps. 136, in which each verse ends with the refrain 'For his mercy endureth for ever'. Responsorial psalmody has come into its own once again since the introduction of the new vernacular liturgy permitted after the Second Vatican Council.

Responsories have a structure resembling rondo-form and this involves the repetition of a part or the whole of the chant after the lead has been given by the solo cantor. Short responsories are sung towards the end of the Day Hours (prime, terce, sext and none, vespers and compline: *see* **Canonical Hours**). The longer responsories are sung after each of the lessons in the nocturns of matins (vigils). They are highly florid chants of great beauty and antiquity. Some of the best-known responsories follow the lessons in the Holy Week* office of *Tenebrae**. Another well-known responsory is the *Libera me* from the Office of the Dead, which also used to be sung at the end of funerals, at the absolution. The first responsory for Advent Sunday takes the form of an elaborate dialogue with successive repetitions of sections of the chant, followed by a complete repetition of the whole.

Helmut Hucke, 'Responsorium', *Die Musik in Geschichte und Gegenwart*, vol. 11, 1963, cols. 313–325.

MARY BERRY

Retable

see **Reredos**

Revisions, Liturgical

A liturgy expresses in words and actions a Christian community's relationship to God and its dependence upon him. It will therefore have, in the words of Thomas à Kempis, two eyes – one which looks on eternity and one which looks on time. There is the eternal God in his unchanging majesty, and there is the constantly changing human world. The preface to the 1549 prayer book clearly recognized the need for liturgies to change; and in his preface to the Great Bible Cranmer had strong words of criticism for those not willing to accept it. The preface to 1662 also argued the case for liturgical change: side by side with the need to preserve established doctrine and laudable practice, there must also be change in the interests of devotion, clarity, intelligibility, and the needs of contemporary society.

Throughout the late seventeenth, the eighteenth and the nineteenth centuries a

succession of groups and individuals sought to revise the prayer book for a variety of reasons, but all without success. Some desired a revision on latitudinarian lines, in order to 'comprehend' within the established church many Dissenters: others, like the non-Jurors, wished to bring the prayer book closer to what they believed to be primitive liturgical patterns: others pleaded for more contemporary language; while others – particularly after the findings of the religious census of 1851, came to recognize that the church was facing a missionary situation, particularly in the new industrial areas, which the prayer book was inadequate to meet. In the second half of the nineteenth century, however, two parliamentary measures were passed which effected modest but useful improvements in the situation. The 1871 Lectionary Measure provided for the first time for the specific needs of Sunday congregations and also rejected the Cranmerian system of 'one lesson, one chapter', making lessons shorter and more intelligible. The Act of Uniformity Amendment Act of 1872 left the text of the prayer book unchanged but provided for its more flexible use, with a permissive shortening of the daily offices, freedom to use mattins, litany and holy communion separately, and provision for special services. Meanwhile, other parts of the Anglican Communion had begun to produce their own rites and prayer books. Scotland produced its own eucharistic liturgy in 1764 – a liturgy approximating more closely to 1549 than to 1662, although for other services it continued to use 1662. America followed suit in 1790 with a complete prayer book, containing elements of the Scottish 1764 rite and 1662: it was a conscious attempt to produce a 'contemporary' book, geared to the American situation. This was in fact preceded in 1784 by John Wesley's radical revision of 1662 for American Methodist congregations – *The Sunday Service of the Methodists in North America*. In the nineteenth century, following its disestablishment and separation from the Church of England, the Church of Ireland produced a very modest revision of the prayer book in 1879; while America produced a further revision in 1892 based on the principles of enrichment and flexibility.

The twentieth century opened with significant developments in this country. In 1906 the Report of the Royal Commission on Ecclesiastical Discipline recognized that 'the law of public worship in the Church of England is too narrow for the religious life of the present generation . . . In an age which has witnessed an extraordinary revival of spiritual life and activity, the church has had to work under regulations for a different condition of things, without that power of self-adjustment which is inherent in the conception of a living church.' It also claimed that the machinery for discipline had broken down, and rigid conformity to the rubrics of the prayer book was no longer possible. It therefore recommended that the Convocations should be asked to undertake 'such modifications in the existing law relating to the conduct of Divine Service (i.e. the rubrics*) as may secure the greater elasticity which a reasonable recognition of the comprehensiveness of the Church of England and of its present needs seems to demand'. It also recommended an amendment of the law so as to give wider scope for the exercise of a regulative authority, particularly in regard to additional and special services. So began the process of prayer book revision culminating in the proposed book of 1927–28. But what began as an exercise primarily involving rubrics, later developed into a full-scale revision of services. This development was due to a number of causes. 1. Successive Lambeth Conferences from 1867 onwards made it clear that liturgical revision had become an increasingly important issue throughout the Anglican Communion. The 1897 Conference, for example, had affirmed that no single prayer book could supply every possible need of worshippers in a variety of local circumstances: while the 1920 Conference not only laid down the general principles governing a revision of the prayer book, but also made specific proposals for the revision of the eucharist and daily office. A number of Anglican churches began work on revision before the First World War – Canada 1908, Ireland and Scotland 1909, and South Africa 1911. 2. What came to be known as the parish communion began to make its way as the principal Sunday service, pioneered by such people as Walter Frere, Charles Gore and John Wordsworth; and for this purpose the 1662 rite as it stood was clearly un-

satisfactory. 3. The unsatisfactoriness of the 1662 rite also became abundantly clear with the remarkable flowering of English liturgical scholarship in the early twentieth century. 4. Considerable dissatisfaction with the prayer book was voiced during the First World War. One of the reports emerging from the National Mission of Repentance and Hope in 1916 highlighted the decline in church attendance and the failure of the prayer book to meet the spiritual needs of many people – a criticism also voiced by many eminent army chaplains serving at the front. 5. With the passing of the Enabling Act of 1919, the National Assembly of the Church of England came into being: the laity now gained a more active voice in church affairs, and the church was given a bigger share in parliamentary legislative procedures.

In the late 1920s England, Scotland, Ireland, America, Canada, and South Africa all completed work on their new prayer books, and India followed suit in the early 1930s. Unfortunately the new English book twice failed to secure the necessary parliamentary approval in 1927 and 1928, thereby creating a crisis in church-state relations. The bishops refused to accept the defeat. They published the book and stated that they would not view its use as 'inconsistent with loyalty to the Church of England'. The Church of England therefore began what was in fact a period of unofficial 'experiment' which lasted until 1966. Two successive commissions on church-state relations sat, one under Lord Cecil in 1930 and another under Sir Walter Moberly in 1949, while a thorough revision of canon law took place between 1939 and 1947. From these activities emerged the machinery by which the Church of England was eventually given freedom by parliament to deal with liturgical revision. Under the Prayer Book (alternative and other services) Measure 1966 the church could experiment with services alternative to those in 1662 for a limited period of years with a view to their authorization; while under the Church of England (worship and doctrine) Measure 1974 it secured freedom from parliamentary control in matters of worship and doctrine, provided that the 1662 prayer book was also retained.

In the post-war years the entire Anglican Communion found itself part of a liturgical activity which involved all churches except the Eastern Orthodox Church. All were influenced in varying degrees by the Liturgical Movement*, and revision became increasingly an ecumenical exercise. Churches looked to the primitive church for their models, but at the same time sought to meet the needs of local or national communities. Thus, while the Lambeth Conference of 1948 still regarded 1662 as 'so strong a bond of unity throughout the whole Anglican Communion', the Lambeth Conference of 1958 no longer accepted this and quoted Article XXXIV as allowing and even enshrining the principle of national uses. After 1958 liturgical revision within the Anglican Communion reached a new level of intensity, undoubtedly encouraged by a number of factors. 1. The level of the 1958 Lambeth Conference itself, which set out more specifically than hitherto the guide-lines on revision. 2. The growing interest of Rome in liturgical revision, indicated by the promulgation of the Papal Encyclical *Mediator Dei* in 1947 – a notable precursor to the work of the Second Vatican Council at which the fruits of the Liturgical Movement may be said to have been garnered (*see* **Books, Liturgical** 3). 3. The work of the Faith and Order Movement on the Ministry and Sacraments, and in particular by its report on *Ways of Worship* in 1951. All this activity was admirably summed up by Professor Charles Davis in 1962: 'One of the results of the Liturgical Movement has been to bring Christians of different communions closer together, because the new understanding of the liturgy is overcoming various distorting prejudices and defective ideas which all the communions of the West have inherited from the Middle Ages and which explain, in part, their divisions. In the Roman Church (and this is, of course, true of other Churches too) the movement has been strongly pastoral in character, and it is the strongest force now working for the renewal of the Christian life among ordinary people.' A notable example of such ecumenical liturgy was the eucharistic rite of the United Church of South India, which first appeared in 1950. Its attempt to learn from primitive patterns and its inclusion of distinctive local Eastern

features created considerable interest, and it became a standard work of reference for churches undertaking liturgical revision. (*See* **Church of South India Worship**.)

In the 1960s and 1970s revision took place in a number of countries at two levels—by individual churches and by ecumenical groups. In the Church of England, for example, the Convocations and the Church Assembly, and later the General Synod, were very active, assisted by a Liturgical Commission, which prepared material for their consideration. Most of the services in the proposed book of 1928 were legally authorized for experimental use as Series 1 services in 1966: these were followed closely by the first set of new experimental services known as Series 2: then came a second set of new services in contemporary language known as Series 3. But from 1963 onwards a Joint Liturgical Group, representing all the main churches in England and Scotland, was also preparing material: and its work, as well as the work of the Church of England, ultimately found its way into the Alternative Service Book 1980. Similar co-operation between other churches in Britain and the Joint Liturgical Group took place in the production of their new service books; and it also occurred overseas, for example in America and Australia. But at the same time some revision was also taking place at an international as distinct from an ecumenical level. The International Consultation on English Texts came into being in 1969 to produce agreed texts of congregational elements – particularly the canticles and creeds (but unfortunately not the Lord's Prayer) – for the new service books of the major English-speaking churches throughout the world. Its work found general acceptance: and liturgical revision therefore transcended both national and denominational limits. Nevertheless dull uniformity was avoided. Within common structures, distinctive local and denominational needs were still met; and individual churches still made their own decisions on the structure and contents of their new rites.

The most interesting liturgy to emerge from this growing consensus has been the Lima eucharistic rite of the World Council of Churches, first used in January 1982. Containing elements from all the main liturgies, it represents the solid fruit of fifty years work and study by all the churches, for it includes contributions by traditions not represented in the World Council of Churches. It is summed up by Dr G. Wainwright: 'For the Churches to have come already so close together is, at the human level, a work of the biblical, liturgical and ecumenical movements, which have in some degree affected almost every church. Two guiding stars have been fixed on by the churches in their common search: they have attended carefully to the church of the New Testament and the early centuries, and they have tried to reckon with the social and cultural circumstances of our time . . . Christian authenticity requires that it be the *original gospel* which is celebrated in *today's world*.'

See also **Books, Liturgical**.

C. O. Buchanan, *Modern Anglican Liturgies 1958–1968*, 1968; *Further Anglican Liturgies 1968–1975*, 1975; G. J. Cuming, *A History of Anglican Liturgy*, 1982; M. Thurian, *Ecumenical Perspectives on Baptism, Eucharist and Ministry*, 1983; M. Thurian and G. Wainwright, *Baptism and Eucharist: Ecumenical Convergence in Celebration*, 1983; G. Wainwright, *Doxology*, 1980.

R. C. D. JASPER

Riddel, Ridle

From the French *rideau*, a riddel is a curtain hung to provide a setting for an altar. Curtains were indeed suspended between the columns of ciboria* from at least the fourth century onwards. In the Middle Ages a riddel was often draped on each side of an altar being attached to a metal rail projecting from the wall. Sometimes prickets for candles were placed at the ends of these rods (*see* Fig. 26). The curtains served a triple purpose: they restricted the draughts that were so plentiful in mediaeval buildings; they provided a frame for the altar and they demarcated what was regarded as the most holy place in the church. The adherents of the Gothic Revival believed that such an arrangement was the standard English custom and was therefore the 'correct' way to enshrine an altar throughout the country; consequently from *c.* 1900 many churches were refurnished to conform to this supposed ideal, irrespective of whether or not such a dis-

position really suited the architecture of a particular building. The curtains were suspended on bars between riddel posts which were often topped with candle holders or the figures of angels. The belief that there is one single 'correct' method of enshrining an altar is demonstrably erroneous.

EDITOR

Rite

A rite is a formal act constituting a religious observance; hence one refers to the sacrificial rites of the OT or to the eucharistic rite.

Rites are a universal phenomenon to be found in all the major religions. In origin

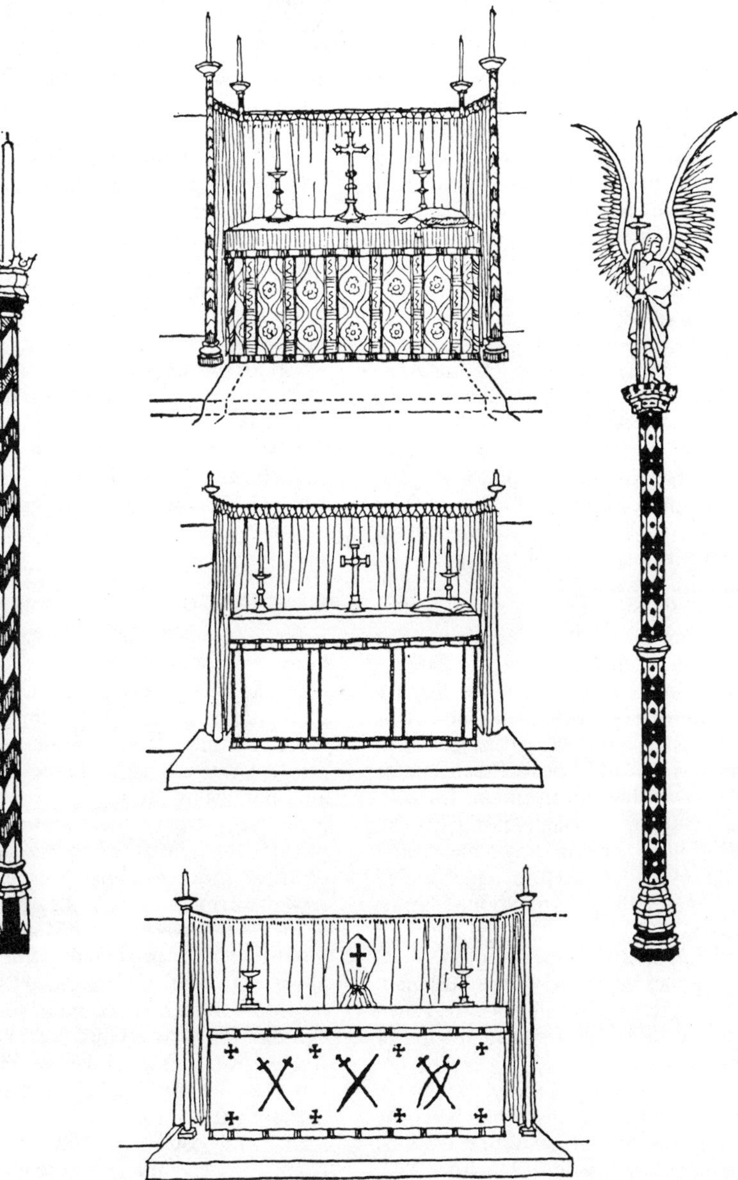

Fig. 26 Altars and riddel posts

they are based upon human actions, e.g. washing underlies baptism, and eating and drinking the Lord's Supper. Hence rites have a natural meaning which has been amplified and enriched by religious associations, without the new and additional meaning being forced arbitrarily upon the original. In other words, rites are not artificial constructions but rest in the natural order and in the sphere of human activities, and unless this connection is preserved they can easily degenerate into magic or intellectualism.

According to Cazeneuve, rites may belong to any one of three types: 1. Those whose object is to establish an intimate contact between humankind and the holy in order that humankind may control the divine power. These belong to the sphere of magic. 2. Those whose object is to isolate humankind from the holy which is regarded as dangerous. These are negative rites, relating to impurity, and are often connected with the idea of taboo. 3. Those whose object is to facilitate humankind's contact with the holy in such a way that it may be preserved and at the same time enter into a relationship with the source of its being.

The corollary of the last type, which is predominant within Christianity, is that rites are frequently regarded as being the work of the gods themselves, i.e. they are considered to have been instituted by the deity and their real agents are the god or gods working in and through them. So within Christianity, the eucharist is held to rest upon a command of Christ and he is the celebrant.

A similar but not identical typology is that of van Gennep. He also specifies three categories: 1. Rites of separation; 2. Rites of transition; 3. Rites of incorporation. Since they are all related to the idea of crossing a threshold (Latin *limen*), he also called them preliminal, liminal and postliminal. These three are usually designated rites of passage in which are to be included puberty rites, weddings and funerals as well as baptism and the eucharist.

At the basis of religious rites are four other concepts: 1. That of *symbolism*. All have a symbolic character whereby the natural object or action symbolizes the divine, e.g. the bread of the eucharist symbolizes Christ who is the bread of life. 2. That of *consecration*. Their main function is to enable the human situation, in its entirety or in certain aspects, to share in a principle which goes beyond it and is its basis. 3. That of *repetition*. The divine power is thereby represented as being brought into the present. Rites are therefore representative actions, not in Schleiermacher's sense of the symbolic representation of the content of faith but in the sense of a representation of the original sacred action. So in the eucharist it is believed that the sacrifice of Christ on the cross is made present through its effects. 4. That of *remembrance*. They are the media for preserving and transmitting the founded tradition of the community and at the same time for sharing experience. This shared experience through the rites sustains the common faith and framework of understanding whereby the community is perpetuated and renewed.

L. Bouyer, *Rite and Man*, ET 1963; J. Cazeneuve, *Les rites et la condition humaine*, 1958; A. van Gennep, *The Rites of Passage*, 1960.

EDITOR

Ritual

Ritual refers to the prescribed form of words which constitute an act of worship. It is therefore not identical with ceremonial* which relates to the actions. Nevertheless in common usage the two are treated as synonymous. Strictly speaking, however, ritual does not include such actions as processions* nor the sign of the cross (*see* **Gestures** 3) and instead refers to the collect, the Lord's Prayer, the preface, etc.

EDITOR

Rogation Days

These days of intercession or prayer were much more frequent in earlier days, some occurring annually and others being arranged to suit local needs. But only four such days have been universally kept for many centuries – April 25 and the three days preceding Ascension Day.

April 25 was chosen to replace with a Christian procession* the pagan Robigalia processions of that date. As this always occurred in the Easter season, it was not a fast day and the procession was festal, like the Easter week processions.

The other three days have their origin in France. In the fifth century, Mamertus introduced three days of fasting and prayer when disaster threatened Vienne and its neighbourhood. This practice spread to other places, but Rome did not adopt it for some while, since it thought fasting incompatible with Paschal joy. When it did adopt these rogation days, the fasting obligation was removed.

The feature of rogation days was the singing of the litanies* of the saints in procession. April 25 was known as the greater litanies and the other three days as the lesser. Conflicting reasons have been given to explain 'greater' and 'lesser'. The litanies used were the same on all four days.

In the recent revision of the Roman liturgy, Ember* and rogation days have been removed from the general calendar and their observance is now a matter of local arrangement.

The practice of processing round the parish before Ascension Day is still retained in some Anglican churches.

J. CONNELLY

Roman Catholic Worship

In the Catholic tradition, both of the East and the West, worship from the earliest days was sacramental, communal and always associated with the proclamation of God's word. It was sacramental in the sense that it was held that the liturgy mediated to the worshipping community the saving power of Christ's redeeming work effected in his passion, death and resurrection. This view implied that the church was 'sacrament' manifesting and making Christ present in the here and now, and in the older Roman tradition (*Gelasian Sacramentary*, 432, ed Mohlberg) the church is called the 'wonderful sacrament'. Worship was communal in the sense that its celebrants were the gathered people who, together with the clergy, celebrated the great events of salvation. The word was proclaimed by the reading of the scriptures, by preaching, but also by the very liturgical texts which unfolded the meaning of the sacramental celebration.

The liturgy, based on those foundations, remained in its main lines, even though from the fifth century onwards ceremonial became more elaborate. But as the sociological composition of the Christian people changed and with the entry of the northern races into the church, especially from the eighth century onwards, an increasing emphasis was laid on the sacramental *action*. Latin was not understood by the new races, and to compensate for the unintelligibility of the word, there was a further elaboration of ceremonial. At the same time, there is observable a tendency to the clericalization of the liturgy which became the preserve of a professional class. For reasons, it is true, of practical rather than theological significance, the cup was withdrawn from the laity (to avoid profanation) and the bread used became unleavened. The gap between the liturgy and the people was not closed by the proliferation of usages and observances of the later Middle Ages, though they did something to mitigate the rigours of a liturgy that had become remote. By the end of the Middle Ages liturgical 'pluralism' had become chaos and reform was necessary.

The reform initiated by the Council of Trent and carried out by the papacy aimed at uniformity, desired by many humanists and made possible by the printing press. The answer to the irreverence and chaos of the last phase of the Middle Ages was a corpus of rubrics that dictated every movement and word of the celebrant. Little enough attention was given to the people who were assumed to be devout onlookers and offerers in their secret hearts of the eucharistic sacrifice. Yet Catholic worship remained warm and devout, much assisted by the art and music of the Baroque era, and the murmured Latin mass with its periods of silence fitted the need of the devout whose spirituality had now become intensely individualistic. Moreover, what was lacking in liturgical worship was made up for by a great variety of popular devotions, expositions* of the blessed sacrament, the rosary*, processions*, the stations of the cross* and others. By the end of the nineteenth century, when most of the laity attended only a low mass*, Catholic worship had become inward-looking, almost cosy, a devotional exercise.

The way of reform was long, slow and painful. But with the coming of the Second Vatican Council (1962–65) a reform was initiated which, it is interesting to observe, takes sacramentality, communal celebration and the proclamation of God's word as the

foundations of its theology of the liturgy as laid out principally in the *Constitution on the Liturgy* of 1963. Here we find that the liturgy 'is the action of Christ the priest and of his body, the church' which is made manifest in a worship made up of 'signs that are perceptible to the senses'. This sacramental liturgy mediates to the worshipping community, and beyond it to the world, the saving power of the mystery of Christ which consists of his passion, death, resurrection and ascension. Through the celebration of the liturgy the church looks on to the *eschaton* and up to heaven and sees the earthly liturgy as the counterpart of the heavenly. The whole Christian people, by virtue of their participation in Christ's priesthood, celebrate the liturgy, 'all liturgical services are celebrations of the church', both people and clergy, and from it they derive as from its source the true Christian spirit. For the liturgy is the summit of the church's activity and the source of all its power, and through its celebration the Christian people are able to make their own the saving mystery of Jesus Christ.

But Christ is known by the word and the liturgy itself, which must be within the people's grasp, must be self-explanatory. Hence liturgical reform must make it possible for the people to share fully in liturgical services; they must always hear God's word for which better provision must be made. If this was to be achieved, it was necessary that the language of the liturgy should be changed from Latin to modern vernaculars*.

These principles have been applied to the whole range of Catholic worship, including not only the eucharist but all the other sacraments, the divine office and the organization of the liturgical year. The reformed liturgy has also affected the style of celebration – the eucharist is normally celebrated facing the people – and necessitated the reordering of old churches and the designing of new ones. In particular, the emphasis on the importance of the word is striking, so much so that one can say 'No celebration without proclamation'.

In addition, new liturgical forms are emerging and the uniformity that was characteristic of post-Tridentine worship is no longer insisted on (*Constitution*, 39, 40). Adaptation is built into the new services.

Popular devotions continue alongside the official liturgy and it is recommended that they should do so but, as the *Constitution* observes (13), they are to be harmonized with the liturgy. Already new forms have emerged (*see* **Bible Services**) and if Catholic worship retains much of the warmth of the past, it has already become markedly biblical. It has been observed that the *Constitution on the Liturgy* does not emphasize mission very strongly, but it must be taken with the other documents of Vatican II, notably with the *Constitution on the Church in the Modern World*, which decisively turned Catholic Christians away from an exclusive concern with their own affairs to their mission in the world.

See also **Books, Liturgical** 3; **Liturgies** 3.

J. D. Crichton, *The Church's Worship*, 1964; J. D. Crichton, H. E. Winstone and J. R. Ainslie (eds), *English Catholic Worship*, 1979; J. A. Jungmann, *The Mass of the Roman Rite*, 1961.

J. D. CRICHTON

Rosary

The name normally refers to a pious exercise which involves bodily, vocal and mental prayer (fingers, lips, minds). It combines repetition of familiar prayers in mantra fashion with meditation on selected mysteries of the faith. The prayers used are fifteen 'decades' (tens) of 'Hail Mary', each decade preceded by an 'Our Father' and concluded by a 'Glory be'. The fifteen 'mysteries', or topics of meditation, are grouped in series of five (which are usually prayed separately): the joyful mysteries (annunciation, visitation, nativity, presentation in the temple, finding in the temple), the sorrowful mysteries (agony in the garden, scourging, crowning with thorns, carrying of the cross, death on the cross), the glorious mysteries (resurrection, ascension, coming of the Holy Spirit, assumption of the Virgin Mary, coronation of the Virgin Mary and the glory of all the saints).

The origin of the devotion has long been popularly associated with St Dominic (d. 1221), whose order has certainly done most to propagate it, but the attribution is unsustainable. The origins are in fact very obscure, but seem to involve a gradual coalescence of Christological and Marian

devotions from the twelfth century onwards.

Illiterate laity and travellers cut off from the divine office were encouraged to resort to the 'poor man's psalter': the recitation of 150 *Pater nosters*, often in blocks of 50, as a substitute for the psalms. Strings of beads, known as 'paternosters', were used to count off these prayers. (Garlands or chaplets of prayers counted on beads go back at least to Roman times and are not confined to Christianity.) A slightly later development seems to have been the parallel practice of 'Our Lady's psalter': in twelfth and thirteenth century England we have examples from St Anselm of Canterbury and St Stephen Langton consisting of 150 quatrains beginning with the word *Ave* and applying to Mary a theme from each psalm in turn. Elsewhere it consisted of 150 'Hail Marys' (only the first half of the present formula) recited in blocks of 10 or 50, often with a genuflexion for each. St Louis, King of France, observed this devotion daily, and in 1440 the statutes of Eton College required the pupils to recite daily 'the complete psalter of the Blessed Virgin, consisting of *Credo*, 15 *Paters*, and 150 *Ave Marias*'.

The first clear evidence for the association of specific meditations with the recitation of the rosary comes from the fifteenth-century Carthusian, Dominic of Prussia, who added short scriptural verses to the 'Jesus' of each 'Hail Mary' (a tradition which persists to this day in the German use of the rosary). In the same century the Breton Dominican, Alain de la Roche (Alanus de Rupe) recommended that the three groups of fifty 'Hail Marys' be said in honour of the incarnation, passion and glorification of Christ respectively. Through the establishment of rosary confraternities (1475 onwards) and the diffusion of books with methods of praying the rosary, he did perhaps more than anyone to propagate and popularize the devotion.

The precise subjects of the fifteen mysteries that have come down to us seem to have been popularized in a series of woodcuts from German Dominican circles in the late fifteenth century. In the following century the present conclusion ('Holy Mary . . .') was added to the 'Hail Mary' (after St Bernardine of Siena?), and the 'Glory be to the Father' added after each decade. A bull of St Pius V in 1569 confirming the devotion, and the introduction of a feast of Our Lady of the Rosary into the Roman calendar in 1573, both helped to establish and standardize its use. It was subsequently encouraged by a succession of popes, and in his document *Marialis Cultus* of 1974, Paul VI endorsed it as a gospel prayer, deriving from and leading to the liturgy.

Paul VI, *Marialis Cultus*, ET = *To Honour Mary*, 1974; M. Ward, *The Splendour of the Rosary*, 1946.

C. J. WALSH

Rostrum

Rostrum means literally the beak of a bird, and by transference it comes to mean the beak-like prow of a ship. Then it was applied to the speaker's platform or tribune in the Roman forum because it was ornamented with the prows of ships taken from the people of Antium (the modern Anzio), in 338 BC. Hence the word has come to mean any platform from which public addresses or lectures are given.

English Nonconformist churches often have a rostrum in front of the pulpit. In larger buildings it is frequently big enough to accommodate the communion table* and chairs, and in Baptist churches it sometimes also serves as a cover for the baptistery*.

K. Lindley, *Chapels and Meeting Houses*, 1969.

C. E. POCKNEE/G. D. W. RANDALL

Rubrics

Rubrics are ceremonial directions for the conduct of a service, and are so-called because in mediaeval books they were written in red (Lat *ruber*) to distinguish them from the text of the services.

In the earliest liturgical books, few or no directions were given, simply the words to be used being provided. In time a special book, known as the *Ordinale*, was produced, being a directory for the arrangement of the altar service. Known also as the *Directorium* or *Pie*, this corresponded to the later rubrics which were included with the texts themselves.

Although at the present day rubrics are frequently not printed in red, the term is still used of the ceremonial directions.

On the so-called 'Black Rubric' *see* **Posture** 3.

EDITOR

Sacramentals

This term first appeared in the writings of theologians and canonists in the twelfth century, but that which it designates had existed long before. Since the NT contains little in the way of directions about how to administer the sacraments, it became the responsibility of the church to determine them. The triple immersion or affusion at baptism and the marking with the sign of the cross together with the kiss of peace at the eucharist (*see* **Gestures** 8) – these are sacramentals. They make explicit the meaning of the sacramental action although they are by no means indispensable to it. They can be used apart from sacraments, e.g. the blessing of palms or the consecration of a church* are sacramentals.

J. D. Crichton, 'Sacramentals', *NDCT*, p.515.

EDITOR

Sacred Heart

A form of devotion to the human and divine love of the incarnate Word expressed in the symbol of the physical heart of Jesus. Though the basic elements and themes of this devotion are indeed to be found in scripture and the fathers, as a devotion it can be traced back only to the more subjective piety of the Middle Ages, perhaps to the cult of the five wounds. St Bonaventure (d. 1274) and Julian of Norwich (d. 1413?) write of it, and in the visions of St Mechtilde and St Gertrude of Helfta at the close of the thirteenth century it achieves great depth and intensity. In the later Middle Ages it was sustained by the Carthusians and the *Devotio Moderna*. In the seventeenth century in France the Jesuits and the Visitandine sisters (following St Francis de Sales) propagated it as a popular devotion and campaigned for its recognition in the official liturgy. St John Eudes (d. 1680) elaborated the theology, but it was the visions of the Visitandine sister St Margaret Mary Alacoque at Paray-le-Monial (1673–75) which succeeded in popularizing the devotion and shaping its practices (particularly the emphasis on reparation for outrages against God's love, especially in the blessed sacrament). But despite its widespread popularity, it was not until 1765 that Rome authorized the mass and office of the feast, which was later extended to the whole church by Pius IX in 1856. It is observed in the Roman calendar as a solemnity on the Friday of the week following Corpus Christi*.

J. A. Jungmann, *Pastoral Liturgy*, 1962; K. Rahner, *Theological Investigations*, III, 1967.

C. J. WALSH

Sacristy

The room or repository in a church in which are kept the vestments, vessels, etc. Sacristies were introduced first in Syria, *c.* 400, as side chambers to the apse*. In the Middle Ages they were often placed on either side of, or behind, the high altar and were sometimes used for reservations*. In current usage, the term is virtually synonymous with vestry*.

EDITOR

Saints, Cult of the

Although the word saints (*hagioi*) was originally used of all Christians (e.g. Rom. 1.7) in the sense of those called to participate in the divine holiness, by AD 200 it was beginning to be restricted to those of heroic virtue who were believed to have entered directly into the company of heaven at death. Such men and women, manifestly filled with the power and holiness of God, were regarded as witnesses to the divine redemptive love in Christ, the supreme form of this testimony being the testimony of blood. Indeed the history of the cult of the saints begins with the veneration of the martyrs (Gk *martus* = witness) originating in the second century. In time the cult developed a variety of liturgical forms and practices.

1. *Commemoration*. In the year 155 Polycarp, Bishop of Smyrna, was brought to the stake, stabbed and his body burned. Then, according to a contemporary account, 'we did gather up his bones – more precious to us than jewels, and finer than pure gold – and we laid them to rest in a spot suitable for the purpose. There we shall assemble, as occasion allows, with glad rejoicings; and with the Lord's permission

we shall celebrate the birthday of his martyrdom. It will serve both as a commemoration of all who have triumphed before, and as a training and preparation for any whose crown may still be to come' (*Mart. Poly*. 18). Here then is the origin of saints' days* and of votive masses* in their honour, e.g. for the Virgin Mary.

From this annual commemoration, it was but a small step to making mention of leading saints at all celebrations of the eucharist. By AD 400 this regular memorial had become habitual in both East and West. Diptychs* found a place in Celtic, Gallican and Mozarabic liturgies and the third paragraph of the Roman canon* – *communicantes* – similarly lists saints by name 'by whose merits and prayers do you grant that in all things we may be defended by the help of your protection'.

The churches of the Reformation would in general accept no such practice. They were jealous of the uniqueness of Christ as sole mediator and intercessor and tended to identify Christocentrism, i.e. the focussing of prayer upon Christ, with Christomonism, i.e. concentration on Christ alone. So invocations in the liturgy were removed from the Anglican 1549 and 1552 BCPs, nor was the later influence of the Oxford Movement to make much difference, as evidenced by ASB (1980).

2. *Prayers*. Belief in the communion of saints and the conviction that unity in Christ is not broken by death encouraged the practice of asking the saints to intercede for those still living on earth. This is evident towards the end of the fourth century, e.g. in the commentary by Cyril or John of Jerusalem on the eucharist: 'Then we commemorate also those who have fallen asleep before us, first, patriarchs, prophets, apostles, martyrs, that at their prayers and intervention God would receive our petition' (*Catech. mystag*. v. 9). Centuries later Thomas Aquinas was to affirm the correctness of calling on the saints to pray for us (*Sum*. IIa. lxxxiii. 2). From the patristic period a litany* of the saints came into use. This consists of invocations of the three persons of the Trinity followed by requests to Mary and a whole series of saints to act as intercessors. The Reformers rejected such invocations, although at the present day within Anglicanism they are sometimes used in devotional exercises.

3. *Services*. To ask the saints to intercede is one thing, to address them as if they have the power to grant favours in their own right is something else. While the former was widespread in the early church, the latter became a feature of popular religion as time passed. Concerned to prevent any form of idolatry, the church authorities differentiated between *latreia*, honour to God alone, and *douleia* or service rendered to someone less than God. But the distinction was lost on many of the laity, and the ways in which they observed the cult of the saints was to earn the opprobrium of the Reformers. This cult combined several elements:

(*a*) *Offerings*. It was the custom of Monica, the mother of Augustine, to take meal-cakes, bread and wine 'to the shrines of the saints on their memorial days'. She was, however, forbidden on the grounds that 'they bore so close a resemblance to the superstitious rites which the pagans held in honour of the dead' (*Conf*. VI. 2). This condemnation had little effect in the long run. Shrines received an immense number of votive offerings and there may be classified into four groups: animate (e.g. animals or birds), inanimate (jewels, precious metals, crutches, artificial limbs), exuvial (diseased bones, stones ejected from the urinary system) and replicative (wax models of afflicted parts of the body). Those presenting these envisaged the saints as able to confer benefits (health, protection in trouble, etc.) and amenable to persuasion by gifts. Votive offerings have continued to be an element in the cult of the saints within the Roman Catholic Church, but they are also to be found in other Christian bodies, e.g. Greek Orthodox Christians, possibly influenced by the West, present their *tamata* (from *tasso*, I vow) both in anticipation of and in thanks for blessings (*see* Plate 48).

(*b*) *Pilgrimages and the veneration of relics*. Visits to shrines became very frequent in the Middle Ages. Pilgrimages* had a penitential aspect as well as culminating in devotions to the sacred relics. There is evidence of dancing (*see* **Dance, Liturgical**) at the shrines in the fourth and fifth centuries, and the remains were adored and kissed, as in Orthodox churches icons are saluted to this day. Candles* were a very frequent offering to light before pictures

Plate 48 Votive offerings *left* Byzantine, sixth-century, Syria *right* Twentieth-century, Greece

and images. The Jewish temple had of course its own seven-branched candlestick (Ex. 25.31ff.) and the seer of the Apocalypse beheld seven burning torches before the throne of God (Rev. 4.5). Moreover it was a pagan practice to put lights on tombs, where they were associated with the idea of apotheosis – suitable therefore for saints. Hence the Second Council of Nicaea (787) asserted the propriety of offering lights and incense* to the images of the saints. Most of these practices were repudiated as idolatrous at the Reformation but continued in the Roman Catholic and Orthodox churches.

4. *Dedications*. Another way of commemorating the saints is to dedicate churches to God in their honour, the particular named individual then becoming the patron saint of the building (*see also* **Dedication** 2). This custom arose from the erection of basilicas* over the tombs of martyrs and hence, for example, St Peter, Rome is so called because it stands above the place where the apostle is believed to have been buried. A patronal festival is then the annual commemoration of the patron saint of a church or cathedral.

P. Brown, *The Cult of the Saints*, 1981; H. Delehaye, *Les origines du culte des martyrs*, [2]1933; R. C. Finucane, *Miracles and Pilgrims*, 1977; A. E. Florakes, *Karafakia-Tamata sto Aigaio*, 1982; M. Perham, *The Communion of Saints*, AC No. 62, 1980; *Prayer and the Departed*, Report of the Archbishops' Commission on Christian Doctrine, 1971.

EDITOR

Saints' Days

'By celebrating the passage of the saints from earth to heaven the Church proclaims the Paschal mystery achieved in those who have suffered and been glorified with Christ; she proposes them to the faithful as examples drawing all to the Father through Christ, and through their merits she pleads for God's favours' (*Liturgical Constitution of Vatican II*, para. 104). In this paragraph the Council sums up the church's reasons for honouring the saints.

The early Christians, like their pagan neighbours, kept the anniversaries of their dead, especially of the martyrs; for the martyrs had conquered in and for Christ and were now with Christ. At these anniversary services the eucharist was celebrated as the completion of the vigil* service.

Lists of the earliest martyrs are practically non-existent, but later generations were exhorted to keep records of the date of the death of the martyrs, the *dies natalis*, and the place of their burial, *depositio*, for the anniversary celebrations depended on these facts. Such celebrations were naturally local at first, for they were held at the martyr's tomb, but some eventually became feast days for the whole church.

Some Christians acknowledged, *confessed*, Christ before men (cf. Matt. 10.32) not by death, but by imprisonment or exile. These were called confessors, *confessores* – a title which was eventually extended to men whose way of life was a confession of Christ and a proclamation of the Paschal mystery. The early confessors came to be honoured alongside the martyrs. Pope

Sylvester, Anthony the Hermit and Martin of Tours seem to have been the first to be so honoured in the West.

Beside the feasts of martyrs and confessors, the Christian calendar contains feasts of those intimately connected with the work of salvation – John the Baptist, Mary, Joseph and the apostles.

See also **All Saints**; **All Souls**; **Calendar**; **Ember Days**; **Fast Days**; **Ferial**; **Rogation Days**.

J. CONNELLY

Salvation Army Worship

In common with other churches the public worship of the Salvation Army always includes praise, prayer, a reading of scripture, together with an exposition of a selected Bible verse or portion. But, in addition, a recognized place is given to Christian testimony and, at the conclusion of a meeting, there is usually an invitation to Christian decision or dedication at what is known as the mercy seat or penitent-form.

Two further features should not be overlooked. One is that women take equal place with men in public worship, whether as leaders or as participants. The other is that the Salvation Army has no fixed liturgy, if by that is meant an order of service from which no deviation may be made. On the contrary, worship may commence with praise, or with prayer, or with a reading of scripture, and there is no pre-determined place for the biblical exhortation. The leader of the meeting is at liberty to alter the order of that meeting in any way which may be for the greater spiritual good of the congregation.

This freedom, however, is not the fortuitous by-product of any casual approach to public worship, but the expression of a considered endeavour to act upon the principle that 'God is Spirit, and those who worship him must worship him in spirit and in truth' (John 4.24, NEB). The fact that there is no set liturgy upon which to lean requires everyone in the congregation to make a personal effort to contribute to the worship of the whole. Yet this, far from giving rise to spiritual tenseness and overstrain frequently results in that joy which is one of the first fruits of the Spirit and in expressing that liberty wherewith the children of God are set free.

Were this not made clear, it might be supposed that the absence of a set structure of worship might lead to a formless informality which, at its worst, could degenerate into a chaos which would defeat the very purpose of worship. But this is averted because, in the first place, Salvationists recognize – in the memorable phrase of van Unnik, quoted by C. F. D. Moule – that worship must always be 'within the magnetic field of the Holy Spirit'. As the Spirit's office is to glorify Christ, the worship which he guides will exalt that Christ as Saviour and Lord of men. Thus no contribution, whether of testimony or of prayer, becomes a private exercise in egoism, and the desire of the preacher is ever to speak 'in demonstration of the Spirit'.

In the second place, the congregation is not passive but active, and this seems to be in harmony with NT practice (I Cor. 14.26). In Salvationist parlance, one will have a prayer to offer, another a word of witness to give, another a 'Hallelujah' or an 'Amen' to utter – yet all will contribute to the edifying of the church. For the reality of Christian worship depends not on the use, or the refusal to use, a formal liturgy, but on the presence of the Holy Spirit.

Music and song play an integral part in the worship of Salvationists. Here again their approach is truly catholic, for their songbook, which draws upon verses which have come down from the mediaeval church as well as the classic hymns of the Reformation, is undergirded by the two Wesleys, Watts and Doddridge, and does not pass by the Tractarians Faber and Newman. In addition, there is a substantial amount of original Salvationist material, some of which could well find a place in other hymn books.

In like manner, the Salvation Army band can draw upon a Bach chorale, or a composition by one of the many gifted Salvationist musicians, to deepen the spirit of worship in a meeting. For such a contribution is not regarded as a programme item which might be applauded if decorum or convention allowed. But, as Walford Davies and Harvey Grace used to insist, there are moments when musical utterance becomes the highest expression of public worship. (*See also* **Music as Worship**)

Finally, it must be added that while worship, directed to the glory of God, is a worthy end in itself, that end is nullified if

public worship does not strengthen the worshipper's public witness. Divine service does not end when the benediction is pronounced; it has only begun. The uniform worn by Salvationists at their meetings – both in and out of doors – is their way of identifying themselves as soldiers of Jesus Christ. They seek the holy place on Sundays so that, by the renewal of grace, they may be more effective Christian soldiers on weekdays.

In the thought and practice of the Salvationist, worship and witness can never be divided – save to the impoverishment of both. As has been well said: 'What we become in the presence of God, that we can be all day long.'

The Handbook of Doctrine, 1969; *The Year Book of the Salvation Army*; B. Boon, *Play the Music, Play*, 1966; *Sing the Happy Song*, 1978.

FREDERICK COUTTS

Sanctification of Time, The

Our appreciation of time is the product of human experience. We perceive it as flowing in one direction only, 'the arrow of time', and the nature of the universe we live in is that we can relate time to observable physical phenomena in such a way as to provide ourselves with a quantitative measure of it by which to relate all the events of our lives and the history of our civilization, and all the rich variety of human cultures, past and present. Though not always the case on a cosmic or sub-atomic level, at a terrestial and human level time is linear and constant in its passage, an essential component in the framework of all human activity, individual and corporate.

If God, therefore, is to involve himself with humanity in a way that is specific, historic and identifiable, then he must do it at a particular point in time, and this is precisely one of the facets of the doctrine of the incarnation, that the birth, life, death and resurrection of Jesus of Nazareth occurred at a specific time in human history. This point is in no way vitiated by the fact that we cannot now put a precise date to these events in terms of our modern calendrical chronology, though we can locate them to within a very few years. The same observations are true about the central event of the Old Testament, the Exodus, even if its actual date can be determined with far less precision.

Christian liturgical celebration, like Jewish celebration of the Passover before it, is therefore celebration of events that happened in time, and has a triple relationship to those times. It celebrates them as they happened in history; it makes available the spiritual power of these past events in the celebration in the present and, because of the eschatological doctrine of the ultimate consumation of all things in Christ, the celebration is seen as an anticipation of that consumation and as a pointer towards it. The early Christian acclamation *Maranatha* – 'Our Lord, Come' – points to this.

At different times and places, different individuals and groups have put more stress on one aspect or another of this triple relationship. Dom Gregory Dix (in chapter 11 of *The Shape of the Liturgy*, 1945) argued with his customary force that the predominant note of pre-Nicene celebration was eschatological expectation, and that only after the peace of the church did it settle down to a much more historically minded 'this worldly' celebration of its redemption as it had happened in Christ Jesus. He accounted for the pre-Nicene calendrical simplicity and the post-Nicene tendency to historicization and elaboration in this way. More recent research has shown that this theory cannot be sustained in detail, and that all three outlooks were present in both pre- and post-Nicene worship. Nevertheless there must have been a change in the psychology of worship between the period when Christians were an illegal and persecuted sect, being saved out of a world that had rejected them into the church, a foretaste of the heavenly bliss that awaited them and into which they could be catapulted through martyrdom at any time, and when they were the approved religion of the empire, when the stress was on the making Christian of the order of this world. The tension between sanctification for the world to come and sanctification in this world, so that through the church the world might be sanctified, has always inevitably been there, within and between Christian groups, and certainly no more so than in the twentieth century.

In origin God sanctified time by being incarnate in the historical process; all liturgy, therefore, being a memorial of the

incarnation, continues the sanctification of time, the potential making holy of all temporal processes.

But just as the incarnation makes all time holy, by a specific focussing of the holy at a particular point in time liturgy makes the whole of a Christian's life potentially holy, and that of the church, by setting aside certain times for itself. As a matter of history, the pre-Nicene foci for this were the Sunday eucharist and the annual Pasch, and the whole of the development and evolution of the Christian calendar* over the centuries can be seen as a continuation and elaboration of this process. The variety of events celebrated during the church's year, with its rhythm of feast and fast, ensures that adequate attention is given to all aspects of the Christian mystery in a balanced way.

Likewise the evolution of the combination of the times of private prayer and the public non-eucharistic worship of the church of the early centuries into the elaborate pattern of daily worship of monastic communities is a way of sanctifying the whole day by prayer at particular times during it (*see* **Canonical Hours**). And while there is a considerable contrast between the length and complexity of formal monastic prayer and the simplest lay observance, there is no fundamental difference in purpose between them.

All Christian devotional life, be it monastic prayer, the daily office of the secular clergy (the appropriateness of the essentially monastic pattern of this can be questioned) or any rule of life concerning corporate worship and private prayer, has the same aim, making holy the passage of time that life itself may be made holy.

P. F. Bradshaw, *Daily Prayer in the Early Church*, 1981; J. D. Crichton, *Christian Celebration: The Prayer of the Church*; 1976; D. Cutts and H. Miller, *Whose Office? Daily Prayer for the People of God*, 1982; Bernard Lovell, *In the Centre of Immensities*, 1979; G. Wainwright, *Eucharist and Eschatology*, 1971.

See also under **Calendar**.

R. F. BUXTON

Sanctuary

In relation to religious architecture, the term sanctuary may be applied in three different ways: 1. Originally it designated that part of a church which was reserved for the clergy, which was often fenced off by chancels* or balustrades. 2. It may also be used of the limited area immediately around an altar*, often demarcated by an altar-rail*. These two uses can lead to confusion, because while according to the first the term describes the whole of an area, according to the second it refers to a subdivision of the whole. 3. Occasionally it is employed of the church building as a whole.

EDITOR

Sanctus

An anthem which in most eucharistic liturgies forms part of the thanksgiving with which the eucharistic prayer or anaphora* commences.

W. JARDINE GRISBROOKE

see also **Music in the Mass of the Roman Rite; Ordinary.**

School Worship (England and Wales)

Under the 1944 Education Act all county schools in England and Wales, both voluntary and fully maintained, are required to begin each school day with an act of worship. Section 25.1 of the Act reads: 'Subject to the provisions of this section, the school day in every county school and in every voluntary school shall begin with collective worship on the part of all pupils in attendance at the school, and the arrangements made therefore shall provide for a single act of worship attended by all such pupils unless, in the opinion of the local education authority or, in the case of a voluntary school, of the managers or governors thereof, the school premises are such as to make it impracticable to assemble them for this purpose.' Section 25.4 provides for pupils to be withdrawn from school worship at the request of their parents and section 26.1 requires that the collective worship 'shall not, in any county school, be distinctive of any particular religious denomination'.

Before 1870, when the Forster Education Act created the School Boards, almost all schools in England and Wales were church property. It was normal to begin and end each school day with what were generally called 'religious observances', and from 1870 to 1944 the Board schools or (as they became in 1902) the Local Education Authority schools continued this practice. This took place, however, under local regulations and

not under Act of Parliament. It must not be thought that the 1944 Act led to an increase in the numbers of schools holding a daily act of worship. This, as we have seen, was all but universal before 1944. Rather, the Act was seen as giving support and confirmation to something which the schools were already doing. One must also remember that the 1944 Act required the LEAs to give attention to the spiritual needs of pupils, and the daily act of worship was intended to be part of that provision.

Religious observances in the schools of the nineteenth century usually consisted of Bible readings, hymns and prayers, often taken from prescribed collections, and in the years following the First World War the expressions 'school worship' and 'school assembly' became more prevalent. Many of the agreed syllabuses from the 1920s included short articles on the conduct of school worship and this practice, although not required by law, has continued to the present day. During the 1930s special collections of spiritual and devotional readings for use in school assembly proliferated, together with numerous hymn books and prayer books for the use of the schools. This literature continues to flourish into the 1980s and a complete bibliography would list many hundreds of titles.

With the increasing secularization and pluralism of British society in the 1950s and 1960s, school worship entered a period of strain. As both staff and pupils became more varied in religious and secular outlook it became increasingly difficult to think of schools as Christian communities, and the assumption of religious unanimity which seemed to be required by a collective act of worship on the part of all pupils (not 'on behalf of') became increasingly questionable. Although the number of pupils withdrawn by their parents under section 25.1 remained small, schools became increasingly uneasy about the issue. The rise during the 1960s and 1970s of a new philosophy of education which emphasized the autonomy of the pupil and the objectivity of the teacher led to more questions, since it became increasingly difficult to defend school worship against the charge of indoctrination. The changes in classroom religious education during this period were of great significance. The subject was no longer thought of as Christian nurture but as providing for an understanding of the religions of humanity such as would enable pupils not only to deal intelligently with religious questions in contemporary society but also to become more reflective and independent in their own thinking and feeling about religion. A separation gradually appeared between classroom religious education and the daily act of worship, since the classroom work did not make assumptions about previous commitment but the collective act of worship appeared to rest upon just such an assumption. The widening of the religious education syllabuses during the 1970s so as to include not only world religions but (as was frequently the case) the secular alternatives to religion created further difficulties of compatibility between religious education departments and the school assemblies for which they were traditionally responsible. The increased size and complexity of secondary schools has meant that fewer and fewer schools are able to accommodate pupils in a hall suitable for a daily assembly. Some enquiries suggest that only about 10% of secondary schools have this facility.

As a result of these various pressures the pattern of school assembly, particularly in secondary schools, is extremely diverse. Assemblies take place in year groups, house groups, in upper and lower school and on various sites, so that a religious education department may find itself organizing not merely one but up to 15 or 20 assemblies weekly. On the other hand, in many schools assemblies are no longer held every day, and even where some kind of assembly is held every day, an individual pupil will perhaps attend only two or three times a week rather than the five times anticipated by the Act. Moreover, the content of school assemblies continues to become more diverse. The Southampton enquiry indicated that even in primary schools only 61% of schools always use prayers in their assemblies and in the secondary sector this fell to 28%. On the other hand, the Southampton enquiry also revealed that only in 4% of the schools was prayer never used. The Southampton enquiry showed that about one fifth of all the schools could not be described as holding acts of collective worship. The Francis survey of Gloucestershire primary schools showed that less than half the schools would describe their assemblies as being either implicitly or ex-

plicitly Christian. Only one quarter of the Gloucestershire county primary schools meet for school assembly every day, one third of the Anglican controlled primary schools and even in the case of the Anglican aided primary schools the number does still not rise above half. A striking feature of the Gloucestershire survey was that primary pupils are almost as likely to encounter an explicitly Christian assembly in the county schools as in the Anglican voluntary or aided schools. Because of a more denominationally controlled admission policy, Catholic schools generally retain explicit Christian acts of worship during assemblies, whereas in the Anglican aided and controlled schools the increasing numbers, especially in the large cities, with a majority of pupils from religious traditions other than Christian, school assemblies are becoming increasingly problematic. But even in Gloucestershire, the Francis survey showed that only 22% of pupils in Anglican aided primary schools will hear the Bible read in assembly as often as twice a week.

While in many schools the act of worship has either become purely formal and stagnant, headteachers continuing with the traditional format in the absence of clear guidance about alternatives, and in others the most frequent assembly consists of nothing more than a moralizing talk from a senior member of staff together with administrative notices, in a minority of schools teachers with courage and vision are creating assemblies in which educational, social and spiritual questions are catching the interest and winning the participation of both staff and pupils.

It seems likely that the focus of interest in worship has shifted from the assembly to the religious education syllabus. Although, as has been said, religious education lessons no longer assume or seek to create religious commitment, it is probably true to say that the study of explicit worship is more widespread in such classes than it has ever been. The study of baptism and of holy communion, visits to places of worship and projects on types of spirituality including prayer, pilgrimage and sacrifice, are widespread today in both primary and secondary schools. The fact that this work is frequently on a multi-faith basis increases its relevance for the spiritual education of pupils. Although it cannot be said that pupils are being encouraged actually to worship, except by imagination and empathy, the importance of this trend in religious education classroom practice should not be underestimated.

It is not easy to predict the future of the school assembly in England and Wales. While no political party at present is proposing changes to the legislation, alternative structures are being widely discussed within the profession. A 1984 report of the National Association of Head Teachers recommends that new legislation should simply require that pupils be assembled together 'at least once a week' and that 'it shall be the responsibility of the governors in consultation with the head of each school to determine the nature and frequency of acts of worship'. It is also often suggested that greater flexibility could be introduced without substantially changing the existing legislation by permitting schools to hold assemblies at times other than at the beginning of each school day, and by no longer requiring that an assembly should be held every day. It is also possible that greater flexibility could be introduced by requiring schools to assemble for the celebration and the sharing of values, beliefs and commitments, the detailed arrangements being left to the discretion of the headteacher and staff. The spirituality of education as a process, and the spirituality of children and young people, which should be developed through education, must be interpreted as being something wider than worship and wider, indeed, than religion itself. School worship seems likely to fall into further uncertainty and decay unless it can be reinterpreted along some such more general humanitarian lines, thus creating assemblies which will preserve the community life of schools while affirming the value of a spiritual commitment on the part of pupils. Such assemblies would be consistent with a Christian philosophy of education, although certainly not its unique and sole possession.

L. J. Francis, *Assessing the Partnership 1944–84, an Interim Report on Religious Education, Assemblies and Church Primary Schools in Gloucestershire* (Culham College Institute Occasional Paper No. 5), 1984; W. A. Gent, *Living Centre, Assembly in the Secondary School*, 1984; 'Resources for the

Arterial Assembly – A Review Article', *British Journal of Religious Education*, 6, 2, 1984, pp.98–102; J. M. Hull, *School Worship: An Obituary*, 1975; *Studies in Religion and Education*, 1984, pp.3–24; National Association of Head Teachers, *Report to National Conference 1984 of the Religious Education and Assemblies Working Party*, 1984; P. C. Souper and W. K. Kay, *The School Assembly Debate 1942–1982*, University of Southampton, 1982; *The School Assembly in Hampshire, Report of a Pilot Study*, University of Southampton 1982; *Worship in the Independent Day School*, University of Southampton 1983.

JOHN M. HULL

Screen

This article deals only with screens in Western Christendom. For the screen in the Eastern Orthodox Church, *see* **Iconostasis**.

1. There were screens in the Roman and other basilicas*, which separate the altar* from the nave*. These screens were constructed of stone and had carved or decorated panels rising from the floor about four feet in height. Above this were columns of marble or porphyry which supported an architrave or beam from which votive lamps were sometimes suspended. Thus the altar was visible through the columns of the screen. On the nave side immediately outside the screen were the singers or the *schola cantorum*. Many of these screens were pulled down in the Baroque era.

2. The chancel* screen in the English parish church developed in the Middle Ages from the narrow opening in the wall that separated the nave and the altar. By the fifteenth century, the English parish church had developed in style, and in the large parish churches there was frequently a wooden screen both carved and decorated with colour of great beauty. This screen extended not only across the main chancel but also across the aisles* thus forming chapels for lesser altars, e.g. the one in Southwold, Suffolk. Where this was the case there were lesser *Parclose* screens, separating the side chapels from the high altar as we can see at Southwold.

Above the chancel screen there was a loft with parapets and above this a beam, the rood beam (OE ród = cross), upon which were tenoned the crucifix with the figures of the Blessed Virgin Mary and St John. Hence the old term for this screen was rood screen. Unlike the Roman basilica, such churches usually accommodated the choir inside the screen in proximity to the altar.

3. In cathedrals and the larger conventional churches there was a solid stone screen known as the *pulpitum* with an opening in the centre, which filled one bay of the arcade west of the choir. On the nave-side there were usually lesser altars on either side of the opening. The loft on the top of the pulpitum usually supported the pipe organ, as we can still see at the cathedral church at Norwich, while on occasions singers used the loft. Also on festivals the gospel was sung from this loft.

4. In the larger churches where there was the body of a notable saint, e.g. St Albans Cathedral, England, from the end of the fourteenth century, the increasing number of pilgrims coming to pray at the shrine of the saint necessitated separating the shrine by a solid screen from the high altar as we can still see at Westminster Abbey and Winchester Cathedral. On the west side the screen rose above the high altar and this side was usually decorated with tabernacle-work with statues of the saints. A canopy was projected out from the screen over the altar and a hanging pyx* was suspended from this containing the reserved sacrament.

In the seventeenth and eighteenth centuries it was sometimes the custom to place wrought-iron gates across the chancel entrance instead of a screen.

See also **Reredos**.

F. E. Howard and F. H. Crossley, *English Church Woodwork*, [2]1927; A. A. King and C. E. Pocknee, *Eucharistic Reservation in the Western Church*, 1965; C. E. Pocknee, *The Christian Altar*, 1963; G. D. W. Randall, *Church Furnishing and Decoration in England and Wales*; 1980; A. Vallance, *English Church Screens*, 1936; *Greater English Church Screens*, 1947.

C. E. POCKNEE/G. D. W. RANDALL

Secret

see **Silent Prayer; *Super Oblata***

Secularization and Worship

Secularization is an imprecise term, since it can be used with a variety of meanings. It may refer, for example, to a process of

social differentiation, involving the division of labour and the separation of home and work as well as a continuing specialization of social groups and institutions. Again, it can be applied to a shift of responsibility from ecclesiastical authority to worldly authority; so the secularization of the monasteries at the Reformation involved the transfer of property from church ownership to private tenure. For the purposes of this entry, however, the term is employed to refer to the process of change from a sacral to a secular universe.

A sacral universe is one in which the functioning of nature and society is explained in terms of the divine. In the sacral universe, man is at the mercy of nature; not only is he dependent upon it, but he finds himself largely unable to control it. Nature appears to be superior and sovereign, while man is weak and helpless. Nature is the central factor in his life, but in a pre-technical age, he is powerless to impose his will upon it. Unable to master nature, man then has to seek divine assistance, in order even to live. Nature appears to have almost divine features; it is an epiphany of God himself and the workings of nature are understood as the workings of God.

Within this sacral universe religion has a dual function. It acts as a preserver of society and it provides rituals to protect man against a world which he dominates neither intellectually nor materially. Worship is then a *cultus publicus*, securing the public well-being and fulfilling the supreme end of the state. It safeguards man from the uncontrollable forces of nature and channels the divine assistance in his direction.

With secularization man enters a secular universe. This is one in which the functioning of nature and society is explained in terms of themselves. No longer is recourse had to the divine in order to understand either the material world or man. The natural sciences seek out the 'laws' of nature, their inter-relationships and their workings; sociology analyses society, while man himself is investigated in terms of biology, psychology, etc. In the secular universe man is no longer at the mercy of nature, rather he is its master. Through the development of technology, man can control his environment; to a large extent he is therefore liberated from nature, in the sense that he has ceased to be dependent upon its changes and chances. This newly-won domination, precarious though it may be in the face of pollution and the need for conservation, results in a reversal of roles. Whereas previously man was in submission to natural forces, now he can bend them to his will. This change in the relationship of man and nature leads to a new concept of man in the universe. Man and his power become fundamental values which direct his efforts towards research into development and progress. So man fast becomes the lord of nature, dominating it by scientific and technological means. So far from being static and rigid, society now enters into a process of change – change that is constant and never ending. Society becomes also pluriform with different cultures and subcultures existing side by side. The mobility which technology brings breaks open the uniformity of society.

The result is that within the secular universe, religion loses the functions it exercised previously in the sacral universe. When change is the keynote, religion can no longer perform the role of preserver of society; if it tries to do so, it will be regarded as a bulwark against progress and a supporter of social stagnation. Moreover, when society is pluriform, there can be no *cultus publicus*. All religions tend to become *cultus privati*, with the abandonment of the public sector of life and with concentration upon forms of individual piety. When human beings dominate the universe, they no longer need rituals to protect themselves. If in former days it seemed reasonable to sprinkle water on an ox that was ill, today few would think of doing this to a tractor that has broken down.

Consequently the association of the words secularization and worship points, in the first instance, to a crisis of worship, because the passage from the sacral to the secular universe (secularization) renders those liturgical forms created within and for the sacral universe void of meaning and relevance within the new context of existence in the modern world. This crisis is intensified by another factor comprehended under secularization as social differentiation. Today, with the progress of urbanization, social life is very different from what it was in mediaeval Christendom. This latter was integrated with a civilization

based largely upon agriculture and village units. The village was a social unity; it was a territorial area of restricted dimensions within which everyone knew everyone else. Its population found its residence, its work and its play all within its boundaries. There was an unavoidable interchange which promoted interest in other people, over and above any utilitarian project in which they may have been engaged. Worship, in this situation, was the occasion when those who knew one another gathered together and strengthened the ties that bound their already existing community, i.e. it was an assembly of a pre-existing community. The Sunday service was an important occasion for going out of the house and encountering one's fellow villagers; hence the importance, too, of conversation and inter-personal contacts, before, during and after the service. This pattern of life and worship favoured stability, respect for tradition and for nature and it allowed for the development of primary relations.

In the modern urban situation, however, specialization and diversification lead to the dispersal of man's social functions over a very wide area indeed. The husband goes to work in one quarter, the wife may work or shop in another, the children may go to school in a third, while the family as a whole will seek entertainment elsewhere. The consequence is that in a residential area personal relations may be non-existent and without this direct contact and sharing of interests, ideas and news, there exists no local community within which anyone can be integrated. The result of this transformation is that relations between fellow citizens become less and less primary, i.e. face-to-face, and more and more functional. What is the effect of the demise of the village and the neighbourhood-based community upon worship? Clearly worship in this new context can no longer be understood in terms of the gathering of a pre-existing village type community. So worship loses its communal dimension and its necessary basis in inter-personal relations.

It now has to be affirmed that the association of the words secularization and worship points, in the second instance, to the need for a reformulation of the meaning and function of the latter in the light of the former. The inherited forms of worship are rooted in the view that it is an activity whereby we retire for a time from the secular world and, leaving all that is common behind, penetrate into another, sacred, world, where we enter the presence of the all-holy God and sing his praises in company with the heavenly choir of angels, archangels and saints. So worship is a special, religious activity, performed in special holy buildings; it may strengthen us to fulfil the divine purpose within our daily lives but it is, in itself, something separate from our daily lives in the world. In contrast to this, if worship today is to have any meaning in the face of secularization, it has to be redefined as an activity which springs out of life in the world; it is a celebration of that life. Instead of involving a divorce from the secular, it takes the secular or common as its basis, and so the cultic action is a means whereby we express the unity of the sacred and the secular. It does not need for its performance holy shrines, and while it is essentially a coming to awareness of and a response to God, this is achieved through that which is human and secular.

'Secular' worship, then, has a festive character in that it is a highlight in everyday existence and is based upon world involvement and not upon world rejection. It is an encounter with the divine and expresses and makes explicit the unity of the sacred and the secular by showing how the holy is a dimension of the whole of life. It is a sensitivizing process, shaping our perception of the divine so as to open the secular to the holy and assist us to find the holy in everyday life. In a world of rapid change, it must also be a vehicle of social criticism and so a celebration of hope, bringing the hoped-for future into contact with the present and providing a stimulus for re-shaping the world. It points to the service of others; it expresses the love of neighbour and it comprises commitment and acceptance of responsibility for one another.

Since worship must have a communal basis, it has to be celebrated primarily in small groups, involving face-to-face encounters, social interaction, participation, mutuality, reciprocity and corporateness. It then fosters inter-personal relations and functions in terms of personalization and community identity. It is a shared activity, which is both intelligible to all and is related to past and future.

The norm of the worshipping community

then becomes the primary group and the large liturgical assembly has to be redefined as a gathering of groups. The small group is a key factor in promoting participation in the large one; an occasional coming together allows for integration in the greater whole.

The meaning and function of worship as thus redefined in the light of secularization corresponds closely with that to be found in the NT, which, after all, belongs to the period before the emergence of Christendom. The disintegration of the latter, although producing a crisis, allows for a more radical interpretation of worship, in the sense that it compels theologians to reassess their roots. Clearly this understanding has to be embodied in new forms, but that is a subject to be considered elsewhere (*see* **Experimental Forms of Worship**).

It will by now be very evident that secularization is to be distinguished from secularism. The latter involves the belief that the secular is entirely autonomous; further, it is commonly associated with atheism and therefore rejects the view that anything can be related to a divine being – worship is then an otiose activity and talk of worship and secularism is meaningless. In one sense secularism is but one of many religions and not among the major ones. Reaction to it in the West, however, has led to a renewed quest by many for a sacral universe, with quite a number of such universes (stemming not only from mediaeval Christianity but also from Islam, Hinduism, etc.) competing for recognition. In this situation it may well be the task of Christian worship, redefined in the light of secularization, to uphold all that is good in secularization itself as a historical process under God.

H. G. Cox, *Religion in the Secular City*, 1984; J. G. Davies, *Every Day God*, 1973; *New Perspectives on Worship Today*, 1978; W. Vos (ed), *Worship and Secularization* (Studia Liturgica 7, 2/3), 1970; J. F. White, *The Worldliness of Worship*, 1967; *Worship in the City of Man*, 1966.

EDITOR

Sentences

Short passages of scripture read out during services. They have two separate purposes. First, they may serve as an introduction to or commentary upon the next stage in the act of worship. So the sentences in the 1552 BCP for use at the beginning of morning and evening prayer preface the confession and absolution with scriptural thoughts of penitence and of the assurance of forgiveness. Similarly the sentences used in association with the funeral procession declare the nature of death and the hope of resurrection. The sentences that accompany the offertory* frequently stress the necessity of almsgiving. The second purpose for which sentences may be used is to relate a particular act of worship with seasons, festivals, saints' days and other special occasions such as those provided in abundance in ASB (1980).

EDITOR

Septuagesima

see **Quinquagesima**

Sepulchre

see **Easter Garden**

Sequence

see **Chants of the Proper of the Mass; Music in the Mass of the Roman Rite**

Sermon

The preaching of a sermon in the liturgy is rooted in the synagogue practice (cf. Luke 4.16ff.; Acts 13.14ff.) of following the readings of scripture by exposition. Paul is related to have discoursed at Troas before breaking the bread (Acts 20.7ff.) and, although not specified, the prior reading of scripture is probably to be presumed. Preaching by prophets or by tongue-speakers was a feature of the assemblies at Corinth (I Cor. 14). The Fourth Gospel says that the Paraclete 'will take of mine and declare it to you' (John 16.14f.), suggesting that in the Christian assemblies the Jesus tradition, as well as the OT scriptures, became preaching material. The evident intention of Paul that his letters should be read in the assembly (I Cor. 16.22–24; cf. Col. 4.16) led to the reading and expositions of 'apostolic' writings also.

In the pre-Nicene church the bishop succeeded the prophet as the preacher of the sermon after the reading of the lections, as he also recited the great eucharist prayer (cf. *Mart. Pol.* 16 where the bishop is called a 'prophetic teacher'). (For a second-

century bishop's understanding of his preaching *see* Irenaeus, *Adv. Haer.* I, x, 2.) An example of such liturgical preaching has survived in Melito of Sardis' homily *On the Passion*.

After Nicaea the sermon continued to be a normal part of the liturgy. Thus, for Egypt, Serapion (*c.* 340) instructs the bishop to pray for the Holy Spirit to assist him in proclaiming the message of the scriptures to the congregation.

During the Dark Ages a number of factors (mass conversions, the multiplication of presbyteral masses, the decay in educational standards, the Western development of low mass) contributed to the decay of preaching, so that the sermon ceased to be a normal part of the liturgy.

Mediaeval revivals of preaching (e.g., the friars) occurred largely outside the context of the liturgy, and it was devotional and moralistic rather than expository. The conservative Reformers sought to re-establish a liturgical sermon (cf. Luther's 'postils' and the rubric of the BCP requiring a sermon), but although there was much expository preaching in the Reformation churches, its integral relation to the liturgy was obscured in Protestant orthodoxy, pietism and rationalism. In reaction, the nineteenth-century liturgical revival in Anglicanism was often accompanied by a depreciation of preaching. Only with the twentieth-century Liturgical Movement* has the sermon come to be understood once more as an integral part of the liturgy in which the word of God read in the lections is proclaimed for the present and becomes the material of the thanksgiving (cf. Vatican II, *Constitution on the Sacred Liturgy*, IV.35).

G. M. Bass, *The Renewal of Liturgical Preaching*, 1967; Y. Brilioth, *Landmarks in the History of Preaching*, 1950; G. Dix, *The Shape of the Liturgy*, [2]1945; John Killinger, *Fundamentals of Preaching*, 1985; D. Ritschl, *A Theology of Proclamation*, 1960.

R. H. FULLER

Server

Though not ordained, the server performs many of the functions which originally belonged to the office of acolyte*. However, in recent years, when the involvement of the congregation in most services has increased in both the Roman Catholic and Anglican Churches, the role is less important than it was. If there is no sacristan, the server may prepare the altar and sanctuary before the eucharist, and if there is no one else to do so, he or she makes or leads the responses, brings the bread and wine to the celebrant at the offertory and usually helps at the ablutions, etc. In the Church of England, the term is loosely used to describe any lay person who assists the officiant at any service.

P. HINCHLIFF

Seventh-day Adventist Worship

According to Seventh-day Adventist belief and practice, public worship is the corporate assembly of the community of faith for the adoration and praise of God, for thanksgiving, sacrifice and communion. 'The duty to worship God is based upon the fact that He is the Creator' (E. G. White, *The Great Controversy between Christ and Satan*, 1900, p.436). Worship is the wholehearted response of the creature to his Creator and Redeemer, otherwise the coming together of worshippers is of no avail (*see* Matt. 15.8, 9). Worship involves an attitude of mind and heart which enables man to love God with all his being. Adventists recall that Christ said this was the fulfilment of the first great commandment. True worship is the fruit of the working of the Holy Spirit and is tied to conduct based on willing obedience to all God's requirements, for 'without obedience to his commandments, no worship can be pleasing to God' (White, loc. cit.; *see* Matt. 15.3–9; I John 5.3 and Prov. 28.9). The experience of worship must merge into a worshipping life.

Unlike most other Christians, Seventh-day Adventists assemble for the weekly divine worship service on the Sabbath, the seventh day of the week. They believe that the biblical Sabbath is a weekly memorial of God's creative act as recorded in the OT and of Christ's redemptive or re-creative act in the NT. The importance of the Sabbath as a day of rest and worship is that it keeps ever present the true reason why worship is due to God – because he is the Creator and Redeemer. The Sabbath, therefore, in Adventist theology, lies at the very foundation of Christian worship and continues to have heterocentric significance for modern man. The historical process which

brought about a change in the *day* of worship also modified the *way* of worship (*see* N. F. Pease, *And Worship Him*, 1967, pp.25–35). While Adventists have no quarrel with the dictum *lex adorandi est lex credendi*, they further believe that the worship of the church never rises higher than its theology, for worship is also a reflection of theology.

Because Adventist worship is 'free', charismatic, rather than liturgical, the emphasis is on extempore prayer, circumstantial, spontaneous inspiration, rather than on a formal liturgy and set prayers. However, the *Seventh-day Adventist Church Manual*, 1981, does provide three suggested orders of worship and guidelines. On certain occasions, such as marriage, burial and ordination services and the Lord's Supper, the service is more formal (*see* **Burial** 14; **Marriage** 14; **Ordination** 14).

Ceremonial is usually quite limited. Vestments are not used, except occasionally academic gowns and choir and baptismal robes. In some churches there is a choir procession. When the platform party (consisting customarily of the minister and one or more lay elders) steps up to the pulpit it kneels in silent prayer, while the congregation stands or remains seated (in some churches the congregation kneels). Adventists believe that usually the most appropriate and reverential attitude in prayer is shown in the bending of the knee. In public worship both ministers and congregation kneel for prayer facing the pulpit, whence go forth messages from God's holy word.

After an organ prelude, the service may begin with a scriptural or musical call to worship or a hymn. Invocation, hymns, one scripture lesson (either from the OT or the NT), pastoral prayer, offering, special music and sermon follow in one order or another. After the benediction is pronounced there may be an organ postlude. While the pastoral prayer represents perhaps the 'holiest exercise of the whole service' (*Seventh-day Adventist Church Manual*, p.113), the reading and expounding of the scriptures constitute the central act of Adventist divine worship. For this reason the pulpit* is normally in the centre of the rostrum*, with the communion table* in front.

The Seventh-day Adventist Church generally pays less attention than do more liturgical churches in worship services to the 'church year'. However, for over half a century it has had its own yearly calendar, with considerable emphasis on evangelistic outreach. Approximately forty special days, weeks and offerings are included.

The ethos of Seventh-day Adventist worship is best conveyed in the idea of a closely knit *koinonia* of believers, meeting for adoration, consecration and communion and desiring in unity to pattern their lives in closer harmony with the will of God and increase the church's evangelistic witness in preparation for the Second Advent of Christ. The intention of the service is to make the power of saving grace a joint reality in the life of the congregation.

See also **Books Liturgical** 15; **Liturgies** 15.

W. R. Beach, *Dimensions in Salvation*, 1963, pp.183–92; Harold B. Hannum, *Music and Worship*, 1969; 'Highways of Worship', *Sabbath School Lesson Quarterly*, Adult Division, No.307, First quarter, 1972; *Manual for Ministers*, 1977; C. Raymond Holmes, *Sing a New Song! Worship Renewal for Adventists Today*, 1984; E. G. White, *The Desire of Ages*, 1946, pp.157–89; E. G. White, *Testimonies for the Church*, V, 1948, pp.491–500.

B. B. BEACH

Sexagesima

see **Quinquagesima**

Sext

see **Canonical Hours**

Shaker Worship

The origins of the Shaker movement go back to the mid-eighteenth century in England which witnessed a series of Quaker revivals. Near Manchester a group was formed of which Ann Lee became the leader in 1766. Increasing persecution led her to contemplate emigration and on 19 May 1774 Mother Lee, as she was now known, with six male and two female companions, set sail from Liverpool for the United States. They settled initially in the woods of Waterliet near Albany, New York. Their numbers increased, partly through the missionary journeys of Mother Lee and partly by the accession of converts from an independent religious revival near New

Lebanon where, in 1878, three years after Mother Lee's death, the first Shaker settlement was established. Under the new leadership of Joseph Meacham and Lucy Wright, the 'United Society of Believers in Christ's Second Appearing' spread rapidly, and in the decade before the American Civil War there were some 6,000 members in 18 different settlements, but today they are virtually extinct.

Shaker worship was remarkable in that it consisted largely of dancing to verses and music of their own composition, interspersed with scripture readings, exhortations and extempore prayer. One Shaker recipe for a service reads: 'Sing a little, dance a little, exhort a little, preach a little, and a good many littles will make a great deal.'

The Shakers believed that the millenium had dawned and that liturgical dance* was now the appropriate form of worship. Whereas the basic steps were only two – a skip and a shuffle – the patterns of movement they devised could be highly complex. There were square order shuffles, circular dances, continuous ring marches, etc. (*see* Plate 49). These involved not only legs and feet but also arms, hands and heads, e.g. shaking of the open palms downwards was considered to be a means of ridding oneself of sin. These movements were regarded as essential to enable the worshippers to enter 'into the spirit of the sentiments contained in the songs' (*see* **Movement-prayers**).

E. D. Andrews, *The Gift to be Simple. Songs, Dances and Rituals of the Ancient Shakers*, 1962; J. G. Davies, P. van Zyl & F. M. Young, *A Shaker Dance Service Reconstructed*, 1984.

EDITOR

Shinto Worship

Shinto, the traditional national religion of Japan, is of particular importance in the comparative study of worship in that of all the world's 'greater' religions it is the one nearest to a 'natural' religion; in the sense in which a Westerner understands the terms, it has no founder, no canonical scriptures, no creeds, and no developed dogmatic theology. The word *shinto* itself means 'the way of the gods', but the word *kami*, translated as 'god' or 'gods', has a much wider connotation than the translation

Plate 49 Shaker mountain meeting on the Holy Hill of Zion, Harvard, Mass.

normally bears in Western languages; in the words of a distinguished Shinto scholar, 'the term is an honorific for noble, sacred spirits which implies a sense of adoration for their virtues and authority. All beings have such spirits, so in a sense all beings can be called *kami*.' Shinto worship, then, is the worship of divinity perceived in and through the whole of creation; in Western terms it is both pantheistic and polytheistic. The whole of life, properly lived, is regarded as an act of worship; its worshipful character is ensured by specific ceremonial acts of worship at particular times, and in particular places, notably by the daily devotions which a devout Shintoist performs before the domestic shrine (*kami-dana*, literally 'god-shelf') in his home, and his participation in the services celebrated on the many festivals in public temples or shrines, as well as by more informal devotional visits to the latter on other occasions.

There are about 100,000 Shinto shrines in Japan. While there is no linguistic ground for the common practice of translating *jinja* as 'shrine' rather than as 'temple', it does perhaps make clearer the essential nature of these sanctuaries, which are regarded primarily as divine dwelling-places, and only consequently as places of meeting for worship. The original shrines appear to have been 'natural' holy places – sacred mountains, sacred forests and so forth – without added buildings; the persistence of the *himorogi*, or small enclosure containing a sacred tree, appears to witness to the next stage in the development of the shrine. The great majority of shrines today, however, take the form of an enclosure containing a complex, simple or elaborate, of buildings; where possible, surroundings of natural beauty and impressiveness are chosen, and even in the great modern conurbations the attempt is made to provide a shrine with an attractive garden enclosure.

The centre of the shrine is the symbol of the *kami* to whom it is dedicated (which may take any of a number of forms, but is usually not a representative image), in which the spirit or power of the *kami* is believed to dwell in a particular manner for the benefit of the worshippers, and which is enshrined in the *honden* or sanctuary. The other principal buildings common to most shrines are the *heiden* or hall of offerings, and the *haiden* or hall of prayer. Other buildings of various kinds are also found in the enclosure; a structure which is universal is the *torii* or sacred gateway which marks each of the public entrances to the enclosure.

Shinto worship comprises a great and rich variety of observances, ranging from the extremely simple to the extremely elaborate. The regular forms of worship, however, whether simple or elaborate, always include four essential elements – purification, offering, prayer, and a sacred meal. They are seen at their simplest in the daily private devotions at home: the worshipper washes his hands and rinses his mouth, places a fresh food offering before the symbol of the *kami*, stands or sits before the shrine, and prays briefly as he will, bowing before and after; the food offering is removed and served at a later meal. When he wishes to pay his devotions at a shrine, the worshipper washes with particular care and puts on clean linen. On arrival at the shrine he removes his outdoor clothes, and purifies his mouth and hands with holy water, proceeds to the hall of prayer, places an offering (today usually money) in the box provided, and prays, as at home, as he will; he may also request the celebration of a votive office by one of the priests, for which he makes a small offering. Offices of this kind are frequently requested, on all kinds of occasions, both by individuals and by groups. The regular shrine services, which commonly centre round morning and evening offerings of food, follow approximately the same pattern as the domestic devotions of the faithful, although each of their constituent parts is, of course, more formal and more elaborate. Most elaborate of all are the observances of festivals, of which there are a great number, and which, as many of them are of a local character, vary greatly from place to place in accordance with the traditions of different shrines. Those taking part, especially the officiating priests, prepare themselves by rituals of purification, and by a period of abstinence and recollection which can vary from half an hour to a week or more; the offerings of food are numerous and complicated, and presented with solemn ceremony accompanied by the playing of sacred music; and often sacred dances are performed. Processions, either within the

shrine enclosure or through the streets, are a prominent feature of many festivals, as are also traditional entertainments of various kinds, which are regarded both as an offering to the *kami* and as a carnival for the worshippers.

There are many important and interesting features of Shinto worship, but two basic characteristics of the whole of its rich variety of liturgical observance stand out. The first is the essential simplicity and 'naturalness' of Shinto rites, even of the most elaborate; the second is their high aesthetic quality – beauty, as both a manifestation of divinity and a tribute to it, is sought for, and commonly achieved, in order to express both the transcendence and the immanence of the divine and the power of the divine to transfigure the whole of life.

J. Herbert, *Shinto*, 1967.

W. JARDINE GRISBROOKE

Sick, Visitation of the

The Sarum 'order for visiting a sick man' begins with nine prayers for the sick man's recovery, for which scriptural precedents are freely invoked; it is nowhere suggested that his illness is due to sin. At first there is no hint that recovery is unlikely, but before long he is told that he is 'about to go the way of all flesh' (hence the name viaticum*). So when he has professed his faith, he is exhorted to have hope and charity, and to make a full confession, since soon he will not be able to do so. No penance is given: instead, he is to give alms. Two absolutions and two more collects for renewal and restoration to the church end the service, which may be followed immediately by extreme unction*. After this, the priest administers communion; if the sick man is too ill to receive in a seemly way, the priest assures him, 'only believe, and you have eaten'.

Popular opinion in the Middle Ages regarded unction as recognition of terminal illness rather than as a means to health, and attached gross superstitions to it. But the service was certainly intended for chronic illness also, and one bishop suggested that weekly communion and yearly unction was sufficient.

As usual, Cranmer greatly abbreviated the mediaeval rite, keeping, for instance, only two of the nine collects. These are followed by an exhortation to acceptance of suffering, based on Heb. 12.5–10, which also provides the epistle. This introduces a new view of illness, that it is God's will for purposes of discipline. The sick man's faith is tested by putting the creed to him in interrogatory form, as in baptism; after which the minister is to exhort him to forgive others, make reparation, make his will, and discharge all his debts. All this is included in being 'in charity with all the world', but no mention of hope is kept. The sick man is then to 'make a special confession, if he feel his conscience troubled with any weighty matter': as in the communion service, it is not regarded as normal and mandatory. The absolution still speaks of Christ's 'authority committed to me'. Unction (of forehead or breast only) is accompanied by a collect assembled from four separate Sarum prayers, on the themes of recovery, forgiveness, and grace to withstand temptations.

Two methods are suggested for the communion of the sick: the priest should either reserve sufficient 'at the open communion', or say the whole service in the house in the short form appointed for weekdays. In the latter case there is a proper psalm, collect, epistle, and gospel. Rubrics lay down that there must always be 'some of his own house, or else of his neighbours' to communicate with the sick man. If he is unable to receive, he must be instructed that 'if he do truly repent . . . and steadfastly believe that Jesus Christ hath suffered . . . for him . . ., he doth eat and drink spiritually . . .'.

Bucer regarded the service as 'agreeing sufficiently with holy scripture', and commended the practice of communicating the sick directly from the Lord's Table, rather than from the reserved sacrament. Peter Martyr, on the other hand, would only approve the use of the complete service in the house. His view prevailed, and the first method is omitted in the 1552 BCP. Unction, being too closely bound up with superstitious ideas, also disappears completely. Curiously enough, the absolution remains untouched.

The service seems never to have become generally acceptable, and Canon 67 of 1604 says that the minister shall instruct and comfort the sick 'in their distress according to the Order of the Communion Book, if he be no preacher; or if he be a preacher,

then as he shall think most needful and convenient'. Individual services have survived by Lancelot Andrewes, John Cosin, Jeremy Taylor, and Denis Granville, which shows that the liberty offered by the canon was readily accepted, and there is abundant evidence of confession *in articulo mortis* throughout the seventeenth century.

In 1662, in response to Puritan criticisms, the minister is directed to *move* the sick man to make his confession, and absolution is only to be given 'if he humbly and heartily desire it'. The second collect was enlarged to stress the need for faith and repentance, and the third to include prayer for the presence of the Spirit. Most important of all, four new prayers by Robert Sanderson were added. In these there is no suggestion that illness is God's will, and the titles imply that the service may be used in cases of chronic illness as well as terminal.

Even these changes proved insufficient, and demands for an improved office continued to be made. In the 1928 BCP the service was printed in five sections, as suggested by W. H. Frere. The first exhortation is replaced by a list of subjects upon which the minister may make an exhortation of his own. New material includes a form of confession, a litany, two prayers from Sarum and 'Go forth upon thy journey, Christian soul'. An appendix suggests twenty-five collects, sixteen psalms, and forty passages of scripture as especially useful. Provision was made for reservation*. In this form the service is enormously improved, and was adopted by other revisions; but, as has been pointed out, the result really belongs to a manual for parish priests rather than to a BCP. This may well be true of any attempt to provide for a private occasion of this character.

The ASB contains no provision for ministry to the sick, but this lack was made good in 1983 by the issue of an independent set of services and prayers under the title *Ministry to the Sick*. The booklet is in several sections: Communion with the Sick; The Celebration of Holy Communion in the presence of the Sick (Rites A and B); The Distribution of Communion to those not present at a Celebration (Rites A and B); The Laying on of Hands with Prayer, and Anointing; A Commendation at the Time of Death; Prayers with the Sick; Psalms and Readings. These titles are self-explanatory, but it may be noted that provision is made for all the customary types of 'sick communion': a complete communion service; taking the consecrated elements from a service direct to the sick person; and communion from the reserved sacrament. There is no special form of absolution, a modernization of the BCP form having been rejected by the General Synod.

The American service is simpler in form, consisting of Ministry of the Word, Laying on of Hands and Anointing, Holy Communion, Prayers for and for use by the Sick, and Ministration at the Time of Death.

The traditional Roman rite (in the *Rituale Romanum* of 1614) provided for the visitation of the sick and the sacraments usually administered during sickness: holy communion, penance*, anointing (cf. 'unction'), viaticum (communion of the dying), though this last was placed before the anointing. This ritual was superseded in 1972 by the Order of the Anointing of the Sick and their Pastoral Care.

According to the Order, visits to the sick should be frequent, and the priest or other ministers, relatives, and friends are urged to support the sick person spiritually and to help him/her to pray. No set service is provided, but Bible readings, psalms, and other prayers are suggested, and samples are given. At the end of the visit the priest lays his hands on the sick person. During the course of the visits holy communion, penance, and anointing are given. The new Order makes it quite clear that anointing is not the sacrament of the dying, but of those whose health 'is seriously impaired by sickness or old age'. The last sacrament is holy communion, called viaticum, which has a special formula for the administration. Readings, psalms, and other prayers are provided for the dying and for the use of those who assist them.

F. E. Brightman, *The English Rite*, 1915, I, pp.cxxv, cxxvi, clxiv, ccxx, ccxxi; II, pp.818–847; J. D. Crichton, *Christian Celebration: The Sacraments*, 1981, pp.168–91; A. J. Collins, *Manuale Sarum*, 1960, pp.97–114; M. J. Hatchett, *Commentary on the American Prayer Book*, 1979, pp.459–71; William Maskell, *Monumenta Ritualia Ecclesiae Anglicanae*, 1846, I, pp.66–95; *Pastoral Care of the Sick*, ET 1983.

G. J. CUMING

Sign, Symbol

Signs are physical objects, events, or human actions which point beyond themselves in such a way as to express some further reality, occurrence, or human conception. They may be linguistic or non-verbal; they may include natural phenomena or human artifacts, activities, gestures, or bodily postures. Verbal signs may include speech or writing. *Symbols* are often said to function at a deeper level than signs, of which they represent a particular sub-class. Some claim that symbols draw not simply on interpretive conventions, as signs do, but on pre-conscious processes and experiences. At very least, the symbol is more closely and more deeply associated with what it symbolizes, often resting on historical or collective experiences which pre-date conscious recollection. Thus traffic signals function as signs on the basis of conventions arbitrarily accepted within the community which govern the use and understanding of red and green. But the American flag (according to Paul Tillich and Mircea Eliade) functions as a symbol because it more directly participates in the historical identity, honour and dignity of the nation.

Such distinctions between signs and symbols, however, remain controversial. The problem is further complicated because different sets of issues arise in theology, psychology, semiotics, the philosophy of language, and in the biblical writings. In modern theology Paul Tillich follows the psychological theories of G. G. Jung which locate the special power of symbols in pre-conscious attitudes, or even in the collective unconscious of the human race. Symbols, unlike signs, cannot be created at will. Symbols are born when they resonate at the deepest level with experiences or truths which are important for the corporate life and identity of a community. Operative symbols often maintain an integrating and stabilizing power for the community, but they may also lose this power, and wither away into mere poetic-symbolic metaphors. In psychology G. G. Jung and Karl Jaspers regard symbols as vitally important bridges between the conscious and unconscious. They provide foci through which pre-conscious longings, anxieties, and feelings may be articulated and ordered. To try to live without symbols is to reduce whole persons to the one level of cerebral consciousness. In the phenomenology of religions Mircea Eliade calls attention to the role of symbols in actualizing in the present patterns of action and belief that are also rooted in the past. Symbol, like myth, re-actualizes past events and patterns especially in the 'here and now' of liturgy.

Different issues and classifications often arise in semiology, but these also remain relevant to theology and liturgy. C. S. Peirce regards symbols, along with icons and indices, as one of three sub-classes of signs. But he defines symbol as that which operates on the basis of human convention or agreement (Tillich's signs); while he uses the term icon for signs which participate directly in the reality of that to which they point (Tillich's symbols). Indices, in Peirce's writings, are more akin to causal symptoms. For example, a fever may be an index (cause-effect sign) of some specific illness. Paul Ricoeur accords a more creative role to symbols than to signs within the sermiotic system. In his earlier writings he stresses the capacity of symbols to convey more than one possible meaning. The symbol, therefore, stimulates the mind into the productive activity of interpretive thought. 'There is more in a symbol than in any of its conceptual equivalents ... Symbols give rise to an endless exegesis ... No concept can exhaust the requirement of further thinking borne by symbols ...' (*Interpretation Theory*, 1976, p.57). In his more recent work Ricoeur examines the constraints placed upon what would otherwise be an open-ended symbolic meaning by the symbol's contextualization within text, plot, or narrative.

The biblical writings do not distinguish, at least in their own use of terms, the functions of signs from those of symbols. But signs themselves (Hebrew *'oth*, Greek *semeion*) function in various ways. The sign of blood on a doorpost (Ex. 12.13) serves as a mark of identification; a cairn of stones (Josh. 4.6) serves as a memorial sign of a past event. Ezekiel's drawing of the siege of Jerusalem serves as a warning sign of God's impending judgment (4.3). Many acts serve as signs or symbols even where *'oth* or *semeion* does not explicitly occur. For example, Jeremiah purchases a field at Anathoth (32.6–25) as a sign of the promise

of restoration. While the New Testament writings discourage a faith which would be based primarily on visible signs themselves (Mark 8.11–13; par. Matt. 12.38, 39; John 4.48; I Cor. 1.22), a positive evaluation is offered particularly in the Fourth Gospel of the role of physical acts and events which point beyond themselves to the truth of God in Christ (John 20.30; Acts 2.43; II Cor. 12.12). Because the reality of God transcends human thought and language, Jesus pointed to this reality both by word and deed. Thus the healing of a blind man is one tangible pointer to the meaning of the claim that Christ is the light of the world. John 2–12, which has been called 'the Book of Signs', correlates a series of such concrete acts on the part of Jesus with discourses on the greater realities to which they point. This is particularly prominent in John because it is an implicate of a theology of 'the word made flesh' (1.14) that there is no sharp dualism betweeen physical and non-physical, or between word and deed. The episode of the foot-washing (John 13.3–9) is no less a semantic marker than the words which relate to it.

Several principles emerge for liturgy. 1. The liturgy is not confined to words. Physical posture*, gesture*, or act, belongs no less to the total speech-act of confession, praise, repentance, or greeting, than the speaking of words. Modern speech-act theory reinforces the closeness and interrelatedness of the two aspects. 2. Every speech-act in liturgy presupposes certain agreements, conventions, or shared beliefs within the community which govern the use and interpretation of signs and symbols. Especially when such symbols exercise considerable power in shaping beliefs and attitudes, it is important to pay attention to the controlling contexts of these symbols in the texts and narratives out of which they arise. 3. Because they relate to pre-conscious springs of feeling and attitude, symbols may operate even more powerfully than conceptual discourse, which often addresses only cognitive consciousness. For this reason it is also crucial to distinguish symbols of the transcendent from that to which they point. For example, pastoral and psychological problems arise if an entire theology of God is dominated by certain selected symbols which are accorded an unduly privileged status, e.g. God as father or as judge. The answer is not to abandon symbols but to encourage an adequately pluriform range. For example, symbols of God as healer and liberator would serve to modify the absoluteness accorded to the first. 4. Liturgy provides such variety through its use of historical sources and especially through a disciplined lectionary. Not only the psalms, but also sometimes neglected sources such as apocalyptic literature provide an abundance of deeply-resonating symbols: 'the river of the water of life . . .'; or 'tree of life . . . for the healing of the nations' (Rev. 22.1,2). 5. Finally, symbols provide a focus for the values which define corporate and individual religious life. Their incorporation within habituated patterns of worship, therefore, strengthens appropriate patterns of response, and re-affirms religious and human identity.

R. E. Brown, *The Gospel According to John*, 1, 1971, pp.523–32; G. Cope, *Symbolism in the Bible and Church*, 1959; F. W. Dillistone, *Traditional Symbols and the Contemporary World*, 1973; M. Douglas, *Natural Symbols*, 1970; T. Fawcett, *The Symbolic Language of Religion*, 1971; S. Hook (ed), *Religious Experience and Truth*, 1961 (esp. essays by Paul Tillich, pp.3–11, 301–22); C. G. Jung, *Man and His Symbols* (1964); W. Nicol, *The Semeia in the Fourth Gospel*, 1972; A. M. Olson, *Myth, Symbol, and Reality*, 1980; H. H. Price, *Thinking and Experience*, [2]1969, pp.144–297; P. Ricoeur, *The Symbolism of Evil*, 1967; *The Conflict of Interpretations*, 1974, pp.269–498; *Essays on Biblical Interpretation*, 1981; R. Scholes, *Semiotics and Interpretation*, 1982.

ANTHONY C. THISELTON

Silent Prayer

Silent prayer within the liturgy falls into three categories: 1. periods of silent prayer which are integral to the structure of the service; 2. the silent, or nearly silent (technically 'secret'), recitation of certain prescribed prayers of private devotion by one or other of the ministers; 3. the similar recitation of prayers which should properly be recited aloud, or at least were originally so recited.

The second of these categories calls for little comment: such prayers are to be found in most of the historic liturgies, in which

they were inserted in the Middle Ages. The most outstanding example of the third category is the eucharistic prayer itself, large parts of which are recited secretly in many of the historic liturgies.

This custom appears to have arisen from the desire to express and evoke an attitude towards the eucharistic mystery of awe and fear, the use of the secret voice being psychologically effective to this end. Such an attitude certainly existed to some extent from the very beginnings of Christian worship, as is clear from I Cor. 11.26–33, but it was in fourth- and fifth-century Syria that it came to dominate the approach to the eucharist, and it is in a Syrian document of the end of the fifth century, *The Liturgical Homilies of Narsai*, that we have the first definite evidence for the largely silent recitation of the anaphora *. By the second half of the sixth century the practice had become widespread, although it was as yet by no means universal: in 565 the Emperor Justianian found it necessary to legislate against it. His legislation produced no lasting effect, and by the end of the eighth century the practice had become the established usage in the Byzantine rite. The first definite evidence of it in the West is found in the second Roman *Ordo* of almost exactly the same date. It became and remained the normal usage in the Roman rite until 1966, when the recitation of the canon aloud was again prescribed.

The silent recitation of the eucharistic prayer is undoubtedly a corrupt practice, but however undesirable it may be liturgically, the spread and persistence of the practice bear witness to an evident devotional need for silence and for its psychological fruits in worship. This need should, however, be provided for in other ways.

Among the possibilities are the provision of a space for silent prayer between any bidding to prayer and the formal prayer following it, of a space for silent meditation after readings from scriptures and after communion, and of a space for silent recollection between major sections of any service. Some of these provisions have been included in several reformed liturgies of recent years, and in an age of far too little silence they can be of great devotional and psychological value. The effective timing and 'control' of these silences, on which in practice not a little of their value depends, calls for sensitivity and good judgment on the part of the officiating priest or minister.

See also ***Super Oblata***.

W. JARDINE GRISBROOKE

Sitting

see **Posture** 4

Sociology of Worship

Although the sociology of worship is applicable to all religious traditions, such is the variety within Christianity that the same questions can be comparatively raised there too. For the purposes of clarity, this entry will focus empirically on Christianity with examples drawn from Britain and the United States.

What constitutes worship in the empirical sense is theologically debated, as is its relation to the sacred and secular. For sociologists, the debate around worship is more to do with what is religion – is worship an essential component? Sociologists have rather less difficulty in identifying worship because for them it is *religious ritual*. Their concern therefore is with corporate worship as ritual activity and their focus is limited to its social dimensions. No matter how religion is defined or theoretically conceived, worship constitutes a major analytical category in sociological analyses of religion.

Worship is religious ritual. Ritual * is the symbolic expression and articulation of meaning in a social situation. What distinguishes religious ritual from other ritual is its sacred reference point, highlighted by the vertical 'I-thou' (Buber) relation in addition to the horizontal 'we' relation.

When differentiated in terms of the social situation, worship falls into four distinct categories:

1. *Regular worship* ranging from that which in a very structured way encapsulates the life-cycle of Christ into the annual cycle (the liturgical calendar) to that which is relatively unstructured such as Quaker meetings. (E.g. Sunday, Christmas, Easter.)

2. *Life-cycle worship* incorporating the individual into the life of the religious organization, ranging from a close biological link, as in infant baptism, to none, as in adult baptism or confirmation. (E.g. baptism, marriage, confirmation, funerary rites.)

3. *Civic worship* relating to important events in the life of the nation state and endorsing national unity. (E.g. American Presidential Inaugurations and Memorial Day ceremonies; Coronations and Remembrance Sunday* ceremonies in Britain.)

4. *Topical worship* conducted spontaneously and relating to current issues of importance for individuals and society and which often point to divisions within society. (E.g. the Birmingham, Alabama, Prayer Pilgrimage in 1963; the Society for the Protection of the Unborn Child Eucharist in Trafalgar Square, London, at an anti-abortion rally; and Peace Movement ceremonies at missile sites held in the 1980s in both America and England.)

While the four categories are analytically distinct, in reality worship can comprise one or more of the four types simultaneously. This depends in part on the type of religious organization and its relationship with wider society.

Worship grows out of the process of institutionalizing religion: it objectifies what was subjective and spontaneous in the early members' experience. Propositions (dogma/myth) are presented in symbolic ceremonial context to give them meaning, through the medium of metaphor. Worship enacts the central theme of the life and death of Christ (root metaphor), and in doing so metaphorically it shields the participants from the horrors of actually experiencing the original experience, but at the same time elicits an empathic understanding through relatively stylized and exegetical re-enactment of selected events. This dramatic presentation at regular intervals has the effect of making participants feel they belong to the whole, giving them a religious identity. Because propositions and ceremonial bear the imprint of organizational theological interpretations, participants' denominational identity is reinforced as well as the more general Christian identity. At the same time worship points the way participants as Christians and as denominational members are to live out their other various identities in society. Rituals integrate the individual into the group.

Propositions and ceremonial* together make explicit the social structure, i.e. the expected relations between individuals and groups, both within the religious organization and outside. Worship addresses and structures contemporary experience by linking it to the original experience: experience is generated by, expressed by and controlled by worship. Feelings are articulated in worship to produce lasting attitudes. Attention is focussed on what are considered important aspects in the relationship between sacred and secular. Through ritual, individuals are brought together, located in their organization, and together in their organization are located in society. Through ritual, by such restoration, reinforcement and/or redirection of identity (Mol), religious organizations control the individual.

As far as the intended purpose of the ritual goes, sociologists and religious specialists would both look to the 'official' (organizational) view for the answer. Apart from this, however, sociologists raise very different sorts of questions.

The first line of inquiry relates to the identification of social patterns in worship attendance, particularly in relation to the first two worship categories, regular and life-cycle (see Glock, Martin, Wilson). We find that 10–12% of the adult population in England and 44% in America attended regular Sunday worship in the mid-1960s, and that in the case of both countries this rate represents a decrease when compared with those for the preceding decade. Interpretation of these patterns is debated in the framework of secularization and centres on the centrality or otherwise of worship in religion, which categories of worship should be examined, and which sub-categories within a particular type of worship are significant.

Can we say that England is more secular than the States, and that both are more secular than they were? Even if worship were an essential component of religion, which attendance statistic measures a society's secularity? In both countries, but most noticeably in England where there is an established church, life-cycle worship rates are higher than those for regular worship. The official view tends to regard regular worship (i.e. committed membership) as the appropriate criterion, but we are still left with the question as to which particular sub-category of regular worship is the more accurate measure. To accept the

official view, we need evidence that non-committed participation in the other three worship categories is totally non-religious in character. To do this, we need to explore the meaning the ritual has for the participants, and its significance for the society in question.

If we break down the figures for the different kinds of regular and life-cycle worship by denomination, we find that there is less variation in attendance for both English and American sectarian groups where tight control is exercised over the membership (and therefore the official line prevails), than in denominations or churches where membership is less controlled (and therefore 'popular' pew-view and/or diffuse, generalized 'folk' or civil religiosity can more easily co-exist with the 'official' line). Another factor, apart from internal organizational structure, contributes to the variation between worship attendance rates, viz. the relationship between religious organization and the state. When we compare denomination and church groups in America and England, we find that although there is variation between the different worship category attendance rates in both situations, this is pronounced in the case of the established Church of England (figures for the mid-1960s):

Regular:	Sunday	10–12%
Life-cycle:	Had been baptized a Christian	80%
	Married in a Christian ceremony	69%
	Received a Christian burial	over 90%

In England, self-assignation as Christians and believing in God is 85–90%, which is very close to the percentage receiving Christian burial. Self-assignation as C of E is identical to the numbers who had been baptized C of E – 66%. What is particularly interesting about burial and infant baptism is the fact that the consciousness of the focal participant is absent, but action is taken on their behalf by significant others. For sociologists, this points to another kind of religiosity – folk and/or popular – operating simultaneously with the official one, and one which does not see regular worship as essential but rather worship connected with biological entry into and departure from this world.

When regular worship attendance figures are broken down by class and/or ethnicity, we find that a significant self-selection into distinctive class or ethnic sub-cultural groups occurs, one which cannot be accounted for solely in terms of neighbourhood composition. This happens between denominations: e.g. in England, the C of E is predominantly white and middle-class, the Salvation Army white and working-class, and the Independent Churches black, while in America there is a strong correlation between Protestantism and high social status. Such class and/or ethnic divisions also occur within denominations: e.g. in America, there are separate Roman Catholic national parishes for Armenian, Croatian, Italian, Polish, Portuguese, Ukrainian and other American subcultural groups, while separate Lutheran bodies and Synods exist for Danish, Finnish, German, Hungarian, Icelandic, Norwegian, Swedish and other ethnic groups; in England, ethnic groups similarly predominate in black or white Pentecostalist congregations. How can we explain this patterning?

To interpret these findings, we need to ask if there is anything in worship itself that produces or reinforces these social differences. Here we come to the second line of major inquiry – the analysis of the ritual itself. Worship is studied as a social process, extending in time to before and after worship activity, and in space beyond the place of worship. Three main areas are studied: 1. social efficacy; 2. identity reinforcement; 3. social structuring. It is in this context also that topical and civic worship categories are analysed.

1. *Social efficacy*. The official 'message' presented is analysed and compared with 'pew-view'. Participants come to worship with their own beliefs, expectations, etc., and these can distort and, in some cases, negate the official presentation (see Bryant in Newton). Similarly, in superstitiously-motivated life-cycle worship, participants' folk religiosity can be endorsed. Resistance in the pews to liturgical change can be indicative, however, of the efficacy of the superseded ritual, reflecting pew lag in the transitional change-over phase. Incongruity can also be expected when the official presentation is ambiguous, pluralist, or contradictory. Furthermore, there are many

openings (individualist loopholes) in ritual structure which religious specialists cannot totally control, e.g. silence, preaching and especially lay preaching, testimonies, witnessing, announcements, etc. In these ways, individuals can relocate themselves (and sometimes others) out of the organizational framework, but very often informal controls operate here to prevent this (see McGuire). Silence is particularly interesting because it is often associated with the numinous and as such is considered part of the vertical 'I-thou' dimension.

2. *Identity reinforcement.* In analysing the ritual process, key factors can be identified which consolidate identities over and above the religious: e.g. language and music are both important aspects of cultural identity. In England, criticism of the ASB in terms of the loss of 'our heritage' is pertinent here: unwittingly, a certain kind of Englishness was being reinforced by the Book of Common Prayer. The replacement of Latin by the vernacular* has introduced possibilities in England for cultural identity reinforcement, and even further opportunities in America for subcultural identity reinforcement, in the place of the universal Roman Catholic religious identity generated by Latin that transcended cultural boundaries. Similarly, in pluralist society the use of the ethnic tongue reinforces subcultural identities reflected in intra-denominational divisions in America, mentioned earlier (see Groves in Newton illustrating this problem in the Greek Orthodox Church in America). Civic ritual most explicitly reinforces national identity (see Shils and Young on the coronation) and additionally reinforces civil religion in the case of America, where separation between religion and state is constitutionally laid down (see Warner on Memorial Day ceremonies). Important secular relationships, e.g. as reflected in choice of godparents and 'guests' at baptism, are sacralized, as is the secular status of the focal participant: family and community identities are reinforced here (see Bossy). When life-cycle worship is conducted within the context of regular worship, then 'family' as a value is reinforced and metaphorically so as the 'family of Christ' as well as the biological family by virtue of the key members present. In an established church, such as the Church of England, life-cycle worship reinforces the national identity of the 'folk' – to be C of E is to be English. A similar situation with regard to life-cycle worship happens in areas where there is in effect a regional church, such as Methodism in certain areas of England, except here it is regional identity that is reinforced.

3. *Social structuring.* The content of worship, both propositional and ceremonial, is analysed in terms of the social relationships it implicitly or explicitly structures. This includes not only the symbolic aspects designed by the religious specialists, e.g. kiss of peace, priest facing congregation representing corporateness and egalitarianism in recent C of E and Roman Catholic liturgical reforms, but the empirical reality expressed in terms of the social positions of those who play key roles, e.g. the exclusion of women, social background of clergy/lay leaders, etc., and how roles are allocated prior to worship, link into the ranking structure of wider society, reinforcing or challenging it. Statements contained in the ritual are related to the wider social structure, e.g. explicit and implicit political alignments can be identified (see Duquoc, Guichard et al.). When explicit statements are made, controversies arise on occasions within the congregation and/or denomination. It is this sort of analysis that is particularly helpful in understanding topical worship (see Campbell and Pettigrew on the desegregation issue).

R. Bocock, *Ritual in Industrial Society: A Sociological Analysis of Ritualism in Modern England*, 1974; J. Bossy, 'Blood and Baptism: Kinship, Community and Christianity in Western Europe from the Fourteenth to the Seventeenth Centuries', *Sanctity and Secularity: The Church and The World* ed D. Baker, 1973; E. Q. Campbell and T. F. Pettigrew, 'Racial and Moral Crisis: The Role of Little Rock Ministers', *Religion, Culture and Society* ed L. Schneider, 1964; D. Clark, *Between Pulpit and Pew: Folk Religion in a North Yorkshire Fishing Village*, 1982; C. Duquoc, J. Guichard et al, *Politique et vocabulaire liturgique*, 1975; K. Flanagan, 'Competitive Assemblies of God: Lies and Mistakes in Liturgy', *Research Bulletin 1981*, ISWRA; C. Y. Glock, *Re-*

ligion in Sociological Perspective: Essays in the Empirical Study of Religion, 1973; D. Martin, *A Sociology of English Religion*, 1967; D. Martin and P. Mullen (eds), *No Alternative: The Prayer Book Controversy*, 1981; M. B. McGuire, *Control of Charisma: A Sociological Interpretation of the Catholic Pentecostal Movement*, 1981; H. Mol, *Identity and the Sacred*, Oxford 1976; D. Newton (ed), *Liturgy and Change*, ISWRA, 1983; S. E. Mead, *The Nation with the Soul of a Church*, 1975; E. Shils and M. Young, 'The Meaning of the Coronation', *Sociological Review*, 1, 1953, pp.63–81; V. Turner, *The Ritual Process*, 1969; W. Lloyd Warner, 'An American Sacred Ceremony', *Readings in Sociology: A Biographical Approach* ed P. Berger, 1974; B. Wilson, *Religion in Secular Society*, 1966.

DENISE NEWTON

South India Church Worship

see **Church of South India Worship**

Spirituals

The Negro Spiritual was born in the American Negro Christian community. Opinions regarding its origin and function vary, but not because of different data available and different research methods used. The determining factor is how a researcher evaluates the innovative, creative and artistic potential of black people. (Striking examples of this are the entries on 'Spiritual' in the old and the new Grove Dictionaries.)

Thus the spiritual is considered as a misinterpreted hymn of the white Christians (G. P. Jackson), as a 'confession of faith' of the Negro church (T. Lehmann and many others), as the clearest exponent of the Negro's real self, as an oral document of historical events in the history of the American Negro (M. M. Fisher), as a protest against social injustice, as an adaptation of African songs (W. E. B. DuBois), as originating in the camp meetings* of the white revival movement, as the product of Negro bards like 'singing Johnson' and 'Ma White' (J. W. Johnson), and a blending of American and European melodies with African rhythm (E. M. v. Hornbostel).

P. Oliver takes a middle-of-the-road position by pointing to a 'considerable exchange between black and white' and stating that 'the spiritual as a folk form has declined in popularity'. The second statement is clearly wrong, the first one needs qualifying. American church hymns owe the black singers a great debt. That black singers and composers have been influenced by white texts and melodies should not be denied. However, what makes the Negro spiritual a *Negro* spiritual is its black history, content and form. These are admirably described and analysed by James H. Cone: 'Black music is unity music. It unites the joy and the sorrow, the love and the hate, the hope and the despair of black people; and it moves the people toward the direction of total liberation. It shapes and defines black being and creates cultural structures for black expression. Black music is unifying because it confronts the individual with the truth of black existence and affirms that black being is possible only in a communal context' (*The Spirituals and the Blues*, 1972, p.5).

The spiritual is at the roots of at least four musical trends today. 1. The different styles of jazz, including the blues (a 'secularized spiritual'). 2. It has been taken up, greatly changed and adapted to the white ear in the Pentecostal churches, particularly in the U S A, where Pentecostalism originated in a Negro church in Los Angeles and where some of the earliest Pentecostal hymn writers were Negroes. 3. It is further cultivated in a manner faithful to the original tradition in the American Negro Pentecostal churches and in some Negro Baptist churches. 4. Attempts have been made to adapt it to European and American traditional church music (an example is Michael Tippett, *A Child of Our Time*, 1944). There is great controversy whether the Negro spiritual has a place in a non-Negro church service, a controversy which becomes even sharper if the spirituals are translated into French or German, or if they are sung in English in a non-English congregation.

Recently church musicians recognized that it was useless to introduce the songs of a contemporary, yet foreign, sub-culture. Some of them therefore discovered a popular (not a pop-) musical language in the sub-culture of their own language groups and created new masses, ballads and community hymns (e.g. in Czechoslovakia, East and

West Germany, Scandinavia). Some of these songs were created not by church musicians, but by folk-singers and chansonniers who took up biblical topics in their chansons (Latin America, France).

J. C. Downey and P. Oliver, 'Spirituals', *The New Grove Dictionary of Music and Musicians*, 18, 1980, pp.1–7; W. E. B. DuBois, *The Souls of Black Folk*, 1903 (many reprints); M. M. Fisher, *Negro Slave Songs in the United States*, 1953; E. M. v. Hornbostel, 'African Negro Music', *Africa*, 1, 1928, pp.30–62; G. P. Jackson, 'Spirituals', *Grove's Dictionary of Music and Musicians*, VIII, 1954, pp.8–12; J. W. Johnson and J. R. Johnson, *The Book of American Negro Spirituals*, 1925; T. Lehmann, *Negro Spirituals, Geschichte und Theologie*, 1965.

W. J. HOLLENWEGER

Standing

see **Posture** 5

Stations of the Cross

The name denotes both fourteen selected representations of incidents in the last journey of Christ and the devotion which consists in pausing at them in sequence for prayer and meditation.

The devotion probably arose out of the practice recorded from early times of pilgrims to Jerusalem following the 'way of the cross' from Pilate's house to Calvary, and wishing to re-enact it when they returned home. Devotion to the holy places and to Christ's passion received an extra fillip with the return of the Crusaders, who often erected tableaux of places they had visited in the Holy Land. And when the Franciscans were given custody of the holy places in 1342 they saw it as part of their mission to promote the devotion and to encourage the erection of series of such tableaux. From their own churches the practice spread widely into parish churches too.

The subjects of these 'stations' varied widely, as did the number (anything from five to over thirty). The number fourteen seems to have appeared first in the sixteenth century in the Low Countries, and when the devotion was regulated by Clement XII in 1731 it stabilized at this number, comprising nine gospel scenes and five from popular tradition. By the nineteenth century virtually all Roman Catholic churches tended to have a set of fourteen ranged around the internal walls (or occasionally out of doors in the church grounds).

The devotion can be used privately by individual worshippers, silently and informally, with or without texts (of which dozens of unofficial collections exist). More public forms are celebrated, with a vested priest, acolytes and cross-bearer doing the circuit, the congregation following or remaining in their pews. In this case verses of the mediaeval hymn *Stabat mater*, in the vernacular, have often been sung between stations, and meditations such as those of St Alphonsus Liguori (d.1787) were particularly popular in Britain. With the liturgical revival in the mid-twentieth century, the use of the devotion has probably waned somewhat, though it can still be encountered widely in Lent and Passiontide and at certain places of pilgrimage. With the recovered theology of the paschal mystery stressing the integral unity of Christ's death and resurrection, a fifteenth station representing the resurrection has frequently been added to the series, and more exclusively scriptural meditations composed. As the devotion has always been strictly extra-liturgical, no official texts have ever been provided.

C. J. WALSH

Stole

see **Vestments** 1(*d*)

Stoup

A vessel for holding holy water placed near the entrance of churches, into which the faithful who enter dip the fingers of the right hand, blessing themselves with the sign of the cross. Holy water stoups (also called stocks) are probably derived from the fountains in the atrium* of the older basilicas* (e.g. old St Peter's, Rome) in which those who were entering the church washed their hands and faces. They seem to have come into more general use from the ninth century, when the custom of sprinkling the people with holy water known as the *Asperges** before the Sunday mass became widespread. The blessing of the water into which salt was thrown crosswise

with an invocation took place before this ceremony, and the stoups at the entrance to the church were replenished. The significance of the ceremony of holy water was to remind the worshipper of the promises made at his baptism and that the water had cleansed not only his body but also his soul for which Christ shed his blood.

In English mediaeval churches the stoup is usually found in a niche inside the porch in the form of a stone basin. But in France and Italy stoups are found inside the church itself, often standing on a stem or pillar. Holy water stoups are in use in the Roman Catholic Church and in the churches of the Anglican Communion there has been a revival of their use.

F. Bond, *The Chancel of English Churches*, 1916.

C. E. POCKNEE

Subdeacon

The office probably originated in Western Christendom about the middle of the third century and its function seems chiefly to have been to provide assistance to the deacon*. The principal liturgical duties of the subdeacon were to read the epistle and to prepare the elements and vessels for the offertory*. The office was regarded as one of the minor orders in the West until the thirteenth century (and still is so regarded in the East). From that date it came to be treated in the West as the lowest of the major orders and those admitted to it were bound to celibacy. It was, however, little more than a stage through which candidates for the priesthood were required to pass and the vestigial liturgical duties of the subdeacon at high mass were performed by a priest, deacon or even layman. In 1972 the office was suppressed in the Roman Catholic church in the reorganization of the 'lesser ministries' and the obligation of celibacy was transferred to the diaconate.

In some parts of the Anglican Communion the office has been revived in the present century where it is hardly distinguishable from that of reader* with additional authority to administer the chalice, a curious device since the administration of the elements does not seem to have been a traditional part of the subdeacon's duties.

P. HINCHLIFF

Suffrages

Suffrages (Lat *suffragia*, prayers seeking favour or support) are found in the divine office in the historic Western rites, and in some rites derived from them, e.g. in morning and evening prayer in the BCP. They are always petitionary, sometimes intercessory; they are usually couched in general, but sometimes in particular terms; they are normally in the form of versicles and responses, commonly include the Lord's Prayer, and usually conclude with a collect or collects.

Suffrages were no part of the original Roman offices; they were added to them when the latter were adopted in the Frankish Lands, where they were probably part of the Gallican offices, and were then accepted at Rome. In the latest reform of the Roman breviary suffrages have been replaced by *preces* (translated in the English version as 'intercessions', which is somewhat misleading, as by no means all of them are intercessory in character), in the form of a litany* which varies according to the hour, day, feast and season.

The suffrages in the morning and evening offices of the BCP, comprising the material from the creed to the third collect, are typical; they are largely derived from those found in the Sarum books. Those in the longer forms for morning and evening prayer in the ASB, although different in detail, follow the same pattern.

W. JARDINE GRISBROOKE

Sunday

The Lord's Day is the foundation of the entire structure of the Christian year. In the Jewish system, the days of the week were known simply as the first day, the second day, and so on. The last day of the week had a title, the Sabbath, and, dependent on this, Friday was called the preparation. The Sabbath set the pattern of a weekly day of worship, but in Christianity it was 'the first day of the week' (Acts 20.7) which took this position. By the end of the first century that designation had given place to one which more adequately conveyed the day's significance – the Lord's Day. The use of the name Sunday dates from about the middle of the second century. In 321 the official recognition by the Roman state of Sunday as the day of Christian worship

and as a day of public rest meant that the Sabbath had now been incorporated into and transformed by the Christian tradition.

As the Sabbath provided the model of a weekly day of worship, so its general influence is demonstrated by the fact that for a considerable period the Christian Sunday began about 6 p.m. on the Saturday evening. Centuries passed before the old semitic reckoning from sunset yielded completely to the Roman conception of the day as beginning at midnight. About the middle of the fourth century the *Testament of our Lord* refers to the evening as the beginning of the day. The 'eves' of the great festivals represent the survival of the beginning of the semitic day, the 'eve' being part of the festival itself. When this reckoning disappeared from common use, it remained in connection with the most important days of the Christian year.

The relationship between the Lord's Day and the Sabbath of the old covenant serves as the context within which to emphasize the immense difference between these liturgical days. The gospel narrative of the resurrection furnishes the true normative use of the designation 'the first day of the week' as a proper name for the Christian day of worship. When we remember that primitive worship took place at an early hour of the morning, the binding link between Sunday and the resurrection becomes more obvious. Late in the fourth century at Jerusalem the central service of Christendom, consisting of the reading and preaching of the word and the celebration of the sacrament, was held at daybreak. Thus the true note of the Lord's Day must always be joy, thanksgiving, victory. It is surely from the Lordship of Jesus Christ, made manifest in the resurrection on 'the first day of the week' (Mark 16.2), that the title 'the Lord's Day' is ultimately derived. The early church never lost this conception of Sunday as the sign of the inbreaking of the eternal order of God, and it remained a day of praise and triumph. Fasting and the penitential observance of kneeling in prayer were strictly forbidden.

The profound revolution which substituted the Christian Sunday for the Jewish Sabbath took place within the first generation of the church's life. Certainly by the middle of the sixth decade when Paul, writing to the Corinthian church, refers to 'the first day of every week' (I Cor. 16.2), the Lord's Day must long have been supreme. As the celebration of the resurrection on the first day of the week, it is a kind of weekly Easter.

In later years its prime importance was perhaps overshadowed by other calendrical developments, in particular the sanctorale. Recent liturgical and calendrical revision has restored it to its proper importance, something Reformed and Free Churches have done from the Reformation onwards, both by the stress they put on it and by their suppression of other observances. In an age when weekday liturgical observance is only followed by a tiny minority of people, this emphasis on Sunday liturgy is surely right for both practical as well as theological reasons.

A. Adam, *The Liturgical Year*, 1981; C. Jones, G. Wainwright and E. Yarnold (eds), *The Study of Liturgy*, 1978; A. A. McArthur, *The Evolution of the Christian Year*, 1953; H. B. Porter, *The Day of Light: The Biblical and Liturgical Meaning of Sunday*, 1960; W. Rordorf, *Sunday*, 1968.

R. F. BUXTON

Sunday School

see **Children and Worship**

Super Oblata

Since the mid-fifth century, the offertory* ceremony in the Roman rite has been concluded with a prayer called originally, and again since 1969, the *oratio super oblata* ('prayer over the offerings'), but for many centuries called the *secreta* ('secret'). As the latter name first appears in France and Germany, where the custom of saying the prayer in a low voice (*secreto*) originated, it probably refers to this custom, although other meanings are possible. At Rome it was anciently sung, and the singing or saying aloud of it has been restored in the new *Ordo Missae* of 1969.

The prayer, which varies according to the day, is in form a variant of the collect type; its basic content is always a prayer for the divine acceptance of the gifts just placed on the altar within the context of the eucharistic mystery about to be accomplished. A prayer parallel to the *oratio super oblata*

in function and content is found in a corresponding place in most of the historic liturgies.

See also **Silent Prayer**

J. A. Jungmann, *The Mass of the Roman Rite*, II, 1955, pp.90–97.

W. JARDINE GRISBROOKE

Superintendent

The Greek term *episcopos*, from which bishop is derived, means overseer. In the Reformation period, when a term was wanted which would express the element of oversight while avoiding the hierarchical and prelatical overtones of bishop*, the title superintendent seemed an obvious choice. Many of the churches of the Reformation used the term. In German Lutheranism there were superintendents until the 1920s, when the title of bishop was revived. In the Church of Scotland, five superintendents were appointed in 1561 and they, with three bishops who threw in their lot with the Reformation, exercised oversight over other clergy. The superintendent was required to minister in a congregation of his own besides overseeing the work of other men. The office was subsequently discontinued, and there has been a good deal of controversy about whether it was intended as a reformed and permanent, if limited, episcopate or whether it was a temporary expedient made necessary as ministers could not be found for every parish. In the Methodist Church the superintendent minister is the minister in charge of a circuit.

P. HINCHLIFF

Surplice

see **Vestments** 2(*c*)

Symbol

see **Sign, Symbol**

Synaxis

The name *synaxis* (Greek 'meeting' or 'assembly'), anciently used in the Christian church of any meeting for public worship, is today normally used only of that service which is the most ancient and archetypal of them all, the office of readings and prayers which precedes the celebration of the eucharist*, and which has indeed, from a very early date, come to be reckoned as a part of the eucharistic liturgy.

The close relationship of *synaxis* to *synagogue* (Greek 'gathering' and hence 'gathering place'), although it is intrinsically no more than a grammatical one, serves to underline the essential character of the first part of the eucharistic liturgy, as an inheritance from, and development of, the worship of the synagogue. The earliest Christians, as we learn from the Acts of the Apostles, continued to worship in the synagogue, while celebrating the eucharist in their own houses; when they were expelled from the synagogue they prefixed the essential elements of the synagogue service to the eucharist, and made one service of the two (except on certain occasions when the eucharist was preceded by some other function, e.g. the baptismal vigil at Easter).

The synagogue service was composed basically of three elements – reading from the scriptures, psalmody, and prayer, and these three are from the beginning the constant basic elements of the Christian synaxis, which is characterized by Jungmann as essentially a biblical instruction. It appears originally to have opened abruptly with the readings, preceded by no more than the exchange of a mutual greeting between the president (bishop or presbyter) and the assembly. Neither the number nor the order of the readings can be definitely gathered from the earliest evidence, but it seems likely, from a comparison with the synagogue, and from the evidently archaic arrangements of the synaxis which survive in some of the Eastern rites, as well as on certain days in the Roman and Byzantine rites, that there were originally at least four readings in a normal synaxis – from the law, the prophets, the epistles, and the gospels. From earliest times the readings appear to have been followed by a sermon expounding them. From the fourth century onwards there was a universal and rapid tendency towards disuse of the readings from the OT, and nearly everywhere in Christendom the ordinary synaxis came to include only two readings, the epistle and the gospel. During the Middle Ages the sermon also came to be a less frequent feature of the synaxis than in earlier times.

The earliest form of psalmody at the synaxis of which we have any evidence is

the singing of selected psalms in a responsorial manner (i.e. the psalm sung by a soloist, and an unvarying refrain sung after each verse by the congregation: *see* **Responsorial Psalmody**) between the readings. This survives in all the historic rites, although commonly in a very reduced form (e.g. the Gradual – since 1969 replaced by a return to a more extended responsorial psalm – and Alleluia of the Roman rite, and the *prokeimenon* and Alleluia of the Byzantine rite) (*see* **Liturgies** 2).

The element of prayer in the early synaxis took the form of more or less extended intercessions which followed the readings and sermon. The oldest formal arrangement of these is probably that still found in the Roman rite on Good Friday – a series of biddings by the deacon, each followed by a period of silent prayer by the congregation and a collect by the president or a concelebrant presbyter; a parallel form still exists in the Alexandrine rite. From the late fourth century onwards a litany* became a more common form in most parts of the Christian world; in the Roman rite the older form was replaced by a litany (elsewhere in the service) late in the fifth century, and by the seventh century this also had fallen out of use, with the result that with the spread of the Roman rite in the former Gallican lands the common prayers of the synaxis disappeared for many centuries over the greater part of Western Christendom, although in the Middle Ages a substitute was found for them in the 'bidding of the bedes' (*see* **Bidding Prayer**).

While between the fourth and eighth centuries there was an almost universal tendency to reduce the quantity of readings and psalmody, there was a simultaneous universal tendency to add secondary matter to the synaxis: notably, parallel introductory rites developed everywhere during this period. The order and contents of these vary considerably, but there are constant features, such as the Introit or entrance psalm, an introductory hymn of prayer and praise – e.g. the *Gloria in excelsis* or great doxology* in the Roman rite and the *Trisagion** in the Byzantine rite – and an introductory prayer by the president – e.g. the collect of the day in all the Western rites and the prayer which accompanies the *Trisagion* in the Byzantine rite. During the Middle Ages a further parallel development led to the widespread prefixing of preparatory rites of various kinds to the introductory rite itself – e.g. the enarxis* of the Byzantine rite, and the preparatory prayers and confession of the Roman rite.

Modern revisions of the synaxis, whether in the great historic rites themselves or in the post-Reformation liturgies (in most of which the principal features of the synaxis, so far as they had been preserved during the Middle Ages, survived in a recognizable form), tend to concentrate on the restoration of the integrity of its primary elements – readings, psalmody and common prayers – and the rationalization (and in part elimination) of the secondary and tertiary growths of introductory and preparatory matter. In particular there is an all but universal move towards the recovery of the OT material – reading and psalmody – which had come over the centuries to be greatly abbreviated or even, in some post-Reformation liturgies, completely eliminated.

The original relationship between the synaxis and the divine office is an obscure and complex problem, but there seems little doubt that the morning and evening services of the early centuries (corresponding to the matins and lauds and the vespers of the later office) bore considerably more resemblance to their common synagogal origins with the synaxis than do their later forms: a brief consideration of this question will be found under the heading **Cathedral Office**.

Further information on the synaxis and its component parts will be found in most books dealing with Christian worship in general, and epecially in those dealing with the eucharistic liturgies of the several rites. For a good summary, see P. G. Cobb, 'The Liturgy of the Word in the Early Church', being Part II, Ch. III, section 5, in C. Jones, G. Wainwright and E. Yarnold (eds), *The Study of Liturgy*, 1978. For the Roman rite, see: J. D. Crichton, *Christian Celebration: The Mass*, 1971, pp.69–81; L. Eisenhofer and J. Lechner, *The Liturgy of the Roman Rite*, ET 1961, pp.271–334; J. A. Jungmann, *The Mass of the Roman Rite*, ET 1955, I, pp.320–494. For the Byzantine rite, see: C. Kucharek, *The Byzantine-Slav Liturgy of St John Chrysostom*, 1971, pp. 381–465; J. Mateos, *La Célébration de la Parole dans la*

Liturgie Byzantine, 1971. For the common prayers, see: P. de Clerck, *La 'Prière Universelle' dans les liturgies anciennes: Témoignages patristiques et textes liturgiques*, 1977.

E. JARDINE GRISBROOKE

Syrian Worship

See **East Syrian Worship**; **West Syrian Worship**

Tabernacle

This term has been employed to describe a number of disparate objects.

1. It has been used to describe the silk 'tent' or canopy which covered the pyx* suspended over the altar in mediaeval England and France.

2. The term is applied to niches with a carved canopy which housed the statue of a saint.

3. The term was also used in the Middle Ages for a type of altar-piece with carved niches and having hinged wings.

4. Its more usual application is to the vessel in which the sacrament is reserved. Since Vatican II it has been normal in the Roman Catholic Church for this to stand in a separate chapel of reservation used as a place of private prayer, from which communion can be taken to the sick. A similar arrangement is sometimes found in Anglican churches, as is the alternative custom in small churches where a separate chapel cannot be provided, of placing it in an aumbry* on a side wall, or sometimes in the wall behind the main altar, though in the latter case it is contrary to contemporary Roman Catholic regulations to place it in the centre of the wall. Formerly tabernacles were always round, but nowadays a coffer shape is usually preferred. They should be covered with a veil, but this regulation is frequently ignored. The term tabernacle to denote this kind of receptacle for the reserved sacrament was introduced by the reforming bishop of Verona, Matthew Giberti, about 1525; his ideas were later endorsed by the Council of Trent.

A. A. King, *Eucharistic Reservation in the Western Church*, 1965.

G. D. W. RANDALL/J. D. CRICHTON

Table Prayers

see **Ante-communion**

Tenebrae

A quasi-popular term, found in the Roman books not before the twelfth century, for matins and lauds of the last three days of Holy Week*. The reason was that to allow the easier participation of the people, these offices were anticipated to the evening before the day to which they referred (thus *Tenebrae* of Maundy Thursday was sung on the evening of Wednesday). The term came into use most probably because the lights (candles) were gradually extinguished in the course of the office and all departed in darkness (*tenebrae*) and silence.

Matins and lauds of these days were originally simply the ordinary offices sung by monastic or quasi-monastic communities serving the Roman basilicas and other collegiate churches throughout Europe (*see* **Canonical Hours**). In their form they reveal certain primitive features of the Roman cathedral office*. Thus, there were no hymns, no invitatory, no introductory versicles and responses and the *Gloria Patri* at the end of each psalm was suppressed. Matins consisted of nine psalms and nine readings (lamentations, patristic readings and NT), the old Roman pattern. The lamentations were sung to a chant of peculiar poignancy and all the readings were divided by responsories* of great musical beauty. They almost certainly derive from the Roman *schola cantorum* of the seventh, eighth and ninth centuries.

These offices are a prolonged meditation on the events of salvation running from the Last Supper to the entombment. The note of betrayal is sounded in Thursday *Tenebrae*, the judgment, crucifixion and death of Christ on Friday and his burial and the expectation of his resurrection on Saturday.

A unique feature of the offices of these days was the triangular candlestick which stood in the choir and on which fifteen candles of natural, dark-coloured wax were placed. They were extinguished one by one after each psalm (nine for matins and five for lauds) until one only remained. During the *Benedictus* this was hidden either behind the altar or elsewhere in the church and when the signal for departure (*strepitus*) was

given it was replaced on the top of the candlestick. This has been understood as an anticipated sign of the resurrection, but probably was no more than a way of providing light for the congregation to depart.

The offices of the last three days of Holy Week have been brought into line with the reformed Divine Office of 1971. Since they are no longer recited in the evening the term *Tenebrae* is now obsolete.

They consist of the Office of Readings and lauds or morning prayer. The former, replacing the old matins, has an invitatory, a hymn, three psalms, two readings (one from the scriptures, one patristic) and a concluding collect. Morning prayer has a hymn, two psalms, one canticle (OT), a short reading, a special antiphon (*Christus factus est*; Phil. 2.8b, 9), *Benedictus* with antiphon, intercessions and concluding collect.

A few of the responsories and some antiphons remain but the strait-jacketing of these offices has unfortunately eliminated a considerable number of ancient and important texts through which much of the message of the offices was conveyed. Much to be regretted is the virtual elimination of the lamentations which were sung to a peculiarly poignant chant.

J. D. Crichton, *Christian Celebration: The Prayer of the Church*, [2]1981; M. Righetti, *Manuale di Storia Liturgica*, II, 1955, pp.154–8.

J. D. CRICHTON

Terce

see **Canonical Hours**

Thanksgiving

see **Prayer** 5

Thanksgiving (USA)

The celebration of Thanksgiving in the United States, the most characteristic American festival, has an origin and history largely independent of the English Harvest Thanksgiving*. Its origin is in the Puritans' observance of occasional days of fast and thanksgiving in order to conform to the providential will of God. Troubles were understood as signs of the wrath of God and probable causes discussed, sometimes accompanied by a day of humiliation. Good times or the passing of a threat were marked by a day of thanksgiving with prayers, psalm-singing and feasting. With their transference to America, these practices became more informal and communal, and were more closely associated with the rhythms of nature. Only later was a regular day of thanksgiving for harvest proclaimed by civil government.

The early seventeenth-century Puritans in England and Holland, from which the earliest settlers in America were drawn, sought mainly to cleanse the Church of England of its 'unbiblical' polity and practices. The church was to be the godly joined together in covenant after a 'sifting' and a day of humiliation, who were to return thanks for the benefits with which God blessed them. They were to live in obedience to the providential will of God as individuals and families, observing only the biblical 'feasts of Christ' (Christmas, Good Friday and Easter) and such days of fast and thanksgiving as were appropriate.

When the Pilgrims arrived at Cape Cod in 1620, survival itself was difficult, and without an ordained ministry religious practices were simple; correspondingly there was greater emphasis on personal and family piety and less on formal observances apart from Sunday worship. The recognized need for humility and thankfulness remained, but no days were set apart for the biblical feasts or for humiliation and thanksgiving. The difficult winter which followed at Plymouth, when nearly half the Pilgrims died and there was civil unrest, was accompanied by a personal awareness of the benevolence of God: when 'it pleased God the mortality began to cease amongst them . . . it was the Lord which upheld them'. And when 'by the goodness of God' they found that they 'had all things in good plenty' the following autumn, they joined the Indians in three days of 'special rejoicing' at Plymouth, during which there was feasting and recreation. This was not apparently a 'day of thanksgiving', however; no religious service is mentioned and recreations would not have been allowed on days of worship. So this 'first' thanksgiving is properly seen as an informal communal rejoicing in the gifts of God, rather than as a specific day of thanksgiving to God.

The Congregational polity of early New England churches, by which individual churches were not subject to external ec-

clesiastical control, inhibited the spread of regular times of fast and thanksgiving, in effect leaving them to local arrangement until they were enacted by civil authority some fifty years later. In the mid-eighteenth century there was still some argument about the 'Pharisaism' of special days publicly appointed, but after the Continental Congress proclaimed a national day of thanksgiving, agreement became more widespread. The Episcopal Church included a form of prayer and thanksgiving in its 1786 Proposed Prayer Book and in the 1789 Book and subsequent revisions. Thanksgiving Day was officially proclaimed as a national holiday by President Abraham Lincoln in 1863; traditionally the last Thursday in November, Thanksgiving is now (by act of Congress in 1941) the fourth Thursday of that month.

Vestiges of the mixed origins of Thanksgiving Day remain in its observance. There is a proclamation by the President, and some allusion to the Pilgrim fathers of the nation, but the day is primarily a family occasion centred on Thanksgiving Dinner (with turkey and pumpkin pie). Most churches observe the day by mid-morning worship comprised of readings, hymns and prayers, in which they seek to restore it as a religious occasion.

William Bradford, *Of Plymouth Plantation 1620–1647*, ed S. E. Morison, 1959; G. D. Langdon, Jr, *Pilgrim Colony*, 1966; W. deL. Love, Jr, *The Fast and Thanksgiving Days of New England*, 1895.

D. W. HARDY

Theology of Worship

The worship of God is a primary activity of the church, requiring no justification beyond itself. It accomplishes indeed 'man's chief end', which according to the Westminster Catechism is 'to glorify God and enjoy him for ever'. Phenomenologically, worship takes place in cultic acts. Such rites are intended as the vehicle of an inward and total devotion; they both form and express the believers who carry them out. The apostle Paul used cultic terminology both of the ethical conduct expected of Christians (Rom. 12.1f.; I Cor. 6.18–20; II Cor. 6.16ff.) and of his own evangelistic activities (Rom. 1.9; 15.15f.; Phil. 2.17; II Tim. 4.6). Liturgists are interested specifically in rites, and more particularly in the corporate worship of the church.

Worship is a faithful human response to the revelation of God's being, character, beneficence and will. In worship, God is adored simply as God, God's character is praised, thanks are given for God's acts, and conformity to God's will is sought. Worship is the requital of God's love in a personal encounter, a communion which is reciprocal but asymmetrical, involving a 'sacrifice of praise' (Heb. 13.15) on the part of the created and redeemed. God precedes humanity not only in the mighty deeds of creation and redemption but also in calling for, and in some sense enabling, the ever renewed response of worship. German theologians like to pun on 'divine service' (*Gottesdienst*), saying that God serves us before we serve God. Finally worship is participation in the life of God in the mode appropriate to created being.

Characteristically, Christian worship is trinitarian in theme and structure. The eucharistic prayer is normally offered to the Father (the 'Abba' of Jesus; in Cappadocian terms, the 'Fount of Deity') through Christ in the Holy Spirit (cf. Eph. 2.18). This is not felt to be in contradiction with doxology addressed to all three divine persons: the Nicene-Constantinopolitan Creed confesses as Lord not only the Son but also the Holy Spirit, 'who with the Father and the Son together is worshipped and glorified'. This praise is offered 'in the church' (Eph. 3.20f.) whose 'principal manifestation', *praecipua manifestatio*, the liturgical assembly is (Vatican II, Constitution on the Liturgy, 41). The etymology of *leitourgia* has sometimes been exploited to stress that worship is 'the work of the whole people' in the sense that it calls for the 'active participation' of the whole assembly, each member in its role (ibid., 14; 26–30). Another interpretation makes of the liturgy a 'public service' rendered by the church on behalf of a world which is no longer, or not yet, able or willing to worship God in agreement with the vocation of humanity (J. J. von Allmen, *Worship: Its Theology and Practice*, 1965). The eschatological nature of worship is shown in its 'playfulness' (R. Guardini, *The Spirit of the Liturgy*, ET 1930), its resolution of work and rest: the service of God is perfect freedom (Book of Common Prayer, second

collect of morning prayer).

At their most elementary, liturgy and doctrine coincide: 'Jesus is Lord' is both an acclamation and an assertion. But as each develops with its own functions and in its own circumstances, the two risk growing apart. In its loving address to God, worship tends towards exuberance and abandon; theology, on the other hand, operates in controversy and responds to intellectual challenge, making fine distinctions and drawing conclusions by argument. Yet worship and theology continue to interact, and church dogma mediates between them. The fourth century provides a classic case that has been decisive for Christian identity. Worship had very early been accorded to Christ: apart from the acts of obeisance (*proskunesis*) in the synoptic gospels and the 'My Lord and my God' of Thomas (John 20.28), the NT contains hymns in praise of Christ's sovereignty (Phil. 2.5–11; Rev. 1.5f.; 5.13; cf. II Tim. 4.18; II Peter 3.18). Against the Arians the Nicenes argued that the reduction of Christ to a creature would turn Christians into idolaters (Athanasius, *Letter to Adelphius*, 3f.; cf. Gregory Nazianzus, *Oration XL on Holy Baptism*, 42; Gregory of Nyssa, *On the Holy Spirit against Macedonius*). Athanasius and the Cappadocians also appealed, in support of the Trinity, to the threefold name confessed in the saving mystery of baptism (Athanasius, *Letter to Serapion* I. 29f.; Gregory of Nyssa, *Sermon on the Baptism of Christ*; Basil, *On the Holy Spirit*, 24–26; cf. Theodore of Mopsuestia, *Catechetical Homily* XIV, 14–21; Ambrose, *On the Mysteries* V. 28). Against the Macedonians, Basil of Caesarea was able to point to an existing tradition of addressing doxologies to the Holy Spirit alongside the Father and the Son (*On the Holy Spirit*, 71–75). Eventually the conciliar creed of Nicaea and Constantinople served not only to regulate the bishops' teaching on God but also became adopted into the eucharistic liturgies of both Byzantium and the West as a doxological text: liturgy and doctrine there coincide once more.

The familiar tag *lex orandi, lex credendi* ('the law of praying [sets] the law of believing') has its verbal origins in the fifth century, although the mode of argument is substantially earlier. Before even such argumentation in the Arian controversy, Irenaeus and Tertullian had invoked against the Gnostics' depreciation of matter the sacramental practice of the church with bodily gesture, water and oil, bread and wine. Between 435 and 442 the lay monk Prosper of Aquitaine, in a work that became associated with Pope Celestine I, argued against semi-pelagianism that the apostolic injunction to *pray* for the whole human race (I Tim. 2.1–4) – which the church obeys in its intercessions – proves the obligation to *believe* that all faith, even the beginnings of good will as well as growth and perseverance, is from start to finish a work of grace. To show the need for grace from the very beginning, Prosper appeals also to prebaptismal exorcisms and exsufflations, as Augustine had already done in establishing that children are born with original sin. While liturgy is thus claimed to establish doctrine, doctrine may also have a return effect on the liturgy. In the area of soteriology, many collects in the ancient Western sacramentaries appear to have been deliberately composed with an anti-pelagian intent and yet a due acknowledgment of the place of works in the salvation of believers. That should not be thought of as an alien imposition on the liturgy, for in its profoundest structures worship shows Christians ascribing salvation to God's grace alone yet themselves engaged in the active response of faith.

Worship is a first-order theology. In the words of Evagrius of Pontus: 'If you are a theologian, you will truly pray; and if you truly pray, you are a theologian.' In the liturgies of *St Mark* and *St Basil*, the doxologies* addressed to God at the *Sanctus** are called 'theologies'. Yet the initial gift and act of faith already contain an element of understanding, the *intellectus fidei*. So there should be no discontinuity between primary theology and second-order, or reflective, theology, or faith seeking (further or self-) understanding (*fides quaerens intellectum*). Nevertheless, reflective theology may have to act critically upon particular manifestations of worship. Thus the Reformation intended to correct developed liturgical practices that were the outcrop of distorted views on God, man and salvation. The Reformers acted in the name of the scriptures which, though they themselves were to a great extent liturgically composed, defined and transmitted, never-

theless had a special authority in view of their canonical status. Protestants have usually held, too, that the Catholic magisterium would have done better to nip Marian devotion in the bud rather than allowing it into the liturgy and eventually appealing to liturgical practice when defining the Marian dogmas. At all times, reflective theology has the duty to advise the pastoral office in its regulation of the more or less spontaneous popular developments that seek expression in the official liturgy.

The Protestant Reformers issued their own orders for public worship. In the circumstances these understandably had a somewhat aggressive doctrinal thrust. As a result, Protestant services have tended to an undue stress on the didactic over the latreutic. Yet there is a properly formative role for the liturgy. At the beginning of the modern Liturgical Movement*, Dom Lambert Beauduin recognized the worship assembly as the primary place in which people learned and grew in the faith. That may be seen as an extension of the mystagogical catechesis of the patristic church.

Among contemporary theologians with a strong interest in worship, emphasis varies as to how far the liturgy itself should control not only the theme but also the structure and texture of their work. A. Schmemann's theology of baptism, *Of Water and the Spirit* (1974), is a direct commentary on the Byzantine rite of initiation, just as he had expounded the eucharist in *For the Life of the World* ([2]1973, ch 2). In his *Theological Dimensions of the Liturgy* (ET 1976), C. Vagaggini locates the rites and prayers within a framework of salvation history and the classical tractates of Catholic theology. D. W. Hardy and D. Ford, in their *Jubilate: Theology in Praise* (1984), take no account of the ritual action and scarcely cite a liturgical text. D. Ritschl, while recognizing that the Christian 'story' is liturgically transmitted, holds that worship is a 'last word' and should not become a starting-point for further 'scholastic deductions' (*Zur Logik der Theologie*, 1984). On the other hand, G. Ebeling makes the fundamental act of prayer the basis of his whole relational ontology (*Dogmatik des christlichen Glaubens*, 1979). It seems proper that systematic theology should draw on and serve the worship of the church, just as it has also other sources and responsibilities in the evangelistic enterprise, the ethical endeavours of Christians, and the engagement with the history of ideas and culture. When it reaches into silence, worship may remind theology of its own apophatic dimension.

One final feature in the current theology of worship should be noted. After the secular reductionism of the 1960s, liturgists in the 1970s and 80s have tended to maintain a stress on the humanity of worship but have regained the sense of rites and signs as vehicles of transcendence from and towards God. They find tools in phenomenology, cultural anthropology and semiotics but recognize the divine component in the system, structure or pattern of 'communication' which is Christian liturgy. Names to be mentioned here include R. Grainger (*The Language of the Rite*, 1974), W. Jetter (*Symbol und Ritual. Anthropologische Elemente im Gottesdienst*, 1978), J. G. Davies (*New Perspectives on Worship Today*, 1978), L. M. Chauvet (*Du symbolique au symbole*, 1979), P. Cornehl (e.g. 'Theorie des Gottesdienstes – ein Prospekt' in *Theologische Quartalschrift* 159, 1979, pp.178–95), G. S. Worgul (*From Magic to Metaphor: A Validation of the Christian Sacraments*, 1980), K. H. Bieritz (*Im Blickpunkt: Gottesdienst*, 1983), D. N. Power (*Unsearchable Riches: The Symbolic Nature of Liturgy*, 1984).

P. Brunner, *Worship in the Name of Jesus*, ET 1968; K. Federer, *Liturgie und Glaube. Eine theologiegeschichtliche Untersuchung*, 1950; A. Kavanagh, *On Liturgical Theology*, 1984; E. J. Lengeling, *Liturgie. Dialog zwischen Gott und Mensch*, 1981; A. Schmemann, *Introduction to Liturgical Theology*, 1966; N. Smart, *The Concept of Worship*, 1972; G. Wainwright, *Doxology*, 1980.

GEOFFREY WAINWRIGHT

Three Hours Devotion

In fourth-century Jerusalem the custom originated by which the events of redemption were celebrated each year on what were believed to be their original sites, and in their original chronological sequence. Accordingly the three hours of Jesus' passion were observed by a service from the sixth to the ninth hour on the day now called Good Friday*. The bishop presided and

the service included readings from all passages of scripture which relate to the passion, interspersed with prayers and ending with the passion story from St John's Gospel. Although many features of the Jerusalem observances, e.g. Palm Sunday*, were adopted throughout Christendom, this particular observance was not, probably because it intruded on the liturgical activities which had already developed in the West, notably the preparation of catechumens* for baptism. The three hours devotion as it is known today originated in Peru as an extra-liturgical devotion as recently as the late seventeenth century and has since been adopted in many Roman Catholic and Anglican churches. In Peru it consisted in essence of addresses on the seven words from the cross, and this remains the common basis of the service today. But it interferes with the proper observance of the traditional liturgy, and in the Church of England the attempt is sometimes made to observe the three hours with a complete use of the official liturgy, mattins*, litany*, and ante-communion*, and to end with evensong. Changing social patterns, however, make it very uncertain whether it is any longer desirable to adhere to the hours in question, which are commonly understood to be twelve noon to three o'clock, as a means of presenting the Lord's passion either to the church or to the world.

J. G. Davies, *Holy Week*, 1963; J. W. Tyrer, *Historical Survey of Holy Week*, 1932.

E. C. WHITAKER

Thurible

More commonly termed in English censer. A metal pan designed to hold heated charcoal upon which powdered or granulated perfumed gums, the most common being *olibanum*, are sprinkled. The most usual form of the censer is now a pan having a cover which is pierced with a number of apertures so that the fumes of the incense* may be exuded as the censer is swung to and fro on the chains to which it is attached. The use of incense in pagan religions as well as in OT rites and also in association with the deification of the Roman emperors probably accounts for its rejection by Christians in the first three centuries. It is unlikely, therefore, that the reference to a censer in Rev. 8.5 reflects the custom of Christian worship at the end of the apostolic era. About AD 200, Tertullian in North Africa rejects the use of incense because of its association with emperor worship (*Apol.* 30).

The first definite evidence for the use of incense in Christian worship is at the end of the fourth century in *The Pilgrimage of Egeria*, describing the services in Holy Week and Easter at the Church of the Holy Sepulchre. Jerusalem. Pseudo–Dionysius the Areopagite also refers to the act of censing about AD 500. The earliest use of the censer was in processions, when it was carried before the bishop at the entrance of the ministers, and also in the procession which preceded the reading of the gospel at the mass. In both these instances its use was probably honorific. This custom may have been derived from imperial usage, since it was customary for torches and incense to be carried before the emperor, and when the bishop acquired a status as a court dignitary in the fourth century this custom may have applied to him. As time went on, the use of the censer was elaborated to include the censing of the ministers and congregation as well as the elements of bread and wine as they were carried in and offered at the altar. After the thirteenth century, with the introduction of the new ceremony of the elevation of the host, the consecrated element was censed as it was lifted up by the celebrant. The censer was also used at the offices of lauds and vespers on festivals.

The use of censers did not entirely cease after the Reformation in England, as the records from the reign of Elizabeth I clearly show, and the use of a censer was maintained at Ely cathedral until 1752. Also a pan with a handle for the use of incense was part of the ceremonies in the coronation processions of all the Stuart kings including James II.

In the Eastern Orthodox Church the censer is used with considerable elaboration not only in the celebration of the eucharistic liturgy, but also in the rites associated with baptisms, marriages and funerals.

There is an enormous and famous thurible suspended from the roof of the Cathedral of Santiago de Compostela, Spain, which requires several men to set it

in motion, and which fills the whole building with incense.

Another form of the censer is to be seen in the cathedral at Lyons, France, where at the pontifical high mass large urns are in use on either side of the altar which are replenished with incense at certain stages of the progress of the liturgy. The grains of incense are usually kept in a metal container known as a 'boat' on account of its shape.

M. Andrieu, *Les Ordines Romani du haut moyen age*, 5 vols, 1931–61, E. G. C. Atchley, *History of the Use of Incense*, 1909; J. Wickham Legg, *Church Ornaments and their Civil Antecedents*, 1917.

C. E. POCKNEE/G. D. W. RANDALL

Thurifer

The person who, in processions or on liturgical occasions, carries the thurible* or censer (a metal brazier hanging from chains and fitted with a lid) in which incense* is burnt.

P. HINCHLIFF

Tower

The most familiar use of this term is in denoting a stone, brick or wooden structure attached to a church building, often containing one or more bells. The term has also been applied to a tower-like vessel used at the eucharist in the Gallican rites. There is some difference of opinion among ecclesiologists as to whether this tower housed the reserved sacrament or whether the bread it contained was for consecration at the eucharist. The poem written by Venantius Fortunatus (*Carm.* XX) would seem to indicate that the tower given by Felix, Bishop of Bourges, *c.* 573, was for the purpose of reservation*.

C. E. POCKNEE

Tract

see **Chants of the Proper of the Mass**

Transept

The transept is the transverse part of a church at right angles to the nave and usually inserted between it and the chancel*.

Transepts originally filled two functions and can therefore be classified as 1. a *transept-martyrium*, which provided a large space around the tomb of a saint; 2. a *transept-prothesis*, which provided an area for the tables on which the congregation placed the gifts at the offertory*.

A second classification, by form instead of function, allows transepts to be divided into six groups (*see* Figs. 27–31): 1. *Continuous transept*. The transverse space is undivided, the colonnades being cut short to leave an open rectangle, e.g. St Peter's, Rome. 2. *Cross transept*. The colonnades are turned at right angles into the wings and

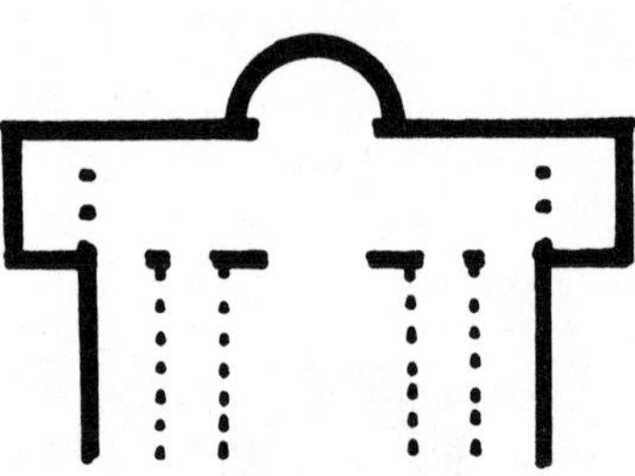

Fig. 27 St Peter's, Rome, Italy

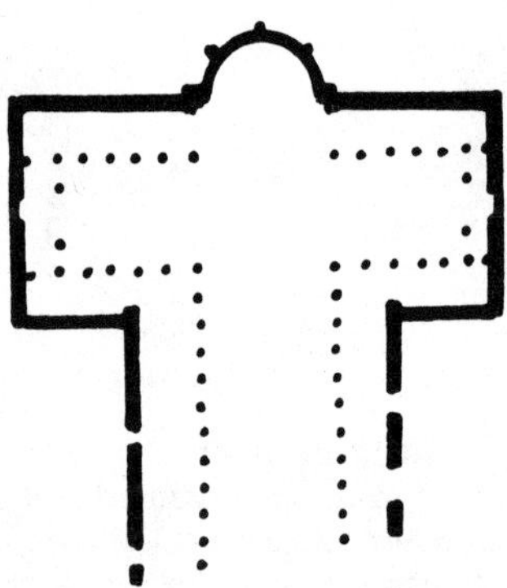

Fig. 28 St Menas, Abu Mina, Egypt

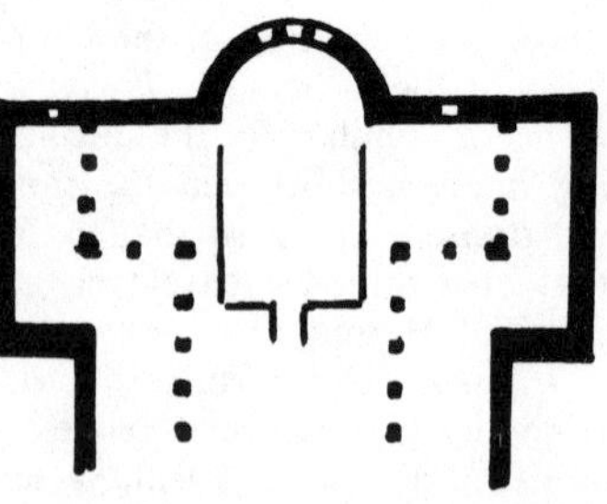

Fig. 29 Basilica A, Philippi, Macedonia

Fig. 30 Church of the Nativity, Bethlehem, Israel

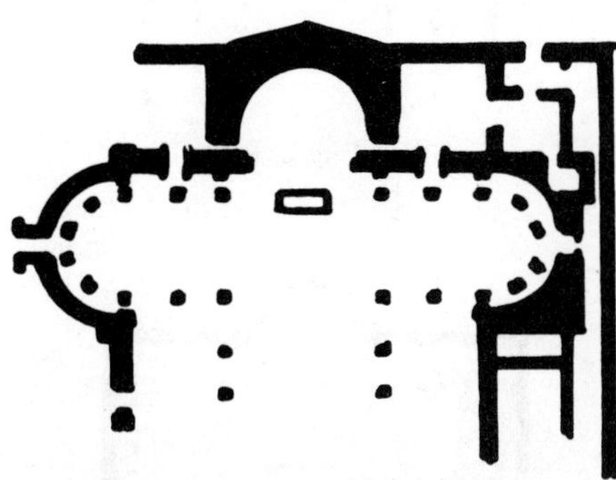

Fig. 31 Hermopolis (Ashmunein), Egypt

then envelop them on three sides, e.g. St Menas, Abu Mina. In a reduced cross transept, the colonnades are bent at right angles and then turn through another to join the east wall, e.g. Basilica A, Philippi. 3. *Trefoil transept*. The two extremities of the transept are provided with apses, and these, with the sanctuary, produce an integrated design with three semi-circles, e.g. the Church of the Nativity, Bethlehem. 4. *Triconch transept*. This is similar to the former, but nothing intervenes between the sanctuary and the transept apses, so that the plan is like that of a three-leaved clover, e.g. the Cathedral of Hermopolis (Ashmunein). 5. *Dwarf transept*. This form is not discernible from the plan, since it relates to the elevation and designates a transverse space whose wings are lower in height than the nave. 6. *Tripartite transept*. This, too, refers to the elevation, when the wings are shut off by arcades from the central area.

EDITOR

Transfiguration

This commemoration of the event recorded in Mark 9.2–8 and parallels takes place on 6 August. It derives from the Eastern church and became general in the West in the fifteenth century. It is independent of and not related to the rest of the liturgical year.

R. F. BUXTON

Trinity Sunday

The first Sunday after Pentecost*. This festival is different in character from those which commemorate the historical events of salvation, being concerned with theological ideas concerning the ontology of God himself. It originated in the West in the tenth century and spread slowly. Late in the eleventh century Pope Alexander II was not persuaded that the festival was a valid development, but Rome finally adopted it in the fourteenth century.

Some parts of the church came to name the Sundays following until Advent as 'after Trinity' rather than 'after Pentecost'. The Sarum Rite was among these and this was copied by the Books of Common Prayer.

R. F. BUXTON

Trisagion

The name (Greek, lit. 'the thrice-holy') of a hymn in the Byzantine rite which is sung after the little entrance* at the pre-eucharistic synaxis*, its place and purpose corresponding to the *Gloria in excelsis* (*see* **Doxology**) in the Roman rite. Also used at many other points in the services of the Byzantine rite, it consists of the invocation 'Holy God, Holy and Mighty, Holy and Immortal, have mercy upon us' three times, followed by the lesser doxology and in some contexts a final repetition of the invocation.

The Byzantine form of the *Trisagion* is occasionally met with in the historic Western rites also, notably in the Roman rite on Good Friday at the veneration of the cross*. Another form of the *Trisagion*, of a more festal character, appears to have been in use in the ancient Hispano-Gallican

liturgy, as an acclamation before the singing of the gospel.

The *Trisagion* should *not* be confused with the *Sanctus**; the use of the Latin name of the *Trisagion* – *Tersanctus* – as a title for the latter by some writers is misleading, although it is possible that the actual name *Trisagion* did in fact originate as a title for the *Sanctus* at some remote date before the hymn now called *Trisagion* existed.

H. Holloway, *A Study of the Byzantine Liturgy*, 1933, pp.59–62; C. Kucharek, *The Byzantine-Slav Liturgy of St John Chrysostom*, 1971, pp.399–405; J. Mateos, *La Célébration de la Parole dans la Liturgie Byzantine*, 1971, pp.98–110.

W. JARDINE GRISBROOKE

Tunicle

see **Vestments** 1(*g*)

Unction

The anointing of persons and things is ancient and widely used in a great many religions, not merely in those of the Mediterranean basin. Various substances (oil, fat, blood, water, saliva) were used at different times and in different places with various significance. Of these, consecration or the making of a person or thing sacred seems to have been the dominant one.

This was so in the OT. Things, Jacob's stone (Gen. 28.18), the ark and tabernacle furniture were consecrated with oil (Ex. 30.25ff.). Kings were the special object of unction (I Sam. 10.1ff.; 16.13; etc.) as also were priests (Lev. 8.12, high priest; Lev. 8.30, other priests). There is a possible reference to the anointing of prophets (Ps. 105.15), though the injunction to anoint Elisha (I Kings 19.16) seems never to have been carried out. None the less, the consecration with oil with which 'priests, kings and prophets' were anointed by God was destined to have a long history in the Christian liturgy.

In the NT there is a reference to the apostles' healing with oil (Mark 6.13) and what in the Catholic tradition is regarded as a ritual use of oil for healing in James 5.14–15. However, the key-factor in the use of unction in the liturgy seems to have been the figure of Jesus, the Messiah ('Anointed', *Christos*), who was 'anointed' at his incarnation (Heb. 1.9), for his messianic ministry at baptism (Mark 1.9–11 and par.), and who was conscious of the presence of the Spirit with him in his saving work (Luke 4.16–22). After his death and resurrection he becomes the source of the Spirit (Acts 2.33) whom he sends upon his church. This coming of the Spirit to the individual Christian is symbolized in the liturgy both by the laying-on of hands and in a great variety of ways by unction. The precise purpose (whether gift, grace or ministry) intended by unction has to be discerned both from the circumstances in which it is given and the words that accompany it. However, the overriding significance of anointing is that it conveys the Spirit of Christ who is at once the source of the Spirit and the exemplar of the life of the Christian.

The relationship between the anointing and the Spirit-filled Christ can be seen in a very striking manner in the post-baptismal unction, usually called chrismation. Apart from the Syrian Church which at first most probably did not have it (E. C. Whitaker, *Documents of the Baptismal Liturgy*, [2]1970, Introduction), all liturgies with remarkable unanimity have had this rite. The oil used is *chrisma* (from the same verb *chrio* as *Christos*) and it signifies the positive side of baptism, the conformation of the Christian to Christ, his participation in the priestly, royal and prophetic quality of Christ and the giving of the Spirit (cf. the prayer of consecration, Roman Pontifical, liturgy of the chrism mass). But as in the OT unction signified richness and abundance of life, the chrism acquired a very rich symbolism. This is particularly noteworthy in the Eastern Church where from the fourth century onwards chrism was called *myron* (Cyril of Jerusalem, *Cat. Myst.*, III, 2, 3, 7) on account of the many aromatic ingredients that went to its composition. It was accordingly interpreted as 'the good odour of Christ' (cf. II Cor. 2.15) which should perfume the life of the Christian who has died and risen with Christ and who henceforth should live with him (*Apostolic Constitutions*, VII, 44). To this the Council of Laodicaea adds that it makes the candidate a sharer in the kingdom of God (can.48). To this the anointing with chrism in confirmation, when it came to be combined with the imposition

of hands, adds the significance of completion and the giving of the fullness of the Spirit (*Ap. Trad.*, 22.1, 2).

The pre-baptismal anointing is more closely related to the culture of the Graeco-Roman world where the anointing of athletes before the *agōn* was well known. This rite, which is found in every baptismal liturgy until the sixteenth century, signifies the strengthening of the candidate for the struggle with the powers of darkness he will meet in the waters into which he will be plunged. Originally, he was anointed all over as were the ancient wrestlers so that the opponent could not get a firm grip on him – a symbolism that was known to St Gregory the Great. This anointing was really an exorcism* and this fact gave its name to the oil which in more recent centuries has been called the 'oil of catechumens'.

In spite of James 5.14–15, the use of unction for the healing of the sick is not attested until the first decades of the third century (*Ap. Trad.* V). The oil is blessed after the eucharistic prayer and is very clearly intended for healing. The prayer envisages the sick persons as not only being anointed with it but also as drinking it. This is found also in the *Sacramentary* of Serapion (*c.* 350, ed Funk, 1905, II, pp.178–81) where the terms are strongly medical (the oil is a healing *medicine*) but there is also an element of exorcism in the prayer. This is not surprising since both in OT and in the Graeco-Roman world physical illness was connected with sin and evil. The emphasis on healing in the liturgical tradition is marked, and the main elements of the prayer of the *Apostolic Tradition* have remained in the Roman Pontifical to this day. The modern version of the prayer has omitted the mention of people touching and drinking the oil but this was a very common practice. They used to bring their phials of oil to church (not only on Maundy Thursday) and when ill anoint themselves or get others to do so for them. Several ecclesiastical writers recommend them to do so, no doubt to eliminate superstitious practices.

At first there was no particular order of anointings and some texts suggest that the oil should be applied where the pain was greatest. It was only when the anointing of the sick became entangled with current penitential practice in the tenth century that the anointing of the separate senses to remove sin committed through them became customary.

Until recent times the unction of the sick was delayed until the danger of death was proximate. Thanks to historical research which was able to separate unction from the sacrament of penance* with which it had become closely associated, the trend towards an earlier anointing began. Unction of the sick was seen more clearly to be a sacrament whose purpose was to restore health, if that should be the will of God. This trend received official expression in the Order for the *Pastoral Care and the Anointing of the Sick* (1972). Basing its teaching on James 5.14, 15, the Order makes clear that it is not a sacrament of the dying but of those 'whose health is seriously impaired by sickness or old age' (no. 8). It may be administered in successive illnesses, during the same illness if there is a fresh crisis, and before surgery 'whenever serious illness is the reason for the surgery'. The Order sees the purpose of the sacrament as the strengthening of 'the whole person' in faith, in trust in God, in the ability to accept suffering in a Christian spirit and the restoration of health.

The use of unction in the ordination* of bishops and priests undoubtedly came in under the influence of the Carolingian practice of anointing kings. Behind this is the influence of the OT, which was dominant in all the liturgy of that time. It was easy to make the transference from the anointing of kings in the OT (and one or two texts in the consecration of the oils suggested it) to the anointing of monarchs. Once this transference was made, it was felt that bishops and priests, too, must be anointed. The rites are first found in the Romano-German pontifical of the end of the tenth century. The bishop was anointed on the head but the text suggests that his whole body was regarded as being anointed. He became a sacred, even a sacrosanct person. The hands of the priest were anointed and made sacred for the celebration of the eucharist and the handling of the sacred elements.

Unction was and is used in rites that are not strictly sacramental, notably in the dedication* of a church. This ritual, until recently very elaborate, saw the physical church as a symbol of the Christian people

and the anointings with chrism were parallel to the initiation rites of baptism and confirmation. In the 1977 Roman Catholic rite there is less emphasis on this aspect of things, although the anointing of the walls of the church and of the altar is retained. The emphasis now is on the dedication of the people for their ministry in the world.

Cabrol, 'Huiles', *DACL*, VI, cols 2777–91; J. D. Crichton, *Christian Celebration: The Sacraments*, [2]1979, pp.168–91; *The Dedication of a Church*, 1980; Bruno Kleinheyer, *Die Priesterweihe im Römischen Ritus*, 1961 (for priesthood only); H. Leclerq, 'Onction', *DACL*, XII, cols 2116–30; 'Onction dans l'Ordination', ibid., cols 2130–47; A. G. Martimort (ed), *L'Eglise en Prière*, 1961, Part 3 on the sacraments, where the meaning of unction in connection with various sacraments is given; cf. pp.169–83 for dedications of church, etc.; L. L. Mitchell, *Baptismal Anointing*, 1966; Placid Murray, 'The Liturgical History of Extreme Unction', *Studies in Pastoral Liturgy* ed Vincent Ryan, 1963, pp.18–38; *Pastoral Care of the Sick*, Rites of Anointing and Viaticum, ET 1983; Mario Righetti, *Storia Liturgica*, [2]1959, IV (on the sacraments, dedication of churches, etc).

J. D. CRICHTON

Unitarian Worship

In his definitive *History of Unitarianism*, E. M. Wilbur suggests that the basic characteristic of Unitarianism, in all its manifestations, is a sturdy devotion to freedom, reason and tolerance.

Unitarianism, at its best, is a form of rational mysticism, solidly Christian in origin and ethos, but firmly based on a genuine belief in tolerance and on an agreement to differ. This has resulted in considerable variations in forms of church government and modes of worship. In the United Kingdom, the central denominational authority is now called a General Assembly, a reminder of the Presbyterian origins of English Unitarianism. But while the churches in Northern Ireland are truly Presbyterian, in Britain, as in the United States, Unitarian church polity is strictly congregational, and in Transylvania, the Unitarian churches, though not really episcopal, have always been presided over by a succession of bishops stretching back to the Reformation. At King's Chapel, Boston, Massachusetts, one of the oldest American congregations, a revised BCP is still in regular use. But American Unitarianism as a whole is now characterized by very radical and diverse forms of free worship, which often finds inspiration in non-Christian and humanist sources.

In England, the free or open service of traditional Nonconformity has co-existed for over two centuries with a vigorous liturgical tradition. The English Presbyterians, from whom Unitarians are in the main descended, were particularly attached to liturgical worship, partly because they always retained a certain nostalgia for the established church, and partly because they came to believe that the use of extempore prayer* could easily degenerate into unseemly 'enthusiasm'. Some traces of Calvinist influence remained in their worship, notably in the retention of the Great Prayer. But in the eighteenth century, when the Presbyterians became increasingly identified with the cause of Rational Dissent (which did much to determine the subsequent development of Unitarianism) they began to produce prayer books of their own. Even Joseph Priestley published *Forms of Prayer for the use of Unitarian Societies* (1783) and the flow was not stemmed by later theological change. From 1741 to our own day, well over a hundred liturgies appeared. They illustrate the development of doctrine common to all congregations, the majority of which always preferred conceived prayer. The Rational Dissenters were profoundly influenced by Locke's philosophy, Hartley's psychology, Newton's mathematical cosmology, and the radical social ideals of the Enlightenment. Their service books were scriptural in language, and often incorporated responses for minister and people. They were dignified and devout, and, in accordance with the spirit of the age, entirely devoid of 'enthusiasm'.

Anglican influence on Unitarian worship was strongly reinforced by the advent of Theophilus Lindsey, who, under the influence of Priestley and the notable Anglican Semi-Arian, Samuel Clarke, had come to embrace advanced Unitarian opinions. After the failure of the Feathers Tavern Petition, he resigned his living at

Catterick and left the Church of England. Though it was his original intention to inaugurate a reformed Anglican Church with a revised BCP, he in fact became the founder of the first avowedly Unitarian church in the country. The church which he opened in 1774 at Essex Street in London (on a site which is now the headquarters of the Unitarian denomination) used what he called *The Book of Common Prayer reformed according to the Plan of the Late Dr Samuel Clarke*. This later went through repeated revisions and soon attained an enormous popularity among the Presbyterians, who were now venturing into the Bible-based Unitarianism. It injected into the Unitarian tradition a strong influence based on non-eucharistic sources, deriving ultimately from the daily offices of mediaeval Catholicism, Lindsey's services being mainly in the form of mattins and evensong. He also followed Clarke in addressing all prayers to God the Father only. This became one of the most tenacious characteristics of Unitarian worship, which also increasingly reflected a purely humanistic christology. The virgin birth was rejected as unhistorical and Satan was expelled from the litany.

In the nineteenth century, under the influence of James Martineau, the older biblical Unitarianism was gradually ousted by a new and deeper spiritual piety, and in 1862, Thomas Sadler, with the support of Martineau, published *Common Prayer for Christian Worship*. This has rightly been reckoned as one of the finest of all Unitarian liturgies. The last two services by Martineau himself are historic. Here for the first time, Nonconformity had produced a liturgical editor of rare genius. The haunting beauty of the prayers, the timely responses, and the scripturally inspired canticles, attain poetic felicity and prophetic power.

But like Lindsey before him, Martineau disliked the perpetual termination of all prayers with the formula 'through Jesus Christ our Lord' and in *Ten Services of Public Prayer*, a revised liturgy published in 1879, he deleted these words and the redemptive and intercessory functions of Jesus were repudiated.

The Martineau tradition persisted into the twentieth century. *Orders of Worship*, edited by Mortimer Rowe and published by the Unitarian General Assembly in 1932, shows continuing Anglican influence. One of the services reproduces most of Martineau's ninth and tenth services, and another is almost wholly indebted to the BCP. In each service, scriptural sentences are followed by a call to worship, a prayer, and, in most cases, a morning or evening collect. Then there is the Lord's Prayer and an 'Open thou our lips' or a 'Lift up your hearts'. There is provision for chanted psalms or canticles, a variety of litanies, and, for each service, a different selection of prayers, including silent prayer and concluding collect.

Orders of Worship became very popular within the denomination and was at one time probably in regular use in a majority of the congregations in England. Many of its fine prayers were also adopted by those congregations which preferred non-liturgical worship. *Prayers of Faith and Fellowship*, published by the General Assembly in 1952, was designed to provide additional material for free worship.

Recent years have seen a steady turning away from the prayer book tradition within Unitarianism. *Orders of Worship* has fallen into disuse and it has been estimated that only about one eighth of the congregations now regularly use set liturgies. However, in 1976, Upper Chapel, Sheffield, under the guidance of its minister, Peter Godfrey, published *Unitarian Orders of Worship* as a new alternative to *Orders of Worship*, and some of its contents, if not the book itself, are now used by other congregations.

For modern Unitarian usage in the matter of sacraments and rites of passage, one has to turn to *A Book of Occasional Services* (1932), edited by Mortimer Rowe, and *In Life and Death* (1952), edited by Kenneth Twinn. Despite the Anabaptist antecedents of continental Unitarianism and the large part played by the General Baptists in the formation of the Unitarian tradition in Britain, the sacrament most commonly observed by Unitarians is infant baptism. This is surprising in some ways, for Unitarians have long since rejected the idea of original sin and have no clearly defined doctrine of the church. The rite is most usually regarded as an act of thanksgiving and dedication for parents. In the older liturgies, the triune formula was retained, but most Unitarians now find this

unacceptable. The most recent service books, mentioned above, suggest several alternatives, but celebrants are in any case entirely free to use words of their own choosing. Holy Communion or the Lord's Supper was at one time universally regarded as an essential part of Unitarian worship – though over-frequent observance was usually deprecated. The ceremony has always been interpreted primarily as a memorial rite, and as the service books testify, there is no rigidly prescribed form, still less any clearly defined eucharistic doctrine. Regular observance among Unitarian congregations has steadily declined during the present century, but a celebration is still held at the annual meetings of the General Assembly in Britain.

As has already been suggested, most regular Unitarian worship in Britain is at present of the free 'hymn sandwich' variety – though there does seem to be an increasing trend towards the use of responsive readings and acts of praise or prayer involving the congregation. *Songs for Living*, published by the General Assembly in 1972 (edited by Sydney Knight) and intended mainly for Sunday School use, has an extended set of 'Words for Worship'. The American Unitarian publication *Hymns for the Celebration of Life* (1964) also includes litanies and responses derived from a wide variety of sources. One of the most firmly established features of modern Unitarianism is the regular use of extra-biblical readings alongside, or instead of, the more traditional scripture 'lessons'. *Every Nation Kneeling* (1954), edited by Will Hayes, an ambitious unofficial publication containing fourteen services with provision for congregational participation, is one of the clearest expressions of the Unitarian conviction that inspiration is to be sought not only within the Judaeo-Christian tradition, but also in all the great world faiths.

The quest for more meaningful worship has led in recent years to some experimentation, involving the use of simple rituals, recorded music, silence, meditation and visual aids. The General Assembly Worship Sub-Committee regularly publishes suggestions for new services for special occasions. It is above all in the Unitarian-Universalist Churches of the United States that one finds the greatest pursuit of novelty, with worship involving liturgical dance*, adaptations of ancient Catholic ritual, oriental meditation, consciousness-raising and other off-beat modern techniques. The 'Flower Communion', now frequently observed in both Britain and the United States, has no eucharistic significance, but is an imaginative celebration of natural beauty which originated with the Czech Unitarians. Unitarianism as a whole still reflects much of the tradition of Rational Dissent. The supreme sacrament is the spoken word and the sermon retains its importance as one of the basic constituents of worship. Nowadays, the preaching may often be unpretentious, but most congregations still expect to be informed and challenged by the competent exposition of theological, social or literary themes, and, especially in America, the sermon is often followed by discussion.

It is this aspect of the Unitarian tradition which has led to the common view that its worship is excessively cold and formal. The older type of piety may indeed have been too shy and unobtrusive, but at least since the time of Martineau, Unitarians have often succeeded in combining rationalism with a deep spirituality. It is not without significance that a favourite modern book of prayers by A. Powell Davies, an American Unitarian, was published in Britain under the title of *The Language of the Heart* (1969) and that two recent General Assembly publications of original worship material, *Reflections* (1979) and *Echoes* (1982), contain some impressive religious poetry.

The warmth of Unitarian devotion, especially at the more popular level, is reflected above all in its hymnology. Though the earlier Presbyterians may have preferred metrical psalms and scriptural paraphrases, the singing of hymns has long been an essential part of Unitarian worship both free and liturgical. Martineau's influential hymnals established a tradition for a comprehensive catholicity of taste, with hymns taken from all branches of Christendom, and Unitarians soon became skilled in writing their own hymns. The considerable Unitarian contribution to general hymnology, especially that of the so-called Transcendentalist hymn-writers of America, must not be overlooked. Hymns by such Unitarian writers as Martineau, Sarah Adams, J. P. Hopps, F. L. Hosmer,

S. Longfellow, S. Johnson, J. W. Chadwick and O. W. Holmes are now found in the books of all denominations.

Unitarians were at one time much inclined to subject non-Unitarian hymns to extensive textual emendation, but they are now increasingly coming to recognize the symbolic nature of religious language and are even prepared to sing 'O come let us adore him, Christ the Lord'!

Most British congregations now use *Hymns of Worship* (1927 and 1951) or *Hymns of Worship Revised* (1962). *Hymns for Living* (1985), edited by Sydney Knight, a completely new hymnal, reflecting radical modern trends (including degenderization), has been adopted in some places.

Horton Davies, *Worship and Theology in England*, Vols 3 and 4, 1961–2; Duncan McGuffie, *The Hymn Sandwich: A Brief History of Unitarian Worship*, 1982; A. E. Peaston, *The Prayer Book Reform Movement in the Eighteenth Century*, 1940; *The Prayer Book Tradition in the Free Churches*, 1946; D. G. Wigmore Beddoes, *Yesterday's Radicals*, 1971.

A. J. LONG

United Reformed Church Worship

Britain's first union across denominational barriers took place in 1972 when the Congregational Church in England and Wales merged with the Presbyterian Church of England to form the United Reformed Church in England and Wales. The union was extended in 1981 by the accession of the Churches of Christ of Great Britain and Ireland, and the United Reformed Church in the United Kingdom came into being. Three distinct streams of liturgical life were thus brought together: the broad variety and theoretical worshipping freedom of the Congregationalists, the completer and more circumscribed forms of the Presbyterians or Reformed and the fullest weekly diet as found in the Churches of Christ. As yet it is too early for scholarly studies to be forthcoming and the unification of the three components is little advanced; although the liturgical promise of the union may be regarded as unique in contemporary British churchmanship, the potential has still to be realized.

It is at the URC's characteristic conciliar events that the fusion of the strands can be most easily detected, whereas the separate congregations have largely retained the ethos and practices which they enjoyed before their mother churches united.

In the Free Churches hymnaries are the most formative liturgical instruments: the three hymn books brought to the URC, i.e. *Congregational Praise* (1951), *The Church Hymnary* (1973) and *The Christian Hymnary* (1938), all still in use in the uniting congregations, thus remain the most important liturgical documents of the URC.

In the late 1970s an attempt was made to produce a completely new hymnary jointly with the Methodist Church. This failed, being set aside in 1980. In 1984 the congregations of the URC were canvassed for their views on a replacement for the existing assortment, although the URC had produced a notable supplement, *New Church Praise*, in 1975, containing 109 hymns. *NCP* is catholic, modern – though not obsessionally so – and with much new music. It contains no jingles. Its success has been only partial. Many find it too rarefied. However, the compilers openly acknowledged the transient and supplementary nature of their work. Other supplements, many of them in ecumenical use, commonly alternate with the traditional hymnals, e.g. *A Hundred Hymns for Today*, *Partners in Praise*. Hymn-writing has flourished in the URC, and is probably the most commonly experienced source of new theological speech among these congregations. The best-known recent writers of hymns include Fred Kaan (b. 1929), F. Pratt Green (b. 1903) and Brian Wren (b. 1936).

The separate service books of the uniting churches of the URC have in part been replaced by *A Book of Services* (1980). This hand-book (it is in no way prescriptive) is on the one side traditional in a broad sense and not markedly denominational in ethos. The services are entirely in modern English, and provide for more congregational response than was common previously. On the other hand its contents reflect the Scheme of Union in anticipation of certain conciliar events, such as ordinations, District and Provincial Assemblies. *A Book of Services* provided a form for the Blessing of Children and Dedication of Parents where baptism of the child is not sought –

in anticipation of the union with the Churches of Christ. There is an order for healing services and suggestions for the Blessing of a Civil Marriage. It contains nothing of a controversial nature, such as an earlier proposed form for the release from marriage vows. Other material in liturgical use in the URC may be found in the *Manual of the United Reformed Church* ([2]1981). Here there was a new readiness to set down and require statements of belief, fixed for the time being, (see especially Part 7, 'The Basis of Union'). Besides hymns, *NCP* contains a very full form for celebration of the eucharist which is meant to be acceptable in almost any Christian tradition, and which, in particular, goes far beyond the rather thin sources inherited from Congregationalism, the major stream of the URC. Enquiry, however, suggests that this order is not much used.

So soon after the union, it is hard to generalize about URC worship. But it seems right to note the growth of the public ministry of healing, even though this remains a divisive matter and its relationship to Sunday public worship is difficult. The short time under review has also seen changes in the place of children in worship*. First, there are many fewer, leading both to uncertainty as to how to shape worship and to anxious change and experiment. Secondly, educators among the churches are pointing to a slowly growing readiness not to treat children so much as spectators or guests at adult worship and so to develop worship for an all-age congregation, including communion, though this latter practice is a subject of heated debate – wherever the issue is raised. In general, modes of worship in the URC have been influenced by a number of factors which have led to a certain blurring, though not necessarily at the boundaries, between the three uniting traditions. Many writers of liturgical material within the URC have regretted the growth in the use of choruses at the expense of the careful statements of the Wesley–Watts tradition of hymnody. Anxiety about diminishing numbers has led in some cases to a search for solutions in wholesale change in received ways of worshipping, Pentecostalism often providing the inspiration. The use of a number of hymn supplements, differing from place to place within the URC, has already been noted. A number of different Bible translations are also in use (e.g. RSV, NEB, *Good News for Modern Man, The Jerusalem Bible*). The implications of the use of often quite different translations and paraphrases for biblical authority in preaching in the URC have yet to be worked out or, possibly, their existence even recognized.

Close as they are, the last few years do not seem to have been a period of any great distinction in the liturgical life of the relatively young URC. Understanding of the purpose and the language of worship, its relation to secularity and the self-understanding of the worshipping congregation are in flux. In the end, the influences that might clarify where the URC is going in its worship may be found in certain, but not all, ecumenical events. One will, for instance, look in vain for a new, URC, liturgically-influenced building style, since almost all new buildings since 1972 have been to house Local Ecumenical Projects. Strikingly, a project in Balsall Heath, Birmingham, which is jointly Anglican and URC (Churches of Christ) has a baptistery with a font beside it. The union of 1972 was not based upon liturgical reform, being in this respect a conservative event. The discussions in preparation for the English Covenant yielded nothing of interest in this respect. However, the accession of the numerically small Churches of Christ in 1981 brought more than the larger union of 1972, namely the weekly celebration of the Lord's Supper and believer's baptism (not rebaptism). If there is to be a new focus of self-understanding in the URC, then it is not so likely to be found in the domination by one of the three traditions, or the effect of the foundered English Covenant, or, indeed, in anything especially British, but rather in the 1982 Lima Document of the WCC, the Faith and Order Paper no. 111 on Baptism, Eucharist and Ministry. The very openness of the URC's future in respect of its worship could mean that it is better able to respond to the new recognition of the ancient liturgical identity of a more universally understood church, as evinced in the proceedings of the Sixth Assembly of the WCC at Vancouver in 1983.

See also **Books, Liturgical** 6, 7, 14; **Christian Church Worship**; **Congregationalist**

Worship; **Liturgies** 6, 7, 14; **Presbyterian Worship**.

H. R. TONKS

Utensils

see **Aumbry**; **Alms-dish**; **Bells**; **Candles**; **Chalice and Paten**; **Chrismatory**; **Ciborium**; **Cruet**; **Fan**; **Monstrance**; **Paschal Candle**; **Pyx**; **Stoup**; **Tabernacle**; **Thurible**; **Tower**

Veil

1. A veil or curtain was drawn before the altar at certain points in the liturgy from the fourth century onwards; and some of the Greek fathers liken this veil to that which hung before the holy of holies in the temple at Jerusalem. This custom has continued until today in the lesser Eastern churches such as the Armenian and the Coptic. But the need for this veil has been obviated in the Eastern Orthodox rite with the development of the solid iconostasis*.

2. In the West this veiling has not developed to the same extent as in the East. But during the season of Lent in the Middle Ages in England and elsewhere, the altar was shrouded from the congregation by the Lenten veil drawn across the sanctuary, which was only drawn aside at the reading of the gospel at the parish mass on Sundays. This veil is not to be confused with another veil which hung before the crucifix on the rood beam during Lent. Both these veils were made of unbleached linen or holland; they formed part of the general shrouding with this material which took place in all churches at the beginning of Lent and continued until the eve of Easter Day. This shrouding is known as the Lenten array (*see* Plate 50). It covered every crucifix, statue, and reredos*, including the three figures on the rood beam. The veils often had emblems of red, black or blue stencilled on them; and the emblem frequently gave a hint of the object that it veiled. The Lenten array has been revived in a number of the cathedrals and parish churches in Britain. In the modern Roman rite it is customary in some places to veil all crucifixes, statues and pictures with purple-toned veiling from the eve of Palm Sunday (called *Dominica in Palmis de Passione Domini*) until the vigil of Easter. It is no longer obligatory.

A. A. King, *The Rites of Eastern Christendom*, 2 vols, 1947; C. E. Pocknee, *The Christian Altar*, 1963; *Cross and Crucifix*, 1962; H. B. Walters, *London Churches at the Reformation*, 1939.

C. E. POCKNEE/G. D. W. RANDALL

Veneration of the Cross

Part of the solemn liturgy of Good Friday* in the Roman rite in which the whole congregation moves forward to venerate a crucifix*.

The rite originated in Jerusalem with the veneration of relics of the 'true cross' on Good Friday morning before the synaxis* (described in detail by the pilgrim Egeria, late fourth century). The custom was incorporated into the Roman liturgy by the

Plate 50
Lenten array and veiling, Southwark cathedral, London

Syrian Pope Sergius I at the end of the seventh century, after relics of the 'true cross' were transferred to the church of Santa Croce in Gerusalemme in Rome. It subsequently spread to other churches which obtained relics, and then, with the Roman rite, extended to churches which had no relics but substituted first a plain cross then later a crucifix. In England, where an early description of the rite can be found in the tenth century *Regularis Concordia*, it became very popular in the Middle Ages as 'Creeping to the Cross'.

The texts which have accompanied the veneration since Carolingian times at least are, for the Roman rite, unusually lyrical, dramatic and hybrid. The principal element is the 'reproaches': centos of scripture, rather freely treated, which are put into the mouth of Christ hanging on the cross, reproaching the whole human race for its ingratitude, betrayal and refusal of his love, and calling us to conversion, all in poignant words of moving intensity. The verses are interspersed with responses of the people, originally in Latin and Greek, which include the only surviving use in the Western liturgy of the *Trisagion**. In very different mood from the reproaches, the procession to the cross is accompanied also by the magnificent hymn of Venantius Fortunatus (sixth century), *Pange lingua gloriosi*, proclaiming the triumph and victory of the cross. (His other great hymn in similar vein, *Vexilla regis prodeunt*, has often been used at this point too.)

In the current version of the rite, a large crucifix (whose figure may be veiled) is carried through the congregation by the celebrant, flanked by acolytes with candles. Three times on the way to the sanctuary he stops, (unveils part of the figure) and elevates the cross to the congregation, singing: 'This is the wood of the cross on which hung the Saviour of the world', to which the people sing in reply: 'Come, let us worship.' While the acolytes hold the cross, he then kneels to reverence it, followed by the whole congregation in turn.

A comparable rite, consisting of solemn procession, elevation and veneration of the cross, takes place in the East on the feast of the Holy Cross (14 September) and on the third Sunday of Lent. In the Church of England a version for optional use is proposed in the report of the Liturgical Commission, *Lent, Holy Week, Easter*, 1984.

C. J. WALSH

Vernacular

Liturgy is of its nature social worship, and therefore must involve the use of audible communication between members of the worshipping community. *A priori* one would expect that the speech used would be in a language intelligible to all present, i.e. a vernacular. This is the natural, sensible and practical means of intercommunication.

History shows that all liturgies did, in fact, come into being in vernacular forms. No religious body using a liturgy has ever deliberately chosen to start with a liturgy in an unintelligible language. (Glossolalia constitutes no exception since it never hardened into liturgical forms.) Yet history shows also another fact which seems surprising: nearly all religions have come to, or passed through, a stage where they employed, either wholly or in part, a liturgy which worshippers understood with difficulty or not at all. The language was antiquated, dead or even foreign. There has been a contradiction between what would seem the natural thing and what actually happened.

No single cause suffices to explain this phenomenon; but some of the factors which produced it are these: 1. Mankind is innately conservative in matters of religion. For religious things are holy things; they are thought to partake in some way of the unchangeableness of the divinity in whose honour they are said or done; it is felt to be improper to change them. Once a liturgy has settled down into a definite form, this form tends to persist from generation to generation as a precious heritage. Yet it is an inescapable fact that living languages change. Therefore if the language of a liturgy remains unchanged it becomes archaic; in time it becomes a dead language. 2. An antiquated or dead language, precisely because it is not a vernacular, comes to be considered as a sacred language. Its exclusive use in liturgy is rationalized in terms of the reverence due to the divinity, who, it is felt, ought not to be addressed in the language used for fellow men and women (equals) but only in a very special and sacred style or language. Any attempt

to change this sacral language is denounced as impious desecration. 3. A dead language is totally unintelligible. Its use in liturgy produces in the popular mind a mystification which, when allied to its 'sacredness', results in a 'sense of mystery' (more correctly described as a 'sense of the numinous'). As this is a very important element in any religion the fact that an unknown tongue fosters it militates against change. 4. It has often happened that some nation has been evangelized by foreign missionaries who already possess a traditional liturgy; this they have imposed, without any change in language, upon their converts. Thus, even if the language is living or merely archaic for the missionaries, it starts off among the converts as something unintelligible and foreign.

For these and other reasons there exists in all liturgies a tension between the need for intelligibility and the tendency to become stabilized, sacralized and mysterious. It is only when this tendency has become excessive that a reaction may set in and cause a demand for the use of the vernacular.

The Christian religion was faced with a choice at its very beginning, for it originated among the Jews. But they, in their temple liturgy and in their scriptures, employed the Hebrew language, a tongue that was archaic and hardly understood except by the learned. In the synagogues, though, Jewish worship, while partly in Hebrew, was largely in Aramaic, the then vernacular which was closely allied to Hebrew. Throughout the diaspora the Aramaic was replaced by Greek, then the common language outside Palestine. Faced with a choice of a dead or a living language, the Christian church unhesitatingly chose the latter. In Palestine the early Christian liturgy took shape in Aramaic; outside Palestine in Greek. But, though Greek was widely spoken in urban areas, it had never completely driven out native languages which were the vernaculars of country people. So when the Gentiles began to be converted they worshipped in their own tongues – Syriac, Armenian, Coptic and many others.

The early church had no inhibitions whatever about changing its liturgical language or translating scriptures into vernaculars. The classic instance of this flexibility is Rome itself where the liturgy started in Greek. This was because the first converts were the poor and humble, almost all from the Greek-speaking slave class. By the third century, however, many Christians were speaking Latin; during the next hundred years Greek died out in Rome. So the Greek liturgy was gradually replaced by Latin until Latin was the sole language for worship. However, in the seventh century many Greek merchants and craftsmen immigrated into Rome and formed quite a large colony there. This resulted in a partial return to Greek in public worship: the scriptures at mass and at vigils were read in Greek as well as in Latin; baptism and other sacraments were administered in either language. This practice continued as long as there was any need for both vernaculars. When Greek died out again only Latin (the remaining vernacular) sufficed. The original policy of the church was undoubtedly to use vernacular languages in worship, and this policy has remained unchanged in the East.

In the West conditions were different, and a different policy ultimately prevailed. The East was fairly well civilized and its languages were developed; even though Greek became spoken almost everywhere, the other languages survived. But when the Romans conquered the West, its peoples were still uncivilized, and there were no developed languages. By the time Christianity began to spread into the West nearly all the inhabitants of the Roman empire spoke Latin, even if only vulgar Latin. For Latin had now become the vernacular; it had driven out all the undeveloped native languages which hardly survived anywhere. Different liturgical rites, such as the Roman, the Gallican, the Celtic did indeed arise, but they were all in Latin from their very beginning. No other possibility existed.

This complete hegemony of Latin explains why the West has differed from the East in its policy about liturgical language. Latin was kept even when it ceased in later centuries to be the vernacular. As living languages always do, it gradually changed in different parts of the empire; there arose dialects which, after centuries of development, have ended up as Italian, French, Spanish and Portuguese. Yet Latin was retained as the language of the liturgy because it, too, had matured and given rise to Christian literature. All educated persons

in the West remained able to speak and write Latin fluently until at least the fifteenth century. It was the language of culture, of government, of theology and even of commerce. But it was not the language of the common people who now could not understand the liturgy.

From time to time the need for the people to understand their worship was perceived and voiced, but the demands for a vernacular liturgy were usually small, localized and without result. A notable exception, however, was the missionary activity of St Cyril and St Methodius who, in the ninth century, evangelized the Slavonic peoples of Moravia. The whole story is immensely complicated, involving political intrigues, the Photian schism, forged documents and contradictory rulings by successive popes; but it all ended up with the establishment of a vernacular liturgy in the Slavonic tongue. In time permission was granted for the use of Dalmatian, Croatian, Slovenian and Czech (all of them Slavic languages). These are genuine vernaculars even today, though the tongue used by Cyril and Methodius, called Staro-Slav, is now archaic and thus but partially intelligible.

In the fourteenth century the Dominicans who had a house in Constantinople were allowed to celebrate their own (Latin) rite in the local Greek; others, working among the Armenians in Cilicia, translated the Dominican liturgy into Armenian. Missionaries in Georgia were likewise permitted to translate their Latin rite into the local vernacular.

In the sixteenth century came the great upheaval of the Reformation. Almost all Protestant Reformers demanded the use of the vernacular in the liturgy, but their reasons for this always involved dogmatic contentions judged by the Council of Trent to be heretical. The question was very thoroughly discussed at the Council; many of the bishops saw clearly that the replacement of Latin by vernacular languages (at least in parts of the liturgy) was in itself desirable. That is why the Council was careful not to condemn the vernacular as such; it decreed that its introduction was not at that time expedient. Because the language question was, in those days, so inextricably bound up with dogmatic positions, the Council could hardly have decided otherwise. Hence, for the next four centuries, Latin continued to be the official liturgical language of the Western patriarchate of the Roman Catholic Church.

The Protestants, of course, took to the vernacular very quickly for some (usually for all) of their worship. Some of the churches dating from that era have vernacular liturgies of which the prayer-texts are 400 years old. As a result these texts have reached the stage of being archaic, and many voices are being raised in favour of modernization. There are new versions of prayers, new translations of holy scripture being used in public worship with or without authorization; a process of liturgical reform is going on in nearly all the churches, and this usually entails a reform of rites and of texts now expressed in twentieth-century language, that is, in the current vernacular. These churches are acting before the original languages of their liturgies have become dead languages.

In the Roman Catholic Church the liturgical language had certainly reached the stage of being a dead language; its liturgical movement, which began with an aesthetic and archaeological phase about a century ago, became pastoral early in the present century. By the time of Pius XII it had become a reforming movement and its leaders were urging (against much powerful opposition) that the Latin liturgy should not only be reformed but also put, wholly or in part, into the vernacular. Partial concessions were granted to several countries and missionary dioceses; the movement grew in intensity and influence till the whole question was examined at the Second Vatican Council convened by Pope John XXIII. The upshot has been a radical reform which has included a complete adoption of the vernacular everywhere. Indeed it has been calculated that from 1964–1978 the new liturgical books were translated into 343 languages.

J. Gilbert, *Le Lingue nella Liturgia dopo il Concilio Vaticano* II, *Notitiae*, 15, nn. 7, 8, 9, 1979.

CLIFFORD HOWELL, SJ

Vespers

see **Canonical Hours**

Vestments

There are four basic types of ecclesiastical vesture. First, the garments which are worn

for the cultus, i.e. at the eucharist and at other sacramental ceremonies – these are vestments in a strict sense. Secondly, there is vesture which may be worn on other liturgical occasions. Thirdly, there are various items of clothing which indicate rank or specific role – including those of religious orders. Fourthly, there are garments which are, or have been, customary clerical dress on non-liturgical occasions – the civilian dress of the clergy.

A cross-division of these types also has to be made between the vesture of different sectors of the whole church – Eastern Orthodox Churches, the Roman Catholic Church and various Reformed Western Churches. Further, it is necessary to consider in outline the historical succession of comparable garments and to trace derivation and development when this has occurred.

In addition to a purely descriptive account of vestments, it is also desirable to consider their significance as a means of communication – both liturgical and theological, and even political and personal.

The organization of such a mass of material creates many problems in the matter of presentation, and some framework of reference is necessary. At the risk of over-simplification, it is possible to state that ecclesiastical vesture can be studied from the proposition that there are two main garments and many accessories. The basic garments are: 1. an *indoor tunic*; 2. an *outdoor cloak*. The classical Christian form of the tunic is the white *alb*, while the cloak exists as both the *chasuble* and the *cope*. Derivatives and variations of the tunic include the following garments: tunicle, dalmatic, rochet, surplice and cotta. Obviously, in clement weather, indoor clothing may also be worn outside without an over-garment, just as, conversely, for ceremonial reasons, outdoor robes may be worn indoors. It should also be remembered that, though worn under a chasuble or cope, the tunic is an outer-garment rather than an under-garment.

The ecclesiastical accessories correspond generally to the accessories of convenience which are normally found in association with civilian dress at any period (e.g. handkerchief and napkin), and also with the rank insignia of the ceremonial dress of the officers of any institution or society. Ecclesiastical accessories, like the garments themselves, are conveniently considered under the following headings:

1. Liturgical: (*a*) eucharistic or generally sacramental; (*b*) 'choir' or generally for other services of worship.

2. Non-liturgical: (*a*) ceremonial; (*b*) civilian.

Since any classification is being imposed upon a range of costume which has developed 'organically' under a variety of influences, there are likely to be some items of dress which are difficult to classify or include in any general scheme. This qualification applies to those which are characteristic of a particular locality or period, and which belong mainly to the non-liturgical dress of dignitaries (e.g. Anglican apron and gaiters): for this reason, apart from pontificalia, they need not be discussed in this context. Several further considerations may be noted before a systematic description and discussion of the liturgical garments. First, the Christian vestments are derived primarily from the civilian dress of the late Roman empire and owe nothing directly to the vesture of the Jewish priesthood: the original differentiation and development from lay attire took place from the fourth to the ninth centuries. Secondly, they have undergone some changes corresponding to differences in the actual mode of conducting the rites and to the addition or omission of particular ceremonies. Thirdly, they have been subject to fashion, and to the availability of various types of material used for their manufacture and embellishment. In this connection the influence of the commercial church furnishers and haberdashers is not without significance. Fourthly, the changes in style reflect to some extent various ecclesiological and sacramental doctrines concerning the status and role of the ministers of the church and the nature of worship in general. Fifthly, like most ceremonial garments, some of their features have lost their original usefulness and survive as vestigial appendages which are no more than visual reminders of the continuity of Christian worship and which, ultimately, may be abandoned (e.g. the maniple). Sixthly, vestments (in common with other 'church furnishings')

have undergone periods of rejection and revival in the Western church and, at times, have become objects of controversy and symbols of party: their use may also be subject to law – both internal ecclesiastical regulations and external national enactments.

Each item of vesture will now be considered within the following scheme:

1. *Vestments of the cultus*: alb, amice, girdle, stole, maniple, chasuble, dalmatic and tunicle.

2. *Other liturgical and clerical garments*: cope, cassock, surplice, tippet and hood, almuce, mozetta, pallium, chimere, rochet, humeral veil and mitre.

3. *Eastern Orthodox vesture.*

1. *Vestments of the cultus*

(*a*) *Alb.* The ecclesiastical alb is directly derived from the *tunica alba* of classical times. It is now usually a long white tunic reaching to the feet, made of linen, and belted with a girdle or cincture at the waist: it has close-fitting sleeves and is collarless.

In antiquity such a garment existed in two forms – short and long. The knee-length Greek *chiton* was more like a modern shirt and was sometimes sleeveless. The long type, *chiton poderes* or *tunica talaris*, has either narrow sleeves (corresponding to the alb) or wide sleeves (corresponding to both the dalmatic and the surplice). If made of linen, the garment might be called *tunica linea*. On occasion two tunics might be worn – one as an undergarment and the other as an outer garment.

In the NT the word *chiton* is used in the saying: 'If a man wants to sue you for your shirt (*chiton*), let him have your coat (*himation*) as well' (Matt. 5.40). It is also used of the seamless tunic worn by Jesus (John 19.23) in contrast to his other garments (*himatia*) which were shared by the soldiers, and *chiton* is also implied in the description of the visionary personage of Revelation as being 'robed to his feet' (*chiton poderes*) (1.13).

The long white tunic was sometimes decorated with *clavi*, i.e. full-length thin strips of purple or russet material – either a single stripe down the middle (front and back), *latus clavus*, or one such stripe over each shoulder. This elementary decoration probably served to cover and strengthen joins in the material, and was discontinued if the alb was to be worn under a dalmatic. Tunics so embellished were generally worn without a girdle and thus their character of verticality was emphasized. In addition, some early tunics carry similar decoration around the hem near the ground and thus suggest a basis for the mediaeval application of apparels.

The long white tunic which was worn generally by professional people did not really begin to become a specifically Christian vestment until the beginning of the fifth century. For example, in a transitional stage, Jerome (341–420) distinguishes between everyday clothing and a special 'suit of clean clothes' for wear in church. The mosaics at Ravenna show that by the sixth century it had become customary for bishops to wear not only the *paenula* (or chasuble) but also a wide-sleeved *tunica* (or dalmatic) over a narrow-sleeved alb (*see* Fig. 32). In S. Vitale, this is quite clear in the case of Archbishop Maximianus – the narrow sleeve of the under-tunic shows at his wrist; moreover, the edges of the wide surplice-like sleeves of his 'dalmatic' are embellished with double purple stripes which correspond with the two full-length clavi. Similarly, in S. Apollinare in Classe

Fig. 32 Sixth-century mosaics at Ravenna, showing the Emperor Justinian (*left*) and Archbishop Maximianus

the narrow sleeves of the bishop's alb are plainly seen to emerge from the broader sleeves of his dalmatic (*see* Plate 51).

Incidentally, the sleeves of the alb (or, more correctly in the East, the *sticherion*) are also decorated with double bands of what appears to be golden embroidery, corresponding to the later Eastern *epimanikia* (detachable cuffs) and, more remotely, to wrist apparels of the alb in the West. This vestment, which is common to all the clergy in the Ravenna mosaics, is remarkably like the long mediaeval surplice in shape, but because of its context and its decoration is best understood as the forerunner of the later tunicle and dalmatic.

All ranks of the clergy wore the plain alb until the eleventh century, but at about this period two changes occurred in the West. First, a wide-sleeved and somewhat shorter version of the alb, namely the surplice, began to replace it as the clerical vestment for non-eucharistic worship, and also for wear by clergy and monks in choir. Secondly, there grew up a custom of applying apparels (*paramenta*), i.e. oblong pieces of richer material or embroidery attached to the cuffs, and also front and back in the middle near the ground: these *alba parata* were, perhaps, being forbidden by implication in the *First English Prayer Book* which orders 'a white Albe plain' to be worn by the priest.

The alb, plain or with apparels, and with only minor changes in fashion (e.g. amplitude of cut, use of lace or other decoration), has continued to be worn until the present day and, in a sense, is to be thought of as the archetypal 'white robe' of Christianity.

(*b*) *Amice*. The amice is a rectangular piece of linen which originated as a neckerchief used to protect other vestments from sweat. The Latin name *amictus* is derived from *amicio* which means 'to wrap around'. The Ravenna and other mosaics show that such a neck-cloth was not worn before the sixth century, and in the Eastern Orthodox churches it has never become an official vestment.

In the West, the amice slowly became adopted as an essential mass vestment from the eighth century onwards. The *Ordo Romanus Primus* refers to the amice (*anagolagium*) as being part of the pope's

Plate 51 Pallium worn by Bishop Apollinaris. The sixth-century apse mosaic in S. Apollinare in Classe depicts the bishop vested in a tight-sleeved under-tunic or alb decorated on the forearms with coloured bands, and over this a wide-sleeved dalmatic with vertical *clavi*. His top garment is a chasuble or *phelonion*, with the episcopal pallium draped from the neck and shoulders. He stands in the *orans* posture of prayer, with arms outstretched and hands upraised.

vesture, but *Ordo IV* (*c*.800) indicates that subdeacons wore amices only when the pontiff was vested in a dalmatic. Other names used of the amice are *humerale* (shawl), *superhumerale* and *anaboladium*.

Originally, as was natural, the amice was not assumed until the alb had been put on. This earlier mode survives in the liturgies of Lyons and Milan, but generally the amice is now the first vestment to be donned. The latter custom derives from the tenth century when a longer hair style was fashionable and, in order to protect the other garments during vesting, the amice was first put on like a helmet and kept there until all the other vestments were in place. Thus the amice is provided with long tapes which are tied around the waist in order to keep it over the hair until vesting is complete. This procedure is further facilitated if a long narrow apparel is attached to the front of the amice so that when the 'helmet' is pushed back from the head the apparel forms a kind of collar. Mediaeval apparels accorded in colour with the stole and maniple and contrasted with that of the chasuble or dalmatic.

In spite of the mediaeval development of the amice into a hood, its origin as a protective neckerchief is attested by the admonition at the ordination of a subdeacon that he receives the amice as the *castigatio vocis*.

(*c*) *Girdle*. It was normal to wear a girdle of some sort with the classical *tunica* simply for the sake of convenience in moving about. Thus, when the long *tunica alba* emerged as a Christian vestment it was accompanied by the customary *cingulum* and was recognized as such in the eighth century. Worn with a very full alb, the girdle is not visible and may be referred to as the *subcingulum* – especially in connection with the attachment to it of a deacon's napkin. In the Eastern Orthodox churches the deacon wears an ungirdled *sticharion*, and the corresponding belt, *zone*, is worn only by priests and bishops.

In the past, the girdle has taken the form of a broad belt or cincture of white or coloured material. Today it is usually a long white rope with tasselled ends. It is put on immediately after the alb and the ends of the stole are customarily tucked under or through it.

(*d*) *Stole*. The stole is a strip of material about four inches (ten centimetres) wide and up to twenty-six feet (eight metres) long. It may be made of white or coloured textiles and may be plain or embroidered. It is worn over one or both shoulders in distinctive ways by bishops, priests and deacons. It is normally worn immediately over the alb and under any other outer vestment, though there are some exceptions.

The remote origin of the stole is obscure: it may have been some sort of napkin or kerchief or, alternatively, it is more likely to have been a ceremonial garland worn in honour at a festival. However, there can be no doubt that its Christian use derives directly from a scarf worn by Roman officials as an ensign of rank, and there is much to be said for the view that the stole and the pallium (*see below*) have a common origin as a status symbol.

Under the civil law in the Theodosian Codex (AD 395) senators and consuls were ordered to wear a coloured scarf or pall over alb and paenula as a badge of office (cf. a mayor's chain). There seems little doubt that by this time the dignitaries of the church had adopted a similar ensign: bishops wore a pallium (*see* Plate 51) (equivalent to the Eastern *omophorion*) over the chasuble, while priests and deacons wore a corresponding scarf known as the orarium. This orarium was forbidden to subdeacons by the Council of Laodicea (*c*.372), and is certainly the same vesture which, in the ninth century, is referred to as the *stola* received by deacons at ordination.

In the East the corresponding vestment of the deacon is still called the *orarion* and is a long narrow strip hanging down, back and front, from the left shoulder, while that of the priest is joined together in front and slipped over the neck – hence the name *epitrachelion*.

Much confusion has been caused by the fact that in the classical period, the Latin *stola* was the name of a long outer garment and, further, that this name corresponds to the NT use of stole for a similar flowing or festal raiment (e.g. Mark 16.5; Luke 15.22; Rev. 6.11). In a very remote way it is possible that the Roman scarf (or pallium) itself is derived from an earlier toga-like garment (also called pallium) which came to be closely folded length-wise and worn

as a sign of rank, but even this possible derivation in no way connects the ecclesiastical stole with the classical *stola* or biblical stole. It is not known why the name was changed from the traditional orarium to *stola* from the ninth century onwards and, regrettable though it may be, there is now no alternative but to continue to use the word which was universally accepted by the thirteenth century.

Historically there have been many different ways of wearing the stole, but today the general Western practice is as follows: a deacon wears a stole as a sash over the left shoulder, fastening or looping it below the right arm; a priest wears the stole round the back of his neck and, when it is over an alb, crosses it on the breast, while over a surplice, the ends are allowed to hang down vertically; a bishop always wears a stole in the latter manner.

The current Western custom that the bishop should wear a stole hanging straight down from both shoulders is not supported by the Byzantine mosaics at Ravenna where, with one exception, the bishops there depicted all wear a pallium over a chasuble instead of a stole beneath it: the exception is Archbishop Ecclesius (in the apse of S. Vitale) who appears to be wearing both. (The validity of this evidence has been doubted, and it has been suggested that the mosaic in question was inaccurately remade in the twelfth century.)

Apart from being worn at the eucharist, the stole is commonly worn in the Roman Catholic Church when the priest is administering the other sacraments, preaching, and hearing confessions.

In the course of time its form has been modified and its decoration varied. It remained long and narrow until the late Middle Ages, when it was shortened and the ends were made wider to accommodate more extensive decoration. From about the tenth century it became customary to embellish stoles with embroidery – usually with simple geometric patterns: sometimes fringes were attached to the ends. In the Baroque period stoles became very short indeed and very heavily decorated. Stoles also came to be made of coloured material – originally, like orphreys (*see below*) and apparels, in contrast to the colour of the chasuble or other vestment, but in the post-Reformation period when the sequence of liturgical colours* was stabilized, stoles were worn in the same colour as the chasuble or dalmatic.

During the Gothic revival stoles were again lengthened and commonly decorated with three crosses – one in the middle and one at each end. In the Evangelical sector of the Anglican Church, the stole is the only item of the early suit of liturgical vestments which is generally found acceptable.

(*e*) *Maniple*. The maniple of today is a strip of material some two to four inches wide (6–10 cms.), varying in length up to three feet (1 metre) or thereabouts: it is looped over the left wrist with some sort of fastening beneath. The maniple normally matches the stole both in material and decoration; its use is now discouraged in the Roman Catholic Church and it is not even mentioned in the new missal.

There is no doubt that this vestment derives directly from the rank ornament of a consul, the *mappa*, which he held in his right hand and waved as a signal for the games to begin: correspondingly, in the seventh century, the maniple of the pope was used as a signal for the beginning of a stational mass.

The *mappa* itself originated as a folded handkerchief or napkin which, since pockets were not a feature of classical clothing, was normally carried in the hand. Thus, a purely practical rectangle of linen developed into an ensign of rank and authority in the empire and in the church, and in the course of this development was known variously as *manipulus*, *mappula*, *sudarium*, *mantile*, *fano*, *manuale* and *sestace*.

For a long time the maniple continued to be carried in the hand (e.g. Archbishop Stigand in the Bayeux Tapestry) and, so far as deacons and subdeacons were concerned, may well have served practical purposes well into the mediaeval period. However, it eventually became solely an ornament worn on the wrist, and other cloths were used to wipe the sacramental vessels and the hands and faces of the ministers.

Further, in the Middle Ages the maniple was commonly worn by all clerics, but it was subsequently restricted to those of at least the rank of subdeacon.

(*f*) *Chasuble*. Chasuble and cope (*see below*) alike are derived from an outer cloak, *burrhus*, *paenula*, or *lacerna*, generally worn in the Graeco-Roman world by

all classes and both sexes. It was made from a semi-circle (or more usually two quadrants) of about twelve feet (four metres) in diameter of woollen material; the two edges could be either sewn together to form a conical or tent-shaped cloak (a hole being left for the head), or joined together by a clasp to form an enveloping cape – in either case the garment would fall to cover the hands. The former type became known as a *casula*, or 'little house', from which the name chasuble is derived, while the latter type is the forerunner of the cope, or *cappa*, signifying 'topmost' garment. The 'overcoat' left by Paul at Troas is called *phelones* (II Tim. 4.13), and related words are used in the Eastern Orthodox churches for the vestment which corresponds to the chasuble – *phelonica*, *felon*, *phenolion*, *phelonion* and *phainoles* – various equivalents of the Latin *paenula*.

The *paenula*-type chasuble has undergone many changes in the course of its ecclesiastical history (*see* Fig. 33) – mainly by way of reduction in size and increase in decoration, but also through being (so to speak) turned through a right-angle. The two quadrants of material which comprised the original chasuble were joined by two seams which appeared vertically in the middle of the front and back of the garment when worn: these seams were strengthened and hidden by narrow strips of braid which, since they often were woven with gold thread, came to be known as *orphreys* (*auriphrygia* or *Phrygian* gold). Subsequently the conical chasuble was cut away at the sides to give greater freedom to the arms, and eventually it was found to be more convenient to make this reduced chasuble by joining two shield-shaped pieces of material in such a way that the seams came along the shoulders and down the sides. The seams of such chasubles are not usually decorated, but non-functional vertical orphreys are often applied and provided with 'arms' to form a kind of cross – back and front.

Starting from a semi-circular design, it is obvious that this shape is easily modified, *e.g.* by increasing or reducing the extent of the notional circle by making the semi-circle a semi-oval, or by making the front smaller than the back.

Illustrations of various kinds from the sixth century onwards (by which time the chasuble had become a specifically ecclesiastical vestment) show that such modifications were made, but that, in general, the full conical chasuble with its characteristic crescent-shaped folds persisted until the thirteenth century. One variation was that there was at times a tendency to make the bottom of the front more pointed (e.g. the *phelonion* of S. Apollinare in the apse mosaic at Classe – *see* Plate 51), and in the eleventh century there appears to have been a temporary fashion for cutting away a considerable part of the front – not unlike the subsequent development of the *phelonion* in the Eastern Orthodox churches.

From the tenth and eleventh centuries in the West chasubles began to be made of much richer materials, when the church became wealthier and as silks became less expensive. Until this time they had been made principally of fine wool and had been worn generally by the clergy. The eighth-century *Ordo Romanus Primus* documents the gradual emergence of the chasuble as the distinctive outer garment of the presiding celebrant at the eucharist: at the stational mass only the pontiff retained his *paenula* for the whole of the mass. And in the ninth century Amalarius of Metz reports that at the mass in Rome the deacon removed his *paenula* before the gospel and thenceforth rolled it in such a way that he could wear it with his stole over the left shoulder and under his right arm – the so-called 'broad stole'.

By the thirteenth century, then, the chasuble was established as a rich 'high-priestly' ornament (*see* Plate 52), but one which had not lost the essential character of the original garment. At this time, however, the ceremonial of the elevation (*see* **Gestures** 4) of the host was introduced into the eucharist. This meant that the president had to raise his hands high above his head in order that the congregation might see the eucharistic bread since, by this time, he no longer faced the worshippers but had his back to them. Therefore, either the front of the chasuble had to be thrown back over the shoulders, or the vestment had to be redesigned with cut-away sides giving greater freedom to the arms (*see* Plate 53). The latter practice prevailed and was carried a stage further still in the Baroque style of the Counter-Reformation (*see* Plate 54).

From the late mediaeval period, the

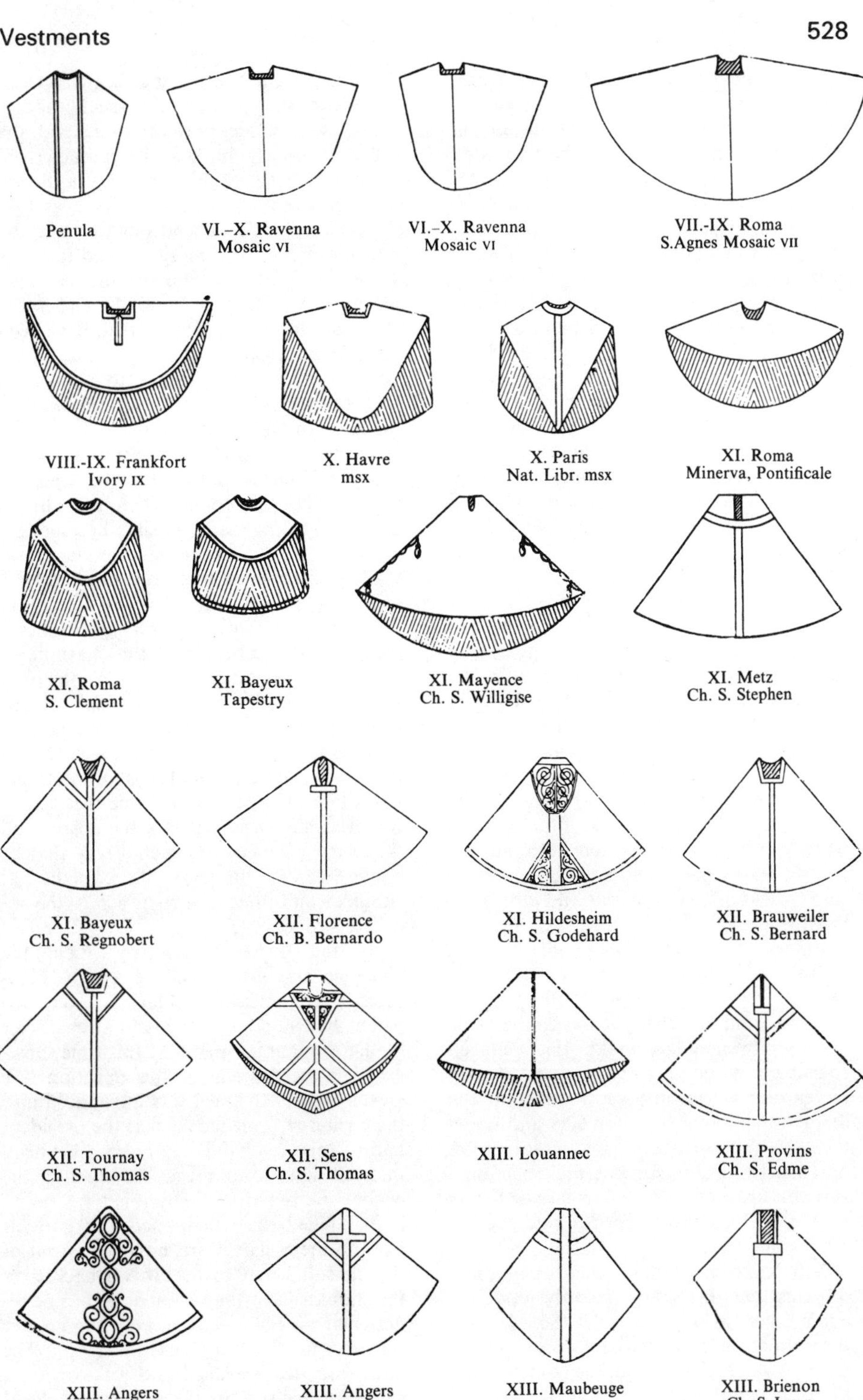

Fig. 33 HISTORY OF THE CHASU

XIII. Reims

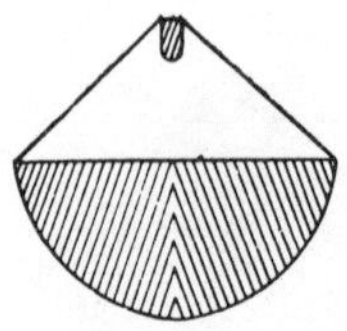
XIII. Reims
Ch. for Deacon

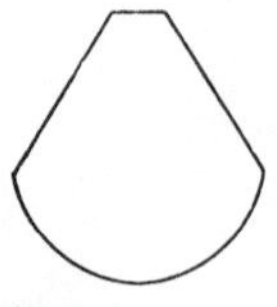
XIII. Brunswick
mus.

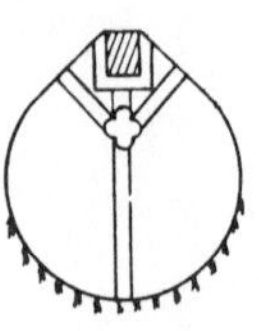
XIII. Dreux
v. Montfaucon

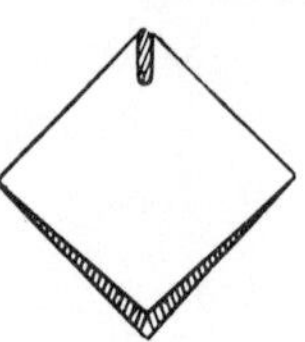
XIII. Brussels
v. Bollandists

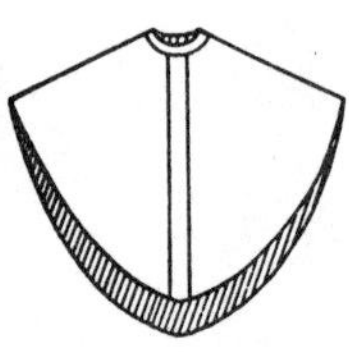
XIV. Aix la Chapelle

XIV. Roma
S. M. Transtav. tomb

XIV. Brussels
v. Bollandists

XIV. Cologn
Dominican Church

XIV. Vatican
Pontifical

XV. Roma
S. Peter a Vinc. tomb

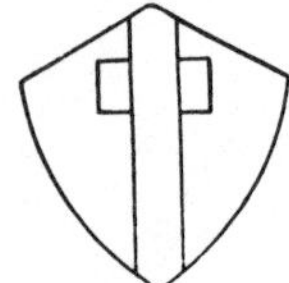
XV. V. Baluze

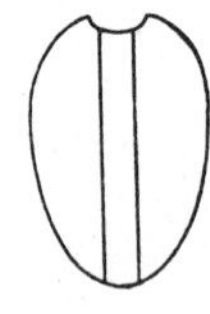
XV. Coire

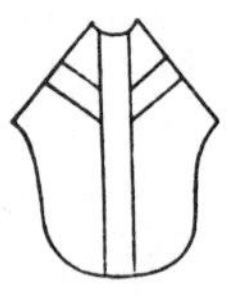
XV Dantzig
N. Dame

XV. Binche
Ch. S. Ursmer

XVI. Bern
Museum

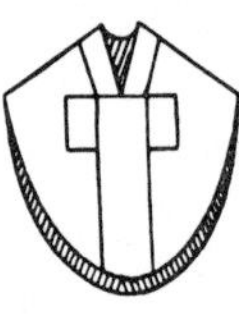
XVI. Roma
Pict. Titian

XVI. Roma
Pict. Tintoretto

XVI. Florence
Cathedral

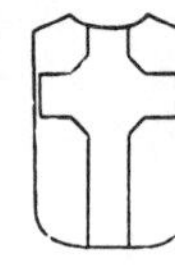
XVI. Brussels
Museum

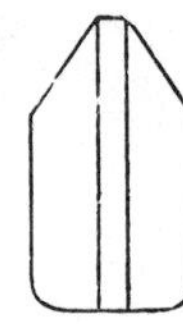
XVI. Brussels
Museum

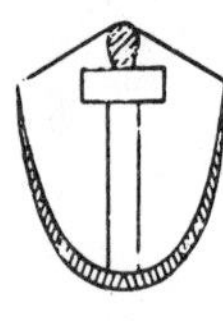
XVII. Roma
Pict Sacchi

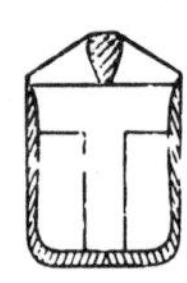
XVII. Roma
Pantheon

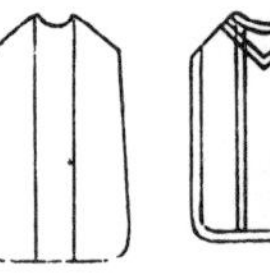
XVII. Brussels
Museum

XVIII. Brussels
Museum

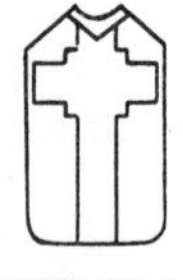
XVIII. Rheims
Cathedral

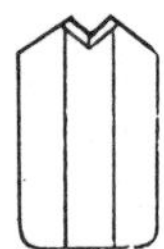
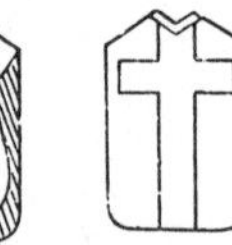
Roman Shape

Roman Shape
Cross at the back

French

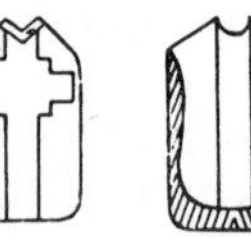
Belgian

Austrian

Spanish

Brazilian

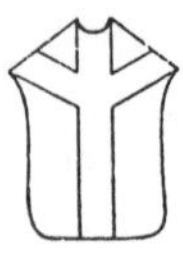
Polish

Austrian

Gothic

Large Gothic

BY THE MONUMENTS

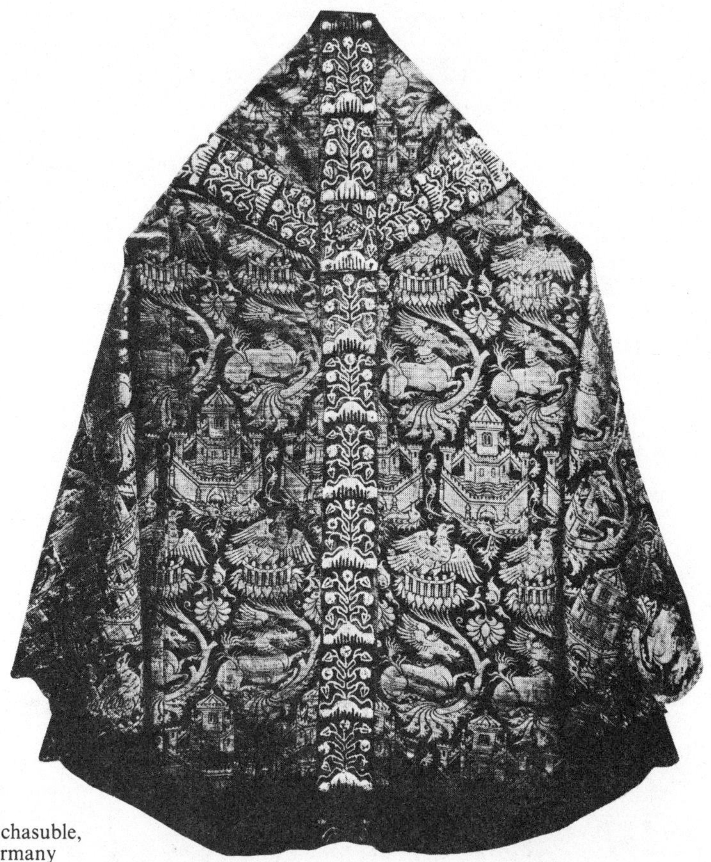

Plate 52 Full Gothic chasuble, fourteenth-century, Germany

embellishment of the vestment with embroidery was vastly extended and this, together with an increased regard for liturgical colours, endangered the very character of the vesture. The front of the chasuble was cut away even more and the way was prepared for the Baroque 'ornament' which, by the seventeenth century, had really ceased to be a garment and had become merely a vehicle for the display of the highly developed art of embroidery with rich silks, velvets, metallic threads, pearls and jewels.

Such vestments continue in use, but the nineteenth-century Romantic Movement includes much ecclesiastical harking back to the fashions of the mediaeval period – real or supposed. This neo-mediaevalism of the Cambridge Ecclesiologists and of the Ritualists led to the advocacy of the so-called Gothic chasuble together with matching stole and maniple, and their mass-production by commercial interests in a period of rapidly expanding population and religious revival. These 'reproduction antiques' have been accepted as the only alternative to the Baroque style up to the middle of the twentieth century, but recently further research and new designs have begun to replace them.

(*g*) *Dalmatic and tunicle*. The dalmatic, like the tunicle, is essentially a variant form of the *tunica alba* or alb: the name *tunica dalmatica* would seem to indicate an origin in the region of Dalmatia. As a wide-sleeved over-tunic it was a popular garment in second century Rome and, in a somewhat shortened version, appears to be the garment worn by some praying figures in catacomb frescoes.

By the fourth century the dalmatic was commonly worn over an alb as part of the distinctive 'uniform' of both bishops and

Plate 53 Elevation in the eastward position at a mediaeval mass. Priest vested in a very full alb (girdle covered) with apparels on skirt and cuffs and on amice; stole not visible but maniple worn on left wrist. Chasuble thrown back for the elevation. Characteristic mediaeval altar with front and reredos. (*The Mass of St Giles*, Flemish diptych *c*.1495. National Gallery, London.)

Plate 54 The Clare chasuble. Originally a full Gothic chasuble made and embroidered at the end of the thirteenth century – a splendid example of the *Opus Anglicanum*. Cut down to a Baroque shape in the seventeenth or eighteenth century. (Victoria and Albert Museum, London.)

deacons, as may be clearly seen in the mosaic of Maximianus in S. Vitale. The dalmatic did not, however, become a vestment until the ninth century or thereabouts. At this time it was formally accepted in the West that over the alb at the eucharist the priest wore a chasuble, the deacon a dalmatic, and the subdeacon a tunicle. In the Latin rite the dalmatic is bestowed upon the deacon at his ordination and, correspondingly, a simpler version of it, the tunicle, belongs to the subdeacon. The bishop continued to wear the dalmatic under the chasuble and, in the ninth century, some bishops adopted the practice of wearing a tunicle under the dalmatic on solemn occasions.

Originally, the dalmatic was made of white linen or wool, and, like the alb (*see* above), was decorated with two coloured strips, *clavi*, running from front to back over the shoulders: the original tunicle lacked such *clavi*. Later, the dalmatic was shortened to knee-length, the sleeves were cut broader still and slits were introduced at the sides. From the tenth century onwards the dalmatic, and to a somewhat lesser extent the tunicle, came to be made of richer materials and to be more elaborately decorated with apparels, orphreys, fringes and tassels. Thus, like the chasuble, dalmatic and tunicle tended to become ornaments rather than garments. They have, indeed, been regarded as festal vestments not to be worn in penitential seasons.

In Eastern Orthodox churches, a dalmatic-like vestment, the *sakkos* (*see below*), is worn only by bishops and, since the

sixteenth century, has replaced the chasuble (*phelonion*) as the liturgical outer garment of Greek metropolitans and all Russian bishops.

(It may also be noted that during the coronation ceremony, the English sovereign is vested in a dalmatic.)

2. *Other liturgical garments*

(*a*) *Cope*. The cope, like the chasuble (*see above*), is a ceremonial version of an outdoor cloak commonly worn in the Roman empire. Basically it is a semicircular piece of cloth worn around the shoulders and held together at the front by a clasp (morse). Apart from a curious deviation in the Church of England (*see below*), the cope is worn at non-eucharistic ceremonies (e.g. baptism, marriage, procession) in place of the chasuble: it may also replace the dalmatic or tunicle since its use is not restricted to bishops and priests.

The forerunner of the ecclesiastical cope was known by the name *cappa* (signifying 'topmost' garment) by the end of the sixth century, and other names by which it was known include *pluviale* ('rain-coat'), *planeta* (possibly from the Greek word meaning 'to wander' or travel around) and *amphibalus* (a Gallican term).

The original *paenula* or *cappa* was often fitted with a hood, and as a functional garment made of thick black material (*cappa nigra*) continued to be worn in choir as a protection against cold throughout the Middle Ages. As increasingly the *cappa* became a ceremonial garment (probably from the sixth century onwards), so the hood ceased to be functional and eventually was reduced to a triangular or shield-shaped decoration on the back.

The employment of silks and other expensive materials, together with the use of embroidery and other means of embellishment of the cope, has run parallel to that of the chasuble. A certain variation in style has occurred, but apart from the reduction of the hood to a vestigial flap, there has been no substantial change in its form. In the West the cope is a general ecclesiastical robe of splendour and has never been a distinctive clerical vestment. There is no liturgical equivalent to the cope in the Eastern Orthodox churches, though cope-like mantles are worn on occasion by some bishops.

At the time of the Reformation in England, the BCP of 1549 ordered the parish priest at the eucharist to wear 'a vestment (i.e. chasuble, stole and maniple) or cope': this rubric was withdrawn in 1552, but in Canon XXIV (1604) it was ruled that the principal minister at the communion in cathedrals and collegiate churches should wear a coloured cope over a plain alb. This custom is still observed in some cathedrals and ex-collegiate churches in spite of the fact that a cope is an extremely inconvenient garment in which to perform the eucharistic actions and gestures. Oddly enough, in the S. Vitale mosaic of Melchizedek offering bread, the priest-king appears to be attired in a 'cut-away' cope: this is probably an imagined Jewish vestment, though it may reflect some aspects of sixth-century Christian ceremonial clothing.

Also in S. Vitale the Emperor Justinian is shown wearing a hoodless ceremonial *paenula* fastened with a clasp on his right shoulder, thus leaving his right arm free (*see* Fig. 32). Some modern copes may be worn in this way as well as in the more customary manner.

(*b*) *Cassock*. The cassock is now an ankle-length tunic with long narrow sleeves; it is usually girt at the waist with a belt or cincture, but may be buttoned from neck to foot; it may be of any colour (*see* **Colours, Liturgical**). Its form and use demonstrate the difficulty of classifying the garments worn by the clergy: thus, it is universally worn under the eucharistic vestments and all other liturgical garments, but it is not itself a vestment. Again, although it is an under-garment, as the Latin name *subtanea* (soutaine) indicates, it is also worn as an over-garment for wear indoors and outdoors. Further, the cassock is not an exclusively clerical garment and may be worn by servers, choristers, vergers and other ecclesiastical persons.

The word in English is derived from Italian *cassaca*, or French *casaque*, possibly themselves derived from the name of a barbarian tunic known in the second century as *caracalla*. A long tunic, *vestis talaris*, was part of normal civilian dress in the late Roman empire, but when under barbarian influence (*c*. sixth century) lay fashions became shorter and more military, the clergy retained the ankle-length coat. Its

use was ordered by the Council of Braga (572) and, in one form or another, it has subsequently been an important element in the distinctive attire of the clergy. Thus, the Anglican Canon LXXIV (1604) forbade beneficed clergy to go out in public 'in their doublet and hose without coats or cassocks' and, together with gown, hood, scarf and square cap, this comprised the outdoor dress of the clergy until the beginning of the nineteenth century. (Correspondingly, Roman Catholic clergy were forbidden by law to wear cassocks in public in England.) Cassocks have from time to time been fitted with hoods or capes and, unless worn with an academic hood, are often still so designed. In the mediaeval period in cold regions cassocks were lined with fur or sheepskin (*pellicia*), hence the wide-sleeved full alb worn over the bulky lined cassock acquired the name 'surplice'. Very full cassocks with a train were fashionable for prelates in the fifteenth and sixteenth centuries but are no longer favoured. In contrast, in the eighteenth century the cassock was shortened to form an 'apron' for horse-riding bishops, deans and archdeacons and, together with corresponding gaiters, forms an outfit still affected by some dignitaries. The ministers of the Reformed churches (apart from some Methodists) do not normally cover their civilian clothes with a cassock, but prefer simply to wear a version of the mediaeval gown (known as 'Geneva' gown) with or without an academic hood, for liturgical or other ceremonial occasions. Gowns and hoods are not, of course, exclusively items of ministerial attire and are worn as ceremonial dress not only by churchmen but by academics and lawyers: it is often the case that two linen strips called 'bands' are worn in place of a tie or stock when a cassock or gown is worn. The decline in the practice of wearing a cassock as distinctive outdoor dress by clergy of the Church of England coincided with the separation of the neckerchief into collar and tie shortly before the middle of the nineteenth century. At about this time the back-fastening so-called Roman collar was devised to be worn with a black stock and without a tie. Until recently it was universally worn as a 'label' by ministers of virtually all denominations, sects and faiths, and the cut of the neck of cassocks was adjusted to accommodate it. Since about 1965 increasing numbers of clergy have abandoned the clerical collar and in their outdoor everyday attire are as indistinguishable from their fellows as were their predecessors in the first five centuries or so in the life of the church.

(*c*) *Surplice*. The surplice is a wide-sleeved ample version of the linen alb which was adopted in northern countries in the twelfth century for wear over fur-lined cassocks, hence the name: *superpelliceum* = over a fur garment. The actual shape of the surplice (as distinct from the name) is much earlier, as may be seen in the sixth-century mosaics of the bishops in S. Apollinare in Classe; apart from the decorative *clavi*, their albs are identical in form with the mediaeval surplice.

From the twelfth century onwards the surplice became the distinctive dress of the lower clergy and was worn by priests outside the mass: today it is commonly worn over the cassock by both clerics and laymen in choir or otherwise assisting in the conduct of worship.

Originally ankle-length, the surplice was progressively shortened and by the eighteenth century on the continent barely reached the waist and had short sleeves: in this form it is known as the *cotta*. In the Roman Catholic Church it has also been trimmed with lace from the sixteenth century onwards. The surplice now exists in many different styles and, from time to time, attempts are made to restore its original simplicity and amplitude.

In the Church of England it has been a prescribed eucharistic vestment since Elizabethan times.

(*d*) *Tippet and hood*. The long black scarf worn by Anglican clergy over the surplice. The exact origin of this ecclesiastical accessory is as obscure as its Latin name *liripipium* (liripipe or typet), though it is probable that it derives from an appendage of the mediaeval hood – either the 'poke' which hung down at the back or extensions of the cape which hung down at the front. In either case, hood and scarf would appear to be separated parts of the same garment – just as collar and tie are derived from the single neckerchief. In the fifteenth century the hood was commonly worn over the surplice and then, having been adopted by the universities as a token of graduation and given distinctive colours and linings,

was further accepted in its academic form in the emergent Anglican Church as part of the choir habit of the clergy. The 1549 BCP recommends the hood as 'seemly' for preachers and the 1604 Canons (XXV and LVIII) order it for all graduate ministers. Correspondingly, non-graduates are ordered to wear a tippet instead of a hood in church. For outdoor wear Canon LXXIV orders all clergy to wear the tippet over a gown.

(*e*) *Almuce*. This garment originated as a protection for the head and shoulders against the winter cold of mediaeval churches and, in the course of time, became a mark of rank or distinction. Originally either a lined hood or a fur scarf worn over the surplice, it emerged as a fur-lined hood with two ends hanging down in front and was regarded as part of the choir habit. The colour and the type of fur of the almuce came to have hierarchical significance – grey squirrel being the highest ranking and reserved for bishops and cathedral canons. Its use was discontinued in the Established Church under Elizabeth I when it became customary to wear a black tippet or scarf.

A transitional stage may be noted at St Paul's Cathedral when in 1549 it is recorded that minor canons wore 'tippets like other priests' instead of their almuces.

The name almuce (Latin *almutia*) sometimes appears as 'amess' or even 'amice', and confusion with the eucharistic amice must be avoided.

(*f*) *Mozetta*. A short hooded cape of coloured silk (red, white, purple or black) or fur worn over a rochet (*see below*) by pope, cardinals, bishops, abbots and other dignitaries of the Roman Catholic Church. It is worn by papal privilege signifying jurisdiction and is part of the ceremonial dress of bishops and canons in England on non-liturgical occasions. Probably derived from the almuce (*see above*) which it has largely replaced.

(*g*) *Pallium*. A narrow band of white woollen material, marked with six dark crosses, and worn in one way or another around the neck and over the shoulders by patriarchs, archbishops and some other bishops. In the Roman Catholic Church it is now usually in the form of a circular band with two hanging strips back and front, but in the Ravenna mosaics the bishops all wear a straight band looped over the shoulders with the ends hanging down back and front from the left shoulder (*see* Plate 51): it is still so worn in the Eastern Orthodox Churches and is called the *omophorion*.

In the Codex of Theodosius (395), a scarf or pall of several colours is ordered to be worn over the *paenula* by senators as an ensign of their rank; shortly afterwards this civil ornament became a distinctive badge of episcopal status. In the West the custom grew of reserving the pallium to archbishops who received it directly from the pope as a sign of their jurisdiction: the pope also acquired discretion to confer it on other bishops.

(It is a matter of dispute whether or not the 'scarf-pallium' is derived from the classical 'wrap-around' toga-like pallium: some writers believe that the latter was folded to form a narrow bundle and then reduced to the size of an ornament.)

(*h*) *Chimere*. A silk or satin sleeveless gown, black or scarlet, now worn by Anglican bishops and doctors of divinity. The name may be derived from the Spanish *zamarra*, and by the twelfth century the chimere was a short cloak worn by bishops when riding horseback. In a longer version it soon became part of the customary attire of bishops on both liturgical and civil occasions.

(*i*) *Rochet*. A variant form of the alb with narrow sleeves, or without sleeves, which was in general use by clerics, sacristans, servers, etc., up to the thirteenth century. Later it became the prerogative of bishops, cardinals and canons regular.

Contrary to its origin as a convenient sleeveless 'dust-coat', the rochet of Anglican bishops (as worn under the chimere) acquired full lawn sleeves gathered at the wrist: in the eighteenth century the sleeves became so voluminous that they were commonly sewn to the chimere.

(*j*) *Humeral Veil*. First mentioned in the Roman *ordines* of the eighth and ninth centuries, the humeral veil was a silk shawl worn around the shoulders (*humerus* = shoulder) and covering the hands, the latter being an ancient sign of reverence. The subdeacon at high mass was required to be so vested from the offertory until after the Lord's Prayer. It was widely used in the nineteenth century and in extra-liturgical devotions may be worn in processions of

the Blessed Sacrament and at Benediction*.

(*k*) *Mitre*. The origin of the mitre is obscure, but by the eleventh century it had emerged as the distinctive liturgical hat of bishops. Its shape has undergone many changes, starting from a simple conical cap of white linen with two lappets (or fanons) hanging down at the back. Subsequently, in the twelfth century, there was a front-to-back dent in this cap, but a century later the dented cap was being worn the other way round and the present form of a tall divided hat began to develop. In the thirteenth century three types of mitre are recognized in Roman ceremonial corresponding with different degrees of ceremony – *mitra pretiosa* (jewelled), *mitra aurifrigiata* (decorated without jewels) and *mitra simplex*.

The wearing of a mitre is not entirely restricted to bishops in the West, and some abbots and cardinals have been granted the privilege.

The Eastern Orthodox form of the mitre (*mitra*) resembles the Byzantine imperial crown and is sometimes worn by archpriests.

3. *Eastern Orthodox vesture*. Deriving from the same source, the vestments and ornaments of the Eastern Orthodox churches are basically similar to those of the West. The differences arise either from the 'fixing' of a particular form or style in the East in contrast to Gothic and subsequent developments in the West, or to minor additions or variations following the Great Schism which have no parallel in the West. Broadly speaking, the vestments in use in the Eastern Orthodox churches are all 'eucharistic', and with only minor modifications are worn at all services; i.e., such garments as cope, surplice, tippet, hood, etc., have never come into existence.

Most of the corresponding Eastern vestments have been mentioned in the above account and the same order will be followed in this summary:

(*a*) *Corresponding vestments*

Sticharion or Stikir. The liturgical tunic, equivalent to the alb, but usually of coloured material.

Zone. Equivalent of the girdle but usually fitted with a clasp.

Epitrachelion. Corresponding to the stole, but a broad band with the ends joined together from the chest downwards to leave an opening for the head. Usually made of silk or brocade and ornamented with metal and jewels. Worn by bishops and priests.

Orarion. A narrow band of silk, also corresponding to the stole, but worn by deacons over the left shoulder with ends either hanging straight down back and front or arranged otherwise.

Phelonion. Equivalent to the Western chasuble and worn by all bishops and priests. From the eleventh century the white *phelonion* of a patriarch began to be embroidered all over with crosses (*polystaurion*), and from the fourteenth century this decoration was used for the vestments of all bishops. In the Russian church the *phelonion* is cut away at the front from the breast downwards while at the back it falls to the feet and covers the arms at the sides. Since the fall of Constantinople in 1453 the *phelonion* has been replaced by the *sakkos* (*see below*) in the Byzantine rite by all bishops.

(*b*) *Western vesture without equivalent in Eastern Orthordox churches*

Amice.

Maniple (but see *epimanikia*).

Cope (a modern form of *phelonion* in the Armenian and Syrian churches is open at the front like a cope).

Dalmatic (but see *sakkos*).

(*c*) *Eastern vesture without equivalent in the West*

Epimanikia. Cuffs of embroidered silk worn over the sleeves of the sticharion of bishops and priests and known from the eleventh century. They take the place of the Western maniple but are not really its equivalent.

Epigonation. A lozenge-shaped ornament suspended from the zone on the right side in the Greek and Armenian churches (*see* Fig. 34) (cf. the decoration worn by Emperor Justinian and his courtiers in the mosaic in Ravenna, S. Vitale). It probably originated as a functional handkerchief and, in this sense, would correspond to the Western maniple.

Sakkos. An ample tunic with short wide sleeves and slit at the sides (*see* Fig. 35). Such a garment was one of the ceremonial vestments of the Byzantine emperors and it may well have a common origin with the

Western dalmatic. As a liturgical vestment it appears at first to have been a mark of imperial favour for selected patriarchs, but by the thirteenth century it was worn by all patriarchs and metropolitans at Christmas, Easter and Whitsun. After the fall of Constantinople it gradually came to be worn generally by all bishops.

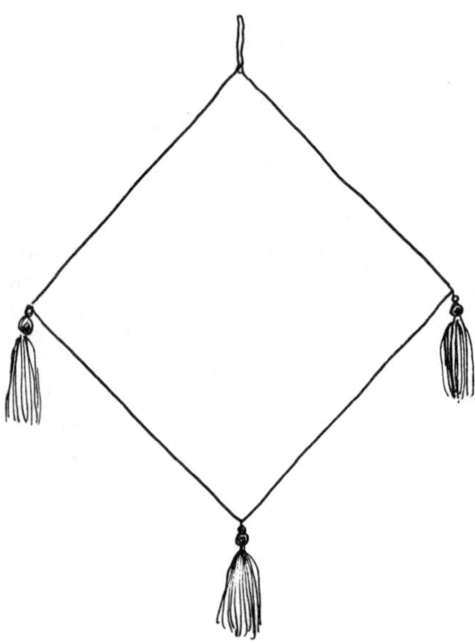

Fig.26 Epigonation

Fig. 27 Sakkos

The outdoor dress of Eastern Orthodox clerics is basically cassock, gown and hat: priest-monks and bishops wear a veil on the hat. There is considerable variety from one country to another in the type of hat. Black is the most usual colour, but some patriarchs wear white and other hierarchs wear Roman purple belts.

4. *The role of vestments.* Liturgical vestments comprise a special case of ceremonial clothing and are, therefore, part of a complex pattern of communication. They serve both to express the nature of the occasion when they are worn and to distinguish the respective role and rank of each participant. Until the church began to be 'imperialized' under Constantine, the ministers (bishops, presbyters and deacons) wore their everyday civilian clothing in the acts of worship of the community: at the Reformation, and again recently, attempts have been made to revert to the principle that contemporary lay clothes should be worn by all at the eucharist and other services. Thus, characteristically, clothing becomes an item in a movement of protest – in these cases against alleged distortions of both sacramental doctrine and hierarchical authoritarianism. And in this way, vestments (themselves derived from ordinary clothing) become badges of party in ecclesiastical conflicts.

This 'political' significance of vestments is, of course, in addition to the allegorical meanings which have been attributed to them and to their more profoundly religious significance associated with concepts of transcendence, incarnation, majesty, priesthood, mystery, revelation, sacrifice and communion. However, on all sides, it is recognized that whatever particular meanings vestments may have acquired, there must, from time to time, be an appraisal of the symbolism of vesture and its relevance and effectiveness in the total communication pattern of worship. Psychologically, it seems that people who engage in the corporate performance of ritual desire that some, if not all, of the participants should wear special clothing. The question then tends to resolve itself into: What type of special clothing? In the church the emphasis has tended to be upon the expression of historical continuity; hence, each succeeding style has been a modification or a

Plate 55 Roman Catholic priest in lay dress for liturgy. At this experimental mass in a Jesuit high school chapel in Amsterdam the priest wore lay clothes for the synaxis but put on a grey gown for the eucharist itself.

revival of a previous one. Thus, any sector of the church is faced with the further question: To what point in the historical development of vesture shall we seek to return? Roman Catholics, some Anglicans and some Lutherans favour modern versions of Gothic, Gothic-revival and even Baroque styles, while Protestants generally are content with the everyday gown as worn by Renaissance Puritans.

There are, then, three basic choices: first, to dispense with ceremonial clothing; secondly, to modernize or modify a particular historic style; thirdly, to attempt to design vestments which express a renewed understanding of Christian liturgical celebrations (*see* Plates 55, 56, 57). The first choice perhaps needs to be made from time to time in order to highlight the underlying problems, but only a minority of worshippers is ever likely to accept the absence of all special clothing as a permanent solution.

The second choice finds clear expression in the most recent Roman Catholic regulations: the *Ordo Missae* (1969) states unequivocally that 'the vestment common to all ministers is the alb' and that, if

Plate 56 Basilican mass in modern vestments. The vestment worn by all the sacred ministers is the wide-sleeved *tunika* designed by Sr Flüeler at Stans, Switzerland. The celebration is in the modern college chapel at Sarnen.

necessary, it should be tied at the waist with a cincture. Also optional is the amice, and the maniple is not mentioned at all. A surplice may replace the alb: a stole may be worn with it, but not a chasuble, dalmatic or tunicle. A cope may be worn in processions and some other services. Vestments may be made of either traditional materials or natural regional fabrics; artificial fabrics may be used for vestments provided they are 'in keeping with the dignity of the sacred action and the person wearing them'. The 'instruction' assumes that the traditional vestments (except the maniple) will be worn for the celebration of the mass and that they will constitute an external demonstration of the diversity of function of members of the body of Christ in worship: the possibility that the ministers should wear ordinary lay clothes is not considered.

This attitude, welcome though it is, does not really go far enough at a time when there is a confluence of the Liturgical Movement* and the Ecumenical Movement, creating a situation in which all 'sides' may be willing to accept similar well-designed simple robes. Increasingly, Roman Catholics realize that most of their customary vestments now have little meaning, while some Protestants recognize the fact that quasi-academic gowns are not entirely appropriate for the *celebration* of sacraments. The restoration of greater lay participation in the ceremonies provides an opportunity for a fresh appraisal of the *functional* character of vestments in a purely practical sense of convenience for movement, posture and gesture as well as in the symbolic senses of cultic hierarchy and historical continuity.

Outstanding in the field of re-designed vestments is the work of Sr Flüeler (*see* Plate 56): she has designed and made a new form of wide-sleeved *tunika* which may be worn directly over the civilian clothing of the minister. In a single off-white garment – at once dignified and practical – the functions of both alb and cassock are combined: as a free-falling tunic it is essentially an outer garment and, therefore, does not require a chasuble to be worn over it because it already has the 'enshrouding' quality of sacred vesture, though, obviously, either a chasuble or a cope may be worn over it, if desired (*see* Plate 57). A long stole has been designed to wear with the *tunika* in such a way that a pleasing draped effect can be obtained and, further, a number of variations of the basic garment have been designed to make possible a distinction between the various ranks of ministers. It is easy to imagine that such new garments would be perfectly acceptable to most Protestants and, thus, it would be possible to use a vestment as an aid to Christian unity and not as a badge of division. This is already happening in an Anglican-Methodist shared church in Birmingham where the vesture of the ministers is identical, namely, an inexpensive version of the off-white combined cassock-alb now commercially available in England.

Plate 57 Modern alb (*tunika*), stole and chasuble. The wide-sleeved alb functions as both cassock and alb and may be worn directly over everyday clothes: the *tunika* is made from commercially produced material but the stole is hand-woven. The chasuble is optional and the vestments appear 'complete' without it; alternatively, a cope may be worn with the fastening either at the centre or on the right shoulder. Vestments designed by Sr Flüeler at Stans.

Archbishop's Commission, *The Canon Law of the Church of England*, 1947; G. R. Balleine, *A History of the Evangelical Party*,

1908/51; J. Braun, *Die Liturgische Gewandung im Occident und Orient nach Ursprung und Entwicklung, Verwandung und Symbolik*, 1907; O. Chadwick, *The Victorian Church*, 1966; H. J. Clayton, *The Ornaments of the Ministers as shown on Monumental Brasses*, 1919; H. J. Clayton, *Cassock and Gown*, 1929; Convocation of Canterbury, *The Ornaments of the Church and its Ministers: Upper House Report 416*, 1908; P. Dearmer, *The Ornaments of the Ministers*, 1908/20; *The Linen Ornaments of the Church*, 1929; A. Flüeler, *Das Sakrale Gewand*, 1964; A. K. Fortescue, *The Vestments of the Roman Rite*, 1912; A. K. Fortescue and J. B. O'Connell, *The Ceremonies of the Roman Rite*, 1917; H. Gee, *The Elizabethan Prayer Book and Ornaments*, 1902; J. A. Hardon, *Modern Catholic Dictionary*, 1981; J. A. Jungmann, *The Mass of the Roman Rite*, rev ed, 1959; J. W. Legg, *Church Ornaments and their Civil Antecedents*, 1917; R. Lesage, *Vestments and Church Furniture*, 1960; J. Mayo, *A History of Ecclesiastical Dress*, 1984; J. T. Micklethwaite, *The Ornaments of the Rubric*, 1897; H. Norris, *Church Vestments*, 1949; *Ordo Missae*, 1969; C. E. Pocknee, *Liturgical Vesture*, 1960; *The Christian Altar*, 1963; F. Procter and W. H. Frere, *The Book of Common Prayer*, new rev ed 1961.

GILBERT COPE

Vestry

A side room in a church where the clergy and/or choir may vest or dress. The term is virtually synonymous with sacristy*.

EDITOR

Viaticum

Communion administered to or received by one who is dying or in danger of death. Derived directly from the Latin, the term means provision for a journey, i.e. the journey into eternity.

See also **Sick, Visitation of the**.

EDITOR

Vigil

A vigil (Lat *vigilia*, watch, wakefulness) is a service on the eve prior to a festival. In the early days of the church vigils preceded not only the great festivals, such as Easter (*see* **Paschal Vigil**) and Pentecost*, but also Sundays* and Martyrs' days. These vigils had no parallels in synagogue worship, but they may in part have originated from the Jewish practice of reckoning a day from sunset to sunset. So, according to Lev. 23.32, 'from evening to evening shall you keep your sabbath'. In part it may also reflect the widespread belief that the Second Coming is to take place at midnight.

In the patristic period such vigils could be scenes of immodest behaviour and they were often restricted to the hours before nightfall. The services consisted of prayers and psalms and occasionally a sermon. As a form of preparation for a feast, they eventually became associated with fasting but not before the ninth century.

See also **Watch-Night**.

EDITOR

Vigil, Easter

see **Paschal Vigil**

Visitation

see **Mariological Feasts**

Votive Mass

A mass provided for a special occasion. Variable prayers were drawn up relating to different subjects, e.g. for travellers, for the sick. One fine mediaeval composition was for 'the Five Wounds of our Lord Jesus Christ'. In time votive mass came to have an extended meaning designating any mass said as a special act of devotion, such as masses of the Trinity, of the Holy Cross, etc.

EDITOR

Vows, Renewal of Baptismal

see **Baptismal Vows, Renewal of**

Watch-Night

Watch-night is the British Methodist form of vigil*, now generally confined to the New Year's Eve.

The watch-night began in spontaneous meetings held by enthusiastic Methodists in Kingswood (a mining area near Bristol), who often spent 'the greater part of the night in prayer, and praise, and thanksgiving'. Discovering these unofficial gatherings, probably in the early spring of 1742,

John Wesley adopted and regularized the idea (*see* **Covenant Service**).

Within a few months the watch-night had become a regular event at the main Methodist centres (Bristol, London, Newcastle), held from about 8.30 p.m. to about 12.30 a.m. on the Friday nearest the full moon, so that attenders walked safely home through moonlit streets. It was also held on public and Methodist fast-days, and especially on New Year's Eve. (This may have been suggested by folk-customs of 'seeing in' the New Year; where such folk-customs are still lively, the watch-night remains popular.) Through the nineteenth century, the watch-night came to be restricted to the New Year, possibly because such a service, to be psychologically effective, needs some defined moment to aim at (namely, the 'seeing in' of the year). In some areas, Anglican and Free Churches adopted this New Year watch-night. At present, services of a 'vigil'-type for great festivals (Christmas midnight communion) and nights of intercession for world need appear to be winning favour in Methodism, while the New Year's Eve service is losing it.

The first watch-nights were preaching-services designed to deepen the spiritual life. Later themes are light and darkness, newness of Christian life, shortness of human life and imminence of judgment, or 'solemn praise to God for continuing his great work in our land' (John Wesley, *Journal*, 31 December 1777).

L. F. Church, *More about the Early Methodist People*, 1949; Charles Wesley, *Hymns for the Watch-Night*, 1744; *Hymns for New Year's Day*, 1750, 1766; John Wesley, *Journal*, ed N. Curnock, 8 vols, 1909–16; *Plain Account of the People called Methodists*, 1749. *See also* Arnold Bennett, *The Old Wives' Tale*, ch v.

DAVID TRIPP

West Syrian Worship

The West Syrian Church, known to many as 'Jacobite' (after Jacob Baradeus, the sixth-century reorganizer of the West Syrian Church) and as Monophysite (after the erroneous idea prevailing in Byzantium and the Latin West that the West Syrians believed only in the divine nature of Christ), historically inherited the Semitic, Palestinian tradition of Christianity, though not uninfluenced by the Hellenistic milieu in which they lived.

The Syrian tradition broke up soon into four families – the East Syrian (Edessa), the West Syrian (Antioch), the Melchite (Greek), and the Maronite (Lebanon).

Liturgical rites. The West Syrian Church has probably the richest and most diverse heritage in respect of eucharistic anaphorae* and canonical offices. In addition to these there are the rites of baptism and chrismation of which three different forms are known. Ordination rites also vary substantially; the whole liturgical corpus also includes rites of matrimony (separate rites for first and second marriages), burial (different for clergy, laymen, women and children), anointing of the sick (not extreme unction – again different for clergy and laity), profession of monks, consecration of churches and altars, translation of relics, etc.

The eucharistic liturgy. The liturgy is nowadays celebrated mostly in the vernacular* – Arabic in the Middle East, English in America, Malayalam in India and so on – though certain portions may still be said by the priest in Syriac. The officiating priest and the people alternate in practically all the prayers, and the deacon plays an important part, admonishing and directing the people to stand with fear, pray and understand the nature of the event that is going on in the liturgy. Choirs have not been allowed to usurp the place of the congregation as in certain other Eastern liturgies.

Some scholars have spoken of a hundred different West Syrian anaphorae, though I can trace only about seventy. Some of these, especially the principal Anaphora of St James, go back in their basic structure to the Jerusalem church of apostolic times. Other anaphorae come from the second (Ignatius of Antioch) to the fourteenth centuries, if we take the names of the anaphorae at face value. New liturgies continued to be created in every century up to the fourteenth, though production was most prolific from the fourth to the seventh. The twelfth century produced at least six new anaphorae and about the same number was produced in the thirteenth. With the thirteenth century the development reached its peak in Gregory Bar-Hebreus and has remained more or less static ever since.

Two peculiarities of the West Syrian rite

are 1. the liturgy of incense between the liturgy of the word and the liturgy of the eucharist proper; 2. the prayer of adieu to the altar at the end of the liturgy. The liturgy of incense, which recalls the offering of incense in the Temple (Ex. 30.1–10), seems to have replaced the dismissal of the catechumens, and comprises a general absolution of the priest and people before the offering of the eucharistic sacrifice. It also represents a sort of offertory; incense* symbolizes the good works and prayers which are well-pleasing to God. It symbolizes also the prayers of the departed saints which mix with those of the congregation, as a true spiritual offering of praise and adoration.

The epiclesis occurs in all the seventy known liturgies, though the form of the epiclesis varies verbally from anaphora to anaphora, as also does the verbal content of the 'words of institution'.

Not all the seventy anaphorae are in common use. The ones most commonly used in India are St James (on all principal feasts, for the first eucharist offered by a priest, or offered at a new altar), Dionysius Bar Salibhi, St John Chrysostom and St John the Evangelist.

The canonical offices for ordinary days are called the *Shimo*, and have recently been translated into English by the Benedictine Fr Griffiths. The more elaborate office, the *Fenqith*, has been recently translated into English by Francis Acharya, a Cistercian monk at the Kurisumala Ashram in Kerala, under the title *Prayer with the Harp of the Spirit* (1982). It is rarely used even in the Syriac. The Syriac text of the *Fenqith* is available in an Indian edition (3 vols) as well as in a Mosul edition (1886–1896).

One major feature of the eucharistic liturgy and the daily offices is the *Sedro*, a long meditative-homiletical prayer, preceded by a proemion which seems to be an elaborated form of the *Gloria*. These prayers are rich in theological content, and play a considerable role in the religious education of the faithful, especially in the absence of biblical preaching.

An introduction and critical text of the Syriac anaphorae with Latin translation have been published by the Pontifical Oriental Institute in Rome (*Anaphorae Syriacae*, 1953). The ninth-century commentary of Moses Bar Kepha on the Syrian liturgies was published with an English translation by R. H. Connolly and H. W. Codrington (*Two Commentaries on the Jacobite Liturgy*).

The people communicate rather rarely, the legal minimum of once per year being observed by most, usually on Holy Thursday (*see* **Maundy Thursday**). Communion is in both kinds, usually by intinction* for the laity. The priest usually administers, though the deacon is allowed to serve communion to the laity.

Reservation of the sacrament for adoration is forbidden; it may be reserved in case of need for the sick, and for those who fast till the evening.

Confession before communion is often demanded, though this is not necessary for those who communicate frequently. Fasting from the previous midnight is required.

The lections during the liturgy of the word are three, one from the Acts or catholic epistles (representing the twelve), then from the Pauline epistles, and then finally the gospel, which is read with great ceremony by the officiating priest. Sermons had gone out of use, but are coming back more recently as priests become better trained.

The creed recited is the Niceno-Constantinopolitan, introduced into the liturgy by Peter the Fuller in the fifth century as an anti-Chalcedonian measure.

Two of the West Syrian anaphorae, those of Matthew the Shepherd and Sixtus of Rome, lack the actual words of institution. The latter says: 'He, when he was prepared for his saving passion, by the bread which by him was blessed, broken and divided among his holy Apostles, gave us his propitiatory body for life eternal; in a like manner, also by the cup . . .'

The canon* of the mass, with words of institution, anamnesis and epiclesis is said aloud by the priest, with responses from the people.

A. Fortescue, *The Lesser Eastern Churches*, 1913; W. de Vries, *Sakramententheologie bei den Syrischen Monophysiten*, 1940; I. Ziade, 'Syrienne' (église), *DTC*, XIV, cols. 3017–88.

PAULOS GREGORIOS

Westward Position

see **Posture** 2

Whitsunday

The English title for Pentecost*, so-called from its association with the white robes of baptism.

EDITOR

Women, Ordination of

see **Ordination of Women**

Women and Worship

The current women's movement, like the similar movement of the nineteenth century, has included in its critique an examination of the position of women in the church in general and in the church's worship in particular. Several issues have emerged as a result of this renewed awareness of the role that the church has played and continues to play in the oppression of women as a group.

1. Historically continuous with the nineteenth-century women's rights movement is a concern for equal access for women into existing ecclesial structures. In relation to worship, this concern has focussed especially on the presence of women as leaders in worship in general and as ordained clergy in particular. The struggle of women to gain official recognition of their ministry by the church has, in many cases, been successful, and it has also generated extensive research and publications on the history and theology of women's leadership in the church (*see* **Ordination of Women**). Moreover, this struggle characteristically has been motivated not only by a concern for public recognition of the call to ministry of individual women, but also by the conviction that such a recognition would itself constitute a powerful witness to the fullness of a church of women and men, equal in the sight of God by virtue of their baptism. At the same time, the physical presence of women at altar and pulpit also challenges presuppositions about the nature of God and the adequacy of exclusively male language to speak of God.

2. A more contemporary concern has been the use of language in such a way that women are, implicitly or explicitly, included. The conventional practice in English of using male referents as 'generic', i.e., referring to the whole human race, has been sharply challenged by those who point out that such usage perpetuates the misconception that males are normative human beings and women secondary, derivative, or deviant. While this critique is by no means universally accepted, it has been more and more widely adopted by the scholarly community at large and by the publishing community specifically, especially in the USA, and every evidence suggests that it will eventually be accepted. The use of 'inclusive' language, in reference to people, in liturgical books, hymnals, resources, and Bible translations has growing support within many church bodies, and linguistic changes are beginning to appear in revised liturgical books and new translations of scripture (*see* **Inclusive Language**).

3. Although often perceived as an aspect of 'inclusive' language, use of language about God is most usefully treated as a separate (though not unrelated) issue. The predominantly (if not exclusively) male image of God which is portrayed in the traditional language of prayer, scripture and hymns (to say nothing about visual images) raises questions about the extent to which women are created 'in the image of God'. Such andocentric language has also undoubtedly been used to reinforce the notion that men are not only normative representatives of the human race, but also more adequate than women as representatives of God. Proposals for change range from the elimination or avoidance of any gender-specific language about God, through the use of only feminine pronouns and titles, to the attempt to balance male and female language and titles. Efforts to alter masculine language encounter most difficulty with language referring to God as Father, references to Jesus, and trinitarian formulae. The first is a problem not only because of the theological import of the term, but also because of its emotional resonance for many Christians. The second is a historical difficulty, and the third is a doctrinal and ecumenical problem. Solutions will require serious re-examination of the underlying theological issues in order to recast the language in a way that is accessible to contemporary sensibilities while remaining faithful to the tradition the church has received. The very understanding of 'tradition' itself has, of course, been challenged on the basis of its exclusion and denigration of women. At the present time

there is no consensus about a solution among those committed to a change in traditional androcentric language about God, nor will there be an easy one.

4. More fundamental, perhaps, even than critiques of language or admission to leadership, is the question of the ability of traditional structures of Christian or Jewish worship to tolerate the inclusion of women in full equality with men. For some, the Christian and Jewish traditions are fundamentally sexist and therefore must be rejected *in toto* by women, and replaced by new feminist religions which appropriate traditions from ancient non-Christian goddess worship. Sometimes called *Wicca*, such worship includes meditation and trance and spell-casting, and emphasizes the equality of all human beings and their continuity with the natural world.

Others deny that Christianity (and/or Judaism) is inherently and irreversibly sexist, and are committed to the reformation of the church by the full inclusion of women and recognition of women's contributions, both past and present. Some would understand this not as a reformist position, but as a 'radical' position, i.e., calling the church back to its 'roots', which have been revealed to have been far more egalitarian than has been assumed.

5. For those who have remained in the church while critical of its treatment of women, yet another concern is the content of worship; in particular, the way in which references to or images of women are included or excluded. At issue here are the predominance of negative images of women (Eve as originator of sin, Israel as harlot or unfaithful wife, etc.) and of positive images which reinforce the secondary status of women (Mary as docile and asexual; obedience to male authority as primary measure of female virtue, etc.). The avoidance in lectionary readings and preaching texts of scriptural material which depicts women as agents of God in history (Miriam, Hannah; Mary Magdalene as 'first witness to the resurrection' rather than reformed harlot, etc.) is noted, as is the dearth of similar examples from more recent history. The Roman Catholic Church, with its sanctoral cycle, has more resources for this than most Protestants, although even there male saints predominate.

Carol Christ and Judith Plaskow (eds), *Womanspirit Rising*, 1979; Rosemary Radford Ruether, *Sexism and God-Talk: Toward a Feminist Theology*, 1983; Elisabeth Schüssler Fiorenza, *In Memory of Her: A Feminist Theological Reconstruction of Christian Origins*, 1983.

MARJORIE PROCTER-SMITH

Words of Administration

The words of administration are those that accompany the giving of the sacramental bread and wine to the communicants at the eucharist. The earliest recorded formula is that preserved by Hippolytus (*Ap. Trad.* 23.5) concerning the bread: 'The bread of heaven in Christ Jesus', to which the recipient responds with 'Amen'. The same answer is made to the words of the priest in the Ambrosian rite – 'The Body of Christ' – and in the *Apostolic Constitutions*, where the formulae are: 'The Body of Christ . . . The Blood of Christ, the Cup of Life.' In the Byzantine liturgy the formula reads: 'The servant of God N partakes of the precious and holy Body and Blood of our Lord and Saviour Jesus Christ for forgiveness of his sins and life eternal.' The form in the Roman mass is that of a blessing, adopted in the eighth century: 'The Body of our Lord Jesus Christ preserve thy soul unto everlasting life.' Indeed, the words in all orders are variations and expansions of those current in the patristic period; so, for example, those in the rite of the Church of South India are: 'The Body of our Lord Jesus Christ, the Bread of Life . . . the Blood of our Lord Jesus Christ, the True Vine.' Within the Church of England, there was a fusion in 1559 of the 1549 words, which were close to the old formulae, and those of 1552, which were substituted in accordance with the view of the European Reformers and avoided calling the elements the body and the blood of Christ.

The BCP of the American Episcopal Church (1979) prints three formulae: that of 1559, that of Hippolytus and one similar to the eighth-century Roman one, namely 'The Body (Blood) of our Lord Jesus Christ keep you in everlasting life.' The ASB (1980) has reverted to the Ambrosian wording with as an alternative the third one of the American BCP, substituting eternal for everlasting.

EDITOR

D0405940